T0189557

Lecture Notes in Computer Science 12107

More information about this series at http://www.springer.com/series/7410

Anne Canteaut · Yuval Ishai (Eds.)

Advances in Cryptology – EUROCRYPT 2020

39th Annual International Conference on the Theory
and Applications of Cryptographic Techniques
Zagreb, Croatia, May 10–14, 2020
Proceedings, Part III

 Springer

Editors
Anne Canteaut 🆔
Équipe-projet COSMIQ
Inria
Paris, France

Yuval Ishai
Computer Science Department
Technion
Haifa, Israel

ISSN 0302-9743   ISSN 1611-3349   (electronic)
Lecture Notes in Computer Science
ISBN 978-3-030-45726-6   ISBN 978-3-030-45727-3   (eBook)
https://doi.org/10.1007/978-3-030-45727-3

LNCS Sublibrary: SL4 – Security and Cryptology

This Springer imprint is published by the registered company Springer Nature Switzerland AG
The registered company address is: Gewerbestrasse 11, 6330 Cham, Switzerland

Preface

Eurocrypt 2020, the 39th Annual International Conference on the Theory and Applications of Cryptographic Techniques, was held in Zagreb, Croatia, during May 10–14, 2020.[1] The conference was sponsored by the International Association for Cryptologic Research (IACR). Lejla Batina (Radboud University, The Netherlands) and Stjepan Picek (Delft University of Technology, The Netherlands) were responsible for the local organization. They were supported by a local organizing team consisting of Marin Golub and Domagoj Jakobovic (University of Zagreb, Croatia). Peter Schwabe acted as the affiliated events chair and Simona Samardjiska helped with the promotion and local organization. We are deeply indebted to all of them for their support and smooth collaboration.

The conference program followed the now established parallel-track system where the works of the authors were presented in two concurrently running tracks. The invited talks and the talks presenting the best paper/best young researcher spanned over both tracks.

We received a total of 375 submissions. Each submission was anonymized for the reviewing process and was assigned to at least three of the 57 Program Committee (PC) members. PC members were allowed to submit at most two papers. The reviewing process included a rebuttal round for all submissions. After extensive deliberations the PC accepted 81 papers. The revised versions of these papers are included in these three volume proceedings, organized topically within their respective track.

The PC decided to give the Best Paper Award to the paper "Optimal Broadcast Encryption from Pairings and LWE" by Shweta Agrawal and Shota Yamada and the Best Young Researcher Award to the paper "Private Information Retrieval with Sublinear Online Time" by Henry Corrigan-Gibbs and Dmitry Kogan. Both papers, together with "Candidate iO from Homomorphic Encryption Schemes" by Zvika Brakerski, Nico Döttling, Sanjam Garg, and Giulio Malavolta, received invitations for the *Journal of Cryptology*.

The program also included invited talks by Alon Rosen, titled "Fine-Grained Cryptography: A New Frontier?", and by Alice Silverberg, titled "Mathematics and Cryptography: A Marriage of Convenience?".

We would like to thank all the authors who submitted papers. We know that the PC's decisions can be very disappointing, especially rejections of very good papers which did not find a slot in the sparse number of accepted papers. We sincerely hope that these works eventually get the attention they deserve.

We are also indebted to the members of the PC and all external reviewers for their voluntary work. The PC work is quite a workload. It has been an honor to work with

---

[1] This preface was written before the conference took place, under the assumption that it will take place as planned in spite of travel restrictions related to the coronavirus.

everyone. The PC's work was simplified by Shai Halevi's submission software and his support, including running the service on IACR servers.

Finally, we thank everyone else – speakers, session chairs, and rump-session chairs – for their contribution to the program of Eurocrypt 2020. We would also like to thank the many sponsors for their generous support, including the Cryptography Research Fund that supported student speakers.

May 2020   Anne Canteaut
                                                                                   Yuval Ishai

Eurocrypt 2020

The 39th Annual International Conference on the Theory and Applications of Cryptographic Techniques

Sponsored by *the International Association for Cryptologic Research (IACR)*

May 10–14, 2020
Zagreb, Croatia

General Co-chairs

Lejla Batina	Radboud University, The Netherlands
Stjepan Picek	Delft University of Technology, The Netherlands

Program Co-chairs

Anne Canteaut	Inria, France
Yuval Ishai	Technion, Israel

Program Committee

Divesh Aggarwal	National University of Singapore, Singapore
Benny Applebaum	Tel Aviv University, Israel
Fabrice Benhamouda	Algorand Foundation, USA
Elette Boyle	IDC Herzliya, Israel
Zvika Brakerski	Weizmann Institute of Science, Israel
Anne Broadbent	University of Ottawa, Canada
Nishanth Chandran	MSR India, India
Yilei Chen	Visa Research, USA
Aloni Cohen	Boston University, USA
Ran Cohen	Boston University and Northeastern University, USA
Geoffroy Couteau	CNRS, IRIF, Université de Paris, France
Joan Daemen	Radboud University, The Netherlands
Luca De Feo	IBM Research Zurich, Switzerland
Léo Ducas	CWI Amsterdam, The Netherlands
Maria Eichlseder	Graz University of Technology, Austria
Thomas Eisenbarth	University of Lübeck and WPI, Germany
Thomas Fuhr	ANSSI, France
Romain Gay	Cornell Tech, USA
Benedikt Gierlichs	KU Leuven, Belgium
Rishab Goyal	UT Austin, USA

Vipul Goyal	Carnegie Mellon University, USA
Tim Güneysu	Ruhr-Universität Bochum and DFKI, Germany
Jian Guo	Nanyang Technological University, Singapore
Mohammad Hajiabadi	UC Berkeley, USA
Carmit Hazay	Bar-Ilan University, Israel
Susan Hohenberger	Johns Hopkins University, USA
Pavel Hubáček	Charles University Prague, Czech Republic
Abhishek Jain	Johns Hopkins University, USA
Marc Joye	Zama, France
Bhavana Kanukurthi	IISc Bangalore, India
Nathan Keller	Bar-Ilan University, Israel
Susumu Kiyoshima	NTT Research, USA
Eyal Kushilevitz	Technion, Israel
Gregor Leander	Ruhr-Universität Bochum, Germany
Tancrède Lepoint	Google, USA
Tal Malkin	Columbia University, USA
Alexander May	Ruhr-Universität Bochum, Germany
Bart Mennink	Radboud University, The Netherlands
Kazuhiko Minematsu	NEC Corporation, Japan
María Naya-Plasencia	Inria, France
Ryo Nishimaki	NTT Secure Platform Laboratories, Japan
Cécile Pierrot	Inria and Université de Lorraine, France
Sondre Rønjom	University of Bergen, Norway
Ron Rothblum	Technion, Israel
Alessandra Scafuro	North Carolina State University, USA
Peter Schwabe	Radboud University, The Netherlands
Adam Smith	Boston University, USA
François-Xavier Standaert	KU Leuven, Belgium
Yosuke Todo	NTT Secure Platform Laboratories, Japan
Gilles Van Assche	STMicroelectronics, Belgium
Prashant Nalini Vasudevan	UC Berkeley, USA
Muthuramakrishnan Venkitasubramaniam	University of Rochester, USA
Frederik Vercauteren	KU Leuven, Belgium
Damien Vergnaud	Sorbonne Université and Institut Universitaire de France, France
Eylon Yogev	Technion, Israel
Yu Yu	Shanghai Jiao Tong University, China
Gilles Zémor	Université de Bordeaux, France

External Reviewers

Aysajan Abidin
Ittai Abraham
Thomas Agrikola
Navid Alamati
Nils Albartus
Martin Albrecht
Ghada Almashaqbeh
Joël Alwen
Miguel Ambrona
Ghous Amjad
Nicolas Aragon
Gilad Asharov
Tomer Ashur
Thomas Attema
Nuttapong Attrapadung
Daniel Augot
Florian Bache
Christian Badertscher
Saikrishna
  Badrinarayanan
Shi Bai
Josep Balasch
Foteini Baldimtsi
Marshall Ball
Zhenzhen Bao
James Bartusek
Lejla Batina
Enkhtaivan Batnyam
Carsten Baum
Gabrielle Beck
Christof Beierle
Amos Beimel
Sebastian Berndt
Dan J. Bernstein
Francesco Berti
Ward Beullens
Rishabh Bhadauria
Obbattu Sai Lakshmi
  Bhavana
Jean-Francois Biasse
Begül Bilgin
Nina Bindel
Nir Bitansky

Olivier Blazy
Naresh Boddu
Koen de Boer
Alexandra Boldyreva
Xavier Bonnetain
Carl Bootland
Jonathan Bootle
Adam Bouland
Christina Boura
Tatiana Bradley
Marek Broll
Olivier Bronchain
Ileana Buhan
Mark Bun
Sergiu Bursuc
Benedikt Bünz
Federico Canale
Sébastien Canard
Ran Canetti
Xavier Caruso
Ignacio Cascudo
David Cash
Gaëtan Cassiers
Guilhem Castagnos
Wouter Castryck
Hervé Chabanne
André Chailloux
Avik Chakraborti
Hubert Chan
Melissa Chase
Cong Chen
Hao Chen
Jie Chen
Ming-Shing Chen
Albert Cheu
Jérémy Chotard
Arka Rai Choudhuri
Kai-Min Chung
Michele Ciampi
Benoit Cogliati
Sandro Coretti-Drayton
Jean-Sébastien Coron
Adriana Suarez Corona

Alain Couvreur
Jan-Pieter D'Anvers
Bernardo David
Thomas Decru
Claire Delaplace
Patrick Derbez
Apoorvaa Deshpande
Siemen Dhooghe
Denis Diemert
Itai Dinur
Christoph Dobraunig
Yevgeniy Dodis
Jack Doerner
Jelle Don
Nico Döttling
Benjamin Dowling
John Schank
Markus Duermuth
Orr Dunkelman
Fréderic Dupuis
Iwan Duursma
Sébastien Duval
Stefan Dziembowski
Aner Moshe Ben Efraim
Naomi Ephraim
Thomas Espitau
Andre Esser
Brett Hemenway Falk
Antonio Faonio
Serge Fehr
Patrick Felke
Rex Fernando
Dario Fiore
Ben Fisch
Marc Fischlin
Nils Fleischhacker
Cody Freitag
Benjamin Fuller
Ariel Gabizon
Philippe Gaborit
Steven Galbraith
Chaya Ganesh
Juan Garay

Rachit Garg
Pierrick Gaudry
Nicholas Genise
Essam Ghadafi
Satrajit Ghosh
Kristian Gjøsteen
Aarushi Goel
Junqing Gong
Alonso Gonzalez
Lorenzo Grassi
Jens Groth
Aurore Guillevic
Berk Gulmezoglu
Aldo Gunsing
Chun Guo
Qian Guo
Siyao Guo
Shai Halevi
Shuai Han
Abida Haque
Phil Hebborn
Brett Hemenway
Shoichi Hirose
Dennis Hofheinz
Justin Holmgren
Akinori Hosoyamada
Senyang Huang
Paul Huynh
Kathrin Hövelmanns
Andreas Hülsing
Ilia Iliashenko
Laurent Imbert
Takanori Isobe
Tetsu Iwata
Håkon Jacobsen
Tibor Jager
Aayush Jain
Samuel Jaques
Jéremy Jean
Yanxue Jia
Zhengzhong Jin
Thomas Johansson
Kimmo Järvinen
Saqib Kakvi
Daniel Kales
Seny Kamara

Gabe Kaptchuk
Martti Karvonen
Shuichi Katsumata
Raza Ali Kazmi
Florian Kerschbaum
Dakshita Khurana
Jean Kieffer
Ryo Kikuchi
Eike Kiltz
Sam Kim
Elena Kirshanova
Fuyuki Kitagawa
Dima Kogan
Lisa Kohl
Markulf Kohlweiss
Ilan Komargodski
Yashvanth Kondi
Venkata Koppula
Lucas Kowalczyk
Karel Kral
Ralf Kuesters
Ashutosh Kumar
Ranjit Kumaresan
Srijita Kundu
Peter Kutasp
Thijs Laarhoven
Gijs Van Laer
Russell Lai
Virginie Lallemand
Baptiste Lambin
Julien Lavauzelle
Phi Hung Le
Eysa Lee
Hyung Tae Lee
Jooyoung Lee
Antonin Leroux
Gaëtan Leurent
Xin Li
Xiao Liang
Chengyu Lin
Huijia (Rachel) Lin
Wei-Kai Lin
Eik List
Guozhen Liu
Jiahui Liu
Qipeng Liu

Shengli Liu
Tianren Liu
Pierre Loidreau
Alex Lombardi
Patrick Longa
Sébastien Lord
Julian Loss
George Lu
Atul Luykx
Vadim Lyubashevsky
Fermi Ma
Varun Madathil
Roel Maes
Bernardo Magri
Saeed Mahloujifar
Christian Majenz
Eleftheria Makri
Giulio Malavolta
Mary Maller
Alex Malozemoff
Nathan Manohar
Daniel Masny
Simon Masson
Takahiro Matsuda
Noam Mazor
Audra McMillan
Lauren De Meyer
Peihan Miao
Gabrielle De Micheli
Ian Miers
Brice Minaud
Pratyush Mishra
Ahmad Moghimi
Esfandiar Mohammadi
Victor Mollimard
Amir Moradi
Tal Moran
Andrew Morgan
Mathilde de la Morinerie
Nicky Mouha
Tamer Mour
Pratyay Mukherjee
Marta Mularczyk
Koksal Mus
Pierrick Méaux
Jörn Müller-Quade

Yusuke Naito
Mridul Nandi
Samuel Neves
Ngoc Khanh Nguyen
Anca Nitulescu
Ariel Nof
Sai Lakshmi Bhavana
    Obbattu
Maciej Obremski
Tobias Oder
Frédérique Oggier
Miyako Ohkubo
Mateus de Oliveira
    Oliveira
Tron Omland
Maximilian Orlt
Michele Orrù
Emmanuela Orsini
Morten Øygarden
Ferruh Ozbudak
Carles Padro
Aurel Page
Jiaxin Pan
Omer Paneth
Lorenz Panny
Anat Paskin-Cherniavsky
Alain Passelègue
Sikhar Patranabis
Michaël Peeters
Chris Peikert
Alice Pellet-Mary
Olivier Pereira
Léo Perrin
Edoardo Persichetti
Thomas Peters
George Petrides
Thi Minh Phuong Pham
Duong-Hieu Phan
Krzysztof Pietrzak
Oxana Poburinnaya
Supartha Podder
Bertram Poettering
Antigoni Polychroniadou
Claudius Pott
Bart Preneel
Robert Primas

Luowen Qian
Willy Quach
Ahmadreza Rahimi
Somindu Ramannai
Matthieu Rambaud
Hugues Randriam
Shahram Rasoolzadeh
Divya Ravi
Mariana P. Raykova
Christian Rechberger
Ling Ren
Joost Renes
Leonid Reyzin
Joao Ribeiro
Silas Richelson
Peter Rindal
Francisco
    Rodríguez-Henríquez
Schuyler Rosefield
Mélissa Rossi
Mike Rosulek
Dragos Rotaru
Lior Rotem
Arnab Roy
Paul Rösler
Reihaneh Safavi-Naini
Amin Sakzad
Simona Samardjiska
Antonio Sanso
Yu Sasaki
Pascal Sasdrich
Or Sattath
John Schanck
Sarah Scheffler
Tobias Schneider
Markus Schofnegger
Peter Scholl
Jan Schoone
André Schrottenloher
Sven Schäge
Adam Sealfon
Jean-Pierre Seifert
Gregor Seiler
Sruthi Sekar
Okan Seker
Karn Seth

Yannick Seurin
Ido Shahaf
Ronen Shaltiel
Barak Shani
Sina Shiehian
Omri Shmueli
Jad Silbak
Thierry Simon
Luisa Sinischalchi
Veronika Slivova
Benjamin Smith
Yifan Song
Pratik Soni
Jessica Sorrell
Nicholas Spooner
Akshayaram Srinivasan
Damien Stehlé
Ron Steinfeld
Noah
    Stephens-Davidowitz
Martin Strand
Shifeng Sun
Ridwan Syed
Katsuyuki Takashima
Titouan Tanguy
Stefano Tessaro
Enrico Thomae
Jean-Pierre Tillich
Benjamin Timon
Junichi Tomida
Deniz Toz
Rotem Tsabary
Daniel Tschudi
Yiannis Tselekounis
Yi Tu
Dominique Unruh
Bogdan Ursu
Vinod Vaikuntanathan
Kerem Varici
Philip Vejre
Marloes Venema
Daniele Venturi
Fernando Virdia
Vanessa Vitse
Damian Vizár
Chrysoula Vlachou

Mikhail Volkhov
Satyanarayana Vusirikala
Hendrik Waldner
Alexandre Wallet
Michael Walter
Haoyang Wang
Meiqin Wang
Weijia Wang
Xiao Wang
Yohei Watanabe
Hoeteck Wee
Mor Weiss
Weiqiang Wen
Benjamin Wesolowski
Jan Wichelmann
Daniel Wichs

Friedrich Wiemer
Christopher Williamson
Jonas Wloka
Wessel van Woerden
Lennert Wouters
David J. Wu
Shai Wyborski
Brecht Wyseur
Keita Xagawa
Xiang Xie
Chaoping Xing
Sophia Yakoubov
Shota Yamada
Takashi Yamakawa
Avishay Yanai
Kang Yang

Kevin Yeo
Arkady Yerukhimovich
Øyvind Ytrehus
Aaram Yun
Mohammad Zaheri
Mark Zhandry
Jiayu Zhang
Liangfeng Zhang
Ren Zhang
Zhenfei Zhang
Zhongxiang Zheng
Hong-Sheng Zhou
Vassilis Zikas
Giorgos Zirdelis
Vincent Zucca

Contents – Part III

Quantum II

Asymmetric Cryptanalysis

(One) Failure Is Not an Option: Bootstrapping the Search for Failures in Lattice-Based Encryption Schemes

Jan-Pieter D'Anvers[1(✉)], Mélissa Rossi[2,3,4,5(✉)], and Fernando Virdia[6(✉)]

[1] imec-COSIC, KU Leuven, Leuven, Belgium
janpieter.danvers@esat.kuleuven.be
[2] ANSSI, Paris, France
[3] ENS Paris, CNRS, PSL University, Paris, France
melissa.rossi@ens.fr
[4] Thales, Gennevilliers, France
[5] Inria, Paris, France
[6] Information Security Group, Royal Holloway,
University of London, Egham, UK
fernando.virdia.2016@rhul.ac.uk

Abstract. Lattice-based encryption schemes are often subject to the possibility of decryption failures, in which valid encryptions are decrypted incorrectly. Such failures, in large number, leak information about the secret key, enabling an attack strategy alternative to pure lattice reduction. Extending the "failure boosting" technique of D'Anvers et al. in PKC 2019, we propose an approach that we call "*directional* failure boosting" that uses previously found "failing ciphertexts" to accelerate the search for new ones. We analyse in detail the case where the lattice is defined over polynomial ring modules quotiented by $\langle X^N + 1 \rangle$ and demonstrate it on a simple Mod-LWE-based scheme parametrized *à la* Kyber768/Saber. We show that for a given secret key (single-target setting), the cost of searching for additional failing ciphertexts after one or more have already been found, can be sped up dramatically. We thus demonstrate that, in this single-target model, these schemes should be designed so that it is hard to even obtain one decryption failure. Besides, in a wider security model where there are many target secret keys (multi-target setting), our attack greatly improves over the state of the art.

J.-P. D'Anvers—The research of D'Anvers was supported the European Commission through the Horizon 2020 research and innovation programme Cathedral ERC Advanced Grant 695305, by the CyberSecurity Research Flanders with reference number VR20192203 and by the Semiconductor Research Corporation (SRC), under task 2909.001.

M. Rossi—The research of Rossi was supported by the European Union's H2020 Programme under PROMETHEUS project (grant 780701). It was also supported by the French Programme d'Investissement d'Avenir under national project RISQ P14158.

F. Virdia—The research of Virdia was supported by the EPSRC and the UK government as part of the Centre for Doctoral Training in Cyber Security at Royal Holloway, University of London (EP/P009301/1).

A. Canteaut and Y. Ishai (Eds.): EUROCRYPT 2020, LNCS 12107, pp. 3–33, 2020.
https://doi.org/10.1007/978-3-030-45727-3_1

Keywords: Cryptanalysis · Lattice-based cryptography · Reaction attacks · Decryption errors

1   Introduction

Algebraic lattices are a powerful tool in cryptography, enabling the many sophisticated constructions such as digital signatures [6,36], zero-knowledge proofs [38,42], FHE [25] and others. Applications of main interest are public-key encryptions (PKE) [37,43] and key encapsulation mechanisms (KEM).

The computational problems defined over lattices are believed to be hard to solve, even with access to large-scale quantum computers, and hence many of these constructions are considered to be quantum-safe. As industry starts to make steps forward into the concrete development of small quantum computers, the US National Institute of Standards and Technology (NIST) begun an open standardization effort, with the aim of selecting quantum-safe schemes for public-key encryption and digital signatures [40]. At the time of writing, the process is in its second round, and 9 out of 17 candidates for PKE or KEM base their security on problems related to lattices, with or without special structure.

One commonly occurring characteristic of lattice-based PKE or KEM schemes is that of lacking perfect correctness. This means that sometimes, ciphertexts generated honestly using a valid public key may lead to decryption failures under the corresponding private key. Throughout this paper we'll refer to such ciphertexs as "failures", "decryption failures", or "failing ciphertexts". While in practice, schemes are parametrised in such a way that decryption failures do not undermine overall performance, these can be leveraged as a vehicle for key recovery attacks against the key pair used to generate them. Such an attack was described by Jaulmes and Joux [30] against NTRU, after which is was extended in [29] and [24]. A similar attack on Ring-LWE based schemes was later presented by Fluhrer [22] and extended by Băetu et al. [5].

However, the aforementioned attacks all use specially crafted ciphertexts and can therefore be prevented with a transformation that achieves chosen ciphertext security. This can for example be obtained by means of an off-the-shelf compiler [23,28] that stops the adversary from being able to freely malleate honestly generated ciphertexts.

The NIST Post-Quantum Standardization Process candidate Kyber [8] noted that it was possible to search for ciphertexts with higher failure probability than average. D'Anvers et al. [16] extended this idea to an attack called "failure boosting", where ciphertexts with higher failure probability are generated to speedup the search for decryption failures, and provided an analysis of the effectiveness of the attack on several NIST candidates. At the same time, Guo et al. [27] described an adaptive attack against the IND-CCA secure ss-ntru-pke variant of NTRUEncrypt [10], which used an adaptive search for decryption failures exploiting information from previously collected ciphertexts.

Our Contributions. In this paper, we present a novel attack technique called "*directional* failure boosting", aimed at enhancing the search for decryption failures in public-key encryption schemes based on the protocol by

Lyubashevsky et al. [37], in the single-target setting. Our technique is an improvement of the "failure boosting" technique of D'Anvers et al. [16].

We consider a simple (but realistically parametrized) scheme based on the Mod-LWE problem as a case study and make some necessary orthogonality and independance assumptions that are reasonable in our range of parameters. We show that in this setting, the work and number of decryption queries needed to obtain multiple failing ciphertexts is only marginally larger than those necessary to obtain the first decryption failure. For example, obtaining 30 decryption failures requires only 25% more quantum work and only 58% more queries than obtaining one decryption failure. As previously shown in [16] and [27], we recall that having many decryption failures enables more efficient lattice reduction which leads to key recovery attacks. As a result, we conclude that when protecting against decryption failure attacks, in the single target setting, designers should make sure that an adversary can not feasibly obtain even a single decryption failure.

Our attack outperforms previously proposed attacks based on decryption failures. In particular, it improves over the multitarget attack of Guo et al. [27] on ss-ntru-pke, lowering the attack's quantum complexity from $2^{139.5}$ to $2^{96.6}$.

Paper Outline. In Sect. 2, we introduce some preliminaries about notation and structures. In Sect. 3, we describe the general idea of lattice-based encryption and how decryption failures are generated. In Sect. 4, we recall the original failure boosting technique from [12]. In Sect. 5, we describe our directional failure boosting technique. In Sect. 6, we show[1] how this method impacts the total work and queries overhead. Finally in Sect. 7, we discuss the results by comparing them with the literature and conclude with possible future work.

2 Preliminaries

Let $\mathbb{Z}_q$ be the ring of integers modulo q. For N a power of 2, we define R_q the ring $\mathbb{Z}_q[X]/(X^N+1)$, and $R_q^{l_1 \times l_2}$ the ring of $l_1 \times l_2$ matrices over R_q. Vectors and polynomials will be indicated with bold lowercase letters, eg. $\mathbf{v}$, while matrices will be written in bold uppercase letters, eg. $\mathbf{M}$. Denote with $\lfloor \cdot \rfloor$ flooring to the nearest lower integer, and with $\lfloor \cdot \rceil$ rounding to the nearest integer. These operations are extended coefficient-wise for vectors and polynomials. Throughout, we abuse notation and identify elements in $\mathbb{Z}_q$ with their representatives in $[-q/2, q/2)$, and elements in R_q with their representatives of degree $< N$, with index i indicating the coefficient of X^i. This allows us to define the ℓ_2-norm $\|\mathbf{x}\|_2$ of a polynomial $\mathbf{x} \in R_q$, so that $\|\mathbf{x}\|_2 = \sqrt{\sum_i \mathbf{x}_i^2}$ where $\mathbf{x}_i \in [-q/2, q/2)$, and extend this to vectors of polynomials $\mathbf{y} \in R_q^{l \times 1}$ as $\|\mathbf{y}\|_2 = \sqrt{\sum_i \|\mathbf{y}_i\|_2^2}$. Identically, we define and extend the ℓ_∞-norm.

Let $x \leftarrow X$ denote sampling x according to the probability distribution X. We extend this notation for coefficient-wise sampling of a vector $\mathbf{x} \in R_q^{l \times 1}$ as $\mathbf{x} \leftarrow$

---

[1] The software is available at: https://github.com/KULeuven-COSIC/PQCRYPTO-decryption-failures.

$X(R_q^{l \times 1})$, and similarly for a matrix. We denote with $\mathbf{x} \leftarrow X(R_q^{l \times 1}; r)$ sampling $\mathbf{x} \in R_q^{l \times 1}$ pseudorandomly from the seed r with each coefficient following the distribution X. In algorithms, we also use $x \leftarrow Alg()$ to mean that the value x is assigned to be the output of a probabilistic algorithm Alg.

Let $\mathcal{U}$ be the uniform distribution over $\mathbb{Z}_q$ and let $\mathcal{N}_{\mu,\sigma}$ be the normal distribution with mean μ and standard deviation σ, so that the probability density function of $x \leftarrow \mathcal{N}_{\mu,\sigma}$ is defined as:

$$f_{\mathcal{N}_{\mu,\sigma}}(x) = \frac{1}{\sigma\sqrt{2\pi}} e^{-(x-\mu)^2/2\sigma^2}. \tag{1}$$

The discrete Gaussian distribution $\mathcal{D}_{\mu,\sigma}$ is a discrete restriction to $\mathbb{Z}_q$ of $\mathcal{N}_{\mu,\sigma}$, so that an integer x is sampled with a probability proportional to $e^{-(x-\mu)^2/2\sigma^2}$ and its remainder modulo q in $[-q/2, q/2)$ is returned.

For an event A we define $P[A]$ as its probability. For an element which does not correspond to an event, a ciphertext ct for example, we abusively write $P[ct]$ to denote the probability of the event $ct' = ct$ where ct' is drawn from a distribution which will be clear in the context. We will denote with $\mathbb{E}[A]$ the expected value of a variable drawn from a distribution A.

Security Definitions. Let $\Pi = (\mathsf{KeyGen}, \mathsf{Enc}, \mathsf{Dec})$ be a public-key encryption scheme, with message space $\mathcal{M}$, and let $K = (\mathsf{KeyGen}, \mathsf{Encaps}, \mathsf{Decaps})$ be a key encapsulation mechanism (KEM). When a decapsulation or a decryption oracle is provided, we assume that the maximum number of ciphertexts that can be queried to it for each key pair is 2^K; in practice, $K = 64$ is often considered [40, §4.A.2]. In this work, we keep the maximum number of queries as a parameter with no specific value, in order to provide a better granularity in the security assessement. Indeed, to mount an attack, the adversary trades off between number of queries and the work.

Definition 1 (IND-CPA$_{A,\Pi}(k)$ game [33]). *Let A be an adversary and $\Pi = (\mathsf{KeyGen}, \mathsf{Enc}, \mathsf{Dec})$ be a public-key encryption scheme. The experiment IND-CPA$_{A,\Pi}(1^k)$ runs as follows:*

1. $(pk, sk) \leftarrow \mathsf{KeyGen}(1^k)$
2. *A is given pk. After evaluating $\mathsf{Enc}(pk, \cdot)$ as desired, it outputs $(m_0, m_1) \in \mathcal{M} \times \mathcal{M}$.*
3. *A random bit $b \leftarrow_\$ \{0, 1\}$ is sampled, and $c \leftarrow \mathsf{Enc}(pk, m_b)$ is passed to A.*
4. *A keeps evaluating $\mathsf{Enc}(pk, \cdot)$ as desired, until it returns a bit b'.*
5. *The experiment outputs 1 if $b = b'$ and 0 otherwise.*

Definition 2 (IND-CCA$_{A,K}(k)$ game [33]). *Let A be an adversary and $K = (\mathsf{KeyGen}, \mathsf{Encaps}, \mathsf{Decaps})$ be a key encapsulation mechanism. The experiment IND-CCA$_{A,K}(1^k)$ runs as follows:*

1. $(pk, sk) \leftarrow \mathsf{KeyGen}(1^k)$
2. $(c, k) \leftarrow \mathsf{Encaps}(pk)$
3. *$b \leftarrow_\$ \{0, 1\}$. If $b = 0$, set $\hat{k} = k$, else let $\hat{k} \leftarrow \{0, 1\}^n$.*

4. *A is given* $(pk, c, \hat{k})$, *and access to a decapsulation oracle* Decaps$(sk, \cdot)$. *After evaluating* Encaps$(pk, \cdot)$ *and querying* Decaps$(sk, \cdot)$ *as desired (except for decapsulation queries on c), it returns* $b' \in \{0, 1\}$.
5. *The experiment outputs 1 if* $b = b'$ *and 0 otherwise.*

Definition 3 (PKE and KEM security [23]). *A public-key encryption scheme* Π *(resp. a key encapsulation mechanism K) is* (t, ϵ)-*GAME secure if for every t-time adversary A, we have that*

$$\left| \Pr[GAME_{A,\Pi}(k) = 1] - \frac{1}{2} \right| \leq \epsilon \quad \left(resp. \left| \Pr[GAME_{A,K}(k) = 1] - \frac{1}{2} \right| \leq \epsilon \right)$$

For a security parameter 1^k, *we usually mean* $t \approx poly(k)$ *and* $\epsilon \leq negl(k)$. *If GAME is IND-CPA (resp. IND-CCA) we say that* Π *(resp. K) is* (t, ϵ)-*secure against chosen-plaintext attacks (resp.* (t, ϵ)-*secure against adaptive chosen-ciphertext attacks).*

3 Lattice-Based Encryption

The Module-LWE (or Mod-LWE) problem [34] is a mathematical problem that can be used to build cryptographic primitives such as encryption [7,13], key exchange [13] and signatures [20]. It is a generalization of both the Learning With Errors (or LWE) problem [43], and the Ring-LWE problem [37,47].

Definition 4 (Mod-LWE [34]). *Let* n, q, k *be positive integers,* χ *be a probability distribution on* $\mathbb{Z}$ *and* $\mathbf{s}$ *be a secret module element in* R_q^k. *We denote by* $\mathcal{L}$ *the probability distribution on* $R_q^k \times R_q$ *obtained by choosing* $\mathbf{a} \in R_q^k$ *uniformly at random, choosing* $e \in R$ *by sampling each of its coefficients according to* χ *and considering it in* R_q, *and returning* $(\mathbf{a}, c) = (\mathbf{a}, \langle \mathbf{a}, \mathbf{s} \rangle + e) \in R_q^k \times R_q$.
Decision-Mod-LWE is the problem of deciding whether pairs $(\mathbf{a}, c) \in R_q^k \times R_q$ *are sampled according to* $\mathcal{L}$ *or the uniform distribution on* $R_q^k \times R_q$.
Search-Mod-LWE is the problem of recovering $\mathbf{s}$ *from* $(\mathbf{a}, c) = (\mathbf{a}, \langle \mathbf{a}, \mathbf{s} \rangle + e) \in R_q^k \times R_q$ *sampled according to* $\mathcal{L}$.

3.1 Passively and Actively Secure Encryption

Lyubashevsky et al. [37] introduced a simple protocol to build passively secure encryption from the Ring-LWE problem, inspired by Diffie-Hellman key exchange [19] and ElGamal public-key encryption [21]. Naturally, the protocol can also be adapted to work based on plain and Module LWE assumptions. A general extension of the protocol for all aforementioned assumptions is described in Algorithms 1, 2, and 3, where $r \in \mathcal{R} = \{0, 1\}^{256}$, and where the message space is defined as $\mathcal{M} = \{$polynomials in R_q with coefficients in $\{0, 1\}\}$.

In order to obtain active security, designers usually use an off-the-shelf CCA compiler, usually a (post-quantum) variant [18,28,31,44,48] of the Fujisaki-Okamoto transform [23] (FO). These come with proofs of security in the

Algorithm 1: PKE.KeyGen()	**Algorithm 2:** PKE.Enc$(pk =$ $(\mathbf{b}, \mathbf{A}), \mathbf{m} \in \mathcal{M}; r)$
1 $\mathbf{A} \leftarrow \mathcal{U}(R_q^{l \times l})$ 2 $\mathbf{s}, \mathbf{e} \leftarrow \mathcal{D}_{0,\sigma_s}(R_q^{l \times 1}) \times \mathcal{D}_{0,\sigma_e}(R_q^{l \times 1})$ 3 $\mathbf{b} := \mathbf{As} + \mathbf{e}$ 4 **return** $(pk = (\mathbf{b}, \mathbf{A}), sk = \mathbf{s})$	1 $\mathbf{s}', \mathbf{e}' \leftarrow \mathcal{D}_{0,\sigma_s}(R_q^{l \times 1}; r) \times \mathcal{D}_{0,\sigma_e}(R_q^{l \times 1}; r)$ 2 $\mathbf{e}'' \leftarrow \mathcal{D}_{0,\sigma_e}(R_q; r)$ 3 $\mathbf{b}' := \mathbf{A}^T \mathbf{s}' + \mathbf{e}'$ 4 $\mathbf{v}' := \mathbf{b}^T \mathbf{s}' + \mathbf{e}'' + \lfloor q/2 \rfloor \cdot \mathbf{m}$ 5 **return** $ct = (\mathbf{v}', \mathbf{b}')$

Algorithm 3: PKE.Dec$(sk = \mathbf{s}, ct = (\mathbf{v}', \mathbf{b}'))$
1 $\mathbf{m}' := \lfloor \lfloor 2/q \rfloor (\mathbf{v}' - \mathbf{b}'^T \mathbf{s}) \rceil$ 2 **return** $\mathbf{m}'$

Algorithm 4: KEM.Encaps(pk)
1 $m \leftarrow \mathcal{U}(\{0,1\}^{256})$ 2 $(\overline{K}, r) := \mathcal{G}(pk, m)$ 3 $ct := $ PKE.Enc(pk, m, r) 4 $K := \mathcal{H}(\overline{K}, r)$ 5 **return** (ct, K)

(quantum) random oracle model, with explicit bounds about the loss of security caused by the transformation. We show such transformed KEM Decapsulation and Encapsulation in Algorithms 4 and 5.

In the case of FO for lattice-based schemes, the randomness used during the encryption is generated by submitting the message (and sometimes also the public key) to a random oracle. As this procedure is repeatable with knowledge of the message, one can check the validity of ciphertexts during decapsulation. Hence, an adversary wanting to generate custom ephemeral secrets $\mathbf{s}', \mathbf{e}', \mathbf{e}''$ in order to fabricate weak ciphertexts, would need to know a preimage of the appropriate random coins for the random oracle. Therefore, their only option is to mount a (Grover's) search by randomly generating ciphertexts corresponding to different messages $\mathbf{m}$, and testing if their predicted failure probability is above a certain threshold.

Remark 1. Several lattice-based candidates submitted to the NIST Post-Quantum Cryptography Standardization Process use a variant of the protocol by Lyubashevsky et al. [37]. Deviating from the original design, most candidates perform an additional rounding of the ciphertext $\mathbf{v}'$, in order to reduce bandwidth. The designers of New Hope [3] and LAC [35] choose to work directly over rings (or equivalently, they choose a module of rank $l = 1$) and add error correction on the encapsulated message, while the designers of Kyber [7] and Saber [13] choose a module of rank $l > 1$ and perform an additional rounding of $\mathbf{b}'$ (and $\mathbf{b}$ in case of Saber). We here focus on the basic version given in Algorithms 1 to 3 and leave the study of the effect of compression to further work.

Algorithm 5: KEM.Decaps(sk, pk, ct, K)

1 $m' := \text{PKE.Dec}(sk, ct)$
2 $(\overline{K}, r') := \mathcal{G}(pk, m')$
3 $ct' := \text{PKE.Enc}(pk, m'; r')$
4 **if** $ct = ct'$ **then**
5 $\quad$ **return** $K := (\overline{K}, r')$
6 **else**
7 $\quad$ **return** $K := \perp$ // Could return a pseudo-random string to
$\qquad$ implicitly reject

Table 1. Comparison between our target scheme and Saber and Kyber 768, as parametrised in Round 2 of the NIST PQC standardization process. The classical (resp. quantum) security is evaluated using the Core-SVP [3] methodology, assuming the cost of BKZ with block size β to be $2^{0.292\beta}$ (resp. $2^{0.265\beta}$).

	l	N	q	σ_s	σ_e	$P[F]$	Classical	Quantum
Chosen parameters	3	256	8192	2.00	2.00	2^{-119}	2^{195}	2^{177}
Saber	3	256	8192	1.41	2.29	2^{-136}	2^{203}	2^{185}
Kyber 768	3	256	3329	1.00	1.00/1.38[†]	2^{-164}	2^{181}	2^{164}

[†]Standard deviation of the error term in the public key and ciphertext respectively

We selected the parameters of the studied encryption scheme to ensure a similar failure probability and security to Kyber and Saber. These parameters can be found in Table 1. The security estimates are generated using the Core-SVP methodology [3] and the LWE estimator[2] [2], while the failure probability of Kyber and Saber is given as reported in their respective the NIST round 2 documentations [14,46]. The failure probability of our chosen parameters is determined by calculating the variance of the error term and assuming the distribution to be Gaussian.

Remark 2. We do not consider the case of "plain" LWE based schemes like FrodoKEM [39] or Round5 [4]. Nonetheless, we believe that the attack methodology would easily translate to the LWE setting as the failure condition and failure probabilities are similar to the investigated case.

3.2 Decryption Failures

Following the execution of the protocol, both messages $\mathbf{m}'$ and $\mathbf{m}$ are the same if the coefficients of the error term $\mathbf{e}^T\mathbf{s}' - \mathbf{s}^T\mathbf{e}' + \mathbf{e}''$ are small enough; more exactly if $\|\mathbf{e}^T\mathbf{s}' - \mathbf{s}^T\mathbf{e}' + \mathbf{e}''\|_\infty \leq q/4$. This expression can be simplified by defining the vector $\mathbf{S}$ as the vertical concatenation of $-\mathbf{s}$ and $\mathbf{e}$, the vector $\mathbf{C}$ as the concatenation of $\mathbf{e}'$ and $\mathbf{s}'$, and by replacing $\mathbf{e}''$ with $\mathbf{G}$, as shown below:

---

[2] The estimator can be found at https://bitbucket.org/malb/lwe-estimator.

$$S = \begin{bmatrix} -s \\ e \end{bmatrix} \quad C = \begin{bmatrix} e' \\ s' \end{bmatrix} \quad G = e''. \tag{2}$$

Here, S contains the secret elements of the secret key, and C and G consist of elements used to construct the ciphertexts[3]. Using these vectors, the error expression can be rewritten: a failure occurs when $\|S^T C + G\|_\infty > q/4$.

The standard deviation of the terms in the polynomial $S^T C$ equals $\sqrt{2N}\sigma_s\sigma_e$, versus a standard deviation of σ_e for the terms of G. Therefore, the influence of G on the failure rate is limited, i.e. $\|S^T C + G\|_\infty \approx \|S^T C\|_\infty$. Let $q_t := q/4$ denote the failure threshold, we will use

$$\|S^T C\|_\infty > q_t \tag{3}$$

as an approximation of the failure expression throughout our analysis. However, with some extra work, one can rewrite a more accurate Eq. 3 as $\|S^T C\|_\infty > q_t - \|G\|_\infty$, and instead of considering q_t to be fixed, taking the distribution of $q_t - \|G\|_\infty$ as shown in [16]. For the ease of the implementation and due to the low influence of G on the failure rate, we prefer to stick with Eq. 3. We now introduce a more handy way of writing the failure condition (Eq. 3) by only using vectors in $\mathbb{Z}_q$.

Definition 5 (Coefficient vector). *For $S \in R_q^{l \times 1}$, we denote by $\overline{S} \in \mathbb{Z}_q^{lN \times 1}$, the representation of S where each polynomial is decomposed as a list of its coefficients in[4] $\mathbb{Z}_q$.*

Definition 6 (Rotations). *For $r \in \mathbb{Z}$ and $C \in R_q^{l \times 1}$, we denote by $C^{(r)} \in R_q^{l \times 1}$, the following vector of polynomials*

$$C^{(r)} := X^r \cdot C(X^{-1}) \mod X^N + 1.$$

Correspondingly, $\overline{C^{(r)}} \in \mathbb{Z}_q^{lN \times 1}$ denotes its coefficient vector.

It is easy to show that $\overline{C^{(r)}}$ is constructed as to ensure that for $r \in [0, ..., N - 1]$, the rth coordinate of $S^T C$ is given by the scalar product $\overline{S}^T \overline{C^{(r)}}$. In other words, one is now able to decompose $S^T C$ as a sum of scalar products:

$$S^T C = \sum_{r \in [0, N-1]} \overline{S}^T \overline{C^{(r)}} \cdot X^r. \tag{4}$$

One can observe that this construction is only valid for the modulo $X^N + 1$ ring structure, but it could be adapted for other ring structures. Note that for any $r \in \mathbb{Z}$, $C^{(r+N)} = -C^{(r)}$ and $C^{(r+2N)} = C^{(r)}$. Besides, taking into account the extension of the norms to vectors of polynomials (defined in Sect. 2), one can make the following remark.

---

[3] When talking about ciphertexts throughout the paper, we will sometimes refer to their underlying elements C and G.

[4] Recall that, in this paper, all the elements in $\mathbb{Z}_q$ are represented as integers belonging in $[-q/2, q/2]$.

Remark 3. Note that for any $r \in \mathbb{Z}$, $\|\overline{\mathbf{C}^{(r)}}\|_2 = \|\overline{\mathbf{C}}\|_2 = \|\mathbf{C}\|_2$ and $\|\overline{\mathbf{C}^{(r)}}\|_\infty = \|\overline{\mathbf{C}}\|_\infty = \|\mathbf{C}\|_\infty$.

The decomposition in Eq. 4 will allow a geometric interpretation of the failures as it will be shown in the rest of the paper. First, let us introduce a brief example to illustrate Definitions 5 and 6.

Example 1. For a secret $\mathbf{S}$ and a ciphertext $\mathbf{C}$ in $\mathbb{Z}_q^{2\times1}[X]/(X^3+1)$:

$$\mathbf{S} = \begin{bmatrix} s_{0,0} + s_{0,1}X + s_{0,2}X^2 \\ s_{1,0} + s_{1,1}X + s_{1,2}X^2 \end{bmatrix}, \quad \mathbf{C} = \begin{bmatrix} c_{0,0} + c_{0,1}X + c_{0,2}X^2 \\ c_{1,0} + c_{1,1}X + c_{1,2}X^2 \end{bmatrix} \tag{5}$$

we get the following vectors:

$$\overline{\mathbf{S}} = \begin{bmatrix} s_{0,0} \\ s_{0,1} \\ s_{0,2} \\ s_{1,0} \\ s_{1,1} \\ s_{1,2} \end{bmatrix}, \quad \overline{\mathbf{C}^{(0)}} = \begin{bmatrix} c_{0,0} \\ -c_{0,2} \\ -c_{0,1} \\ c_{1,0} \\ -c_{1,2} \\ -c_{1,1} \end{bmatrix} \quad \overline{\mathbf{C}^{(1)}} = \begin{bmatrix} c_{0,1} \\ c_{0,0} \\ -c_{0,2} \\ c_{1,1} \\ c_{1,0} \\ -c_{1,2} \end{bmatrix} \quad \overline{\mathbf{C}^{(2)}} = \begin{bmatrix} c_{0,2} \\ c_{0,1} \\ c_{0,0} \\ c_{1,2} \\ c_{1,1} \\ c_{1,0} \end{bmatrix} \quad \overline{\mathbf{C}^{(3)}} = \begin{bmatrix} -c_{0,0} \\ c_{0,2} \\ c_{0,1} \\ -c_{1,0} \\ c_{1,2} \\ c_{1,1} \end{bmatrix} \cdots$$

In case of a failure event, $\mathbf{S}^T\mathbf{C}$ satisfies Eq. 3. Therefore, at least one element among all the coefficients

$$\overline{\mathbf{S}}^T \cdot \overline{\mathbf{C}^{(0)}}, \ldots, \overline{\mathbf{S}}^T \cdot \overline{\mathbf{C}^{(2N-1)}}$$

is larger than q_t.

Definition 7 (Failure event). *A failure event will be denoted with F, while we use S to indicate a successful decryption.*
More precisely, for $r \in [0, 2N-1]$, we denote by F_r the failure event where

$$\overline{\mathbf{S}}^T \cdot \overline{\mathbf{C}^{(r)}} > q_t.$$

The event F_r gives a twofold information: it provides the location of the failure in the $\mathbf{S}^T\mathbf{C}$ polynomial and it also provides the sign of the coefficient that caused the failure.

An Assumption on the Failing Ciphertexts. In the rest of the paper, in order to predict the results of our attack, we will make the following orthogonality assumption.

Assumption 1. *Let $n \ll 2Nl$, and $\mathbf{C}_0, \cdots, \mathbf{C}_n$ be ciphertexts that lead to failure events $F_{r_0}, \cdots, F_{r_n}$. The vectors $\overline{\mathbf{C}_0^{(r_0)}}, \cdots, \overline{\mathbf{C}_n^{(r_n)}}$ are considered orthogonal when projected on the hyperplane orthogonal to $\overline{\mathbf{S}}$.*

This assumption is an approximation that is supported by the fact that vectors in high dimensional space have a strong tendency towards orthogonality, as can be seen in Fig. 2.

4   Failure Boosting Attack Technique

Failure boosting is a technique introduced in [16] to increase the failure rate of (Ring/Mod)-LWE/LWR based schemes by honestly generating ciphertexts and only querying weak ones, i.e. those that have a failure probability above a certain threshold $f_t > 0$. This technique is especially useful in combination with Grover's algorithm [26], in which case the search for weak ciphertexts can be sped up quadratically. Failure boosting consists of two phases: a precomputation phase, and a phase where the decryption oracle is queried.

Precomputation Phase. The adversary does an offline search for weak ciphertexts with the following procedure:

1. Generate a key encapsulation (see Footnote 3) $ct = (\mathbf{C}, \mathbf{G})$.
2. If $P[F \mid ct] \geq f_t$, keep ct in a weak ciphertext list, otherwise go to Step 1.

In Step 2, $P[F \mid ct]$ is defined as the failure probability given a certain ciphertext ct. It is computed as follows.

$$P[F \mid ct] := \sum_{\mathbf{S}} P\left[\|\mathbf{S}^T \mathbf{C} + \mathbf{G}\|_\infty > q_t \mid \mathbf{S} \right] \cdot P[\mathbf{S}] \tag{6}$$

Given the probability of generating ciphertexts $P[ct] = P[\mathbf{C}, \mathbf{G}]$, the probability of finding such a weak ciphertext can be expressed as follows:

$$\alpha_{f_t} = \sum_{\forall ct : P[F \mid ct] > f_t} P[ct]. \tag{7}$$

An adversary thus needs to perform on average $\alpha_{f_t}^{-1}$ work to obtain one weak ciphertext, or $\sqrt{\alpha_{f_t}^{-1}}$ assuming Grover's search achieves a full speed-up.

Decryption Oracle Query Phase. After the precomputation phase, an adversary has a probability β_{f_t} that a weak ciphertext results in a failure, where β_{f_t} can be calculated as a weighted average of the failure probabilities of weak ciphertexts:

$$\beta_{f_t} = \frac{\sum_{\forall ct : P[F \mid ct] > f_t} P[ct] \cdot P[F \mid ct]}{\sum_{\forall ct : P[F \mid ct] > f_t} P[ct]}. \tag{8}$$

Thus to obtain one decryption failure with probability $1 - e^{-1}$, an adversary needs to perform approximately $\beta_{f_t}^{-1}$ queries and therefore $\alpha_{f_t}^{-1} \beta_{f_t}^{-1}$ work (or $\sqrt{\alpha_{f_t}^{-1} \beta_{f_t}^{-1}}$ using a quantum computer).

The better an adversary can predict $P[F \mid ct]$, the more efficient failure boosting will be. Having no information about the secret except its distribution, an adversary is bound to standard failure boosting, where the failure probability is estimated based on $\|\mathbf{C}\|_2$ and $\|\mathbf{G}\|_2$. For a graphical intuition, a two dimensional toy example is depicted in Fig. 1a below, where the red arrow represents the secret vector $\overline{\mathbf{S}}$. Ciphertexts with $\overline{\mathbf{C}}$ that lie in the dashed area will provoke

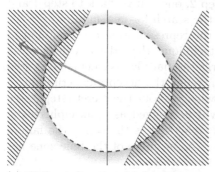 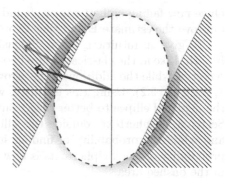

(a) Without directional information, as in [16], the weak ciphertexts (in blue) are defined as the ciphertexts with a probability higher than f_t.

(b) With directional information, the weak ciphertexts (in blue) are found according to a refined acceptance criterion, here represented as an ellipse.

Fig. 1. Simplified diagram trying to provide an intuition on the effect of directional failure boosting. The red arrow represents the secret vector $\overline{\mathbf{S}}$. Ciphertexts with $\overline{\mathbf{C}}$ that lie in the dashed area will provoke a failure as the inner product with $\overline{\mathbf{S}}$ will exceed the threshold q_t. Ciphertexts outside the blue circle are considered weak. (Color figure online)

a failure as the inner product with $\overline{\mathbf{S}}$ will exceed the threshold q_t. The blue circle is a circle of ciphertexts that have a certain failure probability f_t as estimated by an adversary who does not know the secret. During the failure boosting procedure, we will generate random ciphertexts, and only select the ciphertexts with a higher failure probability than f_t, i.e. that are outside the blue circle. One can graphically see in Fig. 1a that these ciphertexts will have a higher failure probability and a higher norm. We refer to [16] for a full description of the failure boosting technique. Note that Fig. 1a is an oversimplified 2-dimension example that does not take into account the polynomial structure and the high dimensionality of the space.

5   Directional Failure Boosting

Once $n \geq 1$ decryption failures $\mathbf{C}_0, \ldots, \mathbf{C}_{n-1}$ are found, additional information about the secret key $\mathbf{S}$ becomes available, and can be used to refine the failure estimation for new ciphertexts and thus speed up failure boosting. We now introduce an iterative two-step method to perform directional failure boosting.

Step 1. An estimate, denoted $\overline{\mathbf{E}}$, of the 'direction' of the secret $\overline{\mathbf{S}}$ in $\mathbb{Z}_q^{lN}$ is obtained from $\mathbf{C}_0, \ldots, \mathbf{C}_{n-1}$.

Step 2. The estimate $\overline{\mathbf{E}}$ is used to inform the search for weak ciphertexts and improve the failure probability prediction for a new ciphertext $\mathbf{C}_n$. One is able to refine the criterion $P[F \mid ct] \geq f_t$ with computing $P[F \mid ct, \overline{\mathbf{E}}] \geq f_t$ instead.

Once new failing ciphertexts are found in step 2, one can go back to step 1 and improve the estimate $\overline{\mathbf{E}}$ and thus bootstrap the search for new failures.

To give an intuition, a two dimensional toy representation can be found in Fig. 1b. Like in the classical failure boosting technique, the red arrow depicts the secret $\overline{\mathbf{S}}$, while the additional blue arrow marks estimate $\overline{\mathbf{E}}$ (as calculated in step 1, see Sect. 5.2). Using this estimate, we can refine the acceptance criterion to the depicted ellipse to better reflect our knowledge about the secret (step 2, see Sect. 5.3). Ciphertexts outside this ellipse will be flagged as weak ciphertexts, and while the probability of finding such a ciphertext is the same, the failure probability of weak ciphertexts is now higher. As in, more of the blue zone lies in the dashed area.

5.1 Distributions

We now introduce some probability distributions that will be useful in following sections.

Scaled χ-distribution. The scaled χ-distribution $\chi_{n,\sigma}$ is the distribution of the ℓ_2-norm of a vector with n coefficients, each following the normal distribution $\mathcal{N}_{0,\sigma}$. Denoting with Γ the gamma function, the probability density function of $\chi_{n,\sigma}$ is given by:

$$f_{\chi_{n,\sigma}}(x) = \frac{\left(\frac{x}{\sigma}\right)^{n-1} e^{-\frac{x^2}{2\sigma^2}}}{2^{\left(\frac{n}{2}-1\right)} \Gamma\left(\frac{n}{2}\right)} \quad \text{for } x \geq 0, \tag{9}$$

which has mean [32, §18.3] $\mathbb{E}_\chi[x] = \sqrt{2}\frac{\Gamma((n+1)/2)}{\Gamma(n/2)}\sigma \approx \sqrt{n}\sigma$.

We will approximate the probability distribution of $\|\mathbf{x}\|_2$ where $\mathbf{x} \leftarrow \mathcal{D}_{0,\sigma}(R_q^{l \times 1})$ with a discretized version of the $\chi_{(l \cdot N),\sigma}$-distribution, which will be denoted with $\chi_{(l \cdot N),\sigma}^D$. Using this distribution, the probability density function of $\|\mathbf{x}\|_2$ is calculated as:

$$P[\|\mathbf{x}\|_2 = x] = C \cdot \left(\frac{x}{\sigma}\right)^{l \cdot N - 1} e^{-\frac{x^2}{2\sigma^2}} \quad \text{for } x \in \left\{0, \ldots, \left\lfloor \frac{q}{2}\sqrt{lN} \right\rfloor\right\}, \tag{10}$$

with C a normalization constant.

Angle Distribution. The distribution of angles between n-dimensional vectors in $\mathbb{R}^n$ with coefficients drawn from a normal distribution $\mathcal{N}_{0,\sigma}$ can be modelled using the following probability density function [9]:

$$f_{\Theta_n}(\theta) = \sin^{n-2}(\theta) / \int_0^\pi \sin^{n-2}(t)dt, \quad \text{for } \theta \in [0, \pi]. \tag{11}$$

Due to the high dimensionality of the vector space used in this paper, vectors will have a very strong tendency towards orthogonality, i.e. θ is close to $\pi/2$, as can be seen in Fig. 2.

For computational reasons, we will use a discretized version Θ_n^D of this distribution to model the distribution of the angles between discrete vectors, if no

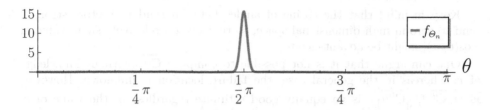

Fig. 2. Probability density function (pdf) of the angle between two random vectors in 1536-dimensional space. As the dimension increases, the pdf tends to the Dirac delta function centered at $\frac{\pi}{2}$.

extra directional information is present. Given a uniformly spaced list of angles between 0 and π, we assign to each angle a probability

$$P[\theta] = C \sin^{n-2}(\theta) \tag{12}$$

with C a normalization constant. The higher the number of angles in this list, the better this distribution approximates the continuous distribution Θ_n.

Order Statistics. The maximal order statistic of a distribution X in n dimensions, is the distribution of the maximum of n samples drawn from this distribution. We will denote this distribution with $M(X, n)$. For a discrete distribution X, the probability mass function of $M(X, n)$ can be computed as:

$$f_{M(X,n)}(x) = P[x \geq y | y \leftarrow X]^n - P[x > y | y \leftarrow X]^n \tag{13}$$
$$\approx n \cdot P[x = y | y \leftarrow X] \cdot P[x > y | y \leftarrow X]^{n-1}, \tag{14}$$

where the latter approximation gets better for smaller probabilities.

5.2 Step 1: Estimating the Direction $\overline{\mathbf{E}}$

Informally, $\overline{\mathbf{E}}$ should be a vector that has approximately the same direction as $\overline{\mathbf{S}}$. Denoting the angle between $\overline{\mathbf{E}}$ and $\overline{\mathbf{S}}$ as θ_{ES}, the bigger $|\cos(\theta_{ES})|$, the closer our estimate is to $\pm\overline{\mathbf{S}}$ and the better our estimate of failure probability will be. Since we focus on estimating the direction of $\overline{\mathbf{S}}$, $\overline{\mathbf{E}}$ will always be normalized.

In this section, we derive an estimate $\overline{\mathbf{E}}$ of the direction of the secret $\overline{\mathbf{S}}$ given $n \geq 1$ ciphertexts $\mathbf{C}_0, \ldots, \mathbf{C}_{n-1}$. Our goal is to find $\overline{\mathbf{E}}$ such that $|\cos(\theta_{ES})|$ is as big as possible. We will first discuss the case where the adversary has one ciphertext, then the case where she has two, followed by the more general case where she has n ciphertexts.

One Ciphertext. Assume that a unique failing ciphertext $\mathbf{C}$ is given. For a failure event F_r, $\overline{\mathbf{E}} = \overline{\mathbf{C}^{(r)}} / \left\| \overline{\mathbf{C}^{(r)}} \right\|_2$ is a reasonable choice as $\cos(\theta_{ES})$ is bigger than average. This can be seen as follows:

$$|\cos(\theta_{ES})| = \frac{|\overline{\mathbf{S}}^T \cdot \overline{\mathbf{E}}|}{\|\overline{\mathbf{S}}\|_2 \|\overline{\mathbf{E}}\|_2} = \frac{|\overline{\mathbf{S}}^T \cdot \overline{\mathbf{C}^{(r)}}|}{\|\overline{\mathbf{S}}\|_2 \left\| \overline{\mathbf{C}^{(r)}} \right\|_2} > \frac{q_t}{\|\overline{\mathbf{S}}\|_2 \left\| \overline{\mathbf{C}^{(r)}} \right\|_2}. \tag{15}$$

Keep in mind that the cosine of angles between random vectors strongly tend to zero in high dimensional space, so that even a relatively small value of $|\cos(\theta_{ES})|$ might be advantageous.

One can argue that it is not possible to compute $\overline{\mathbf{C}^{(r)}}$ without knowledge of r; whereas in the general case, the failure location is unknown. However, $\overline{\mathbf{E}} = \overline{\mathbf{C}^{(0)}}/\left\|\overline{\mathbf{C}^{(0)}}\right\|_2$ is an equally good estimate regardless of the value of r. Indeed, $\overline{\mathbf{C}^{(0)}}$ approximates a rotation of the secret $\overline{\mathbf{S}'} := \overline{X^{-r} \cdot \mathbf{S}}$ instead of $\overline{\mathbf{S}}$, which can be seen using the equality $\overline{\mathbf{A}}^T \cdot \overline{\mathbf{B}} = \overline{X^i \mathbf{A}}^T \cdot \overline{X^i \mathbf{B}}$:

$$\overline{\mathbf{S}}^T \cdot \overline{\mathbf{C}^{(r)}} = \overline{X^{-r} \cdot \mathbf{S}}^T \cdot \overline{X^{-r} X^r \mathbf{C}^{(0)}}$$
$$= \overline{X^{-r} \cdot \mathbf{S}}^T \cdot \overline{\mathbf{C}^{(0)}}. \tag{16}$$

Furthermore, multiplicating a polynomial in R_q with a power of X does not change its infinity norm, as the multiplication only results in the rotation or negation of coefficients. Thus, using an estimate of the direction of $\overline{X^{-r} \cdot \mathbf{S}}$ is as good as an estimate of the direction of $\overline{\mathbf{S}}$ when predicting the failure probability of ciphertexts, and we can use $\overline{\mathbf{E}} = \overline{\mathbf{C}^{(0)}}/\left\|\overline{\mathbf{C}^{(0)}}\right\|_2$.

Two Ciphertexts. Now, assume that two linearly independent failing ciphertexts $\mathbf{C}_0$ and $\mathbf{C}_1$, resulting from failure events F_{r_0} and F_{r_1} respectively, are given. Taking $\overline{\mathbf{E}}$ as the normalized version of an average $\overline{\mathbf{C}}_{av} = \left(\overline{\mathbf{C}_0^{(0)}} + \overline{\mathbf{C}_1^{(0)}}\right)/2$ may not necessarily result in a good estimate. For example, if $\mathbf{C}_0$ comes from a failure event F_0 and $\mathbf{C}_1$ from a failure event F_N, the two directions cancel each other out as the ciphertexts $\overline{\mathbf{C}_0^{(0)}}$ and $\overline{\mathbf{C}_1^{(0)}}$ are in opposite directions.

Keeping the convention that $\overline{\mathbf{C}_0^{(0)}}$ approximates a rotation of the secret $\overline{\mathbf{S}'} = \overline{X^{-r_0} \cdot \mathbf{S}}$, we will compute the relative error position $\delta_{1,0} = r_1 - r_0$ and show that is enough to build a correct estimate $\overline{\mathbf{E}}$ as $\overline{\mathbf{E}} = \overline{\mathbf{C}_{rav}}/\left\|\overline{\mathbf{C}_{rav}}\right\|_2$ where:

$$\overline{\mathbf{C}_{rav}} := \left(\overline{\mathbf{C}_0^{(0)}} + \overline{\mathbf{C}_1^{(\delta_{1,0})}}\right)/2. \tag{17}$$

The reason why such $\overline{\mathbf{E}}$ is a good estimator of $\overline{\mathbf{S}'}$ can be seen as follows:

$$\cos(\theta_{ES'}) = \frac{1}{2\left\|\overline{\mathbf{C}_{rav}}\right\|_2 \left\|\overline{\mathbf{S}'}\right\|_2} \cdot \left(\overline{X^{-r_0} \cdot \mathbf{S}}^T \cdot \overline{\mathbf{C}_0^{(0)}} + \overline{X^{-r_0} \cdot \mathbf{S}}^T \cdot \overline{X^{r_1 - r_0} \mathbf{C}_1^{(0)}}\right)$$
$$= \frac{1}{2\left\|\overline{\mathbf{C}_{rav}}\right\|_2 \left\|\overline{\mathbf{S}'}\right\|_2} \cdot \left(\overline{\mathbf{S}}^T \cdot \overline{\mathbf{C}_0^{(r_0)}} + \overline{\mathbf{S}}^T \cdot \overline{\mathbf{C}_1^{(r_1)}}\right) > \frac{q_t}{\left\|\overline{\mathbf{C}_{rav}}\right\|_2 \left\|\overline{\mathbf{S}'}\right\|_2}.$$

Remark 4. In practice ciphertexts with smaller norm will on average be better aligned with the secret, as $\cos(\theta_{CS'}) > q_t/(\left\|\overline{\mathbf{C}}\right\|_2 \left\|\overline{\mathbf{S}'}\right\|_2)$. Therefore they carry more information than ciphertexts with larger norm. To compensate for this effect we will calculate $\overline{\mathbf{C}_{rav}}$ as $:= \left(\overline{\mathbf{C}_0^{(0)}}/\left\|\overline{\mathbf{C}_0^{(0)}}\right\|_2 + \overline{\mathbf{C}_1^{(\delta_{1,0})}}/\left\|\overline{\mathbf{C}_1^{(\delta_{1,0})}}\right\|_2\right)/2$.

While it is possible to further refine the calculation of $\overline{\mathbf{E}}$ using extra directional information, this heuristic is good enough for our purposes.

Computation of the Relative Position $\delta_{1,0}$. One can use the fact that both $\overline{\mathbf{C}_0^{(0)}}$ and $\overline{\mathbf{C}_1^{(\delta_{1,0})}}$ are expected to be directionally close to $\overline{\mathbf{S}'}$. Thus, the cosine of the angle between $\overline{\mathbf{C}_0^{(0)}}$ and $\overline{\mathbf{C}_1^{(\delta_{1,0})}}$ should be larger than usual. Therefore, $\delta_{1,0}$ can be estimated with the following distinguisher:

$$\delta'_{1,0} := \underset{r \in [0, 2N-1]}{\mathrm{argmax}} \, \mathcal{C}(r) \text{ where } \mathcal{C}(r) := \frac{\overline{\mathbf{C}_0^{(0)}}^T \cdot \overline{\mathbf{C}_1^{(r)}}}{\left\|\overline{\mathbf{C}_0^{(0)}}\right\|_2 \left\|\overline{\mathbf{C}_1^{(r)}}\right\|_2}. \tag{18}$$

The next paragraph estimates the efficiency of using Eq. 18 as a distinguisher for deriving $\delta_{1,0}$. We will show that, for Table 1 parameters, we expect

$$P[\delta'_{1,0} = \delta_{1,0}] \approx 89\%. \tag{19}$$

Experiments run by simulating the sampling 10^4 failing ciphertexts (refer to the full version of our paper [15] for the generation technique), and using Eq. 18 for finding $\delta_{1,0}$ between pairs of them, return $P_{\mathrm{Exp}}[\delta'_{1,0} = \delta_{1,0}] \approx 84.8\%$, in sufficiently good agreement.

To obtain the value (19), the idea is to estimate the distribution of a correct guess $\mathcal{C}(\delta_{1,0})$ and an incorrect guess $\max_{r \neq \delta_{1,0}} \mathcal{C}(r)$ and quantify the discrepancy. First, we decompose the ciphertexts in a component parallel to $\overline{\mathbf{S}'}$, denoted with $\parallel$, and a component orthogonal, denoted with $\perp$, we rewrite $\mathcal{C}(r)$ as follows:

$$\mathcal{C}(r) = \frac{\overline{\mathbf{C}_{0,\parallel}^{(0)}} \cdot \overline{\mathbf{C}_{1,\parallel}^{(r)}} + \overline{\mathbf{C}_{0,\perp}^{(0)}} \cdot \overline{\mathbf{C}_{1,\perp}^{(r)}}}{\left\|\overline{\mathbf{C}_0^{(0)}}\right\|_2 \left\|\overline{\mathbf{C}_1^{(r)}}\right\|_2} \tag{20}$$

In the first term, the scalar product of two parallel elements equals the product of their norms (up to their sign). For the second term, we apply the scalar product definition and intoduce t as the angle between $\overline{\mathbf{C}_{0,\perp}^{(0)}}$ and $\overline{\mathbf{C}_{1,\perp}^{(r)}}$.

$$\mathcal{C}(r) = \pm \frac{\left\|\overline{\mathbf{C}_{0,\parallel}^{(0)}}\right\|_2}{\left\|\overline{\mathbf{C}_0^{(0)}}\right\|_2} \cdot \frac{\left\|\overline{\mathbf{C}_{1,\parallel}^{(r)}}\right\|_2}{\left\|\overline{\mathbf{C}_1^{(r)}}\right\|_2} \pm \frac{\left\|\overline{\mathbf{C}_{0,\perp}^{(0)}}\right\|_2}{\left\|\overline{\mathbf{C}_0^{(0)}}\right\|_2} \cdot \frac{\left\|\overline{\mathbf{C}_{1,\perp}^{(r)}}\right\|_2}{\left\|\overline{\mathbf{C}_1^{(r)}}\right\|_2} \cdot \cos(t) \tag{21}$$

$$= \cos\left(\theta_{S'C_0^{(0)}}\right) \cos\left(\theta_{S'C_1^{(r)}}\right) + \sin\left(\theta_{S'C_0^{(0)}}\right) \sin\left(\theta_{S'C_1^{(r)}}\right) \cos(t) \tag{22}$$

The vectors $\overline{\mathbf{C}_{0,\perp}^{(0)}}$ and $\overline{\mathbf{C}_{1,\perp}^{(r)}}$ are orthogonal to $\overline{\mathbf{S}'}$. This means that they live in the $2Nl-1$ dimensional space orthogonal to $\overline{\mathbf{S}'}$. The high dimension of the space will strongly drive the vectors towards orthogonality as can be seen in Fig. 2. Using Assumption 1, the angle t between $\overline{\mathbf{C}_{0,\perp}^{(0)}}$ and $\overline{\mathbf{C}_{1,\perp}^{(r)}}$ is then assumed to follow the distribution of random angles between vectors in a $2Nl-1$ dimensional space (See Eq. 11).

Now, let us study the distribution of $\mathcal{C}(r)$ depending of the value $r \in [0, 2N-1]$. One can refer to Fig. 3 for a graphical interpretation based on the parameters of Table 1.

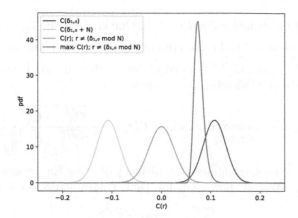

Fig. 3. Distributions used for finding $\delta_{1,0}$ (Color figure online)

- If $r = \delta_{1,0}$, the expected value of $\mathcal{C}(r)$ will be higher than average. Indeed, by definition of F_{r_1} and F_{r_0} the cosines forming the first term are positive. The distribution of $\mathcal{C}(r)$ can then be estimated using Eq. 22 (blue curve).
- If $r = \delta_{1,0} + N \mod 2N$, the distribution of $\mathcal{C}(r)$ is equal to the distribution of $-\mathcal{C}(\delta_{1,0})$ and will be closer to -1 (orange curve).
- If $r \neq \delta_{1,0} \mod N$, $\mathcal{C}(r)$ can be assumed to follow the distribution of random angles in a $2Nl$ dimensional space Θ_{2Nl}, as given in Eq. 11 (green curve).
- The pdf of $\max_{r \neq \delta_{1,0}} \mathcal{C}(r)$ is then calculated as $M(\Theta_{2Nl}, 2N - 1)$ by definition of the maximal order statistic (red curve).

Figure 3 assembles the probability density functions of the above distributions in a plot. The probability of selecting the correct $\delta'_{1,0}$ using $\underset{r \in [0, 2N-1]}{\operatorname{argmax}} \mathcal{C}(r)$, can then be computed as:

$$P[\delta'_{1,0} = \delta_{1,0}] = P\left[\max_{r \neq \delta_{1,0}} \mathcal{C}(r) < \mathcal{C}(\delta_{1,0})\right].$$

For our toy scheme's parameters, this results in Eq. 19.

Multiple Ciphertexts. In this section, we assume that n linearly independent failing ciphertexts $\mathbf{C}_0, \dots, \mathbf{C}_{n-1}$, resulting from failure events $F_{r_0}, \dots, F_{r_{n-1}}$ respectively, are given. We introduce a generalized method to recover the relative positions $\delta_{1,0}, \dots, \delta_{n-1,0}$, based on "loopy belief propagation" [41]. Once these relative positions are found, they can be combined in an estimate $\overline{\mathbf{E}}$ with $\overline{\mathbf{E}} = \overline{\mathbf{C}_{\text{rav}}} / \left\| \overline{\mathbf{C}_{\text{rav}}} \right\|_2$ where

$$\overline{\mathbf{C}_{\text{rav}}} := \left(\overline{\mathbf{C}_0^{(0)}} / \left\| \overline{\mathbf{C}_0^{(0)}} \right\|_2 + \sum_{i \in [1, n-1]} \overline{\mathbf{C}_i^{(\delta_{i,0})}} / \left\| \overline{\mathbf{C}_i^{(\delta_{i,0})}} \right\|_2 \right) / n. \tag{23}$$

To find the correct rotations, we construct a weighted graph that models the probability of different relative rotations, and we will use loopy belief propagation to obtain the most probable set of these rotations:

- The nodes represent the obtained failing ciphertexts: $(\mathbf{C}_i)_{i \in [0,n-1]}$. In total, there are n nodes.
- Each node $\mathbf{C}_i$ where $i \neq 0$ is associated a list with $2N$ probability values called *beliefs* and denoted $(b_i(0), \cdots, b_i(2N-1))$ that together define a probability distribution over $[0, 2N-1]$. The rth item in the list represents our belief that the correct relative position $\delta_{0,1}$ equals r. The correct rotation of the 0th node will be fixed to 0 (i.e. $b_0(0) = 1$ and $b_0(i) = 0$ for all other i) as only the relative rotations of the ciphertexts is important. These node weights are initialized as follows:

$$b_i(r) := P\left[\delta_{i,0} = r\right] \quad (= P\left[F_r \text{ for } \mathbf{C}_i | F_0 \text{ for } \mathbf{C}_0\right])$$

- For two nodes $\mathbf{C}_i$ and $\mathbf{C}_j$, the value of the vertex called *message*, models the influence of the beliefs in the rotations s of node j towards the beliefs in rotation r of node i, which can be formalized as follows:

$$m_{i,j}(r,s) := P\left[\delta_{i,j} = r - s\right] \quad (= P\left[F_{r-s} \text{ for } \mathbf{C}_i | F_0 \text{ for } \mathbf{C}_j\right])$$

Loopy belief propagation tries to find the node values r for each node, so that the probabilities over the whole graph are maximized. This is done in an iterative fashion by updating the node beliefs according to the messages coming from all other nodes. Our goal is eventually to find $r = \delta_{i,0}$ for each node i.

Example 2. For example, with $N = 3$ and $n = 3$, the graph contains the nodes $\mathbf{C}_0$, $\mathbf{C}_1$, and $\mathbf{C}_2$. In Fig. 4, we represent how such a graph could look like where we arbitrarly instantiate the messages and beliefs. We can see that if one chooses the $r_i = \text{argmax}_r b_i(r)$ for each node, one would have chosen $r_1 = 1$ and $r_2 = 3$. Nevertheless, we notice that the influence of the other probabilities allows for a better choice (underlined in blue in the figure): $r_1 = 2, r_2 = 3$.

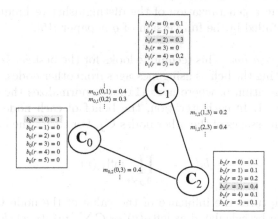

Fig. 4. Example of the graph for finding the relative rotations where $N = 3$ and $n = 3$. The beliefs are in the rectangles, the circles represent the nodes and some messages are represented between the nodes. (Color figure online)

Algorithm 6: GetRotation()

1 **for** $i \in [1, n-1]$ **do** // initialization
2   **foreach** r **do**
3         $\lfloor$ $b_i(r) := P[\delta_{0,i} = r]$

4 **for** # *of iterations* **do** // update phase
5   **for** $i \in [1, n)$ **do**
6   **for** $j \in [1, n)$ **if** $i \neq j$ **do**
7   **foreach** r **do**
8               $\lfloor$ $\mathsf{infl}_{ji}(r) := \sum_s m_{i,j}(r, s) \cdot b_j(s)$ // influence of node j on node i
9            $\lfloor$ normalize(infl_{ji})
10   **foreach** r **do**
11           $\lfloor$ $b_i(r) := \prod_{j=0, j \neq i}^n \mathsf{infl}_{ji}(r)$ // calculate new belief
12   normalize(b_i)

13 **for** $i \in [1, n)$ **do** // finally
14     $r_i := \operatorname{argmax}_{r \in [0, 2N-1]} b_i(r)$ // pick the r_i with highest belief
15 **return** $(r_i)_{i \in [1, n-1]}$

Table 2. Probability of finding the correct relative rotations and thus building the correct estimate $\overline{\mathbf{E}}$ with the knowledge of 2, 3, 4 and 5 failing ciphertexts.

	2 ciphertexts	3 ciphertexts	4 ciphertexts	5 ciphertexts
$P[r_i = \delta_{i,0} \ \forall i \in [1, n-1]]$	84.0%	95.6%	>99.0%	>99.0%

Vertex Probabilities. As discussed, the edge between two nodes $\mathbf{C}_i$ with rotation r and $\mathbf{C}_j$ with rotation s is weighted with $P[\delta_{i,j} = r - s]$. This probability can be computed using a generalization of the distinguisher technique used for two ciphertexts as detailed in the full version of our paper [15].

Loopy Belief Propagation. This technique looks for the best set $(r_1, \ldots, r_{n-1})$ by iteratively correcting the beliefs using messages from other nodes. This procedure is detailed in Algorithm 6, where normalize(f) normalizes the list $b()$ so that $\sum_{x \in supp(b)} b(x) = 1$. In each iteration, the belief of each node $\mathbf{C}_i$ is updated according to the messages of the other nodes $\mathbf{C}_j$. For each i the belief is updated as follows:

$$b_i(r) = \prod_{j=0, j \neq i}^{n} \mathsf{infl}_{ji}(r) \tag{24}$$

where $\mathsf{infl}_{ji}(r)$ captures the influence of the value of the node $\mathbf{C}_j$ to node $\mathbf{C}_i$. This influence can be calculated as $\mathsf{infl}_{ji}(r) \leftarrow C \sum_x m_{i,j}(r, x) \cdot b_j(x)$, with C as normalizing constant.

Experimental Verification. With Table 1 parameters, we obtained the correct values $r_i = \delta_{i,0}$ for all $i \in [1, n-1]$ after 3 iterations with the probabilities as reported in Table 2, by generating 1000 times each number of ciphertexts and trying to find the correct values of the r_i.

Remark 5 (Consistency with the previous section). Note that this procedure also incorporates the setting where one has only 2 failing ciphertexts, which would yield exactly the same results as in the previous paragraph.

Finally, once all the rotations are found, recall that the estimate is obtained by $\overline{\mathbf{E}} = \overline{\mathbf{C}_{\mathrm{rav}}} / \left\| \overline{\mathbf{C}_{\mathrm{rav}}} \right\|_2$ where

$$\overline{\mathbf{C}_{\mathrm{rav}}} = \left(\overline{\mathbf{C}_0^{(0)}} / \left\| \overline{\mathbf{C}_0^{(0)}} \right\|_2 + \sum_{i \in [1, n-1]} \overline{\mathbf{C}_i^{(r_i)}} / \left\| \overline{\mathbf{C}_i^{(r_i)}} \right\|_2 \right) / n. \tag{25}$$

5.3 Step 2: Finding Weak Ciphertexts

In this section, we are given an estimate $\overline{\mathbf{E}}$ and we refine the acceptance criterion. Instead of accepting if $P[F \mid ct] \geq f_t$, our condition is slightly changed.

1. Generate a key encapsulation $ct = (\mathbf{C}, \mathbf{G})$ with derived key K.
2. If $P[F \mid \overline{\mathbf{E}}, ct] \geq f_t$, keep ct in a weak ciphertext list, otherwise go to to Step 1.

In Step 2, $P[F \mid \overline{\mathbf{E}}, ct]$ is defined as the failure probability, given a certain ciphertext ct and a certain estimate $\overline{\mathbf{E}}$. In the following, we explain a way to compute it.

First, for $r \in [0, 2N - 1]$, we will estimate the probability that a ciphertext leads to an error in the rth location. Decomposing the vectors $\overline{\mathbf{S}}$ and $\overline{\mathbf{C}}$ in a component orthogonal to $\overline{\mathbf{E}}$, denoted with subscript $\perp$, and a component parallel to $\overline{\mathbf{E}}$, denoted with subscript $\parallel$, we obtain the failure expression:

$$P[F_r \mid \overline{\mathbf{E}}, \mathbf{C}] = P[\overline{\mathbf{S}}^T \cdot \overline{\mathbf{C}^{(r)}} > q_t \mid \overline{\mathbf{E}}, \mathbf{C}] = P[\overline{\mathbf{S}}_\parallel^T \cdot \overline{\mathbf{C}^{(r)}_\parallel} + \overline{\mathbf{S}}_\perp^T \cdot \overline{\mathbf{C}^{(r)}_\perp} > q_t \mid \overline{\mathbf{E}}, \mathbf{C}]$$

$$= P \left[\left(\begin{array}{c} \left\| \overline{\mathbf{S}} \right\|_2 \left\| \overline{\mathbf{C}^{(r)}} \right\|_2 \cos(\theta_{SE}) \cos(\theta_{C^{(r)}E}) + \\ \left\| \overline{\mathbf{S}} \right\|_2 \left\| \overline{\mathbf{C}^{(r)}} \right\|_2 \sin(\theta_{SE}) \sin(\theta_{C^{(r)}E}) \cos(t) \end{array} \right) > q_t \mid \overline{\mathbf{E}}, \mathbf{C} \right]$$

$$= P \left[\cos(t) > \frac{q_t - \left\| \overline{\mathbf{S}} \right\|_2 \left\| \overline{\mathbf{C}^{(r)}} \right\|_2 \cos(\theta_{SE}) \cos(\theta_{C^r E})}{\left\| \overline{\mathbf{S}} \right\|_2 \left\| \overline{\mathbf{C}^{(r)}} \right\|_2 \sin(\theta_{SE}) \sin(\theta_{C^r E})} \mid \overline{\mathbf{E}}, \mathbf{C} \right]$$

where θ_{SE} and $\theta_{C^{(r)}E}$ are the angles of $\overline{\mathbf{S}}$ and $\overline{\mathbf{C}^{(r)}}$ with the estimate $\overline{\mathbf{E}}$ respectively, and where t is the angle between $\overline{\mathbf{S}}_\perp$ and $\overline{\mathbf{C}^{(r)}_\perp}$. We assume no other knowledge about the direction of the secret apart from the directional estimate $\overline{\mathbf{E}}$. In this case, using Assumption 1, t can be estimated as a uniform angle in a $2Nl - 1$ dimensional space. Then t is assumed to follow the probability distribution Θ_{2Nl-1} (defined in Eq. 11).

The values $\overline{\mathbf{E}}$, $\|\mathbf{C}\|_2$ and $\cos(\theta_{C^{(r)}E})$ are known, meanwhile the values $\|\mathbf{S}\|$ and θ_{SE} can be modelled using their probability distribution. Thus, we can approximate $P[F_i \mid \overline{\mathbf{E}}, \mathbf{C}]$ with $P[F_i \mid \overline{\mathbf{E}}, \|\overline{\mathbf{C}}\|_2, \cos(\theta_{C^{(r)}E})]$.

Assumption 2. *We assume that failures at different locations are independent.*

Assumption 2 is a valid assumption for schemes without error correcting codes, as discussed in [17]. We can then calculate the failure probability of a certain ciphertext as:

$$P[F \mid \overline{\mathbf{E}}, \mathbf{C}] = 1 - \prod_{r=0}^{2N} \left(1 - P[F_r \mid \overline{\mathbf{E}}, \|\overline{\mathbf{C}}\|_2, \cos(\theta_{C^{(r)}E})]\right) \tag{26}$$

As this expression gives us a better prediction of the failure probability of ciphertexts by using the information embedded in $\overline{\mathbf{E}}$, we can more accurately (Grover) search for weak ciphertexts and thus reduce the work to find the next decryption failure. Moreover, the better $\overline{\mathbf{E}}$ approximates the direction of $\overline{\mathbf{S}}$, the easier it becomes to find a new decryption failure.

5.4   Finalizing the Attack with Lattice Reduction

Once multiple failures are found, the secret key can be recovered with lattice reduction techniques as presented in [17, §4] and in [27, Step 3 of the attack]. The following Section simply outlines how their technique transposes to our framework. As shown in Sect. 5, an estimate $\overline{\mathbf{E}}$ of the direction of a rotated version of $\overline{\mathbf{S}'} = X^r \mathbf{S}$ with an unknown value r is provided. Therefore, similarly to [27], an attacker can obtain an estimation of $\overline{\mathbf{S}'}$ (and not only its direction) by rescaling

$$\overline{\mathbf{E}'} := \overline{\mathbf{E}} \cdot nq_t \cdot \left(\left\|\mathbf{C}_0^{(0)} + \sum_{i \in [1,n-1]} \overline{\mathbf{C}_i^{(r_i)}}\right\|_2\right)^{-1},$$

using the approximation $\overline{\mathbf{E}'}^T \cdot 1/n \left(\mathbf{C}_0^{(0)} + \sum_{i \in [1,n-1]} \overline{\mathbf{C}_i^{(r_i)}}\right) \approx q_t$.

Then, for each possible $r \in [0, 2N-1]$, an attacker can perform lattice reduction and recover candidates for $\mathbf{s}, \mathbf{e}$ that are accepted if they verify $\mathbf{b} = \mathbf{As} + \mathbf{e}$. One caveat is that an attacker may have to run a lattice reduction up to $2N$ times. Since $\overline{\mathbf{E}'} - \overline{\mathbf{S}'}$ is small, the attacker can construct an appropriate lattice basis encoding $\overline{\mathbf{E}'} - \overline{\mathbf{S}'}$ as a unique shortest target vector, and solves the corresponding Unique-SVP problem with the BKZ algorithm [1,3,11,45]. The block size of BKZ will depend on the accuracy of the estimate $\overline{\mathbf{E}}$. Indeed, the standard deviation of $\overline{\mathbf{E}'}_i - \overline{\mathbf{S}'}_i$ is of the order of $\sigma_s \cdot \sin(\theta_{S'E})$ (assuming that $\theta_{S'E}$ is small and $\|\overline{\mathbf{S}'}\|_2 \approx \|\overline{\mathbf{E}'}\|_2$). Thus, when many decryption failures are available, $\sin(\theta_{S'E})$ gets very small and the complexity of this step is dominated by the work required for constructing $\overline{\mathbf{E}}$. For example, in the case of our toy scheme, if $\cos(\theta_{S'E}) > 0.985$, using [2], the BKZ block size becomes lower than 363 which leads to less than 2^{100} quantum work (in the Core-SVP [3] 0.265β model). As we will see in Sect. 6.3, this is less than the work required to find the first failure.

Remark 6. One can think that the failures obtained by directional failure boosting will not be totally independent. It is true that the failing ciphertexts are roughly following the same direction. But applying our Assumption 1, in high dimensions, for a reasonable number n of failures ($n \ll 2lN$), the hypercone in which the failures belong is large enough that linear dependency will happen with very low probability.

6   Efficiency of Directional Failure Boosting

In this section, we experimentally verify the efficiency of the directional failure boosting technique. We first quantify the accuracy of the estimate $\overline{\mathbf{E}}$ computed according to Sect. 5.2. We then derive the necessary work required to run the directional failure boosting technique and the optimal number of queries. For the rest of the section, we focus on minimizing the total work for finding failures and we will assume there is no upper limit to the number of decryption queries.

Our key takeaway is that, for Table 1 parameters, the more failing ciphertexts have been found, the easier it becomes to obtain the next one, and that most of the effort is concentrated in finding the first failure. The final work and query overheads are stored in Table 4.

6.1   Accuracy of the Estimate

Let $\mathbf{C}_0, ..., \mathbf{C}_{n-1}$ be n previously found failing ciphertexts and we take the estimate defined according to Eq. 25. Similarly to Sect. 5.2, we define $\overline{\mathbf{S}'} = \overline{X^{-r_0} \cdot \mathbf{S}}$ as the secret vector for an unknown F_{r_0}. To estimate the accuracy of $\overline{\mathbf{E}}$, we compute $\cos(\theta_{S'E}) = \frac{\overline{\mathbf{S}'}^T \cdot \overline{\mathbf{E}}}{\left\|\overline{\mathbf{S}'}\right\|_2} = \frac{\overline{\mathbf{S}'}^T \cdot \overline{\mathbf{C}_{\text{rav}}}}{\left\|\overline{\mathbf{S}'}\right\|_2 \left\|\overline{\mathbf{C}_{\text{rav}}}\right\|_2}$ as

$$\cos(\theta_{S'E}) = \frac{\overline{\mathbf{S}'}^T \cdot \left(\frac{\overline{\mathbf{C}_0^{(0)}}}{\left\|\overline{\mathbf{C}_0^{(0)}}\right\|_2} + \sum_{i=1}^{n-1} \frac{\overline{\mathbf{C}_i^{(r_i)}}}{\left\|\overline{\mathbf{C}_i^{(r_i)}}\right\|_2} \right)}{n \left\|\overline{\mathbf{S}'}\right\|_2 \left\|\overline{\mathbf{C}_{\text{rav}}}\right\|_2} \tag{27}$$

$$= \frac{\cos\left(\theta_{C_0^{(0)} S'}\right) + \sum_{i=1}^{n-1} \cos\left(\theta_{C_i^{(r_i)} S'}\right)}{\left\| \frac{\overline{\mathbf{C}_0^{(0)}}}{\left\|\overline{\mathbf{C}_0^{(0)}}\right\|_2} + \sum_{i=1}^{n-1} \frac{\overline{\mathbf{C}_i^{(r_i)}}}{\left\|\overline{\mathbf{C}_i^{(r_i)}}\right\|_2} \right\|_2} \tag{28}$$

First, we make the following approximation.

Approximation 1. *We approximate the cosine with the secret $\overline{\mathbf{S}'}$ by its expected value denoted* $\cos(\theta_{CS'}) := \mathbb{E}\left[\cos\left(\theta_{C_i^{(r_i)} S'}\right)\right]$. *In other words, for all $i \in [1, n-1]$ we assume*

$$\cos(\theta_{CS'}) = \cos\left(\theta_{C_i^{(r_i)} S'}\right) = \cos\left(\theta_{C_0^{(0)} S'}\right).$$

To estimate the denominator of Eq. 28, we split the ciphertexts in a component parallel to the secret $\overline{\mathbf{C}_{i,\|}^{(r_i)}}$ and a component orthogonal $\overline{\mathbf{C}_{i,\perp}^{(r_i)}}$ to the secret. Following Assumption 1, we will assume orthogonality between the various $\overline{\mathbf{C}_{i,\perp}^{(r_i)}}$. As the norm of the sum of parallel vectors is the sum of their norm, and the norm

Table 3. Accuracy of the estimate derived from several failures. Expected value of $\cos(\theta_{S'E})$ according to Eq. 29. The closer to 1, the more accurate $\overline{\mathbf{E}}$ is.

n	1	2	3	5	10	20	30	50	100
Theoretical	0.328	0.441	0.516	0.613	0.739	0.841	0.885	0.926	0.961
Experimental	0.318	0.429	0.502	0.600	0.727	0.832	0.878	0.921	0.958

of the sum of orthogonal vectors can be calculated using Pythagoras' theorem, we can approximate $\cos(\theta_{S'E})$ as follows:

$$\cos(\theta_{S'E}) \approx \frac{n\cos(\theta_{CS'})}{\sqrt{n^2\cos(\theta_{CS'})^2 + n\sin(\theta_{CS'})^2}} = \frac{\cos(\theta_{CS'})}{\sqrt{\cos(\theta_{CS'})^2 + \sin(\theta_{CS'})^2/n}} \tag{29}$$

One can see from this equation that $\cos(\theta_{S'E})$ gets closer to 1 when n increases.

Experimental Verification. The first line of Table 3 gives the expected values of $\cos(\theta_{S'E})$ for various n, according to Eq. 29, with $\cos(\theta_{CS'})$ set to $q_t / \mathbb{E}[\|\overline{\mathbf{S}}\|]\mathbb{E}[\|\overline{\mathbf{C}^{(0)}}\|]$, which is a good approximation of $\cos(\theta_{CS'})$ as $\cos(\theta_{CS'}) > q_t / \|\overline{\mathbf{S}}\|\|\mathbf{C}^{(0)}\|$ and because angles tend to orthogonality in high dimensional space.

Then, to verify the theory, we implemented a method to simulate the distribution of random failing ciphertexts. This technique is described in the full version of our paper [15]. Once the simulated failing ciphertexts are found, we combine them to build $\overline{\mathbf{E}}$ using their correct rotations, and we compute $\cos(\theta_{S'E})$. The latter experiment was repeated 100 times and the average values are reported in line two of Table 3.

6.2   Estimating α_{i,f_t} and β_{i,f_t}

To estimate the effectiveness of directional failure boosting given a certain number i of previously collected failing ciphertexts, we need to find the optimal weak ciphertext threshold f_t for each i. This corresponds to considering how much time to spend for one precalculation $\sqrt{\alpha_{i,f_t}^{-1}}$ and the average failure probability of weak ciphertexts β_{i,f_t} after the precalculation. Let us recall the definition of α_{n,f_t} and β_{n,f_t}, derived from Eqs. 7 and 8, where $\mathbf{C}_0, ..., \mathbf{C}_{n-1}$ are the n previously found failing ciphertexts.

$$\alpha_{i,f_t} = \sum_{\forall ct: P[F|ct,\mathbf{C}_0,...,\mathbf{C}_{n-1}]>f_t} P[ct] \tag{30}$$

$$\beta_{i,f_t} = \frac{\sum_{\forall ct: P[F|ct,\mathbf{C}_0,...,\mathbf{C}_{n-1}]>f_t} P[ct] \cdot P[F|ct,\mathbf{C}_0,...,\mathbf{C}_{n-1}] > f_t]}{\sum_{\forall ct: P[F|ct,\mathbf{C}_0,...,\mathbf{C}_{n-1}]>f_t} P[ct]}. \tag{31}$$

To find the optimal values, we need to calculate Eqs. 30 and 31 as functions of f_t. This requires us to list the probability of all ciphertexts $ct := (\mathbf{C}, \mathbf{G})$, and their failure probability $P[F|ct, \mathbf{C}_0, ..., \mathbf{C}_{t-1}]$. As discussed in [16], exhaustively computing both values is not practically feasible, and therefore we will make some assumptions to get an estimate.

A first simplification is to cluster ciphertexts that have similar $\|\mathbf{C}\|_2$ and $|\theta_{C^{(0)}E}| \cdots |\theta_{C^{(N-1)}E}|$ and thus a similar failure probability. To further reduce the list size, we only take into account the largest value of $|\cos(\theta_{C^{(i)}E})|$ denoted

$$\text{maxcos}(\theta_{\text{CE}}) := \max_i(|\cos(\theta_{C^{(i)}E})|,$$

which results in a slight underestimation of the effectiveness of the attack. In other words,

$$P[ct] \text{ becomes } P[\|\mathbf{C}\|_2, \text{maxcos}(\theta_{\text{CE}})],$$
$$P[F|ct, \mathbf{C}_0, ..., \mathbf{C}_{n-1}] \text{ becomes } P[F \mid \|\mathbf{C}\|_2, \text{maxcos}(\theta_{\text{CE}})].$$

Assuming independence between the norm of $\mathbf{C}$ and its angle with $\overline{\mathbf{E}}$, $P[\|\mathbf{C}\|_2, \text{maxcos}(\theta_{\text{CE}}))]$ can be estimated using the distributions defined with Eqs. 10 and 13 as follows:

$$P[\|\mathbf{C}\|_2, \text{maxcos}(\theta_{\text{CE}})] = \underbrace{P[\|\mathbf{C}\|_2]}_{\chi_{Nl,\sigma}} \cdot \underbrace{P[\text{maxcos}(\theta_{\text{CE}})]}_{M(\Theta_{2Nl}, 2N)}. \tag{32}$$

Denoting with r the position of the maximum angle, we can rewrite $P[F \mid \|\mathbf{C}\|_2, \text{maxcos}(\theta_{\text{CE}})]$ as follows:

$$P[F \mid \|\mathbf{C}\|_2, \text{maxcos}(\theta_{\text{CE}})] = 1 - \prod_i \left(1 - P[F_i \mid \|\mathbf{C}\|_2, |\cos(\theta_{C^{(r)}E})|]\right), \tag{33}$$

$$= 1 - \left(\begin{array}{c}\left(1 - P[F_r \mid \|\mathbf{C}\|_2, |\cos(\theta_{C^{(r)}E})|]\right) \cdot \\ \prod_{i \neq r}\left(1 - P[F_i \mid \|\mathbf{C}\|_2, |\cos(\theta_{C^{(i)}E})| \leq |\cos(\theta_{C^{(r)}E})|]\right)\end{array}\right), \tag{34}$$

where $1 - P[F_r \mid \|\mathbf{C}\|_2, |\cos(\theta_{C^{(r)}E})|]$ can be estimated using Eq. 26, and $P[F_i \mid \|\mathbf{C}\|_2, |\cos(\theta_{C^{(i)}E})| \leq |\cos(\theta_{C^{(r)}E})|]$ using an integral over Eq. 26. The estimated failure probability of ciphertexts given $\|\mathbf{C}\|_2$ and $\cos(\theta_{CE})$ for the parameters listed in Table 1 is depicted in Fig. 5a.

Verification Experiment. We verified these results experimentally by generating $5 \cdot 10^6$ failing ciphertexts and $5 \cdot 10^6$ successful ciphertexts, and calculating their norm and angle with 1000 estimates, or in this case other ciphertexts. The failing ciphertexts were produced using the methodology detailed in the full version of our paper [15]. Once they are generated, we estimate their failure probability with a procedure also detailed in the full version of our paper [15]. We combined these results into Fig. 5b. These experimental results confirm our theoretical estimates given in Fig. 5a.

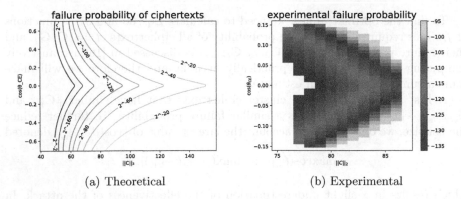

(a) Theoretical   (b) Experimental

Fig. 5. Failure probability of ciphertexts as a function of $\|\mathbf{C}\|_2$ and $\cos(\theta_{CE})$. A zoomed version of (a) for easier comparison can be found the full version of our paper [15].

With the estimation of $P\left[F \mid \|\mathbf{C}\|_2, \mathrm{maxcos}(\theta_{\mathrm{CE}})\right]$ and $P[\|\|\mathbf{C}\|_2, \mathrm{maxcos}(\theta_{\mathrm{CE}})]$, α_{i,f_t} and β_{i,f_t} can be estimated as functions of i and f_t. Let us now define the optimal threshold f_t as a function of i as :

$$f_i := \mathrm{argmin}_{f_t}\ \left(\sqrt{\alpha_{i,f_t}} \cdot \beta_{i,f_t}\right)^{-1}.$$

6.3   Total Amount of Work and Queries

In this section, we will derive the optimal work and queries for an adversary to perform, in order to obtain n ciphertexts with probability $1 - e^{-1}$. We introduce the following notation: to find the $(i+1)^{\mathrm{th}}$ ciphertext, the adversary performs Q_i queries. Using a Poisson distribution, the success probability of finding the $(i+1)^{\mathrm{th}}$ ciphertext in Q_i queries is $1 - e^{-Q_i\beta_{i,f_i}}$. The probability of obtaining n failures can then be calculated as the product of the success probabilities of finding ciphertexts 0 to $n-1$:

$$P_n = \prod_{i=0}^{n-1}(1 - e^{-Q_i\beta_{i,f_i}}). \tag{35}$$

This is a slight underestimation of the success probability of the attack, because if an adversary finds a failing ciphertext in less than Q_i samples, she can query more ciphertexts in the next stages $i+1, \ldots, n$. However, this effect is small due to the large value of Q_i.

The total amount of precomputation quantum work, and the total amount of queries to obtain the n failing ciphertexts by performing Q_i tries for each ciphertext, can be expressed as

$$\mathcal{W}_n^{\mathrm{tot}} := \sum_{i=0}^{n-1}\underbrace{\frac{Q_i}{\sqrt{\alpha_{i,f_i}}}}_{:=W_i} \qquad \mathcal{Q}_n^{\mathrm{tot}} := \sum_{i=0}^{n-1}Q_i. \tag{36}$$

Table 4. Quantum work $\mathcal{W}_n^{\text{tot}}$ and queries $\mathcal{Q}_n^{\text{tot}}$ required to find n failing ciphertexts with probability $1 - e^{-1}$. Finding the first ciphertext requires the heaviest amount of computation. After the third failing ciphertext is found, the following ones are essentially for free.

Ciphertexts n	1	2	3	5	10	20	30
$\log_2(\mathcal{W}_n^{\text{tot}})$	112.45	112.77	112.78	112.78	112.78	112.78	112.78
$\log_2(\mathcal{W}_n^{\text{tot}}/\mathcal{W}_1^{\text{tot}})$	—	0.32	0.33	0.33	0.33	0.33	0.33
$\log_2(\mathcal{Q}_n^{\text{tot}})$	102.21	102.86	102.87	102.87	102.87	102.87	102.87
$\log_2(\mathcal{Q}_n^{\text{tot}}/\mathcal{Q}_1^{\text{tot}})$	—	0.65	0.66	0.66	0.66	0.66	0.66

Recall that for now we assume there is no upper limit to the number of decryption queries that can be made, and we focus on minimizing the amount of work. The values of Q_i that minimizes the total quantum work $\mathcal{W}_n^{\text{tot}}$ can be found using the following Lagrange multiplier, minimizing the total amount of work to find n failures with probability $1 - e^{-1}$ using the above probability model:

$$L(Q_0, \cdots, Q_{n-1}, \lambda) = \sum_{t=0}^{n-1} \frac{Q_i}{\sqrt{\alpha_{i, f_i}}} + \lambda \left((1 - e^{-1}) - \prod_{i=0}^{n-1} (1 - e^{-Q_i \beta_{i, f_i}}) \right) \quad (37)$$

By equating the partial derivative of L in $Q_0, \cdots, Q_{n-1}$ and λ to zero and solving the resulting system of equations, we obtain the optimal values of $Q_0, \cdots, Q_{n-1}$ to mount our attack.

The resulting total work and queries of obtaining n ciphertext using directional failure boosting are given in Table 4 and Fig. 6. One can see that the majority of the work lies in obtaining the first ciphertext, and that obtaining more than one ciphertext can be done in less than double the work and queries, or less than one extra bit of complexity. For schemes with a lower failure probability, failing ciphertexts will be more correlated to the secret, so that the directional information is higher and directional failure boosting will be more effective.

In conclusion, the security of a scheme with low failure probability under a single target decryption failure attack can be approximated by the amount of work and queries that an adversary needs to do in order to obtain the first decryption failure. We emphasize the fact that obtaining many failures for a low overhead threatens the security of the scheme (See Sect. 5.4).

7 Discussion and Variants

7.1 Comparison with D'Anvers et al. [16]

In Fig. 7, the total work and queries needed to obtain n ciphertexts with probability $1 - e^{-1}$ is plotted for both the traditional failure boosting, and our directional failure boosting approach. For a fair comparison between both results, we adapted the method for estimating the total work and queries with success probability $1 - e^{-1}$ using the traditional failure boosting of [16]. For more information about our method, we refer to the full version of our paper [15].

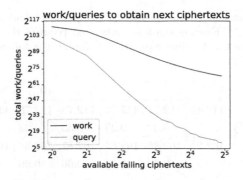

Fig. 6. Quantum work W_i and number of decryption queries Q_i required to find a new failing ciphertext, given the i failing ciphertexts found previously.

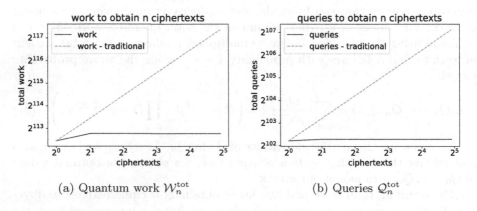

(a) Quantum work $\mathcal{W}_n^{\text{tot}}$ (b) Queries $\mathcal{Q}_n^{\text{tot}}$

Fig. 7. Quantum work $\mathcal{W}_n^{\text{tot}}$ and number of decryption queries $\mathcal{Q}_n^{\text{tot}}$ required to obtain n failing ciphertexts with probability $1 - e^{-1}$, given the number of previously found failing ciphertexts.

7.2 Minimizing the Number of Queries Instead

In case there is a maximal number of decryption queries is imposed, say 2^K, the same attack strategy can be followed. However, to limit the number of queries $\mathcal{Q}_n^{\text{tot}}$ necessary in the attack, a stronger preprocessing $\sqrt{\alpha_{i,f_t}^{-1}}$ might be necessary to increase the failure probability β_{i,f_t} of weak ciphertexts over 2^{-K}. The only change to accomplish this is selecting the threshold f_t for each i appropriately. Note that for most practical schemes (e.g. Kyber, Saber, New Hope), increasing the failure probability β_{0,f_t} over 2^{-K} is not practically feasible or would require too much preprocessing $\sqrt{\alpha_{0,f_t}^{-1}}$.

Figure 8 depicts the amount of work $\sqrt{\alpha_{i,f_t}^{-1} \beta_{i,f_t}^{-1}}$ needed to increase the failure probability β_{i,f_t} to a certain failure probability (e.g. 2^{-K}) for the parameters given in Table 1. The various curves correspond to different numbers of available failing ciphertexts. From this figure, one can see that also in this case, the work is dominated by finding the first decryption failure. Another observation is that the attack gets much more expensive as the maximal number of decryption queries 2^K gets smaller.

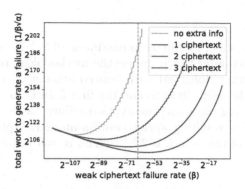

Fig. 8. Quantum work $\mathcal{W}_n^{tot}$ required to find a new failing ciphertext, as a function of the decryption failure probability of a Mod-LWE scheme.

7.3 Application to ss-ntru-pke and Improvement of Guo et al. [27]

In [27], an adaptive multitarget attack is proposed on the ss-ntru-pke version of NTRUEncrypt [10], a Ring-LWE based encryption scheme that claims security against chosen ciphertext attacks. The parameters of this scheme are given in Table 5. The attack performs at most 2^{64} queries on at most 2^{64} targets and has a classical cost of 2^{216} work, and a quantum cost of 2^{140} when speeding up the offline phase with Grover's search. We adapt directional failure boosting to this attack model and propose both a single and multitarget attack.

For the single target attack, our proposed methodology in Subsect. 6.3 needs more than 2^{64} queries to obtain a ciphertext. To mitigate this, we increase the precomputational work $\sqrt{\alpha^{-1}}$ so that the failure probability of weak ciphertexts β increases over a certain f_t, which is chosen as 2^{-57} to make sure the total queries are below 2^{64}. The effect is a bigger overall computation, but a reduction in the number of necessary decryption queries. The rest of the attack proceeds as discussed in Subsect. 6.3. The work or queries needed to obtain an extra ciphertexts with n ciphertexts can be seen in Fig. 9a. The cost of this single target attack is $2^{139.6}$, which is close to the cost of their multitarget attack $2^{139.5}$, as can be seen in Table 6.

Table 5. Parameters of the ss-ntru-pke [10] scheme.

	l	N	q	σ_s	σ_e	$P[F]$	Claimed security
ss-ntru-pke	1	1024	$2^{30} + 2^{13} + 1$	724	724	$>2^{-80}$	2^{198}

Table 6. Comparison of costs for different attacks against ss-ntru-pke [10].

Scheme	Claimed security	Multitarget attack [27]	Our single target attack	Our multitarget attack
ss-ntru-pke	2^{198}	$2^{139.5}$	$2^{139.6}$	$2^{96.6}$

In the multitarget case, we can use a maximum of $2^{64} \cdot 2^{64}$ queries to find the first failing ciphertext, after which we use the methodology of the single target attack to obtain further ciphertext with limited amount of queries. In practice we stay well below the query limit to find the first failure. In this case, the work is dominated by finding the second decryption failure, as we need to do this in under 2^{64} queries. The resulting work to obtain an extra ciphertext is depicted in Fig. 9b. The cost of this attack is $2^{96.6}$, which is well below the cost of $2^{139.5}$ reported by Guo et al.

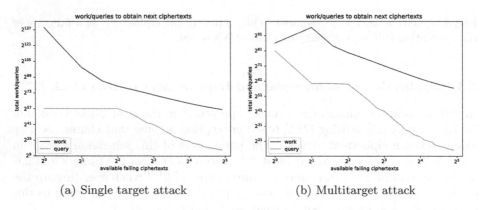

(a) Single target attack   (b) Multitarget attack

Fig. 9. Quantum work $\mathcal{W}_n^{\text{tot}}$ and number of decryption queries $\mathcal{Q}_n^{\text{tot}}$ required to find a new failing ciphertext for ss-ntru-pke, given the ones found previously.

Acknowledgements. We thank Henri Gilbert and Alessandro Budroni for the interesting discussions about decryption errors, and for providing advice during the writeup of this paper.

References

1. Albrecht, M.R., Göpfert, F., Virdia, F., Wunderer, T.: Revisiting the expected cost of solving uSVP and applications to LWE. In: Takagi, T., Peyrin, T. (eds.) ASIACRYPT 2017, Part I. LNCS, vol. 10624, pp. 297–322. Springer, Cham (2017). https://doi.org/10.1007/978-3-319-70694-8_11
2. Albrecht, M.R., Player, R., Scott, S.: On the concrete hardness of learning with errors. JMC **9**(3), 169–203 (2015)
3. Alkim, E., Ducas, L., Pöppelmann, T., Schwabe, P.: Post-quantum key exchange – a New Hope. In: USENIX Security 2016 (2016)

4. Baan, H., et al.: Round2: KEM and PKE based on GLWR. IACR ePrint 2017/1183 (2017)
5. Băetu, C., Durak, F.B., Huguenin-Dumittan, L., Talayhan, A., Vaudenay, S.: Misuse attacks on post-quantum cryptosystems. In: Ishai, Y., Rijmen, V. (eds.) EUROCRYPT 2019, Part II. LNCS, vol. 11477, pp. 747–776. Springer, Cham (2019). https://doi.org/10.1007/978-3-030-17656-3_26
6. Bai, S., Galbraith, S.D.: An improved compression technique for signatures based on learning with errors. In: Benaloh, J. (ed.) CT-RSA 2014. LNCS, vol. 8366, pp. 28–47. Springer, Cham (2014). https://doi.org/10.1007/978-3-319-04852-9_2
7. Bos, J., et al.: CRYSTALS - Kyber: a CCA-secure module-lattice-based KEM. IACR ePrint 2017/634 (2017)
8. Bos, J., et al.: CRYSTALS – Kyber: a CCA-secure module-lattice-based KEM (2017)
9. Cai, T., Fan, J., Jiang, T.: Distributions of angles in random packing on spheres. J. Mach. Learn. Res. **14**(1), 1837–1864 (2013)
10. Chen, C., Hoffstein, J., Whyte, W., Zhang, Z.: NTRUEncrypt. Technical report, NIST (2017)
11. Chen, Y., Nguyen, P.Q.: BKZ 2.0: better lattice security estimates. In: Lee, D.H., Wang, X. (eds.) ASIACRYPT 2011. LNCS, vol. 7073, pp. 1–20. Springer, Heidelberg (2011). https://doi.org/10.1007/978-3-642-25385-0_1
12. D'Anvers, J.-P., Guo, Q., Johansson, T., Nilsson, A., Vercauteren, F., Verbauwhede, I.: Decryption failure attacks on IND-CCA secure lattice-based schemes. In: Lin, D., Sako, K. (eds.) PKC 2019, Part II. LNCS, vol. 11443, pp. 565–598. Springer, Cham (2019). https://doi.org/10.1007/978-3-030-17259-6_19
13. D'Anvers, J.-P., Karmakar, A., Sinha Roy, S., Vercauteren, F.: Saber: module-LWR based key exchange, CPA-secure encryption and CCA-secure KEM. In: Joux, A., Nitaj, A., Rachidi, T. (eds.) AFRICACRYPT 2018. LNCS, vol. 10831, pp. 282–305. Springer, Cham (2018). https://doi.org/10.1007/978-3-319-89339-6_16
14. D'Anvers, J.-P., Karmakar, A., Roy, S.S., Vercauteren, F.: SABER, Round 2 submission. Technical report, NIST (2019)
15. D'Anvers, J.-P., Rossi, M., Virdia, F.: *(one) failure is not an option*: bootstrapping the search for failures in lattice-based encryption schemes. Cryptology ePrint Archive, Report 2019/1399 (2019). https://eprint.iacr.org/2019/1399
16. D'Anvers, J.-P., Vercauteren, F., Verbauwhede, I.: On the impact of decryption failures on the security of LWE/LWR based schemes. IACR ePrint 2018/1089 (2018)
17. D'Anvers, J.-P., Vercauteren, F., Verbauwhede, I.: The impact of error dependencies on Ring/Mod-LWE/LWR based schemes. IACR ePrint 2018/1172 (2018)
18. Dent, A.W.: A designer's guide to KEMs. In: Paterson, K.G. (ed.) Cryptography and Coding 2003. LNCS, vol. 2898, pp. 133–151. Springer, Heidelberg (2003). https://doi.org/10.1007/978-3-540-40974-8_12
19. Diffie, W., Hellman, M.: New directions in cryptography. IEEE Trans. Inf. Theory **22**(6), 644–654 (1976)
20. Ducas, L., et al.: CRYSTALS-dilithium: a lattice-based digital signature scheme. TCHES **2018**(1), 238–268 (2018)
21. ElGamal, T.: A public key cryptosystem and a signature scheme based on discrete logarithms. IEEE Trans. Inf. Theory **31**(4), 469–472 (1985)
22. Fluhrer, S.: Cryptanalysis of ring-LWE based key exchange with key share reuse. IACR ePrint 2016/085 (2016)
23. Fujisaki, E., Okamoto, T.: Secure integration of asymmetric and symmetric encryption schemes. J. Cryptol. **26**(1), 80–101 (2013)

24. Gama, N., Nguyen, P.Q.: New chosen-ciphertext attacks on NTRU. In: Okamoto, T., Wang, X. (eds.) PKC 2007. LNCS, vol. 4450, pp. 89–106. Springer, Heidelberg (2007). https://doi.org/10.1007/978-3-540-71677-8_7

25. Gentry, C., Boneh, D.: A Fully Homomorphic Encryption Scheme. Stanford University, Stanford (2009)

26. Grover, L.K.: A fast quantum mechanical algorithm for database search. In: Proceedings of the Twenty-Eighth Annual ACM Symposium on Theory of Computing, STOC 1996. ACM, New York (1996)

27. Guo, Q., Johansson, T., Nilsson, A.: A Generic Attack on Lattice-based Schemes using Decryption Errors with Application to ss-ntru-pke. IACR ePrint 2019/043 (2019)

28. Hofheinz, D., Hövelmanns, K., Kiltz, E.: A modular analysis of the Fujisaki-Okamoto transformation. In: Kalai, Y., Reyzin, L. (eds.) TCC 2017, Part I. LNCS, vol. 10677, pp. 341–371. Springer, Cham (2017). https://doi.org/10.1007/978-3-319-70500-2_12

29. Howgrave-Graham, N., et al.: The impact of decryption failures on the security of NTRU encryption. In: Boneh, D. (ed.) CRYPTO 2003. LNCS, vol. 2729, pp. 226–246. Springer, Heidelberg (2003). https://doi.org/10.1007/978-3-540-45146-4_14

30. Jaulmes, É., Joux, A.: A chosen-ciphertext attack against NTRU. In: Bellare, M. (ed.) CRYPTO 2000. LNCS, vol. 1880, pp. 20–35. Springer, Heidelberg (2000). https://doi.org/10.1007/3-540-44598-6_2

31. Jiang, H., Zhang, Z., Chen, L., Wang, H., Ma, Z.: Post-quantum IND-CCA-secure KEM without additional hash. IACR ePrint 2017/1096

32. Johnson, N.L., Kotz, S., Balakrishnan, N.: Continuous Univariate Distributions. Houghton Mifflin, Boston (1970)

33. Katz, J., Lindell, Y.: Introduction to Modern Cryptography, 2nd edn. Chapman & Hall/CRC, Boca Raton (2014)

34. Langlois, A., Stehlé, D.: Worst-case to average-case reductions for module lattices. Des. Codes Crypt. 75(3), 565–599 (2014). https://doi.org/10.1007/s10623-014-9938-4

35. Lu, X., Liu, Y., Jia, D., Xue, H., He, J., Zhang, Z.: LAC. Technical report, NIST (2017)

36. Lyubashevsky, V.: Fiat-Shamir with aborts: applications to lattice and factoring-based signatures. In: Matsui, M. (ed.) ASIACRYPT 2009. LNCS, vol. 5912, pp. 598–616. Springer, Heidelberg (2009). https://doi.org/10.1007/978-3-642-10366-7_35

37. Lyubashevsky, V., Peikert, C., Regev, O.: On ideal lattices and learning with errors over rings. In: Gilbert, H. (ed.) EUROCRYPT 2010. LNCS, vol. 6110, pp. 1–23. Springer, Heidelberg (2010). https://doi.org/10.1007/978-3-642-13190-5_1

38. Micciancio, D., Vadhan, S.P.: Statistical zero-knowledge proofs with efficient provers: lattice problems and more. In: Boneh, D. (ed.) CRYPTO 2003. LNCS, vol. 2729, pp. 282–298. Springer, Heidelberg (2003). https://doi.org/10.1007/978-3-540-45146-4_17

39. Naehrig, M., et al.: FrodoKEM. Technical report, NIST (2017)

40. NIST: Submission requirements and evaluation criteria for the Post-Quantum Cryptography standardization process (2016)

41. Pearl, J.: Probabilistic Reasoning in Intelligent Systems: Networks of Plausible Inference. Elsevier, Amsterdam (2014)

42. Peikert, C., Vaikuntanathan, V.: Noninteractive statistical zero-knowledge proofs for lattice problems. In: Wagner, D. (ed.) CRYPTO 2008. LNCS, vol. 5157, pp. 536–553. Springer, Heidelberg (2008). https://doi.org/10.1007/978-3-540-85174-5_30

43. Regev, O.: On lattices, learning with errors, random linear codes, and cryptography. In: STOC. ACM (2005)

44. Saito, T., Xagawa, K., Yamakawa, T.: Tightly-Secure Key-Encapsulation Mechanism in the Quantum Random Oracle Model. IACR ePrint 2017/1005 (2017)

45. Schnorr, C.-P., Euchner, M.: Lattice basis reduction: improved practical algorithms and solving subset sum problems. Math. Program. **66**(1–3), 181–199 (1994). https://doi.org/10.1007/BF01581144

46. Schwabe, P., et al.: Crystals-Kyber, Round 2 submission. Technical report, NIST, Post-Quantum Standardization Process Round 2 (2019)

47. Stehlé, D., Steinfeld, R., Tanaka, K., Xagawa, K.: Efficient public key encryption based on ideal lattices. In: Matsui, M. (ed.) ASIACRYPT 2009. LNCS, vol. 5912, pp. 617–635. Springer, Heidelberg (2009). https://doi.org/10.1007/978-3-642-10366-7_36

48. Targhi, E.E., Unruh, D.: Post-quantum security of the Fujisaki-Okamoto and OAEP transforms. In: Hirt, M., Smith, A. (eds.) TCC 2016, Part II. LNCS, vol. 9986, pp. 192–216. Springer, Heidelberg (2016). https://doi.org/10.1007/978-3-662-53644-5_8

Key Recovery from Gram–Schmidt Norm Leakage in Hash-and-Sign Signatures over NTRU Lattices

Pierre-Alain Fouque[1], Paul Kirchner[1], Mehdi Tibouchi[2(✉)],
Alexandre Wallet[2], and Yang Yu[1(✉)]

[1] Univ Rennes, CNRS, IRISA, Rennes, France
pa.fouque@gmail.com, paul.kirchner@irisa.fr, yang.yu0986@gmail.com
[2] NTT Corporation, Tokyo, Japan
{mehdi.tibouchi.br,alexandre.wallet.th}@hco.ntt.co.jp

Abstract. In this paper, we initiate the study of side-channel leakage in hash-and-sign lattice-based signatures, with particular emphasis on the two efficient implementations of the original GPV lattice-trapdoor paradigm for signatures, namely NIST second-round candidate FALCON and its simpler predecessor DLP. Both of these schemes implement the GPV signature scheme over NTRU lattices, achieving great speed-ups over the general lattice case. Our results are mainly threefold.

First, we identify a specific source of side-channel leakage in most implementations of those schemes, namely, the one-dimensional Gaussian sampling steps within lattice Gaussian sampling. It turns out that the implementations of these steps often leak the Gram–Schmidt norms of the secret lattice basis.

Second, we elucidate the link between this leakage and the secret key, by showing that the entire secret key can be efficiently reconstructed solely from those Gram–Schmidt norms. The result makes heavy use of the algebraic structure of the corresponding schemes, which work over a power-of-two cyclotomic field.

Third, we concretely demonstrate the side-channel attack against DLP (but not FALCON due to the different structures of the two schemes). The challenge is that timing information only provides an approximation of the Gram–Schmidt norms, so our algebraic recovery technique needs to be combined with pruned tree search in order to apply it to approximate values. Experimentally, we show that around 2^{35} DLP traces are enough to reconstruct the entire key with good probability.

1 Introduction

Lattice-Based Signatures. Lattice-based cryptography has proved to be a versatile way of achieving a very wide range of cryptographic primitives with strong security guarantees that are also believed to hold in the postquantum setting. For a while, it was largely confined to the realm of theoretical cryptography, mostly concerned with asymptotic efficiency, but it has made major

© International Association for Cryptologic Research 2020
A. Canteaut and Y. Ishai (Eds.): EUROCRYPT 2020, LNCS 12107, pp. 34–63, 2020.
https://doi.org/10.1007/978-3-030-45727-3_2

strides towards practicality in recent years. Significant progress has been made in terms of practical constructions, refined concrete security estimates and fast implementations. As a result, lattice-based schemes are seen as strong contenders in the NIST postquantum standardization process.

In terms of practical *signature schemes* in particular, lattice-based constructions broadly fit within either of two large frameworks: Fiat–Shamir type constructions on the one hand, and hash-and-sign constructions on the other.

Fiat–Shamir lattice based signatures rely on a variant of the Fiat–Shamir paradigm [16] developed by Lyubashevsky, called "Fiat–Shamir with aborts" [31], which has proved particularly fruitful. It has given rise to numerous practically efficient schemes [2,8,23] including the two second round NIST candidates Dilithium [10,33] and qTESLA [5].

The hash-and-sign family has a longer history, dating back to Goldreich–Goldwasser–Halevi [22] signatures as well as NTRUSign [24]. Those early proposals were shown to be insecure [12,19,21,40], however, due to a statistical dependence between the distribution of signatures and the signing key. That issue was only overcome with the development of lattice trapdoors by Gentry, Peikert and Vaikuntanathan [20]. In the GPV scheme, signatures follow a distribution that is provably independent of the secret key (a discrete Gaussian supported on the public lattice), but which is hard to sample from without knowing a secret, short basis of the lattice. The scheme is quite attractive from a theoretical standpoint (for example, it is easier to establish QROM security for it than for Fiat–Shamir type schemes), but suffers from large keys and a potentially costly procedure for discrete Gaussian sampling over a lattice. Several follow-up works have then striven to improve its concrete efficiency [13,34,37,42,49], culminating in two main efficient and compact implementations: the scheme of Ducas, Lyubashevsky and Prest (DLP) [11], and its successor, NIST second round candidate FALCON [47], both instantiated over NTRU lattices [24] in power-of-two cyclotomic fields. One can also mention NIST first round candidates pqNTRUSign [52] and DRS [44] as members of this family, the latter of which actually fell prey to a clever statistical attack [51] in the spirit of those against GGH and NTRUSign.

Side-Channel Analysis of Lattice-Based Signatures. With the NIST postquantum standardization process underway, it is crucial to investigate the security of lattice-based schemes not only in a pure algorithmic sense, but also with respect to implementation attacks, such as side-channels. For lattice-based signatures constructed using the Fiat–Shamir paradigm, this problem has received a significant amount of attention in the literature, with numerous works [4,6,7,14,43,50] pointing out vulnerabilities with respect to timing attacks, cache attacks, power analysis and other types of side-channels. Those attacks have proved particularly devastating against schemes using discrete Gaussian sampling, such as the celebrated BLISS signature scheme [8]. In response, several countermeasures have also been proposed [27,28,39], some of them provably secure [3,4], but the side-channel arms race does not appear to have subsided quite yet.

In contrast, the case of hash-and-sign lattice-based signatures, including DLP and FALCON, remains largely unexplored, despite concerns being raised regarding their vulnerability to side-channel attacks. For example, the NIST status report on first round candidates, announcing the selection of FALCON to the second round, notes that "more work is needed to ensure that the signing algorithm is secure against side-channel attacks". The relative lack of cryptanalytic works regarding these schemes can probably be attributed to the fact that the relationship between secret keys and the information that leaks through side-channels is a lot more subtle than in the Fiat–Shamir setting.

Indeed, in Fiat–Shamir style schemes, the signing algorithm uses the secret key very directly (it is combined linearly with other elements to form the signature), and as a result, side-channel leakage on sensitive variables, like the random nonce, easily leads to key exposure. By comparison, the way the signing key is used in GPV type schemes is much less straightforward. The key is used to construct the trapdoor information used for the lattice discrete Gaussian sampler; in the case of the samplers [13,20,30] used in GPV, DLP and FALCON, that information is essentially the Gram–Schmidt orthogonalization (GSO) of a matrix associated with the secret key. Moreover, due to the way that GSO matrix is used in the sampling algorithm, only a small amount of information about it is liable to leak through side-channels, and how that small amount relates to the signing key is far from clear. To the best of our knowledge, neither the problem of identifying a clear side-channel leakage, nor that of relating that such a leakage to the signing key have been tackled in the literature so far.

Our Contributions. In this work, we initiate the study of how side-channel leakage impacts the security of hash-and-sign lattice-based signature, focusing our attention to the two most notable practical schemes in that family, namely DLP and FALCON. Our contributions towards that goal are mainly threefold.

First, we identify a specific leakage of the implementations of both DLP and FALCON (at least in its original incarnation) with respect to timing side-channels. As noted above, the lattice discrete Gaussian sampler used in signature generation relies on the Gram–Schmidt orthogonalization of a certain matrix associated with the secret key. Furthermore, the problem of sampling a discrete Gaussian distribution supported over the lattice is reduced to sampling one-dimensional discrete Gaussians with standard deviations computed from the norms of the rows of that GSO matrix. In particular, the one-dimensional sampler has to support varying standard deviations, which is not easy to do in constant time. Unsurprisingly, the target implementations both leak that standard deviation through timing side-channels; specifically, they rely on rejection sampling, and the acceptance rate of the corresponding loop is directly related to the standard deviation. As a result, timing attacks will reveal the Gram–Schmidt norms of the matrix associated to the secret key (or rather, an approximation thereof, to a precision increasing with the number of available samples).

Second, we use algebraic number theoretic techniques to elucidate the link between those Gram–Schmidt norms and the secret key. In fact, we show that the secret key can be entirely reconstructed from the knowledge of those Gram–Schmidt norms (at least if they are known *exactly*), in a way which crucially relies on the algebraic structure of the corresponding lattices.

Since both DLP and FALCON work in an NTRU lattice, the signing key can be expressed as a pair (f, g) of small elements in a cyclotomic ring $\mathcal{R} = \mathbb{Z}[\zeta]$ (of power-of-two conductor, in the case of those schemes). The secret, short basis of the NTRU lattice is constructed by blocks from the multiplication matrices of f and g (and related elements F, G) in a certain basis of $\mathcal{R}$ as a $\mathbb{Z}$-algebra (DLP uses the usual power basis, whereas FALCON uses the power basis in *bit-reversed order*; this apparently small difference interestingly plays a crucial role in this work). It is then easily seen that the Gram matrix of the first half of the lattice basis is essentially the multiplication matrix associated with the element $u = f\bar{f} + g\bar{g}$, where the bar denotes the complex conjugation $\bar{\zeta} = \zeta^{-1}$. From that observation, we deduce that knowing the Gram–Schmidt norms of lattice basis is essentially equivalent to knowing the leading principal minors of the multiplication matrix of u, which is a real, totally positive element of $\mathcal{R}$.

We then give general efficient algorithms, both for the power basis (DLP case) and for the bit-reversed order power basis (FALCON case), which recover an arbitrary totally positive element u (up to a possible automorphism of the ambient field) given the leading principal minors of its multiplication matrix. The case of the power basis is relatively easy: we can actually recover the coefficients iteratively one by one, with each coefficient given as a solution of quadratic equation over $\mathbb{Q}$ depending only on the minors and the previous coefficients. The bit-reversed order power basis is more contrived, however; recovery is then carried out recursively, by reduction to the successive subfields of the power-of-two cyclotomic tower.

Finally, to complete the recovery, we need to deduce f and g from u. We show that this can be done using the public key $h = g/f \bmod q$: we can use it to reconstruct both the relative norm $f\bar{f}$ of f, and the ideal $(f) \subset \mathcal{R}$. That data can then be plugged into the Gentry–Szydlo algorithm [21] to obtain f in polynomial time, and hence g. Those steps, though simple, are also of independent interest, since they can be applied to the side-channel attack against BLISS described in [14], in order to get rid of the expensive factorization of an algebraic norm, and hence make the attack efficient for all keys (instead of a small percentage of weak keys as originally stated).

Our third contribution is to actually collect timing traces for the DLP scheme and mount the concrete key recovery. This is not an immediate consequence of the previous points, since our totally positive element recovery algorithm a priori requires the *exact* knowledge of Gram–Schmidt norms, whereas side-channel leakage only provides approximations (and since some of the squared Gram–Schmidt norms are rational numbers of very large height, recovering them exactly would require an unrealistic number of traces). As a result, the recovery algorithm has to be combined with some pruned tree search in order to account for approximate inputs. In practice, for the larger parameters of DLP signatures (with a claimed security level of 192 bits), we manage to recover the key with good probability using 2^{33} to 2^{35} DLP timing traces.

Carrying out such an experiment in the FALCON setting, however, is left as a challenging open problem for further work. This is because adapting the bit-reversed order totally positive recovery algorithm to deal with approximate inputs appears to be much more difficult (instead of sieving integers whose square lies in some specified interval, one would need to find the *cyclotomic* integers whose square lies in some target set, which does not even look simple to describe).

The source code of the attack is available at https://github.com/yuyang-crypto/Key_Recovery_from_GSnorms.

Related Work. As noted above, the side-channel security of Fiat–Shamir lattice-based signature has been studied extensively, including in [4,6,7,14,43,50]. However, the only implementation attacks we are aware of against hash-and-sign schemes are fault analysis papers [15,35]: side-channel attacks have not been described so far to the best of our knowledge.

Aside from the original implementations of DLP and FALCON, which are the focus of this paper, several others have appeared in the literature. However, they usually do not aim for side-channel security [36,41] or only make the *base* discrete Gaussian sampler (with fixed standard deviation) constant time [29], but do not eliminate the leakage of the varying standard deviations. As a result, those implementations are also vulnerable to the attacks of this paper.

This is not the case, however, for Pornin's very recent, updated implementation of FALCON, which uses a novel technique proposed by Prest, Ricosset and Rossi [48], combined with other recent results on constant time *rejection sampling* for discrete Gaussian distribution [4,53] in order to eliminate the timing leakage of the lattice discrete Gaussian sampler. This technique applies to discrete Gaussian sampling over $\mathbb{Z}$ with varying standard deviations, when those deviations only take values in a small range. It is then possible to eliminate the dependence on the standard deviation in the rejection sampling by scaling the target distribution to match the acceptance rate of the maximal possible standard deviation. The small range ensures that the overhead of this countermeasure is relatively modest. Thanks to this countermeasure, we stress that the most recent official implementation of FALCON is *already protected* against the attacks of this paper. Nevertheless, we believe our results underscore the importance of applying such countermeasures.

Organization of the Paper. Following some preliminary material in Sect. 2, Sect. 3 is devoted to recalling some general facts about signature generation for hash-and-sign lattice-based schemes. Section 4 then gives a roadmap of our attack strategy, and provides some details about the final steps (how to deduce the secret key from the totally positive element $u = f\bar{f} + g\bar{g}$. Section 5 describes our main technical contribution: the algorithms that recover u from the Gram–Schmidt norms, both in the DLP and in the FALCON setting. Section 6 delves into the details of the side-channel leakage, showing how the implementations of the Gaussian samplers of DLP and FALCON do indeed reveal the Gram–Schmidt norms through timing side-channels. Finally, Sect. 7 presents our concrete experiments against DLP, including the tree search strategy to accommodate approximate Gram–Schmidt norms and experimental results in terms of timing and number of traces.

Notation. We use bold lowercase letters for vectors and bold uppercase for matrices. The zero vector is $\mathbf{0}$. We denote by $\mathbb{N}$ the non-negative integer set and by log the natural logarithm. Vectors are in row form, and we write $\mathbf{B} = (\mathbf{b}_0, \ldots, \mathbf{b}_{n-1})$ to denote that $\mathbf{b}_i$ is the i-th row of $\mathbf{B}$. For a matrix $\mathbf{B} \in \mathbb{R}^{n \times m}$, we denote by $\mathbf{B}_{i,j}$ the entry in the i-th row and j-th column of $\mathbf{B}$, where $i \in \{0, \ldots, n-1\}$ and $j \in \{0, \ldots, m-1\}$. For $I \subseteq [0, n), J \subseteq [0, m)$, we denote by $\mathbf{B}_{I \times J}$ the submatrix $(\mathbf{B}_{i,j})_{i \in I, j \in J}$. In particular, we write $\mathbf{B}_I = \mathbf{B}_{I \times I}$. Let $\mathbf{B}^t$ denote the transpose of $\mathbf{B}$.

Given $\mathbf{u} = (u_0, \ldots, u_{n-1})$ and $\mathbf{v} = (v_0, \ldots, v_{n-1})$, their inner product is $\langle \mathbf{u}, \mathbf{v} \rangle = \sum_{i=0}^{n-1} u_i v_i$. The ℓ_2-norm of $\mathbf{v}$ is $\|\mathbf{v}\| = \sqrt{\langle \mathbf{v}, \mathbf{v} \rangle}$ and the ℓ_∞-norm is $\|\mathbf{v}\|_\infty = \max_i |v_i|$. The determinant of a square matrix $\mathbf{B}$ is denoted by $\det(\mathbf{B})$, so that $\det\left(\mathbf{B}_{[0,i]}\right)$ is the i-th leading principal minor of $\mathbf{B}$.

Let D be a distribution. We write $z \hookleftarrow D$ when the random variable z is sampled from D, and denote by $D(x)$ the probability that $z = x$. The expectation of a random variable z is $\mathbb{E}[z]$. We write $\mathcal{N}(\mu, \sigma^2)$ the normal distribution of mean μ and variance σ^2. We let $U(S)$ be the uniform distribution over a finite set S. For a real-valued function f and any countable set S in the domain of f, we write $f(S) = \sum_{x \in S} f(x)$.

2 Preliminaries

A lattice $\mathcal{L}$ is a discrete additive subgroup of $\mathbb{R}^m$. If it is generated by $\mathbf{B} \in \mathbb{R}^{n \times m}$, we also write $\mathcal{L} := \mathcal{L}(\mathbf{B}) = \{\mathbf{x}\mathbf{B} \mid \mathbf{x} \in \mathbb{Z}^n\}$. If $\mathbf{B}$ has full row rank, then we call $\mathbf{B}$ a basis and n the rank of $\mathcal{L}$.

2.1 Gram Schmidt Orthogonalization

Let $\mathbf{B} = (\mathbf{b}_0, \ldots, \mathbf{b}_{n-1}) \in \mathbb{Q}^{n \times m}$ of rank n. The Gram-Schmidt orthogonalization of $\mathbf{B}$ is $\mathbf{B} = \mathbf{L}\mathbf{B}^*$, where $\mathbf{L} \in \mathbb{Q}^{n \times n}$ is lower-triangular with 1 on its diagonal and $\mathbf{B}^* = (\mathbf{b}_0^*, \ldots, \mathbf{b}_{n-1}^*)$ is a matrix with pairwise orthogonal rows. We call $\|\mathbf{b}_i^*\|$ the i-th Gram-Schmidt norm of $\mathbf{B}$, and let $\|\mathbf{B}\|_{GS} = \max_i \|\mathbf{b}_i^*\|$.

The Gram matrix of $\mathbf{B}$ is $\mathbf{G} = \mathbf{B}\mathbf{B}^t$, and satisfies $\mathbf{G} = \mathbf{L}\mathbf{D}\mathbf{L}^t$ where $\mathbf{D} = \operatorname{diag}\left(\|\mathbf{b}_i^*\|^2\right)$. This is also known as the Cholesky decomposition of $\mathbf{G}$, and such a decomposition exists for any symmetric positive definite matrix. The next proposition follows from the triangular structure of $\mathbf{L}$.

Proposition 1. *Let $\mathbf{B} = \mathbb{Q}^{n \times m}$ of rank n and $\mathbf{G}$ its Gram matrix. Then for all integer $0 \leq k \leq n-1$, we have $\det\left(\mathbf{G}_{[0,k]}\right) = \prod_{i=0}^{k} \|\mathbf{b}_i^*\|^2$.*

Let $\mathbf{M} = \begin{pmatrix} \mathbf{A} & \mathbf{B} \\ \mathbf{C} & \mathbf{D} \end{pmatrix}$, where $\mathbf{A} \in \mathbb{R}^{n \times n}$, $\mathbf{D} \in \mathbb{R}^{m \times m}$ are invertible matrices, then $\mathbf{M}/\mathbf{A} = \mathbf{D} - \mathbf{C}\mathbf{A}^{-1}\mathbf{B} \in \mathbb{R}^{m \times m}$ is called the Schur complement of $\mathbf{A}$. It holds that

$$\det(\mathbf{M}) = \det(\mathbf{A})\det(\mathbf{M}/\mathbf{A}). \tag{1}$$

2.2   Parametric Statistics

Let D_p be some distribution determined by parameter p. Let $\mathbf{X} = (X_1, \ldots, X_n)$ be a vector of observed samples of $X \hookleftarrow D_p$. The *log-likelihood function* with respect to $\mathbf{X}$ is

$$\ell_{\mathbf{X}}(p) = \sum_{i=1}^{n} \log(D_p(X_i)).$$

Provided the log-likelihood function is bounded, a *maximum likelihood estimator* for samples $\mathbf{X}$ is a real $MLE(\mathbf{X})$ maximizing $\ell_{\mathbf{X}}(p)$. The *Fisher information* is

$$\mathcal{I}(p) = -\mathbb{E}\left[\frac{d^2}{dp^2}\ell_{\mathbf{X}}(p)\right].$$

Seen as a random variable, it is known (e.g. [26, Theorem 6.4.2]) that $\sqrt{n}(MLE(\mathbf{X}) - p)$ converges in distribution to $\mathcal{N}(0, \mathcal{I}(p)^{-1})$. When the target distribution is a geometric, maximum likelihood estimators and the Fisher information are well-known. The second statement of the next lemma directly comes from a Gaussian tail bound.

Lemma 1. *Let Geo_p denote a geometric distribution with parameter p, and $\mathbf{X} = (X_1, \cdots, X_n)$ be samples from Geo_p. Then we have $MLE(\mathbf{X}) = \frac{n}{\sum_{i=1}^{n} X_i}$ and $\sqrt{n}(MLE(\mathbf{X}) - p)$ converges in distribution to $\mathcal{N}(0, p^2(1-p))$. In particular, when N is large, then for any $\alpha \geq 1$, we have $|MLE(\mathbf{X}) - p| \leq \alpha \cdot p\sqrt{\frac{1-p}{N}}$ except with probability at most $2\exp(-\alpha^2/2)$.*

2.3   Discrete Gaussian Distributions

Let $\rho_{\sigma,\mathbf{c}}(\mathbf{x}) = \exp\left(-\frac{\|\mathbf{x}-\mathbf{c}\|^2}{2\sigma^2}\right)$ be the n-dimensional Gaussian function with center $\mathbf{c} \in \mathbb{R}^n$ and standard deviation σ. When $\mathbf{c} = \mathbf{0}$, we just write $\rho_{\sigma}(\mathbf{x})$. The discrete Gaussian over a lattice $\mathcal{L}$ with center $\mathbf{c}$ and standard deviation parameter σ is defined by the probability function

$$D_{\mathcal{L},\sigma,\mathbf{c}}(\mathbf{x}) = \frac{\rho_{\sigma,\mathbf{c}}(\mathbf{x})}{\rho_{\sigma,\mathbf{c}}(\mathcal{L})}, \forall \mathbf{x} \in \mathcal{L}.$$

In this work, the case $\mathcal{L} = \mathbb{Z}$ is of particular interest. It is well known that $\int_{-\infty}^{\infty} \rho_{\sigma,c}(x)dx = \sigma\sqrt{2\pi}$. Notice that $D_{\mathbb{Z},\sigma,c}$ is equivalent to $i + D_{\mathbb{Z},\sigma,c-i}$ for an arbitrary $i \in \mathbb{Z}$, hence it suffices to consider the case where $c \in [0, 1)$. The half discrete integer Gaussian, denoted by $D_{\mathbb{Z},\sigma,c}^+$, is defined by

$$D_{\mathbb{Z},\sigma,c}^+(x) = \frac{\rho_{\sigma,c}(x)}{\rho_{\sigma,c}(\mathbb{N})}, \forall x \in \mathbb{N}.$$

We again omit the center when it is $c = 0$. For any $\epsilon > 0$, the (scaled)[1] smoothing parameter $\eta_\epsilon'(\mathbb{Z})$ is the smallest $s > 0$ such that $\rho_{1/s\sqrt{2\pi}}(\mathbb{Z}) \leq 1 + \epsilon$. In practice, ϵ is very small, say 2^{-50}. The smoothing parameter allows to quantify precisely how the discrete Gaussian differs from the standard Gaussian function.

Lemma 2 ([38], implicit in Lemma 4.4). *If $\sigma \geq \eta_\epsilon'(\mathbb{Z})$, then $\rho_\sigma(c + \mathbb{Z}) \in [\frac{1-\epsilon}{1+\epsilon}, 1]\rho_\sigma(\mathbb{Z})$ for any $c \in [0, 1)$.*

Corollary 1. *If $\sigma \geq \eta_\epsilon'(\mathbb{Z})$, then $\rho_\sigma(\mathbb{Z}) \in [1, \frac{1+\epsilon}{1-\epsilon}]\sqrt{2\pi}\sigma$.*

Proof. Notice that $\int_0^1 \rho_\sigma(\mathbb{Z} + c)\mathrm{d}c = \int_{-\infty}^\infty \rho_\sigma(x)\mathrm{d}x = \sqrt{2\pi}\sigma$, the proof is completed by Lemma 2. □

2.4 Power-of-Two Cyclotomic Fields

For the rest of this article, we let $n = 2^\ell$ for some integer $\ell \geq 1$. We let ζ_n be a $2n$-th primitive root of 1. Then $\mathcal{K}_n = \mathbb{Q}(\zeta_n)$ is the n-th power-of-two cyclotomic field, and comes together with its ring of algebraic integers $\mathcal{R}_n = \mathbb{Z}[\zeta_n]$. It is also equipped with n field automorphisms forming the Galois group which is commutative in this case. It can be seen that $\mathcal{K}_{n/2} = \mathbb{Q}(\zeta_{n/2})$ is the subfield of $\mathcal{K}_n$ fixed by the automorphism $\sigma(\zeta_n) = -\zeta_n$ of $\mathcal{K}_n$, as $\zeta_n^2 = \zeta_{n/2}$. This leads to a tower of field extensions and their corresponding rings of integers

$$\begin{array}{ccccc}
\mathcal{K}_n \supseteq & \mathcal{K}_{n/2} \supseteq & \cdots \supseteq & \mathcal{K}_1 = \mathbb{Q} \\
\cup & \cup & \cdots & \cup \\
\mathcal{R}_n \supseteq & \mathcal{R}_{n/2} \supseteq & \cdots \supseteq & \mathcal{R}_1 = \mathbb{Z}
\end{array}$$

Given an extension $\mathcal{K}_n | \mathcal{K}_{n/2}$, the relative trace $\mathrm{Tr} : \mathcal{K}_n \to \mathcal{K}_{n/2}$ is the $\mathcal{K}_{n/2}$-linear map given by $\mathrm{Tr}(f) = f + \sigma(f)$. Similarly, the relative norm is the multiplicative map $\mathrm{N}(f) = f \cdot \sigma(f) \in \mathcal{K}_{n/2}$. Both maps send integers in $\mathcal{K}_n$ to integers in $\mathcal{K}_{n/2}$. For all $f \subset \mathcal{K}_n$, it holds that $f = (\mathrm{Tr}(f) + \zeta_n\mathrm{Tr}(\zeta_n^{-1}f))/2$.

We are also interested in the field automorphism $\zeta_n \mapsto \zeta_n^{-1} = \bar{\zeta}_n$, which corresponds to the complex conjugation. We call *adjoint* the image $\bar{f}$ of f under this automorphism. The fixed subfield $\mathcal{K}_n^+ := \mathbb{Q}(\zeta_n + \zeta_n^{-1})$ is known as the *totally real subfield* and contains the *self-adjoint* elements, that is, such that $f = \bar{f}$. Another way to describe self-adjoint elements is to say that all their complex embeddings[2] are in fact reals. Elements whose embeddings are all positive are called *totally positive elements*, and we denote their set by $\mathcal{K}_n^{++}$. A standard example of such an element is given by $f\bar{f}$ for any $f \in \mathcal{K}_n$. It is well-known that the Galois automorphisms act as permutation of these embeddings, so that a totally positive element stays positive under the action of the Galois group.

---

[1] The scaling factor is $(\sqrt{2\pi})^{-1}$ before the smoothing parameter $\eta_\epsilon(\mathbb{Z})$ in [38].

[2] Each root of $x^n + 1$ describes one complex embedding by mean of evaluation.

Representation of Cyclotomic Numbers. We also have $\mathcal{K}_n \simeq \mathbb{Q}[x]/(x^n + 1)$ and $\mathcal{R}_n \simeq \mathbb{Z}[x]/(x^n + 1)$, so that elements in cyclotomic fields can be seen as polynomials. In this work, each $f = \sum_{i=0}^{n-1} f_i \zeta_n^i \in \mathcal{K}_n$ is identified with its coefficient vector $(f_0, \cdots, f_{n-1})$. Then the inner product of f and g is $\langle f, g \rangle = \sum_{i=0}^{n-1} f_i g_i$, and we write $\|f\|$, resp. $\|f\|_\infty$, the ℓ_2-norm, resp. ℓ_∞-norm, of f. In this representation, it can be checked that $\bar{f} = (f_0, -f_{n-1}, \ldots, -f_1)$ and that $\langle f, gh \rangle = \langle f\bar{g}, h \rangle$ for all $f, g, h \in \mathcal{K}_n$. In particular, the constant coefficient of $f\bar{g}$ is $\langle f, g \rangle = \langle f\bar{g}, 1 \rangle$. A self-adjoint element f has coefficients $(f_0, f_1, \ldots, f_{n/2-1}, 0, -f_{n/2-1}, \ldots, -f_1)$.

Elements in $\mathcal{K}_n$ can also be represented by their matrix of multiplication in the basis $1, \zeta_n, \ldots, \zeta_n^{n-1}$. In other words, the map $\mathcal{A}_n : \mathcal{K}_n \to \mathbb{Q}^{n \times n}$ defined by

$$
\mathcal{A}_n(f) = \begin{pmatrix} f_0 & f_1 & \cdots & f_{n-1} \\ -f_{n-1} & f_0 & \cdots & f_{n-2} \\ \vdots & \vdots & \ddots & \vdots \\ -f_1 & -f_2 & \cdots & f_0 \end{pmatrix} = \begin{pmatrix} f \\ \zeta_n \cdot f \\ \vdots \\ \zeta_n^{n-1} \cdot f \end{pmatrix}
$$

is a ring isomorphism. We have $fg = g \cdot \mathcal{A}_n(f)$. We can also see that $\mathcal{A}_n(\bar{f}) = \mathcal{A}_n(f)^t$ which justifies the term "adjoint". We deduce that the matrix of a self-adjoint element is symmetric. It can be observed that a totally positive element $A \in \mathcal{K}_n$ corresponds to the symmetric positive definite matrix $\mathcal{A}_n(A)$.

For efficiency reasons, the scheme FALCON uses another representation corresponding to the tower structure. If $f = (f_0, \ldots, f_{n-1}) \in \mathcal{K}_n$, we let $f_e = \mathrm{Tr}(f)/2 = (f_0, f_2, \ldots, f_{n-2})$ and $f_o = \mathrm{Tr}(\zeta_n^{-1}f)/2 = (f_1, f_3, \ldots, f_{n-1})$. Let $\mathbf{P}_n \in \mathbb{Z}^{n \times n}$ be the permutation matrix corresponding to the bit-reversal order. We define $\mathcal{F}_n(f) = \mathbf{P}_n \mathcal{A}_n(f) \mathbf{P}_n^t$. In particular, it is also symmetric positive definite when f is a totally positive element. As shown in [13], it holds that

$$
\mathcal{F}_n(f) = \begin{pmatrix} \mathcal{F}_{n/2}(f_e) & \mathcal{F}_{n/2}(f_o) \\ \mathcal{F}_{n/2}(\zeta_{n/2}f_o) & \mathcal{F}_{n/2}(f_e) \end{pmatrix}. \tag{2}
$$

2.5   NTRU Lattices

Given $f, g \in \mathcal{R}_n$ such that f is invertible modulo some $q \in \mathbb{Z}$, we let $h = f^{-1}g \bmod q$. The NTRU lattice determined by h is $\mathcal{L}_{\mathrm{NTRU}} = \{(u, v) \in \mathcal{R}_n^2 : u + vh = 0 \bmod q\}$. Two bases of this lattice are of particular interest for cryptography:

$$
\mathbf{B}_{\mathrm{NTRU}} = \begin{pmatrix} q & 0 \\ -h & 1 \end{pmatrix} \text{ and } \mathbf{B}_{f,g} = \begin{pmatrix} g & -f \\ G & -F \end{pmatrix},
$$

where $F, G \in \mathcal{R}_n$ such that $fG - gF = q$. Indeed, the former basis acts usually as the public key, while the latter is the secret key, also called the trapdoor basis, when f, g, F, G are short vectors. In practice, these matrices are represented using either the operator $\mathcal{A}_n$ [11] or $\mathcal{F}_n$ [47]:

$$
\mathbf{B}_{f,g}^{\mathcal{A}} = \begin{pmatrix} \mathcal{A}_n(g) & \mathcal{A}_n(-f) \\ \mathcal{A}_n(G) & \mathcal{A}_n(-F) \end{pmatrix} \quad \text{and} \quad \mathbf{B}_{f,g}^{\mathcal{F}} = \begin{pmatrix} \mathcal{F}_n(g) & \mathcal{F}_n(-f) \\ \mathcal{F}_n(G) & \mathcal{F}_n(-F) \end{pmatrix}.
$$

3   Hash-and-Sign over NTRU Lattices

Gentry, Peikert and Vaikuntanathan introduced in [20] a generic and provably secure hash-and-sign framework based on trapdoor sampling. This paradigm has then been instantiated over NTRU lattices giving rise to practically efficient cryptosystems: DLP [11] and FALCON [47] signature schemes.

In the NTRU-based hash-and-sign scheme, the secret key is a pair of short polynomials $(f, g) \in \mathcal{R}_n^2$ and the public key is $h = f^{-1}g \bmod q$. The *trapdoor basis* $\mathbf{B}_{f,g}$ (of $\mathcal{L}_{\mathrm{NTRU}}$) derives from (f, g) by computing $F, G \in \mathcal{R}_n$ such that $fG - gF = q$. In both the DLP signature and FALCON, the trapdoor basis has a bounded Gram–Schmidt norm: $\|\mathbf{B}_{f,g}\|_{GS} \leq 1.17\sqrt{q}$ for compact signatures.

The signing and verification procedure is described on a high level as follows:

Sign$(m, \mathsf{sk} = \mathbf{B}_{f,g})$	**Verify**$(m, s, \mathsf{pk} = h)$
Compute $c = \mathsf{hash}(m) \in \mathcal{R}_n$;	Compute $c = \mathsf{hash}(m) \in \mathcal{R}_n$;
Using sk, sample a short (s_1, s_2)	Compute $\mathbf{s} = (c - sh \bmod q, s)$;
such that $s_1 + s_2 h = c \bmod q$;	If $\|\mathbf{s}\|$ is not small enough, reject.
Return $s = s_2$.	Accept.

Lattice Gaussian samplers [20,42] are nowadays a standard tool to generate signatures provably statistically independent of the secret basis. However, such samplers are also a notorious target for side-channel attacks. This work makes no exception and attacks non constant-time implementations of the lattice Gaussian samplers at the heart of both DLP and FALCON, that are based on the KGPV sampler [30] or its ring variant [13]. Precisely, while previous attacks target to Gaussian with *public* standard deviations, our attack learns the *secret-dependent* Gaussian standard deviations involved in the KGPV sampler.

3.1   The KGPV Sampler and Its Variant

The KGPV sampler is a randomized variant of Babai's nearest plane algorithm [1]: instead of rounding each center to the closest integer, the KGPV sampler determines the integral coefficients according to some integer Gaussians. It is shown in [20] that under certain smoothness condition, the algorithm outputs a sample from a distribution negligibly close to the target Gaussian. Its formal description is illustrated in Algorithm 3.1.

Note that in the KGPV sampler (or its ring variant), the standard deviations of integer Gaussians are inversely proportional to the Gram–Schmidt norms of the input basis. In the DLP scheme, $\mathbf{B}$ is in fact the trapdoor basis $\mathbf{B}_{f,g}^A \in \mathbb{Z}^{2n \times 2n}$.

The Ducas–Prest Sampler. FALCON uses a variant of the KGPV algorithm which stems naturally from Ducas–Prest's fast Fourier nearest plane algorithm [13]. It exploits the tower structure of power-of-two cyclotomic rings. Just like the KGPV sampler, the Ducas-Prest sampler fundamentally relies on integer Gaussian sampling to output Gaussian vectors. We omit its algorithmic description, as it is not needed in this work. Overall, what matters is to understand that the standard

---

Algorithm 3.1. The KGPV algorithm $\mathsf{KGPV}(\sigma, \mathbf{B}, \mathbf{c})$

Input: a basis $\mathbf{B} = (\mathbf{b}_0, \cdots, \mathbf{b}_{n-1})$ of a lattice $\mathcal{L}$, $\mathbf{c} \in \mathbb{Q}^n$ and $\sigma \geq \|\mathbf{B}\|_{GS} \cdot \eta_\epsilon(\mathbb{Z})$.
Output: $\mathbf{z} \in \mathbb{Z}^n$ such that $\mathbf{zB}$ follows a distribution close to $D_{\mathcal{L}, \sigma, \mathbf{cB}^*}$.

   Precomputation:
1: compute $\mathbf{B} = \mathbf{LB}^*$
2: $(\boldsymbol{\mu}_0, \cdots, \boldsymbol{\mu}_{n-1}) \leftarrow \mathbf{L} - \mathbf{I}_n$
3: **for** $i = n - 1, \cdots, 0$ **do**
4:    $\sigma_i \leftarrow \sigma/\|\mathbf{b}_i^*\|$
5: **end for**
   Sampling:
6: $\mathbf{z} \leftarrow \mathbf{0}, \mathbf{c}' \leftarrow \mathbf{c}$
7: **for** $i = n - 1, \cdots, 0$ **do**
8:    $z_i \leftarrow \mathsf{GaussianIntegerSampler}(\sigma_i, c_i')$
9:    $\mathbf{c}' \leftarrow \mathbf{c}' - z_i \boldsymbol{\mu}_i$
10: **end for**
11: return $\mathbf{z}$

---

deviations of involved integer Gaussians are also in the form $\sigma_i = \sigma/\|\mathbf{b}_i^*\|$, but that $\mathbf{B} = \mathbf{B}_{f,g}^{\mathcal{F}}$ in this context.

4 Side-Channel Attack Against Trapdoor Samplers: A Roadmap

Our algorithm proceeds as follows:

1. Side-channel leakage: extract the $\|\mathbf{b}_i^*\|$'s associated to $\mathbf{B}_{f,g}^{\mathcal{A}}$, resp. $\mathbf{B}_{f,g}^{\mathcal{F}}$ via the timing leakage of integer Gaussian sampler in the DLP scheme, reps. FALCON.

2. Totally positive recovery: from the given $\|\mathbf{b}_i^*\|$'s, recover a Galois conjugate u of $f\bar{f} + g\bar{g} \in \mathcal{K}_n^{++}$.

3. Final recovery: compute f from u and the public key $g/f \mod q$.

Steps 1 and 2 of the attack are the focus of Sects. 6 and 5 respectively. Below we describe how the third step is performed. First we recover the element $f\bar{g}$, using the fact that it has small coefficients. More precisely, the jth coefficient is $\langle f, \zeta_n^j g \rangle$ where f and $\zeta_n^j g$ are independent and identically distributed according to $D_{\mathbb{Z}^n, r}$, with $r = 1.17\sqrt{\frac{q}{2n}}$. By [32, Lemma 4.3], we know that all these coefficients are of size much smaller than $q/2$ with high probability. Now, we can compute $v = u\bar{h}(1 + h\bar{h})^{-1} \mod q$, where $h = f^{-1}g \mod q$ is the public verification key. We readily see that $v = f\bar{g} \mod q$ if and only if $u = f\bar{f} + g\bar{g}$. If u is a conjugate of $f\bar{f} + g\bar{g}$, then most likely the coefficients of v will look random in $(-q/2, q/2)$. This can mostly be interpreted as the NTRU assumption, that is, h being indistinguishable from a random element modulo q. When this happens, we just consider another conjugate of u, until we obtain a distinguishably small element, which must then be $f\bar{g}$ (not just in reduction modulo q, but in fact over the integers).

Once this is done, we can then deduce the reduction modulo q of $f\bar{f} \equiv f\bar{g}/\bar{h}$ (mod q), which again coincides with $f\bar{f}$ over the integers with high probability (if we again lift elements of $\mathbb{Z}_q$ to $(-q/2, q/2]$, except for the constant coefficient, which should be lifted positively). This boils down to the fact that with high probability $f\bar{f}$ has its constant coefficient in $(0, q)$ and the others are in $(-q/2, q/2)$. Indeed, the constant coefficient of $f\bar{f}$ is $\|f\|^2$, and the others are $\langle f, \zeta_n^j f \rangle$'s with $j \geq 1$. By some Gaussian tail bound, we can show $\|f\|^2 \leq q$ with high probability. As for $\langle f, \zeta_n^j f \rangle$'s, despite the dependency between f and $\zeta_n^j f$, we can still expect $|\langle f, \zeta_n^j f \rangle| < q/2$ for all $j \geq 1$ with high probability. We leave details in the full version [17] for interested readers.

Next, we compute the ideal (f) from the knowledge of $f\bar{f}$ and $f\bar{g}$. Indeed, as f and g are co-prime from the key generation algorithm, we directly have $(f) = (f\bar{f}) + (f\bar{g})$. At this point, we have obtained both the ideal (f) and the relative norm $f\bar{f}$ of f on the totally real subfield. That data is exactly what we need to apply the Gentry–Szydlo algorithm [21], and finally recover f itself in polynomial time. Note furthermore that the practicality of the Gentry–Szydlo algorithm for the dimensions we consider ($n = 512$) has been validated in previous work [14].

Comparison with Existing Method. As part of their side-channel analysis of the BLISS signature scheme, Espitau *et al.* [14] used the Howgrave-Graham–Szydlo algorithm to recover an NTRU secret f from $f\bar{f}$. They successfully solved a small proportion ($\approx 7\%$) of NTRU instances with $n = 512$ in practice. The Howgrave-Graham–Szydlo algorithm first recovers the ideal (f) and then calls the Gentry–Szydlo algorithm as we do above. The bottleneck of this method is in its reliance on integer factorization for ideal recovery: the integers involved can become quite large for an arbitrary f, so that recovery cannot be done in classical polynomial time in general. This is why only a small proportion of instances can be solved in practice.

However, the technique we describe above bypasses this expensive factorization step by exploiting the arithmetic property of the NTRU secret key. In particular, it is immediate to obtain a two-element description of (f), so that the Gentry-Szydlo algorithm can be run as soon as $f\bar{f}$ and $f\bar{g}$ are computed. This significantly improves the applicability and efficiency of Espitau *et al.*'s side-channel attack against BLISS [14]. The question of avoiding the reliance on Gentry–Szydlo algorithm by using the knowledge of $f\bar{g}$ and $f\bar{f}$ remains open, however.

5 Recovering Totally Positive Elements

Totally positive elements in $\mathcal{K}_n$ correspond to symmetric positive definite matrices with an inner structure coming from the algebra of the field. In particular, it is enough to know only one line of the matrix to recover the corresponding field element. Hence it can be expected that being given the diagonal part of the LDL decomposition also suffices to perform a recovery. In this section, we show that this is indeed the case provided we know *exactly* the diagonal.

Recall on the one hand that the $\mathcal{A}_n$ representation is the skew circulant matrix in which each diagonal consists of the same entries. On the other hand, the $\mathcal{F}_n$ representation does not follow the circulant structure, but it is compatible with the tower of rings structure, i.e. its sub-matrices are the $\mathcal{F}_{n/2}$ representations of elements in the subfield $\mathcal{K}_{n/2}$. Each operator leads to a distinct approach, which is described in Sects. 5.1 and 5.2 respectively.

While the algorithms of this section can be used independently, they are naturally related to hash-and-sign over NTRU lattices. Let $\mathbf{B}$ be a matrix representation of some secret key $(g, -f)$, and $\mathbf{G} = \mathbf{B}\mathbf{B}^t$. Then the diagonal part of $\mathbf{G}$'s LDL decomposition contains the $\|\mathbf{b}_i^*\|$'s, and $\mathbf{G}$ is a matrix representation of $f\bar{f} + g\bar{g} \in \mathcal{K}_n^{++}$. As illustrated in Sect. 4, the knowledge of $u = f\bar{f} + g\bar{g}$ allows to recover the secret key in polynomial time. Therefore results in this section pave the way for a better use of secret Gram-Schmidt norms.

In practice however, we will obtain only *approximations* of the $\|\mathbf{b}_i^*\|$'s. The algorithms of this section must then be tweaked to handle the approximation error. The case of $\mathcal{A}_n$ is dealt with in Sect. 7.1. While we do not solve the "approximate" case of $\mathcal{F}_n$, we believe our "exact" algorithms to be of independent interest to the community.

5.1   Case of the Power Basis

The goal of this section is to obtain the next theorem. It involves the heuristic argument that some rational quadratic equations always admits exactly one integer root, which will correspond to a coefficient of the recovered totally positive element. Experimentally, when it happens that there are two integer roots and the wrong one is chosen, the algorithm "fails" with overwhelming probability at the next step: the next discriminant does not lead to integer roots.

Theorem 1. *Let $u \in \mathcal{R}_n \cap \mathcal{K}_n^{++}$. Write $\mathcal{A}_n(u) = \mathbf{L} \cdot \mathrm{diag}(\lambda_i)_i \cdot \mathbf{L}^t$. There is a (heuristic) algorithm* Recovery$_\mathcal{A}$ *that, given λ_i's, computes u or $\sigma(u)$. It runs in $\tilde{O}(n^3 \log \|u\|_\infty)$.*

The complexity analysis is given in the full version [17]. In Sect. 7.2, a version tweaked to handle approximations of the λ_i's is given, and may achieve quasi-quadratic complexity. It is in any case very efficient in practice, and it is used in our attack against DLP signature.

We now describe Algorithm 5.1. By Proposition 1, $\prod_{j=0}^{i} \lambda_i = \det\left(\mathcal{A}_n(u)_{[0,i]}\right)$ is an integer, thus we take $m_i = \prod_{j=0}^{i} \lambda_i$ instead of λ_i as input for integrality. It holds that $u_0 = \det\left(\mathcal{A}_n(u)_{[0,0]}\right) = \lambda_0$. By the self-adjointness of u, we only need to consider the first $n/2$ coefficients. For any $0 \le i < n/2 - 1$, we have

$$\mathcal{A}_n(u)_{[0,i+1]} = \begin{pmatrix} & & & u_{i+1} \\ & \mathcal{A}_n(u)_{[0,i]} & & \vdots \\ & & & u_1 \\ u_{i+1} & \cdots & u_1 & u_0 \end{pmatrix}.$$

Algorithm 5.1. Recovery$_{\mathcal{A}}(m_0, \ldots, m_{n-1})$

Input: $m_0, \ldots, m_{n-1} \in \mathbb{Z}_+$.
Output: $u \in \mathcal{R}_n$ such that u is totally positive and the principal minors of $\mathcal{F}_n(u)$ are
    m_i's $(0 \leq i < n)$.
1: $u_0 \leftarrow m_0$
2: $u_1 \leftarrow$ any root of $u_0 - \frac{m_1}{m_0} - \frac{X^2}{u_0}$
3: **for** $i = 1$ to $n/2 - 2$ **do**
4:    Build $\mathcal{A}_n(u)_{[0,i]}$ from $u_i, \ldots, u_0$
5:    $\mathbf{v}_i \leftarrow (X, u_i, \ldots, u_1)$
6:    Solve $\mathcal{A}_n(u)_{[0,i]} \cdot \mathbf{w}_i^t = \mathbf{v}_i^t$ for $\mathbf{w}_i$
7:    $E \leftarrow u_0 - m_{i+1}/m_i - \mathbf{v}_i \cdot \mathbf{w}_i^t$.
8:    Compute the roots $\{r_1, r_2\}$ of E
9:    $u_{i+1} \leftarrow \{r_1, r_2\} \cap \mathbb{Z}$
10: **end for**
11: **return** $(u_0, u_1, \ldots, u_{n/2-1}, 0, -u_{n/2-1}, \ldots, -u_1)$.

Let $\mathbf{v}_i = (u_{i+1}, \ldots, u_1)$. By the definition of the Schur complement and Proposition 1, we see that

$$\frac{\det\left(\mathcal{A}_n(u)_{[0,i+1]}\right)}{\det\left(\mathcal{A}_n(u)_{[0,i]}\right)} = u_0 - \mathbf{v}_i \mathcal{A}_n(u)_{[0,i]}^{-1} \mathbf{v}_i^t,$$

where the left-hand side is actually λ_{i+1}, and the right-hand side gives a quadratic equation in u_{i+1} with rational coefficients that can be computed from the knowledge of $(u_0, \ldots, u_i)$. When $i = 0$, the equation is equivalent to $\lambda_0 \lambda_1 = u_0^2 - u_1^2$: there are two candidates of u_1 up to sign. Once u_1 is chosen, for $i \geq 1$, the quadratic equation should have with very high probability a unique integer solution, i.e. the corresponding u_{i+1}. This leads to Algorithm 5.1. Note that the sign of u_1 determines whether the algorithm recovers u or $\sigma(u)$. This comes from the fact that $\mathcal{A}_n(u) = \mathrm{diag}((-1)^i)_{i \leq n} \cdot \mathcal{A}_n(\sigma(u)) \cdot \mathrm{diag}((-1)^i)_{i \leq n}$.

5.2   Case of the Bit-Reversed Order Basis

In this section, we are given the diagonal part of the LDL decomposition $\mathcal{F}_n(u) = \mathbf{L}' \mathrm{diag}(\lambda_i) \mathbf{L}'^t$, which rewrites as $(\mathbf{L}'^{-1}\mathbf{P}_n)\mathcal{A}_n(u)(\mathbf{L}'^{-1}\mathbf{P}_n)^t = \mathrm{diag}(\lambda_i)$. Since the triangular structure is shuffled by the bit-reversal representation, recovering u from the λ_i's is not as straightforward as in the previous section. Nevertheless, the compatibility of the $\mathcal{F}_n$ operator with the tower of extension can be exploited. It gives a recursive approach that stems from natural identities between the trace and norm maps relative to the extension $\mathcal{K}_n \mid \mathcal{K}_{n/2}$, crucially uses the self-adjointness and total positivity of u, and fundamentally relies on computing square roots in $\mathcal{R}_n$.

Theorem 2. *Let $u \in \mathcal{R}_n \cap \mathcal{K}_n^{++}$. Write $\mathcal{F}_n(u) = \mathbf{L}' \cdot \mathrm{diag}(\lambda_i)_i \cdot \mathbf{L}'^t$. There is a (heuristic) algorithm that, given the λ_i's, computes a conjugate of u. It runs in $\widetilde{O}(n^3 \log \|u\|_\infty)$.*

The recursiveness of the algorithm and its reliance on square roots will force it to always work "up to Galois conjugation". In particular, at some point we will assume heuristically that only one of the conjugates of a value computed within the algorithm is in a given coset of the subgroup of relative norms in the quadratic subfield. Since that constraint only holds with negligible probability for random values, the heuristic is essentially always verified in practice. Recall that we showed in Sect. 4 how to recover the needed conjugate in practice by a distinguishing argument.

The rest of the section describes the algorithm, while the complexity analysis is presented in the full version [17]. First, we observe from

$$\text{Tr}(u) + \zeta_n \text{Tr}(\zeta_n^{-1}u) = 2u = 2\bar{u} = \overline{\text{Tr}(u)} + \zeta_n^{-1}\overline{\text{Tr}(\zeta_n^{-1}u)}$$

that $\text{Tr}(u)$ is self-adjoint. The positivity of u implies that $\text{Tr}(u) \in \mathcal{K}_{n/2}^{++}$. From Eq. (2), we know that the $n/2$ first minors of $\mathcal{F}_n(u)$ are the minors of $\mathcal{F}_{n/2}(\text{Tr}(u)/2)$. The identity above also shows that $\text{Tr}(\zeta_n^{-1}u)$ is a square root of the element $\zeta_{n/2}^{-1}\text{Tr}(\zeta_n^{-1}u)\overline{\text{Tr}(\zeta_n^{-1}u)}$ in $\mathcal{K}_{n/2}$. Thus, if we knew $\text{Tr}(\zeta_n^{-1}u)\overline{\text{Tr}(\zeta_n^{-1}u)}$, we could reduce the problem of computing $u \in \mathcal{K}_n$ to computations in $\mathcal{K}_{n/2}$, more precisely, recovering a totally positive element from "its minors" and a square root computation.

It turns out that $\text{Tr}(\zeta_n^{-1}u)\overline{\text{Tr}(\zeta_n^{-1}u)}$ can be computed by going down the tower as well. One can see that

$$\text{Tr}(u)^2 - 4\text{N}(u) = \text{Tr}(\zeta_n^{-1}u)\overline{\text{Tr}(\zeta_n^{-1}u)}, \tag{3}$$

where $\text{N}(u)$ is totally positive since u (and therefore $\sigma(u)$) is. This identity[3] can be thought as a "number field version" of the $\mathcal{F}_n$ representation. Indeed, recall that $u_e = (1/2)\text{Tr}(u)$ and $u_o = (1/2)\text{Tr}(\zeta_n^{-1}u)$. Then by block determinant formula and the fact that $\mathcal{F}_n$ is a ring isomorphism, we see that

$$\det \mathcal{F}_n(u) = \prod_{i=0}^{n-1} \lambda_i = \det(\mathcal{F}_{n/2}(u_e)^2 - \mathcal{F}_{n/2}(u_o\overline{u_o})).$$

This strongly suggests a link between the successive minors of $\mathcal{F}_n(u)$ and the element $\text{N}(u)$. The next lemma makes this relation precise, and essentially amounts to taking Schur complements in the above formula.

Lemma 3. *Let $u \in \mathcal{K}_n^{++}$ and $\hat{u} = \frac{2\text{N}(u)}{\text{Tr}(u)} \in \mathcal{K}_{n/2}^{++}$. Then for $0 < k < n/2$, we have*

$$\det\left(\mathcal{F}_n(u)_{[0,k+\frac{n}{2})}\right) = \det\left(\mathcal{F}_{n/2}(u_e)\right)\det\left(\mathcal{F}_{n/2}(\hat{u})_{[0,k)}\right).$$

Proof. Let $\mathbf{G} = \mathcal{F}_n(u)$ and $\mathbf{B} = \mathcal{F}_{n/2}(u_o)_{[0,\frac{n}{2})\times[0,k)}$ in order to write

$$\mathbf{G}_{[0,\frac{n}{2}+k)} = \begin{pmatrix} \mathcal{F}_{n/2}(u_e) & \mathbf{B} \\ \mathbf{B}^t & \mathcal{F}_{n/2}(u_e)_{[0,k)} \end{pmatrix},$$

---

[3] This describes the discriminant of $T^2 - \text{Tr}(u)T + \text{N}(u)$ whose roots are u and $\sigma(u)$ in $\mathcal{K}_n$. It is then not surprising that $\text{Tr}(\zeta_n^{-1}u)\overline{\text{Tr}(\zeta_n^{-1}u)}$ is a square only in $\mathcal{K}_n$.

Algorithm 5.2. TowerRecovery$_\mathcal{F}(m_0, \ldots, m_{n-1})$

Input: $m_0, \ldots, m_{n-1}$.
Output: $u \in \mathcal{R}_n$ such that u is totally positive and the principal minors of $\mathcal{F}_n(u)$ are
 m_i's $(0 \le i < n)$.
1: **if** $n = 2$ **then**
2:   **return** m_0.
3: **end if**
4: $u^+ \leftarrow$ TowerRecovery$_\mathcal{F}(m_0, \ldots, m_{\frac{n}{2}-1})$ $\{u^+$ is $\mathrm{Tr}(u)/2\}$
5: $\widetilde{u} \leftarrow$ TowerRecovery$_\mathcal{F}(\frac{m_{n/2}}{m_{n/2-1}}, \ldots, \frac{m_{n-1}}{m_{n/2-1}})$ $\{\widetilde{u}$ is a conjugate of $\widehat{u} = \frac{2\mathrm{N}(u)}{\mathrm{Tr}(u)}\}$
6: Find τ such that $u^+ \cdot \tau(\widetilde{u})$ is a relative norm.
7: $\widehat{u} \leftarrow \tau(\widetilde{u})$
8: $s \leftarrow u^+ \cdot (u^+ - \widehat{u})$
9: $u^- \leftarrow$ TowerRoot$(\zeta_{n/2}^{-1} s)$ $\{u^-$ is a conjugate of $\pm \mathrm{Tr}(\zeta_n^{-1} u)/2\}$
10: **return** $u^+ + \zeta_n u^-$

---

with $\mathbf{B}^t = \mathcal{F}_{n/2}(\overline{u_o})_{[0,k) \times [0, \frac{n}{2})}$. Let $\mathbf{S} = \mathbf{G}_{[0, \frac{n}{2}+k)}/\mathcal{F}_{n/2}(u_e) = \mathcal{F}_{n/2}(u_e)_{[0,k)} - \mathbf{B}\mathcal{F}_{n/2}(u_e)^{-1}\mathbf{B}^t$. Since $\mathcal{F}_n$ is a ring isomorphism, a routine computation shows that $\mathbf{S} = \mathcal{F}_{n/2}(\widehat{u})_{[0,k)}$. The proof follows from Eq. (1). $\qquad\qquad\square$

Lemma 3 tells us that knowing $\mathrm{Tr}(u)$ and the principal minors of $\mathcal{F}_n(u)$ is enough to recover those of $\mathcal{F}_{n/2}(\widehat{u})$, so that the computations in $\mathcal{K}_n$ are again reduced to computing a totally positive element in $\mathcal{K}_{n/2}$ from its minors. Then from Eq. (3), we can obtain $\mathrm{Tr}(\zeta_n^{-1}u)\overline{\mathrm{Tr}(\zeta_n^{-1}u)}$. The last step is then to compute a square root of $\zeta_{n/2}^{-1}\mathrm{Tr}(\zeta_n^{-1}u)\overline{\mathrm{Tr}(\zeta_n^{-1}u)}$ in $\mathcal{K}_{n/2}$ to recover $\pm\mathrm{Tr}(\zeta_n^{-1}u)$. In particular, this step will lead to u or its conjugate $\sigma(u)$. As observed above, this translates ultimately in recovering only a conjugate of u.

Lastly, when $n = 2$, that is, when we work in $\mathbb{Q}(i)$, a totally positive element is in fact in $\mathbb{Q}_+$. This leads to Algorithm 5.2, which is presented in the general context of $\mathcal{K}_n$ to fit the description above, for the sake of simplicity. The algorithm TowerRoot of Step 9 computes square roots in $\mathcal{K}_n$ and a quasi-quadratic version for integers is presented and analyzed in the next section.

The whole procedure is constructing a binary tree as illustrated in Fig. 1. The algorithm can be made to rely essentially only on algebraic integers, which also helps in analyzing its complexity. This gives the claim of Theorem 2 (see the full version [17] for details). At Step 6, the algorithm finds the (heuristically unique) conjugate $\widehat{u}$ of $\widetilde{u}$ such that $\widehat{u} \cdot u^+$ is a relative norm (since we must have $\widehat{u} \cdot u^+ = \mathrm{N}(u)$ by the above). In practice, in the integral version of this algorithm, we carry out this test not by checking for being a norm, but as an integrality test.

5.2.1 Computing Square Roots in Cyclotomic Towers

In this section, we will focus on computing square roots of algebraic integers: given $s = t^2 \in \mathcal{R}_n$, compute t. The reason for focusing on integers is that both our Algorithm 5.2 and practical applications deal only with algebraic integers.

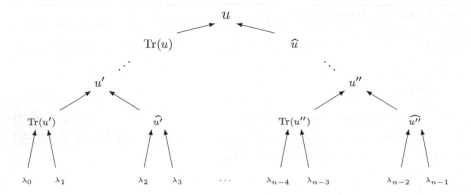

Fig. 1. Binary tree built by TowerRecovery$_\mathcal{F}$.

A previous approach was suggested in [25], relying on finding primes with small splitting pattern in $\mathcal{R}_n$, computing square roots in several finite fields and brute-forcing to find the correct candidate. A hassle in analyzing this approach is to first find a prime larger enough than an arbitrary input, and that splits in, say, two factors in $\mathcal{R}_n$. Omitting the cost of finding such a prime, this algorithm can be shown to run in $\widetilde{O}(n^2 (\log \|s\|_\infty)^2)$. Our recursive approach does not theoretically rely on finding a correct prime, and again exploits the tower structure to achieve the next claim.

Theorem 3. *Given a square s in $\mathcal{R}_n$, there is a deterministic algorithm that computes $t \in \mathcal{R}_n$ such that $t^2 = s$ in time $\widetilde{O}(n^2 \log \|s\|_\infty)$.*

Recall that the subfield $\mathcal{K}_{n/2}$ is fixed by the automorphism $\sigma(\zeta_n) = -\zeta_n$. For any element t in $\mathcal{R}_n$, recall that $t = \frac{1}{2}(\mathrm{Tr}(t) + \zeta_n \mathrm{Tr}(\zeta_n^{-1}t))$, where Tr is the trace relative to this extension. We can also see that

$$\mathrm{Tr}(t)^2 = \mathrm{Tr}(t^2) + 2\mathrm{N}(t) = \mathrm{Tr}(s) + 2\mathrm{N}(t),$$

$$\mathrm{Tr}(\zeta_n^{-1}t)^2 = \zeta_n^{-2}(\mathrm{Tr}(t^2) - 2\mathrm{N}(t)) = \zeta_{n/2}^{-1}(\mathrm{Tr}(s) - 2\mathrm{N}(t)), \qquad (4)$$

for the relative norm. Hence recovering $\mathrm{Tr}(t)$ and $\mathrm{Tr}(\zeta_n^{-1}t)$ can be done by computing the square roots of elements in $\mathcal{R}_{n/2}$ determined by s and $\mathrm{N}(t)$. The fact that $\mathrm{N}(s) = \mathrm{N}(t)^2$ leads to Algorithm 5.3.

Notice that square roots are only known up to sign. This means that an algorithm exploiting the tower structure of fields must perform several sign checks to ensure that it will lift the correct root to the next extension. For our algorithm, we only need to check for the sign of $\mathrm{N}(t)$ (the signs of $\mathrm{Tr}(t)$ and $\mathrm{Tr}(\zeta_n^{-1}t)$ can be determined by checking if their current values allow to recover s). This verification happens at Step 6 of Algorithm 5.3, where after computing the square root of $\mathrm{N}(s)$, we know $(-1)^b\mathrm{N}(t)$ for some $b \in \{0,1\}$. It relies on noticing that from Eq. (4), $T_b := \mathrm{Tr}(s) + 2 \cdot (-1)^b\mathrm{N}(t)$ is a square in $\mathcal{K}_{n/2}$ if and only if $b = 0$, in which case $T_b = \mathrm{Tr}(t)^2$. (Else, $\zeta_n^{-2}T_b$ is the square $\mathrm{Tr}(\zeta_n^{-1}t)^2$ in $\mathcal{K}_{n/2}$.) This observation can be extended to a sign check that runs in $\widetilde{O}(n \cdot \log \|s\|_\infty)$. The detailed analysis is given in the full version [17].

Algorithm 5.3. TowerRoot(s)

Input: $s = t^2$ for some $t \in \mathcal{R}_n$.
Output: $t \in \mathcal{R}_n$.
1: **if** $s \in \mathbb{Z}$ **then**
2:     **return** IntegerSqrt(s)
3: **end if**
4: $S \leftarrow \mathrm{N}(s)$ and $S' \leftarrow \mathrm{Tr}(s)$
5: $T \leftarrow$ TowerRoot(S) $\{T = (-1)^b \mathrm{N}(t)\}$
6: **if** CheckSqr($S' + 2T$) = False **then**
7:     $T \leftarrow -T$
8: **end if**
9: $T^+ \leftarrow$ TowerRoot($S' + 2T$) $\{T^+ = (-1)^{b_0} \mathrm{Tr}(t)\}$
10: $T^- \leftarrow$ TowerRoot($\zeta_{n/2}^{-1}(S' - 2T)$) $\{T^- = (-1)^{b_1} \mathrm{Tr}(\zeta_n^{-1} t)\}$
11: **if** $(1/4)(T^+ + \zeta_n T^-)^2 = s$ **then**
12:     **return** $(1/2)(T^+ + \zeta_n T^-)$
13: **else**
14:     **return** $(1/2)(T^+ - \zeta_n T^-)$
15: **end if**

In practice, we can use the following approach: since n is small, we can easily precompute a prime integer p such that $p - 1 \equiv n \mod 2n$. For such a prime, there is a primitive n^{th} root ω of unity in $\mathbb{F}_p$, and such a root cannot be a square in $\mathbb{F}_p$ (else $2n$ would divide $p-1$). Checking squareness then amounts to checking which of $T_b(\omega)$ or $\omega^{-2}T_b(\omega)$ is a square mod p by computing a Legendre symbol. While we need such primes for any power of 2 that is smaller than n, in any case, this checks is done in quasi-linear time. Compared to [25], the size of p here does not matter.

Let us denote by $\mathsf{SQRT}(n, S)$ the complexity of Algorithm 5.3 for an input $s \in \mathcal{R}_n$ with coefficients of size $S = \log \|s\|_\infty$. Using e.g. FFT based multiplication of polynomials, $\mathrm{N}(s)$ can be computed in $\widetilde{O}(nS)$, and has bitsize at most $2S + \log n$. Recall that the so-called canonical embedding of any $s \in \mathcal{K}_n$ is the vector $\tau(s)$ of its evaluations at the roots of $x^n + 1$. It is well-known that it satisfies $\|\tau(s)\| = \sqrt{n}\|s\|$, so that $\|\tau(s)\|_\infty \leq n\|s\|_\infty$ by norm equivalence. If $s = t^2$ we see that $\|\tau(s)\|_\infty = \|\tau(t)\|_\infty^2$. Using again norm equivalence, we obtain $\|t\|_\infty \leq \sqrt{n}\|s\|_\infty^{1/2}$. In the case of $\mathrm{N}(s) = \mathrm{N}(t)^2$, we obtain that $\mathrm{N}(t)$ has size at most $S + \log n$. The cost of CheckSqr is at most $\widetilde{O}(nS)$, so we obtain

$$\mathsf{SQRT}(n, S) = \mathsf{SQRT}\left(\frac{n}{2}, 2S + \log n\right) + 2\mathsf{SQRT}\left(\frac{n}{2}, S + \log n\right) + \widetilde{O}(nS).$$

A tedious computation (see the full version [17] for details) gives us Theorem 3.

6   Side-Channel Leakage of the Gram–Schmidt Norms

Our algorithms in Sect. 5 rely on the knowledge of the exact Gram-Schmidt norms $\|\mathbf{b}_i^*\|$. In this section, we show that in the original implementations of

DLP and FALCON, approximations of $\|\mathbf{b}_i^*\|$'s can be obtained by exploiting the leakage induced by a non constant-time rejection sampling.

In previous works targeting the rejection phase, the standard deviation of the sampler was a public constant. This work deals with a different situation, as both the centers and the standard deviations used by the samplers of DLP and FALCON are secret values determined by the secret key. These samplers output Gaussian vectors by relying on an integer Gaussian sampler, which performs rejection sampling. The secret standard deviation for the ith integer Gaussian is computed as $\sigma_i = \sigma/\|\mathbf{b}_i^*\|$ for some fixed σ, so that exposure of the σ_i's means the exposure of the Gram-Schmidt norms. The idea of the attack stems from the simple observation that the acceptance rate of the sampler is essentially a linear function of its current σ_i. In this section, we show how, by a timing attack, one may recover all acceptance rates from sufficiently many signatures by computing a well-chosen maximum likelihood estimator. Recovering approximations of the $\|\mathbf{b}_i^*\|$'s then follows straightforwardly.

6.1   Leakage in the DLP Scheme

We first target the Gaussian sampling in the original implementation [46], described in Algorithms 6.1 and 6.2. It samples "shifted" Gaussian integers by relying on three layers of Gaussian integer sampling with rejection. More precisely, the target Gaussian distribution at the "top" layer has a center which depends on secret data and varies during each call. To deal with the varying center, the "shifted" sample is generated by combining zero-centered sampler and rejection sampling. Yet the zero-centered sampler has the same standard deviation as the "shifted" one, and the standard deviation depends on the secret key. At the "intermediate" layer, also by rejection sampling, the sampler rectifies a public zero-centered sample to a secret-dependent one.

At the "bottom" layer, the algorithm IntSampler actually follows the BLISS sampler [8] that is already subject to side-channel attacks [7,14,43]. We stress again that our attack does not target this algorithm, so that the reader can assume a constant-time version of it is actually used here. The weakness we are exploiting is a non constant-time implementation of Algorithm 6.2 in the "intermediate" layer. We now describe how to actually approximate the σ_i's using this leakage.

Algorithm 6.1. DLP base sampler $\mathsf{DLPIntSampler}(\sigma_i, c)$

Input: $c \in [0,1)$ and $\sigma_i \geq \eta_\epsilon(\mathbb{Z})$.
Output: $z \in \mathbb{Z}$ following $D_{\mathbb{Z},\sigma_i,c}$.
 1: $z \leftarrow \mathsf{DLPCenteredIntSampler}(\sigma_i)$
 2: $b \leftarrow U(\{0,1\})$
 3: $z \leftarrow z + b$
 4: return z with probability $\frac{\rho_{\sigma_i,c}(z)}{\rho_{\sigma_i}(z)+\rho_{\sigma_i}(z-1)}$, otherwise restart.

Algorithm 6.2. DLP centered base sampler DLPCenteredIntSampler(σ_i)

Input: $\sigma_i \geq \eta_\epsilon(\mathbb{Z})$.
Output: $z \in \mathbb{Z}$ following $D_{\mathbb{Z},\sigma_i}$.

1: $k \leftarrow \lceil \frac{\sigma_i}{\hat{\sigma}} \rceil$ where $\hat{\sigma} = \sqrt{\frac{1}{2\log(2)}}$
2: $z \leftarrow$ IntSampler($k\hat{\sigma}$)
3: return z with probability $\frac{\rho_{\sigma_i}(z)}{\rho_{k\hat{\sigma}}(z)}$, otherwise restart.

Let $\hat{\sigma} = \sqrt{\frac{1}{2\log(2)}}$ be the standard deviation of the Gaussian at the "bottom" layer and $k_i = \lceil \frac{\sigma_i}{\hat{\sigma}} \rceil$. It can be verified that the average acceptance probability of Algorithm 6.2 is $AR(\sigma_i) = \frac{\rho_{\sigma_i}(\mathbb{Z})}{\rho_{k\hat{\sigma}}(\mathbb{Z})}$. As required by the KGPV algorithm, we know that $k_i \hat{\sigma} \geq \sigma_i \geq \eta'_\epsilon(\mathbb{Z})$ and by Corollary 1 we have $AR(\sigma_i) \in \frac{\sigma_i}{k_i \hat{\sigma}} \cdot \left[\frac{1-\epsilon}{1+\epsilon}, 1 \right]$. Since ϵ is very small in this context, we do not lose much by assuming that $AR(\sigma_i) = \frac{\sigma_i}{k_i \hat{\sigma}}$.

Next, for a given σ_i, the number of trials before Algorithm 6.2 outputs its result follows a geometric distribution $\text{Geo}_{AR(\sigma_i)}$. We let $\overline{AR}_i$ be maximum likelihood estimators for the $AR(\sigma_i)$'s associated to N executions of the KGPV sampler, that we compute using Lemma 1. We now want to determine the k_i's to compute $\overline{\sigma}_i = k_i \hat{\sigma} \overline{AR}_i$. Concretely, for the suggested parameters, we can set $k_i = 3$ for all i at the beginning and measure $\overline{AR}_i$. Because the first half of the σ_i's are in a small interval and increase slowly, it may be the case at some step that $\overline{AR}_{i+1}$ is significantly smaller than $\overline{AR}_i$ (say, $1.1 \cdot \overline{AR}_{i+1} < \overline{AR}_i$). This means that $k_{i+1} = k_i + 1$, and we then increase by one all the next k_i's. This approach can be done until $\overline{AR}_n$ is obtained, and works well in practice. Lastly, Lemma 1 tells us that for large enough α and p, taking $N \geq 2^{2(p+\log \alpha)}$ implies $|\overline{\sigma}_i - \sigma_i| \leq 2^{-p} \cdot \sigma_i$ for all $0 \leq i < 2n$ with high probability.

From [11], the constant σ is publicly known. This allows us to have approximations $\overline{b}_i = \frac{\sigma}{\overline{\sigma}_i}$, which we then expect are up to p bits of accuracy on $\|\mathbf{b}_i^*\|$.

6.2 Leakage in the Falcon Scheme

We now describe how the original implementation of FALCON presents a similar leakage of Gram–Schmidt norms via timing side-channels. In contrast to the previous section, the integer sampler of FALCON is based on one public half-Gaussian sampler and some rejection sampling to reflect sensitive standard deviations and centers. The procedure is shown in Algorithm 6.3.

Our analysis does not target the half-Gaussian sampler $D_{\mathbb{Z},\hat{\sigma}}^+$ where $\hat{\sigma} = 2$, so that we omit its description. It can be implemented in a constant-time way [29], but this has no bearing on the leakage we describe.

We first consider c_i and σ_i to be fixed. Following Algorithm 6.3, we let $p(z, b) = \exp\left(\frac{z^2}{2\hat{\sigma}^2} - \frac{(b+(2b-1)z-c_i)^2}{2\sigma_i^2} \right)$ be the acceptance probability and note that

Algorithm 6.3. FALCON base sampler FalconIntSampler(σ_i, c)

Input: $c \in [0,1)$ and $\sigma_i \geq \eta_\epsilon(\mathbb{Z})$.
Output: $z' \in \mathbb{Z}$ following $D_{\mathbb{Z}, \sigma_i, c}$.
1: $z \hookleftarrow D_{\mathbb{Z}, \hat{\sigma}}^+$ where $\hat{\sigma} = 2$
2: $b \hookleftarrow U(\{0, 1\})$
3: return $z' = b + (2b - 1)z$ with probability $\exp\left(\frac{z^2}{2\hat{\sigma}^2} - \frac{(b+(2b-1)z-c)^2}{2\sigma_i^2}\right)$, otherwise restart.

$$p(z, 0) = \frac{1}{\rho_{\hat{\sigma}}(z)} \exp\left(-\frac{(-z-c)^2}{2\sigma_i^2}\right) \text{ and } p(z, 1) = \frac{1}{\rho_{\hat{\sigma}}(z)} \exp\left(-\frac{(z+1-c)^2}{2\sigma_i^2}\right).$$

Then the average acceptance probability for fixed c and σ_i satisfies

$$\mathbb{E}_{z,b}[p(z, b)] = \frac{1}{2\rho_{\hat{\sigma}}(\mathbb{N})} \sum_{z \in \mathbb{N}} \left(\exp\left(-\frac{(-z-c)^2}{2\sigma_i^2}\right) + \exp\left(-\frac{(z+1-c)^2}{2\sigma_i^2}\right)\right)$$

$$= \frac{\rho_{\sigma_i}(\mathbb{Z} - c)}{2\rho_{\hat{\sigma}}(\mathbb{N})}.$$

As $\hat{\sigma} \geq \sigma_i \geq \eta'_\epsilon(\mathbb{Z})$ for a very small ϵ, we can again use Lemma 2 to have that $\rho_{\sigma_i}(\mathbb{Z}-c) \approx \rho_{\sigma_i}(\mathbb{Z})$. This allows us to consider the average acceptance probability as a function $AR(\sigma_i)$, independent of c. Using that $2\rho_{\hat{\sigma}}^+(\mathbb{N}) = \rho_{\hat{\sigma}}(\mathbb{Z})+1$ combined with Corollary 1, we write $AR(\sigma_i) = \frac{\sigma_i \sqrt{2\pi}}{1+2\sqrt{2\pi}}$. Then an application of Lemma 1 gives the needed number of traces to approximate σ_i up to a desired accuracy.

7   Practical Attack Against the DLP Scheme

For the methods in Sect. 6, measure errors seem inevitable in practice. To mount a practical attack, we have to take into account this point. In this section, we show that it is feasible to compute a totally positive element even with noisy diagonal coefficients of its LDL decomposition.

First we adapt the algorithm Recovery$_A$ (Algorithm 5.1) to the noisy input in Sect. 7.1. To determine each coefficient, we need to solve a quadratic inequality instead of an equation due to the noise. As a consequence, each quadratic inequality may lead to several candidates of the coefficient. According to if there is a candidate or not, the algorithm extends prefixes hopefully extending to a valid solution or eliminates wrong prefixes. Thus the algorithm behaves as a tree search.

Then we detail in Sect. 7.2 some implementation techniques to accelerate the recovery algorithm in the context of the DLP scheme. While the algorithm is easy to follow, adapting it to practical noisy case is not trivial.

At last, we report experimental results in Sect. 7.3. As a conclusion, given the full timing leakage of about 2^{34} signatures, one may practically break the DLP parameter claimed for 192-bit security with a good chance. We bring some theoretical support for this value in Sect. 7.4.

Algorithm 7.1. Recovery$_\mathcal{A}(\delta, \{\overline{d_i}\}_i, \text{prefix})$

Input: $\delta \in [0, \frac{1}{2})$, prefix $= (\overline{A_0}, \cdots, \overline{A_{l-1}}) \in \mathbb{Z}^l$ and for all i
    $\overline{d_i} = d_i + \epsilon_i$ where $d_i = \det(\mathcal{A}_n(A)_{[0,i]}) / \det(\mathcal{A}_n(A)_{[0,i-1]})$ and $|\epsilon_i| \leq \delta$.
Output: a list of candidates of A in which each candidate A'
    (1) takes prefix as the first l coefficients;
    (2) satisfies $|\overline{d_i} - d_i'| < \delta$ where $d_i' = \det(\mathcal{A}_n(A')_{[0,i]}) / \det(\mathcal{A}_n(A')_{[0,i-1]})$.
1: $S \leftarrow \emptyset$
2: **if** $l = \frac{n}{2}$ **then**
3:     $S \leftarrow \{\overline{A_0} + \sum_{i=1}^{\frac{n}{2}-1} \overline{A_i}(X^i + X^{-i})\}$
4: **else**
5:     $\mathbf{T} \leftarrow (\overline{A_{|i-j|}})_{i,j \in [0,l)}$, $\mathbf{t} \leftarrow (0, \overline{A_{l-1}}, \cdots, \overline{A_1})$
6:     $Q_a \leftarrow \mathbf{T}_{0,0}^{-1}$, $Q_b \leftarrow \sum_{i=1}^{l-1} \mathbf{T}_{0,i}^{-1} t_i$, $Q_c \leftarrow \mathbf{t}^t \mathbf{T}^{-1} \mathbf{t} - \overline{A_0} + \overline{d_l}$
7:     $S_l \leftarrow \{x \in \mathbb{Z} : |Q_a x^2 + 2Q_b x + Q_c| < \delta\}$ {all possible A_l}
8:     **for** $a \in S_l$ **do**
9:        prefix$' \leftarrow (\text{prefix}, a) \in \mathbb{Z}^{l+1}$
10:       $S \leftarrow S \bigcup \text{Recovery}_\mathcal{A}(\delta, \{\overline{d_i}\}_i, \text{prefix}')$
11:     **end for**
12: **end if**
13: **return** S

7.1 Totally Positive Recovery with Noisy Inputs

Section 5.1 has sketched the exact recovery algorithm. To tackle the measure errors, we introduce a new parameter to denote the error bound. The modified algorithm proceeds in the same way: given a prefix $(A_0, \cdots, A_{l-1})$, it computes all possible A_l's satisfying the error bound condition and extends or eliminates the prefix according to if it can lead to a valid solution. A formal algorithmic description is provided in Algorithm 7.1. For convenience, we use the (noisy) diagonal coefficients (i.e. secret Gram-Schmidt norms) of the LDL decomposition as input. In fact, Proposition 1 has shown the equivalence between the diagonal part and principal minors. In addition, we include prefix in the input for ease of description. The initial prefix is prefix $= \overline{A_0} = \lfloor \overline{d_0} \rceil$. Clearly, the correct A must be in the final candidate list.

7.2 Practical Tweaks in the DLP Setting

Aiming at the DLP signature, we implemented our side-channel attack. By the following techniques, one can boost the practical performance of the recovery algorithm significantly and reduce the number of required signatures.

Fast Computation of the Quadratic Equation. Exploiting the Toeplitz structure of $\mathcal{A}_n(A)$, we propose a fast algorithm to compute the quadratic equation, i.e. (Q_a, Q_b, Q_c), that requires only $O(l)$ multiplications and additions. The idea is as follows. Let $\mathbf{T}_i = \mathcal{A}_n(A)_{[0,i]}$. Let $\mathbf{u}_i = (A_1, \cdots, A_i)$ and $\mathbf{v}_i = (A_i, \cdots, A_1)$, then

$$\mathbf{T}_i = \begin{pmatrix} \mathbf{T}_{i-1} & \mathbf{v}_i^t \\ \mathbf{v}_i & A_0 \end{pmatrix} = \begin{pmatrix} A_0 & \mathbf{u}_i \\ \mathbf{u}_i^t & \mathbf{T}_{i-1} \end{pmatrix}.$$

Let $\mathbf{r}_i = \mathbf{v}_i \mathbf{T}_{i-1}^{-1}$, $\mathbf{s}_i = \mathbf{u}_i \mathbf{T}_{i-1}^{-1}$ which is the reverse of $\mathbf{r}_i$ and $d_i = A_0 - \langle \mathbf{v}_i, \mathbf{r}_i \rangle = A_0 - \langle \mathbf{u}_i, \mathbf{s}_i \rangle$. A straightforward computation leads to that

$$\mathbf{T}_i^{-1} = \begin{pmatrix} \mathbf{T}_{i-1}^{-1} + \mathbf{r}_i^t \mathbf{r}_i / d_i & -\mathbf{r}_i^t / d_i \\ -\mathbf{r}_i / d_i & 1/d_i \end{pmatrix}.$$

Let $f_i = \langle \mathbf{r}_i, \mathbf{u}_i \rangle = \langle \mathbf{s}_i, \mathbf{v}_i \rangle$, then the quadratic equation of A_i is

$$d_i = A_0 - \langle \mathbf{v}_i, \mathbf{r}_i \rangle = A_0 - (A_i - f_{i-1})^2 / d_{i-1} - \langle \mathbf{v}_{i-1}, \mathbf{r}_{i-1} \rangle.$$

Remark that d_i is the square of the last Gram-Schmidt norm. Because $\overline{d_i}$, a noisy d_i, is the input, combining $f_{i-1}, \mathbf{v}_{i-1}, \mathbf{r}_{i-1}$ would determine all possible A_i's. Once A_i is recovered, one can then compute $\mathbf{r}_i, \mathbf{s}_i$ according to

$$\mathbf{s}_i = \left(-\frac{A_i - f_{i-1}}{d_{i-1}} \mathbf{r}_{i-1} + \mathbf{s}_{i-1}, \; \frac{A_i - f_{i-1}}{d_{i-1}} \right)$$

and further compute d_i, f_i. As the recovery algorithm starts with $i = 1$ (i.e. prefix $= A_0$), we can compute the sequences $\{d_i\}, \{f_i\}, \{\mathbf{r}_i\}, \{\mathbf{s}_i\}$ on the fly.

Remark 1. The input matrix is very well conditioned, so we can use a precision of only $O(\log n)$ bits.

Remark 2. The above method implies an algorithm of complexity $\widetilde{O}(n^2)$ for the exact case (Sect. 5.1).

Pruning. We expect that when a mistake is made in the prefix, the error committed in the Gram-Schmidt will be larger. We therefore propose to prune prefixes when $\sum_{k=i}^{j} e_k^2 / \sigma_k^2 \geq B_{j-i}$ for some i, j where e_k is the difference between the measured k-th squared Gram-Schmidt norm and the one of the prefix. The bound B_l is selected so that for e_k a Gaussian of standard deviation σ_k, the condition is verified except with probability $\tau / \sqrt{l}$. The failure probability τ is geometrically decreased until the correct solution is found.

Verifying Candidates. Let $A = f\overline{f} + g\overline{g}$, then $f\overline{f} = A(1 + h\overline{h}) \bmod q$. As mentioned in Sect. 4, all coefficients except the constant one of $f\overline{f}$ would be much smaller the modulus q. This can be used to check if a candidate is correct. In addition, both $A(x)$ and $A(-x)$ are the final candidates, we also check $A(1 + h(-x)\overline{h}(-x))$ to ensure that the correct $A(-x)$ will not to be eliminated. Once either $A(x)$ or $A(-x)$ is found, we terminate the algorithm.

The Use of Symplecticity. As observed in [18], the trapdoor basis $\mathbf{B}_{f,g}$ is q-symplectic and thus $\|\mathbf{b}_i^*\| \cdot \|\mathbf{b}_{2n-1-i}^*\| = q$. Based on that, we combine the samples of the i-th and $(2n - 1 - i)$-th Gaussians to approximate $\|\mathbf{b}_i^*\|$. This helps to refine the approximations and thus to reduce the number of signatures enabling a practical attack.

7.3   Experimental Results

We validate the recovery algorithm on practical DLP instances. Experiments are conducted on the parameter set claimed for 192-bit security in which

$$n = 512, \quad q \approx 2^{10}, \quad \sigma = 2.2358\sqrt{q}, \quad \|\mathbf{b}_i^*\| \le 1.17\sqrt{q}.$$

The leakage data we extracted is the number of iterations of centered Gaussian samplings (Algorithm 6.2). To obtain it, we added some instrumentation to Prest's C++ implementation [46]. The centered Gaussian samplings only depend on the secret key itself not the hashed message. Hence, instead of executing complete signing, we only perform centered Gaussian samplings. We mean by *sample size* the number of collected Gaussian samples. In fact, considering the rejection sampling in Algorithm 6.1, one requires about $N/2$ signatures to generate N samples per centered Gaussian.

We tested our algorithm on ten instances, and result is shown in Table 1. Producing the dataset of $2^{36.5}$ samples for a given key took about 36 hours on our 48-core machine (two weeks for all 10 distinct keys).

In one instance, the recovery algorithm found millions of candidate solutions with Gram-Schmidt norms closer to the noisy ones than the correct solution, in the sense that they had a larger τ. This indicates that the recovery algorithm is relatively close to optimality.

Table 1. Experimental validation of the recovery of $f\bar{f} + g\bar{g}$. The first column and row indicate the time limit and the logarithm of used sample size respectively. The remaining data shows how many instances out of 10 are solved correctly within the time limit and with given number of samples.

	36.5	36.0	35.5	35.0	34.5	34.0
<1 s	8	7	4	3	0	0
<10 s	9	8	6	4	1	0
$<10^2$ s	10	9	7	4	3	1
$<10^3$ s	10	10	8	4	4	1
$<10^4$ s	10	10	8	5	4	1
$<10^5$ s	10	10	8	6	4	2
$<5 \cdot 10^5$ s	10	10	9	7	4	3

7.4   Precision Required on the Gram–Schmidt Norms

We try here to give a closed formula for the number of samples needed. We recall that the relative error with respect to the Gram-Schmidt norm (squared) is $\Theta(1/\sqrt{N})$ where N is the number of samples.

A fast recovery corresponds to the case where only one root is close to an integer; and in particular increasing by one the new coefficient must change by $\Omega(1/\sqrt{N})$ the Gram-Schmidt norm. This is not an equivalence because there is another root of the quadratic form, but we will assume this is enough.

Let b_1 be the first row of $\left(\mathcal{A}_n(f)\ \mathcal{A}_n(g)\right)$, and b_i the i-th row for $i \geq 2$. We define pb_i as the projection of b_1 orthogonally to $b_2, \ldots, b_{i-1}$. We expect that $\|pb_i\| \approx \sqrt{\frac{2n-i+2}{2n}}\|b_1\|$. Consider the Gram matrix of the family $b_1, \ldots, b_{i-1}, b_i \pm \frac{pb}{\|b_1\|^2}$. We have indeed changed only the top right/bottom left coefficients by ± 1, beside the bottom right coordinate. Clearly this does not change the i-th Gram-Schmidt vector; so the absolute change in the i-th Gram-Schmidt norm squared is

$$\left\| b_i \pm \frac{pb_i}{\|b_1\|^2} \right\|^2 - \|b_i\|^2 \approx \pm \frac{\langle b_i, pb_i \rangle}{\|b_1\|^2}.$$

The Gram-Schmidt norm squared is roughly $\|pb_i\|^2$.

Getting only one solution at each step with constant probability corresponds to

$$\langle b_i, pb_i \rangle \geq \frac{\|b_i\|\|pb_i\|}{\sqrt{2n-i+2}}$$

(assuming the scalar product is distributed as a Gaussian) which means a total number of samples of

$$N = \Theta\left(\frac{\sqrt{2n-i+2}\|pb_i\|\|b_1\|^2}{\|b_i\|\|pb_i\|} \right)^2 = \Theta(n\|b_1\|^2) = \Theta(nq^2).$$

This gives roughly 2^{29} samples, which is similar to what the search algorithm requires.

Getting only one solution at each step with probability $1 - 1/n$ corresponds to

$$\langle b_i, pb_i \rangle \geq \frac{\|b_i\|\|pb_i\|}{n\sqrt{2n-i+2}}$$

and $N = \Theta(n^3 q^2)$. This would be 2^{57} samples.

8   Conclusion and Future Work

In this paper, we have investigated the side-channel security of the two main efficient hash-and-sign lattice-based signature schemes: DLP and FALCON (focusing on their original implementations, although our results carry over to several later implementations as well). The two main takeaways of our analysis are that:

1. the Gram–Schmidt norms of the secret basis leak through timing side-channels; and
2. knowing the Gram–Schmidt norms allows to fully recover the secret key.

Interestingly, however, there is a slight mismatch between those two results: the side-channel leakage only provides *approximate* values of the Gram–Schmidt norms, whereas secret key recovery a priori requires *exact* values. We are able to bridge this gap in the case of DLP by combining the recovery algorithm with a pruned tree search. This lets us mount a concrete attack against DLP that recovers the key from 2^{33} to 2^{35} DLP traces in practice for the high security parameters of DLP (claiming 192 bits of security).

However, the gap remains in the case of FALCON: we do not know how to modify our recovery algorithm so as to deal with approximate inputs, and as a result apply it to a concrete attack. This is left as a challenging open problem for future work.

Also left for future work on the more theoretical side is the problem of giving an intrinsic description of our recovery algorithms in terms of algebraic quantities associated with the corresponding totally positive elements (or equivalently, to give an algebraic interpretation of the LDL decomposition for algebraically structured self-adjoint matrices). In particular, in the FALCON case, our approach shows that the Gram–Schmidt norms characterize the Galois conjugacy class of a totally positive element. This strongly suggests that they should admit a nice algebraic description, but it remains elusive for now.

The final recovery in our attack, that is computing f from $f\bar{f} + g\bar{g}$, heavily relies on the property of NTRU. We need further investigations to understand the impact of Gram-Schmidt norm leakage in hash-and-sign schemes over other lattices. But for non-structured lattices, there appears to be a strong obstruction to at least a full key recovery attack, simply due to the dimension of the problem: there are only n Gram-Schmidt norms but $O(n^2)$ secret coefficients to be recovered.

On a positive note, we finally recall that the problem of finding countermeasures against the leakage discussed in this paper is fortunately *already solved*, thanks to the recent work of Prest, Ricosset and Rossi [48]. And that countermeasure has very recently been implemented into FALCON [45], so the leak can be considered as patched! The overhead of that countermeasure is modest in the case of FALCON, thanks to the small range in which the possible standard deviations occur; however, it could become more costly for samplers that need to accommodate a wider range of standard deviations.

An alternate possible countermeasure could be to use Peikert's convolution sampling [42] in preference to the KGPV approach, as it eliminates the need for varying standard deviations, and is easier to implement even without floating point arithmetic [9]. It does have the drawback of sampling wider Gaussians, however, and hence leads to less compact parameter choices.

Acknowledgements. This work is supported by the European Union Horizon 2020 Research and Innovation Program Grant 780701 (PROMETHEUS). This work has also received a French government support managed by the National Research Agency in the "Investing for the Future" program, under the national project RISQ P141580-2660001/DOS0044216, and under the project TYREX granted by the CominLabs excellence laboratory with reference ANR-10-LABX-07-01.

References

1. Babai, L.: On Lovász' lattice reduction and the nearest lattice point problem. Combinatorica **6**(1), 1–13 (1986)
2. Bai, S., Galbraith, S.D.: An improved compression technique for signatures based on learning with errors. In: Benaloh, J. (ed.) CT-RSA 2014. LNCS, vol. 8366, pp. 28–47. Springer, Cham (2014). https://doi.org/10.1007/978-3-319-04852-9_2
3. Barthe, G., et al.: Masking the GLP lattice-based signature scheme at any order. In: Nielsen, J.B., Rijmen, V. (eds.) EUROCRYPT 2018, Part II. LNCS, vol. 10821, pp. 354–384. Springer, Cham (2018). https://doi.org/10.1007/978-3-319-78375-8_12
4. Barthe, G., Belaïd, S., Espitau, T., Fouque, P.A., Rossi, M., Tibouchi, M.: GALAC-TICS: Gaussian sampling for lattice-based constant-time implementation of cryptographic signatures, revisited. In: Cavallaro, L., Kinder, J., Wang, X., Katz, J. (eds.) ACM CCS 2019, pp. 2147–2164. ACM Press (2019)
5. Bindel, N., et al.: qTESLA. Technical report, National Institute of Standards and Technology (2019). https://csrc.nist.gov/projects/post-quantum-cryptography/round-2-submissions
6. Bootle, J., Delaplace, C., Espitau, T., Fouque, P.-A., Tibouchi, M.: LWE without modular reduction and improved side-channel attacks against BLISS. In: Peyrin, T., Galbraith, S. (eds.) ASIACRYPT 2018, Part I. LNCS, vol. 11272, pp. 494–524. Springer, Cham (2018). https://doi.org/10.1007/978-3-030-03326-2_17
7. Groot Bruinderink, L., Hülsing, A., Lange, T., Yarom, Y.: Flush, gauss, and reload – a cache attack on the BLISS lattice-based signature scheme. In: Gierlichs, B., Poschmann, A.Y. (eds.) CHES 2016. LNCS, vol. 9813, pp. 323–345. Springer, Heidelberg (2016). https://doi.org/10.1007/978-3-662-53140-2_16
8. Ducas, L., Durmus, A., Lepoint, T., Lyubashevsky, V.: Lattice signatures and bimodal Gaussians. In: Canetti, R., Garay, J.A. (eds.) CRYPTO 2013, Part I. LNCS, vol. 8042, pp. 40–56. Springer, Heidelberg (2013). https://doi.org/10.1007/978-3-642-40041-4_3
9. Ducas, L., Galbraith, S., Prest, T., Yu, Y.: Integral matrix gram root and lattice Gaussian sampling without floats. In: Canteaut, A., Ishai, Y. (eds.) EUROCRYPT 2020. LNCS, vol. 12107, pp. 608–637. Springer, Cham (2020)
10. Ducas, L., et al.: CRYSTALS-Dilithium: a lattice-based digital signature scheme. IACR TCHES **2018**(1), 238–268 (2018). https://tches.iacr.org/index.php/TCHES/article/view/839
11. Ducas, L., Lyubashevsky, V., Prest, T.: Efficient identity-based encryption over NTRU lattices. In: Sarkar, P., Iwata, T. (eds.) ASIACRYPT 2014, Part II. LNCS, vol. 8874, pp. 22–41. Springer, Heidelberg (2014). https://doi.org/10.1007/978-3-662-45608-8_2
12. Ducas, L., Nguyen, P.Q.: Learning a zonotope and more: cryptanalysis of NTRUSign countermeasures. In: Wang, X., Sako, K. (eds.) ASIACRYPT 2012. LNCS, vol. 7658, pp. 433–450. Springer, Heidelberg (2012). https://doi.org/10.1007/978-3-642-34961-4_27
13. Ducas, L., Prest, T.: Fast Fourier orthogonalization. In: ISSAC, pp. 191–198 (2016)
14. Espitau, T., Fouque, P.A., Gérard, B., Tibouchi, M.: Side-channel attacks on BLISS lattice-based signatures: exploiting branch tracing against strongSwan and electromagnetic emanations in microcontrollers. In: Thuraisingham, B.M., Evans, D., Malkin, T., Xu, D. (eds.) ACM CCS 2017, pp. 1857–1874. ACM Press, October/November 2017

15. Espitau, T., Fouque, P., Gérard, B., Tibouchi, M.: Loop-abort faults on lattice-based signature schemes and key exchange protocols. IEEE Trans. Comput. **67**(11), 1535–1549 (2018). https://doi.org/10.1109/TC.2018.2833119

16. Fiat, A., Shamir, A.: How to prove yourself: practical solutions to identification and signature problems. In: Odlyzko, A.M. (ed.) CRYPTO 1986. LNCS, vol. 263, pp. 186–194. Springer, Heidelberg (1987). https://doi.org/10.1007/3-540-47721-7_12

17. Fouque, P.A., Kirchner, P., Tibouchi, M., Wallet, A., Yu, Y.: Key Recovery from Gram-Schmidt Norm Leakage in Hash-and-Sign Signatures over NTRU Lattices. IACR Cryptology ePrint Archive, report 2019/1180 (2019)

18. Gama, N., Howgrave-Graham, N., Nguyen, P.Q.: Symplectic lattice reduction and NTRU. In: Vaudenay, S. (ed.) EUROCRYPT 2006. LNCS, vol. 4004, pp. 233–253. Springer, Heidelberg (2006). https://doi.org/10.1007/11761679_15

19. Gentry, C., Jonsson, J., Stern, J., Szydlo, M.: Cryptanalysis of the NTRU signature scheme (NSS) from Eurocrypt 2001. In: Boyd, C. (ed.) ASIACRYPT 2001. LNCS, vol. 2248, pp. 1–20. Springer, Heidelberg (2001). https://doi.org/10.1007/3-540-45682-1_1

20. Gentry, C., Peikert, C., Vaikuntanathan, V.: Trapdoors for hard lattices and new cryptographic constructions. In: Ladner, R.E., Dwork, C. (eds.) 40th ACM STOC, pp. 197–206. ACM Press, May 2008

21. Gentry, C., Szydlo, M.: Cryptanalysis of the revised NTRU signature scheme. In: Knudsen, L.R. (ed.) EUROCRYPT 2002. LNCS, vol. 2332, pp. 299–320. Springer, Heidelberg (2002). https://doi.org/10.1007/3-540-46035-7_20

22. Goldreich, O., Goldwasser, S., Halevi, S.: Public-key cryptosystems from lattice reduction problems. In: Kaliski Jr., B.S. (ed.) CRYPTO 1997. LNCS, vol. 1294, pp. 112–131. Springer, Heidelberg (1997). https://doi.org/10.1007/BFb0052231

23. Güneysu, T., Lyubashevsky, V., Pöppelmann, T.: Practical lattice-based cryptography: a signature scheme for embedded systems. In: Prouff, E., Schaumont, P. (eds.) CHES 2012. LNCS, vol. 7428, pp. 530–547. Springer, Heidelberg (2012). https://doi.org/10.1007/978-3-642-33027-8_31

24. Hoffstein, J., Howgrave-Graham, N., Pipher, J., Silverman, J.H., Whyte, W.: NTRUSign: digital signatures using the NTRU lattice. In: Joye, M. (ed.) CT-RSA 2003. LNCS, vol. 2612, pp. 122–140. Springer, Heidelberg (2003). https://doi.org/10.1007/3-540-36563-X_9

25. Hoffstein, J., Lieman, D., Silverman, J.H.: Polynomial rings and efficient public key authentication (1999)

26. Hogg, R.V., McKean, J.W., Craig, A.T.: Introduction to Mathematical Satistics, 8th edn. Pearson, London (2018)

27. Hülsing, A., Lange, T., Smeets, K.: Rounded Gaussians - fast and secure constant-time sampling for lattice-based crypto. In: Abdalla, M., Dahab, R. (eds.) PKC 2018, Part II. LNCS, vol. 10770, pp. 728–757. Springer, Cham (2018). https://doi.org/10.1007/978-3-319-76581-5_25

28. Karmakar, A., Roy, S.S., Reparaz, O., Vercauteren, F., Verbauwhede, I.: Constant-time discrete Gaussian sampling. IEEE Trans. Comput. **67**(11), 1561–1571 (2018)

29. Karmakar, A., Roy, S.S., Vercauteren, F., Verbauwhede, I.: Pushing the speed limit of constant-time discrete Gaussian sampling. A case study on the Falcon signature scheme. In: DAC 2019 (2019)

30. Klein, P.N.: Finding the closest lattice vector when it's unusually close. In: Shmoys, D.B. (ed.) 11th SODA, pp. 937–941. ACM-SIAM, January 2000

31. Lyubashevsky, V.: Fiat-Shamir with aborts: applications to lattice and factoring-based signatures. In: Matsui, M. (ed.) ASIACRYPT 2009. LNCS, vol. 5912, pp. 598–616. Springer, Heidelberg (2009). https://doi.org/10.1007/978-3-642-10366-7_35

32. Lyubashevsky, V.: Lattice signatures without trapdoors. In: Pointcheval, D., Johansson, T. (eds.) EUROCRYPT 2012. LNCS, vol. 7237, pp. 738–755. Springer, Heidelberg (2012). https://doi.org/10.1007/978-3-642-29011-4_43

33. Lyubashevsky, V., et al.: CRYSTALS-DILITHIUM. Technical report, National Institute of Standards and Technology (2019). https://csrc.nist.gov/projects/post-quantum-cryptography/round-2-submissions

34. Lyubashevsky, V., Prest, T.: Quadratic time, linear space algorithms for Gram-Schmidt orthogonalization and Gaussian sampling in structured lattices. In: Oswald, E., Fischlin, M. (eds.) EUROCRYPT 2015, Part I. LNCS, vol. 9056, pp. 789–815. Springer, Heidelberg (2015). https://doi.org/10.1007/978-3-662-46800-5_30

35. McCarthy, S., Howe, J., Smyth, N., Brannigan, S., O'Neill, M.: BEARZ attack FALCON: implementation attacks with countermeasures on the FALCON signature scheme. In: Obaidat, M.S., Samarati, P. (eds.) SECRYPT, pp. 61–71 (2019)

36. McCarthy, S., Smyth, N., O'Sullivan, E.: A practical implementation of identity-based encryption over NTRU lattices. In: O'Neill, M. (ed.) IMACC 2017. LNCS, vol. 10655, pp. 227–246. Springer, Cham (2017). https://doi.org/10.1007/978-3-319-71045-7_12

37. Micciancio, D., Peikert, C.: Trapdoors for lattices: simpler, tighter, faster, smaller. In: Pointcheval, D., Johansson, T. (eds.) EUROCRYPT 2012. LNCS, vol. 7237, pp. 700–718. Springer, Heidelberg (2012). https://doi.org/10.1007/978-3-642-29011-4_41

38. Micciancio, D., Regev, O.: Worst-case to average-case reductions based on Gaussian measures. SIAM J. Comput. 37(1), 267–302 (2007)

39. Micciancio, D., Walter, M.: Gaussian sampling over the integers: efficient, generic, constant-time. In: Katz, J., Shacham, H. (eds.) CRYPTO 2017, Part II. LNCS, vol. 10402, pp. 455–485. Springer, Cham (2017). https://doi.org/10.1007/978-3-319-63715-0_16

40. Nguyen, P.Q., Regev, O.: Learning a parallelepiped: cryptanalysis of GGH and NTRU signatures. In: Vaudenay, S. (ed.) EUROCRYPT 2006. LNCS, vol. 4004, pp. 271–288. Springer, Heidelberg (2006). https://doi.org/10.1007/11761679_17

41. Oder, T., Speith, J., Höltgen, K., Güneysu, T.: Towards practical microcontroller implementation of the signature scheme Falcon. In: Ding, J., Steinwandt, R. (eds.) PQCrypto 2019. LNCS, vol. 11505, pp. 65–80. Springer, Cham (2019). https://doi.org/10.1007/978-3-030-25510-7_4

42. Peikert, C.: An efficient and parallel Gaussian sampler for lattices. In: Rabin, T. (ed.) CRYPTO 2010. LNCS, vol. 6223, pp. 80–97. Springer, Heidelberg (2010). https://doi.org/10.1007/978-3-642-14623-7_5

43. Pessl, P., Bruinderink, L.G., Yarom, Y.: To BLISS-B or not to be: attacking strongSwan's implementation of post-quantum signatures. In: Thuraisingham, B.M., Evans, D., Malkin, T., Xu, D. (eds.) ACM CCS 2017, pp. 1843–1855. ACM Press, October/November 2017

44. Plantard, T., Sipasseuth, A., Dumondelle, C., Susilo, W.: DRS. Technical report, National Institute of Standards and Technology (2017). https://csrc.nist.gov/projects/post-quantum-cryptography/round-1-submissions

45. Pornin, T.: New Efficient, Constant-Time Implementations of Falcon, August 2019. https://falcon-sign.info/falcon-impl-20190802.pdf

46. Prest, T.: Proof-of-concept implementation of an identity-based encryption scheme over NTRU lattices (2014). https://github.com/tprest/Lattice-IBE
47. Prest, T., et al.: FALCON. Technical report, National Institute of Standards and Technology (2019). https://csrc.nist.gov/projects/post-quantum-cryptography/round-2-submissions
48. Prest, T., Ricosset, T., Rossi, M.: Simple, fast and constant-time Gaussian sampling over the integers for Falcon. In: Second PQC Standardization Conference (2019)
49. Stehlé, D., Steinfeld, R.: Making NTRU as secure as worst-case problems over ideal lattices. In: Paterson, K.G. (ed.) EUROCRYPT 2011. LNCS, vol. 6632, pp. 27–47. Springer, Heidelberg (2011). https://doi.org/10.1007/978-3-642-20465-4_4
50. Tibouchi, M., Wallet, A.: One bit is all it takes: a devastating timing attack on BLISS's non-constant time sign flips. Cryptology ePrint Archive, Report 2019/898 (2019). https://eprint.iacr.org/2019/898
51. Yu, Y., Ducas, L.: Learning strikes again: the case of the DRS signature scheme. In: Peyrin, T., Galbraith, S. (eds.) ASIACRYPT 2018, Part II. LNCS, vol. 11273, pp. 525–543. Springer, Cham (2018). https://doi.org/10.1007/978-3-030-03329-3_18
52. Zhang, Z., Chen, C., Hoffstein, J., Whyte, W.: pqNTRUSign. Technical report, National Institute of Standards and Technology (2017). https://csrc.nist.gov/projects/post-quantum-cryptography/round-1-submissions
53. Zhao, R.K., Steinfeld, R., Sakzad, A.: FACCT: FAst, Compact, and Constant-Time Discrete Gaussian Sampler over Integers. IACR Cryptology ePrint Archive, report 2018/1234 (2018)

An Algebraic Attack on Rank Metric Code-Based Cryptosystems

Magali Bardet[1,2], Pierre Briaud[2], Maxime Bros[3], Philippe Gaborit[3],
Vincent Neiger[3(✉)], Olivier Ruatta[3], and Jean-Pierre Tillich[2(✉)]

[1] LITIS, University of Rouen Normandie, Mont-Saint-Aignan, France
[2] Inria, 2 rue Simone Iff, 75012 Paris, France
jean-pierre.tillich@inria.fr
[3] Univ. Limoges, CNRS, XLIM, UMR 7252, 87000 Limoges, France
vincent.neiger@unilim.fr

Abstract. The Rank metric decoding problem is the main problem considered in cryptography based on codes in the rank metric. Very efficient schemes based on this problem or quasi-cyclic versions of it have been proposed recently, such as those in the submissions ROLLO and RQC currently at the second round of the NIST Post-Quantum Cryptography Standardization Process. While combinatorial attacks on this problem have been extensively studied and seem now well understood, the situation is not as satisfactory for algebraic attacks, for which previous work essentially suggested that they were ineffective for cryptographic parameters. In this paper, starting from Ourivski and Johansson's algebraic modelling of the problem into a system of polynomial equations, we show how to augment this system with easily computed equations so that the augmented system is solved much faster via Gröbner bases. This happens because the augmented system has solving degree r, $r + 1$ or $r + 2$ depending on the parameters, where r is the rank weight, which we show by extending results from Verbel *et al.* (PQCrypto 2019) on systems arising from the MinRank problem; with target rank r, Verbel *et al.* lower the solving degree to $r + 2$, and even less for some favorable instances that they call "superdetermined". We give complexity bounds for this approach as well as practical timings of an implementation using `magma`. This improves upon the previously known complexity estimates for both Gröbner basis and (non-quantum) combinatorial approaches, and for example leads to an attack in 200 bits on ROLLO-I-256 whose claimed security was 256 bits.

Keywords: Post-quantum cryptography · NIST-PQC candidates · Rank metric code-based cryptography · Gröbner basis

1 Introduction

Rank Metric Code-Based Cryptography. In the last decade, rank metric code-based cryptography has proved to be a powerful alternative to more traditional code-based cryptography based on the Hamming metric. This thread of

© International Association for Cryptologic Research 2020
A. Canteaut and Y. Ishai (Eds.): EUROCRYPT 2020, LNCS 12107, pp. 64–93, 2020.
https://doi.org/10.1007/978-3-030-45727-3_3

research started with the GPT cryptosystem [37] based on Gabidulin codes [36], which are rank metric analogues of Reed-Solomon codes. However, the strong algebraic structure of those codes was successfully exploited for attacking the original GPT cryptosystem and its variants with the Overbeck attack [53] (see for example [51] for one of the latest related developments). This has to be traced back to the algebraic structure of Gabidulin codes that makes masking extremely difficult; one can draw a parallel with the situation in the Hamming metric where essentially all McEliece cryptosystems based on Reed-Solomon codes or variants of them have been broken. However, recently a rank metric analogue of the NTRU cryptosystem from [44] has been designed and studied, starting with the pioneering paper [38]. Roughly speaking, the NTRU cryptosystem relies on a lattice that has vectors of rather small Euclidean norm. It is precisely those vectors that allow an efficient decoding/deciphering process. The decryption of the cryptosystem proposed in [38] relies on LRPC codes that have rather short vectors in the dual code, but this time for the rank metric. These vectors are used for decoding in the rank metric. This cryptosystem can also be viewed as the rank metric analogue of the MDPC cryptosystem [50] that relies on short vectors in the dual code for the Hamming metric.

This new way of building rank metric code-based cryptosystems has led to a sequence of proposals [5,6,38,40], culminating in submissions to the NIST post-quantum competition [1,2], whose security relies solely on the decoding problem in rank metric codes with a ring structure similar to the ones encountered right now in lattice-based cryptography. Interestingly enough, one can also build signature schemes using the rank metric; even though early attempts which relied on masking the structure of a code [9,41] have been broken [24], a promising recent approach [8] only considers random matrices without structural masking.

Decoding in Rank Metric. In other words, in rank metric code-based cryptography we are now only left with assessing the difficulty of the decoding problem for the rank metric. The rank metric over $\mathbb{F}_q^N$, where $\mathbb{F}_q$ is the finite field of cardinality q and $N = mn$ is a composite integer, consists in viewing elements in this ambient space as $m \times n$ matrices over $\mathbb{F}_q$ and considering the distance $d(\boldsymbol{X}, \boldsymbol{Y})$ between two such matrices $\boldsymbol{X}$ and $\boldsymbol{Y}$ as

$$d(\boldsymbol{X}, \boldsymbol{Y}) = \mathrm{Rank}\,(\boldsymbol{Y} - \boldsymbol{X}).$$

A (linear matrix) code $\mathcal{C}$ in $\mathbb{F}_q^{m \times n}$ is simply a $\mathbb{F}_q$-linear subspace in $\mathbb{F}_q^{m \times n}$, generated by K matrices $\boldsymbol{M}_1, \ldots, \boldsymbol{M}_K$. The decoding problem for the rank metric at distance r is as follows: given a matrix $\boldsymbol{Y}$ in $\mathbb{F}_q^{m \times n}$ at distance $\leq r$ from $\mathcal{C}$, recover an element $\boldsymbol{M}$ in $\mathcal{C}$ at distance $\leq r$ from $\boldsymbol{Y}$. This is precisely the MinRank problem given as input $\boldsymbol{Y}$ and $\boldsymbol{M}_1, \ldots, \boldsymbol{M}_K$:

Problem 1 (MinRank).
Input: an integer $r \in \mathbb{N}$ and $K + 1$ matrices $\boldsymbol{Y}, \boldsymbol{M}_1, \ldots, \boldsymbol{M}_K \in \mathbb{F}_q^{m \times n}$.
Output: field elements $x_1, x_2, \ldots, x_K \in \mathbb{F}_q$ such that

$$\text{Rank}\left(\boldsymbol{Y} - \sum_{i=1}^{K} x_i \boldsymbol{M}_i\right) \leq r.$$

As observed in [20], the MinRank problem is NP-complete and the best known algorithms solving it have exponential complexity bounds.

Matrix Codes Specified as $\mathbb{F}_{q^m}$-Linear Codes. However, the trend in rank metric code-based cryptography has been to consider a particular form of linear matrix codes: they are linear codes of length n over an extension $\mathbb{F}_{q^m}$ of degree m of $\mathbb{F}_q$, that is, $\mathbb{F}_{q^m}$-linear subspaces of $\mathbb{F}_{q^m}^n$. In the rest of this section, we fix a basis $(\beta_1, \ldots, \beta_m)$ of $\mathbb{F}_{q^m}$ an $\mathbb{F}_q$-vector space. Then such codes can be interpreted as matrix codes over $\mathbb{F}_q^{m \times n}$ by viewing a vector $\boldsymbol{x} = (x_1, \ldots, x_n) \in \mathbb{F}_{q^m}^n$ as a matrix $\text{Mat}(\boldsymbol{x}) = (X_{ij})_{i,j}$ in $\mathbb{F}_q^{m \times n}$, where $(X_{ij})_{1 \leq i \leq m}$ is the column vector formed by the coordinates of x_j in the basis $(\beta_1, \ldots, \beta_m)$, that is, $x_j = X_{1j}\beta_1 + \cdots + X_{mj}\beta_m$.

Then the "rank" metric d on $\mathbb{F}_{q^m}^n$ is the rank metric on the associated matrix space, namely

$$d(\boldsymbol{x}, \boldsymbol{y}) := |\boldsymbol{y} - \boldsymbol{x}|, \quad \text{where we define } |\boldsymbol{x}| := \text{Rank}\,(\text{Mat}(\boldsymbol{x})).$$

An $\mathbb{F}_{q^m}$-linear code $\mathcal{C}$ of length n and dimension k over $\mathbb{F}_{q^m}$ specifies a matrix code $\text{Mat}(\mathcal{C}) := \{\text{Mat}(\boldsymbol{c}) : \boldsymbol{c} \in \mathcal{C}\}$ in $\mathbb{F}_q^{m \times n}$ of dimension $K := mk$ over $\mathbb{F}_q$: it is readily verified that a basis of this $\mathbb{F}_q$-subspace is given by $(\text{Mat}(\beta_i \boldsymbol{c}_j))_{1 \leq i \leq m, 1 \leq j \leq k}$ where $(\boldsymbol{c}_1, \ldots, \boldsymbol{c}_k)$ is a basis of $\mathcal{C}$ over $\mathbb{F}_{q^m}$.

There are several reasons for this trend. On the one hand, the families of matrix codes for which an efficient decoding algorithm is known are families of $\mathbb{F}_{q^m}$-linear codes. On the other hand, $\mathbb{F}_{q^m}$-linear codes have a much shorter description than general matrix codes. Indeed, a matrix code in $\mathbb{F}_q^{m \times n}$ of dimension $K = km$ can be specified by a basis of it, which uses $Kmn \log(q) = km^2 n \log(q)$ bits, whereas a matrix code obtained from an $\mathbb{F}_{q^m}$-linear code of dimension k over $\mathbb{F}_{q^m}$ can be specified by a basis $(\boldsymbol{c}_1, \ldots, \boldsymbol{c}_k)$ of it, which uses $kmn \log(q)$ bits and thus saves a factor m.

Progress in the design of efficient algorithms for decoding $\mathbb{F}_{q^m}$-linear codes suggests that their additional structure may not have a significant impact on the difficulty of solving the decoding problem. For instance, a generic matrix code over $\mathbb{F}_q^{m \times n}$ of dimension $K = mk$ can be decoded using the information set decoder of [39] within a complexity of the order of q^{kr} when the errors have rank at most r and $m \geq n$, compared to q^{kr-m} for the decoding of a linear code over $\mathbb{F}_{q^m}^n$ in the same regime, using a similar decoder [10]. Moreover, even if the decoding problem is not known to be NP-complete for these $\mathbb{F}_{q^m}$-linear codes, there is a randomised reduction to an NP-complete problem [42] (namely to decoding in the Hamming metric). Hereafter, we will use the following terminology.

Problem 2 ((m, n, k, r)-decoding problem).
Input: an $\mathbb{F}_{q^m}$-basis $(\boldsymbol{c}_1, \ldots, \boldsymbol{c}_k)$ of a subspace $\mathcal{C}$ of $\mathbb{F}_{q^m}^n$, an integer $r \in \mathbb{N}$, a vector $\boldsymbol{y} \in \mathbb{F}_{q^m}^n$ at distance at most r of $\mathcal{C}$ (i.e. $|\boldsymbol{y} - \boldsymbol{c}| \leq r$ for some $\boldsymbol{c} \in \mathcal{C}$).
Output: $\boldsymbol{c} \in \mathcal{C}$ and $\boldsymbol{e} \in \mathbb{F}_{q^m}^n$ such that $\boldsymbol{y} = \boldsymbol{c} + \boldsymbol{e}$ and $|\boldsymbol{e}| \leq r$.

The region of parameters which is of interest for the NIST submissions corresponds to $m = \Theta(n)$, $k = \Theta(n)$ and $r = \Theta(\sqrt{n})$.

Gröbner Basis Techniques for Decoding in the Rank Metric. The aforementioned algorithm from [10] for solving the decoding problem follows a combinatorial approach pioneered in [52], which is related to decoding techniques for the Hamming metric. Another approach consists in viewing the decoding problem as a particular case of MinRank and using the algebraic techniques designed for this problem; namely these techniques use a suitable algebraic modelling of a MinRank instance into a system of multivariate polynomial equations, and then solve this system with Gröbner basis techniques. Several modellings have been considered, such as the Kipnis-Shamir modelling [45] and the minors modelling (described for example in [34]); the complexity of solving MinRank using these modellings has been investigated in [33,34]. The Kipnis-Shamir modelling boils down to a polynomial system which is *affine bilinear*. This means that each equation has degree at most 2 and the set of variables can be partitioned into two sets $\{x_1, \ldots, x_s\} \cup \{y_1, \ldots, y_t\}$ such that all monomials of degree 2 involved in the equations are of the form $x_i y_j$; in other words, the equations are formed by a quadratic part which is bilinear plus an affine part. Although the complexity of solving this system can be bounded by that of solving bilinear systems, which is studied in [35], the complexity estimates thus obtained are very pessimistic, as observed experimentally in [21]. A theoretical explanation of why Gröbner basis techniques perform much better on the Kipnis-Shamir modelling than on generic bilinear systems was later given in [56]. It was also demonstrated there that the Kipnis-Shamir approach is more efficient than the minors approach on several multivariable encryption or signature schemes relying on the MinRank problem. However, the speed-up obtained for the Kipnis-Shamir modelling in the latter reference mostly comes from the "superdetermined" case considered therein. When applied to the (m, n, k, r)-decoding problem, this corresponds to the case where $m = n$ and $km < nr$; this condition is not met in the decoding problem instances we are interested in.

Another algebraic approach to solve the (m, n, k, r)-decoding problem was suggested in [39, §V.]. It is based on a new modelling specific to $\mathbb{F}_{q^m}$-linear codes which fundamentally relies on the underlying $\mathbb{F}_{q^m}$-linear structure and on q-polynomials. Also, it results in a system of polynomial equations that are sparse and have large degree. This approach seems to be efficient only if rk is not much larger than n.

Our Contribution. If one compares the best known complexity estimates, the algebraic techniques appear to be less efficient than the combinatorial ones, such as [39,52], and [10] for the parameters of the rank metric schemes proposed to the NIST [3,7] or of other rank metric code-based cryptosystems [49]. In [55], Levy-dit-Vehel and Perret pioneered the use of Gröbner basis techniques to solve the polynomial system arising in the Ourivski-Johansson algebraic modelling [52], with promising practical timings. In this paper, we follow on from this approach and show how this polynomial system can be augmented with additional equations that are easy to compute and bring on a substantial speed-up in the Gröbner basis computation for solving the system. This new algebraic algorithm results in the best practical efficiency and complexity bounds that are currently known for the decoding problem; in particular, it significantly improves upon the above-mentioned combinatorial approaches.

There are several reasons why the Ourivski-Johansson algebraic modelling improves upon the Kipnis-Shamir one. First, it has the same affine bilinear structure and a similar number of equations, but it involves much fewer variables. Indeed, for the case of interest to us where m and k are in $\Theta(n)$ and r is in $\Theta(n^{1/2})$, the Kipnis-Shamir modelling involves $\Theta(n^2)$ equations and variables, while the Ourivski-Johansson one involves $\Theta(n^2)$ equations and $\Theta(n^{3/2})$ variables. Second, this modelling naturally leads to what corresponds to reducing by one the value of r, as explained in Sect. 3. Third, and most importantly, the main properties that ensure that the Kipnis-Shamir modelling behaves much better with respect to Gröbner basis techniques than generic bilinear systems also hold for the Ourivski-Johansson modelling. In essence, this is due to a *solving degree* which is remarkably low: at most $r + 2$ for the former modelling and at most $r + 1$ for the latter. Recall that the solving degree indicates the maximum degree reached during a Gröbner basis computation; it is known to be a strong predictor of the complexity of the most expensive step in a Gröbner basis computation and has been widely used for this purpose with confirmations via numerical experiments, see for instance [26–29, 43, 56].

To prove the third point, we start from the result about degree falls at the core of [56], which is based on work from [35], and we extend it to a more general setting which includes the Ourivski-Johansson modelling. In our case, these degree falls mean that from the initial system of quadratic equations $f_i = 0$ of the Ourivski-Johansson modelling, we are able to build many new equations of degree r that are combinations $\sum_i f_i g_{ij} = 0$ where the g_{ij}'s are polynomials of degree $r - 1$ involved in the j-th new equation. We also prove that, when the parameters satisfy the condition

$$m\binom{n-k-1}{r} \geq \binom{n}{r} - 1, \tag{1}$$

by using that these polynomials $\sum_i f_i g_{ij}$ can be expressed as linear combinations of only a few other polynomials, we can perform suitable linear combinations of the equations $\sum_i f_i g_{ij} = 0$'s giving $\binom{n-1}{r-1} - 1$ equations of degree $r - 1$. All these polynomial combinations are easily computed from the initial quadratic equations. By adding these equations and then performing Gröbner basis computations on the augmented system, we observe that experimentally the Gröbner basis algorithm behaves as expected from the degree fall heuristic:

- if (1) holds, this degree is r and the overall complexity is $\mathcal{O}\left(\left(\frac{((m+n)r)^r}{r!}\right)^\omega\right)$ operations in $\mathbb{F}_q$.

- if (1) does not hold, the maximum degree reached in the Gröbner basis computation is $r + 1$ (in some intermediate cases), or $r + 2$, leading to an overall complexity of at most $\mathcal{O}\left(\left(\frac{((m+n)r)^{r+1}}{(r+1)!}\right)^{\omega}\right)$ (resp. $\mathcal{O}\left(\left(\frac{((m+n)r)^{r+2}}{(r+2)!}\right)^{\omega}\right)$) operations in $\mathbb{F}_q$, where ω is the exponent of matrix multiplication.

Note that for a majority of parameters proposed in [3,7], the condition (1) holds. Taking for ω the smallest value currently achievable in practice, which is $\omega \approx 2.8$ via Strassen's algorithm, this leads to an attack on the cryptosystems proposed in the aforementioned NIST submissions which is in all cases below the claimed classical security levels.

2   Notation

In the whole paper, we use the following notation and definitions:

- Matrices and vectors are written in boldface font $\boldsymbol{M}$.
- For a matrix $\boldsymbol{M}$ its entry in row i and column j is denoted by $\boldsymbol{M}[i,j]$.
- The transpose of a matrix $\boldsymbol{M}$ is denoted by $\boldsymbol{M}^{\mathsf{T}}$.
- For a given ring $\mathcal{R}$, the space of matrices with m rows and n columns and coefficients in $\mathcal{R}$ is denoted by $\mathcal{R}^{m \times n}$.
- For $\boldsymbol{M} \in \mathcal{R}^{m \times n}$, we denote by $vec_{row}(\boldsymbol{M})$ the column vector formed by concatenating the rows of $\boldsymbol{M}$, i.e. $vec_{row}(\boldsymbol{M}) = \left(\boldsymbol{M}_{\{1\},*} \cdots \boldsymbol{M}_{\{n\},*}\right)^{\mathsf{T}}$.
- For $\boldsymbol{M} \in \mathcal{R}^{m \times n}$, we denote by $vec_{col}(\boldsymbol{M})$ the column vector formed by concatenating the columns of $\boldsymbol{M}$, i.e. $vec_{col}(\boldsymbol{M}) = vec_{row}(\boldsymbol{M}^{\mathsf{T}})$.
- $\{1..n\}$ stands for the set of integers from 1 to n, and for any subset $J \subset \{k+1..n\}$, we denote by $J - k$ the set $J - k = \{j - k : j \in J\} \subset \{1..n - k\}$.
- For two subsets $I \subset \{1..m\}$ and $J \subset \{1..n\}$, we write $\boldsymbol{M}_{I,J}$ for the submatrix of $\boldsymbol{M}$ formed by its rows (resp. columns) with index in I (resp. J).
- We use the shorthand notation $\boldsymbol{M}_{*,J} = \boldsymbol{M}_{\{1..m\},J}$ and $\boldsymbol{M}_{I,*} = \boldsymbol{M}_{I,\{1..n\}}$, where $\boldsymbol{M}$ has m rows and n columns.
- $\mathbb{F}_q$ is a finite field of size q, and $\alpha \in \mathbb{F}_{q^m}$ is a primitive element, so that $(1, \alpha, \ldots, \alpha^{m-1})$ is a basis of $\mathbb{F}_{q^m}$ as an $\mathbb{F}_q$-vector space. For $\beta \in \mathbb{F}_{q^m}$, we denote by $[\alpha^{i-1}]\beta$ its ith coordinate in this basis.
- For $\boldsymbol{v} = (v_1, \ldots, v_n) \in \mathbb{F}_{q^m}^n$. The $support$ of $\boldsymbol{v}$ is the $\mathbb{F}_q$-vector subspace of $\mathbb{F}_{q^m}$ spanned by the vectors $v_1, \ldots, v_n$. Thus this support is the column space of the matrix $\mathrm{Mat}(\boldsymbol{v})$ associated to $\boldsymbol{v}$ (for any choice of basis), and its dimension is precisely $\mathrm{Rank}(\mathrm{Mat}(\boldsymbol{v}))$.
- An $[n, k]$ $\mathbb{F}_{q^m}$-linear code is an $\mathbb{F}_{q^m}$-linear subspace of $\mathbb{F}_{q^m}^n$ of dimension k endowed with the rank metric.

3   Algebraic Modellings of the Decoding Problem

In what follows, parameters are chosen in the cryptographically relevant region mentioned in the introduction, say $m = \Theta(n)$, $k = \Theta(n)$ and $r = \Theta(\sqrt{n})$. Decoding instances will then have a single solution e. For simplicity, we assume that the rank of e is exactly r; in general one can run the algorithm for increasing values of the target rank up to r, until a solution is found, and the most expensive step will correspond to the largest considered rank. We consider here the (m, n, k, r)-decoding problem for the code $\mathcal{C}$ and assume we have received $y \in \mathbb{F}_{q^m}^n$ at distance r from $\mathcal{C}$ and look for $c \in \mathcal{C}$ and e such that $y = c + e$ and $|e| = r$.

3.1   Solving the MinRank Instance Using Kipnis-Shamir's Modelling

As explained in Sect. 1, a possible approach to perform the decoding is to solve the underlying MinRank instance with $km + 1$ matrices in $\mathbb{F}_q^{m \times n}$; this is done by introducing $M_0 := \mathrm{Mat}(y)$ and $M_1, \dots, M_{km}$ which is an $\mathbb{F}_q$-basis of $\mathrm{Mat}(\mathcal{C})$. Several methods have been developed, and so far the Kipnis-Shamir modelling [45] seems to be the most efficient to solve this MinRank instance. We want to find $(z_0, \dots, z_{km})$ in $\mathbb{F}_q^{mk+1}$ such that $\mathrm{Rank}(\sum_{i=0}^{km} z_i M_i) = r$. $(z_0, z_1, \dots, z_{km})$ is a solution to the MinRank problem if and only if the right kernel of $\sum_{i=0}^{km} z_i M_i$ contains a subspace of dimension $n - r$ of $\mathbb{F}_q^n$. With high probability, a basis of such a space can be written in systematic form, that is, in the form $\left(\begin{smallmatrix} I_{n-r} \\ K \end{smallmatrix} \right)$. Thus we have to solve the system

$$\left(\sum_{i=0}^{km} z_i M_i \right) \left(\begin{matrix} I_{n-r} \\ K \end{matrix} \right) = 0, \tag{2}$$

over $\mathbb{F}_q$, where K is an $r \times (n-r)$ matrix of indeterminates. This system is affine bilinear and has $m(n - r)$ equations and $km + 1 + r(n - r)$ variables, which are $z_0, z_1, \dots, z_{km}$ and the $r(n - r)$ entries of K; each equation has a bilinear part as well as a linear part which only involves the variables z_i.

3.2   Syndrome Modelling

We recall here the modelling considered in [2,7]. Let H be a parity-check matrix of $\mathcal{C}$, i.e.

$$\mathcal{C} = \{c \in \mathbb{F}_{q^m}^n : cH^\top = 0\}.$$

The (m, n, k, r)-decoding problem can be algebraically described by the system $eH^\top = s$ where $e \in \mathbb{F}_{q^m}^n$ has rank r and $s \in \mathbb{F}_{q^m}^{(n-k)}$ is given by $s := yH^\top$. Let $(S_1, \dots, S_r) \in \mathbb{F}_{q^m}^r$ be a basis of the support of e; then, $e = (S_1 \quad \cdots \quad S_r)C$, where $C \in \mathbb{F}_q^{r \times n}$ is the matrix of the coordinates of e in the basis $(S_1, \dots, S_r)$. Then expressing the elements S_i in the basis $(1, \alpha, \dots, \alpha^{m-1})$ of $\mathbb{F}_{q^m}$ over $\mathbb{F}_q$ yields $(S_1 \quad \cdots \quad S_r) = (1 \quad \alpha \quad \cdots \quad \alpha^{m-1})S$ for some matrix $S \in \mathbb{F}_q^{m \times r}$. Thus, the system is rewritten as

$$\left(1 \, \alpha \cdots \alpha^{m-1} \right) SCH^\top = s, \text{ over } \mathbb{F}_{q^m} \text{ with solutions in } \mathbb{F}_q. \tag{3}$$

This polynomial system, that we refer to as the *syndrome modelling*, has $m(n-k)$ equations and $mr + nr$ variables when it is written over $\mathbb{F}_q$. It is affine bilinear (without terms of degree 1) with respect to the two sets of variables coming from the support and from the coordinates of the error. Besides, this system admits $(q^r - 1)(q^r - q) \cdots (q^r - q^{r-1})$ solutions since this is the number of bases of the support. These solutions to the system all correspond to the same unique solution e of the initial decoding problem. We can easily impose a unique solution by fixing some of the unknowns as in the Kipnis-Shamir modelling, or as has been done in the Ourivski-Johansson modelling that we will present next. It is worthwhile to note that this kind of modelling has, as the Kipnis-Shamir modelling, $\Theta\left(n^2\right)$ equations for our choice of parameters but significantly fewer variables since we now have only $\Theta\left(n^{3/2}\right)$ unknowns. The Ourivski-Johansson's modelling will be a related modelling that gives a further improvement.

3.3 Ourivski-Johansson's Modelling

We now describe the algebraic modelling considered in the rest of this paper, which is basically Ourivski and Johansson's one [52]. It can be viewed as an homogenising trick. Instead of looking for $c \in \mathcal{C}$ and e of rank r that satisfy $y = c + e$, or what is the same for $c \in \mathcal{C}$ such that $|c + y| = r$, we look for $c \in \mathcal{C}$ and $\lambda \in \mathbb{F}_{q^m}$ such that

$$|c + \lambda y| = r. \tag{4}$$

It is precisely here that the $\mathbb{F}_{q^m}$-linearity of $\mathcal{C}$ is used in a crucial way. Once we have found such a c and λ, we have found a $c + \lambda y$ such that $c + \lambda y = \mu e$ for some non-zero $\mu \in \mathbb{F}_{q^m}$ from which we deduce easily e. The point of proceeding this way is that there are $q^m - 1$ solutions to (4) and that this allows us to fix more unknowns in the algebraic system. Another point of view [52, Sec. 2] is to say that we introduce the code $\tilde{\mathcal{C}} := \mathcal{C} + \langle y \rangle$ and that we look for a rank r word in $\tilde{\mathcal{C}}$, since all such words are precisely the multiples λe for nonzero $\lambda \in \mathbb{F}_{q^m}$ of the error e we are looking for. Let $\tilde{G} = \left(I_{k+1} \; R\right)$ (resp. $\tilde{H} = \left(-R^{\mathsf{T}} \; I_{n-k-1}\right)$) be the generator matrix in systematic form (resp. a parity-check matrix) of the extended code $\tilde{\mathcal{C}}$; note that for a vector v, we have $v \in \tilde{\mathcal{C}}$ if and only if $v\tilde{H}^{\mathsf{T}} = 0$. Using the notation $e = (1 \; \alpha \; \cdots \; \alpha^{m-1})SC$ as above, and writing $C = (C_1 \; C_2)$ with $C_1 \in \mathbb{F}_q^{r \times (k+1)}$ and $C_2 \in \mathbb{F}_q^{r \times (n-k-1)}$, the fact that $e \in \tilde{\mathcal{C}}$ yields the system

$$\left(1 \; \alpha \cdots \alpha^{m-1}\right) S \left(C_2 - C_1 R\right) = 0, \quad \text{over } \mathbb{F}_{q^m} \text{ with solutions in } \mathbb{F}_q. \tag{5}$$

Since all multiples λe are solutions of this system, we can specify the first column of C to $(1 \; 0 \; \cdots \; 0)^{\mathsf{T}}$. In this way, there is a single λe satisfying these constraints: the one where λ is the inverse of the first coordinate of e (assuming it is nonzero, see below). The system still admits several solutions which correspond to different bases of the support of λe. To fix one basis of this support, similarly to what is done in [52, Sec. 3], we can specify $S_1 = 1$, or equivalently, set the first column of S to be $(1 \; 0 \; \cdots \; 0)^{\mathsf{T}}$, and take an $r \times r$ invertible submatrix of S and specify it to be the identity matrix; thus the system has a single solution.

Doing so, the resulting system is affine bilinear (without constant term), with $(n - k - 1)m$ equations and $(m - 1)r + nr$ variables, and has a unique solution.

For the sake of presentation, in Sect. 5 we present our results assuming that the first coordinate of e is nonzero and that the top $r \times r$ block of S is invertible; these results are easily extended to the general case. Under these assumptions, our system can be rewritten as follows:

$$\mathcal{F} = \left\{ (1 \; \alpha \; \cdots \; \alpha^{m-1}) \left(\frac{I_r}{0 \mid S'} \right) \left(C_2 - \left(\frac{1}{0} \middle| C_1' \right) R \right) \right\}, \tag{6}$$

where S' is the $(m - r) \times (r - 1)$ submatrix $S_{\{r+1..m\},\{2..r\}}$ and C_1' is the $r \times k$ submatrix $C_{*,\{2..k+1\}}$. We call the entries of S' the *support variables* whereas the entries of C_1' and C_2 are called the *coefficient variables*. In Sect. 6.2 we give a procedure to handle the general case, by making several attempts to find the invertible block of S and a nonzero component of e.

4   Gröbner Bases and Degree Falls

We refer to [23] for basic definitions and properties of monomial orderings and Gröbner bases.

Field Equations and Monomial Ordering. Since we are looking for solutions in $\mathbb{F}_q$, we augment the polynomial system we want to solve with the field equations, that is, the equation $x_i^q - x_i = 0$ for each variable x_i arising in the system. In our case, as the system we consider in practice has mainly only one solution in $\mathbb{F}_q$ (see Sect. 6), the ideal of the system with the field equations is radical, and for any monomial ordering the reduced Gröbner basis is the set of linear polynomials $\{x_i - a_i\}_i$, where $\{x_i\}_i$ are the variables and $a_i \in \mathbb{F}_q$ is the i-th coordinate of the solution. The classical approach consists in computing the Gröbner basis with respect to a degree-reverse lexicographic order (grevlex), that will keep the degree of the polynomials as small as possible during the computation, and behaves usually better than other monomial orderings in terms of complexity.

Generic Gröbner Bases Algorithms and Their Link with Linear Algebra. Since the first descriptions of algorithms to compute Gröbner bases [18], far more efficient algorithms have been developed. On the one hand, substantial practical speed-ups were achieved by incorporating and accelerating fast linear algebra operations such as Gaussian elimination on the Macaulay matrices, which are sparse and structured (see Faugère's F4 algorithm [31], variants of the XL algorithm [22], and for instance GBLA [17]). We recall that the Macaulay matrix in degree d of a homogeneous system $(f_i)_i$ is the matrix whose columns correspond to the monomials of degree d sorted in descending order w.r.t. a chosen monomial ordering, whose rows correspond to the polynomials $t f_i$ for all i where t is a monomial of degree $d - \deg(f_i)$, and whose entry in row $t f_i$ and column u is the coefficient of the monomial u in the polynomial $t f_i$. In the case of a system containing field equations, we consider compact Macaulay matrices, where all monomials are reduced w.r.t. the field equations. For an affine system, the Macaulay matrix in degree d contains all polynomials $\{tf_i\}$ for $\deg(tf_i) \leq d$ and the columns are the monomials of degree less than or equal to d.

The approaches from F4 or XL are similar in that they both compute row echelon forms of some submatrices of Macaulay matrices for some given degree; in fact, it was proven in [11] that the XL algorithm computes a so-called d-Gröbner basis, which is a basis of the initial system where all computations in degree larger than d are ignored, and that one can rephrase the original XL algorithm in terms of the original F4 algorithm.

Now, many variants of these algorithms have been designed to tackle specific families of polynomial systems, and it seems that none of them performs always better than the others. In our experimental considerations, we rely on the implementation of the F4 algorithm which is available in magma V2.22-2 and is recognised for its efficiency.

On the other hand, improvements have been obtained by refining criteria which allow one to avoid useless computations (avoiding to consider monomials that cannot appear, a priori detection of reductions to zero as in the F5 algorithm [32] and other signature-based algorithms that followed, see [30] for a survey).

Complexity Analysis for Homogeneous Systems. For *homogeneous* systems, and for a graded monomial ordering, the complexity of these algorithms in terms of arithmetic operations is dominated by the cost of the row echelon forms on all Macaulay matrices up to degree d, where d is the largest degree of a polynomial in the reduced Gröbner basis[1]. This degree d is bounded by the *index of regularity*, or *degree of regularity*, which only depends on the ideal generated by the system, not on the specific generators forming the system. Some algorithms may need to go beyond degree d to check that no new polynomials will be produced, like the XL Algorithm or the F4 Algorithm without the F5 criteria, but those computations may be avoided if one knows in advance the degree of regularity of the system. This parameter can be precisely estimated for different families of generic systems, using the notions of regularity, of semi-regularity in the over-determined case, and of bi-regularity in the bilinear case [12,14,15,35]. However, those bounds may be very pessimistic for other specific (sub-)families of systems, and deriving estimations in this situation is difficult a priori, in particular for affine systems.

Definition 1. *Let $(f_i)_i$ be (non necessarily homogeneous) polynomials in a polynomial ring $\mathcal{R}$. A syzygy is a vector $(s_i)_i$, $s_i \in \mathcal{R}$ such that $\sum_i s_i f_i = 0$. The degree of the syzygy is defined as $\max_i(\deg(f_i) + \deg(s_i))$. The set of all syzygies of $(f_i)_i$ is an $\mathcal{R}$-module called the syzygy module of $(f_i)_i$.*

For a given family of systems, there are syzygies that occur for any system in the family. For instance, for any system $(f_i)_i$, the syzygy module contains the

---

[1] If the system contains redundant polynomials of degree larger than d, additional operations are needed to check that those polynomials reduce to zero w.r.t. the Gröbner basis, but this has usually a negligible cost.

$\mathcal{R}$-module spanned by the so-called *trivial syzygies* $(e_j f_i - e_i f_j)_{i,j}$, where e_i is the coordinate vector with 1 at index i. A system is called *regular* if its syzygy module is generated by these trivial syzygies.

Let us consider the particular case of a zero-dimensional system $(f_i)_i$ of homogeneous polynomials, generating an ideal I. As the system is homogenous and has a finite number of solutions, then it must have only 0 as a solution (with maybe some multiplicities). In this case, the degree of regularity of the system is the lowest integer d_{reg} such that all monomials of degree d_{reg} are in the ideal of leading terms of I (see [12,15]). Such a system is called *semi-regular* if the set of its syzygies of degree less than $d_{\text{reg}}(I)$ is exactly the set of trivial syzygies of degree less than $d_{\text{reg}}(I)$. Note that there may be non-trivial syzygies in degree $d_{\text{reg}}(I)$, which may be different for each system. As a consequence, all polynomials occurring in the computation of a Gröbner basis have degree $\leq d_{\text{reg}}$ and the arithmetic complexity is bounded by the cost of the row echelon form on the Macaulay matrices in degree $\leq d_{\text{reg}}$.

Complexity Analysis for Affine Systems. For affine systems, things are different. The degree of regularity can be defined in the same way w.r.t. the Gröbner basis for a grevlex ordering. But it is not any more related to the complexity of the computation: for instance, a system with only one solution will have a degree of regularity equal to 1. We need another parameter to control the complexity of the computation.

Let $(f_i)_i$ be a system of affine polynomials, and f_i^h the homogeneous part of highest degree of f_i. Let $I = \langle \{f_i\}_i \rangle$ and $I^h = \langle \{f_i^h\}_i \rangle$, and let d_{reg}^h be the degree of regularity of I^h. What may happen is that, during the computation of the basis in some degree d, some polynomials of degree less than d may be added to the basis. This will happen any time a syzygy $(s_i^h)_i$ for $(f_i^h)_i$ of degree d is such that there exists no syzygy $(s_i)_i$ for $(f_i)_i$ where s_i^h is the homogeneous part of highest degree of s_i. In that case, $\sum_i s_i^h f_i$ is a polynomial of degree less than d (the homogeneous part of highest degree cancels), that will not be reduced to zero during the Gröbner basis computation since this would give a syzygy $(s_i)_i$ for $(f_i)_i$ with homogeneous part $(s_i^h)_i$. This phenomenon is called a *degree fall* in degree d, and we will call such syzygies (s_i^h) that cannot be extended to syzygies for $(f_i)_i$ in the same degree *partial syzygies*; the corresponding polynomial $\sum_i s_i^h f_i$ is called the *residue*.

In cryptographic applications, the *first degree fall* d_{ff} has been widely used as a parameter controlling the complexity in algebraic cryptanalysis, for instance in the study of some HFE-type systems [25,29,43] and Kipnis-Shamir systems [56]. This first degree fall is simply the smallest d such that there exists a degree fall in degree d on $(f_i)_i$, and this quantity does depend on $(f_i)_i$: it might be different for another set of generators of the same ideal. Still, this notion takes on its full meaning while computing a Gröbner basis for a graded ordering, if we admit that the algorithm terminates shortly after reaching the first degree fall and without considering polynomials of higher degree. This can happen for some families of systems, as explained in the next paragraph, but there are examples of systems where the first degree fall d_{ff} is not the maximal degree reached during the computation, in which case it is not related to the complexity of the computation.

If the system $(f_i^h)_i$ is semi-regular, then the computation in degree less than d_{reg}^h will act as if the polynomials where homogeneous: there cannot be degree falls, as they would correspond to syzygies for the system $(f_i^h)_i$ that is assumed to be semi-regular. In degree d_{reg}^h, degree falls will occur for the first time, but at this point the remainder of the computation is negligible compared to the previous ones: by definition of d_{reg}^h, all monomials of degree d_{reg}^h are leading terms of polynomials in the basis, and the remaining steps in the computation will necessarily deal with polynomials of degree at most d_{reg}^h. Hence, the computations are almost the same as the ones for $(f_i^h)_i$, and the complexity is controlled by d_{reg}^h, which is here the *first degree fall* for the system $(f_i)_i$.

The behavior of the computation may be very different if degree falls occur in a much smaller degree. A good example of what may happen for particular families of systems is the affine bilinear case. It is proven in [35, Prop. 5] that a generic affine bilinear system of m equations $(f_1, \ldots, f_m) \in \mathbb{K}[x_1, \ldots, x_{n_x}, y_1, \ldots, y_{n_y}]$ in $n_x + n_y \geq m$ variables is regular. In particular, the Macaulay bound $d_{\text{reg}} \leq n_x + n_y + 1$ applies [46]. However, it was also proven in [35, Thm. 6] that for a zero-dimensional affine bilinear system ($m = n_x + n_y$), d_{reg} satisfies a much sharper inequality $d_{\text{reg}} \leq \min(n_x + 1, n_y + 1)$. The reason is that (homogeneous) bilinear systems are not regular, but the syzygy module of those systems is well understood [35]. In particular, there are syzygies for $(f_i^h)_i$ coming from Jacobian matrices, that are partial syzygies for $(f_i)_i$ and produce degree falls.

For affine systems, that are mainly encountered in cryptographic applications, and in particular for systems coming from a product of matrices whose coefficients are the variables of the system, the Jacobian matrices have a very particular shape that is easily described, and leads to a series of degree falls that reduces the degree of regularity of those systems. This is explained in detail in Sect. 5.

5 Degree Falls and Low Degree Equations

5.1 Degree Falls from the Kernel of the Jacobian

Fundamental Results from [35,56]. It has been realized in [56] that the first degree fall in the Kipnis and Shamir modelling can be traced back to partial syzygies obtained from low degree vectors in the kernel of the Jacobian of the bilinear part of a system either with respect to the kernel variables or the linear variables. This argument can also be adapted to our case and Jacobians with respect to the support variables are relevant here. To understand the relevance of the Jacobians for bilinear affine systems over some field $\mathbb{K}$ in general, consider a bilinear affine system $\mathcal{F} = \{f_1, \ldots, f_M\} \subset \mathbb{K}[s_1, \ldots, s_{t_s}, c_1, \ldots, c_{t_c}]$ of M equations in t_s variables s and t_c variables c. We denote by $\mathcal{F}^h := \{f_1^h, \ldots, f_M^h\}$ the bilinear part of these equations. In other words each f_i can be written as

$$f_i = f_i^h + r_i,$$

where each r_i is affine and $f_i{}^h$ is bilinear with respect to $\{s_1, \ldots, s_{t_s}\} \cup \{c_1, \ldots, c_{t_c}\}$. We define the Jacobian matrices associated to $\mathcal{F}^h$ as

$$\mathrm{Jac}_S(\mathcal{F}^h) = \begin{pmatrix} \frac{\partial f_1^h}{\partial s_1} & \cdots & \frac{\partial f_1^h}{\partial s_{t_s}} \\ \vdots & \vdots & \vdots \\ \frac{\partial f_M^h}{\partial s_1} & \cdots & \frac{\partial f_M^h}{\partial s_{t_s}} \end{pmatrix} \quad \text{and} \quad \mathrm{Jac}_C(\mathcal{F}^h) = \begin{pmatrix} \frac{\partial f_1^h}{\partial c_1} & \cdots & \frac{\partial f_1^h}{\partial c_{t_c}} \\ \vdots & \vdots & \vdots \\ \frac{\partial f_M^h}{\partial c_1} & \cdots & \frac{\partial f_M^h}{\partial c_{t_c}} \end{pmatrix}.$$

Note that $\mathrm{Jac}_S(\mathcal{F}^h)$ is a matrix with linear entries in $\mathbb{K}[c_1, \ldots, c_{t_c}]$ whereas $\mathrm{Jac}_C(\mathcal{F}^h)$ is a matrix with linear entries in $\mathbb{K}[s_1, \ldots, s_{t_s}]$. As shown in [56][Prop. 1 & 2] vectors in the left kernel of these Jacobians yield partial syzygies. This is essentially a consequence of the following identities that are easily verified:

$$\mathrm{Jac}_S(\mathcal{F}^h) \begin{pmatrix} s_1 \\ \vdots \\ s_{t_s} \end{pmatrix} = \begin{pmatrix} f_1^h \\ \vdots \\ f_M^h \end{pmatrix} \quad \text{and} \quad \mathrm{Jac}_C(\mathcal{F}^h) \begin{pmatrix} c_1 \\ \vdots \\ c_{t_c} \end{pmatrix} = \begin{pmatrix} f_1^h \\ \vdots \\ f_M^h \end{pmatrix}.$$

For instance, a vector $(g_1, \ldots, g_M)$ in the left kernel of $\mathrm{Jac}_C(\mathcal{F}^h)$ is a syzygy for $\mathcal{F}^h$, as it satisfies

$$\sum_{i=1}^M g_i f_i^h = (g_1 \cdots g_M) \begin{pmatrix} f_1^h \\ \vdots \\ f_M^h \end{pmatrix} = (g_1 \cdots g_M) \mathrm{Jac}_C(\mathcal{F}^h) \begin{pmatrix} c_1 \\ \vdots \\ c_{t_c} \end{pmatrix} = 0.$$

This gives typically a degree fall for $\mathcal{F}$ at degree $2 + \max(\deg g_i)$, with the corresponding residue given by

$$\sum_{i=1}^M g_i f_i = \sum_{i=1}^M g_i f_i^h + \sum_{i=1}^M g_i r_i = \sum_{i=1}^M g_i r_i.$$

These Jacobians are matrices with entries that are linear forms. The kernel of such matrices is well understood as shown by the next result.

Theorem 1 ([35]). *Let M be an $M \times t$ matrix of linear forms in $\mathbb{K}[s_1, \ldots, s_{t_s}]$. If $t < M$, then generically the left kernel of M is generated by vectors whose coefficients are maximal minors of M, specifically vectors of the form*

$$V_J = (\ldots, \underbrace{0}_{j \notin J}, \ldots, \underbrace{(-1)^{l+1} \det(M_{J \setminus \{j\}, *})}_{j \in J, j = j_l}, \ldots)_{1 \leq j \leq M}$$

where $J = \{j_1 < j_2 < \cdots < j_{t+1}\} \subset \{1, \ldots, M\}, \#J = t + 1$.

A direct use of this result however yields degree falls that occur for very large degrees, namely at degrees $t_s + 2$ or $t_c + 2$. In the case of the Kipnis-Shamir modelling, the syndrome modelling or the Ourivski-Johansson modelling, due to the particular form of the systems, degree falls occur at much smaller degrees than for generic bilinear affine systems. Roughly speaking, the reason is that the Jacobian of a system coming from a matrix product splits as a tensor product, as we now explain. This has been realized in [56] for the Kipnis-Shamir modelling, and here we slightly generalize this result in order to use it for more general modellings, and in particular for the Ourivski-Johansson modelling.

Jacobian Matrices of Systems Coming from Matrix Products. Consider a system $AXY = 0$ where $A = (a_{i,s})_{1 \leq i \leq m, 1 \leq s \leq p}$, $X = (x_{s,t})_{1 \leq s \leq p, 1 \leq t \leq r}$ and $Y = (y_{t,j})_{1 \leq t \leq r, 1 \leq j \leq n}$. The variables considered for this Jacobian matrix are the $x_{s,t}$. The matrices A and Y may have polynomial coefficients, but they do not involve the $x_{s,t}$ variables. Below, we use the Kronecker product of two matrices, for example $A \otimes Y^\mathsf{T} = (a_{i,s} Y^\mathsf{T})_{1 \leq i \leq m, 1 \leq s \leq p}$. We use the notations

$$vec_{row}(A) = (A_{\{1\},*} \cdots A_{\{n\},*})^\mathsf{T} \text{ and } vec_{col}(A) = vec_{row}(A^\mathsf{T}).$$

Lemma 1. *The Jacobian matrix of the system $AXY = 0_{m \times n}$ with respect to the variables X can be written, depending on the order of the equations and variables:*

$$\mathrm{Jac}_{vec_{col}(X)}(vec_{col}(AXY)) = Y^\mathsf{T} \otimes A \in \mathbb{K}[A, Y]^{nm \times rp}$$
$$\mathrm{Jac}_{vec_{row}(X)}(vec_{row}(AXY)) = A \otimes Y^\mathsf{T} \in \mathbb{K}[A, Y]^{nm \times rp}.$$

Proof. For $1 \leq i \leq m$, $1 \leq j \leq n$, the equation in row i and column j of AXY is

$$f_{i,j} = \sum_{s=1}^{p} \sum_{t=1}^{r} a_{i,s} x_{s,t} y_{t,j}.$$

We then have, for $1 \leq s \leq p$ and $1 \leq t \leq r$, $\frac{\partial f_{i,j}}{\partial x_{s,t}} = a_{i,s} y_{t,j}$ so that in row order,

$$\mathrm{Jac}_{x_{s,1},\ldots,x_{s,r}}(\{f_{i,1}, \ldots, f_{i,n}\}) = \left(\frac{\partial f_{i,j}}{\partial x_{s,t}}\right)_{\substack{1 \leq j \leq n \\ 1 \leq t \leq r}} = a_{i,s} (y_{t,j})_{\substack{1 \leq j \leq n \\ 1 \leq t \leq r}} = a_{i,s} Y^\mathsf{T}.$$

The result follows from the definition of the Kronecker product of matrices. The proof when the equations and variables are in column order is similar. □

Application to the Kipnis-Shamir Modelling. Recall the system:

$$\left(\sum_{i=1}^{km} x_i M_i\right) \begin{pmatrix} I_{n-r} \\ K \end{pmatrix} = 0_{m,n-r}, \tag{7}$$

where $M_i \in \mathbb{F}_q^{m \times n}$ and K is an $r \times (n-r)$ matrix of indeterminates. If we write each $M_i = (M_i' \ M_i'')$ with $M_i' \in \mathbb{F}_q^{m \times (n-r)}$ and $M_i'' \in \mathbb{F}_q^{m \times r}$, then we have

$$\sum_{i=1}^{km} x_i (M_i' + M_i'' K) = 0_{m,n-r} \tag{KS}$$

The bilinear and linear parts of the system are respectively $\sum_{i=1}^{km} x_i \mathbf{M}''_i \mathbf{K}$ and $\sum_{i=1}^{km} x_i \mathbf{M}'_i$. Using Lemma 1 (with equations in column order), when we compute the Jacobian with respect to the entries of $\mathbf{K}$ (the so-called kernel variables in [56]), we obtain

$$\mathrm{Jac}_{vec_{col}(\mathbf{K})}\left(vec_{col}\left(\sum_{i=1}^{km} x_i \mathbf{M}''_i \mathbf{K}\right)\right) = \sum_{i=1}^{km} x_i (\mathbf{I}_{n-r} \otimes \mathbf{M}''_i) = \mathbf{I}_{n-r} \otimes \left(\sum_{i=1}^{km} x_i \mathbf{M}''_i\right).$$

The kernel of $\mathrm{Jac}_{vec_{col}(\mathbf{K})}$ is generated by the vectors $(\mathbf{v}_1, \ldots, \mathbf{v}_{n-r})$ with $\mathbf{v}_l$ in the left kernel of $\mathbf{M} = \sum_{i=1}^{km} x_i \mathbf{M}''_i$, that should be generated by $\binom{m}{r+1}$ vectors of minors, according to Theorem 1. Hence the kernel of $\mathrm{Jac}_{vec_{col}(\mathbf{K})}$ is generated by $\binom{m}{r+1}(n-r)$ vectors. It is here that we see the point of having this tensor product form. These kernel vectors have entries that are polynomials of degree r by using Theorem 1. This gives degree falls at degree $r+2$ and yields partial syzygies that have degree $r+1$. These considerations are a slightly different way of understanding the results given in [56, §3]. The syndrome modelling displays a similar behavior, i.e. a degree fall at $r+2$ for the very same reason as can be readily verified. Let us apply now Lemma 1 to the Ourivski-Johansson modelling.

Application to the Ourivski-Johansson Modelling. The system here is

$$\mathcal{F} = \left\{ (1 \; \alpha \; \cdots \; \alpha^{m-1}) \left(\begin{array}{c|c} \mathbf{I}_r \\ \hline \mathbf{0} & \mathbf{S}' \end{array}\right) \left(\mathbf{C}_2 - \left(\begin{array}{c|c} 1 \\ \mathbf{0} \end{array}\right| \mathbf{C}'_1\right) \mathbf{R}\right) \right\}, \qquad (8)$$

where $\mathbf{S}'$ is the $(m-r) \times (r-1)$ matrix $\mathbf{S}_{\{r+1..m\},\{2..r\}}$ and $\mathbf{C}'_1$ is the $r \times k$ matrix $\mathbf{C}_{*,\{2..k+1\}}$. We add to $\mathcal{F}$ the field equations $\mathcal{F}_q = \{s_{i,j}^q - s_{i,j}, r+1 \leq i \leq m, 2 \leq j \leq r, c_{i,j}^q - c_{i,j}, 1 \leq i \leq r, 2 \leq j \leq n\}$.

With high probability, this system has a unique solution. As we used the field equations, the ideal $\langle \mathcal{F}, \mathcal{F}_q \rangle$ is radical. The system has $n_S = (m-r)(r-1)$ variables $\mathbf{S}$, $n_C = (n-1)r$ variables $\mathbf{C}$, and $n-k-1$ equations over $\mathbb{F}_{q^m}$, hence $n_{eq} = (n-k-1)m$ equations over $\mathbb{F}_q$, plus the field equations.

Consider the system $\mathcal{F}^h$ formed by the bilinear parts of the equations in $\mathcal{F}$. A simple computation shows that

$$\mathcal{F}^h = \left\{ \alpha^r \left(1 \; \alpha \; \cdots \; \alpha^{m-r-1}\right) \mathbf{S}'(\mathbf{C}''_2 - \mathbf{C}''_1 \mathbf{R}') \right\},$$

where $\mathbf{C}''_2 = \mathbf{C}_{\{2..r\},\{k+2..n\}}$, $\mathbf{C}''_1 = \mathbf{C}_{\{2..r\},\{2..k+1\}}$ and $\mathbf{R}' = \mathbf{R}_{\{2..k+1\},*}$.

If we take the equations and variables in row order, and use Lemma 1, then

$$\mathrm{Jac}_{vec_{row}(\mathbf{S})}(vec_{row}(\mathcal{F}^h)) = \alpha^r \left(1 \; \alpha \; \cdots \; \alpha^{m-r-1}\right) \otimes \left(\mathbf{C}''_2 - \mathbf{C}''_1 \mathbf{R}'\right)^\mathsf{T} \qquad (9)$$

The elements in the left kernel of $\mathrm{Jac}_{vec_{row}(\mathbf{S})}(vec_{row}(\mathcal{F}^h))$ are those in the right kernel of $\mathbf{C}''_2 - \mathbf{C}''_1 \mathbf{R}'$, and applying Theorem 1, they belong to the module generated by the vectors $\mathbf{V}_J$ for any $J = \{j_1 < j_2 < \cdots < j_r\} \subset \{1, \ldots, n-k-1\}$ of size r defined by

$$\mathbf{V}_J = (\ldots, \underbrace{\mathbf{0}}_{j \notin J}, \ldots, \underbrace{(-1)^{l+1} \det(\mathbf{C}''_2 - \mathbf{C}''_1 \mathbf{R}'_{*,J\setminus\{j\}})}_{j=j_l \in J}, \ldots)_{1 \leq j \leq n-k-1}.$$

Each V_J gives a syzygy for $\mathcal{F}^h$ and when applying it to $\mathcal{F}$ it yields a degree fall in degree $r + 1$ because the entries of V_J are homogeneous polynomials of degree $r - 1$. The inner product of V_J with the vector of the equations gives an equation of degree $\leq r$ since the homogeneous part of highest degree cancels, as has been observed at the beginning of this section. Now the affine part of the equations $\mathcal{F}$ is $\left(1\ \alpha\ \cdots\ \alpha^{r-1}\right)(C_2 - C_1 R)$.

Writing $\tilde{H} = \left(-R^\mathsf{T}\ I_{n-k-1}\right)$, then

$$\det(C_2'' - C_1'' R'_{*,J\setminus\{j\}}) = \det((C\tilde{H}^\mathsf{T})_{\{2..r\},J\setminus\{j\}}).$$

Using the reverse of Laplace's formula expressing a determinant in terms of minors, we can compute the inner product of the vector V_J with the ith row of $C_2 - C_1 R = C\tilde{H}^\mathsf{T}$, that is 0 for $2 \leq i$ and $\det((C\tilde{H}^\mathsf{T})_{*,J})$ for $i = 1$.

The product gives

$$V_J \left(\left(1\ \alpha\ \cdots\ \alpha^{r-1}\right)(C_2 - C_1 R)\right)^\mathsf{T} = V_J (C_2 - C_1 R)^\mathsf{T} \left(1\ \alpha\ \cdots\ \alpha^{r-1}\right)^\mathsf{T}$$
$$= \det(C_2 - C_1 R)_{*,J}. \tag{10}$$

This yields a corresponding equation that will be reduced to zero by a degree-$(r + 1)$ Gröbner basis of $\mathcal{F}$. Hence the partial syzygies of degree r coming from the degree fall in the $(r + 1)$-Macaulay matrix are exactly the maximal minors of $C_2 - C_1 R$. We have thus proven that

Theorem 2. *The equations* MaxMinors$(C_2 - C_1 R) = 0$, *that are the maximal minors of the matrix $C_2 - C_1 R$, belong to the ideal $\langle \mathcal{F}, \mathcal{F}_q \rangle$. Moreover, they are reduced to zero by a degree $(r + 1)$-Gröbner basis of $\{\mathcal{F}, \mathcal{F}_q\}$.*

Remark 1. If we are only interested in the first part of the theorem about the maximal minors, then there is a simple and direct proof which is another illustration of the role of the matrix form of the system. Indeed, let (S^*, C^*) be a solution of $\{\mathcal{F}, \mathcal{F}_q\}$, then the nonzero vector $\left(1\ S_2^*\ \cdots\ S_m^*\right) = \left(1\ \alpha\ \cdots\ \alpha^{m-1}\right)S^*$ belongs to the left kernel of the matrix $C_2^* - C_1^* R$. Hence this matrix has rank less than r, and the equations MaxMinors$(C_2 - C_1 R) = 0$ are satisfied for any solution of the system $\{\mathcal{F}, \mathcal{F}_q\}$, which means that the equations belong to the ideal $\langle \mathcal{F}, \mathcal{F}_q \rangle$ as this ideal is radical.

5.2 Analysis of the Ideal MaxMinors$(C_2 - C_1 R)$

The previous theorem allows us to obtain directly degree r equations without having to compute first the Macaulay matrix in degree $r + 1$. This is a significant saving when performing the Gröbner basis computation. A nice feature of these equations is that they only involve one part of the unknowns, namely the coefficient variables.

Moreover all these equations can be expressed by using a limited number of polynomials as we now show. Some of them will be of degree r, some of them will be of degree $r - 1$. If we perform Gaussian elimination on these equations by treating these polynomials as variables and trying to eliminate the ones corresponding to the polynomials of degree r first, then if the number of equations we had was greater than the number of polynomials of degree r, we would expect to find equations of degree $r - 1$. Roughly speaking, when this phenomenon happens we just have to add all the equations of degree $r - 1$ we obtain in this way to the Ourivski-Johansson modelling and the Gröbner basis calculation will not go beyond degree r.

Let us analyse precisely the behavior we just sketched. The shape of the equations MaxMinors($C_2 - C_1 R$) $= 0$ is given by the following proposition, where by convention $\det(M_{\emptyset,\emptyset}) = 1$ and the columns of R are indexed by $\{k + 2..n\}$:

Proposition 1. MaxMinors($C_2 - C_1 R$) *is a set of* $\binom{n-k-1}{r}$ *polynomials* P_J, *indexed by* $J \subset \{k + 2..n\}$ *of size* r:

$$P_J = \sum_{\substack{T_1 \subset \{1..k+1\}, T_2 \subset J \\ \text{such that } T = T_1 \cup T_2 \text{ has size } \#T = r}} (-1)^{\sigma_J(T_2)} \det(R_{T_1, J \setminus T_2}) \det(C_{*,T}).$$

where $\sigma_J(T_2)$ *is an integer depending on* T_2 *and* J.

If $1 \notin T$, *the polynomial* $\det(C_{*,T})$ *is homogeneous of degree* r *and contains* $r!$ *monomials; if* $1 \in T$, $\det(C_{*,T})$ *is homogeneous of degree* $r - 1$ *and contains* $(r - 1)!$ *monomials.*

Proof. The matrix $C_2 - C_1 R$ has size $r \times (n - k - 1)$, hence there are $\binom{n-k-1}{r}$ different minors $P_J = \det(C(\begin{smallmatrix} -R \\ I_{n-k-1} \end{smallmatrix})_{*,J})$. To compute them, we use the Cauchy-Binet formula for the determinant of a product of non-square matrices:

$$\det(AB) = \sum_{T \subset \{1..p\}, \#T = r} \det(A_{*,T}) \det(B_{T,*})$$

where $A \in \mathbb{K}^{r \times p}$, $B \in \mathbb{K}^{p \times r}$, and $p \geq r$. We apply this formula to P_J, and use the fact that, for $T = T_1 \cup T_2$ with $T_1 \subset \{1..k+1\}$ and $T_2 \subset \{k+2..n\}$,

$$\det \left(\begin{pmatrix} -R \\ I_{n-k-1} \end{pmatrix}_{T_1 \cup T_2, J} \right) = 0 \text{ if } T_2 \not\subset J$$

$$= (-1)^{\sigma_J(T_2)} \det(R_{T_1, J \setminus T_2}) \text{ if } T_2 \subset J,$$

using the Laplace expansion of this determinant along the last rows, with $\sigma_J(T_2) = d(k+r) + (d-1)d/2 + \sum_{t \in T_2} Pos(t, J)$ where $Pos(t, J)$ is the position of t in J, and $d = \#J - \#T_2$.   □

Each polynomial P_J can be expanded into m equations over $\mathbb{F}_q$, the polynomial $P_J[i]$ being the coefficient of P_J in α^{i-1}. When computing a grevlex Gröbner basis of the system of the $P_J[i]$'s over $\mathbb{F}_q$, with an algorithm like F4 using linear algebra, the first step consists in computing a basis of the $P_J[i]$'s over $\mathbb{F}_q$.

It appears that there may be a degree fall in this first step, in degree r, that produces equations of degree $r - 1$. The following heuristic explains when this degree fall occurs.

Heuristic 1 – Overdetermined case: *when* $m\binom{n-k-1}{r} \geq \binom{n}{r} - 1$*, generically, a degree-*r *Gröbner basis of the projected system* $\mathrm{MaxMinors}(C_2 - C_1 R) = 0$ *of* $m\binom{n-k-1}{r}$ *equations over* $\mathbb{F}_q$ *contains* $\binom{n-1}{r-1} - 1$ *equations of degree* $r - 1$*, that are obtained by linear combinations of the initial equations.*
- Intermediate case: *when* $\binom{n}{r} - 1 > m\binom{n-k-1}{r} > \binom{n-1}{r}$*, generically a degree-*r *Gröbner basis of the projected system* $\mathrm{MaxMinors}(C_2 - C_1 R) = 0$ *contains* $m\binom{n-k-1}{r} - \binom{n-1}{r}$ *equations of degree* $r - 1$*, that are obtained by linear combinations of the initial equations.*
- Underdetermined case: *When* $m\binom{n-k-1}{r} \leq \binom{n-1}{r}$*, then generically a degree-*r *Gröbner basis of the system contains* $m\binom{n-k-1}{r}$ *polynomials that are all of degree* r*.*

Remark 2. Here overdetermined/underdetermined refers to the system of maximal minors given by the set of equations $\mathrm{MaxMinors}(C_2 - C_1 R) = 0$

Remark 3. The degree-r Gröbner bases also contain polynomials of degree r in the overdetermined and intermediate cases, but we will not compute them, as experimentally they bring no speed-up to the computation, see Sect. 6.1.

Proposition 2. *Computing the polynomials in a degree-*r *Gröbner basis of the projected equations* $\mathrm{MaxMinors}$ *amounts to solving a linear system with* $\nu = m\binom{n-k-1}{r}$ *equations in* $\mu = \binom{n}{r}$ *variables, which costs* $O(\min(\mu, \nu)^{\omega-2}\mu\nu)$ *operations in the base field, where* ω *is the exponent of matrix multiplication (see Sect. 6.2).*

Proof. It is possible to view the system $\mathrm{MaxMinors}(C_2 - C_1 R)$ projected over $\mathbb{F}_q$ as a linear system of $\mu = m\binom{n-k-1}{r}$ equations, whose variables are the $\nu = \binom{n}{r}$ unknowns $x_T = \det(C_{*,T})$ for all $T \subset \{1..n\}$ of size r. The matrix associated to this linear system is a matrix M of size $\mu \times \nu$ whose coefficient in row $(i, J) : i \in \{1..m\}, J \subset \{k+2..n\}, \#J = r$, and column x_T is, with $T_2 = T \cap \{k+2..n\}$:

$$M[(i, J), x_T] = \begin{cases} [\alpha^{i-1}](-1)^{\sigma_J(T_2)} \det(R_{T \cap \{1..k+1\}, J \setminus T_2}) & \text{if } T_2 \subset J, \\ 0 & \text{otherwise.} \end{cases} \quad (11)$$

where $[\alpha^{i-1}]\beta$ is the ith component of $\beta \in \mathbb{F}_{q^m}$ viewed in the vector space $\mathbb{F}_q^m$ with generator basis $(1 \, \alpha \ldots \alpha^{m-1})$.

A basis of the vector space generated by the equations $\mathrm{MaxMinors}(C_2 - C_1 R) = 0$ is given by $\tilde{M} \cdot T$ where $\tilde{M}$ is the row echelon form of M and T is the column vector formed by the polynomials $\det(C_{*,T}) : \#T = r$. As we are searching for equations of degree $r - 1$, we order the variables x_T such that the ones with $1 \in T$ that correspond to polynomials $\det(C_{*,T})$ of degree $r - 1$ are the rightmost entries of the matrix. □

Heuristic 1 can be stated in terms of the matrix M. In the overdetermined case, that is when $m\binom{n-k-1}{r} \geq \binom{n}{r} - 1$, we expect matrix M to have rank $\binom{n}{r} - 1$ with high probability. This rank can not be larger, as the (left) kernel space of the matrix has dimension 1 (this comes from the fact that the equations are homogeneous). Hence, $\tilde{M} \cdot T$ produces $\binom{n-1}{r}$ equations of degree r, and $\binom{n-1}{r-1} - 1$ equations of degree $r - 1$, that have all the shape $\det(C_{*,T})$ or $\det(C_{*,T}) - \det(C_{*,T_0})$ where T_0 corresponds to the free variable x_{T_0} of the linear system, $1 \in T_0$. In the intermediate and underdetermined cases, we also expect matrix M to be full rank in general, and to be also full rank on the columns corresponding to the c_T's of degree r.

6   Experimental Results, Complexity Bounds, and Security

6.1   Experimental Results

We did various computations for different values of the parameters (m, n, k, r). We got our best complexity results by doing the following steps:

1. compute the set of equations $\mathcal{F}$ which comes from $\left(1 \; \alpha \; \cdots \; \alpha^{m-1}\right) S\left(C_2 - C_1 R\right)$ specialised as in (6),
2. compute the system MaxMinors$(C_2 - C_1 R)$,
3. compute the matrix M from (11) and its echelon form $\tilde{M}$, let $\mathcal{J}$ be the set of the resulting equations of degree $r - 1$ in the C variables,
4. if $\mathcal{J}$ is empty, then let $\mathcal{J}$ be the set of equations coming from $\tilde{M}$ of degree r in the C variables,
5. compute G a reduced degree-d Gröbner basis of the system $\{\mathcal{F}, \mathcal{J}, \mathcal{F}_q\}$, where

$$d = \begin{cases} r & \text{in the overdetermined case,} \\ r \text{ or } r + 1 & \text{in the intermediate case,} \\ r + 2 & \text{in the underdetermined case.} \end{cases}$$

The computations are done using magma v2.22-2 on a machine with an Intel® Xeon® 2.00 GHz processor. Here are the notation used in all tables:

- $n_S = (r - 1)(m - r)$: the number of variables in S
- $n_C = r(n - 1)$: the number of variables in C
- $n_{eq} = m(n - k - 1)$: the number of equations in $\mathcal{F}$
- $d : n_{syz}$: the number of equations in $\mathcal{J}$, where d denotes the degree of the equations and n_{syz} the number of them:
  - $r - 1 : \binom{n-1}{r-1} - 1$ in the overdetermined case
  - $r - 1 : m\binom{n-k-1}{r} - \binom{n-1}{r}$ in the intermediate case
  - $r : m\binom{n-k-1}{r}$ in the underdetermined case
- T_{syz}: time of computing the n_{syz} equations of degree $r - 1$ or r in $\mathcal{J}$

- T_{Gbsyz}: time of the Gröbner basis computation of $\{\mathcal{J}, \mathcal{F}_q\}$
- T_{Gb}: time of the Gröbner basis computation of $\{\mathcal{F}, \mathcal{J}, \mathcal{F}_q\}$
- d_{ff}: the degree where we observe the first degree fall
- d_{max}: the maximal degree where some new polynomial is produced by the F4 algorithm
- "Max Matrix size": the size of the largest matrix reduced during the F4 computation, given by magma. We did not take into account the useless steps (the matrices giving no new polynomials)

Table 1 gives our timings on the parameters proposed in [55]. For each set of parameters, the first row of the table gives the timing for the direct computation of a Gröbner basis of $\{\mathcal{F}, \mathcal{F}_q\}$ whereas the second row gives the timings for the Gröbner basis of $\{\mathcal{F}, \mathcal{J}, \mathcal{F}_q\}$. We can see that, apart from very small parameters, the computation of the equations MaxMinors($C_2 - C_1 R$) is negligible compared to the time of the Gröbner basis computation.

Among the proposed parameters, only the $(15, 15, 8, 3)$ was in the case where the system MaxMinors is underdetermined. In that case, the most consuming part of the computation is the Gröbner basis of the system MaxMinors, that depends only on the C variables. Once this computation is done, the remaining Gröbner basis of $\{\mathcal{F}, \mathcal{J}, \mathcal{F}_q\}$ has a negligible cost.

Table 2 gives timing for different values of k and r, with $m = 14$ and $n = 18$ fixed. For $r = 2$, the values $k \in \{1..11\}$ correspond to the overdetermined case, the value $k = 12$ to the intermediate one, and $k = 13$ to the underdetermined case. The values $k \in \{1..11\}$ behave all like $k = 11$. As for the parameters from [55], the hardest cases are the ones when the system MaxMinors is underdetermined, where the maximal degree reached during the computation is $r + 2$. For the overdetermined cases, the maximal degree is r, and for the intermediate cases, it may be r or $r + 1$.

For $r = 3$, the overdetermined cases are $k \in \{1..8\}$, $k = 9$ is intermediate and $k \in \{10..11\}$ are underdetermined. Values of $k \geq 12$ do not allow a unique decoding for $r = 3$, the Gilbert-Varshamov bound being 2 for those values.

For $r = 4$ the tradeoffs are $1 \leq k \leq 6$, $k = 7$ and $8 \leq k \leq 9$ for the three cases, and for $r = 5$, $1 \leq k \leq 5$, $k = 6$ and $7 \leq k \leq 8$. We could not perform the computations for the intermediate and underdetermined cases, due to a lack of memory. We also observe that the first degree fall (d_{ff}) does not always predict the complexity of the computation.

Table 3 gives the timings for a fixed $r = 3$, a ratio $n = 2k$ and various values of k. Again, we can observe that for defavorable cases $(k = 6, 7)$ the maximal degree is $r + 2$ or $r + 1$ rather than r, making the computation harder for small values of k than for larger.

Table 1. We compare the behavior of the Gröbner basis computation for the parameters considered in [48], with and without adding to the system the equations $\mathcal{J}$.

m	n	k	r	n_S	n_C	n_{eq}	n_{syz}	T_{syz}	T_{Gbsyz}	T_{Gb}	d_{ff}	d_{max}	Max Mat Size
25	30	15	2	23	58	350				0.4 s	3	3	18550 ×19338
							1:28	0.4 s		0.02 s	2	2	1075 × 749
30	30	16	2	28	58	390				0.5 s	3	3	22620 × 25288
							1:28	0.4 s		0.02 s	2	2	1260 × 899
30	50	20	2	28	98	870				2.2 s	3	3	67860 × 57898
							1:48	3.8 s		0.07 s	2	2	2324 × 1499
50	50	26	2	48	98	1150				7.4 s	3	3	112700 × 120148
							1:48	3.5 s		0.2 s	2	2	3589 × 2499
15	15	7	3	24	42	105				60.1 s	4	4	77439 × 153532
							2:90	0.2 s		0.06 s	3	3	8860 × 13658
15	15	8	3	24	42	90		–			4	≥5	–
							3:300	0.3 s	162 s	0.2 s	4	5	191515 × 457141
20	20	10	3	34	57	180				450 s	4	4	233672 × 543755
							2:170	1.0 s		0.2 s	3	3	22124 × 35087

Table 2. $m = 14$ and $n = 18$.

k	r	n_{syz}	n_S	n_C	n_{eq}	$T_{Syz.}$	T_{Gbsyz}	T_{Gb}	d_{ff}	d_{max}	Max Matrix size	Mem
11	2	1:16	12	34	84	<0.1s		<0.1s	2	2	322 × 251	34 Mo
12	2	1:4	12	34	70	<0.1s		<0.1s	3	3	1820 × 2496	34 Mo
13	2	2:84	12	34	56	<0.1s	32 s	0 s	3	4	231187 × 141064	621 Mo
8	3	2:135	22	51	126	0.6 s		0.1 s	3	3	13179 × 18604	34 Mo
9	3	2:104	22	51	112	0.5 s		0.7 s	3	3	10907 × 18743	67 Mo
4	4	3:679	30	68	182	12.1 s		53.7 s	2	4	314350 × 650610	1.3 Go
5	4	3:679	30	68	168	9.4 s		59.3 s	4	4	314350 × 650610	2.0 Go
6	4	3:679	30	68	154	7.1 s		69.4 s	4	4	281911 × 679173	3.6 Go
2	5	4:2379	36	85	210	138.8 s		27.5 s	2	4	416433 × 669713	1.1 Go
5	5	4:2379	36	85	196	44.8 s		5h08	2	5	7642564 × 30467163	253.6 Go

Table 3. The parameters are $r = 3$, $m = n$, $k = \frac{n}{2}$.

k	n_{syz}	n_S	n_C	n_{eq}	T_{syz}	T_{Gbsyz}	T_{Gb}	d_{max}	Memory
6	3:120	18	33	60	0.2 s	117 s	0.02 s	5	4.9 Go
7	3:280	22	39	84	0.1 s	9.7 s	0.1 s	4	0.3 Go
8	2:104	26	45	112	0.2 s		0.1 s	3	.04 Go
17	2:527	62	99	544	34.3 s		4.7 s	3	0.3 Go
27	2:1377	102	159	1404	650.2 s		161.3 s	3	2.7 Go
37	2:2627	142	219	2664	5603.6 s		3709.4 s	3	15.0 Go
47	2:4277	182	279	4324	26503.9 s		26022.6 s	3	83.0 Go

6.2 Complexity Analysis and Security over $\mathbb{F}_2$

Now, we give an upper bound on the complexity of our algebraic approach to solve the (m, n, k, r)-decoding problem using the modelling of Sect. 3.3. The complexity is estimated in terms of the number of operations in $\mathbb{F}_2$ that the algorithm uses. This allows us to update the number of bits of security for several cryptosystems, as showed in Table 4: Loidreau's one [49], ROLLO [7], and RQC [3]. Note that the restriction to $\mathbb{F}_2$ is only there because we want to derive security values. If one works over a larger field $\mathbb{F}_q$, a similar analysis can be derived. The only change in this case is to consider the relevant number of monomials. Note also that even if Algorithm 1 works over any field, its success probability given in Proposition 3 depends on q.

Remark that, in Table 4, for the sets of parameters which do not satisfy Eq. (1), which correspond to underdetermined instances, we assume that the system can be solved at $d = r + 1$. It is a conservative choice: in the experiments of Sect. 6.1, the maximal degree is often r for the underdetermined cases.

The complexity bound follows from the fact that the Gröbner basis algorithm works with Macaulay matrices of degree δ for increasing values of δ up to d, the degree for which the Gröbner basis is found (see Sect. 4 for a more detailed description). At each of these steps, the algorithm performs a Gaussian elimination algorithm on a Macaulay matrix which has at most $\binom{(m-r)(r-1)+(n-1)r}{\delta}$ columns and fewer rows than columns. The number of columns is the number of squarefree monomials of degree δ in $(m - r)(r - 1) + (n - 1)r$ variables.

Table 4. Security in bits for several cryptosystems with respect to our attack, computed using Eq. (12) with $\omega = 2.807$, $d = r$ or $d = r + 1$. The values in bold correspond the most likely maximal degree, i.e. r if Eq. (1) holds and $r + 1$ otherwise. The last column gives the previous best known security values, based on the attack in [10].

Cryptosystem	Parameters (m, n, k, r)	$d = r$	$d = r + 1$	Previous
Loidreau	$(128, 120, 80, 4)$	**96.3**	117.1	256
ROLLO-I-128	$(79, 94, 47, 5)$	**114.9**	134.5	128
ROLLO-I-192	$(89, 106, 53, 6)$	**142.2**	162.5	192
ROLLO-I-256	$(113, 134, 67, 7)$	174.0	**195.3**	256
ROLLO-II-128	$(83, 298, 149, 5)$	**132.3**	155.4	128
ROLLO-II-192	$(107, 302, 151, 6)$	**161.5**	185.0	192
ROLLO-II-256	$(127, 314, 157, 7)$	191.6	**215.4**	256
ROLLO-III-128	$(101, 94, 47, 5)$	**117.1**	137.2	128
ROLLO-III-192	$(107, 118, 59, 6)$	**145.7**	166.6	192
ROLLO-III-256	$(131, 134, 67, 7)$	175.9	**197.5**	256
RQC-I	$(97, 134, 67, 5)$	**121.1**	142.0	128
RQC-II	$(107, 202, 101, 6)$	**154.2**	176.5	192
RQC-III	$(137, 262, 131, 7)$	188.4	**211.9**	256

In general, Gaussian elimination of a $\mu \times \nu$ matrix of rank ρ over a field has a complexity of $O(\rho^{\omega-2}\mu\nu) \subseteq O(\max(\mu,\nu)^\omega)$ operations in that field [19,54]. Here, ω is the exponent of matrix multiplication, with naive bounds $2 \leq \omega \leq 3$. The best currently known value for ω is $\omega \approx 2.37$ [47], by an improvement of Coppersmith-Winograd's algorithm. In terms of practical performances, the best known method is based on Strassen's algorithm, which allows one to take $\omega \approx 2.807$, and when the base field is a finite field, this exponent is indeed observed in practice for matrices with more than a few hundreds rows and columns.

The Macaulay matrices encountered in the Gröbner basis computations we consider are usually very sparse and exhibit some structure. Some Gaussian elimination algorithms have been designed specifically for matrices over $\mathbb{F}_2$ [4], also for sparse matrices [16], and even to take advantage of the specific structure of Macaulay matrices (see [17]; we expect Magma's closed-source implementation of F$_4$ to use similar techniques). However, none of these optimized algorithms has been proven to reach a complexity which is asymptotically better than the one mentioned above, apart from speed-ups by constant factors.

As a result, we bound the complexity of the step of degree δ in the Gröbner basis computation by that of performing Gaussian elimination on a $\mu \times \nu$ matrix over $\mathbb{F}_2$, with $\mu \leq \nu = \binom{(m-r)(r-1)+(n-1)r}{\delta}$; the overall computation then costs

$$\mathcal{O}\left(\left(\sum_{\delta=0}^{d}\binom{(m-r)(r-1)+(n-1)r}{\delta}\right)^\omega\right) \tag{12}$$

operations in $\mathbb{F}_2$. Let us now focus on the case $m = n = 2k$ and $r \approx \sqrt{n}$. Then the complexity of our approach is as in Eq. (12) with $d = r$. Using a similar analysis, the approach based on Kipnis-Shamir's modelling has a complexity of

$$\mathcal{O}\left(\left(\sum_{\delta=0}^{r+2}\binom{km+r(n-r)}{\delta}\right)^\omega\right)$$

operations. Asymptotically, the dominant term in the former bound is of the order of $2^{\frac{3}{2}\omega r \log_2(n)}$, to be compared to $2^{2\omega r \log_2(n)}$ in the Kipnis-Shamir bound. Also, the aforementioned combinatorial attacks ([10]) would have a complexity of the order of $2^{\frac{1}{2}rn}$ when $m = n = 2k$.

Finally, note that the complexity bound stated above was derived under assumptions: in Sect. 3.3, we presented the modelling along with some assumptions which allowed us to specialize variables a priori and still ensure that the algorithm of Sect. 5 yields the solution λe. In general, the assumption might not hold, that is, the specific specialization made in Sect. 3.3 could be wrong. We use Algorithm 1 in order to specialize more variables: it first uses the specialization detailed in Sect. 3.3, and if that one fails, follows on with other similar specializations. This algorithm uses the subroutine $\mathtt{Solve}(S, C, R)$, which augments the system as explained in Sect. 5 and returns a solution to Eq. (5) if one is found and $\emptyset$ otherwise.

Input: Matrix $\boldsymbol{R}$
Output: A solution to the system in (5) or $\emptyset$
$\boldsymbol{S} = m \times r$ matrix of variables
$\boldsymbol{C} = r \times n$ matrix of variables
Set the first column and the first row of $\boldsymbol{S}$ to $[1 \ 0 \ \cdots \ 0]$
Set a randomly selected column of $\boldsymbol{C}$ to $[1 \ 0 \ \cdots \ 0]^{\mathsf{T}}$
Choose at random $\lfloor \frac{m-1}{r-1} \rfloor$ disjoint subsets $T_i \subseteq \{2, \ldots, m\}$ of cardinality $r-1$
for $i \leftarrow 1$ **to** $\lfloor \frac{m-1}{r-1} \rfloor$ **do**
$\quad$ Set the $(r-1) \times (r-1)$ submatrix $\boldsymbol{S}_{T_i, \{2, \ldots, r\}}$ to $\boldsymbol{I}_{r-1}$
$\quad$ sol $=$ Solve$(\boldsymbol{S}, \boldsymbol{C}, \boldsymbol{R})$
$\quad$ **if** sol $\neq \emptyset$ **then return** sol
return $\emptyset$

Algorithm 1: (m, n, k, r)-Decoding

For positive integers a and b with $a \leq b$, we denote by $p_{q,a,b} := \prod_{i=0}^{a-1} \left(1 - q^{i-b}\right)$ the probability that a uniformly random matrix in $\mathbb{F}_q^{a \times b}$ has full rank.

Proposition 3. *Fix integers* m, n, k, r, *and let* $c \in \{1, \ldots, \lfloor \frac{m-1}{r-1} \rfloor\}$. *Suppose that a* (m, n, k, r)-*rank decoding instance is chosen uniformly at random, and that the input matrix* $\boldsymbol{R}$ *is built from this instance. Then, the probability that Algorithm 1 makes at most* c *calls to* Solve$(\boldsymbol{S}, \boldsymbol{C}, \boldsymbol{R})$ *before finding a solution is greater than*

$$\frac{1 - q^{-r}}{1 - q^{-n}} \left(1 - \frac{\left(1 - p_{q,r-1,r-1}\right)^c}{p_{q,r-1,m-1}}\right).$$

The proof is differed to Appendix.

If one applies this proposition to the cryptosystems mentioned in Table 4, with at most 5 calls to Solve$(\boldsymbol{S}, \boldsymbol{C}, \boldsymbol{R})$, Algorithm 1 will return a solution with a probability always greater than 0.8; note that for these instances the quantity $\lfloor \frac{m-1}{r-1} \rfloor$ is greater than 15, and around 20 for most of them.

In the event where Algorithm 1 returns $\emptyset$ after $\lfloor \frac{m-1}{r-1} \rfloor$ calls to Solve$(\boldsymbol{S}, \boldsymbol{C}, \boldsymbol{R})$, one can run it again until a solution is found. The probabilities mentioned in the previous paragraph show that for parameters of interest a second run of the algorithm is very rarely needed.

7 Conclusion

In this paper we introduce a new approach for solving the Rank Metric Decoding problem with Gröbner basis techniques. Our approach is based on adding partial syzygies to a newer version of a modelling due to Ourivski and Johansson.

Overall our analysis shows that our attack, for which we give a general estimation, clearly outperforms all previous attacks in rank metric for a classical (non quantum) attacker. In particular we obtain an attack below the claimed security level for all rank-based schemes proposed to the NIST Post-Quantum

Cryptography Standardization Process. Note that there has been some very recent progress [13] on the modelling and the attack proposed here. This results in even less complex attacks and in the removal of the Gröbner basis computation step: it is replaced by solving a linear system. Although our attack and its recent improvement really improve on previous attacks for rank metric, they meanwhile suffer from two limitations.

First these attacks do not benefit from a direct Grover quantum speedup, unlike combinatorial attacks. For the NIST parameters (with the exception of Rollo-I-192 for the latest attack [13]) the best quantum attacks still remain quantum attacks based on combinatorial attacks, because of the Grover speed-up. Second, these attacks need an important amount of memory for large parameters.

Acknowledgements. This work has been supported by the French ANR projects CBCRYPT (ANR-17-CE39-0007) and the MOUSTIC project with the support from the European Regional Development Fund (ERDF) and the Regional Council of Normandie. The authors would like to thank the anonymous reviewers for their valuable comments and suggestions, as well as Ray Perlner and Daniel Smith for useful discussions.

Appendix: Proof of Proposition 3

Let n, m, k, r be positive integers such that n and m are both greater than r. Let E be a $\mathbb{F}_q$-vector space of $\mathbb{F}_{q^m}$ of dimension r spanned by $\{E_1, E_2, \ldots, E_r\}$ and let $e \in \mathbb{F}_{q^m}^n$ whose components generate E. By definition, there exists a non-zero coordinate e_j of e, and hereafter one focuses on the vector space $\lambda E = \langle \lambda E_1, \lambda E_2, \ldots, \lambda E_r \rangle$ where $\lambda = e_j^{-1}$.

Given a basis $(1, \alpha, \ldots, \alpha^{m-1})$ of $\mathbb{F}_{q^m}$ over $\mathbb{F}_q$, one can write a basis of λE as a matrix $S \in \mathbb{F}_q^{m \times r}$. By construction, $1 \in \lambda E$, so that we can set the first column and the first row of S to the vectors $[1\ 0\ \cdots\ 0]^\mathsf{T}$ and $[1\ 0\ \cdots\ 0]$. We write $\widehat{S}$ for the remaining $(m-1) \times (r-1)$ block of S. One can also express the coordinates of the components of λe (with respect to the basis $\{\lambda E_1, \lambda E_2, \ldots, \lambda E_r\}$) as a matrix $C \in \mathbb{F}_q^{r \times n}$. By construction, the j-th column of C is the vector $[1\ 0\ \cdots\ 0]^\mathsf{T}$.

Lemma 2 estimates the probability to come across an index j such that e_j is non-zero. Once such an index is found, Lemma 3 computes the probability that Algorithm 1 succeeds in finding a non-singular block in $\widehat{S}$.

Lemma 2. *With the same notation and hypotheses as above, if an index j is chosen uniformly at random in $\{1, \ldots, n\}$, then e_j will be non-zero with probability $(1 - q^{-r})/(1 - q^{-n})$.*

Proof. A component e_j of e will be non-zero if and only if its corresponding column of coordinates in the matrix C is non-zero. If the components of e were chosen uniformly at random in the vector space E of dimension r, the probability for a random component to be equal to zero would be exactly q^{-r}. This is not the case since there is a constraint on C, more precisely it has to be of rank r.

Taking this into account, we can count the number of full rank matrices in $\mathbb{F}_q^{r \times n}$ that have a zero column. The ratio between those matrices and all the full rank matrices in $\mathbb{F}_q^{r \times n}$ is exactly the probability for a column chosen at random in C to be zero:

$$\prod_{i=0}^{r-1} \frac{q^{n-1} - q^i}{q^n - q^i} = \frac{q^{n-r} - 1}{q^n - 1}.$$

One concludes the proof by taking the complementary event.   □

Lemma 3. *Let $c \in \{1, \ldots, \lfloor \frac{m-1}{r-1} \rfloor\}$; with the same notation and hypotheses as above, if E and e are chosen uniformly at random, and if the inverse of a nonzero coordinate of e, λ, is given, then at least one of the c disjoint blocks B_i in $\widehat{S}$ is not singular with probability greater than*

$$1 - \frac{(1 - p_{q,r-1,r-1})^c}{p_{q,r-1,m-1}}$$

Proof. Since λ is a fixed nonzero element in $\mathbb{F}_{q^m}$ and since E is uniformly random, the vector space λE is also uniformly random. Therefore $\widehat{S}$ is a matrix chosen uniformly at random among all the full rank matrices in $\mathbb{F}_q^{(m-1) \times (r-1)}$. The probability that all the c blocks B_i in $\widehat{S}$ are singular is then bounded from above by

$$\frac{\left(q^{(r-1)^2} - q^{(r-1)^2} p_{q,r-1,r-1} \right)^c q^{(r-1)(m-1-c(r-1))}}{q^{(m-1)(r-1)} p_{q,r-1,m-1}}, \tag{13}$$

which is the ratio between the number of matrices in $\mathbb{F}_q^{(m-1) \times (r-1)}$ with c singular disjoint blocks and the total amount of full rank matrices in $\mathbb{F}_q^{(m-1) \times (r-1)}$. It is an upper bound since the number of matrices with c singular blocks includes matrices that are not of full rank.

The reader can check that the term (13) is equal to

$$\frac{(1 - p_{q,r-1,r-1})^c}{p_{q,r-1,m-1}}.$$

The probability that at least one of the B_i's is non-singular is obtained using the complementary probability.   □

In Algorithm 1, the first requirement not to return fail is to find an index j such that e_j is non-zero; Lemma 3 gives the probability of this event, that is to say $(1 - q^{-r})/(1 - q^{-n})$. Once this index is found, the associated vector space λE is distributed uniformly among all the vector spaces of $\mathbb{F}_{q^m}$ of dimension r since E is chosen at random. Using Lemma 2, one has a lower bound on the probability that at least one of the c block B_i's is non singular. Thus the probability of Proposition 3 is

$$\frac{1 - q^{-r}}{1 - q^{-n}} \left(1 - \frac{(1 - p_{q,r-1,r-1})^c}{p_{q,r-1,m-1}} \right).$$

□

References

1. Aguilar Melchor, C., et al.: Ouroboros-R. First round submission to the NIST post-quantum cryptography call, November 2017. https://pqc-ouroborosr.org
2. Aguilar Melchor, C., et al.: Rank quasi cyclic (RQC). First round submission to the NIST post-quantum cryptography call, November 2017. https://pqc-rqc.org
3. Aguilar Melchor, C., et al.: Rank quasi cyclic (RQC). Second round submission to the NIST post-quantum cryptography call, April 2019. https://pqc-rqc.org
4. Albrecht, M., Bard, G.: The M4RI Library - Version 20140914. The M4RI Team (2014). http://m4ri.sagemath.org
5. Aragon, N., et al.: LAKE - Low rAnk parity check codes Key Exchange. First round submission to the NIST post-quantum cryptography call, November 2017. https://csrc.nist.gov/CSRC/media/Projects/Post-Quantum-Cryptography/documents/round-1/submissions/LAKE.zip
6. Aragon, N., et al.: LOCKER - LOw rank parity ChecK codes EncRyption. First round submission to the NIST post-quantum cryptography call, November 2017. https://csrc.nist.gov/CSRC/media/Projects/Post-Quantum-Cryptography/documents/round-1/submissions/LOCKER.zip
7. Aragon, N., et al.: ROLLO (merger of Rank-Ouroboros, LAKE and LOCKER). Second round submission to the NIST post-quantum cryptography call, March 2019. https://pqc-rollo.org
8. Aragon, N., Blazy, O., Gaborit, P., Hauteville, A., Zémor, G.: Durandal: a rank metric based signature scheme. In: Ishai, Y., Rijmen, V. (eds.) EUROCRYPT 2019. LNCS, vol. 11478, pp. 728–758. Springer, Cham (2019). https://doi.org/10.1007/978-3-030-17659-4_25
9. Aragon, N., Gaborit, P., Hauteville, A., Ruatta, O., Zémor, G.: RankSign - a signature proposal for the NIST's call. First round submission to the NIST post-quantum cryptography call, November 2017. https://csrc.nist.gov/CSRC/media/Projects/Post-Quantum-Cryptography/documents/round-1/submissions/RankSign.zip
10. Aragon, N., Gaborit, P., Hauteville, A., Tillich, J.P.: A new algorithm for solving the rank syndrome decoding problem. In: 2018 IEEE International Symposium on Information Theory, ISIT 2018, Vail, CO, USA, 17–22 June 2018, pp. 2421–2425. IEEE (2018). https://doi.org/10.1109/ISIT.2018.8437464
11. Ars, G., Faugère, J.-C., Imai, H., Kawazoe, M., Sugita, M.: Comparison between XL and Gröbner basis algorithms. In: Lee, P.J. (ed.) ASIACRYPT 2004. LNCS, vol. 3329, pp. 338–353. Springer, Heidelberg (2004). https://doi.org/10.1007/978-3-540-30539-2_24
12. Bardet, M.: Étude des systèmes algébriques surdéterminés. Applications aux codes correcteurs et à la cryptographie. Ph.D. thesis, Université Paris VI, December 2004. http://tel.archives-ouvertes.fr/tel-00449609/en/
13. Bardet, M., et al.: Algebraic attacks for solving the Rank Decoding and MinRank problems without Gröbner basis. arXiv e-prints arXiv:2002.08322, February 2020
14. Bardet, M., Faugère, J.C., Salvy, B.: On the complexity of the F_5 Gröbner basis algorithm. J. Symb. Comput. **70**, 49–70 (2015)
15. Bardet, M., Faugère, J.C., Salvy, B., Yang, B.Y.: Asymptotic expansion of the degree of regularity for semi-regular systems of equations. In: MEGA 2005 - Effective Methods in Algebraic Geometry, pp. 1–14 (2005)

16. Bouillaguet, C., Delaplace, C.: Sparse Gaussian elimination modulo p: an update. In: Gerdt, V.P., Koepf, W., Seiler, W.M., Vorozhtsov, E.V. (eds.) CASC 2016. LNCS, vol. 9890, pp. 101–116. Springer, Cham (2016). https://doi.org/10.1007/978-3-319-45641-6_8
17. Boyer, B., Eder, C., Faugère, J., Lachartre, S., Martani, F.: GBLA: Gröbner basis linear algebra package. In: Proceedings of the ACM on International Symposium on Symbolic and Algebraic Computation, ISSAC 2016, Waterloo, ON, Canada, 19–22 July 2016, pp. 135–142 (2016). https://doi.org/10.1145/2930889.2930914
18. Buchberger, B.: Ein Algorithmus zum Auffinden der Basiselemente des Restklassenringes nach einem nulldimensionalen Polynomideal. Ph.D. thesis, Universitat Innsbruck (1965)
19. Bunch, J.R., Hopcroft, J.E.: Triangular factorization and inversion by fast matrix multiplication. Math. Comput. **28**(125), 231–236 (1974)
20. Buss, J.F., Frandsen, G.S., Shallit, J.O.: The computational complexity of some problems of linear algebra. J. Comput. Syst. Sci. **58**(3), 572–596 (1999)
21. Cabarcas, D., Smith-Tone, D., Verbel, J.A.: Key recovery attack for ZHFE. In: Lange, T., Takagi, T. (eds.) PQCrypto 2017. LNCS, vol. 10346, pp. 289–308. Springer, Cham (2017). https://doi.org/10.1007/978-3-319-59879-6_17
22. Courtois, N., Klimov, A., Patarin, J., Shamir, A.: Efficient algorithms for solving overdefined systems of multivariate polynomial equations. In: Preneel, B. (ed.) EUROCRYPT 2000. LNCS, vol. 1807, pp. 392–407. Springer, Heidelberg (2000). https://doi.org/10.1007/3-540-45539-6_27
23. Cox, D., Little, J., O'Shea, D.: Ideals, Varieties, and Algorithms: An Introduction to Computational Algebraic Geometry and Commutative Algebra. Undergraduate Texts in Mathematics. Springer, New York (2001). https://doi.org/10.1007/978-0-387-35651-8
24. Debris-Alazard, T., Tillich, J.-P.: Two attacks on rank metric code-based schemes: RankSign and an IBE scheme. In: Peyrin, T., Galbraith, S. (eds.) ASIACRYPT 2018. LNCS, vol. 11272, pp. 62–92. Springer, Cham (2018). https://doi.org/10.1007/978-3-030-03326-2_3
25. Ding, J., Hodges, T.J.: Inverting HFE systems is quasi-polynomial for all fields. In: Rogaway, P. (ed.) CRYPTO 2011. LNCS, vol. 6841, pp. 724–742. Springer, Heidelberg (2011). https://doi.org/10.1007/978-3-642-22792-9_41
26. Ding, J., Kleinjung, T.: Degree of regularity for HFE-. Cryptology ePrint Archive, Report 2011/570 (2011). http://eprint.iacr.org/2011/570
27. Ding, J., Schmidt, D.: Solving degree and degree of regularity for polynomial systems over a finite fields. In: Fischlin, M., Katzenbeisser, S. (eds.) Number Theory and Cryptography. LNCS, vol. 8260, pp. 34–49. Springer, Heidelberg (2013). https://doi.org/10.1007/978-3-642-42001-6_4
28. Ding, J., Yang, B.-Y.: Degree of regularity for HFEv and HFEv-. In: Gaborit, P. (ed.) PQCrypto 2013. LNCS, vol. 7932, pp. 52–66. Springer, Heidelberg (2013). https://doi.org/10.1007/978-3-642-38616-9_4
29. Dubois, V., Gama, N.: The degree of regularity of HFE systems. In: Abe, M. (ed.) ASIACRYPT 2010. LNCS, vol. 6477, pp. 557–576. Springer, Heidelberg (2010). https://doi.org/10.1007/978-3-642-17373-8_32
30. Eder, C., Faugère, J.C.: A survey on signature-based algorithms for computing Gröbner bases. J. Symb. Comput. **80**, 719–784 (2017). https://doi.org/10.1016/j.jsc.2016.07.031. http://www.sciencedirect.com/science/article/pii/S0747717116300785
31. Faugère, J.C.: A new efficient algorithm for computing Gröbner bases (F4). J. Pure Appl. Algebra **139**(1–3), 61–88 (1999)

32. Faugère, J.C.: A new efficient algorithm for computing Gröbner bases without reduction to zero: F5. In: Proceedings ISSAC 2002, pp. 75–83. ACM Press (2002)
33. Faugère, J.-C., Levy-dit-Vehel, F., Perret, L.: Cryptanalysis of MinRank. In: Wagner, D. (ed.) CRYPTO 2008. LNCS, vol. 5157, pp. 280–296. Springer, Heidelberg (2008). https://doi.org/10.1007/978-3-540-85174-5_16
34. Faugère, J., Safey El Din, M., Spaenlehauer, P.: Computing loci of rank defects of linear matrices using Gröbner bases and applications to cryptology. In: International Symposium on Symbolic and Algebraic Computation, ISSAC 2010, Munich, Germany, 25–28 July 2010, pp. 257–264 (2010). https://doi.org/10.1145/1837934.1837984
35. Faugère, J.C., Safey El Din, M., Spaenlehauer, P.J.: Gröbner bases of bihomogeneous ideals generated by polynomials of bidegree (1,1): algorithms and complexity. J. Symb. Comput. **46**(4), 406–437 (2011)
36. Gabidulin, E.M.: Theory of codes with maximum rank distance. Problemy Peredachi Informatsii **21**(1), 3–16 (1985)
37. Gabidulin, E.M., Paramonov, A.V., Tretjakov, O.V.: Ideals over a noncommutative ring and their application in cryptology. In: Davies, D.W. (ed.) EUROCRYPT 1991. LNCS, vol. 547, pp. 482–489. Springer, Heidelberg (1991). https://doi.org/10.1007/3-540-46416-6_41
38. Gaborit, P., Murat, G., Ruatta, O., Zémor, G.: Low rank parity check codes and their application to cryptography. In: Proceedings of the Workshop on Coding and Cryptography, WCC 2013, Bergen, Norway (2013). www.selmer.uib.no/WCC2013/pdfs/Gaborit.pdf
39. Gaborit, P., Ruatta, O., Schrek, J.: On the complexity of the rank syndrome decoding problem. IEEE Trans. Inf. Theory **62**(2), 1006–1019 (2016)
40. Gaborit, P., Ruatta, O., Schrek, J., Zémor, G.: New results for rank-based cryptography. In: Pointcheval, D., Vergnaud, D. (eds.) AFRICACRYPT 2014. LNCS, vol. 8469, pp. 1–12. Springer, Cham (2014). https://doi.org/10.1007/978-3-319-06734-6_1
41. Gaborit, P., Ruatta, O., Schrek, J., Zémor, G.: RankSign: an efficient signature algorithm based on the rank metric. In: Mosca, M. (ed.) PQCrypto 2014. LNCS, vol. 8772, pp. 88–107. Springer, Cham (2014). https://doi.org/10.1007/978-3-319-11659-4_6. https://arxiv.org/pdf/1606.00629.pdf
42. Gaborit, P., Zémor, G.: On the hardness of the decoding and the minimum distance problems for rank codes. IEEE Trans. Inf. Theory **62**(12), 7245–7252 (2016)
43. Granboulan, L., Joux, A., Stern, J.: Inverting HFE is quasipolynomial. In: Dwork, C. (ed.) CRYPTO 2006. LNCS, vol. 4117, pp. 345–356. Springer, Heidelberg (2006). https://doi.org/10.1007/11818175_20
44. Hoffstein, J., Pipher, J., Silverman, J.H.: NTRU: a ring-based public key cryptosystem. In: Buhler, J.P. (ed.) ANTS 1998. LNCS, vol. 1423, pp. 267–288. Springer, Heidelberg (1998). https://doi.org/10.1007/BFb0054868
45. Kipnis, A., Shamir, A.: Cryptanalysis of the HFE public key cryptosystem by relinearization. In: Wiener, M. (ed.) CRYPTO 1999. LNCS, vol. 1666, pp. 19–30. Springer, Heidelberg (1999). https://doi.org/10.1007/3-540-48405-1_2
46. Lazard, D.: Gröbner bases, Gaussian elimination and resolution of systems of algebraic equations. In: van Hulzen, J.A. (ed.) EUROCAL 1983. LNCS, vol. 162, pp. 146–156. Springer, Heidelberg (1983). https://doi.org/10.1007/3-540-12868-9_99
47. Le Gall, F.: Powers of tensors and fast matrix multiplication. In: Proceedings ISSAC 2014, pp. 296–303. ACM, New York (2014). https://doi.org/10.1145/2608628.2608664

48. Levy-dit-Vehel, F., Perret, L.: Algebraic decoding of rank metric codes. Talk at the Special Semester on Gröbner Bases - Workshop D1, pp. 1–19 (2006). https://ricamwww.ricam.oeaw.ac.at/specsem/srs/groeb/download/Levy.pdf
49. Loidreau, P.: A new rank metric codes based encryption scheme. In: Lange, T., Takagi, T. (eds.) PQCrypto 2017. LNCS, vol. 10346, pp. 3–17. Springer, Cham (2017). https://doi.org/10.1007/978-3-319-59879-6_1
50. Misoczki, R., Tillich, J.P., Sendrier, N., Barreto, P.S.L.M.: MDPC-McEliece: new McEliece variants from moderate density parity-check codes (2012). http://eprint.iacr.org/2012/409
51. Otmani, A., Talé-Kalachi, H., Ndjeya, S.: Improved cryptanalysis of rank metric schemes based on Gabidulin codes. Des. Codes Cryptogr. **86**(9), 1983–1996 (2018). https://doi.org/10.1007/s10623-017-0434-5
52. Ourivski, A.V., Johansson, T.: New technique for decoding codes in the rank metric and its cryptography applications. Probl. Inf. Transm. **38**(3), 237–246 (2002). https://doi.org/10.1023/A:1020369320078
53. Overbeck, R.: A new structural attack for GPT and variants. In: Dawson, E., Vaudenay, S. (eds.) Mycrypt 2005. LNCS, vol. 3715, pp. 50–63. Springer, Heidelberg (2005). https://doi.org/10.1007/11554868_5
54. Storjohann, A.: Algorithms for matrix canonical forms. Ph.D. thesis, Swiss Federal Institute of Technology - ETH (2000)
55. Lévy-dit Vehel, F., Perret, L.: Algebraic decoding of codes in rank metric. In: Communication at YACC06, Porquerolles, France, June 2006
56. Verbel, J., Baena, J., Cabarcas, D., Perlner, R., Smith-Tone, D.: On the complexity of "superdetermined" minrank instances. In: Ding, J., Steinwandt, R. (eds.) PQCrypto 2019. LNCS, vol. 11505, pp. 167–186. Springer, Cham (2019). https://doi.org/10.1007/978-3-030-25510-7_10

Low Weight Discrete Logarithm and Subset Sum in $2^{0.65n}$ with Polynomial Memory

Andre Esser[✉] and Alexander May

Ruhr University Bochum, Bochum, Germany
{andre.esser,alex.may}@rub.de

Abstract. We propose two heuristic polynomial memory collision finding algorithms for the low Hamming weight discrete logarithm problem in any abelian group G. The first one is a direct adaptation of the Becker-Coron-Joux (BCJ) algorithm for subset sum to the discrete logarithm setting. The second one significantly improves on this adaptation for all possible weights using a more involved application of the representation technique together with some new Markov chain analysis. In contrast to other low weight discrete logarithm algorithms, our second algorithm's time complexity interpolates to Pollard's $|G|^{\frac{1}{2}}$ bound for general discrete logarithm instances.

We also introduce a new heuristic subset sum algorithm with polynomial memory that improves on BCJ's $2^{0.72n}$ time bound for random subset sum instances $a_1, \ldots, a_n, t \in \mathbb{Z}_{2^n}$. Technically, we introduce a novel nested collision finding for subset sum – inspired by the NestedRho algorithm from Crypto '16 – that recursively produces collisions. We first show how to instantiate our algorithm with run time $2^{0.649n}$. Using further tricks, we are then able to improve its complexity down to $2^{0.645n}$.

Keywords: Low weight dlog · Subset sum · Representations · Nested Rho

1 Introduction

The subset sum problem is one of the most fundamental problems in cryptography. It was early used in the 80's for the construction of cryptosystems [8,21], suffered from lattice-based attacks [18,23], and found a revival in the last two decades [11,19] since even LWE (SIS) [25] and LPN [2] instances can be formulated as (vectorial) versions of subset sum.

In this paper, we study subset sum instances $a_1, \ldots, a_n, t \in \mathbb{Z}_{2^n}$. These are known as density-1 instances in the cryptographic literature, and they

A. May—Funded by DFG under Germany's Excellence Strategy - EXC 2092 CASA - 390781972.

A. Canteaut and Y. Ishai (Eds.): EUROCRYPT 2020, LNCS 12107, pp. 94–122, 2020.
https://doi.org/10.1007/978-3-030-45727-3_4

enjoy some useful hardness properties [16]. The invention of the polynomial memory $2^{0.72n}$-algorithm by Becker, Coron and Joux (BCJ) [4] initiated a renewed interest in the subset sum problem itself [1,3] and its vectorial versions [5,15]. Polynomial memory algorithms are of crucial importance to cryptanalysis, since they allow for very efficient implementations, and therefore are often used for record computations [7,10]. Moreover, if we aim at implementing cryptanalytic quantum algorithms [6] in the near future, we have to focus on the development of low memory algorithms.

Our Contributions

Discrete Logarithms. It is not hard to see that also the famous *discrete logarithm problem* (DLP) reduces to the subset sum problem. Let $g^\alpha = \beta$ be a discrete logarithm instance in some abelian group G generated by g with order $2^{n-1} \leq |G| < 2^n$. Then we can easily compute the values $a_i := g^{2^{i-1}}$. Any subset $I \subset \{1, \ldots, n\}$ of all a_i that combines in G to β immediately reveals the bits of the discrete logarithm α. Moreover, if we know a priori that α has low Hamming weight ωn, $\omega \leq \frac{1}{2}$, then we have to find some I of small size $|I| = \omega n$, a fact from which subset sum algorithms usually benefit.

While the security of discrete log-based schemes is usually not directly based on the hardness of low weight DLP, their side channel resistance is linked to low weight DLP. Assume that we obtain via some side channel a faulty version $\tilde{\alpha}$ of a discrete logarithm α. Further assume that $\tilde{\alpha}$ is obtained from α by flipping ωn one bits to zero, but not flipping any zero bits to one (a quite usual setting for e.g. cold boot attacks [14]). Then $\frac{\beta}{g^{\tilde{\alpha}}} = g^{\alpha - \tilde{\alpha}} =: g^{\alpha'}$ forms a low weight DLP with $\mathrm{wt}(\alpha') = \omega n$. In this setting, any low weight DLP algorithm serves as an error correction algorithm for reconstructing α from $\tilde{\alpha}$.

For both DLP settings – the general discrete logarithm problem as well as its low weight variant – there exist algorithms matching the square root time lower bound for generic algorithms [26,27]. But only for the general DLP we have Pollard's Rho algorithm with polynomial memory that matches the time lower bound $|G|^{\frac{1}{2}}$. Whether there exists a low memory algorithm for the low weight DLP was left as an open question by Galbraith and Gaudry [12,13]. We do a significant step towards answering this question in the affirmative by giving a heuristic algorithm that achieves the time lower bound $|G|^{\frac{H(\omega)}{2}}$, where H is the binary entropy function. While there is a variant of the Baby-Step Giant Step algorithm, which also achieves time $|G|^{\frac{H(\omega)}{2}}$, our algorithm consumes way less memory. To quantify, our algorithm consumes always less than $|G|^{0.23}$ memory, while Baby-Step Giant-Step for $\omega = \frac{1}{2}$ consumes as much as $|G|^{\frac{1}{2}}$ memory. Additionally, we are able to instantiate our algorithm with polynomial memory only, where it outperforms all other known low-weight DLP algorithms in that memory regime for the whole range of weights $0 \leq \omega \leq \frac{1}{2}$.

In more detail, we show the following discrete log results.

– The BCJ subset sum algorithm works in a more general setting that we call group subset sum, from which we directly obtain a BCJ adaptation to the low weight discrete logarithm setting via the above reduction. This adaptation already improves on the best known folklore low weight discrete log algorithm (see e.g. Chapter 14.8.1 in [12]), which is an application of van Oorschot-Wiener's collision finding [28].

- We introduce an improved low weight discrete logarithm algorithm, inspired by the BCJ adaptation, that makes use of the special form $a_i = g^{2^{i-1}}$ of our subset sum instance. Our idea is to represent weight-ωn discrete logarithms α as the sum of two integers of smaller weight $\phi(\omega)$ by exploiting the fact of carry propagation. Technically, we introduce a Markov chain analysis for finding the optimal weight $\phi(\omega)$.

- By not insisting on polynomial memory, we tune our algorithm via Parallel Collision search [29] to reach the time complexity $|G|^{\frac{H(\omega)}{2}}$ of the low weight DLP variant of Baby-Step Giant-Step, while consuming only $|G|^{H(\omega)-H(\phi(\omega))}$ memory.

Our results for polynomial space algorithms are illustrated in Fig. 1.

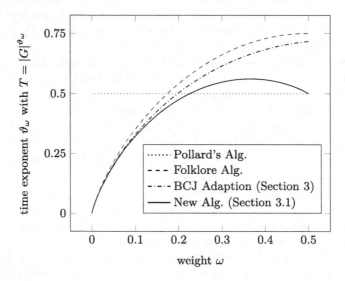

Fig. 1. Comparison of runtime exponents ϑ_ω for low weight DLP algorithms

Subset Sums. Previous polynomial memory subset sum algorithms based on collision finding, such as the folklore algorithm or the BCJ algorithm, are non-optimal in the following sense. In a first step, these algorithms output collisions that correspond to potential solutions $\mathbf{e}' = (e'_1, \ldots, e'_n) \in \{0, 1\}^n$ such that the subset sum identity $\sum_i e'_i a_i = t$ holds only for a constant fraction of all n bits. In a second step, the algorithms brute-force potential solutions $\mathbf{e}'$ until by chance the identity holds on all bits.

We replace this collision-and-brute-force approach by a two-layer nested collision finding that is inspired by the NestedRho algorithm from Dinur, Dunkelman, Keller and Shamir [9], which was introduced in the context of finding the mode of a distribution. More precisely, we find in layer-1 potential solutions $\mathbf{e}'$ that satisfy the subset sum identity on $n/2$ bits, where in layer-2 our algorithm produces only candidates that also satisfy the subset sum identity on the remaining $n/2$ bits. Therefore, our algorithm always returns some $\mathbf{e}'$ satisfying $\sum_i e_i' a_i = t \bmod 2^n$. Moreover, each iteration costs us time roughly $2^{n/2}$.

As a collision finding technique this is optimal, since for a search space of size 2^n we need to perform $\Omega(2^{n/2})$ operations to obtain collisions at all (with good probability). Unfortunately, our collision-finding algorithm does not solve the subset sum problem in time $2^{n/2}$, since it produces potential solutions $\mathbf{e}_i' \in \{0, 1, 2, 3, 4\}^n$.

However, we show that after $2^{0.149n}$ iterations of our algorithm we expect to find some $\mathbf{e}_i' \in \{0, 1\}^n$ that solves subset sum. This leads to a subset sum algorithm with complexity $2^{0.649n}$. Using additional tricks, we further improve to $2^{0.645n}$.

One might hope that our improvements for subset sum then in turn lead to improvements for the low Hamming weight discrete logarithm problem. However, for instantiating our two-layer subset sum collision finding we make use of the canonical group homomorphism $(\mathbb{Z}_{2^n}, +) \rightarrow (\mathbb{Z}_{2^{n/2}}, +)$, a subgroup structure that usually does not exist for discrete logarithm groups $(G, \cdot)$ (see [20] for results in composite groups).

Our paper is organized as follows. In Sect. 3 we introduce the general group subset sum problem, which we solve via the BCJ algorithm, and derive our first low weight discrete logarithm algorithm. Our second low weight DLP algorithm is described, analyzed, and experimentally validated in Sect. 3.1. Our $2^{0.649n}$ subset sum algorithm is given in Sects. 4 and 4.1, and experimentally verified in Sect. 4.3, the improvement to $2^{0.645n}$ can be found in Sect. 4.2.

2   Preliminaries

It is well-known that a collision in an n-to-n bit function f can be computed using roughly $2^{\frac{n}{2}}$ function evaluations and only a polynomial amount of memory. Common collision search algorithms [17,22,24] achieve this by computing a chain of invocations of f from a random starting point x, that is the iteration $f(x), f^2(x) := f(f(x)), f^3(x), \ldots$, until a repetition occurs, which in turn is found via some cycle finding algorithm (see also Fig. 2). Let $f^\ell(x)$ be the first repeated value in the chain and $f^{\ell+\mu}$ its second appearance. We denote by $\mathtt{Rho}(f, x)$ the output of some collision search procedure on f started at point x, that is the pair of colliding inputs. In other words

$$\mathtt{Rho}(f, x) := (f^{\ell-1}(x), f^{\ell+\mu-1}(x)).$$

The name $\mathtt{Rho}$ stems from the usual illustration from Fig. 2 of a colliding chain's shape for iterated collision search.

In [28] van Oorschot and Wiener extended this idea of collision search to collisions between two functions f_1 and f_2. The van Oorschot-Wiener construction defines a new function $\tilde{f}$ that alternates between applications of f_1 and

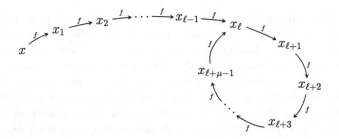

Fig. 2. Application of Rho to function f with starting point x.

f_2 depending on the input. The output of a collision search in $\tilde{f}$ yields then a collision between f_1 and f_2 with probability $\frac{1}{2}$, whereas with probability $\frac{1}{2}$ it produces a collision between the same functions f_1 and f_1, or f_2 and f_2. If we obtain a collision between the same functions, we may (in a deterministic fashion) manipulate the start point x, until we obtain a collision between f_1 and f_2. On expectation, this only doubles the run time (in case that collisions are independent for different start points, which we address below). Therefore, in the following we assume without loss of generality that we always obtain collisions for f_1, f_2 and define

$$\text{Rho}(f_1, f_2, x) := (x_1, x_2) \text{ with } f_1(x_1) = f_2(x_2).$$

Obviously, by restricting the collision search to the function $\tilde{f}$ not all collisions between f_1 and f_2 can be found anymore. However, on expectation this concerns only a constant fraction of all collision and hence we safely ignore this in our analysis.

All the algorithms considered in this work perform exponentially many invocations of the Rho algorithm on different starting points using the same function f. This causes some technical dependency problems. For instance in Fig. 2 Rho$(f, \cdot)$ produces the same output collision for any start point $x, x_1, \ldots, x_{\ell-1}$. This problem was already identified in the work of [4,9], who both introduced similar notions to break dependencies, called flavours in [9]. We adapt this notion to our purpose.

Definition 2.1 (Flavour of a function). *Let f be a function with $f : \mathcal{T} \to \mathcal{T}$, where $\mathcal{T} \subseteq \{0,1\}^n$. Let $P_k : \mathcal{T} \to \mathcal{T}$ be a family of bijective functions addressed by k. Then the kth flavour of f is defined as*

$$f^{[k]}(\mathbf{x}) := P_k(f(\mathbf{x})).$$

Notice that for all k, a collision $(\mathbf{x}_1, \mathbf{x}_2)$ in $f^{[k]}$ satisfies

$$f^{[k]}(\mathbf{x}_1) = f^{[k]}(\mathbf{x}_2) \iff P_k(f(\mathbf{x}_1)) = P_k(f(\mathbf{x}_2)) \iff f(\mathbf{x}_1) = f(\mathbf{x}_2).$$

Thus, $(\mathbf{x}_1, \mathbf{x}_2)$ is also a collision in f itself. However, different flavours $f^{[k]}$ invoke different function graphs. We use flavours of f to heuristically obtain independence of the Rho$(f, \cdot)$ invocations. Namely, we assume that different Rho$(f, \cdot)$

invocations independently produce uniformly distributed collisions in f. A similar heuristic was also used in [9], and the authors verified their heuristic experimentally.

We analyze our algorithms in $\tilde{\Theta}$-notation, where $\tilde{\Theta}(2^n)$ suppresses polynomial factors in n. By $H(x)$ we refer to the binary entropy function defined as $H(x) := -x\log(x) - (1-x)\log(1-x)$, where all logarithms are base 2. Using Stirling's formula, we estimate binomial coefficients as

$$\binom{n}{m} = \tilde{\Theta}\left(2^{nH\left(\frac{m}{n}\right)}\right).$$

For $a, b \in \mathbb{N}$ with $1 \leq a < b$ we let $[a, b] := \{a, a+1, \ldots, b\}$ and conveniently write $[b] := [1, b]$. For a vector $\mathbf{y} \in \{0, 1\}^n$ we denote by $\text{wt}(\mathbf{y}) := |\{i \in [n] \mid y_i = 1\}|$ the Hamming weight of $\mathbf{y}$ while for an integer $a \in \mathbb{N}$, $\text{wt}(a)$ denotes the Hamming weight of the binary representation of a.

We denote by $\mathbb{Z}_N$ the ring of integers modulo N. We call $(\mathbf{x}_1, \ldots, \mathbf{x}_k) \in (\mathbb{Z}^n)^k$ a representation of $\mathbf{x} = \mathbf{x}_1 + \ldots + \mathbf{x}_k$ over $\mathbb{Z}^n$.

3   A Generalized View on the BCJ Subset Sum Algorithm

In this section we define a generalized *group subset sum problem* and show that the BCJ algorithm also succeeds on this generalization. This abstraction contains the usual subset sum problem in $\mathbb{Z}_{2^n}$ as well as our new application, the low weight *discrete logarithm problem* (DLP), as special cases. As a first result we obtain a BCJ-type algorithm solving the low weight DLP using only a polynomial amount of memory — in any group, generically.

Definition 3.1 (Group Subset Sum). *Let $(G, \cdot)$ be an abelian group with order $|G|$ satisfying $2^{n-1} \leq |G| < 2^n$. In the group subset sum problem we are given $a_1, \ldots, a_n, t \in G$ together with $\omega, 0 < \omega \leq \frac{1}{2}$ such that there exists some solution $\mathbf{e} = (e_1, \ldots, e_n) \in \{0, 1\}^n$ satisfying*

$$\prod_{i=1}^{n} a_i^{e_i} = t \text{ in } G \text{ with } \text{wt}(\mathbf{e}) = \omega n.$$

Our goal is to recover $\mathbf{e}$ (or some other weight-ωn solution $\mathbf{e}'$).

Notice that by Definition 3.1 our group subset sum problem has some desired solution $\mathbf{e}$. In cryptographic applications, such a solution exists by construction and is usually unique. Moreover, the weight ω is generally known. If ω is unknown, one may iterate over all $\mathcal{O}(n)$ choices. As the change to target $t' = t^{-1} \cdot \prod_{i=1}^{n} a_i$ with complimentary solution $(1, \ldots, 1) - \mathbf{e}$ yields an instance with solution weight $(1 - \omega)n$, there is no loss in generality assuming $\omega \leq \frac{1}{2}$. Additionally, one usually knows the generators of G such that one can define the a_i via generators.

Let us now look at two interesting special cases of group subset sum.

Subset Sum. Let $(a_1, \ldots, a_n, t)$ be a subset sum instance. By considering $G = (\mathbb{Z}_{2^n}, +)$ the product $\prod_{i=1}^{n} a_i^{e_i} = t$ in G rewrites directly to the usual subset sum identity

$$\sum_{i=1}^{n} e_i a_i = t \bmod 2^n.$$

Low Weight DLP. Let $(G, \cdot)$ be a cyclic group generated by g. Let $g^\alpha = \beta$ be a discrete logarithm instance in G. Let us define $a_i = g^{2^{i-1}}$ for $1 \leq i \leq n$ and $t = \beta$. Let $\mathbf{e}$ be a solution of the group subset sum problem, that is

$$t = \prod_{i=1}^{n} a_i^{e_i} = \prod_{i=1}^{n} g^{e_i 2^{i-1}} = g^{\sum_{i=1}^{n} e_i 2^{i-1}}. \tag{1}$$

Thus, $\mathbf{e} = (e_1, \ldots, e_n)$ immediately implies a solution $\alpha = \sum_{i=1}^{n} e_i 2^{i-1}$ to the DLP. Moreover, low weight group subset sum solutions $\mathbf{e}$ imply low weight discrete logarithms α.

Folklore Algorithm. Let us first translate the folklore algorithm for low weight DLP – as for example described in [12] – into the notion of the group subset sum problem. We take $\mathcal{T} := \{\mathbf{x} \in \{0,1\}^{\frac{n}{2}} \mid \text{wt}(\mathbf{x}) = \frac{\omega n}{2}\}$ with $|\mathcal{T}| = \tilde{\Theta}(|G|^{\frac{1}{2}H(\omega)})$. Let us define a hash function $\pi : G \to \mathcal{T}$. Further, we define functions f, f_t as

$$f, f_t : \mathcal{T} \to \mathcal{T} \ , \text{ where}$$

$$f(\mathbf{x}) = \pi \left(\prod_{i=1}^{\frac{n}{2}} a_i^{x_i} \right) \text{ and } f_t(\mathbf{x}) = \pi \left(t \cdot \prod_{i=1}^{\frac{n}{2}} a_{\frac{n}{2}+i}^{-x_i} \right).$$

Now we search for collisions $(\mathbf{x}_1, \mathbf{x}_2)$ between f and f_t until $\mathbf{x} = \mathbf{x}_1 \| \mathbf{x}_2$ solves the group subset sum problem. Note, that there is a unique decomposition of the desired solution $\mathbf{e} = \mathbf{x}_1 \| \mathbf{x}_2$ and hence a single collision $(\mathbf{x}_1, \mathbf{x}_2)$ giving rise to $\mathbf{e}$. This in turn requires us to find all collisions between f and f_t. However, we expect f, f_t to have $|\mathcal{T}|$ collisions, where finding each collision costs $\tilde{\Theta}(|\mathcal{T}|^{\frac{1}{2}})$ function evaluations. In total, we achieve expected runtime

$$T = \tilde{\Theta}(|\mathcal{T}|^{\frac{3}{2}}) = \tilde{\Theta}(|G|^{\frac{3}{4}H(\omega)}). \tag{2}$$

The runtime exponent $\frac{3}{4}H(\omega)$ is depicted in Fig. 3.

A pseudocode description of the folklore algorithm in the group subset sum setting is given by Algorithm 1, where we instantiate f_1, f_2 via their function definitions f, f_t.

Algorithm 1. GROUP SUBSET SUM SOLVER

Input: functions $f_1, f_2 \colon \mathcal{D} \to \mathcal{D}$, group subset sum instance $(a_1, \ldots, a_n, t) \in G^{n+1}$
Output: solution $\mathbf{e} \in \{0,1\}^n$ satisfying $\prod_{i=1}^n a_i^{e_i} = t$
1: **repeat**
2:    choose random flavour k
3:    choose random starting point $\mathbf{s} \in \mathcal{D}$
4:    $(\mathbf{x}, \mathbf{y}) \leftarrow \mathtt{Rho}(f_1^{[k]}, f_2^{[k]}, \mathbf{s})$
5:    $\mathbf{e}' \leftarrow \mathbf{x} + \mathbf{y}$
6: **until** $\mathbf{e}' \in \{0,1\}^n$ and $\prod_{i=1}^n a_i^{e_i'} = t$
7: **return** $\mathbf{e}'$

Remark 3.1. We find collisions via the Rho procedure defined in Sect. 2 (see Algorithm 1). To (heuristically) guarantee independence of the collisions, we choose a random flavour k (see Definition 2.1) each time we invoke Rho. This means instead of searching for collisions between f and f_t themselves, we search for collisions between their flavoured versions $f^{[k]}$ and $f_t^{[k]}$. Analogously, we have to proceed for the subsequently described algorithms, our BCJ adaptation and our new algorithm in Sect. 3.1. However, for ease of notation we skip the flavours in our descriptions.

BCJ Algorithm. The idea of the memoryless BCJ algorithm is to split the solution vector $\mathbf{e}$ with $\mathrm{wt}(\mathbf{e}) = \omega n$ in two vectors $\mathbf{e}_1, \mathbf{e}_2 \in \{0,1\}^n$ each of weight $\frac{\omega n}{2}$, which add up to $\mathbf{e}$. Let $(\mathbf{a}, t)$ be a group subset sum instance and $\mathcal{T} := \{\mathbf{x} \in \{0,1\}^n \mid \mathrm{wt}(\mathbf{x}) = \frac{\omega n}{2}\}$, where $|\mathcal{T}| = \tilde{\Theta}(2^{H(\frac{\omega}{2})n}) = \tilde{\Theta}(|G|^{H(\frac{\omega}{2})})$.

Let us define a hash function $\pi \colon G \to \mathcal{T}$ and the two functions

$$f, f_t \colon \mathcal{T} \to \mathcal{T} \ , \ \text{where}$$

$$f(\mathbf{x}) = \pi \left(\prod_{i=1}^n a_i^{x_i} \right) \ \text{and} \ f_t(\mathbf{x}) = \pi \left(t \cdot \prod_{i=1}^n a_i^{-x_i} \right).$$

Note that any representation $(\mathbf{e}_1, \mathbf{e}_2)$ of our desired solution $\mathbf{e}$, i.e. $\mathbf{e} = \mathbf{e}_1 + \mathbf{e}_2$, satisfies

$$\prod_{i=1}^n a_i^{(\mathbf{e}_1)_i} = t \cdot \prod_{i=1}^n a_i^{-(\mathbf{e}_2)_i}, \tag{3}$$

and therefore also $f(\mathbf{e}_1) = f_t(\mathbf{e}_2)$. The algorithm now simply searches for collisions $(\mathbf{e}_1', \mathbf{e}_2')$ between f and f_t, until $\mathbf{e}_1' + \mathbf{e}_2'$ yields a solution to the subset sum instance. Algorithm 1 provides a pseudocode description of our BCJ adaptation by using the function definitions of f and f_t to instantiate f_1 and f_2.

Runtime Analysis. Notice that while our hash function $\pi \colon G \to \mathcal{T}$ allows us to iterate the functions f, f_t, it also introduces many useless collisions $(\mathbf{x}, \mathbf{y})$ with

$$\pi \left(\prod_{i=1}^n a_i^{x_i} \right) = \pi \left(t \cdot \prod_{i=1}^n a_i^{-y_i} \right) \ \text{but} \ \prod_{i=1}^n a_i^{x_i} \neq t \cdot \prod_{i=1}^n a_i^{-y_i}.$$

However, we already know that any representation $(\mathbf{e}_1, \mathbf{e}_2)$ of the desired solution $\mathbf{e}$ satisfies Eq. (3) and thus defines a useful collision. Hence, we can simply compute the probability p that a randomly drawn collision is useful. We expect f, f_t to have $|\mathcal{T}|$ collisions, while the number of representations of $\mathbf{e}$ as weight-$\frac{\omega}{2}n$ vectors $\mathbf{e}_1, \mathbf{e}_2 \in \{0,1\}^n$ is $\binom{\omega n}{\frac{\omega}{2}n} = \tilde{\Theta}(2^{\omega n}) = \tilde{\Theta}(|G|^\omega)$. This implies

$$p = \tilde{\Theta}\left(\frac{|G|^\omega}{|\mathcal{T}|}\right).$$

Hence, after an expected number of p^{-1} iterations we find our desired solution $\mathbf{e}$. Since finding a single collision takes on expectation $\tilde{\Theta}(|\mathcal{T}|^{\frac{1}{2}})$ function evaluations and $|\mathcal{T}| = \tilde{\Theta}(|G|^{H(\frac{\omega}{2})})$, we obtain a total runtime of

$$T = \tilde{\Theta}(|\mathcal{T}|^{\frac{1}{2}} \cdot p^{-1}) = \tilde{\Theta}(|\mathcal{T}|^{\frac{3}{2}} \cdot |G|^{-w}) = \tilde{\Theta}(|G|^{\frac{3}{2}H(\omega/2)-\omega}). \qquad (4)$$

In Fig. 3 we show our new runtime exponent $\frac{3}{2}H(\omega/2) - \omega$ (called BCJ Adaption), which always improves on the folklore algorithm over the whole range of ω.

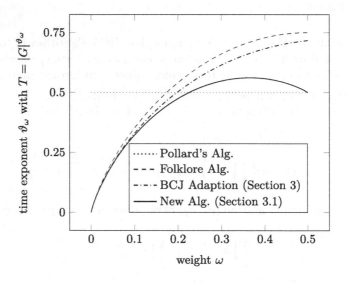

Fig. 3. Comparison of runtime exponents ϑ_ω for low weight DLP algorithms

For group subset sum problems of weight $\frac{n}{2}$, we achieve runtime $|G|^{\frac{3}{2}H(\frac{1}{4})-\frac{1}{2}} = |G|^{0.72}$. This implies a polynomial-space subset algorithm with runtime $2^{0.72n}$, the remarkable result of Becker, Coron and Joux. For the discrete logarithm setting, the result $|G|^{0.72}$ is less remarkable, since Pollard's algorithm already achieves runtime $|G|^{\frac{1}{2}}$. However, for weights $\omega \leq 0.197$ our BCJ adaption improves on Pollard's runtime.

In the subsequent Sect. 3.1 we further improve on the BCJ adaptation by using the special form $a_i = g^{2^{i-1}}$ in the low weight DLP. Notice that so far representations $(\mathbf{e}_1, \mathbf{e}_2) \in \{0,1\}^n$ of $\mathbf{e}$ in the analysis of the BCJ algorithm fulfill $\mathbf{e}_1 + \mathbf{e}_2 \in \{0,1\}^n$. In other words, in $\mathbf{e}_1, \mathbf{e}_2$ we never have 1-coordinates that add up. However, we also know by Eq. (1) that the vectors $\mathbf{e}_1, \mathbf{e}_2$ can be treated as bit-representations of numbers. Hence, if in the ith position, $i < n$, we have a 1-entry in both vectors, then we obtain

$$a_i^2 = (g^{2^{i-1}})^2 = g^{2^i} = a_{i+1}.$$

That is, we can make good use of carry bits to further increase the number of representations of our solution by looking at the total number of sums $\mathbf{e} = \mathbf{e}_1 + \mathbf{e}_2$ not only over $\{0,1\}^n$ but over the integers (modulo $|G|$).

3.1 Improved Low Weight DLP Algorithm

Let G be a cyclic group generated by g with order $2^{n-1} \leq |G| < 2^n$. Let $g^\alpha = \beta$ with $wt(\alpha) = \omega n \leq \frac{n}{2}$ be a low weight DLP in G. Our idea is to represent $\alpha = \alpha_1 + \alpha_2 \mod |G|$ with $\alpha_1, \alpha_2 \in \mathbb{Z}_{|G|}$ both of a certain weight. For ease of notation, we will only concentrate on representations (α_1, α_2) with $\alpha_1 + \alpha_2 < |G|$ such that we can ignore reductions modulo $|G|$. With this simplification, we only lose a constant (namely $\frac{1}{2}$) fraction of all representations, which does not affect asymptotics.

Thus, we first have to determine for which weight of $\phi n = wt(x_1) = wt(x_2)$, $x_1, x_2 \in \mathbb{Z}_{|G|}$ we expect that $wt(x_1 + x_2) = \omega n$. This seems to be a rather natural and fundamental problem to study, but to our surprise we could not find any treatment in the literature. In the following we provide a (heuristic) Markov chain analysis for computing ϕ as a function of ω, which we experimentally validate.

Computation of ϕ via Markov Chain. Let us model the bitwise summation $x_1 + x_2$ as a Markov chain. Since in every bit position we also have to take into account a carry bit, every state of our Markov chain contains three bits (b_1, b_2, b_3). Here we denote by b_1 the carry bit and by b_2, b_3 the corresponding bit from x_1 respectively x_2.

To make ourselves a bit more familiar with the notion, let us look at the following example from Fig. 4. Let us start in state $(0,0,0)$. As $0 + 0 + 0 = 0$, this state produces carry bit 0 and depending on the subsequent bits of x_1, x_2 we may enter one of the four states $(0,0,0), (0,1,0), (0,0,1)$ or $(0,1,1)$.

As x_1, x_2 are uniformly drawn from the set of vectors with weight ϕn, a single bit position in these vectors takes value 1 with probability ϕ. In our analysis, we ignore the effect that the random variables for the bit positions are not independent (since they have to sum to ϕn). This heuristic should only insignificantly affect our asymptotic treatment.

Hence, in our example we stay in state $(0,0,0)$ with probability $(1 - \phi)^2$, move to either $(0,0,1)$ or $(0,1,0)$ with probability $\phi(1-\phi)$, and move to $(0,1,1)$ with probability ϕ^2.

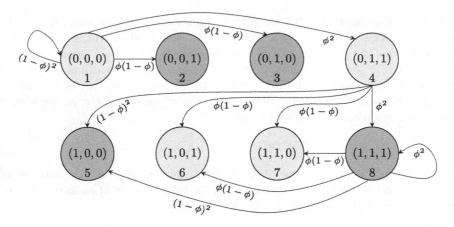

Fig. 4. Possible state transitions from states $(0,0,0)$, $(0,1,1)$ and $(1,1,1)$, where edge labels are transition probabilities and the first bit indicates the carry. Further state transitions are omitted for the sake of clarity.

The complete Markov process is defined by the following transition matrix $M = (m_{i,j})_{1 \le i,j \le 8}$, where $m_{i,j}$ is the transition probability from state i to j, where the labels i, j are defined in Fig. 4.

$$M := \begin{pmatrix} (1-\phi)^2 & \phi(1-\phi) & \phi(1-\phi) & \phi^2 & 0 & 0 & 0 & 0 \\ (1-\phi)^2 & \phi(1-\phi) & \phi(1-\phi) & \phi^2 & 0 & 0 & 0 & 0 \\ (1-\phi)^2 & \phi(1-\phi) & \phi(1-\phi) & \phi^2 & 0 & 0 & 0 & 0 \\ 0 & 0 & 0 & 0 & (1-\phi)^2 & \phi(1-\phi) & \phi(1-\phi) & \phi^2 \\ (1-\phi)^2 & \phi(1-\phi) & (\phi)(1-\phi) & \phi^2 & 0 & 0 & 0 & 0 \\ 0 & 0 & 0 & 0 & (1-\phi)^2 & \phi(1-\phi) & \phi(1-\phi) & \phi^2 \\ 0 & 0 & 0 & 0 & (1-\phi)^2 & \phi(1-\phi) & \phi(1-\phi) & \phi^2 \\ 0 & 0 & 0 & 0 & (1-\phi)^2 & \phi(1-\phi) & \phi(1-\phi) & \phi^2 \end{pmatrix}$$

Note that the states $2, 3, 5$ and 8 produce a 1 in the corresponding bit of the sum $x_1 + x_2$, while the other states produce a 0. Since $\mathrm{wt}(x_1 + x_2) = \omega n$, we should (asymptotically) produce a 1 with probability ω. Thus, we should be in either of the states $2, 3, 5$ or 8 with probability ω.

Markov chain theory tells us that M reaches a *stationary distribution* $\pi = (\pi_1, \ldots, \pi_8)$ satisfying $\pi M = \pi$. For each $1 \le i \le 8$, the Markov process (asymptotically) reaches state i with probability π_i. Thus, from the linear equations

$$\pi M = \pi, \quad \pi_1 + \ldots + \pi_8 = 1 \text{ and } \pi_2 + \pi_3 + \pi_5 + \pi_8 = \omega$$

we obtain an expression for ϕ as a function of ω. Computing the stationary distribution yields

$$\pi = (-\phi^4 + 2\phi^3 - 2\phi + 1, \quad \phi^4 - \phi^3 - \phi^2 + \phi, \quad \phi^4 - \phi^3 - \phi^2 + \phi, \quad -\phi^4 + \phi^2,$$
$$\phi^4 - 2\phi^3 + \phi^2, \quad -\phi^4 + \phi^3, \quad -\phi^4 + \phi^3, \quad \phi^4).$$

Hence, it follows that $\omega = 4\phi^4 - 4\phi^3 - \phi^2 + 2\phi$. Solving for ϕ yields our desired function that we illustrate in Fig. 5a. In Fig. 5b we experimentally verify the accuracy of our asymptotic analysis for concrete sums of 500-bit integers x_1, x_2.

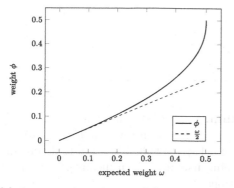
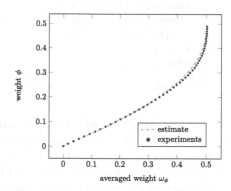

(a) Asymptotic estimate of the expected weight ωn

(b) Experimentally averaged value of ω for $n = 500$ (sample size per ϕ is 1000)

Fig. 5. Asymptotic estimate and experimentally obtained values for the weight ωn of the sum of two n-bit numbers with weight ϕn

Our Low Weight Discrete Logarithm Algorithm. Recall that $g^\alpha = \beta$ with $\mathrm{wt}(\alpha) = \omega \leq \frac{1}{2}$, where g generates a group G of order $2^{n-1} \leq |G| < 2^n$. We represent $\alpha = \alpha_1 + \alpha_2$ with $\mathrm{wt}(\alpha_1) = \mathrm{wt}(\alpha_2) = \phi$, where we compute ϕ as a function of ω as described in the previous paragraph.

Let us define $\mathcal{T} := \{x \in \mathbb{Z}_{2^n} \mid \mathrm{wt}(x) = \phi(\omega)n\}$, where $|\mathcal{T}| = \tilde{\Theta}(2^{H(\phi(\omega))n}) = \tilde{\Theta}(|G|^{H(\phi(\omega))})$. Further, we define a hash function $\pi : G \to \mathcal{T}$ and the two functions

$$f, f_\beta : \mathcal{T} \to \mathcal{T} \ , \ \text{where}$$
$$f(x) = \pi\left(g^x\right) \text{ and } f_t(x) = \pi\left(\beta g^{-x}\right).$$

Any representation (α_1, α_2) of our discrete logarithm α, i.e. $\alpha = \alpha_1 + \alpha_2$, satisfies

$$g^{\alpha_1} = \beta g^{-\alpha_2}, \tag{5}$$

and therefore also $f(\alpha_1) = f_\beta(\alpha_2)$. Our algorithm searches for collisions (x_1, x_2) between f and f_β, until $x_1 + x_2$ yields a solution to the discrete logarithm problem. Algorithm 2 gives a pseudocode description of our new algorithm.

Algorithm 2. DISCRETE LOGARITHM SOLVER

Input: functions $f, f_\beta : \mathcal{T} \to \mathcal{T}$, generator g of G, $\beta \in G$
Output: $\alpha = \mathrm{dlog}_g \beta$ satisfying $g^\alpha = \beta$
1: **repeat**
2:     choose random flavour k
3:     choose random starting point $s \in \mathcal{T}$
4:     $(x, y) \leftarrow \mathtt{Rho}(f^{[k]}, f_\beta^{[k]}, s)$
5:     $\alpha' \leftarrow x + y$
6: **until** $g^{\alpha'} = \beta$
7: **return** α'

Heuristic Analysis of Our Algorithm. The hash function $\pi : G \to \mathcal{T}$ produces a lot of useless collisions $f(x_1) = f_\beta(x_2)$ for which $g^{x_1} \neq \beta g^{-x_2}$. However, for any representation (α_1, α_2) of α Eq. (5) holds. In order to determine the probability p of a collision (x_1, x_2) being useful – which means $g^{x_1} = \beta g^{-x_2}$ – we compute the number of representations.

We search for our weight-ωn discrete logarithm α by computing sums of weight-$\phi(\omega)n$ numbers $(x_1, x_2) \in \mathcal{T}^2$. Let us heuristically assume that the weights of the resulting sums $x_1 + x_2$ concentrate around weight ωn. Namely, we assume that a polynomial fraction of all sums attains weight ωn. Such concentration results hold for similar distributions like the binomial distribution, and we validate our concentration heuristic experimentally. From Fig. 6 we conclude that quite sharply a $\frac{1}{\sqrt{n}}$-fraction of our experiments hits their expectation, exactly the same concentration result that we obtain from the binomial distribution.

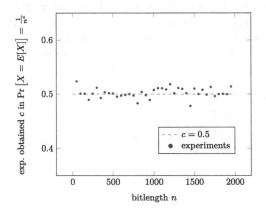

Fig. 6. Experimentally averaged value c in $\Pr\left[X = \mathbb{E}[X]\right] = \frac{1}{n^c}$, when adding two n-bit numbers of weight $\lfloor 0.3n \rfloor$, where X is a random variable for the weight of their sum (sample size per n is 5000).

We further assume that the polynomial fraction of sums $x_1 + x_2$ with weight ωn takes uniformly distributed values among all numbers of weight ωn. Therefore, any random sum $x_1 + x_2$ of weight ωn equals α with probability

$\binom{n}{\omega n}^{-1} = \tilde{\Theta}(G^{-H(\omega)})$. This implies that heuristically we obtain $\tilde{\Theta}(|T|^2|G|^{-H(\omega)})$ many representations. As we expect a total of $|T|$ collisions, the probability p of a useful collision is

$$p = \tilde{\Theta}\left(\frac{|T|^2|G|^{-H(\omega)}}{|T|}\right) = \tilde{\Theta}(|T| \cdot |G|^{-H(\omega)}).$$

Finding each collision heuristically takes time $|T|^{\frac{1}{2}}$. Since $|T| = \tilde{\Theta}(|G|^{H(\phi(\omega))})$, we expect to find the low weight discrete logarithm α in time

$$T = \tilde{\Theta}(|T|^{\frac{1}{2}} \cdot p^{-1}) = \tilde{\Theta}(|T|^{-\frac{1}{2}}|G|^{H(\omega)}) = \tilde{\Theta}(|G|^{H(\omega)-\frac{1}{2}H(\phi(\omega))}). \qquad (6)$$

The run time exponent of Eq. (6) is depicted in Fig. 3 (as New Alg.). While our low weight DLP algorithm significantly improves over the folklore algorithm and the BCJ adaptation, it does not yet achieve the square root of the search space S. Namely, if S denotes the set of all weight-ωn numbers, i.e. $|S| = \binom{n}{\omega n} = \tilde{\Theta}(|G|^{H(\omega)})$, then we might hope for a polynomial space algorithm with time complexity $|S|^{\frac{1}{2}}$, as a possible generalization of Pollard's algorithm to the low weight discrete logarithm regime.

In Fig. 7 we illustrate all runtime exponents to the base $|S|$. That is for Pollard's algorithm, the folklore algorithm (Eq. (2)), the BCJ algorithm (Eq. (4)), and our new algorithm (Eq. (6)) we depict their exponents

$$\frac{1}{2H(\omega)}, \quad \frac{3}{4}, \quad \frac{\frac{3}{2}H(\omega/2) - \omega}{H(\omega)}, \quad \frac{H(\omega) - \frac{1}{2}H(\phi(\omega))}{H(\omega)}.$$

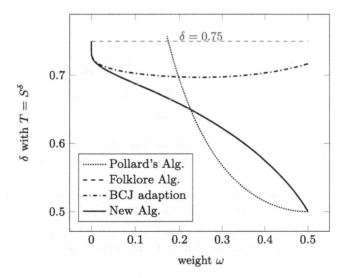

Fig. 7. Runtime exponent of the search space for low hamming weight DLP

The folklore algorithm has a constant exponent $\frac{3}{4}$ in the search space. Pollard's algorithm is superior for large weights $\omega \geq 0.174$, but also gets arbitrarily bad in the search space for small ω. Our BCJ adaptation achieves the first improvement over $\frac{3}{4}$ for *arbitrary* weights ω. However, BCJ only reaches a minimal exponent of $\delta = 0.697$ (achieved at $\omega = 0.248$). Eventually, our new algorithm improves on the BCJ algorithm for all weights, where we obtain an interpolation between $\frac{3}{4}$ for arbitrary small weights and the desired optimum $\frac{1}{2}$ for $\omega = \frac{1}{2}$. Additionally, our new algorithm is superior to Pollard's algorithm for all weights $\omega \leq 0.225$.

Experimental Verification of Our Algorithm. For experimental convenience, we implemented our algorithm in the multiplicative group $G = \mathbb{Z}_p^*$. We chose bit-length $n = 40$, and p as the largest prime smaller than 2^{40}. We generated 40 random small weight DLP instances for each weight $\omega n \in \{2, 3, \ldots, 20\}$. We measured T_f, the amount of calls to our function f, and averaged T_f over all 40 instances.[1]

Figure 8 shows the results of our computations. Here the dots are the values obtained in our experiments, while the dashed line is our asymptotic prediction $40(H(\omega) - \frac{1}{2}H(\phi(\omega)))$, shifted by 2.92 to take some (in the analysis neglected) polynomial run time factor into account.

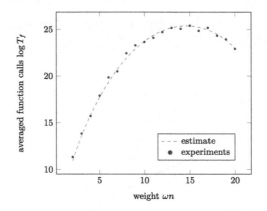

Fig. 8. Experimentally averaged number of function calls (in logarithmic scale) needed to solve a 40-bit discrete logarithm problem of weight ωn. Sample size per ωn is 40.

Time-Memory Tradeoff for Reaching the Square Root Bound. Let $|S| = \binom{n}{\omega n} = \tilde{\Theta}(|G|^{H(\omega)})$ be the low weight DLP search space as defined before. As we have seen, it remains open to reach square root complexity $|S|^{\frac{1}{2}}$ with a polynomial space algorithm, but our new algorithm makes a significant step towards this goal.

---

[1] Implementation available at https://github.com/LwDLPandSubsetSum/lwDLP-and-NestedSubsetSum.

Let us at this point forget about our polynomial space restriction (for the first and only time in this paper). Then Coppersmith's Baby-Step Giant-Step variant for low weight DLP(see [12], Chap. 13) achieves both time and space complexity $T_{\mathrm{BSGS}} = M_{\mathrm{BSGS}} = \tilde{\Theta}(|S|^{\frac{1}{2}})$.

Fortunately, our BCJ adaption as well as our new algorithm also allow for a time-memory tradeoff using van Oorschot-Wiener's Parallel Collision Search (PCS) [29]. Let C be the time complexity to find a collision with polynomial memory, then PCS finds 2^m collisions in time $\tilde{\Theta}(2^{\frac{m}{2}}C)$ using $\tilde{\Theta}(2^m)$ memory.

In the following, we minimize the run time of BCJ and our new algorithm by applying PCS.

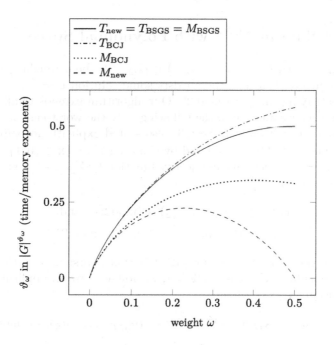

Fig. 9. Time-memory tradeoffs when applying PCS to our algorithms.

BCJ Tradeoff. From the analysis in Sect. 3, our BCJ adaptation requires to find an expected number of $\tilde{\Theta}(|G|^{H(\omega/2)-\omega})$ collisions, each at the cost of $\tilde{\Theta}(|G|^{\frac{H(\omega/2)}{2}})$. Thus, using memory $M_{\mathrm{BCJ}} = \tilde{\Theta}(|G|^{H(\omega/2)-\omega})$ BCJ's time complexity decreases to

$$T_{\mathrm{BCJ}} = \tilde{\Theta}(|G|^{\frac{H(\omega/2)-\omega}{2}} \cdot |G|^{\frac{H(\omega/2)}{2}}) = \tilde{\Theta}(|G|^{H(\frac{\omega}{2})-\frac{\omega}{2}}).$$

The time exponent is illustrated in Fig. 9 as dash-dotted line, the memory exponent as dotted line, both as a function of ω.

New Algorithm Tradeoff. Following the analysis in Sect. 3.1 our new algorithm requires to find $\tilde{\Theta}(|G|^{H(\omega)-H(\phi(\omega))})$ collisions, each at the cost of $\tilde{\Theta}(|G|^{\frac{H(\phi(\omega))}{2}})$. Hence, using memory $M_{\text{new}} = \tilde{\Theta}(|G|^{H(\omega)-H(\phi(\omega))})$ via PCS yields a runtime of

$$T_{\text{new}} = \tilde{\Theta}(|G|^{\frac{H(\omega)-H(\phi(\omega))}{2}} \cdot |G|^{\frac{H(\phi(\omega))}{2}}) = \tilde{\Theta}(|G|^{\frac{H(\omega)}{2}}) = \tilde{\Theta}(|S|^{\frac{1}{2}}).$$

Therefore – as opposed to the BCJ adaptation – our new low weight DLP algorithm achieves the optimal time bound $\tilde{\Theta}(|S|^{\frac{1}{2}})$ for collision search algorithms. In comparison to Coppersmith's Baby-Step Giant-Step algorithm it does not require full memory $\tilde{\Theta}(|S|^{\frac{1}{2}})$, but only memory $\tilde{\Theta}(|G|^{H(\omega)-H(\phi(\omega))})$. We illustrate the exponent $H(\omega) - H(\phi(\omega))$ as a dashed line in Fig. 9.

4   Subset Sum in $2^{0.65n}$ with Polynomial Space

Motivation. Let $(\mathbf{a}, t) = (a_1, \ldots, a_n, t) \in (\mathbb{Z}_{2^n})^{n+1}$ be a weight-$\frac{1}{2}$ instance of the subset sum problem, i.e., there exists some solution $\mathbf{e} = (e_1, \ldots, e_n)$ with $\text{wt}(\mathbf{e}) = \frac{n}{2}$ satisfying $\langle \mathbf{a}, \mathbf{e} \rangle = t \mod 2^n$. Our algorithm extends to all weights ω, but for simplicity we analyze in the following only the worst-case $\omega = \frac{1}{2}$.

The folklore algorithm from Sect. 3 (also stated explicitly for subset sum in [4]) has runtime $2^{\frac{3}{4}n}$. This is achieved by choosing $\mathcal{T} := \{\mathbf{x} \in \{0,1\}^{\frac{n}{2}} \mid \text{wt}(\mathbf{x}) = \frac{n}{4}\}$ with $|\mathcal{T}| = \tilde{\Theta}(2^{\frac{n}{2}})$, defining an injective function $h : \mathbb{Z}_{2^{n/2}} \to \mathcal{T}$ and searching for collisions between

$$f(\mathbf{x}) = h(\langle (a_1, \ldots, a_{n/2}), \mathbf{x} \rangle \mod 2^{\frac{n}{2}}) \text{ and}$$
$$f_t(\mathbf{x}) = h(t - \langle (a_{n/2+1}, \ldots, a_n), \mathbf{x} \rangle \mod 2^{\frac{n}{2}}).$$

With the notation from Sect. 3 our hash function π first applies the canonical group homomorphism $(\mathbb{Z}_{2^n}, +) \to (\mathbb{Z}_{2^{n/2}}, +)$, followed by an application of h.

Any collision $(\mathbf{x}_1, \mathbf{x}_2)$ satisfies

$$h(\langle (a_1, \ldots, a_{n/2}), \mathbf{x}_1 \rangle \mod 2^{\frac{n}{2}}) = h(t - \langle (a_{n/2+1}, \ldots, a_n), \mathbf{x}_2 \rangle \mod 2^{\frac{n}{2}}).$$

Since h is injective, we conclude that $\langle \mathbf{a}, \mathbf{x}_1 \| \mathbf{x}_2 \rangle = t \mod 2^{\frac{n}{2}}$. Thus $\mathbf{x} = \mathbf{x}_1 \| \mathbf{x}_2$ is a *potential solution* that matches t already on $\frac{n}{2}$ bits, see also Fig. 10. Any potential solution can be found in time $2^{\frac{n}{4}}$ via collision search. However, it costs us on expectation $2^{\frac{n}{2}}$ iterations to find a useful solution that also matches t on the remaining $\frac{n}{2}$ bits. Put differently, we use a square-root cycle finding algorithm to find potential solutions, whereas we use a naive brute-force routine to identify a useful solution. The conflicting problem is that π hashes down to $\frac{n}{2}$ bits to allow for an iterative function application, but thereby inherently introduces $2^{\frac{n}{2}}$ useless collisions.

Our High-Level Idea. Our goal is to use a nested collision search to first find potential solutions that match on $\frac{n}{2}$ bits, and then among these collisions use another collision search for identifying some useful solution. This introduces a

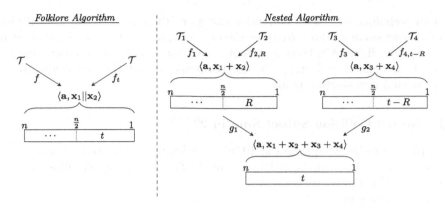

Fig. 10. Basic structure of the folklore and our new algorithm for solving subset sum.

two-layer approach, see also Fig. 10, for which we need to split our solution $\mathbf{e}$ into four summands $\mathbf{e} = \mathbf{x}_1 + \ldots + \mathbf{x}_4$. Obviously, $\langle \mathbf{a}, \mathbf{e} \rangle = t \bmod 2^n$ implies

$$\langle \mathbf{a}, \mathbf{x}_1 + \mathbf{x}_2 \rangle = t - \langle \mathbf{a}, \mathbf{x}_3 + \mathbf{x}_4 \rangle \bmod 2^{\frac{n}{2}}.$$

On layer 1, our algorithm fixes some $R \in \mathbb{Z}_{2^{n/2}}$ and finds collisions $(\mathbf{x}_1, \mathbf{x}_2)$ satisfying $\langle \mathbf{a}, \mathbf{x}_1 + \mathbf{x}_2 \rangle = R \bmod 2^{\frac{n}{2}}$ as well as collisions $(\mathbf{x}_3, \mathbf{x}_4)$ satisfying $\langle \mathbf{a}, \mathbf{x}_3 + \mathbf{x}_4 \rangle = t - R \bmod 2^{\frac{n}{2}}$.

On layer 2, we search among the collisions $(\mathbf{x}_1, \mathbf{x}_2)$ and $(\mathbf{x}_3, \mathbf{x}_4)$ via some nested collision search for some collision that satisfies the identity $\langle \mathbf{a}, \mathbf{x}_1 + \ldots + \mathbf{x}_4 \rangle$ also on the remaining $\frac{n}{2}$ bits.

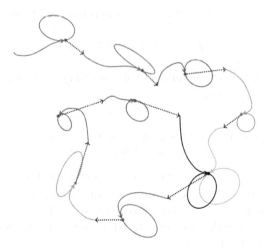

Fig. 11. Structure of the nested Rho algorithm, where different flavours of the function are represented by different colours. (Color figure online)

Our technique for subset sum induces a giant Rho structure (layer 2 collision search) over smaller Rho structures (layer 1 collision search), as illustrated in Fig. 11. Here different colours represent a collision search on different function flavours, as defined in Sect. 2. The dotted arrows depict the transition from a collision to a new starting point.

4.1 Nested Collision Subset Sum in $2^{0.649n}$

To explain our algorithm from Fig. 10 in more detail, we have to first specify the domains $\mathcal{T}_1, \ldots, \mathcal{T}_4$ of the layer-1 functions $f_1, f_{2,R}, f_3, f_{4,t-R}$. We illustrate the domains in Fig. 12.

Let us denote by

$$\mathcal{B}(n, \beta) := \{\mathbf{x} \in \{0,1\}^n \mid \mathrm{wt}(\mathbf{x}) = \beta n\}$$

the set of n dimensional vectors with relative (to n) weight β. For some $\gamma \in [0,1]$ we define

$$\mathcal{T}_1 = 0^{\frac{1}{4}(1-\gamma)n} \times 0^{\frac{1}{4}(1-\gamma)n} \times 0^{\frac{1}{4}(1-\gamma)n} \times \mathcal{B}\left(\frac{1}{4}(1-\gamma)n, \frac{1}{2}\right) \times \mathcal{B}\left(\gamma n, \frac{1}{8}\right)$$

$$\mathcal{T}_2 = 0^{\frac{1}{4}(1-\gamma)n} \times 0^{\frac{1}{4}(1-\gamma)n} \times \mathcal{B}\left(\frac{1}{4}(1-\gamma)n, \frac{1}{2}\right) \times 0^{\frac{1}{4}(1-\gamma)n} \times \mathcal{B}\left(\gamma n, \frac{1}{8}\right)$$

$$\mathcal{T}_3 = 0^{\frac{1}{4}(1-\gamma)n} \times \mathcal{B}\left(\frac{1}{4}(1-\gamma)n, \frac{1}{2}\right) \times 0^{\frac{1}{4}(1-\gamma)n} \times 0^{\frac{1}{4}(1-\gamma)n} \times \mathcal{B}\left(\gamma n, \frac{1}{8}\right)$$

$$\mathcal{T}_4 = \mathcal{B}\left(\frac{1}{4}(1-\gamma)n, \frac{1}{2}\right) \times 0^{\frac{1}{4}(1-\gamma)n} \times 0^{\frac{1}{4}(1-\gamma)n} \times 0^{\frac{1}{4}(1-\gamma)n} \times \mathcal{B}\left(\gamma n, \frac{1}{8}\right).$$

$$(7)$$

Notice that $|\mathcal{B}(n, \beta)| = \binom{n}{\beta n} = \tilde{\Theta}(2^{H(\beta)n})$. Therefore, all $\mathcal{T}_i$ satisfy

$$|\mathcal{T}_i| = \tilde{\Theta}(2^{(\frac{1-\gamma}{4} + H(\frac{1}{8})\gamma)n}).$$

Since we want to have function domain $\frac{n}{2}$ for both layers, we set γ as the solution of $\frac{1-\gamma}{4} + H(\frac{1}{8})\gamma = \frac{1}{2}$, that is

$$\gamma \approx 0.8516. \qquad (8)$$

Recall that we represent our subset sum solution $\mathbf{e}$ as $\mathbf{e} = \mathbf{e}_1 + \ldots + \mathbf{e}_4$ with $(\mathbf{e}_1, \ldots, \mathbf{e}_4) \in \mathcal{T}_1 \times \ldots \times \mathcal{T}_4$. By our definition of the $\mathcal{T}_i$ we may write $\mathbf{e} \in \left(\{0,1\}^{\frac{(1-\gamma)n}{4}}\right)^4 \times \{0,1\}^{\gamma n}$, where each of its 5 parts has relative weight $\frac{1}{2}$. Such a weight distribution of $\mathbf{e}$ can be enforced by an initial permutation on the a_i.

Let us fix some $R \in \mathbb{Z}_{2^{n/2}}$, and let $h_i : \mathbb{Z}_{2^{n/2}} \to \mathcal{T}_i$, $i = 1, \ldots, 4$, be injective functions. Layer-1 collisions are defined as elements $(\mathbf{x}_1, \mathbf{x}_2) \in \mathcal{T}_1 \times \mathcal{T}_2$ and $(\mathbf{x}_3, \mathbf{x}_4) \in \mathcal{T}_3 \times \mathcal{T}_4$ satisfying

$$\langle \mathbf{a}, \mathbf{x}_1 + \mathbf{x}_2 \rangle = R \bmod 2^{\frac{n}{2}} \quad \text{and} \quad \langle \mathbf{a}, \mathbf{x}_3 + \mathbf{x}_4 \rangle = t - R \bmod 2^{\frac{n}{2}}. \qquad (9)$$

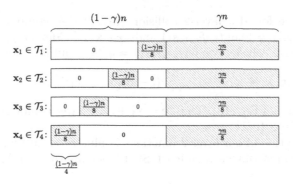

Fig. 12. Weight distribution of vectors from first level domains. Shaded areas contain weight, white areas are all zero.

Therefore, we define the following four first layer functions $f_{i,.} : \mathcal{T}_i \to \mathbb{Z}_{2^{n/2}}$ with

$$f_1(\mathbf{x}) = \langle \mathbf{a}, \mathbf{x} \rangle \bmod 2^{\frac{n}{2}}, \quad f_{2,R}(\mathbf{x}) = R - \langle \mathbf{a}, \mathbf{x} \rangle \bmod 2^{\frac{n}{2}} \text{ and}$$

$$f_3(\mathbf{x}) = \langle \mathbf{a}, \mathbf{x} \rangle \bmod 2^{\frac{n}{2}}, \quad f_{4,t-R}(\mathbf{x}) = t - R - \langle \mathbf{a}, \mathbf{x} \rangle \bmod 2^{\frac{n}{2}}.$$

As a consequence, layer-1 collisions $f_1(\mathbf{x}_1) = f_{2,R}(\mathbf{x}_2)$ and $f_3(\mathbf{x}_3) = f_{4,t-R}(\mathbf{x}_4)$ satisfy Eq. (9). Also notice that by Eq. (9) any pair of layer-1 collisions $(\mathbf{x}_1, \mathbf{x}_2) \in \mathcal{T}_1 \times \mathcal{T}_2$, $(\mathbf{x}_3, \mathbf{x}_4) \in \mathcal{T}_3 \times \mathcal{T}_4$ satisfies

$$\langle \mathbf{a}, \mathbf{x}_1 + \mathbf{x}_2 + \mathbf{x}_3 + \mathbf{x}_4 \rangle = t \bmod 2^{\frac{n}{2}}.$$

Layer-2 collisions are now defined as pairs of layer-1 collisions $(\mathbf{x}_1, \mathbf{x}_2) \in \mathcal{T}_1 \times \mathcal{T}_2$ and $(\mathbf{x}_3, \mathbf{x}_4) \in \mathcal{T}_3 \times \mathcal{T}_4$ satisfying

$$\langle \mathbf{a}, \mathbf{x}_1 + \mathbf{x}_2 + \mathbf{x}_3 + \mathbf{x}_4 \rangle = t \bmod 2^n.$$

Since we already know that by construction layer-1 collisions satisfy the identity $\langle \mathbf{a}, \mathbf{x}_1 + \mathbf{x}_2 + \mathbf{x}_3 + \mathbf{x}_4 \rangle = t$ on the lower $n/2$ bits, it suffices to check for layer-2 collisions the identity on the upper $n/2$ bits, which we denote by

$$\langle \mathbf{a}, \mathbf{x}_1 + \mathbf{x}_2 + \mathbf{x}_3 + \mathbf{x}_4 \rangle_{[n/2+1,n]} = t_{[n/2+1,n]}. \tag{10}$$

Recall from Sect. 2 that $(\mathbf{x}_1, \mathbf{x}_2) = \texttt{Rho}(f_1, f_{2,R}, x)$ denotes the application of a collision finding algorithm on f_1, f_2 with starting point x. The starting point $x \in \mathbb{Z}_{2^{n/2}}$ fully determines the collision $(\mathbf{x}_1, \mathbf{x}_2) \in \mathcal{T}_1 \times \mathcal{T}_2$ found by $\texttt{Rho}$. Before we apply functions f_1 respectively $f_{2,R}$ iteratively on x, we map x (and all function outputs) via h_1 respectively h_2 to their domains $\mathcal{T}_1$ respectively $\mathcal{T}_2$. An analogous mapping is done for the collision search between f_3 and $f_{4,t-R}$.

Let us define the layer-2 functions $g_1, g_2 : \mathbb{Z}_{2^{n/2}} \to \mathbb{Z}_{2^{n/2}}$ as

$$g_1(x) := \langle \mathbf{a}, \mathbf{x}_1 + \mathbf{x}_2 \rangle_{[n/2+1,n]} \quad , \text{ where } (\mathbf{x}_1, \mathbf{x}_2) = \texttt{Rho}(f_1, f_{2,R}, x) \text{ and}$$

$$g_2(x) := (t - \langle \mathbf{a}, \mathbf{x}_3 + \mathbf{x}_4 \rangle)_{[n/2+1,n]}, \text{ where } (\mathbf{x}_3, \mathbf{x}_4) = \texttt{Rho}(f_3, f_{4,t-R}, x).$$

Assume that we found a layer-2 collision (s_1, s_2). We compute from (s_1, s_2) the values $(\mathbf{x}_1, \mathbf{x}_2) = \mathrm{Rho}(f_1, f_{2,R}, s_1)$ and $(\mathbf{x}_3, \mathbf{x}_4) = \mathrm{Rho}(f_3, f_{4,t-R}, s_2)$. Since (s_1, s_2) is a layer-2 collision we have $g_1(s_1) = g_2(s_2)$ and therefore

$$\langle \mathbf{a}, \mathbf{x}_1 + \mathbf{x}_2 \rangle_{[n/2+1,n]} = (t - \langle \mathbf{a}, \mathbf{x}_3 + \mathbf{x}_4 \rangle)_{[n/2+1,n]}.$$

This identity implies Eq. (10). Thus, $\mathbf{e} = \mathbf{x}_1 + \ldots + \mathbf{x}_4$ is a solution to the subset sum problem if $\mathbf{e} \in \{0,1\}^n$.

The computation of our layer-2 functions is illustrated in Fig. 13. Our whole algorithm NESTED COLLISION SUBSET SUM is summarized in Algorithm 3.

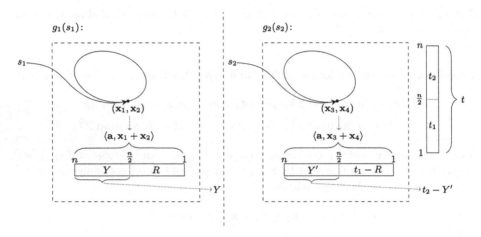

Fig. 13. Computation of layer-2 functions $g_1(s_1)$ and $g_2(s_2)$, where $(\mathbf{x}_1, \mathbf{x}_2) = \mathrm{Rho}(f_1, f_{2,R}, s_1)$ and $(\mathbf{x}_3, \mathbf{x}_4) = \mathrm{Rho}(f_3, f_{4,t-R}, s_2)$.

Algorithm 3. NESTED COLLISION SUBSET SUM

Input: subset sum instance $(\mathbf{a}, t) = (a_1, \ldots, a_n, t) \in \mathbb{Z}_{2^n}^{n+1}$
Output: solution $\mathbf{e} \in \{0,1\}^n$ satisfying $\langle \mathbf{a}, \mathbf{e} \rangle = t \bmod 2^n$
1: **repeat**
2:      Randomly permute the a_i.
3:      Choose $R, z \in \mathbb{Z}_{2^{n/2}}$ randomly.
4:      $(s_1, s_2) \leftarrow \mathrm{Rho}(g_1, g_2, z)$
5:      Compute $(\mathbf{x}_1, \mathbf{x}_2) = \mathrm{Rho}(f_1, f_{2,R}, s_1)$.
6:      Compute $(\mathbf{x}_3, \mathbf{x}_4) = \mathrm{Rho}(f_3, f_{4,t-R}, s_2)$.
7:      Set $\mathbf{e} = \mathbf{x}_1 + \mathbf{x}_2 + \mathbf{x}_3 + \mathbf{x}_4$.
8: **until** $\mathbf{e} \in \{0,1\}^n$

Remark 4.1. We have to guarantee independence of the collisions returned by Rho on input g_1, g_2 for different starting points. This can be done (heuristically) by using flavoured inner functions (see Sect. 2). More formally, we have to change the definitions to

$$g_1(x) := \langle \mathbf{a}, \mathbf{x}_1 + \mathbf{x}_2 \rangle_{[n/2+1,n]} \quad , \text{ where } (\mathbf{x}_1, \mathbf{x}_2) = \text{Rho}(f_1^{[x]}, f_{2,R}^{[x]}, x) \text{ and}$$

$$g_2(x) := (t - \langle \mathbf{a}, \mathbf{x}_3 + \mathbf{x}_4 \rangle)_{[n/2+1,n]}, \text{ where } (\mathbf{x}_3, \mathbf{x}_4) = \text{Rho}(f_3^{[x]}, f_{4,t-R}^{[x]}, x).$$

In the following, we omit flavours for ease of notation.

Run Time Analysis of Nested Collision Subset Sum. The cost of any iteration of the **repeat**-loop in NESTED COLLISION SUBSET SUM is dominated by the function call to $\text{Rho}(g_1, g_2, z)$, which itself recursively calls $\text{Rho}(f_1, f_{2,R}, \cdot)$ and $\text{Rho}(f_3, f_{4,t-R}, \cdot)$. Each invocation of collision finding in the layer-1 functions costs time $|\mathcal{T}_i|^{\frac{1}{2}} = \tilde{\Theta}(2^{\frac{n}{4}})$. Since $g_i : \mathbb{Z}_{2^{\frac{n}{2}}} \to \mathbb{Z}_{2^{\frac{n}{2}}}$, a collision search in the layer-2 functions requires on expectation $\tilde{\Theta}(2^{\frac{n}{4}})$ function evaluations of the g_i. Hence in total each iteration in NESTED COLLISION SUBSET SUM requires time $\tilde{\Theta}(2^{\frac{n}{2}})$.

Notice that each iteration computes some potential solution $\mathbf{e}'$ satisfying $\langle \mathbf{a}, \mathbf{e}' \rangle = t$, no matter whether the permutation of the a_i induced the correct weight distribution on $\mathbf{e}$. However, such an $\mathbf{e}'$ is usually not in $\{0,1\}^n$, and therefore does not solve our subset sum instance.

Let us look at some fixed iteration of NESTED COLLISION SUBSET SUM. Let E_1 be the event that our initial permutation yields the correct weight distribution in this iteration. Then

$$p_1 := \Pr[E_1] = \frac{\binom{(1-\gamma)n/4}{(1-\gamma)n/8}^4 \binom{\gamma n}{\gamma n/2}}{\binom{n}{n/2}} = \frac{1}{\text{poly}(n)} - \tilde{\Theta}(1). \tag{11}$$

Let $(\mathbf{e}_1, \ldots, \mathbf{e}_4)$ be a representation of our subset sum solution $\mathbf{e}$ satisfying $\langle \mathbf{a}, \mathbf{e}_1 + \mathbf{e}_2 \rangle = R \mod 2^{\frac{n}{2}}$ (for the choice of R in line 3 of Algorithm 3). Then we call $(\mathbf{e}_1, \mathbf{e}_2)$ a *useful collision* of $f_1, f_{2,R}$. By construction, $(\mathbf{e}_3, \mathbf{e}_4)$ is automatically a useful collision of $f_3, f_{4,t-R}$ satisfying $\langle \mathbf{a}, \mathbf{e}_3 + \mathbf{e}_4 \rangle = t - R \mod 2^{n/2}$. Now, for all useful collisions $(\mathbf{e}_1, \mathbf{e}_2)$ of $f_1, f_{2,R}$ and $(\mathbf{e}_3, \mathbf{e}_4)$ of $f_3, f_{4,t-R}$ there exists some collision (s_1', s_2') of g_1, g_2 satisfying $(\mathbf{e}_1, \mathbf{e}_2) = \text{Rho}(f_1, f_{2,R}, s_1')$ and $(\mathbf{e}_3, \mathbf{e}_4) = \text{Rho}(f_3, f_{4,t-R}, s_2')$. Thus, useful collisions of $f_1, f_{2,R}$ and $f_3, f_{4,t-R}$ are in 1:1-correspondence with the collisions of g_1, g_2 that yield a representation of the solution. Hence, we can compute the probability of success in one iteration given E_1 as the fraction of useful collisions with respect to R among all collisions of g_1, g_2, where the latter is $\tilde{\Theta}(2^{\frac{n}{2}})$.

Let E_2 be the event that there exist useful collisions for our choice of R. Let E_3 be the event that our collision finding yields a representation $(\mathbf{x}_1, \ldots, \mathbf{x}_4)$ of the solution $\mathbf{e}$. Then we succeed in this iteration with probability $p := \Pr[E_1 \cap E_2 \cap E_3] = \Pr[E_1] \cdot \Pr[E_2 \mid E_1] \cdot \Pr[E_3 \mid E_2 \cap E_1]$. It remains to compute $p_2 := \Pr[E_2 \mid E_1]$ and $p_3 := \Pr[E_3 \mid E_2 \cap E_1]$. Let us start with probability p_2.

Let us calculate the number of different R values for which we obtain useful collisions. We first observe that different representations $(\mathbf{e}_1, \ldots, \mathbf{e}_4)$ might share the same value $\mathbf{e}_1 + \mathbf{e}_2$ and hence the same inner product $\langle \mathbf{a}, \mathbf{e}_1 + \mathbf{e}_2 \rangle$. Thus, we have to count the number of distinct representations $(\mathbf{e}_1', \mathbf{e}_2') = (\mathbf{e}_1 + \mathbf{e}_2, \mathbf{e}_3 + \mathbf{e}_4)$ of $\mathbf{e}$. By the definition of our function domains in Eq. (7) and in Fig. 12 this number is

$$\binom{\frac{\gamma n}{2}}{\frac{\gamma n}{4}} = \tilde{\Theta}\left(2^{\frac{\gamma n}{2}}\right).$$

Hence, the probability of choosing an $R \in \mathbb{Z}_{2^{n/2}}$ for which useful collisions exist is

$$p_2 := \tilde{\Theta}\left(\frac{2^{\frac{\gamma n}{2}}}{2^{\frac{n}{2}}}\right) = \tilde{\Theta}\left(2^{\frac{(\gamma-1)n}{2}}\right).$$

Note that for a good choice of R there directly exist several useful collisions, since any fixed $(\mathbf{e}_1', \mathbf{e}_2') = (\mathbf{e}_1 + \mathbf{e}_2, \mathbf{e}_3 + \mathbf{e}_4)$ is represented via multiple $(\mathbf{e}_1, \ldots, \mathbf{e}_4)$. More precisely every $\mathbf{e}_1'$ (resp. $\mathbf{e}_2'$) is represented by

$$\binom{\frac{\gamma n}{4}}{\frac{\gamma n}{8}} = \tilde{\Theta}\left(2^{\frac{\gamma n}{4}}\right)$$

different $(\mathbf{e}_1, \mathbf{e}_2)$ (resp. $(\mathbf{e}_3, \mathbf{e}_4)$). Note that any of these $(\mathbf{e}_1, \mathbf{e}_2)$ and $(\mathbf{e}_3, \mathbf{e}_4)$ form useful collisions of $f_1, f_{2,R}$ and $f_3, f_{4,t-R}$. Furthermore, any of the $2^{\frac{\gamma n}{2}}$ combinations of $(\mathbf{e}_1, \mathbf{e}_2)$ and $(\mathbf{e}_3, \mathbf{e}_4)$ is a representation of $\mathbf{e}$. Therefore, we obtain a total of $2^{\frac{\gamma n}{2}}$ distinct collisions in g_1, g_2 that represent $\mathbf{e}$. Thus in case that we made a good choice of R, a random collision is a representation of the solution with probability

$$p_3 := \tilde{\Theta}\left(\frac{2^{\frac{\gamma n}{2}}}{2^{\frac{n}{2}}}\right) = \tilde{\Theta}\left(2^{\frac{(\gamma-1)n}{2}}\right).$$

Eventually, we expect $p^{-1} = (p_1 p_2 p_3)^{-1} = 2^{(1-\gamma)n} = 2^{0.149n}$ iterations with cost each $\tilde{\Theta}(2^{\frac{n}{2}})$, resulting in total expected runtime

$$T = \tilde{\Theta}(2^{(\frac{3}{2}-\gamma)n}) = 2^{0.649n}.$$

Alternative Run Time Analysis of Nested Collision Subset Sum. We already saw that each iteration of NESTED COLLISION SUBSET SUM takes time $\tilde{\Theta}(2^{n/2})$ and we have to iterate until we find some $\mathbf{e} \in \{0,1\}^n$. We call $(\mathbf{x}_1, \mathbf{x}_2, \mathbf{x}_3, \mathbf{x}_4) \in \mathcal{T}_1 \times \ldots \times \mathcal{T}_4$ *consistent* iff $\mathbf{e} = \mathbf{x}_1 + \mathbf{x}_2 + \mathbf{x}_3 + \mathbf{x}_4 \in \{0,1\}^n$.

Now observe that a random tuple $(\mathbf{x}_1, \mathbf{x}_2, \mathbf{x}_3, \mathbf{x}_4) \in \mathcal{T}_1 \times \ldots \times \mathcal{T}_4$ is consistent with probability

$$p = \frac{\binom{\gamma n}{\gamma n/8}\binom{7\gamma n/8}{\gamma n/8}\binom{6\gamma n/8}{\gamma n/8}\binom{5\gamma n/8}{\gamma n/8}}{\binom{\gamma n}{\gamma n/8}^4}$$

$$= \tilde{\Theta}\left(2^{\left(\frac{7}{8}H\left(\frac{1}{7}\right)+\frac{3}{4}H\left(\frac{1}{6}\right)+\frac{5}{8}H\left(\frac{1}{5}\right)-3H\left(\frac{1}{8}\right)\right)\gamma n}\right) \geq 2^{-0.149n}.$$

Let us assume that the representations of $\mathbf{e}$ distribute uniformly in $\mathcal{T}_1 \times \ldots \times \mathcal{T}_4$ and that NESTED COLLISION SUBSET SUM finds random collisions. Then we need on expection p^{-1} iterations until we find $\mathbf{e} \in \{0,1\}^n$, resulting in a total runtime of

$$T = p^{-1} \cdot \tilde{\Theta}(2^{n/2}) = 2^{0.649n}.$$

This view on the runtime of NESTED COLLISION SUBSET SUM motivates the improved algorithm in the subsequent section that increases the probability of obtaining a consistent vector $\mathbf{e}$ at the cost of an initial exponential time permutation step.

4.2   Improved Nested Collision Subset Sum in $2^{0.645n}$

Recall from Eq. (7) and Fig. 12 that in $\mathbf{x}_1 + \ldots + \mathbf{x}_4$ the left-most coordinates are always in $\{0,1\}^{(1-\gamma)n}$. In other words, inconsistencies are always due to the last γn coordinates. Therefore, our goal is to shift less weight in the last γn coordinates. Namely, we modify the weight distribution of $\mathbf{e}$ such that the last γn coordinates have relative weight $\frac{\beta}{2}$ for some $2 - \frac{1}{\gamma} \leq \beta \leq 1$. We depict our new weight distribution in Fig. 14. Since we cannot shift arbitrary weight into the left-most coordinates, the lower bound on β guarantees $\frac{(1-\gamma)n}{4} \geq \frac{(1-\gamma\beta)n}{8}$.

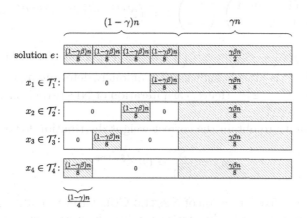

Fig. 14. Weight distribution of vectors from new layer-1 domains. Shaded areas contain weight, white areas are all zero.

More formally, we change the layer-1 domains to

$$\mathcal{T}_1' = 0^{\frac{1}{4}(1-\gamma)n} \times 0^{\frac{1}{4}(1-\gamma)n} \times 0^{\frac{1}{4}(1-\gamma)n} \times \mathcal{B}\left(\frac{1}{4}(1-\gamma)n, \frac{1-\gamma\beta}{2(1-\gamma)}\right) \times \mathcal{B}\left(\gamma n, \frac{\beta}{8}\right)$$

$$\mathcal{T}_2' = 0^{\frac{1}{4}(1-\gamma)n} \times 0^{\frac{1}{4}(1-\gamma)n} \times \mathcal{B}\left(\frac{1}{4}(1-\gamma)n, \frac{1-\gamma\beta}{2(1-\gamma)}\right) \times 0^{\frac{1}{4}(1-\gamma)n} \times \mathcal{B}\left(\gamma n, \frac{\beta}{8}\right)$$

$$\mathcal{T}_3' = 0^{\frac{1}{4}(1-\gamma)n} \times \mathcal{B}\left(\frac{1}{4}(1-\gamma)n, \frac{1-\gamma\beta}{2(1-\gamma)}\right) \times 0^{\frac{1}{4}(1-\gamma)n} \times 0^{\frac{1}{4}(1-\gamma)n} \times \mathcal{B}\left(\gamma n, \frac{\beta}{8}\right)$$

$$\mathcal{T}_4' = \mathcal{B}\left(\frac{1}{4}(1-\gamma)n, \frac{1-\gamma\beta}{2(1-\gamma)}\right) \times 0^{\frac{1}{4}(1-\gamma)n} \times 0^{\frac{1}{4}(1-\gamma)n} \times 0^{\frac{1}{4}(1-\gamma)n} \times \mathcal{B}\left(\gamma n, \frac{\beta}{8}\right).$$

This changes the domain sizes to

$$|\mathcal{T}_i'| = \binom{(1-\gamma)n/4}{(1-\gamma\beta)n/8}\binom{\gamma n}{\frac{\gamma\beta n}{8}}.$$

In the analysis from Sect. 4.1, we set γ such that the search space of 2^n splits into $2^{\frac{n}{2}}$ for both layer-1 and layer-2 collisions. However, observe that our new *weight-shifted subset sum problem* has no longer search space of size 2^n, but only of size

$$\mathcal{S} = \binom{(1-\gamma)n/4}{(1-\gamma\beta)n/8}^4\binom{\gamma n}{\frac{\gamma\beta n}{2}} = \tilde{\Theta}\left(2^{\left((1-\gamma)H\left(\frac{1-\gamma\beta}{2(1-\gamma)}\right)+\gamma H\left(\frac{\beta}{2}\right)\right)n}\right).$$

Let $\delta := (1-\gamma)H\left(\frac{1-\gamma\beta}{2(1-\gamma)}\right) + \gamma H\left(\frac{\beta}{2}\right)$ be the exponent of $\mathcal{S}$. Thus, computing $\langle \mathbf{a}, \mathbf{e} \rangle = t \bmod 2^{\delta n}$ is already sufficient for uniquely determining $\mathbf{e}$. Analogous to Sect. 4.1 we set $|\mathcal{T}_i'| = 2^{\frac{\delta}{2}n}$. Hence, each iteration of NESTED COLLISION SUBSET SUM costs time $\tilde{\Theta}(2^{\frac{\delta}{2}n})$.

The probability to obtain the correct weight distribution for $\mathbf{e}$ is

$$p_1 := \frac{\mathcal{S}}{\binom{n}{\frac{n}{2}}} = \tilde{\Theta}(2^{(\delta-1)n}).$$

Let us look at a fixed iteration of NESTED COLLISION SUBSET SUM with some choice of R. Assume that in this iteration $\mathbf{e}$ has the correct weight distribution. Any representation $(\mathbf{e}_1, \dots, \mathbf{e}_4)$ of $\mathbf{e}$ is useful in this iteration if $\langle \mathbf{a}, \mathbf{e}_1 + \mathbf{e}_2 \rangle = R \bmod 2^{\frac{\delta}{2}n}$. Since we shift less weight into the γn right-most coordinates, the amount of distinct representations $(\mathbf{e}_1', \mathbf{e}_2') = (\mathbf{e}_1 + \mathbf{e}_2, \mathbf{e}_3 + \mathbf{e}_4)$ decreases to

$$\binom{\frac{\gamma\beta n}{2}}{\frac{\gamma\beta n}{4}} = \tilde{\Theta}\left(2^{\frac{\gamma\beta n}{2}}\right).$$

Hence the probability of choosing an $R \in \mathbb{Z}_{2^{\delta n/2}}$ for which useful representations exist becomes

$$p_2 := \tilde{\Theta}\left(\frac{2^{\frac{\gamma\beta n}{2}}}{2^{\frac{\delta n}{2}}}\right) = \tilde{\Theta}\left(2^{\frac{(\gamma\beta-\delta)n}{2}}\right).$$

For a good choice of R there exists at least one representation $(e_1', e_2') = (e_1 + e_2, e_3 + e_4)$ of the solution with $\langle a, e_1' \rangle = R \bmod 2^{\frac{\delta n}{2}}$, and the number of ways we can represent $(e_1', e_2') = (e_1 + e_2, e_3 + e_4)$ is

$$\binom{\frac{\gamma\beta n}{4}}{\frac{\gamma\beta n}{8}}^2 = \tilde{\Theta}\left(2^{\frac{\gamma\beta n}{2}}\right).$$

Since g has a total of $\tilde{\Theta}(2^{\frac{\delta n}{2}})$ collisions, a random collision is a representation of the solution with probability

$$p_3 := \tilde{\Theta}\left(\frac{2^{\frac{\gamma\beta n}{2}}}{2^{\frac{\delta n}{2}}}\right) = \tilde{\Theta}\left(2^{\frac{(\gamma\beta-\delta)n}{2}}\right).$$

With probability $p = p_1 p_2 p_3$ we have the correct weight distribution, choose a good R, and find a useful representation. Thus, we need on expectation p^{-1} iterations with running time $\tilde{\Theta}(2^{\frac{\delta}{2}n})$ each. This results in a total run time of

$$T = \tilde{\Theta}\left(2^{(1-\delta+\delta-\gamma\beta+\frac{\delta}{2})n}\right) = \tilde{\Theta}\left(2^{(1-\gamma\beta+\frac{\delta}{2})n}\right).$$

Optimization yields $\beta = 0.964$, from which we obtain $\gamma = 0.8832$ and $\delta = 0.9928$. This gives us $p_1 = 2^{-0.0072n}$, $p_2 = p_3 = 2^{-0.0707n}$ and a total expected run time of

$$T = 2^{0.645n}.$$

4.3 Experiments for Our $2^{0.649n}$ Subset Sum Algorithm

We implemented our NESTED COLLISION SUBSET SUM algorithm (Algorithm 3)[2] and summarize the results of our experiments in Table 1.

Table 1. Amount of function calls T_f in logarithmic scale to solve a random subset sum instance in dimension n using our NESTED COLLISION SUBSET SUM algorithm. Sample size per n is 30.

n	16	24	32	40	48
$\log T_f$	16.80	21.91	26.97	32.01	37.25

The computed regression line in Fig. 15 is $\log T_f(n) = 0.637n + 6.678$. The parameter 6.678 shows that the implementation of our algorithm incorporates some quite large polynomial run time overhead. However, more importantly the experimental slope 0.637 demonstrates that our asymptotic run time exponent of 0.649 is already achieved in small dimension.

---

[2] Implementation available at https://github.com/LwDLPandSubsetSum/lwDLP-and-NestedSubsetSum.

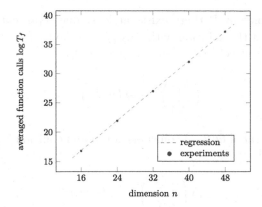

Fig. 15. Experimentally averaged number of function calls (in logarithmic scale) needed to solve a subset sum instance in dimension n of weight $n/2$. Sample size per n is 30.

References

1. Abboud, A., Bringmann, K., Hermelin, D., Shabtay, D.: Seth-based lower bounds for subset sum and bicriteria path. In: Proceedings of the Thirtieth Annual ACM-SIAM Symposium on Discrete Algorithms, pp. 41–57. Society for Industrial and Applied Mathematics (2019)
2. Alekhnovich, M.: More on average case vs approximation complexity. In: 44th Annual Symposium on Foundations of Computer Science, Cambridge, MA, USA, 11–14 October 2003, pp. 298–307. IEEE Computer Society Press (2003)
3. Bansal, N., Garg, S., Nederlof, J., Vyas, N.: Faster space-efficient algorithms for subset sum and k-sum. In: Hatami, H., McKenzie, P., King, V. (eds.) 49th Annual ACM Symposium on Theory of Computing, Montreal, QC, Canada, 19–23 June 2017, pp. 198–209. ACM Press (2017)
4. Becker, A., Coron, J.-S., Joux, A.: Improved generic algorithms for hard knapsacks. In: Paterson, K.G. (ed.) EUROCRYPT 2011. LNCS, vol. 6632, pp. 364–385. Springer, Heidelberg (2011). https://doi.org/10.1007/978-3-642-20465-4_21
5. Becker, A., Joux, A., May, A., Meurer, A.: Decoding random binary linear codes in $2^{n/20}$: how $1 + 1 = 0$ improves information set decoding. In: Pointcheval, D., Johansson, T. (eds.) EUROCRYPT 2012. LNCS, vol. 7237, pp. 520–536. Springer, Heidelberg (2012). https://doi.org/10.1007/978-3-642-29011-4_31
6. Bernstein, D.J., Jeffery, S., Lange, T., Meurer, A.: Quantum algorithms for the subset-sum problem. In: Gaborit, P. (ed.) PQCrypto 2013. LNCS, vol. 7932, pp. 16–33. Springer, Heidelberg (2013). https://doi.org/10.1007/978-3-642-38616-9_2
7. Bos, J.W., Kaihara, M., Kleinjung, T., Lenstra, A.K., Montgomery, P.L.: Solving 112-bit prime ECDLP on game consoles using sloppy reduction. Int. J. Appl. Cryptogr. **2**(ARTICLE), 212–228 (2012)
8. Chor, B., Rivest, R.L.: A knapsack type public key cryptosystem based on arithmetic in finite fields (preliminary draft). In: Blakley, G.R., Chaum, D. (eds.) CRYPTO 1984. LNCS, vol. 196, pp. 54–65. Springer, Heidelberg (1985). https://doi.org/10.1007/3-540-39568-7_6

9. Dinur, I., Dunkelman, O., Keller, N., Shamir, A.: Memory-efficient algorithms for finding needles in haystacks. In: Robshaw, M., Katz, J. (eds.) CRYPTO 2016, Part II. LNCS, vol. 9815, pp. 185–206. Springer, Heidelberg (2016). https://doi.org/10.1007/978-3-662-53008-5_7

10. Esser, A., Kübler, R., May, A.: LPN decoded. In: Katz, J., Shacham, H. (eds.) CRYPTO 2017, Part II. LNCS, vol. 10402, pp. 486–514. Springer, Cham (2017). https://doi.org/10.1007/978-3-319-63715-0_17

11. Faust, S., Masny, D., Venturi, D.: Chosen-ciphertext security from subset sum. In: Cheng, C.-M., Chung, K.-M., Persiano, G., Yang, B.-Y. (eds.) PKC 2016, Part I. LNCS, vol. 9614, pp. 35–46. Springer, Heidelberg (2016). https://doi.org/10.1007/978-3-662-49384-7_2

12. Galbraith, S.D.: Mathematics of Public Key Cryptography. Cambridge University Press, Cambridge (2012)

13. Galbraith, S.D., Gaudry, P.: Recent progress on the elliptic curve discrete logarithm problem. Des. Codes Crypt. **78**(1), 51–72 (2015). https://doi.org/10.1007/s10623-015-0146-7

14. Halderman, J.A., et al.: Lest we remember: cold-boot attacks on encryption keys. Commun. ACM **52**(5), 91–98 (2009)

15. Herold, G., May, A.: LP solutions of vectorial integer subset sums – cryptanalysis of Galbraith's binary matrix LWE. In: Fehr, S. (ed.) PKC 2017, Part I. LNCS, vol. 10174, pp. 3–15. Springer, Heidelberg (2017). https://doi.org/10.1007/978-3-662-54365-8_1

16. Impagliazzo, R., Naor, M.: Efficient cryptographic schemes provably as secure as subset sum. J. Cryptol. **9**(4), 199–216 (1996)

17. Knuth, D.E: The Art of Computer Programming, Volume II: Seminumerical Algorithms, 3rd edn. Addison-Wesley (1998). http://www.worldcat.org/oclc/312898417. ISBN: 0201896842

18. Lagarias, J.C., Odlyzko, A.M.: Solving low-density subset sum problems. J. ACM (JACM) **32**(1), 229–246 (1985)

19. Lyubashevsky, V., Palacio, A., Segev, G.: Public-key cryptographic primitives provably as secure as subset sum. In: Micciancio, D. (ed.) TCC 2010. LNCS, vol. 5978, pp. 382–400. Springer, Heidelberg (2010). https://doi.org/10.1007/978-3-642-11799-2_23

20. May, A., Ozerov, I.: A generic algorithm for small weight discrete logarithms in composite groups. In: Joux, A., Youssef, A. (eds.) SAC 2014. LNCS, vol. 8781, pp. 278–289. Springer, Cham (2014). https://doi.org/10.1007/978-3-319-13051-4_17

21. Merkle, R., Hellman, M.: Hiding information and signatures in trapdoor knapsacks. IEEE Trans. Inf. Theory **24**(5), 525–530 (1978)

22. Nivasch, G.: Cycle detection using a stack. Inform. Process. Lett. **90**(3), 135–140 (2004)

23. Odlyzko, A.M.: The rise and fall of knapsack cryptosystems. Cryptol. Comput. Number Theory **42**, 75–88 (1990)

24. Pollard, J.M.: A monte carlo method for factorization. BIT Numer. Math. **15**(3), 331–334 (1975). https://doi.org/10.1007/BF01933667

25. Regev, O.: On lattices, learning with errors, random linear codes, and cryptography. In: Gabow, H.N., Fagin, R. (eds.) 37th Annual ACM Symposium on Theory of Computing, Baltimore, MA, USA, 22–24 May 2005, pp. 84–93. ACM Press, Baltimore (2005)

26. Shanks, D.: Five number-theoretic algorithms. In: Proceedings of the Second Manitoba Conference on Numerical Mathematics (Winnipeg), 1973 (1973)

27. Stinson, D.: Some baby-step giant-step algorithms for the low hamming weight discrete logarithm problem. Math. Comput. **71**(237), 379–391 (2002)
28. Van Oorschot, P.C., Wiener, M.J.: Parallel collision search with application to hash functions and discrete logarithms. In: Proceedings of the 2nd ACM Conference on Computer and Communications Security, pp. 210–218. ACM (1994)
29. van Oorschot, P.C., Wiener, M.J.: Parallel collision search with cryptanalytic applications. J. Cryptol. **12**(1), 1–28 (1999)

Verifiable Delay Functions

Continuous Verifiable Delay Functions

Naomi Ephraim[1]($\boxtimes$), Cody Freitag[1]($\boxtimes$), Ilan Komargodski[2], and Rafael Pass[1]

[1] Cornell Tech, New York, NY 10044, USA
{nephraim,cfreitag,rafael}@cs.cornell.edu
[2] NTT Research, Palo Alto, CA 94303, USA
ilan.komargodski@ntt-research.ac.il

Abstract. We introduce the notion of a *continuous verifiable delay function* (cVDF): a function g which is (a) iteratively sequential—meaning that evaluating the iteration $g^{(t)}$ of g (on a random input) takes time roughly t times the time to evaluate g, even with many parallel processors, and (b) (iteratively) verifiable—the output of $g^{(t)}$ can be efficiently verified (in time that is essentially independent of t). In other words, the iterated function $g^{(t)}$ is a verifiable delay function (VDF) (Boneh et al., CRYPTO '18), having the property that intermediate steps of the computation (i.e., $g^{(t')}$ for $t' < t$) are publicly and continuously verifiable.

We demonstrate that cVDFs have intriguing applications: (a) they can be used to construct *public randomness beacons* that only require an initial random seed (and no further unpredictable sources of randomness), (b) enable *outsourceable VDFs* where any part of the VDF computation can be verifiably outsourced, and (c) have deep complexity-theoretic consequences: in particular, they imply the existence of *depth-robust moderately-hard* Nash equilibrium problem instances, i.e. instances that can be solved in polynomial time yet require a high sequential running time.

Our main result is the construction of a cVDF based on the repeated squaring assumption and the soundness of the Fiat-Shamir (FS) heuristic for *constant-round proofs*. We highlight that when viewed as a (plain) VDF, our construction requires a weaker FS assumption than previous ones (earlier constructions require the FS heuristic for either super-logarithmic round proofs, or for arguments).

1 Introduction

A fundamental computational task is to simulate "real time" via computation. This was first suggested by Rabin [42] in 1983, who introduced a notion called *randomness beacon* to describe an ideal functionality that publishes unpredictable and independent random values at fixed intervals. This concept has received a substantial amount of attention since its introduction, and even more so in recent years due to its many applications to more efficient and reliable consensus protocols in the context of blockchain technologies.

© International Association for Cryptologic Research 2020
A. Canteaut and Y. Ishai (Eds.): EUROCRYPT 2020, LNCS 12107, pp. 125–154, 2020.
https://doi.org/10.1007/978-3-030-45727-3_5

One natural approach, which is the focus of this work, is to implement a randomness beacon by using an *iteratively sequential function*.[1] An iteratively sequential function g inherently takes some time ℓ to compute and has the property that there are no shortcuts to compute sequential iterations of it. That is, computing the t-wise composition of g for any t should take roughly time $t \cdot \ell$, even with parallelism. Using an iteratively sequential function g with an initial seed x, we can construct a randomness beacon where the output at interval t is computed as the hash of

$$g^{(t)}(x) = \underbrace{g \circ g \circ \ldots \circ g}_{t \text{ times}}(x).$$

After $t \cdot \ell$ time has elapsed (at which point we know the first t values), the beacon's output should be unpredictable sufficiently far in the future.[2] The original candidate iteratively sequential function is based on (repeated) squaring in a finite group of unknown order [13,43]. It is also conjectured that any secure hash function (such as SHA-256) gives an iteratively sequential function; this was suggested in [30] and indeed, as shown in [36], a random oracle is iteratively sequential.

Continuous VDFs. The downside of using an iteratively sequential function as a randomness beacon is that to verify the current value of the beacon, one needs to recompute its entire history which is time consuming by definition. In particular, a party that joins late will never be able to catch up. Rather, we would like the output at each step to be both *publicly* and *efficiently* verifiable. It is also desirable for the randomness beacon to be generated without any private state so that *anyone* can compute it, meaning that each step can be computed based solely on the output of the preceding step. Indeed, if we have an iteratively sequential function that is also *(iteratively) verifiable*—in the sense that one can efficiently verify the output of $g^{(t)}(x)$ in time polylog(t)—then such a function could be used to obtain a *public randomness beacon*. In this paper, we introduce and construct such a function and refer to it as a *continuous verifiable delay function* (cVDF). As the name suggests, it can be viewed as enabling continuous evaluation and verification of a verifiable delay function (VDF) [10] as we describe shortly.[3]

Continuous VDFs are related to many previously studied time-based primitives. One classical construction is the time-lock puzzle of Rivest, Shamir, and Wagner [43]. Their construction can be viewed as an iteratively sequential function that is *privately verifiable* with a trapdoor—unfortunately, this trapdoor

---

[1] We use the terminology from [10]; these have also been referred to as sequential functions [36].

[2] If g is perfectly iteratively sequential, meaning that t iterations cannot be computed in time faster than *exactly* $t \cdot \ell$, then after t steps of g the *next* value would be unpredictable. However, if t iterations cannot be computed in time faster than $(1 - \epsilon) \cdot t \cdot \ell$, we can only guarantee that the $(\epsilon \cdot t)$-th value into the future is unpredictable.

[3] Our notion of a cVDF (just like the earlier notion of a "plain" VDF) also allows for the existence of some trusted public parameters.

not only enables quickly verifying the output of iterations of the function, but in fact also enables quickly computing the iterations. New publicly verifiable time-based primitives have since emerged, including proofs of sequential work (PoSW) [18,21,36] and verifiable delay functions (VDF) [10,11,23,40,45]. While these primitives are enough for many applications, they fall short of implementing a public randomness beacon (on their own). In more detail, a PoSW enables generating a publicly verifiable proof of *some* computation (rather than a specific function with a unique output) that is guaranteed to have taken a long time. This issue was overcome through the introduction of VDFs [10], which are functions that require some "long" time T to compute (where T is a parameter given to the function), yet the answer to the computation can be efficiently verified given a proof that can be jointly generated with the output (with only small overhead).

In fact, one of the motivating applications for constructing VDFs was to obtain a public randomness beacon. A natural approach toward this goal is to simply iterate the VDF at fixed intervals. However, this construction does not satisfy our desired efficiency for verifiability. In particular, even though the VDF enables fast verification of each invocation, we still need to store all proofs for the intermediate values to verify the final output of the iterated function, and thus the proof size and verification time grow linearly with the number of invocations t. While a recent construction of Wesolowski [45] enables aggregating these intermediate proofs to obtain a single short proof, the verification time still grows linearly with t (in contrast, a cVDF enables continuously iterating a function such that the output of t iterations can be efficiently verified in time essentially independent of t, for any t). While a VDF does not directly give a public randomness beacon, it does, however, enable turning a "high-entropy beacon" (e.g., continuous monitoring of stock market prices) into an unbiased and unpredictable beacon as described in [10]. In contrast, using a cVDF enables dispensing altogether with the high-entropy beacon—we simply need a *single* initial seed x.

Continuous VDFs are useful not only for randomness beacons, but also for standard applications of VDFs. Consider a scenario where some entity is offering a $5M reward for evaluating a single VDF with time parameter 5 years (i.e., it is supposed to take five years to evaluate it). Alice starts evaluating the VDF, but after two years runs out of money and can no longer continue the computation. Ideally, she would like to sell the work she has completed for $2M. Bob is willing to buy the intermediate state, verify it, and continue the computation. The problem, however, is that there is no way for Bob to verify Alice's internal state. In contrast, had Alice used a cVDF, she would simply be iterating an iteratively sequential function, and we would directly have the guarantee that at any intermediate state of the computation can be verified and Alice can be compensated for her effort. In other words, cVDF enable verifiably outsourcing VDF computation.

Finally, as we show, cVDFs are intriguing also from a complexity-theoretic point of view. The existence of cVDFs imply that PPAD [39] (the class for which the task of finding a Nash equilibrium in a two-party game is complete) is hard—in fact, the existence of cVDFs imply the existence of a relaxed-SVL [5,15] instance with *tight* hardness (which yields improved hardness results also for PPAD). Additionally, the existence of cVDFs imply that there is a constant d such that for large enough c, there is a distribution over Nash equilibrium problem instances of size n that can be solved in time n^c but cannot be solved in depth $n^{c/d}$ (and arbitrary polynomial size)—that is, the existence of "easy" Nash equilibrium problem instances that requires high *sequential* running time. In other words, cVDFs imply that it is possible to sample "moderately-hard" Nash equilibrium problem instances that require a large time to solve, even with many parallel processors.

1.1   Our Results

Our main result is the construction of a cVDF based on the repeated squaring assumption in a finite group of unknown order and a variant of the Fiat-Shamir (FS) heuristic for *constant-round proof* systems. Informally, the iteratively sequential property of our construction comes from the repeated squaring assumption which says that squaring in this setting is an iteratively sequential function. We use the Fiat-Shamir assumption to obtain the continuous verifiability property of our construction. More precisely, we apply the Fiat-Shamir heuristic on a constant-round proof system where the verifier may be inefficient. We note that by the classic results of [26] this holds in the random oracle model.

Theorem 1.1 (Informal, see Corollary 6.3). *Under the repeated squaring assumption and the Fiat-Shamir assumption for constant-round proof systems with inefficient verifiers, there exists a cVDF.*

We remark that to obtain a plain VDF we only need the "standard" Fiat-Shamir assumption for constant-round proof systems (with efficient verifiers).

A cVDF readily gives a public randomness beacon. As discussed above, the notions of cVDFs and public randomness beacons are closely related. The main difference between the two is that the output of a randomness beacon should not only be unpredictable before a certain time, but should also be indistinguishable from random. Thus, we obtain our public randomness beacon by simply "hashing" the output of the cVDF. We show that this indeed gives a public randomness beacon by performing the hashing using a pseudo-random generators (PRGs) for unpredictable sources (which exist either in the random oracle model or from extremely lossy functions [46]).

Theorem 1.2 (Informal). *Assuming the existence of cVDFs and PRGs for unpredictable sources, there exists a public randomness beacon.*

Comparison with (Plain) VDFs. The two most related VDF constructions are that of Pietrzak [40] and that of Wesolowski [45], as these are based on repeated squaring. In terms of assumptions, Pietrzak's protocol [40] assumes the Fiat-Shamir heuristic for a proof system with a *super-constant* number of rounds and Wesolowski's [45] assumes the Fiat-Shamir heuristic for a constant-round *argument system*. It is known that, in general, the Fiat-Shamir heuristic is not true for super-constant round protocols (even in the random oracle model[4]), and not true for constant-round arguments [6,27]. As such, both of these constructions rely on somewhat non-standard assumptions. In contrast, our VDF relies only on the Fiat-Shamir heuristic for a constant-round proof system—no counter examples are currently known for such proof systems.

We additionally note that before applying the Fiat-Shamir heuristic (i.e., a VDF in the random oracle model), our VDF satisfies computational uniqueness while Pietrzak's satisfies statistical uniqueness. He achieves this by working over the group of signed quadratic residues. We note that we can get statistical uniqueness in this setting using the same idea. Lastly, we emphasize that the concrete proof length and verification time are polynomially higher in our case than that of both Pietrzak and Wesolowski. For a detailed comparison of the parameters, see Sect. 2.3.

PPAD Hardness. PPAD [39] is an important subclass in TFNP [38] (the class of total search problems), most notably known for its complete problem of finding a Nash equilibrium in bimatrix games [14,19]. Understanding whether PPAD contains hard problems is a central open problem and the most common approach for proving hardness was pioneered by Abbot, Kane, and Valiant [5]. They introduced a problem, which [9] termed SINK-OF-VERIFIABLE-LINE (SVL), and showed that it reduces to END-OF-LINE (EOL), a complete problem for PPAD. In SVL, one has to present a function f that can be iterated and each intermediate value can be efficiently verified, but the output of T iterations (where T is some super-polynomial value, referred to as the length of the "line") is hard to compute in polynomial time.

In a beautiful recent work, Choudhuri et al. [15] defined the RELAXED-SINK-OF-VERIFIABLE-LINE (rSVL) problem, and showed that it reduces to EOL, as well. rSVL is a generalization of SVL where one is required to find either the output after many iterations (as in SVL) or an off-chain value that verifies. Choudhuri et al. [15] gave a hard rSVL instance assuming the security of the Fiat-Shamir transformation applied to the sum-check protocol [35] (which is a *polynomial-round* protocol).

The notion of an (r)SVL instance is very related to our notion of a cVDF. The main differences are that a cVDF requires that the gap between the honest computation and the malicious one is tight and that security holds for adversaries that have access to multiple processors running in parallel. As such, the existence of a cVDF (which handles super-polynomially many iterations) directly implies an rSVL instances with "optimal" hardness—namely, one where the number of computational steps required to solve an instance of the problem with a "line" of length T is $(1 - \epsilon) \cdot T$.

---

[4] Although, [40] shows that it does hold in the random oracle model for his particular protocol.

Theorem 1.3 (Informal). *The existence of a cVDF supporting superpolynomially many iterations implies an optimally-hard rSVL instance (which in turn implies that PPAD is hard (on average)).*

Theorem 1.1 readily extends to give a cVDF supporting super-polynomially many iterations by making a Fiat-Shamir assumption for $\omega(1)$-round proof systems. As a consequence, we get an optimally-hard instance of rSVL based on this Fiat-Shamir assumption for $\omega(1)$-round proofs[5] and the repeated squaring assumption. By following the reductions from rSVL to EOL and to finding a Nash equilibrium, we get (based on the same assumptions) hard PPAD and Nash equilibrium instances. We remark that in comparison to the results of Choudhuri et al., we only rely on the Fiat-Shamir assumption for $\omega(1)$-round protocols, whereas they rely on it for a polynomial-round, or at the very least an $\omega(\log n)$-round proof systems (if additionally assuming that #SAT is sub-exponentially hard). On the other hand, we additionally require a computational assumption—namely, the repeated squaring assumption, whereas they do not.[6]

Our method yields PPAD instances satisfying another interesting property: we can generate PPAD (and thus Nash equilibrium problem) instances that can be solved in polynomial time, yet they also require a high sequential running time—that is, they are "depth-robust" moderately-hard instances. As far as we know, this gives the first evidence that PPAD (and thus Nash equilibrium problems) requires high sequential running time to solve (even for easy instances!).

Theorem 1.4 (Informal). *The existence of a cVDF implies a distribution of depth-robust moderately-hard PPAD instances. In particular, there exists a constant d such that for all sufficiently large constants c, there is a distribution over Nash equilibrium problem instances of size n that can be solved in time n^c but cannot be solved in depth $n^{c/d}$ and arbitrary polynomial time.[7]*

Combining Theorems 1.1 and 1.4, we get a depth-robust moderately-hard PPAD instance based on the Fiat-Shamir assumption for constant-round proof systems with inefficient verifiers and the repeated squaring assumption.

1.2   Related Work

In addition to the time lock puzzle of [43] mentioned above, an alternative construction is by Bitansky et al. [8] assuming a strong form of randomized

---

[5] As mentioned above, in general, the Fiat-Shamir assumption is false for super-constant-round proofs. But we state a restricted form of a Fiat-Shamir assumption for super-constant-round proofs with *exponentially small soundness error* which holds in the random oracle model, due to the classic reduction from [26].

[6] We also note that Choudhuri et al. show how to instantiate the hash function in their Fiat-Shamir transformation assuming a class of fully homomorphic encryption schemes has almost-optimal security against quasi-polynomial time adversaries. We leave such instantiations in our context for future work.

[7] If we additionally assume that the repeated squaring assumption is sub-exponentially hard, then the resulting instance cannot be solved in depth $n^{c/d}$ and sub-exponential time.

encodings and the existence of inherently sequential functions. While the time-lock puzzle of [43] is only privately verifiable, Boneh and Naor [12] showed a method to prove that the time-lock puzzle has a solution. Jerschow and Mauve [29] and Lenstra and Wesolowski [33] constructed iteratively sequential functions based on Dwork and Naor's slow function [22] (which is based on hardness of modular exponentiations).

PPAD Hardness. The complexity class PPAD (standing for *Polynomial Parity Arguments on Directed graphs*), introduced by Papadimitriou [39], is one of the central classes in TFNP. It contains the problems that can be shown to be total by a parity argument. This class is famous most notably since the problem of finding a Nash equilibrium in bimatrix games is complete for it [14,19]. The class is formally defined by one of its complete problems END-OF-LINE (EOL).

Bitansky, Paneth, and Rosen [9] introduced the SINK-OF-VERIFIABLE-LINE (SVL) problem and showed that it reduces to the EOL problem (based on Abbot et al. [5] who adapted the reversible computation idea of Bennet [7]). They additionally gave an SVL instance which is hard assuming sub-exponentially secure indistinguishability obfuscation and one-way functions. These underlying assumptions were somewhat relaxed over the years yet remain in the class of obfuscation-type assumptions which are still considered very strong [25,31,32].

Hubáček and Yogev [28] observed that the SINK-OF-VERIFIABLE-LINE actually reduces to a more structured problem, which they termed END-OF-METERED-LINE (EOML), which in turn resides in CLS (standing for *Continuous Local Search*), a subclass of PPAD. As a corollary, all of the above hardness results for PPAD actually hold for CLS.

In an exciting recent work, Choudhuri et al. [15] introduced a relaxation of SVL, termed RELAXED-SVL (rSVL) which still reduces to EOML and therefore can be used to prove hardness of PPAD and CLS. They were able to give a hard rSVL instance based on the sum-check protocol of [35] assuming soundness of the Fiat-Shamir transformation and that #SAT is hard.

Verifiable Delay Functions. VDFs were recently introduced and constructed by Boneh, Bonneau, Bünz, and Fisch [10]. Following that work, additional constructions were given in [23,40,45]. The constructions of Pietrzak [40] and Wesolowski [45] are based on the repeated squaring assumption plus the Fiat-Shamir heuristic, while the construction of De Feo et al. [23] relies on elliptic curves and bilinear pairings. We refer to Boneh et al. [11] for a survey.

VDFs have numerous applications to the design of reliable distributed systems; see [10, Section 2]. Indeed, they are nowadays widely used in the design of reliable and resource efficient blockchains (e.g., in the consensus mechanism of the Chia blockchain [1]) and there is a collaboration [4] between the Ethereum Foundation [2], Protocol Labs [3], and various academic institutions to design better and more efficient VDFs.

Proofs of Sequential Work. Proofs of sequential work, suggested by Mahmoody, Moran, and Vadhan [36], are proof systems where on input a random challenge and time parameter t one can generate a publicly verifiable proof making t sequential computations, yet it is computationally infeasible to find a valid proof in significantly less than t sequential steps. Mahmoody et al. [36] gave the first construction and Cohen and Pietrzak [18] gave a simple and practical construction (both in the random oracle model). A recent work of Döttling et al. [21] constructs an *incremental* PoSW based on [18]. The techniques underlying Döttling et al's construction are related in spirit to ours though the details are very different. See Sect. 2 for a comparison. All of the above constructions of PoSWs do not satisfy uniqueness, which is a major downside for many applications (see [10] for several examples). Indeed, VDFs were introduced exactly to mitigate this issue. Since our construction satisfies (computational) uniqueness, we actually get the first unique incremental PoSW.

Concurrent Works. In a concurrent and independent work, Choudhuri et al. [16] show PPAD-hardness based on the Fiat-Shamir heuristic and the repeated squaring assumption. Their underlying techniques are related to ours since they use a similar tree-based proof merging technique on top of Pietrzak's protocol [40]. However, since they use a ternary tree (while we use a high arity tree) their construction cannot be used to get a continuous VDF (and its applications). Also, for PPAD-hardness, their construction requires Fiat-Shamir for protocols with $\omega(\log \lambda)$ rounds (where λ is the security parameter) while we need Fiat-Shamir for $\omega(1)$-round protocols.

VDFs were also studied in two recent independent works by Döttling et al. [20] and Mahmoody et al. [37]. Both works show negative results for black-box constructions of VDFs in certain regimes of parameters in the random oracle model. The work of Döttling et al. [20] additionally shows that certain VDFs with a somewhat inefficient evaluator can be generically transformed into VDFs where the evaluator has optimal sequential running time. Whether such a transformation exists for cVDFs is left for future work.

2 Technical Overview

We start by informally defining a cVDF. At a high level, a cVDF specifies an iteratively sequential function Eval where each iteration of the function gives a step of computation. Let x_0 be any starting point and $x_t = \mathsf{Eval}^{(t)}(x_0)$ be the tth step or state given by the cVDF. We let B be an upper bound on the total number of steps in the computation, and assume that honest parties have some bounded parallelism polylog(B) while adversarial parties may have parallelism poly(B). For each step $t \leq B$, we require the following properties to hold:

- **Completeness:** x_t can be verified as the tth state in time polylog(t).
- **Adaptive Soundness:** Any value $x_t' \neq x_t$ computed by an adversarial party will not verify as the tth state (even when the starting point x_0 is chosen adaptively). That is, each state is (computationally) unique.
- **Iteratively Sequential:** Given an honestly sampled x_0, adversarial parties cannot compute x_t in time $(1 - \epsilon) \cdot t \cdot \ell$, where ℓ is the time for an honest party to compute a step of the computation.

We require adaptive soundness due to the distributed nature of a cVDF. In particular, suppose a new party starts computing the cVDF after t steps have elapsed. Then, x_t is the effective starting point for that party, and they may compute for t' more steps to obtain a state $x_{t+t'}$. We want to ensure that soundness holds for the computation from x_t to $x_{t+t'}$, so that the next party that starts at $x_{t+t'}$ can trust the validity of $x_{t+t'}$. Note that the above definition does not contain any proofs, but instead the states are verifiable by themselves. In terms of plain VDFs, this verifiability condition is equivalent to the case where the VDF is unique, meaning that the proofs are empty or included implicitly in the output.

To construct a cVDF, we start with a plain VDF. For simplicity in this overview, we assume that this underlying VDF is unique.

A First Attempt. The naïve approach for using a VDF to construct a cVDF is to iterate the VDF as a chain of computations. For any "base difficulty" T, which will be the time to compute a single step, we can use a VDF to do the computation from x_0 to x_T with an associated proof of correctness $\pi_{0 \to T}$. Then, we can start a new VDF instance starting at x_T and compute until x_{2T} with a proof of correctness $\pi_{T \to 2T}$. At this point, anyone can verify that x_{2T} is correct by verifying both $\pi_{0 \to T}$ and $\pi_{T \to 2T}$. We can continue this process indefinitely.

This solution has the property that after t steps, another party can pick up the current value $x_{t \cdot T}$, verify it by checking each of the proofs computed so far, and then continue the VDF chain. In other words, there is no unverified internal state after t steps of the computation. Still, this naïve solution has the following major drawback (violating completeness). The final proof $\pi_{(t-1) \cdot T \to t \cdot T}$ only certifies that computing a step from $x_{(t-1) \cdot T}$ results in $x_{t \cdot T}$ and does not guarantee anything about the computation from x_0 to $x_{(t-1) \cdot T}$. As such, we need to retain and check all proofs $\pi_{0 \to T}, \ldots, \pi_{(t-1) \cdot T \to t \cdot T}$ computed so far to be able to verify $x_{t \cdot T}$. Therefore, both the proof size and verification time scale linearly with t. We note that this idea is not new (e.g., see [10]), but nevertheless it does not solve our problem. Wesolowski [45] partially addresses this issue by showing how to aggregate proofs so the proof size does not grow, but the verification time in his protocol still grows.

One possible idea to overcome the blowup mentioned above is to use generic proof merging techniques. These can combine two different proofs into one that certifies both but whose size and verification time are proportional to that of a single one. Such techniques were given by Valiant [44] and Chung et al. [17]. However, being generic, they rely on strong assumptions and do not give the properties that we need (for example, efficiency and uniqueness). We next look at a promising—yet failed—attempt to overcome this.

A Logarithmic Approach. Since we can implement the above iterated strategy for *any* fixed interval T, we can simply run $\log B$ many independent iterated VDF chains in parallel at the intervals $T = 1, 2, 4, \ldots, 2^{\log B}$. Now say that we want to prove that x_{11} is the correct value eleven steps from the starting point x_0. We just need to verify the proofs $\pi_{0 \to 8}$, $\pi_{8 \to 10}$, and $\pi_{10 \to 11}$. For any number of steps t, we can now verify x_t by verifying only $\log(t)$ many proofs, so we have resolved the major drawbacks! Furthermore, the prover can maintain a small state at each step of the computation by "forgetting" the smaller proofs. For example, after completing a proof $\pi_{0\to 2T}$ of size $2T$, the prover no longer needs to store the proofs $\pi_{0\to T}$ and $\pi_{T\to 2T}$.

Unfortunately, we have given up the distributed nature of a continuous VDF. Specifically, completeness fails to hold. Each "step" of the computation that the prover does to compute x_t with its associated proofs is no longer an independent instance of a single VDF computation. Rather, upon computing x_t, the current prover has some internal state for all of the computations which have not yet completed at step t. Since a VDF only provides a way to prove that the output of each VDF instance is correct, then a new party who wants to pick up the computation has no way to verify the internal states of the unfinished VDF computations. As a result, this solution only works in the case where there is one trusted party maintaining the state of all the current VDF chains over a long period of time. In contrast, a cVDF ensures that there is no internal state at each step of the computation (or equivalently that the internal state is unique and can be verified as part of the output).

At an extremely high level, our continuous VDF builds off of this failed attempt when applied to the protocol of Pietrzak [40]. We make use of the algebraic structure of the underlying repeated squaring computation to ensure that the internal state of the prover is verifiable at every step and can be efficiently continued.

2.1   Adapting Pietrzak's VDF

We next give a brief overview of Pietrzak's sumcheck-style interactive protocol for repeated squaring and the resulting VDF. Let $N = p \cdot q$ where p and q are safe primes and consider the language

$$\mathcal{L}_{N,B} = \{(x,y,t) \mid x,y \in \mathbb{Z}_N^* \text{ and } y = x^{2^t} \bmod N \text{ and } t \le B\}$$

that corresponds to valid repeated squaring instances with at most B exponentiations (where we think of B as smaller than the time to factor N). In order for the prover to prove that $(x,y,t) \in \mathcal{L}_{N,B}$ (corresponding to t steps of the computation), it first computes $u = x^{2^{t/2}}$. It is clearly enough to then prove that $u = x^{2^{t/2}}$ and that $u^{2^{t/2}} = y$. However, recursively proving both statements separately is too expensive. The main observation of Pietrzak is that using a random challenge r from the verifier, one can merge both statements into a single one $u^r y = (x^r u)^{2^{t/2}}$ which is true if and only if the original two statements are true (with high probability over r). We emphasize that proving that $u^r y = (x^r u)^{2^{t/2}}$ has the same form as our original statement, but with difficulty $t/2$. This protocol readily gives a VDF by applying the Fiat-Shamir heuristic [24] on the $\log_2 B$ round interactive proof.

From the above, it is clear that the only internal state that the prover needs to maintain in Pietrzak's VDF consists of the midpoint $u = x^{2^{t/2}}$ and the output $y = x^{2^t}$. Thus, if we want another party to be able to pick up the computation at any time, we need to simultaneously prove the correctness of u in addition to y. Note that proving the correctness of u just requires another independent VDF instance of difficulty $t/2$. This results in a natural recursive tree-based structure where each computation of t steps consists of proving three instances of size $t/2$: $u = x^{2^{t/2}}$, $y = u^{2^{t/2}}$, and $u^r y = (x^r u)^{2^{t/2}}$. Consequently, once these three instances are proven, it directly gives a proof for the "parent" instance $x^{2^t} = y$. Note that this parent proof *only* need to consist of u, y, and a proof that $u^r y = (x^r u)^{2^{t/2}}$ (in particular, it does not require proofs of the first two sub-computations, since they are certified by the proof of the third).

This suggests a high-level framework for making the construction continuous: starting at the root where we want to compute x^{2^t}, recursively compute and prove each of the three sub-instances. Specifically, each step of the cVDF will be a step in the traversal of this tree. At any point when all three sub-instances of a node have been proven, merge the proofs into a proof of the parent node and "forget" the proofs of the sub-instances. This has the two desirable properties we want for a cVDF—first, at any point a new party can verify the state before continuing the computation, since the state only contains the nodes that have been completed; second, due to the structure of the proofs, the proof size at any node is bounded roughly by the height of the tree and hence avoids a blowup in verification time.

Proof Merging. The above approach heavily relies on the proof merging technique discussed above, namely that proofs of sub-instances of a parent node can be efficiently merged into a proof at that parent node. We obtain this due to the structure of the proofs in Pietrzak's protocol. We note that similar proof merging techniques for specific settings were recently given by Döttling et al. [21] (in the context of incremental PoSW) and Choudhuri et al. [15] (in the context of constructing a hard rSVL instance). While their constructions are conceptually similar to ours, our construction for a cVDF introduces many challenges in order to achieve both uniquely verifiable states and a tight gap between honest and malicious evaluation. Döttling et al. [21] build on the Cohen and Pietrzak [18] PoSW and use a tree-based construction to make it incremental. At a high level, [18] is a PoSW based on a variant of Merkle trees, where the public verification procedure consists of a challenge for opening a random path in the tree and checking consistency. The main idea of Döttling et al. is to traverse the tree in a certain way and remember a small intermediate state which enables them to continue the computation incrementally. Moreover, they provide a proof at each step by creating a random challenge which "merges" previously computed challenges. The resulting construction is only a PoSW (where neither the output nor the proof are unique) and therefore does not suffice for our purpose. Choudhuri et al. [15] show how to merge proofs in the context of the #SAT sum-check protocol. There, they modify the #SAT proof system to be incremental by performing many additional recursive sub-computations, which is sufficient for their setting but in ours would cause a large gap between honest and malicious evaluation. We note that our method of combining proofs by proving a related statement is reminiscent of the approach of [15].

Before discussing the technical details of our tree-based construction, we first go over modifications we make to Pietrzak's interactive protocol. Specifically, we discuss adaptive soundness, and we show how to achieve tight sequentiality (meaning that for any T, computing the VDF with difficulty T cannot be done significantly faster than T) in order to use it for our cVDF.

Achieving Adaptive Soundness. In order to show soundness, we requires the verifier to be able to efficiently check that the starting point of any computation is a valid generator of QR_N. To achieve this, we use the fact that there is an efficient way to test if x generates QR_N *given the square root of x* (see Fact 3.6). As a result, we work with the square roots of elements in our protocol, which slightly changes the language. Namely, x, y are now square roots and $(x, y, t) \in \mathcal{L}_{N,B}$ if $(x^2)^{2^t} = y^2 \mod N$.[8] We note that, following [40], working in QR_N^+, the group of signed quadratic residues, would also give adaptive soundness (without including the square roots). This holds as soundness of Pietrzak's protocol can be based on the low order assumption, and QR_N^+ has no low order elements [11].[9]

Bounding the Fraction of Intermediate Proofs. Recall that to compute $y = x^{2^t}$ using the VDF of Pietrzak for our proposed cVDF, the honest party recursively proves three different computations of $t/2$ squarings, so that each step will be verifiable. This results in computing for *at least* time $t^{\log_2 3}$, since it corresponds to computing the leaves of a ternary tree of depth $\log_2(t)$, and each leaf requires a squaring. Note that this does not even consider the overhead of computing each proof, only the squarings. However, an adversary (even without parallelism) can shortcut this method and compute the underlying VDF to prove that $y = x^{2^t}$ by computing roughly t squarings (and then computing the proof, which has relatively low overhead).

We deal with this issue by reducing the fraction of generating the intermediate proofs in Pietrzak's protocol. Our solution is to (somewhat paradoxically) modify Pietrzak's protocol to keep additional state, which we will need to verify. Specifically, we observe that t squarings can be split into k different segments. To prove that $y = x^{2^t}$, the prover splits the computation into k segments each with difficulty t/k:

$$x_1 = x^{2^{t/k}}, \quad x_2 = x^{2^{2t/k}}, \quad \ldots, \quad x_{k-1} = x^{2^{(k-1)t/k}}, \quad x_k = x^{2^t} = y.$$

Using a random challenge $(r_1, \ldots, r_k)$ from the verifier, we are able to combine these k segments into a single statement $(\prod_{i=1}^{k}(x_{i-1})^{r_i})^{t/k} = \prod_{i=1}^{k}(x_i)^{r_i}$ (where $x_0 = x$) which is true if and only if *all* of the segments are true (with high probability over the challenge). We call the combined statement the *sketch*.[10] Now

---

[8] Giving the square root x is the cause of our computational uniqueness guarantee, since a different square root for x^2 would verify. As mentioned, working over QR_N^+ would prevent this attack and give information theoretic uniqueness, as in [40].

[9] We thank the anonymous EUROCRYPT reviewers for pointing out that Pietrzak's protocol satisfies adaptive soundness using QR_N^+.

[10] The name sketch is inspired by the notion of a sketch in algorithms, which refers to a random linear projection.

in the recursive tree-based structure outlined above, a computation of t steps consists of proving $k + 1$ instances of size t/k. By choosing k to be proportional to the security parameter λ, the total fraction of extra proofs in the honest computation of t steps is now sublinear in t. As an additional benefit when $k = \lambda$, we note that the interactive protocol has $\log_\lambda B \in O(1)$ rounds if B is a fixed polynomial in λ (as opposed to $O(\log \lambda)$ rounds when $k = 2$ corresponding to Pietrzak's protocol). Applying the Fiat-Shamir heuristic to a constant-round protocol is a more standard assumption.[11]

Bounding the Overhead of Each Step. Even though we have bounded the total fraction of extra nodes that the honest party has to compute, this does not suffice to achieve the tight gap between honest and adversarial computation for our proposed cVDF. Specifically, the honest computation has an additive (fixed) polynomial overhead λ^d—for example, to check validity of the inputs and sometimes compute the sketch node—an adversary does not have to do so at each step. To compensate for this, we make each base step of the cVDF larger: namely, we truncate the tree. The effect of this is that a single step now takes time $\lambda^{d'}$ for $d' > d$.

2.2   Constructing a Continuous VDF

As outlined above, our main insight is designing a cVDF based on a tree structure where each intermediate state of the computation can be verified and proofs of the computation can be efficiently merged. More concretely, the steps of computation correspond to a specific traversal of a $(k+1)$-ary tree of height $h = \log_k B$. Each node in the tree is associated to a statement (x, y, t, π) for the underlying VDF, where $y = x^{2^t}$ and π is the corresponding proof of correctness. We call x the node's input, y its output, π the proof, and t the difficulty. The difficulty is determined by its height in the tree, namely, a node at distance l from the root has difficulty $t = k^{h-l}$ (so nodes closer to the leaves take less time to compute).

In more detail, the tree is defined as follows. Starting at the root with input x_0 and difficulty $t = k^h$, we divide it into k segments $x_1, \ldots, x_k$, analogous to our VDF construction. These form the inputs and outputs of its first k children: its ith child will have input x_{i-1} and output x_i, and requires a proof that $(x_{i-1})^{t/k} = x_i$. Its $(k + 1)$-st child corresponds to the sketch, namely a node where the k statements of the siblings are merged into a single statement. Recursively splitting statements this way gives the statement at each node in the tree, until reaching the leaves where squaring can be done directly. Note that with this structure, only the leaves require computation—the statement of nodes at greater heights can be deduced from the statements of their children (which gives us a way to efficiently merge proofs "up" the tree as we described above).

As a result, we would like each step of computation in the cVDF to correspond to computing the statement of a single leaf. Accomplishing this requires being

---

[11] We are talking about an instantiation of the VDF in the plain model using a concrete hash function. The resulting VDF is provably secure in the random oracle model for any k.

able to compute the input x of the leaf from the previous state (from which y can be computed via squaring). By the structure of our tree, we observe that this only requires knowing a (small) subset of nodes that were *already* computed, which we call the *frontier*. The frontier of a leaf s, denoted frontier(s), contains all the left siblings of its ancestors, including the left siblings of s itself.[12] Therefore, a state in the computation contains a leaf label s and the statements associated with the nodes in frontier(s), which contains at most $k \cdot \log_k(B)$ nodes. A single step of our continuous VDF, given a state $v = (s, \text{frontier}(s))$, first verifies v and then computes the next state $v' = (s', \text{frontier}(s'))$ where s' is the next leaf after s. See Fig. 1 for an illustration of computing the next state.

This is the basic template for our continuous VDF. Next, we discuss some of the challenges that come up related to efficiency and security.

Ensuring the Iteratively Sequential Property. Recall that we want to obtain a tight gap between honest and malicious evaluation of the continuous VDF for *any* number of steps. A priori, it seems that computing a sketch for each node in the tree adds a significant amount of complexity to the honest evaluation. To illustrate this, suppose a malicious evaluator wants to compute the statement (x, y, t, π) at the root. This can be done by skipping the sketch nodes for intermediate states and only computing a proof for the final output $y = x^{2^t}$, which in total involves t squarings (corresponding to computing the leaves of a k-ary tree of height $\log_k t$) along with the sketch node for the root. However, for an honest evaluator, this requires computing $(k+1)^{\log_k t}$ leaf nodes (corresponding to every leaf in a $(k+1)$-ary tree of height $\log_k t$). Therefore, the ratio is $\alpha = ((k+1)/k)^{\log_k t}$. In order to get the tight gap, we choose k to be proportional to the security parameter so that $\alpha = (1 + o(1)) \cdot t$. This change is crucial (as we eluded towards above), as otherwise if k is a constant, the relative overhead would be significant. Indeed, in Pietrzak's protocol, $k = 2$ and computing the sketch node constitutes a constant fraction of the computation.

2.3   The Efficiency of Our Construction

In this section, we briefly compare the efficiency of our constructions to previous ones which are based on repeated squaring. Specifically, we discuss Wesolowki's VDF [45] (denoted WVDF), Pietrzak's VDF [40] (denoted PVDF), in comparison to our cVDF using a tree of arity k (denoted k-cVDF) and the VDF underlying it (denoted k-VDF), which is simply Pietrzak's VDF with arity k.

For proof length corresponding to t squares, the WVDF proof is just a single group element, and the PVDF proof consists of $\log_2(t)$ group elements. For the k-VDF, generalizing Pietrzak's VDF to use a tree with arity k results in a proof with $(k-1) \cdot \log_k(t)$ group elements. Finally, the k-cVDF output consists of a frontier with at most $(k-1)$ proofs for a k-VDF in each of $\log_k(t)$ levels of the tree, resulting in $(k-1)^2(\log_k(t))^2$ group elements. In all cases, verifying a proof

---

[12] The term frontier is standard in the algorithms literature. Many other names have been used to describe this notion, such as dangling nodes in [17] and unfinished nodes in [21].

with n group elements requires doing $O(n \cdot \lambda)$ squares. For prover efficiency, the honest prover can compute the proof in the time to do $t(1 + o(t))$ squares (when $t \in \text{poly}(\lambda)$ and $k \in \Omega(\log \lambda)$ for the k-cVDF).

In the full cVDF construction, we set k to be equal to λ for simplicity, but as the above shows, different values of k give rise to different efficiency trade-offs.

3   Preliminaries

In this section, we give relevant definitions and notation. Additional preliminaries, including definitions of interactive protocols and the Fiat-Shamir heuristic, are deferred to the full version.

3.1   Verifiable, Sequential, and Iteratively Sequential Functions

In this section, we define different properties of functions which will be useful in subsequent sections when we define unique VDFs (Definition 5.1) and continuous VDFs (Definition 6.1). All of our definitions will be in the public parameter model. We start by defining a verifiable function.

Definition 3.1 (Verifiable Functions). *Let $B \colon \mathbb{N} \to \mathbb{N}$. A B-sound verifiable function is a tuple of algorithms* (Gen, Eval, Verify) *where* Gen *is PPT,* Eval *is deterministic, and* Verify *is deterministic polynomial-time, satisfying the following property:*

- **Perfect Completeness.** *For every $\lambda \in \mathbb{N}$,* pp $\in \text{Supp}\big(\text{Gen}(1^\lambda)\big)$, *and $x \in \{0,1\}^*$, it holds that*

$$\text{Verify}(1^\lambda, \text{pp}, x, \text{Eval}(1^\lambda, \text{pp}, x)) = 1.$$

- **B-Soundness.** *For every non-uniform algorithm $\mathcal{A} = \{\mathcal{A}_\lambda\}_{\lambda \in \mathbb{N}}$ such that* $\text{size}(A_\lambda) \in \text{poly}(B(\lambda))$ *for all $\lambda \in \mathbb{N}$, there exists a negligible function* negl *such that for every $\lambda \in \mathbb{N}$ it holds that*

$$\Pr\left[\begin{array}{l} \text{pp} \leftarrow \text{Gen}(1^\lambda) \\ (x,y) \leftarrow \mathcal{A}_\lambda(\text{pp}) \end{array} : \text{Verify}(1^\lambda, \text{pp}, x, y) = 1 \wedge \text{Eval}(1^\lambda, \text{pp}, x) \neq y \right] \leq \text{negl}(\lambda).$$

Next, we define a sequential function. At a high level, this is a function f implemented by an algorithm Eval that takes input (x, t), such that computing $f(x, t)$ requires time roughly t, even with parallelism. Our formal definition is inspired by [10]. Intuitively, it requires that any algorithm $\mathcal{A}_{0,\lambda}$ which first pre-processes the public parameters cannot output a circuit $\mathcal{A}_1$ satisfying the following. Upon receipt of a freshly sampled input x, $\mathcal{A}_1$ outputs a value y and a difficulty t, where y is the output of Eval on x for difficulty t, where t is sufficiently larger than its depth. This captures the notion that $\mathcal{A}_1$ manages to compute y in less than t time, even with large width.

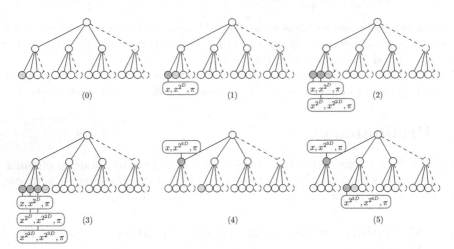

Fig. 1. The first six states of our continuous VDF with $k = 3$ and base difficulty $D = k^{d'}$ for a constant d'. In each tree, the segment nodes are given by solid lines and the sketch nodes by dashed lines. The yellow node is the current leaf, and the pink nodes are its frontier. The values in blue are contain (x, y, π) for the corresponding node. The proofs π at leaf nodes with input x and output y correspond to the underlying VDF proof that $x^{2^D} = y$, and the proofs at each higher node consist of its segments (outputs of k first children) and of the proof of the sketch node (the $(k+1)$st child). (Color figure online)

Definition 3.2. *Let $D, B, \ell \colon \mathbb{N} \to \mathbb{N}$ and let $\epsilon \in (0, 1)$. A (D, B, ℓ, ϵ)-sequential function is a tuple* (Gen, Sample, Eval) *where* Gen *and* Sample *are PPT,* Eval *is deterministic, and the following properties hold:*

- **Honest Evaluation.** *There exists a uniform circuit family $\{C_{\lambda,t}\}_{\lambda,t\in\mathbb{N}}$ such that $C_{\lambda,t}$ computes* Eval$(1^\lambda, \cdot, (\cdot, t))$, *and for all sufficiently large $\lambda \in \mathbb{N}$ and $D(\lambda) \leq t \leq B(\lambda)$, it holds that* depth$(C_{\lambda,t}) = t \cdot \ell(\lambda)$ *and* width$(C_{\lambda,t}) \in$ poly(λ).
- **Sequentiality.** *For all non-uniform algorithms $\mathcal{A}_0 = \{\mathcal{A}_{0,\lambda}\}_{\lambda\in\mathbb{N}}$ such that* size$(\mathcal{A}_{0,\lambda}) \in$ poly$(B(\lambda))$ *for all $\lambda \in \mathbb{N}$, there exists a negligible function* negl *such that for every $\lambda \in \mathbb{N}$,*

$$\Pr\left[\begin{matrix} \mathsf{pp} \leftarrow \mathsf{Gen}(1^\lambda) \\ \mathcal{A}_1 \leftarrow \mathcal{A}_{0,\lambda}(\mathsf{pp}) \\ x \leftarrow \mathsf{Sample}(1^\lambda, \mathsf{pp}) \\ (t, y) \leftarrow \mathcal{A}_1(x) \end{matrix} : \begin{matrix} \mathsf{Eval}(1^\lambda, \mathsf{pp}, (x, t)) = y \\ \wedge\ \mathsf{depth}(\mathcal{A}_1) \leq (1 - \epsilon) \cdot t \cdot \ell(\lambda) \\ \wedge\ t \geq D(\lambda) \end{matrix}\right] \leq \mathsf{negl}(\lambda).$$

Next, we define an iteratively sequential function. This is a function f implemented by an algorithm Eval, such that the t-wise composition of f cannot be computed faster than computing f sequentially t times, even using parallelism. We also require that the length of the output of f is bounded, so that it does not grow with the number of compositions.

Definition 3.3 (Iteratively Sequential Function). *Let* $D, B, \ell \colon \mathbb{N} \to \mathbb{N}$ *be functions and let* $\epsilon \in (0,1)$. *A tuple of algorithms* (Gen, Sample, Eval) *is a* (D, B, ℓ, ϵ)-*iteratively sequential function if* Gen *and* Sample *are PPT,* Eval *is deterministic, and the following properties hold.*

- **Length Bounded.** *There exists a polynomial* m *such that for every* $\lambda \in \mathbb{N}$ *and* $x \in \{0,1\}^*$, *it holds that* $\left| \mathsf{Eval}(1^\lambda, \mathsf{pp}, x) \right| \leq m(\lambda)$. *We define* $\mathsf{Eval}^{(\cdot)}$ *to be the function that takes as input* $1^\lambda, \mathsf{pp}$, *and* (x, T) *and represents the* T-*wise composition given by*

$$\mathsf{Eval}^{(T)}(1^\lambda, \mathsf{pp}, x) \stackrel{\mathsf{def}}{=} \underbrace{\mathsf{Eval}(1^\lambda, \mathsf{pp}, \cdot) \circ \ldots \circ \mathsf{Eval}(1^\lambda, \mathsf{pp}, \cdot)}_{T \ times}(x)$$

  and note that this function is also length bounded.
- **Iteratively sequential.** *The tuple* (Gen, Sample, $\mathsf{Eval}^{(\cdot)}$) *is a* (D, B, ℓ, ϵ)-*sequential function.*

Remark 3.4 (Decoupling size and depth). We note that one can also consider a generalization of a (D, B, ℓ, ϵ)-sequential function to a $(D, U, B, \ell, \epsilon)$-sequential function (and thus iteratively sequential functions), where the size of $\mathcal{A}_{0,\lambda}$ remains bounded by $\mathrm{poly}(B(\lambda))$, but the parameter t output by $\mathcal{A}_1$ must be at most $U(\lambda)$.

3.2   Repeated Squaring Assumption

The repeated squaring assumption (henceforth, the RSW assumption[13]) roughly says that there is no parallel algorithm that can perform t squarings modulo an RSA integer N significantly faster than just performing t squarings sequentially. This implicitly assumes that N cannot be factored efficiently. This assumption has been very useful for various applications (e.g., time-lock puzzles [43], reliable benchmarking [13], and timed commitments [12,34] and to date there is no known strategy that beats the naive sequential one.

Define RSW = (RSW.Gen, RSW.Sample, RSW.Eval) as follows.

- $N \leftarrow \mathsf{RSW.Gen}(1^\lambda)$:
  Sample random primes p', q' from $[2^\lambda, 2^{\lambda+1})$ such that $p = 2p' + 1$ and $q = 2q' + 1$ are prime, and output $N = p \cdot q$.
- $x \leftarrow \mathsf{RSW.Sample}(1^\lambda, N)$:
  Sample and output a random element $g \leftarrow \mathbb{Z}_N^*$.
- $y \leftarrow \mathsf{RSW.Eval}(1^\lambda, N, g)$:
  Output $y = g^2 \bmod N$.

Assumption 3.5 (RSW Assumption). *Let* $D, B \colon \mathbb{N} \to \mathbb{N}$. *The* (D, B)-*RSW assumption is that there exists a polynomial* $\ell \in \mathbb{N} \to \mathbb{N}$ *and constant* $\epsilon \in (0,1)$ *such that* RSW *is a* (D, B, ℓ, ϵ)-*iteratively sequential function.*

---

[13] The assumption is usually called the RSW assumption after Rivest, Shamir, and Wagner who used it to construct time-lock puzzles [43].

Note that the RSW assumption implies that factoring is hard. Namely, no adversary can factor an integer $N = p \cdot q$ where p and q are large "safe" primes (a prime p is safe if $p - 1$ has two factors, 2 and p', for some prime number $p' \in [2^\lambda, 2^{\lambda+1})$).

3.3 Number Theory Facts

For $N \in \mathbb{N}$ and any $x \in \mathbb{Z}_N$, we use the notation $|x|_N$ to denote $\min \{x, N - x\}$. Next, we state three standard useful facts. The proofs are deferred to the full version.

Fact 3.6. *Let* $N \in \mathrm{Supp}\left(\mathsf{RSW.Gen}(1^\lambda)\right)$. *Then, for* $\mu \in \mathbb{Z}_N^\star$, *it holds that* $\langle \mu \rangle = \mathsf{QR}_N$ *if and only if there exists an* $x \in \mathbb{Z}_N^\star$ *such that* $\mu = x^2$ *and* $\gcd(x \pm 1, N) = 1$.

Fact 3.7 ([41]). *There exists a polynomial time algorithm* $\mathcal{A}$ *such that for any* $\lambda \in \mathbb{N}$, N *in the support of* $\mathsf{RSW.Gen}(1^\lambda)$, *and* $\mu, x, x' \in \mathbb{Z}_N$, *if* $\mu = x^2 = x'^2$ *and* $x' \notin \{x, -x\}$, *then* $\mathcal{A}(1^\lambda, N, (\mu, x, x'))$ *outputs* (p, q) *such that* $N = p \cdot q$.

Fact 3.8. *Let* $N \in \mathrm{Supp}\left(\mathsf{RSW.Gen}(1^\lambda)\right)$ *and let* $\langle x \rangle = \mathsf{QR}_N$. *Then, for any* $i \in \mathbb{N}$, *it holds that* $\langle x^{2^i} \rangle = \mathsf{QR}_N$.

4 Interactive Proof for Repeated Squaring

In this section, we give an interactive proof for a language representing t repeated squarings. As discussed in Sect. 2, this protocol is based on that of [40]. We start with an overview. The common input includes an integer t and two values $\widehat{x}_0, \widehat{y} \in \mathbb{Z}_N^\star$, where, for the purpose of this overview, the goal is for the prover to convince the verifier that $\widehat{y} = (\widehat{x}_0)^{2^t} \bmod N$. The protocol is defined recursively.

Starting with a statement $(\widehat{x}_0, \widehat{y}, t)$, where we assume for simplicity that t is a power of k, the prover splits x_0 into k "segments", where each segment is t/k "steps" of the computation of $(\widehat{x}_0)^{2^t} \bmod N$. The ith segment is recursively defined as the value $(\widehat{x}_{i-1})^{2^{t/k}}$. In other words, $\widehat{x}_i = (\widehat{x}_0)^{2^{i \cdot t/k}}$ for all $i \in \{0, 1, \ldots, k\}$. If one can verify the values of $\widehat{x}_1, \ldots, \widehat{x}_k$, then one can also readily verify that $\widehat{y} = (\widehat{x}_0)^{2^t} \bmod N$. To verify the values of $\widehat{x}_1, \ldots, \widehat{x}_k$ efficiently we rely on interaction and require the prover to convince the verifier that the values $\widehat{x}_1, \ldots, \widehat{x}_k$ are consistent (in some sense) under a random linear relation. To this end, the prover and verifier engage in a second protocol to prove a modified statement $(\widehat{x}_0', \widehat{y}', t/k)$ which combines all the segments and should only be true if all segments are true (with high probability). The modified statement is proved in the same way, where the exponent t/k is divided by k with each new statement. This process is continued $\log_k t$ times until the statement to verify can be done by direct computation.

For soundness of our protocol, we need to bound the probability of a cheating prover jumping from a false statement in the beginning of the protocol to a true statement in one of the subsequent protocols. One technical point is that to accomplish this, we work in the subgroup QR_N of $\mathbb{Z}_N^\star$ and thus we want the starting point $\widehat{x}_0$ to generate QR_N. To accommodate this, we let the prover provide a square root of every group element as a witness to the fact that it is in QR_N (actually, by Fact 3.8, this will imply that all group elements generate QR_N). Therefore, rather than working with $\widehat{x}_0$ and $\widehat{y}$ directly, we work with their square roots x_0 and y, respectively. Hence, the common input consists of an integer t and (x_0, y), where the goal is actually to prove that $y^2 = (x_0^2)^{2^t} = x_0^{2^{t+1}} \bmod N$.

Note that, in general, the square root x_0 is not unique in $\mathbb{Z}_N^\star$ for a given square x_0^2. Indeed, there are 4 square roots $\pm x_0, \pm x_0'$. In our protocol, the computationally bounded prover can compute only two of them, either $\pm x_0$ or $\pm x_0'$, as otherwise, by Fact 3.7 we could use the prover to factor N. Among the two square roots that the prover can compute, we canonically decide that the prover must use the smaller one. This gives rise to our definition of a *valid* element x: $x^2 \bmod N$ generates QR_N and $x = |x|_N$, formally defined in Definition 4.1.

4.1   Protocol

Before presenting the protocol, we first define the language. Toward that goal, we start with the formal definition of a valid element.

Definition 4.1 (Valid element). *For any $N \in \mathbb{N}$ and $x \in \{0,1\}^*$, we say that x is a* valid element *if $x \in \mathbb{Z}_N^\star$, $\langle x^2 \rangle = \mathsf{QR}_N$, and $x = |x|_N$. We say that a sequence of elements $(x_1, \ldots, x_\ell)$ is a* valid sequence *if each element x_i is a valid element.*

By Fact 3.6, whenever N is in the support of $\mathsf{RSW.Gen}(1^\lambda)$, validity can be tested in polynomial time by verifying that $x = |x|_N$, and that $\gcd(x \pm 1, N) = 1$ (and outputting 1 if and only if all checks pass). This algorithm naturally extends to one that receives as input a sequence of pairs and verifies each separately.

The language for our interactive proof, $\mathcal{L}_{N,B}$, is parametrized by integers $N \in \mathsf{Supp}\left(\mathsf{RSW.Gen}(1^\lambda)\right)$ and $B = B(\lambda)$, and it is defined as:

$$\mathcal{L}_{N,B} = \left\{ (x_0, y, t) : \begin{array}{l} y^2 = (x_0)^{2^{t+1}} \bmod N \text{ if } x_0 \text{ is valid and } t \leq B, \\ y = \bot \text{ otherwise} \end{array} \right\}.$$

Intuitively, $\mathcal{L}_{N,B}$ should be thought of as the language of elements x_0, y where x_0 is valid and $x_0^{2^{t+1}} = y^2 \bmod N$. To be well-defined on any possible statement with $x_0, y \in \mathbb{Z}_N^\star$ and $t \in \mathbb{N}$, we include statements with invalid elements x_0 in the language. Since the verifier can test validity efficiently, this language still enforces that valid elements represent repeated squaring.

Our protocol $\Pi_{\lambda,k,d}$, given in Fig. 2, is parametrized by the security parameter λ, as well as integers $k = k(\lambda)$ and $d = d(\lambda)$, where k is the number of segments into which we split each statement and d is a "cut-off" parameter that defines the base of the recursive protocol.

INTERACTIVE PROOF $\Pi_{\lambda,k,d} = (P, V)$ ON COMMON INPUT (x_0, y, t)

Prover $P \to$ Verifier V:

1. If x_0 is an invalid element (Definition 4.1), $t \leq k^d$, or $t > B$, send $\mathsf{msg}_P = \bot$ to V.
2. Otherwise, for $i \in [k-1]$, compute $x_i = \left| x_0^{2^{i \cdot t/k}} \right|_N$.
3. Send $\mathsf{msg}_P = (x_1, \ldots, x_{k-1})$ to V.

Verifier $V \to$ Prover P:

1. If x_0 is an invalid element or $t > B$, output 1 if $\mathsf{msg}_P = y = \bot$ and 0 otherwise.
2. If $|y|_N$ is invalid, output 0.
3. If $t \leq k^d$, output 1 if both $y^2 = (x_0)^{2^{t+1}} \bmod N$ and $\mathsf{msg}_P = \bot$ and output 0 otherwise.
4. Output 0 if msg_P is an invalid sequence.
5. Send $\mathsf{msg}_V = (r_1, \ldots, r_k) \leftarrow [2^\lambda]^k$ to P.

Prover $P \leftrightarrow$ Verifier V:

1. Let $x_0' = \left| \prod_{i=1}^k x_{i-1}^{r_i} \right|_N$ and $y' = \left| \prod_{i=1}^k x_i^{r_i} \right|_N$, where $x_k = y$. Note that both P and V can efficiently compute x_0', y' given $\mathsf{msg}_P, \mathsf{msg}_V$, and the common inputs. If x_0' is invalid, let $y' = \bot$.
2. Output the result of $\Pi_{\lambda,k,d}$ on common input $(x_0', y', t/k)$.

Fig. 2. Interactive proof $\Pi_{\lambda,k,d}$ for $\mathcal{L}_{N,B}$

We show the following theorem, stating that $\Pi_{\lambda,k,d}$ is an interactive proof for the language $\mathcal{L}_{N,B}$, by showing completeness and soundness. Furthermore, we prove an additional property which roughly shows that any cheating prover cannot deviate in a specific way from the honest prover strategy even for statements in the language. Due to lack of space, the proof is deferred to the full version.

Theorem 4.2. *For any* $\lambda \in \mathbb{N}$, $k = k(\lambda)$, $d = d(\lambda)$, $B = B(\lambda)$, *and* $N \in$ Supp $\big(\mathsf{RSW.Gen}(1^\lambda)\big)$, *the protocol* $\Pi_{\lambda,k,d}$ *(given in Fig. 2) is a* $(\log_k(B) - d) \cdot 3/2^\lambda$*-sound interactive proof for* $\mathcal{L}_{N,B}$.

5   Unique Verifiable Delay Function

In this section, we use the Fiat-Shamir heuristic to transform the interactive proof for the language $\mathcal{L}_{N,B}$ corresponding to repeated squaring (given in Sect. 4) into a unique VDF.

Definition 5.1 (Unique Verifiable Delay Function). *A* (D, B, ℓ, ϵ)*-unique verifiable delay function (uVDF) is a tuple* (Gen, Sample, Eval, Verify) *where* Eval *outputs a value* y *and a proof* π, *such that* (Gen, Sample, Eval) *is a* (D, B, ℓ, ϵ)*-sequential function and* (Gen, Eval, Verify) *is a* B*-sound verifiable function.*

5.1   Construction

For parameters k, d we define $(P_{\mathsf{FS}}, V_{\mathsf{FS}})$ to be the result of applying the Fiat-Shamir transformation to the protocol $\Pi_{\lambda,k,d}$ for $\mathcal{L}_{N,B}$ relative to some hash family $\mathcal{H}$. At a high level, this construction computes repeated squares and then uses P_{FS} and V_{FS} to prove and verify that this is done correctly.

We start by defining helper algorithms in Fig. 3 based on the interactive protocol of Sect. 4. For notational convenience, we explicitly write algorithms FS-Prove and FS-Verify, which take $\mathsf{pp} = (N, B, k, d, \mathsf{hash})$ as input, as well as $((x_0, t), y)$, where (N, B, k, d) correspond to the parameters of the non-interactive protocol and language, hash is the hash function sampled from the hash family $\mathcal{H}$ when applying the FS transform to $\Pi_{\lambda,k,d}$, and $((x_0, t), y)$ correspond to the statements of the language. We additionally define an efficient algorithm Sketch that outputs the statement for the recursive step in the interactive proof $\Pi_{\lambda,k,d}$.

We emphasize that the algorithms in Fig. 3 are a restatement of the interactive protocol from Sect. 4 after applying the FS transform, given here only for ease of reading.

$\mathsf{Sketch}(\mathsf{pp}, (x_0, t), y, \mathsf{msg})$:
1. Parse $\mathsf{msg} = (x_1, \ldots, x_{k-1})$ and let $x_k = y$.
2. Let $(r_1, \ldots, r_k) = \mathsf{hash}(\mathsf{pp}, (x_0, t), y, \mathsf{msg})$.
3. Let $x_0' = \left| \prod_{i=1}^{k} x_{i-1}^{r_i} \right|_N$ and $y' = \left| \prod_{i=1}^{k} x_i^{r_i} \right|_N$.
4. If x_0' is invalid, let $y' = \bot$.
5. Output (x_0', y').

$\mathsf{FS\text{-}Prove}(\mathsf{pp}, (x_0, t), y)$:
1. If x_0 is an invalid element (Definition 4.1), $t \le k^d$, or $t > B$, output $\bot$.
2. Let $\mathsf{msg} = (x_1, \ldots, x_{k-1})$ where $x_i = \left| (x_0)^{2^{i \cdot t/k}} \right|_N$.
3. Compute $(x_0', y') = \mathsf{Sketch}(\mathsf{pp}, (x_0, t), y, \mathsf{msg})$.
4. Output $\pi = (\mathsf{msg}, \pi')$ where $\pi' = \mathsf{FS\text{-}Prove}(\mathsf{pp}, (x_0', t/k), y')$.

$\mathsf{FS\text{-}Verify}(\mathsf{pp}, (x_0, t), y, \pi)$:
1. If x_0 is an invalid element or $t > B$, output 1 if $y = \pi = \bot$ and 0 otherwise.
2. If $|y|_N$ is an invalid element, output 0.
3. If $t \le k^d$, output 1 if both $y^2 = (x_0)^{2^{t+1}} \bmod N$ and $\pi = \bot$ and output 0 otherwise.
4. Parse π as (msg, π'), and output 0 if msg is an invalid sequence.
5. Compute $(x_0', y') = \mathsf{Sketch}(\mathsf{pp}, (x_0, t), y, \mathsf{msg})$.
6. Output $\mathsf{FS\text{-}Verify}(\mathsf{pp}, (x_0', t/k), y', \pi')$.

Fig. 3. Helper algorithms for VDF for $\mathsf{pp} = (N, B, k, d, \mathsf{hash})$.

Next, we give a construction uVDF of a unique VDF consisting of algorithms (uVDF.Gen, uVDF.Sample, uVDF.Eval, uVDF.Verify) relative to a function $B \colon \mathbb{N} \to \mathbb{N}$.

- pp ← uVDF.Gen(1^λ):
  Sample $N \leftarrow$ RSW.Gen(1^λ), hash ← $\mathcal{H}$, let $k = \lambda$, $B = B(\lambda)$, and let d be
  a constant which will be specified in the proof of sequentiality (in the full
  version), and output pp $= (N, B, k, d, \mathsf{hash})$.
- $x_0 \leftarrow$ uVDF.Sample(1^λ, pp):
  Sample and output a random element $x_0 \leftarrow \mathbb{Z}_N^\star$ such that $\gcd(x_0 \pm 1, N) = 1$
  and $x_0 = |x_0|_N$.[14]
- $(y, \pi) \leftarrow$ uVDF.Eval(1^λ, pp, (x_0, t)):
  If x_0 is an invalid element, output $(\bot, \bot)$. If $t \le k^d$, compute $y = \left|x_0^{2^t}\right|_N$ and
  output $(y, \bot)$.
  Otherwise, compute $x_i = \left|(x_0)^{i \cdot t/k}\right|_N$ for $i \in [k]$ and let msg $= (x_1, \ldots, x_{k-1})$
  and $y = x_k$. Let $(x_0', y') = \mathsf{Sketch}(\mathsf{pp}, (x_0, t), y, \mathsf{msg})$. Finally, output (y, π)
  where $\pi = (\mathsf{msg}, \pi')$ and $\pi' = \mathsf{FS\text{-}Prove}(\mathsf{pp}, (x_0', t/k), y')$.
- $b \leftarrow$ uVDF.Verify(1^λ, pp, (x_0, t), (y, π)):
  If x_0 is an invalid element or $t > B$, output 1 if $y = \pi = \bot$ and 0
  if this is not the case. If y is invalid, then output 0. Otherwise, output
  $\mathsf{FS\text{-}Verify}(\mathsf{pp}, (x_0, t), y, \pi)$.

We prove the following theorem. Due to lack of space, the proof is deferred to
the full version.

Theorem 5.2. *Let $D, B, \alpha \colon \mathbb{N} \to \mathbb{N}$ be functions satisfying $D(\lambda) \in \omega(\lambda^2)$,
$B(\lambda) \in 2^{O(\lambda)}$, and $\alpha(\lambda) \le \lceil \log_\lambda(B(\lambda)) \rceil$. Suppose that the α-round strong
FS assumption holds and the (D, B)-RSW assumption holds for polynomial
$\ell \colon \mathbb{N} \to \mathbb{N}$ and constant $\epsilon \in (0, 1)$. Then, for any constants $\delta > 0$ and $\epsilon' > \frac{\epsilon + \delta}{1 + \delta}$
it holds that uVDF is a $(D, B, (1 + \delta) \cdot \ell, \epsilon')$-unique verifiable delay function.*

6 Continuous Verifiable Delay Function

In this section, we construct a cVDF. Intuitively, this is an iteratively sequential
function where every intermediate state is verifiable. Throughout this section,
we denote by $\mathsf{Eval}^{(\cdot)}$ the composed function which takes as input 1^λ, pp, and
(x, T), and runs the T-wise composition of $\mathsf{Eval}(1^\lambda, \mathsf{pp}, \cdot)$ on input x.

We first give the formal definition of a cVDF. In the following definition,
the completeness requirement says that if v_0 is an honestly generated starting
state, then the Verify will accept the state given by $\mathsf{Eval}^{(T)}(1^\lambda, \mathsf{pp}, v_0)$ for any T.
Note that when coupled with soundness, this implies that completeness holds
with high probability for any intermediate state generated by a computationally
bounded adversary.

Definition 6.1 (Continuous Verifiable Delay Function). *Let $B, \ell \colon \mathbb{N} \to \mathbb{N}$
and $\epsilon \in (0, 1)$. A (B, ℓ, ϵ)-continuous verifiable delay function (cVDF) is a*

---

[14] We note that x_0 uniformly from $\mathbb{Z}_N^\star$ is sufficient due to the following. By Fact 3.6,
it holds that uVDF.Sample will succeed whenever $\langle x_0^2 \rangle = \mathsf{QR}_N$. Furthermore, x_0^2 is a
random element of QR_N, and therefore is a generator with probability $1 - (p' + q')/(p' \cdot q') \ge 1 - 4/2^\lambda$. Also note that x_0 is distributed according to RSW.Sample($1^\lambda, N$).

tuple (Gen, Sample, Eval, Verify) *such that* (Gen, Sample, Eval) *is a* $(1, B, \ell, \epsilon)$-*iteratively sequential function,* (Gen, Eval$^{(\cdot)}$, Verify) *is a B-sound function, and it satisfies the following completeness property:*

- **Completeness from Honest Start.** *For every* $\lambda \in \mathbb{N}$, pp *in the support of* Gen(1^λ), v_0 *in the support of* Sample$(1^\lambda, pp)$, *and* $T \in \mathbb{N}$, *it holds that* Verify$(1^\lambda, pp, (v_0, T), \mathsf{Eval}^{(T)}(1^\lambda, pp, v_0)) = 1$.

The main result of this section is stated next.

Theorem 6.2 (Continuous VDF). *Let* $D, B, \alpha \colon \mathbb{N} \to \mathbb{N}$ *be functions satisfying* $B(\lambda) \leq 2^{\lambda^{1/3}}$, $\alpha(\lambda) = \lceil \log_\lambda(B(\lambda)) \rceil$, *and* $D(\lambda) \geq \lambda^{d'}$ *for all* $\lambda \in \mathbb{N}$ *and for a specific constant* d'. *Suppose that the α-round strong FS assumption holds and the (D, B)-RSW assumption holds for a polynomial* $\ell \colon \mathbb{N} \to \mathbb{N}$ *and constant* $\epsilon \in (0, 1)$. *Then, for any constant* $\delta > 0$ *and* $\epsilon' > \frac{\epsilon+\delta}{1+\delta}$, *it holds that* cVDF *is a* $(B, (1+\delta) \cdot D(\lambda) \cdot \ell, \epsilon')$-*cVDF.*

In the case where we want to have a fixed polynomial bound on the number of iterations, we obtain the following corollary.

Corollary 6.3 (Restatement of Theorem 1.1). *For any polynomials* B, D *where* $D(\lambda) \geq \lambda^{d'}$ *for a specific constant* d', *suppose the $O(1)$-round strong FS assumption holds and the (D, B)-RSW assumption holds for a polynomial* $\ell \colon \mathbb{N} \to \mathbb{N}$ *and constant* $\epsilon \in (0, 1)$. *Then, for any constant* $\delta > 0$ *and* $\epsilon' > \frac{\epsilon+\delta}{1+\delta}$, *it holds that* cVDF *is a* $(B, (1+\delta) \cdot D(\lambda) \cdot \ell, \epsilon')$-*cVDF.*

Remark 6.4 (Decoupling size and depth). The definition of a (B, ℓ, ϵ)-cVDF naturally extends to a (U, B, ℓ, ϵ)-cVDF, where we require (Gen, Sample, Eval) to be a $(1, U, B, \ell, \epsilon)$-iteratively sequential function; see Remark 3.4. Our construction will satisfy this for all functions U such that $U(\lambda) \leq B(\lambda)$ for all $\lambda \in \mathbb{N}$ Moreover, in this case, the above corollary can be based on the strong Fiat-Shamir assumption for $\lceil \log_\lambda(U(\lambda)) \rceil$ rounds (rather than for $\lceil \log_\lambda(B(\lambda)) \rceil$ rounds).

We prove Theorem 6.2 by using the unique VDF uVDF from Sect. 5 as a building block. We start with some definitions which will be helpful in the construction.

Definition 6.5 (Puzzle tree). *A* (pp$_\mathsf{uVDF}$, d', g)-*puzzle tree for* pp$_\mathsf{uVDF}$ = $(N, B, k, d, \mathsf{hash})$ *is a* $(k+1)$-*ary tree that has the following syntax.*

- *Each node is labeled by a string* $s \in \{0, 1, \dots, k\}^*$, *where the root is labeled with the empty string* null, *and for a node labeled* s, *its ith child is labeled* $s\|i$ *for* $i \in \{0, 1, \dots, k\}$. *We let* $[s]_i$ *denote the ith character of* s *for* $i \in \mathbb{N}$.[15]
- *We define the height of the tree as* $h = \lceil \log_k(B) \rceil - d'$ *which determines difficulty at each node. Specifically, each node* s *is associated with the difficulty* $t = k^{h+d'-|s|}$.[16]

---

[15] For ease of notation, we store s as a $(k+1)$-ary string and when doing integer operations, they are implicitly done in base $(k+1)$.

[16] Note that since the tree has height h, this implies that each leaf has difficulty $t = k^{d'}$.

- *Each node s has a value $\mathsf{val}(s) = (x, y, \pi)$, where we call x the input, y the output, and π the proof.*

The inputs, outputs, and proofs of each node are defined as follows:

- *The root has input g. In general, for a node s with input x and difficulty t, its first k children are called segment nodes and its last child is called a sketch node. Each segment node $s\|i$ has input $x_i = \left|x^{2^{i \cdot t/k}}\right|_N$ and the sketch node $s\|k$ has input x' where $(x', *) = \mathsf{Sketch}(\mathsf{pp}_{\mathsf{uVDF}}, (x, t), x_k, (x_1, \ldots, x_{k-1}))$ (given in Fig. 3).*
- *For a node s with input x and difficulty t, its output and proof are given by $(y, \pi) = \mathsf{uVDF}.\mathsf{Eval}(\mathsf{pp}_{\mathsf{uVDF}}, (x, t))$.*

We note that whenever we refer to a node s, we mean the node labeled by s, and when we refer to a pair (s', value), this corresponds to a node and associated value (where value may not necessarily be equal to the true value $\mathsf{val}(s)$).

Definition 6.6 (Left/Middle/Right Nodes). *For a node with label s in a $(\mathsf{pp}_{\mathsf{uVDF}}, d', g)$-puzzle tree with $s = s'\|i$ for $i \in \{0, 1, \ldots, k\}$, we call s a leftmost child if $i = 0$, a rightmost child if $i = k$, and a middle child otherwise. Additionally, we define the left (resp. right) siblings of s to be the set of nodes $s'\|j$ for $0 \le j < i$ (resp. $i < j \le k$).*

Next, we define a frontier. At a high level, for a leaf s, the frontier of s will correspond to the state of the continuous VDF upon reaching s. Specifically, it will contain all nodes whose values have been computed at that point, but whose parents' values have not yet been computed.

Definition 6.7 (Frontier). *For a node s in a $(\mathsf{pp}_{\mathsf{uVDF}}, d', g)$-puzzle tree, the frontier of s, denoted $\mathsf{frontier}(s)$, is the set of pairs $(s', \mathsf{val}(s'))$ for nodes s' that are left siblings of any of the ancestors of s. We note that s is included as one of its ancestors.[17]*

Next, we define what it means for a set to be consistent. At a high level, for a set of nodes and values, consistency ensures that the relationship of their given inputs and outputs across different nodes is in accordance with the definition of a puzzle tree. If a set is consistent, it does not imply that the input-output pairs are correct, but it implies that they "fit" together logically. Note that consistency does not check proofs.

Definition 6.8 (Consistency). *Let S be a set of pairs (s, value) for nodes s and values value in a $((N, B, k, d, \mathsf{hash}), d', g)$-puzzle tree. We say that $(s', (x, y))$ is consistent with S if the following hold:*

---

[17] It may be helpful to observe that for a leaf node $s = [s]_1\|[s]_2\|\cdots\|[s]_h$, the frontier contains $[s]_i$ nodes at level i for $i \in [h]$.

1. *The input x of s' is (a) the output given for its left sibling if its left sibling is in S and s' is a middle child, (b) given by the sketch of its left siblings' values if all of its left siblings are in S and s' is a rightmost child, or (c) defined recursively as its parent's input if s' is a leftmost child (where the base of the recursion is the root with input g).*
2. *The output y of s' is (a) given by the sketch of its left siblings' values if all of its left siblings are in S and s' is a rightmost child, or (b) given recursively by its parent's output if s' is a kth child (where, upon reaching the root recursively, we then accept any output for s').*

We say that S is a consistent set if every node in S is consistent with S.

6.1   Construction

Before giving the cVDF construction, we give a detailed overview. At a high level, the cVDF will iteratively compute each leaf node in a $(\mathsf{pp}_{\mathsf{uVDF}}, d', g)$-puzzle tree, where $\mathsf{pp}_{\mathsf{uVDF}} = (N, B, k, d, \mathsf{hash})$ are the public parameters of the underlying uVDF and g is the starting point of the tree given by uVDF.Sample.

The heart of our construction is the cVDF.Eval functionality which takes a state v corresponding to a leaf s in the tree and computes the next state v' corresponding to the next leaf. Each state v will be of the form (g, s, F), where s is the current leaf in the tree and F is the frontier of s. Then, cVDF.Eval$(1^\lambda, \mathsf{pp}, (g, s, \mathsf{frontier}(s)))$ will output $(g, s + 1, \mathsf{frontier}(s + 1))$. There are three phases of the algorithm cVDF.Eval. First, it checks that its input is well-formed. It then computes $\mathsf{val}(s)$ using $\mathsf{frontier}(s)$, and then computes $\mathsf{frontier}(s + 1)$ using both $\mathsf{frontier}(s)$ and $\mathsf{val}(s)$. These are discussed next.

Checking That v Is Well-Formed. Recall that $v = (g, s, F)$ corresponds to the node s in the tree. This state v is correct if running cVDF.Eval for s steps (where s is interpreted as an integer in base $(k+1)$) starting at the leaf 0^h results in $(g, s, \mathsf{frontier}(s))$. Therefore, before computing the next state, cVDF.Eval needs to verify that the state it was given is correct. To do this, we run cVDF.Verify with input state $(g, 0^h, \bot)$ and output state (g, s, F), and check that this is s steps of computation.

Computing the Value of s. To compute $\mathsf{val}(s)$, we have the following observation: for every node, its input is a function of the input of its parent and the outputs of its left siblings. Indeed, if s is a middle child, its input is the output of the sibling to its left (given in F). If s is a rightmost child, its input is the sketch of the values of its left siblings (also given in F). If s is a leftmost child, its input is input of its parent, defined recursively. Therefore, we compute its input based on F in this manner. Then, we compute its output by running uVDF.Eval on its input (Fig. 4).

Computing the Frontier of $s + 1$. The final phase of cVDF.Eval is to compute the next frontier using $\mathsf{val}(s)$ and $\mathsf{frontier}(s)$. To do this, we consider the closest common ancestor a of s and $s + 1$ and note that by definition, $\mathsf{frontier}(a) \subset \mathsf{frontier}(s+1)$. Moreover, its straightforward to see that $\mathsf{frontier}(s+1) \backslash \mathsf{frontier}(a)$

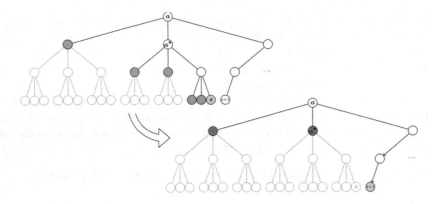

Fig. 4. An example of computing frontier($s + 1$) from frontier(s) for $k = 2$ with nodes s, $s + 1$, $a^\star$, and a given. In both graphs, the yellow node is the current node at that point in the computation, and the nodes in gray are those whose proofs have already been merged to proofs at their parents. In the left graph, the frontier of s is shown in pink. The right graph is the result of merging values to obtain the frontier of s', which is shown in blue. (Color figure online)

only contains a node $a^\star$ and its left siblings, where $a^\star$ is the child of a along the path to s. Note that when s and $(s+1)$ are siblings, then $a^\star = s$, and otherwise, it can be shown that $a^\star$ is the closest ancestor of s that is not a rightmost child.

Therefore, to compute frontier($s + 1$), we start by computing the value of node $a^\star$. If $a^\star = s$, then we have already computed it, and otherwise it's input and output are known from its children's values in F. Specifically, its input is the input of its first child, and its output is the output of its kth child. These are in F because of the definition of $a^\star$, which implies that each of its descendants along the path to s must be rightmost children. To compute its proof, observe that the values of s and its siblings are all known, so they can be efficiently merged into a proof of its parent. If the parent is $a^\star$, then we are done. If not, we can similarly merge values into a proof of the grandparent of s. We can continue this process until we reach $a^\star$. We show how to do this by traversing the path from s up to $a^\star$ and by iteratively "merging" values up the tree. An example depicting $s, s + 1, a, a^\star$ is given in Fig. 4.

Formal construction. Next, we give the formal details of our construction cVDF = (cVDF.Gen, cVDF.Sample, cVDF.Eval, cVDF.Verify).

- pp $\leftarrow$ cVDF.Gen(1^λ):
  Sample $pp_{uVDF} \leftarrow$ uVDF.Gen(1^λ) where $pp_{uVDF} = (N, B, k, d, \text{hash})$. Let d' be a constant, which will be specified in the proof of iterative sequentiality (in the full version), and set tree height $h = \lceil \log_k(B) \rceil - d'$. Output pp $= (pp_{uVDF}, d', h)$.
- $v \leftarrow$ cVDF.Sample(1^λ, pp):
  Sample $g \leftarrow$ uVDF.Sample(1^λ, pp_{uVDF}) and output $v = (g, 0^h, \emptyset)$.

- $v' \leftarrow \mathsf{cVDF.Eval}(1^\lambda, \mathsf{pp}, v)$:

  Check that v is well-formed:
  1. Parse v as (g, s, F), where s is a leaf label in a $(\mathsf{pp}_{\mathsf{uVDF}}, g)$-puzzle tree and F is a frontier. Output $\perp$ if v cannot be parsed this way.
  2. Run $\mathsf{cVDF.Verify}(1^\lambda, \mathsf{pp}, ((g, 0^h, \emptyset), s), (g, s, F))$ to verify v. Output $\perp$ if it rejects.

Compute the value of s:

1. Compute the input x of node s as the output of the sibling to its left (given in F) if s is a middle child, a sketch of its left siblings' values (given in F) if s is a rightmost child, or recursively as its parent's input if s is a leftmost child.
2. Compute its output and proof as $(y, \pi) = \mathsf{uVDF.Eval}(1^\lambda, \mathsf{pp}_{\mathsf{uVDF}}, (x, k^{d'}))$.

Compute the frontier of $s + 1$:

1. Let a be the closest common ancestor of s and $s+1$, and let $a^\star$ be the ancestor of s that is a child a.
2. If $a^\star = s$, compute its value as $(x^\star, y^\star, \pi^\star) = (x, y, \pi)$.
3. If $a^\star$ is a strict ancestor of s, let $x^\star$ be the input of its leftmost child in F, let $y^\star$ be the output of its kth child in F, and let $\pi^\star$ be $\perp$ if $x^\star$ is invalid and otherwise the outputs of its first $k - 1$ children in F along with the proof, computed recursively, of its child along the path to s.
4. Form the next frontier F' by removing all descendants of $a^\star$ from F, and adding $(a^\star, (x^\star, y^\star, \pi^\star))$.

Finally, output $(g, s + 1, F')$.

- $b \leftarrow \mathsf{cVDF.Verify}(1^\lambda, \mathsf{pp}, (v, T), v')$:
  Check that v is well-formed:
  Parse v as (g, s, F) where $g \in \mathbb{Z}_N^\star$, s is a leaf node, and F is a frontier. If v cannot be parsed this way, then output 1 if $v' = \perp$ and 0 otherwise.
  If $(g, s, F) \neq (g, 0^h, \emptyset)$, then verify the state v by recursively running this verification algorithm, i.e., $\mathsf{cVDF.Verify}(1^\lambda, \mathsf{pp}, ((g, 0^h, \emptyset), s), (g, s, F))$. If this rejects, then output 1 if $v' = \perp$ and 0 otherwise.
  Check that v' is correct:
  Output 1 if the following checks succeed, and 0 otherwise:
  1. Parse v' as $(g, s + T, F')$ where F' is a frontier.
  2. Check that the set of nodes in F' is the set of nodes in $\mathsf{frontier}(s')$ (considering only node labels and not values).
  3. Check that F' is a consistent set.[18]
  4. For each element $(s', (x, y, \pi)) \in F'$, check that $\mathsf{uVDF.Verify}(1^\lambda, \mathsf{pp}_{\mathsf{uVDF}}, (x, t), (y, \pi))$ accepts, where $t = k^{h+d'-|s'|}$.

---

[18] This can be done efficiently, since consistency of every element in F' can be checked by looking at k nodes in each of the h levels of the tree and performing at most one sketch.

Theorem 6.9. *Let $D, B \colon \mathbb{N} \to \mathbb{N}$ where $B(\lambda) \leq 2^{\lambda^{1/3}}$, $D(\lambda) = \lambda^{d'}$ for all $\lambda \in \mathbb{N}$ and specific constant d'. Assume that (1) the (D, B)-RSW assumption holds for an $\epsilon \in (0, 1)$ and a polynomial ℓ, and (2) for any constants $\epsilon', \delta \in (0, 1)$, uVDF (given in Sect. 5) is a $(D, B, (1 + \delta) \cdot \ell, \epsilon')$-unique VDF. Then cVDF is a $(B, (1 + \delta') \cdot D \cdot \ell, \epsilon'')$-cVDF for any $\epsilon'' > \frac{\epsilon + \delta'}{1 + \delta'}$ and $\delta' > \delta$.*

The proof is deferred to the full version. As a corollary, by combining Theorem 5.2 with Theorem 6.9, we obtain Theorem 6.2: a continuous VDF under the Fiat-Shamir and the repeated squaring assumptions.

Acknowledgements. We thank Ian Miers for suggesting the name *continuous* VDFs and Eylon Yogev for discussions regarding our PPAD hardness results.

This work was supported in part by NSF Award SATC-1704788, NSF Award RI-1703846, AFOSR Award FA9550-18-1-0267, and by NSF Award DGE-1650441. This research is based upon work supported in part by the Office of the Director of National Intelligence (ODNI), Intelligence Advanced Research Projects Activity (IARPA), via 2019-19-020700006. The views and conclusions contained herein are those of the authors and should not be interpreted as necessarily representing the official policies, either expressed or implied, of ODNI, IARPA, or the U.S. Government. The U.S. Government is authorized to reproduce and distribute reprints for governmental purposes notwithstanding any copyright annotation therein.

References

1. Chia network. https://chia.net/. Accessed 17 May 2019
2. Ethereum foundation. https://www.ethereum.org/. Accessed 17 May 2019
3. Protocol labs. https://protocol.ai/. Accessed 17 May 2019
4. VDF research effort. https://vdfresearch.org/. Accessed 17 May 2019
5. Abbot, T., Kane, D., Valiant, P.: On algorithms for Nash equilibria (2004). http://web.mit.edu/tabbott/Public/final.pdf. Accessed 18 Sept 2019
6. Barak, B.: How to go beyond the black-box simulation barrier. In: 42nd IEEE Symposium on Foundations of Computer Science, FOCS, pp. 106–115 (2001)
7. Bennett, C.H.: Time/space trade-offs for reversible computation. SIAM J. Comput. **18**(4), 766–776 (1989)
8. Bitansky, N., Goldwasser, S., Jain, A., Paneth, O., Vaikuntanathan, V., Waters, B.: Time-lock puzzles from randomized encodings. In: Innovations in Theoretical Computer Science, ITCS, pp. 345–356 (2016)
9. Bitansky, N., Paneth, O., Rosen, A.: On the cryptographic hardness of finding a Nash equilibrium. In: Guruswami, V. (ed.) IEEE 56th Symposium on Foundations of Computer Science, FOCS, pp. 1480–1498 (2015)
10. Boneh, D., Bonneau, J., Bünz, B., Fisch, B.: Verifiable delay functions. In: Shacham, H., Boldyreva, A. (eds.) CRYPTO 2018. LNCS, vol. 10991, pp. 757–788. Springer, Cham (2018). https://doi.org/10.1007/978-3-319-96884-1_25
11. Boneh, D., Bünz, B., Fisch, B.: A survey of two verifiable delay functions. IACR Cryptology ePrint Archive 2018, 712 (2018)
12. Boneh, D., Naor, M.: Timed commitments. In: Bellare, M. (ed.) CRYPTO 2000. LNCS, vol. 1880, pp. 236–254. Springer, Heidelberg (2000). https://doi.org/10.1007/3-540-44598-6_15

13. Cai, J., Lipton, R.J., Sedgewick, R., Yao, A.C.: Towards uncheatable benchmarks. In: 8th Structure in Complexity Theory Conference, pp. 2–11. IEEE Computer Society (1993)

14. Chen, X., Deng, X., Teng, S.: Settling the complexity of computing two-player Nash equilibria. J. ACM **56**(3), 14:1–14:57 (2009)

15. Choudhuri, A.R., Hubáček, P., Kamath, C., Pietrzak, K., Rosen, A., Rothblum, G.N.: Finding a Nash equilibrium is no easier than breaking Fiat-Shamir. In: 51st ACM SIGACT Symposium on Theory of Computing, STOC, pp. 1103–1114 (2019)

16. Choudhuri, A.R., Hubáček, P., Kamath, C., Pietrzak, K., Rosen, A., Rothblum, G.N.: PPAD-hardness via iterated squaring modulo a composite. IACR Cryptology ePrint Archive 2019, 667 (2019)

17. Chung, K., Lin, H., Pass, R.: Constant-round concurrent zero knowledge from P-certificates. In: 54th IEEE Symposium on Foundations of Computer Science, FOCS, pp. 50–59 (2013)

18. Cohen, B., Pietrzak, K.: Simple proofs of sequential work. In: Nielsen, J.B., Rijmen, V. (eds.) EUROCRYPT 2018. LNCS, vol. 10821, pp. 451–467. Springer, Cham (2018). https://doi.org/10.1007/978-3-319-78375-8_15

19. Daskalakis, C., Goldberg, P.W., Papadimitriou, C.H.: The complexity of computing a Nash equilibrium. Commun. ACM **52**(2), 89–97 (2009)

20. Döttling, N., Garg, S., Malavolta, G., Vasudevan, P.N.: Tight verifiable delay functions. IACR Cryptology ePrint Archive 2019, 659 (2019)

21. Döttling, N., Lai, R.W.F., Malavolta, G.: Incremental proofs of sequential work. In: Ishai, Y., Rijmen, V. (eds.) EUROCRYPT 2019. LNCS, vol. 11477, pp. 292–323. Springer, Cham (2019). https://doi.org/10.1007/978-3-030-17656-3_11

22. Dwork, C., Naor, M.: Pricing via processing or combatting junk mail. In: Brickell, E.F. (ed.) CRYPTO 1992. LNCS, vol. 740, pp. 139–147. Springer, Heidelberg (1993). https://doi.org/10.1007/3-540-48071-4_10

23. De Feo, L., Masson, S., Petit, C., Sanso, A.: Verifiable delay functions from supersingular isogenies and pairings. IACR Cryptology ePrint Archive 2019, 166 (2019)

24. Fiat, A., Shamir, A.: How to prove yourself: practical solutions to identification and signature problems. In: Odlyzko, A.M. (ed.) CRYPTO 1986. LNCS, vol. 263, pp. 186–194. Springer, Heidelberg (1987). https://doi.org/10.1007/3-540-47721-7_12

25. Garg, S., Pandey, O., Srinivasan, A.: Revisiting the cryptographic hardness of finding a nash equilibrium. In: Robshaw, M., Katz, J. (eds.) CRYPTO 2016. LNCS, vol. 9815, pp. 579–604. Springer, Heidelberg (2016). https://doi.org/10.1007/978-3-662-53008-5_20

26. Goldreich, O., Krawczyk, H.: On the composition of zero-knowledge proof systems. In: Paterson, M.S. (ed.) ICALP 1990. LNCS, vol. 443, pp. 268–282. Springer, Heidelberg (1990). https://doi.org/10.1007/BFb0032038

27. Goldwasser, S., Kalai, Y.T.: On the (in)security of the Fiat-Shamir paradigm. In: 44th IEEE Symposium on Foundations of Computer Science, FOCS, pp. 102–113 (2003)

28. Hubáček, P., Yogev, E.: Hardness of continuous local search: query complexity and cryptographic lower bounds. In: 28th ACM-SIAM Symposium on Discrete Algorithms, SODA, pp. 1352–1371 (2017)

29. Jerschow, Y.I., Mauve, M.: Non-parallelizable and non-interactive client puzzles from modular square roots. In: 6th International Conference on Availability, Reliability and Security, ARES1, pp. 135–142. IEEE Computer Society (2011)

30. Kaliski, B.: PKCS #5: password-based cryptography specification version 2.0 (2000)

31. Kitagawa, F., Nishimaki, R., Tanaka, K.: Obfustopia built on secret-key functional encryption. In: Nielsen, J.B., Rijmen, V. (eds.) EUROCRYPT 2018. LNCS, vol. 10821, pp. 603–648. Springer, Cham (2018). https://doi.org/10.1007/978-3-319-78375-8_20

32. Komargodski, I., Segev, G.: From Minicrypt to Obfustopia via private-key functional encryption. In: Coron, J.-S., Nielsen, J.B. (eds.) EUROCRYPT 2017. LNCS, vol. 10210, pp. 122–151. Springer, Cham (2017). https://doi.org/10.1007/978-3-319-56620-7_5

33. Lenstra, A.K., Wesolowski, B.: Trustworthy public randomness with sloth, unicorn, and trx. IJACT 3(4), 330–343 (2017)

34. Lin, H., Pass, R., Soni, P.: Two-round and non-interactive concurrent non-malleable commitments from time-lock puzzles. In: 58th IEEE Symposium on Foundations of Computer Science (FOCS), pp. 576–587 (2017)

35. Lund, C., Fortnow, L., Karloff, H.J., Nisan, N.: Algebraic methods for interactive proof systems. J. ACM 39(4), 859–868 (1992)

36. Mahmoody, M., Moran, T., Vadhan, S.P.: Publicly verifiable proofs of sequential work. In: Innovations in Theoretical Computer Science, ITCS, pp. 373–388 (2013)

37. Mahmoody, M., Smith, C., Wu, D.J.: A note on the (im)possibility of verifiable delay functions in the random oracle model. ePrint p. 663 (2019)

38. Megiddo, N., Papadimitriou, C.H.: On total functions, existence theorems and computational complexity. Theor. Comput. Sci. 81(2), 317–324 (1991)

39. Papadimitriou, C.H.: On the complexity of the parity argument and other inefficient proofs of existence. J. Comput. Syst. Sci. 48(3), 498–532 (1994)

40. Pietrzak, K.: Simple verifiable delay functions. In: 10th Innovations in Theoretical Computer Science Conference, ITCS, pp. 60:1–60:15 (2019)

41. Rabin, M.O.: Digitalized signatures and public key functions as intractable as factoring. Technical report, TR-212, LCS, MIT, Cambridge, MA (1979)

42. Rabin, M.O.: Transaction protection by beacons. J. Comput. Syst. Sci. 27(2), 256–267 (1983)

43. Rivest, R.L., Shamir, A., Wagner, D.A.: Time-lock puzzles and timed-release crypto (1996, manuscript)

44. Valiant, P.: Incrementally verifiable computation or proofs of knowledge imply time/space efficiency. In: Canetti, R. (ed.) TCC 2008. LNCS, vol. 4948, pp. 1–18. Springer, Heidelberg (2008). https://doi.org/10.1007/978-3-540-78524-8_1

45. Wesolowski, B.: Efficient verifiable delay functions. In: Ishai, Y., Rijmen, V. (eds.) EUROCRYPT 2019. LNCS, vol. 11478, pp. 379–407. Springer, Cham (2019). https://doi.org/10.1007/978-3-030-17659-4_13

46. Zhandry, M.: The magic of ELFs. In: Robshaw, M., Katz, J. (eds.) CRYPTO 2016. LNCS, vol. 9814, pp. 479–508. Springer, Heidelberg (2016). https://doi.org/10.1007/978-3-662-53018-4_18

Generic-Group Delay Functions Require Hidden-Order Groups

Lior Rotem, Gil Segev[(✉)], and Ido Shahaf[(✉)]

School of Computer Science and Engineering, Hebrew University of Jerusalem,
91904 Jerusalem, Israel
{lior.rotem,segev,ido.shahaf}@cs.huji.ac.il

Abstract. Despite the fundamental importance of delay functions, underlying both the classic notion of a time-lock puzzle and the more recent notion of a verifiable delay function, the only known delay function that offers both sufficient structure for realizing these two notions and a realistic level of practicality is the "iterated squaring" construction of Rivest, Shamir and Wagner. This construction, however, is based on rather strong assumptions in groups of hidden orders, such as the RSA group (which requires a trusted setup) or the class group of an imaginary quadratic number field (which is still somewhat insufficiently explored from the cryptographic perspective). For more than two decades, the challenge of constructing delay functions in groups of known orders, admitting a variety of well-studied instantiations, has eluded the cryptography community.

In this work we prove that there are no constructions of generic-group delay functions in cyclic groups of known orders: We show that for any delay function that does not exploit any particular property of the representation of the underlying group, there exists an attacker that completely breaks the function's sequentiality when given the group's order. As any time-lock puzzle and verifiable delay function give rise to a delay function, our result holds for these two notions we well, and explains the lack of success in resolving the above-mentioned long-standing challenge. Moreover, our result holds even if the underlying group is equipped with a d-linear map, for any constant $d \geq 2$ (and even for super-constant values of d under certain conditions).

1 Introduction

The classic notion of a time-lock puzzle, introduced by Rivest, Shamir and Wagner [RSW96], and the recent notion of a verifiable delay function, introduced by Boneh et al. [BBB+18], are instrumental to a wide variety of exciting

L. Rotem, G. Segev and I. Shahaf—Supported by the European Union's Horizon 2020 Framework Program (H2020) via an ERC Grant (Grant No. 714253).

L. Rotem—Supported by the Adams Fellowship Program of the Israel Academy of Sciences and Humanities.

I. Shahaf—Supported by the Clore Israel Foundation via the Clore Scholars Programme.

© International Association for Cryptologic Research 2020
A. Canteaut and Y. Ishai (Eds.): EUROCRYPT 2020, LNCS 12107, pp. 155–180, 2020.
https://doi.org/10.1007/978-3-030-45727-3_6

applications, such as randomness beacons, resource-efficient blockchains, proofs of replication and computational timestamping. Underlying both notions is the basic notion of a cryptographic delay function: For a delay parameter T, evaluating a delay function on a randomly-chosen input should require at least T sequential steps (even with a polynomial number of parallel processors and with a preprocessing stage), yet the function can be evaluated on any input in time polynomial in T (e.g., $2T$ or T^4).[1]

A delay function can be easily constructed by iterating a cryptographic hash function, when modeled as a random oracle for proving its sequentiality. However, the complete lack of structure that is offered by this construction renders its suitability for realizing time-lock puzzles or verifiable delay functions rather unclear. Specifically, for time-lock puzzles, iterating a cryptographic hash function in general does not enable sufficiently fast generation of input-output pairs. Similarly, for verifiable delay functions, iterating a cryptographic hash function in general does not able sufficiently fast verification (although, asymptotically, such verification can be based on succinct non-interactive arguments for NP languages [Kil92, Mic94, GW11], as suggested by Döttling et al. [DGM+19] and Boneh et al. [BBB+18]).

The only known construction of a delay function that offers both a useful structure for realizing time-lock puzzles or verifiable delay functions and a realistic level of practicality is the "iterated squaring" construction underlying the time-lock puzzle of Rivest et al. [RSW96], which was recently elegantly extended by Pietrzak [Pie19] and Wesolowski [Wes19] to additionally yield a verifiable delay function. The iterated squaring construction, however, is based on rather strong assumptions in groups of hidden orders such as the RSA group or the class group of an imaginary quadratic number field. Unfortunately, RSA groups require a trusted setup stage as the factorization of the RSA modulus serves as a trapdoor enabling fast sequential evaluation [RSW96, Pie19, Wes19], and the class group of an imaginary quadratic number field is not as well-studied from the cryptographic perspective as other, more standard, cryptographic groups [BBF18, Sec. 6].

Thus, a fundamental goal is to construct delay functions in groups of known orders, giving rise to a variety of well-studied instantiations. In such groups, the security of delay functions can potentially be proved either based on long-standing cryptographic assumptions or within the generic-group model as a practical heuristic.

1.1   Our Contributions

In this work we prove that there are no constructions of generic-group delay functions in cyclic groups of known orders: Roughly speaking, we show that for any delay function that does not exploit any particular property of the representation of the underlying group, there exists an attacker that breaks the

---

[1] We refer the reader to Sect. 2 for a formal definition of a delay function, obtained as a natural relaxation of both a time-lock puzzle and a verifiable delay function.

function's sequentiality when given the group's order. As any time-lock puzzle and verifiable delay function give rise to a delay function, our result holds for these two notions as well. Moreover, our impossibility result holds even if the underlying group is equipped with a d-linear map, for any constant $d \geq 2$ and even for super-constant values of d under certain conditions as discussed below.

Our result: Attacking delay functions in known-order groups. Generic-group algorithms have access to an oracle for performing the group operation and for testing whether two group elements are equal, and the efficiency of such algorithms is measured mainly by the number of oracle queries that they issue [Nec94, Sho97, BL96, MW98, Mau05]. In the context of generic-group delay functions, we view generic-group algorithms as consisting of parallel processors, and we measure the number of such processors together with the number of sequential queries that are issued by each such processor. In addition, we measure the amount of any internal computation that is performed by our attacker, and this enables us to prove an impossibility result that is not only of theoretical significance in the generic-group model, but is also of practical significance.

The following theorem presents our main result in an informal and simplified manner that focuses on prime-order groups without d-linear maps, and on delay functions whose public parameters, inputs and outputs consist only of group elements[2]:

Theorem (informal & simplified). *Let* DF *be a generic-group delay function whose public parameters, inputs and outputs consist of* $k_{pp}(\lambda, T)$, $k_{in}(\lambda, T)$ *and* $k_{out}(\lambda, T)$ *group elements, respectively, where* $\lambda \in \mathbb{N}$ *is the security parameter and* $T \in \mathbb{N}$ *is the delay parameter. Let* $Q_{eqEval}(\lambda, T)$ *denote the number of equality queries issued by the function's honest evaluation algorithm. Then, there exists a generic-group attacker* $\mathcal{A}$ *that takes as input the* λ-bit *order* p *of the group such that:*

- *$\mathcal{A}$ correctly computes the function on any input.*
- *$\mathcal{A}$ consists of* $(k_{pp} + k_{in}) \cdot \max\{k_{out}, Q_{eqEval}\}$ *parallel processors, each of which issues at most* $O((k_{pp} + k_{in}) \cdot \log p)$ *sequential oracle queries.*

For interpreting our theorem, first note that our attacker does not require a preprocessing stage, and is able to correctly compute the function on any input (these rule out even an extremely weak notion of sequentiality).

Second, note that the number $(k_{pp} + k_{in}) \cdot \max\{k_{out}, Q_{eqEval}\}$ of parallel processors used by our attacker is at most polynomial in the security parameter λ and in the delay parameter T, and that the number $O((k_{pp} + k_{in}) \cdot \log p)$ of sequential queries issued by each processor is polynomial in λ and essentially independent of the delay parameter T. Specifically, for delay functions underlying time-lock puzzles and verifiable delay functions, the parameters k_{pp}, k_{in} and

---

[2] As discussed in Sect. 1.3, we prove our result also to groups of composite order, to groups equipped with a d-linear map, and to delay functions whose public parameters, inputs and outputs consist of both group elements and arbitrary additional values.

k_{out} are all polynomials in λ and $\log T$ (for the iterated squaring delay function, for example, it holds that $k_{pp} = Q_{eqEval} = 0$ and $k_{in} = k_{out} = 1$).[3] Therefore, in these cases the number of sequential queries issued by each processor is at most polynomial in λ and $\log T$.

An additional interpretation of our result is as follows. The term $\max\{k_{out}, Q_{eqEval}\}$ lower bounds the time to compute Eval without parallelism (even though it could be much smaller – as for the iterated squaring function). Optimally, an α speedup, that is, computing the function α times faster than without parallelism, is obtained by using α parallel processors. We show that an (at least) α speedup can be obtained by using $O(\alpha \cdot (k_{pp} + k_{in})^2 \cdot \log p)$ parallel processors.

1.2   Related Work

Various cryptographic notions that share a somewhat similar motivation with delay functions have been proposed over the years, such as the above-discussed notions of time-lock puzzles and verifiable delay functions (e.g., [RSW96, BGJ+16, BBB+18, BBF18, Pie19, Wes19, EFK+19, DMP+19]), as well as other notions such as sequential functions and proofs of sequential work (e.g., [MMV11, MMV13, CP18]). It is far beyond the scope of this work to provide an overview of these notions, and we refer the reader to the work of Boneh et al. [BBB+18] for an in-depth discussion of these notions and of the relations among them.

A generic-group candidate for a function that requires more time to evaluate than to verify was proposed by Dwork and Naor [DN92] based on extracting square roots modulo a prime number p (see also the work of Lenstra and Wesolowski [LW15] on composing several such functions). However, the time required to sequentially evaluate this function, as well as the gap between the function's sequential evaluation time and its verification time, both seem limited to $O(\log p)$, and thus cannot be flexibly adjusted via a significantly larger delay parameter T. As noted by Boneh et al. [BBB+18], this does not meet the notion of a verifiable delay function (or our less-strict notion of a delay function).

In the random-oracle model, Döttling, Garg, Malavolta and Vasudevan [DGM+19], and Mahmoody, Smith and Wu [MSW19] proved impossibility results for certain classes of verifiable delay functions (and, thus, in particular, for certain classes of delay functions). Before describing their results, we note that whereas Döttling et al. and Mahmoody et al. captured restricted classes of verifiable delay functions within the random-oracle model, our work captures all constructions of delay functions (a more relaxed notion) within the incomparable generic-group model. Most importantly, in the random-oracle model a delay function can be easily constructed by iterating the random oracle (however, as discussed above, this does not seem practically useful for realizing time-lock puzzles or verifiable delay functions).

---

[3] For time-lock puzzles this follows from the requirement that an input-output pair can be generated in time polynomial in λ and $\log T$, and for verifiable delay functions this follows from the requirement that the verification algorithm runs in time polynomial in λ and $\log T$.

The work of Döttling et al. rules out constructions of verifiable delay functions with a *tight* gap between the assumed lower bound on their sequential evaluation time and their actual sequential evaluation time. Specifically, they proved that there is no construction that cannot be evaluated using less than T sequential oracle queries (even with parallel processors), but can be evaluated using $T + O(T^\delta)$ sequential oracle queries (for any constant $\delta > 0$ where T is the delay parameter). Note, however, that this does not rule out constructions that cannot be evaluated using less than T sequential oracle queries but can be evaluated, say, using $4T$ or $T \log T$ sequential oracle queries. In addition to their impossibility result, Döttling et al. showed that any verifiable delay function with a prover that runs in time $O(T)$ and has a natural self-composability property can be generically transformed into a verifiable delay function with a prover that runs in time $T + O(1)$ based on succinct non-interactive arguments for NP languages [Kil92, Mic94, GW11].

The work of Mahmoody et al. rules out constructions of verifiable delay functions that are *statistically* sound with respect to *any* oracle[4]. That is, they consider verifiable delay functions whose soundness property holds for *unbounded* adversaries and holds completely independently of the oracle. As noted by Mahmoody et al. this suffices, for example, for ruling out verifiable delay functions that are permutations. However, for such functions that are not permutations, this strong soundness property does not necessarily hold – as the security of constructions in the random-oracle model is on based the randomness of the oracle (and does not hold with respect to any oracle).

1.3   Overview of Our Approach

In this section we give an informal technical overview of our approach. We start by reviewing the generic-group model in which our lower bound is proven, and then move on to describe our attack, first in simplified settings and then gradually building towards our full-fledged attack. Finally, we illustrate how this attack can be extended to rule out generic-group delay functions in groups equipped with multilinear maps.

The Framework. We prove our impossibility result within the generic-group model introduced by Maurer [Mau05], which together with the incomparable model introduced by Shoup [Sho97], seem to be the most commonly-used approaches for capturing generic group computations. At a high level, in both models algorithms have access to an oracle for performing the group operation and for testing whether two group elements are equal. The difference between the two models is in the way that algorithms specify their queries to the oracle. In Maurer's model algorithms specify their queries by pointing to two group elements that have appeared in the computation so far (e.g., the 4th and the 7th group elements), whereas in Shoup's model group elements have an explicit

---

[4] In fact, as pointed out by Mahmoody et al. their impossibility result holds also for proofs of sequential work.

representation (sampled uniformly at random from the set of all injective mappings from the group to sufficiently long strings) and algorithms specify their queries by providing two strings that have appeared in the computation so far as encoding of group elements.

Jager and Schwenk [JS08] proved that the complexity of any computational problem that is defined in a manner that is independent of the representation of the underlying group (e.g., computing discrete logarithms) in one model is essentially equivalent to its complexity in the other model. However, not all generic cryptographic constructions are independent of the underlying representation.

More generally, these two generic-group models are rather incomparable. On one hand, the class of cryptographic schemes that are captured by Maurer's model is a subclass of that of Shoup's model – although as demonstrated by Maurer his model still captures all schemes that only use the abstract group operation and test whether two group elements are equal. On the other hand, the same holds also for the class of adversaries, and thus in Maurer's model we have to break the security of a given scheme using an adversary that is more restricted when compared to adversaries in Shoup's model. In fact, Shoup's model is "sufficiently non-generic" to accommodate delay functions such as the iterated-hashing construction. Delay functions of such flavor, however, rely on the randomness of the representation of group elements, which may or may not be sufficient in specific implementations of concrete groups, and are not based solely on the underlying algebraic hardness as in Maurer's model. Furthermore, as discussed earlier, delay functions that exploit such randomness are somewhat unstructured, and thus seem limited in their applicability to the design of time-lock puzzles and VDFs (for time-lock puzzles insufficient structure may not enable sufficiently fast generation of input-output pairs, and for VDFs insufficient structure may not enable sufficiently fast verification). We refer the reader to Sect. 2.1 for a formal description of Maurer's generic-group model.

Generic-group delay functions. A generic-group delay function in a cyclic group of order N is defined by an evaluation algorithm Eval, which receives the public parameters pp and an input $\mathbf{x}$, and returns an output $\mathbf{y}$. For the sake of this overview, we assume that pp, $\mathbf{x}$ and $\mathbf{y}$ consist of k_{pp}, k_{in} and k_{out} group elements, respectively (we refer the reader to Sect. 5 for a detailed account of how we handle additional explicit bit-strings as part of the public parameters, input and output). As a generic algorithm, Eval's access to these group elements is implicit and is provided via oracle access as follows. At the beginning of its execution, a table $\mathbf{B}$ is initialized with $\mathbb{Z}_N$ elements which correspond to the elements in pp and in $\mathbf{x}$. Eval can then access the table via two types of queries: (1) group operation queries, which place the sum of the two $\mathbb{Z}_N$ elements in the entries pointed to by Eval in the next vacant entry of the table; and (2) equality queries, which return 1 if and only if the two $\mathbb{Z}_N$ elements in the entries pointed to by Eval are equal. At the end of its execution, in order to implicitly output group elements, Eval outputs the indices of entries in the table in which the output group elements are positioned. We refer the reader to Sect. 2.2 for a more formal presentation of generic-group delay functions.

A simplified warm-up. Our goal is to construct an attacker, which (implicitly) receives the public parameters pp and an input $\mathbf{x}$, and computes the corresponding output $\mathbf{y}$ in a sequentially-fast manner. As a starting point, consider an oversimplified and hypothetical scenario in which the attacker is provided not only with oracle access to the table $\mathbf{B}$, but also with the explicit $\mathbb{Z}_N$ elements which are in the table and that correspond to pp and to $\mathbf{x}$. In this case, an attacker can simply emulate the execution of Eval locally without any queries to the oracle, where instead of the oracle table $\mathbf{B}$, the attacker keeps a local table of $\mathbb{Z}_N$ elements: Group oracle queries are emulated via integer addition modulo N, and equality queries are answered in accordance with integer equality. At the end of this emulation, the attacker holds the $\mathbb{Z}_N$ elements that correspond to the output elements of Eval. A key observation is that translating each of these $\mathbb{Z}_N$ elements into the appropriate group element – i.e., placing this $\mathbb{Z}_N$ element in the table $\mathbf{B}$ – requires only $O(\log N) = O(\lambda)$ oracle queries (e.g., via the standard square-then-multiply method).[5] Moreover, for any number k_{out} of group elements in the function's output, the number of sequential oracle queries remains only $O(\lambda)$ when using k_{out} parallel processors – one per each output element.

As an intermediate step towards our full-fledged attack, consider a somewhat less hypothetical scenario, in which the attacker only gets implicit access to the group elements in pp and in $\mathbf{x}$, but Eval does not issue any equality queries. Observe that this setting already captures the widely-used iterated squaring delay function discussed above. The main idea behind our attack in this setting is to replace each of the input group elements to Eval with a formal variable, and then to symbolically compute each output element as a polynomial in these variables. Note that in general, these are not fixed polynomials, but rather depend on the equality pattern resulting from Eval's equality queries. Here, however, we are assuming that Eval does not issue any such queries. Concretely, when there are no equality queries, computing the output polynomials does not require any oracle queries by a similar emulation to the one described above, where values in the local table are stored as polynomials, and the group operation is replaced with polynomial addition. Once we have each of the output elements expressed as a polynomial, we can implicitly evaluate it at $(\mathsf{pp}, \mathbf{x})$, starting with implicit access to the elements in $(\mathsf{pp}, \mathbf{x})$, using $k_{\mathsf{pp}} + k_{\mathsf{in}}$ parallel processors each of which performing $O(\log N + \log(k_{\mathsf{pp}} + k_{\mathsf{in}})) = O(\lambda)$ sequential group operations.[6]

Handling equality queries. On the face of it, the attack described in the previous paragraph is not applicable when Eval does issue equality queries, since it is unclear how to answer such queries in the polynomial-based emulation of

---

[5] We assume that the first entry of the table $\mathbf{B}$ is always occupied with the number 1, which is always a generator for $\mathbb{Z}_N$.

[6] Note that implicitly evaluating each monomial using roughly $\log N$ sequential group operations requires knowing the precise order N of the group. Without knowing N, this polynomial may have coefficients which are exponentially large in the delay parameter T, and evaluating each monomial can take up to $\mathsf{poly}(T)$ sequential group operations.

Eval. One possibility is to answer each equality query in the affirmative if and only if the two elements pointed to by Eval are identical as polynomials in the formal variables replacing the input elements. Indeed, if the two polynomials are identical, it is necessarily the case that the two elements are equal. Unfortunately, the opposite is incorrect, and it is possible (and indeed to be expected) that the two elements will be equal even though their corresponding polynomials are not identical, resulting in a false negative answer and thus the emulation will deviate from the true execution of Eval.

The main observation underlying our attack is that even though the number Q_{eqEval} of equality queries that Eval issues might be quite large (potentially as large as the delay parameter T), at most $|\mathsf{factors}(N)| \cdot (k_{\mathsf{pp}} + k_{\mathsf{in}})$ of the non-trivial queries can be affirmatively answered, where $\mathsf{factors}(N)$ denotes the multi-set of prime factors of N (where the number of appearances of each primes factor is its multiplicity – e.g., $\mathsf{factors}(100) = \{2, 2, 5, 5\}$), and by trivial queries we mean queries for which equality or inequality follows from the previous query/answer pattern. This is the case because at each point during the execution of Eval, the set of possible values for $(\mathsf{pp}, \mathbf{x})$, given the equality pattern so far, is a coset of some subgroup $H \leq \mathbb{Z}_N^{k_{\mathsf{pp}}+k_{\mathsf{in}}}$ relative to $(\mathsf{pp}, \mathbf{x})$: The possible values for $(\mathsf{pp}, \mathbf{x})$ are a set of the form $\{(\mathsf{pp}, \mathbf{x}) + (\mathsf{pp}', \mathbf{x}') | (\mathsf{pp}', \mathbf{x}') \in H\}$, where initially $H = \mathbb{Z}_N^{k_{\mathsf{pp}}+k_{\mathsf{in}}}$. Moreover, if q is a non-trivial equality query answered affirmatively, H is the said subgroup before q is issued and H' is the subgroup after q is answered, then due to the non-triviality of q, it is necessarily the case that $H' < H$ (i.e., H' is a proper subgroup of H). In particular, the order of H' is smaller than the order of H and divides it. Hence, since $|\mathsf{factors}(|\mathbb{Z}_N^{k_{\mathsf{pp}}+k_{\mathsf{in}}}|)| = (k_{\mathsf{pp}} + k_{\mathsf{in}}) \cdot |\mathsf{factors}(N)|$, the observation follows by induction.

Utilizing the Power of Parallelism. We translate this observation into an attack on the sequentiality of any generic-group delay function by carefully utilizing the power of parallelism in the following manner. Our attacker keeps track of an initially empty set $\mathcal{L}$ of linear equations in the formal variables that replace pp and $\mathbf{x}$, and runs for $(k_{\mathsf{pp}} + k_{\mathsf{in}}) \cdot |\mathsf{factors}(N)| + 1$ iterations.[7] In each iteration, the attacker runs the polynomial-based emulation described above, with the exception that now equality queries are answered affirmatively if and only if equality follows from the equations in $\mathcal{L}$. The attacker then checks, by querying the oracle, if any of the negatively-answered queries in the emulation should have been answered affirmatively, and if so, the equality that follows from this query is added to $\mathcal{L}$ – this step can be executed using $Q_{\mathsf{eqEval}} \cdot (k_{\mathsf{pp}} + k_{\mathsf{in}})$ parallel processors, each of which issuing $O(\log N + \log(k_{\mathsf{pp}} + k_{\mathsf{in}})) = O(\lambda)$ sequential queries.

Since we make sure that the true $(\mathsf{pp}, \mathbf{x})$ is always in the solution set of $\mathcal{L}$, there will be no false positive answers, and in each iteration there are only two possibilities: Either there exists a false negative answer (which we will then add

---

[7] We emphasize that our attack does not require knowing the factorization of N. Since $|\mathsf{factors}(N)| \leq \log N$, one can replace $|\mathsf{factors}(N)|$ with $\log N$ when determining the number of iterations.

to $\mathcal{L}$ as an equality) or all queries are answered correctly. On the one hand, if all queries are answered correctly, then the emulation in this iteration is accurate and we are done – all that is left is to translate the output polynomials of this emulation into implicit group elements, which we already discussed how to do. On the other hand, if there exists a false negative answer, then we learn a new equation that does not follow from the equations already in $\mathcal{L}$. By our observation, we can learn at most $|\mathsf{factors}(N)| \cdot (k_{\mathsf{pp}} + k_{\mathsf{in}})$ new such equations, so there must be an iteration in which we successfully emulate the execution of Eval and compute the correct output of the function.

Attacking generic delay functions in multilinear groups. We extend our attack so that it computes the output of any generic delay function in groups that are equipped with a d-linear map and on any input, while issuing at most $O((k_{\mathsf{pp}} + k_{\mathsf{in}} + 1)^d \cdot |\mathsf{factors}(N)| \cdot \lambda)$ sequential queries. In such groups, in addition to the group operation and equality queries, generic algorithms can also issue d-linear map queries, supplying (implicitly) d elements in the source group and receiving as a reply implicit access to the resulting element of the target group. In our polynomial-based emulation of Eval described above, we replace such queries with polynomial multiplication, resulting in polynomials of degree at most d. Since these polynomials may be non-linear, and the analysis of our attack heavily relied on the fact that the learned equations are linear, this analysis no longer applies.

We address this situation by carefully employing a linearization procedure. Roughly speaking, in our polynomial-based emulation of Eval, the attacker now replaces each possible product of at most d formal variables (out of the formal variables that replace the group elements in pp and in $\mathbf{x}$) with a single new formal variable. After applying this linearization procedure, the learned equations are once again linear (in the new formal variables), but by applying it, we lose information about the possible set of assignments to the elements in $(\mathsf{pp}, \mathbf{x})$, given the learned equations in $\mathcal{L}$. As a result, it might be that a certain equality which follows from the equations in $\mathcal{L}$, no longer follows from them after applying the linearization procedure (to both the equality and the equations in $\mathcal{L}$). The main observation that makes our attack successful nevertheless is that if a certain equality follows from $\mathcal{L}$ after applying the linearization procedure, it necessarily followed from $\mathcal{L}$ before applying the procedure as well. Hence, it is still the case that there are no false positive answers in the emulation, and that in each iteration we either add a new equation to $\mathcal{L}$ or compute the correct output.

This linearization procedure comes at a cost. After applying it, we have $(k_{\mathsf{pp}} + k_{\mathsf{in}} + 1)^d$ different formal variables instead of just $k_{\mathsf{pp}} + k_{\mathsf{in}}$ as before. Thus, in order for our analysis from the linear setting to apply, our attacker needs to run for roughly $(k_{\mathsf{pp}} + k_{\mathsf{in}} + 1)^d \cdot |\mathsf{factors}(N)|$ iterations, explaining the exponential dependency on d in its sequential query complexity. Note however that the attack still computes the output with less than T sequential queries as long as $d \leq O(\log T / (\log \lambda \cdot \log(k_{\mathsf{pp}} + k_{\mathsf{in}})))$, and in particular whenever d is constant.

Our attacker's internal computation. In order to rule out constructions of delay functions whose sequentiality is proven within the generic-group model, it suffices to present an attacker which is efficient relative to the security parameter and the delay parameter in terms of its number of parallel processors and generic-group operations, regardless of the amount of additional internal computation required by the attacker. Nevertheless, we show that our attacker requires an overhead which is only polynomial in terms of its internal computation. Consequently, when our attack is applied to any "heuristically secure" construction in any cyclic group of known order, the number of sequential group operations it performs is essentially independent of T, and the additional computation – which is independent of the specific group in use – is at most $\mathsf{poly}(\lambda, T)$. Put differently, either this additional computation can be sped-up using parallelism and then the construction is insecure; or it cannot be sped-up and thus yields an inherently-sequential computation that does not rely on the underlying group.

Specifically, the most significant operation that is performed by our attacker which is non-trivial in terms of its computational cost is checking in each iteration whether or not a given linear equation over $\mathbb{Z}_N$ follows from the linear equations already in the set $\mathcal{L}$. When considering groups of prime order, this can be done simply by testing for linear independence among the vectors of coefficients corresponding to these equations. When considering groups of composite order this is a bit more subtle, and can be done for example by relying on fast algorithms for computing the Smith normal form of integer matrices (e.g., [Sto96]) and without knowing the factorization of the order of the group – see Appendix A for more details.

1.4 Paper Organization

The remainder of this paper is organized as follows. First, in Sect. 2 we present the basic notation used throughout the paper, and formally describe the framework we consider for generic-group delay functions. In Sect. 3 we prove our main impossibility result for generic delay functions, and in Sect. 4 we extend it to generic multilinear groups. Finally, in Sect. 5 we discuss several additional extensions, and in Appendix A we show that our attacker is efficient not only with respect to its number of parallel processors and generic group operations, but also in its additional internal computation.

2 Preliminaries

In this section we present the basic notions and standard cryptographic tools that are used in this work. For a distribution X we denote by $x \leftarrow X$ the process of sampling a value x from the distribution X. Similarly, for a set $\mathcal{X}$ we denote by $x \leftarrow \mathcal{X}$ the process of sampling a value x from the uniform distribution over $\mathcal{X}$. For an integer $n \in \mathbb{N}$ we denote by $[n]$ the set $\{1, \ldots, n\}$. A function $\nu : \mathbb{N} \to \mathbb{R}^+$ is *negligible* if for any polynomial $p(\cdot)$ there exists an integer N such that for all $n > N$ it holds that $\nu(n) \leq 1/p(n)$.

2.1 Generic Groups and Algorithms

As discussed in Sect. 1.1, we prove our results within the generic-group model introduced by Maurer [Mau05]. We consider computations in cyclic groups of order N (all of which are isomorphic to $\mathbb{Z}_N$ with respect to addition modulo N), for a λ-bit integer N that is generated by a order generation algorithm $\mathsf{OrderGen}(1^\lambda)$, where $\lambda \in \mathbb{N}$ is the security parameter (and N may or may not be prime).

When considering such groups, each computation Maurer's model is associated with a table $\mathbf{B}$. Each entry of this table stores an element of $\mathbb{Z}_N$, and we denote by V_i the group element that is stored in the ith entry. Generic algorithms access this table via an oracle $\mathcal{O}$, providing black-box access to $\mathbf{B}$ as follows. A generic algorithm $\mathcal{A}$ that takes d group elements as input (along with an optional bit-string) does not receive an explicit representation of these group elements, but instead, has oracle access to the table $\mathbf{B}$, whose first d entries store the $\mathbb{Z}_N$ elements corresponding to the d group element in $\mathcal{A}$'s input. That is, if the input of an algorithm A is a tuple $(g_1, \ldots, g_d, x)$, where $g_1, \ldots, g_d$ are group elements and x is an arbitrary string, then from A's point of view the input is the tuple $(\widehat{g_1}, \ldots, \widehat{g_d}, x)$, where $\widehat{g_1}, \ldots, \widehat{g_d}$ are pointers to the group elements $g_1, \ldots, g_d$ (these group elements are stored in the table $\mathbf{B}$), and x is given explicitly. All generic algorithms in this paper will receive as their first input a generator of the group; we capture this fact by always assuming that the first entry of $\mathbf{B}$ is occupied by $1 \in \mathbb{Z}_N$, and we will sometimes forgo noting this explicitly. The oracle $\mathcal{O}$ allows for two types of queries:

- **Group operation queries:** On input $(i, j, +)$ for $i, j \in \mathbb{N}$, the oracle checks that the ith and jth entries of the table $\mathbf{B}$ are not empty, computes $V_i + V_j \bmod N$ and stores the result in the next available entry. If either the ith or the jth entries are empty, the oracle ignores the query.
- **Equality queries:** On input $(i, j, =)$ for $i, j \in \mathbb{N}$, the oracle checks that the ith and jth entries in $\mathbf{B}$ are not empty, and then returns 1 if $V_i = V_j$ and 0 otherwise. If either the ith or the jth entries are empty, the oracle ignores the query.

In this paper we consider interactive computations in which multiple algorithms pass group elements (as well as non-group elements) as inputs to one another. This is naturally supported by the model as follows: When a generic algorithm $\mathcal{A}$ outputs k group elements (along with a potential bit-string σ), it outputs the indices of k (non-empty) entries in the table $\mathbf{B}$ (together with σ). When these outputs (or some of them) are passed on as inputs to a generic algorithm $\mathcal{C}$, the table $\mathbf{B}$ is re-initialized, and these values (and possibly additional group elements that $\mathcal{C}$ receives as input) are placed in the first entries of the table. Additionally, we rely on the following conventions:

1. Throughout the paper we refer to values as either "explicit" ones or "inexplicit" ones. Explicit values are all values whose representation (e.g., binary strings of a certain length) is explicitly provided to the generic algorithms under consideration. Inexplicit values are all values that correspond to group elements and that are stored in the table $\mathbf{B}$ – thus generic algorithms can

access them only via oracle queries. We will sometimes interchange between providing group elements as input to generic algorithms inexplicitly, and providing them explicitly. Note that moving from the former to the latter is well defined, since a generic algorithm $\mathcal{A}$ that receives some of its input group elements explicitly can always simulate the computation as if they were received as part of the table $\mathbf{B}$.

2. For a group element g, we will differentiate between the case where g is provided explicitly and the case where it is provided implicitly via the table $\mathbf{B}$, using the notation g in the former case, and the notation $\hat{g}$ in the latter.

3. As is common in the generic group model, we identify group elements that are given as input to a generic algorithm with formal variables, the results of addition queries (i.e., the content of the entries in the table $\mathbf{B}$) with linear polynomials in these variables, and positively-answered equality queries between distinct polynomials with linear equations.

2.2   Generic-Group Delay Functions

A generic-group delay function is a triplet $\mathsf{DF} = (\mathsf{Setup}, \mathsf{Sample}, \mathsf{Eval})$ of oracle-aided algorithms satisfying the following properties:

- Setup is a randomized algorithm that has oracle access to the group oracle $\mathcal{O}$, receives as input the group order $N \in \mathbb{N}$ and a sequentiality parameter $T \in \mathbb{N}$, and outputs public parameters $\mathsf{pp} = (\mathsf{pp}_G, \mathsf{pp}_s)$ where pp_G is an ordered list of group elements and $\mathsf{pp}_s \in \{0,1\}^*$ is an explicit string.
- Sample is a randomized algorithm that has oracle access to the group oracle $\mathcal{O}$, receives as input N and T as above, as well as the public parameters pp, and outputs $x = (x_G, x_s) \in \mathcal{X}_{\mathsf{pp}}$ (the domain $\mathcal{X}_{\mathsf{pp}}$ may be a function of the public parameters pp), where x_G is an ordered list of group elements and $x_s \in \{0,1\}^*$ is an explicit string.
- Eval is a deterministic algorithm that has oracle access to the group oracle $\mathcal{O}$, receives as input N,T and pp as above, as well as an input $x \in \mathcal{X}_{\mathsf{pp}}$, and outputs $y = (y_G, y_s)$, where y_G is an ordered list of group elements and $y_s \in \{0,1\}^*$ in an explicit string.

Motivated by notions of time-lock puzzles and verifiable delay functions, we consider delay functions where the lengths of the public parameters, inputs, and outputs are polynomial in λ and $\log T$. For time-lock puzzles this follows from the requirement that an input-output pair can be generated in time polynomial in λ and $\log T$, and for verifiable delay functions this follows from the requirement that the verification algorithm runs in time polynomial in λ and $\log T$.

In terms of security, we require that for a delay parameter T, no algorithm should be successful with a non-negligible probability in evaluating a delay function on a randomly-chosen input – even with any polynomial number of parallel processors and with a preprocessing stage.

Definition 2.1 (Sequentiality). *Let $T = T(\lambda)$ and $p = p(\lambda)$ be functions of the security parameter $\lambda \in \mathbb{N}$. A delay function $\mathsf{DF} = (\mathsf{Setup}, \mathsf{Sample}, \mathsf{Eval})$ is (T,p)-sequential if for every polynomial $q = q(\cdot, \cdot)$ and for every pair of* *oracle-aided algorithms* $(\mathcal{A}_0, \mathcal{A}_1)$, *where* $\mathcal{A}_0$ *issues at most* $q(\lambda, T)$ *oracle queries, and* $\mathcal{A}_1$ *consists of at most* $p(\lambda)$ *parallel processors, each of which issues at most* T *oracle queries, there exists a negligible function* $\nu(\cdot)$ *such that*

$$\Pr\left[y' = y \;\middle|\; \begin{array}{l} N \leftarrow \mathsf{OrderGen}(1^\lambda), \mathsf{pp} \leftarrow \mathsf{Setup}^{\mathcal{O}}(N, T) \\ \mathsf{st} \leftarrow \mathcal{A}_0^{\mathcal{O}}(N, T, \mathsf{pp}), x \leftarrow \mathsf{Sample}^{\mathcal{O}}(N, T, \mathsf{pp}) \\ y \leftarrow \mathsf{Eval}^{\mathcal{O}}(N, T, \mathsf{pp}, x) \\ y' \leftarrow \mathcal{A}_1^{\mathcal{O}}(\mathsf{st}, N, T, \mathsf{pp}, x) \end{array} \right] \leq \nu(\lambda)$$

for all sufficiently large $\lambda \in \mathbb{N}$.

3   Our Impossibility Result

In this section we prove our impossibility result for generic-group delay functions in cyclic groups of known orders. For ease of presentation, here we consider functions whose public parameters, inputs and outputs consist of group elements and do not additionally contain any explicit bit-strings (see Sect. 5 for extending our approach to this case).

In what follows we denote by $\mathsf{factors}(N)$ the multi-set of prime factors of the λ-bit group order N (where the number of appearances of each prime factor is its multiplicity – e.g., $\mathsf{factors}(100) = \{2, 2, 5, 5\}$). We prove the following theorem:

Theorem 3.1. *Let* $\mathsf{DF} = (\mathsf{Setup}, \mathsf{Sample}, \mathsf{Eval})$ *be a generic-group delay function whose public parameters, inputs and outputs consist of* $k_{\mathsf{pp}}(\lambda, T)$, $k_{\mathsf{in}}(\lambda, T)$ *and* $k_{\mathsf{out}}(\lambda, T)$ *group elements, respectively, where* $\lambda \in \mathbb{N}$ *is the security parameter and* $T \in \mathbb{N}$ *is the delay parameter. Let* $Q_{\mathsf{eqEval}}(\lambda, T)$ *denote the number of equality queries issued by the algorithm* Eval. *Then, there exists a generic-group algorithm* $\mathcal{A}$ *that consists of* $(k_{\mathsf{pp}} + k_{\mathsf{in}}) \cdot \max\{k_{\mathsf{out}}, Q_{\mathsf{eqEval}}\}$ *parallel processors, each of which issues at most* $O((k_{\mathsf{pp}} + k_{\mathsf{in}}) \cdot |\mathsf{factors}(N)| \cdot \lambda)$ *sequential oracle queries, such that*

$$\Pr\left[\mathbf{y}' = \mathbf{y} \;\middle|\; \begin{array}{l} N \leftarrow \mathsf{OrderGen}(1^\lambda), \widehat{\mathsf{pp}} \leftarrow \mathsf{Setup}^{\mathcal{O}}(N, T) \\ \widehat{\mathbf{x}} \leftarrow \mathsf{Sample}^{\mathcal{O}}(N, T, \widehat{\mathsf{pp}}) \\ \widehat{\mathbf{y}} \leftarrow \mathsf{Eval}^{\mathcal{O}}(N, T, \widehat{\mathsf{pp}}, \widehat{\mathbf{x}}) \\ \widehat{\mathbf{y}'} \leftarrow \mathcal{A}^{\mathcal{O}}(N, T, \widehat{\mathsf{pp}}, \widehat{\mathbf{x}}) \end{array} \right] = 1$$

for all $\lambda \in \mathbb{N}$ *and* $T \in \mathbb{N}$, *where the probability is taken over the internal randomness of* $\mathsf{OrderGen}$, Setup *and* Sample.

The proof of Theorem 3.1 relies on the following notation. We will at times substitute the group elements $\widehat{\mathsf{pp}} = (\widehat{\mathsf{pp}_1}, \ldots, \widehat{\mathsf{pp}_{k_{\mathsf{pp}}}})$ and $\widehat{\mathbf{x}} = (\widehat{x_1}, \ldots, \widehat{x_k})$ that are given as input to Eval, with formal variables $\mathsf{PP} = (\mathsf{PP}_1, \ldots, \mathsf{PP}_{k_{\mathsf{pp}}})$ and $\mathbf{X} = (X_1, \ldots, X_{k_{\mathsf{in}}})$. When this is the case, instead of writing $\mathsf{Eval}^{\mathcal{O}}(N, T, \widehat{\mathsf{pp}}, \widehat{\mathbf{x}})$ we will write $\mathsf{Eval}^{\mathbb{Z}_N[\mathsf{PP}, \mathbf{X}]|\mathcal{L}}(N, T, \mathsf{PP}, \mathbf{X})$, where $\mathcal{L}$ is a set of linear equations in PP and in $\mathbf{X}$. This latter computation is obtained from the original one by the following emulation:

– Group elements are represented via polynomials in the formal variables PP and $\mathbf{X}$. The computation keeps track of the elements via a local table, which replaces the table $\mathbf{B}$ of the oracle $\mathcal{O}$ (recall Sect. 2). This table is ininitialized so that its first $1 + k_{pp} + k_{in}$ entries are inhabited with the monomials $1, PP_1, \ldots, PP_{k_{pp}}, X_1, \ldots, X_{k_{in}}$.

- Group operations are simulated via polynomial addition; i.e., when Eval issues a group operation query with two elements that are represented in the local table by two polynomials $p_1(PP, \mathbf{X})$ and $p_2(PP, \mathbf{X})$, the result is the polynomial $p_1(PP, \mathbf{X}) + p_2(PP, \mathbf{X})$, which is then placed in the next vacant entry of the table.
- Each equality query is answered affirmatively if and only if equality follows from the equations in $\mathcal{L}$ (in particular, when $\mathcal{L} = \emptyset$, equality queries are answered affirmatively if and only if the two polynomials at hand are identical).
- The output $\mathbf{y}(PP, \mathbf{X}) = (y_1(PP, \mathbf{X}), \ldots, y_{k_{out}}(PP, \mathbf{X}))$ of this computation is a vector of polynomials in PP and in $\mathbf{X}$. We denote by $\mathbf{y}(pp, \mathbf{x}) = (y_1(pp, \mathbf{x}), \ldots, y_{k_{out}}(pp, \mathbf{x}))$ the vector obtained by evaluating each entry of $\mathbf{y}(PP, \mathbf{X})$ at the point $(pp, \mathbf{x}) \in \mathbb{Z}_N^{k_{pp}+k_{in}}$.

We now turn to present the proof of Theorem 3.1.

Proof. Let $\mathsf{DF} = (\mathsf{Setup}, \mathsf{Sample}, \mathsf{Eval})$ be a generic-group delay function, and consider the following adversary $\mathcal{A}$:

The adversary $\mathcal{A}$

The adversary $\mathcal{A}$ on input $(N, T, \widehat{pp}, \widehat{\mathbf{x}})$ and oracle access to $\mathcal{O}$ is defined as follows:

1. Initialize a set $\mathcal{L} = \emptyset$ of linear equations in the formal variables $PP = (PP_1, \ldots, PP_{k_{pp}})$ and $\mathbf{X} = (X_1, \ldots, X_{k_{in}})$.
2. Repeat the following steps for $t = (k_{pp} + k_{in}) \cdot |\mathsf{factors}(N)| + 1$ iterations:
   (a) Compute $\mathbf{y}'(PP, \mathbf{X}) = \mathsf{Eval}^{\mathbb{Z}_N[PP, \mathbf{X}]|\mathcal{L}}(N, T, PP, \mathbf{X})$. Let m denote the number of equality queries that are negatively answered in the computation, and let $\ell_1(PP, \mathbf{X}), \ldots, \ell_m(PP, \mathbf{X})$ be the linear equations that would have followed from each of these queries had it been affirmatively answered.
   (b) For each $i \in [m]$, if $\ell_i(pp, \mathbf{x})$ holds then add $\ell_i(PP, \mathbf{X})$ to $\mathcal{L}$. If at least one linear equation was added to $\mathcal{L}$ then skip step 2(c) and continue to the next iteration.
   (c) Compute and output $\widehat{\mathbf{y}'(pp, \mathbf{x})}$, then terminate.
3. Output $\bot$.

Query completed. Steps 1 and 2(a) require no oracle queries. Step 2(b) requires $m \cdot (k_{pp} + k_{in})$ parallel processors, each issuing $O(\log N)$ sequential queries for checking whether $\ell_i(pp, \mathbf{x})$ hold for any $i \in [m]$ (and it holds that $m \leq Q_{eqEval}$). Step 2(c) is executed at most once and requires $k_{out} \cdot (k_{pp} + k_{in})$ parallel processors, each issuing $O(\log N)$ queries.

Finally, note that for a composite order N, the attacker $\mathcal{A}$ is not required to compute the factorization of N in order to determine the number of iterations. Specifically, for a λ-bit modulos N it always holds that $|\mathsf{factors}(N)| < \lambda$, and $\mathcal{A}$ can use this upper bound for determining an upper bound on the number of iterations.

Fix an iteration $j \in [t]$ where $t = (k_{\sf pp} + k_{\sf in}) \cdot |{\sf factors}(N)| + 1$, let $\mathcal{L}_j$ denote the state of the set $\mathcal{L}$ of linear equations at the beginning of the jth iteration, and consider the two computations $\mathbf{y} = {\sf Eval}^{\mathcal{O}}(N, T, \widehat{\sf pp}, \widehat{\mathbf{x}})$ and $\mathbf{y}'_j({\sf PP}, \mathbf{X}) = {\sf Eval}^{\mathbb{Z}_N[{\sf PP}, \mathbf{X}] \| \mathcal{L}_j}(N, T, {\sf PP}, \mathbf{X})$. By the condition specified in step 2(b) for adding a linear equation ℓ to $\mathcal{L}$, any $\ell \in \mathcal{L}_j$ is satisfied by $({\sf pp}, \mathbf{x})$ (i.e., $\ell({\sf pp}, \mathbf{x})$ holds). Therefore, every equality query that is negatively answered in the computation of $\mathbf{y}$ is also negatively answered in the computation of $\mathbf{y}'_j({\sf PP}, \mathbf{X})$. Hence, one of the following two cases must happen:

- Case I: All equality queries in both computations are answered the same way. In this case, the output of both computations is the same vector of linear polynomials in terms of the inputs, and it holds that $\mathbf{y} = \mathbf{y}'_j({\sf pp}, \mathbf{x})$. Furthermore, since all negatively answered queries in the computation of $\mathbf{y}'_j({\sf PP}, \mathbf{X})$ are also negatively answered in the computation of $\mathbf{y}$, then for all $i \in [m]$ the linear equation $\ell_i({\sf pp}, \mathbf{x})$ is not satisfied. Therefore, step 2(c) is reached in this case and $\mathcal{A}$ succeeds in outputting $\mathbf{y}$.
- Case II: There exists an equality query that is positively answered in the computation of $\mathbf{y}$ but is negatively answered in the computation of $\mathbf{y}'_j({\sf PP}, \mathbf{X})$. This means that there exists an $i \in [m]$ for which $\ell_i({\sf pp}, \mathbf{x})$ holds, but $\ell_i({\sf PP}, \mathbf{X})$ is not implied by the linear equations in $\mathcal{L}_j$. Thus, ℓ_i is added to $\mathcal{L}$ and the algorithm skips to the next iteration.

So far we have shown that $\mathcal{A}$ outputs $\mathbf{y}$ (i.e., the correct output) whenever step 2(c) is reached. We now complete the proof by showing that step 3 is never reached (i.e., that step 2(c) is always reached). Suppose towards contradiction that $t = (k_{\sf pp} + k_{\sf in}) \cdot |{\sf factors}(N)| + 1$ iterations are performed, but none of them reaches step 2(c). For every $j \in [t]$ recall that $\mathcal{L}_j$ denotes the state of the set $\mathcal{L}$ at the beginning of the jth iteration, and denote by $\mathcal{L}_{t+1}$ the state of $\mathcal{L}$ when reaching step 3. Then, it holds that $\mathcal{L}_1 \subsetneq \mathcal{L}_2 \subsetneq \cdots \subsetneq \mathcal{L}_{t+1}$, since for every $j \in [t]$ the set $\mathcal{L}_{j+1}$ contains at least one linear equation that is not implied by $\mathcal{L}_j$. Also, as already mentioned, for every $j \in [t+1]$ and $\ell \in \mathcal{L}_j$ the linear equation $\ell({\sf pp}, \mathbf{x})$ is satisfied. For a system of linear equations $\mathcal{M}$ with k variables over $\mathbb{Z}_N$, if there exists a solution $\mathbf{z} \in \mathbb{Z}_N^k$ to the system $\mathcal{M}$ then the set of solutions forms a coset of a subgroup of $\mathbb{Z}_N^k$. That is, there exists a subgroup H of $\mathbb{Z}_N^k$ such the the set of solutions to $\mathcal{M}$ is $\mathbf{z} + H$. Therefore, there exist subgroups $H_1, \ldots, H_{t+1}$ of $\mathbb{Z}_N^{k_{\sf pp} + k_{\sf in}}$ such that for every $j \in [t+1]$ it holds that

$$\left\{ ({\sf pp}', \mathbf{x}') \in \mathbb{Z}_N^{k_{\sf pp} + k_{\sf in}} \middle| \forall \ell({\sf PP}, \mathbf{X}) \in \mathcal{L}_j : \ell({\sf pp}', \mathbf{x}') \text{ is satisfied} \right\} = ({\sf pp}, \mathbf{x}) + H_j .$$

Then, it holds that $H_1 > H_2 > \cdots > H_{t+1}$ (i.e., H_{j+1} is a proper subgroup of H_j for every $j \in [t]$). Therefore, the order of every H_{j+1} divides that of H_j, and it holds that

$$ {\sf factors}(|H_{t+1}|) \subsetneq {\sf factors}(|H_t|) \subsetneq \cdots \subsetneq {\sf factors}(|H_1|) \subseteq {\sf factors}(|\mathbb{Z}_N^{k_{\sf pp} + k_{\sf in}}|). $$

Since

$$ |{\sf factors}(|\mathbb{Z}_N^{k_{\sf pp} + k_{\sf in}}|)| = |{\sf factors}(N^{k_{\sf pp} + k_{\sf in}})| = t - 1, $$

it is impossible to have t proper containments in the above chain and we reach a contradiction.   ∎

4   Extending Our Impossibility Result to the Multilinear Setting

In this section we extend our impossibility result to groups that are equipped with a d-linear map. Similarly to our proof in Sect. 3, once again we begin by considering functions whose public parameters, inputs and outputs consist of group elements and do not additionally contain any explicit bit-strings (see Sect. 5 for extending our proof to this case).

Recall that we denote by $\mathsf{factors}(N)$ the multi-set of prime factors of the λ-bit group order N (where the number of appearances of each prime factor is its multiplicity – e.g., $\mathsf{factors}(100) = \{2, 2, 5, 5\}$). We prove the following theorem (from which Theorem 3.1 follows by setting $d = 1$):

Theorem 4.1. *Let $d = d(\lambda)$ be a function of the security parameter $\lambda \in \mathbb{N}$, and let $\mathsf{DF} = (\mathsf{Setup}, \mathsf{Sample}, \mathsf{Eval})$ be a generic d-linear-group delay function whose public parameters, inputs and outputs consist of $k_{\mathsf{pp}}(\lambda, T)$, $k_{\mathsf{in}}(\lambda, T)$ and $k_{\mathsf{out}}(\lambda, T)$ group elements, respectively, where $T \in \mathbb{N}$ is the delay parameter. Let $Q_{\mathsf{eqEval}}(\lambda, T)$ denote the number of equality queries issued by the algorithm Eval. Then, there exists a generic-group algorithm $\mathcal{A}$ that consists of $\binom{k_{\mathsf{pp}} + k_{\mathsf{in}} + d}{d} \cdot \max\{k_{\mathsf{out}}, Q_{\mathsf{eqEval}}\}$ parallel processors, each of which issues at most $O(\binom{k_{\mathsf{pp}} + k_{\mathsf{in}} + d}{d} \cdot |\mathsf{factors}(N)| \cdot \lambda)$ sequential oracle queries, such that*

$$\Pr\left[\mathbf{y}' = \mathbf{y} \; \middle| \; \begin{array}{l} N \leftarrow \mathsf{OrderGen}(1^\lambda), \widehat{\mathsf{pp}} \leftarrow \mathsf{Setup}^{\mathcal{O}}(N, T) \\ \widehat{\mathbf{x}} \leftarrow \mathsf{Sample}^{\mathcal{O}}(N, T, \widehat{\mathsf{pp}}) \\ \widehat{\mathbf{y}} \leftarrow \mathsf{Eval}^{\mathcal{O}}(N, T, \widehat{\mathsf{pp}}, \widehat{\mathbf{x}}) \\ \widehat{\mathbf{y}}' \leftarrow \mathcal{A}^{\mathcal{O}}(N, T, \widehat{\mathsf{pp}}, \widehat{\mathbf{x}}) \end{array} \right] = 1$$

for all $\lambda \in \mathbb{N}$ and $T \in \mathbb{N}$, where the probability is taken over the internal randomness of $\mathsf{OrderGen}$, Setup and Sample. Moreover, $\mathcal{A}$ issues at most $O\left(\binom{k_{\mathsf{pp}} + k_{\mathsf{in}} + d}{d}\right)$ multilinear map queries, which may all be issued in parallel.

Theorem 4.1 is in fact identical to Theorem 3.1 expect for replacing the term $k_{\mathsf{pp}} + k_{\mathsf{in}}$ with the term $\binom{k_{\mathsf{pp}} + k_{\mathsf{in}} + d}{d}$, where d is the level of linearity, and note that $\binom{k_{\mathsf{pp}} + k_{\mathsf{in}} + d}{d} \leq (k_{\mathsf{pp}} + k_{\mathsf{in}} + 1)^d$ (i.e., the efficiency of our attacker degrades exponentially with the level of linearity). This shows that there are no constructions of generic-group delay functions in cyclic groups of known orders that are equipped with a d-linear map, for any d such that $\binom{k_{\mathsf{pp}} + k_{\mathsf{in}} + d}{d}$ is polynomial in the security parameter $\lambda \in \mathbb{N}$. For example, this holds for any constant d, and for functions whose public parameters and inputs consist of a constant number of group elements this holds for any $d = O(\log \lambda)$.

In what follows we first naturally extend the framework of generic groups and algorithms, described in Sect. 2.1, to the multilinear setting (see Sect. 4.1), and then prove Theorem 4.1 (see Sect. 4.2).

4.1 Generic Multilinear Groups

In order to generalize our impossibility result to rule out generic constructions in groups that are equipped with a multilinear map, we first extend the model of Maurer [Mau05] (recall Sect. 2.1) to support such groups. For simplicity of presentation, we start by defining the model and proving our impossibility result assuming that the multilinear map is symmetric. Then, in Sect. 5 we discuss how to naturally extend the model and the proof to accommodate asymmetric maps as well.

Let $d = d(\lambda)$ be a function of the security parameter $\lambda \in \mathbb{N}$. In what follows, we consider computations in a source group of order N with a d-linear map into a target group of the same order, for a λ-bit integer N generated by the order generation algorithm $\mathsf{OrderGen}(1^\lambda)$. For the purpose of capturing generic computations in such groups, we consider a model which is obtained from Maurer's model by the following modifications:

1. Each element in the table $\mathbf{B}$ is now a pair in $\{\mathsf{source}, \mathsf{target}\} \times \mathbb{Z}_N$; meaning, it consists of a label which specifies whether this element is from the source group or from the target group, together with a $\mathbb{Z}_N$ element as before. All generic algorithms we consider now receive as input a generator for the source group; we capture this fact by always initializing $\mathbf{B}$ with the element $(\mathsf{source}, 1)$ in its first entry (we will forgo noting this explicitly).[8]
2. When the oracle receives a group operation query of the form $(i, j, +)$, it first verifies that the label of the element in the ith entry of the table $\mathbf{B}$ is the same as the label of the element in the jth entry (and that both entries are non-empty). If that is the case, then the oracle places $(\mathsf{label}, V_i + V_j)$ in the next vacant entry of the table, where label is the label of the elements at hand, and V_i and V_j are the $\mathbb{Z}_N$ elements in the ith entry and in the jth entry of $\mathbf{B}$, respectively.
3. When the oracle receives an equality query of the form $(i, j, =)$, it first verifies that the label of the element in the ith entry of the table $\mathbf{B}$ is the same as the label of the element in the jth entry (and that both entries are non-empty). If that is the case, then the oracle returns 1 if $V_i = V_j$ and 0 otherwise.
4. We add a third type of queries, which we refer to as *multilinear map queries*: On input $(i_1, \ldots, i_d, \times)$, the oracle first verifies that for each $j \in [d]$ the i_jth entry contains the label source. If so, it places $(\mathsf{target}, \prod_{j \in [d]} V_{i_j})$, where for every $j \in [d]$, V_{i_j} is the $\mathbb{Z}_N$ element in the i_jth entry of $\mathbf{B}$ and the multiplication is with respect to addition modulo N.

---

[8] The generator $(\mathsf{target}, 1)$ for the target group can be obtained using a single multilinear map query, as described below.

The definition of generic-group delay functions remains the same as in Sect. 2.2, other than the fact that all algorithms (i.e., Setup, Sample and Eval, as well as the adversarial algorithms $\mathcal{A}_0$ and $\mathcal{A}_1$ from Definition 2.1) get oracle access to the extended oracle described in this section, and two additional inputs: (1) The arity d of the map; and (2) the labels of the group elements that are placed in the table $\mathbf{B}$ when the algorithm starts its execution.

4.2   Proof of Theorem 4.1

We define the computation $\mathsf{Eval}^{\mathbb{Z}_N[\mathsf{Lin}_d(\mathsf{PP},\mathbf{X})]|\mathcal{L}}(N, T, \mathsf{PP}, \mathbf{X})$ to be obtained from the original computation $\mathsf{Eval}^{\mathcal{O}}(N, T, \widehat{\mathsf{pp}}, \widehat{\mathbf{x}})$ by a similar emulation to that from Sect. 3, with the following differences:

- The tuples PP and $\mathbf{X}$ consist of pairs of a label and a variable $\mathsf{PP} = ((\mathsf{grp}_1^{\mathsf{pp}}, \mathsf{PP}_1), \ldots, (\mathsf{grp}_{k_{\mathsf{pp}}}^{\mathsf{pp}}, \mathsf{PP}_{k_{\mathsf{pp}}}))$ and $\mathbf{X} = ((\mathsf{grp}_1^{\mathsf{x}}, X_1), \ldots, (\mathsf{grp}_{k_{\mathsf{in}}}^{\mathsf{x}}, X_{k_{\mathsf{in}}}))$, where each label is either source or target, and is determined according to the corresponding label of the original input $(\mathsf{pp}, \mathbf{x})$.[9] We assume without loss of generality that the source variables in both PP and $\mathbf{X}$ appear before the target variables, denote the number of source variables in these tuples by $k_{\mathsf{pp}}^{\mathsf{src}}$ and $k_{\mathsf{in}}^{\mathsf{src}}$, respectively, and denote their total number by $k^{\mathsf{src}} = k_{\mathsf{pp}}^{\mathsf{src}} + k_{\mathsf{in}}^{\mathsf{src}}$.
- We define new variables

$$\mathbf{Z} = \mathsf{Lin}_d(\mathsf{PP}, \mathbf{X}) = \{Z_{\alpha_1, \ldots, \alpha_{k^{\mathsf{src}}}} | \alpha_1 + \cdots + \alpha_{k^{\mathsf{src}}} \leq d\}$$
$$\cup \{\mathsf{PP}_1, \ldots, \mathsf{PP}_{k_{\mathsf{pp}}}, X_1, \ldots, X_{k_{\mathsf{in}}}\},$$

where each variable of the form $Z_{\alpha_1, \ldots, \alpha_{k^{\mathsf{src}}}}$ is associated with the product $\mathsf{PP}_1^{\alpha_1} \cdots \mathsf{PP}_{k_{\mathsf{pp}}^{\mathsf{src}}}^{\alpha_{k_{\mathsf{pp}}^{\mathsf{src}}}} \cdot X_1^{\alpha_{k_{\mathsf{pp}}^{\mathsf{src}}+1}} \cdots X_{k_{\mathsf{in}}^{\mathsf{src}}}^{\alpha_{k^{\mathsf{src}}}}$. Additionally, for the standard basis $e_1, \ldots, e_{k^{\mathsf{src}}}$ we identify the variables $Z_{e_1}, \ldots, Z_{e_{k^{\mathsf{src}}}}$ with the source variables $\mathsf{PP}_1, \ldots, \mathsf{PP}_{k_{\mathsf{pp}}^{\mathsf{src}}}, X_1, \ldots, X_{k_{\mathsf{in}}^{\mathsf{src}}}$, respectively (thus, the union in the above definition of $\mathbf{Z}$ is not disjoint). The number of variables in $\mathbf{Z}$ is at most $g_d(k_{\mathsf{pp}} + k_{\mathsf{in}})$ where $g_d(k) = \binom{k+d}{d}$ (the number of non-negative integer solutions to $\alpha_1 + \cdots + \alpha_k \leq d$).

- Each entry in the local table maintained by the computation (recall Sect. 3) includes a label – either source or target – in addition to a formal polynomial as before. The table is initialized so that its first $1 + k_{\mathsf{pp}} + k_{\mathsf{in}}$ entries are inhabited with the pairs $(\mathsf{source}, 1), (\mathsf{grp}_1^{\mathsf{pp}}, \mathsf{PP}_1), \ldots, (\mathsf{grp}_{k_{\mathsf{pp}}}^{\mathsf{pp}}, \mathsf{PP}_{k_{\mathsf{pp}}}), (\mathsf{grp}_1^{\mathsf{x}}, X_1), \ldots, (\mathsf{grp}_{k_{\mathsf{in}}}^{\mathsf{x}}, X_{k_{\mathsf{in}}})$. These labels are used in accordance with the oracle definition from Sect. 4.1: When group operation or equality queries are issued, the computation first makes the necessary label consistency checks; and when a group operation query is executed, the result polynomial is stored in the local table with the appropriate label.

---

[9] Typically, the labels are predetermined by the scheme, but if this is not the case then the labels can be recovered from the input.

- Multilinear map queries are simulated as follows. First, we check that all d polynomials that are the input to the query are stored in the local table with the label source (otherwise, the query is ignored). If so, then let $p_1(\mathbf{Z}), \ldots, p_d(\mathbf{Z})$ be the polynomials given as input to the query. By the queries allowed, it is guaranteed that $p_1, \ldots, p_d$ are linear polynomials which only involve the variables $\mathsf{PP}^{\mathsf{src}} = (\mathsf{PP}_1, \ldots, \mathsf{PP}_{k_{\mathsf{pp}}^{\mathsf{src}}})$ and $\mathbf{X}^{\mathsf{src}} = (X_1, \ldots, X_{k_{\mathsf{in}}^{\mathsf{src}}})$. We compute the polynomial $p(\mathsf{PP}^{\mathsf{src}}, \mathbf{X}^{\mathsf{src}}) = \prod_{i \in [d]} p_i(\mathsf{PP}^{\mathsf{src}}, \mathbf{X}^{\mathsf{src}})$, and then we replace each product of variables $\mathsf{PP}_1^{\alpha_1} \cdots \mathsf{PP}_{k_{\mathsf{pp}}^{\mathsf{src}}}^{\alpha_{k_{\mathsf{pp}}^{\mathsf{src}}}} \cdot X_1^{\alpha_{k_{\mathsf{pp}}^{\mathsf{src}}+1}} \cdots X_{k_{\mathsf{in}}^{\mathsf{src}}}^{\alpha_{k^{\mathsf{src}}}}$ with the single variable $Z_{\alpha_1, \ldots, \alpha_{k^{\mathsf{src}}}}$ to receive a linear polynomial $p'(\mathbf{Z})$. Finally, we store $(\mathsf{target}, p'(\mathbf{Z}))$ in the next vacant entry of the local table.
- Valid equality queries (i.e., when the entries to be compared have the same label) are answered as in Theorem 4.1. If $p_1(\mathbf{Z})$ and $p_2(\mathbf{Z})$ are to be compared, then the query is answered affirmatively if and only if the equality $p_1(\mathbf{Z}) = p_2(\mathbf{Z})$ follows from the equations in $\mathcal{L}$ (which are linear in $\mathbf{Z}$).
- For $\mathsf{pp} \in \mathbb{Z}_N^{k_{\mathsf{pp}}}$ and $\mathbf{x} \in \mathbb{Z}_N^{k_{\mathsf{in}}}$ we define

$$\mathsf{Products}_{\leq d}(\mathsf{pp}, \mathbf{x}) = \left\{ \mathsf{pp}_1^{\alpha_1} \cdots \mathsf{pp}_{k_{\mathsf{pp}}^{\mathsf{src}}}^{\alpha_{k_{\mathsf{pp}}^{\mathsf{src}}}} \cdot x_1^{\alpha_{k_{\mathsf{pp}}^{\mathsf{src}}+1}} \cdots x_{k_{\mathsf{in}}^{\mathsf{src}}}^{\alpha_{k^{\mathsf{src}}}} \,\Big|\, \alpha_1 + \cdots + \alpha_{k^{\mathsf{src}}} \leq d \right\}$$
$$\cup \left\{ \mathsf{pp}_1, \ldots, \mathsf{pp}_{k_{\mathsf{pp}}}, x_1, \ldots, x_{k_{\mathsf{in}}} \right\}.$$

That is, $\mathsf{Products}_{\leq d}(\mathsf{pp}, \mathbf{x})$ contains all elements of $(\mathsf{pp}, \mathbf{x})$ and all products of at most d elements from the source variables of $(\mathsf{pp}, \mathbf{x})$. Given pointers $(\widehat{\mathsf{pp}}, \widehat{\mathbf{x}})$, we can compute $\widehat{\mathbf{w}} = \{\widehat{(\mathsf{target}, z)} | z \in \mathsf{Products}_{\leq d}(\mathsf{pp}, \mathbf{x})\}$ by using multilinear map queries. Then, given a linear polynomial $p(\mathbf{Z})$, we can compute $\overline{(\mathsf{target}, p(\mathsf{Products}_{\leq d}(\mathsf{pp}, \mathbf{x})))}$ using $\mathbf{w}$, and if $p(\mathbf{Z})$ involves only the source variables $\mathsf{PP}_1, \ldots, \mathsf{PP}_{k_{\mathsf{pp}}^{\mathsf{src}}}, X_1, \ldots, X_{k_{\mathsf{in}}^{\mathsf{src}}}$ then we can compute $\overline{(\mathsf{source}, p(\mathsf{Products}_{\leq d}(\mathsf{pp}, \mathbf{x})))}$.
- The output of the computation is of the form $\mathbf{y}'(\mathbf{Z}) = ((\mathsf{grp}_1, y_1'(\mathbf{Z})), \ldots, (\mathsf{grp}_{k_{\mathsf{out}}}, y_{k_{\mathsf{out}}}'(\mathbf{Z})))$ where $\mathsf{grp}_i \in \{\mathsf{source}, \mathsf{target}\}$ and $y_i'(\mathbf{Z})$ is a linear polynomial for every $i \in [k_{\mathsf{out}}]$. Moreover, if $\mathsf{grp}_i = \mathsf{source}$ then $y_i'(\mathbf{Z})$ is guaranteed to involve only the source variables $\mathsf{PP}_1, \ldots, \mathsf{PP}_{k_{\mathsf{pp}}^{\mathsf{src}}}, X_1, \ldots, X_{k_{\mathsf{in}}^{\mathsf{src}}}$. Therefore, given pointers $(\widehat{\mathsf{pp}}, \widehat{\mathbf{x}})$, for every $i \in [k_{\mathsf{out}}]$ we can compute $\overline{(\mathsf{grp}_i, y_i'(\mathbf{z}))}$ where $\mathbf{z} = \mathsf{Products}_{\leq d}(\mathsf{pp}, \mathbf{x})$, and we denote

$$\widehat{\mathbf{y}'(\mathbf{z})} = (\overline{(\mathsf{grp}_1, y_1'(\mathbf{z}))}, \ldots, \overline{(\mathsf{grp}_{k_{\mathsf{out}}}, y_{k_{\mathsf{out}}}'(\mathbf{z}))}).$$

We now turn to present the proof of Theorem 4.1.

Proof. Let $\mathsf{DF} = (\mathsf{Setup}, \mathsf{Sample}, \mathsf{Eval})$ be a generic d-linear-group delay function, and consider the following adversary $\mathcal{A}$:

The adversary $\mathcal{A}$

The adversary $\mathcal{A}$ on input $(N, T, \widehat{\mathsf{pp}}, \widehat{\mathbf{x}})$ and oracle access to $\mathcal{O}$ is defined as follows:

1. Initialize a set $\mathcal{L} = \emptyset$ of linear equations in the formal variables $\mathsf{Lin}_d(\mathsf{PP}, \mathbf{X}) = \mathbf{Z}$, where $\mathsf{PP} = (\mathsf{PP}_1, \ldots, \mathsf{PP}_{k_{\mathsf{pp}}})$ and $\mathbf{X} = (X_1, \ldots, X_{k_{\mathsf{in}}})$.
2. Compute $\widehat{\mathbf{w}} = \{\widehat{(\mathsf{target}, z)} | z \in \mathsf{Products}_{\leq d}(\mathsf{pp}, \mathbf{x})\}$.

---

3. Repeat the following steps for $t = g_d(k_{pp} + k_{in}) \cdot |\mathsf{factors}(N)| + 1$ iterations:
   (a) Compute $\mathbf{y}'(\mathbf{Z}) = \mathsf{Eval}^{\mathbb{Z}_N [\mathsf{Lin}_d(\mathsf{PP},\mathbf{X})] \| \mathcal{L}}(N, T, \mathsf{PP}, \mathbf{X})$. Let m denote the number of equality queries that are negatively answered in the computation, and let $\ell_1(\mathbf{Z}), \ldots, \ell_m(\mathbf{Z})$ be the linear equations that would have followed from each of these queries had it been affirmatively answered.
   (b) For each $i \in [m]$, if $\ell_i(\mathsf{Products}_{\leq d}(\mathsf{pp}, \mathbf{x}))$ holds then add $\ell_i(\mathbf{Z})$ to $\mathcal{L}$. If at least one linear equation was added to $\mathcal{L}$ then skip step 3(c) and continue to the next iteration.
   (c) Compute and output $\mathbf{y}'(\mathsf{Products}_{\leq d}(\mathsf{pp}, \mathbf{x}))$, then terminate.
4. Output $\perp$.

Query Complexity. Steps 1 and 3(a) require no oracle queries. Step 2 requires at most $g_d(k_{pp} + k_{in})$ parallel processors, each issuing a single multilinear map query. Step 3(b) requires $m \cdot g_d(k_{pp} + k_{in})$ parallel processors, each issuing $O(\log N)$ sequential queries for checking whether $\ell_i(\mathsf{Products}_{\leq d}(\mathsf{pp}, \mathbf{x}))$ hold (using the pre-computed $\widehat{\mathbf{w}}$) for any $i \in [m]$ (and it holds that $m \leq Q_{\mathsf{eqEval}}$). Step 3(c) is executed at most once and requires $k_{out} \cdot g_d(k_{pp} + k_{in})$ parallel processors, each issuing $O(\log N)$ queries (using the precomputed $\widehat{\mathbf{w}}$).

Finally, note that for a composite order N, the attacker $\mathcal{A}$ is not required to compute the factorization of N in order to determine the number of iterations. Specifically, for a λ-bit modulos N it always holds that $|\mathsf{factors}(N)| < \lambda$, and $\mathcal{A}$ can use this upper bound for determining an upper bound on the number of iterations.

Fix an iteration $j \in [t]$ where $t = g_d(k_{pp} + k_{in}) \cdot |\mathsf{factors}(N)| + 1$, let $\mathcal{L}_j$ denote the state of the set $\mathcal{L}$ of linear equations at the beginning of the jth iteration, and consider the two computations $\mathbf{y} = \mathsf{Eval}^{\mathcal{O}}(N, T, \widehat{\mathsf{pp}}, \widehat{\mathbf{x}})$ and $\mathbf{y}'_j(\mathbf{Z}) = \mathsf{Eval}^{\mathbb{Z}_N [\mathsf{Lin}_d(\mathsf{PP},\mathbf{X})] \| \mathcal{L}_j}(N, T, \mathsf{PP}, \mathbf{X})$. By the condition specified in step 3(b) for adding a linear equation ℓ to $\mathcal{L}$, any $\ell \in \mathcal{L}_j$ is satisfied by $\mathbf{z} = \mathsf{Products}_{\leq d}(\mathsf{pp}, \mathbf{x})$ (i.e., $\ell(\mathbf{z})$ holds). Therefore, every equality query that is negatively answered in the computation of $\mathbf{y}$ is also negatively answered in the computation of $\mathbf{y}'_j(\mathbf{Z})$. Hence, one of the following two cases must happen:

- Case I: All equality queries in both computations are answered the same way. In this case, the output of both computations is the same vector of linear polynomials in terms of $\mathbf{z} = \mathsf{Products}_{\leq d}(\mathsf{pp}, \mathbf{x})$ and $\mathbf{Z} = \mathsf{Lin}_d(\mathsf{PP}, \mathbf{X})$, respectively, and also each coordinate in the output has the same $\{\mathsf{source}, \mathsf{target}\}$ label, so it holds that $\mathbf{y} = \mathbf{y}'_j(\mathbf{z})$. Furthermore, since all negatively answered queries in the computation of $\mathbf{y}'_j(\mathbf{Z})$ are also negatively answered in the computation of $\mathbf{y}$, then for all $i \in [m]$ the linear equation $\ell_i(\mathbf{z})$ is not satisfied. Therefore, step 3(c) is reached in this case and $\mathcal{A}$ succeeds in outputting $\mathbf{y}$.
- Case II: There exists an equality query that is positively answered in the computation of $\mathbf{y}$ but is negatively answered in the computation of $\mathbf{y}'_j(\mathbf{Z})$. This means that there exists an $i \in [m]$ for which $\ell_i(\mathbf{z})$ holds, but $\ell_i(\mathbf{Z})$ is not implied by the linear equations in $\mathcal{L}_j$. Thus, ℓ_i is added to $\mathcal{L}$ and the algorithm skips to the next iteration.

So far we have shown that $\mathcal{A}$ outputs $\mathbf{y}$ (i.e., the correct output) whenever step 3(c) is reached. We now complete the proof by showing that step 4 is never reached (i.e., that step 3(c) is always reached). Suppose towards contradiction that $t = g_d(k_{\text{pp}} + k_{\text{in}}) \cdot |\text{factors}(N)| + 1$ iterations are performed, but none of them reaches step 3(c). For every $j \in [t]$ recall that $\mathcal{L}_j$ denotes the state of the set $\mathcal{L}$ at the beginning of the jth iteration, and denote by $\mathcal{L}_{t+1}$ the state of $\mathcal{L}$ when reaching step 4. Then, it holds that $\mathcal{L}_1 \subsetneq \mathcal{L}_2 \subsetneq \cdots \subsetneq \mathcal{L}_{t+1}$, since for every $j \in [t]$ the set $\mathcal{L}_{j+1}$ contains at least one linear equation that is not implied by $\mathcal{L}_j$. Also, as already mentioned, for every $j \in [t+1]$ and $\ell \in \mathcal{L}_j$ the linear equation $\ell(\mathbf{z})$ is satisfied. For a system of linear equations $\mathcal{M}$ with k variables over $\mathbb{Z}_N$, if there exists a solution $\mathbf{z} \in \mathbb{Z}_N^k$ to the system $\mathcal{M}$ then the set of solutions forms a coset of a subgroup of $\mathbb{Z}_N^k$. That is, there exists a subgroup H of $\mathbb{Z}_N^k$ such the the set of solutions to $\mathcal{M}$ is $\mathbf{z} + H$. Therefore, there exist subgroups $H_1, \ldots, H_{t+1}$ of $\mathbb{Z}_N^{g_d(k_{\text{pp}} + k_{\text{in}})}$ such that for every $j \in [t+1]$ it holds that

$$\left\{ \mathbf{z}' \in \mathbb{Z}_N^{g_d(k_{\text{pp}} + k_{\text{in}})} \middle| \forall \ell(\mathbf{Z}) \in \mathcal{L}_j \; : \; \ell(\mathbf{z}') \text{ is satisfied} \right\} = \mathbf{z} + H_j \; .$$

Then, it holds that $H_1 > H_2 > \cdots > H_{t+1}$ (i.e., H_{j+1} is a proper subgroup of H_j for every $j \in [t]$). Therefore, the order of every H_{j+1} divides that of H_j, and it holds that

$$\text{factors}(|H_{t+1}|) \subsetneq \text{factors}(|H_t|) \subsetneq \cdots \subsetneq \text{factors}(|H_1|) \subseteq \text{factors}(|\mathbb{Z}_N^{g_d(k_{\text{pp}} + k_{\text{in}})}|).$$

Since

$$|\text{factors}(|\mathbb{Z}_N^{g_d(k_{\text{pp}} + k_{\text{in}})}|)| = |\text{factors}(N^{g_d(k_{\text{pp}} + k_{\text{in}})})| = t - 1,$$

it is impossible to have t proper containments in the above chain and we reach a contradiction. ∎

5 Additional Extensions

In this section we first discuss two extensions of our results, showing that our proofs extend to delay functions whose public parameters, inputs and outputs may include arbitrary bit-strings (in addition to group elements), and to asymmetric multilinear maps. Then, we pose an open problem regarding incremental computation of Smith normal forms.

Allowing explicit bit-strings as part of pp, x and y. Our proofs from Sects. 3 and 4 readily extend to the case where the public parameters pp, the input $\mathbf{x}$ and the output $\mathbf{y}$ may include arbitrary bit-strings, in addition to group elements. We review the necessary adjustments for our proof from Sect. 3, and note that essentially identical adjustments can be applied to our proof in the multilinear setting as well. Concretely:

- In addition to N, T, $\widehat{\text{pp}}$ and $\widehat{\mathbf{x}}$, the evaluation algorithm Eval now receives as input two bit-strings, pp_s and x_s, denoting the bit-string parts of pp and of the input $\mathbf{x}$, respectively, and outputs a bit-string y_s in addition to $\widehat{\mathbf{y}}$. The computation $\text{Eval}^{\mathbb{Z}_N[\text{PP},\mathbf{X}]|\mathcal{L}} (N, T, (\text{PP}, \text{pp}_s), (\mathbf{X}, x_s))$ is then defined via an emulation of the computation $\text{Eval}^{\mathcal{O}} (N, T, (\widehat{\text{pp}}, \text{pp}_s), (\widehat{\mathbf{x}}, x_s))$ similarly to Sect. 3: The local table maintained by the emulation and the way queries are emulated are defined as in Sect. 3, and the output of this emulation is now a pair $(\mathbf{y}(\mathsf{PP}, \mathbf{X}), y_s)$, where $\mathbf{y}(\mathsf{PP}, \mathbf{X})$ is a vector of k_{out} polynomials $y_1(\mathsf{PP}, \mathbf{X}), \ldots, y_{k_{\mathsf{out}}}(\mathsf{PP}, \mathbf{X})$ in PP and in $\mathbf{X}$, and y_s is an explicit bit-string.

– The adversary $\mathcal{A}$ now receives the bit-strings pp_s and x_s, in addition to its inputs from Sect. 3. In Step 2(a) it now runs the emulation $\mathsf{Eval}^{\mathbb{Z}_N[\mathsf{PP}, \mathbf{X}]|\mathcal{L}}(N, T, (\mathsf{PP}, \mathsf{pp}_s), (\mathbf{X}, x_s))$ to obtain its output $(\mathbf{y}'(\mathsf{PP}, \mathbf{X}), y_s')$. In Step 2(c) it computes $\widehat{\mathbf{y}'(\mathsf{pp}, \mathbf{x})}$ and outputs $\left(\widehat{\mathbf{y}'(\mathsf{pp}, \mathbf{x})}, y_s'\right)$. The main additional observation is that for each iteration $j \in [(k_{\mathsf{pp}} + k_{\mathsf{in}}) \cdot |\mathsf{factors}(N)| + 1]$, if all equality queries in the emulation $\mathsf{Eval}^{\mathbb{Z}_N[\mathsf{PP}, \mathbf{X}]|\mathcal{L}}(N, T, (\mathsf{PP}, \mathsf{pp}_s), (\mathbf{X}, x_s))$ in that iteration are answered consistently with the equality pattern in $\mathsf{Eval}^{\mathcal{O}}(N, T, (\widehat{\mathsf{pp}}, \mathsf{pp}_s), (\widehat{\mathbf{x}}, x_s))$, then the bit-string component y_s' outputted by the emulation in this iteration is the same as the bit-string component y_s outputted by the original computation $\mathsf{Eval}^{\mathcal{O}}(N, T, (\widehat{\mathsf{pp}}, \mathsf{pp}_s), (\widehat{\mathbf{x}}, x_s))$. Hence, when Case I from our analysis is reached, it is still the case that the adversary is successful in outputting the correct output.

Asymmetric multilinear maps. Our impossibility result from Sect. 4 can be adjusted in order to rule out the existence of generic-group delay functions in groups with *asymmetric* multilinear maps; i.e., collections of $d + 1$ groups – d source groups and a single target group, each of which is of order N – which are equipped with a d-linear operation mapping d elements, an element from each source group, into an element in the target group.

First, the model has to be extended to support such groups. This is done in a natural manner, by considering $d + 1$ labels (instead of 2): $\mathsf{source}_1, \ldots, \mathsf{source}_d$ and target. Now, each entry in the table $\mathbf{B}$ is pair of the form (label, a), where label is one of the aforementioned labels, and $a \in \mathbb{Z}_N$; and we assume that the table $\mathbf{B}$ is always initialized with the pairs $(\mathsf{source}_1, 1), \ldots, (\mathsf{source}_d, 1)$ in its first d entries, respectively. Upon receiving a multilinear operation query, the oracle now verifies that the labels in the entries (implicitly) given as input to the oracle are indeed $\mathsf{source}_1, \ldots, \mathsf{source}_d$.

The proof is then obtained from the proof of Theorem 4.1 by adjusting it to this generalized generic model. Roughly speaking, the main adjustment is that now the linearization procedure needs to take into consideration the particular group of each input element. More concretely, the new formal variables introduced by this linearization (denoted by $\mathbf{Z}$ in the proof of Theorem 4.1) do not include all products of degree at most d of the formal variables replacing the source group elements in the public parameters and in the input. Instead, they include all products of at most d elements, with *distinct labels* from $\{\mathsf{source}_1, \ldots, \mathsf{source}_d\}$. Hence, the number of new formal variables introduced by the linearization phase is now at most $((k_{\mathsf{pp}} + k_{\mathsf{in}})/d + 1)^d$, rather than $\binom{k_{\mathsf{pp}} + k_{\mathsf{in}} + d}{d}$.

Incremental computation of Smith normal forms. As discussed in Sect. 1.3 and described in detail in Appendix A, our attacker is efficient not only in its number of parallel processors and generic group operations but also in its additional internal computation. Specifically, in each iteration our attacker performs a single invocation of any algorithm for computing Smith normal form. However, throughout the attack the matrices to which we apply such an algorithm are not independent of each other, but rather each matrix is obtained from the previous one by adding one more row and column. Thus, any algorithm that can compute Smith normal forms in an incremental manner may lead to substantial improvements in the practical running time of our attacker. Finally, we note that efficiently realizing our attacker's internal computation is not essential for our result in the generic-group model, and that basing our approach on fast algorithms for Smith normal forms is just one concrete possibility.

A   Fast Internal Computation via Smith Normal Forms

As discussed in Sect. 1.3, the most significant operation that is performed by our attacker which is non-trivial in terms of its computational cost is checking in each iteration whether or not a given linear equation follows from the linear equations already in the set $\mathcal{L}$. When considering groups of prime order, this can be done simply by testing for linear independence among the vectors of coefficients corresponding to these equations. When considering groups of composite order, this is a bit more subtle, and in what follows we show that this can be done for example by relying on fast algorithms for computing the Smith normal form of integer matrices (e.g., [Sto96]) and without knowing the factorization of the order of the group.

The Smith normal form. The Smith normal form is a canonical diagonal form for equivalence of matrices over a principal ideal ring R. For any $\mathbf{A} \in R^{n \times m}$ there exist square invertible matrices $\mathbf{S}$ and $\mathbf{T}$ over R such that $\mathbf{D} = \mathbf{SAT}$ is the all-zeros matrix except for the first r terms $s_1, \ldots, s_r$ on its main diagonal, where $s_i | s_{i+1}$ for every $0 \leq i \leq r - 1$. The matrix $\mathbf{D}$ is called the Smith normal form of $\mathbf{A}$ and it is unique up to multiplications of its non-zero terms by units. The Smith normal form was first proven to exist by Smith [Smi61] for matrices over the integers, and in this case each s_i is positive, $r = \mathrm{rank}(\mathbf{A})$ and $|\det(\mathbf{S})| = |\det(\mathbf{T})| = 1$. For our purposes we consider Smith forms of integer matrices, and we will not be relying on the fact that $s_i | s_{i+1}$ for every $0 \leq i \leq r - 1$.

A fast algorithm for computing Smith normal forms over the integers was presented by Storjohann [Sto96]. His algorithm requires $\tilde{O}\left(n^{\omega-1}m \cdot \mathsf{M}\left(n \log \|\mathbf{A}\|\right)\right)$ bit operations for computing the Smith normal form of a matrix $\mathbf{A} \in \mathbb{Z}^{n \times m}$, where ω is the exponent for matrix multiplication over rings (i.e., two $n \times n$ matrices can be multiplied in $O(n^\omega)$ ring operations), $\mathsf{M}(t)$ bounds the number of bit operations required for multiplying two $\lceil t \rceil$-bit integers, and $\|\mathbf{A}\| = \max |\mathbf{A}_{i,j}|$.

Efficiently realizing our attacker. Let $\mathcal{L}$ be a set of linear equations over $\mathbb{Z}_N$ in the formal variables $\mathbf{Z} = (Z_1, \ldots, Z_k)$, and let $\ell(\mathbf{Z})$ be an additional such linear equation. Then, we would like to determine whether or not there exists $\mathbf{z} \in \mathbb{Z}_N^k$ such that $\ell'(\mathbf{z})$ holds for every $\ell'(\mathbf{Z}) \in \mathcal{L}$ but $\ell(\mathbf{z})$ does not hold (i.e., ℓ is not implied by $\mathcal{L}$).

Denote $\mathcal{L} = \{\langle \mathbf{a}^{(i)}, \mathbf{Z} \rangle = b_i \mod N : i \in [t]\}$, where $t = |\mathcal{L}|$, $\mathbf{a}^{(i)} \in \mathbb{Z}^k$ and $b_i \in \mathbb{Z}$ for every $i \in [t]$ (that is, we identify $\mathbb{Z}_N$ with $\{0, \ldots, N-1\} \subseteq \mathbb{Z}$).

First, we convert our equations to equations over $\mathbb{Z}$ by adding new variables $\mathbf{W} = (W_1, \ldots, W_t)$ and for each $i \in [t]$ we convert the equation $\langle \mathbf{a}^{(i)}, \mathbf{Z} \rangle = b_i$ mod N into the equation

$$\langle \mathbf{a}^{(i)}, \mathbf{Z} \rangle + N \cdot W_i = b_i \; .$$

In matrix notation we let

$$\mathbf{A} = \begin{bmatrix} \mathbf{a}^{(1)} \\ \vdots & N \cdot I_{t \times t} \\ \mathbf{a}^{(t)} \end{bmatrix} \in \mathbb{Z}^{(k+t) \times t}, \; \mathbf{b} = \begin{bmatrix} b_1 \\ \vdots \\ b_t \end{bmatrix} \in \mathbb{Z}^t, \; \mathbf{v} = \begin{bmatrix} \mathbf{Z} \\ \mathbf{W} \end{bmatrix} \in \mathbb{Z}^{k+t},$$

and then our system of linear equations is $\mathbf{Av} = \mathbf{b}$. Next, we compute the Smith normal form of $\mathbf{A}$, that is, we find matrices $\mathbf{S} \in \mathbb{Z}^{(k+t) \times (k+t)}$ and $\mathbf{T} \in \mathbb{Z}^{t \times t}$ that are invertible over $\mathbb{Z}$ (i.e., $|\det \mathbf{S}| = |\det \mathbf{T}| = 1$), such that the matrix $\mathbf{D} = \mathbf{SAT}$ is zero everywhere except for the first r terms on its main diagonal for some $0 \leq r \leq t$. Now, by multiplying from left by $\mathbf{S}$, our system is the same as $\mathbf{SATT}^{-1}\mathbf{v} = \mathbf{Sb}$, and denoting $\mathbf{u} = \mathbf{T}^{-1}\mathbf{v}$ and $\mathbf{c} = \mathbf{Sb}$, we obtain the equivalent system $\mathbf{Du} = \mathbf{c}$. Let $d_1, \ldots, d_r$ be the non-zero diagonal values of $\mathbf{D}$. If there exists $i \in [r]$ such that d_i does not divide c_i, or $r \leq i \leq k+t$ such that $c_i \neq 0$ then the system does not have any solution. Otherwise, the general solution for the system $\mathbf{Du} = \mathbf{c}$ is of the form $\mathbf{u} = (u_1, \ldots, u_{k+t}) = (c_1/d_1, \ldots, c_r/d_r, y_1, \ldots, y_s)$, where $s = k + t - r$ and the y coordinates can take any value.

Now, let $\ell(\mathbf{Z})$ be another linear equation in $\mathbb{Z}_N$, and denote it by $\langle \mathbf{a}', \mathbf{Z} \rangle = b'$ mod N, where $\mathbf{a}' \in \mathbb{Z}^k$ and $b' \in \mathbb{Z}$ (recall that we identify $\mathbb{Z}_N$ with $\{0, \ldots, N - 1\} \subseteq \mathbb{Z}$ as mentioned above). We may substitute $\mathbf{Z} = \mathbf{T}'\mathbf{u}$, where $\mathbf{T}' \in \mathbb{Z}^{k \times t}$ consists of the first k rows of $\mathbf{T}$. Then, we obtain the linear equation $\langle \mathbf{a}', \mathbf{T}'\mathbf{u} \rangle = b'$ mod N. Substituting the general solution $\mathbf{u} = (c_1/d_1, \ldots, c_r/d_r, y_1, \ldots, y_s)$, we obtain a linear equation of the form $\sum_{i=1}^{s} \alpha_i y_i = \beta$ mod N. If $\beta = 0$ mod N and $\alpha_i = 0$ mod N for all $i \in [s]$ then every $z \in \mathbb{Z}^k$ satisfying $\mathcal{L}$ also satisfies $\ell(\mathbf{Z})$. Otherwise, if $\beta \neq 0$ mod N then the solution corresponding to $(y_1, \ldots, y_s) = (0, \ldots, 0)$ satisfies $\mathcal{L}$ but does not satisfy $\ell(\mathbf{Z})$, and if $\beta = 0$ mod N but there exists $i \in [s]$ such that $\alpha_i \neq 0$ mod N then the solution corresponding to $(y_1, \ldots, y_s) = e_i$ satisfies $\mathcal{L}$ but does not satisfy $\ell(\mathbf{Z})$.

References

[BBB+18] Boneh, D., Bonneau, J., Bünz, B., Fisch, B.: Verifiable delay functions. In: Shacham, H., Boldyreva, A. (eds.) CRYPTO 2018. LNCS, vol. 10991, pp. 757–788. Springer, Cham (2018). https://doi.org/10.1007/978-3-319-96884-1_25

[BBF18] Boneh, D., Bünz, B., Fisch, B.: A survey of two verifiable delay functions. Cryptology ePrint Archive, Report 2018/712 (2018)

[BGJ+16] Bitansky, N., Goldwasser, S., Jain, A., Paneth, O., Vaikuntanathan, V., Waters, B.: Time-lock puzzles from randomized encodings. In: Proceedings of the 7th Conference on Innovations in Theoretical Computer Science, pp. 345–356 (2016)

[BL96]   Boneh, D., Lipton, R.J.: Algorithms for black-box fields and their application to cryptography. In: Koblitz, N. (ed.) CRYPTO 1996. LNCS, vol. 1109, pp. 283–297. Springer, Heidelberg (1996). https://doi.org/10.1007/3-540-68697-5_22

[CP18]   Cohen, B., Pietrzak, K.: Simple proofs of sequential work. In: Nielsen, J.B., Rijmen, V. (eds.) EUROCRYPT 2018. LNCS, vol. 10821, pp. 451–467. Springer, Cham (2018). https://doi.org/10.1007/978-3-319-78375-8_15

[DGM+19]   Döttling, N., Garg, S., Malavolta, G., Vasudevan, P.N.: Tight verifiable delay functions. Cryptology ePrint Archive, Report 2019/659 (2019)

[DMP+19]   De Feo, L., Masson, S., Petit, C., Sanso, A.: Verifiable delay functions from supersingular isogenies and pairings. Cryptology ePrint Archive, Report 2019/166 (2019)

[DN92]   Dwork, C., Naor, M.: Pricing via processing or combatting junk mail. In: Brickell, E.F. (ed.) CRYPTO 1992. LNCS, vol. 740, pp. 139–147. Springer, Heidelberg (1993). https://doi.org/10.1007/3-540-48071-4_10

[EFK+19]   Ephraim, N., Freitag, C., Komargodski, I., Pass, R.: Continuous verifiable delay functions. Cryptology ePrint Archive, Report 2019/619 (2019)

[GW11]   Gentry, C., Wichs, D.: Separating succinct non-interactive arguments from all falsifiable assumptions. In: Proceedings of the 43rd Annual ACM Symposium on Theory of Computing, pp. 99–108 (2011)

[JS08]   Jager, T., Schwenk, J.: On the equivalence of generic group models. In: Baek, J., Bao, F., Chen, K., Lai, X. (eds.) ProvSec 2008. LNCS, vol. 5324, pp. 200–209. Springer, Heidelberg (2008). https://doi.org/10.1007/978-3-540-88733-1_14

[Kil92]   Kilian, J.: A note on efficient zero-knowledge proofs and arguments. In: Proceedings of the 24th Annual ACM Symposium on Theory of Computing, pp. 723–732 (1992)

[LW15]   Lenstra, A.K., Wesolowski, B.: A random zoo: sloth, unicorn, and trx. Cryptology ePrint Archive, Report 2015/366 (2015)

[Mau05]   Maurer, U.: Abstract models of computation in cryptography. In: Smart, N.P. (ed.) Cryptography and Coding 2005. LNCS, vol. 3796, pp. 1–12. Springer, Heidelberg (2005). https://doi.org/10.1007/11586821_1

[Mic94]   Micali, S.: CS proofs. In: Proceedings of the 35th Annual IEEE Symposium on the Foundations of Computer Science, pp. 436–453 (1994)

[MMV11]   Mahmoody, M., Moran, T., Vadhan, S.: Time-lock puzzles in the random oracle model. In: Rogaway, P. (ed.) CRYPTO 2011. LNCS, vol. 6841, pp. 39–50. Springer, Heidelberg (2011). https://doi.org/10.1007/978-3-642-22792-9_3

[MMV13]   Mahmoody, M., Moran, T., Vadhan, S.P.: Publicly verifiable proofs of sequential work. In: Proceedings of the 4th Conference on Innovations in Theoretical Computer Science, pp. 373–388 (2013)

[MSW19]   Mahmoody, M., Smith, C., Wu, D.J.: A note on the (im)possibility of verifiable delay functions in the random oracle model. Cryptology ePrint Archive, Report 2019/663 (2019)

[MW98]   Maurer, U., Wolf, S.: Lower bounds on generic algorithms in groups. In: Nyberg, K. (ed.) EUROCRYPT 1998. LNCS, vol. 1403, pp. 72–84. Springer, Heidelberg (1998). https://doi.org/10.1007/BFb0054118

[Nec94]   Nechaev, V.I.: Complexity of a determinate algorithm for the discrete logarithm. Math. Notes **55**(2), 91–101 (1994). https://doi.org/10.1007/BF02113297

[Pie19] Pietrzak, K.: Simple verifiable delay functions. In: Proceedings of the 10th Conference on Innovations in Theoretical Computer Science, pp. 60:1–60:15 (2019)

[RSW96] Rivest, R.L., Shamir, A., Wagner, D.A.: Time-lock puzzles and timed-release crypto (1996)

[Sho97] Shoup, V.: Lower bounds for discrete logarithms and related problems. In: Fumy, W. (ed.) EUROCRYPT 1997. LNCS, vol. 1233, pp. 256–266. Springer, Heidelberg (1997). https://doi.org/10.1007/3-540-69053-0_18

[Smi61] Smith, H.J.S.: On systems of linear indeterminate equations and congruences. Philos. Trans. R. Soc. **151**(1), 293–326 (1861)

[Sto96] Storjohann, A.: Near optimal algorithms for computing Smith normal forms of integer matrices. In: Proceedings of the International Symposium on Symbolic and Algebraic Computation, pp. 267–274 (1996)

[Wes19] Wesolowski, B.: Efficient verifiable delay functions. In: Ishai, Y., Rijmen, V. (eds.) EUROCRYPT 2019. LNCS, vol. 11478, pp. 379–407. Springer, Cham (2019). https://doi.org/10.1007/978-3-030-17659-4_13

Signatures

Sigma Protocols for MQ, PKP and SIS, and Fishy Signature Schemes

Ward Beullens[✉]

imec-COSIC KU Leuven,
Kasteelpark Arenberg 10 - bus 2452, 3001 Heverlee, Belgium
Ward.Beullens@esat.kuleuven.be

Abstract. This work presents sigma protocols to prove knowledge of:
- a solution to a system of quadratic polynomials,
- a solution to an instance of the Permuted Kernel Problem and
- a witness for a variety of lattice statements (including SIS).

Our sigma protocols have soundness error $1/q'$, where q' is any number bounded by the size of the underlying finite field. This is much better than existing proofs, which have soundness error $2/3$ or $(q'+1)/2q'$. The prover and verifier time our proofs are $O(q')$. We achieve this by first constructing so-called *sigma protocols with helper*, which are sigma protocols where the prover and the verifier are assisted by a trusted third party, and then eliminating the helper from the proof with a "cut-and-choose" protocol. We apply the Fiat-Shamir transform to obtain signature schemes with security proof in the QROM. We show that the resulting signature schemes, which we call the "MUltivariate quaDratic FIat-SHamir" scheme (MUDFISH) and the "ShUffled Solution to Homogeneous linear SYstem FIat-SHamir" scheme (SUSHSYFISH), are more efficient than existing signatures based on the MQ problem and the Permuted Kernel Problem. Our proof system can be used to improve the efficiency of applications relying on (generalizations of) Stern's protocol. We show that the proof size of our SIS proof is smaller than that of Stern's protocol by an order of magnitude and that our proof is more efficient than existing post-quantum secure SIS proofs.

Keywords: Zero-knowledge · Post-Quantum digital signatures · SIS · Multivariate cryptography · Permuted Kernel Problem · Silly acronyms

1 Introduction

Zero-knowledge proofs of knowledge and more specifically Sigma protocols are a technique in cryptography that allows a prover to prove to a verifier that they know a value x that satisfies some relation, without revealing any additional information about x [19]. Sigma protocols are useful to build a wide variety of cryptographic applications, including digital signatures, group/ring signatures,

© International Association for Cryptologic Research 2020
A. Canteaut and Y. Ishai (Eds.): EUROCRYPT 2020, LNCS 12107, pp. 183–211, 2020.
https://doi.org/10.1007/978-3-030-45727-3_7

e-voting protocols, and privacy-preserving cryptocurrencies. In some cases these sigma protocols are not completely sound, meaning that a cheating prover can convince a verifier he knows some value, without actually knowing it. If a prover can do this with a probability at most ϵ, then ϵ is said to be the *soundness error* of the sigma protocol. The soundness of a sigma protocol can be amplified; by repeating the protocol k times the soundness error of the entire protocol becomes ϵ^k. Therefore, if one repeats a protocol with soundness error ≤ 1 often enough, one can obtain a sound protocol. However, if a large number of repetitions is required, this makes the protocol less efficient and makes applications of the protocol less practical. This is the case for Stern's protocol [34] and the sigma protocols underlying some post-quantum signature schemes [10,12,14]. The goal of this paper is to develop new variants of these sigma protocols that have a smaller soundness error, such that fewer repetitions are necessary and such that the overall efficiency of the protocols is improved.

Zero-Knowledge Based Post-Quantum Signatures. One way to construct a signature scheme is to first construct a zero-knowledge identification scheme and then make it into a non-interactive signature scheme with a transformation such as the Fiat-Shamir transform [17] or the Unruh transform [35]. Looking at the NIST Post-Quantum Standardization project, three of the Round II signature schemes, MQDSS, Picnic, and Dilithium use this approach. MQDSS [13] uses a zero-knowledge proof that, given a multivariate quadratic map $\mathcal{P} : \mathbb{F}_q^n \to \mathbb{F}_q^m$ proves knowledge of a solution $\mathbf{s} \in \mathbb{F}_q^n$ such that $\mathcal{P}(\mathbf{s}) = \mathbf{0}$. Picnic [12] uses an identification scheme constructed using the "MPC-in-the-head" technique [20] that relies on symmetric primitives. Dilithium is a lattice-based signature scheme that relies on the Fiat-Shamir with aborts technique [29]. Another example is PKP-DSS [10], which uses a zero-knowledge proof introduced by Shamir in 1989 for proving knowledge of a solution of an instance of the Permuted Kernel Problem (PKP) [33]. This means that, given a matrix $\mathbf{A} \in \mathbb{F}_q^{m \times n}$ and a vector $\mathbf{v} \in \mathbb{F}_q^n$, the proof system can prove knowledge of a permutation $\pi \in S_n$ such that $\mathbf{A}\mathbf{v}_\pi = 0$, where $\mathbf{v}_\pi$ is the vector obtained by permuting the entries of the vector $\mathbf{v}$ with the permutation π. A drawback of these schemes (with exception of Dilithium) is that the underlying identification schemes have a large soundness error, so a large number of parallel repetitions are required to get a secure signature scheme. This increases the signature sizes and the signing and verification times. For example, the protocol underlying the Picnic signature scheme has a soundness error of $\frac{2}{3}$ and hence requires $k = 219$ repetitions to get the soundness error down to less than 2^{-128}.

Recently, Katz et al. [24] improved on the approach of Picnic by building a zero-knowledge proof from MPC in the preprocessing model, where the parties can use some auxiliary data that was generated during a preprocessing phase. The advantage of moving to the new MPC protocol is that it allows for secure computation with dishonest majority with an arbitrary number of parties n, which results in a zero-knowledge proof with a soundness error of $\frac{1}{n}$. Hence, fewer parallel rounds are required to get a secure signature scheme. A "cut-and-choose" protocol is used to deal with the preprocessing phase, which makes signing and verification slower compared to the original Picnic scheme. This new signature scheme is called Picnic2 and is, together with the original Picnic scheme, one of the Round 2 candidates of the NIST PQC standardization project.

Stern's Protocol. In 1993, Stern proposed a code based sigma protocol [34]. For a publicly known parity check matrix $\mathbf{H} \in \mathbb{F}_2^{m \times n}$, syndrome $\mathbf{s} \in \mathbb{F}_2^m$ and weight t, Stern's zero-knowledge proof can prove knowledge of an error vector $\mathbf{e} \in \mathbb{F}_2^n$ with hamming weight t such that $\mathbf{He} = \mathbf{s}$. Internally, Stern's protocol is very similar to Shamir's protocol for PKP, and in fact, Stern's protocol generalizes easily to proving knowledge of a witness of the inhomogeneous PKP (IPKP) relation. The motivation behind Stern's protocol was to obtain a code-based identification scheme (and hence also a signature scheme with the Fiat-Shamir transform). However, Stern's protocol has been used extensively in lattice-based cryptography, because the IPKP relation can be bootstrapped to prove knowledge of a solution to the SIS problem, knowledge of an LWE secret and more complex lattice statements such as proving that a given LWE ciphertext is a valid encryption of a known message satisfying certain constraints [28]. This led to the construction of many advanced primitives from lattices, such as identity-based identification schemes, group signatures (with verifier local revocation), logarithmic size ring signatures and group encryption [25–28]. Improving Stern's protocol is an important and long-standing open problem because this would improve the efficiency of all these constructions.

Contributions. In this paper we generalize the idea behind Picnic2 [24] to something we call "sigma protocols with helper". Concretely, a sigma protocol with helper is a 3-party protocol between a prover, a verifier and a trusted third party called the "helper". The protocol begins with the helper who honestly generates some auxiliary information that he sends to the verifier. The helper also sends the randomness seed that he used to generate his randomness to the prover. Then, the protocol resumes like a normal sigma protocol. A sigma protocol with helper is similar to a sigma protocol in the Common Reference String (CRS) model, except that the trusted third party sends some secret information (the randomness seed) to the prover and that the trusted third party needs to participate in every execution, rather than just doing the trusted setup once.

We then construct a sigma protocol with helper to prove knowledge of a solution of a system of quadratic equations and a sigma protocol with helper for proving knowledge of a solution of an inhomogeneous PKP instance (i.e. the same relation as the Shamir and Stern protocols). Our proofs have soundness error $\frac{1}{q'}$ and prover time $\Theta(q')$, where q' is any number bounded by the size of the finite fields that are used. This soundness error is much better than existing proofs which have soundness error $\frac{1}{2} + \frac{1}{2q}$ or soundness error $2/3$. We then show how to remove the helper with a "cut-and-choose" protocol, analogous to the approach used by Katz et al. [24]. This transformation gives rise to standard sigma protocols (i.e. without helper) which can then be transformed into signature schemes using the Fiat-Shamir transform or used as a more efficient variant of Stern's protocol as a building block for advanced privacy-preserving constructions.

Note that, even though the soundness error is q', it is not possible to do one-shot proofs if the field size is exponential because the prover time is $\Theta(q')$. However, we can still realize a large practical improvement over existing proofs: The proof size of existing proofs is $\mathcal{O}(\lambda X)$, where λ is the security parameter and X is the proof size of a single iteration of the protocol. In comparison, the proof size of our proofs is $\mathcal{O}(\frac{\lambda}{\log q'}(X + \log q' * |\text{seed}|))$, because the number of iterations is now $O(\frac{\lambda}{\log q'})$, and each iteration incurs an overhead of $\log q'|\text{seed}|$ (a path in a Merkle tree of size q'). In practice, the proof size is often dominated by the $\mathcal{O}(\lambda|\text{seed}|)$ term even for small values of q'. Since X is usually much larger than $|\text{seed}| = \lambda$, this gives a large improvement in practice. X and $|\text{seed}|$ are both linear in λ, so the improvement factor remains the same at higher security levels.

We apply the Fiat-Shamir transform to our Sigma protocol for the MQ relation to get a signature scheme whose security reduces to the problem of finding a solution to a random system of multivariate quadratic polynomials. We call this the "MUltivarite quaDratic FIat-SHamir" scheme (MUDFISH). MUDFISH is more efficient than MQDSS, the existing signature scheme based on the same hard problem. At NIST security level 1, the MUDFISH signatures are roughly half as big as the MQDSS signatures, while our constant-time MUDFISH implementation is roughly twice as fast as the optimized MQDSS implementation that was submitted to the NIST PQC standardization project. Using the Fiat-Shamir transform on our sigma protocol for the PKP relation, we obtain the "ShUffled Solution to Homogeneous linear SYstem FIat-SHamir" scheme (SUSHSYFISH), a signature scheme whose security reduces to finding a solution of a random PKP instance. SUSHSYFISH has smaller signatures than PKP-DSS, the existing scheme based on the PKP problem while being only slightly slower. Moreover, unlike MQDSS and PKP-DSS, the MUDFISH and SUSHSYFISH signature schemes are based on sigma protocols (i.e. 3-round proofs) rather than 5-round proofs, which results in tighter security proofs in the ROM and even allows us to use the recent results of Don et al. [16] to prove their security in the QROM. A comparison of the signature sizes and signing speed of MUDFISH and multiple instantiations of SUSHSYFISH with those of existing Post-Quantum Fiat-Shamir signatures is given in Fig. 1. Our implementation is available on GitHub [9].

We can improve the lattice-based constructions such as identity-based identification schemes, group signatures (with verifier local revocation), logarithmic size ring signatures and group encryption that rely on Stern's protocol [25–28], by replacing Sterns protocol by our more efficient proof for IPKP. In particular, we make a case study for the SIS problem, where we see that with our proof system, the proof size is a factor 10 smaller than with Stern's protocol. And smaller than proof sizes arising from other post-quantum exact proofs for SIS, such as using "MPC-in-the-head" techniques [5] or an algebraic approach [11].

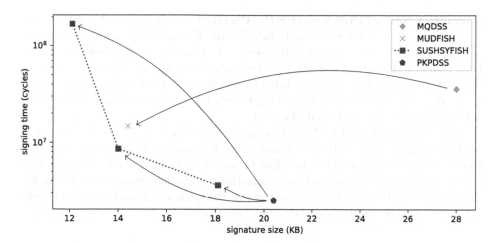

Fig. 1. Comparison of MUDFISH and SUSHSYFISH to existing signatures based on the MQ problem (MQDSS) and PKP problem (PKP-DSS). Cycle counts of picnic and MQDSS are taken from the NIST Round2 submission packages (the optimized, but not AVX2 optimized implementations, updated to take the attack of Kales and Zaverucha into account [23]), cycle counts for PKP-DSS are taken from [10].

Roadmap. In Sect. 2 we lay out some basic preliminaries required for the remainder of the paper. In Sect. 3 we formalize the notion of a sigma protocol with helper, then we construct sigma protocols with helper for the MQ problem and the Permuted Kernel Problem in Sects. 4 and 5. In Sect. 6 we show how to convert a sigma protocol with helper in a normal zero-knowledge proof (without helper). Then, we convert our zero-knowledge proofs into signature schemes in Sect. 8, where we also briefly discuss our proof-of-concept implementations. Finally, in Sect. 9 we show how to use the IPKP proof to construct a zero-knowledge proof for the SIS relation, and we compare our SIS proof to existing SIS proofs.

2 Preliminaries

2.1 Hard Problems

We introduce (variants of) the Permuted Kernel Problem (PKP), the Multivariate quadratic problem (MQ) and the Short Integer Solution problem (SIS), three computationally hard problems that are used in the remainder of the paper.

Permuted Kernel Problem (PKP/IPKP). Given a matrix $\mathbf{A} \in \mathbb{F}_q^{m \times n}$ and a vector $\mathbf{v} \in \mathbb{F}_q^n$ defined over a finite field $\mathbb{F}_q$, the Permuted Kernel Problem is to find a permutation $\pi \in S_n$, such that $\mathbf{A}\mathbf{v}_\pi = 0$, where $\mathbf{v}_\pi$ is the vector obtained by permuting the entries of $\mathbf{v}$ with the permutation π, that is, the vector defined by $(\mathbf{v}_\pi)_i = v_{\pi(i)}$. There is also a inhomogeneous version of the problem, where given $\mathbf{A} \in \mathbb{F}_q^{m \times n}$, $\mathbf{v} \in \mathbb{F}_q^n$ and a target vector $\mathbf{t} \in \mathbb{F}_q^m$, the task is to find a permutation $\pi \in S_n$, such that $\mathbf{A}\mathbf{v}_\pi = \mathbf{t}$.

The permuted kernel problem is a classical NP-Hard problem that was first introduced in cryptography by Shamir, who designed an identification scheme, whose security reduces to the problem of solving a random PKP instance [33]. Several works have introduced new algorithms and time-memory trade-offs for solving the PKP [3,18,21,30], but solving the problem remains prohibitively difficult, even for small parameters (see Table 3).

Subgroup IPKP. The Subgroup Inhomogeneous Permuted Kernel Problem (SIPKP) is the same as the IPKP problem, with the additional constraint that the solution is a member of a certain subgroup of S_n. Concretely, a solution to the a SIPKP instance $(\mathbf{A}, \mathbf{v}, \mathbf{t}, H)$, with $\mathbf{A} \in \mathbb{F}_q^{m \times n}, \mathbf{v} \in \mathbb{F}_q^n, \mathbf{t} \in \mathbb{F}_q^m$ and H a subgroup of S_n is a permutation $\pi \in H$ such that $\mathbf{A}\mathbf{v}_\pi = \mathbf{t}$.

Multivariate Quadratic (MQ). Given a multivariate quadratic map $\mathcal{P} : \mathbb{F}_q^n \to \mathbb{F}_q^m$ of m quadratic polynomials in n variables defined over a finite field $\mathbb{F}_q$, the MQ problem asks to find a solution $\mathbf{s} \in \mathbb{F}_q^n$ such that $\mathcal{P}(\mathbf{s}) = 0$. The best known methods for solving this problem rely on Grobner basis methods or linearization methods in combination with guessing a number of the variables [8,22]. This is the central problem underlying most of multivariate cryptography, and for random systems $\mathcal{F}$, the hardness of the problem is well understood.

Short Integer Solution (SIS/ISIS). The well known Short Integer Solution problem, introduced in the seminal work of Ajtai [1] asks to, given a matrix $\mathbf{A} \in \mathbb{Z}_q^{n \times m}$, and a bound β, find a vector $\mathbf{x}$, such that $\mathbf{A}\mathbf{x} = 0$ whose norm is bounded by $||\mathbf{x}|| \leq \beta$. There is also a inhomogeneous version of the problem (ISIS), where, given $\mathbf{A} \in \mathbb{Z}_q^{n \times m}$, $\mathbf{t} \in \mathbb{Z}_q^n$ and a bound β the task is to find $\mathbf{x} \in \mathbb{Z}_q^m$ such that $\mathbf{A}\mathbf{x} = \mathbf{t}$, again subject to $||\mathbf{x}|| \leq \beta$. The problem enjoys reductions from worst case lattice problems, and is one of the fundamental problems underlying lattice-based cryptography.

2.2 Commitment Schemes

Many sigma protocols, including ours, depend heavily on secure non-interactive commitment schemes. In the remainder of the paper we assume a non-interactive commitment function $\mathsf{Com} : \{0,1\}^\lambda \times \{0,1\}^* \to \{0,1\}^{2\lambda}$, that takes as input λ uniformly random bits bits, where λ is the security parameter, and a message $m \in \{0,1\}^*$ and outputs a 2λ bit long commitment $\mathsf{Com}(\mathsf{bits}, m)$.

Intuitively, the commitment scheme should not reveal anything the message it commits to, and it should not be possible to open the commitment to some different message. These properties are formalized as follows:

Definition 1 (Computational binding). *For an adversary $\mathcal{A}$ we define its advantage for the commitment binding game as*

$$\mathsf{Adv}_{\mathsf{Com}}^{\mathsf{Binding}}(\mathcal{A}) = \Pr[\mathsf{Com}(\mathsf{bits}, m) = \mathsf{Com}(\mathsf{bits}', m') | (\mathsf{bits}, m, \mathsf{bits}', m') \leftarrow \mathcal{A}(1^\lambda)]$$

We say that Com is computationally binding if for all polynomial time algorithms $\mathcal{A}$, the advantage $\mathsf{Adv}_{\mathsf{Com}}^{\mathsf{Binding}}(\mathcal{A})$ is a negligible function of the security parameter λ.

Definition 2 (Computational hiding). *For an adversary $\mathcal{A}$ we define the advantage for the commitment hiding game for a pair of messages m, m' as*

$$\mathsf{Adv}_{\mathsf{Com}}^{\mathsf{Hiding}}(\mathcal{A}, m, m') = \left| \Pr_{\mathsf{bits} \leftarrow \{0,1\}^\lambda}[1 = \mathcal{A}(\mathsf{Com}(\mathsf{bits}, m)] - \Pr_{\mathsf{bits} \leftarrow \{0,1\}^\lambda}[1 = \mathcal{A}(\mathsf{Com}(\mathsf{bits}, m')] \right|$$

We say that Com is computationally hiding if for all polynomial time algorithms $\mathcal{A}$, and every pair of messages m, m' the advantage $\mathsf{Adv}_{\mathsf{Com}}^{\mathsf{Hiding}}(\mathcal{A}, m, m')$ is a negligible function of the security parameter λ.

In our implementations, we use SHAKE256 as commitment function. If we model SHAKE256 as a quantum random oracle, then it satisfies the computational binding and hiding properties.

3 Sigma Protocols with Helper

This paper introduces two Sigma protocols with helper, which are like normal sigma protocols, with the addition of a trusted third party (called the helper) that runs a setup algorithm based on a random seed at the beginning of each execution of the protocol. The helper then sends some auxiliary information to the verifier and sends the seed value that was used to seed the setup algorithm to the prover. A more formal definition is as follows:

Definition 3 (Sigma protocol with helper). *A protocol is a sigma protocol with helper for relation R with challenge space C if it is of the form of Fig. 2 and satisfies:*

- **Completeness.** *If all parties (Helper, Prover and Verifier) follow the protocol on input $(x, w) \in R$, then the verifier always accepts.*
- **2-Special soundness.** *From an adversary A that outputs with noticeable probability two valid transcripts $(x, \mathsf{aux}, \mathsf{com}, ch, \mathsf{rsp})$ and $(x, \mathsf{aux}, \mathsf{com}, ch', \mathsf{rsp}')$ with $ch \neq ch'$ and where $\mathsf{aux} = Setup(\mathsf{seed})$ for some seed value seed (not necessarily known to the extractor) one can efficiently extract a witness w such that $(x, w) \in R$.*
- **Special honest-verifier zero-knowledge.** *There exists a PPT simulator S that on input x, a random seed value seed and a random challenge ch outputs a transcript $(x, \mathsf{aux}, \mathsf{com}, ch, \mathsf{rsp})$ with $\mathsf{aux} = Setup(\mathsf{seed})$ that is computationally indistinguishable from the probability distribution of transcripts of honest executions of the protocol on input (x, w) for some w such that $(x, w) \in R$, conditioned on the auxiliary information being equal to aux and the challenge being equal to ch.*

4 Proving Knowledge of a Solution to a System of Quadratic Equations

Two zero-knowledge proofs to prove knowledge of a solution of a system of multivariate quadratic equations over a finite field $\mathbb{F}_q$ were proposed by Sakumoto et al. [32]. The first proof is a 3-round protocol which has soundness error $\frac{2}{3}$, while the second proof is a 5-round protocol with soundness error $\frac{1}{2} + \frac{1}{2q}$, where q is the size of the finite field over which the system of polynomials is defined. The MQDSS [13] signature scheme is obtained by applying the Fiat-Shamir transform to the 5-round protocol of Sakumoto et al. Because the soundness error of $\frac{1}{2} + \frac{1}{2q}$ is rather big, and because the Fiat-Shamir transformation does not tightly preserve security for 5-round protocols [23] a large number (e.g. 184 for the NIST security level I parameter set) of parallel rounds is required to obtain a secure signature scheme.

In this section, we present a sigma protocol with helper to prove knowledge of a solution of a system of multivariate quadratic equations. The scheme improves the knowledge error to only $1/q$, but this comes at the cost of having an honest party that helps the prover and the verifier in their execution of the protocol. Similar to the schemes of Sakumoto et al. the new protocol relies on the fact that if $\mathcal{F} : \mathbb{F}_q^n \to \mathbb{F}_q^n$ is a multivariate quadratic map of m polynomials in n variables, then the polar form of $\mathcal{F}$, which is defined as

$$\mathcal{G}(\mathbf{x}, \mathbf{y}) := \mathcal{F}(\mathbf{x} + \mathbf{y}) - \mathcal{F}(\mathbf{x}) - \mathcal{F}(\mathbf{y}) \tag{1}$$

is linear in both $\mathbf{x}$ and $\mathbf{y}$.

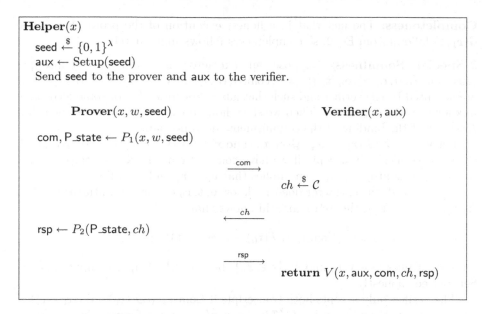

Fig. 2. The structure of a sigma protocol with trusted setup.

To prove knowledge of a secret $\mathbf{s}$ such that $\mathcal{F}(\mathbf{s}) = \mathbf{v}$ the protocol goes as follows: During the first phase the helper picks a random vector $\mathbf{r_0}$ and commits to linear secret sharings $\mathbf{t} + \mathbf{t}_c = c\mathbf{r_0}, \mathbf{e} + \mathbf{e}_c = c\mathcal{F}(\mathbf{r_0})$ for each $c \in \mathbb{F}_q$. These commitments are public auxiliary information which the helper sends to the verifier. The helper also sends the seed that he used to generate his randomness to the prover. Then, the prover publishes the masked secret $\mathbf{r_1} = \mathbf{s} - \mathbf{r_0}$ and commits to the value of $\mathbf{e} + \mathcal{G}(\mathbf{r_1}, \mathbf{t})$. Finally the verifier challenges the prover to reveal $\mathbf{e}_\alpha$ and $\mathbf{t}_\alpha$ for a random choice of $\alpha \in \mathbb{F}_q$ and checks whether the following equation, which is equivalent to Eq. 1, holds.

$$\mathbf{e} + \mathcal{G}(\mathbf{r_1}, \mathbf{t}) = c\left(\mathcal{F}(\mathbf{s}) - \mathcal{F}(\mathbf{r_1})\right) - \mathbf{e}_c - \mathcal{G}(\mathbf{r_1}, \mathbf{t}_c), \quad \forall c \in \mathbb{F}_q \qquad (2)$$

A more detailed version of the protocol is displayed in Fig. 3.

Theorem 1. *Suppose the used commitment scheme is computationally binding and computationally hiding, then the protocol of Fig. 3 is a sigma protocol with trusted setup as in Definition 3 with challenge space $\mathbb{F}_q$.*

Proof. We prove completeness, 2-special soundness and special honest-verifier zero knowledge separately:

Completeness: The fact that in a honest execution of the protocol $\mathbf{x} = \mathbf{c} + \mathcal{G}(\mathbf{r}_1, \mathbf{t})$ follows from Eq. 2, so completeness follows immediately.

2-Special Soundness: Suppose an extractor is given two transcripts $(\mathsf{aux}, \mathsf{com}, \alpha, (\mathbf{r}, \mathbf{r}_\alpha, \mathbf{r}_1, \mathbf{e}_\alpha, \mathbf{t}_\alpha))$, $(\mathsf{aux}, \mathsf{com}, \alpha, (\mathbf{r}', \mathbf{r}'_\alpha, \mathbf{r}'_1, \mathbf{e}_{\alpha'}, \mathbf{t}_{\alpha'}))$ with $\alpha \neq \alpha'$ that are accepted by the verifier and such that $\mathsf{aux} = \mathsf{Setup}(\mathsf{seed})$ (for some seed value unknown to the extractor). Then we show how to extract a witness $\mathbf{s}$ such that $\mathcal{P}(\mathbf{s}) = \mathbf{v}$ if the binding of the commitments does not fail.

Let $\mathbf{x} := \alpha(\mathbf{v} - \mathcal{F}(\mathbf{r}_1)) - \mathbf{e}_\alpha - \mathcal{G}(\mathbf{r}_1, \mathbf{t}_\alpha)$ and $\mathbf{x}' := \alpha'(\mathbf{v} - \mathcal{F}(\mathbf{r}'_1)) - \mathbf{e}_{\alpha'} - \mathcal{G}(\mathbf{r}'_1, \mathbf{t}_{\alpha'})$, then the verifier only accepts if we have $\mathsf{com} = \mathsf{Com}(\mathbf{r}, \mathbf{r}_1, \mathbf{x}) = \mathsf{Com}(\mathbf{r}', \mathbf{r}'_1, \mathbf{x}')$, so the binding property of Com implies that $\mathbf{r}_1 = \mathbf{r}'_1$ and $\mathbf{x} = \mathbf{x}'$.

Even though the extractor does not know $\mathbf{e}, \mathbf{t}, \mathbf{r}_0$ or the commitment random strings $\{r_c \,|\, c \in \mathbb{F}_q\}$, the extractor still knows that

$$\mathsf{aux} = \{\mathsf{Com}(\tilde{r}_c, (c\mathcal{F}(\mathbf{r}_0) - \mathbf{e}, c\mathbf{r}_0 - \mathbf{t})) \,|\, c \in \mathbb{F}_q\}$$

for *some* values of $\mathbf{e}, \mathbf{t}, \mathbf{r}_0$ and $\{\tilde{r}_c \,|\, c \in \mathbb{F}_q\}$, because the helper computed $\mathsf{aux} = \mathsf{Setup}(\mathsf{seed})$ honestly.

The verifier only accepts both transcripts if $\mathsf{Com}(\tilde{r}_\alpha, (\alpha\mathcal{F}(\mathbf{r}_0) - \mathbf{e}, \alpha\mathbf{r}_0 - \mathbf{t})) = \mathsf{Com}(r_\alpha, (\mathbf{e}_\alpha, \mathbf{t}_\alpha))$ and $\mathsf{Com}(\tilde{r}_{\alpha'}, (\alpha'\mathcal{F}(\mathbf{r}_0) - \mathbf{e}, \alpha'\mathbf{r}_0 - \mathbf{t})) = \mathsf{Com}(r'_\alpha, (\mathbf{e}_{\alpha'}, \mathbf{t}_{\alpha'}))$, so the binding property of Com implies that

$$\alpha\mathcal{F}(\mathbf{r}_0) - \mathbf{e} = \mathbf{e}_\alpha, \qquad\qquad \alpha\mathbf{r}_0 - \mathbf{t} = \mathbf{t}_\alpha,$$
$$\alpha'\mathcal{F}(\mathbf{r}_0) - \mathbf{e} = \mathbf{e}_{\alpha'} \quad\text{and}\quad \alpha'\mathbf{r}_0 - \mathbf{t} = \mathbf{t}_{\alpha'}.$$

Substituting this into $\mathbf{x} = \mathbf{x}'$ we get

$$\alpha(\mathbf{v} - \mathcal{F}(\mathbf{r}_1)) + \mathbf{e} - \alpha\mathcal{F}(\mathbf{r}_0) - \mathcal{G}(\mathbf{r}_1, \alpha\mathbf{r}_0 - \mathbf{t}) = \alpha'(\mathbf{v} - \mathcal{F}(\mathbf{r}_1)) + \mathbf{e} - \alpha'\mathcal{F}(\mathbf{r}_0) - \mathcal{G}(\mathbf{r}_1, \alpha'\mathbf{r}_0 - \mathbf{t}),$$

which simplifies to

$$(\alpha - \alpha')\,(\mathcal{F}(\mathbf{r}_1) + \mathcal{F}(\mathbf{r}_0) + \mathcal{G}(\mathbf{r}_0, \mathbf{r}_1) - \mathbf{v}) =$$
$$(\alpha - \alpha')\,(\mathcal{F}(\mathbf{r}_0 + \mathbf{r}_1) - \mathbf{v})) = 0,$$

so $\mathbf{r}_0 + \mathbf{r}_1 = \frac{\mathbf{t}_\alpha - \mathbf{t}_{\alpha'}}{\alpha - \alpha'} + \mathbf{r}_1$ is a solution to $\mathcal{F}(\mathbf{x}) = \mathbf{v}$. Notice that all the values on the right hand side of this equation are included in the 2 transcripts, so extracting the solution from the two transcripts is trivial.

Special Honest-Verifier Zero-Knowledge: Define a simulator $\mathcal{S}$, that on input $\mathbf{v}$, a random seed value seed and a random challenge $\alpha \in \mathbb{F}_q$ does the following things:

1. recompute aux, r_α, e_α and t_α from seed.
2. pick a uniformly random vector $\mathbf{u} \in \mathbb{F}_q^n$.
3. compute $f_{\alpha, e_\alpha, t_\alpha}(\mathbf{u})$, where $f_{\alpha, e_\alpha, t_\alpha}(\mathbf{x}) := \alpha(\mathbf{v} - \mathcal{F}(\mathbf{x})) - e_\alpha - \mathcal{G}(\mathbf{x}, t_\alpha)$.
4. produce commitment randomness r and a commitment com' to $(\mathbf{u}, f_{\alpha, e_\alpha, t_\alpha}(\mathbf{u}))$.
5. output $(aux, com', \alpha, (r, r_\alpha, \mathbf{u}, e_\alpha, t_\alpha))$.

Then the Simulator is identical to an honest prover, except for step 2, where the honest prover sets $\mathbf{u}$ equal to $\mathbf{s} - \mathbf{r}_0$ rather than a uniformly random value. It is clear that $(\alpha, r, r_\alpha, \mathbf{u}, e_\alpha, t_\alpha)$ and $(\alpha, r, r_\alpha, \mathbf{s} - \mathbf{r}_0, e_\alpha, t_\alpha)$ are both uniformly distributed in $\mathbb{F}_q \times \{0, 1\}^{2\lambda} \times (\mathbb{F}_q^n)^3$ and hence follow the same distribution. Since com and com_α are completely determined by $(\alpha, r, r_\alpha, \mathbf{s} - \mathbf{r}_0, e_\alpha, t_\alpha)$ it follows that $(com_\alpha, com', \alpha, r, r_\alpha, \mathbf{u}, e_\alpha, t_\alpha)$ and $(com_\alpha, com, \alpha, r, r_\alpha, \mathbf{s} - \mathbf{r}_0, e_\alpha, t_\alpha)$ also follow the same distribution. Finally, since the commitments $com_{c \neq \alpha}$ are never opened, it follows from the hiding property of the commitment scheme with the standard hybrid argument that $(aux, com', \alpha, r, r_\alpha, \mathbf{u}, e_\alpha, t_\alpha)$ and $(aux, com, \alpha, r, r_\alpha, \mathbf{s} - \mathbf{r}_0, e_\alpha, t_\alpha)$ are computationally indistinguishable.

5 Proving Knowledge of a Solution to a (inhomogeneous) PKP Instance

In this section we give a Sigma protocol with helper with challenge space $\mathbb{F}_p$ to prove knowledge of a solution for an inhomogeneous PKP instance, i.e. given $\mathbf{A}, \mathbf{v}, \mathbf{t}$ our proof system proves knowledge of a permutation π such that $\mathbf{A}\mathbf{v}_\pi = \mathbf{t}$. The soundness error of our proof is only $1/p$, which is much better than the 5-round proof of Shamir, which has a soundness error of $\frac{1}{2} + \frac{1}{2p}$ [33], and Stern's 3-round protocol, which has a soundness error of $2/3$ [34].

To prove knowledge of a solution π to the instance $(\mathbf{A}, \mathbf{v}, \mathbf{t})$ the protocol goes as follows: The helper picks a random vector $\mathbf{r} \in \mathbb{F}_p^n$, and a random permutation $\sigma \in S_n$, it then commits to $\mathbf{r} + c\mathbf{v}_\sigma$ for all values of $c \in \mathbb{F}_p$. The helper sends these commitments as public auxiliary information to the verifier, and he sends the seed that he used to generate his randomness to the prover. Then the prover sends $\rho = \pi\sigma^{-1}$ to the verifier and commits to the value of $\mathbf{A}\mathbf{r}_{\pi\sigma^{-1}}$. Finally, the verifier challenges the prover to reveal $\mathbf{x} = \mathbf{r} + \alpha\mathbf{v}_\sigma$ for a random choice of α. Once the prover reveals $\mathbf{x}$ the verifier checks if $\mathbf{A}\mathbf{x}_\rho - \alpha\mathbf{t} = \mathbf{A}(\mathbf{r}_{\pi\sigma^{-1}} + \alpha\mathbf{v}_\pi) - \alpha\mathbf{t} = \mathbf{A}\mathbf{r}_{\pi\sigma^{-1}}$. For a more detailed description of the protocol we refer to Fig. 4.

Theorem 2. *Suppose the used commitment scheme is computationally binding and computationally hiding, then the protocol of Fig. 4 is a sigma protocol with trusted setup as in Definition 3 with challenge space $\mathbb{F}_p$.*

Proof. We prove completeness, 2-special soundness and special honest-verifier zero knowledge separately:

Helper($\mathcal{F}$)

seed $\xleftarrow{\$} \{0,1\}^\lambda$

Generate $\mathbf{e} \in \mathbb{F}_q^m$ and $\mathbf{t}, \mathbf{r}_0 \in \mathbb{F}_q^n$ from seed.

for each c in $\mathbb{F}_q$ **do**

$\quad \mathbf{e}_c \leftarrow c\mathcal{F}(\mathbf{r}_0) - \mathbf{e}$

$\quad \mathbf{t}_c \leftarrow c\mathbf{r}_0 - \mathbf{t}$

$\quad$ Generate commitment randomness $r_c \in \{0,1\}^\lambda$ from seed.

$\quad \mathsf{com}_c \leftarrow \mathsf{Com}(r_c, (\mathbf{e}_c, \mathbf{t}_c))$

end for

aux $\leftarrow [\mathsf{com}_c|$ **for** $c \in \mathbb{F}_q]$

Send seed to the prover and aux to the verifier.

Prover($\mathcal{F}, \mathbf{s}, \mathsf{seed}$)	**Verifier($\mathcal{F}, \mathbf{v}, \mathsf{aux}$)**

Regenerate $\mathbf{e}, \mathbf{t}, \mathbf{r}_0$ from seed.

$\mathbf{r}_1 \leftarrow \mathbf{s} - \mathbf{r}_0$

$r \leftarrow \{0,1\}^\lambda$

$\mathsf{com} \leftarrow \mathsf{Com}(r, (\mathbf{r}_1, \mathbf{e} + \mathcal{G}(\mathbf{r}_1, \mathbf{t})))$

$$\xrightarrow{\mathsf{com}}$$

$$\alpha \xleftarrow{\$} \mathbb{F}_q$$

$$\xleftarrow{\alpha}$$

Recompute $\mathbf{r}_\alpha, \mathbf{e}_\alpha, \mathbf{t}_\alpha$ from seed.

$$\xrightarrow{(r, r_\alpha, \mathbf{r}_1, \mathbf{e}_\alpha, \mathbf{t}_\alpha)}$$

$\mathbf{x} \leftarrow \alpha(\mathbf{v} - \mathcal{F}(\mathbf{r}_1)) - \mathbf{e}_\alpha - \mathcal{G}(\mathbf{r}_1, \mathbf{t}_\alpha)$

$b_1 \leftarrow \mathsf{com} = \mathsf{Com}(r, (\mathbf{r}_1, \mathbf{x}))$

$b_2 \leftarrow \mathsf{com}_\alpha = \mathsf{Com}(r, (\mathbf{e}_\alpha, \mathbf{t}_\alpha))$

return $b_1 \wedge b_2$

Fig. 3. A sigma protocol with helper for proving knowledge of a solution to the MQ problem.

Completeness: In an honest execution of the protocol we have

$$\mathbf{y} = \mathbf{A}\mathbf{x}_\rho - \alpha\mathbf{t} = \mathbf{A}\left(\mathbf{r}_{\pi\sigma^{-1}} + \alpha\mathbf{v}_\pi\right) - \alpha\mathbf{t},$$

so if π is a solution to the PKP instance $(\mathbf{A}, \mathbf{v}, \mathbf{t})$, then $\mathbf{A}\mathbf{v}_\pi = \mathbf{t}$, which means $\mathbf{y} = \mathbf{A}\mathbf{r}_{\pi\sigma^{-1}}$ and hence the completeness follows from the completeness of the commitment scheme.

2-Special Soundness: Given two transcripts $(\mathsf{aux}, \mathsf{com}, \alpha, (\mathsf{r}, \mathsf{r}_\alpha, \rho, \mathbf{x}))$ and $(\mathsf{aux}, \mathsf{com}, \alpha', (\mathsf{r}', \mathsf{r}'_\alpha, \rho', \mathbf{x}'))$ with $\alpha \neq \alpha'$ that are accepted by the verifier and such that $\mathsf{aux} = \mathsf{Setup}(\mathsf{seed})$, for some value of seed (not necessarily known to the extractor). Then, if the binding of the commitment scheme does not fail (which, by assumption, happens with overwhelming probability), one can efficiently extract a witness π such that $\mathbf{A}\mathbf{v}_\pi = \mathbf{t}$.

Let $\mathbf{y} := \mathbf{A}\mathbf{x}_\rho - \alpha\mathbf{t}$ and $\mathbf{y}' := \mathbf{A}\mathbf{x}'_{\rho'} - \alpha'\mathbf{t}$, then the verifier only accepts if we have $\mathsf{com} = \mathsf{Com}(\mathsf{r}, (\rho, \mathbf{y})) = \mathsf{Com}(\mathsf{r}', (\rho', \mathbf{y}'))$, so the binding property of Com implies that $\rho = \rho'$ and $\mathbf{y} = \mathbf{y}'$.

Note that even though the extractor does not know $\mathbf{r}, \sigma$ or any of the commitment randomness strings r_c, he still knows that aux is of the form

$$\mathsf{aux} = \{\mathsf{Com}(\mathsf{r}_c, \mathbf{r} + c\mathbf{v}_\sigma) \mid c \in \mathbb{F}_q\}$$

for *some* values of $\mathbf{r}, \sigma$ and $\{\mathsf{r}_c\}_{c \in \mathbb{F}_q}$, because the helper computed $\mathsf{aux} = \mathsf{Setup}(\mathsf{seed})$ honestly.

The verifier only accepts both transcripts if $\mathsf{Com}(\mathsf{r}_\alpha, \mathbf{r} + \alpha\mathbf{v}_\sigma) = \mathsf{Com}(\mathsf{r}_\alpha, \mathbf{x})$ and $\mathsf{Com}(\mathsf{r}_{\alpha'}, \mathbf{r} + \alpha'\mathbf{v}_\sigma) = \mathsf{Com}(\mathsf{r}_{\alpha'}, \mathbf{x}')$, so the binding property of Com implies that $\mathbf{x} = \mathbf{r} + \alpha\mathbf{v}_\sigma$, and that $\mathbf{x}' = \mathbf{r} + \alpha'\mathbf{v}_\sigma$.

Putting everything together we get

$$\mathbf{A}\left(\mathbf{r}_\rho + \alpha\mathbf{v}_{\rho\sigma}\right) - \alpha\mathbf{t} = \mathbf{A}\left(\mathbf{r}_\rho + \alpha'\mathbf{v}_{\rho\sigma}\right) - \alpha'\mathbf{t}$$

which simplifies to

$$(\alpha - \alpha')\left(\mathbf{A}\mathbf{v}_{\rho\sigma} - \mathbf{t}\right) = 0,$$

so $\rho\sigma$ is a solution to the instance of the permuted kernel problem. The value of ρ is known to the extractor because it is included in the transcripts, and the value of σ can be deduced from $\alpha, \alpha', \mathbf{x}, \mathbf{x}'$ and $\mathbf{v}$, because $\mathbf{x} - \mathbf{x}' = (\alpha - \alpha')\mathbf{v}_\sigma$. (If the entries of $\mathbf{v}$ are not unique, multiple values of σ are possible, but they will all give valid solutions to the PKP problem.)

Special Honest-Verifier Zero Knowledge: Define a simulator $\mathcal{S}$, that on input $\mathbf{A}, \mathbf{v}$, a random seed value seed and a random challenge $\alpha \in \mathbb{F}_p$ does the following things:

1. recompute $\mathsf{aux}, \mathsf{r}_\alpha$ and $\mathbf{x} = \mathbf{r} + \alpha\mathbf{v}_\sigma$ from seed.
2. pick a uniformly random permutation $\tau \in S_n$.
3. produce commitment randomness r, and a commitment com' to $(\tau, \mathbf{A}\mathbf{x}_\tau)$.
4. output $(\mathsf{aux}, \mathsf{com}', \alpha, (\mathsf{r}, \mathsf{r}_\alpha, \tau, \mathbf{A}\mathbf{x}_\tau))$.

Then the Simulator is identical to an honest prover, except for step 2, where the honest prover sets ρ equal to $\pi\sigma^{-1}$ rather than a uniformly random value. It is clear that $(\alpha, \mathsf{r}, \mathsf{r}_\alpha, \tau, \mathbf{A}\mathbf{x}_\tau)$ and $(\alpha, \mathsf{r}, \mathsf{r}_\alpha, \rho, \mathbf{A}\mathbf{x}_\rho)$ are both uniformly distributed in $\mathbb{F}_q \times \{0,1\}^{2\lambda} \times S_n \times \mathbb{F}_q^n$ and hence follow the same distribution. Since com and com_α are completely determined by $(\alpha, \mathsf{r}, \mathsf{r}_\alpha, \rho, \mathbf{A}\mathbf{x}_\rho)$ it follows that $(\mathsf{com}_\alpha, \mathsf{com}', \alpha, \mathsf{r}, \mathsf{r}_\alpha, \tau, \mathbf{A}\mathbf{x}_\tau)$ and $(\mathsf{com}_\alpha, \mathsf{com}, \alpha, \mathsf{r}, \mathsf{r}_\alpha, \rho, \mathbf{A}\mathbf{x}_\rho)$

also follow the same distribution. Finally, since the commitments $\mathsf{com}_{c \neq \alpha}$ are never opened, it follows from the hiding property of the commitment scheme and the standard hybrid argument that $(\mathsf{aux}, \mathsf{com}', \alpha, (\mathsf{r}, \mathsf{r}_\alpha, \tau, \mathbf{Ax}_\tau))$ and $(\mathsf{aux}, \mathsf{com}, \alpha, (\mathsf{r}, \mathsf{r}_\alpha, \rho, \mathbf{Ax}_\rho))$ are computationally indistinguishable.

6   Removing the Helper

In this section, we show how to transform a Sigma protocol with helper into a standard zero-knowledge proof of knowledge (without helper). We use the same "Cut-and-choose" approach that was used by Katz et al. to get rid of the preprocessing phase [24].

The idea is to let the prover pick k seeds $\mathsf{seed}_1, \cdots, \mathsf{seed}_k$ and generate k sets of auxiliary information $\mathsf{aux}_i = \mathrm{Setup}\,(\mathsf{seed}_i)$ which the prover sends to the verifier, along with the first messages of the protocol $\mathsf{com}_i = P_1(x, w, \mathsf{seed}_i)$ for all i from 1 to k. The verifier then picks a random index I and a single challenge $ch \in \mathcal{C}$ and sends this to the prover. The prover then sends seed_i for $i \neq I$ as well as a response rsp to the challenge at index I. Using the seeds, the verifier then checks if all the auxiliary information $\mathsf{aux}_{i \neq I}$ was generated properly and checks if rsp is a correct response to the challenge at index I. The details of the protocol are displayed in Fig. 5. We prove that this is a honest-verifier zero knowledge protocol with soundness error $\max(\frac{1}{k}, \frac{1}{|\mathcal{C}|})$.

Theorem 3. *Let (Setup, P_1, P_2, V) be a sigma protocol with helper and challenge space $\mathcal{C}$, if the used commitment scheme is hiding, then the protocol of Fig. 5 is an honest-verifier zero knowledge proof of knowledge with challenge space $\{1, \cdots, k\} \times \mathcal{C}$ and $\max(k, |\mathcal{C}|) + 1$-special soundness (and hence it has soundness error $\max(\frac{1}{k}, \frac{1}{|\mathcal{C}|})$).*

Proof. We prove completeness, special soundness and special honest-verifier zero knowledge separately.

Completeness: Follows immediately from the completeness of the underlying Sigma protocol with trusted setup.

$(\max(k, |\mathcal{C}|) + 1)$-**special Soundness:** If there are $\max(k, |\mathcal{C}|) + 1$ valid transcripts then there are at least two valid transcripts with different values of I, which implies that all k setups were done honestly. The pigeon hole principle says there are at least two accepted transcripts with the same value of I, but different ch, so the extractor can use special soundness of the underlying Sigma protocol with trusted setup to extract a witness w.

Helper(v)

seed $\overset{\$}{\leftarrow} \{0,1\}^{\lambda}$

Generate $\mathbf{r} \in \mathbb{F}_p^n$ and $\sigma \in S_n$ from seed.

for each c in $\mathbb{F}_p$ **do**

    Generate commitment randomness $r_c \in \{0,1\}^{\lambda}$ from seed.

    $\mathsf{com}_c \leftarrow \mathsf{Com}(r_c, \mathbf{r} + c\mathbf{v}_\sigma)$

end for

$\mathsf{aux} \leftarrow [\mathsf{com}_c| \text{ for } c \in \mathbb{F}_p]$

Send seed to the prover and aux to the verifier.

Prover(A, v, π, seed)	**Verifier(A, v, t, aux)**

Regenerate $\mathbf{r}, \sigma$ from seed.

$\rho \leftarrow \pi\sigma^{-1}$

$r \leftarrow \{0,1\}^{\lambda}$

$\mathsf{com} \leftarrow \mathsf{Com}(r, (\rho, \mathbf{A}\mathbf{r}_\rho))$

$$\xrightarrow{\quad \mathsf{com} \quad}$$

$$\alpha \overset{\$}{\leftarrow} \mathbb{F}_q$$

$$\xleftarrow{\quad \alpha \quad}$$

Recompute r_α and

$\mathbf{x} = \mathbf{r} + \alpha\mathbf{v}_\sigma$ from seed.

$$\xrightarrow{\quad (r, r_\alpha \rho, \mathbf{x}) \quad}$$

$$\mathbf{y} \leftarrow \mathbf{A}\mathbf{x}_\rho - \alpha\mathbf{t}$$
$$b_1 \leftarrow \mathsf{com} = \mathsf{Com}(r, (\rho, \mathbf{y}))$$
$$b_2 \leftarrow \mathsf{com}_\alpha = \mathsf{Com}(r_\alpha, \mathbf{x})$$
$$\textbf{return } b_1 \wedge b_2$$

Fig. 4. A sigma protocol with helper for proving knowledge of a solution to the inhomogeneous PKP problem.

Special Honest-Verifier Zero-Knowledge: On input (I, ch), the simulator generates all the setups honestly, and commits to random dummy values to create the commitments $\mathsf{com}_{i \neq I}$. The simulator then uses the simulator of the underlying sigma protocol with trusted setup to simulate the transcript at index I. Indistinguishability follows from the hiding property of the commitment scheme and the honest-verifier zero-knowledge property of the underlying sigma protocol with trusted setup.

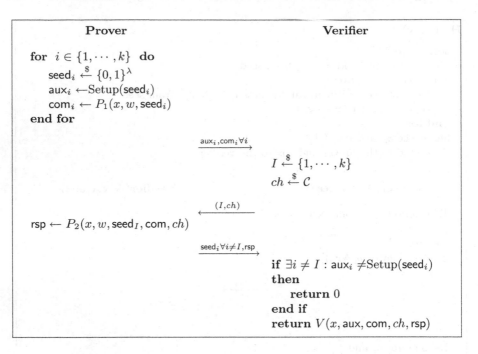

Fig. 5. A zero knowledge proof (without trusted setup) from a Sigma protocol with trusted setup.

7   Optimizations

In this section, we describe optimizations for the MQ and PKP zero-knowledge proofs with trusted setup, as well as for the transformation that removes the trusted setup. The first two optimizations are applications of standard techniques and the last optimization was proposed by Katz et al. [24], and proven secure by Baum and Nof [5].

Hashing and Merkle Trees. In both the MQ proof and the PKP proof the auxiliary information consists of q commitments com_i for $i \in \mathbb{F}_q$, but only one of these commitments, com_α, is opened in each honest execution of the protocol. To reduce the communication cost (and hence the signature size after the Fiat-Shamir transform) we can build a Merkle tree on these commitments and only send the root of the tree. Then the prover includes in his response the $\lceil \log_2(q) \rceil$ nodes of the Merkle tree required to reconstruct the root of the Merkle tree.

When we are doing the transformation to get rid of the trusted party, we do not have to send all the k roots separately. Instead, it suffices to send a hash of all the roots to the verifier. Then, during verification, the verifier recomputes all the roots (either from seed_i if $i \neq I$, or through the verification algorithm if $i = I$) and hashes the roots to verify that they were correct.

The prover sends k commitments com_i, but only the commitment com_I is used. Therefore, similar to the first optimization, the prover can build a Merkle tree on his commitments and send the root to the verifier. Then, he includes com_I and some nodes of the Merkle tree in his response, so the verifier can recompute the root and authenticate com_I.

Sending Fewer Seeds. The prover chooses k seed values and sends all but one of these seeds to the verifier. We can use a tree strategy to reduce the communication cost. The prover constructs a binary tree of seed values. First, he picks the value of the root at random. Then, the value of each internal node is used to seed a PRNG which generates the values of its two children. In the end, the leaf nodes act as the $seed_i$ values. Now, instead of sending $k - 1$ seed values, the prover can send $\lceil \log_2(k) \rceil$ node values in the tree and the prover can recompute the $k - 1$ seeds himself (but not $seed_I$).

Smaller Challenge Space. For some applications, the finite field $\mathbb{F}_q$ is so large that it would not be practical to compute Merkle trees of size q. In that case, we can simply reduce the challenge space to some subset of $\mathbb{F}_q$ of size $q' \leq q$. The soundness error of the scheme then becomes $1/q'$ instead of $1/q$.

Beating Parallel Repetition. The basic scheme has soundness error $\frac{1}{q'}$, so to reach a soundness error of $2^{-\lambda}$ we would need to perform $r = \left\lceil \frac{\lambda}{log_2(q')} \right\rceil$ parallel executions of the protocol. The optimization of Katz et al. [24] gives a more efficient approach: The idea is that instead of letting the verifier choose 1 out of k setups to execute, we now let him choose τ out of M setups to execute. Now suppose a cheating prover does $e \leq \tau$ out of the M setups incorrectly. Since he cannot produce $seed_i$ values for the cheated setups, he can only convince the verifier if all the setups in which he cheated end up being executed. This happens with probability $\binom{M-e}{\tau-e} \cdot \binom{M}{\tau}^{-1}$. Then, the prover still needs to generate responses for $\tau - e$ honest setups, which he can do with probability at most $\left(\frac{1}{q'}\right)^{\tau-e}$. Therefore the soundness error of the adapted scheme is bounded by

$$\max_{0 \leq e \leq \tau} \frac{\binom{M-e}{\tau-e}}{\binom{M}{\tau}q'^{\tau-e}}.$$

For a more formal proof we refer to [5].

Example 1. Suppose $q = 128$, then without the optimization, we would need 19 parallel executions of the basic protocol to reach a soundness error of 2^{-128}, which amounts to $19*128 = 2432$ setups and 19 executions of the protocol. With the optimization, it turns out that 916 setups and 20 executions are sufficient. So, in this case, the optimization reduces the number of setups by a factor 2.6 at the cost of a single extra execution.

8   Signature Schemes

In this section, we apply the Fiat-Shamir transformation to the zero-knowledge proofs for MQ and PKP (after applying the transformation of Sect. 6) to obtain 2 signature schemes. We call these schemes the "MUltivariate quaDratic FIat-SHamir" scheme (MUDFISH) and the "ShUffled Solution to Homogeneous linear SYstem FIat-SHamir" scheme (SUSHSYFISH). First, we observe that the recent results on Post-Quantum Fiat-Shamir by Don et al. [15] apply and thus that our signature scheme are provably secure in the QROM (with non-tight reductions). We then give some generic optimizations for the signature scheme and parameter choices for MUDFISH and SUSHSYFISH. We provide a proof-of-concept implementation to show that MUDFISH and SUSHSYFISH are more efficient than existing signature schemes based on the MQ and PKP assumptions (i.e. MQDSS and PKP-DSS respectively) in terms of signature size and speed (on the NIST reference platform).

8.1   Fiat-Shamir Transform

The Fiat-Shamir transform allows us to convert the sigma protocols for MQ and PKP into signatures. The idea is that instead of letting the verifier choose the challenge at random, we derive the challenge deterministically from the commitment and the message that we want to sign. Concretely, to sign a message m, the signer executes the first part of the identification scheme to produce a commitment com, then he derives a challenge ch by applying a random oracle to com$|m$. Finally, the signer completes his part of the identification scheme to produce the response rsp. The signature is then simply (com, resp). To verify a signature (com, resp) for a message m, the verifier simply computes ch by querying the random oracle at com$|m$, and then he accepts the signature if and only if (com, ch, resp) is a valid transcript of the identification protocol. Using the results of [15], it is straightforward to prove that MUDFISH and SUSHSYFISH are strongly unforgeable in the QROM.

Theorem 4. *Assume that a hash function modeled as a Quantum Random Oracle is used as commitment scheme and that a Quantum random oracle model is used as PRG, then the non-optimized variants of MUDFISH and SUSHSYFISH signature schemes are strongly existentially unforgeable in the QROM.*

Proof. (The argument is similar to the proof for the FS variant of Picnic, see Sect. 6.1 of [15].) First, we prove that the Setup function is collapsing: If we model the commitment functions as Quantum random oracles, then they are collapsing [36]. In both the MUDFISH and SUSHYFISH schemes, the Setup algorithm consists of expanding a randomness seed, computing some values based on the output of the PRG, and committing to them. In both cases, the PRG output is more than three times longer than the input, so this function is injective with overwhelming probability. Also, it is easily verified that the computing of the values from the output of the PRG is injective. Since the concurrent composition of collapsing functions is collapsing [16] and composing a collapsing function with an injective function preserves collapsingness, it follows that the entire Setup algorithm is collapsing.

Since the responses of the sigma protocol only consist of openings of commitments (which are preimages to Com), and preimages to the Setup function it follows from the collapsingness of Com and Setup that the MUDFISH and SUSHSYFISH sigma protocols have quantum computationally unique responses. Moreover, the protocols have k-special soundness, so theorem 25 of [15] says that the non-optimized versions of MUDFISH and SUSHSYFISH are quantum computational proofs of knowledge. Together with their theorem 22, this implies that MUDFISH and SUSHSYFISH are sEUF-CMA secure.

8.2 MUDFISH

Parameter Choices. For ease of implementation, we have chosen to use the same finite field $\mathbb{F}_4$ for all the parameter sets. To have a fair comparison with the MQDSS scheme, and to avoid the technicalities of choosing secure parameters for the MQ problem, we use the parameters proposed in the MQDSS submission to the NIST PQC standardization project. These parameter choices for the MQ problem are displayed in Table 1.

We still need to pick parameters for the ZK proof (i.e. τ, the number of executions and M, the number of setups). The choice of τ and M allows for a trade-off: If one is willing to increase τ, which mainly impacts signature size, then one can decrease M, which mainly impacts signing and verification time.

Table 1. Parameters for the MQ problem used by MUDFISH, and the complexity of solving them with the Crossbred algorithm. The parameter sets and the complexity estimates are taken from Table 8.4 of [14].

NIST PQC security level	q	$n = m$	Best classical attack	Best quantum attack	
			Gates	Gates	Depth
I	4	88	2^{156}	2^{93}	2^{83}
III	4	128	2^{230}	2^{129}	2^{119}
V	4	160	2^{290}	2^{158}	2^{147}

Table 2. Parameters for MUDFISH, key and signature sizes and performance measurements (average over 1000 signatures).

NIST PQC security level	Parameters				$|pk|$ (B)	$|sk|$ (B)	$|sig|$ (KB)	KeyGen (Mc)	Sign (Mc)	Verify (Mc)
	q	n	M	τ						
I	4	88	191	68	38	16	14.4	2.3	14.8	15.3
III	4	128	256	111	56	24	32.9	7.2	51.3	49.6
V	4	160	380	136	72	32	55.6	14.2	140.4	139.3

Implementation Results. The signing and verification algorithms require to do a lot of setups and executions of the ZK proof on independent data. We take advantage of this by fitting data from 64 independent rounds into one word. Hence, we can do 64 setups or 64 executions of the protocol in parallel on a 64-bit machine. Since the MUDFISH algorithm is inherently constant-time, there was no performance penalty for making the implementation constant-time. Our proof-of-concept implementation uses SHAKE256 as hash function and to expand randomness. The performance results of the implementation are displayed in Table 2. We see that MUDFISH is more efficient than MQDSS: Comparing the parameter sets that achieve NIST security level I, the signatures of MUDFISH are only half as big as those of MQDSS. At the same time, the signing and verification speed of our proof-of-concept implementation of MUDFISH is a factor 2.5 and 1.8 faster than those of the optimized implementation of MQDSS submitted to the second round of the NIST PQC standardization project. We leave the task of making an AVX2 optimized implementation of MUDFISH and comparing its performance to the AVX2 optimized implementation of MQDSS for future work.

8.3 SUSHSYFISH

Parameter Choices. An advantage of building cryptography on PKP is that the best attack algorithms are quite simple and easy to analyze. We use the PKP parameter sets proposed by Faugère et al. [10] to achieve the NIST security levels 1, 3 and 5. The choice of the remaining parameters q', τ and M allows for a trade-off between signature size and signing and verification speed. For each of the NIST PQC security levels 1, 3 and 5 we propose a parameter set which aims to be fast ($q' = 4$), a parameter sets which aims to have small signatures $q' = 128$ and an intermediate parameter set $q' = 16$.

Table 3. Parameters for SUSHSYFISH, key and signature sizes and performance measurements (average over 1000 signatures).

NIST PQC security level		q	n	m	q'	M	τ	|pk| (B)	|sk| (B)	|sig| (KB)	KeyGen (Mc)	Sign (Mc)	Verify (Mc)
I	Fast	997	61	28	4	191	68	72	16	18.1	0.1	3.6	1.7
	Middle	997	61	28	16	250	36	72	16	14.0	0.1	8.6	6.0
	Compact	997	61	28	128	916	20	72	16	12.1	0.1	170	169
III	Fast	1409	87	42	4	256	111	108	24	43.7	0.1	7.3	3.3
	Middle	1409	87	42	16	452	51	108	24	30.8	0.1	22.7	16.5
	Compact	1409	87	42	128	1357	30	108	24	27.1	0.1	365	342
V	Fast	1889	111	55	4	380	136	142	32	72.8	0.2	12.1	5.8
	Middle	1889	111	55	16	643	67	142	32	54.9	0.2	25.7	18.0
	Compact	1889	111	55	128	2096	39	142	32	47.5	0.2	602	567

Making the Implementation Constant-Time. Most of the SUSHSYFISH algorithm is inherently constant-time, except for some operations involving permutations such as composing permutations, applying a permutation to a vector and sampling random permutations. Naive implementations of these operations involve accessing memory at secret indices, which could make the implementation vulnerable to cache timing attacks. In our implementation, we leverage the *djbsort* constant-time sorting software library [7] to do these operations in constant-time. For example, to apply a permutation $\pi \in S_n$ to a vector $\mathbf{v} \in \mathbb{F}_p^n$ we first construct a list of integers x_i, such that the high-order bits of x_i correspond to π_i, and such that the low-order bits of x_i correspond to v_i. We then call the *djbsort* library to sort this list of integers in constant-time, and we extract the low-order bits from the sorted list, which correspond to $\mathbf{v}_\pi$. Since the performance bottleneck of SUSHSYFISH is hashing, a slight increase in the cost of the operations involving permutations has a negligible effect on the total performance of the signature scheme.

Implementation Results. Our implementation uses SHAKE256 as hash function and to expand randomness. The signing and verification times are dominated by the use of SHAKE256, and hence there is a lot of potential for speedups by choosing different symmetric primitives or by parallelizing independent calls of the SHAKE function. The key and signature sizes and the performance measurements for the 9 proposed parameter sets are displayed in Table 3. We see that SUSHSYFISH has smaller signatures than PKP-DSS while being only slightly slower. For NIST PQC security level I, the performance of the "Fast" SUSHSY-FISH parameter set is the close to the performance of PKP-DSS: Signatures are 12% smaller, while with the current implementations signing and verification are 44% and 80% slower respectively. The "Middle" and "Fast" parameter sets offer more compact signatures at the cost of slower signing and verification.

Comparison to Previous Works. In this section, we compare the MUD-FISH and SUSHSYFISH non-interactive zero-knowledge proof systems to existing methods for proving knowledge of a solution to the MQ or PKP problem. We compare to MQDSS [14] and PKP-DSS [10] that are dedicated proof systems for MQ and PKP respectively, and we compare to Ligero [2] and Aurora [6], which are generic ZK-proof systems capable of proving knowledge of a witness for any NP statement. To compare with generic ZK systems we construct a verification circuit with a minimal number of multiplication gates (since linear gates are for free). For the MQ problem, the verification circuit just evaluates the multivariate system, which requires $n(n + 1)/2$ secret multiplications. Using a permutation network [37], we can encode a permutation as a sequence of bits, where each bit controls if a switch in the network is active or not. With this representation, we can verify if a permutation is a solution of a PKP problem with a small number of non-linear gates. If the permutation network has k switches the verification can be done with $2k$ non-linear gates; k multiplications for applying the k switches and an additional k multiplications to verify that the witness consists of bits.

Table 4. Comparison of proof sizes of various ZK-proof systems for proving knowledge of a solution of an MQ instance. For the MQDSS system the number of iterations is 315, 478 and 637 respectively. At security level λ, the hashes and commitments are 2λ bits long. The parameter choices do not compensate for the non-tightness of the Fiat-Shamir transform, instead they only guarantee λ bits of soundness for the interactive version of the protocols.

Sec. level	Parameters $\mathbb{F}, n$	Circuit size	Proof size (KB)			
			MQDSS	Ligero	Aurora	**Mudfish**
128	GF(4), 88	3916	40	199	59	**14**
192	GF(4), 128	8256	43	421	90	**33**
256	GF(4), 160	12880	154	721	358	**56**

Table 5. Comparison of proof sizes of various ZK-proof systems for proving knowledge of a solution of a PKP instance.

Sec. level	Parameters $\mathbb{F}, n, m$	Circuit size	Proof size (KB)			
			PKP-DSS	Ligero	Aurora	**Sushsyfish**
128	GF(997), 61, 28	606	20	251	46	**12**
192	GF(1409), 87, 42	964	43	385	88	**27**
256	GF(1889), 111, 55	1300	77	539	239	**48**

Tables 4 and 5 show that our proof systems have significantly lower proof sizes compared to existing solutions.

9   Zero Knowledge Proofs for Lattice Statements

Stern's zero-knowledge protocol has been used extensively in lattice-based cryptography because it can be used to prove a wide variety of statements. It has been used to construct, among other things, identity-based identification schemes, group signatures (with verifier local revocation), logarithmic size ring signatures and group encryption [25–28]. The way this works is to transform the lattice statement into an instance of the IPKP problem, in such a way that from a solution to the IPKP instance one can efficiently derive a witness for the lattice statement and conversely, that given a witness for the statement one can efficiently compute a solution to the IPKP instance. Then, one just uses Stern's protocol to prove knowledge of a solution to the IPKP instance, which is equivalent to proving knowledge of a witness of the lattice statement. However, it is often the case that witnesses for the lattice statement correspond to IPKP solutions that lie in a certain subgroup $H \subset S_n$. If this is the case, then the prover needs to prove that he knows a solution π to the IPKP instance subject to $\pi \in H$. Luckily, Stern's protocol (and as we will see also our IPKP proof) can be easily adapted to prove knowledge of an IPKP solution that lies in any subgroup H (assuming one can sample uniformly from H and efficiently verify membership of H).

In the remainder of this section, we prove that our IPKP proof can handle proving that a solution lies in a subgroup $H \subset S_n$, which implies that we can improve all the applications of Sterns protocol by replacing Stern's proof by our more efficient protocol. Then, we will focus on proving knowledge of a solution to the inhomogeneous SIS problem. We briefly illustrate how the ISIS problem can be embedded into IPKP with the decomposition-extension technique of Ling et al. [28]. Then, we compare the efficiency of our IPKP proof against the efficiency of Stern's protocol for proving knowledge of a solution of an ISIS problem. Finally, we compare our approach to some recent works that use different techniques to prove knowledge of a solution of an ISIS instance.

9.1 Generalizing to Subgroup IPKP

It is trivial to generalize the protocol of Sect. 5 to prove knowledge of a solution π of an IPKP instance with the additional constraint that π lies in a subgroup $H \subset S_n$, assuming that one can efficiently sample uniformly from H and efficiently test if a group element is a member of H. The only modification required is that the prover now samples σ from H instead of from S_n and that the verifier checks that ρ lies in H.

Theorem 5. *The modified version of the protocol for IPKP of Sect. 5 is a sigma protocol with helper as in Definition 3 with challenge space $\mathbb{F}_q$.*

Proof. **Completeness.** If π is a solution of the IPKP instance, then since the unmodified protocol is complete, the verifier will accept a transcript unless the additional check that ρ lies in H fails. However, if $\pi \in H$, then also $\rho = \pi\sigma^{-1}$ lies in H, because σ is sampled from H. Therefore, the verifier will accept with probability 1 if π is a solution to the SIPKP problem.

2-Special Soundness. The extractor from the security proof of the IPKP proof system extracts $\rho\sigma$, which is a solution to the IPKP problem. We only need to show that $\rho\sigma \in H$. The verifier only accepts if $\rho \in H$, and we know that $\sigma \in H$, because it is sampled from H by the honest helper. Therefore the extracted solution to the IPKP solution is also a solution to the SIPKP problem.

Honest-Verifier Zero-Knowledge. The proof is the same as in the proof of Theorem 2, except that the simulator samples τ uniformly from H instead of from S_n.

Remark 1. The proof of Theorem 2 does not use any specific properties of the action of S_n apart from the property that $\mathbf{v}_\sigma + \mathbf{w}_\sigma = (\mathbf{v} + \mathbf{w})_\sigma$, which is required for correctness. Therefore, it is clear that the proof system generalizes to any representation of a finite group G on $\mathbb{F}_q^n$. In particular, we can also consider the group of signed permutations with it natural representation on $\mathbb{F}_q^n$.

9.2 Embedding ISIS into IPKP

To illustrate the embedding first suppose that $(\mathbf{A}, \mathbf{t}) \in \mathbb{F}_q^{m \times n} \times \mathbb{F}_q^m$ is an instance of the ISIS problem where a solution is a vector $\mathbf{s} \in \mathbb{F}_q^n$ such that $\mathbf{As} = \mathbf{t}$ and the coefficients of $\mathbf{s}$ are 0 or 1. In that case we define the extended matrix $\mathbf{A}' = \begin{pmatrix} \mathbf{A} & \mathbf{0}_{m \times n} \end{pmatrix}$ and a vector $\mathbf{v} \in \mathbb{F}_q$ whose first n entries are 1 and whose last n entries are equal to 0. Then finding a solution to the ISIS instance $(\mathbf{A}, \mathbf{t})$ is equivalent to finding a solution to the IPKP instance $(\mathbf{A}', \mathbf{v}, \mathbf{t})$: Given a solution $\mathbf{s}$ to the ISIS instance it is trivial to find a permutation π such that the first half of $\mathbf{v}_\pi$ equals $\mathbf{s}$, which is then a solution to the IPKP instance. Conversely, if π is a solution to the IPKP instance, then the first half of $\mathbf{v}_\pi$ is a solution to the ISIS instance. Therefore, proving knowledge of π is equivalent to proving knowledge of $\mathbf{s}$.

To improve the efficiency of the proof system we can restrict the IPKP solutions to the subgroup of S_{2n} generated by the transpositions $(i \quad i + n)$ for $0 \le i < n$. This approach reduces the proof size because elements of the subgroup can be represented with only n bits, rather than the $\log_2((2n)!) \approx 2n \log_2(2n)$ bits required to represent an arbitrary permutation of $2n$ elements.

More generally, if the coefficients of $\mathbf{s}$ are required to lie in a range of size B, one can use the decomposition-extension technique [28] to transform an instance of the ISIS problem into an equivalent instance of the IPKP with a matrix $\mathbf{A}'$ with $2n\lceil \log_2 B \rceil$ columns [28]. Moreover, we can restrict to a subgroup of size $2^{2\lceil \log_2 B \rceil}$ to reduce the proof size.

9.3 Concrete Examples and Comparison to Previous Works

To compare the concrete efficiency of our work with the recent work of Bootle et al. [11] and Baum and Nof [5] we apply our proof system to the following two SIS parameters sets:

1. $q \approx 2^{32}, m = 512, n = 2048, \beta = 1$: This is the parameter set considered by Bootle et al [11]. This parameter set is relevant for FHE schemes and group signature schemes.
2. $q \approx 2^{61}, m = 1024, n = 4092$, binary solution: This is one of the parameter sets considered by Baum and Nof. [5], they claim that this parameter set is relevant for applications such as somewhat homomorphic encryption.

Let $\mathbf{A} \in \mathbb{F}_q^{512 \times 2048}$ be an instance of the SIS problem from the first parameter set, define the matrix $\mathbf{A}' = \begin{pmatrix} \mathbf{A} & \mathbf{0}_{512 \times 2048} \end{pmatrix}$ and let $\mathbf{v} \in \{0, 1\}^{4096}$ be the vector whose first 2048 entries are equal to 1 and whose remaining 2048 entries are equal to 0. Then finding a solution to the SIS instance $\mathbf{A}$ is equivalent to finding a solution to the generalized PKP instance that asks to find a signed permutation π such that $\mathbf{A}'\mathbf{v}_\pi = \mathbf{0}$. Moreover, this still holds if we restrict the solutions of the PKP problem to lie in the subgroup H generated by sign swaps and the transpositions $\{(i \quad i+2048)|$ for i from 1 to 2048$\}$. This subgroup has 8^{2048} elements, and we can represent each element by $3 * 2048$ bits.

Therefore, to prove knowledge of a short integer solution it suffices to prove knowledge of a signed permutation π in H such that $\mathbf{A}'\mathbf{v}_\pi = 0$. We choose parameters $\tau = 14, M = 4040, q' = 2^{10}$ to achieve a soundness error less than 2^{-128}. The proof size is dominated by the vectors and signed permutations in the proof, of which there is one per execution. A vector can be represented with $4069 \log_2(q)$ bits and each permutation in H can be represented with $2048 * 3$ bits. Therefore the total proof size is roughly equal to

$$14 \cdot (4069 \cdot 32 + 2048 \cdot 3) \text{ bits } = 233 \text{ KB.}$$

Observe that (in a field of characteristic > 2) if $\overline{1}$ is the vector with a 1 in each entry, then

$$A\mathbf{s} = \mathbf{t} \iff A(2\mathbf{s} - \overline{1}) = 2\mathbf{t} + A\overline{1},$$

which means that binary SIS is equivalent to a SIS instance where the entries of $\mathbf{s}$ are restricted to $\{-1, 1\}$. Therefore, for the second parameter set, we can embed the binary SIS problem into a generalized PKP problem of the form $A\overline{1}_\pi = \mathbf{t}'$ with π in the group with 2^{4092} elements generated by sign flips. If we again pick $\tau = 14, M = 4040, q' = 2^{10}$ to achieve a soundness error less than 2^{-128} the total proof size is approximately

$$14 \cdot (4092 \cdot 61 + 4092) \text{ bits } = 444 \text{ KB}$$

Comparison to Previous Works. Table 6 makes a comparison of the proof sizes of our proof system with that of previous works. First of all, an application of Stern's protocol to the generalized PKP problems derived from the two parameter sets results in proofs of 2.3 MB and 4.3 MB respectively. This is an order of magnitude larger than our proof system for both parameter sets. The work of Bootle et al. [11] uses algebraic techniques rather than combinatorial ones and achieves a proof size of 384 KB for the first parameter set, which is 65% larger than our proofs.

The proof system of Baum and Nof uses MPC-in-the-head techniques and has a proof size of 4.0 MB for the second parameter set. This is almost an order of magnitude larger than our proofs. Baum and Nof also include timings of the implementation of their protocol. An implementation with 80 bits of statistical security for the second SIS parameter takes 2.4 s, with a proof size of 7.5 MB. (Note that this proof size is larger than for their 128 bits variant, because this choice was optimized for speed rather than proof size.) If we choose the parameters for our proof scheme as $q' = 2^4, M = 149, \tau = 23$ to reach 80 bits of statistical security and optimize for speed, our proof size would be 1.4 MB (still 5 times smaller). Extrapolating from our SUSHSYFISH measurements, we claim that with these parameter choices our proof system will be significantly faster than the system of Baum and Nof.

Compared to the generic sub-linear Zero-Knowledge systems Ligero and Aurora [6] our proof systems are asymptotically worse, and for the large examples in Table 6 aiming at applications such as FHE we also perform significantly worse in terms of concrete proof sizes. However, for smaller applications, such as proving knowledge of a secret key that corresponds to a MLWE-encryption public key. ($q \approx 2^{13}, n = 1024, m = 512, \beta = 3$) we expect our proof size to be smaller than those of Ligero and similar to those of Aurora. Moreover, an important advantage of our proof system, as well as Stern's protocol and the method of Baum and Nof is that they do not require $\mathbb{F}_q$ (or a field extension thereof) to be NTT friendly, this is in contrast to Ligero, Aurora and the work of Bootle et al.

Table 6. Proof sizes of various protocols for our two SIS parameter sets aiming at 128 bits of security. The hashes and commitments are 256 bits long. The parameter choices do not compensate for the non-tightness of the Fiat-Shamir transform, instead they only guarantee 128 bits of soundness for the interactive version of the protocols.

	$q = 2^{32}$, $m = 512, n = 2048$	$q = 2^{61}$, $m = 1024, n = 4096$
Ours	233 KB	444 KB
Stern [28,34]	2.3 MB	4.3 MB
Bootle et al. [11]	384 KB	/
Baum and Nof [5]	/	4.0 MB
Aurora [6]	71 KB	71 KB
Ligero [2]	157 KB	200 KB

The work of Del Pino et al. [31] uses so-called bulletproofs to achieve much smaller proof sizes for SIS (for example 1.25 KB for $q \approx 2^{13}, m = 2048, n = 4096$) at the cost of longer running times. However, one cannot make a direct comparison with our work and the other works in Table 6, because bulletproofs rely on the discrete logarithm problem and are hence not post-quantum secure. Also, there has been a lot of work on "relaxed" proofs for SIS, where the extractor does not output the witness that is known to the prover, but instead some other solution that is somewhat short, but bigger than the witness [4,29]. For some applications, such as post-quantum signatures [29], this is not a problem, but for other applications, exact proofs are required.

Acknowledgements. I would like to thank Simona Samardjiska for helping estimate the complexity of the Joux-Vitse algorithm and Muthu Venkitasubramaniam and Nicholas Ward for providing proof sizes of the Ligero and Aurora proof systems respectively. I would also like to thank the anonymous reviewer for the suggestion to generalize PKP to signed permutations. This work was supported in part by the Research Council KU Leuven: C16/15/058. In addition, this work was supported by the European Commission through the Horizon 2020 research and innovation programme under grant agreement H2020-DS-LEIT-2017-780108 FENTEC, by the Flemish Government through FWO SBO project SNIPPET S007619N and by the IF/C1 on Cryptanalysis of post-quantum cryptography. Ward Beullens is funded by an FWO fellowship.

References

1. Ajtai, M.: Generating hard instances of lattice problems. In: Proceedings of the Twenty-Eighth Annual ACM Symposium on Theory of Computing, pp. 99–108. ACM (1996)
2. Ames, S., Hazay, C., Ishai, Y., Venkitasubramaniam, M.: Ligero: lightweight sublinear arguments without a trusted setup. In: Proceedings of the 2017 ACM SIGSAC Conference on Computer and Communications Security, pp. 2087–2104 (2017)
3. Baritaud, T., Campana, M., Chauvaud, P., Gilbert, H.: On the security of the permuted kernel identification scheme. In: Brickell, E.F. (ed.) CRYPTO 1992. LNCS, vol. 740, pp. 305–311. Springer, Heidelberg (1993). https://doi.org/10.1007/3-540-48071-4_21
4. Baum, C., Bootle, J., Cerulli, A., del Pino, R., Groth, J., Lyubashevsky, V.: Sublinear lattice-based zero-knowledge arguments for arithmetic circuits. In: Shacham, H., Boldyreva, A. (eds.) CRYPTO 2018. LNCS, vol. 10992, pp. 669–699. Springer, Cham (2018). https://doi.org/10.1007/978-3-319-96881-0_23
5. Baum, C., Nof, A.: Concretely-efficient zero-knowledge arguments for arithmetic circuits and their application to lattice-based cryptography. Technical report, Cryptology ePrint Archive, Report 2019/532 (2019). https://eprint. iacr. org . . .
6. Ben-Sasson, E., Chiesa, A., Riabzev, M., Spooner, N., Virza, M., Ward, N.P.: Aurora: transparent succinct arguments for R1CS. In: Ishai, Y., Rijmen, V. (eds.) EUROCRYPT 2019. LNCS, vol. 11476, pp. 103–128. Springer, Cham (2019). https://doi.org/10.1007/978-3-030-17653-2_4
7. Bernstein, D.: The djbsort software library for sorting arrays of integers or floating-point numbers in constant time. https://sorting.cr.yp.to/
8. Bettale, L., Faugere, J.C., Perret, L.: Hybrid approach for solving multivariate systems over finite fields. J. Math. Cryptol. $3(3)$, 177–197 (2009)
9. Beullens, W.: FISH (2019). https://github.com/WardBeullens/FISH
10. Beullens, W., Faugère, J.C., Koussa, E., Macario-Rat, G., Patarin, J., Perret, L.: PKP-based signature scheme. Cryptology ePrint Archive, Report 2018/714 (2018). https://eprint.iacr.org/2018/714
11. Bootle, J., Lyubashevsky, V., Seiler, G.: Algebraic techniques for short(er) exact lattice-based zero-knowledge proofs. In: Boldyreva, A., Micciancio, D. (eds.) CRYPTO 2019. LNCS, vol. 11692, pp. 176–202. Springer, Cham (2019). https://doi.org/10.1007/978-3-030-26948-7_7
12. Chase, M., et al.: Post-quantum zero-knowledge and signatures from symmetric-key primitives. In: Proceedings of the 2017 ACM SIGSAC Conference on Computer and Communications Security, pp. 1825–1842. ACM (2017)
13. Chen, M.-S., Hülsing, A., Rijneveld, J., Samardjiska, S., Schwabe, P.: From 5-pass $\mathcal{MQ}$-based identification to $\mathcal{MQ}$-based signatures. In: Cheon, J.H., Takagi, T. (eds.) ASIACRYPT 2016. LNCS, vol. 10032, pp. 135–165. Springer, Heidelberg (2016). https://doi.org/10.1007/978-3-662-53890-6_5
14. Chen, M.S., Hülsing, A., Rijneveld, J., Samardjiska, S., Schwabe, P.: MQDSS-submission to the NIST post-quantum cryptography project (2017)
15. Don, J., Fehr, S., Majenz, C., Schaffner, C.: Security of the Fiat-Shamir transformation in the quantum random-oracle model. In: Boldyreva, A., Micciancio, D. (eds.) CRYPTO 2019. LNCS, vol. 11693, pp. 356–383. Springer, Cham (2019). https://doi.org/10.1007/978-3-030-26951-7_13
16. Fehr, S.: Classical proofs for the quantum collapsing property of classical hash functions. In: Beimel, A., Dziembowski, S. (eds.) TCC 2018. LNCS, vol. 11240, pp. 315–338. Springer, Cham (2018). https://doi.org/10.1007/978-3-030-03810-6_12

17. Fiat, A., Shamir, A.: How to prove yourself: practical solutions to identification and signature problems. In: Odlyzko, A.M. (ed.) CRYPTO 1986. LNCS, vol. 263, pp. 186–194. Springer, Heidelberg (1987). https://doi.org/10.1007/3-540-47721-7_12

18. Georgiades, J.: Some remarks on the security of the identification scheme based on permuted kernels. J. Cryptol. 5(2), 133–137 (1992)

19. Goldwasser, S., Micali, S., Rackoff, C.: The knowledge complexity of interactive proof systems. SIAM J. Comput. 18(1), 186–208 (1989)

20. Ishai, Y., Kushilevitz, E., Ostrovsky, R., Sahai, A.: Zero-knowledge from secure multiparty computation. In: Proceedings of the Thirty-Ninth Annual ACM Symposium on Theory of Computing, pp. 21–30. ACM (2007)

21. Jaulmes, É., Joux, A.: Cryptanalysis of PKP: a new approach. In: Kim, K. (ed.) PKC 2001. LNCS, vol. 1992, pp. 165–172. Springer, Heidelberg (2001). https://doi.org/10.1007/3-540-44586-2_12

22. Joux, A., Vitse, V.: A crossbred algorithm for solving Boolean polynomial systems. In: Kaczorowski, J., Pieprzyk, J., Pomykała, J. (eds.) NuTMiC 2017. LNCS, vol. 10737, pp. 3–21. Springer, Cham (2018). https://doi.org/10.1007/978-3-319-76620-1_1

23. Kales, D., Zaverucha, G.: Forgery attacks on MQDSSv2. 0 (2019)

24. Katz, J., Kolesnikov, V., Wang, X.: Improved non-interactive zero knowledge with applications to post-quantum signatures. In: Proceedings of the 2018 ACM SIGSAC Conference on Computer and Communications Security, pp. 525–537. ACM (2018)

25. Langlois, A., Ling, S., Nguyen, K., Wang, H.: Lattice-based group signature scheme with verifier-local revocation. In: Krawczyk, H. (ed.) PKC 2014. LNCS, vol. 8383, pp. 345–361. Springer, Heidelberg (2014). https://doi.org/10.1007/978-3-642-54631-0_20

26. Libert, B., Ling, S., Mouhartem, F., Nguyen, K., Wang, H.: Zero-Knowledge Arguments for Matrix-Vector Relations and Lattice-Based Group Encryption. In: Cheon, J.H., Takagi, T. (eds.) ASIACRYPT 2016. LNCS, vol. 10032, pp. 101–131. Springer, Heidelberg (2016). https://doi.org/10.1007/978-3-662-53890-6_4

27. Libert, B., Ling, S., Nguyen, K., Wang, H.: Zero-knowledge arguments for lattice-based accumulators: logarithmic-size ring signatures and group signatures without trapdoors. In: Fischlin, M., Coron, J.-S. (eds.) EUROCRYPT 2016. LNCS, vol. 9666, pp. 1–31. Springer, Heidelberg (2016). https://doi.org/10.1007/978-3-662-49896-5_1

28. Ling, S., Nguyen, K., Stehlé, D., Wang, H.: Improved zero-knowledge proofs of knowledge for the ISIS problem, and applications. In: Kurosawa, K., Hanaoka, G. (eds.) PKC 2013. LNCS, vol. 7778, pp. 107–124. Springer, Heidelberg (2013). https://doi.org/10.1007/978-3-642-36362-7_8

29. Lyubashevsky, V.: Fiat-Shamir with aborts: applications to lattice and factoring-based signatures. In: Matsui, M. (ed.) ASIACRYPT 2009. LNCS, vol. 5912, pp. 598–616. Springer, Heidelberg (2009). https://doi.org/10.1007/978-3-642-10366-7_35

30. Patarin, J., Chauvaud, P.: Improved algorithms for the permuted kernel problem. In: Stinson, D.R. (ed.) CRYPTO 1993. LNCS, vol. 773, pp. 391–402. Springer, Heidelberg (1994). https://doi.org/10.1007/3-540-48329-2_33

31. del Pino, R., Lyubashevsky, V., Seiler, G.: Short discrete log proofs for FHE and ring-LWE ciphertexts. In: Lin, D., Sako, K. (eds.) PKC 2019. LNCS, vol. 11442, pp. 344–373. Springer, Cham (2019). https://doi.org/10.1007/978-3-030-17253-4_12

32. Sakumoto, K., Shirai, T., Hiwatari, H.: Public-key identification schemes based on multivariate quadratic polynomials. In: Rogaway, P. (ed.) CRYPTO 2011. LNCS, vol. 6841, pp. 706–723. Springer, Heidelberg (2011). https://doi.org/10.1007/978-3-642-22792-9_40
33. Shamir, A.: An efficient identification scheme based on permuted kernels (extended abstract). In: Brassard, G. (ed.) CRYPTO 1989. LNCS, vol. 435, pp. 606–609. Springer, New York (1990). https://doi.org/10.1007/0-387-34805-0_54
34. Stern, J.: A new identification scheme based on syndrome decoding. In: Stinson, D.R. (ed.) CRYPTO 1993. LNCS, vol. 773, pp. 13–21. Springer, Heidelberg (1994). https://doi.org/10.1007/3-540-48329-2_2
35. Unruh, D.: Non-interactive zero-knowledge proofs in the quantum random oracle model. In: Oswald, E., Fischlin, M. (eds.) EUROCRYPT 2015. LNCS, vol. 9057, pp. 755–784. Springer, Heidelberg (2015). https://doi.org/10.1007/978-3-662-46803-6_25
36. Unruh, D.: Computationally binding quantum commitments. In: Fischlin, M., Coron, J.-S. (eds.) EUROCRYPT 2016. LNCS, vol. 9666, pp. 497–527. Springer, Heidelberg (2016). https://doi.org/10.1007/978-3-662-49896-5_18
37. Waksman, A.: A permutation network. J. ACM (JACM) 15(1), 159–163 (1968)

Signatures from Sequential-OR Proofs

Marc Fischlin, Patrick Harasser$^{(\boxtimes)}$, and Christian Janson

Cryptoplexity, Technische Universität Darmstadt, Darmstadt, Germany
{marc.fischlin,patrick.harasser,christian.janson}@cryptoplexity.de

Abstract. OR-proofs enable a prover to show that it knows the witness for one of many statements, or that one out of many statements is true. OR-proofs are a remarkably versatile tool, used to strengthen security properties, design group and ring signature schemes, and achieve tight security. The common technique to build OR-proofs is based on an approach introduced by Cramer, Damgård, and Schoenmakers (CRYPTO'94), where the prover splits the verifier's challenge into random shares and computes proofs for each statement in parallel.

In this work we study a different, less investigated OR-proof technique, highlighted by Abe, Ohkubo, and Suzuki (ASIACRYPT'02). The difference is that the prover now computes the individual proofs sequentially. We show that such sequential OR-proofs yield signature schemes which can be proved secure in the non-programmable random oracle model. We complement this positive result with a black-box impossibility proof, showing that the same is unlikely to be the case for signatures derived from traditional OR-proofs. We finally argue that sequential-OR signature schemes can be proved secure in the quantum random oracle model, albeit with very loose bounds and by programming the random oracle.

Keywords: Sequential-OR proofs · Zero-knowledge · Signatures · Non-programmable random oracle model · Quantum random oracle model

1 Introduction

In a zero-knowledge Σ-protocol between a prover P and a verifier V, the prover holds a statement x and a witness w for x, and the verifier only x. Both parties engage in an interactive execution, resulting in an initial commitment com sent by the prover, a verifier random challenge ch, and a final response resp computed by the prover. With such a proof, P shows to V that x is true (in proof systems), or that it knows a witness w for x (in proofs of knowledge). At the same time, the zero-knowledge property guarantees that nothing beyond this fact is revealed.

1.1 OR-Proofs

Now assume that one has two interactive proof systems of the above form for two statements x_0 and x_1, and a witness w_b for x_b, $b \in \{0,1\}$. The goal is to combine

© International Association for Cryptologic Research 2020
A. Canteaut and Y. Ishai (Eds.): EUROCRYPT 2020, LNCS 12107, pp. 212–244, 2020.
https://doi.org/10.1007/978-3-030-45727-3_8

$P_{\text{par-OR}}(1^\lambda; (x_0, x_1), (b, w))$:

11: $\text{com}_b, \leftarrow_{\$} P_b(1^\lambda; x_b, w)$

12: $\text{ch}_{1-b} \leftarrow_{\$} \{0, 1\}^{\ell(\lambda)}$

13: $(\text{com}_{1-b}, \text{resp}_{1-b}, \text{ch}_{1-b}) \leftarrow_{\$}$

$\qquad \leftarrow_{\$} S_{1-b}(1^\lambda; x_{1-b}, \text{ch}_{1-b})$

14: $\textbf{return } (\text{com}_0, \text{com}_1)$

$P_{\text{par-OR}}(1^\lambda; (x_0, x_1), (b, w), (\text{com}_0, \text{com}_1), \text{ch})$:

21: $\text{ch}_b \leftarrow \text{ch} \oplus \text{ch}_{1-b}$

22: $\text{resp}_b \leftarrow_{\$} P_b(1^\lambda; x_b, w, \text{com}_b, \text{ch}_b)$

23: $\textbf{return } (\text{ch}_0, \text{ch}_1, \text{resp}_0, \text{resp}_1)$

Fig. 1. Description of the prover algorithm $P_{\text{par-OR}}$ from the parallel-OR construction by Cramer et al. [23] in the standard model. On the left, generation of the first message $\text{com} = (\text{com}_0, \text{com}_1)$. On the right, computation of the final response $\text{resp} = (\text{ch}_0, \text{ch}_1, \text{resp}_0, \text{resp}_1)$ answering the verifier challenge ch.

them into a single protocol which proves the logical OR of x_0 and x_1; that is, the prover should be able to convince a verifier that it holds a witness for one of the two statements, ideally without revealing which one. The first instantiation of such general OR-proofs, sometimes called CDS-OR proofs, was given by Cramer, Damgård, and Schoenmakers [23]. Their construction works under the assumption that the two protocols are special honest-verifier zero-knowledge, meaning that a simulator S, given x and a random challenge ch at the outset, is able to generate a verifier view $(\text{com}, \text{resp}, \text{ch})$ without knowing a witness for x, in such a way that this view is indistinguishable from a genuine interaction between the real prover and an honest verifier using the given challenge. The prover in the CDS-OR protocol from [23] is described in Fig. 1. For reasons that will become apparent soon, we call such CDS-OR proofs also *parallel-OR* proofs.

An important observation is that the resulting protocol is witness indistinguishable, i.e., it does not reveal for which statement the prover holds a witness. Moreover, since the resulting protocol is again a Σ-protocol, one can apply the Fiat-Shamir transform [32] to it and obtain a non-interactive version or a signature scheme in the random oracle model. Also, the construction easily generalizes to the case of 1-out-of-n proofs.

1.2 Applications of OR-Proofs

OR-proofs have turned out to be a very powerful tool in the design of efficient protocols. Early on they have been identified as a means to thwart man-in-the-middle attacks [22] and, similarly in spirit, to give designated-verifier proofs [43]. The idea in both cases is to have the verifier send its public key to the prover, who then shows that the statement x it originally wanted to prove is true or that it knows the verifier's secret key. This proof is still convincing for the verifier (who knows it is the only holder of its secret key), but not transferable to other parties. Garay et al. [38] apply the same idea to make zero-knowledge proofs simulation-sound and non-malleable, by putting a verification key into a common reference string (CRS). The prover then shows that the original statement x is true or that it knows the secret to the verification key in the CRS.

The idea of giving a valid proof when knowing a witness for only one of several statements can also be used in the context of group signatures [19] and ring signatures [56]. Given a set of public keys $x_1, \ldots, x_n$, where the signer knows only one witness w_i (their own secret key), an OR-proof allows to sign anonymously on behalf of the entire group, and witness indistinguishability implies that the identity of the signer remains hidden. This design strategy appears explicitly for example in the group signature scheme of Camenisch [13].

The OR-technique has also proved very useful in deriving tightly-secure schemes. This approach has appeared in several works in the literature [6,39,42]. The idea is to first derive tightly-secure signature schemes from the OR-combination of some Σ-protocols. These schemes are then used within higher-level solutions (like key exchange protocols), passing on the tight security guarantees to these protocols.

1.3   Non-programmable Random Oracles

Another important feature of the OR-technique is that it facilitates the design of schemes in the non-programmable random oracle model. The general random oracle model comes with several remarkable technical properties, rooted in the formalization of the hash function as a truly random, oracle-based function. One of the most extraordinary consequences of this formalization is the programmability property of the random oracle, saying that one can adaptively choose the answers to random oracle queries made by the adversary. Indeed, the ability to change answers on the fly is a necessary feature of security proofs of some signature schemes [33,35,37,61]. In practice, however, hash functions are not programmable and their values are fixed. Therefore, one would ideally prefer to forgo the programming of random oracle replies.

The fact that the OR-technique can be used to bypass the programmability issues with the random oracle model can already be observed in the early constructions of Σ-protocols, namely, the Okamoto variant [52] of the Schnorr signature scheme [57] and the Guillou-Quisquater variant [41] of the Fiat-Shamir signature protocol [32]. In these variants, based on number-theoretic specifics, one uses "embedded" OR-proofs which allow to simulate signatures without having to program the random oracle, as opposed to [32,57] and explicitly carried out in [55]: One can then simply use the known witness to generate signatures.

Unfortunately, the security proofs of the signature schemes in [41,52] still need programming at another step. Namely, in order to show that the adversary cannot forge signatures, one rewinds the execution and re-programs the random oracle in order to extract a witness (a technique called forking in [55]). This also comes with a loose security bound. Abdalla et al. [1] overcome the forking technique by considering passively-secure identification schemes, where the adversary is allowed to see transcripts of honest executions. Still, they program the random oracle when simulating signatures.

Later, Abdalla et al. [2] used the notion of lossy identification schemes to give non-forking security proofs for signatures derived via the Fiat-Shamir heuristic. Lossiness here roughly means that valid statements x are indistinguishable from so-called lossy ones, for which it is statistically impossible to find convincing proofs. This idea has later been adopted by lattice-based and LWE-based signature schemes such as [7,49] (in the classical random oracle model) or the TESLA signature scheme [4] (in the quantum random oracle model [10]). Still, all approaches program the random oracle in order to be able to simulate signatures.

1.4 Sequential-OR Proofs

The above construction is the classical technique to combine Σ-protocols and prove OR-statements, but it is not the only possible solution. Indeed, there is at least one other way to prove the disjunction of two or more statements in the random oracle model, which in its spirit already appears in a work by Rivest, Shamir, and Tauman [56]. Here, we follow the exposition given by Abe, Ohkubo, and Suzuki [3] in the context of group signature schemes, and call this approach the *sequential-OR* technique.

In this construction, the non-interactive prover computes the individual proofs sequentially, starting with the commitment com_b for the statement x_b for which it knows the witness w_b. Next it derives the challenge ch_{1-b} for the proof of x_{1-b} (with unknown witness) as the hash value of com_b. This in turn allows the OR-prover to simulate a view $(\mathsf{com}_{1-b}, \mathsf{resp}_{1-b}, \mathsf{ch}_{1-b})$ for x_{1-b} with this predetermined challenge, as done in parallel-OR proofs. The simulated commitment com_{1-b} again yields the challenge ch_b for the first proof through the hash function, which the prover now can answer with a valid response resp_b since it knows the witness w_b. The details of the prover in the sequential-OR protocol from [3] are described in Fig. 2.

Note that this technique generalizes to the 1-out-of-n case (we provide all details in the full version [34]). In fact, Abe et al. [3] and follow-up works like [8,47], use this more general version of the sequential-OR technique to build group signature schemes, yet still programming the random oracle to fork and extract. The paradigm proposed by Abe et al. has also been applied in the area of cryptocurrencies, in particular Monero [58] and Mimblewimble [44,54]. There, in order to prevent overflow attacks, it is necessary to prove that committed values fall within a specific range. One instance of such range proofs uses a special type of ring signature, called borromean ring signature [50], which is based on ideas presented in [3]. Observe that, in the aforementioned range proofs, borromean signatures have since been superseded by more efficient bulletproofs [12].

1.5 Our Results

At first glance, the sequential-OR technique does not seem to give any significant advantage over the parallel version. Both protocols are based on the idea that one can easily give a proof for a statement for which the witness is known, and simulate the proof for the other statement where the challenge is known in advance. This, however, misses one important point if we combine these two approaches with the idea of lossy statements as in the work by Abdalla et al. [2]:

$P_{seq-OR}(1^\lambda; (x_0, x_1), (b, w))$:

11: $com_b \leftarrow_\$ P_b(1^\lambda; x_b, w)$

12: $ch_{1-b} \leftarrow \mathcal{H}(b, x_0, x_1, com_b)$

13: $(com_{1-b}, resp_{1-b}, ch_{1-b}) \leftarrow_\$ S_{1-b}(1^\lambda; x_{1-b}, ch_{1-b})$

14: $ch_b \leftarrow \mathcal{H}(1 - b, x_0, x_1, com_{1-b})$

15: $resp_b \leftarrow_\$ P_b(1^\lambda; x_b, w, com_b, ch_b)$

16: **return** $(com_0, com_1, resp_0, resp_1)$

Fig. 2. Description of the prover algorithm P_{seq-OR} from the sequential-OR construction by Abe et al. [3] in the random oracle model.

We show that signatures derived from sequential-OR proofs are secure in the non-programmable random oracle model, whereas those originating from parallel-OR proofs do not seem to have a security proof in this model.

The signature scheme in the sequential-OR case is based on two valid statements x_0 and x_1 (the public keys), for which we know one of the two witnesses w_b (one of the secret keys). A signature for a message m is basically a sequential-OR proof, where m is included in the hash evaluations. In contrast to the proof in [3], which is based on forking, we can now reduce unforgeability to a decisional problem about the languages. This allows us to avoid rewinding and re-programming the random oracle.

The idea of our proof in the sequential-OR case can be illustrated by looking at the honest signer first. If one was able to observe the signer's random oracle queries, then their order reveals which witness the signer is using: The signer first queries the commitment com_b of the instance x_b for which it knows the witness w_b. We will use the same idea against the adversary, helping us to decide if some random input x_{1-b} is in the language or not. If x_{1-b} is not in the language, and thus does not have a witness, the special soundness of the Σ-protocol guarantees that the adversary will never make the first query about this part, since it will then not be able to answer the random challenge.[1] Hence, by merely observing the adversary's queries, we can decide membership of x_{1-b}. We use the other part x_b in the key and its witness w_b to simulate signatures without programming the random oracle. But we need to make sure that the adversary is not biased by our signatures. This follows from the witness indistinguishability of the proofs (against an adversary who cannot observe random oracle queries).

We next argue that it is in general hard to show that the parallel-OR technique of Cramer et al. [23] yields a secure signature scheme in the non-programmable random oracle model. Our result assumes a black-box reduction R transforming any (PPT or unbounded) adversary against the signature scheme into a solver of some hard problem, and makes a mild assumption about the zero-knowledge simulators of the languages (namely, that they work independently of

---

[1] One can think of this as a very lossy mode.

how the statements x are generated). Remarkably, we do not make any stipulations about the reduction's executions of the adversary instances: The reduction can run an arbitrary (bounded) number of instances of the adversary, and there are no restrictions on the inputs of these instances or their scheduling. However, the reduction R can only use the external random oracle.

Our approach is based on the meta-reduction technique [11,40,53]. That is, we start with an unbounded adversary A, who breaks the signature scheme easily with its super-polynomial power by computing a secret key and signing as the honest prover would. This means that the reduction R also solves the underlying problem when interacting with A. Afterwards, we show how to simulate A efficiently, resulting in an efficient algorithm solving the problem directly. This implies that there cannot exist such a reduction R in the first place.

The crucial difference between the sequential and the parallel version of the OR-technique is that in the latter case observing the random oracle queries of the adversary does *not* reveal which witness is being used. By the zero-knowledge property one cannot distinguish real and simulated sub-proofs in the parallel case. Indeed, our negative result relies exactly on this zero-knowledge property, taking advantage of the fact that the random oracle is external to the reduction.

1.6   Further Related Work

The issue of non-programmability of random oracles also appears in recent works related to Canetti's universal composability (UC) framework [15]. In this model, random oracles can be cast as an ideal functionality $\mathcal{F}_{RO}$, and protocols can be developed in the hybrid setting where $\mathcal{F}_{RO}$ is present. A technical consequence of this design choice is that the random oracle is programmable, and a compositional consequence is that one would need a fresh random oracle for each protocol instance. Therefore, the global random oracle model [18], based on ideas of global set-ups [16,26], defines a random oracle functionality $\mathcal{G}_{sRO}$ which can be used by all protocols, obliterating also the programmability of the random oracle in this model.

We stress, however, that protocols designed in the global random oracle model are not necessarily secure for non-programmable random oracles. The discrepancy lies in the distinction between the model and the security proof: In the global random oracle model, one may no longer be able to program the random oracle when devising a simulator *in the model*, but a reduction may still program the random oracle *in the security proof* showing that the simulator is good. Indeed, this can be observed in the security reductions in [14] proving that all signature schemes which have a stand-alone proof of unforgeability in the "isolated" random oracle model, including schemes with a security reduction via programming, remain secure in the strict global random oracle model $\mathcal{G}_{sRO}$.

The impossibility of proving the security of specific types of signatures derived via the Fiat-Shamir transform in the non-programmable random oracle model has already been discussed in prior works, e.g., [33,36]. These works usually make some restrictions on the reduction being ruled out (like key preservation or being single-instance) , whereas we do not need any such condition. We remark here that our impossibility result for parallel-OR signatures does likely not follow in a general way from these results, since the same approach fails in the sequential-OR case.

In terms of OR-proofs, Ciampi et al. [20], based on an earlier approach by Lindell [46], *use* the OR-technique to build non-interactive zero-knowledge proofs from Σ-protocols in the non-programmable random oracle model. For technical reasons they also need a common reference string, which is used to form the OR-language. Note that this is orthogonal to our goal here, where we aim to *build* OR-proofs for two languages in the non-programmable random oracle model. In another work, Ciampi et al. [21] consider extensions of parallel-OR proofs where (some of) the languages are not specified yet when the execution starts. This includes the solution in the common reference string model in [20].

1.7 Extension to the Quantum Random Oracle Model

The results discussed so far are in the classical random oracle model. In terms of the quantum random oracle model (QROM), introduced by Boneh et al. [10], the situation regarding OR-proofs is less scrutinized. Our approach in the (classical) sequential-OR case is based on the observability of queries to the random oracle, a technique that usually does not carry over to the QROM because of superposition queries. In the parallel-OR case, we have seen that observability may not even help in the classical setting.

Fortunately, there have been two recent results regarding the security of Fiat-Shamir protocols in the QROM [27,48], bypassing previous negative results concerning the Fiat-Shamir transform in this model [5,24]. These works both yield a non-tight bound, but give an immediate solution for the parallel-OR case in the QROM. There, one first combines the two interactive proofs via the parallel-OR construction to get an interactive Fiat-Shamir proof, and then applies these techniques. We show in Sect. 6 that one can also prove security of signatures derived from the sequential-OR construction in the QROM via the measure-and-reprogram technique described in [27]. The price we pay is that we inherit the loose security bound from the solution in [27] and we, like all currently known constructions in the QROM, need to program the quantum random oracle.

2   Preliminaries

2.1   Basic Notation

We denote by $\mathbb{N} = \mathbb{Z}_{\geq 0}$ the set of non-negative integers, and by $\lambda \in \mathbb{N}$ the security parameter (often written in unary notation as 1^λ). A function $\mu \colon \mathbb{N} \to \mathbb{R}$ is called *negligible* if, for every constant $c \in \mathbb{R}_{>0}$, there exists $\lambda_c \in \mathbb{N}$ such that, for every $\lambda \in \mathbb{N}$ with $\lambda \geq \lambda_c$, we have $\mu(\lambda) \leq \lambda^{-c}$. For a random variable X, we write $x \leftarrow_{\$} X$ to denote that x is a random variate of X. For a finite set S of size $|S|$, we use $s \leftarrow_{\$} S$ as a shorthand for $s \leftarrow_{\$} U_S$, where U_S is a random variable uniformly distributed over S. The arrow $\leftarrow$ will be used for assignment statements. We denote the length of a string $x \in \{0,1\}^*$ by $|x|$, and we write ε for the empty string. We consider an injective, efficiently computable, efficiently reversible, and length-increasing encoding function $(\{0,1\}^*)^* \to \{0,1\}^*$. This allows us to represent sequences of strings again as strings, and will be tacitly used throughout the paper.

In this work we use the computational model of probabilistic oracle Turing machines, also called algorithms. We assume that they are equipped with a separate security parameter tape containing the value 1^λ. The running time of algorithms, which is intended to be bounded by the worst case, is a function of the security parameter input length only. A uniform algorithm is called *probabilistic polynomial-time (PPT)* if its running time is bounded by a polynomial, whereas a non-uniform algorithm is *PPT* if it corresponds to an infinite sequence of Turing machines, indexed by the security parameter λ, whose description sizes and running times are bounded by a polynomial in λ. Queries to the oracles always count as one operation each. For an algorithm A, we denote by $\mathsf{A}^{\mathcal{O}}(1^\lambda; x)$ the random variable representing the output of A when run on security parameter λ and input $x \in \{0,1\}^*$, with access to oracles $\mathcal{O} = (\mathcal{O}_1, \ldots, \mathcal{O}_t)$.

We use $\perp$ as a special symbol to denote rejection or an error, and we assume that $\perp \notin \{0,1\}^*$. Both inputs and outputs of algorithms can be $\perp$, and we convene that if any input to an algorithm is $\perp$, then its output is $\perp$ as well. Double square brackets $[\![\cdot]\!]$ enclosing boolean statements return the bit 1 if the statement is true, and 0 otherwise.

2.2   Random Oracle Model

Let $\ell \colon \mathbb{N} \to \mathbb{N}$ be a polynomial-time computable function. For a security parameter $\lambda \in \mathbb{N}$, a *random oracle* (RO) [9,17] is an oracle $\mathcal{H}$ that implements a function randomly chosen from the space of all functions $\{0,1\}^* \to \{0,1\}^{\ell(\lambda)}$, to which all parties have access. In other words, it is an oracle that answers every query with a truly random response chosen from the range $\{0,1\}^{\ell(\lambda)}$. For every repeated query the random oracle consistently returns the same output.

Constructions established and statements proved in the presence of a RO are said to hold in the *random oracle model* (ROM). Throughout the paper, whenever a security game is set in the ROM, we assume that at the beginning of the experiment a random oracle is sampled uniformly from the aforementioned function space, and then used throughout the experiment. In this setting, it will sometimes be necessary to record queries to the random oracle $\mathcal{H}$, and we will do so via a set $Q_{\mathcal{H}}$: If $(i, x) \in Q_{\mathcal{H}}$, this means that the i-th query to $\mathcal{H}$ was x.

We also define the "zero oracle" as a function $\mathcal{Z} \colon \{0,1\}^* \to \{0,1\}^{\ell(\lambda)}$, with $\mathcal{Z}(x) = 0^{\ell(\lambda)}$ for all $x \in \{0,1\}^*$. This allows us to state our definitions simultaneously in the standard model and in the ROM: Parties will be given access to a generic oracle $\mathcal{O}$, and it is understood that $\mathcal{O} := \mathcal{Z}$ if the definition is formulated in the standard model, and $\mathcal{O} := \mathcal{H}$ if it is in the ROM.

The quantum analogue of the above is the so-called *quantum random oracle model* (QROM), introduced by Boneh et al. [10]. Here, a quantum algorithm may query the random oracle $\mathcal{H}$ in superposition, i.e., submit superposition queries of the form $\sum_x \alpha_x |x\rangle |0\rangle$ and obtain the output $\sum_x \alpha_x |x\rangle |\mathcal{H}(x)\rangle$. We refer to [51] for further background and conventions regarding quantum information.

2.3 Languages and Relations

A *language* is a subset $L \subseteq \{0,1\}^*$. In this work, we assume that every language L is equipped with a uniform PPT algorithm G_L (called *instance generator*) which, on input $(1^\lambda; b)$ with $b \in \{0,1\}$, returns an element $x \in L$ if $b = 1$ (*yes-instance*), and an element $x \notin L$ if $b = 0$ (*no-instance*). Usually, the complexity of x is closely related to the security parameter λ, e.g., $|x| = \lambda$, but we can allow for other (polynomial) dependencies as well.

A *binary relation* is a subset $R \subseteq \{0,1\}^* \times \{0,1\}^*$ which is *polynomially bounded*, i.e., there exists a polynomial p such that, for every $(x,w) \in R$, we have $|w| \leq p(|x|)$. If $(x,w) \in R$, we call x an *R-instance* and w an *R-witness* of x. For every $x \in \{0,1\}^*$, we denote the set of all *R*-witnesses of x by $W_R(x) := \{w \mid (x,w) \in R\}$ (if x is not an *R*-instance, then $W_R(x) = \emptyset$). Note that every binary relation R defines a language $L_R := \{x \mid \exists w : (x,w) \in R\}$. Just like before for languages, we also assume that every binary relation R is equipped with a uniform PPT algorithm G_R (called *instance generator*) which, on input $(1^\lambda; b)$ with $b \in \{0,1\}$, returns a pair $(x,w) \in R$ if $b = 1$ (*yes-instance*), and an element $x \notin L_R$ if $b = 0$ (*no-instance*). Observe that from an instance generator G_R for a binary relation R we get an instance generator G_{L_R} for L_R by simply running G_R and returning the first component only if $b = 1$.

An *$\mathcal{NP}$-relation* is a binary relation that is *polynomial-time recognizable*, i.e., $R \in \mathcal{P}$. Observe that if R is an $\mathcal{NP}$-relation, then $L_R \in \mathcal{NP}$, and vice-versa if $L \in \mathcal{NP}$, then the set R_L of all string pairs $(x,w) \in \{0,1\}^* \times \{0,1\}^*$ with $x \in L$ and w an $\mathcal{NP}$-witness for x (w.r.t. a fixed polynomial and Turing machine) is an $\mathcal{NP}$-relation. In this situation, we have of course $L_{R_L} = L$ and $R_{L_R} \supseteq R$.

We next define the OR-combination of two relations and its instance generator. Here and in the following, we present all definitions and constructions with respect to the OR of two relations only, but all results extend to the more general 1-out-of-n case. A yes-instance of the OR-relation is a pair of values (x_0, x_1), each in its respective language, together with a witness w of either value. A no-instance of the OR-relation is again a pair of values, where at least one is not in the corresponding language, while the other may or may not belong to its language. The convention that a yes-instance has both inputs in their respective languages corresponds to the setting of group signature schemes, where all parties choose their public keys honestly; only in security reductions one may diverge from this. It is also in general necessary to ensure completeness of the OR-protocol, since the simulator for x_{1-b} is only guaranteed to output a valid transcript for yes-instances.

Definition 1. *Let R_0 and R_1 be two binary relations. Define the* OR-relation *of R_0 and R_1 as the binary relation*

$$R_{\mathsf{OR}} := \left\{ ((x_0, x_1), (b, w)) \mid b \in \{0,1\} \wedge (x_b, w) \in R_b \wedge x_{1-b} \in L_{R_{1-b}} \right\},$$

equipped with the instance generator $\mathsf{G}_{R_{\mathsf{OR}}}$ defined in Fig. 3. We denote the corresponding OR-language *by $L_{\mathsf{OR}} := L_{R_{\mathsf{OR}}}$.*

Observe that, for binary relations R_0 and R_1, the relation R_{OR} is indeed a binary relation, and that $L_{\mathsf{OR}} = L_{R_0} \times L_{R_1}$.

We now recall two hardness notions a binary relation R may satisfy. Intuitively, R is *decisionally hard* if no PPT distinguisher can decide if it is given an R-instance or a no-instance. It is *computationally hard* if no PPT adversary can efficiently compute an R-witness w for a given R-instance x.

Definition 2. *Let R be a binary relation. We say that R is:*

1. *Decisionally Hard if, for every PPT distinguisher* D, *there exists a negligible function $\mu : \mathbb{N} \to \mathbb{R}$ such that, for every $\lambda \in \mathbb{N}$ and every $z \in \{0,1\}^*$,*

$$\left| \Pr\left[\mathbf{Exp}_{\mathsf{D},R}^{\mathsf{DHR},0}(\lambda, z) = 1 \right] - \Pr\left[\mathbf{Exp}_{\mathsf{D},R}^{\mathsf{DHR},1}(\lambda, z) = 1 \right] \right| \leq \mu(\lambda),$$

where $\mathbf{Exp}_{\mathsf{D},R}^{\mathsf{DHR},0}(\lambda, z)$ and $\mathbf{Exp}_{\mathsf{D},R}^{\mathsf{DHR},1}(\lambda, z)$ are defined in Fig. 3.

2. *Computationally Hard if, for every PPT algorithm* A, *there exists a negligible function $\mu : \mathbb{N} \to \mathbb{R}$ such that, for every $\lambda \in \mathbb{N}$ and every $z \in \{0,1\}^*$,*

$$\Pr\left[\mathbf{Exp}_{\mathsf{A},R}^{\mathsf{CHR}}(\lambda, z) = 1 \right] \leq \mu(\lambda),$$

where $\mathbf{Exp}_{\mathsf{A},R}^{\mathsf{CHR}}(\lambda, z)$ is defined in Fig. 3.

It is readily verified that two binary relations R_0 and R_1 are computationally hard if and only if R_{OR} is computationally hard. Furthermore, if an $\mathcal{NP}$-relation R is decisionally hard, it is also computationally hard.

2.4   Interactive Protocols

An *interactive protocol* Π between two parties, called *prover* and *verifier*, is a pair of uniform algorithms $\Pi = (\mathsf{P}, \mathsf{V})$. We write $\mathsf{P}^{\mathcal{O}}(1^\lambda; x, w) \leftrightarrows \mathsf{V}^{\mathcal{O}}(1^\lambda; x, z)$ to denote the interaction between P and V on security parameter λ, common input x, respective auxiliary inputs w and z, and with access to oracle $\mathcal{O}$.

Algorithms P and V compute the next-message function of the corresponding party. In more detail, $\mathsf{P}^{\mathcal{O}}(1^\lambda; \beta_i, \mathsf{st_P})$ is the random variable which returns the prover's next message α_{i+1} and its updated state $\mathsf{st_P}$, both computed on input the security parameter λ, the last incoming message β_i, and the current state $\mathsf{st_P}$. Here we assume that $\mathsf{st_P}$ contains all the information necessary for P to perform its computation, including at least the common input, its auxiliary input, and the messages exchanged thus far. Similar considerations hold for V.

$\mathsf{G}_{R_{\mathsf{OR}}}(1^\lambda; b)$:	$\mathbf{Exp}_{\mathsf{D},R}^{\mathsf{DHR},b}(\lambda, z)$:
11: **if** $b = 0$ **then**	31: $x \leftarrow_\$ \mathsf{G}_R(1^\lambda; 0)$
12: $b', b'' \leftarrow_\$ \{0, 1\}$	32: **if** $b = 1$ **then**
13: $x_{b'} \leftarrow_\$ \mathsf{G}_{L_{b'}}(1^\lambda; 0)$	33: $(x, w) \leftarrow_\$ \mathsf{G}_R(1^\lambda; 1)$
14: $x_{1-b'} \leftarrow_\$ \mathsf{G}_{L_{R_{1-b'}}}(1^\lambda; b'')$	34: $b' \leftarrow_\$ \mathsf{D}^{\mathcal{O}}(1^\lambda; x, z)$
15: **return** (x_0, x_1)	35: **return** b'
16: **else**	
17: $b' \leftarrow_\$ \{0, 1\}$	$\mathbf{Exp}_{\mathsf{A},R}^{\mathsf{CHR}}(\lambda, z)$:
18: $(x_0, w_0) \leftarrow_\$ \mathsf{G}_{R_0}(1^\lambda; 1)$	41: $(x, w) \leftarrow_\$ \mathsf{G}_R(1^\lambda; 1)$
19: $(x_1, w_1) \leftarrow_\$ \mathsf{G}_{R_1}(1^\lambda; 1)$	42: $w^* \leftarrow_\$ \mathsf{A}^{\mathcal{O}}(1^\lambda; x, z)$
20: **return** $((x_0, x_1), (b', w_{b'}))$	43: **return** $[\![(x, w^*) \in R]\!]$

Fig. 3. Definition of the instance generator $\mathsf{G}_{R_{\mathsf{OR}}}$ of the relation R_{OR}, and of the experiments $\mathbf{Exp}_{\mathsf{D},R}^{\mathsf{DHR},b}(\lambda, z)$ and $\mathbf{Exp}_{\mathsf{A},R}^{\mathsf{CHR}}(\lambda, z)$ from Definition 2. Recall that $\mathcal{O}$ is either a random oracle or the trivial all-zero oracle.

We write $\mathrm{trans}\big[\mathsf{P}^{\mathcal{O}}(1^\lambda; x, w) \leftrightarrows \mathsf{V}^{\mathcal{O}}(1^\lambda; x, z)\big] = (A_1, B_1, \ldots, A_t, B_t, A_{t+1})$ for the *transcript* of the interaction between P and V. This is the random variable which returns a sequence of messages $(\alpha_1, \beta_1, \ldots, \alpha_t, \beta_t, \alpha_{t+1})$, where $(\alpha_{i+1}, \mathsf{st_P}) \leftarrow_\$ \mathsf{P}^{\mathcal{O}}(1^\lambda; \beta_i, \mathsf{st_P})$ and $(\beta_j, \mathsf{st_V}) \leftarrow_\$ \mathsf{V}^{\mathcal{O}}(1^\lambda; \alpha_j, \mathsf{st_V})$ for every $0 \le i \le t$ and $1 \le j \le t$. Here we assume that $\mathsf{st_P}$, $\mathsf{st_V}$ and β_0 are initialized to $\mathsf{st_P} \leftarrow (x, w)$, $\mathsf{st_V} \leftarrow (x, z)$ and $\beta_0 \leftarrow \varepsilon$. The *view* of V in the interaction with P, denoted $\mathrm{view_V}\big[\mathsf{P}^{\mathcal{O}}(1^\lambda; x, w) \leftrightarrows \mathsf{V}^{\mathcal{O}}(1^\lambda; x, z)\big]$, is the random variable $(A_1, A_2, \ldots, A_t, A_{t+1}, R_\mathsf{V})$, where R_V is the random variable representing V's random coins.

The interaction between prover and verifier terminates with V computing a decision $v \leftarrow_\$ \mathsf{V}^{\mathcal{O}}(1^\lambda; \alpha_{t+1}, \mathsf{st_V})$, where $v \in \{0, 1\}$, on whether to accept or reject the transcript. This is also called V's *local output*, and the corresponding random variable will be denoted by $\mathrm{out_V}\big[\mathsf{P}^{\mathcal{O}}(1^\lambda; x, w) \leftrightarrows \mathsf{V}^{\mathcal{O}}(1^\lambda; x, z)\big]$.

We say that a protocol $\Pi = (\mathsf{P}, \mathsf{V})$ is *efficient* if V is a PPT algorithm. For a binary relation R, we say that Π has an *efficient prover w.r.t.* R if P is a PPT algorithm and, on security parameter λ, it receives common and auxiliary inputs x and w such that $(x, w) \leftarrow_\$ \mathsf{G}_R(1^\lambda; 1)$. Note that we will only consider protocols which are efficient, have an efficient prover w.r.t. a specified binary relation R, and where the honest verifier is independent of its auxiliary input (we can therefore assume $z = \varepsilon$ in this case). We call these *protocols w.r.t.* R.

We call Π *public-coin (PC)* if all the messages the honest verifier sends to P consist of disjoint segments of its random tape, and if V's local output is computed as a deterministic function of the common input and the transcript, that is $v \leftarrow \mathsf{V}^{\mathcal{O}}(1^\lambda; x, \alpha_1, \beta_1, \ldots, \alpha_t, \beta_t, \alpha_{t+1})$. In this situation we say that a transcript is *accepting for* x if $v = 1$.

$\mathbf{Exp}_{V^*,D,\Pi}^{\mathsf{CWI},b}(\lambda, x, w, w', z, z')$:	$\mathbf{Exp}_{D,\Pi}^{\mathsf{SCZK},b}(\lambda, x, w, z)$:
11: $y \leftarrow w$	21: $(\mathsf{ch}, \mathsf{st_D}) \leftarrow_\$ \mathsf{D}_0^{\mathcal{O}}(1^\lambda; x, z)$
12: **if** $b = 1$ **then**	22: $\mathsf{st_P} \leftarrow (x, w)$
13: $y \leftarrow w'$	23: $(\mathsf{com}, \mathsf{st_P}) \leftarrow_\$ \mathsf{P}^{\mathcal{O}}(1^\lambda; \mathsf{st_P})$
14: $v^* \leftarrow_\$ \mathsf{out}_{V^*}\left[\mathsf{P}^{\mathcal{O}}(1^\lambda; x, y) \leftrightarrows V^{*\mathcal{O}}(1^\lambda; x, z)\right]$	24: $(\mathsf{resp}, \mathsf{st_P}) \leftarrow_\$ \mathsf{P}^{\mathcal{O}}(1^\lambda; \mathsf{ch}, \mathsf{st_P})$
15: $d \leftarrow_\$ \mathsf{D}^{\mathcal{O}}(1^\lambda; x, z, z', v^*)$	25: $v \leftarrow (\mathsf{com}, \mathsf{resp}, \mathsf{ch})$
16: **return** d	26: **if** $b = 1$ **then**
	27: $v \leftarrow_\$ \mathsf{S}^{\mathcal{O}}(1^\lambda; x, \mathsf{ch})$
	28: $d \leftarrow_\$ \mathsf{D}_1^{\mathcal{O}}(1^\lambda; x, z, v, \mathsf{st_D})$
	29: **return** d

Fig. 4. Definition of the experiments $\mathbf{Exp}_{V^*,D,\Pi}^{\mathsf{CWI},b}(\lambda, x, w, w', z, z')$ and $\mathbf{Exp}_{D,\Pi}^{\mathsf{SCZK},b}(\lambda, x, w, z)$ from Definitions 3 and 4.

We now recall the notion of computational witness indistinguishability [31], which is the property of general interactive protocols that is most relevant to our work. Intuitively, this notion captures the idea that protocol runs for a fixed R-instance but different witnesses should be indistinguishable. For the sake of completeness, we state the precise definitions of the completeness, soundness, honest-verifier zero-knowledge (HVCZK), and computational witness hiding (CWH) properties in the full version [34].

Definition 3. *Let R be a binary relation, and let $\Pi = (\mathsf{P}, \mathsf{V})$ be a protocol w.r.t. R. We say that Π is Computationally Witness Indistinguishable (CWI) if, for every uniform PPT algorithm V^* and every PPT distinguisher D, there exists a negligible function $\mu: \mathbb{N} \to \mathbb{R}$ such that, for every $\lambda \in \mathbb{N}$, every $x \leftarrow_\$ \mathsf{G}_{L_R}(1^\lambda; 1)$, every $w, w' \in W_R(x)$, and every $z, z' \in \{0,1\}^*$,*

$$\left| \Pr\left[\mathbf{Exp}_{V^*,D,\Pi}^{\mathsf{CWI},0}(\lambda, x, w, w', z, z') = 1 \right] - \right.$$
$$\left. \Pr\left[\mathbf{Exp}_{V^*,D,\Pi}^{\mathsf{CWI},1}(\lambda, x, w, w', z, z') = 1 \right] \right| \leq \mu(\lambda),$$

where $\mathbf{Exp}_{V^*,D,\Pi}^{\mathsf{CWI},b}(\lambda, x, w, w', z, z')$ is defined in Fig. 4.

Note that we will later require a stronger version of CWI, which we term multi-query computational witness indistinguishability (mqCWI) and define formally in the full version [34]. This is basically an oracle extension of ordinary CWI, where the distinguisher can query arbitrarily many protocol executions before guessing which witness was used to generate them. One can prove via a simple hybrid argument that CWI and mqCWI are equivalent, albeit with a polynomial loss in the distinguishing advantage.

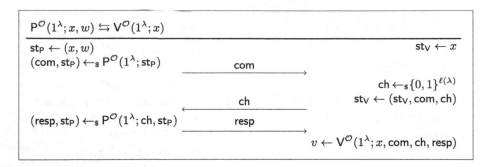

Fig. 5. Representation of a 3PC protocol w.r.t. a binary relation R.

2.5   3PC-Protocols and Σ-Protocols

Let R be a binary relation. We will be mainly interested in so-called *3PC-protocols w.r.t. R*, i.e., protocols w.r.t. R which are public-coin, and where the two parties exchange exactly three messages. We also assume that, on security parameter λ, the only message sent by the verifier to the prover has fixed length $\ell(\lambda)$, for a function $\ell \colon \mathbb{N} \to \mathbb{N}$ called the *length function* associated to the protocol. A graphical representation of such a protocol is given in Fig. 5.

In this particular context, we call the three messages exchanged between prover and verifier the *commitment*, the *challenge*, and the *response*, and denote them by $\mathsf{com} := \alpha_1$, $\mathsf{ch} := \beta_1$, and $\mathsf{resp} := \alpha_2$, respectively. Furthermore, we say that two accepting transcripts $(\mathsf{com}, \mathsf{ch}, \mathsf{resp})$ and $(\mathsf{com}', \mathsf{ch}', \mathsf{resp}')$ for an element x constitute a *transcript collision for x* if $\mathsf{com} = \mathsf{com}'$ and $\mathsf{ch} \neq \mathsf{ch}'$.

We now recall the critical notion of special computational zero-knowledge. Intuitively, it means that there exists a simulator which, for any maliciously chosen challenge given in advance, is able to create an authentic-looking transcript.

Definition 4. *Let R be a binary relation, and let $\Pi = (\mathsf{P}, \mathsf{V})$ be a 3PC protocol w.r.t. R. We say that Π is* Special Computational Zero-Knowledge (SCZK), *if there exists a uniform PPT algorithm S with the following property: For every two-stage PPT distinguisher $\mathsf{D} = (\mathsf{D}_0, \mathsf{D}_1)$, there exists a negligible function $\mu \colon \mathbb{N} \to \mathbb{R}$ such that, for every $\lambda \in \mathbb{N}$, every $(x, w) \leftarrow_\$ \mathsf{G}_R(1^\lambda; 1)$, and every $z \in \{0, 1\}^*$,*

$$\left| \Pr\left[\mathbf{Exp}_{\mathsf{D}, \Pi}^{\mathsf{SCZK}, 0}(\lambda, x, w, z) = 1 \right] - \Pr\left[\mathbf{Exp}_{\mathsf{D}, \Pi}^{\mathsf{SCZK}, 1}(\lambda, x, w, z) = 1 \right] \right| \leq \mu(\lambda),$$

where $\mathbf{Exp}_{\mathsf{D}, \Pi}^{\mathsf{SCZK}, b}(\lambda, x, w, z)$ is defined in Fig. 4.

The definitions of other properties of 3PC protocols, like optimal and special soundness, are included in the full version [34]. Roughly, optimal soundness says that for every $x \notin L$ and every commitment, there is at most one challenge which can lead to a valid response. Special soundness says that for $x \in L$, any transcript collision yields a witness, and for $x \notin L$ no collisions can be found. We are now in a position to define the notion of a Σ-protocol.

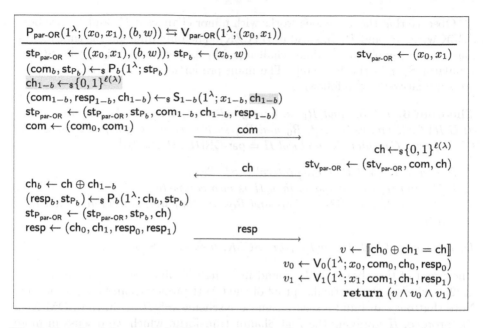

Fig. 6. Details of the parallel-OR construction by Cramer et al. [23]. Parts specific to the case where both Π_0 and Π_1 are SCZK (in comparison to HVCZK) are highlighted in gray.

Definition 5. *Let R be a binary relation. A Σ-protocol w.r.t. R is a 3PC protocol Π w.r.t. R which is complete, specially sound, and SCZK.*

3 Parallel-OR Proofs

In this section we recall the classical *parallel-OR* construction of Cramer et al. [23], which works for two arbitrary 3PC HVCZK protocols.

Let R_0 and R_1 be binary relations, and consider two 3PC HVCZK protocols $\Pi_0 = (\mathsf{P}_0, \mathsf{V}_0)$, $\Pi_1 = (\mathsf{P}_1, \mathsf{V}_1)$ w.r.t. R_0 and R_1 (with HVCZK-simulators S_0 and S_1), such that the two length functions $\ell_0 = \ell_1 =: \ell$ coincide (this is no real restriction, as the challenge length of such a protocol can be increased via parallel repetition). The construction, first presented in [23] and depicted in Fig. 6, allows to combine Π_0 and Π_1 into a new 3PC HVCZK protocol $\mathsf{par\text{-}OR}[\Pi_0, \Pi_1, \mathsf{S}_0, \mathsf{S}_1] = (\mathsf{P}_{\mathsf{par\text{-}OR}}, \mathsf{V}_{\mathsf{par\text{-}OR}})$ w.r.t. the binary relation R_{OR}. Note that the simulators of the two protocols become an integral part of the scheme.

The key idea of the construction is to split the challenge ch sent by $\mathsf{V}_{\mathsf{par\text{-}OR}}$ into two random parts, $\mathsf{ch} = \mathsf{ch}_0 \oplus \mathsf{ch}_1$, and to provide accepting transcripts for both inputs x_0 and x_1 with the corresponding challenge share. If the prover knows a witness w for x_b, it can use the HVCZK-simulator S_{1-b} of Π_{1-b} to generate a simulated view $(\mathsf{com}_{1-b}, \mathsf{resp}_{1-b}, \mathsf{ch}_{1-b})$ for x_{1-b}, and then compute a genuine transcript $(\mathsf{com}_b, \mathsf{ch}_b, \mathsf{resp}_b)$ for x_b using the witness w it knows.

Observe that the same idea works with minor changes if Π_0 and Π_1 are both SCZK w.r.t. R_0 and R_1 (instead of HVCZK). The only difference is that $\mathsf{P}_{\mathsf{par\text{-}OR}}$ must now sample a random challenge ch_{1-b} before running the SCZK-simulator S_{1-b} in the first step. The main properties of $\mathsf{par\text{-}OR}[\Pi_0, \Pi_1, \mathsf{S}_0, \mathsf{S}_1]$ are summarized in the following.

Theorem 6. *Let R_0 and R_1 be binary relations, and let Π_0 and Π_1 be two 3PC HVCZK protocols w.r.t. R_0 and R_1, such that the length functions satisfy $\ell_0 = \ell_1 =: \ell$. Consider the protocol $\Pi = \mathsf{par\text{-}OR}[\Pi_0, \Pi_1, \mathsf{S}_0, \mathsf{S}_1]$. Then:*

1. *Π is a 3PC CWI HVCZK protocol w.r.t. R_{OR}.*
2. *If Π_0 and Π_1 are complete, then Π is also complete.*
3. *If R_0 and R_1 are $\mathcal{NP}$-relations and R_{OR} is computationally hard, then Π is CWH.*

Furthermore, if both Π_0 and Π_1 are SCZK, then Π is SCZK.

The proof of the above can be found in a slightly different syntactical version in [25], whereas the particular proof of the CWH property can be found in [59]. Note that one can build a secure signature scheme $\mathsf{sFS}[\Pi, \mathcal{H}]$ in the ROM from the protocol Π applying the Fiat-Shamir transform, which we discuss in more detail in the full version [34].

4   Sequential-OR Proofs

In this section, we discuss an alternative OR-proof technique which we call *sequential-OR*. This technique was first used in the context of group signature schemes by Abe et al. [3]. On a high level, in the sequential-OR variant the prover derives two sub-proofs, where data from one proof is used to derive the challenge for the other one.

4.1   Protocol

Similarly to Sect. 3, we denote by R_0 and R_1 two binary relations, and consider two 3PC SCZK protocols $\Pi_0 = (\mathsf{P}_0, \mathsf{V}_0)$ and $\Pi_1 = (\mathsf{P}_1, \mathsf{V}_1)$ w.r.t. R_0 and R_1 and simulators S_0 and S_1, such that the two length functions $\ell_0 = \ell_1 =: \ell$ coincide. Furthermore, let $\mathcal{H}$ be a random oracle. The sequential-OR construction enables one to merge the two protocols Π_0 and Π_1 into a non-interactive protocol $\mathsf{seq\text{-}OR}[\Pi_0, \Pi_1, \mathsf{S}_0, \mathsf{S}_1, \mathcal{H}] = (\mathsf{P}_{\mathsf{seq\text{-}OR}}, \mathsf{V}_{\mathsf{seq\text{-}OR}})$ w.r.t. the binary relation R_{OR}. The formal details of the protocol are summarized in Fig. 7.

The key idea of the construction is to compute the challenge for the instance the prover indeed does know the witness of, based on the commitment for which it does not know the witness (derived via the SCZK-simulator). In more detail, on input the security parameter $\lambda \in \mathbb{N}$, consider a yes-instance for the OR-relation $((x_0, x_1), (b, w)) \leftarrow_\$ \mathsf{G}_{R_{\mathsf{OR}}}(1^\lambda; 1)$. The protocol $\mathsf{seq\text{-}OR}[\Pi_0, \Pi_1, \mathsf{S}_0, \mathsf{S}_1, \mathcal{H}]$ starts with the prover $\mathsf{P}_{\mathsf{seq\text{-}OR}}$ and verifier $\mathsf{V}_{\mathsf{seq\text{-}OR}}$ receiving (x_0, x_1) as common

$$P^{\mathcal{H}}_{\text{seq-OR}}(1^\lambda; (x_0, x_1), (b, w)) \leftrightarrows V^{\mathcal{H}}_{\text{seq-OR}}(1^\lambda; (x_0, x_1))$$

$\text{stp}_{\text{seq-OR}} \leftarrow ((x_0, x_1), (b, w)), \ \text{stp}_{P_b} \leftarrow (x_b, w)$ $\qquad\qquad\qquad$ $\text{stv}_{\text{seq-OR}} \leftarrow (x_0, x_1)$

$(\text{com}_b, \text{stp}_{P_b}) \leftarrow_\$ P_b(1^\lambda; \text{stp}_{P_b})$

$\text{ch}_{1-b} \leftarrow \mathcal{H}(b, x_0, x_1, \text{com}_b)$

$(\text{com}_{1-b}, \text{resp}_{1-b}, \text{ch}_{1-b}) \leftarrow_\$ S_{1-b}(1^\lambda; x_{1-b}, \text{ch}_{1-b})$

$\text{ch}_b \leftarrow \mathcal{H}(1 - b, x_0, x_1, \text{com}_{1-b})$

$(\text{resp}_b, \text{stp}_{P_b}) \leftarrow_\$ P_b(1^\lambda; \text{ch}_b, \text{stp}_{P_b})$

$\text{stp}_{\text{seq-OR}} \leftarrow (\text{stp}_{\text{seq-OR}}, \text{stp}_{P_b}, \text{com}_{1-b}, \text{resp}_{1-b})$

$\text{resp} \leftarrow (\text{com}_0, \text{com}_1, \text{resp}_0, \text{resp}_1)$ $\qquad\qquad$ $\xrightarrow{\ \text{resp}\ }$

$\qquad\qquad\qquad\qquad\qquad\qquad\qquad\qquad\qquad\qquad\qquad\qquad$ $\text{ch}_1 \leftarrow \mathcal{H}(0, x_0, x_1, \text{com}_0)$

$\qquad\qquad\qquad\qquad\qquad\qquad\qquad\qquad\qquad\qquad\qquad\qquad$ $\text{ch}_0 \leftarrow \mathcal{H}(1, x_0, x_1, \text{com}_1)$

$\qquad\qquad\qquad\qquad\qquad\qquad\qquad\qquad\qquad\qquad\qquad$ $v_0 \leftarrow V_0(1^\lambda; x_0, \text{com}_0, \text{ch}_0, \text{resp}_0)$

$\qquad\qquad\qquad\qquad\qquad\qquad\qquad\qquad\qquad\qquad\qquad$ $v_1 \leftarrow V_1(1^\lambda; x_1, \text{com}_1, \text{ch}_1, \text{resp}_1)$

$\qquad\qquad\qquad\qquad\qquad\qquad\qquad\qquad\qquad\qquad\qquad\qquad\qquad\qquad$ **return** $(v_0 \wedge v_1)$

Fig. 7. Details of the sequential-OR construction by Abe et al. [3].

input. Additionally, $P_{\text{seq-OR}}$ receives the witness (b, w) as auxiliary input. The protocol then proceeds in the following way:

1. $P_{\text{seq-OR}}$ sets $\text{stp}_{P_b} \leftarrow (x_b, w)$ and computes $(\text{com}_b, \text{stp}_{P_b}) \leftarrow_\$ P_b(1^\lambda; \text{stp}_{P_b})$. It then computes the challenge ch_{1-b} evaluating the random oracle $\mathcal{H}$ on the common input (x_0, x_1) and the previously generated commitment com_b. It also includes the bit b from the witness for domain separation. Next, it runs the SCZK-simulator S_{1-b} to obtain a simulated view $(\text{com}_{1-b}, \text{resp}_{1-b}, \text{ch}_{1-b}) \leftarrow_\$ S_{1-b}(1^\lambda; x_{1-b}, \text{ch}_{1-b})$. It then obtains the challenge ch_b for the first proof by evaluating $\mathcal{H}$ on the common input (x_0, x_1), the commitment com_{1-b} from the simulator, and the bit $1 - b$. Finally, $P_{\text{seq-OR}}$ computes $(\text{resp}_b, \text{stp}_{P_b}) \leftarrow_\$ P_b(1^\lambda; \text{ch}_b, \text{stp}_{P_b})$ using the witness for x_b, and sends $\text{resp} \leftarrow (\text{com}_0, \text{com}_1, \text{resp}_0, \text{resp}_1)$ to $V_{\text{seq-OR}}$.

2. $V_{\text{seq-OR}}$ first re-computes both challenge values using the random oracle $\mathcal{H}$. It then accepts the proof if and only if *both* transcripts verify correctly, i.e., $V_0(1^\lambda; x_0, \text{com}_0, \text{ch}_0, \text{resp}_0) = 1$ and $V_1(1^\lambda; x_1, \text{com}_1, \text{ch}_1, \text{resp}_1) = 1$.

In the following theorem, we establish the main properties of the protocol seq-OR$[\Pi_0, \Pi_1, S_0, S_1, \mathcal{H}]$.

Theorem 7. *Let R_0 and R_1 be binary relations, and let Π_0 and Π_1 be two 3PC SCZK protocols w.r.t. R_0 and R_1, such that the length functions satisfy $\ell_0 = \ell_1 =: \ell$. Consider the protocol $\Pi = $ seq-OR$[\Pi_0, \Pi_1, S_0, S_1, \mathcal{H}]$. Then the following holds in the ROM:*

1. *Π is a 1-move CWI protocol w.r.t. R_{OR}.*
2. *If Π_0 and Π_1 are complete, then Π is also complete.*
3. *If R_0 and R_1 are $\mathcal{NP}$-relations and R_{OR} is computationally hard, then Π is CWH.*

A detailed proof of Theorem 7 as well as an extension of the above technique to the more general 1-out-of-n case can be found in the full version [34].

KGen(1^λ):

11: $((x_0, x_1), (b, w)) \leftarrow_\$ G_{R_{OR}}(1^\lambda; 1)$
12: vk $\leftarrow (x_0, x_1)$
13: sk $\leftarrow (b, w)$
14: **return** (vk, sk)

Verify$^{\mathcal{H}}(1^\lambda; m, \sigma, \text{vk})$:

41: **parse** $\sigma = (\text{com}_0, \text{com}_1, \text{resp}_0, \text{resp}_1)$
42: ch$_1 \leftarrow \mathcal{H}(0, \text{vk}, \text{com}_0, m)$
43: ch$_0 \leftarrow \mathcal{H}(1, \text{vk}, \text{com}_1, m)$
44: $v_0 \leftarrow V_0(1^\lambda; x_0, \text{com}_0, \text{ch}_0, \text{resp}_0)$
45: $v_1 \leftarrow V_1(1^\lambda; x_1, \text{com}_1, \text{ch}_1, \text{resp}_1)$
46: **return** $(v_0 \wedge v_1)$

Sign$^{\mathcal{H}}(1^\lambda; m, \text{vk}, \text{sk})$:

21: **parse** vk $= (x_0, x_1)$
22: **parse** sk $= (b, w)$
23: stp$_b \leftarrow (x_b, w)$
24: $(\text{com}_b, \text{stp}_b) \leftarrow_\$ P_b(1^\lambda; \text{stp}_b)$
25: ch$_{1-b} \leftarrow \mathcal{H}(b, \text{vk}, \text{com}_b, m)$
26: $(\text{com}_{1-b}, \text{resp}_{1-b}, \text{ch}_{1-b}) \leftarrow_\$$
     $\leftarrow_\$ S_{1-b}(1^\lambda; x_{1-b}, \text{ch}_{1-b})$
27: ch$_b \leftarrow \mathcal{H}(1 - b, \text{vk}, \text{com}_{1-b}, m)$
28: $(\text{resp}_b, \text{stp}_b) \leftarrow_\$ P_b(1^\lambda; \text{ch}_b, \text{stp}_b)$
29: $\sigma \leftarrow (\text{com}_0, \text{com}_1, \text{resp}_0, \text{resp}_1)$
30: **return** σ

Fig. 8. Description of the signature scheme $\Gamma = (\text{KGen}, \text{Sign}, \text{Verify})$ obtained from the protocol seq-OR$[\Pi_0, \Pi_1, S_0, S_1, \mathcal{H}]$ by appending the message m being signed to all random oracle queries.

4.2 Sequential-OR Signatures

We now show how one can use the sequential-OR proof technique (see Fig. 7) to build a secure signature scheme $\Gamma = (\text{KGen}, \text{Sign}, \text{Verify})$ in the *non-programmable* ROM. On a high level, the signer runs a normal execution of the protocol seq-OR$[\Pi_0, \Pi_1, S_0, S_1, \mathcal{H}]$, but always includes the message m being signed when it queries the random oracle to obtain the challenges. Signatures in this scheme consist of the commitments and responses generated during the protocol execution, and verification can be achieved by re-computing the challenges (again, including the message) and checking whether the two transcripts verify. The formal details of the scheme can be found in Fig. 8, and we provide a detailed description in the following.

The signature scheme's key generation algorithm runs the instance generator $((x_0, x_1), (b, w)) \leftarrow_\$ G_{R_{OR}}(1^\lambda; 1)$ of the relation R_{OR}, which returns an R_{OR}-instance (x_0, x_1) and a witness w for x_b. The pair (x_0, x_1) then constitutes the public verification key, and (b, w) is set to be the secret signing key.

Signing a message m starts with running P_b on the instance x_b with the corresponding known witness (contained in the signing key), which results in a commitment com$_b$. The next step is to compute the challenge ch$_{1-b}$ for the instance the prover does not know the witness for, and this is done querying the random oracle $\mathcal{H}$, as done before. The only difference is that now the message m is appended to the oracle's input. Next, the signer runs the SCZK-simulator of Π_{1-b} on the instance x_{1-b} and this challenge, generating a simulated view $(\text{com}_{1-b}, \text{resp}_{1-b}, \text{ch}_{1-b})$. To complete the signature, it is still necessary to derive the missing response resp$_b$. In order to do so, first the random oracle is invoked to output ch_b from com_{1-b} (again, the message m is appended to its argument), and on input this challenge the prover computes the response $resp_b$. Finally, the signature is $(com_0, com_1, resp_0, resp_1)$.

The verification algorithm checks whether the signature is valid for the given message. The signature is parsed in its components, and the algorithm queries the random oracle twice (including the message) to obtain the challenges ch_0 and ch_1, as computed by the signing algorithm. It then verifies whether $(com_0, ch_0, resp_0)$ and $(com_1, ch_1, resp_1)$ are accepting transcripts for x_0 and x_1, respectively. If both transcripts verify correctly then the verification algorithm accepts the signature, and rejects otherwise.

Theorem 8. *Let R_0 and R_1 be decisional hard relations, and let Π_0 and Π_1 be two 3PC optimally sound SCZK protocols w.r.t. R_0 and R_1, such that the length functions satisfy $\ell_0 = \ell_1 =: \ell$. Consider the signature scheme Γ obtained from the protocol $\Pi = \text{seq-OR}[\Pi_0, \Pi_1, S_0, S_1, \mathcal{H}]$ as depicted in Fig. 8. Then Γ is an UF-CMA-secure signature scheme in the non-programmable random oracle model. More precisely, for any PPT adversary A against the UF-CMA-security of Γ making at most $q_{\mathcal{H}}$ queries to the random oracle $\mathcal{H}$, there exist PPT algorithms C, V^*, D_0 and D_1 such that*

$$\mathbf{Adv}^{\text{UF-CMA}}_{\text{A},\Gamma}(\lambda) \leq \mathbf{Adv}^{\text{mqCWI}}_{\text{V}^*,\text{C},\Pi}(\lambda) + \mathbf{Adv}^{\text{DHR}}_{\text{D}_0,R_0}(\lambda) + \mathbf{Adv}^{\text{DHR}}_{\text{D}_1,R_1}(\lambda)$$
$$+ 2 \cdot (q_{\mathcal{H}}(\lambda) + 2)^2 \cdot 2^{-\ell(\lambda)}.$$

In particular, for a perfectly witness indistinguishable proof system, where $\mathbf{Adv}^{\text{mqCWI}}_{\text{V}^*,\text{C},\Pi}(\lambda) \leq q_s(\lambda) \cdot \mathbf{Adv}^{\text{CWI}}_{\text{V}^*,\text{C},\Pi}(\lambda) = 0$ (here and in the following, q_s denotes the number of queries the adversary makes to the signature oracle), the bound becomes tightly related to the underlying decisional problem. This holds for example if we have a perfect zero-knowledge simulator. We remark that our proof also works if the relations are not optimally sound but instead c-optimally sound, i.e., for every $x \notin L_R$ and every commitment, there is a small set of at most c challenges for which a valid response can be found. In this case we get the term $c(\lambda) \cdot 2^{-\ell(\lambda)}$ in place of $2^{-\ell(\lambda)}$ in the above bound.

The complete proof of Theorem 8 can be found in the full version [34], but we still give a proof sketch here. We show that the obtained signature scheme Γ is secure via a sequence of game hops. The general approach is based on the following idea:

1. Assume that we have an adversary A which creates a forgery $(com_0^*, com_1^*, resp_0^*, resp_1^*)$ for message m^*. We can modify A into an adversary B which will always query both $(0, x_0, x_1, com_0^*, m^*)$ and $(1, x_0, x_1, com_1^*, m^*)$ to the random oracle when computing the forgery, simply by making the two additional queries if necessary.
2. Since the adversary is oblivious about which witness w_b is being used to create signatures, B will submit the query $(1 - b, x_0, x_1, com_{1-b}^*, m^*)$ first, before making any query about $(b, x_0, x_1, com_b^*, m^*)$, with probability roughly $1/2$, and will still succeed with non-negligible probability.

3. If we next replace x_{1-b} with a no-instance (which is indistinguishable for B because R_{1-b} is decisionally hard) we obtain the contradiction that B's advantage must be negligible now, because finding a forgery when querying com^*_{1-b} first should be hard by the optimal soundness property of Π_{1-b}, since x_{1-b} is a no-instance.

In more detail, in the first step we transition from the classical unforgeability game G_0 for the signature scheme Γ to a game G_1 where the adversary is additionally required to query both $(0, x_0, x_1, \text{com}^*_0, m^*)$ and $(1, x_0, x_1, \text{com}^*_1, m^*)$ to the random oracle. It is always possible to make this simplifying assumption: Indeed, given any adversary A against the UF-CMA-security of Γ, we can modify it into an adversary B which works exactly like A, but whose last two operations before returning the forgery as computed by A (or aborting) are the two required oracle queries, in the order given above. It is clear that B is a PPT algorithm, that it makes at most $q_{\mathcal{H}} + 2$ random oracle queries, and that the probabilities of adversaries A winning game G_0 and B winning game G_1 are the same.

We remark that it is also possible, albeit a bit lengthy, to prove that a successful adversary A against G_0 would already make both oracle queries with overwhelming probability, so that one could replace this first step with a more cumbersome security proof ruling out adversaries that do not make both queries. We choose here not to do so, because it would make the proof much longer and worsen the overall bound on the advantage of A.

Next, we define a game G_2 which is the same as game G_1, with the change that the adversary is required to query $(1 - b, x_0, x_1, \text{com}^*_{1-b}, m^*)$ to the random oracle *before* submitting any query of the form $(b, x_0, x_1, \text{com}^*_b, m^*)$. By witness indistinguishability this should happen with roughly the same probability as the other case (with the opposite order), because from the adversary's perspective the signatures do not reveal which witness w_b is used by the signer. Indeed, we show that the difference between both games is (up to a factor $\frac{1}{2}$) negligibly close. This is shown by building a distinguisher against a multi-query extension of the CWI property (see the full version [34] for its definition), and proving that the difference coincides with the distinguishing advantage of this distinguisher in the mqCWI experiment. As a result, the winning probability of B in game G_1 is approximately twice its winning probability in game G_2.

Finally, we move to a game G_3 which is identical to G_2, with the difference that the $(1 - b)$-th instance is switched to a no-instance. Since the relations are decisionally hard, we can build another distinguisher playing the DHR experiment, showing that the winning probabilities are again roughly the same.

To conclude the proof we argue that the probability of the adversary winning game G_3 can be bounded using the fact that Π_{1-b} is optimally sound. Indeed, by the winning condition in the game, the adversary needs to provide the commitment com^*_{1-b} early on. By the fact that the $(1 - b)$-th instance is a no-instance, we know that for every such commitment there exists at most one challenge (derived querying $\mathcal{H}$ on com^*_b later in the game) for which there exists a response such that the transcript for x_{1-b} verifies correctly. Since the adversary must ask com^*_{1-b} in one of the random oracle queries, there are at most $q_{\mathcal{H}} + 2$ commitments com^*_{1-b} it can check. For every such commitment it can try at most $q_{\mathcal{H}} + 2$ other oracle queries to find the matching challenge, so that we can bound B's winning probability in G_3 by $(q_{\mathcal{H}}(\lambda) + 2)^2 \cdot 2^{-\ell(\lambda)+1}$.

4.3 Example: Post-Quantum Ring Signatures

We discuss here briefly that our sequential-OR technique can be applied to build lattice-based ring signatures. We exemplify this for the case of the Dilithium signature scheme [28]. We stress that our solution may be less efficient than optimized lattice-based constructions such as [30] (but which, again, relies on programming the random oracle and yields a loose reduction). Our aim is to demonstrate that one can use the sequential-OR approach in principle to immediately obtain a solution with security guarantees in the non-programmable classical ROM (with tight security relative to the underlying lattice problem) and also in the QROM (with loose security at this point).

We briefly recall the Dilithium signature scheme [29]. The scheme works over a ring $R_q = \mathbb{Z}_q[X]/(X^n + 1)$. The public key consists of (a size-reduced version of) $t = As_1 + s_2$, where the matrix $A \in R_q^{k \times \ell}$ and the vectors s_1, s_2 become part of the secret key. The signature $\sigma = (z, h, c)$ of a message m consists of a short response value $z = y + cs_1$, where y is chosen randomly and $c = \mathsf{H}(\mu, w_1)$ is a (deterministically post-processed) hash value of a salted hash μ of the message m and the commitment of $w = Ay$ in form of its higher-order bits w_1. The value h is a hint required for verification. When generating a signature, the process may not always create a sufficiently short value z, in which case the generation is started from scratch.

The security proof of Dilithium [45] is based on the presumably hard problem to distinguish genuine public keys $(A, As_1 + s_2)$ from (A, t) for random t. As such we have our required decisional hard relation. Optimal soundness, in the sense that for random public keys there exists at most one challenge for which one can find a valid answer for a given commitment, has been also shown to hold with overwhelming probability in [45]. The zero-knowledge property in [45] reveals, by inspecting the construction of the simulator, that the construction is special zero-knowledge with perfectly indistinguishable distribution. The witness indistinguishability of the sequential-OR protocol hence follows from Theorem 7.

We can now apply Theorem 8 to conclude that the sequential-OR version is a secure signature scheme (in the non-programmable random oracle model). Note that it is irrelevant for us how many trials the signature generation takes, since we are merely interested in the point in time when we actually observe the right random oracle queries. With Theorem 10 we can also conclude that the protocol is secure in the quantum random oracle model.

5 Impossibility of Parallel-OR Signatures in the Non-programmable Random Oracle Model

In this section we show that it may be hard to prove the unforgeability of the parallel-OR signature scheme $\Gamma = \mathsf{sFS}[\mathsf{par\text{-}OR}[\Pi_0, \Pi_1, \mathsf{S}_0, \mathsf{S}_1], \mathcal{H}]$ in the non-programmable ROM (all formal details about the definition of Γ can be found in the full version [34]). On a high level, this means that we must rule out the existence of an efficient reduction R which has access to a random oracle but is not allowed to program it, and which transforms any (bounded or unbounded) successful adversary A against the unforgeability of Γ into an algorithm C solving some problem G assumed to be hard with non-negligible advantage.

Our proof will proceed in two steps. First, assuming by contradiction that such a reduction R indeed does exist, we will construct a specific unbounded adversary A which breaks the unforgeability of Γ with overwhelming probability. By the properties of R, this means that the *unbounded* algorithm C resulting from the interaction between R and A must successfully break instances of G in the non-programmable ROM with non-negligible probability. Then, we show how to efficiently simulate to R its interaction with A, thereby yielding an *efficient* algorithm B against G in the standard model with roughly the same advantage as C. This is impossible by the hardness of G, which means that R cannot exist.

In the following paragraphs we discuss which kinds of reductions R we are able to rule out, define what types of problems G the algorithms B and C play against, and discuss a pointwise version of zero-knowledge which the base protocols must satisfy for our result to work. We then come to the main result of this section.

Reduction. The efficient reductions R we consider have oracle access to the random oracle $\mathcal{H}$, as well as a (bounded) number of adversary instances A_i which themselves have oracle access to $\mathcal{H}$. The latter guarantees that the reduction cannot program the random oracle for the adversarial instances, but we stress that R gets to see all the queries made by any instance A_i. We let each adversarial instance be run on the same security parameter λ as the reduction itself.

Recall that, in the first step of our proof, the adversary A is unbounded. Therefore, we can assume that A incorporates a truly random function which it uses if random bits are required. With this common derandomization technique, we can make some simplifying assumptions about the reduction: Without loss of generality, R runs the instances of the adversary in sequential order, starting with A_1. It also never revisits any of the previous instances $A_1, \ldots, A_i$ once it switches to the next instance A_{i+1} by inputting a verification key vk_{i+1}. Furthermore, we can disallow any resets of the adversarial instances: The reduction can simply re-run the next instance up to the desired reset point and then diverge from there on.

Games. The hard problems that algorithms B and C are trying to solve are non-interactive ("oracle-free") problems, like distinguishing between different inputs. Formally, we consider games of the form $G = (I, V, \alpha)$ consisting of an instance generation algorithm I and a verification algorithm V, where $(\mathsf{inst}, \mathsf{st}) \leftarrow_{\$} I(1^{\lambda})$ generates a challenge inst of the game and some state information st. On input a potential solution sol computed by some algorithm, the deterministic algorithm $V(1^{\lambda}; \mathsf{inst}, \mathsf{sol}, \mathsf{st})$ returns 0 or 1, depending on whether sol is a valid solution of inst. The constant α allows to measure the advantage of an algorithm trying to win the game over some trivial guessing strategy (e.g., $\alpha = \frac{1}{2}$ for distinguishing games). We say that an algorithm B has advantage ϵ winning the game $G = (I, V, \alpha)$ if

$$\Pr\left[V(1^\lambda; \mathsf{inst}, \mathsf{sol}, \mathsf{st}) = 1 \;:\; (\mathsf{inst}, \mathsf{st}) \leftarrow_\$ I(1^\lambda), \mathsf{sol} \leftarrow_\$ B(1^\lambda; \mathsf{inst})\right] \geq \alpha + \epsilon(\lambda).$$

For us, the canonical problem to reduce security of the signature scheme to would be the distinguishing game against the hard instance generator for the underlying language. However, our theorem holds more generally for other problems.

The All-Powerful Adversary. In our setting, the reduction $R^{\mathcal{H}, A_1^{\mathcal{H}}, A_2^{\mathcal{H}}, \cdots}(1^\lambda; \mathsf{inst})$ has black-box access to a successful adversary A against Γ, receives as input some instance inst of a game $G = (I, V, \alpha)$, and is supposed to output a valid solution sol, winning the game with non-negligible advantage ϵ, while interacting with A. Recall that R must be able to convert any (efficient or unbounded) adversary A into a solver for G; in particular, this must be the case for the following all-powerful forger A, which we will consider throughout the proof:

1. Upon receiving a verification key $\mathsf{vk} = (x_0, x_1)$ as input, the adversary first queries its singing oracle for a signature on the message $m_{\mathsf{vk}} = \mathsf{vk}$.
2. When receiving the signature σ, adversary A verifies the signature and aborts if this check fails.
3. Else, adversary A uses its power to compute the lexicographic first witness w of x_0 (if it exists), or of x_1 (if it exists, and no witness for x_0 has been found). If no witness can be found, then A aborts. Otherwise, let $b \in \{0, 1\}$ be such that A has found a witness for x_b.
4. Adversary A picks a random λ-bit message m^* and runs the signing algorithm with secret key $\mathsf{sk} = (b, w)$ to create a signature σ^*. This requires one random oracle query over the message $(x_0, x_1, \mathsf{com}_0^*, \mathsf{com}_1^*, m^*)$. The randomness necessary to create the signature and the message m^* is computed by applying the inner random function to (vk, σ).
5. The adversary outputs (m^*, σ^*) as its forgery.

Note that since the adversary includes the public key vk in the messages m_{vk}, our result would also hold if the signing process itself did not include vk; according to our specification it currently does.

We observe that A obviously wins the UF-CMA experiment of Γ with overwhelming probability. We denote by $C^{\mathcal{H}}(1^\lambda; \mathsf{inst})$ the adversary against G in the non-programmable ROM obtained by letting R interact with A (see the left-hand side of Fig. 9). By the properties of R, the advantage of C against G in the non-programmable ROM must be non-negligible.

Zero-Knowledge. Recall that we defined the zero-knowledge property for protocols w.r.t. relations R that have an efficient instance generator. Here, we need a stronger notion: Zero-knowledge must hold pointwise for every $(x, w) \in R$. The reason is that we will rely on the zero-knowledge property to argue that the reduction R does not learn any useful information from the signatures created by the all-powerful adversary A. The problem here is that the reduction may choose the instance $vk_i = (x_0, x_1)$ in the execution of the i-th adversary adaptively and in dependence of the behavior of A in previous instances. The reduction may then also base its final output on this choice.

We therefore say that a protocol $\Pi = (P, V)$ w.r.t. a relation R is *pointwise HVCZK*, if there exist a uniform PPT algorithm S and a polynomial p with the following property: For every PPT distinguisher D, there exists a negligible function $\mu \colon \mathbb{N} \to \mathbb{R}$ such that, for every $\lambda \in \mathbb{N}$, every $(x, w) \in R$ with $|x|, |w| \leq p(\lambda)$, and every $z \in \{0, 1\}^*$, D can distinguish verifier views $view_V[P^{\mathcal{O}}(1^\lambda; x, w) \leftrightarrows V^{\mathcal{O}}(1^\lambda; x)]$ in the honest interaction between P and V from the simulator's output $S(1^\lambda; x)$ with advantage at most $\mu(\lambda)$, even if D receives z as auxiliary input.

Note that in the definition above, the relation and the language are still fixed, only the sampling process may vary. This seems to be a reasonable assumption which applies to known protocols, as the zero-knowledge simulator is usually independent of the generation process for the statement.

Impossibility Result. We now show that, if there exists a black-box reduction R as described above, our all-powerful adversary A induces an efficient algorithm B winning the game directly, such that the advantages of B and C are roughly the same. This is impossible by the assumed hardness of G, so that R cannot exist.

Theorem 9. *Let R_0 and R_1 be binary relations, and let Π_0 and Π_1 be two 3PC optimally sound pointwise HVCZK protocols w.r.t. R_0 and R_1, such that the length functions satisfy $\ell_0 = \ell_1 =: \ell$. Denote by $\Pi = \mathsf{par\text{-}OR}[\Pi_0, \Pi_1, S_0, S_1]$ the corresponding parallel-OR protocol, and let $\Gamma = \mathsf{sFS}[\Pi, \mathcal{H}]$ be the parallel-OR signature scheme derived from Π in the ROM.*

Assume that there exists a PPT black-box reduction R from the unforgeability of Γ to winning a game $G = (I, V, \alpha)$. Then there exists a PPT algorithm B which wins the game G with non-negligible advantage in the standard model.

The idea is as follows. Algorithm B receives as input a challenge inst of the game G, and must compute a valid solution sol with non-negligible probability. The strategy of B is to run the reduction R on inst as a subroutine, and to efficiently simulate to R its interaction with A. To do so, B must be able to answer the two types of queries that R can make: Random oracle evaluations and forgery queries to A. The former are handled via lazy sampling, i.e., B simulates a random oracle to R. If on the other hand R requests a forgery for a verification key $vk = (x_0, x_1)$, B at first follows the definition of A and requests a signature for m_{vk}. This initial signature request ensures that the verification key vk must be such that $x_0 \in L_0$ or $x_1 \in L_1$ or both. Indeed, the reduction cannot program the random oracle (which is controlled by B) and, by special soundness of Π_0 and Π_1, finding a valid signature when both $x_0 \notin L_0$ and $x_1 \notin L_1$ is infeasible for parallel-OR signatures. Hence, in the original experiment A will always be able to find a witness (b, w) for vk if it receives a valid signature.

Next, A will compute a forgery for the message m^*. Here B, instead of using w from the witness (b, w) to run P_b and compute com_b^* and $resp_b^*$ in its forgery,

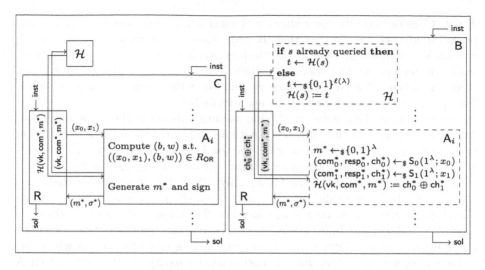

Fig. 9. Representation of the reduction R interacting with adversarial instances A_i in the ROM (left) and of the efficient solver B running R (right). The components simulated by B are dashed, and the queries of which R gets informed are highlighted in gray.

uses the zero-knowledge simulator S_b for this part as well. Now both parts of the signature of m^* are independent of the actual witness. The algorithm B can now program the random oracle $\mathcal{H}$ it is simulating to R, so that $\mathcal{H}(vk, com^*, m^*)$ matches the XOR of the two challenges obtained from the two simulators.[2] By the strong zero-knowledge property of the base protocols, and since m^* contains sufficient randomness to make sure that we can still set the random oracle for R at this point, this is indistinguishable for the reduction. Finally, if at some point R returns a solution to the given instance, algorithm B terminates with the same output. In conclusion, we can now efficiently simulate A's behavior to R, so that the reduction together with this simulation technique yields our efficient algorithm B against game G (see the right-hand side of Fig. 9).

Let us stress that the impossibility result above does not hold for sequential-OR signatures. The difference lies in the observability of the reduction in both cases. In the parallel-OR case we still need to tell R which query $\mathcal{H}(vk, com_0^*, com_1^*, m^*)$ the adversary has made to compute the forgery. But we have already argued that the simulated value com_b^* is indistinguishable from the prover's value com_b^* in the forgery, so that this query does not give any additional information to R. In the sequential-OR case, however, we would need to inform R which query A makes first, revealing which witness it has computed.

---

[2] One could indeed argue why we are here allowed to program the random oracle in light of the discussion about non-programmability. One may think of this here as a restriction of the reduction, that it needs to be able to cope with such external oracles. Technically, it gives the required advantage over the reduction to make the meta-reduction argument work.

Proof. Consider an efficient reduction R interacting with instances of our all-powerful adversary A. Assume that the reduction calls at most q_A instances of A and makes at most $q_\mathcal{H}$ calls to the random oracle. Since R is polynomial-time, both parameters are polynomially bounded. We can also assume that R never runs an instance for the same key vk and then the same signature σ twice, because it will just receive the same answers as before.

We start by making some simplifying assumptions about the reduction. First, we can assume that R only provides A with a valid signature to some verification key vk = (x_0, x_1) if $x_0 \in L_0$ or $x_1 \in L_1$ (or both). Indeed, since Π_0 and Π_1 are optimally sound, if both values are not in their language, then each commitment com_0 for x_0 and com_1 for x_1 only allows for at most one challenge, ch_0 and ch_1, to have a valid response. But then, the probability that a random oracle query $\mathcal{H}(\mathsf{vk}, \mathsf{com}_0, \mathsf{com}_1, m_\mathsf{vk})$ matches the unique value $\mathsf{ch}_0 \oplus \mathsf{ch}_1$ is at most $2^{-\ell(\lambda)}$. The probability that such a random oracle query exists at all, either made by R or, if not, later made by any instance of the adversary A when verifying the signature, is therefore at most $(q_\mathcal{H}(\lambda) + q_A(\lambda)) \cdot 2^{-\ell(\lambda)}$. Given that A aborts if the signature it receives is not valid, we can from now on assume that each public key vk for which R requests a forgery (and must provide a signature) allows A to compute a witness (b, w), and that R itself leaves the instance immediately if verification fails.

Second, we may assume that, whenever A creates a forgery for m^*, the random oracle has not been queried by any party yet about any value terminating in m^*. Indeed, since A applies the internal random function to compute m^* from vk and σ, and we assume that the reduction never runs the adversary twice on the same values, this can only happen if two random messages m^* of the adversary collide, or if the reduction has made such a query by chance. The probability for this is at most $(q_\mathcal{H}(\lambda) + q_A(\lambda))^2 \cdot 2^{-\lambda}$. Hence, we can from now on assume that this does not happen. In other words, if R stumbles upon such a value it immediately aborts.

We now define the algorithm B as explained in the overview above. On input $(1^\lambda; \mathsf{inst})$, B runs the reduction on security parameter 1^λ and instance inst as a subroutine, and simulates to R its interaction with A. The random oracle queries made by R are answered via lazy sampling. If on the other hand R calls an adversarial instance for a forgery under vk = (x_0, x_1), B does the following:

1. It first requests a signature of m_vk = vk under vk to its signature oracle (provided by the reduction), and checks if the corresponding signature is valid. If not, it aborts the simulation of the current instance of A.
2. Assuming that R has provided a valid signature of m_vk under vk, B does not compute a witness (b, w) for vk (as A would do). It still picks a random message $m^* \in \{0, 1\}^\lambda$ and fresh coins for the signing process, though.
3. To compute the forgery for m^*, instead of invoking $\mathsf{P}_b(1^\lambda; x_b, w)$ to generate com_b, B now runs the two simulators $\mathsf{S}_0(1^\lambda; x_0)$ and $\mathsf{S}_1(1^\lambda; x_1)$ to compute simulated views $(\mathsf{com}_0^*, \mathsf{resp}_0^*, \mathsf{ch}_0^*)$ and $(\mathsf{com}_1^*, \mathsf{resp}_1^*, \mathsf{ch}_1^*)$.
4. Algorithm B saves $\mathcal{H}(\mathsf{vk}, \mathsf{com}_0^*, \mathsf{com}_1^*, m^*) := \mathsf{ch}_0^* \oplus \mathsf{ch}_1^*$ into the lookup table it keeps to simulate the random oracle to R, and informs R that the adversary A

it is simulating has made a query $(\mathsf{vk}, \mathsf{com}_0^*, \mathsf{com}_1^*, m^*)$ to the random oracle, with answer $\mathsf{ch}_0^* \oplus \mathsf{ch}_1^*$.

5. Finally, B sends m^* and $\sigma^* = (\mathsf{com}_0^*, \mathsf{com}_1^*, \mathsf{resp}_0^*, \mathsf{resp}_1^*)$ to R as the forgery computed by the simulated instance of A.

Note that B is now efficient: The only potentially exponential step involving the witness search has been eliminated. We must now argue that B's success probability in the standard model is close to the one of C in the ROM. This is done by carrying out a reduction to the pointwise zero-knowledge property of the protocols Π_0 and Π_1, where zero-knowledge must hold for every $(x, w) \in R$, even in the presence of some auxiliary information $z \in \{0, 1\}^*$ that may contain further information about (x, w). The proof is done via a hybrid argument for hybrids $\mathsf{Hyb}_0, \ldots, \mathsf{Hyb}_{q_\mathsf{A}}$, where Hyb_i answers R's forgery requests by running the (unbounded) algorithm A up to, and including, the i-th adversarial instance (as C would do), and then efficiently simulates A for the remaining instances (as B would do). Then the extreme hybrid $\mathsf{Hyb}_{q_\mathsf{A}}$ corresponds to the original inefficient algorithm C, whereas the extreme hybrid Hyb_0 coincides with B's simulation.

The jump from hybrid Hyb_{i-1} to hybrid Hyb_i substitutes the honestly generated proof for x_b (where x_b is the instance that A finds a witness for) in the i-th adversarial instance with a simulated one, so that we can construct a reduction to the pointwise HVCZK property of Π_b. The main idea is to let the reduction interact with the inefficient forger A for the first i instances, up to the point where A_i has determined the witness (b, w) for x_b, and save all the state information into the auxiliary input z. This allows us to pick up the reduction later. We then leverage the pointwise HVCZK property of Π_b, with instance $(x_b, w) \in R_b$: The zero-knowledge distinguisher D_b receives a genuine or simulated view for x_b and the state information z, and continues to run the reduction, but now using B's simulation for the remaining instances (so that D_b is efficient).

More formally, we use the pointwise HVCZK property of Π_b for the distinguisher D_b, the instance $(x_b, w) \in R_b$, and the auxiliary information z defined as follows. We let $(\mathsf{inst}, \mathsf{sol}) \leftarrow_\$ \mathsf{I}(1^\lambda)$ generate an instance of G, pick a random tape r for the reduction and a random index i between 1 and q_A for the jump in the hybrids, and then run the reduction (interacting with A) on input inst, up to the point where A has computed a witness for one of the two instances in the i-th execution (on input $\mathsf{vk} = (x_0, x_1)$) and has generated the message m^*. All random oracle queries are answered via lazy sampling and a table H is maintained to record previously answered queries. Let S store all forgery attempts of A. Then we let $(x_b, w) \in R_b$ be the instance and the corresponding witness found by A, and we set $z = (\mathsf{inst}, \mathsf{st}, r, i, x_{1-b}, b, w, m^*, H, S)$. Note that if no witness can be found by A, or if A has stopped in this instance prematurely, then we simply set x_b and w to some fixed elements of the relation R_0 and the output z as before. In any case, z is of polynomial size and can be processed by an efficient distinguisher, because $q_\mathcal{H}$ and q_A are polynomially bounded.

The (efficient) distinguisher D_b against the pointwise HVCZK property of Π_b receives x_b, a real or simulated view $(\mathsf{com}_b^*, \mathsf{resp}_b^*, \mathsf{ch}_b^*)$ for x_b, and the auxiliary information $z = (\mathsf{inst}, \mathsf{st}, r, i, x_{1-b}, b, w, m^*, H, S)$. With these data D_b can re-run the reduction up to the interaction of R with the i-th adversarial instance and then inject the given transcript $(\mathsf{com}_b^*, \mathsf{ch}_b^*, \mathsf{resp}_b^*)$ into this instance (the transcript for x_{1-b} needed to complete the forgery is obtained via the simulator $\mathsf{S}_{1-b}(1^\lambda; x_{1-b})$). Algorithm D_b now completes the execution of the reduction, using lazy sampling and the table H to continue the consistent simulation of random oracle queries. In particular, in all subsequent signature forgeries it will use B's efficient simulation technique, calling the simulators S_0 and S_1 to create the two transcripts and programming the random oracle accordingly. Note that the order of execution of these two simulators is irrelevant, because D_b only needs to inform the reduction about a single random oracle query. Finally, D_b takes the reduction's output sol and returns the decision bit $\mathsf{V}(1^\lambda; \mathsf{inst}, \mathsf{sol}, \mathsf{st})$.

Observe that D_b runs in polynomial time, because it does not need to invoke any super-polynomial subroutines like A. If D_b receives a real view $(\mathsf{com}_b^*, \mathsf{resp}_b^*, \mathsf{ch}_b^*)$ in the i-th instance, then ch_b^* is truly random and independent, and therefore programming the (simulated) random oracle to $\mathcal{H}(\mathsf{vk}, \mathsf{com}_0^*, \mathsf{com}_1^*, m^*) := \mathsf{ch}_0^* \oplus \mathsf{ch}_1^*$ is perfectly sound. Hence, for real transcripts D_b simulates the hybrid Hyb_i with the first i instances according to C's strategy, and the following instances with the simulated mode of B.

If on the other hand the transcript is simulated by S_b, then both parts of the signature are simulated. This means that both ch_0^* and ch_1^* are indistinguishable from random strings to an efficient adversary, which again implies that programming $\mathcal{H}(\mathsf{vk}, \mathsf{com}_0^*, \mathsf{com}_1^*, m^*) := \mathsf{ch}_0^* \oplus \mathsf{ch}_1^*$ is sound for R. In this case, only the first $i - 1$ instances follow C's method; starting form the i-th adversarial instance we have two simulated proofs, each simulated individually. Hence, this corresponds to the $(i - 1)$-th hybrid Hyb_{i-1}.

Let $\mu_b \colon \mathbb{N} \to \mathbb{R}$ be the negligible function bounding the distinguishing advantage of D_b in the pointwise HVCZK experiment of Π_b. It follows via a standard hybrid argument that any change in the reduction's behavior translates into a distinguisher against the pointwise HVCZK property of Π_0 and Π_1 (times the number of queries q_A). The advantage of our algorithm B in breaking the game is thus at least

$$\epsilon(\lambda) - (q_\mathcal{H}(\lambda) + q_A(\lambda))^2 \cdot 2^{-\lambda} - (q_\mathcal{H}(\lambda) + q_A(\lambda)) \cdot 2^{-\ell(\lambda)} - q_A(\lambda)\big(\mu_0(\lambda) + \mu_1(\lambda)\big),$$

where ϵ is the advantage of C. Since ϵ is non-negligible by assumption, so must be B's advantage. But this contradicts the presumed hardness of G.   □

6   Security in the Quantum Random Oracle Model

In this section we give an outline of the security proof for signatures derived from the sequential-OR construction in the QROM. More details can be found in the full version [34].

While treating quantum random oracles is a clear qualitative extension in terms of the security guarantees (especially if we work with quantum-resistant primitives), we have to sacrifice two important features of our proof in the classical case. One is that the bound we obtain is rather loose. The other point is that we need to program the random oracle in the security reduction. Both properties are currently shared by all proofs in the quantum random oracle model, e.g., programmability appears in form of using pairwise independent hash functions or semi-constant distributions (see [60]). Hopefully, progress in this direction will also carry over to the case of sequential-OR signatures.

Our starting point is the "measure-and-reprogram" technique of Don et al. [27] for Fiat-Shamir protocols in the QROM. They show that it is possible to turn a quantum adversary A into an algorithm R^{A} such that R^{A} measures one of the $q_{\mathcal{H}}$ quantum queries of A to the random oracle, yielding some classical query com'. The choice of this query is made at random. Algorithm R^{A} returns either correctly $\mathcal{H}(\mathsf{com}')$ or an independent and random value Θ to this now classical query, the choice being made at random. Algorithm R^{A} continues the execution of A but always returns Θ for com' from then on. Algorithm R^{A} eventually returns the output $(\mathsf{com}, \mathsf{resp})$ of A.

Don et al. [27] now show that, for any quantum adversary A making at most $q_{\mathcal{H}}$ quantum random oracle queries, there exists a (quantum) algorithm R^{A} such that, for every fixed com_0 and every predicate Λ, there exists a negligible function $\mu_{\mathsf{com}_0} : \mathbb{N} \to \mathbb{R}$ such that

$$\Pr\Big[\mathsf{com} = \mathsf{com}_0 \wedge \Lambda(1^{\lambda}; \mathsf{com}, \Theta, \mathsf{resp}) : (\mathsf{com}, \mathsf{resp}) \leftarrow_{\$} \mathsf{R}^{\mathsf{A},\mathcal{H}}(1^{\lambda}; \Theta)\Big]$$

$$\geq \frac{1}{O(q_{\mathcal{H}}(\lambda)^2)} \cdot \Pr\left[\begin{array}{c} \mathsf{com} = \mathsf{com}_0 \wedge \\ \Lambda(1^{\lambda}; \mathsf{com}, \mathcal{H}(\mathsf{com}), \mathsf{resp}) \end{array} : (\mathsf{com}, \mathsf{resp}) \leftarrow_{\$} \mathsf{A}^{\mathcal{H}}(1^{\lambda})\right] - \mu_{\mathsf{com}_0}(\lambda),$$

where $\sum_{\mathsf{com}_0} \mu_{\mathsf{com}_0}(\lambda) = \frac{1}{q_{\mathcal{H}}(\lambda) \cdot 2^{\ell(\lambda)+1}}$ for the output size ℓ of the random oracle.

We will apply the above measure-and-reprogram technique twice in order to capture the two (classical) queries in which the adversary asks for the two commitments com_0^{*} and com_1^{*} for the forgery. However, we do not know if the strategy can be safely applied multiple times in general. Fortunately, we can apply the technique in our setting once without actually reprogramming the random oracle, only turning one of the queries into a classical one, and then view this as a special adversary B which still works with the given random oracle model. In doing so we lose a factor of approximately $1/q^2$ in the success probability, where $q(\lambda) = q_{\mathcal{H}}(\lambda) + 2 + 2q_s(\lambda)$ counts the number of hash queries made by both the adversary and the signature scheme. Then we can apply the technique once more to B, losing another factor $1/q^2$. Finally, we need to take into account that we actually obtain the matching commitments in the two measured queries, costing us another factor $1/q$. Eventually, we get an algorithm R which makes two classical queries about the two commitments in the forgery with high probability, but with a loose factor of $1/q^5$ compared to the original success probability of the forger.

Note that we now have a forger making two classical queries about the commitments $\mathsf{com}_{a^*}^{*}$ and $\mathsf{com}_{1-a^*}^{*}$ in the forgery in this order, but where we reprogram the random oracle reply in the second query about $\mathsf{com}_{1-a^*}^{*}$ to Θ. In our sequential-OR construction this value Θ describes the (now reprogrammed) challenge for the first commitment. In particular, the forgery then satisfies $\mathsf{V}_{a^*}(1^{\lambda}; x_{a^*}, \mathsf{com}_{a^*}^{*}, \Theta, \mathsf{resp}_{a^*}^{*}) = 1$ for the commitment $\mathsf{com}_{a^*}^{*}$ chosen *before* Θ is determined. If x_{a^*} was a no-instance, this should be infeasible by the optimal soundness property. The last step in the argument is then similar to the classical setting, showing that if R is forced to use the "wrong order" and queries about a no-instance first with sufficiently high probability, its success probability will be small by the witness indistinguishability of the protocol and the decisional hardness of the problems (but this time against quantum algorithms).

Overall, we get:

Theorem 10. *Let R_0 and R_1 be decisional hard relations against quantum algorithms, and let Π_0 and Π_1 be two 3PC optimally sound SCZK protocols w.r.t. R_0 and R_1, where zero-knowledge holds with respect to quantum distinguishers, such that the length functions satisfy $\ell_0 = \ell_1 =: \ell$. Consider the signature scheme Γ obtained from the protocol $\Pi = \mathsf{seq\text{-}OR}[\Pi_0, \Pi_1, \mathsf{S}_0, \mathsf{S}_1, \mathcal{H}]$ as depicted in Fig. 8. Then Γ is an UF-CMA-secure signature scheme in the quantum random oracle model. More precisely, for any polynomial-time quantum adversary A against the UF-CMA-security of Γ making at most $q_\mathcal{H}$ quantum queries to the random oracle $\mathcal{H}$ and at most q_s signature queries, there exist a negligible function $\mu \colon \mathbb{N} \to \mathbb{R}$ and polynomial-time quantum algorithms C, V^*, D_0 and D_1 such that*

$$\mathbf{Adv}_{\mathsf{A}, \Gamma}^{\mathsf{UF\text{-}CMA}}(\lambda) \le O((q_\mathcal{H}(\lambda) + q_s(\lambda) + 2)^5) \cdot \left(\mathbf{Adv}_{\mathsf{V}^*, \mathsf{C}, \Pi}^{\mathsf{mqCWI}}(\lambda) + \mathbf{Adv}_{\mathsf{D}_0, R_0}^{\mathsf{DHR}}(\lambda) \right.$$
$$\left. + \mathbf{Adv}_{\mathsf{D}_1, R_1}^{\mathsf{DHR}}(\lambda) + 2^{-\ell(\lambda)+1} \right) + \mu(\lambda).$$

Acknowledgments. We thank the anonymous reviewers for valuable comments. We thank Serge Fehr and Tommaso Gagliardoni for helpful discussions. This work was funded by the Deutsche Forschungsgemeinschaft (DFG) – SFB 1119 – 236615297.

References

1. Abdalla, M., An, J.H., Bellare, M., Namprempre, C.: From identification to signatures via the Fiat-Shamir transform: minimizing assumptions for security and forward-security. In: Knudsen, L.R. (ed.) EUROCRYPT 2002. LNCS, vol. 2332, pp. 418–433. Springer, Heidelberg (2002). https://doi.org/10.1007/3-540-46035-7_28

2. Abdalla, M., Fouque, P.-A., Lyubashevsky, V., Tibouchi, M.: Tightly secure signatures from lossy identification schemes. J. Cryptol. **29**(3), 597–631 (2016). https://doi.org/10.1007/s00145-015-9203-7

3. Abe, M., Ohkubo, M., Suzuki, K.: 1-out-of-n signatures from a variety of keys. In: Zheng, Y. (ed.) ASIACRYPT 2002. LNCS, vol. 2501, pp. 415–432. Springer, Heidelberg (2002). https://doi.org/10.1007/3-540-36178-2_26

4. Alkim, E., et al.: Revisiting TESLA in the quantum random oracle model. In: Lange, T., Takagi, T. (eds.) PQCrypto 2017. LNCS, vol. 10346, pp. 143–162. Springer, Cham (2017). https://doi.org/10.1007/978-3-319-59879-6_9

5. Ambainis, A., Rosmanis, A., Unruh, D.: Quantum attacks on classical proof systems: the hardness of quantum rewinding. In: 55th FOCS, pp. 474–483 (2014)

6. Bader, C., Hofheinz, D., Jager, T., Kiltz, E., Li, Y.: Tightly-secure authenticated key exchange. In: Dodis, Y., Nielsen, J.B. (eds.) TCC 2015, Part I. LNCS, vol. 9014, pp. 629–658. Springer, Heidelberg (2015). https://doi.org/10.1007/978-3-662-46494-6_26

7. Bai, S., Galbraith, S.D.: An improved compression technique for signatures based on learning with errors. In: Benaloh, J. (ed.) CT-RSA 2014. LNCS, vol. 8366, pp. 28–47. Springer, Cham (2014). https://doi.org/10.1007/978-3-319-04852-9_2

8. Baum, C., Lin, H., Oechsner, S.: Towards practical lattice-based one-time linkable ring signatures. In: Naccache, D., et al. (eds.) ICICS 2018. LNCS, vol. 11149, pp. 303–322. Springer, Cham (2018). https://doi.org/10.1007/978-3-030-01950-1_18

9. Bellare, M., Rogaway, P.: Random oracles are practical: a paradigm for designing efficient protocols. In: ACM CCS, vol. 93, pp. 62–73 (1993)

10. Boneh, D., Dagdelen, Ö., Fischlin, M., Lehmann, A., Schaffner, C., Zhandry, M.: Random oracles in a quantum world. In: Lee, D.H., Wang, X. (eds.) ASIACRYPT 2011. LNCS, vol. 7073, pp. 41–69. Springer, Heidelberg (2011). https://doi.org/10.1007/978-3-642-25385-0_3

11. Boneh, D., Venkatesan, R.: Breaking RSA may not be equivalent to factoring. In: Nyberg, K. (ed.) EUROCRYPT 1998. LNCS, vol. 1403, pp. 59–71. Springer, Heidelberg (1998). https://doi.org/10.1007/BFb0054117

12. Bünz, B., Bootle, J., Boneh, D., Poelstra, A., Wuille, P., Maxwell, G.: Bulletproofs: short proofs for confidential transactions and more. In: 2018 IEEE Symposium on Security and Privacy, pp. 315–334 (2018)

13. Camenisch, J.: Efficient and generalized group signatures. In: Fumy, W. (ed.) EUROCRYPT 1997. LNCS, vol. 1233, pp. 465–479. Springer, Heidelberg (1997). https://doi.org/10.1007/3-540-69053-0_32

14. Camenisch, J., Drijvers, M., Gagliardoni, T., Lehmann, A., Neven, G.: The wonderful world of global random oracles. In: Nielsen, J.B., Rijmen, V. (eds.) EUROCRYPT 2018, Part I. LNCS, vol. 10820, pp. 280–312. Springer, Cham (2018). https://doi.org/10.1007/978-3-319-78381-9_11

15. Canetti, R.: Universally composable security: a new paradigm for cryptographic protocols. In: 42nd FOCS, pp. 136–145 (2001)

16. Canetti, R., Dodis, Y., Pass, R., Walfish, S.: Universally composable security with global setup. In: Vadhan, S.P. (ed.) TCC 2007. LNCS, vol. 4392, pp. 61–85. Springer, Heidelberg (2007). https://doi.org/10.1007/978-3-540-70936-7_4

17. Canetti, R., Goldreich, O., Halevi, S.: The random oracle methodology, revisited (preliminary version). In: 30th ACM STOC, pp. 209–218 (1998)

18. Canetti, R., Jain, A., Scafuro, A.: Practical UC security with a global random oracle. In: ACM CCS 2014, pp. 597–608 (2014)

19. Chaum, D., van Heyst, E.: Group signatures. In: Davies, D.W. (ed.) EUROCRYPT 1991. LNCS, vol. 547, pp. 257–265. Springer, Heidelberg (1991). https://doi.org/10.1007/3-540-46416-6_22

20. Ciampi, M., Persiano, G., Scafuro, A., Siniscalchi, L., Visconti, I.: Improved OR-composition of sigma-protocols. In: Kushilevitz, E., Malkin, T. (eds.) TCC 2016, Part II. LNCS, vol. 9563, pp. 112–141. Springer, Heidelberg (2016). https://doi.org/10.1007/978-3-662-49099-0_5

21. Ciampi, M., Persiano, G., Scafuro, A., Siniscalchi, L., Visconti, I.: Online/offline OR composition of sigma protocols. In: Fischlin, M., Coron, J.-S. (eds.) EUROCRYPT 2016, Part II. LNCS, vol. 9666, pp. 63–92. Springer, Heidelberg (2016). https://doi.org/10.1007/978-3-662-49896-5_3

22. Cramer, R., Damgård, I.: Fast and secure immunization against adaptive man-in-the-middle impersonation. In: Fumy, W. (ed.) EUROCRYPT 1997. LNCS, vol. 1233, pp. 75–87. Springer, Heidelberg (1997). https://doi.org/10.1007/3-540-69053-0_7

23. Cramer, R., Damgård, I., Schoenmakers, B.: Proofs of partial knowledge and simplified design of witness hiding protocols. In: Desmedt, Y.G. (ed.) CRYPTO 1994. LNCS, vol. 839, pp. 174–187. Springer, Heidelberg (1994). https://doi.org/10.1007/3-540-48658-5_19

24. Dagdelen, Ö., Fischlin, M., Gagliardoni, T.: The Fiat–Shamir transformation in a quantum world. In: Sako, K., Sarkar, P. (eds.) ASIACRYPT 2013, Part II. LNCS, vol. 8270, pp. 62–81. Springer, Heidelberg (2013). https://doi.org/10.1007/978-3-642-42045-0_4

25. Damgård, I.: On Σ-protocols. Lecture Notes, Department for Computer Science, University of Aarhus (2002)

26. Dodis, Y., Shoup, V., Walfish, S.: Efficient constructions of composable commitments and zero-knowledge proofs. In: Wagner, D. (ed.) CRYPTO 2008. LNCS, vol. 5157, pp. 515–535. Springer, Heidelberg (2008). https://doi.org/10.1007/978-3-540-85174-5_29

27. Don, J., Fehr, S., Majenz, C., Schaffner, C.: Security of the Fiat-Shamir transformation in the quantum random-oracle model. In: Boldyreva, A., Micciancio, D. (eds.) CRYPTO 2019, Part II. LNCS, vol. 11693, pp. 356–383. Springer, Cham (2019). https://doi.org/10.1007/978-3-030-26951-7_13

28. Ducas, E. et al.: CRYSTALS-Dilithium: a lattice-based digital signature scheme. IACR TCHES 2018, vol. 1, pp. 238–268 (2018). https://tches.iacr.org/index.php/TCHES/article/view/839

29. Ducas, L., et al.: Crystals-Dilithium: algorithm specifications and supporting documentation (2019). https://pq-crystals.org/dilithium/index.shtml

30. Esgin, M.F., Steinfeld, R., Liu, J.K., Liu, D.: Lattice-based zero-knowledge proofs: new techniques for shorter and faster constructions and applications. In: Boldyreva, A., Micciancio, D. (eds.) CRYPTO 2019, Part I. LNCS, vol. 11692, pp. 115–146. Springer, Cham (2019). https://doi.org/10.1007/978-3-030-26948-7_5

31. Feige, U., Shamir, A.: Witness indistinguishable and witness hiding protocols. In: 22nd ACM STOC, pp. 416–426 (1990)

32. Fiat, A., Shamir, A.: How to prove yourself: practical solutions to identification and signature problems. In: Odlyzko, A.M. (ed.) CRYPTO 1986. LNCS, vol. 263, pp. 186–194. Springer, Heidelberg (1987). https://doi.org/10.1007/3-540-47721-7_12

33. Fischlin, M., Fleischhacker, N.: Limitations of the meta-reduction technique: the case of Schnorr signatures. In: Johansson, T., Nguyen, P.Q. (eds.) EUROCRYPT 2013. LNCS, vol. 7881, pp. 444–460. Springer, Heidelberg (2013). https://doi.org/10.1007/978-3-642-38348-9_27

34. Fischlin, M., Harasser, P., Janson, C.: Signatures from sequential-OR proofs. IACR Cryptology ePrint Archive (2020). https://eprint.iacr.org/2020/271

35. Fischlin, M., Lehmann, A., Ristenpart, T., Shrimpton, T., Stam, M., Tessaro, S.: Random oracles with(out) Programmability. In: Abe, M. (ed.) ASIACRYPT 2010. LNCS, vol. 6477, pp. 303–320. Springer, Heidelberg (2010). https://doi.org/10.1007/978-3-642-17373-8_18

36. Fukumitsu, M., Hasegawa, S.: Impossibility on the provable security of the Fiat-Shamir-Type signatures in the non-programmable random oracle model. In: Bishop, M., Nascimento, A.C.A. (eds.) ISC 2016. LNCS, vol. 9866, pp. 389–407. Springer, Cham (2016). https://doi.org/10.1007/978-3-319-45871-7_23

37. Fukumitsu, M., Hasegawa, S.: Black-box separations on Fiat-Shamir-type signatures in the non-programmable random oracle model. IEICE Trans. **101-A**(1), 77–87 (2018)

38. Garay, J.A., MacKenzie, P., Yang, K.: Strengthening zero-knowledge protocols using signatures. In: Biham, E. (ed.) EUROCRYPT 2003. LNCS, vol. 2656, pp. 177–194. Springer, Heidelberg (2003). https://doi.org/10.1007/3-540-39200-9_11

39. Gjøsteen, K., Jager, T.: Practical and tightly-secure digital signatures and authenticated key exchange. In: Shacham, H., Boldyreva, A. (eds.) CRYPTO 2018, Part II. LNCS, vol. 10992, pp. 95–125. Springer, Cham (2018). https://doi.org/10.1007/978-3-319-96881-0_4

40. Goldwasser, S., Micali, S., Rivest, R.L.: A digital signature scheme secure against adaptive chosen-message attacks. SIAM J. Comput. **17**(2), 281–308 (1988)

41. Guillou, L.C., Quisquater, J.-J.: A practical zero-knowledge protocol fitted to security microprocessor minimizing both transmission and memory. In: Barstow, D., et al. (eds.) EUROCRYPT 1988. LNCS, vol. 330, pp. 123–128. Springer, Heidelberg (1988). https://doi.org/10.1007/3-540-45961-8_11

42. Hofheinz, D., Jager, T.: Tightly secure signatures and public-key encryption. In: Safavi-Naini, R., Canetti, R. (eds.) CRYPTO 2012. LNCS, vol. 7417, pp. 590–607. Springer, Heidelberg (2012). https://doi.org/10.1007/978-3-642-32009-5_35

43. Jakobsson, M., Sako, K., Impagliazzo, R.: Designated verifier proofs and their applications. In: Maurer, U. (ed.) EUROCRYPT 1996. LNCS, vol. 1070, pp. 143–154. Springer, Heidelberg (1996). https://doi.org/10.1007/3-540-68339-9_13

44. Jedusor, T.E.: MimbleWimble (2016). https://download.wpsoftware.net/bitcoin/wizardry/mimblewimble.txt

45. Kiltz, E., Lyubashevsky, V., Schaffner, C.: A concrete treatment of Fiat-Shamir signatures in the quantum random-oracle model. In: Nielsen, J.B., Rijmen, V. (eds.) EUROCRYPT 2018, Part III. LNCS, vol. 10822, pp. 552–586. Springer, Cham (2018). https://doi.org/10.1007/978-3-319-78372-7_18

46. Lindell, Y.: An efficient transform from sigma protocols to NIZK with a CRS and non-programmable random oracle. In: Dodis, Y., Nielsen, J.B. (eds.) TCC 2015, Part I. LNCS, vol. 9014, pp. 93–109. Springer, Heidelberg (2015). https://doi.org/10.1007/978-3-662-46494-6_5

47. Liu, J.K., Wei, V.K., Wong, D.S.: Linkable spontaneous anonymous group signature for ad hoc groups (extended abstract). In: Wang, H., Pieprzyk, J., Varadharajan, V. (eds.) ACISP 2004. LNCS, vol. 3108, pp. 325–335. Springer, Heidelberg (2004). https://doi.org/10.1007/978-3-540-27800-9_28

48. Liu, Q., Zhandry, M.: Revisiting post-quantum Fiat-Shamir. In: Boldyreva, A., Micciancio, D. (eds.) CRYPTO 2019, Part II. LNCS, vol. 11693, pp. 326–355. Springer, Cham (2019). https://doi.org/10.1007/978-3-030-26951-7_12

49. Lyubashevsky, V.: Lattice signatures without trapdoors. In: Pointcheval, D., Johansson, T. (eds.) EUROCRYPT 2012. LNCS, vol. 7237, pp. 738–755. Springer, Heidelberg (2012). https://doi.org/10.1007/978-3-642-29011-4_43

50. Maxwell, G., Poelstra, A.: Borromean ring signatures (2015). https://pdfs.semanticscholar.org/4160/470c7f6cf05ffc81a98e8fd67fb0c84836ea.pdf

51. Nielsen, M.A., Chuang, I.L.: Quantum Computation and Quantum Information: 10th Anniversary Edition, 10th edn. Cambridge University Press, New York (2011)

52. Okamoto, T.: Provably secure and practical identification schemes and corresponding signature schemes. In: Brickell, E.F. (ed.) CRYPTO 1992. LNCS, vol. 740, pp. 31–53. Springer, Heidelberg (1993). https://doi.org/10.1007/3-540-48071-4_3

53. Paillier, P., Vergnaud, D.: Discrete-log-based signatures may not be equivalent to discrete log. In: Roy, B. (ed.) ASIACRYPT 2005. LNCS, vol. 3788, pp. 1–20. Springer, Heidelberg (2005). https://doi.org/10.1007/11593447_1
54. Poelstra, A.: MimbleWimble (2016). https://download.wpsoftware.net/bitcoin/wizardry/mimblewimble.pdf
55. Pointcheval, D., Stern, J.: Security arguments for digital signatures and blind signatures. J. Cryptol. 13(3), 361–396 (2000). https://doi.org/10.1007/s001450010003
56. Rivest, R.L., Shamir, A., Tauman, Y.: How to leak a secret. In: Boyd, C. (ed.) ASIACRYPT 2001. LNCS, vol. 2248, pp. 552–565. Springer, Heidelberg (2001). https://doi.org/10.1007/3-540-45682-1_32
57. Schnorr, C.-P.: Efficient signature generation by smart cards. J. Cryptol. 4(3), 161–174 (1991). https://doi.org/10.1007/BF00196725
58. van Saberhagen, N.: CryptoNote v 2.0 (2013). https://cryptonote.org/whitepaper.pdf
59. Venturi, D.: Zero-knowledge proofs and applications (2015). http://wwwusers.di.uniroma1.it/~venturi/misc/zero-knowledge.pdf
60. Zhandry, M.: Secure identity-based encryption in the quantum random oracle model. In: Safavi-Naini, R., Canetti, R. (eds.) CRYPTO 2012. LNCS, vol. 7417, pp. 758–775. Springer, Heidelberg (2012). https://doi.org/10.1007/978-3-642-32009-5_44
61. Zhang, Z., Chen, Y., Chow, S.S.M., Hanaoka, G., Cao, Z., Zhao, Y.: Black-box separations of hash-and-sign signatures in the non-programmable random oracle model. In: Au, M.-H., Miyaji, A. (eds.) ProvSec 2015. LNCS, vol. 9451, pp. 435–454. Springer, Cham (2015). https://doi.org/10.1007/978-3-319-26059-4_24

Attribute-Based Encryption

Compact Adaptively Secure ABE from k-Lin: Beyond NC^1 and Towards NL

Huijia Lin$^{(\boxtimes)}$ and Ji Luo$^{(\boxtimes)}$ (ID)

University of Washington, Seattle, USA
{rachel,luoji}@cs.washington.edu

Abstract. We present a new general framework for constructing *compact* and *adaptively secure* attribute-based encryption (ABE) schemes from k-Lin in asymmetric bilinear pairing groups. Previously, the only construction [Kowalczyk and Wee, Eurocrypt '19] that simultaneously achieves compactness and adaptive security from static assumptions supports policies represented by *Boolean formulae*. Our framework enables supporting more expressive policies represented by *arithmetic branching programs*.

Our framework extends to ABE for policies represented by uniform models of computation such as Turing machines. Such policies enjoy the feature of being applicable to attributes of arbitrary lengths. We obtain the first compact adaptively secure ABE for deterministic and non-deterministic finite automata (DFA and NFA) from k-Lin, previously unknown from any static assumptions. Beyond finite automata, we obtain the first ABE for large classes of uniform computation, captured by deterministic and non-deterministic *logspace* Turing machines (the complexity classes L and NL) based on k-Lin. Our ABE scheme has compact secret keys of size linear in the description size of the Turing machine M. The ciphertext size grows linearly in the input length, but also linearly in the time complexity, and exponentially in the space complexity. Irrespective of compactness, we stress that our scheme is the first that supports large classes of Turing machines based solely on standard assumptions. In comparison, previous ABE for general Turing machines all rely on strong primitives related to indistinguishability obfuscation.

1 Introduction

Attribute-based encryption (ABE) [32] is an advanced form of public-key encryption that enables fine-grained access control. The encryption algorithm using the master public key mpk can encrypt a message m with a descriptive attribute x,[1] producing a ciphertext $\mathsf{ct}_x(m)$. The key generation algorithm using the master secret key msk can produce a secret key sk_y associated with an access policy y. Decrypting $\mathsf{ct}_x(m)$ using sk_y reveals the message m if the attribute x satisfies the policy y; otherwise, no information about m is revealed. The security

---

[1] Some works call x a set of attributes, and each bit or component of x an attribute. We treat the attribute as a single vector.

© International Association for Cryptologic Research 2020
A. Canteaut and Y. Ishai (Eds.): EUROCRYPT 2020, LNCS 12107, pp. 247–277, 2020.
https://doi.org/10.1007/978-3-030-45727-3_9

requirement of ABE stipulates resilience to collusion attacks—any group of users holding secret keys for different policies learn nothing about the plaintext as long as none of them is individually authorized to decrypt the ciphertext.

A primary goal of research on ABE is designing ABE schemes for expressive classes of policies, usually defined by computation models or complexity classes. A beautiful and fruitful line of works have constructed ABE for many different policy classes. For non-uniform computation, we have ABE for Boolean [32,44] or arithmetic formulae, branching/span programs [13,23,31,37,45,47,48,53,54], and circuits [14,19,30]. For uniform computation, we have ABE for deterministic finite automata [1,5,12,13,29,58], non-deterministic finite automata [4], and even Turing machines [3,8]. These constructions, however, achieve different trade-offs between security, efficiency, and underlying computational assumptions. It is rare to have a construction that simultaneously achieves the following natural desirata on all fronts:

- *Security*: (full) adaptive security (as opposed to selective or semi-adaptive security);
- *Efficiency*: having compact secret key and ciphertext, whose sizes grow linearly with the description size of the policy and the length of the attribute, respectively;
- *Assumptions*: relying on standard and simple assumptions, such as LWE and k-Lin or SXDH in bilinear pairing groups (in particular, it is preferable to avoid the use of strong primitives such as indistinguishability obfuscation, and instance-dependent assumptions such as q-type assumptions, whose strength can be weakened by adversarially chosen parameters).

All previous constructions of ABE fail to achieve at least one of the desirable properties, except for the recent construction of ABE for *Boolean formulae* from the k-Lin assumption by Kowalczyk and Wee [44]. This raises the question:

Can we construct ABE schemes with all the desirable properties above for more expressive classes of policies than Boolean formulae?

When it comes to uniform computation, the state of affairs is even less satisfactory. All constructions of ABE for general Turing machines are based on strong primitives such as indistinguishability obfuscation and multilinear map. Without these powerful tools, existing schemes can only handle the weak computation model of finite automata.

Can we construct ABE schemes based on standard assumptions for more expressive uniform computations than finite automata?

Our Result. Via a unified framework, we construct *compact and adaptively secure* ABE schemes based on the k-Lin assumption in asymmetric prime-order bilinear pairing groups for the following classes of policies:

Arithmetic Branching Programs. ABPs capture many functions of interest, including arithmetic computations like sparse polynomials, mean, and variance, as well as combinatorial computations like string-matching, finite automata, and decision trees. It is also known that Boolean/arithmetic formulae and Boolean branching programs can all be converted into ABPs with polynomial blow-up in description size. Thus, ABPs can be viewed as a more powerful computational model than them.

Previous ABE schemes for ABPs only provide selective security [30,37] or do not have compact ciphertexts [23].[2] In addition to achieving both adaptive security and compactness, our scheme is the first one that handles ABPs directly without converting it to circuits or arithmetic span programs, which leads to an efficiency improvement in the size of the secret keys from up to quadratic to linear in the size of the ABP.[3]

*(Non-)Deterministic Logspace Turing Machines (*L *and* NL*).* Here, a secret key is associated with a Turing machine M, and the attribute in a ciphertext specifies an input $\mathbf{x}$, a polynomial time bound T, and a logarithmic space bound S. Decryption succeeds if and only if M accepts $\mathbf{x}$ within time T and space S. Our scheme is *unbounded* in the sense that the public parameters do not restrict the sizes of the Turing machine M and input $\mathbf{x}$, nor the time/space bounds T, S. Furthermore, it enjoys the advantage of ABE for uniform computation that a secret key for M can decrypt ciphertexts with arbitrarily long inputs and arbitrary time/space bounds. This stands in contrast with ABE for non-uniform computation (like ABPs), where a program or circuit f takes inputs of a specific length n, and a secret key for f decrypts only ciphertext of length-n inputs. Achieving this feature is precisely the challenge in constructing ABE for uniform models of computation.

Our scheme is the first ABE for large classes of Turing machine computation, captured by the complexity classes L and NL, *without using the heavy machineries* of multilinear map, extractable witness encryption, or indistinguishability obfuscation as in previous works [3,9,27,41]. In addition, our scheme is adaptively secure and *half-compact*. The secret keys are compact, of size $O(|M|)$ linear in the description size of M, while the ciphertext size depends linearly in $|\mathbf{x}|TS2^S$ (both ignoring fixed polynomial factors in the security parameter).

Removing the dependency on 2^S or T is an interesting open problem that requires technical breakthrough. In particular, removing the dependency on 2^S would give an ABE for polynomial-time Turing machine computation from pairing, a long sought-after goal that has remained elusive for more than a decade. Removing the dependency of encryption time on T even only in the 1-key

---

[2] More precisely, they construct ABE for read-once branching programs. For general branching programs, one can duplicate each component in the attribute for the number of times it is accessed [43]. As such, the ciphertext size grows linearly with the size of the branching program.

[3] An ABP is specified by a directed graph, with edges weighted by affine functions of the input. The size of an ABP is measured by the number of vertices (instead of edges) in the graph.

1-ciphertext setting implies a succinct message-hiding encoding [42],[4] which is only known from strong primitives like indistinguishability obfuscation or functional encryption [18,21,41,42]. Removing the dependency of ciphertext size on T might be an easier task, but would need new techniques different from ours.

Finite Automata. As a special case of ABE for L and NL, we obtain ABE for deterministic finite automata (DFA) and non-deterministic finite automata (NFA).[5] This simply follows from the fact that DFA and NFA can be represented as simple deterministic and non-deterministic Turing machines with space complexity 1 and time complexity N that always move the input tape pointer to the right and never use the work tape.

Previous schemes for DFA based on pairing either achieve only selective security [5,29,58] or rely on q-type assumptions [1,12,13]. The only direct construction of ABE for NFA [4] based on LWE, however, is symmetric-key and only selectively secure. We settle the open problem of constructing adaptively secure ABE for DFA from static assumptions [29] and that of constructing ABE for NFA that is public-key, adaptively secure, or based on assumptions other than LWE [4].

New Techniques for Constructing Adaptively Secure ABE. Constructing adaptively secure ABE is a challenging task. Roughly speaking, previous constructions proceed in two steps. First, a secure core secret-key ABE component for a single ciphertext and a single secret key—termed 1-ABE—is designed. Then, Dual System Encryption framework, originally proposed in [57] and refined in [1,12,13,22,59], provides guidance on how to lift 1-ABE to the public-key and multi-secret-key setting. The main technical challenge lies in the first step: Adaptively secure schemes prior to that of Kowalczyk and Wee [44] either impose a read-once restriction on the attribute[6] [45,59] or rely on q-type assumptions [1,12,16,48]. Kowalczyk and Wee [44] elegantly applied the "partial selectivization" framework [6,38] for achieving adaptive security in general to constructing 1-ABE. In particular, they used a variant of the secret-sharing scheme for Boolean formulae in [38] whose selective simulation security can be proven via a sequence of hybrids, each only requiring *partial* information of the input to be chosen selectively. Then, to show adaptive security, the reduction can *guess* this partial information while incurring only a polynomial security loss.

---

[4] Message-hiding encodings [42] are a weaker variant of randomized encodings that allow encoding a public computation f, x with a secret message m such that the encoding reveals m if and only if $f(x) = 1$. Such encodings are *succinct* if the time to encode is much smaller than the running time of the computation. A pair of ABE secret key for predicate f and ciphertext for attribute x and message m is a message-hiding encoding.

[5] DFA and NFA both characterize regular languages, yet a DFA recognizing a language could have exponentially more states than an NFA recognizing the same language. In this work, by ABE for DFA/NFA, we mean ABE schemes that run in time polynomial in the description size of the finite automata.

[6] As mentioned in Footnote 2, read-once restriction can be circumvented by duplicating attribute components at the cost of losing ciphertext compactness.

However, secret-sharing schemes as needed in [44] are only known for Boolean formulae. When dealing with computation over arithmetic domains of potentially exponential size, we have the additional challenge that it is hard to guess even a single component of the input, except with exponentially small probability, rendering the partial selectivization framework ineffective. When dealing with uniform computation, we further encounter the challenge that neither the secret key nor the ciphertext is as large as the secret-sharing, making it impossible to directly use information-theoretically secure secret-sharing schemes. We develop new techniques to overcome these challenges.

1. First, we present a generic framework for constructing adaptively secure 1-ABE from (i) an information theoretic primitive called *arithmetic key garbling*, and (ii) a computational primitive called *function-hiding inner-product functional encryption* (IPFE) [17,40,49,56]. Our arithmetic key garbling schemes are partial garbling schemes [37] with special structures, which act as the counterpart of secret-sharing schemes for arithmetic computation. Our framework is modular: It decomposes the task of constructing 1-ABE to *first* designing an arithmetic key garbling scheme for the computation class of interest, and *second* applying a generic transformation depending solely on structural properties of the garbling and agnostic of the underlying computation. In particular, the security proof of the transformation does not attempt to trace the computation, unlike [29,44].

2. Second, we formulate structural properties of arithmetic key garbling schemes—called piecewise security—sufficient for achieving adaptive security. The properties are natural and satisfied by the garbling scheme for ABPs in [37]. For logspace Turing machine computation, we present a simple arithmetic key garbling scheme for L and NL, inspired by the garbling schemes in [11,19].

3. Third, we present a new method of lifting 1-ABE to full-fledged ABE using function-hiding IPFE. Our method can be cast into the dual system encryption framework, but is natural on its own, without seeing through the lens of dual system encryption. One feature of IPFE is that it provides a conceptually simple abstraction which allows moving information between ABE keys and ciphertexts easily, and hides away lower-level details on how to guarantee security. This feature makes it a convenient tool in many other parts of the security proof as well.

4. Lastly, to overcome the unique challenge related to ABE for uniform computation, we further enhance our generic method to be able to use partial garbling generated with *pseudorandomness* so that the total size of the secret keys and ciphertexts can be smaller than the garbling.

Organization. In Sect. 2, we give an overview of our framework for constructing compact adaptively secure ABE schemes for ABPs, logspace Turing machines, and finite automata, using as tools IPFE and arithmetic key garbling schemes (AKGS, a refinement of partial garbling schemes). After introducing basic notations and definitions in Sect. 3, we define AKGS and its security in Sect. 4.

In Sect. 5, we show how to construct 1-ABE (the core component of our ABE schemes) for ABPs from an AKGS. Due to space constraints, the security proof of our 1-ABE for ABPs, the construction of full-fledged ABE for ABPs, and ABE for L and NL are provided in the full version.

2 Technical Overview

We now give an overview of our technique, starting with introducing the two key tools arithmetic key garbling schemes and IPFE. Below, by bilinear pairing groups, we mean asymmetric prime-order bilinear pairing groups, denoted as $(G_1, G_2, G_T, g_1, g_2, e)$ and implicitly, $g_T = e(g_1, g_2)$. We use $[\![a]\!]_b$ to represent the encoding g_b^a of a in group G_b.

Arithmetic Key Garbling Scheme. We use a refinement of the notion of partial garbling schemes [37] (which in turn is based on the notion of garbling and randomized encoding [10,36,61]). An *arithmetic key garbling scheme* (AKGS) is an information-theoretic partial garbling scheme for computing $\alpha f(\mathbf{x}) + \beta$ that hides the *secrets* $\alpha, \beta \in \mathbb{Z}_p$, but not $f, \mathbf{x}$:

- A garbling procedure $(\mathbf{L}_1, \ldots, \mathbf{L}_m) \leftarrow \mathsf{Garble}(f, \alpha, \beta; \mathbf{r})$ turns f and two secrets α, β (using randomness $\mathbf{r}$) into m affine *label functions* $L_1, \ldots, L_m$, described by their coefficient vectors $\mathbf{L}_1, \ldots, \mathbf{L}_m$ over $\mathbb{Z}_p$. The label functions specify how to encode an input $\mathbf{x}$ to produce the *labels* for computing $f(\mathbf{x})$ with secrets α, β:

$$\widehat{f(\mathbf{x})}_{\alpha, \beta} = (\ell_1, \ldots, \ell_m), \text{ where } \ell_j = L_j(\mathbf{x}) = \langle \mathbf{L}_j, (1, \mathbf{x}) \rangle \text{ over } \mathbb{Z}_p. \quad (1)$$

- A *linear* evaluation procedure $\gamma \leftarrow \mathsf{Eval}(f, \mathbf{x}, \ell_1, \ldots, \ell_m)$ recovers the sum $\gamma = \alpha f(\mathbf{x}) + \beta$ weighted by the function value $f(\mathbf{x})$.

AKGS is a *partial* garbling as it only hides information of the secrets α and β beyond the weighted sum $\alpha f(\mathbf{x}) + \beta$, and does not hide $(f, \mathbf{x})$, captured by a simulation procedure $(\ell'_1, \ldots, \ell'_m) \xleftarrow{\$} \mathsf{Sim}(f, \mathbf{x}, \alpha f(\mathbf{x}) + \beta)$ that produces the same distribution as the honest labels.

Ishai and Wee [37] proposed a partial garbling scheme for ABPs, which directly implies an AKGS for ABPs. It is also easy to observe that the (fully secure) garbling scheme for arithmetic formulae in [11] can be weakened [19] to an AKGS. Later, we will introduce additional structural and security properties of AKGS needed for our 1-ABE construction. These properties are natural and satisfied by both schemes [11,37].

Inner-Product Functional Encryption. A *function-hiding* (secret-key) inner-product functional encryption (IPFE)[7] enables generating many secret keys $\mathsf{isk}(\mathbf{v}_j)$ and ciphertexts $\mathsf{ict}(\mathbf{u}_i)$ associated with vectors $\mathbf{v}_j$ and $\mathbf{u}_i$ such that decryption yields all the inner products $\{\langle \mathbf{u}_i, \mathbf{v}_j \rangle\}_{i,j} \pmod{p}$ and nothing else.

---

[7] Some works use "inner-product encryption" (IPE) to refer to IPFE [17,25,49,50] and some others [24,39,52–55] use it for inner-product *predicate* encryption.

In this work, we need an *adaptively secure* IPFE, whose security holds even against adversaries choosing all the vectors adaptively. Such an IPFE scheme can be constructed based on the k-Lin assumption in bilinear pairing groups [50,60]. The known scheme also has nice structural properties that will be instrumental to our construction of ABE:

- $\mathsf{isk}(\mathbf{v}) \xleftarrow{\$} \mathsf{IPFE.KeyGen}(\mathsf{msk}, [\![\mathbf{v}]\!]_2)$ operates *linearly* on $\mathbf{v}$ (in the exponent of G_2) and the size of the secret key $\mathsf{isk}(\mathbf{v})$ grows linearly with $|\mathbf{v}|$.
- $\mathsf{ict}(\mathbf{u}) \xleftarrow{\$} \mathsf{IPFE.Enc}(\mathsf{msk}, [\![\mathbf{u}]\!]_1)$ also operates *linearly* on $\mathbf{u}$ (in the exponent of G_1) and the size of the ciphertext $\mathsf{ict}(\mathbf{u})$ grows linearly with $|\mathbf{u}|$.
- $\mathsf{IPFE.Dec}(\mathsf{sk}(\mathbf{v}), \mathsf{ct}(\mathbf{u}))$ simply invokes pairing to compute the inner product $[\![\langle \mathbf{u}, \mathbf{v} \rangle]\!]_T$ in the exponent of the target group.

2.1 1-ABE from Arithmetic Key Garbling and IPFE Schemes

1-ABE is the technical heart of our ABE construction. It works in the setting where a single ciphertext $\mathsf{ct}(\mathbf{x})$ for an input vector $\mathbf{x}$ and a single secret key $\mathsf{sk}(f, \mu)$ for a policy $y = f_{\neq 0}$ and a secret μ are published. Decryption reveals μ if $f(\mathbf{x}) \neq 0$; otherwise, μ is hidden.[8]

1-ABE. To hide μ conditioned on $f(\mathbf{x}) = 0$, our key idea is using IPFE to compute an AKGS garbling $\widehat{f(\mathbf{x})}_{\mu,0}$ of $f(\mathbf{x})$ with secrets $\alpha = \mu$ and $\beta = 0$. The security of AKGS guarantees that only $\mu f(\mathbf{x})$ is revealed, which information theoretically hides μ when $f(\mathbf{x}) = 0$.

The reason that it is possible to use IPFE to compute the garbling is attributed to the *affine input-encoding* property of AKGS—the labels $\ell_1, \ldots, \ell_m$ are the output of affine functions $L_1, \ldots, L_j$ of $\mathbf{x}$ as described in Eq. (1). Since f, α, β are known at key generation time, the ABE key can be a collection of IPFE secret keys, each encoding the coefficient vector $\mathbf{L}_j$ of one label function L_j. On the other hand, the ABE ciphertext can be an IPFE ciphertext encrypting $(1, \mathbf{x})$. When put together for decryption, they reveal exactly the labels $L_1(\mathbf{x}), \ldots, L_m(\mathbf{x})$, as described below on the left.

Honest Algorithms		Hybrid for Selective Security	
$\mathsf{ct}(\mathbf{x})$: $\quad\quad\quad$ $\mathsf{ict}(\ (1, \mathbf{x}) \parallel \mathbf{0}\ )$		$\mathsf{ct}(\mathbf{x})$: $\quad\quad\quad$ $\mathsf{ict}(\ (1, \mathbf{x}) \parallel 1 \parallel \mathbf{0}\ )$	
$\mathsf{sk}(f, \mu)$: $j \in [m]$: $\mathsf{isk}_j(\ \ \mathbf{L}_j \ \ \parallel \mathbf{0}\ )$		$\mathsf{sk}(f, \mu)$: $j \in [m]$: $\mathsf{isk}_j(\ \ \mathbf{0} \ \ \parallel \ell_j \parallel \mathbf{0}\ )$	

We note that the positions or slots at the right end of the vectors encoded in isk and ict are set to zero by the honest algorithms—$\mathbf{0}$ denotes a vector (of unspecified length) of zeros. These slots provide programming space in the security proof.

It is extremely simple to prove selective (or semi-adaptive) security, where the input $\mathbf{x}$ is chosen before seeing the sk. By the function-hiding property of IPFE, it is indistinguishable to switch the secret keys and the ciphertext to

---

[8] We can also handle policies of the form $f_{=0}$ so that μ is revealed if and only if $f(\mathbf{x}) = 0$. For simplicity, we focus on one case in this overview.

encode any vectors that preserve the inner products. This allows us to hardwire honestly generated labels $\widehat{f(\mathbf{x})}_{\mu,0} = \{\ell_j \leftarrow \langle \mathbf{L}_j, (1, \mathbf{x}) \rangle\}_{j \in [m]}$ in the secret keys as described above on the right. The simulation security of AKGS then implies that only $\mu f(\mathbf{x})$ is revealed, i.e., nothing about μ is revealed.

Achieving Adaptive Security. When it comes to adaptive security, where the input $\mathbf{x}$ is chosen *after* seeing sk, we can no longer hardwire the honest labels $\widehat{f(\mathbf{x})}_{\mu,0}$ in the secret key, as $\mathbf{x}$ is undefined when sk is generated, and hence cannot invoke the simulation security of AKGS. Our second key idea is relying on a stronger security property of AKGS, named *piecewise security*, to hardwire simulated labels into the secret key in a piecemeal fashion.

Piecewise security of AKGS requires the following two properties: (*i*) reverse sampleability—there is an efficient procedure RevSamp that can *perfectly* reversely sample the first label ℓ_1 given the output $\alpha f(\mathbf{x}) + \beta$ and all the other labels $\ell_2, \ldots, \ell_m$, and (*ii*) marginal randomness—each ℓ_j of the following labels for $j > 1$ is uniformly distributed over $\mathbb{Z}_p$ even given all subsequent *label functions* $\mathbf{L}_{j+1}, \ldots, \mathbf{L}_m$. More formally,

$$\{\ell_1 \leftarrow \langle \mathbf{L}_1, (1, \mathbf{x}) \rangle, \quad \mathbf{L}_2, \ldots, \mathbf{L}_m\} \equiv \{\ell_1' \xleftarrow{\$} \mathsf{RevSamp}(\cdots), \quad \mathbf{L}_2, \ldots, \mathbf{L}_m\}, \quad (2)$$

$$\{\ell_j \leftarrow \langle \mathbf{L}_j, (1, \mathbf{x}) \rangle, \mathbf{L}_{j+1}, \ldots, \mathbf{L}_m\} \equiv \{\ell_j' \xleftarrow{\$} \mathbb{Z}_p \qquad\quad , \mathbf{L}_{j+1}, \ldots, \mathbf{L}_m\}. \quad (3)$$

In Eq. (2), $\ell_1' \xleftarrow{\$} \mathsf{RevSamp}(f, \mathbf{x}, \alpha f(\mathbf{x}) + \beta, \ell_2, \ldots, \ell_m)$. These properties are natural and satisfied by existing AKGS for ABPs and arithmetic formulae [11,37].

Adaptive Security via Piecewise Security. We are now ready to prove adaptive security of our 1-ABE. The proof strategy is to first hardwire ℓ_1 in the ciphertext and sample it reversely as $\ell_1 \xleftarrow{\$} \mathsf{RevSamp}(f, \mathbf{x}, 0, \ell_2, \ldots, \ell_m)$, where $\ell_j = \langle \mathbf{L}_j, (1, \mathbf{x}) \rangle$ for $j > 1$ and $\mu f(\mathbf{x}) = 0$ by the constraint, as described in hybrid $k = 1$ below. The indistinguishability follows immediately from the function-hiding property of IPFE and the reverse sampleability of AKGS. Then, we gradually replace each remaining label function $\mathbf{L}_j$ for $j > 1$ with a randomly sampled label $\ell_j \xleftarrow{\$} \mathbb{Z}_p$ in the secret key, as described in hybrids $1 \le k \le m+1$. It is easy to observe that in the final hybrid $k = m + 1$, where all labels $\ell_2, \ldots, \ell_m$ are random and ℓ_1 reversely sampled *without* μ, the value μ is information-theoretically hidden.

HYBRID $1 \le k \le m+1$	HYBRID $k : 1$ OR $k : 2$

$\mathsf{sk}(f, \mu)$: $\mathsf{isk}_1(\quad \mathbf{0} \quad \| \ 1 \ \| \ 0 \ \| \ 0 \ )$

$\qquad 1 < j < k: \mathsf{isk}_j(\quad \mathbf{0} \quad \| \ 0 \ \| \ \ell_j \ \| \ 0 \ )$

$\qquad\qquad\qquad \mathsf{isk}_k(\ \mathbf{L}_k \ \| \ 0 \ \| \ 0 \ \| \ 0 \ )$ $\mathsf{isk}_k(\quad \mathbf{0} \quad \| \ 0 \ \| \ 0 \ \| \ 1 \ )$

$\qquad j > k: \mathsf{isk}_j(\ \mathbf{L}_j \ \| \ 0 \ \| \ 0 \ \| \ 0 \ )$

$\mathsf{ct}(\mathbf{x})$: $\mathsf{ict}(\ (1, \mathbf{x}) \ \| \ \ell_1 \ \| \ 1 \ \| \ 0 \ )$ $\mathsf{ict}(\ (1, \mathbf{x}) \ \| \ \ell_1 \ \| \ 1 \ \| \ \ell_k \ )$

$\ell_1 \xleftarrow{\$} \mathsf{RevSamp}(\cdots)$, FOR $1 < j < k: \ell_j \xleftarrow{\$} \mathbb{Z}_p$ $\ell_k \leftarrow \langle \mathbf{L}_k, (1, \mathbf{x}) \rangle$ OR $\ell_k \xleftarrow{\$} \mathbb{Z}_p$

To move from hybrid k to $k + 1$, we want to switch the kth IPFE secret key isk_k from encoding the label function $\mathbf{L}_k$ to a simulated label $\ell_k \xleftarrow{\$} \mathbb{Z}_p$. This is possible via two moves. First, by the function-hiding property of IPFE, we can hardwire the honest $\ell_k = \langle \mathbf{L}_k, (1, \mathbf{x}) \rangle$ in the ciphertext as in hybrid $k : 1$ (recall that at encryption time, $\mathbf{x}$ is known). Then, by the marginal randomness property of AKGS, we switch to sample ℓ_k as random in hybrid $k : 2$. Lastly, hybrid $k : 2$ is indistinguishable to hybrid $k + 1$ again by the function-hiding property of IPFE.

1-ABE for ABPs. Plugging in the AKGS for ABPs by Ishai and Wee [37], we immediately obtain 1-ABE for ABPs based on k-Lin. The size of the garbling grows linearly with the number of vertices $|V|$ in the graph describing the ABP, i.e., $m = O(|V|)$. Combined with the fact that IPFE has linear-size secret keys and ciphertexts, our 1-ABE scheme for ABPs has secret keys of size $O(m|\mathbf{x}|) = O(|V||\mathbf{x}|)$ and ciphertexts of size $O(|\mathbf{x}|)$. This gives an efficiency improvement over previous 1-ABE or ABE schemes for ABPs [23,37], where the secret key size grows linearly with the number of edges $|E|$ in the ABP graph, due to that their schemes first convert ABPs into an arithmetic span program, which incurs the efficiency loss.

Discussion. Our method for constructing 1-ABE is generic and modular. In particular, it has the advantage that the proof of adaptive security is agnostic of the computation being performed and merely carries out the simulation of AKGS in a mechanic way. Indeed, if we plug in an AKGS for arithmetic formulae or any other classes of non-uniform computation, the proof remains the same. (Our 1-ABE for logspace Turing machines also follows the same blueprint, but needs additional ideas.) Furthermore, note that our method departs from the partial selectivization technique used in [44], which is not applicable to arithmetic computation as the security reduction cannot afford to guess even one component of the input $\mathbf{x}$. The problem is circumvented by using IPFE to hardwire the labels (i.e., ℓ_1, ℓ_k) that depend on $\mathbf{x}$ in the ciphertext.

2.2   Full-Fledged ABE via IPFE

From 1-ABE for the 1-key 1-ciphertext setting to full-fledged ABE, we need to support publishing multiple keys and make encryption public-key. It turns out that the security of our 1-ABE scheme directly extends to the many-key 1-ciphertext (still secret-key) setting via a simple hybrid argument. Consider the scenario where a ciphertext ct and multiple keys $\{\mathsf{sk}_q(f_q, \mu_q)\}_{q \in [Q]}$ that are unauthorized to decrypt the ciphertext are published. Combining the above security proof for 1-ABE with a hybrid argument, we can gradually switch each secret key sk_q from encoding honest label functions encapsulating μ_q to ones encapsulating an independent secret $\mu'_q \xleftarrow{\$} \mathbb{Z}_p$. Therefore, all the secrets $\{\mu_q\}_{q \in [Q]}$ are hidden.

The security of our 1-ABE breaks down once two ciphertexts are released. Consider publishing just a single secret key $\mathsf{sk}(f, \mu)$ and two ciphertexts

$\mathsf{ct}_1(\mathbf{x}_1), \mathsf{ct}_2(\mathbf{x}_2)$. Since the label functions $L_1, \ldots, L_m$ are encoded in sk, decryption computes two AKGS garblings $\widehat{f(\mathbf{x}_1)}_{\mu,0}$ and $\widehat{f(\mathbf{x}_2)}_{\mu,0}$ generated using the *same* label functions. However, AKGS security does not apply when the label functions are reused.

What we wish is that IPFE decryption computes two garblings $\widehat{f(\mathbf{x}_1)}_{\mu,0} = (L_1(\mathbf{x}_1), \ldots, L_m(\mathbf{x}_1))$ and $\widehat{f(\mathbf{x}_2)}_{\mu,0} = (L'_1(\mathbf{x}_2), \ldots, L'_m(\mathbf{x}_2))$ using *independent* label functions. This can be achieved in a *computational* fashion relying on the fact that the IPFE scheme encodes the vectors and the decryption results in the exponent of bilinear pairing groups. Hence we can rely on computational assumptions such as SXDH or k-Lin, combined with the function-hiding property of IPFE to argue that the produced garblings are computationally independent. We modify the 1-ABE scheme as follows:

- If SXDH holds in the pairing groups, we encode in the ciphertext $(1, \mathbf{x})$ multiplied by a random scalar $s \xleftarrow{\$} \mathbb{Z}_p$. As such, decryption computes $(sL_1(\mathbf{x}), \ldots, sL_m(\mathbf{x}))$ *in the exponent*. We argue that the label functions $sL_1, \ldots, sL_m$ are computationally random *in the exponent*: By the function-hiding property of IPFE, it is indistinguishable to multiply s not with the ciphertext vector, but with the coefficient vectors in the secret key as depicted below on the right; by DDH (in G_2) and the linearity of Garble (i.e., the coefficients $\mathbf{L}_j$ depend linearly on the secrets α, β and the randomness $\mathbf{r}$ used by Garble), $s\mathbf{L}_j$ are the coefficients of pseudorandom label functions.

ALGORITHMS BASED ON SXDH | HYBRID

			$\approx \mathbf{L}'_j$ (fresh)
$\mathsf{sk}(f, \mu):$	$j \in [m]: \mathsf{isk}_j(\ \ \mathbf{L}_j\ \ \| \ \mathbf{0}\ )$	$\mathsf{isk}_j(\ \mathbf{L}_j\ \|\ s\mathbf{L}_j\ \|\ \mathbf{0}\ )$
$\mathsf{ct}(\mathbf{x}):$	$\mathsf{ict}(\ s(1, \mathbf{x})\ \|\ \mathbf{0}\ )$	$\mathsf{ict}(\ \mathbf{0}\ \|\ (1, \mathbf{x})\ \|\ \mathbf{0}\ )$

- If k-Lin holds in the pairing groups, we encode in the secret key k independent copies of label functions $L_1^t, \ldots, L_m^t$ for $t \in [k]$, and in the ciphertexts k copies of $(1, \mathbf{x})$ multiplied with independent random scalars $\mathbf{s}[t]$ for $t \in [k]$. This way, decryption computes a random linear combination of the garblings $(\sum_{t \in [k]} \mathbf{s}[t] L_1^t(\mathbf{x}), \ldots, \sum_{t \in [k]} \mathbf{s}[t] L_m^t(\mathbf{x}))$ in the exponent, which via a similar hybrid as above corresponds to pseudorandom label functions in the exponent.

ALGORITHMS BASED ON k-LIN

$\mathsf{sk}(f, \mu):$	$j \in [m]: \mathsf{isk}_j(\ \ \ \mathbf{L}_j^1$	$\| \cdots \|$	$\mathbf{L}_j^k$	$\|$	$\mathbf{0}$	$)$
$\mathsf{ct}(\mathbf{x}):$	$\mathsf{ict}(\ \mathbf{s}[1](1, \mathbf{x})$	$\| \cdots \|\ \mathbf{s}[k](1, \mathbf{x})\ \|$			$\mathbf{0}$	$)$

HYBRID

					$\approx \mathbf{L}'_j$ (fresh)	
$\mathsf{sk}(f, \mu):$	$j \in [m]: \mathsf{isk}_j(\ \ \ \mathbf{L}_j^1$	$\| \cdots \|$	$\mathbf{L}_j^k$	$\|$	$\sum_{t \in [k]} \mathbf{s}[t] \mathbf{L}_j^t\ \|\ \mathbf{0}$	$)$
$\mathsf{ct}(\mathbf{x}):$	$\mathsf{ict}(\ \ \ \mathbf{0}$	$\| \cdots \|$	$\mathbf{0}$	$\|$	$(1, \mathbf{x})\ \ \ \| \ \mathbf{0}$	$)$

The above modification yields a secret-key ABE secure in the many-ciphertext many-key setting. The final hurdle is how to make the scheme public-key, which we resolve using slotted IPFE.

Slotted IPFE. Proposed in [50], *slotted* IPFE is a hybrid between a secret-key function-hiding IPFE and a public-key IPFE. Here, a vector $\mathbf{u} \in \mathbb{Z}_p^n$ is divided into two parts $(\mathbf{u}_{\mathrm{pub}}, \mathbf{u}_{\mathrm{priv}})$ with $\mathbf{u}_{\mathrm{pub}} \in \mathbb{Z}_p^{n_{\mathrm{pub}}}$ in the public slot and $\mathbf{u}_{\mathrm{priv}} \in \mathbb{Z}_p^{n_{\mathrm{priv}}}$ in the private slot $(n_{\mathrm{pub}} + n_{\mathrm{priv}} = n)$. Like a usual secret-key IPFE, the encryption algorithm IPFE.Enc using the master secret key msk can encrypt to both the public and private slots, i.e., encrypting any vector $\mathbf{u}$. In addition, there is an IPFE.SlotEnc algorithm that uses the master public key mpk, but can only encrypt to the public slot, i.e., encrypting vectors such that $\mathbf{u}_{\mathrm{priv}} = \mathbf{0}$. Since anyone can encrypt to the public slot, it is impossible to hide the public slot part $\mathbf{v}_{\mathrm{pub}}$ of a secret-key vector $\mathbf{v}$. As a result, slotted IPFE guarantees function-hiding only w.r.t. the private slot, and the weaker indistinguishability security w.r.t. the public slot. Based on the construction of slotted IPFE in [49], we obtain adaptively secure slotted IPFE based on k-Lin.

The aforementioned secret-key ABE scheme can be easily turned into a public-key one with slotted IPFE: The ABE encryption algorithm simply uses IPFE.SlotEnc and mpk to encrypt to the public slots. In the security proof, we move vectors encrypted in the public slot of the challenge ciphertext to the private slot, where function-hiding holds and the same security arguments outlined above can be carried out.

Discussion. Our method can be viewed as using IPFE to implement dual system encryption [57]. We believe that IPFE provides a valuable abstraction, making it conceptually simpler to design strategies for moving information between the secret key and the ciphertext, as done in the proof of 1-ABE, and for generating independent randomness, as done in the proof of full ABE. The benefit of this abstraction is even more prominent when it comes to ABE for logspace Turing machines.

2.3   1-ABE for Logspace Turing Machines

We now present ideas for constructing 1-ABE for L, and then its extension to NL and how to handle DFA and NFA as special cases for better efficiency. Moving to full-fledged ABE follows the same ideas in the previous subsection, though slightly more complicated, which we omit in this overview.

1-ABE for L enables generating a single secret key $\mathsf{sk}(M, \mu)$ for a Turing machine M and secret μ, and a ciphertext $\mathsf{ct}(\mathbf{x}, T, S)$ specifying an input $\mathbf{x}$ of length N, a polynomial time bound $T = \mathrm{poly}(N)$, and a logarithmic space bound $S = O(\log N)$ such that decryption reveals $\mu M|_{N,T,S}(\mathbf{x})$, where $M|_{N,T,S}(\mathbf{x})$ represents the computation of running $M(\mathbf{x})$ for T steps with a work tape of size S, which outputs 1 if and only if the computation lands in an accepting state after T steps and has *never* exceeded the space bound S. A key feature of ABE for uniform computation is that a secret key $\mathsf{sk}(M, \mu)$ can decrypt ciphertexts with inputs of unbounded lengths and unbounded time/(logarithmic) space bounds.

(In contrast, for non-uniform computation, the secret key decides the input length and time/space bounds.) Our 1-ABE for L follows the same blueprint of combining AKGS with IPFE, but uses new ideas in order to implement the unique feature of ABE for uniform computation.

Notations for Turing Machines. We start with introducing notations for logspace Turing machines (TM) over the binary alphabet. A TM $M = (Q, q_{acc}, \delta)$ consists of Q states, with the initial state being 1 and an accepting state[9] $q_{acc} \in [Q]$, and a transition function δ. The computation of $M|_{N,T,S}(\mathbf{x})$ goes through a sequence of $T + 1$ *configurations* $(\mathbf{x}, (i, j, \mathbf{W}, q))$, where $i \in [N]$ is the input tape pointer, $j \in [S]$ the work tape pointer, $\mathbf{W} \in \{0,1\}^S$ the content of the work tape, and $q \in [Q]$ the state. The initial *internal* configuration is thus $(i = 1, j = 1, \mathbf{W} = \mathbf{0}_S, q = 1)$, and the transition from one internal configuration $(i, j, \mathbf{W}, q)$ to the next $(i', j', \mathbf{W}', q')$ is governed by the transition function δ and the input $\mathbf{x}$. Namely, if $\delta(q, \mathbf{x}[i], \mathbf{W}[j]) = (q', w', \Delta i, \Delta j)$,

$$(i, j, \mathbf{W}, q) \to (i' = i + \Delta i, \ j' = j + \Delta j, \ \mathbf{W}' = \mathsf{overwrite}(\mathbf{W}, j, w'), \ q').$$

In other words, the transition function δ on input state q and bits $\mathbf{x}[i]$, $\mathbf{W}[j]$ on the input and work tape under scan, outputs the next state q', the new bit $w' \in \{0,1\}$ to be written to the work tape, and the directions $\Delta i, \Delta j \in \{0, \pm 1\}$ to move the input and work tape pointers. The next internal configuration is then derived by updating the current configuration accordingly, where $\mathbf{W}' = \mathsf{overwrite}(\mathbf{W}, j, w')$ is a vector obtained by overwriting the jth cell of $\mathbf{W}$ with w' and keeping the other cells unchanged.

AKGS for Logspace Turing Machines. To obtain an AKGS for L, we represent the TM computation algebraically as a sequence of matrix multiplications over $\mathbb{Z}_p$, for which we design an AKGS. To do so, we represent each internal configuration as a basis vector $\mathbf{e}_{(i,j,\mathbf{W},q)}$ of dimension $NS2^SQ$ with a single 1 at position $(i, j, \mathbf{W}, q)$. We want to find a *transition matrix* $\mathbf{M}(\mathbf{x})$ (depending on δ and $\mathbf{x}$) such that moving to the next state $\mathbf{e}_{(i',j',\mathbf{W}',q')}$ simply involves (right) multiplying $\mathbf{M}(\mathbf{x})$, i.e., $\mathbf{e}_{(i,j,\mathbf{W},q)}^{\mathsf{T}} \mathbf{M}(\mathbf{x}) = \mathbf{e}_{(i',j',\mathbf{W}',q')}^{\mathsf{T}}$. It is easy to verify that the correct transition matrix is

$$\mathbf{M}(\mathbf{x})[(i, j, \mathbf{W}, q), (i', j', \mathbf{W}', q')] = \mathsf{CanTransit}[(i, j, \mathbf{W}), (i', j', \mathbf{W}')]$$
$$\times \mathbf{M}_{\mathbf{x}[i], \mathbf{W}[j], \mathbf{W}'[j], i'-i, j'-j}[q, q'], \qquad (4)$$

$$\mathsf{CanTransit}[(i, j, \mathbf{W}), (i', j', \mathbf{W}')] = 1 \quad \text{iff } \mathbf{W}'[\neq j] = \mathbf{W}[\neq j] \text{ and}$$
$$i' - i, j' - j \in \{0, \pm 1\},$$
$$\mathbf{M}_{x,w,w',\Delta i,\Delta j}[q, q'] = 1 \quad \text{iff } \delta(q, x, w') = (q', w', \Delta i, \Delta j). \qquad (5)$$

Here, $\mathsf{CanTransit}[(i, j, \mathbf{W}), (i'j', \mathbf{W}')]$ indicates whether it is possible, irrespective of δ, to move from an internal configuration with $(i, j, \mathbf{W})$ to one with $(i', j', \mathbf{W}')$. If possible, then $\mathbf{M}_{\mathbf{x}[i], \mathbf{W}[j], \mathbf{W}'[j], \Delta i, \Delta j}[q, q']$ indicates whether δ permits moving

---

[9] For simplicity, in this overview, we assume there is only one accepting state.

from state q with current read bits $x = \mathbf{x}[i], w = \mathbf{W}[j]$ to state q' with overwriting bit $w' = \mathbf{W}'[j]$ and moving directions $\Delta i = i' - i, \Delta j = j' - j$. Armed with this, the TM computation can be done by right multiplying the matrix $\mathbf{M}(\mathbf{x})$ for T times with the initial configuration $\mathbf{e}_{(1,1,0,1)}^{\mathsf{T}}$, reaching the final configuration $\mathbf{e}_{(i_T,j_T,\mathbf{W}_T,q_T)}^{\mathsf{T}}$, and then testing whether $q_T = q_{\mathrm{acc}}$. More precisely,

$$M|_{N,T,S}(\mathbf{x}) = \mathbf{e}_{(1,1,0,1)}^{\mathsf{T}} \big(\mathbf{M}(\mathbf{x}) \big)^T \mathbf{t} \text{ for } \mathbf{t} = \mathbf{1}_{NS2^S} \otimes \mathbf{e}_{q_{\mathrm{acc}}}.$$

To construct AKGS for L, it boils down to construct AKGS for matrix multiplication. Our construction is inspired by the randomized encoding for arithmetic NC^1 scheme of [11] and the garbling mechanism for multiplication gates in [19]. Let us focus on garbling the computation $M|_{N,T,S}(\mathbf{x})$ with secrets $\alpha = \mu$ and $\beta = 0$ (the case needed in our 1-ABE). The garbling algorithm Garble produces the following affine label functions of $\mathbf{x}$:

$$\ell_{\mathrm{init}} = L_{\mathrm{init}}(\mathbf{x}) = \mathbf{e}_{(1,1,0,1)}^{\mathsf{T}} \mathbf{r}_0,$$

$$t \in [T]: \quad \boldsymbol{\ell}_t = (\ell_{t,z}) = \big(L_{t,z}(\mathbf{x}) \big)_z = -\boxed{\mathbf{r}_{t-1}} + \mathbf{M}(\mathbf{x})\mathbf{r}_t,$$

$$\ell_{T+1} = (\ell_{T+1,z})_z = \big(L_{T+1,z}(\mathbf{x}) \big)_z = -\boxed{\mathbf{r}_T} + \mu\mathbf{t}.$$

Here, $z = (i, j, \mathbf{W}, q)$ runs through all $NS2^SQ$ possible internal configurations and $\mathbf{r}_t \xleftarrow{\$} \mathbb{Z}_p^{[N] \times [S] \times \{0,1\}^S \times [Q]}$. The evaluation proceeds inductively, starting with $\ell_{\mathrm{init}} = \mathbf{e}_{(1,1,0,1)}^{\mathsf{T}} \mathbf{r}_0$, going through $\mathbf{c}_{(i_t,j_t,\mathbf{W}_t,q_t)}^{\mathsf{T}} \mathbf{r}_t$ for every $t \in [T]$ using the identity below, and completing after T steps by combining $\mathbf{e}_{(i_T,j_T,\mathbf{W}_T,q_T)}^{\mathsf{T}} \mathbf{r}_T$ with ℓ_{T+1} to get $\mathbf{e}_{(i_T,j_T,\mathbf{W}_T,q_T)}^{\mathsf{T}} \mu\mathbf{t} = \mu M|_{N,T,S}(\mathbf{x})$ as desired:

$$\mathbf{e}_{(i_{t+1},j_{t+1},\mathbf{W}_{t+1},q_{t+1})}^{\mathsf{T}} \mathbf{r}_{t+1} = \mathbf{e}_{(i_t,j_t,\mathbf{W}_t,q_t)}^{\mathsf{T}} \mathbf{r}_t + \mathbf{e}_{(i_t,j_t,\mathbf{W}_t,q_t)}^{\mathsf{T}} \underbrace{(-\mathbf{r}_t + \mathbf{M}(\mathbf{x})\mathbf{r}_{t+1})}_{\ell_{t+1}}.$$

We now show that the above AKGS is *piecewise secure*. First, ℓ_{init} is reversely sampleable. Since Eval is linear in the labels and ℓ_{init} has coefficient 1, given all but the first label ℓ_{init}, one can reversely sample ℓ_{init}, the value uniquely determined by the linear equation[10] imposed by the correctness of Eval. Second, the marginal randomness property holds because every label $\boldsymbol{\ell}_t$ is random due to the random additive term $\mathbf{r}_{t-1}$ that is not used in subsequent label functions $L_{t',z}$ for all $t' > t$ and z, nor in the non-constant terms of $L_{t,z}$'s—we call $\mathbf{r}_{t-1}$ the *randomizers* of $\boldsymbol{\ell}_t$ (highlighted in the box). Lastly, we observe that the size of the garbling is $(T+1)NS2^SQ + 1$.

1-ABE for L. We now try to construct 1-ABE for L from AKGS for L, following the same blueprint of using IPFE. Yet, applying the exact same method for non-uniform computation fails for multiple reasons. In 1-ABE for non-uniform computation, the ciphertext ct contains a single IPFE ciphertext ict encoding

---

[10] This means RevSamp is deterministic, and we can reversely sample ℓ_{init} *in the exponent* and when the randomness is not uniform, which is important for our construction.

$(1, \mathbf{x})$, and the secret key sk contains a set of IPFE secret keys isk_j encoding all the label functions. However, in the uniform setting, the secret key $\mathsf{sk}(M, \mu)$ depends only on the TM M and the secret μ, and is supposed to work with ciphertexts $\mathsf{ct}(\mathbf{x}, T, S)$ with unbounded $N = |\mathbf{x}|, T, S$. Therefore, at key generation time, the size of the AKGS garbling, $(T + 1)NS2^SQ + 1$, is *unknown*, let alone generating and encoding all the label functions. Moreover, we want our 1-ABE to be compact, with secret key size $|\mathsf{sk}| = O(Q)$ linear in the number Q of states and ciphertext size $|\mathsf{ct}| = O(TNS2^S)$ (ignoring polynomial factors in the security parameter). The total size of secret key and ciphertext is much smaller than the total number of label functions, i.e., $|\mathsf{sk}| + |\mathsf{ct}| \ll (T + 1)NS2^SQ + 1$.

To overcome these challenges, our idea is that instead of encoding the label functions in the secret key or the ciphertext (for which there is not enough space), we let the secret key and the ciphertext jointly generate the label functions. For this idea to work, the label functions cannot be generated with true randomness which cannot be "compressed", and must use pseudorandomness instead. More specifically, our 1-ABE secret key $\mathsf{sk}(M, \mu)$ contains $\sim Q$ IPFE secret keys $\{\mathsf{isk}(\mathbf{v}_j)\}_j$, while the ciphertext $\mathsf{ct}(\mathbf{x}, T, S)$ contains $\sim TNS2^S$ IPFE ciphertexts $\{\mathsf{ict}(\mathbf{u}_i)\}_i$, such that decryption computes in the exponent $\sim TNS2^SQ$ cross inner products $\langle \mathbf{u}_i, \mathbf{v}_j \rangle$ that correspond to a garbling of $M|_{N,T,S}(\mathbf{x})$ with secret μ. To achieve this, we rely crucially on the special *block structure* of the transition matrix $\mathbf{M}$ (which in turn stems from the structure of TM computation, where the same transition function is applied in every step). Furthermore, as discussed above, we replace every truly random value $\mathbf{r}_t[i, j, \mathbf{W}, q]$ with a product $\mathbf{r}_\mathbf{x}[t, i, j, \mathbf{W}]\mathbf{r}_\mathsf{f}[q]$, which can be shown pseudorandom in the exponent based on SXDH.[11]

Block Structure of the Transition Matrix. Let us examine the transition matrix again (cf. Eqs. (4) and (5)):

$$\mathbf{M}(\mathbf{x})[(i, j, \mathbf{W}, q), (i', j', \mathbf{W}', q')] = \mathsf{CanTransit}[(i, j, \mathbf{W}), (i', j', \mathbf{W}')]$$
$$\times \mathbf{M}_{\mathbf{x}[i], \mathbf{W}[j], \mathbf{W}'[j], i'-i, j'-j}[q, q'].$$

We see that that every block $\mathbf{M}(\mathbf{x})[(i, j, \mathbf{W}, \llcorner), (i', j', \mathbf{W}', \llcorner)]$ either is the $Q \times Q$ zero matrix or belongs to a small set $\mathcal{T}$ of a constant number of *transition blocks*:

$$\mathcal{T} = \big\{ \mathbf{M}_{x, w, w', \Delta i, \Delta j} \,\big|\, x, w, w' \in \{0, 1\}, \Delta i, \Delta j \in \{0, \pm 1\} \big\}.$$

Moreover, in the $\mathsf{i} = (i, j, \mathbf{W})^{\text{th}}$ "block row", $\mathbf{M}(\mathbf{x})[(\mathsf{i}, \llcorner), (\llcorner, \llcorner, \llcorner, \llcorner)]$, each transition block $\mathbf{M}_{x, w, w', \Delta i, \Delta j}$ either does not appear at all if $x \neq \mathbf{x}[i]$ or $w' \neq \mathbf{W}[j]$,

---

[11] Our scheme readily extends to be based on k-Lin. However, that makes the scheme more complex to present. We choose to present this scheme using SXDH in this paper.

or appears once as the block $\mathbf{M}(\mathbf{x})[(\mathsf{i}, \lrcorner), (\mathsf{i}', \lrcorner)]$, where i' is the triplet obtained by updating i appropriately according to $(w', \Delta i, \Delta j)$:

$$\mathsf{i}' \overset{\text{def}}{=} \mathsf{i} \boxplus (w', \Delta i, \Delta j) = (i + \Delta i,\ j + \Delta j,\ \mathbf{W}' = \mathsf{overwrite}(\mathbf{W}, j, w')),$$
$$\mathbf{M}(\mathbf{x})[(\mathsf{i}, \lrcorner), (\mathsf{i}', \lrcorner)] = \mathbf{M}_{\mathbf{x}[i], \mathbf{W}[j], w', \Delta i, \Delta j}.$$

Thus we can "decompose" every label $\ell_t[\mathsf{i}, q]$ as an inner product $\langle \mathbf{u}_{t,\mathsf{i}}, \mathbf{v}_q \rangle$ as

$$
\begin{aligned}
\ell_t[\mathsf{i}, q] &= -\mathbf{r}_{t-1}[\mathsf{i}, q] + \mathbf{M}(\mathbf{x})[(\mathsf{i}, q)(\lrcorner, \lrcorner, \lrcorner, \lrcorner)]\mathbf{r}_t \\
&= -\mathbf{r}_{t-1}[\mathsf{i}, q] + \sum_{w', \Delta i, \Delta j} \left(\mathbf{M}_{\mathbf{x}[i], \mathbf{W}[j], w', \Delta i, \Delta j} \mathbf{r}_t[\mathsf{i}', \lrcorner]\right)[q] \quad (\mathsf{i}' = \mathsf{i} \boxplus (w', \Delta i, \Delta j)) \\
&= -\mathbf{r}_{\mathbf{x}}[t-1, i]\mathbf{r}_{\mathbf{f}}[q] + \sum_{w', \Delta i, \Delta j} \mathbf{r}_{\mathbf{x}}[t, i'] \left(\mathbf{M}_{\mathbf{x}[i], \mathbf{W}[j], w', \Delta i, \Delta j} \mathbf{r}_{\mathbf{f}}\right)[q] \\
&= \langle \mathbf{u}_{t,\mathsf{i}}, \mathbf{v}_q \rangle, \qquad\qquad \left(\mathbf{r}_{t''}[\mathsf{i}'', q''] = \mathbf{r}_{\mathbf{x}}[t'', i'']\mathbf{r}_{\mathbf{f}}[q'']\right)
\end{aligned}
$$

where vectors $\mathbf{u}_{t,\mathsf{i}}$ and $\mathbf{v}_q$ are as follows, with $\mathbb{1}\{\cdots\}$ indicating if the conditions (its argument) are true:

$$
\begin{aligned}
\mathbf{u}_{t,\mathsf{i}} &= (\ \mathbf{r}_{\mathbf{x}}[t-1, i] \ \| \ \cdots \ \| \ \mathbf{r}_{\mathbf{x}}[t, i'] \cdot \mathbb{1}\{x = \mathbf{x}[i], w = \mathbf{W}[j]\} \ \| \ \cdots \ \| \ \mathbf{0}), \\
\mathbf{v}_q &= (\quad -\mathbf{r}_{\mathbf{f}}[q] \quad \| \ \cdots \ \| \qquad (\mathbf{M}_{x, w, w', \Delta i, \Delta j} \mathbf{r}_{\mathbf{f}})[q] \qquad \| \ \cdots \ \| \ \mathbf{0}).
\end{aligned}
$$

Similarly, we can "decompose" $\ell_{\mathsf{init}} = \mathbf{e}_{1,1,0,1}^{\mathsf{T}} \mathbf{r}_0$ as $\langle \mathbf{r}_{\mathbf{x}}[0, 1, 1, 0], \mathbf{r}_{\mathbf{f}}[1] \rangle$. (For simplicity in the discussion below, we omit details on how to handle ℓ_{T+1}.) Given such decomposition, our semi-compact 1-ABE scheme follows immediately by using IPFE to compute the garbling:

Honest Algorithms

$$
\begin{aligned}
\mathsf{sk}(M, \mu): \mathsf{isk}_{\mathsf{init}}(\quad \mathbf{r}_{\mathbf{f}}[1] \quad \| \ \mathbf{0}\ ), \quad &\forall q: \quad \mathsf{isk}_q(\ \mathbf{u}_{t,\mathsf{i}} \ \| \ \mathbf{0}\ ) \\
\mathsf{ct}(\mathbf{x}, T, S): \mathsf{ict}_{\mathsf{init}}(\ \mathbf{r}_{\mathbf{x}}[0, 1, 1, 0] \ \| \ \mathbf{0}\ ), \quad &\forall t, \mathsf{i}: \ \mathsf{ict}_{t,\mathsf{i}}(\ \mathbf{v}_q \ \| \ \mathbf{0}\ )
\end{aligned}
$$

Decrypting the pair $\mathsf{isk}_{\mathsf{init}}, \mathsf{ict}_{\mathsf{init}}$ (generated using one master secret key) gives exactly the first label ℓ_{init}, while decrypting $\mathsf{isk}_q, \mathsf{ict}_{t,\mathsf{i}}$ (generated using another master secret key) gives the label $\ell_t[\mathsf{i}, q]$ in the exponent, generated using pseudorandomness $\mathbf{r}_t[\mathsf{i}, q] = \mathbf{r}_{\mathbf{x}}[t, i]\mathbf{r}_{\mathbf{f}}[q]$. Note that the honest algorithms encode $\mathbf{r}_{\mathbf{f}}[q]$ (in $\mathbf{v}_q$) and $\mathbf{r}_{\mathbf{x}}[t, i]$ (in $\mathbf{u}_{t,\mathsf{i}}$) in IPFE secret keys and ciphertexts that use the *two* source groups G_1 and G_2 respectively. As such, we cannot directly use the SXDH assumption to argue the pseudorandomness of $\mathbf{r}_t[\mathsf{i}, q]$. In the security proof, we will use the function-hiding property of IPFE to move both $\mathbf{r}_{\mathbf{x}}[t, i]$ and $\mathbf{r}_{\mathbf{f}}[q]$ into the same source group before invoking SXDH.

Adaptive Security. To show adaptive security, we follow the same blueprint of going through a sequence of hybrids, where we first hardcode ℓ_{init} and sample it reversely using RevSamp, and next simulate the other labels $\ell_t[\mathsf{i}, q]$ one by one. Hardwiring ℓ_{init} is easy by relying on the function-hiding property of IPFE. However, it is now more difficult to simulate $\ell_t[\mathsf{i}, q]$ because (i) before simulating $\ell_t[\mathsf{i}, q]$, we need to switch its *randomizer* $\mathbf{r}_{t-1}[\mathsf{i}, q] = \mathbf{r}_{\mathbf{x}}[t-1, i]\mathbf{r}_{\mathbf{f}}[q]$ to truly random $\mathbf{r}_{t-1}[i,q] \xleftarrow{\$} \mathbb{Z}_p$, which enables us to simulate the label $\ell_t[i,q]$ as random; and (ii) to keep simulation progressing, we need to switch the random $\ell_t[i,q]$ back to a pseudorandom value $\ell_t[i,q] = \mathbf{s}_{\mathsf{x}}[t,i]\mathbf{s}_{\mathsf{f}}[q]$, as otherwise, there is not enough space to store all $\sim TNS2^S Q$ random labels $\ell_t[i,q]$.

We illustrate how to carry out above proof steps in the simpler case where the adversary queries for the ciphertext first and the secret key second. The other case where the secret key is queried first is handled using similar ideas, but the technicality becomes much more delicate.

In hybrid (t,i), the first label ℓ_{init} is reversely sampled and hardcoded in the secret key $\mathsf{isk}_{\mathsf{init}}$, i.e., $\mathsf{ict}_{\mathsf{init}}$ encrypts $(1 \parallel 0)$ and $\mathsf{isk}_{\mathsf{init}}$ encrypts $(\ell_{\mathsf{init}} \parallel 0)$ with $\ell_{\mathsf{init}} \leftarrow \mathsf{RevSamp}(\cdots)$. All labels $\ell_{t'}[i',q]$ with $(t',i') < (t,i)$ have been simulated as $\mathbf{s}_{\mathsf{x}}[t',i']\mathbf{s}_{\mathsf{f}}[q]$—observe that the ciphertext $\mathsf{ict}_{t',i'}$ encodes only $\mathbf{s}_{\mathsf{f}}[t',i']$ in the second slot, which is multiplied by $\mathbf{s}_{\mathsf{f}}[q]$ in the second slot of isk_q. On the other hand, all labels $\ell_{t'}[i',q]$ with $(t',i') \geq (t,i)$ are generated honestly as the honest algorithms do.

$$\text{Hybrid } (t,i),\ \boxed{\; (t,i):1 \;},\ \text{and}\ \boxed{(t,i)+1}$$

$\mathsf{ct}(\mathbf{x},T,S){:}$	$(t',i') < (t,i)$: $\mathsf{ict}_{t',i'}($	0	$\parallel$	$\mathbf{s}_{\mathsf{x}}[t',i']$	$\parallel$	0	$)$		
	$(t',i') = (t,i)$: $\mathsf{ict}_{t,i}$ ($ $\mathbf{u}_{t,i}$ $\boxed{0}\boxed{0}$	$\parallel$ 0 $\boxed{0}$	$\boxed{\mathbf{s}_{\mathsf{x}}[t,i]}$	$\parallel$ 0	$\boxed{1}$	$\boxed{0}$	$)$		
	$(t',i') > (t,i)$: $\mathsf{ict}_{t',i'}($	$\mathbf{u}_{t',i'}$	$\parallel$	0	$\parallel$	0	$)$		
$\mathsf{sk}(M,\mu){:}$	$q \in [Q]$: $\mathsf{isk}_q($	$\mathbf{v}_q$	$\parallel$	$\mathbf{s}_{\mathsf{f}}[q]$	$\parallel$ 0	$\boxed{\ell_t[i,q]}\,\boxed{0}$	$)$		

Moving from hybrid (t,i) to its successor $(t,i)+1$, the only difference is that labels $\ell_t[i,q]$ are switched from being honestly generated $\langle \mathbf{u}_{t,i}, \mathbf{v}_q \rangle$ to pseudorandom $\mathbf{s}_{\mathsf{x}}[t,i]\mathbf{s}_{\mathsf{f}}[q]$, as depicted above with values in the solid line box (the rest of the hybrid is identical to hybrid (t,i)). The transition can be done via an intermediate hybrid $(t,i):1$ with values in the dash line box. In this hybrid, all labels $\ell_t[i,q]$ produced as inner products of all $\mathbf{v}_q$'s and $\mathbf{u}_{t,i}$ are temporarily hardcoded in the secret keys isk_q, using the third slot (which is zeroed out in all the other $\mathbf{u}_{(t',i')\neq(t,i)}$'s). Furthermore, $\mathbf{u}_{t,i}$ is removed from $\mathsf{ict}_{t,i}$. As such, the random scalar $\mathbf{r}_{\mathsf{x}}[t-1,i]$ (formerly embedded in $\mathbf{u}_{t,i}$) no longer appears in the exponent of group G_1, and $\ell_{\mathsf{init}} \leftarrow \mathsf{RevSamp}(\cdots)$ can be performed using $\mathbf{r}_{\mathsf{x}}[t-1,i], \mathbf{r}_{\mathsf{f}}[q], \mathbf{r}_{t-1}[i,q]$ in the exponent of G_2. Therefore, we can invoke the SXDH assumption in G_2 to switch the randomizers $\mathbf{r}_{t-1}[i,q] = \mathbf{r}_{\mathsf{x}}[t-1,i]\mathbf{r}_{\mathsf{f}}[q]$ to be truly random, and hence so are the labels $\ell_t[i,q] \xleftarrow{\$} \mathbb{Z}_p$. By a similar argument, this intermediate hybrid $(t,i):1$ is also indistinguishable to $(t,i)+1$, as the random $\ell_t[i,q]$ can be switched to $\mathbf{s}_{\mathsf{x}}[t,i]\mathbf{s}_{\mathsf{f}}[q]$ in hybrid $(t,i)+1$, relying again on SXDH and the function-hiding property of IPFE. This concludes our argument of security in the simpler case where the ciphertext is queried first.

AKGS and 1-ABE for NL. Our construction of AKGS and 1-ABE essentially works for NL without modification, because the computation of a non-deterministic logspace Turing machine $M = ([Q], q_{\mathsf{acc}}, \delta)$ on an input $\mathbf{x}$ can also be represented as a sequence of matrix multiplications. We briefly describe how by pointing out the difference from L. The transition function δ of a non-deterministic TM dost not instruct a unique transition, but rather specifies a set of legitimate transitions. Following one internal configuration $(i, j, \mathbf{W}, q)$, there are potentially many legitimate successors:

$$(i, j, \mathbf{W}, q) \rightarrow \{(i' = i + \Delta i, j' = j + \Delta j, \mathbf{W}' = \text{overwrite}(\mathbf{W}, j, w'), q')$$
$$\mid (q', w', \Delta i, \Delta j) \in \delta(q, \mathbf{x}[i], \mathbf{W}[j])\}.$$

The computation is accepting if and only if *there exists* a path with T legitimate transitions starting from $(1, 1, \mathbf{0}, 1)$, through $(i_t, j_t, \mathbf{W}_t, q_t)$ for $t \in [T]$, and landing at $q_T = q_{\text{acc}}$.

Naturally, we modify the transition matrix as below to reflect all legitimate transitions. The only difference is that each transition block determined by δ may map a state q to multiple states q', as highlighted in the solid line box:

$$\mathbf{M}(\mathbf{x})[(i, j, \mathbf{W}, q), (i', j', \mathbf{W}', q')] = \text{CanTransit}[(i, j, \mathbf{W}), (i', j', \mathbf{W}')]$$
$$\times \mathbf{M}_{\mathbf{x}[i], \mathbf{W}[j], \mathbf{W}'[j], i'-i, j'-j}[q, q'],$$
$$\mathbf{M}_{x, w, w', \Delta i, \Delta j}[q, q'] = 1 \quad \text{iff} \quad (q', w', \Delta i, \Delta j) \boxed{\in} \delta(q, x, w').$$

Let us observe the effect of right multiplying $\mathbf{M}(\mathbf{x})$ to an $\mathbf{e}_{i,q}$ indicating configuration (i, q): $\mathbf{e}_{i,q}^{\mathsf{T}} \mathbf{M}(\mathbf{x})$ gives a vector $\mathbf{c}_1$ such that $\mathbf{c}_1[i', q'] = 1$ if and only if (i', q') is a legitimate next configuration. Multiplying $\mathbf{M}(\mathbf{x})$ one more time, $\mathbf{e}_{i,q}^{\mathsf{T}} (\mathbf{M}(\mathbf{x}))^2$ gives $\mathbf{c}_2$ where $\mathbf{c}_2[i', q']$ is the number of length-2 paths of legitimate transitions from (i, q) to (i', q'). Inductively, $\mathbf{e}_{i,q}^{\mathsf{T}} (\mathbf{M}(\mathbf{x}))^t$ yields $\mathbf{c}_t$ that counts the number of length-t paths from (i, q) to any other internal configuration (i', q'). Therefore, we can *arithmetize* the computation of M on $\mathbf{x}$ as

$$M|_{N,T,S}(\mathbf{x}) = \mathbf{e}_{(1,1,\mathbf{0},1)}^{\mathsf{T}} (\mathbf{M}(\mathbf{x}))^T \mathbf{t} \text{ for } \mathbf{t} = \mathbf{1}_{NS2^S} \otimes \mathbf{e}_{q_{\text{acc}}}. \tag{6}$$

Right multiplying $\mathbf{t}$ in the end sums up the number of paths to (i, q_{acc}) for all i in $\mathbf{c}_T$ (i.e., accepting paths).

If the computation is not accepting—there is no path to any (i, q_{acc})—the final sum would be 0 as desired. If the computation is accepting—there is a path to some (i, q_{acc})—then the sum should be non-zero (up to the following technicality). Now that we have represented NL computation as matrix multiplication, we immediately obtain AKGS and 1-ABE for NL using the same construction for L.

A Technicality in the Correctness for NL. The correctness of our scheme relies on the fact that when the computation is accepting, the matrix multiplication formula (Eq. (6)) counts correctly the total number of length-T accepting paths. However, a subtle issue is that in our 1-ABE, the matrix multiplications are carried out over $\mathbb{Z}_p$, where p is the order of the bilinear pairing groups. This means if the total number of accepting paths happens to be a multiple of p, the sequence of matrix multiplications mod p carried out in 1-ABE would return 0, while the correct output should be non-zero. This technicality can be circumvented if p is entropic with $\omega(\log n)$ bits of entropy and the computation $(M, \mathbf{x}, T, S)$ is independent of p. In that case, the probability that the number of accepting paths is a multiple of p is negligible. We can achieve this by letting the setup algorithm of 1-ABE sample the bilinear pairing groups from a distribution with entropic order. Then, we have statistical correctness for computations $(M, \mathbf{x}, T, S)$ chosen statically ahead of time (independent of p). We believe such *static* correctness is sufficient for most applications where correctness is meant for non-adversarial behaviors. However, if the computation $(M, \mathbf{x}, T, S)$ is chosen *adaptively* to make the number of accepting paths a multiple of p, then an accepting computation will be mistakenly rejected. We stress that security is unaffected since if an adversary chooses M and $(\mathbf{x}, T, S)$ as such, it only learns less information.

The Special Cases of DFA and NFA. DFA and NFA are special cases of L and NL, respectively, as they can be represented as Turing machines with a work tape of size $S = 1$ that always runs in time $T = N$, and the transition function δ always moves the input tape pointer to the right. Therefore, the internal configuration of a finite automaton contains only the state q, and the transition matrix $\mathbf{M}(x)$ is determined by δ and the current input bit x under scan. Different from the case of L and NL, here the transition matrix no longer keeps track of the input tape pointer since its move is fixed—the tth step uses the transition matrix $\mathbf{M}(\mathbf{x}[t])$ depending on $\mathbf{x}[t]$. Thus, the computation can be represented as follows:

$$M(\mathbf{x}) = \mathbf{e}_1^{\mathsf{T}} \prod_{t=1}^{N} \mathbf{M}(\mathbf{x}[t]) \cdot \mathbf{e}_{q_{\text{acc}}} = \mathbf{e}_1^{\mathsf{T}} \prod_{t=1}^{N} \left(\mathbf{M}_0(1 - \mathbf{x}[t]) + \mathbf{M}_1 \mathbf{x}[t] \right) \cdot \mathbf{e}_{q_{\text{acc}}},$$

$$\mathbf{M}_b[q, q'] = \mathbb{1}\{\delta(q, b) = q'\}.$$

Our construction of AKGS directly applies:

$$\ell_{\text{init}} = L_{\text{init}}(\mathbf{x}) = \mathbf{e}_1^{\mathsf{T}} \mathbf{r}_0,$$

$$t \in [N]: \quad \ell_t = \left(L_{t,q}(\mathbf{x}) \right)_{q \in [Q]} = -\mathbf{r}_{t-1} + \boxed{\mathbf{M}(\mathbf{x}[t])} \, \mathbf{r}_t, \quad \left(\mathbf{r}_{t-1}, \mathbf{r}_t \xleftarrow{\$} \mathbb{Z}_p^Q \right)$$

$$\ell_{N+1} = \left(L_{N+1,q}(\mathbf{x}) \right)_{q \in [Q]} = -\mathbf{r}_N + \mu \mathbf{e}_{q_{\text{acc}}}.$$

When using pseudorandomness $\mathbf{r}_t[q] = \mathbf{r}_{\text{f}}[q] \mathbf{r}_{\text{x}}[t]$, the labels $\ell_t[q]$ can be computed as the inner products of $\mathbf{v}_q = (-\mathbf{r}_{\text{f}}[q] \,\|\, (\mathbf{M}_0 \mathbf{r}_{\text{f}})[q] \,\|\, (\mathbf{M}_1 \mathbf{r}_{\text{f}})[q] \,\|\, \mathbf{0})$ and $\mathbf{u}_t = (\mathbf{r}_{\text{x}}[t-1] \,\|\, (1 - \mathbf{x}[t])\mathbf{r}_{\text{x}}[t] \,\|\, \mathbf{x}[t]\mathbf{r}_{\text{x}}[t] \,\|\, \mathbf{0})$. Applying our 1-ABE construction with respect to such "decomposition" gives *compact* 1-ABE for DFA and NFA with secret keys of size $O(Q)$ and ciphertexts of size $O(N)$.

Discussion. Prior to our work, there have been constructions of ABE for DFA based on pairing [1, 5, 12, 13, 29, 58] and ABE for NFA based on LWE [4]. However, no previous scheme achieves adaptive security unless based on q-type assumptions [12, 13]. The work of [20] constructed ABE for DFA, and that of [7] for random access machines, both based on LWE, but they only support inputs of bounded length, giving up the important advantage of uniform computation of handling unbounded-length inputs. There are also constructions of ABE (and even the stronger generalization, functional encryption) for Turing machines [3, 9, 28, 41] based on strong primitives such as multilinear map, extractable witness encryption, and indistinguishability obfuscation. However, these primitives are non-standard and currently not well-understood.

In terms of techniques, our work is most related to previous pairing-based ABE for DFA, in particular, the recent construction based on k-Lin [29]. These ABE schemes for DFA use a linear secret-sharing scheme for DFA first proposed in [58], and combining the secret key and ciphertext produces a secret-sharing in the exponent, which reveals the secret if and only if the DFA computation is accepting. Proving (even selective) security is complicated. Roughly speaking, the work of [29] relies on an *entropy propagation technique* to trace the DFA computation and propagate a few random masks "down" the computation path, with which they can argue that secret information related to states that are *backward reachable* from the final accepting states is hidden. The technique is implemented using the "nested two-slot" dual system encryption [23,33,46,47,54,57] combined with a combinatorial mechanism for propagation.

Our AKGS is a generalization of Waters' secret-sharing scheme to L and NL, and the optimized version for DFA is identical to Waters' secret-sharing scheme. Furthermore, our 1-ABE scheme from AKGS and IPFE is more modular. In particular, our proof (similar to our 1-ABE for non-uniform computation) does not reason about or trace the computation, and simply relies on the structure of AKGS. Using IPFE enables us to design sophisticated sequences of hybrids without getting lost in the algebra, as IPFE helps separating the logic of changes in different hybrids from how to implement the changes. For instance, we can easily manage multiple slots in the vectors encoded in IPFE for holding temporary values and generating pseudorandomness.

3 Preliminaries

Indexing. Let S be any set, we write $S^{\mathcal{I}}$ for the set of vectors whose entries are in S and indexed by $\mathcal{I}$, i.e., $S^{\mathcal{I}} = \{(\mathbf{v}[i])_{i \in \mathcal{I}} \mid \mathbf{v}[i] \in S\}$. Suppose $\mathfrak{s}_1, \mathfrak{s}_2$ are two index sets with $\mathfrak{s}_1 \subseteq \mathfrak{s}_2$. For any vector $\mathbf{v} \in \mathbb{Z}_p^{\mathfrak{s}_1}$, we write $\mathbf{u} = \mathbf{v}|^{\mathfrak{s}_2}$ for its zero-extension into $\mathbb{Z}_p^{\mathfrak{s}_2}$, i.e., $\mathbf{u} \in \mathbb{Z}_p^{\mathfrak{s}_2}$ and $\mathbf{u}[i] = \mathbf{v}[i]$ if $i \in \mathfrak{s}_1$ and 0 otherwise. Conversely, for any vector $\mathbf{v} \in \mathbb{Z}_p^{\mathfrak{s}_2}$, we write $\mathbf{u} = \mathbf{v}|_{\mathfrak{s}_1}$ for its canonical projection onto $\mathbb{Z}_p^{\mathfrak{s}_1}$, i.e., $\mathbf{u} \in \mathbb{Z}_p^{\mathfrak{s}_1}$ and $\mathbf{u}[i] = \mathbf{v}[i]$ for $i \in \mathfrak{s}_1$. Lastly, let $\mathbf{u}, \mathbf{v} \in \mathbb{Z}_p^{\mathfrak{s}}$, denote by $\langle \mathbf{u}, \mathbf{v} \rangle$ their inner product, i.e., $\sum_{i \in \mathfrak{s}} \mathbf{u}[i]\mathbf{v}[i]$.

Coefficient Vector. We conveniently associate an affine function $f : \mathbb{Z}_p^{\mathcal{I}} \to \mathbb{Z}_p$ with its coefficient vector $\mathbf{f} \in \mathbb{Z}_p^{\mathfrak{s}}$ (written as the same letter in boldface) for $\mathfrak{s} = \{\mathsf{const}\} \cup \{\mathsf{coef}_i \mid i \in \mathcal{I}\}$ such that $f(\mathbf{x}) = \mathbf{f}[\mathsf{const}] + \sum_{i \in \mathcal{I}} \mathbf{f}[\mathsf{coef}_i]\mathbf{x}[i]$.

3.1 Bilinear Pairing and Matrix Diffie-Hellman Assumption

Throughout the paper, we use a sequence of bilinear pairing groups

$$\mathcal{G} = \{(G_{\lambda,1}, G_{\lambda,2}, G_{\lambda,\mathrm{T}}, g_{\lambda,1}, g_{\lambda,2}, e_\lambda)\}_{\lambda \in \mathbb{N}},$$

where $G_{\lambda,1}, G_{\lambda,2}, G_{\lambda,\mathrm{T}}$ are groups of prime order $p = p(\lambda)$, and $G_{\lambda,1}$ (resp. $G_{\lambda,2}$) is generated by $g_{\lambda,1}$ (resp. $g_{\lambda,2}$). The maps $e_\lambda : G_{\lambda,1} \times G_{\lambda,2} \to G_{\lambda,\mathrm{T}}$ are

- *bilinear:* $e_\lambda(g_{\lambda,1}^a, g_{\lambda,2}^b) = \left(e_\lambda(g_{\lambda,1}, g_{\lambda,2})\right)^{ab}$ for all a, b; and
- *non-degenerate:* $e_\lambda(g_{\lambda,1}, g_{\lambda,2})$ generates $G_{\lambda,T}$.

Implicitly, we set $g_{\lambda,T} = e(g_{\lambda,1}, g_{\lambda,2})$. We require the group operations as well as the bilinear maps be efficiently computable.

Bracket Notation. Fix a security parameter, for $i = 1, 2, T$, we write $[\![\mathbf{A}]\!]_i$ for $g_{\lambda,i}^{\mathbf{A}}$, where the exponentiation is element-wise. When bracket notation is used, group operation is written additively, so $[\![\mathbf{A} + \mathbf{B}]\!]_i = [\![\mathbf{A}]\!]_i + [\![\mathbf{B}]\!]_i$ for matrices $\mathbf{A}, \mathbf{B}$. Pairing operation is written multiplicatively so that $[\![\mathbf{A}]\!]_1 [\![\mathbf{B}]\!]_2 = [\![\mathbf{AB}]\!]_T$. Furthermore, numbers can always operate with group elements, e.g., $[\![\mathbf{A}]\!]_1 \mathbf{B} = [\![\mathbf{AB}]\!]_1$.

Matrix Diffie-Hellman Assumption. In this work, we rely on the MDDH assumptions defined in [26], which is implied by k-Lin.

Definition 1 (MDDH$_k$ [26]). *Let $k \geq 1$ be an integer constant. For a sequence of pairing groups $\mathcal{G}$ of order $p(\lambda)$, MDDH$_k$ holds in G_i ($i = 1, 2, T$) if*

$$\{([\![\mathbf{A}]\!]_i, [\![\mathbf{s}^\mathsf{T}\mathbf{A}]\!]_i)\}_{\lambda \in \mathbb{N}} \approx \{([\![\mathbf{A}]\!]_i, [\![\mathbf{c}^\mathsf{T}]\!]_i)\}_{\lambda \in \mathbb{N}} \text{ for } \mathbf{A} \xleftarrow{\$} \mathbb{Z}_{p(\lambda)}^{k \times (k+1)}, \mathbf{s} \xleftarrow{\$} \mathbb{Z}_{p(\lambda)}^k, \mathbf{c} \xleftarrow{\$} \mathbb{Z}_{p(\lambda)}^{k+1}.$$

3.2 Attribute-Based Encryption

Definition 2. *Let $\mathcal{M} = \{M_\lambda\}_{\lambda \in \mathbb{N}}$ be a sequence of message sets. Let $\mathcal{P} = \{\mathcal{P}_\lambda\}_{\lambda \in \mathbb{N}}$ be a sequence of families of predicates, where $\mathcal{P}_\lambda = \{P : X_P \times Y_P \to \{0, 1\}\}$. An attribute-based encryption (ABE) scheme for message space $\mathcal{M}$ and predicate space $\mathcal{P}$ consists of 4 efficient algorithms:*

- Setup($1^\lambda, P \in \mathcal{P}_\lambda$) *generates a pair of master public/secret key* (mpk, msk).
- KeyGen(1^λ, msk, $y \in Y_P$) *generates a secret key* sk$_y$ *associated with y.*
- Enc(1^λ, mpk, $x \in X_P, g \in M_\lambda$) *generates a ciphertext* ct$_{x,g}$ *for g associated with x.*
- Dec(1^λ, sk, ct) *outputs either $\perp$ or a message in M_λ.*

Correctness requires that for all $\lambda \in \mathbb{N}$, all $P \in \mathcal{P}_\lambda, g \in M_\lambda$, and all $y \in Y_P, x \in X_P$ such that $P(x, y) = 1$,

$$\Pr\left[\begin{array}{l} (\mathsf{mpk}, \mathsf{msk}) \xleftarrow{\$} \mathsf{Setup}(1^\lambda, P) \\ \mathsf{sk} \xleftarrow{\$} \mathsf{KeyGen}(1^\lambda, \mathsf{msk}, y) : \mathsf{Dec}(1^\lambda, \mathsf{sk}, \mathsf{ct}) = g \\ \mathsf{ct} \xleftarrow{\$} \mathsf{Enc}(1^\lambda, \mathsf{mpk}, x, g) \end{array}\right] = 1.$$

The basic security requirement of an ABE scheme stipulates that no information about the message can be inferred as long as each individual secret key the adversary receives does not allow decryption. The adversary is given the master public key and allowed arbitrarily many secret key and ciphertexts queries. For the secret key queries, the adversary is given the secret key for a policy of its choice. For the ciphertext queries, the adversary is either given a correct encryption to the message or an encryption of a random message. It has to decide whether the encryptions it receives are correct or random. We stress that in the *adaptive* setting considered in this work, the secret key and ciphertext queries can arbitrarily interleave and depend on responses to previous queries. The definition is standard in the literature, and we refer the readers to [32] or the full version for details.

3.3 Function-Hiding Slotted Inner-Product Functional Encryption

Definition 3 (pairing-based slotted IPFE). *Let $\mathcal{G}$ be a sequence of pairing groups of order $p(\lambda)$. A slotted inner-product functional encryption (IPFE) scheme based on $\mathcal{G}$ consists of 5 efficient algorithms:*

- Setup$(1^\lambda, \mathfrak{s}_{\mathrm{pub}}, \mathfrak{s}_{\mathrm{priv}})$ *takes as input two disjoint index sets, the public slot $\mathfrak{s}_{\mathrm{pub}}$ and the private slot $\mathfrak{s}_{\mathrm{priv}}$, and outputs a pair of master public key and master secret key* (mpk, msk)*. The whole index set $\mathfrak{s}$ is $\mathfrak{s}_{\mathrm{pub}} \cup \mathfrak{s}_{\mathrm{priv}}$.*
- KeyGen$(1^\lambda, \mathsf{msk}, [\![\mathbf{v}]\!]_2)$ *generates a secret key $\mathsf{sk}_{\mathbf{v}}$ for $\mathbf{v} \in \mathbb{Z}_{p(\lambda)}^{\mathfrak{s}}$.*
- Enc$(1^\lambda, \mathsf{msk}, [\![\mathbf{u}]\!]_1)$ *generates a ciphertext $\mathsf{ct}_{\mathbf{u}}$ for $\mathbf{u} \in \mathbb{Z}_{p(\lambda)}^{\mathfrak{s}}$ using the master secret key.*
- Dec$(1^\lambda, \mathsf{sk}_{\mathbf{v}}, \mathsf{ct}_{\mathbf{u}})$ *is supposed to compute $[\![\langle \mathbf{u}, \mathbf{v} \rangle]\!]_{\mathrm{T}}$.*
- SlotEnc$(1^\lambda, \mathsf{mpk}, [\![\mathbf{u}]\!]_1)$ *generates a ciphertext ct for $\mathbf{u}|^{\mathfrak{s}}$ when given input $\mathbf{u} \in \mathbb{Z}_{p(\lambda)}^{\mathfrak{s}_{\mathrm{pub}}}$ using the master public key.*

Decryption correctness *requires that for all $\lambda \in \mathbb{N}$, all index set $\mathfrak{s}$, and all vectors $\mathbf{u}, \mathbf{v} \in \mathbb{Z}_{p(\lambda)}^{\mathfrak{s}}$,*

$$\Pr\left[\begin{array}{l} \mathsf{msk} \xleftarrow{\$} \mathsf{Setup}(1^\lambda, \mathfrak{s}) \\ \mathsf{sk} \xleftarrow{\$} \mathsf{KeyGen}(1^\lambda, \mathsf{msk}, [\![\mathbf{v}]\!]_2) : \mathsf{Dec}(1^\lambda, \mathsf{sk}, \mathsf{ct}) = [\![\langle \mathbf{u}, \mathbf{v} \rangle]\!]_{\mathrm{T}} \\ \mathsf{ct} \xleftarrow{\$} \mathsf{Enc}(1^\lambda, \mathsf{msk}, [\![\mathbf{u}]\!]_1) \end{array}\right] = 1.$$

Slot-mode correctness *requires that for all $\lambda \in \mathbb{N}$, all disjoint index sets $\mathfrak{s}_{\mathrm{pub}}, \mathfrak{s}_{\mathrm{priv}}$, and all vector $\mathbf{u} \in \mathbb{Z}_{p(\lambda)}^{\mathfrak{s}_{\mathrm{pub}}}$, the following distributions should be identical:*

$$\left\{ \begin{array}{l} (\mathsf{mpk}, \mathsf{msk}) \xleftarrow{\$} \mathsf{Setup}(1^\lambda, \mathfrak{s}_{\mathrm{pub}}, \mathfrak{s}_{\mathrm{priv}}) \\ \mathsf{ct} \xleftarrow{\$} \mathsf{Enc}(1^\lambda, \mathsf{msk}, [\![\mathbf{u}|^{\mathfrak{s}}]\!]_1) \end{array} : (\mathsf{mpk}, \mathsf{msk}, \mathsf{ct}) \right\},$$

$$\left\{ \begin{array}{l} (\mathsf{mpk}, \mathsf{msk}) \xleftarrow{\$} \mathsf{Setup}(1^\lambda, \mathfrak{s}_{\mathrm{pub}}, \mathfrak{s}_{\mathrm{priv}}) \\ \mathsf{ct} \xleftarrow{\$} \mathsf{SlotEnc}(1^\lambda, \mathsf{mpk}, [\![\mathbf{u}]\!]_1) \end{array} : (\mathsf{mpk}, \mathsf{msk}, \mathsf{ct}) \right\}.$$

Slotted IPFE generalizes both secret-key and public-key IPFEs: A secret-key IPFE can be obtained by setting $\mathfrak{s}_{\mathrm{pub}} = \varnothing$ and $\mathfrak{s}_{\mathrm{priv}} = \mathfrak{s}$; a public-key IPFE can be obtained by setting $\mathfrak{s}_{\mathrm{pub}} = \mathfrak{s}$ and $\mathfrak{s}_{\mathrm{priv}} = \varnothing$.

We now define the adaptive *function-hiding* property.

Definition 4 (function-hiding slotted IPFE). *Let* (Setup, KeyGen, Enc, Dec, SlotEnc) *be a slotted IPFE. The scheme is* function-hiding *if $\mathsf{Exp}_{\mathrm{FH}}^0 \approx \mathsf{Exp}_{\mathrm{FH}}^1$, where $\mathsf{Exp}_{\mathrm{FH}}^b$ for $b \in \{0, 1\}$ is defined as follows:*

- **Setup.** *Run the adversary* $\mathcal{A}(1^\lambda)$ *and receive two disjoint index sets* $\mathfrak{S}_{\mathrm{pub}}, \mathfrak{S}_{\mathrm{priv}}$ *from* $\mathcal{A}$*. Let* $\mathfrak{S} = \mathfrak{S}_{\mathrm{pub}} \cup \mathfrak{S}_{\mathrm{priv}}$*. Run* $(\mathsf{mpk}, \mathsf{msk}) \xleftarrow{\$} \mathsf{Setup}(1^\lambda, \mathfrak{S}_{\mathrm{pub}}, \mathfrak{S}_{\mathrm{priv}})$ *and return* mpk *to* $\mathcal{A}$*.*
- **Challenge.** *Repeat the following for arbitrarily many rounds determined by* $\mathcal{A}$*: In each round,* $\mathcal{A}$ *has 2 options.*
  - $\mathcal{A}$ *can submit* $[\![\mathbf{v}_j^0]\!]_2, [\![\mathbf{v}_j^1]\!]_2$ *for a secret key, where* $\mathbf{v}_j^0, \mathbf{v}_j^1 \in \mathbb{Z}_p^5$*. Upon this query, run* $\mathsf{sk}_j \xleftarrow{\$} \mathsf{KeyGen}(1^\lambda, \mathsf{msk}, [\![\mathbf{v}_j^b]\!]_2)$ *and return* sk_j *to* $\mathcal{A}$*.*
  - $\mathcal{A}$ *can submit* $[\![\mathbf{u}_i^0]\!]_1, [\![\mathbf{u}_i^1]\!]_1$ *for a ciphertext, where* $\mathbf{u}_i^0, \mathbf{u}_i^1 \in \mathbb{Z}_p^5$*. Upon this query, run* $\mathsf{ct}_i \xleftarrow{\$} \mathsf{Enc}(1^\lambda, \mathsf{msk}, [\![\mathbf{u}_i^b]\!]_1)$ *and return* ct_i *to* $\mathcal{A}$*.*
- **Guess.** $\mathcal{A}$ *outputs a bit* b'*. The outcome is* b' *if* $\mathbf{v}_j^0|_{\mathfrak{S}_{\mathrm{pub}}} = \mathbf{v}_j^1|_{\mathfrak{S}_{\mathrm{pub}}}$ *for all* j *and* $\langle \mathbf{u}_i^0, \mathbf{v}_j^0 \rangle = \langle \mathbf{u}_i^1, \mathbf{v}_j^1 \rangle$ *for all* i, j*. Otherwise, the outcome is 0.*

Applying the techniques in [49,50] to the IPFE of [2,60], we obtain adaptively secure function-hiding slotted IPFE:

Lemma 5 ([2,49,50,60])**.** *Let* $\mathcal{G}$ *be a sequence of pairing groups and* $k \geq 1$ *an integer constant. If* MDDH_k *holds in both* G_1, G_2*, then there is an (adaptively) function-hiding slotted IPFE scheme based on* $\mathcal{G}$*.*

4   Arithmetic Key Garbling Scheme

Arithmetic key garbling scheme (AKGS) is an information-theoretic primitive related to randomized encodings [11] and partial garbling schemes [37]. It is the information-theoretic core in our construction of one-key one-ciphertext ABE (more precisely 1-ABE constructed in Sect. 5). Given a function $f : \mathbb{Z}_p^{\mathcal{I}} \to \mathbb{Z}_p$ and two secrets $\alpha, \beta \in \mathbb{Z}_p$, an AKGS produces label functions $L_1, \ldots, L_m : \mathbb{Z}_p^{\mathcal{I}} \to \mathbb{Z}_p$ that are affine in $\mathbf{x}$. For any $\mathbf{x}$, one can compute $\alpha f(\mathbf{x}) + \beta$ from $L_1(\mathbf{x}), \ldots, L_m(\mathbf{x})$ together with f and $\mathbf{x}$, while all other information about α, β are hidden.

Definition 6 (AKGS, adopted from Definition 1 in [37])**.** *An arithmetic key garbling scheme (AKGS) for a function class* $\mathcal{F} = \{f\}$*, where* $f : \mathbb{Z}_p^{\mathcal{I}} \to \mathbb{Z}_p$ *for some* $p, \mathcal{I}$ *specified by* f*, consists of two efficient algorithms:*

- $\mathsf{Garble}(f \in \mathcal{F}, \alpha \in \mathbb{Z}_p, \beta \in \mathbb{Z}_p)$ *is randomized and outputs* m *affine functions* $L_1, \ldots, L_m : \mathbb{Z}_p^{\mathcal{I}} \to \mathbb{Z}_p$ *(called* label functions*, which specifies how input is encoded as labels). Pragmatically, it outputs the coefficient vectors* $\mathbf{L}_1, \ldots, \mathbf{L}_m$*.*
- $\mathsf{Eval}(f \in \mathcal{F}, \mathbf{x} \in \mathbb{Z}_p^{\mathcal{I}}, \ell_1 \in \mathbb{Z}_p, \ldots, \ell_m \in \mathbb{Z}_p)$ *is deterministic and outputs a value in* $\mathbb{Z}_p$ *(the input* $\ell_1, \ldots, \ell_m$ *are called* labels*, which are supposed to be the values of the label functions at* $\mathbf{x}$*).*

Correctness requires that for all $f : \mathbb{Z}_p^{\mathcal{I}} \to \mathbb{Z}_p \in \mathcal{F}, \alpha, \beta \in \mathbb{Z}_p, \mathbf{x} \in \mathbb{Z}_p^{\mathcal{I}}$,

$$\Pr\left[\begin{array}{c} (\mathbf{L}_1, \ldots, \mathbf{L}_m) \xleftarrow{\$} \mathsf{Garble}(f, \alpha, \beta) \\ \ell_j \leftarrow L_j(\mathbf{x}) \text{ for } j \in [m] \end{array} : \mathsf{Eval}(f, \mathbf{x}, \ell_1, \ldots, \ell_m) = \alpha f(\mathbf{x}) + \beta\right] = 1.$$

We also require that the scheme have deterministic shape*, meaning that* m *is determined solely by* f*, independent of* α, β*, and the randomness in* Garble*. The number of label functions,* m*, is called the* garbling size *of* f *under this scheme.*

Definition 7 (linear AKGS). *An AKGS* (Garble, Eval) *for $\mathcal{F}$ is* linear *if the following conditions hold:*

- Garble(f, α, β) *uses a* **uniformly random** *vector* $\mathbf{r} \xleftarrow{\$} \mathbb{Z}_p^{m'}$ *as its randomness, where m' is determined solely by f, independent of α, β.*
- *The coefficient vectors* $\mathbf{L}_1, \ldots, \mathbf{L}_m$ *produced by* Garble$(f, \alpha, \beta; \mathbf{r})$ *are linear in* $(\alpha, \beta, \mathbf{r})$.
- Eval$(f, \mathbf{x}, \ell_1, \ldots, \ell_m)$ *is linear in* $(\ell_1, \ldots, \ell_m)$.

Later in this paper, AKGS refers to linear AKGS by default.

The basic security notion of AKGS requires the existence of an efficient simulator that draws a sample from the real labels' distribution given $f, \mathbf{x}, \alpha f(\mathbf{x}) + \beta$. We emphasize, as it's the same case in [37], that AKGS does *not* hide $\mathbf{x}$ and hides all other information about α, β except the value $\alpha f(\mathbf{x}) + \beta$.

Definition 8 ((usual) simulation security, Definition 1 in [37]). *An AKGS* (Garble, Eval) *for $\mathcal{F}$ is* secure *if there exists an efficient algorithm* Sim *such that for all $f : \mathbb{Z}_p^{\mathcal{I}} \to \mathbb{Z}_p \in \mathcal{F}, \alpha, \beta \in \mathbb{Z}_p, \mathbf{x} \in \mathbb{Z}_p^{\mathcal{I}}$, the following distributions are identical:*

$$\left\{ \begin{array}{l} (\mathbf{L}_1, \ldots, \mathbf{L}_m) \xleftarrow{\$} \mathsf{Garble}(f, \alpha, \beta) \\ \quad \ell_j \leftarrow L_j(\mathbf{x}) \text{ for } j \in [m] \end{array} : (\ell_1, \ldots, \ell_m) \right\},$$
$$\{ (\ell_1, \ldots, \ell_m) \xleftarrow{\$} \mathsf{Sim}(f, \mathbf{x}, \alpha f(\mathbf{x}) + \beta) : (\ell_1, \ldots, \ell_m) \}.$$

As discussed in Sect. 2.1, the usual simulation security suffices for selective (or semi-adaptive) security. To achieve adaptive security, we need the following stronger property.

Definition 9 (piecewise security). *An AKGS* (Garble, Eval) *for $\mathcal{F}$ is* piecewise secure *if the following conditions hold:*

- *The first label is* reversely sampleable *from the other labels together with f and $\mathbf{x}$. This reconstruction is perfect even given all the other label functions. Formally, there exists an efficient algorithm* RevSamp *such that for all $f : \mathbb{Z}_p^{\mathcal{I}} \to \mathbb{Z}_p \in \mathcal{F}, \alpha, \beta \in \mathbb{Z}_p, \mathbf{x} \in \mathbb{Z}_p^{\mathcal{I}}$, the following distributions are identical:*

$$\left\{ \begin{array}{l} (\mathbf{L}_1, \ldots, \mathbf{L}_m) \xleftarrow{\$} \mathsf{Garble}(f, \alpha, \beta) \\ \quad \ell_1 \leftarrow L_1(\mathbf{x}) \end{array} : (\ell_1, \mathbf{L}_2, \ldots, \mathbf{L}_m) \right\},$$
$$\left\{ \begin{array}{l} (\mathbf{L}_1, \ldots, \mathbf{L}_m) \xleftarrow{\$} \mathsf{Garble}(f, \alpha, \beta) \\ \quad \ell_j \leftarrow L_j(\mathbf{x}) \text{ for } j \in [m], j > 1 \\ \quad \ell_1 \xleftarrow{\$} \mathsf{RevSamp}(f, \mathbf{x}, \alpha f(\mathbf{x}) + \beta, \ell_2, \ldots, \ell_m) \end{array} : (\ell_1, \mathbf{L}_2, \ldots, \mathbf{L}_m) \right\}.$$

- *For the other labels, each is* marginally random *even given all the label functions after it. Formally, this means for all $f : \mathbb{Z}_p^{\mathcal{I}} \to \mathbb{Z}_p \in \mathcal{F}, \alpha, \beta \in \mathbb{Z}_p, \mathbf{x} \in \mathbb{Z}_p^{\mathcal{I}}$*

and all $j \in [m], j > 1$, the following distributions are identical:

$$\left\{ \begin{array}{c} (\mathbf{L}_1, \ldots, \mathbf{L}_m) \xleftarrow{\$} \mathsf{Garble}(f, \alpha, \beta) \\ \ell_j \leftarrow L_j(\mathbf{x}) \end{array} : (\ell_j, \mathbf{L}_{j+1}, \ldots, \mathbf{L}_m) \right\},$$

$$\left\{ \begin{array}{c} (\mathbf{L}_1, \ldots, \mathbf{L}_m) \xleftarrow{\$} \mathsf{Garble}(f, \alpha, \beta) \\ \ell_j \xleftarrow{\$} \mathbb{Z}_p \end{array} : (\ell_j, \mathbf{L}_{j+1}, \ldots, \mathbf{L}_m) \right\}.$$

As piecewise security is stronger, it implies the usual simulation security:

Lemma 10. *A piecewise secure AKGS for some function class is also secure for the same function class.*

5   1-ABE for ABPs

Arithmetic branching program (ABP) is a computation model introduced by Nisan [51] and later studied in [15,34–37]. It is defined by a directed acyclic graph (V, E) with distinguished vertices $s, t \in V$ where every edge $e \in E$ is labeled by an affine function w_e of the input $\mathbf{x}$, and the output is computed as

$$f(\mathbf{x}) = \sum_{\substack{s\text{-}t \text{ path} \\ e_1 \cdots e_i}} \prod_{j=1}^{i} w(e_j)(\mathbf{x}).$$

Our ABE for ABPs relies on an AKGS for ABPs, which we derive as a special case of the partial garbling scheme for ABPs in [37].

Lemma 11. *There is a piecewise secure AKGS for ABPs. Moreover, the garbling size of an ABP coincides with the number of vertices in the graph.*

Below, we define and construct 1-ABE, a precursor to our full-fledged ABE, using a piecewise secure AKGS for the matching function class. It captures the key ideas for achieving adaptive security using AKGS and function-hiding IPFE, while keeping the ciphertext compact. (For technical reasons, it is more convenient to define it as a key encapsulation mechanism.)

Definition 12. *Let $\mathcal{G}$ be a sequence of pairing groups of order $p(\lambda)$. A 1-ABE scheme based on $\mathcal{G}$ has the same syntax as an ABE scheme in Definition 2, except that*

- *There is no message space $\mathcal{M}$.*
- Setup *outputs a master secret key* msk, *without a* mpk.
- KeyGen$(1^\lambda, \mathsf{msk}, y, \mu)$ *outputs a secret key* sk *for policy y that encapsulates a pad $\mu \in \mathbb{Z}_{p(\lambda)}$.*
- Enc$(1^\lambda, \mathsf{msk}, x)$ *uses* msk *and outputs a ciphertext* ct *for attribute x without encrypting a message.*
- Dec$(\mathsf{sk}, \mathsf{ct})$ *outputs $\perp$ or some $[\![\mu']\!]_T$.*

- *Correctness requires that $\mu = \mu'$ if the decapsulation should be successful, i.e., $P(x, y) = 1$.*

Such a scheme is 1-key 1-ciphertext secure *(or simply secure) if* $\mathsf{Exp}^0_{\text{1-sk,1-ct}} \approx \mathsf{Exp}^1_{\text{1-sk,1-ct}}$, *where* $\mathsf{Exp}^b_{\text{1-sk,1-ct}}$ *is defined as follows:*

- **Setup.** *Run the adversary $\mathcal{A}(1^\lambda)$ and receive a predicate P from it.*
- **Query I.** *$\mathcal{A}$ can submit a key query y. Upon this query, sample two random pads $\mu^0, \mu^1 \xleftarrow{\$} \mathbb{Z}_{p(\lambda)}$, run $\mathsf{sk} \xleftarrow{\$} \mathsf{KeyGen}(1^\lambda, \mathsf{msk}, y, \mu^0)$, and return (sk, μ^b) to $\mathcal{A}$.*
- **Challenge.** *$\mathcal{A}$ submits a challenge attribute x. Upon the challenge, run $\mathsf{ct} \xleftarrow{\$} \mathsf{Enc}(1^\lambda, \mathsf{msk}, x)$, and return ct to $\mathcal{A}$.*
- **Query II.** *Same as Query I.*
- **Guess.** *$\mathcal{A}$ outputs a bit b'. The outcome of the experiment is b' if the adversary makes only a single key query for some y and $P(x, y) = 0$. Otherwise, the outcome is 0.*

For any function class $\mathcal{F}$ (e.g., arithmetic branching programs), we show how to construct a 1-ABE for the class of zero-test predicates in $\mathcal{F}$ (i.e., predicates of form $f_{\neq 0}, f_{=0}$ that computes whether $f(\mathbf{x})$ evaluates to zero or non-zero), using a piecewise secure AKGS for $\mathcal{F}$ and a function-hiding secret-key IPFE scheme.

Construction 13 (1-ABE). We describe the construction for any fixed value of the security parameter λ and suppress the appearance of λ below for simplicity of notations. Let (Garble, Eval) be an AKGS for a function class $\mathcal{F}$, $\mathcal{G}$ pairing groups of order p, and (IPFE.Setup, IPFE.KeyGen, IPFE.Enc, IPFE.Dec) a secret-key IPFE based on $\mathcal{G}$. We construct a 1-ABE scheme based on $\mathcal{G}$ for the predicate space $\mathcal{P}$ induced by $\mathcal{F}$:

$$X_n = \mathbb{Z}_p^n, \quad Y_n = \{f_{\neq 0}, f_{=0} \mid f \in \mathcal{F}, f : \mathbb{Z}_p^n \to \mathbb{Z}_p\},$$
$$\mathcal{P} = \{P_n : X_n \times Y_n \to \{0, 1\}, (\mathbf{x}, y) \mapsto y(\mathbf{x}) \mid n \in \mathbb{N}\}.$$

The 1-ABE scheme (Setup, KeyGen, Enc, Dec) operates as follows:

- Setup(1^n) takes the attribute length in unary (i.e., P_n is encoded as 1^n) as input. It generates an IPFE master secret key $\mathsf{msk} \xleftarrow{\$} \mathsf{IPFE.Setup}(\mathfrak{S}_{\text{1-ABE}})$ for the index set $\mathfrak{S}_{\text{1-ABE}} = \{\mathsf{const}, \mathsf{coef}_1, \ldots, \mathsf{coef}_n, \mathsf{sim}_1, \mathsf{sim}_*\}$. The algorithm returns msk as the master secret key.

  Note: *The positions indexed by $\mathsf{const}, \mathsf{coef}_1, \ldots, \mathsf{coef}_n$ in the secret key encode the coefficient vectors $\mathbf{L}_j$ of the label functions L_i produced by garbling f with secrets α, β, and these positions encode $(1, \mathbf{x})$ in the ciphertext. The positions indexed by $\mathsf{sim}_1, \mathsf{sim}_*$ are set to zero by the honest algorithms, and are only used in the security proof.*

- KeyGen($\mathsf{msk}, y \in Y_n, \mu \in \mathbb{Z}_p$) samples $\eta \xleftarrow{\$} \mathbb{Z}_p$ and garbles the function f underlying y as follows:

$$\begin{cases} \alpha \leftarrow \mu, & \beta \leftarrow 0, & \text{if } y = f_{\neq 0}; \\ \alpha \leftarrow \eta, & \beta \leftarrow \mu, & \text{if } y = f_{=0}; \end{cases} \quad (\mathbf{L}_1, \ldots, \mathbf{L}_m) \xleftarrow{\$} \mathsf{Garble}(f, \alpha, \beta).$$

It generates an IPFE key $\mathsf{isk}_j \xleftarrow{\$} \mathsf{IPFE.KeyGen}(\mathsf{msk}, [\![\mathbf{v}_j]\!]_2)$ for the following vector $\mathbf{v}_j$ encoding each label function L_j:

vector	const	coef_i	sim_1	$\mathsf{sim}_\star$
$\mathbf{v}_j$	$\mathbf{L}_j[\mathsf{const}]$	$\mathbf{L}_j[\mathsf{coef}_i]$	0	0

The algorithm returns $\mathsf{sk}_y = (y, \mathsf{isk}_1, \dots, \mathsf{isk}_m)$ as the secret key.

- $\mathsf{Enc}(\mathsf{msk}, \mathbf{x} \in \mathbb{Z}_p^n)$ generates an IPFE ciphertext $\mathsf{ict} \xleftarrow{\$} \mathsf{IPFE.Enc}(\mathsf{msk}, [\![\mathbf{u}]\!]_1)$ encrypting the vector $\mathbf{u}$ that contains $1, \mathbf{x}$:

vector	const	coef_i	sim_1	$\mathsf{sim}_\star$
$\mathbf{u}$	1	$\mathbf{x}[i]$	0	0

It returns $\mathsf{ct} = (\mathbf{x}, \mathsf{ict})$ as the ciphertext.

- $\mathsf{Dec}(\mathsf{sk}, \mathsf{ct})$ parses sk as $(y, \mathsf{isk}_1, \dots, \mathsf{isk}_m)$ and ct as $(\mathbf{x}, \mathsf{ict})$, and returns $\bot$ if $y(\mathbf{x}) = 0$. Otherwise, it does the following:

$$\text{for } j \in [m]: \quad [\![\ell_j]\!]_T \leftarrow \mathsf{IPFE.Dec}(\mathsf{isk}_j, \mathsf{ict}),$$

$$[\![\mu']\!]_T \leftarrow \begin{cases} \frac{1}{f(\mathbf{x})}\mathsf{Eval}(f, \mathbf{x}, [\![\ell_1]\!]_T, \dots, [\![\ell_m]\!]_T), & \text{if } y = f_{\neq 0}; \\ \mathsf{Eval}(f, \mathbf{x}, [\![\ell_1]\!]_T, \dots, [\![\ell_m]\!]_T), & \text{if } y = f_{=0}. \end{cases}$$

The algorithm returns $[\![\mu']\!]_T$ as the decapsulated pad.

Note: *We show the correctness of the scheme. First, by the correctness of IPFE and the definition of vectors $\mathbf{v}_j, \mathbf{u}$, we have $\ell_j = \langle \mathbf{u}, \mathbf{v}_j \rangle = L_j(\mathbf{x})$ for all $j \in [m]$. Next, by the linearity of Eval in $\ell_1, \dots, \ell_m$, we can evaluate the garbling in the exponent of the target group and obtain $\mathsf{Eval}(f, \mathbf{x}, \ell_1, \dots, \ell_m) = \alpha f(\mathbf{x}) + \beta$ in the exponent. In the two cases where decapsulation should succeed, we have*

$$\alpha f(\mathbf{x}) + \beta = \begin{cases} \mu f(\mathbf{x}), & \text{if } y = f_{\neq 0} \text{ and } f(\mathbf{x}) \neq 0; \\ \mu, & \text{if } y = f_{=0} \text{ and } f(\mathbf{x}) = 0. \end{cases}$$

In both cases, the μ' above equals to μ. Therefore, Dec correctly decapsulates the pad.

Theorem 14. *Suppose in Construction 13, the AKGS is* piecewise secure *and the IPFE scheme is* function-hiding, *then the constructed 1-ABE scheme is 1-key 1-ciphertext secure.*

We refer the readers to the full version for the formal proof.

Acknowledgments. The authors were supported by NSF grants[12] CNS-1528178, CNS-1929901, CNS-1936825 (CAREER). The authors thank Hoeteck Wee for helpful discussions and the anonymous reviewers for insightful comments.

References

1. Agrawal, S., Chase, M.: Simplifying design and analysis of complex predicate encryption schemes. In: Coron, J.-S., Nielsen, J.B. (eds.) EUROCRYPT 2017, Part I. LNCS, vol. 10210, pp. 627–656. Springer, Cham (2017). https://doi.org/10.1007/978-3-319-56620-7_22

2. Agrawal, S., Libert, B., Stehlé, D.: Fully secure functional encryption for inner products, from standard assumptions. In: Robshaw, M., Katz, J. (eds.) CRYPTO 2016, Part III. LNCS, vol. 9816, pp. 333–362. Springer, Heidelberg (2016). https://doi.org/10.1007/978-3-662-53015-3_12

3. Agrawal, S., Maitra, M.: FE and iO for turing machines from minimal assumptions. In: Beimel, A., Dziembowski, S. (eds.) TCC 2018, Part II. LNCS, vol. 11240, pp. 473–512. Springer, Cham (2018). https://doi.org/10.1007/978-3-030-03810-6_18

4. Agrawal, S., Maitra, M., Yamada, S.: Attribute based encryption (and more) for nondeterministic finite automata from LWE. In: Boldyreva, A., Micciancio, D. (eds.) CRYPTO 2019, Part II. LNCS, vol. 11693, pp. 765–797. Springer, Cham (2019). https://doi.org/10.1007/978-3-030-26951-7_26

5. Agrawal, S., Maitra, M., Yamada, S.: Attribute based encryption for deterministic finite automata from DLIN. In: Hofheinz, D., Rosen, A. (eds.) TCC 2019, Part II. LNCS, vol. 11892, pp. 91–117. Springer, Cham (2019). https://doi.org/10.1007/978-3-030-36033-7_4

6. Ananth, P., Chen, Y.-C., Chung, K.-M., Lin, H., Lin, W.-K.: Delegating RAM computations with adaptive soundness and privacy. In: Hirt, M., Smith, A. (eds.) TCC 2016, Part II. LNCS, vol. 9986, pp. 3–30. Springer, Heidelberg (2016). https://doi.org/10.1007/978-3-662-53644-5_1

7. Ananth, P., Fan, X., Shi, E.: Towards attribute-based encryption for RAMs from LWE: sub-linear decryption, and more. Cryptology ePrint Archive, Report 2018/273 (2018). https://eprint.iacr.org/2018/273

8. Ananth, P., Sahai, A.: Projective arithmetic functional encryption and indistinguishability obfuscation from degree-5 multilinear maps. In: Coron, J.-S., Nielsen, J.B. (eds.) EUROCRYPT 2017, Part I. LNCS, vol. 10210, pp. 152–181. Springer, Cham (2017). https://doi.org/10.1007/978-3-319-56620-7_6

9. Ananth, P.V., Sahai, A.: Functional encryption for turing machines. In: Kushilevitz, E., Malkin, T. (eds.) TCC 2016, Part I. LNCS, vol. 9562, pp. 125–153. Springer, Heidelberg (2016). https://doi.org/10.1007/978-3-662-49096-9_6

10. Applebaum, B., Ishai, Y., Kushilevitz, E.: Cryptography in NC^0. In: 45th FOCS, pp. 166–175. IEEE Computer Society Press, October 2004

11. Applebaum, B., Ishai, Y., Kushilevitz, E.: How to garble arithmetic circuits. In: Ostrovsky, R. (ed.) 52nd FOCS, pp. 120–129. IEEE Computer Society Press, October 2011

---

[12] The views expressed are those of the authors and do not reflect the official policy or position of the Department of Defense, the National Science Foundation, or the U.S. Government.

12. Attrapadung, N.: Dual system encryption via doubly selective security: framework, fully secure functional encryption for regular languages, and more. In: Nguyen, P.Q., Oswald, E. (eds.) EUROCRYPT 2014. LNCS, vol. 8441, pp. 557–577. Springer, Heidelberg (2014). https://doi.org/10.1007/978-3-642-55220-5_31

13. Attrapadung, N.: Dual system encryption framework in prime-order groups via computational pair encodings. In: Cheon, J.H., Takagi, T. (eds.) ASIACRYPT 2016, Part II. LNCS, vol. 10032, pp. 591–623. Springer, Heidelberg (2016). https://doi.org/10.1007/978-3-662-53890-6_20

14. Attrapadung, N.: Dual system framework in multilinear settings and applications to fully secure (compact) ABE for unbounded-size circuits. In: Fehr, S. (ed.) PKC 2017, Part II. LNCS, vol. 10175, pp. 3–35. Springer, Heidelberg (2017). https://doi.org/10.1007/978-3-662-54388-7_1

15. Beimel, A., Gal, A.: On arithmetic branching programs. In: Proceedings of the 13th Annual IEEE Conference on Computational Complexity, pp. 68–80 (1998)

16. Bethencourt, J., Sahai, A., Waters, B.: Ciphertext-policy attribute-based encryption. In: 2007 IEEE Symposium on Security and Privacy (SP 2007), pp. 321–334, May 2007

17. Bishop, A., Jain, A., Kowalczyk, L.: Function-hiding inner product encryption. In: Iwata, T., Cheon, J.H. (eds.) ASIACRYPT 2015, Part I. LNCS, vol. 9452, pp. 470–491. Springer, Heidelberg (2015). https://doi.org/10.1007/978-3-662-48797-6_20

18. Bitansky, N., Garg, S., Lin, H., Pass, R., Telang, S.: Succinct randomized encodings and their applications. In: Servedio, R.A., Rubinfeld, R. (eds.) 47th ACM STOC, pp. 439–448. ACM Press, June 2015

19. Boneh, D., et al.: Fully key-homomorphic encryption, arithmetic circuit ABE and compact garbled circuits. In: Nguyen, P.Q., Oswald, E. (eds.) EUROCRYPT 2014. LNCS, vol. 8441, pp. 533–556. Springer, Heidelberg (2014). https://doi.org/10.1007/978-3-642-55220-5_30

20. Boyen, X., Li, Q.: Attribute-based encryption for finite automata from LWE. In: Au, M.-H., Miyaji, A. (eds.) ProvSec 2015. LNCS, vol. 9451, pp. 247–267. Springer, Cham (2015). https://doi.org/10.1007/978-3-319-26059-4_14

21. Canetti, R., Holmgren, J., Jain, A., Vaikuntanathan, V.: Succinct garbling and indistinguishability obfuscation for RAM programs. In: Servedio, R.A., Rubinfeld, R. (eds.) 47th ACM STOC, pp. 429–437. ACM Press, June 2015

22. Chen, J., Gay, R., Wee, H.: Improved dual system ABE in prime-order groups via predicate encodings. In: Oswald, E., Fischlin, M. (eds.) EUROCRYPT 2015, Part II. LNCS, vol. 9057, pp. 595–624. Springer, Heidelberg (2015). https://doi.org/10.1007/978-3-662-46803-6_20

23. Chen, J., Gong, J., Kowalczyk, L., Wee, H.: Unbounded ABE via bilinear entropy expansion, revisited. In: Nielsen, J.B., Rijmen, V. (eds.) EUROCRYPT 2018, Part I. LNCS, vol. 10820, pp. 503–534. Springer, Cham (2018). https://doi.org/10.1007/978-3-319-78381-9_19

24. Chen, J., Gong, J., Wee, H.: Improved inner-product encryption with adaptive security and full attribute-hiding. In: Peyrin, T., Galbraith, S. (eds.) ASIACRYPT 2018, Part II. LNCS, vol. 11273, pp. 673–702. Springer, Cham (2018). https://doi.org/10.1007/978-3-030-03329-3_23

25. Datta, P., Dutta, R., Mukhopadhyay, S.: Functional encryption for inner product with full function privacy. In: Cheng, C.-M., Chung, K.-M., Persiano, G., Yang, B.-Y. (eds.) PKC 2016, Part I. LNCS, vol. 9614, pp. 164–195. Springer, Heidelberg (2016). https://doi.org/10.1007/978-3-662-49384-7_7

26. Escala, A., Herold, G., Kiltz, E., Ràfols, C., Villar, J.: An algebraic framework for Diffie-Hellman assumptions. In: Canetti, R., Garay, J.A. (eds.) CRYPTO 2013, Part II. LNCS, vol. 8043, pp. 129–147. Springer, Heidelberg (2013). https://doi.org/10.1007/978-3-642-40084-1_8

27. Goldwasser, S., Kalai, Y.T., Popa, R.A., Vaikuntanathan, V., Zeldovich, N.: How to run turing machines on encrypted data. In: Canetti, R., Garay, J.A. (eds.) CRYPTO 2013, Part II. LNCS, vol. 8043, pp. 536–553. Springer, Heidelberg (2013). https://doi.org/10.1007/978-3-642-40084-1_30

28. Goldwasser, S., Kalai, Y.T., Popa, R.A., Vaikuntanathan, V., Zeldovich, N.: Reusable garbled circuits and succinct functional encryption. In: Boneh, D., Roughgarden, T., Feigenbaum, J. (eds.) 45th ACM STOC, pp. 555–564. ACM Press, June 2013

29. Gong, J., Waters, B., Wee, H.: ABE for DFA from k-Lin. In: Boldyreva, A., Micciancio, D. (eds.) CRYPTO 2019, Part II. LNCS, vol. 11693, pp. 732–764. Springer, Cham (2019). https://doi.org/10.1007/978-3-030-26951-7_25

30. Gorbunov, S., Vaikuntanathan, V., Wee, H.: Attribute-based encryption for circuits. In: Boneh, D., Roughgarden, T., Feigenbaum, J. (eds.) 45th ACM STOC, pp. 545–554. ACM Press, June 2013

31. Gorbunov, S., Vinayagamurthy, D.: Riding on asymmetry: efficient ABE for branching programs. In: Iwata, T., Cheon, J.H. (eds.) ASIACRYPT 2015, Part I. LNCS, vol. 9452, pp. 550–574. Springer, Heidelberg (2015). https://doi.org/10.1007/978-3-662-48797-6_23

32. Goyal, V., Pandey, O., Sahai, A., Waters, B.: Attribute-based encryption for fine-grained access control of encrypted data. In: Juels, A., Wright, R.N., di Vimercati, S.C. (eds.) ACM CCS 2006, pp. 89–98. ACM Press, October/November 2006. Available as Cryptology ePrint Archive Report 2006/309

33. Hofheinz, D., Koch, J., Striecks, C.: Identity-based encryption with (almost) tight security in the multi-instance, multi-ciphertext setting. In: Katz, J. (ed.) PKC 2015. LNCS, vol. 9020, pp. 799–822. Springer, Heidelberg (2015). https://doi.org/10.1007/978-3-662-46447-2_36

34. Ishai, Y., Kushilevitz, E.: Private simultaneous messages protocols with applications. In: Proceedings of the 5th ISTCS, pp. 174–183 (1997)

35. Ishai, Y., Kushilevitz, E.: Randomizing polynomials: a new representation with applications to round-efficient secure computation. In: 41st FOCS, pp. 294–304. IEEE Computer Society Press, November 2000

36. Ishai, Y., Kushilevitz, E.: Perfect constant-round secure computation via perfect randomizing polynomials. In: Widmayer, P., Ruiz, F.T., Bueno, R.M., Hennessy, M., Eidenbenz, S., Conejo, R. (eds.) ICALP 2002. LNCS, vol. 2380, pp. 244–256. Springer, Heidelberg (2002). https://doi.org/10.1007/3-540-45465-9_22

37. Ishai, Y., Wee, H.: Partial garbling schemes and their applications. In: Esparza, J., Fraigniaud, P., Husfeldt, T., Koutsoupias, E. (eds.) ICALP 2014, Part I. LNCS, vol. 8572, pp. 650–662. Springer, Heidelberg (2014). https://doi.org/10.1007/978-3-662-43948-7_54

38. Jafargholi, Z., Kamath, C., Klein, K., Komargodski, I., Pietrzak, K., Wichs, D.: Be adaptive, avoid overcommitting. In: Katz, J., Shacham, H. (eds.) CRYPTO 2017, Part I. LNCS, vol. 10401, pp. 133–163. Springer, Cham (2017). https://doi.org/10.1007/978-3-319-63688-7_5

39. Katz, J., Sahai, A., Waters, B.: Predicate encryption supporting disjunctions, polynomial equations, and inner products. J. Cryptol. **26**(2), 191–224 (2013)

40. Kim, S., Lewi, K., Mandal, A., Montgomery, H., Roy, A., Wu, D.J.: Function-hiding inner product encryption is practical. In: Catalano, D., De Prisco, R. (eds.) SCN 2018. LNCS, vol. 11035, pp. 544–562. Springer, Cham (2018). https://doi.org/10.1007/978-3-319-98113-0_29

41. Kitagawa, F., Nishimaki, R., Tanaka, K., Yamakawa, T.: Adaptively secure and succinct functional encryption: improving security and efficiency, simultaneously. In: Boldyreva, A., Micciancio, D. (eds.) CRYPTO 2019, Part III. LNCS, vol. 11694, pp. 521–551. Springer, Cham (2019). https://doi.org/10.1007/978-3-030-26954-8_17

42. Koppula, V., Lewko, A.B., Waters, B.: Indistinguishability obfuscation for turing machines with unbounded memory. In: Servedio, R.A., Rubinfeld, R. (eds.) 47th ACM STOC, pp. 419–428. ACM Press, June 2015

43. Kowalczyk, L., Liu, J., Malkin, T., Meiyappan, K.: Mitigating the one-use restriction in attribute-based encryption. In: Lee, K. (ed.) ICISC 2018. LNCS, vol. 11396, pp. 23–36. Springer, Cham (2019). https://doi.org/10.1007/978-3-030-12146-4_2

44. Kowalczyk, L., Wee, H.: Compact adaptively secure ABE for NC^1 from k-Lin. In: Ishai, Y., Rijmen, V. (eds.) EUROCRYPT 2019, Part I. LNCS, vol. 11476, pp. 3–33. Springer, Cham (2019). https://doi.org/10.1007/978-3-030-17653-2_1

45. Lewko, A., Okamoto, T., Sahai, A., Takashima, K., Waters, B.: Fully secure functional encryption: attribute-based encryption and (hierarchical) inner product encryption. In: Gilbert, H. (ed.) EUROCRYPT 2010. LNCS, vol. 6110, pp. 62–91. Springer, Heidelberg (2010). https://doi.org/10.1007/978-3-642-13190-5_4

46. Lewko, A.B., Waters, B.: New techniques for dual system encryption and fully secure HIBE with short ciphertexts. In: Micciancio, D. (ed.) TCC 2010. LNCS, vol. 5978, pp. 455–479. Springer, Heidelberg (2010). https://doi.org/10.1007/978-3-642-11799-2_27

47. Lewko, A., Waters, B.: Unbounded HIBE and attribute-based encryption. In: Paterson, K.G. (ed.) EUROCRYPT 2011. LNCS, vol. 6632, pp. 547–567. Springer, Heidelberg (2011). https://doi.org/10.1007/978-3-642-20465-4_30

48. Lewko, A., Waters, B.: New proof methods for attribute-based encryption: achieving full security through selective techniques. In: Safavi-Naini, R., Canetti, R. (eds.) CRYPTO 2012. LNCS, vol. 7417, pp. 180–198. Springer, Heidelberg (2012). https://doi.org/10.1007/978-3-642-32009-5_12

49. Lin, H.: Indistinguishability obfuscation from SXDH on 5-linear maps and locality-5 PRGs. In: Katz, J., Shacham, H. (eds.) CRYPTO 2017, Part I. LNCS, vol. 10401, pp. 599–629. Springer, Cham (2017). https://doi.org/10.1007/978-3-319-63688-7_20

50. Lin, H., Vaikuntanathan, V.: Indistinguishability obfuscation from DDH-like assumptions on constant-degree graded encodings. In: Dinur, I. (ed.) 57th FOCS, pp. 11–20. IEEE Computer Society Press, October 2016

51. Nisan, N.: Lower bounds for non-commutative computation (extended abstract). In: 23rd ACM STOC, pp. 410–418. ACM Press, May 1991

52. Okamoto, T., Takashima, K.: Hierarchical predicate encryption for inner-products. In: Matsui, M. (ed.) ASIACRYPT 2009. LNCS, vol. 5912, pp. 214–231. Springer, Heidelberg (2009). https://doi.org/10.1007/978-3-642-10366-7_13

53. Okamoto, T., Takashima, K.: Fully secure functional encryption with general relations from the decisional linear assumption. In: Rabin, T. (ed.) CRYPTO 2010. LNCS, vol. 6223, pp. 191–208. Springer, Heidelberg (2010). https://doi.org/10.1007/978-3-642-14623-7_11

54. Okamoto, T., Takashima, K.: Fully secure unbounded inner-product and attribute-based encryption. In: Wang, X., Sako, K. (eds.) ASIACRYPT 2012. LNCS, vol. 7658, pp. 349–366. Springer, Heidelberg (2012). https://doi.org/10.1007/978-3-642-34961-4_22

55. Shen, E., Shi, E., Waters, B.: Predicate privacy in encryption systems. In: Reingold, O. (ed.) TCC 2009. LNCS, vol. 5444, pp. 457–473. Springer, Heidelberg (2009). https://doi.org/10.1007/978-3-642-00457-5_27

56. Tomida, J., Abe, M., Okamoto, T.: Efficient functional encryption for inner-product values with full-hiding security. In: Bishop, M., Nascimento, A.C.A. (eds.) ISC 2016. LNCS, vol. 9866, pp. 408–425. Springer, Cham (2016). https://doi.org/10.1007/978-3-319-45871-7_24

57. Waters, B.: Dual system encryption: realizing fully secure IBE and HIBE under simple assumptions. In: Halevi, S. (ed.) CRYPTO 2009. LNCS, vol. 5677, pp. 619–636. Springer, Heidelberg (2009). https://doi.org/10.1007/978-3-642-03356-8_36

58. Waters, B.: Functional encryption for regular languages. In: Safavi-Naini, R., Canetti, R. (eds.) CRYPTO 2012. LNCS, vol. 7417, pp. 218–235. Springer, Heidelberg (2012). https://doi.org/10.1007/978-3-642-32009-5_14

59. Wee, H.: Dual system encryption via predicate encodings. In: Lindell, Y. (ed.) TCC 2014. LNCS, vol. 8349, pp. 616–637. Springer, Heidelberg (2014). https://doi.org/10.1007/978-3-642-54242-8_26

60. Wee, H.: Attribute-hiding predicate encryption in bilinear groups, revisited. In: Kalai, Y., Reyzin, L. (eds.) TCC 2017, Part I. LNCS, vol. 10677, pp. 206–233. Springer, Cham (2017). https://doi.org/10.1007/978-3-319-70500-2_8

61. Yao, A.C.-C.: How to generate and exchange secrets (extended abstract). In: 27th FOCS, pp. 162–167. IEEE Computer Society Press, October 1986

Adaptively Secure ABE for DFA
from k-Lin and More

Junqing Gong[1,2(✉)] and Hoeteck Wee[2(✉)]

[1] East China Normal University, Shanghai, China
[2] CNRS, ENS and PSL, Paris, France
{jgong,wee}@di.ens.fr

Abstract. In this work, we present:
- the first adaptively secure ABE for DFA from the k-Lin assumption in prime-order bilinear groups; this resolves one of open problems posed by Waters [CRYPTO'12];
- the first ABE for NFA from the k-Lin assumption, provided the number of accepting paths is smaller than the order of the underlying group; the scheme achieves selective security;
- the first compact adaptively secure ABE (supporting unbounded multi-use of attributes) for branching programs from the k-Lin assumption, which generalizes and simplifies the recent result of Kowalczyk and Wee for boolean formula (NC1) [EUROCRYPT'19].

Our adaptively secure ABE for DFA relies on a new combinatorial mechanism avoiding the exponential security loss in the number of states when naively combining two recent techniques from CRYPTO'19 and EURO-CRYPT'19. This requires us to design a selectively secure ABE for NFA; we give a construction which is sufficient for our purpose and of independent interest. Our ABE for branching programs leverages insights from our ABE for DFA.

1 Introduction

Attribute-based encryption (ABE) [12,19] is an advanced form of public-key encryption that supports fine-grained access control for encrypted data. Here, ciphertexts are associated with an attribute x and keys with a policy Γ; decryption is possible only when $\Gamma(x) = 1$. One important class of policies we would like to support are those specified using deterministic finite automata (DFA). Such policies capture many real-world applications involving simple computation on data of unbounded size such as network logging application, tax returns and virus scanners.

Since the seminal work of Waters [21] introducing ABE for DFA and providing the first instantiation from pairings, substantial progress has been made

J. Gong—Supported by NSFC-ISF Joint Scientific Research Program (61961146004) and ERC Project aSCEND (H2020 639554).
H. Wee—Supported by ERC Project aSCEND (H2020 639554).

A. Canteaut and Y. Ishai (Eds.): EUROCRYPT 2020, LNCS 12107, pp. 278–308, 2020.
https://doi.org/10.1007/978-3-030-45727-3_10

in the design and analysis of ABE schemes for DFA [1–5,11], proving various trade-offs between security assumptions and security guarantees. However, two central problems posed by Waters [21] remain open. The first question pertains to security and assumptions:

Q1: Can we build an ABE for DFA with adaptive security from static assumptions in bilinear groups, notably the k-Lin assumption in prime-order bilinear groups?

From both a practical and theoretical stand-point, we would like to base cryptography on weaker and better understood assumptions, as is the case with the k-Lin assumption, while also capturing more realistic adversarial models, as is the case with adaptive security. Prior ABE schemes for DFA achieve either adaptive security from less desirable q-type assumptions [1,4,5,21], where the complexity of the assumption grows with the length of the string x, or very recently, selective security from the k-Lin assumption [2,11]. Indeed, this open problem was reiterated again in the latter work [11], emphasizing a security loss that is polynomial (and not exponential) in the size of the DFA.

The next question pertains to expressiveness:

Q2: Can we build an ABE for nondeterministic finite automata (NFA) with a polynomial dependency on the NFA size?

The efficiency requirement rules out the naive approach of converting a NFA to a DFA, which incurs an exponential blow-up in size. Here, we do not know any construction even if we only require selective security under q-type assumptions. Partial progress was made very recently by Agrawal *et al.* [3] in the more limited secret-key setting, where encryption requires access to the master secret key. Throughout the rest of this work, we refer only to the standard public-key setting for ABE, and where the adversary can make an a-priori unbounded number of secret key queries.

1.1   Our Results

In this work, we address the afore-mentioned open problems:

- We present an adaptively secure ABE for DFA from the k-Lin assumption in prime-order bilinear groups, which affirmatively answers the first open problem. Our scheme achieves ciphertext and key sizes with linear complexity, as well as security loss that is polynomial in the size of the DFA and the number of key queries. Concretely, over the binary alphabet and under the SXDH (=1-Lin) assumption, our ABE for DFA achieves ciphertext and key sizes 2–3 times that of Waters' scheme (cf. Fig. 4), while simultaneously improving on both the assumptions and security guarantees.
- We present a selectively secure ABE for NFA also from the k-Lin assumption, provided the number of accepting paths is smaller than p, where p is the order of the underlying group. We also present a simpler ABE for NFA with the same restriction from the same q-type assumption used in Waters' ABE for DFA. Both ABE schemes for NFA achieve ciphertext and key sizes with linear complexity.

- Finally, we present the first compact adaptively secure ABE for branching programs from the k-Lin assumption, which generalizes and simplifies the recent result of Kowalczyk and Wee [15] for boolean formula (NC1). Here, "compact" is also referred to as "unbounded multi-use of attributes" in [5]; each attribute/input bit can appear in the formula/program an unbounded number of times. Our construction leverages insights from our ABE for DFA, and works directly with any layered branching program and avoids both the pre-processing step in the latter work for transforming boolean formulas into balanced binary trees of logarithmic depth, as well as the delicate recursive pebbling strategy for binary trees.

We summarize the state of the art of ABE for DFA, NFA and branching programs in Figs. 1, 2, 3, respectively.

In the rest of this section, we focus on our three ABE schemes that rely on the k-Lin assumption, all of which follow the high-level proof strategy in [11,15]. We design a series of hybrids that traces through the computation, and the analysis carefully combines (i) a "nested, two-slot" dual system argument [8,13,16–18,20], (ii) a new combinatorial mechanism for propagating entropy along the NFA computation path, and (iii) the piecewise guessing framework [14,15] for achieving adaptive security. We proceed to outline and motivate several of our key ideas. From now on, we use GWW to refer to the ABE for DFA by Gong *et al.* [11].

Adaptively Secure ABE for DFA. Informally, the piecewise guessing framework [14,15] for ABE adaptive security says that if we have a selectively secure ABE scheme where proving indistinguishability of every pair of adjacent hybrids requires only knowing $\log L$ bits of information about the challenge attribute x, then the same scheme is adaptively secure with a security loss of L. Moreover, when combined with the dual system argument, it suffices to consider selective security when the adversary only gets a single key corresponding to a single DFA.

In the GWW security proof, proving indistinguishability of adjacent hybrids requires knowing the subset of DFA states that are reachable from the accept states by "back-tracking" the computation. This corresponds to $\log L = Q$—we need Q bits to specify an arbitrary subset of $[Q]$—and a security loss of 2^Q. Our key insight for achieving adaptive security is that via a suitable transformation to the DFA, we can ensure that the subset of reachable states per input are always singleton sets, which corresponds to $\log L = \log Q$ and a security loss of Q. The transformation is very simple: run the DFA "in reverse"! That is, start from the accept states, read the input bits in reverse order and the transitions also in reverse, and accept if we reach the start state. It is easy to see that this actually corresponds to an NFA computation, which means that we still need to design a selectively secure ABE for NFA. Also, back-tracking along this NFA corresponds to normal computation in the original DFA, and therefore always reaches singleton sets of states during any intermediate computation.

ABE for NFA. Next, we sketch our ABE for NFA, which uses an asymmetric bilinear group (G_1, G_2, G_T, e) of prime order p where $e : G_1 \times G_2 \to G_T$. As in

Waters' ABE for DFA [21], an encryption of $x = (x_1, \ldots, x_\ell) \in \{0,1\}^\ell$ contains random scalars $s_0, \ldots, s_\ell \leftarrow \mathbb{Z}_p$ in the exponent in G_1. In the secret key, we pick a random scalar $d_u \leftarrow \mathbb{Z}_p$ for each state $u \in [Q]$. We can now describe the invariant used during decryption with g_1, g_2 being respective generators of G_1, G_2:

- In Waters' ABE for DFA, if the computation reaches a state $u_i \in [Q]$ upon reading $x_1, \ldots, x_i$, decryption computes $e(g_1, g_2)^{s_i d_{u_i}}$. In particular, the scheme allows the decryptor to compute the ratios

$$e(g_1, g_2)^{s_j d_v - s_{j-1} d_u}, \ \forall j \in [\ell], u \in [Q], v = \delta(u, x_j) \in [Q] \tag{1}$$

  where $\delta : [Q] \times \{0,1\} \to [Q]$ is the DFA transition function.
- The natural way to extend (1) to account for non-deterministic transitions in an NFA is to allow the decryptor to compute

$$e(g_1, g_2)^{s_j d_v - s_{j-1} d_u}, \ \forall j \in [\ell], u \in [Q], v \in \delta(u, x_j) \subseteq [Q] \tag{2}$$

  where $\delta : [Q] \times \{0,1\} \to 2^{[Q]}$ is the NFA transition function. As noted by Waters [21], such an ABE scheme for NFA is broken via a so-called "backtracking attack", which we describe in the full paper.
- In our ABE for NFA, we allow the decryptor to compute

$$e(g_1, g_2)^{s_j \left(\sum_{v \in \delta(u, x_j)} d_v \right) - s_{j-1} d_u}, \ \forall j \in [\ell], u \in [Q] \tag{3}$$

A crucial distinction between (3) and (2) is that the decryptor can only compute *one* quantity for each j, u in the former (as is the case also in (1)), and up to Q quantities in the latter. The ability to compute multiple quantities in (2) is exactly what enables the back-tracking attack.

We clarify that our ABE for NFA imposes an extra restriction on the NFA, namely that the total number of accepting paths[1] be non-zero mod p for accepting inputs; we use $\text{NFA}^{\oplus p}$ to denote such NFAs. In particular, this is satisfied by standard NFA where the total number of accepting paths is less than p for all inputs. This is in general a non-trivial restriction since the number of accepting paths for an arbitrary NFA can be as large as Q^ℓ. Fortunately, for NFAs obtained by running a DFA "in reverse", the number of accepting paths is always either 0 or 1.

Indeed, the above idea, along with a suitable modification of Waters' proof strategy, already yields our selectively secure ABE for $\text{NFA}^{\oplus p}$ under q-type assumptions in asymmetric bilinear groups of prime order p. We defer the details to the full paper.

- To obtain a selectively secure scheme based on k-Lin, we apply the same modifications as in GWW [11]. For the proof of security, entropy propagation is defined via back-tracking the NFA computation, in a way analogous to that for back-tracking the DFA computation.

---

[1] An accepting path on input $x \in \{0,1\}^\ell$ is described by a sequence of states $u_0, \ldots, u_\ell \in [Q]$ where u_0 is the start state, u_ℓ is an accept state and $u_j \in \delta(u_{j-1}, x_j)$ for all $j \in [\ell]$.

reference	assumption	security	$|\mathsf{sk}|$	$|\mathsf{ct}|$
[21]	q-type	selective	$O(Q)$	$O(\ell)$
[5,4,1]	q-type + k-Lin	adaptive ✓	$O(Q)$	$O(\ell)$
[11]	k-Lin ✓	selective	$O(Q)$	$O(\ell)$
[3]	k-Lin ✓	selective*	$O(Q^2)$	$O(\ell^3)$
ours	k-Lin ✓	adaptive ✓	$O(Q)$	$O(\ell)$

Fig. 1. Summary of ABE schemes for DFA. In the table, Q is the number of states in the DFA associated with sk and ℓ is the length of x associated with ct, and where $|\Sigma| = O(1)$.

reference	$|\mathsf{sk}|$	$|\mathsf{ct}|$	type of NFA	public key?	assumption
[2]	$\mathrm{poly}(Q)$	$\mathrm{poly}(\ell)$	standard ✓		LWE ✓
ours	$O(Q)$	$O(\ell)$	NFA$^{\oplus p}$	✓	q-type
	$O(Q)$	$O(\ell)$	NFA$^{\oplus p}$	✓	k-Lin ✓

Fig. 2. Summary of ABE schemes for NFA. In the table, Q is the number of states in the NFA associated with sk and ℓ is the length of x associated with ct.

reference	assumption	compact?
[7]	k-Lin ✓	
[5]	q-type + k-Lin	✓
	k-Lin ✓	
ours	k-Lin ✓	✓

Fig. 3. Summary of adaptively secure ABE schemes for branching programs (BP). Here "compact" is also referred to "unbounded multi-use" in [5].

- To obtain an adaptively secure scheme based on k-Lin, we adapt the selectively secure scheme to the piecewise guessing framework [15]. One naive approach is to introduce a new semi-functional space. In contrast, we introduce one extra components into master public key, secret key and ciphertext, respectively. With the extra components, we can avoid adding a new semi-functional subspace, by reusing an existing subspace as shown in previous unbounded ABE in [8]. Under k-Lin assumption, our technique roughly saves $k \cdot \ell$ elements in the ciphertext and $k \cdot (2|\Sigma| + 2)Q$ elements in the secret key over the general approach. This way, we obtain ciphertext and key sizes that are almost the same as those in the GWW selectively secure scheme.

ABE for Branching Programs. We build our compact adaptively secure ABE for branching program (BP) in two steps analogous to our adaptively secure ABE for DFA. In particular, we first show how to transform branching programs to a subclass of nondeterministic branching programs (NBP) and construct adaptively secure ABE for such class of NBP. Note that the latter is sufficient to capture a special BP with permutation transition function (without transforming BP to NBP) and readily simplify the result of Kowalczyk and Wee [15] for boolean formula (NC1).

1.2 Technical Overview

We start by recalling the standard definitions of DFA and NFA using vector-matrix notation: that is, we describe the start and accept states using the

reference	|ct|	|sk|	assumption	security
[21]	$(2\ell + 3)\|G_1\|$	$(3\|\Sigma\|Q + 4)\|G_2\|$	q-type	selective
[5]	$((2k + 2)\ell + 6k + 6)\|G_1\|$	$((3k + 3)\|\Sigma\|Q + 5k + 5)\|G_2\|$	q-type + k-Lin	adaptive ✓
	$(3\ell + 12)\|G_1\|$	$(6\|\Sigma\|Q + 10)\|G_2\|$	q-type + SXDH	adaptive ✓
[11]	$((3k + 1)\ell + 4k + 1)\|G_1\|$	$((4k + 2)\|\Sigma\|Q + (3k + 1)Q + 2k + 1)\|G_2\|$	k-Lin ✓	selective
	$(4\ell + 5)\|G_1\|$	$(6\|\Sigma\|Q + 4Q + 3)\|G_2\|$	SXDH ✓	selective
ours	$((3k + 1)\ell + 6k + 2)\|G_1\|$	$((4k + 2)\|\Sigma\|Q + (5k + 2)Q + 2k + 1)\|G_2\|$	k-Lin ✓	adaptive ✓
	$(4\ell + 8)\|G_1\|$	$(6\|\Sigma\|Q + 7Q + 3)\|G_2\|$	SXDH ✓	adaptive ✓

Fig. 4. Concrete parameter sizes of pairing-based ABE schemes for DFA. Note that [11,21] are selectively secure whereas our scheme is adaptively secure; [3] is omitted from the table since the ciphertext and key sizes are asymptotically larger, see Fig. 1. In the table, Q is the number of states in the DFA, Σ indicates the alphabet, ℓ is the length of input x. All the schemes work over bilinear groups (G_1, G_2, G_T, e) of prime order p where $e : G_1 \times G_2 \to G_T$. We note that all the schemes shown in the table have mpk of $O(|\Sigma|)$ group elements. In the \|ct\|-column, we omit one G_T element. In the **assumption** column, SXDH means 1-Lin.

character vectors, and specify the transition function via a transition matrix. The use of vector-matrix notation enables a more compact description of our ABE schemes, and also clarifies the connection to branching programs.

NFA, DFA, NFA$^{\oplus_p}$. An NFA Γ is specified using $(Q, \Sigma, \{\mathbf{M}_\sigma\}_{\sigma \in \Sigma}, \mathbf{u}, \mathbf{f})$ where Σ is the alphabet and

$$Q \in \mathbb{N}; \quad \mathbf{M}_\sigma \in \{0, 1\}^{Q \times Q}, \forall \sigma \in \Sigma; \quad \mathbf{u}, \mathbf{f} \in \{0, 1\}^{1 \times Q}.$$

The NFA Γ accepts an input $x = (x_1, \ldots, x_\ell) \in \Sigma^\ell$, denoted by $\Gamma(x) = 1$, if

$$\mathbf{f}\mathbf{M}_{x_\ell} \cdots \mathbf{M}_{x_2}\mathbf{M}_{x_1}\mathbf{u}^\top > 0 \tag{4}$$

and rejects the input otherwise, denoted by $\Gamma(x) = 0$. We will also refer to the quantity $\mathbf{f}\mathbf{M}_{x_\ell} \cdots \mathbf{M}_{x_2}\mathbf{M}_{x_1}\mathbf{u}^\top$ as the number of accepting paths for x. The above relation (4) is equivalent to

$$\mathbf{u}\mathbf{M}_{x_1}^\top \mathbf{M}_{x_2}^\top \cdots \mathbf{M}_{x_\ell}^\top \mathbf{f}^\top > 0$$

The unusual choice of notation is to simplify the description of our ABE scheme. Let $\mathcal{E}_Q$ be the collection of Q elementary row vectors of dimension Q.

- A DFA Γ is a special case of NFA where $\mathbf{u} \in \mathcal{E}_Q$ and each column in every matrix $\mathbf{M}_\sigma$ is an elementary column vector (i.e., contains exactly one 1).
- An NFA$^{\oplus_p}$, parameterized by a prime p, is the same as an NFA except we change the accept criterion in (4) to:

$$\mathbf{f}\mathbf{M}_{x_\ell} \cdots \mathbf{M}_{x_2}\mathbf{M}_{x_1}\mathbf{u}^\top \neq 0 \bmod p$$

Note that this coincides with the standard NFA definition whenever the total number of accepting paths for all inputs is less than p.

Throughout the rest of this work, when we refer to NFA, we mean $\text{NFA}^{\oplus_p}$ unless stated otherwise.

ABE for $\text{NFA}^{\oplus_p}$. Following our overview in Sect. 1.1, an encryption of $x = (x_1, \ldots, x_\ell) \in \Sigma^\ell$ contains random scalars $s_0, \ldots, s_\ell$ in the exponent, where the plaintext is masked by $e(g_1, g_2)^{s_\ell \alpha}$. To generate a secret key for an $\text{NFA}^{\oplus_p}$ Γ, we first pick $\mathbf{d} = (d_1, \ldots, d_Q) \leftarrow \mathbb{Z}_p^Q$ as before. We allow the decryptor to compute the following quantities in the exponent over G_T:

$$\text{(i)} \quad s_\ell(\alpha \mathbf{f} - \mathbf{d}) \tag{5}$$
$$\text{(ii)} \quad s_j \mathbf{d} \mathbf{M}_{x_j} - s_{j-1}\mathbf{d}, \ \forall j \in [\ell] \ \text{(corresponds to (3))}$$
$$\text{(iii)} \quad s_0 \mathbf{d} \mathbf{u}^\top$$

If we write $\mathbf{u}_{j,x}^\top = \mathbf{M}_{x_j} \cdots \mathbf{M}_{x_1} \mathbf{u}^\top$ for all $j \in [\ell]$ and $\mathbf{u}_{0,x} = \mathbf{u}$, then we have

$$s_\ell \alpha \cdot \mathbf{f} \mathbf{u}_{\ell,x}^\top = \overbrace{s_\ell(\alpha \mathbf{f} - \mathbf{d})}^{\text{(i)}} \cdot \mathbf{u}_{\ell,x}^\top + \left(\sum_{j=1}^{\ell} \overbrace{(s_j \mathbf{d} \mathbf{M}_{x_j} - s_{j-1}\mathbf{d})}^{\text{(ii)}} \cdot \mathbf{u}_{j-1,x}^\top \right) + \overbrace{s_0 \mathbf{d} \mathbf{u}_{0,x}^\top}^{\text{(iii)}}$$

This means that whenever $\mathbf{f} \mathbf{u}_{\ell,x}^\top \neq 0 \bmod p$, as is the case when $\Gamma(x) = 1$, the decryptor will be able to recover $e(g_1, g_2)^{s_\ell \alpha}$.

Indeed, it is straight-forward to verify that the following ABE scheme satisfies the above requirements, where $[\cdot]_1, [\cdot]_2, [\cdot]_T$ denote component-wise exponentiations in respective groups G_1, G_2, G_T [10].

$$\mathsf{msk} = \left(w_{\text{start}}, w_{\text{end}}, z, \{w_\sigma\}_{\sigma \in \Sigma}, \alpha \right) \tag{6}$$
$$\mathsf{mpk} = \left([w_{\text{start}}]_1, [w_{\text{end}}]_1, [z]_1, \{[w_\sigma]_1\}_{\sigma \in \Sigma}, [\alpha]_T \right)$$
$$\mathsf{ct}_x = \begin{pmatrix} [s_0]_1, [s_0 w_{\text{start}}]_1 \\ \{ [s_j]_1, [s_{j-1}z + s_j w_{x_j}]_1 \}_{j \in [\ell]} \\ [s_\ell]_1, [s_\ell w_{\text{end}}]_1, [s_\ell \alpha]_T \cdot m \end{pmatrix}$$
$$\mathsf{sk}_\Gamma = \begin{pmatrix} [\mathbf{d}\mathbf{u}^\top + w_{\text{start}} \mathbf{r}\mathbf{u}^\top]_2, [\mathbf{r}\mathbf{u}^\top]_2 \\ \{ [-\mathbf{d} + z\mathbf{r}]_2, [\mathbf{d}\mathbf{M}_\sigma + w_\sigma \mathbf{r}]_2, [\mathbf{r}]_2 \}_{\sigma \in \Sigma} \\ [\alpha \mathbf{f} - \mathbf{d} + w_{\text{end}} \mathbf{r}]_2, [\mathbf{r}]_2 \end{pmatrix}, \quad \mathbf{d}, \mathbf{r} \leftarrow \mathbb{Z}_p^{1 \times Q}$$

In the full paper, we prove that this scheme is selectively secure under ℓ-EBDHE assumption; this is the assumption underlying Waters' selectively secure ABE for DFA [21].

Selective Security from k-Lin. Following the GWW proof strategy which in turn builds on the dual system argument, we design a series of games $\mathsf{G}_0, \ldots, \mathsf{G}_\ell$ such that in G_i, the quantities s_i and $\mathbf{d}$ have some extra entropy in the so-called semi-functional space (which requires first modifying the above scheme). The entropy in $\mathbf{d}$ is propagated from G_0 to G_1, then G_2, and finally to G_ℓ via a combination of a computational and combinatorial arguments. In G_ℓ, we will have sufficient entropy to statistically mask α in the secret key, which allows us to argue that $e(g_1, g_2)^{s_\ell \alpha}$ statistically masks the plaintext. In this overview, we focus on the novel component, namely the combinatorial argument which exploits specific properties of our scheme for $\mathrm{NFA}^{\oplus_p}$; the computational steps are completely analogous to those in GWW.

In more detail, we want to replace $\mathbf{d}$ with $\mathbf{d} + \mathbf{d}'_i$ in G_i, where $\mathbf{d}'_i \in \mathbb{Z}_p^Q$ corresponds to the extra entropy we introduce into the secret keys in the semi-functional space. Note that $\mathbf{d}'_i$ will depend on both the challenge attribute x^* as well as the underlying $\mathrm{NFA}^{\oplus_p}$. We have the following constraints on $\mathbf{d}'_i$'s, arising from the fact that an adversarial distinguisher for $\mathsf{G}_0, \ldots, \mathsf{G}_\ell$ can always compute what a decryptor can compute in (5):

- to mask α in G_ℓ, we set $\mathbf{d}'_\ell = \Delta \mathbf{f}$ where $\Delta \leftarrow \mathbb{Z}_p$, so that

$$\alpha \mathbf{f} - (\mathbf{d} + \mathbf{d}'_\ell) = (\alpha - \Delta)\mathbf{f} - \mathbf{d}$$

perfectly hides α;
- (ii) implies that

$$\overbrace{s_i \mathbf{d} \mathbf{M}_{x_i^*} - s_{i-1}(\mathbf{d} + \mathbf{d}'_{i-1})}^{\mathsf{G}_{i-1}} \approx_s \overbrace{s_i(\mathbf{d} + \mathbf{d}'_i)\mathbf{M}_{x_i^*} - s_{i-1}\mathbf{d}}^{\mathsf{G}_i}$$
$$\implies -s_{i-1}\mathbf{d}'_{i-1} \approx_s s_i \mathbf{d}'_i \mathbf{M}_{x_i^*}$$

to prevent a distinguishing attack[2] between G_{i-1} and G_i by computing $s_i \mathbf{d} \mathbf{M}_{x_i^*} - s_{i-1}\mathbf{d}$ in both games;
- (iii) implies that $s_0(\mathbf{d} + \mathbf{d}'_0)\mathbf{u}^\top = s_0 \mathbf{d} \mathbf{u}^\top$, and therefore, $\mathbf{d}'_0 \mathbf{u}^\top = 0 \bmod p$. This is to prevent a distinguishing attack[3] between the real keys and those in G_0.

In particular, we can satisfy the first two constraints by setting[4]

$$\mathbf{d}'_i = \Delta \cdot \mathbf{f} \mathbf{M}_{x_\ell^*} \cdots \mathbf{M}_{x_{i+1}^*} \ \forall i \in [0, \ell]$$

where $\approx_s$ holds over $\Delta \leftarrow \mathbb{Z}_p$, as long as $s_0, \ldots, s_\ell \neq 0$. Whenever $\Gamma(x^*) = 0$, we have

$$\mathbf{f} \mathbf{M}_{x_\ell^*} \cdots \mathbf{M}_{x_1^*} \mathbf{u}^\top = 0 \bmod p$$

and therefore the third constraint is also satisfied.

Two clarifying remarks. First, the quantity

$$\mathbf{f} \mathbf{M}_{x_\ell^*} \cdots \mathbf{M}_{x_{i+1}^*}$$

used in defining $\mathbf{d}'_i$ has a natural combinatorial interpretation: its u'th coordinate corresponds to the number of paths from the accept states to u, while backtracking along $x_\ell^*, \ldots, x_{i+1}^*$. In the specific case of a DFA, this value is 1 if u is

---

[2] Looking ahead to the proof of security in Sect. 4, this "simplified" attack corresponds roughly to using $\mathsf{ct}_{x^*}^{i-1,i}$ to distinguish $\mathsf{sk}_\Gamma^{i-1,i}$ and sk_Γ^i; this comes up in the proof of $\mathsf{G}_{2.i.2} \approx_c \mathsf{G}_{2.i.3}$ in Lemma 8.

[3] In Sect. 4, this roughly corresponds to distinguish sk_Γ and sk_Γ^0 with $\mathsf{ct}_{x^*}^0$; this comes up in the proof of $\mathsf{G}_1 \approx_c \mathsf{G}_{2.1.0}$ in Lemma 6.

[4] We adopt the standard convention that the product of an empty sequence of matrices is the identity matrix. This means $\mathbf{d}'_\ell = \Delta \cdot \mathbf{f}$.

reachable from an accept state, and 0 otherwise. It is then easy to see that our proof strategy generalizes that of GWW for DFA: the latter adds Δ to d_u in $\mathbf{G}_i$ whenever u is reachable from accept state while back-tracking along the last $\ell - i$ bits of the challenge attribute (cf. [11, Sec. 3.2]). Second, the "naive" (and insecure) ABE for NFA that captures non-deterministic transitions as in (2) introduces more equations in (ii) in (5); this in turn yields more –and ultimately unsatisfiable– constraints on the $\mathbf{d}_i'$'s.

Finally, we remark that our ABE for NFA$^{\oplus_p}$ (and ABE for DFA from GWW as well) can be proved in the semi-adaptive model [9], which is weaker than adaptive security but stronger than both selective and selective* model used in [3].

Adaptive Security for Restricted NFA$^{\oplus_p}$ and DFA. Fix a set $\mathcal{F} \subseteq \mathbb{Z}^Q$. We say that an NFA or an NFA$^{\oplus_p}$ is $\mathcal{F}$-restricted if

$$\forall \ell \in \mathbb{N},\, x \in \Sigma^\ell,\, i \in [0, \ell] \; : \; \mathbf{f} \mathbf{M}_{x_\ell} \cdots \mathbf{M}_{x_{i+1}} \in \mathcal{F}$$

Note that $\mathbf{f} \mathbf{M}_{x_\ell^*} \cdots \mathbf{M}_{x_{i+1}^*}$ corresponding to the challenge attribute x^* is exactly what is used to define $\mathbf{d}_i'$ in the previous paragraph. Moreover, following GWW, knowing this quantity is sufficient to prove indistinguishability of $\mathbf{G}_{i-1}$ and $\mathbf{G}_i$. This means that to prove selective security for $\mathcal{F}$-restricted NFAs, it suffices to know $\log|\mathcal{F}|$ bits about the challenge attribute, and via the piecewise guessing framework, this yields adaptive security with a security loss of $|\mathcal{F}|$. Unfortunately, $|\mathcal{F}|$ is in general exponentially large for general NFAs and DFAs. In particular, DFAs are $\{0, 1\}^Q$-restricted, and naively applying this argument would yield adaptively secure DFAs with a 2^Q security loss.

Instead, we show how to transform DFAs into $\mathcal{E}_Q$-restricted NFA$^{\oplus_p}$, where $\mathcal{E}_Q \subset \{0, 1\}^Q$ is the collection of Q elementary row vectors of dimension Q; this yields adaptively secure ABE for DFAs with a security loss of $|\mathcal{E}_Q| = Q$. Concretely, our adaptively secure ABE for DFA uses an adaptively secure ABE for $\mathcal{E}_Q$-restricted NFA$^{\oplus_p}$, and proceeds

- to encrypt $x = (x_1, \ldots, x_\ell)$, use the ABE for NFA to encrypt $x^\top = (x_\ell, \ldots, x_1)$;[5]
- to generate a secret key for a DFA $\Gamma = (Q, \Sigma, \{\mathbf{M}_\sigma\}, \mathbf{u}, \mathbf{f})$, use the ABE for NFA to generate a key for $\Gamma^\top = (Q, \Sigma, \{\mathbf{M}_\sigma^\top\}, \mathbf{f}, \mathbf{u})$.

Note that we reversed x during encryption, and transposed $\mathbf{M}_\sigma$, and switched $\mathbf{u}, \mathbf{f}$ during key generation. Correctness essentially follows from the equality

$$\overbrace{\mathbf{f} \mathbf{M}_{x_\ell} \cdots \mathbf{M}_{x_1} \mathbf{u}^\top}^{\Gamma(x)} = (\mathbf{f} \mathbf{M}_{x_\ell} \cdots \mathbf{M}_{x_1} \mathbf{u}^\top)^\top = \overbrace{\mathbf{u} \mathbf{M}_{x_1}^\top \cdots \mathbf{M}_{x_\ell}^\top \mathbf{f}^\top}^{\Gamma^\top(x^\top)}.$$

Furthermore $\Gamma^\top = (Q, \Sigma, \{\mathbf{M}_\sigma^\top\}, \mathbf{f}, \mathbf{u})$ is indeed a $\mathcal{E}_Q$-restricted NFA$^{\oplus_p}$. This follows from the fact that for any DFA Γ:

$$\forall \ell \in \mathbb{N},\, x \in \Sigma^\ell,\, i \in [0, \ell] \; : \; (\mathbf{M}_{x_i} \cdots \mathbf{M}_{x_1} \mathbf{u}^\top)^\top \in \mathcal{E}_Q$$

---

[5] We acknowledge that writing $x^\top$ constitutes an abuse of notation, but nonetheless convenient in analogy with $\mathbf{M}_\sigma^\top$.

	policy	security	decryption		proof	
			direction	information	direction	information
GWW [11]	DFA	selective	forward	reachability	backward	reachability
§ 5	DFA	adaptive	backward	reachability	forward	reachability
Naive	NFA	broken	forward	reachability	-	-
§ 4	NFA	selective	forward	# paths	backward	# paths

Fig. 5. Summary of tracing executions underlying GWW, our adaptively secure ABE for DFA, our selectively secure ABE for NFA$^{\oplus p}$ and naive extension of Waters' ABE for DFA.

which is implied by the property of DFA: $\mathbf{u} \in \mathcal{E}_Q$ and each column in every matrix $\mathbf{M}_\sigma$ contains exactly one 1. We give an example of reversing DFA in the full paper.

1.3 Discussion

Tracing Executions. Recall that a DFA is specified using a transition function $\delta : [Q] \times \Sigma \rightarrow [Q]$. A forward computation upon reading σ goes from a state u to $v = \delta(u, \sigma)$, whereas back-tracking upon reading σ goes from v to u if $v = \delta(u, \sigma)$.

- GWW selective ABE for DFA: Decryption follows normal "forward" computation keeping track of whether a state is reachable from the start state, whereas the security proof introduces entropy based on whether a state is reachable from the accept states via "back-tracking".
- Our adaptive ABE for DFA and branching programs: Decryption uses back-tracking and keeps track of whether a state is reachable from the accept states, whereas the security proof introduces entropy based on whether a state is reachable from the start state via forward computation. To achieve polynomial security loss, we crucially rely on the fact that when reading i input bits, exactly one state is reachable from the start state via forward computation.
- Naive and insecure ABE for NFA$^{\oplus p}$: Decryption follows normal forward computation keeping track of whether a state is reachable from the start state.
- Our selective ABE for NFA$^{\oplus p}$: Decryption follows normal forward computation keeping track of the number of paths from the start state, whereas the security proof introduces entropy scaled by the number of paths that are reachable from the accept states via back-tracking.

We summarize the discussion in Fig. 5.

ABE for DFA vs Branching Programs. Our work clarifies that the same obstacle (having to guess a large subset of states that are reached upon back-tracking) arose in constructing adaptive ABE for DFA and compact adaptive ABE for branching programs from k-Lin, and presents a new technique that solves both problems simultaneously in the setting of KP-ABE. Furthermore, our results and techniques can carry over to the CP-ABE settings using more-or-less standard (but admittedly non-black-box) arguments, following e.g. [4, Sec. 8] and [6, Sec. 4]. See the full paper for adaptively secure CP-ABE for DFA and branching programs, respectively.

Interestingly, the very recent work of Agrawal et $al.$ [2,3] shows a related connection: namely that compact and unbounded adaptive KP and CP-ABE for branching programs[6] –for which they do not provide any instantiations– yields compact adaptive KP-ABE (as well as CP-ABE) for DFA. In particular, just getting to KP-ABE for DFA already requires both KP and CP-ABE for branching programs and also incurs a larger polynomial blow-up in the parameters compared to our constructions; furthermore, simply getting to compact, unbounded, adaptive KP-ABE for branching programs would also require most of the technical machinery used in this work, notably the "nested, two-slot" dual system argument and the piecewise guessing framework. Nonetheless, there is significant conceptual appeal to having a generic and modular transformation that also yields both KP-ABE and CP-ABE schemes. That said, at the core of our constructions and analysis is a very simple combinatorial object sketched in Sect. 1.2. We leave the question of properly formalizing this object and building a generic compiler to full-fledged KP-ABE and CP-ABE schemes to further work; in particular, such a compiler should (i) match or improve upon the concrete efficiency of our schemes, as with prior compilers such as [5,7], and (ii) properly decouple the combinatorial arguments that are specific to DFA, NFA and branching programs from the computational arguments that are oblivious to the underlying computational model.

Organization. The next section gives some background knowledge. Section 3 shows the transformation from DFA to $\mathcal{E}$-restricted NFA$^{\oplus p}$. We show our selectively secure ABE for NFA$^{\oplus p}$ in Sect. 4 and upgrade to adaptive security for $\mathcal{E}_Q$-restricted NFA$^{\oplus p}$ in Sect. 5. The latter implies our adaptively secure ABE for DFA. See the full paper for the concrete description and our basic selectively secure ABE for NFA$^{\oplus p}$ from q-type assumption. We also defer our compact adaptively secure ABE for branching programs to the full paper.

2   Preliminaries

Notation. We denote by $s \leftarrow S$ the fact that s is picked uniformly at random from a finite set S; by $U(S)$, we indicate uniform distribution over finite set S. We use $\approx_s$ to denote two distributions being statistically indistinguishable, and $\approx_c$ to denote two distributions being computationally indistinguishable. We use $\langle \mathcal{A}, \mathsf{G} \rangle = 1$ to denote that an adversary $\mathcal{A}$ wins in an interactive game G. We use lower case boldface to denote row vectors and upper case boldcase to denote matrices. We use $\mathbf{e}_i$ to denote the i'th elementary (row) vector (with 1 at the i'th position and 0 elsewhere) and let $\mathcal{E}_Q$ denote the set of all elementary vectors

---

[6] The statement in [3] refers to monotone span programs, which is a more powerful object, but we believe that branching program suffices.

of dimension Q. For matrix $\mathbf{A}$, we use $\mathsf{span}(\mathbf{A})$ to denote the *row* span of $\mathbf{A}$ and use $\mathsf{basis}(\mathbf{A})$ to denote a basis of *column* span of $\mathbf{A}$. Throughout the paper, we use prime number p to denote the order of underlying groups.

2.1 Attribute-Based Encryption

Syntax. An attribute-based encryption (ABE) scheme for some class $\mathcal{C}$ consists of four algorithms:

$\mathsf{Setup}(1^\lambda, \mathcal{C}) \rightarrow (\mathsf{mpk}, \mathsf{msk})$. The setup algorithm gets as input the security parameter 1^λ and class description $\mathcal{C}$. It outputs the master public key mpk and the master secret key msk. We assume mpk defines the message space $\mathcal{M}$.

$\mathsf{Enc}(\mathsf{mpk}, x, m) \rightarrow \mathsf{ct}_x$. The encryption algorithm gets as input mpk, an input x and a message $m \in \mathcal{M}$. It outputs a ciphertext ct_x. Note that x is public given ct_x.

$\mathsf{KeyGen}(\mathsf{mpk}, \mathsf{msk}, \Gamma) \rightarrow \mathsf{sk}_\Gamma$. The key generation algorithm gets as input mpk, msk and $\Gamma \in \mathcal{C}$. It outputs a secret key sk_Γ. Note that Γ is public given sk_Γ.

$\mathsf{Dec}(\mathsf{mpk}, \mathsf{sk}_\Gamma, \mathsf{ct}_x) \rightarrow m$. The decryption algorithm gets as input sk_Γ and ct_x such that $\Gamma(x) = 1$ along with mpk. It outputs a message m.

Correctness. For all input x and Γ with $\Gamma(x) = 1$ and all $m \in \mathcal{M}$, we require

$$\Pr \left[\mathsf{Dec}(\mathsf{mpk}, \mathsf{sk}_\Gamma, \mathsf{ct}_x) = m : \begin{array}{c} (\mathsf{mpk}, \mathsf{msk}) \leftarrow \mathsf{Setup}(1^\lambda, \mathcal{C}) \\ \mathsf{sk}_\Gamma \leftarrow \mathsf{KeyGen}(\mathsf{mpk}, \mathsf{msk}, \Gamma) \\ \mathsf{ct}_x \leftarrow \mathsf{Enc}(\mathsf{mpk}, x, m) \end{array} \right] = 1.$$

Security Definition. For a stateful adversary $\mathcal{A}$, we define the advantage function

$$\mathsf{Adv}_{\mathcal{A}}^{\mathrm{ABE}}(\lambda) := \Pr \left[\beta = \beta' : \begin{array}{c} (\mathsf{mpk}, \mathsf{msk}) \leftarrow \mathsf{Setup}(1^\lambda, \mathcal{C}) \\ (x^*, m_0, m_1) \leftarrow \mathcal{A}^{\mathsf{KeyGen}(\mathsf{mpk}, \mathsf{msk}, \cdot)}(\mathsf{mpk}) \\ \beta \leftarrow \{0, 1\}; \ \mathsf{ct}_{x^*} \leftarrow \mathsf{Enc}(\mathsf{mpk}, x^*, m_\beta) \\ \beta' \leftarrow \mathcal{A}^{\mathsf{KeyGen}(\mathsf{mpk}, \mathsf{msk}, \cdot)}(\mathsf{ct}_{x^*}) \end{array} \right] - \frac{1}{2}$$

with the restriction that all queries Γ that $\mathcal{A}$ sent to $\mathsf{KeyGen}(\mathsf{mpk}, \mathsf{msk}, \cdot)$ satisfy $\Gamma(x^*) = 0$. An ABE scheme is *adaptively secure* if for all PPT adversaries $\mathcal{A}$, the advantage $\mathsf{Adv}_{\mathcal{A}}^{\mathrm{ABE}}(\lambda)$ is a negligible function in λ. The *selective* security is defined analogously except that the adversary $\mathcal{A}$ selects x^* before seeing mpk. A notion between selective and adaptive is so-called *semi-adaptive security* [9] where the adversary $\mathcal{A}$ is allowed to select x^* after seeing mpk but before making any queries.

2.2 Prime-Order Groups

A generator $\mathcal{G}$ takes as input a security parameter 1^λ and outputs a description $\mathbb{G} := (p, G_1, G_2, G_T, e)$, where p is a prime of $\Theta(\lambda)$ bits, G_1, G_2 and G_T are cyclic groups of order p, and $e : G_1 \times G_2 \to G_T$ is a non-degenerate bilinear map. We require that the group operations in G_1, G_2, G_T and the bilinear map e are computable in deterministic polynomial time in λ. Let $g_1 \in G_1$, $g_2 \in G_2$ and $g_T = e(g_1, g_2) \in G_T$ be the respective generators. We employ the *implicit representation* of group elements: for a matrix $\mathbf{M}$ over $\mathbb{Z}_p$, we define $[\mathbf{M}]_1 := g_1^\mathbf{M}, [\mathbf{M}]_2 := g_2^\mathbf{M}, [\mathbf{M}]_T := g_T^\mathbf{M}$, where exponentiation is carried out component-wise. Also, given $[\mathbf{A}]_1, [\mathbf{B}]_2$, we let $e([\mathbf{A}]_1, [\mathbf{B}]_2) = [\mathbf{AB}]_T$. We recall the matrix Diffie-Hellman (MDDH) assumption on G_1 [10]:

Assumption 1 (MDDH$_{k,k'}^d$ Assumption). *Let $k' > k \geq 1$ and $d \geq 1$. We say that the MDDH$_{k,k'}^d$ assumption holds if for all PPT adversaries $\mathcal{A}$, the following advantage function is negligible in λ.*

$$\mathsf{Adv}_\mathcal{A}^{\mathrm{MDDH}_{k,k'}^d}(\lambda) := \big| \Pr[\mathcal{A}(\mathbb{G}, [\mathbf{M}]_1, \boxed{[\mathbf{MS}]_1}) = 1] - \Pr[\mathcal{A}(\mathbb{G}, [\mathbf{M}]_1, \boxed{[\mathbf{U}]_1}) = 1] \big|$$

where $\mathbb{G} := (p, G_1, G_2, G_T, e) \leftarrow \mathcal{G}(1^\lambda)$, $\mathbf{M} \leftarrow \mathbb{Z}_p^{k' \times k}$, $\mathbf{S} \leftarrow \mathbb{Z}_p^{k \times d}$ and $\mathbf{U} \leftarrow \mathbb{Z}_p^{k' \times d}$.

The MDDH assumption on G_2 can be defined in an analogous way. Escala *et al.* [10] showed that

$$k\text{-Lin} \Rightarrow \mathrm{MDDH}_{k,k+1}^1 \Rightarrow \mathrm{MDDH}_{k,k'}^d \ \forall k' > k, d \geq 1$$

with a tight security reduction. We will use $\mathsf{Adv}_\mathcal{A}^{k\text{-LIN}}(\lambda)$ to denote the advantage function w.r.t. k-Lin assumption.

3   DFA, NFA, and Their Relationships

Let p be a global parameter and $\mathcal{E}_Q = \{\mathbf{e}_1, \dots, \mathbf{e}_Q\}$ be the set of all elementary row vectors of dimension Q. This section describes various notions of DFA and NFA and studies their relationships.

Finite Automata. We use $\Gamma = (Q, \Sigma, \{\mathbf{M}_\sigma\}_{\sigma \in \Sigma}, \mathbf{u}, \mathbf{f})$ to describe deterministic finite automata (DFA for short), nondeterministic finite automata (NFA for short), p-bounded NFA (NFA$^{<p}$ for short) and mod-p NFA (NFA$^{\oplus p}$ for short), where $Q \in \mathbb{N}$ is the number of states, vectors $\mathbf{u}, \mathbf{f} \in \{0,1\}^{1 \times Q}$ describe the start and accept states, a collection of matrices $\mathbf{M}_\sigma \in \{0,1\}^{Q \times Q}$ describe the transition function. Let $x = (x_1, \dots, x_\ell)$ denote an input, then,

- for DFA Γ, we have $\mathbf{u} \in \mathcal{E}_Q$, each column in every matrix $\mathbf{M}_\sigma$ is an elementary column vector (i.e., contains exactly one 1) and

$$\Gamma(x) = 1 \iff \mathbf{f}\mathbf{M}_{x_\ell} \cdots \mathbf{M}_{x_1}\mathbf{u}^\top = 1;$$

- for NFA Γ, we have

$$\Gamma(x) = 1 \iff \mathbf{f}\mathbf{M}_{x_\ell} \cdots \mathbf{M}_{x_1}\mathbf{u}^\top > 0;$$

– for NFA$^{<p}$ Γ, we have $\mathbf{f}\mathbf{M}_{x_\ell}\cdots\mathbf{M}_{x_1}\mathbf{u}^\top < p$ and

$$\Gamma(x) = 1 \iff \mathbf{f}\mathbf{M}_{x_\ell}\cdots\mathbf{M}_{x_1}\mathbf{u}^\top > 0;$$

– for NFA$^{\oplus p}$ Γ, we have

$$\Gamma(x) = 1 \iff \mathbf{f}\mathbf{M}_{x_\ell}\cdots\mathbf{M}_{x_1}\mathbf{u}^\top \neq 0 \bmod p.$$

We immediately have: DFA $\subset$ NFA$^{<p}\subset$ NFA $\cap$ NFA$^{\oplus p}$.

$\mathcal{E}_Q$-Restricted NFA$^{\oplus p}$. We introduce the notion of $\mathcal{E}_Q$-restricted NFA$^{\oplus p}$ which is an NFA$^{\oplus p}$ $\Gamma = (Q, \Sigma, \{\mathbf{M}_\sigma\}_{\sigma\in\Sigma}, \mathbf{u}, \mathbf{f})$ with an additional property: for all $\ell \in \mathbb{N}$ and all $x \in \Sigma^\ell$, it holds that

$$\mathbf{f}_{i,x} := \mathbf{f}\mathbf{M}_{x_\ell}\cdots\mathbf{M}_{x_{i+1}} \in \mathcal{E}_Q, \ \forall i \in [0, \ell]$$

Here $\mathbf{M}_{x_\ell}\cdots\mathbf{M}_{x_{i+1}}$ for $i = \ell$ refers to $\mathbf{I}$ of size $Q \times Q$.

Transforming DFA to $\mathcal{E}_Q$-Restricted NFA$^{\oplus p}$. In general, a DFA is not necessarily a $\mathcal{E}_Q$-restricted NFA$^{\oplus p}$. The next lemma says that we can nonetheless transform any DFA into a $\mathcal{E}_Q$-restricted NFA$^{\oplus p}$:

Lemma 1 (DFA to $\mathcal{E}_Q$-restricted NFA$^{\oplus p}$). *For each DFA $\Gamma = (Q, \Sigma, \{\mathbf{M}_\sigma\}_{\sigma\in\Sigma}, \mathbf{u}, \mathbf{f})$, we have NFA$^{\oplus p}$ $\Gamma^\top = (Q, \Sigma, \{\mathbf{M}_\sigma^\top\}_{\sigma\in\Sigma}, \mathbf{f}, \mathbf{u})$ such that*

1. $\Gamma^\top$ is $\mathcal{E}_Q$-restricted;
2. for all $\ell \in \mathbb{N}$ and $x = (x_1, \ldots, x_\ell) \in \Sigma^\ell$, it holds that

$$\Gamma(x) = 1 \iff \Gamma^\top(x^\top) = 1 \quad \text{where } x^\top = (x_\ell, \ldots, x_1) \in \Sigma^\ell. \tag{7}$$

Proof. Recall that the definition of DFA implies two properties:

$$\mathbf{f} \in \{0, 1\}^Q \tag{8}$$

$$\text{and} \quad (\mathbf{M}_{x_i}\cdots\mathbf{M}_{x_1}\mathbf{u}^\top)^\top \in \mathcal{E}_Q, \quad \forall i \in [0, \ell]. \tag{9}$$

Property (9) comes from the facts that $\mathbf{u} \in \mathcal{E}_Q$ and each column in every matrix $\mathbf{M}_\sigma$ is an elementary column vector.

We parse $x^\top = (x_1^\top, \ldots, x_\ell^\top)$ and prove the two parts of the lemma as below.

1. $\Gamma^\top$ is $\mathcal{E}_Q$-restricted since we have

$$\mathbf{u}\mathbf{M}_{x_\ell^\top}^\top\cdots\mathbf{M}_{x_{i+1}^\top}^\top = (\mathbf{M}_{x_{\ell-i}}\cdots\mathbf{M}_{x_1}\mathbf{u}^\top)^\top \in \mathcal{E}_Q, \quad \forall i \in [0, \ell]$$

where the equality is implied by the structure of $\Gamma^\top, x^\top$ and we use property (9).

2. To prove (7), we rely on the fact

$$\Gamma(x) = 1 \iff \mathbf{f}\mathbf{M}_{x_\ell}\cdots\mathbf{M}_{x_1}\mathbf{u}^\top = 1$$

$$\iff \mathbf{f}\mathbf{M}_{x_\ell}\cdots\mathbf{M}_{x_1}\mathbf{u}^\top \neq 0 \bmod p$$

$$\iff \mathbf{u}\mathbf{M}_{x_\ell^\top}^\top\cdots\mathbf{M}_{x_1^\top}^\top\mathbf{f}^\top \neq 0 \bmod p$$

$$\iff \Gamma^\top(x^\top) = 1.$$

The second $\iff$ follows from the fact that $\mathbf{f}\mathbf{M}_{x_\ell}\cdots\mathbf{M}_{x_1}\mathbf{u}^\top \in \{0, 1\}$ which is implied by property (8) and (9) while the third $\iff$ is implied by the structure of $\Gamma^\top, x^\top$. $\qquad\square$

4 Semi-adaptively Secure ABE for NFA$^{\oplus p}$

In this section, we present our ABE for NFA$^{\oplus p}$ in prime-order groups. The scheme achieves semi-adaptive security under the k-Lin assumption. Our construction is based on GWW ABE for DFA [11] along with an extension of the key structure and decryption to NFA; the security proof follows that of GWW with our novel combinatorial arguments regarding our NFA extension. (See Sect. 1.2 for an overview.) We remark that our scheme and proof work well for a more general form of NFA$^{\oplus p}$ where $\mathbf{u}, \mathbf{f}, \mathbf{M}_\sigma$ are over $\mathbb{Z}_p$ instead of $\{0, 1\}$.

4.1 Basis

We will use the same basis as GWW [11]:

$$\mathbf{A}_1 \leftarrow \mathbb{Z}_p^{k \times (2k+1)}, \quad \mathbf{a}_2 \leftarrow \mathbb{Z}_p^{1 \times (2k+1)}, \quad \mathbf{A}_3 \leftarrow \mathbb{Z}_p^{k \times (2k+1)} \tag{10}$$

and use $(\mathbf{A}_1^\| \mid \mathbf{a}_2^\| \mid \mathbf{A}_3^\|)$ to denote the dual basis so that $\mathbf{A}_i \mathbf{A}_i^\| = \mathbf{I}$ (known as *non-degeneracy*) and $\mathbf{A}_i \mathbf{A}_j^\| = \mathbf{0}$ if $i \neq j$ (known as *orthogonality*). For notational convenience, we always consider $\mathbf{a}_2^\|$ as a column vector. We review $\mathrm{SD}_{\mathbf{A}_1 \mapsto \mathbf{A}_1, \mathbf{A}_3}^{G_1}$ and $\mathrm{DDH}_{d,Q}^{G_2}$ assumption from [8] which are parameterized for basis (10) and tightly implied by k-Lin assumption. By symmetry, we may permute the indices for $\mathbf{A}_1, \mathbf{a}_2, \mathbf{A}_3$.

Lemma 2 (MDDH$_{k,2k}$ $\Rightarrow$ SD$_{\mathbf{A}_1 \mapsto \mathbf{A}_1, \mathbf{A}_3}^{G_1}$ [8]). *Under the MDDH$_{k,2k}$ assumption in G_1, there exists an efficient sampler outputting random $([\mathbf{A}_1]_1, [\mathbf{a}_2]_1, [\mathbf{A}_3]_1)$ along with base* $\mathsf{basis}(\mathbf{A}_1^\|)$, $\mathsf{basis}(\mathbf{a}_2^\|)$, $\mathsf{basis}(\mathbf{A}_1^\|, \mathbf{A}_3^\|)$ *(of arbitrary choice) such that the following advantage function is negligible in λ.*

$$\mathsf{Adv}_{\mathcal{A}}^{\mathrm{SD}_{\mathbf{A}_1 \mapsto \mathbf{A}_1, \mathbf{A}_3}^{G_1}}(\lambda) := \big| \Pr[\mathcal{A}(D, [\mathbf{t}_0]_1) = 1] - \Pr[\mathcal{A}(D, [\mathbf{t}_1]_1) = 1] \big|$$

where

$$D := (\ [\mathbf{A}_1]_1, [\mathbf{a}_2]_1, [\mathbf{A}_3]_1, \mathsf{basis}(\mathbf{A}_1^\|), \mathsf{basis}(\mathbf{a}_2^\|), \mathsf{basis}(\mathbf{A}_1^\|, \mathbf{A}_3^\|)\ ),$$
$$\mathbf{t}_0 \leftarrow \boxed{\mathsf{span}(\mathbf{A}_1)}, \quad \mathbf{t}_1 \leftarrow \boxed{\mathsf{span}(\mathbf{A}_1, \mathbf{A}_3)}.$$

More concretely, we have, for all $\mathcal{A}$, there exists $\mathcal{B}$ with $\mathsf{Time}(\mathcal{B}) \approx \mathsf{Time}(\mathcal{A})$ such that $\mathsf{Adv}_{\mathcal{A}}^{\mathrm{SD}_{\mathbf{A}_1 \mapsto \mathbf{A}_1, \mathbf{A}_3}^{G_1}}(\lambda) \leq \mathsf{Adv}_{\mathcal{A}}^{\mathrm{MDDH}_{k,2k}}(\lambda)$.

Lemma 3 (MDDH$_{k,k+d}^d$ $\Rightarrow$ DDH$_{d,Q}^{G_2}$ [8]). *Let $d, Q \in \mathbb{N}$. Under the MDDH$_{k,k+d}^d$ assumption in G_2, the following advantage function is negligible in λ.*

$$\mathsf{Adv}_{\mathcal{A}}^{\mathrm{DDH}_{d,Q}^{G_2}}(\lambda) := \big| \Pr[\mathcal{A}([\mathbf{WB}]_2, [\mathbf{B}]_2, \boxed{[\mathbf{WR}]_2}, [\mathbf{R}]_2) = 1]$$
$$- \Pr[\mathcal{A}([\mathbf{WB}]_2, [\mathbf{B}]_2, \boxed{[\mathbf{WR} + \mathbf{U}]_2}, [\mathbf{R}]_2) = 1] \big|$$

where $\mathbf{W} \leftarrow \mathbb{Z}_p^{d \times k}$, $\mathbf{B} \leftarrow \mathbb{Z}_p^{k \times k}$, $\mathbf{R} \leftarrow \mathbb{Z}_p^{k \times Q}$ and $\mathbf{U} \leftarrow \mathbb{Z}_p^{d \times Q}$. More concretely, we have, for all $\mathcal{A}$, there exists $\mathcal{B}$ with $\mathsf{Time}(\mathcal{B}) \approx \mathsf{Time}(\mathcal{A})$ such that $\mathsf{Adv}_{\mathcal{A}}^{\mathrm{DDH}_{d,Q}^{G_2}}(\lambda) \leq O(1) \cdot \mathsf{Adv}_{\mathcal{A}}^{\mathrm{MDDH}_{k,k+d}^d}(\lambda)$.

Lemma 4 (statistical lemma [8]). *With probability* $1 - 1/p$ *over* $\mathbf{A}_1, \mathbf{a}_2,$ $\mathbf{A}_3, \mathbf{A}_1^{\parallel}, \mathbf{a}_2^{\parallel}, \mathbf{A}_3^{\parallel},$ *the following two distributions are statistically identical.*

$$\{\; \mathbf{A}_1\mathbf{W}, \mathbf{A}_3\mathbf{W}, \boxed{\mathbf{a}_2\mathbf{W}} \;\} \quad and \quad \{\; \mathbf{A}_1\mathbf{W}, \mathbf{A}_3\mathbf{W}, \boxed{\mathbf{w}} \;\}$$

where $\mathbf{W} \leftarrow \mathbb{Z}_p^{(2k+1)\times k}$ *and* $\mathbf{w} \leftarrow \mathbb{Z}_p^{1\times k}$.

4.2 Scheme

Our ABE for $\mathrm{NFA}^{\oplus_p}$ in prime-order groups is described as follows:

– Setup$(1^{\lambda}, \Sigma)$: Run $\mathbb{G} = (p, G_1, G_2, G_T, e) \leftarrow \mathcal{G}(1^{\lambda})$. Sample

$$\mathbf{A}_1 \leftarrow \mathbb{Z}_p^{k\times(2k+1)}, \mathbf{k} \leftarrow \mathbb{Z}_p^{1\times(2k+1)}, \mathbf{W}_{\mathrm{start}}, \mathbf{Z}_b, \mathbf{W}_{\sigma,b}, \mathbf{W}_{\mathrm{end}} \leftarrow \mathbb{Z}_p^{(2k+1)\times k}$$

for all $\sigma \in \Sigma$ and $b \in \{0,1\}$. Output

$$\mathsf{mpk} = (\,[\,\mathbf{A}_1, \mathbf{A}_1\mathbf{W}_{\mathrm{start}}, \{\,\mathbf{A}_1\mathbf{Z}_b, \mathbf{A}_1\mathbf{W}_{\sigma,b}\,\}_{\sigma\in\Sigma, b\in\{0,1\}}, \mathbf{A}_1\mathbf{W}_{\mathrm{end}}\,]_1, [\mathbf{A}_1\mathbf{k}^{\top}]_T\,)$$
$$\mathsf{msk} = (\,\mathbf{k}, \mathbf{W}_{\mathrm{start}}, \{\,\mathbf{Z}_b, \mathbf{W}_{\sigma,b}\,\}_{\sigma\in\Sigma, b\in\{0,1\}}, \mathbf{W}_{\mathrm{end}}\,).$$

– Enc(mpk, x, m) : Let $x = (x_1, \ldots, x_{\ell}) \in \Sigma^{\ell}$ and $m \in G_T$. Pick $\mathbf{s}_0, \mathbf{s}_1, \ldots, \mathbf{s}_{\ell} \leftarrow \mathbb{Z}_p^{1\times k}$ and output

$$\mathsf{ct}_x = \left(\begin{array}{c} [\mathbf{s}_0\mathbf{A}_1]_1, [\mathbf{s}_0\mathbf{A}_1\mathbf{W}_{\mathrm{start}}]_1 \\ \{[\mathbf{s}_j\mathbf{A}_1]_1, [\mathbf{s}_{j-1}\mathbf{A}_1\mathbf{Z}_{j \bmod 2} + \mathbf{s}_j\mathbf{A}_1\mathbf{W}_{x_j, j \bmod 2}]_1\}_{j\in[\ell]} \\ [\mathbf{s}_{\ell}\mathbf{A}_1]_1, [\mathbf{s}_{\ell}\mathbf{A}_1\mathbf{W}_{\mathrm{end}}]_1, [\mathbf{s}_{\ell}\mathbf{A}_1\mathbf{k}^{\top}]_T \cdot m \end{array} \right).$$

– KeyGen$(\mathsf{mpk}, \mathsf{msk}, \Gamma)$: Let $\Gamma = (Q, \Sigma, \{\mathbf{M}_{\sigma}\}_{\sigma\in\Sigma}, \mathbf{u}, \mathbf{f})$. Pick $\mathbf{D} \leftarrow \mathbb{Z}_p^{(2k+1)\times Q}$, $\mathbf{R} \leftarrow \mathbb{Z}_p^{k\times Q}$ and output

$$\mathsf{sk}_{\Gamma} = \left(\begin{array}{c} [\mathbf{D}\mathbf{u}^{\top} + \mathbf{W}_{\mathrm{start}}\mathbf{R}\mathbf{u}^{\top}]_2, [\mathbf{R}\mathbf{u}^{\top}]_2 \\ \{[-\mathbf{D} + \mathbf{Z}_b\mathbf{R}]_2, [\mathbf{D}\mathbf{M}_{\sigma} + \mathbf{W}_{\sigma,b}\mathbf{R}]_2, [\mathbf{R}]_2\}_{\sigma\in\Sigma, b\in\{0,1\}} \\ [\mathbf{k}^{\top}\mathbf{f} - \mathbf{D} + \mathbf{W}_{\mathrm{end}}\mathbf{R}]_2, [\mathbf{R}]_2 \end{array} \right).$$

– Dec$(\mathsf{mpk}, \mathsf{sk}_{\Gamma}, \mathsf{ct}_x)$: Parse ciphertext for $x = (x_1, \ldots, x_{\ell})$ and key for $\Gamma = (Q, \Sigma, \{\mathbf{M}_{\sigma}\}_{\sigma\in\Sigma}, \mathbf{u}, \mathbf{f})$ as:

$$\mathsf{ct}_x = \left(\begin{array}{c} [\mathbf{c}_{0,1}]_1, [\mathbf{c}_{0,2}]_1 \\ \{\,[\mathbf{c}_{j,1}]_1, [\mathbf{c}_{j,2}]_1\,\}_j \\ [\mathbf{c}_{\ell,1}]_1, [\mathbf{c}_{\mathrm{end}}]_1, C \end{array} \right) \quad \text{and} \quad \mathsf{sk}_{\Gamma} = \left(\begin{array}{c} [\mathbf{k}_0^{\top}]_2, [\mathbf{r}_0^{\top}]_2 \\ \{\,[\mathbf{K}_b]_2, [\mathbf{K}_{\sigma,b}]_2, [\mathbf{R}]_2\,\}_{\sigma,b} \\ [\mathbf{K}_{\mathrm{end}}]_2, [\mathbf{R}]_2 \end{array} \right)$$

We define

$$\mathbf{u}_{j,x}^{\top} = \mathbf{M}_{x_j} \cdots \mathbf{M}_{x_1} \mathbf{u}^{\top} \bmod p, \quad \forall j \in [0, \ell] \tag{11}$$

and proceed as follows:

1. Compute

$$B_0 = e([\mathbf{c}_{0,1}]_1, [\mathbf{k}_0^{\top}]_2) \cdot e([\mathbf{c}_{0,2}]_1, [\mathbf{r}_0^{\top}]_2)^{-1};$$

2. For all $j \in [\ell]$, compute

$$[\mathbf{b}_j]_T = e([\mathbf{c}_{j-1,1}]_1, [\mathbf{K}_{j \bmod 2}]_2) \cdot e([\mathbf{c}_{j,1}]_1, [\mathbf{K}_{x_j, j \bmod 2}]_2) \cdot e([-\mathbf{c}_{j,2}]_1, [\mathbf{R}]_2)$$
$$\text{and} \quad B_j = [\mathbf{b}_j \mathbf{u}_{j-1,x}^\top]_T;$$

3. Compute

$$[\mathbf{b}_{\mathrm{end}}]_T = e([\mathbf{c}_{\ell,1}]_1, [\mathbf{K}_{\mathrm{end}}]_2) \cdot e([-\mathbf{c}_{\mathrm{end}}]_1, [\mathbf{R}]_2) \quad \text{and} \quad B_{\mathrm{end}} = [\mathbf{b}_{\mathrm{end}} \mathbf{u}_{\ell,x}^\top]_T;$$

4. Compute

$$B_{\mathrm{all}} = B_0 \cdot \prod_{j=1}^{\ell} B_j \cdot B_{\mathrm{end}} \quad \text{and} \quad B = B_{\mathrm{all}}^{(\mathbf{f} \mathbf{u}_{\ell,x}^\top)^{-1}}$$

and output the message $m' \leftarrow C \cdot B^{-1}$.

Correctness. For $x = (x_1, \ldots, x_\ell)$ and $\Gamma = (Q, \Sigma, \{\mathbf{M}_\sigma\}_{\sigma \in \Sigma}, \mathbf{u}, \mathbf{f})$ such that $\Gamma(x) = 1$, we have:

$$B_0 = [\mathbf{s}_0 \mathbf{A}_1 \mathbf{D} \mathbf{u}^\top]_T = [\mathbf{s}_0 \mathbf{A}_1 \mathbf{D} \mathbf{u}_{0,x}^\top]_T \tag{12}$$

$$\mathbf{b}_j = \mathbf{s}_j \mathbf{A}_1 \mathbf{D} \mathbf{M}_{x_j} - \mathbf{s}_{j-1} \mathbf{A}_1 \mathbf{D} \tag{13}$$

$$B_j = [\mathbf{s}_j \mathbf{A}_1 \mathbf{D} \mathbf{u}_{j,x}^\top - \mathbf{s}_{j-1} \mathbf{A}_1 \mathbf{D} \mathbf{u}_{j-1,x}^\top]_T \tag{14}$$

$$\mathbf{b}_{\mathrm{end}} = \mathbf{s}_\ell \mathbf{A}_1 \mathbf{k}^\top \mathbf{f} - \mathbf{s}_\ell \mathbf{A}_1 \mathbf{D} \tag{15}$$

$$B_{\mathrm{end}} = [\mathbf{s}_\ell \mathbf{A}_1 \mathbf{k}^\top \mathbf{f} \mathbf{u}_{\ell,x}^\top - \mathbf{s}_\ell \mathbf{A}_1 \mathbf{D} \mathbf{u}_{\ell,x}^\top]_T \tag{16}$$

$$B_{\mathrm{all}} = [\mathbf{s}_\ell \mathbf{A}_1 \mathbf{k}^\top \mathbf{f} \mathbf{u}_{\ell,x}^\top]_T \tag{17}$$

$$B = [\mathbf{s}_\ell \mathbf{A}_1 \mathbf{k}^\top]_T \tag{18}$$

Here (16) is trivial; (14) and (18) follow from

$$\mathbf{u}_{j,x}^\top = \mathbf{M}_{x_j} \mathbf{u}_{j-1,x}^\top \bmod p, \ \forall j \in [\ell] \quad \text{and} \quad \Gamma(x) = 1 \iff \mathbf{f} \mathbf{u}_{\ell,x}^\top \neq 0 \bmod p \tag{19}$$

by the definition in (11), the remaining equalities follow [7], more detail can be found in the full paper.

Security. We have the following theorem stating that our construction is selectively secure. We remark that our construction achieves semi-adaptive security as is and the proof is almost the same.

Theorem 1 (Selectively secure ABE for NFA$^{\oplus p}$). *The ABE scheme for NFA$^{\oplus p}$ in prime-order bilinear groups described above is selectively secure (cf. Sect. 2.1) under the k-Lin assumption with security loss $O(\ell \cdot |\Sigma|)$. Here ℓ is the length of the challenge input x^*.*

4.3 Game Sequence

The proof is analogous to GWW's proof. We show the proof in the one-key setting where the adversary asks for at most one secret key; this is sufficient to motivate the proof in the next section. As in [11], it is straightforward to handle many keys, see the full paper for more details. Let $x^* \in \Sigma^\ell$ denote the selective challenge and let $\bar{\ell} = \ell \bmod 2$. Without loss of generality, we assume $\ell > 1$. We begin with some auxiliary distributions.

Auxiliary Distributions. We describe the auxiliary ciphertext and key distributions that we use in the proof. Throughout, the distributions are the same as the original distributions except for the so-called $\mathbf{a}_2$-components which is defined as below.

$\mathbf{a}_2$-*Components.* For a ciphertext in the following form, capturing real and all auxiliary ciphertexts (defined below):

$$\mathsf{ct}_x = \begin{pmatrix} [\mathbf{c}_0]_1, \, [\mathbf{c}_0\mathbf{W}_{\text{start}}]_1 \\ \left\{ [\mathbf{c}_j\mathbf{A}_1]_1, [\mathbf{c}_{j-1}\mathbf{Z}_{j \bmod 2} + \mathbf{c}_j\mathbf{W}_{x_j, j \bmod 2}]_1 \right\}_j \\ [\mathbf{c}_\ell]_1, [\mathbf{c}_\ell\mathbf{W}_{\text{end}}]_1, [\mathbf{c}_\ell\mathbf{k}^\top]_T \cdot m \end{pmatrix} \tag{20}$$

where $\mathbf{c}_j = \mathbf{s}_j\mathbf{A}_1 + s_j\mathbf{a}_2 + \tilde{\mathbf{s}}_j\mathbf{A}_3$ with $\mathbf{s}_j, \tilde{\mathbf{s}}_j \in \mathbb{Z}_p^k$ and $s_j \in \mathbb{Z}_p$, we define its $\mathbf{a}_2$-components, denoted by $\mathsf{ct}_x[2]$, as follows:

$$\mathsf{ct}_x[2] = \begin{pmatrix} [s_0]_1, \, [s_0\mathbf{a}_2\mathbf{W}_{\text{start}}]_1 \\ \left\{ [s_j]_1, [s_{j-1}\mathbf{a}_2\mathbf{Z}_{j \bmod 2} + s_j\mathbf{a}_2\mathbf{W}_{x_j, j \bmod 2}]_1 \right\}_j \\ [s_\ell]_1, [s_\ell\mathbf{a}_2\mathbf{W}_{\text{end}}]_1, [s_\ell\mathbf{a}_2\mathbf{k}^\top]_T \cdot m \end{pmatrix}.$$

For a key in the following form, capturing real and all auxiliary keys (defined below):

$$\mathsf{sk}_\Gamma = \begin{pmatrix} [\mathbf{k}_0^\top]_2, [\mathbf{r}_0^\top]_2 \\ \left\{ [\mathbf{K}_b]_2, [\mathbf{K}_{\sigma,b}]_2, [\mathbf{R}]_2 \right\}_{\sigma,b} \\ [\mathbf{K}_{\text{end}}]_2, [\mathbf{R}]_2 \end{pmatrix} \tag{21}$$

where $\mathbf{k}_0 \in \mathbb{Z}_p^{1 \times (2k+1)}$, $\mathbf{K}_b, \mathbf{K}_{\sigma,b}, \mathbf{K}_{\text{end}} \in \mathbb{Z}_p^{(2k+1) \times Q}$ and $\mathbf{r}_0 \in \mathbb{Z}_p^{1 \times k}, \mathbf{R} \in \mathbb{Z}_p^{k \times Q}$, we define its $\mathbf{a}_2$-components, denoted by $\mathsf{sk}_\Gamma[2]$, as follows:

$$\mathsf{sk}_\Gamma[2] = \begin{pmatrix} [\mathbf{a}_2\mathbf{k}_0^\top]_2, [\mathbf{r}_0^\top]_2 \\ \left\{ [\mathbf{a}_2\mathbf{K}_b]_2, [\mathbf{a}_2\mathbf{K}_{\sigma,b}]_2, [\mathbf{R}]_2 \right\}_{\sigma,b} \\ [\mathbf{a}_2\mathbf{K}_{\text{end}}]_2, [\mathbf{R}]_2 \end{pmatrix}$$

For notation simplicity of $\mathsf{ct}_x[2]$ and $\mathsf{sk}_\Gamma[2]$ with $\mathbf{k}, \mathbf{D}, \mathbf{W}_{\text{start}}, \mathbf{W}_{\text{end}}, \mathbf{Z}_b, \mathbf{W}_{\sigma,b}$, we write

$$\alpha = \mathbf{a}_2\mathbf{k}^\top, \quad \mathbf{d} = \mathbf{a}_2\mathbf{D}, \quad \mathbf{w}_{\text{start}} = \mathbf{a}_2\mathbf{W}_{\text{start}}, \quad \mathbf{w}_{\text{end}} = \mathbf{a}_2\mathbf{W}_{\text{end}}, \quad \mathbf{z}_b = \mathbf{a}_2\mathbf{Z}_b, \quad \mathbf{w}_{\sigma,b} = \mathbf{a}_2\mathbf{W}_{\sigma,b}$$

and call them the $\mathbf{a}_2$-components of $\mathbf{k}^\top, \mathbf{D}, \mathbf{W}_{\text{start}}, \mathbf{W}_{\text{end}}, \mathbf{Z}_b, \mathbf{W}_{\sigma,b}$, respectively. We also omit zeroes and adjust the order of terms in $\mathsf{ct}_x[2]$. Furthermore, for all $\mathbf{A}_1, \mathbf{a}_2, \mathbf{A}_3$, mpk and various forms of $\mathsf{ct}_x, \mathsf{sk}_\Gamma$ we will use in the proof, we have

$$\mathsf{ct}_x[2], \mathsf{sk}_\Gamma[2], \{ \mathbf{A}_i\mathbf{k}^\top, \mathbf{A}_i\mathbf{D}, \mathbf{A}_i\mathbf{W}_{\text{start}}, \mathbf{A}_i\mathbf{W}_{\text{end}}, \mathbf{A}_i\mathbf{Z}_b, \mathbf{A}_i\mathbf{W}_{\sigma,b} \}_{i \in \{1,3\}, \sigma \in \Sigma, b \in \{0,1\}}$$
$$\approx_s \mathsf{ct}_x[2], \mathsf{sk}_\Gamma[2], \{ \mathbf{A}_i\widetilde{\mathbf{k}}^\top, \mathbf{A}_i\widetilde{\mathbf{D}}, \mathbf{A}_i\widetilde{\mathbf{W}}_{\text{start}}, \mathbf{A}_i\widetilde{\mathbf{W}}_{\text{end}}, \mathbf{A}_i\widetilde{\mathbf{Z}}_b, \mathbf{A}_i\widetilde{\mathbf{W}}_{\sigma,b} \}_{i \in \{1,3\}, \sigma \in \Sigma, b \in \{0,1\}}$$

where $\widetilde{\mathbf{k}} \leftarrow \mathbb{Z}_p^{1 \times (2k+1)}, \widetilde{\mathbf{D}} \leftarrow \mathbb{Z}_p^{(2k+1) \times Q}, \widetilde{\mathbf{W}}_{\text{start}}, \widetilde{\mathbf{W}}_{\text{end}}, \widetilde{\mathbf{Z}}_b, \widetilde{\mathbf{W}}_{\sigma,b} \leftarrow \mathbb{Z}_p^{(2k+1) \times k}$ are fresh. This follows from Lemma 4 and the fact that all matrices $\mathbf{W} \in \mathbb{Z}_p^{(2k+1) \times k'}$ with $k' \in \mathbb{N}$ can be decomposed as

$$\mathbf{W} = \mathbf{A}_1^{\|} \cdot \mathbf{A}_1\mathbf{W} + \mathbf{a}_2^{\|} \cdot \mathbf{a}_2\mathbf{W} + \mathbf{A}_3^{\|} \cdot \mathbf{A}_3\mathbf{W}.$$

The property allows us to simulate $\mathsf{mpk}, \mathsf{ct}_x, \mathsf{sk}_\Gamma$ from $\mathsf{ct}_x[2], \mathsf{sk}_\Gamma[2]$ and $\mathbf{A}_1, \mathbf{a}_2, \mathbf{A}_3$ so that we can focus on the crucial argument over $\mathbf{a}_2$-components in the proofs, e.g., those in Sects. 4.4, 4.5 and 4.6.

Ciphertext Distributions. We sample $s_0, s_1, \ldots, s_\ell \leftarrow \mathbb{Z}_p$ and define:

- for $i \in [0, \ell]$: $\mathsf{ct}_{x^*}^i$ is the same as ct_{x^*} except we replace $s_i\mathbf{A}_1$ with $s_i\mathbf{A}_1 + s_i\mathbf{a}_2$;
- for $i \in [\ell]$: $\mathsf{ct}_{x^*}^{i-1,i}$ is the same as ct_{x^*} except we replace $s_{i-1}\mathbf{A}_1, s_i\mathbf{A}_1$ with $s_{i-1}\mathbf{A}_1 + s_{i-1}\mathbf{a}_2, s_i\mathbf{A}_1 + s_i\mathbf{a}_2$.

That is, we have: writing $\tau = i \bmod 2$,

$$\mathsf{ct}_{x^*}^i[2] = \begin{cases} [s_0\mathbf{w}_{\mathrm{start}}]_1, \ [s_0]_1, \ [s_0\mathbf{z}_1]_1 & \text{if } i = 0 \\ [s_i\mathbf{w}_{x_i^*, \tau}]_1, \ [s_i]_1, \ [s_i\mathbf{z}_{1-\tau}]_1 & \text{if } i \in [\ell-1] \\ [s_\ell\mathbf{w}_{x_\ell^*, \bar{\ell}}]_1, \ [s_\ell]_1, \ [s_\ell\mathbf{w}_{\mathrm{end}}]_1, \ [s_\ell\alpha]_T \cdot m_\beta & \text{if } i = \ell \end{cases}$$

$$\mathsf{ct}_{x^*}^{i-1,i}[2] = \begin{cases} [s_0\mathbf{w}_{\mathrm{start}}]_1, \ [s_0]_1, \ [s_0\mathbf{z}_1 + s_1\mathbf{w}_{x_1^*, 1}]_1, \ [s_1]_1, \ [s_1\mathbf{z}_0]_1 \\ \qquad\qquad\qquad\qquad\qquad\qquad\qquad\qquad\qquad \text{if } i = 1 \\ [s_{i-1}\mathbf{w}_{x_{i-1}^*, 1-\tau}]_1, \ [s_{i-1}]_1, \ [s_{i-1}\mathbf{z}_\tau + s_i\mathbf{w}_{x_i^*, \tau}]_1, \ [s_i]_1, \ [s_i\mathbf{z}_{1-\tau}]_1 \\ \qquad\qquad\qquad\qquad\qquad\qquad\qquad\qquad\qquad \text{if } i \in [2, \ell-1] \\ [s_{\ell-1}\mathbf{w}_{x_{\ell-1}^*, 1-\bar{\ell}}]_1, \ [s_{\ell-1}]_1, \ [s_{\ell-1}\mathbf{z}_{\bar{\ell}} + s_\ell\mathbf{w}_{x_\ell^*, \bar{\ell}}]_1, \ [s_\ell]_1, \ [s_\ell\mathbf{w}_{\mathrm{end}}]_1, \ [s_\ell\alpha]_T \cdot m_\beta \\ \qquad\qquad\qquad\qquad\qquad\qquad\qquad\qquad\qquad \text{if } i = \ell \end{cases}$$

They are exactly the same as those used in GWW's proof [11].

Secret Key Distributions. Given $x^* \in \Sigma^\ell$ and $\Gamma = (Q, \Sigma, \{\mathbf{M}_\sigma\}_{\sigma \in \Sigma}, \mathbf{u}, \mathbf{f})$, we define

$$\mathbf{f}_{i,x^*} = \mathbf{f}\mathbf{M}_{x_\ell^*} \cdots \mathbf{M}_{x_{i+1}^*} \bmod p, \ \forall i \in [0, \ell]. \tag{22}$$

For all $i \in [\ell]$, we sample $\Delta \leftarrow \mathbb{Z}_p$ and define:

- sk_Γ^0 is the same as sk_Γ except we replace $\mathbf{D}$ with $\mathbf{D} + \mathbf{a}_2^\parallel \cdot s_0^{-1}\Delta \cdot \mathbf{f}_{0,x^*}$ in the term $[\mathbf{D}\mathbf{u}^\top + \mathbf{W}_{\mathrm{start}}\mathbf{R}\mathbf{u}^\top]_2$;
- sk_Γ^i is the same as sk_Γ except we replace $\mathbf{D}$ with $\mathbf{D} + \mathbf{a}_2^\parallel \cdot s_i^{-1}\Delta \cdot \mathbf{f}_{i,x^*}$ in the term $[\mathbf{D}\mathbf{M}_{x_i^*} + \mathbf{W}_{x_i^*, i \bmod 2}\mathbf{R}]_2$;
- $\mathsf{sk}_\Gamma^{i-1,i}$ is the same as sk_Γ except we replace $-\mathbf{D}$ with $-\mathbf{D} + \mathbf{a}_2^\parallel \cdot s_{i-1}^{-1}\Delta \cdot \mathbf{f}_{i-1,x^*}$ in the term $[-\mathbf{D} + \mathbf{Z}_{i \bmod 2}\mathbf{R}]_2$;
- $\mathsf{sk}_\Gamma^{\ell,*}$ is the same as sk_Γ except we replace $-\mathbf{D}$ with $-\mathbf{D} + \mathbf{a}_2^\parallel \cdot s_\ell^{-1}\Delta \cdot \mathbf{f}_{\ell,x^*}$ in the term $[\mathbf{k}^\top\mathbf{f} - \mathbf{D} + \mathbf{W}_{\mathrm{end}}\mathbf{R}]_2$.

That is, we have: writing $\tau = i \bmod 2$,

$$
\mathsf{sk}_\Gamma^0[2] = \left(
\begin{array}{c}
[(\mathbf{d} + \boxed{s_0^{-1}\Delta \cdot \mathbf{f}_{0,x^*}})\mathbf{u}^\top + \mathbf{w}_{\mathrm{start}}\mathbf{R}\mathbf{u}^\top]_2, [\mathbf{R}\mathbf{u}^\top]_2 \\
\big\{[-\mathbf{d} + \mathbf{z}_b\mathbf{R}]_2, [\mathbf{d}\mathbf{M}_\sigma + \mathbf{w}_{\sigma,b}\mathbf{R}]_2, [\mathbf{R}]_2\big\}_{\sigma\in\Sigma,b\in\{0,1\}} \\
[\alpha\mathbf{f} - \mathbf{d} + \mathbf{w}_{\mathrm{end}}\mathbf{R}]_2, [\mathbf{R}]_2
\end{array}
\right)
$$

$$
\mathsf{sk}_\Gamma^i[2] = \left(
\begin{array}{c}
[\mathbf{d}\mathbf{u}^\top + \mathbf{w}_{\mathrm{start}}\mathbf{R}\mathbf{u}^\top]_2, [\mathbf{R}\mathbf{u}^\top]_2 \\
\big\{[-\mathbf{d} + \mathbf{z}_\tau\mathbf{R}]_2, [(\mathbf{d} + \boxed{s_i^{-1}\Delta \cdot \mathbf{f}_{i,x^*}})\mathbf{M}_{x_i^*} + \mathbf{w}_{x_i^*,\tau}\mathbf{R}]_2, [\mathbf{R}]_2\big\} \\
\big\{[\mathbf{d}\mathbf{M}_\sigma + \mathbf{w}_{\sigma,\tau}\mathbf{R}]_2\big\}_{\sigma\neq x_i^*} \\
\big\{[-\mathbf{d} + \mathbf{z}_{1-\tau}\mathbf{R}]_2, [\mathbf{d}\mathbf{M}_\sigma + \mathbf{w}_{\sigma,1-\tau}\mathbf{R}]_2, [\mathbf{R}]_2\big\}_{\sigma\in\Sigma} \\
[\alpha\mathbf{f} - \mathbf{d} + \mathbf{w}_{\mathrm{end}}\mathbf{R}]_2, [\mathbf{R}]_2
\end{array}
\right)
$$

$$
\mathsf{sk}_\Gamma^{i-1,i}[2] = \left(
\begin{array}{c}
[\mathbf{d}\mathbf{u}^\top + \mathbf{w}_{\mathrm{start}}\mathbf{R}\mathbf{u}^\top]_2, [\mathbf{R}\mathbf{u}^\top]_2 \\
\big\{[-\mathbf{d} + \boxed{s_{i-1}^{-1}\Delta \cdot \mathbf{f}_{i-1,x^*}} + \mathbf{z}_\tau\mathbf{R}]_2, [\mathbf{d}\mathbf{M}_\sigma + \mathbf{w}_{\sigma,\tau}\mathbf{R}]_2, [\mathbf{R}]_2\big\}_{\sigma\in\Sigma} \\
\big\{[-\mathbf{d} + \mathbf{z}_{1-\tau}\mathbf{R}]_2, [\mathbf{d}\mathbf{M}_\sigma + \mathbf{w}_{\sigma,1-\tau}\mathbf{R}]_2, [\mathbf{R}]_2\big\}_{\sigma\in\Sigma} \\
[\alpha\mathbf{f} - \mathbf{d} + \mathbf{w}_{\mathrm{end}}\mathbf{R}]_2, [\mathbf{R}]_2
\end{array}
\right)
$$

$$
\mathsf{sk}_\Gamma^{\ell,*}[2] = \left(
\begin{array}{c}
[\mathbf{d}\mathbf{u}^\top + \mathbf{w}_{\mathrm{start}}\mathbf{R}\mathbf{u}^\top]_2, [\mathbf{R}\mathbf{u}^\top]_2 \\
\big\{[-\mathbf{d} + \mathbf{z}_b\mathbf{R}]_2, [\mathbf{d}\mathbf{M}_\sigma + \mathbf{w}_{\sigma,b}\mathbf{R}]_2, [\mathbf{R}]_2\big\}_{\sigma\in\Sigma,b\in\{0,1\}} \\
[\alpha\mathbf{f} - \mathbf{d} + \boxed{s_\ell^{-1}\Delta \cdot \mathbf{f}_{\ell,x^*}} + \mathbf{w}_{\mathrm{end}}\mathbf{R}]_2, [\mathbf{R}]_2
\end{array}
\right)
$$

They are analogous to those used in GWW's proof [11] with a novel way to change $\mathbf{a}_2$-components[7]. Following the notations in Sect. 1.2, we use $\mathbf{d}_i' = s_i^{-1}\Delta \cdot \mathbf{f}_{i,x^*}$ rather than $\mathbf{d}_i' = \Delta \cdot \mathbf{f}_{i,x^*}$. We remark that they are essentially the same but the former helps to simplify the exposition of the proof. Also, we note that s_i is independent of the challenge input x^* which will be crucial for the adaptive security in the next section.

Game Sequence. As in GWW's proof, we prove Theorem 1 via a series of games summarized in Fig. 6:

- G_0: Identical to the real game.
- G_1: Identical to G_0 except that the challenge ciphertext is $\mathsf{ct}_{x^*}^0$.
- $\mathsf{G}_{2.i.0}$, $i \in [\ell]$: In this game, the challenge ciphertext is $\mathsf{ct}_{x^*}^{i-1}$ and the secret key is sk_Γ^{i-1}.
- $\mathsf{G}_{2.i.1}$, $i \in [\ell]$: Identical to $\mathsf{G}_{2.i.0}$ except that the secret key is $\mathsf{sk}_\Gamma^{i-1,i}$.
- $\mathsf{G}_{2.i.2}$, $i \in [\ell]$: Identical to $\mathsf{G}_{2.i.1}$ except that the challenge ciphertext is $\mathsf{ct}_{x^*}^{i-1,i}$.
- $\mathsf{G}_{2.i.3}$, $i \in [\ell]$: Identical to $\mathsf{G}_{2.i.2}$ except that the secret key is sk_Γ^i.
- $\mathsf{G}_{2.i.4}$, $i \in [\ell]$: Identical to $\mathsf{G}_{2.i.3}$ except that the challenge ciphertext is $\mathsf{ct}_{x^*}^i$.
- G_3: Identical to $\mathsf{G}_{2.\ell.4}$ except that secret key is $\mathsf{sk}_\Gamma^{\ell,*}$.

Note that $\mathsf{G}_{2.1.0}$ is identical to G_1 except that the secret key is sk_Γ^0 and we have $\mathsf{G}_{2.i.0} = \mathsf{G}_{2.i-1.4}$ for all $i \in [2, \ell]$. The remaining of this section will be devoted to

---

[7] We also change the definition of sk_Γ^i, $i \in [0, \ell]$, with the goal of improving the exposition.

proving the indistinguishability of each pair of adjacent games described above. The proofs will be analogous to those for GWW, however, crucially use the property of $\mathbf{f}_{0,x^*}, \ldots, \mathbf{f}_{\ell,x^*}$. Due to lack of space, we focus on proofs using the properties; other proofs are completely analogous to GWW and can be found in the full paper.

Useful Lemmas. Before proceed to the proof, we show the next lemma describing the property of $\mathbf{f}_{0,x^*}, \ldots, \mathbf{f}_{\ell,x^*}$.

Lemma 5 (Property of $\{\mathbf{f}_{i,x^*}\}_{i \in [0,\ell]}$). *For any NFA$^{\oplus p}$ $\Gamma = (Q, \Sigma, \{\mathbf{M}_\sigma\}, \mathbf{u}, \mathbf{f})$ and input $x^* \in \Sigma^\ell$, we have:*

1. $\Gamma(x^*) = 0 \iff \mathbf{f}_{0,x^*} \mathbf{u}^\top = 0 \bmod p$;
2. $\mathbf{f}_{i-1,x^*} = \mathbf{f}_{i,x^*} \mathbf{M}_{x_i^*} \bmod p$ *for all* $i \in [\ell]$;
3. $\mathbf{f}_{\ell,x^*} = \mathbf{f}$.

Proof. The lemma directly follows from the definitions of NFA$^{\oplus p}$ in Sect. 3 and $\mathbf{f}_{0,x^*}, \ldots, \mathbf{f}_{\ell,x^*}$ in (22). $\qquad\square$

4.4 Initializing

It is standard to prove $\mathsf{G}_0 \approx_c \mathsf{G}_1$, see the full paper. We only show the proof sketch for $\mathsf{G}_1 \approx_c \mathsf{G}_{2.1.0}$.

Lemma 6 ($\mathsf{G}_1 = \mathsf{G}_{2.1.0}$). *For all $\mathcal{A}$, we have*

$$\Pr[\langle \mathcal{A}, \mathsf{G}_1 \rangle = 1] = \Pr[\langle \mathcal{A}, \mathsf{G}_{2.1.0} \rangle = 1].$$

Proof. Roughly, we will prove that

$$\left(\mathsf{mpk}, \mathsf{ct}^0_{x^*}, \boxed{\mathsf{sk}_\Gamma} \right) = \left(\mathsf{mpk}, \mathsf{ct}^0_{x^*}, \boxed{\mathsf{sk}^0_\Gamma} \right)$$

where we have

$$\mathsf{sk}_\Gamma[2] = \begin{pmatrix} [\boxed{\mathbf{du}^\top} + \mathbf{w}_{\mathsf{start}} \mathbf{R} \mathbf{u}^\top]_2, [\mathbf{R}\mathbf{u}^\top]_2 \\ \{[-\mathbf{d} + \mathbf{z}_b \mathbf{R}]_2, [\mathbf{dM}_\sigma + \mathbf{w}_{\sigma,b} \mathbf{R}]_2, [\mathbf{R}]_2\}_{\sigma \in \Sigma, b \in \{0,1\}} \\ [\alpha \mathbf{f} - \mathbf{d} + \mathbf{w}_{\mathsf{end}} \mathbf{R}]_2, [\mathbf{R}]_2 \end{pmatrix},$$

$$\mathsf{sk}^0_\Gamma[2] = \begin{pmatrix} [\boxed{(\mathbf{d} + s_0^{-1} \Delta \cdot \mathbf{f}_{0,x^*}) \mathbf{u}^\top} + \mathbf{w}_{\mathsf{start}} \mathbf{R} \mathbf{u}^\top]_2, [\mathbf{R}\mathbf{u}^\top]_2 \\ \{[-\mathbf{d} + \mathbf{z}_b \mathbf{R}]_2, [\mathbf{dM}_\sigma + \mathbf{w}_{\sigma,b} \mathbf{R}]_2, [\mathbf{R}]_2\}_{\sigma \in \Sigma, b \in \{0,1\}} \\ [\alpha \mathbf{f} - \mathbf{d} + \mathbf{w}_{\mathsf{end}} \mathbf{R}]_2, [\mathbf{R}]_2 \end{pmatrix},$$

and

$$\mathsf{ct}^0_{x^*}[2] = \left([s_0 \mathbf{w}_{\mathsf{start}}]_1, [s_0]_1, [s_0 \mathbf{z}_1]_1 \right).$$

This follows from the statement:

$$\overbrace{\{[\boxed{\mathbf{du}^\top} + \mathbf{w}_{\mathsf{start}} \mathbf{R} \mathbf{u}^\top, \mathbf{R}\mathbf{u}^\top\}}^{\mathsf{sk}_\Gamma[2]} = \overbrace{\{[\boxed{(\mathbf{d} + s_0^{-1} \Delta \cdot \mathbf{f}_{0,x^*}) \mathbf{u}^\top} + \mathbf{w}_{\mathsf{start}} \mathbf{R} \mathbf{u}^\top, \mathbf{R}\mathbf{u}^\top\}}^{\mathsf{sk}^0_\Gamma[2]} \text{ given } \mathbf{d}, \overbrace{\mathbf{w}_{\mathsf{start}}}^{\mathsf{ct}^0_{x^*}[2]}$$

which is implied by the fact $\Gamma(x^*) = 0 \iff \mathbf{f}_{0,x^*} \mathbf{u}^\top = 0 \bmod p$ (see Lemma 5). This is sufficient for the proof. $\qquad\square$

Game	ct_{x^*}	$\mathsf{sk}_\Gamma[2]$							Remark
		$? \cdot \mathbf{u}^\top + \mathbf{w}_{\text{start}}\mathbf{R}\mathbf{u}^\top$	$? \cdot \mathbf{M}_{x^*_{i-1}} + \mathbf{w}_{x^*_{i-1},1,1-\tau}\mathbf{R}$	$? + \mathbf{z}_\tau\mathbf{R}$	$? \cdot \mathbf{M}_{x^*_i} + \mathbf{w}_{x^*_i,\tau}\mathbf{R}$	$\alpha\mathbf{f} + ?$	$? + \mathbf{z}_{\text{end}}\mathbf{R}$	
0	ct_{x^*}	sk_Γ	d	d	$-$d	d	$-$d	$-$d	real game
1	$\boxed{\mathsf{ct}^0_{x^*}}$	sk_Γ	d	d	$-$d	d	$-$d	$-$d	SD
2.1.0	$\mathsf{ct}^0_{x^*}$	$\boxed{\mathsf{sk}^0_\Gamma}$	$\mathrm{d} + \boxed{s_0^{-1}\Delta \cdot \boldsymbol{f}_{0,x^*}}$	d	$-$d	d	$-$d	$-$d	Lem 5 - 1
2.i.0	$\mathsf{ct}^{i-1}_{x^*}$	sk^{i-1}_Γ	$\mathrm{d} + s_{i-1}^{-1}\Delta \cdot \boldsymbol{f}_{i-1,x^*}$	d	$-$d	d	$-$d	$-$d	$i \in [2,\ell]$
2.i.1	$\mathsf{ct}^{i-1}_{x^*}$	$\boxed{\mathsf{sk}^{i-1,i}_\Gamma}$	d	$\mathrm{d} + \boxed{s_{i-1}^{-1}\Delta \cdot \boldsymbol{f}_{i-1,x^*}}$	$-$d	d	$-$d	$-$d	change of variables + DDH
2.i.2	$\boxed{\mathsf{ct}^{i-1,i}_{x^*}}$	$\mathsf{sk}^{i-1,i}_\Gamma$	d	d	$-\mathrm{d} + s_{i-1}^{-1}\Delta \cdot \boldsymbol{f}_{i-1,x^*}$	d	$-$d	$-$d	switching lemma
2.i.3	$\mathsf{ct}^i_{x^*}$	sk^i_Γ	d	d	$-$d	$\mathrm{d} + \boxed{s_i^{-1}\Delta \cdot \boldsymbol{f}_{i,x^*}}$	$-$d	$-$d	transition lemma, Lem 5 - 2
2.i.4	$\boxed{\mathsf{ct}^i_{x^*}}$	sk^i_Γ	d	d	$-$d	$\mathrm{d} + s_i^{-1}\Delta \cdot \boldsymbol{f}_{i,x^*}$	$-$d	$-$d	switching lemma
3	$\mathsf{ct}^\ell_{x^*}$	$\boxed{\mathsf{sk}^{\ell,*}_\Gamma}$	d	d	$-$d	d	$-$d	$-\mathrm{d} + \boxed{s_\ell^{-1}\Delta \cdot \boldsymbol{f}_{\ell,x^*}}$	change of variables + DDH

Fig. 6. Game sequence for our selectively secure ABE for $\mathrm{NFA}^{\oplus_p}$ where $i \in [\ell]$. In the table, we only show the $\mathbf{a}_2$-components of secret key. In the **Remark** column, "SD" and "DDH" indicate $\mathrm{SD}^{G_1}_{\mathbf{A}_1 \mapsto \mathbf{A}_1, \mathbf{a}_2}$ and $\mathrm{DDH}^{G_2}_{1,Q}$ assumption, respectively; switching lemma and transition lemma were given in GWW, cf. Lemma 7 and the full paper; "Lemma 5 - x" refers to bullet x in Lemma 5.

4.5 Switching Secret Keys II

This section proves $G_{2.i.2} \approx_c G_{2.i.3}$ for all $i \in [\ell]$ using the the transition lemma from GWW [11].

Lemma 7 (($\mathbf{z}, \mathbf{w}$)-transition lemma [11]). *For all $s_{i-1}, s_i \neq 0$ and $\bar{\Delta} \in \mathbb{Z}_p$, we have*

$$\mathsf{aux},\ s_{i-1}\mathbf{z} + s_i\mathbf{w},\ \ \boxed{s_{i-1}^{-1}\bar{\Delta}} + \mathbf{zr}^\top]_2,\qquad\qquad [\mathbf{wr}^\top]_2, [\mathbf{r}^\top]_2$$
$$\approx_c \mathsf{aux},\ s_{i-1}\mathbf{z} + s_i\mathbf{w},\qquad\qquad [\mathbf{zr}^\top]_2, \boxed{s_i^{-1}\bar{\Delta}} + \mathbf{wr}^\top]_2, [\mathbf{r}^\top]_2$$

where $\mathsf{aux} = ([\mathbf{zB}, \mathbf{wB}, \mathbf{B}]_2)$ *and* $\mathbf{z}, \mathbf{w} \leftarrow \mathbb{Z}_p^{1 \times k}$, $\mathbf{B} \leftarrow \mathbb{Z}_p^{k \times k}$, $\mathbf{r} \leftarrow \mathbb{Z}_p^{1 \times k}$. *Concretely, the advantage function* $\mathsf{Adv}_{\mathcal{B}}^{\mathrm{TRANS}}(\lambda)$ *is bounded by* $O(1) \cdot \mathsf{Adv}_{\mathcal{B}_0}^{k\text{-}\mathrm{LIN}}(\lambda)$ *with* $\mathsf{Time}(\mathcal{B}_0) \approx \mathsf{Time}(\mathcal{B})$.

Lemma 8 ($G_{2.i.2} \approx_c G_{2.i.3}$). *For all $i \in [\ell]$ and all $\mathcal{A}$, there exists $\mathcal{B}$ with* $\mathsf{Time}(\mathcal{B}) \approx \mathsf{Time}(\mathcal{A})$ *such that*

$$\Pr[\langle \mathcal{A}, G_{2.i.2}\rangle = 1] - \Pr[\langle \mathcal{A}, G_{2.i.3}\rangle = 1] \leq \mathsf{Adv}_{\mathcal{B}}^{\mathrm{TRANS}}(\lambda).$$

Overview. This roughly means

$$\left(\mathsf{mpk},\ \mathsf{ct}_{x^*}^{i-1,i},\ \boxed{\mathsf{sk}_{\Gamma}^{i-1,i}}\right) \approx_c \left(\mathsf{mpk},\ \mathsf{ct}_{x^*}^{i-1,i},\ \boxed{\mathsf{sk}_{\Gamma}^{i}}\right);$$

more concretely, we want to prove the following statement over $\mathbf{a}_2$-components:

$$[-\mathbf{d} + \boxed{s_{i-1}^{-1}\Delta \cdot \mathbf{f}_{i-1,x^*} + \mathbf{z}_\tau \mathbf{R}}]_2,\qquad\qquad [\mathbf{dM}_{x_i^*} + \boxed{\mathbf{w}_{x_i^*,\tau}\mathbf{R}}]_2, [\mathbf{R}]_2$$
$$\approx_c \quad [-\mathbf{d} + \boxed{\mathbf{z}_\tau \mathbf{R}}]_2, [\mathbf{dM}_{x_i^*} + \boxed{s_i^{-1}\Delta \cdot \mathbf{f}_{i,x^*}\mathbf{M}_{x_i^*} + \mathbf{w}_{x_i^*,\tau}\mathbf{R}}]_2, [\mathbf{R}]_2$$

given $\mathbf{d}, \Delta, s_{i-1}, s_i, s_{i-1}\mathbf{z}_\tau + s_i\mathbf{w}_{x_i^*,\tau}$ revealed by $\mathsf{ct}_{x^*}^{i-1,i}$. The first row corresponds to $\mathsf{sk}_{\Gamma}^{i-1,i}[2]$ while the second corresponds to $\mathsf{sk}_{\Gamma}^{i}[2]$. This can be handled by the $(\mathbf{z}_\tau, \mathbf{w}_{x_i^*,\tau})$-transition lemma and the fact that $\mathbf{f}_{i-1,x^*} = \mathbf{f}_{i,x^*}\mathbf{M}_{x_i^*} \bmod p$ (see Lemma 5).

Proof. Recall that $\tau = i \bmod 2$. By Lemma 4, it suffices to prove the lemma over $\mathbf{a}_2$-components which roughly means:

$$\mathsf{sk}_{\Gamma}^{i-1,i}[2] = \begin{pmatrix} [\mathbf{du}^\top + \mathbf{w}_{\mathrm{start}}\mathbf{Ru}^\top]_2, [\mathbf{Ru}^\top]_2 \\ [-\mathbf{d} + \boxed{s_{i-1}^{-1}\Delta \cdot \mathbf{f}_{i-1,x^*} + \mathbf{z}_\tau \mathbf{R}}]_2, [\mathbf{dM}_{x_i^*} + \boxed{\mathbf{w}_{x_i^*,\tau}\mathbf{R}}]_2, [\mathbf{R}]_2 \\ \{[\mathbf{dM}_\sigma + \mathbf{w}_{\sigma,\tau}\mathbf{R}]_2\}_{\sigma \neq x_i^*} \\ \{[-\mathbf{d} + \mathbf{z}_{1-\tau}\mathbf{R}]_2, [\mathbf{dM}_\sigma + \mathbf{w}_{\sigma,1-\tau}\mathbf{R}]_2, [\mathbf{R}]_2\}_{\sigma \in \Sigma} \\ [\alpha\mathbf{f} - \mathbf{d} + \mathbf{w}_{\mathrm{end}}\mathbf{R}]_2, [\mathbf{R}]_2 \end{pmatrix}$$

$$\approx_c \begin{pmatrix} [\mathbf{du}^\top + \mathbf{w}_{\mathrm{start}}\mathbf{Ru}^\top]_2, [\mathbf{Ru}^\top]_2 \\ [-\mathbf{d} + \boxed{\mathbf{z}_\tau \mathbf{R}}]_2, [\mathbf{dM}_{x_i^*} + \boxed{s_i^{-1}\Delta \cdot \mathbf{f}_{i,x^*}\mathbf{M}_{x_i^*} + \mathbf{w}_{x_i^*,\tau}\mathbf{R}}]_2, [\mathbf{R}]_2 \\ \{[\mathbf{dM}_\sigma + \mathbf{w}_{\sigma,\tau}\mathbf{R}]_2\}_{\sigma \neq x_i^*} \\ \{[-\mathbf{d} + \mathbf{z}_{1-\tau}\mathbf{R}]_2, [\mathbf{dM}_\sigma + \mathbf{w}_{\sigma,1-\tau}\mathbf{R}]_2, [\mathbf{R}]_2\}_{\sigma \in \Sigma} \\ [\alpha\mathbf{f} - \mathbf{d} + \mathbf{w}_{\mathrm{end}}\mathbf{R}]_2, [\mathbf{R}]_2 \end{pmatrix} = \mathsf{sk}_{\Gamma}^{i}[2]$$

in the presence of

$$
\mathsf{ct}_{x^*}^{i-1,i}[2] = \begin{cases}
[s_0\mathbf{w}_{\mathsf{start}}]_1,\ [s_0]_1,\ [s_0\mathbf{z}_1 + s_1\mathbf{w}_{x_1^*,1}]_1,\ [s_1]_1,\ [s_1\mathbf{z}_0]_1 \\
\qquad\qquad\qquad\qquad\qquad\qquad\qquad\qquad\qquad \text{if } i = 1 \\[2mm]
[s_{i-1}\mathbf{w}_{x_{i-1}^*,1-\tau}]_1,\ [s_{i-1}]_1,\ [s_{i-1}\mathbf{z}_\tau + s_i\mathbf{w}_{x_i^*,\tau}]_1,\ [s_i]_1,\ [s_i\mathbf{z}_{1-\tau}]_1 \\
\qquad\qquad\qquad\qquad\qquad\qquad\qquad\qquad\qquad \text{if } i \in [2, \ell-1] \\[2mm]
[s_{\ell-1}\mathbf{w}_{x_{\ell-1}^*,1-\bar{\ell}}]_1,\ [s_{\ell-1}]_1,\ [s_{\ell-1}\mathbf{z}_{\bar{\ell}} + s_\ell\mathbf{w}_{x_\ell^*,\bar{\ell}}]_1,\ [s_\ell]_1,\ [s_\ell\mathbf{w}_{\mathsf{end}}]_1,\ [s_\ell\alpha]_T \cdot m_\beta \\
\qquad\qquad\qquad\qquad\qquad\qquad\qquad\qquad\qquad \text{if } i = \ell
\end{cases}
$$

One can sample basis $\mathbf{A}_1, \mathbf{a}_2, \mathbf{A}_3, \mathbf{A}_1^\parallel, \mathbf{a}_2^\parallel, \mathbf{A}_3^\parallel$ and trivially simulate mpk, $\mathsf{ct}_{x^*}^{i-1,i}$ and secret key using terms given out above. Furthermore, we prove this using $(\mathbf{z}_\tau, \mathbf{w}_{x_i^*,\tau})$-transition lemma. On input

$$
\mathsf{aux}, [\bar{\Delta}_0 + \mathbf{z}_\tau \mathbf{r}^\top]_2, [\bar{\Delta}_1 + \mathbf{w}_{x_i^*,\tau}\mathbf{r}^\top]_2, [\mathbf{r}^\top]_2
$$

where $(\bar{\Delta}_0, \bar{\Delta}_1) \in \left\{ \boxed{(s_{i-1}^{-1}\bar{\Delta}, 0)},\ (0, s_i^{-1}\bar{\Delta}) \right\}$ and

$$
\mathsf{aux} = (\bar{\Delta}, s_{i-1}, s_i, s_{i-1}\mathbf{z}_\tau + s_i\mathbf{w}_{x_i^*,\tau}, [\mathbf{z}_\tau\mathbf{B}, \mathbf{w}_{x_i^*,\tau}\mathbf{B}, \mathbf{B}]_2)
$$

with $\mathbf{z}_\tau, \mathbf{w}_{x_i^*,\tau} \leftarrow \mathbb{Z}_p^{1\times k}$, $\mathbf{B} \leftarrow \mathbb{Z}_p^{k\times k}$, $\mathbf{r} \leftarrow \mathbb{Z}_p^{1\times k}$ and $\bar{\Delta} \leftarrow \mathbb{Z}_p$, we sample $\alpha \leftarrow \mathbb{Z}_p$, $\mathbf{w}_{\mathsf{start}}, \mathbf{z}_{1-\tau}, \mathbf{w}_{\sigma,1-\tau}, \mathbf{w}_{\mathsf{end}} \leftarrow \mathbb{Z}_p^{1\times k}$ for all $\sigma \in \Sigma$ and $\mathbf{w}_{\sigma,\tau} \leftarrow \mathbb{Z}_p^{1\times k}$ for all $\sigma \neq x_i^*$ and proceed as follows:

(Simulating challenge ciphertext) On input (m_0, m_1), we trivially simulate $\mathsf{ct}_{x^*}^{i-1,i}[2]$ using $s_{i-1}, s_i, s_{i-1}\mathbf{z}_\tau + s_i\mathbf{w}_{x_i^*,\tau}$ in aux and α, $\mathbf{w}_{\mathsf{start}}$, $\mathbf{w}_{\sigma,1-\tau}$, $\mathbf{z}_{1-\tau}$, $\mathbf{w}_{\mathsf{end}}$ as well.

(Simulating secret key) On input Γ, we want to return a secret key for Γ in the form:

$$
\begin{pmatrix}
[\mathbf{d}\mathbf{u}^\top + \mathbf{w}_{\mathsf{start}}\mathbf{R}\mathbf{u}^\top]_2,\ [\mathbf{R}\mathbf{u}^\top]_2 \\
\boxed{[-\mathbf{d} + \Delta_0 \cdot \mathbf{f}_{i-1,x^*} + \mathbf{z}_\tau\mathbf{R}]_2, [\mathbf{d}\mathbf{M}_{x_i^*} + \Delta_1 \cdot \mathbf{f}_{i-1,x^*} + \mathbf{w}_{x_i^*,\tau}\mathbf{R}]_2},\ [\mathbf{R}]_2 \\
\left\{ [\mathbf{d}\mathbf{M}_\sigma + \mathbf{w}_{\sigma,\tau}\mathbf{R}]_2 \right\}_{\sigma \neq x_i^*} \\
\left\{ [-\mathbf{d} + \mathbf{z}_{1-\tau}\mathbf{R}]_2, [\mathbf{d}\mathbf{M}_\sigma + \mathbf{w}_{\sigma,1-\tau}\mathbf{R}]_2, [\mathbf{R}]_2 \right\}_{\sigma \in \Sigma} \\
[\alpha\mathbf{f} - \mathbf{d} + \mathbf{w}_{\mathsf{end}}\mathbf{R}]_2,\ [\mathbf{R}]_2
\end{pmatrix}
$$

where $(\Delta_0, \Delta_1) \in \left\{ \boxed{(s_{i-1}^{-1}\Delta, 0)},\ \boxed{(0, s_i^{-1}\Delta)} \right\}$. Observe that

- when $(\Delta_0, \Delta_1) = \boxed{(s_{i-1}^{-1}\Delta, 0)}$, the distribution is identical to $\boxed{\mathsf{sk}_\Gamma^{i-1,i}[2]}$;
- when $(\Delta_0, \Delta_1) = \boxed{(0, s_i^{-1}\Delta)}$, the distribution is identical to $\boxed{\mathsf{sk}_\Gamma^i[2]}$ since $\mathbf{f}_{i-1,x^*} = \mathbf{f}_{i,x^*}\mathbf{M}_{x_i^*} \bmod p$ (see Lemma 5).

We sample $\mathbf{d} \leftarrow \mathbb{Z}_p^{1\times Q}$ and $\widetilde{\mathbf{R}} \leftarrow \mathbb{Z}_p^{k\times Q}$ and implicitly set

$$
\Delta = \bar{\Delta}, \quad (\Delta_0, \Delta_1) = (\bar{\Delta}_0, \bar{\Delta}_1) \quad \text{and} \quad \mathbf{R} = \mathbf{r}^\top \cdot \mathbf{f}_{i-1,x^*} + \mathbf{B} \cdot \widetilde{\mathbf{R}}.
$$

We then generate the key for Γ as follows:

- We simulate $[\mathbf{R}]_2$ from $[\mathbf{r}^\top]_2$, $[\mathbf{B}]_2$ and $\mathbf{f}_{i-1,x^*}, \tilde{\mathbf{R}}$.
- We rewrite the terms in the dashed box as follows:

$$[-\mathbf{d} + (\bar{\Delta}_0 + \mathbf{z}_\tau \mathbf{r}^\top) \cdot \mathbf{f}_{i-1,x^*} + \mathbf{z}_\tau \mathbf{B} \cdot \tilde{\mathbf{R}}]_2, \; [\mathbf{d}\mathbf{M}_{x_i^*} + (\bar{\Delta}_1 + \mathbf{w}_{x_i^*,\tau} \mathbf{r}^\top) \cdot \mathbf{f}_{i-1,x^*} + \mathbf{w}_{x_i^*,\tau} \mathbf{B} \cdot \tilde{\mathbf{R}}]_2$$

and simulate them using $[\bar{\Delta}_0 + \mathbf{z}_\tau \mathbf{r}^\top]_2$, $[\bar{\Delta}_1 + \mathbf{w}_{x_i^*,\tau} \mathbf{r}^\top]_2$, $[\mathbf{z}_\tau \mathbf{B}]_2$, $[\mathbf{w}_{x_i^*,\tau} \mathbf{B}]_2$ and $\mathbf{d}, \mathbf{f}_{i-1,x^*}, \tilde{\mathbf{R}}$.

- We simulate all remaining terms using $[\mathbf{R}]_2$ and α, $\mathbf{d}$, $\mathbf{w}_{\text{start}}$, $\mathbf{z}_{1-\tau}$, $\{\mathbf{w}_{\sigma,\tau}\}_{\sigma \neq x_i^*}$, $\{\mathbf{w}_{\sigma,1-\tau}\}_{\sigma \in \Sigma}$, $\mathbf{w}_{\text{end}}$.

Observe that, when $(\bar{\Delta}_0, \bar{\Delta}_1) = \boxed{(s_{i-1}^{-1}\bar{\Delta}, 0)}$, we have $(\Delta_0, \Delta_1) = \boxed{(s_{i-1}^{-1}\Delta, 0)}$, then the secret key is $\boxed{\mathsf{sk}_\Gamma^{i-1,i}[2]}$ and the simulation is identical to $\mathsf{G}_{2.i.2}$; when $(\bar{\Delta}_0, \bar{\Delta}_1) = \boxed{(0, s_i^{-1}\bar{\Delta})}$, we have $(\Delta_0, \Delta_1) = \boxed{(0, s_i^{-1}\Delta)}$, then the secret key is $\boxed{\mathsf{sk}_\Gamma^i[2]}$ and the simulation is identical to $\mathsf{G}_{2.i.3}$. This completes the proof. $\square$

4.6   Finalize

We finally prove that the adversary wins G_3 with probability $1/2$.

Lemma 9. $\Pr[\langle \mathcal{A}, \mathsf{G}_3 \rangle = 1] \approx 1/2$.

Proof. First, we argue that the secret key $\mathsf{sk}_\Gamma^{\ell,*}$ in this game perfectly hides the $\mathbf{a}_2$-component of $\mathbf{k}^\top$, i.e., $\alpha = \mathbf{a}_2 \mathbf{k}^\top$. Recall the $\mathbf{a}_2$-components of the secret key:

$$\mathsf{sk}_\Gamma^{\ell,*}[2] = \begin{pmatrix} [\mathbf{d}\mathbf{u}^\top + \mathbf{w}_{\text{start}} \mathbf{R}\mathbf{u}^\top]_2, [\mathbf{R}\mathbf{u}^\top]_2 \\ \{[-\mathbf{d} + \mathbf{z}_b \mathbf{R}]_2, [\mathbf{d}\mathbf{M}_\sigma + \mathbf{w}_{\sigma,b}\mathbf{R}]_2, [\mathbf{R}]_2\}_{\sigma \in \Sigma, b \in \{0,1\}} \\ [\alpha \mathbf{f} - \mathbf{d} + \boxed{s_\ell^{-1}\Delta \cdot \mathbf{f}_{\ell,x^*}} + \mathbf{w}_{\text{end}} \mathbf{R}]_2, [\mathbf{R}]_2 \end{pmatrix}.$$

By the property $\mathbf{f}_{\ell,x^*} = \mathbf{f}$ (see Lemma 5), we can see that $\mathsf{sk}_\Gamma^{\ell,*}[2]$ can be simulated using $\alpha + s_\ell^{-1}\Delta$, which means the secret key perfectly hides $\alpha = \mathbf{a}_2 \mathbf{k}^\top$. Therefore, the unique term involving $\mathbf{k}$ in $\mathsf{ct}_{x^*}^\ell$, i.e., $[s_\ell \mathbf{A}_1 \mathbf{k}^\top + s_\ell \mathbf{a}_2 \mathbf{k}^\top]_T$, is independently and uniformly distributed and thus statistically hides message m_β. $\square$

5   Adaptively Secure ABE for $\mathcal{E}_Q$-Restricted NFA$^{\oplus p}$ and DFA

In this section, we present our adaptively secure ABE for $\mathcal{E}_Q$-restricted NFA$^{\oplus p}$. By our transformation from DFA to $\mathcal{E}_Q$-restricted NFA$^{\oplus p}$ (cf. Lemma 1), this readily gives us an adaptively secure ABE for DFA. We defer the concrete construction to the full paper.

Overview. Our starting point is the selectively secure ABE scheme in Sect. 4. To achieve adaptive security, we handle key queries one by one following standard dual system method [20]; for each key, we carry out the one-key selective proof in Sect. 4 with piecewise guessing framework [15]. However this does not work immediately, we will make some changes to the scheme and proof in Sect. 4.

Recall that, in the one-key setting, the (selective) proof in Sect. 4 roughly tells us

$$(\mathsf{mpk}, \mathsf{sk}_\Gamma, \mathsf{ct}_{x^*}) \approx_c (\mathsf{mpk}, \boxed{\mathsf{sk}_\Gamma^{\ell,*}}, \boxed{\mathsf{ct}_{x^*}^\ell}). \tag{23}$$

The two-key setting, for example, is expected to be handled by hybrid arguments:

$$(\mathsf{mpk}, \mathsf{sk}_{\Gamma_1}, \mathsf{sk}_{\Gamma_2}, \mathsf{ct}_{x^*}) \approx_c (\mathsf{mpk}, \boxed{\mathsf{sk}_{\Gamma_1}^{\ell,*}}, \mathsf{sk}_{\Gamma_2}, \boxed{\mathsf{ct}_{x^*}^\ell}) \approx_c (\mathsf{mpk}, \mathsf{sk}_{\Gamma_1}^{\ell,*}, \boxed{\mathsf{sk}_{\Gamma_2}^{\ell,*}}, \mathsf{ct}_{x^*}^\ell)$$

The first step seems to be feasible with some natural extension but the second one is problematic. Since we can not switch the challenge ciphertext back to ct_{x^*} due to the presence of $\mathsf{sk}_{\Gamma_1}^{\ell,*}$, the argument (23) can not be applied to the second key sk_{Γ_2} literally. In more detail, recall that

$$\mathsf{ct}_{x^*}^\ell[2] = \big([s_\ell \mathbf{w}_{x_\ell^*, \bar{\ell}}]_1, [s_\ell]_1, [s_\ell \mathbf{w}_{\mathrm{end}}]_1 \big) \tag{24}$$

leaks information of $\mathbf{w}_{x_\ell^*, \bar{\ell}}$ and $\mathbf{w}_{\mathrm{end}}$ while we need them to be hidden in some steps of the one-key proof; for example, Lemma in Sect. 4.5 for $\mathsf{G}_{2.i.2} \approx_c \mathsf{G}_{2.i.3}$. We quickly argue that the natural solution of adding an extra subspace for fresh copies of $\mathbf{w}_{x_\ell^*, \bar{\ell}}$ and $\mathbf{w}_{\mathrm{end}}$ blows up the ciphertext and key sizes (see Sect. 1.1 for discussion).

Our approach reuses the existing $\mathbf{a}_2$-components as in [8]. Recall that, our one-key proof (23) uses a series of hybrids with random coins $s_0, s_1, \ldots$ and finally stops at a hybrid with s_ℓ (cf. (23) and (24)). Roughly, we change the scheme by adding an extra random coin s into the ciphertext and move one more step in the proof so that we finally stop at a new hybrid with the new s only. This allows us to release s_ℓ and reuse $\mathbf{w}_{x_\ell^*, \bar{\ell}}, \mathbf{w}_{\mathrm{end}}$ for the next key. More concretely, starting with the scheme in Sect. 4.2, we introduce a new component $[\mathbf{W}]_1 \in G_1^{(2k+1) \times k}$ into mpk:

- during encryption, we pick one more random coin $\mathbf{s} \leftarrow \mathbb{Z}_p^{1 \times k}$ and replace the last three components in ct_x with

$$[\mathbf{s}\mathbf{A}_1]_1, [s_\ell \mathbf{A}_1 \mathbf{W}_{\mathrm{end}} + \mathbf{s}\mathbf{A}_1 \mathbf{W}]_1, [\mathbf{s}\mathbf{A}_1 \mathbf{k}^\top]_T \cdot m;$$

  this connects the last random coin s_ℓ with the newly introduced $\mathbf{s}$; and $\mathbf{s}$ corresponds to s in the proof;
- during key generation, we replace the last two components in sk_Γ with

$$[-\mathbf{D} + \mathbf{W}_{\mathrm{end}}\mathbf{R}]_2, [\mathbf{k}^\top \mathbf{f} + \mathbf{W}\mathbf{R}]_2, [\mathbf{R}]_2;$$

  the decryption will recover $[\mathbf{s}\mathbf{A}_1 \mathbf{k}^\top \mathbf{f} - s_\ell \mathbf{A}_1 \mathbf{D}]_T$ instead of $[s_\ell \mathbf{A}_1 \mathbf{k}^\top \mathbf{f} - s_\ell \mathbf{A}_1 \mathbf{D}]_T$;

– during the proof, we extend the proof in Sect. 4.3 by one more step (see the dashed box):

$$(\mathsf{mpk}, \mathsf{sk}_\Gamma, \mathsf{ct}_{x^*}) \overset{\S4.3}{\approx_c} (\mathsf{mpk}, \boxed{\mathsf{sk}_\Gamma^{\ell,*}}, \boxed{\mathsf{ct}_{x^*}^\ell}) \overset{}{\approx_c} (\mathsf{mpk}, \boxed{\mathsf{sk}_\Gamma^*}, \boxed{\mathsf{ct}_{x^*}^*})$$

so that $\mathsf{ct}_{x^*}^*[2]$ is in the following form:

$$\mathsf{ct}_{x^*}^*[2] = ([s\mathbf{w}]_1, [s]_1, [s\alpha]_1 \cdot m_\beta)$$

which leaks $\mathbf{w} = \mathbf{a}_2 \mathbf{W}$ instead of $\mathbf{w}_{x_\ell^*, \bar\ell}, \mathbf{w}_{\mathrm{end}}$; by this, we can carry out the one-key proof (23) for the next key (with some natural extensions).

Conceptually, we can interpret this as letting the NFA move to a specific dummy state whenever it accepts the input. Such a modification has been mentioned in [4] for simplifying the description rather than improving security and efficiency. In our formal description below, we will rename $\mathbf{W}_{\mathrm{end}}, \mathbf{W}, \mathbf{s}, s$ as $\mathbf{Z}_{\mathrm{end}}, \mathbf{W}_{\mathrm{end}}, \mathbf{s}_{\mathrm{end}}, s_{\mathrm{end}}$, respectively.

5.1   Scheme

Our adaptively secure ABE for $\mathcal{E}_Q$-restricted $\mathrm{NFA}^{\oplus_p}$ in prime-order groups use the same basis as described in Sect. 4.1 and is described as follows:

– Setup$(1^\lambda, \Sigma)$: Run $\mathbb{G} = (p, G_1, G_2, G_T, e) \leftarrow \mathcal{G}(1^\lambda)$. Sample

$$\mathbf{A}_1 \leftarrow \mathbb{Z}_p^{k \times (2k+1)}, \; \mathbf{k} \leftarrow \mathbb{Z}_p^{1 \times (2k+1)}, \; \mathbf{W}_{\mathrm{start}}, \mathbf{Z}_b, \mathbf{W}_{\sigma,b}, \mathbf{Z}_{\mathrm{end}}, \mathbf{W}_{\mathrm{end}} \leftarrow \mathbb{Z}_p^{(2k+1) \times k}$$

for all $\sigma \in \Sigma$ and $b \in \{0,1\}$. Output

$$\mathsf{mpk} = ([\mathbf{A}_1, \mathbf{A}_1 \mathbf{W}_{\mathrm{start}}, \{\mathbf{A}_1 \mathbf{Z}_b, \mathbf{A}_1 \mathbf{W}_{\sigma,b}\}_{\sigma \in \Sigma, b \in \{0,1\}}, \mathbf{A}_1 \mathbf{Z}_{\mathrm{end}}, \mathbf{A}_1 \mathbf{W}_{\mathrm{end}}]_1, [\mathbf{A}_1 \mathbf{k}^\top]_T)$$
$$\mathsf{msk} = (\mathbf{k}, \mathbf{W}_{\mathrm{start}}, \{\mathbf{Z}_b, \mathbf{W}_{\sigma,b}\}_{\sigma \in \Sigma, b \in \{0,1\}}, \mathbf{Z}_{\mathrm{end}}, \mathbf{W}_{\mathrm{end}}).$$

– Enc(mpk, x, m) : Let $x = (x_1, \ldots, x_\ell) \in \Sigma^\ell$ and $m \in G_T$. Pick $\mathbf{s}_0, \mathbf{s}_1, \ldots, \mathbf{s}_\ell, \mathbf{s}_{\mathrm{end}} \leftarrow \mathbb{Z}_p^{1 \times k}$ and output

$$\mathsf{ct}_x = \begin{pmatrix} [\mathbf{s}_0 \mathbf{A}_1]_1, \; [\mathbf{s}_0 \mathbf{A}_1 \mathbf{W}_{\mathrm{start}}]_1 \\ \{[\mathbf{s}_j \mathbf{A}_1]_1, [\mathbf{s}_{j-1} \mathbf{A}_1 \mathbf{Z}_{j \bmod 2} + \mathbf{s}_j \mathbf{A}_1 \mathbf{W}_{x_j, j \bmod 2}]_1\}_{j \in [\ell]} \\ [\mathbf{s}_{\mathrm{end}} \mathbf{A}_1]_1, [\mathbf{s}_\ell \mathbf{A}_1 \mathbf{Z}_{\mathrm{end}} + \mathbf{s}_{\mathrm{end}} \mathbf{A}_1 \mathbf{W}_{\mathrm{end}}]_1, [\mathbf{s}_{\mathrm{end}} \mathbf{A}_1 \mathbf{k}^\top]_T \cdot m \end{pmatrix}.$$

– KeyGen$(\mathsf{mpk}, \mathsf{msk}, \Gamma)$: Let $\Gamma = (Q, \Sigma, \{\mathbf{M}_\sigma\}_{\sigma \in \Sigma}, \mathbf{u}, \mathbf{f})$. Pick $\mathbf{D} \leftarrow \mathbb{Z}_p^{(2k+1) \times Q}$, $\mathbf{R} \leftarrow \mathbb{Z}_p^{k \times Q}$ and output

$$\mathsf{sk}_\Gamma = \begin{pmatrix} [\mathbf{D}\mathbf{u}^\top + \mathbf{W}_{\mathrm{start}} \mathbf{R}\mathbf{u}^\top]_2, [\mathbf{R}\mathbf{u}^\top]_2 \\ \{[-\mathbf{D} + \mathbf{Z}_b \mathbf{R}]_2, [\mathbf{D}\mathbf{M}_\sigma + \mathbf{W}_{\sigma,b} \mathbf{R}]_2, [\mathbf{R}]_2\}_{\sigma \in \Sigma, b \in \{0,1\}} \\ [-\mathbf{D} + \mathbf{Z}_{\mathrm{end}} \mathbf{R}]_2, [\mathbf{k}^\top \mathbf{f} + \mathbf{W}_{\mathrm{end}} \mathbf{R}]_2, [\mathbf{R}]_2 \end{pmatrix}.$$

– Dec(mpk, sk_Γ, ct_x) : Parse ciphertext for $x = (x_1, \ldots, x_\ell)$ and key for $\Gamma = (Q, \Sigma, \{\mathbf{M}_\sigma\}_{\sigma \in \Sigma}, \mathbf{u}, \mathbf{f})$ as

$$\mathsf{ct}_x = \begin{pmatrix} [\mathbf{c}_{0,1}]_1, [\mathbf{c}_{0,2}]_1 \\ \{ [\mathbf{c}_{j,1}]_1, [\mathbf{c}_{j,2}]_1 \}_j \\ [\mathbf{c}_{\mathrm{end},1}]_1, [\mathbf{c}_{\mathrm{end},2}]_1, C \end{pmatrix} \quad \text{and} \quad \mathsf{sk}_\Gamma = \begin{pmatrix} [\mathbf{k}_0^\top]_2, [\mathbf{r}_0^\top]_2 \\ \{ [\mathbf{K}_b]_2, [\mathbf{K}_{\sigma,b}]_2, [\mathbf{R}]_2 \}_{\sigma,b} \\ [\mathbf{K}_{\mathrm{end},1}]_2, [\mathbf{K}_{\mathrm{end},2}]_2, [\mathbf{R}]_2 \end{pmatrix}$$

We define $\mathbf{u}_{j,x}^\top$ for all $j \in [0, \ell]$ as (11) in Sect. 4.2 and proceed as follows:

1. Compute
$$B_0 = e([\mathbf{c}_{0,1}]_1, [\mathbf{k}_0^\top]_2) \cdot e([\mathbf{c}_{0,2}]_1, [\mathbf{r}_0^\top]_2)^{-1};$$

2. For all $j \in [\ell]$, compute
$$[\mathbf{b}_j]_T = e([\mathbf{c}_{j-1,1}]_1, [\mathbf{K}_{j \bmod 2}]_2) \cdot e([\mathbf{c}_{j,1}]_1, [\mathbf{K}_{x_j, j \bmod 2}]_2) \cdot e([-\mathbf{c}_{j,2}]_1, [\mathbf{R}]_2)$$
$$\text{and} \quad B_j = [\mathbf{b}_j \mathbf{u}_{j-1,x}^\top]_T;$$

3. Compute
$$[\mathbf{b}_{\mathrm{end}}]_T = e([\mathbf{c}_{\ell,1}]_1, [\mathbf{K}_{\mathrm{end},1}]_2) \cdot e([\mathbf{c}_{\mathrm{end},1}]_1, [\mathbf{K}_{\mathrm{end},2}]_2) \cdot e([-\mathbf{c}_{\mathrm{end},2}]_1, [\mathbf{R}]_2)$$
$$\text{and} \quad B_{\mathrm{end}} = [\mathbf{b}_{\mathrm{end}} \mathbf{u}_{\ell,x}^\top]_T;$$

4. Compute
$$B_{\mathrm{all}} = B_0 \cdot \prod_{j=1}^{\ell} B_j \cdot B_{\mathrm{end}} \quad \text{and} \quad B = B_{\mathrm{all}}^{(\mathbf{f}\mathbf{u}_{\ell,x}^\top)^{-1}}$$

and output the message $m' \leftarrow C \cdot B^{-1}$.

It is direct to verify the correctness as in Sect. 4.2. See the full paper for more details.

Security. We prove the following theorem stating the adaptive security of the above ABE for $\mathcal{E}_Q$-restricted NFA$^{\oplus_p}$. This readily implies our adaptively secure ABE for DFA thanks to Lemma 1.

Theorem 2 (Adaptively secure ABE for $\mathcal{E}_Q$-restricted NFA$^{\oplus_p}$). *The ABE scheme for $\mathcal{E}_Q$-restricted NFA$^{\oplus_p}$ in prime-order bilinear groups described above is adaptively secure (cf. Sect. 2.1) under the k-Lin assumption with security loss $O(q \cdot \ell \cdot |\Sigma|^3 \cdot Q^2)$. Here ℓ is the length of the challenge input x^* and q is the number of key queries.*

5.2 Proof of Main Theorem

From a high level, we employ the standard dual system proof switching the challenge ciphertext and keys into semi-functional forms in a one-by-one manner. To switch a secret key, we employ the proof technique for one-key selective setting in Sect. 4 in the piecewise guessing framework [14, 15]. We will capture this by a core lemma. Let $x^* \in \Sigma^\ell$ denote the adaptive challenge. We begin with auxiliary distributions and use the notation for $\mathbf{a}_2$-components in Sect. 4.3.

Auxiliary Distributions. We sample $s_{end} \leftarrow \mathbb{Z}_p$, $\Delta \leftarrow \mathbb{Z}_p$ and define semi-functional ciphertext and key:

- $\mathsf{ct}^*_{x^*}$ is the same as ct_{x^*} except we replace $s_{end}\mathbf{A}_1$ with $s_{end}\mathbf{A}_1 + s_{end}\mathbf{a}_2$;
- sk^*_Γ is the same as sk_Γ except we replace $\mathbf{k}^\top$ with $\mathbf{k}^\top + \mathbf{a}_2^\parallel \cdot s_{end}^{-1}\Delta$ in the term $[\mathbf{k}^\top\mathbf{f} + \mathbf{W}_{end}\mathbf{R}]_2$.

That is, we have:

$$\mathsf{ct}^*_{x^*}[2] = \left([s_{end}\mathbf{W}_{end}]_1, [s_{end}]_1, [s_{end}\alpha]_T \cdot m_\beta \right)$$

$$\mathsf{sk}^*_\Gamma[2] = \begin{pmatrix} [\mathbf{du}^\top + \mathbf{w}_{start}\mathbf{Ru}^\top]_2, [\mathbf{Ru}^\top]_2 \\ \{[-\mathbf{d} + \mathbf{z}_b\mathbf{R}]_2, [\mathbf{dM}_\sigma + \mathbf{w}_{\sigma,b}\mathbf{R}]_2, [\mathbf{R}]_2\}_{\sigma \in \Sigma, b \in \{0,1\}} \\ [-\mathbf{d} + \mathbf{z}_{end}\mathbf{R}]_2, [\alpha\mathbf{f} + \boxed{s_{end}^{-1}\Delta \cdot \mathbf{f}} + \mathbf{w}_{end}\mathbf{R}]_2, [\mathbf{R}]_2 \end{pmatrix}$$

Game Sequence and Core Lemma. We prove Theorem 2 via a series of games following standard dual system method [20]:

- G_0: Identical to the real game.
- G_1: Identical to G_0 except that the challenge ciphertext is semi-functional, i.e., $\mathsf{ct}^*_{x^*}$.
- $\mathsf{G}_{2.\kappa}$ for $\kappa \in [0, q]$: Identical to G_1 except that the first κ secret keys are semi-functional, i.e., sk^*_Γ.
- G_3: Identical to $\mathsf{G}_{2.q}$ except that the challenge ciphertext is an encryption of a random message.

Here we have $\mathsf{G}_{2.0} = \mathsf{G}_1$. It is standard to prove $\mathsf{G}_0 \approx_c \mathsf{G}_1$, $\mathsf{G}_{2.q} \approx_s \mathsf{G}_3$ and show that adversary in G_3 has no advantage. We sketch the proofs in the full paper. To prove $\mathsf{G}_{2.\kappa-1} \approx_c \mathsf{G}_{2.\kappa}$ for all $\kappa \in [q]$, we use core lemma:

Lemma 10 (Core lemma). *For all $\mathcal{A}$, there exists $\mathcal{B}$ with* $\mathsf{Time}(\mathcal{B}) \approx \mathsf{Time}(\mathcal{A})$ *and*

$$\mathsf{Adv}^{\mathrm{CORE}}_{\mathcal{A}}(\lambda) = \Pr[\langle\mathcal{A}, \mathsf{H}_0\rangle = 1] - \Pr[\langle\mathcal{A}, \mathsf{H}_1\rangle = 1] \leq O(\ell \cdot |\Sigma|^3 \cdot Q^2) \cdot \mathsf{Adv}^{k\text{-}\mathrm{LIN}}_{\mathcal{B}}(\lambda)$$

where, for all $b \in \{0, 1\}$, we define:

$$\langle\mathcal{A}, \mathsf{H}_b\rangle := \left\{ b' \leftarrow \mathcal{A}^{\mathsf{OEnc}(\cdot), \mathsf{OKey}(\cdot)}(\mathsf{mpk}, \mathsf{aux}_1, \mathsf{aux}_2) \right\}$$

where

$$\mathsf{mpk} = \left([\mathbf{A}_1, \mathbf{A}_1\mathbf{W}_{start}, \{\mathbf{A}_1\mathbf{Z}_b, \mathbf{A}_1\mathbf{W}_{\sigma,b}\}_{\sigma \in \Sigma, b \in \{0,1\}}, \mathbf{A}_1\mathbf{Z}_{end}, \mathbf{A}_1\mathbf{W}_{end}]_1, [\mathbf{A}_1\mathbf{k}^\top]_T\right)$$

$$\mathsf{aux}_1 = \left([\mathbf{k}, \mathbf{B}, \mathbf{W}_{start}\mathbf{B}, \{\mathbf{Z}_b\mathbf{B}, \mathbf{W}_{\sigma,b}\mathbf{B}\}_{\sigma \in \Sigma, b \in \{0,1\}}, \mathbf{Z}_{end}\mathbf{B}, \mathbf{W}_{end}\mathbf{B}]_2\right)$$

$$\mathsf{aux}_2 = \left([\mathbf{r}^\top, \mathbf{W}_{start}\mathbf{r}^\top, \{\mathbf{Z}_b\mathbf{r}^\top, \mathbf{W}_{\sigma,b}\mathbf{r}^\top\}_{\sigma \in \Sigma, b \in \{0,1\}}, \mathbf{Z}_{end}\mathbf{r}^\top, \mathbf{a}_2^\parallel \cdot s_{end}^{-1}\Delta + \mathbf{W}_{end}\mathbf{r}^\top]_2\right)$$

with $\mathbf{W}_{start}, \mathbf{Z}_0, \mathbf{Z}_1, \mathbf{W}_{\sigma,0}, \mathbf{W}_{\sigma,1}, \mathbf{Z}_{end}, \mathbf{W}_{end} \leftarrow \mathbb{Z}_p^{(2k+1)\times k}$, $\mathbf{B} \leftarrow \mathbb{Z}_p^{k\times k}$, $\mathbf{r} \leftarrow \mathbb{Z}_p^{1\times k}$, $s_{end}, \Delta \leftarrow \mathbb{Z}_p$ *and the two oracles work as follows:*

- OEnc(x^*, m): *output* $\mathsf{ct}^*_{x^*}$ *using* s_{end} *in* aux_2;
- OKey(Γ): *output* $\boxed{\mathsf{sk}_\Gamma}$ *if* $b = 0$; *output* $\boxed{\mathsf{sk}^*_\Gamma}$ *using* Δ *and* s_{end} *in* aux_2 *if* $b = 1$;

with the restrictions that (1) $\mathcal{A}$ makes only one query to each oracle; (2) queries Γ and x^* satisfy $\Gamma(x^*) = 0$.

It is direct to see that the core lemma implies $\mathsf{G}_{2.\kappa-1} \approx_c \mathsf{G}_{2.\kappa}$; here aux_1 and aux_2 are sufficient to simulate other $q - 1$ keys which are either sk_Γ or sk^*_Γ, see the full paper for more details.

Acknowledgments. We thank Brent Waters for insightful discussions on adaptive security, as well as the anonymous reviewers for constructive feedback on our write-up.

References

1. Agrawal, S., Chase, M.: Simplifying design and analysis of complex predicate encryption schemes. In: Coron, J.-S., Nielsen, J.B. (eds.) EUROCRYPT 2017, Part I. LNCS, vol. 10210, pp. 627–656. Springer, Cham (2017). https://doi.org/10.1007/978-3-319-56620-7_22
2. Agrawal, S., Maitra, M., Yamada, S.: Attribute based encryption (and more) for nondeterministic finite automata from LWE. In: Boldyreva, A., Micciancio, D. (eds.) CRYPTO 2019. LNCS, vol. 11693, pp. 765–797. Springer, Cham (2019). https://doi.org/10.1007/978-3-030-26951-7_26
3. Agrawal, S., Maitra, M., Yamada, S.: Attribute based encryption for deterministic finite automata from DLIN. In: Hofheinz, D., Rosen, A. (eds.) TCC 2019. LNCS, vol. 11892, pp. 91–117. Springer, Cham (2019). https://doi.org/10.1007/978-3-030-36033-7_4
4. Attrapadung, N.: Dual system encryption via doubly selective security: framework, fully secure functional encryption for regular languages, and more. In: Nguyen, P.Q., Oswald, E. (eds.) EUROCRYPT 2014. LNCS, vol. 8441, pp. 557–577. Springer, Heidelberg (2014). https://doi.org/10.1007/978-3-642-55220-5_31
5. Attrapadung, N.: Dual system encryption framework in prime-order groups via computational pair encodings. In: Cheon, J.H., Takagi, T. (eds.) ASIACRYPT 2016, Part II. LNCS, vol. 10032, pp. 591–623. Springer, Heidelberg (2016). https://doi.org/10.1007/978-3-662-53890-6_20
6. Attrapadung, N., Yamada, S.: Duality in ABE: converting attribute based encryption for dual predicate and dual policy via computational encodings. In: Nyberg, K. (ed.) CT-RSA 2015. LNCS, vol. 9048, pp. 87–105. Springer, Cham (2015). https://doi.org/10.1007/978-3-319-16715-2_5
7. Chen, J., Gay, R., Wee, H.: Improved dual system ABE in prime-order groups via predicate encodings. In: Oswald, E., Fischlin, M. (eds.) EUROCRYPT 2015, Part II. LNCS, vol. 9057, pp. 595–624. Springer, Heidelberg (2015). https://doi.org/10.1007/978-3-662-46803-6_20
8. Chen, J., Gong, J., Kowalczyk, L., Wee, H.: Unbounded ABE via bilinear entropy expansion, revisited. In: Nielsen, J.B., Rijmen, V. (eds.) EUROCRYPT 2018, Part I. LNCS, vol. 10820, pp. 503–534. Springer, Cham (2018). https://doi.org/10.1007/978-3-319-78381-9_19

9. Chen, J., Wee, H.: Semi-adaptive attribute-based encryption and improved delegation for Boolean formula. In: Abdalla, M., De Prisco, R. (eds.) SCN 2014. LNCS, vol. 8642, pp. 277–297. Springer, Cham (2014). https://doi.org/10.1007/978-3-319-10879-7_16

10. Escala, A., Herold, G., Kiltz, E., Ràfols, C., Villar, J.: An algebraic framework for Diffie-Hellman assumptions. In: Canetti, R., Garay, J.A. (eds.) CRYPTO 2013, Part II. LNCS, vol. 8043, pp. 129–147. Springer, Heidelberg (2013). https://doi.org/10.1007/978-3-642-40084-1_8

11. Gong, J., Waters, B., Wee, H.: ABE for DFA from k-Lin. In: Boldyreva, A., Micciancio, D. (eds.) CRYPTO 2019, Part II. LNCS, vol. 11693, pp. 732–764. Springer, Cham (2019). https://doi.org/10.1007/978-3-030-26951-7_25

12. Goyal, V., Pandey, O., Sahai, A., Waters, B.: Attribute-based encryption for fine-grained access control of encrypted data. In: Juels, A., Wright, R.N., Vimercati, S. (eds.) ACM CCS 2006, pp. 89–98. ACM Press, October/November 2006. Available as Cryptology ePrint Archive Report 2006/309

13. Hofheinz, D., Koch, J., Striecks, C.: Identity-based encryption with (almost) tight security in the multi-instance, multi-ciphertext setting. In: Katz, J. (ed.) PKC 2015. LNCS, vol. 9020, pp. 799–822. Springer, Heidelberg (2015). https://doi.org/10.1007/978-3-662-46447-2_36

14. Jafargholi, Z., Kamath, C., Klein, K., Komargodski, I., Pietrzak, K., Wichs, D.: Be adaptive, avoid overcommitting. In: Katz, J., Shacham, H. (eds.) CRYPTO 2017, Part I. LNCS, vol. 10401, pp. 133–163. Springer, Cham (2017). https://doi.org/10.1007/978-3-319-63688-7_5

15. Kowalczyk, L., Wee, H.: Compact adaptively secure ABE for NC^1 from k-Lin. In: Ishai, Y., Rijmen, V. (eds.) EUROCRYPT 2019, Part I. LNCS, vol. 11476, pp. 3–33. Springer, Cham (2019). https://doi.org/10.1007/978-3-030-17653-2_1

16. Lewko, A., Waters, B.: New techniques for dual system encryption and fully secure HIBE with short ciphertexts. In: Micciancio, D. (ed.) TCC 2010. LNCS, vol. 5978, pp. 455–479. Springer, Heidelberg (2010). https://doi.org/10.1007/978-3-642-11799-2_27

17. Lewko, A., Waters, B.: Unbounded HIBE and attribute-based encryption. In: Paterson, K.G. (ed.) EUROCRYPT 2011. LNCS, vol. 6632, pp. 547–567. Springer, Heidelberg (2011). https://doi.org/10.1007/978-3-642-20465-4_30

18. Okamoto, T., Takashima, K.: Fully secure unbounded inner-product and attribute-based encryption. In: Wang, X., Sako, K. (eds.) ASIACRYPT 2012. LNCS, vol. 7658, pp. 349–366. Springer, Heidelberg (2012). https://doi.org/10.1007/978-3-642-34961-4_22

19. Sahai, A., Waters, B.: Fuzzy identity-based encryption. In: Cramer, R. (ed.) EUROCRYPT 2005. LNCS, vol. 3494, pp. 457–473. Springer, Heidelberg (2005). https://doi.org/10.1007/11426639_27

20. Waters, B.: Dual system encryption: realizing fully secure IBE and HIBE under simple assumptions. In: Halevi, S. (ed.) CRYPTO 2009. LNCS, vol. 5677, pp. 619–636. Springer, Heidelberg (2009). https://doi.org/10.1007/978-3-642-03356-8_36

21. Waters, B.: Functional encryption for regular languages. In: Safavi-Naini, R., Canetti, R. (eds.) CRYPTO 2012. LNCS, vol. 7417, pp. 218–235. Springer, Heidelberg (2012). https://doi.org/10.1007/978-3-642-32009-5_14

Side-Channel Security

Tornado: Automatic Generation of Probing-Secure Masked Bitsliced Implementations

Sonia Belaïd[1]([✉]), Pierre-Évariste Dagand[2], Darius Mercadier[2]([✉]),
Matthieu Rivain[1], and Raphaël Wintersdorff[1]([✉])

[1] CryptoExperts, Paris, France
{sonia.belaid,matthieu.rivain}@cryptoexperts.com, raphaelwin@hotmail.com
[2] Sorbonne Université, Paris, France
{pierre-evariste.dagand,darius.mercadier}@lip6.fr

Abstract. Cryptographic implementations deployed in real world devices often aim at (provable) security against the powerful class of side-channel attacks while keeping reasonable performances. Last year at Asiacrypt, a new formal verification tool named tightPROVE was put forward to exactly determine whether a masked implementation is secure in the well-deployed probing security model for any given security order t. Also recently, a compiler named Usuba was proposed to automatically generate bitsliced implementations of cryptographic primitives.

This paper goes one step further in the security and performances achievements with a new automatic tool named Tornado. In a nutshell, from the high-level description of a cryptographic primitive, Tornado produces a functionally equivalent bitsliced masked implementation at any desired order proven secure in the probing model, but additionally in the so-called *register probing model* which much better fits the reality of software implementations. This framework is obtained by the integration of Usuba with tightPROVE⁺, which extends tightPROVE with the ability to verify the security of implementations in the register probing model and to fix them with inserting refresh gadgets at carefully chosen locations accordingly.

We demonstrate Tornado on the lightweight cryptographic primitives selected to the second round of the NIST competition and which somehow claimed to be masking friendly. It advantageously displays performances of the resulting masked implementations for several masking orders and prove their security in the register probing model.

Keywords: Compiler · Masking · Automated verification · Bitslice

1 Introduction

Cryptographic implementations susceptible to power and electromagnetic side-channel attacks are usually protected by *masking*. The general principle of masking is to apply some secret sharing scheme to the sensitive variables processed by

© International Association for Cryptologic Research 2020
A. Canteaut and Y. Ishai (Eds.): EUROCRYPT 2020, LNCS 12107, pp. 311–341, 2020.
https://doi.org/10.1007/978-3-030-45727-3_11

the implementation in order to make the side-channel information either negligible or hard to exploit in practice. Many masked implementations rely on Boolean masking in which a variable x is represented as n random shares $x_1, \ldots, x_n$ satisfying the completeness relation $x_1 \oplus \cdots \oplus x_n = x$ (where $\oplus$ denotes the bitwise addition).

The *probing model* is widely used to analyze the security of masked (software) implementations vs. side-channel attacks. This model was introduced by Ishai, Sahai and Wagner in [26] to construct circuits resistant to hardware probing attacks. It was latter shown that this model and the underlying construction were instrumental to the design of efficient practically-secure masked cryptographic implementations [15,18,19,32]. A masking scheme secure against a t-probing adversary, *i.e.* who can probe t arbitrary variables in the computation, is indeed secure by design against the class of side-channel attacks of order t [17].

Most masking schemes consider the implementation to be protected as a Boolean or arithmetic circuit composed of gates of different natures. These gates are then replaced by *gadgets* processing masked variables. One of the important contributions of [26] was to propose a multiplication gadget secure against t-probing attacks for any t, based on a Boolean masking of order $n = 2t + 1$. This was reduced to the tight order $n = t + 1$ in [32] by constraining the two input sharings to be independent, which could be ensured by the application of a mask refreshing gadget when necessary. The design of secure refresh gadgets and, more generally, the secure composition of gadgets were subsequently subject to many works [5,6,16,18]. Of particular interest, the notion of Non-Interference (NI) and Strong Non-Interference (SNI) introduced in [5] provide a practical framework for the secure composition of gadgets which yields tight probing-secure masked implementations. In a nutshell, such implementations are composed of ISW multiplication and refresh gadgets (from the names of their inventors Ishai, Sahai, and Wagner [26]) achieving the SNI property, and of sharewise addition gadgets. The main technical challenge in such a context is to identify the number of required refresh gadgets and their (optimal) placing in the implementation to obtain a provable t-probing security. Last year at Asiacrypt, a formal verification tool called tightPROVE was put forward by Belaïd, Goudarzi, and Rivain [8] which is able to clearly state whether a tight masked implementation is t-probing secure or not. Given a masked implementation composed of standard gadgets (sharewise addition, ISW multiplication and refresh), tightPROVE either produces a probing-security proof (valid at any order) or exhibits a security flaw that directly implies a probing attack at a given order. Although nicely answering a relevant open issue, tightPROVE still suffers two important limitations. First it only applies to Boolean circuits and does not straightforwardly generalize to software implementation processing ℓ-bit registers (for $\ell > 1$). Secondly, it does not provide a method to place the refresh whenever a probing attack is detected.

In parallel to these developments, many works have focused on the efficient implementation of masking schemes with possibly high orders. For software implementations, it was recently demonstrated in several works that the use of bitslicing makes it possible to achieve (very) aggressive performances. In the bitsliced higher-order masking paradigm, the ISW scheme is applied to secure bitwise **and** instructions which are significantly more efficient than their field-multiplication counterparts involved in the so-called polynomial schemes [25,27]. Moreover, the bitslice strategy allows to compute several instances of a cryptographic primitive in parallel, or alternatively all the s-boxes in parallel within an instance of the primitive. The former setting is simply called (full) bitslice in the present paper while the latter setting is referred to as *n-slice*. In both settings, the high degree of parallelization inherited from the bitslice approach results in important efficiency gains. Verifying the probing security of full bitslice masked implementation is possible with tightPROVE since the different bit slots (corresponding to different instances of the cryptographic primitive) are mutually independent. Therefore, probing an ℓ-bit register in the bitslice implementation is equivalent to probing the corresponding variable in ℓ independent Boolean circuits, and hence tightPROVE straightforwardly applies. For n-slice implementations on the other hand, the different bit slots are mixed together at some point in the implementation which makes the verification beyond the scope of tightPROVE. In practice for masked software implementations, the *register probing model* makes much more sense than the *bit probing model* because a software implementation works on ℓ-bit registers containing several bits that leak all together.

Another limitation of tightPROVE is that it simply verifies an implementation under the form of an abstract circuit but it does not output a secure implementation, nor provide a sound placing of refresh gadgets to make the implementation secure. In practice one could hope for an integrated tool that takes an input circuit in a simple syntax, determine where to place the refresh gadgets and compile the augmented circuit into a masked implementation, for a given masking order on a given computing platform. Usuba, introduced by Mercadier and Dagand in [29], is a high-level programming language for specifying symmetric block ciphers. It provides an optimizing compiler that produces efficient bitsliced implementations. On high-end Intel platforms, Usuba has demonstrated performance on par with several, publicly available cipher implementations. As part of its compilation pipeline, Usuba features an intermediate representation, Usuba_0, that shares many commonalities with the input language of tightPROVE.

It is therefore natural to consider integrating both tools in a single programming environment. We aim at enabling cryptographers to prototype their algorithms in Usuba, letting tightPROVE verify or repair its security and letting the Usuba back-end perform masked code generation.

Our Contributions. The contributions of our work are threefold:

Extended Probing-Security Verification Tool. We tackle the limitations of tightPROVE and propose an extended verification tool, that we shall call tightPROVE$^+$. This tool can verify the security of any masked bitslice implementation in the register probing model (which makes more sense than the bit probing model w.r.t. masked software implementations). Given a masked bitslice/n-slice implementation composed of standard gadgets for bitwise operations, tightPROVE$^+$ either produces a probing-security proof or exhibits a probing attack.

New Integrated Compiler for Masked Bitslice Implementations. We present (and report on the development of) a new compiler Tornado[1] which integrates Usuba and tightPROVE$^+$ in a global compiler producing masked bitsliced implementations proven secure in the bit/register probing model. This compiler takes as input a high-level, functional specification of a cryptographic primitive. If some probing attacks are detected by tightPROVE$^+$, the Tornado compiler introduces refresh gadgets, following a sound heuristic, in order to thwart these attacks. Once a circuit has been identified as secure, Tornado produces bitsliced C code achieving register probing security at a given input order. To account for the limited resources available on embedded systems, Tornado exploits a generalization of bitslicing – implemented by Usuba – to reduce register pressure and implements several optimizations specifically tailored for Boolean masking code.

Benchmarks of NIST Lightweight Cryptography Candidates. We evaluate Tornado on 11 cryptographic primitives from the second round of the ongoing NIST lightweight cryptography standardization process.[2] The choice of cryptographic primitives has been made on the basis that they were self-identified as being amenable to masking. These implementation results give a benchmark of these different candidates with respect to masked software implementation for a number of shares ranging between 1 and 128. The obtained performances are pretty satisfying. For instance, the n-slice implementations of the tested primitives masked with 128 shares takes from 1 to a few dozen megacycles on an Cortex-M4 processor.

2   Technical Background

2.1   Usuba

Usuba is a domain-specific language for describing bitsliced algorithms. It has been designed around the observation that a bitsliced algorithm is essentially a combinational circuit implemented in software. As a consequence, Usuba's design is inspired by high-level synthesis languages, following a dataflow specification style. For instance, the language offers the possibility to manipulate bit-level quantities as well as to apply bitwise transformations to compound quantities. A domain-specific compiler then synthesizes an efficient software implementation manipulating machine words.

Figure 1 shows the Usuba implementation of the ASCON cipher. To structure programs, we use node's (Fig. 1b, c and d), of which table's (Fig. 1a) are a special

---

[1] Tornado ambitions to be the work*horse* of those cryptographers that selflessly protect their ciphers through provably secure *mask*ing and precise bit*slicing*.

[2] https://csrc.nist.gov/Projects/lightweight-cryptography/round-2-candidates.

case of a node specified through its truth table. A node specifies a set of input values, output values as well as a system of equations relating these variables. To streamline the definition of repeating systems (*e.g.*, the 12 rounds of Ascon), Usuba offers bounded loops, which simply desugar into standalone equations. A static analysis ensures that the system of equations admits a solution. The semantics of an Usuba program is thus straightforward: it is the (unique) solution to the system of equations.

```
table Sbox(x:v5) returns (y:v5) {
    0x4,   0xb,   0x1f,  0x14,  0x1a,  0x15,
    0x9,   0x2,   0x1b,  0x5,   0x8,   0x12,
    0x1d,  0x3,   0x6,   0x1c,  0x1e,  0x13,
    0x7,   0xe,   0x0,   0xd,   0x11,  0x18,
    0x10,  0xc,   0x1,   0x19,  0x16,  0xa,
    0xf,   0x17
}
```

```
node AddConstant(state:u64x5,c:u64)
                 returns (stateR:u64x5)
let
    stateR = (state[0,1], state[2] ^ c,
              state[3,4]);
tel
```

(a) S-box specified by its truth table.   (b) Node manipulating a 5-uple

```
node LinearLayer(state:u64x5)
                 returns (stateR:u64x5)
let
    stateR[0] = state[0]
              ^ (state[0] >>> 19)
              ^ (state[0] >>> 28);
    stateR[1] = state[1]
              ^ (state[1] >>> 61)
              ^ (state[1] >>> 39);
    stateR[2] = state[2]
              ^ (state[2] >>> 1)
              ^ (state[2] >>> 6);
    stateR[3] = state[3]
              ^ (state[3] >>> 10)
              ^ (state[3] >>> 17);
    stateR[4] = state[4]
              ^ (state[4] >>> 7)
              ^ (state[4] >>> 41);
tel
```

```
node ascon12(input:u64x5)
             returns (output:u64x5)
vars
    consts:u64[12],
    state:u64x5[13]
let
    consts = (0xf0, 0xe1, 0xd2, 0xc3,
              0xb4, 0xa5, 0x96, 0x87,
              0x78, 0x69, 0x5a, 0x4b);

    state[0] = input;
    forall i in [0, 11] {
        state[i+1] = LinearLayer
                     (Sbox
                     (AddConstant
                     (state[i],consts[i])))
    }
    output = state[12]
tel
```

(c) Node involving rotations and xors   (d) Main node composing the 12 rounds

Fig. 1. Ascon cipher in Usuba

Aside from custom syntax, Usuba features a type system that documents and enforces parallelization strategies. Traditionally, bitslicing [12] consists in treating an m-word quantity as m variables, such that a combinational circuit can be straightforwardly implemented by applying the corresponding bitwise logical operations over the variables. On a 32-bit architecture, this means that 32 circuits are evaluated "in parallel": for example, a 32-bit **and** instruction is seen as 32 Boolean **and** gates. To ensure that an algorithm admits an efficient bitsliced implementation, Usuba only allows bitwise operations and forbids stateful computations [30].

However, bitslicing can be generalized to n-slicing [29] (with $n > 1$). Whereas bitslicing splits an m-word quantity into m individual bits, we can also treat it at a coarser granularity[3], splitting it into k variables of n bits each (preserving the invariant that $m = k \times n$). The register pressure is thus lowered, since we introduce k variables rather than m, and, provided some support from the underlying hardware or compiler, we may use arithmetic operations in addition to the usual Boolean operations. Conversely, certain operations become prohibitively expensive in this setting, such as permuting individual bits. The role of Usuba's type system is to document the parallelization strategy decided by the programmer (*e.g.*, u64x5 means that we chose to treat a 320-bit block at the granularity of 64-bit atoms) and ensure that the programmer only used operations that can be efficiently implemented on a given architecture.

The overall architecture of the Usuba compiler is presented in Fig. 2. It involves two essential steps. Firstly, normalization expands the high-level constructs of the language to a minimal core language called Usuba_0. Usuba_0 is the software equivalent of a netlist: it represents the sliced implementation in a flattened form, erasing tuples altogether. Secondly, optimizations are applied at this level, taking Usuba_0 circuits to (functionally equivalent) Usuba_0 circuits. In particular, scheduling is responsible for ordering the system of equations in such a way as to enable sequential execution as well as maximize instruction-level parallelism. To obtain a C program from a scheduled Usuba_0 circuit, we merely have to replace the Boolean and arithmetic operations of the circuit with the corresponding C operations. The resulting C program is in static single assignment (SSA) form, involving only operations on integer types: we thus solely rely on the C compiler to perform register allocation and produce executable code.

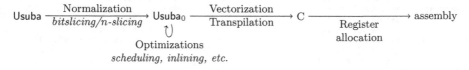

Fig. 2. High-level view of the Usuba compiler

At compile-time, a specific node is designated as the cryptographic primitive of interest (here, `ascon12`): the Usuba compiler is then tasked to produce a C file exposing a function corresponding to the desired primitive. In this case, the bitsliced primitive would have type

```
void Ascon12 (uint32_t plain[320], uint32_t cipher[320])
```

whereas the 64-sliced primitive would have type

```
void Ascon12 (uint64_t plain[5], uint64_t cipher[5])
```

---

[3] The literature [29, Fig. 2] distinguishes *vertical* from *horizontal* n-slicing: lacking the powerful SIMD instructions required by horizontal n-slicing, we focus here solely on vertical n-slicing, which we abbreviate unambiguously to "n-slicing".

Usuba targets C so as to maximize portability: it has been successfully used to deploy cryptographic primitives on Intel, PowerPC, Arm and Sparc architectures. However, a significant amount of optimization is carried by the Usuba compiler: because this programming model is subject to stringent invariants, the compiler is able to perform far-reaching, whole program optimizations that a C compiler would shy away from. For example, it features a custom instruction scheduling algorithm, aimed at minimizing the register pressure of bitsliced code. On high-end Intel architectures featuring Single Instruction Multiple Data (SIMD) extensions, Usuba has demonstrated performance on par with hand-optimized reference implementations [29].

Usuba offers an ideal setting in which to automate Boolean masking. Indeed, ciphers specified in Usuba are presented at a suitable level of abstraction: they consist in combinational circuits, by construction. As a result, the Usuba compiler can perform a systematic source-to-source transformation, automating away the tedious introduction of masking gadgets and refreshes. Besides, the high-level nature of the language allows us to extract a model of an algorithm, analyzable by static analysis tools such as SAT solvers – to check program equivalence, which is used internally to validate the correctness of optimizations – or tightPROVE – to verify probing security.

2.2   tightPROVE

tightPROVE is a verification tool which aims to verify the probing security of a shared Boolean circuit. It takes as input a list of instructions that describes a shared circuit made of specific multiplication, addition and refresh *gadgets* and outputs either a probing security proof or a probing attack. To that end, a security reduction is made through a sequence of four equivalent games. In each of them, an adversary $\mathcal{A}$ chooses a set of probes $\mathcal{P}$ (indices pointing to wires in the shared circuit) in the target circuit C, and a simulator $\mathcal{S}$ wins the game if it successfully simulates the distribution of the tuple of variables carried by the corresponding wires without knowledge of the secret inputs.

Game 0 corresponds to the t-probing security definition: the adversary can choose t probes in a $t + 1$-shared circuit, on whichever wires she wishes. In Game 1, the adversary is restricted to only probe gadget inputs: one probe on an addition or refresh gadget becomes one probe on one input share, one probe on a multiplication gadget becomes one probe on each of the input sharings. In Game 2, the circuit C is replaced by another circuit C' that has a multiplicative depth of one, through a transformation called **Flatten**, illustrated in the original paper [8]. In a nutshell, each output of a multiplication or refresh gadget in the original circuit gives rise to a new input with a fresh sharing in C'. Finally, in Game 3, the adversary is only allowed to probe pairs of inputs of multiplication gadgets. The transition between these games is mainly made possible by an important property of the selected refresh and multiplication gadgets: in addition to being t-probing secure, they are t-*strong non interfering* (t-SNI for short) [5]. Satisfying the latter means that t probed variables in their circuit description can be simulated with less than t_1 shares of each input, where $t_1 \leq t$ denotes the number of internal probes *i.e.* which are not placed on output shares.

Game 3 can be interpreted as a linear algebra problem. In the flattened circuit, the inputs of multiplication gadgets are linear combinations of the circuit inputs. These can be modelled as Boolean vectors that we call *operand vectors*, with ones at indexes of involved inputs. From the definition of Game 3, the $2t$ probes made by the adversary all target these operand vectors for chosen shares. These probes can be distributed into $t + 1$ matrices $M_0, \ldots, M_t$, where $t + 1$ corresponds to the (tight) number of shares, such that for each probe targeting the share i of an operand vector $\mathbf{v}$, with i in $\{0, \ldots, t\}$, $\mathbf{v}$ is added as a row to matrix M_i. Deciding whether a circuit is t-probing secure can then be reduced to verifying whether $\langle M_0^T \rangle \cap \cdots \cap \langle M_t^T \rangle = \emptyset$ (where $\langle \cdot \rangle$ denotes the column space of a matrix). The latter can be solved algorithmically with the following high-level algorithm for a circuit with m multiplications:

For each operand vector $\mathbf{w}$,

1. Create a set $\mathcal{G}_1$ with all the multiplications for which $\mathbf{w}$ is one of the operand vectors.
2. Create a set $\mathcal{O}_1$ with the co-operand vectors of $\mathbf{w}$ in the multiplications in $\mathcal{G}_1$.
3. Stop if $\mathbf{w} \in \langle \mathcal{O}_1 \rangle$ ($\mathcal{O}_1$'s linear span), that is if $\mathbf{w}$ can be written as a linear combination of Boolean vectors from $\mathcal{O}_1$.
4. For i from 2 to m, create new sets $\mathcal{G}_i$ and $\mathcal{O}_i$ by adding to $\mathcal{G}_{i-1}$ multiplications that involve an operand $\mathbf{w}'$ verifying $\mathbf{w}' \in (\mathbf{w} \oplus \langle \mathcal{O}_{i-1} \rangle)$, and adding to $\mathcal{O}_{i-1}$ the other operand vectors of these multiplications. Stop whenever $i = m$ or $\mathcal{G}_i = \mathcal{G}_{i-1}$ or $\mathbf{w} \in \langle \mathcal{O}_i \rangle$.

If this algorithm stops when $\mathbf{w} \in \langle \mathcal{O}_i \rangle$ for some i, then there is a probing attack on $\mathbf{w}$, i.e., from a certain t, the attacker can recover information on $\mathbf{x} \cdot \mathbf{w}$ (where $\mathbf{x}$ denote the vector of plain inputs), with only t probes on the $(t + 1)$-shared circuit. In the other two scenarios, the circuit is proven to be t-probing secure for any value of t.

3   Extending tightPROVE to the Register-Probing Model

3.1   Model of Computation

Notations. In this paper, we denote by $\mathbb{K} = \mathbb{F}_2$ the field with two elements and by $\mathcal{V} = \mathbb{K}^s$ the vector space of dimension s over $\mathbb{K}$, for some given integer s (which will be used to denote the register size). Vectors, in any vector space, are written in bold. $[\![i, j]\!]$ denotes the integer interval $\mathbb{Z} \cap [i, j]$ for any two integers i and j. For a finite set $\mathcal{X}$, we denote by $|\mathcal{X}|$ the cardinality of $\mathcal{X}$ and by $x \leftarrow \mathcal{X}$ the action of picking x from $\mathcal{X}$ independently and uniformly at random. For some (probabilistic) algorithm $\mathcal{A}$, we further denote $x \leftarrow \mathcal{A}(in)$ the action of running algorithm $\mathcal{A}$ on some inputs in (with fresh uniform random tape) and setting x to the value returned by $\mathcal{A}$.

Basic Notions. We call *register-based circuit* any directed acyclic graph, whose vertices either correspond to an input gate, a constant gate outputting an element of $\mathcal{V}$ or a gate processing one of the following functions:

- XOR and AND, the coordinate-wise Boolean addition and multiplication over $\mathbb{K}^s$, respectively. For the sake of intelligibility, we write $\mathbf{a}+\mathbf{b}$ and $\mathbf{a}\cdot\mathbf{b}$ instead of $\mathsf{XOR}(\mathbf{a},\mathbf{b})$ and $\mathsf{AND}(\mathbf{a},\mathbf{b})$ respectively when it is clear from the context that we are performing bitwise operations between elements of $\mathcal{V}$.
- $(\mathsf{ROTL}_r)_{r\in[\![1,s-1]\!]}$, the family of vector Boolean rotations. For all $r \in [\![1,s-1]\!]$,

$$\mathsf{ROTL}_r \colon \mathcal{V} \to \mathcal{V}$$
$$(v_1,\ldots,v_s) \mapsto (v_{r+1},\ldots,v_s,v_1,\ldots,v_r)$$

- $(\mathsf{SHIFTL}_r)_{r\in[\![1,s-1]\!]}$ and $(\mathsf{SHIFTR}_r)_{r\in[\![1,s-1]\!]}$, the families of vector Boolean left and right shifts. For all $r \in [\![1,s-1]\!]$,

$$\mathsf{SHIFTL}_r \colon \mathcal{V} \to \mathcal{V} \qquad\qquad \mathsf{SHIFTR}_r \colon \mathcal{V} \to \mathcal{V}$$
$$(v_1,\ldots,v_s) \mapsto (v_{r+1},\ldots,v_s,0,\ldots,0) \quad (v_1,\ldots,v_s) \mapsto (0,\ldots,0,v_1,\ldots,v_{s-r})$$

A *randomized circuit* is a register-based circuit augmented with gates of fan-in 0 that output elements of $\mathcal{V}$ chosen uniformly at random.

Translation to the Masking World. A d-*sharing of* $\mathbf{x} \in \mathcal{V}$ refers to any random tuple $[\mathbf{x}]_d = (\mathbf{x}_0,\mathbf{x}_1\ldots,\mathbf{x}_{d-1}) \in \mathcal{V}^d$ that satisfies $\mathbf{x} = \mathbf{x}_0+\mathbf{x}_1+\cdots+\mathbf{x}_{d-1}$. A d-sharing $[\mathbf{x}]_d$ is *uniform* if it is uniformly distributed over the subspace of tuples satisfying this condition, meaning that for any $k < d$, any k-tuple of the shares of $\mathbf{x}$ is uniformly distributed over $\mathcal{V}^k$. In the following, we omit the sharing order d when it is clear from the context, so a d-sharing of $\mathbf{x}$ is denoted by $[\mathbf{x}]$. We further denote by **Enc** a probabilistic *encoding* algorithm that maps $\mathbf{x} \in \mathcal{V}$ to a fresh uniform sharing $[\mathbf{x}]$.

In this paper, we call a d-*shared register-based circuit* a randomized register-based circuit working on d-shared variables as elements of $\mathcal{V}$ that takes as inputs some d-sharings $[\mathbf{x}_1],\ldots,[\mathbf{x}_n]$ and performs operations on their shares with the functions described above. Assuming that we associate an index to each edge in the circuit, a *probe* refers to a specific edge index. For such a circuit C, we denote by $C([\mathbf{x}_1],\ldots,[\mathbf{x}_n])_{\mathcal{P}}$ the distribution of the tuple of values carried by the wires of C of indexes in $\mathcal{P}$ when the circuit is evaluated on $[\mathbf{x}_1],\ldots,[\mathbf{x}_n]$.

We consider circuits composed of subcircuits called *gadgets*. Gadgets are d-shared circuits performing a specific operation. They can be seen as building blocks of a more complex circuit. We furthermore say that a gadget is *sharewise* if each output share of this gadget can be expressed as a deterministic function of its input shares of the same sharing index. In this paper, we specifically consider the following gadgets:

- The *ISW-multiplication gadget* $[\otimes]$ takes two d-sharings $[\mathbf{a}]$ and $[\mathbf{b}]$ as inputs and outputs a d-sharing $[\mathbf{c}]$ such that $\mathbf{c} = \mathbf{a} \cdot \mathbf{b}$ as follows:
  1. for every $0 \leq i < j \leq d - 1$, $\mathbf{r}_{i,j} \leftarrow \mathcal{V}$;
  2. for every $0 \leq i < j \leq d - 1$, compute $\mathbf{r}_{j,i} \leftarrow (\mathbf{r}_{i,j} + \mathbf{a}_i \cdot \mathbf{b}_j) + \mathbf{a}_j \cdot \mathbf{b}_i$;
  3. for every $0 \leq i \leq d - 1$, compute $\mathbf{c}_i \leftarrow \mathbf{a}_i \cdot \mathbf{b}_i + \sum_{j \neq i} \mathbf{r}_{i,j}$.
- The *ISW-refresh gadget* $[R]$ is the ISW-multiplication gadget in which the second operand $[\mathbf{b}]$ is set to the constant sharing $(\mathbf{1}, \mathbf{0}, \ldots, \mathbf{0})$, where $\mathbf{0} \in \mathcal{V}$ and $\mathbf{1} \in \mathcal{V}$ denote the all 0 and all 1 vector respectively.
- The *sharewise addition gadget* $[\oplus]$ computes a d-sharing $[\mathbf{c}]$ from sharings $[\mathbf{a}]$ and $[\mathbf{b}]$ such that $\mathbf{c} = \mathbf{a} + \mathbf{b}$ by letting $\mathbf{c}_i = \mathbf{a}_i + \mathbf{b}_i$ for $i \in [\![0, d - 1]\!]$.
- The *sharewise left shift, right shift and rotation gadgets* $([\lll_n], [\ggg_n]$ and $[\lll_n]$ respectively) take a sharing $[\mathbf{a}]$ as input and output a sharing $[\mathbf{c}]$ such that $\mathbf{c} = f(\mathbf{a})$ by letting $\mathbf{c}_i = f(\mathbf{a}_i)$ for $i \in [\![0, d - 1]\!]$, f being the corresponding function described in the section above.
- The *sharewise multiplication by a constant* $[\otimes_k]$ takes a sharing $[\mathbf{a}]$ and a constant $\mathbf{k} \in \mathcal{V}$ as inputs and outputs a sharing $[\mathbf{c}]$ such that $\mathbf{c} = \mathbf{k} \cdot \mathbf{a}$ by letting $\mathbf{c}_i = \mathbf{k} \cdot \mathbf{a}_i$ for $i \in [\![0, d - 1]\!]$.
- The *sharewise addition with a constant* $[\oplus_k]$ takes a sharing $[\mathbf{a}]$ and a constant $\mathbf{k} \in \mathcal{V}$ as input and outputs a sharing $[\mathbf{c}]$ such that $\mathbf{c} = \mathbf{a} + \mathbf{k}$ by letting $\mathbf{c}_i = \mathbf{a}_i$ for $i \in [\![0, d - 1]\!]$ and $\mathbf{c}_0 = \mathbf{a}_0 + \mathbf{k}$. The coordinate-wise logical complement NOT is captured by this definition with $\mathbf{k} = (1, \ldots, 1)$.

3.2 Security Notions

In this section, we recall the *t-probing security* originally introduced in [26] as formalized through a concrete security game in [8]. It is based on two experiments described in Figure 3 from [8] in which an adversary $\mathcal{A}$, modelled as a probabilistic algorithm, outputs of set of t probes $\mathcal{P}$ and n inputs $x_1, \ldots, x_n$ in a set $\mathbb{K}$. In the first experiment, ExpReal, the inputs are encoded and given as inputs to the shared circuit C. The experiment then outputs a random evaluation of the chosen probes $(v_1, \ldots, v_t)$. In the second experiment, ExpSim, the simulator outputs a simulation of the evaluation $C([x_1], \ldots, [x_n])_{\mathcal{P}}$ without the input sharings. It wins the game if and only if the distributions of both experiments are identical.

Definition 1 ([8]). *A shared circuit C is t-probing secure if and only if for every adversary $\mathcal{A}$, there exists a simulator $\mathcal{S}$ that wins the t-probing security game defined in Fig. 3, i.e. the random experiments* ExpReal$(\mathcal{A}, C)$ *and* ExpSim$(\mathcal{A}, \mathcal{S}, C)$ *output identical distributions.*

ExpReal($\mathcal{A}, C$):
1. $(\mathcal{P}, x_1, \ldots, x_n) \leftarrow \mathcal{A}()$
2. $[x_1] \leftarrow \mathbf{Enc}(x_1), \ldots, [x_n] \leftarrow \mathbf{Enc}(x_n)$
3. $(v_1, \ldots, v_t) \leftarrow C([x_1], \ldots, [x_n])_{\mathcal{P}}$
4. Return $(v_1, \ldots, v_t)$

ExpSim($\mathcal{A}, \mathcal{S}, C$):
1. $(\mathcal{P}, x_1, \ldots, x_n) \leftarrow \mathcal{A}()$
2. $(v_1, \ldots, v_t) \leftarrow \mathcal{S}(\mathcal{P})$
3. Return $(v_1, \ldots, v_t)$

Fig. 3. t-probing security game from [8].

In [8], the notion of t-probing security was defined for a Boolean circuit, with $\mathbb{K} = \mathbb{F}_2$, that is with $x_1, \ldots, x_n \in \mathbb{F}_2$ and $v_1, \ldots, v_t \in \mathbb{F}_2$. We further refer to this specialized notion as *t-bit probing security*.

While the notion of t-bit probing security is relevant in a hardware scenario, in the reality of masked software embedded devices, variables are manipulated in registers which contain several bits that leak all together. To capture this model, in this paper, we extend the verification to what we call the *t-register probing model* in which the targeted circuit manipulates variables on registers of size s for some $s \in \mathbb{N}^+$ and the adversary is able to choose t probes as registers containing values in $\mathcal{V} = \mathbb{F}_2^s$. Notice that the t-bit probing model can be seen as a specialization of the t-register probing model with $s = 1$.

Cautionary Note. In software implementations, we may also face transition leakages, modeled as functions of two ℓ-bit variables when they are successively stored in the same register. In that scenario, the masking order t might be halved [2, 31]. While specific techniques can be settled to detect and handle such leakages, we leave it for future work and focus on simple register probing model in this paper, in which one observation reveals the content of a single register.

3.3 Security Reductions in the Register Probing Model

Just like for the bit-probing version of tightPROVE, the security notions are formalized through games. Similar notions are used which only differ in the fact that the probes in the new model now point to wires of register-based circuits, which carry vectors of $\mathcal{V}$. In this section, we present the differences between the security games in the bit-probing model and the register-probing model. The games are still equivalent to one another, and we give a sketch of proof for each transition (as well as a full proof in the full version). We then give a description of the linear algebra problem induced by the last game.

Sequence of Games. Similarly to the bit-probing case, Game 0 corresponds to the probing security definition for a register-based circuit, and still features an adversary $\mathcal{A}$ that chooses a set of probes $\mathcal{P}$ in a circuit C, and a simulator $\mathcal{S}$ that wins the game if it successfully simulates $C([\mathbf{x}_1], \ldots, [\mathbf{x}_n])_{\mathcal{P}}$, for inputs $x_1, \ldots, x_n \in \mathcal{V}$.

Game 1. In Game 1, the adversary returns a set of probes $\mathcal{P}' = \mathcal{P}'_r \cup \mathcal{P}'_m \cup \mathcal{P}'_{sw}$, where $|\mathcal{P}'| = t$ and the sets $\mathcal{P}'_r$, $\mathcal{P}'_m$ and $\mathcal{P}'_{sw}$ contain probes pointing to refresh gadgets' inputs, pairs of probes pointing to multiplication gadgets' inputs and probes pointing to sharewise gadgets' inputs or outputs respectively. $C([\mathbf{x}_1], \ldots, [\mathbf{x}_n])_{\mathcal{P}'}$ is then a q-tuple for $q = 2|\mathcal{P}'_m| + |\mathcal{P}'_r \cup \mathcal{P}'_{sw}|$. Besides the definition set of variables, the only difference with the bit-probing case stands in the fact that the sharewise gadgets are not restricted to addition gadgets.

Game 2. In Game 2, the circuit C is replaced by an equivalent circuit C' of multiplicative depth 1, just like in the bit-probing case. The **Flatten** operation can be trivially adapted to register-based circuits, as the outputs of refresh and multiplication gadgets can still be considered as uniform sharings.

Game 3. In this last game, the adversary is restricted to only position its t probes on multiplication gadgets, *i.e.* $\mathcal{A}$ returns a set of probes $\mathcal{P}'' = \mathcal{P}'_r \cup \mathcal{P}'_m \cup \mathcal{P}'_{sw}$ such that $\mathcal{P}'_{sw} = \mathcal{P}'_r = \emptyset$ and $\mathcal{P}'' = \mathcal{P}'_m$. $C([\mathbf{x}_1], \ldots, [\mathbf{x}_n])_{\mathcal{P}''}$ thus returns a q-tuple for $q = 2t$ since all the elements in $\mathcal{P}''$ are pairs of inputs of multiplication gadgets.

Theorem 1. *Let C be a shared circuit. We have the following equivalences:*

$$\forall \mathcal{A}_0, \exists \mathcal{S}_0, \mathcal{S}_0 \text{ wins Game 0.} \iff \forall \mathcal{A}_1, \exists \mathcal{S}_1, \mathcal{S}_1 \text{ wins Game 1.}$$
$$\iff \forall \mathcal{A}_2, \exists \mathcal{S}_2, \mathcal{S}_2 \text{ wins Game 2.}$$
$$\iff \forall \mathcal{A}_3, \exists \mathcal{S}_3, \mathcal{S}_3 \text{ wins Game 3.}$$

For the sake of clarity, we define one lemma per game transition. The corresponding proofs are available in the full version of this paper, but an informal reasoning that supports these ideas is given in the following, as well as the differences with the proofs established in [8].

Lemma 1. $\forall \mathcal{A}_0, \exists \mathcal{S}_0, \mathcal{S}_0$ *wins Game 0.* $\iff \forall \mathcal{A}_1, \exists \mathcal{S}_1, \mathcal{S}_1$ *wins Game 1.*

Proof (sketch). The proof for the first game transition is based on the fact that multiplication and refresh gadgets are t-SNI gadgets, and that each probe on such gadgets can be replaced by one probe on each input sharing. The reason why this still works in the new model is that the ISW multiplication and refresh gadgets are still SNI for register-based circuits performing bitwise operations on $\mathcal{V}$. This transition can thus be reduced to the original transition.

Lemma 2. $\forall \mathcal{A}_1, \exists \mathcal{S}_1, \mathcal{S}_1$ *wins Game 1.* $\iff \forall \mathcal{A}_2, \exists \mathcal{S}_2, \mathcal{S}_2$ *wins Game 2.*

Proof (sketch). The proof for the second game transition relies on the fact that just as the output of a Boolean multiplication gadget is a random uniform Boolean sharing, the outputs of the multiplication gadgets we consider can be treated as new, fresh input encodings. Thus, a circuit C is t-probing secure if and only if the circuit $C' = Flatten(C)$ is t-probing secure.

Lemma 3. $\forall \mathcal{A}_2, \exists \mathcal{S}_2, \mathcal{S}_2$ *wins Game 2.* $\iff \forall \mathcal{A}_3, \exists \mathcal{S}_3, \mathcal{S}_3$ *wins Game 3.*

Proof (sketch). A cross product of shares $\mathbf{a}_i \cdot \mathbf{b}_j$ *carries informations on both shares* $\mathbf{a}_i$ *and* $\mathbf{b}_j$*, as each of the s slots in the cross product carries information about each share. Thus, placing probes on multiplication gadgets only is optimal from the attacker point of view. The complete proof for Lemma 3 makes use of formal notions which are introduced in the next paragraph.*

Translation to Linear Algebra. From now on, the column space of a matrix M is denoted by $\langle M \rangle$ and the column space of the concatenation of all the matrices in a set E is denoted by $\langle E \rangle$.

From Lemmas 1 and 2, checking the t-probing security of a shared circuit C has been reduced to verifying the t-probing security of a shared circuit $C' = \mathbf{Flatten}(C)$, for which the attacker is restricted to use probes on its multiplication and refresh gadgets' inputs. We can translate this problem into a linear algebra problem that we can solve algorithmically. In the following, let us denote by $\mathbf{x}_{i,j} \in \mathcal{V}$ the jth share of the ith input sharing $[\mathbf{x}_i]$, so that

$$\forall i \in [\![1, N]\!], [\mathbf{x}_i] = (\mathbf{x}_{i,0}, \mathbf{x}_{i,1}, \ldots, \mathbf{x}_{i,t}) \in \mathcal{V}^{t+1}$$

We also denote by $\mathbf{x}_{\|j}$ the concatenation of the jth shares of the input sharings:

$$\forall j \in [\![0, t]\!], \mathbf{x}_{\|j} = \mathbf{x}_{1,j} \| \mathbf{x}_{2,j} \| \ldots \| \mathbf{x}_{N,j} \in \mathbb{K}^{sN}$$

The probed variables in the flattened circuit C' form a q-tuple $(\mathbf{v}_1, \ldots, \mathbf{v}_q) = C'([\mathbf{x}_1], \ldots, [\mathbf{x}_N])_{\mathcal{P}'}$. It can be checked that all these variables are linear combinations of inputs shares' coordinates since (1) the circuit C' has a multiplicative depth of one, (2) the adversary can only place probes on inputs for multiplication and refresh gadgets, and (3) other types of gadgets are linear. Since the gadgets other than multiplication and refresh are sharewise, we can assert that for every $k \in [\![1, q]\!]$, there exists a single share index j for which $\mathbf{v}_k$ only depends on the jth share of the input sharings and thus only depends on $\mathbf{x}_{\|j}$. Therefore there exists a Boolean matrix $A_k \in \mathbb{K}^{sN \times s}$, that we refer to as a *block* from now on, such that

$$\mathbf{v}_k = \mathbf{x}_{\|j} \cdot A_k \in \mathcal{V}.$$

Let us denote by $\mathbf{v}_{\|j}$ the concatenation of all n_j probed variables $\mathbf{v}_i$ with $i \in [\![1, q]\!]$ such that $\mathbf{v}_i$ only depends on share j. Similarly, we denote by $M_j \in \mathbb{K}^{sN \times sn_j}$ the matrix obtained from the concatenation of all the corresponding blocks A_i (in the same order). We can now write

$$\mathbf{v}_{\|0} = \mathbf{x}_{\|0} \cdot M_0, \quad \mathbf{v}_{\|1} = \mathbf{x}_{\|1} \cdot M_1, \quad \ldots, \quad \mathbf{v}_{\|t} = \mathbf{x}_{\|t} \cdot M_t$$

which leads us to the following proposition.

Proposition 1. *For any* $(\mathbf{x}_1, \ldots, \mathbf{x}_N) \in \mathcal{V}^N$*, the q-tuple of probed variables* $(\mathbf{v}_1, \ldots, \mathbf{v}_q) = C([\mathbf{x}_1], [\mathbf{x}_2], \ldots, [\mathbf{x}_N])_{\mathcal{P}'}$ *can be perfectly simulated if and only if the M_j matrices satisfy*

$$\langle M_0 \rangle \cap \langle M_1 \rangle \cap \cdots \cap \langle M_t \rangle = \emptyset.$$

Proof. Let us denote by $\mathbf{x} = (\mathbf{x}_1 \| \mathbf{x}_2 \| \ldots \| \mathbf{x}_N)$ *the concatenation of all the inputs. We split the proof into two parts to handle both implications.*

From Left to Right. Let us assume that there exist a non-null vector $\mathbf{w} \in \mathbb{K}^{sN}$ and vectors $\mathbf{u}_0 \in \mathbb{K}^{sn_0}, \ldots, \mathbf{u}_t \in \mathbb{K}^{sn_t}$ that verify $\mathbf{w} = M_0 \cdot \mathbf{u}_0 = \cdots = M_t \cdot \mathbf{u}_t$. This implies the following sequence of equalities:

$$\sum_{j=0}^{t} \mathbf{v}_{||j} \cdot \mathbf{u}_j = \sum_{j=0}^{t} \mathbf{x}_{||j} \cdot M_j \cdot \mathbf{u}_j = \sum_{j=0}^{t} \mathbf{x}_{||j} \cdot \mathbf{w} = \mathbf{x} \cdot \mathbf{w}$$

which implies that the distribution of $(\mathbf{v}_1, \ldots, \mathbf{v}_q)$ depends on $\mathbf{x}$, and thus cannot be perfectly simulated.

From Right to Left. Since the sharings $[\mathbf{x}_1], \ldots, [\mathbf{x}_N]$ are uniform and independent, the vectors $\mathbf{x}_{||1}, \ldots, \mathbf{x}_{||t}$ are independent uniform random vectors in $\mathbb{K}^{sN}$, and can thus be perfectly simulated without the knowledge of any secret value. As a direct consequence, the distribution of $(\mathbf{v}_{||1}, \ldots, \mathbf{v}_{||t})$ can be simulated. From the definition $\mathbf{v}_{||0} = \mathbf{x}_{||0} \cdot M_0$, each coordinate of $\mathbf{v}_{||0}$ is the result of a product $\mathbf{x}_{||0} \cdot \mathbf{c}$ where $\mathbf{c}$ is a column of M_0. By assumption, there exists $j \in \{1, \ldots, t\}$ such that $\mathbf{c} \notin \langle M_j \rangle$. Since $\mathbf{x}_{||1}, \ldots, \mathbf{x}_{||t}$ are mutually independent, $\mathbf{x}_{||j} \cdot \mathbf{c}$ is a random uniform bit independent of $\mathbf{x}_{||1} \cdot M_1, \ldots, \mathbf{x}_{||j-1} \cdot M_{j-1}, \mathbf{x}_{||j+1} \cdot M_{j+1}, \ldots, \mathbf{x}_{||t} \cdot M_t$, and since $\mathbf{c} \notin \langle M_j \rangle$, it is also independent of $\mathbf{x}_{||j} \cdot M_j$. This means that $\mathbf{x}_{||j} \cdot \mathbf{c}$ is a random uniform bit independent of $\mathbf{v}_{||1}, \ldots, \mathbf{v}_{||t}$, and so is $\mathbf{x}_{||0} \cdot \mathbf{c}$, as $\mathbf{x}_{||0} \cdot \mathbf{c} = \mathbf{x}_{||j} \cdot \mathbf{c} + (\mathbf{x}_{||1} \cdot \mathbf{c} + \cdots + \mathbf{x}_{||j-1} \cdot \mathbf{c} + \mathbf{x}_{||j+1} \cdot \mathbf{c} + \cdots + \mathbf{x}_{||t} \cdot \mathbf{c} + \mathbf{x} \cdot \mathbf{c})$. Since $\mathbf{v}_{||0} = \mathbf{x}_{||0} \cdot M_0$, we can then perfectly simulate $\mathbf{v}_{||0}$. As a result, $(\mathbf{v}_1, \ldots, \mathbf{v}_q)$ can be perfectly simulated. $\qquad\square$

3.4 Verification in the Register Probing Model

In this section, we present a method based on Proposition 1 that checks whether a $(t+1)$-shared circuit C achieves t-register probing security for every $t \in \mathbb{N}^*$. We start by introducing some notations and formalizing the problem, then we give a description of the aforementioned method, along with a pseudocode of the algorithm. The method is finally illustrated with some examples.

Formal Definitions. Now that the equivalence between the t-register probing security game was proven to be equivalent to Game 3, in which the adversary can only probe variables that are inputs of multiplication gadgets in a flattened circuit C', we formally express the verification of the t-register probing security as a linear algebra problem. For a given multiplication gadget of index g, let us denote by $[\mathbf{a}_g]$ and $[\mathbf{b}_g]$ its input sharings, *i.e.*

$$[\mathbf{a}_g] = (\mathbf{x}_{||0} \cdot A_g, \ \ldots, \ \mathbf{x}_{||t} \cdot A_g) \text{ and } [\mathbf{b}_g] = (\mathbf{x}_{||0} \cdot B_g, \ \ldots, \ \mathbf{x}_{||t} \cdot B_g)$$

for some constant blocks A_g and B_g that we now call *operand blocks*. The adversary outputs a set of t pairs of probes $\mathcal{P} = \{(p_1^1, p_2^1), (p_1^2, p_2^2), \ldots, (p_1^t, p_2^t)\}$, where for i in $\{1, \ldots, t\}$, p_1^i and p_2^i are wire indices corresponding to one element of each input sharings of the same multiplication. For all $j \in [\![0, t]\!]$, we define the matrix M_j as the concatenation of all the blocks corresponding to probed shares of share index j.

By Proposition 1, there is a register probing attack on C if and only if $\bigcap_{i=0}^{t}\langle M_j \rangle \neq \emptyset$. For an attack to exist, the matrices must be non-empty, and since these matrices contain $2t$ blocks, at least one of them is made of a single block D that belongs to the set of operand blocks $\{A_g, B_g\}_g$. We can now say that there exists a register probing attack on C if and only if there exists a non-empty subspace S of $\mathbb{K}^{sN}$ such that $S = \bigcap_{i=0}^{t}\langle M_j \rangle \subseteq \langle D \rangle$. In that case, there is an attack on the subset S that we now refer to as the *attack span*.

tightPROVE$^+$. When $s = 1$ (i.e., in the t-bit probing model case), the dimension of $S = \bigcap_{i=0}^{t}\langle M_j \rangle$ is at most 1, so checking whether an operand block W leads to an attack or not reduces to verifying whether there exists a set of probes for which $S = \langle W \rangle$. However, for $s > 1$, there can be many possible subspaces of $\langle W \rangle$ for an operand block W, so that any non-null subspace of $\langle W \rangle \cap S$ leads to an attack. That is why the new method not only has to determine whether there is an attack, but also which subsets of $\langle W \rangle$ could possibly intersect with the attack span S.

Our method loops over all the operand blocks $W \in \{A_g, B_g\}_g$ of multiplication gadgets and checks whether there is a probing attack on a subset of $\langle W \rangle$. For each $W \in \{A_g, B_g\}_g$, we create a layered directed acyclic graph $\mathcal{G}_W$ for which each node is associated with a *permissible attack span* that represents the subspace of $\langle W \rangle$ in which an attack could possibly be found. The permissible attack span in a node is a subset of the permissible attack span in its parent node. Each node is indexed by a layer number i and a unique index b. Besides, the permissible attack span denoted $S_{i,b}$, the node contains some information in the form of three additional sets $\mathcal{G}_{i,b}$, $\mathcal{O}_{i,b}$ and $\mathcal{Q}_{i,b}$. $\mathcal{G}_{i,b}$ is a list of multiplication gadgets which could be used to find an attack. $\mathcal{Q}_{i,b}$ contains the operand blocks of the multiplications in $\mathcal{G}_{i,b}$ that can be combined with other operands to obtain elements of $\langle W \rangle$. And then $\mathcal{O}_{i,b}$, called the set of *free operand blocks*, contains the other operand blocks of $\mathcal{G}_{i,b}$. If there is a way to combine free operands to obtain an element of $\langle W \rangle$, then a probing attack is found.

We start with the first node *root*. We assign to $S_{1,root}$ the span $\langle W \rangle$, to $\mathcal{G}_{1,root}$ the set of multiplications for which W is an operand and to $\mathcal{Q}_{1,root}$ the operand W. $\mathcal{O}_{1,root}$ can then be deduced from $\mathcal{G}_{1,root}$ and $\mathcal{Q}_{1,root}$:

$$\begin{cases} S_{1,root} = \langle W \rangle \\ \mathcal{G}_{1,root} = \{g \mid A_g = W\} \cup \{g \mid B_g = W\} \\ \mathcal{O}_{1,root} = \{B_g \mid A_g = W\} \cup \{A_g \mid B_g = W\} \\ \mathcal{Q}_{1,root} = \{W\} \end{cases}$$

At each step i (from $i = 1$) of the algorithm, for each node b in the ith layer, if $S_{i,b} \cap \langle \mathcal{O}_{i,b} \rangle \neq \emptyset$, the method stops and returns False: the circuit is not tight t-register probing secure for any t. If not, for each node b in the ith layer, for each operand block $A \in \{A_g, B_g\}_g \setminus \mathcal{Q}_{i,b}$, if $S_{i,b} \cap (\langle A \rangle + \langle \mathcal{O}_{i,b} \rangle) \neq \emptyset$ (where $\langle A \rangle + \langle \mathcal{O}_{i,b} \rangle$

denotes the Minkowski sum of $\langle A \rangle$ and $\langle \mathcal{O}_{i,b} \rangle$), then we connect b to a new node b' in the next layer $i+1$, containing the following information:

$$\begin{cases} S_{i+1,b'} = S_{i,b} \cap (\langle A \rangle + \langle \mathcal{O}_{i,b} \rangle) \\ \mathcal{G}_{i+1,b'} = \mathcal{G}_{i,b} \cup \{g \mid A \text{ is an operand block of the multiplication gadget } g\} \\ \mathcal{O}_{i+1,b'} = \mathcal{O}_{i,b} \cup \{B \mid A \text{ is a co-operand block of } B \text{ in a multiplication gadget}\} \\ \mathcal{Q}_{i+1,b'} = \mathcal{Q}_{i,b} \cup \{A\} \end{cases}$$

If no new node is created at step i, then the algorithm stops and returns True: the circuit is tight t-register probing secure for any t. The method eventually stops, as the number of nodes we can create for each graph is finite. Indeed, at each step i, each node b can only produce $|\{A_g, B_g\}_g| - |\mathcal{Q}_{i,b}|$ new nodes, and for each of them the set $\mathcal{Q}$ grows by one. In total, each graph can contain up to $(|\{A_g, B_g\}_g| - 1)!$ nodes.

The pseudocode of Algorithm 1 gives a high-level description of our method. In this algorithm, each edge on the graph corresponds to adding an operand in $\mathcal{Q}$. Multiple operands can be added at once if the corresponding permissible attack span is the same for all of those operands. For the sake of simplicity, we decide to omit this optimization in the algorithm.

Proposition 2. *Algorithm 1 is correct.*

Proof (sketch). The proof is organized in two parts. First, we show that there are no false negatives: if the algorithm returns False, then there is a probing attack on the input circuit C. This is done with a constructive proof. Assuming that the algorithm returns False, we construct from the graph a set of matrices (as defined in Sect. 3.3) such that the intersection of their images is non-empty. Then we prove that there are no false positives by showing that if there is a probing attack on a circuit C, then the algorithm cannot stop as long as no attack is found. Since the algorithm has been proven to terminate, it must return False. □

The complete proof is provided in the full version.

Complete Characterization. The verification algorithm can be slightly modified to output all the existing t-register probing attack paths on the input circuit. This extension mostly amounts to continuing to add new nodes to the graph even when an attack has been detected until no new node can be added, and slightly changing the condition to add a node. The new condition can be written $S_{i,b} \cap (\langle A \rangle^* + \langle \mathcal{O}_{i,b} \rangle) \neq \emptyset$, where $\langle A \rangle^*$ denotes the set of non-null vectors of the column space of A. And with this, it is possible to determine the least attack order, which is the least amount of probes t_{min} that can be used to recover a secret value in a $(t_{min} + 1)$-shared circuit.

Toy Example. We provide in the full version of the paper a comprehensive illustration of tightPROVE$^+$ on a toy example.

Algorithm 1. tightPROVE$^+$

input : A description of a circuit C
output: True or False, along with a proof (and possibly a list of attacks)

foreach *operand W* **do**
$\quad$ /* create root for the new graph $\mathscr{G}_W$ */
$\quad S_{1,root} = \langle W \rangle$
$\quad \mathcal{G}_{1,root} = \{g \mid A_g = W\} \cup \{g \mid B_g = W\}$
$\quad \mathcal{O}_{1,root} = \{B_g \mid A_g = W\} \cup \{A_g \mid B_g = W\}$
$\quad \mathcal{Q}_{1,root} = \{W\}$
$\quad$ **foreach** *step i* **do**
$\quad\quad$ **foreach** *branch b in layer i* **do**
$\quad\quad\quad$ | **if** $S_{i,b} \cap \langle \mathcal{O}_{i,b} \rangle \neq \emptyset$ **then** return False;
$\quad\quad$ **end**
$\quad\quad$ **foreach** *branch b in layer i* **do**
$\quad\quad\quad$ **foreach** *operand $A \notin \mathcal{Q}_{i,b}$* **do**
$\quad\quad\quad\quad$ **if** $S_{i,b} \cap (\langle A \rangle + \langle \mathcal{O}_{i,b} \rangle) \neq \emptyset$ **then**
$\quad\quad\quad\quad\quad$ /* add new branch b' */
$\quad\quad\quad\quad\quad S_{i+1,b'} = S_{i,b} \cap (\langle A \rangle + \langle \mathcal{O}_{i,b} \rangle)$
$\quad\quad\quad\quad\quad \mathcal{G}_{i+1,b'} = \mathcal{G}_{i,b} \cup \{g \mid A \text{ is an operand of the mult. gadget } g\}$
$\quad\quad\quad\quad\quad \mathcal{O}_{i+1,b'} = \mathcal{O}_{i,b} \cup \{B \mid A \text{ is an operand of a mult. gadget}\}$
$\quad\quad\quad\quad\quad \mathcal{Q}_{i+1,b'} = \mathcal{Q}_{i,b} \cup \{A\}$
$\quad\quad\quad\quad$ **end**
$\quad\quad\quad$ **end**
$\quad\quad$ **end**
$\quad$ **end**
end
return True

Concrete Example. We now present an example that shows how tightPROVE$^+$ applies to real-life implementations of cryptographic primitives. We take as example an Usuba implementation of the Gimli [10] cipher, a 384-bit permutation, with 32-bit registers. When applying tightPROVE$^+$ on this circuit, register probing attacks are identified. Let us describe one of them and display the subgraph of the circuit it is based on in Fig. 4.

The subcircuit uses 5 input blocks I_1, I_2, I_3, I_4, I_5. We denote by $[x]$ the sharing obtained after the rotation of I_2 and $[y]$ the one after the rotation of I_1. By probing the multiplication g_1, one can get the values $x_{32,0}$ and $y_{32,1}$ (the first index denotes the bit slot in the register and the second one denotes the share). Due to the left shifts, one can get the values $x_{32,2}$ and $x_{32,1} + y_{32,1}$ by probing g_2. The following values can thus be obtained: $x_{32,0}$, $x_{32,1} = (x_{32,1} + y_{32,1}) + y_{32,1}$, and $x_{32,2}$. This implies that x_{32}, the last slot of the secret value x, can be retrieved with t probes when the circuit is $(t+1)$-shared for any $t \geq 2$.

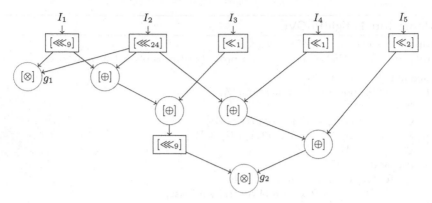

Fig. 4. Graph representation of a sub-circuit of Gimli.

4   Tornado: Automating Slicing and Masking

Given a high-level description of a cryptographic primitive, Tornado synthesizes a masked implementation using the ISW-based multiplication and refresh gadgets. The gadgets are provided as C functions, presented in Fig. 5 and where the macro MASKING_ORDER is instantiated at compile time to the desired masking order. The key role of Usuba is to automate the generation of a sliced implementation, upon which tightPROVE+ is then able to verify either the bit probing or register probing security, or identify the necessary refreshes. By integrating both tools, we derive a masked implementation from the sliced one. This is done by mapping linear operations over all shares, by using isw_mult for bitwise **and** operations and by calling isw_refresh where necessary.

```
static void isw_mult(uint32_t *res,
              const uint32_t *op1,
              const uint32_t *op2) {
  for (int i=0; i<=MASKING_ORDER; i++)
    res[i] = 0;

  for (int i=0; i<=MASKING_ORDER; i++) {
    res[i] ^= op1[i] & op2[i];

    for (int j=i+1; j<=MASKING_ORDER; j++) {
      uint32_t rnd = get_random();
      res[i] ^= rnd;
      res[j] ^= (rnd ^ (op1[i] & op2[j]))
              ^ (op1[j] & op2[i]);
    }
  }
}
```

```
static void isw_refresh(uint32_t *res,
              const uint32_t *in) {
  for (int i=0; i<=MASKING_ORDER; i++)
    res[i] = in[i];

  for (int i=0; i<=MASKING_ORDER; i++) {
    for (int j=i+1; j<=MASKING_ORDER; j++) {
      uint32_t rnd = get_random();
      res[i] ^= rnd;
      res[j] ^= rnd;
    }
  }
}
```

Fig. 5. ISW gadgets.

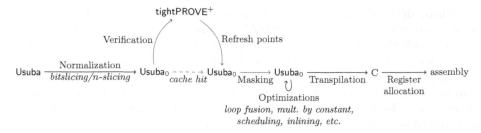

Fig. 6. High-level view of the Tornado compiler.

The overall architecture of the Tornado compiler is shown in Fig. 6. It consists essentially in the integration of Usuba and tightPROVE$^+$ within a single, unified framework. This integration is reasonably simple since the Usuba$_0$ intermediate representation amounts essentially to a register-based circuit extended with a notion of function node (for code reuse), whereas the input language of tightPROVE$^+$ consists in unrolled inlined register-based circuits. We therefore easily obtain an input suitable for tightPROVE$^+$ by inlining all the nodes within the Usuba$_0$ generated by Usuba. We also need to specify the probing model to use when carrying the analysis in tightPROVE$^+$: this corresponds exactly to the typing information specified in Usuba, whether we are considering a bitsliced implementation (in which case we select the bit probing model), or an n-sliced implementation (in which case we select the register probing model, registers whose size is m).

Having sent a register-based circuit to the extended tool tightPROVE$^+$, it may either be accepted as-is or tightPROVE$^+$ may have identified necessary refresh points to achieve bit or register probing security. In the latter case, Tornado maps these refresh points back into the initial, non-inlined Usuba$_0$ code: each refresh point is turned into a custom `refresh` operator that is treated specifically by the Tornado backend (in particular, it cannot be optimized out). Upon emitting C code, this operator turns into a call to the `isw_refresh` gadget of Fig. 5.

4.1   Addition of Refresh Gadgets

In order to make the generation of secure masked implementations fully automatic, we use heuristic methods to determine a set of operands to be refreshed in order to make the resulting circuit secure in the considered probing model.

When a circuit is built from the combination of several instances of the same subcircuit, the description of the subcircuit is analyzed first, assuming that it has random, uniform and independent inputs. If probing attacks are found, an exhaustive search of the placement of refresh gadgets can be done if the size of the subcircuit is not too big. The same placement of refresh is then applied every time this subcircuit appears. Doing so is relevant, as any attack that can be done on a subfunction alone also exists when that subfunction is part of a wider circuit.

Then, tightPROVE⁺ verifies that the resulting circuit is secure. If probing attacks are still found, then tightPROVE⁺ is called in full characterization mode which yields the complete list of multiplications involved in each attack. We then select an operand of the multiplication that appears the most in that list, and apply a refresh to this operand. This step is repeated until no more attacks can be found. This method is bound to stop and yield a secure circuit since, as proven in the original paper describing tightPROVE, refreshing one input per multiplication guarantees that the resulting circuit is secure.

We stress that this method is not optimal in the sense that it does not always find the minimal number of refresh gadgets needed to make a circuit secure, but it provides a sound heuristic. Finding an optimal and efficient method to place refresh gadgets is left open for future research.

4.2 Optimizations

Whereas this compilation scheme is functionally sufficient to guarantee security, further optimizations are beneficial to make it scale to large masking orders on a typical embedded platform. Tornado therefore integrates a modicum of optimizations to optimize stack usage (especially for bitsliced implementations), to reduce the overhead of repeatedly iterating over shares and to minimize the number of masked multiplications. Note that the objective of the present work is not to demonstrate best-in-class performance results: we are instead interested in 1. the asymptotic performance of a given primitive across a sizable choice of masking orders; and 2. the comparative performance of sizable number primitives at a given masking order.

To this end, Tornado has proved to be a valuable tool. We enable the first point by minimizing the impact that the C compiler can have on the quality (or lack thereof) of the resulting code. For example and as the masking order grows, the compiler tends to shy away from certain loop-related optimizations that are beneficial. We therefore systematically carry these optimizations in Tornado. We enable the second point by subjecting all the primitives to the same, predictable (even if imperfect) compilation process tailored to the platform of interest.

We have therefore identified two optimizations that are necessary to scale to large masking orders: aggressive constant propagation for multiplications and loop fusion. Masked multiplication being expensive, we strive to spot the case where the operand of a multiplication is in fact a constant value. We do so through a constant propagation analysis in Usuba₀ followed by a specific compilation rule in this case: we directly multiply all the shares with the constant.

To mask a sequence of instructions, Tornado replaces each of them with a masked gadget. Gadgets for linear operations consist in a loop applying iteratively a basic operation over each share, such as

```
for (int i=0; i<=MASKING_ORDER; i++) A(i);
for (int i=0; i<=MASKING_ORDER; i++) B(i);
for (int i=0; i<=MASKING_ORDER; i++) C(i);
```

where A, B and C are linear operations storing their results in a number of variables linear with MASKING_ORDER. As a result, stack usage increases linearly with the masking order, which means that, when considering implementations as register-hungry as bitslicing ones, even small masking orders can be too heavy. Besides, operating each loop (increment, comparison, branching) impedes an overhead that the C compiler is something heuristically willing to optimize out at small orders, leading to confusing threshold effects when benchmarking. To address both issues, we systematically perform loop fusion, thus obtaining

```
for (int i=0; i<=MASKING_ORDER; i++) {
  A(i); B(i); C(i);
}
```

on the above example, followed by instruction scheduling, which will strive to reduce the live range [29] (and thus the number of temporaries) of, for example, the variables set in A and used in B.

This optimization allows us to reduce stack usage of our bitsliced implementations by 11 kB on average whereas this saves us, on average, 3 kB of stack for our n-sliced implementations (recall that our platform offers a measly 96 kB of SRAM). It also positively impacts performance, with a 16% average speedup for bitslicing and a 21% average speedup for n-slicing.

5   Evaluation

We evaluated Tornado on 11 cryptographic primitives from the second round of the NIST lightweight cryptography competition[4]. The choice of cryptographic primitives was made on the basis that they were self-identified as being amenable to masking. We stress that we do not focus on the full authenticated encryption, message authentication, or hash protocols but on the underlying primitives, mostly block ciphers and permutations.

Table 1 provides an overview of these primitives. Whenever possible, we generate both a bitsliced and an n-sliced implementation for each primitive, which allows us to exercise the bit-probing and the register-probing models of tightPROVE⁺. However, 4 primitives do not admit a straightforward n-sliced implementation. The Subterranean permutation involves a significant amount of bit-twiddling across its 257-bit state, which makes it a resolutely bitsliced primitive (as confirmed by its reference implementation). PHOTON, SKINNY, SPONGENT rely on lookup tables that would be too expansive to emulate in n-sliced mode. In bitslicing, these tables are simply implemented by their Boolean circuit, either provided by the authors (PHOTON, SKINNY) or generated through SAT [34] with the objective of minimizing multiplicative complexity (SPONGENT, with 4 ANDs and 28 XORs). Spook and Elephant respectively rely on the Clyde and SPONGENT primitives, which we therefore include in our evaluation.

---

[4] See   https://csrc.nist.gov/Projects/lightweight-cryptography/round-2-candidates for the list of candidates together with specifications and reference implementations.

Note that the n-sliced implementations, when they exist, are either 32-sliced or 64-sliced. This means in particular that, unlike bitslicing that processes multiple blocks in parallel, these implementations process a single block at once on our 32-bit Cortex M4.

In Subsect. 5.1, we present the results of tightPROVE$^+$ on the considered primitives using the refresh placement strategy explained in Subsect. 4.1. Finally, we benchmark our unmasked implementations against reference implementations in Subsect. 5.2, and compare their masked versions in Subsect. 5.3.

Table 1. Overview of the selected cryptographic primitives.

primitive	state size (bits)	multiplications		mult./bits		n-sliceable	slice size
		n-slice	bitslice	n-slice	bitslice		
ACE [1]	320	384	12288	1.2	38	✓	32
ASCON [23]	320	60	3840	0.19	12	✓	64
Clyde [9]	128	48	1536	0.37	12	✓	32
GIFT [3]	128	160	5120	1.25	40	✓	32
Gimli [11]	384	288	9216	0.75	24	✓	32
PHOTON [4]	256	-	3072	-	12	✗	-
Pyjamask [24]	128	56	1792	0.44	14	✓	32
SKINNY [7]	128	-	6144	-	48	✗	-
SPONGENT [13,14]	160	-	12800	-	80	✗	-
Subterranean [22]	257	-	2056	-	8	✗	-
Xoodoo [20,21]	384	144	4608	0.37	12	✓	32

5.1 tightPROVE$^+$

Table 2 contains the results of tightPROVE$^+$ for the aforementioned primitives. We display the output of our algorithm for each circuit, along with the size of the registers used and the time it takes for tightPROVE$^+$ to output the results. Table 3 provides additional information about the implementations that are not secure in the register probing model. This includes the size of the registers, the time it takes to find the first attack, the time it takes to find all the operands that can be retrieved, then the least attack order, the optimal number of refresh gadgets needed to make the implementation secure in the register probing model, and finally the time tightPROVE$^+$ takes to verify that the refreshed implementation is indeed secure. All calculations were made on an iMac with an intel Core i7 processor (4 GHz) and 16 GB of DDR3 RAM (1600 MHz), with parallel computing on its 8 CPUs.

Following the method described in Sect. 4.1, tightPROVE$^+$ places refresh gadgets for the considered implementations of ACE, Clyde and Gimli. For the two first primitives, there is exactly one subcircuit which is responsible for the identified register probing attacks, which can be fixed by adding only one refresh gadget. This gives us a lower bound for the optimal number of refresh gadgets,

Table 2. Results of tightPROVE$^+$ on all the implementations.

submissions	primitive	time (bitslice)	bit probing security	register size	time (n-slice)	register probing security
block ciphers						
GIFT-COFB, HYENA, SUNDAE-GIFT	GIFT-128	55 H 40 min	✓	32	2 H 15 min	✓
Pyjamask	Pyjamask-128	30 min	✓	32	6 min	✓
SKINNY, ROMULUS	SKINNY-128-256	10 H	✓	-	-	-
Spook	Clyde-128	10 min	✓	32	32 s	✗
permutations						
ACE	ACE	54 H 30 min	✓	32	10 min	✗
ASCON	p^{12}	1 H 45 min	✓	64	1 H 13 min	✓
Elephant	SPONGENT-$\pi[160](1$ round$)$	6 s	✓	-	-	-
Elephant	SPONGENT-$\pi[160](10$ rounds$)$	20 min 40 s	✓	-	-	-
Gimli	Gimli-36	22 H 45 min	✓	32	1 H 10 min	✗
ORANGE, PHOTON-BEETLE	PHOTON-256	2 H	✓	-	-	-
Xoodyak	Xoodoo[12]	2 H 50 min	✓	32	4 H 5 min	✓
others						
Subterranean	blank(8)	17 min	✓	-	-	-

and since tightPROVE$^+$ does not find any further attack after the addition of refresh gadgets, it is also an upper bound. Gimli, however, is made of 6 subsequent identical subcircuits that are subject to register probing attacks, but the method uses 20 refresh gadgets per subcircuits to make the implementation secure. We can thus only conclude that we have an upper bound of 120 for the optimal number of gadgets, and that it is a multiple of 6, but in the current method, we cannot ascertain that it is optimal without setting up an exhaustive search.

5.2 Baseline Performance Evaluation

In the following, we benchmark our implementations – in Usuba and compiled with Tornado – of the NIST submissions against the reference implementation provided by the contestants. This allows us to establish a performance baseline (without masking), thus providing a common frame of reference for the performance of these primitives based on their implementation synthesized from Usuba. In doing so, we have to bear in mind that the reference implementations

Table 3. Complementary information on flawed implementations.

primitive	register size	first attack	all operands	least attack order	refresh gadgets needed	refreshed circuit
Ace	32	10 min	25 min	1	384	70 H
Clyde-128	32	32 s	2 min 10 s	2	6	3 min 10 s
Gimli-36	32	1 H 10 min	66 H 20 min	2	≤ 120	8 H 50 min

provided by the NIST contestants are of varying quality: some appear to have been finely tuned for performance while others focus on simplicity, acting as an executable specification.

In an effort to level the playing field, we ran our benchmark on an Intel i5-6500 @ 3.20 GHz, running Linux 4.15.0-54. The implementations were compiled with Clang 7.0.0 with flags `-O3 -fno-slp-vectorize -fno-vectorize`. These flags prevent Clang from trying to produce vectorized code, which would artificially advantage some implementations at the expense of others because of brittle, hard-to-predict vectorization heuristics. Besides, vectorized instructions remain an exception in the setting of embedded devices (*e.g.*, Cortex M). At the exception of Subterranean (which is bitsliced), the reference implementations follow a n-sliced implementation pattern, representing the state of the primitive through a matrix of 32-bit values, or 64-bit in the case of Ascon. To evaluate bitsliced implementations, we simulate a 32-bit architecture, meaning that the throughput we report corresponds to the parallel encryption of 32 independent blocks.

The results are shown in Table 4. We notice that Usuba often delivers performance that is on par or better than the reference implementations. Note that this does not come at the expense of intelligibility: our Usuba implementations are written in a high-level language, which is amenable to formal reasoning thanks to its straightforward semantic model (unlike any implementation in C). The reference implementations of Skinny and Photon use lookup tables, which do not admit a straightforward implementation in terms of constant-time, combinational operations. As a result, we are unable to implement a constant-time n-sliced version in Usuba and to, in Sect. 5.3, mask such an implementation.

We now turn our attention specifically to a few implementations that exhibit interesting performance with the following observations:

- The reference implementation of Subterranean is an order of magnitude slower than in Usuba because its implementation is bit-oriented (each bit is stored in a distinct 8-bit variable) but only a single block is encrypted at a time. Switching to 32-bit variables and encrypting 32 blocks in parallel, as Usuba does, significantly improves performance.
- The reference implementation of Spongent is slowed down by a prohibitively expensive bit-permutation over 160 bits, which is spread across 20 8-bit variables. Thanks to bitslicing, Usuba turns this permutation into a purely static renaming of variable, which occurs purely at compile-time.

- On ASCON, our n-sliced implementation is twice slower than the reference implementation. Unlike the reference implementation, we have refrained from performing aggressive function inlining and loop unrolling to keep code size in check, since we target embedded systems. However, if we instruct the Usuba compiler to perform these optimizations, the performance of our n-sliced implementation is on par with the reference one.
- ACE reference implementation suffers from significant performance issues, relying on an excessive number of temporary variables to store intermediate results.
- Finally, Gimli offers two reference implementations, one being a high-performance SSE implementation with the other serving as an executable specification on general-purpose registers. We chose the general-purpose one here (which had not been subjected to the same level of optimizations) because our target architecture (Cortex M) does not provide a vectorized instruction set.

Table 4. Comparison of Usuba vs reference implementations.

primitive	Performances (cycles/bytes) (lower is better)		
	Usuba n-slice	Usuba bitslice	reference
ACE	34.25	55.89	276.53
ASCON	9.84	4.94	5.18
Clyde	33.72	21.99	37.69
Gimli	15.77	5.80	44.35
GIFT	565.30	45.51	517.27
PHOTON	-	44.88	214.47
Pyjamask	246.72	131.33	267.35
SKINNY	-	46.87	207.82
SPONGENT	-	146.93	4824.97
Subterranean	-	17.64	355.38
Xoodoo	14.93	6.47	10.14

5.3   Masking Benchmarks

We now turn to the evaluation of the masked implementations produced by Tornado using the Usuba implementations presented in the previous section. Our benchmarks are run on a Nucleo STM32F401RE offering an Arm Cortex-M4 with 512 Kbytes of Flash memory and 96 Kbytes of SRAM. We used the GNU C compiler arm-none-eabi-gcc version 9.2.0 at optimization level -O3.

We considered two modes regarding the Random Number Generator (RNG):

- *Pooling mode*: The RNG generates random numbers at a rate of 32 bits every 64 clock cycles. Fetching a random number can thus take up to 65 clock cycles.

– *Fast mode*: The RNG only takes a few clock cycles to generate a 32-bit random word. The RNG routine thus can simply read a register containing this 32-bit random word without checking for its availability.

Those two modes were chosen because they are the ones used in the submission of Pyjamask, which is the only submission detailing the question of how to get random numbers for a masked implementation.

Of these 11 NIST submissions, only Pyjamask provides a masked implementation. Our implementation is consistently (at every order, and with both the pooling and fast RNGs) 1.8 times slower than their masked implementation. The reason is twofold. First, their reference implementation has been heavily optimized to take advantage of the barrel shifter on the Cortex M4, which we do not exploit. Second, our implementation uses the generic ISW multiplication (Fig. 5) whereas the reference implementation employs a specialized, hand-tuned implementation in assembly.

n-sliced Implementations. Table 5a gives the performances of the *n*-sliced implementations produced by Tornado in terms of cycles per byte. Note that these implementations are provably secure, with refreshing gadgets being inserted if necessary.

Since masking a multiplication has a quadratic cost in the number of shares, we expect performance at high orders to be mostly proportional with the number of multiplications used by the primitives. We thus report the number of multiplications involved in our implementation normalized to the block size (in bytes) of the primitive. This is confirmed by our results with 128 shares (on the Cortex M4). This effect is less pronounced at small orders since the execution time remains dominated by linear operations. Using the pooling RNG increases the cost of multiplications compared to the fast RNG, which results in performances being proportional to the number of multiplications at smaller order than with the fast RNG.

Pyjamask illustrates the influence of the number of multiplications on scaling. Because of its use of dense binary matrix multiplications, it involves a significant number of linear operations for only a few multiplications. As a result, it is slower than Gimli and ACE at order 3, despite the fact that they use respectively 2× and 6× more multiplications. With the fast RNG, the inflection point is reached at order 7 for ACE and order 31 for Gimli, only to improve afterward. Similarly when compared to Clyde, Pyjamask goes from 5× slower at order 3 to 50% slower at order 127 with the fast RNG and 20% slower at order 127 with the pooling RNG. The same analysis applies to GIFT and ACE, where the linear overhead of GIFT is only dominated at order 63 with the pooling RNG and at order 127 with the fast RNG.

One notable exception is ASCON with the fast RNG, compared in particular to Xoodoo and Clyde. Whereas ASCON uses a smaller number of multiplications, it involves a 64-sliced implementation (Table 1), unlike its counterparts that are 32-sliced. Running on our 32-bit Cortex-M4 requires GCC to generate 64-bit emulation code, which induces a significant operational overhead and prevents

Table 5. Performances of Tornado generated n-sliced masked implementations.

primitive	mult./bytes	TRNG	Performances (cycles/bytes) (lower is better)						
			$d = 0$	$d = 3$	$d = 7$	$d = 15$	$d = 31$	$d = 63$	$d = 127$
Ascon	1.375	pooling	49	1.34k	4.57k	20.54k	79.24k	324k	1.30m
		fast	49	1.05k	3.08k	11.61k	42.48k	163k	640k
Xoodoo	1.5	pooling	63	1.71k	6.96k	29.07k	113k	448k	1.73m
		fast	63	889	3.26k	10.84k	39.43k	143k	555k
Clyde	3	pooling	92	1.88k	7.58k	31.43k	121k	483k	1.87m
		fast	92	961	3.53k	11.84k	41.88k	161k	653k
Pyjamask	3	pooling	994	5.93k	17.16k	59.66k	194k	646k	2.27m
		fast	994	4.97k	12.84k	38.40k	108k	297k	950k
Gimli	6	pooling	56	3.97k	17.35k	73.42k	293k	1.17m	4.56m
		fast	56	1.77k	7.14k	24.71k	95.20k	356k	1.40m
Gift	10	pooling	1.12k	15.27k	44.68k	138k	532k	1.82m	6.40m
		fast	1.13k	12.53k	32.27k	77.61k	285k	819k	2.64m
Ace	19.2	pooling	92	7.55k	32.94k	114k	495k	1.96m	7.77m
		fast	92	3.88k	13.29k	40.06k	190k	746k	2.84m

(a) cycles per byte

primitive	mult.	TRNG	Performances (cycles) (lower is better)						
			$d = 0$	$d = 3$	$d = 7$	$d = 15$	$d = 31$	$d = 63$	$d = 127$
Clyde	48	pooling	1.47k	30.08k	121.28k	502.88k	1.94m	7.73m	29.92m
		fast	1.47k	15.38k	56.48k	189.44k	670.08k	2.58m	10.45m
Pyjamask	56	pooling	15.90k	94.88k	274.56k	954.56k	3.10m	10.34m	36.32m
		fast	15.90k	79.52k	205.44k	614.40k	1.73m	4.75m	15.20m
Ascon	60	pooling	1.96k	53.60k	182.80k	821.60k	3.17m	12.96m	52.00m
		fast	1.96k	42.00k	123.20k	464.40k	1.70m	6.52m	25.60m
Xoodoo	144	pooling	3.02k	82.08k	334.08k	1.40m	5.42m	21.50m	83.04m
		fast	3.02k	42.67k	156.48k	520.32k	1.89m	6.86m	26.64m
Gift	160	pooling	17.92k	244.32k	714.88k	2.21m	8.51m	29.12m	102.40m
		fast	18.08k	200.48k	516.32k	1.24m	4.56m	13.10m	42.24m
Gimli	288	pooling	2.69k	190.56k	832.80k	3.52m	14.06m	56.16m	218.88m
		fast	2.69k	84.96k	342.72k	1.19m	4.57m	17.09m	67.20m
Ace	384	pooling	3.68k	302.00k	1.32m	4.56m	19.80m	78.40m	310.80m
		fast	3.68k	155.20k	531.60k	1.60m	7.60m	29.84m	113.60m

(b) cycles per bloc

further optimization by the compiler. When using the pooling RNG however, Ascon is faster than both Xoodoo and Clyde at every order, thanks to its smaller number of multiplications.

For scenarios in which one is not interested in encrypting a lot of data but rather a single block, possibly short, then it makes more sense to look at the performances of a single run of a cipher, rather than its amortized performances over the amount of bytes it encrypts. This is shown in Table 5b. The ciphers that use the least amount of multiplications have the upper hand when masking order increases: Clyde is clearly the fastest primitive at order 127, closely followed by Pyjamask. ASCON, which is the fastest one when looking at the cycles/bytes actually owns its performances to his low number of multiplications compared to its 320-bit block size. Therefore, when looking at a single run, it is actually 1.7× slower than Clyde at order 127. Similarly, Xoodoo performs well on the cycles/bytes metric, but has a block size of 384 bits, making it 2.5× slower.

Bitsliced Implementations. The key limiting factor to execute bitslice code on an embedded device is the amount of memory available. Bitsliced programs tend to be large and to consume a significant amount of stack. Masking such implementations at high orders becomes quickly impractical because of the quadratic growth of the stack usage.

To reduce stack usage and allow us to explore high masking orders, our bitsliced programs manipulate 8-bit variables, meaning that 8 independent blocks can be processed in parallel. This trades memory usage for performance, as we could have used 32-bit variables and improved our throughput by a factor 4. However, doing so would have put an unbearable amount of pressure on the stack, which would have prevented us from considering masking orders beyond 7. Besides, it is not clear whether there is a use-case for such a massively parallel (32 independent blocks) encryption primitive in a lightweight setting. As a result of our compilation strategy, we have been able to mask all primitives with up to 16 shares and, additionally, reach 32 shares for PHOTON, SKINNY, SPONGENT and Subterranean.

As for the n-sliced implementations, we observe a close match between the asymptotic performance of the primitive and their number of multiplications per bits (Table 6), which becomes even more prevalent as order increases and the overhead of linear operations becomes comparatively smaller. Pyjamask remains a good example to illustrate this phenomenon, the inflection point being reached at order 15 with respect to ACE (which uses 3× more multiplications).

The performance of ASCON with the fast RNG, which was slowed down by its suboptimal use of 64-bit registers in n-slicing, is streamlined in bitslicing: here, it exhibits the same number of multiplication per bits as Xoodoo and, indeed, their performance match remarkably well.

Finally, we observe that with the pooling RNG, already at order 15, the performances of our implementations is in accord with their relative number of multiplications per bits. In bitslicing (more evidently than in n-slicing), the number of multiplications is performance critical, even at relatively low masking order.

Table 6. Performances of Tornado generated bitslice masked implementations.

primitive	mult./bits	TRNG	Performances (cycles/bytes) *(lower is better)*				
			$d = 0$	$d = 3$	$d = 7$	$d = 15$	$d = 31$
Subterranean	8	pooling	94	4.46k	19.13k	79.63k	312k
		fast	94	2.15k	7.18k	27.03k	95.19k
Ascon	12	pooling	101	7.33k	30.33k	125k	-
		fast	101	3.07k	11.45k	42.39k	-
Xoodoo	12	pooling	112	6.69k	28.79k	120k	-
		fast	112	3.12k	10.49k	39.35k	-
Clyde	12	pooling	177	7.88k	31.04k	127k	-
		fast	161	3.44k	13.57k	45.34k	-
Photon	12	pooling	193	10.47k	31.77k	126k	476k
		fast	193	7.66k	14.28k	44.99k	154k
Pyjamask	14	pooling	1.59k	20.33k	52.81k	193k	-
		fast	1.59k	16.52k	31.74k	97.88k	-
Gimli	24	pooling	127	12.14k	53.64k	236k	-
		fast	127	5.51k	19.15k	76.91k	-
Ace	38	pooling	336	19.94k	89.12k	395k	-
		fast	336	8.22k	35.29k	123k	-
Gift	40	pooling	358	21.38k	93.92k	405k	-
		fast	358	11.08k	36.79k	136k	-
Skinny	48	pooling	441	34.28k	131k	525k	1.97m
		fast	441	18.19k	61.75k	200k	664k
Spongent	80	pooling	624	44.04k	188k	816k	3.15m
		fast	624	19.45k	64.78k	259k	948k

6   Conclusion

In this paper, we have introduced tightPROVE$^+$, an extension of tightPROVE that operates on the register-probing model. Stepping beyond the bit-probing model allows us to establish provable security in a purely software context. By combining tightPROVE$^+$ with the Usuba programming language, we have obtained an integrated development environment, called Tornado, that streamlines the definition of symmetric ciphers and automates their compilation into provably-secure masked implementations. Thanks to this framework, we have been able to systematically evaluate 11 NIST lightweight cryptography round-2 submissions that are amenable to masking. We have identified 3 ciphers (Ace, Clyde, Gimli) that are not safe in the register probing model and proposed some refresh points to repair them. We have also carried out an extensive performance evaluation, studying the asymptotic behavior of these ciphers across a large range of masking orders.

As part of future work, we intend to further enrich our compiler backend with optimizations specific to embedded architectures (Cortex M and/or Risc-V), systematizing various primitive-specific optimizations documented in the literature [28, 33, 35]. Previous results on Intel architecture [29] has demonstrated that Usuba can produce code whose performance is on par with hand-optimized, assembly implementations.

Acknowledgments. This work is partly supported by the French FUI-AAP25 VeriS-iCC project, the Émergence(s) program of the City of Paris and the EDITE doctoral school.

References

1. Aagaard, M., AlTawy, R., Gong, G., Mandal, K., Rohit, R.: ACE: an authenticated encryption and hash algorithm (2019)
2. Balasch, J., Gierlichs, B., Grosso, V., Reparaz, O., Standaert, F.-X.: On the cost of lazy engineering for masked software implementations. Cryptology ePrint Archive, Report 2014/413 (2014). http://eprint.iacr.org/2014/413
3. Banik, S., et al.: GIFT-COFB (2019)
4. Bao, Z., et al.: PHOTON-Beetle authenticated encryption and hash family (2019)
5. Barthe, G., et al.: Strong non-interference and type-directed higher-order masking. In: Weippl, E.R., Katzenbeisser, S., Kruegel, C., Myers, A.C., Halevi, S. (eds.) ACM CCS 2016, pp. 116–129. ACM Press, New York (2016)
6. Battistello, A., Coron, J.-S., Prouff, E., Zeitoun, R.: Horizontal side-channel attacks and countermeasures on the ISW masking scheme. In: Gierlichs, B., Poschmann, A.Y. (eds.) CHES 2016. LNCS, vol. 9813, pp. 23–39. Springer, Heidelberg (2016). https://doi.org/10.1007/978-3-662-53140-2_2
7. Beierle, C., et al.: SKINNY-AEDA and SKINNY-Hash (2019)
8. Belaïd, S., Goudarzi, D., Rivain, M.: Tight private circuits: achieving probing security with the least refreshing. In: Peyrin, T., Galbraith, S. (eds.) ASIACRYPT 2018, Part II. LNCS, vol. 11273, pp. 343–372. Springer, Cham (2018). https://doi.org/10.1007/978-3-030-03329-3_12
9. Bellizia, D., et al.: Spook: sponge-based leakage-resilient authenticated encryption with a masked tweakable block cipher (2019)
10. Bernstein, D.J., et al.: GIMLI: a cross-platform permutation. In: Fischer, W., Homma, N. (eds.) CHES 2017. LNCS, vol. 10529, pp. 299–320. Springer, Cham (2017). https://doi.org/10.1007/978-3-319-66787-4_15
11. Bernstein, D.J., et al.: GIMLI (2019)
12. Biham, E.: A fast new DES implementation in software. In: Biham, E. (ed.) FSE 1997. LNCS, vol. 1267, pp. 260–272. Springer, Heidelberg (1997). https://doi.org/10.1007/BFb0052352
13. Bogdanov, A., Knežević, M., Leander, G., Toz, D., Varıcı, K., Verbauwhede, I.: SPONGENT: a lightweight hash function. In: Preneel, B., Takagi, T. (eds.) CHES 2011. LNCS, vol. 6917, pp. 312–325. Springer, Heidelberg (2011). https://doi.org/10.1007/978-3-642-23951-9_21
14. Byene, T., Chen, Y.L., Dobraunig, C., Mennink, B.: Elephant v1 (2019)
15. Carlet, C., Goubin, L., Prouff, E., Quisquater, M., Rivain, M.: Higher-order masking schemes for S-boxes. In: Canteaut, A. (ed.) FSE 2012. LNCS, vol. 7549, pp. 366–384. Springer, Heidelberg (2012). https://doi.org/10.1007/978-3-642-34047-5_21
16. Carlet, C., Prouff, E., Rivain, M., Roche, T.: Algebraic decomposition for probing security. In: Gennaro, R., Robshaw, M. (eds.) CRYPTO 2015, Part I. LNCS, vol. 9215, pp. 742–763. Springer, Heidelberg (2015). https://doi.org/10.1007/978-3-662-47989-6_36
17. Coron, J.-S., Prouff, E., Rivain, M.: Side channel cryptanalysis of a higher order masking scheme. In: Paillier, P., Verbauwhede, I. (eds.) CHES 2007. LNCS, vol. 4727, pp. 28–44. Springer, Heidelberg (2007). https://doi.org/10.1007/978-3-540-74735-2_3

18. Coron, J.-S., Prouff, E., Rivain, M., Roche, T.: Higher-order side channel security and mask refreshing. In: Moriai, S. (ed.) FSE 2013. LNCS, vol. 8424, pp. 410–424. Springer, Heidelberg (2014). https://doi.org/10.1007/978-3-662-43933-3_21

19. Coron, J.-S., Roy, A., Vivek, S.: Fast evaluation of polynomials over binary finite fields and application to side-channel countermeasures. In: Batina, L., Robshaw, M. (eds.) CHES 2014. LNCS, vol. 8731, pp. 170–187. Springer, Heidelberg (2014). https://doi.org/10.1007/978-3-662-44709-3_10

20. Daemen, J., Hoert, S., Van Assche, G., Van Keer, R.: Xoodoo cookbook. IACR Cryptology ePrint Archive, 2018:767 (2018)

21. Daemen, J., Hoert, S., Peeters, M., Van Assche, G., Van Keer, R.: Xoodyak, a lightweight cryptographic scheme (2019)

22. Daemen, J., Massolino, P.M.C., Rotella, Y.: The Subterranean 2.0 cipher suite (2019)

23. Dobraunig, C., Eichlseder, M., Mendal, F., Schäffer, M.: The Subterranean 2.0 cipher suite (2019)

24. Goudarzi, D., et al.: Pyjamask (2019)

25. Goudarzi, D., Rivain, M.: How fast can higher-order masking be in software? In: Coron, J.-S., Nielsen, J.B. (eds.) EUROCRYPT 2017, Part I. LNCS, vol. 10210, pp. 567–597. Springer, Cham (2017). https://doi.org/10.1007/978-3-319-56620-7_20

26. Ishai, Y., Sahai, A., Wagner, D.: Private circuits: securing hardware against probing attacks. In: Boneh, D. (ed.) CRYPTO 2003. LNCS, vol. 2729, pp. 463–481. Springer, Heidelberg (2003). https://doi.org/10.1007/978-3-540-45146-4_27

27. Journault, A., Standaert, F.-X.: Very high order masking: efficient implementation and security evaluation. In: Fischer, W., Homma, N. (eds.) CHES 2017. LNCS, vol. 10529, pp. 623–643. Springer, Cham (2017). https://doi.org/10.1007/978-3-319-66787-4_30

28. Kannwischer, M.J., Rijneveld, J., Schwabe, P., Stoffelen, K.: pqm4: testing and benchmarking NIST PQC on ARM cortex-M4. IACR Cryptology ePrint Archive 2019:844 (2019)

29. Mercadier, D., Dagand, P.: Usuba: high-throughput and constant-time ciphers, by construction. In: PLDI, pp. 157–173 (2019)

30. Mercadier, D., Dagand, P., Lacassagne, L., Muller, G.: Usuba: optimizing & trustworthy bitslicing compiler. In: Proceedings of the 4th Workshop on Programming Models for SIMD/Vector Processing, WPMVP@PPoPP 2018, Vienna, Austria, 24 February 2018, pp. 4:1–4:8 (2018)

31. Papagiannopoulos, K., Veshchikov, N.: Mind the gap: towards secure 1st-order masking in software. In: Guilley, S. (ed.) COSADE 2017. LNCS, vol. 10348, pp. 282–297. Springer, Cham (2017). https://doi.org/10.1007/978-3-319-64647-3_17

32. Rivain, M., Prouff, E.: Provably secure higher-order masking of AES. In: Mangard, S., Standaert, F.-X. (eds.) CHES 2010. LNCS, vol. 6225, pp. 413–427. Springer, Heidelberg (2010). https://doi.org/10.1007/978-3-642-15031-9_28

33. Schwabe, P., Stoffelen, K.: All the AES you need on cortex-M3 and M4. In: Avanzi, R., Heys, H. (eds.) SAC 2016. LNCS, vol. 10532, pp. 180–194. Springer, Cham (2017). https://doi.org/10.1007/978-3-319-69453-5_10

34. Stoffelen, K.: Optimizing S-box implementations for several criteria using SAT solvers. In: Peyrin, T. (ed.) FSE 2016. LNCS, vol. 9783, pp. 140–160. Springer, Heidelberg (2016). https://doi.org/10.1007/978-3-662-52993-5_8

35. Stoffelen, K.: Efficient cryptography on the RISC-V architecture. In: Schwabe, P., Thériault, N. (eds.) LATINCRYPT 2019. LNCS, vol. 11774, pp. 323–340. Springer, Cham (2019). https://doi.org/10.1007/978-3-030-30530-7_16

Side-Channel Masking
with Pseudo-Random Generator

Jean-Sébastien Coron[1(✉)], Aurélien Greuet[2], and Rina Zeitoun[2(✉)]

[1] University of Luxembourg, Esch-sur-Alzette, Luxembourg
jean-sebastien.coron@uni.lu
[2] IDEMIA, Courbevoie, France
{aurelien.greuet,rina.zeitoun}@idemia.com

Abstract. High-order masking countermeasures against side-channel attacks usually require plenty of randomness during their execution. For security against t probes, the classical ISW countermeasure requires $\mathcal{O}(t^2 s)$ random bits, where s is the circuit size. However running a True Random Number Generator (TRNG) can be costly in practice and become a bottleneck on embedded devices. In [IKL+13] the authors introduced the notion of *robust* pseudo-random number generator (PRG), which must remain secure even against an adversary who can probe at most t wires. They showed that when embedding a robust PRG within a private circuit, the number of random bits can be reduced to $\tilde{\mathcal{O}}(t^4)$, that is independent of the circuit size s (up to a logarithmic factor). Using bipartite expander graphs, this can be further reduced to $\tilde{\mathcal{O}}(t^{3+\varepsilon})$; however the resulting construction is impractical.

In this paper we describe a construction where the number of random bits is only $\tilde{\mathcal{O}}(t^2)$ for security against t probes, without expander graphs; moreover the running time of each pseudo-random generation goes down from $\tilde{\mathcal{O}}(t^4)$ to $\tilde{\mathcal{O}}(t)$. Our technique consists in using multiple independent PRGs instead of a single one. We show that for ISW circuits, the robustness property of the PRG is not required anymore, which leads to simple and efficient constructions. For example, for AES we only need 48 bytes of randomness to get second-order security ($t = 2$), instead of 2880 in the original Rivain-Prouff countermeasure. As a first feasibility result, we have implemented our countermeasure on an ARM-based embedded device with a relatively slow TRNG, and obtained a 50% speed-up compared to Rivain-Prouff.

1 Introduction

High-Order Masking. Side-channel analysis is a class of attacks which exploits the physical environment of a cryptosystem during its execution, to reveal the secrets being manipulated. The masking countermeasure is an efficient technique to protect sensitive data against this threat. To protect a sensitive data x, the masking technique consists in generating a random variable r and manipulating the masked variable $x' = x \oplus r$ and the random r separately, instead of x directly. In that case, every intermediate variable has the uniform distribution

© International Association for Cryptologic Research 2020
A. Canteaut and Y. Ishai (Eds.): EUROCRYPT 2020, LNCS 12107, pp. 342–375, 2020.
https://doi.org/10.1007/978-3-030-45727-3_12

and any first-order attack is thwarted. However by combining information from both leakage points x' and r, a second-order attack can still be feasible (see for example [OMHT06]).

A natural countermeasure against high-order attacks is to use a high-order masking, where each variable x is split into n Boolean shares $x = x_1 \oplus x_2 \oplus \cdots \oplus x_n$, with $n > t$ for security against t probes. Initially the shares are generated uniformly at random under this condition; for example one can generate $x_1, \ldots, x_{n-1}$ randomly and let $x_n = x \oplus x_1 \oplus \cdots \oplus x_{n-1}$. The shares are then processed separately in masked operations (also called gadgets) that enable to compute the underlying secret variables in a secure way.

The study of circuits resistant against probing attacks was initiated by Ishai, Sahai and Wagner in [ISW03]. They showed how to transform any circuit of size s into a circuit of size $\mathcal{O}(t^2 s)$ secure against any adversary who can probe at most t wires. The ISW construction is based on secret sharing every variable x into $x = x_1 \oplus x_2 \oplus \cdots \oplus x_n$ as above, with $n = 2t + 1$ shares to guarantee security against t probes. Processing a XOR gate is straightforward as the shares can be xored separately. For processing an AND gate $z = xy$, one computes all cross-products $x_i y_j$ in Eq. (1) below, and then uses a randomized algorithm to recombine the n^2 cross-products into an n-sharing of the output z.

$$z = xy = \left(\bigoplus_{i=1}^{n} x_i \right) \cdot \left(\bigoplus_{i=1}^{n} y_i \right) = \bigoplus_{1 \leq i,j \leq n} x_i y_j \qquad (1)$$

Every AND gate is then expanded into a gadget of size $\mathcal{O}(t^2)$ and the resulting circuit has size $\mathcal{O}(t^2 s)$.

The ISW construction was adapted to AES by Rivain and Prouff in [RP10], by working in $\mathbb{F}_{2^8}$ instead of $\mathbb{F}_2$. The authors observed that the non-linear part $S(x) = x^{254}$ of the AES SBox can be efficiently evaluated with only 4 non-linear multiplications over $\mathbb{F}_{2^8}$, and a few linear squarings. Each of those 4 multiplications can in turn be evaluated with the previous ISW gadget based on Eq. (1), by working over $\mathbb{F}_{2^8}$ instead of $\mathbb{F}_2$.

Proving Security. The approach initiated in [ISW03] for proving security against a t-probing adversary is based on simulation; one must show that the view of an adversary probing at most t wires can be perfectly simulated without knowing the secret variables from the original circuit. To this aim, one shows that any set of t probed variables can be perfectly simulated from the knowledge of at most $n - 1$ input shares. Since any subset of $n - 1$ input shares is uniformly and independently distributed, this ensures that the adversary learns nothing from the t probes, since he could simulate them by himself. It was shown in [DDF14] that security against t probes implies security against noisy leakage, under the assumption that every variable leaks independently.

Recently, the notions of (Strong) Non-Interference (NI/SNI) were introduced by Barthe et al. in [BBD+16], to allow easy composition of gadgets. The authors showed that the ISW multiplication gadget does satisfy the stronger t-SNI security definition. They also showed that with some additional mask refreshing, the

Rivain-Prouff countermeasure for the full AES can be made secure with $n = t+1$ shares only, instead of $n = 2t + 1$ shares in [ISW03].

More recently, a new security notion was introduced by Cassiers and Standaert in [CS18], called PINI, that allows even simpler composition of gadgets. Namely it suffices to ensure that all gadgets are PINI, and the composite gadget is then also PINI, which also implies security against t probes. With its power and simplicity, the PINI definition appears to be the "right" notion for gadget security and composition; therefore we will use this definition in this paper, either by proving the PINI property of a gadget directly, or by first proving the t-SNI property and then PINI.

Minimizing Randomness Complexity. High-order masking countermeasures against side-channel attacks usually require plenty of randomness during their execution. The secure AND operation from [ISW03] with $t + 1$ shares requires $t(t + 1)/2$ random bits, and therefore the randomness complexity of the ISW countermeasure is $\mathcal{O}(t^2 s)$, where s is the circuit size. More concretely, the evaluation of the AES SBox in Rivain-Prouff [RP10] requires the execution of 4 secure multiplications and 2 mask refreshing; each of those 6 gadgets requires $t(t+1)/2$ fresh random bytes. For the 16 SBoxes and the 10 rounds of the AES, this amounts to generating $6 \times 16 \times 10 \times t(t + 1)/2 = 480t(t + 1)$ random bytes, which gives 2880 bytes for second-order security ($t = 2$).

However running a True Random Number Generator (TRNG) can be costly in practice and become a major bottleneck on embedded devices such as smartcards. Thus, high-order resistant algorithms can rapidly become impractical when the number of shares grows. The main question is therefore how to minimize the number of TRNG calls while still guaranteeing t-probing security as in [ISW03].

Several attempts have been made to reduce the randomness complexity of private circuits. In [BBP+16], the authors showed a variant of the ISW multiplication with roughly $t^2/4$ randoms instead of $t^2/2$ in ISW. In [FPS17], the authors showed how to re-use randomness within several gadgets, thereby reducing the total amount of randomness needed, for small values of t ($t \leq 7$). However the two above approaches only reduce the randomness complexity by a constant factor; that is, their asymptotic complexity is still $\mathcal{O}(t^2 s)$ for circuit size s, as in the original ISW countermeasure.

A natural idea to reduce the number of calls to the TRNG is to use a pseudo-random generator (PRG) to generate all randoms in the circuit, while only a small seed will be generated by the TRNG. Obviously the PRG circuit should also be secure against probing attacks. We recall below that such approach, initiated by Ishai *et al.* in [IKL+13] with the concept of robust PRG, enables to reduce the randomness complexity of t-private circuits from $\mathcal{O}(t^2 s)$ to $\mathcal{O}(t^4(\log s + \log t))$; with respect to the circuit size s, this is therefore an exponential improvement. Our main contribution is this paper will be to reduce this complexity further down to $\mathcal{O}(t^2(\log s + \log t))$, and to describe a concrete implementation of AES based on this approach. We refer to Table 2 below for the number of bytes required to protect AES against t-th order attacks; we see that for small values of t, we obtain almost two orders of magnitude improvement compared to previous methods.

Robust PRGs and Private Circuits. In [IKL+13], the authors introduced the notion of *robust* pseudo-random number generator (PRG). A robust PRG must remain secure even if an adversary can probe at most t intermediate variables in the PRG circuit. The authors showed that such robust PRG can be used in the ISW countermeasure to minimize the randomness complexity. Namely the resulting circuit uses a short random seed only, and remains secure against t-th order attacks.

Recall that the original ISW countermeasure requires $\mathcal{O}(t^2 s)$ bits of randomness, where s is the circuit size. Following [IKL+13], we first recall how this can be reduced to $\mathcal{O}(t^4(\log t + \log s))$, using a trivial construction of robust PRG. More precisely, the construction is based on r-wise independent PRG. A PRG is said to be r-wise independent if any subset of at most r output bits of the PRG is uniformly and independently distributed. The authors show that the ISW countermeasure can be adapted so that any wire in the ISW circuit depends on at most $\ell = \mathcal{O}(t^2)$ bits of randomness; such parameter ℓ is called the *locality* of the randomness and will play a crucial role in this paper. Since the adversary can probe at most t wires, the adversary's side-channel observation can then depend on at most $t \cdot \ell = \mathcal{O}(t^3)$ bits of randomness. Therefore, instead of using a TRNG, it is sufficient to use an r-wise independent PRG with parameter $r = t \cdot \ell = \mathcal{O}(t^3)$; if the r-wise PRG is secure against t probes, as shown in [IKL+13] the resulting circuit will remain secure against t probes.

It is easy to obtain an r-wise independent PRG by evaluating a degree $r-1$ polynomial on distinct inputs in a finite field $\mathbb{F}$; the r coefficients of the polynomials are initially generated at random in $\mathbb{F}$; this is the seed of the PRG. From r fresh randoms in $\mathbb{F}$, one can then obtain m pseudo-randoms with the r-wise independence property, as long as $m \leq |\mathbb{F}|$. To obtain an r-wise independent PRG with robustness against t probes, as observed in [IKL+13] a trivial construction consists in xoring the output of $t+1$ PRGs, so that at least one PRG has not been probed. One can therefore obtain an r-wise independent PRG robust against t probes by using $r \cdot (t+1) = \mathcal{O}(t^4)$ fresh randoms in $\mathbb{F}$ as input, and such PRG can then generate $m \leq |\mathbb{F}|$ pseudo-randoms in $\mathbb{F}$. Since the original ISW countermeasure requires $m = \mathcal{O}(t^2 s)$ randoms (where s is the circuit size), using $\mathbb{F} = \mathbb{F}_{2^k}$ one can take $k = \mathcal{O}(\log m) = \mathcal{O}(\log t + \log s)$. One therefore needs $\mathcal{O}(t^4(\log t + \log s)) = \tilde{\mathcal{O}}(t^4)$ bits of randomness[1], instead of $\mathcal{O}(t^2 s)$. The number of input random bits is then independent of the circuit size s (up to some logarithmic factor). In summary, any t-private circuit in which each wire depends on at most ℓ bits of randomness can be converted into a t-private circuit using roughly $t^2 \ell$ bits of randomness via the use of robust r-wise PRGs. As written by the authors: "Improving the randomness locality ℓ of private circuits would

---

[1] We use the notation $f(\lambda) = \tilde{\mathcal{O}}(g(\lambda))$ if $f(\lambda) = \mathcal{O}(g(\lambda) \log^k \lambda)$ for some $k \in \mathbb{N}$.

immediately yield a corresponding improvement [in the number of input random bits].".

In [IKL+13], the authors describe an improved construction of robust PRG, based on unbalanced bipartite expander graphs. Using the Guruswami-Umans-Vadhan construction of expander graphs [GUV09], they obtain r-wise independence and resistance against $t = r$ probes with $r^{1+\eta}$ bits of true randomness as input, for any $\eta > 0$. In the context of the ISW countermeasure, this enables to use $\tilde{O}(t^{3+\varepsilon})$ random bits as input for any $\varepsilon > 0$, instead $\tilde{O}(t^4)$.

Our Contribution. Our main contribution is a countermeasure against side-channel attacks where the number of random bits is only $\tilde{O}(t^2)$ for security against t probes, independently of the circuit size (up to a logarithmic factor), and without using expander graphs. Moreover the running time of pseudo-random generation goes down from $\tilde{O}(t^4)$ to $\tilde{O}(t)$. We summarize in Table 1 below the asymptotic complexities of existing techniques and our new techniques. We proceed in two steps.

In the first step, we show how to improve the locality ℓ of private circuits from $\ell = O(t^2)$ down to $\ell = O(t)$. As illustrated in the third line of Table 1 below, reducing ℓ from $O(t^2)$ to $O(t)$ enables to reduce the r-wise independence parameter from $r = O(t^3)$ down to $r = O(t^2)$; the number of input random bits is then now decreased from $\tilde{O}(t^4)$ to $\tilde{O}(t^3)$ with the trivial construction (and from $\tilde{O}(t^{3+\varepsilon})$ to $\tilde{O}(t^{2+\varepsilon})$ with expander graphs). Our technique is as follows. The authors of [IKL+13] obtain $\ell = O(t^2)$ by performing a mask locality refreshing at the end of each ISW multiplication gadget. Instead we modify the ISW multiplication by performing a series of internal locality refreshing. For this we consider successive $i \times i$ ISW submatrices and perform a mask refreshing after the processing of each submatrix; these internal mask refreshing enable to bring the locality down to $\ell = O(t)$. We have also performed a formal verification of our new algorithms, using the CheckMasks tool [Cor18], for both the locality and the security properties; we provide the source code in [Cor19a]. This first step is described in Sect. 3.

In the second step, our technique consists in using multiple independent PRGs instead of a single one. This has two main advantages. The first advantage is that for ISW circuits, one can show that the robustness property of the PRG is not required anymore; this implies that we can use a very simple PRG based on polynomial evaluation as above. The second advantage is that the locality with respect to each subset of randoms generated by each PRG becomes $\ell = O(1)$. Therefore each independent PRG can be r-wise independent with a much smaller parameter $r = O(t)$ instead of $r = O(t^3)$, and therefore requires only $r = O(t)$ randoms in the finite field (since robustness is not needed). In that case, we need $O(t^2)$ independent PRGs and therefore the size of the input randomness is $\tilde{O}(t^3)$; see Line 4 of Table 1. Finally, when using internal locality refreshing as in the first step above, we only need $O(t)$ independent PRGs, and eventually the number of input random bits is reduced to $\tilde{O}(t^2)$, instead of $\tilde{O}(t^{3+\varepsilon})$ with expander graphs in [IKL+13] (see Line 5 of Table 1). We stress that this asymptotic improvement over [IKL+13] is obtained *without* using expander graphs, that is we can use a simple PRG based on polynomial evaluation in a finite field (see Sect. 4).[2]

As mentioned previously, we found that expander graphs PRG are impractical for minimizing the amount of input randomness. However expander graphs can still be useful for optimizing the time generation of each pseudo-random; namely the output locality of an expander graph PRG (i.e., the number of inputs on which each output depends) can be at most polylogarithmic in the seed length (as opposed to linear for a PRG based on polynomial evaluation); hence in Table 1 the pseudo-random time generation is always $\tilde{\mathcal{O}}(1)$. In Sect. 2.3 we give an example of a simple construction based on expander graph that achieves very fast pseudo-random generation, at the cost of significantly more input randomness.

Table 1. Asymptotic efficiency of various constructions. The Locality Refreshing (LR) is performed either at the end of each gadget (Line 2 and Line 4), or sequentially within each gadget (Line 3 and Line 5). The trivial construction of PRG is based on xoring $t + 1$ linear PRGs to get robustness against t probes.

	#PRG	loc. ℓ	r-wise	PRG	TRNG	Time PRG
ISW without PRG [ISW03]	–	–	–	–	$\mathcal{O}(t^2 s)$	–
ISW with Final LR, single PRG [IKL+13]	1	$\mathcal{O}(t^2)$	$\mathcal{O}(t^3)$	Trivial	$\tilde{\mathcal{O}}(t^4)$	$\tilde{\mathcal{O}}(t^4)$
				EG	$\tilde{\mathcal{O}}(t^{3+\varepsilon})$	$\tilde{\mathcal{O}}(1)$
ISW with Internal LR, single PRG (Sect. 3)	1	$\mathcal{O}(t)$	$\mathcal{O}(t^2)$	Trivial	$\tilde{\mathcal{O}}(t^3)$	$\tilde{\mathcal{O}}(t^3)$
				EG	$\tilde{\mathcal{O}}(t^{2+\varepsilon})$	$\tilde{\mathcal{O}}(1)$
ISW with Final LR, multiple PRGs (Sect. 4)	$\mathcal{O}(t^2)$	$\mathcal{O}(1)$	$\mathcal{O}(t)$	Linear	$\tilde{\mathcal{O}}(t^3)$	$\tilde{\mathcal{O}}(t)$
				EG	$\tilde{\mathcal{O}}(t^{3+\varepsilon})$	$\tilde{\mathcal{O}}(1)$
ISW with Internal LR, multiple PRGs (Sect. 4)	$\mathcal{O}(t)$	$\mathcal{O}(1)$	$\mathcal{O}(t)$	Linear	$\tilde{\mathcal{O}}(t^2)$	$\tilde{\mathcal{O}}(t)$
				EG	$\tilde{\mathcal{O}}(t^{2+\varepsilon})$	$\tilde{\mathcal{O}}(1)$

Finally, we describe in Sect. 5 an application of our countermeasure to AES. We show that for AES we only need 48 bytes of randomness to get second-order security ($t = 2$), instead of 2880 in the original Rivain-Prouff countermeasure. We see in Table 2 below that for small values of t, our construction reduces the randomness complexity of masking AES by almost 2 orders of magnitude. In Sect. 5, we also provide the results of a concrete implementation. When implemented on an ARM-based embedded device with a relatively slow TRNG, we obtain a 50% speed-up compared to Rivain-Prouff for $t = 2$. We provide the source code in C in [Cor19b]. Needless to say, we do not claim that in practice our implementation would be secure against a t-th order attack. Namely the implementation is only provided for illustrative purpose, and timing comparisons. Obtaining a secure implementation would require to (at least) carefully examine the assembly code, and perform a leakage test with concrete acquisitions from an oscilloscope.

---

[2] An earlier version of [AIS18] claimed to achieve randomness complexity $\mathcal{O}(t^{1+\varepsilon})$, but the claim was later retracted in the final version.

Table 2. Number of bytes of randomness to get t-th order security for AES.

	$t=2$	$t=3$	$t=4$	$t=5$	$t=6$	$t=7$
Rivain-Prouff [RP10]	2880	5760	9600	14400	20160	26880
Belaïd et al. [BBP+16]	2560	5120	8000	13120	18240	24000
Faust et al. [FPS17]	1415	2530	6082	6699	20712	20726
This paper	48	108	192	300	432	588

2 Definitions and Previous Work

2.1 Private Circuits

In 2003, Ishai, Sahai and Wagner [ISW03] initiated the study of securing circuits against an attacker who can probe a fraction of its wires. They showed how to transform any circuit of size $|C|$ into a larger circuit of size $O(|C| \cdot t^2)$ with the same functionality but secure against a t-probing adversary, based on splitting each variable x into $n = 2t + 1$ shares with $x = x_1 \oplus x_2 \oplus \cdots \oplus x_n$.

Definition 1 (Private circuit). *A private circuit for $f : \{0,1\}^{n_i} \to \{0,1\}^{n_o}$ is a triple (I, C, O) where $I : \{0,1\}^{n_i} \to \{0,1\}^{\hat{n}_i}$ is a randomized input encoder, C is a randomized boolean circuit with input $\hat{\omega} \in \{0,1\}^{\hat{n}_i}$, output $\hat{y} \in \{0,1\}^{\hat{n}_o}$, and randomness $\rho \in \{0,1\}^m$, and $O : \{0,1\}^{\hat{n}_o} \to \{0,1\}^{n_o}$ is an output decoder, such that for any input $\omega \in \{0,1\}^{n_i}$ we have $\Pr[O(C(I(\omega), \rho)) = f(\omega)] = 1$, where the probability is over the randomness of I and ρ.*

For I and O we consider the canonical encoder and decoder: I encodes each input bit ω_i by a vector of $2t + 1$ random bits with parity ω_i, and O takes the parity of each block of $2t + 1$ bits.

Definition 2 (t-privacy). *We say that C is a t-private implementation of f with encoder I and decoder O is t-private (or t-probing secure) if for any $\omega, \omega' \in \{0,1\}^{n_i}$ and any set P of t wires in C, the distributions $C_P(I(\omega), \rho)$ and $C_P(I(\omega'), \rho)$ are identical, where C_P denotes the set of t values on the wires from P.*

2.2 PINI and t-SNI Security

The Probe Isolating Non-Interference (PINI) security notion was introduced in [CS18] to enable easy composition of gadgets. Let n be the number of shares. We let $x_\star = (x_i)_{i=1,\dots n}$ be an n-sharing of x if $x = \bigoplus_{i=1}^n x_i$. Given a subset $I \subset [1, n]$ of share indices, we denote by $x_{|I} := \{x_i : i \in I\}$ the corresponding subset of shares. A gadget with m inputs and ℓ outputs is a circuit with mn input shares grouped into m n-sharings denoted $(x_{\star,1}, \dots x_{\star,m})$, and similarly ℓn output shares denoted $(y_{\star,1}, \dots y_{\star,\ell})$. For a given share index i, we also use the notation $x_{i,\star} = \{x_{i,j} : 1 \le j \le m\}$ to denote all shares with index $1 \le$

$i \leq n$; similarly, we also write $x_{|I,\star} = \{x_{i,\star} : i \in I\}$. Below we recall the Probe Isolating Non-Interference (PINI) definition from [CS18]; we actually use a slightly simplified (and equivalent) definition compared to [CS18]; we explain the difference in the full version of our paper [CGZ19].

Definition 3 (PINI [CS18] (adapted)). *Let G be a gadget with input shares $x_{i,\star}$ and output shares $y_{i,\star}$ for $1 \leq i \leq n$. The gadget G is PINI if for any $t_1 \in \mathbb{N}$, any set of t_1 intermediate variables and any subset $\mathcal{O}$ of output indices, there exists a subset $I \subset [1, n]$ of input indices with $|I| \leq t_1$ such that the t_1 intermediate variables and the output shares $y_{|\mathcal{O},\star}$ can be perfectly simulated from the input shares $x_{|I \cup \mathcal{O},\star}$.*

It is straightforward to show that a PINI gadget with n shares is secure against $t = n - 1$ probes. We recall the proof of PINI composition (under our slightly modified definition) in the full version of our paper [CGZ19].

Proposition 1 (PINI security [CS18]). *Any PINI gadget with n shares is $(n-1)$-probing secure.*

Proposition 2 (PINI composition [CS18]). *Any composite gadget made of PINI composing gadgets is PINI.*

Below we recall the SNI security notion introduced in [BBD+15]. We consider a gadget taking as input two n-tuples $(x_i)_{1 \leq i \leq n}$ and $(y_i)_{1 \leq i \leq n}$ of shares, and outputting a single n-tuple $(z_i)_{1 \leq i \leq n}$. As previously, given a subset $I \subset [1, n]$, we denote by $x_{|I}$ all elements x_i such that $i \in I$.

Definition 4 (t-SNI security). *Let G be a gadget taking as input n shares $(x_i)_{1 < i < n}$ and n shares $(y_i)_{1 \leq i \leq n}$, and outputting n shares $(z_i)_{1 \leq i \leq n}$. The gadget G is said to be t-SNI secure if for any set of t_1 probed intermediate variables and any subset $\mathcal{O}$ of output indices, such that $t_1 + |\mathcal{O}| \leq t$, there exist two subsets I and J of input indices which satisfy $|I| \leq t_1$ and $|J| \leq t_1$, such that the t_1 intermediate variables and the output variables $z_{|\mathcal{O}}$ can be perfectly simulated from $x_{|I}$ and $y_{|J}$.*

Intuitively, the t-SNI security definition provides an "isolation" between the output shares and the input shares, so that the number of input variables required for the simulation is upper-bounded by the number of internal probes t_1, and does not depend on the number of output variables that must be simulated, as long as $t_1 + |\mathcal{O}| \leq t$. There is an analogous definition for a gadget with a single input $(x_i)_{1 \leq i \leq n}$; in that case, the simulation is performed from $x_{|I}$ with $|I| \leq t_1$.

It is easy to see that for a single input gadget, $(n - 1)$-SNI security implies PINI security. Moreover, for a 2-input $(n - 1)$-SNI gadget as considered in Definition 4, as shown in [CS18] we can obtain a PINI gadget by pre-refreshing one of the inputs with a $(n - 1)$-SNI mask refreshing algorithm; this is the double-SNI approach (see Fig. 1). A mask refreshing gadget takes as input the n-sharing of a value x and outputs a randomized n-sharing of the same value x. Therefore, in this paper, our strategy for proving gadget security is either to directly prove the PINI property, or to first prove the t-SNI property and then apply the "double-SNI" strategy. Note that for specific circuits such as the AES SBox, one can use some optimization; for example the full SBox computation can be proven t-SNI and therefore PINI with 4 multiplications and 2 mask refreshing only (instead of 4 mask refreshing as in the naive "double-SNI" strategy).

Proposition 3 (Double-SNI [CS18]). *Let G be a $(n-1)$-SNI gadget taking as input $(a_i)_{1\leq i\leq n}$ and $(b_i)_{1\leq i\leq n}$, and outputting $(c_i)_{1\leq i\leq n}$. Let R be a $(n-1)$-SNI gadget taking as input $(x_i)_{1\leq i\leq n}$ and outputting $(y_i)_{1\leq i\leq n}$. The composite gadget G' taking as input $(x_i)_{1\leq i\leq n}$ and $(b_i)_{1\leq i\leq n}$, and outputting $(c_i)_{1\leq i\leq n}$, with $G'((x_i),(b_i)) = G(R((x_i)),(b_i))$ is PINI.*

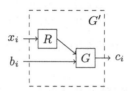

Fig. 1. The double-SNI approach: when both gadgets G and R are $(n-1)$-SNI, the composite gadget G' is PINI.

Finally, we recall in Appendix B the SecMult gadget used in [RP10] for protecting AES against t-th order attacks. It is an extension to $\mathbb{F}_{2^k}$ of the original ISW countermeasure [ISW03] described in $\mathbb{F}_2$. The SecMult gadget was proven t-SNI in [BBD+16]. We also recall in the full version of our paper [CGZ19] the mask refreshing gadget FullRefresh introduced by Duc *et al.* in [DDF14], based on SecMult; it was also proven t-SNI in [BBD+16]. We can therefore use the FullRefresh gadget to apply the above "double-SNI" strategy. Moreover, in this paper, when we describe a variant of SecMult, we apply the same modifications to the FullRefresh gadget; this is straightforward, since the FullRefresh gadget can be seen as a SecMult with one input equal to $(1,0,\ldots,0)$.

2.3 r-wise Independent PRG: Definition and Construction

We recall the definition of an r-wise independent pseudo-random generator (PRG). We denote by U_n the uniform distribution in $\{0,1\}^n$.

Definition 5 (r-wise independent PRG). *A function $G : \{0,1\}^n \to \{0,1\}^m$ is an r-wise independent pseudo-random generator if any subset of r bits of $G(x)$ is uniformly and independently distributed when $x \leftarrow U_n$.*

We can construct an r-wise independent PRG via polynomial evaluation in a finite field $\mathbb{F}$. Letting $\boldsymbol{a} = (a_0,\ldots,a_{r-1}) \in \mathbb{F}^r$, we consider the polynomial:

$$h_{\boldsymbol{a}}(x) = \sum_{i=0}^{r-1} a_i x^i$$

For any $m \leq |\mathbb{F}|$, we can define the function $G : \mathbb{F}^r \to \mathbb{F}^m$ by letting:

$$G(\boldsymbol{a}) = (h_{\boldsymbol{a}}(0), \ldots, h_{\boldsymbol{a}}(m-1))$$

where we assume that we have some indexing of the field elements in $\mathbb{F}$. The function G is an r-wise independent PRG because there is a bijection between the r coefficients of a polynomial of degree at most $r - 1$ and its evaluation at r distinct points x_i.

For $\mathbb{F} = \mathbb{F}_{2^k}$, this gives an r-wise independent PRG taking as input rk bits and outputting at most $k \cdot 2^k$ bits. Namely when working over $\mathbb{F}_{2^k}$ and generating k-bit pseudo-randoms, we can use each individual bit of the k-bit pseudo-random, and the PRG function remains r-wise independent. The parameter k determines the expansion factor of the PRG. For our application to AES in Sect. 5, for simplicity we will work over $\mathbb{F}_{2^{16}}$, using $\mathbb{F}_{2^8}$ as a subfield. For a block-cipher using single bits, one would work in $\mathbb{F}_{2^k}$ and use each of the k bits of $\mathbb{F}_{2^k}$ separately.

A Simple 3-wise Independent PRG. We also consider a very simple PRG that achieves 3-wise independence only. We consider a set of $2d$ random bits x_i and y_i for $1 \leq i \leq d$. We define the following function $G : \{0,1\}^{2d} \to \{0,1\}^{d^2}$:

$$G(x_1, \ldots, x_d, y_1, \ldots, y_d) = (x_i \oplus y_j)_{1 \leq i, j \leq d}$$

The function G can be seen as a PRG based on expander graph; see the full version of our paper [CGZ19].

Lemma 1. *The function G is a 3-wise independent PRG.*

Proof. We must show that any 3 variables $(x_{i_1} \oplus y_{j_1})$, $(x_{i_2} \oplus y_{j_2})$ and $(x_{i_3} \oplus y_{j_3})$ are uniformly and independently distributed.

We distinguish 3 cases. If $\#\{i_1, i_2, i_3\} = 3$, then the three values are independent thanks to randoms x_{i_1}, x_{i_2} and x_{i_3}. If $i_1 = i_2 = i_3$, then we must have $\#\{j_1, j_2, j_3\} = 3$ and the three values are independent thanks to randoms y_{j_1}, y_{j_2} and y_{j_3}. Eventually, if exactly two indices among i_1, i_2 and i_3 are equal, say wlog $i_1 = i_2 \neq i_3$, then we must have $j_1 \neq j_2$ and the randoms y_{j_1}, y_{j_2} and x_{i_3} ensure the independence of the three values. $\square$

2.4 Robust PRG: Definition and Trivial Construction

In [IKL+13], the authors introduced the notion of *robust* pseudo-random number generator (PRG), which should remain secure even if an adversary can probe at most k intermediate variables in the PRG circuit. We recall the definition of (strongly) robust PRG from [IKL+13] below. Under this definition, the output bits of the PRG must remain r-wise independent outside some set T of bounded size, conditioned on the values of any set S of at most k probes in the PRG circuit and the outputs in T.

In this paper we actually use a slightly weaker definition of strong robustness compared to [IKL+13], in which we allow the output bits outside the set T to be only $(r - q|S|)$-wise independent, instead of r-wise independent, where $|S| \leq k$ is the number of probes and q a parameter. In other words, we allow the r-wise independence of the PRG to degrade gracefully with the number of probes. This will give slightly more efficient constructions; in particular, the trivial construction of xoring $k + 1$ PRGs will only require the r-wise independence of each PRG, instead of the $(r + k)$-wise independence in [IKL+13]. Obviously we need to ensure that a robust PRG under our definition can still be embedded in a private circuit with the same parameters as in [IKL+13]; see Theorem 1 below.

Definition 6 (Strong robust PRG [IKL+13] (adapted)). *A circuit implementation C of a PRG $G : \{0,1\}^n \to \{0,1\}^m$ is strong (r, k, q)-robust if given $Y = G(X)$ where $X \leftarrow \{0,1\}^n$, for any set S of at most k probes in C, there is a set T of at most $q|S|$ output bits such that conditioned on any fixing of the values C_S of the wires in S and of Y_T, the values $Y_{\bar{T}}$ of the output bits not in T are $(r - q|S|)$-wise independent and uniformly distributed.*

Trivial Construction. As noted in [IKL+13], we can obtain a strong $(r, k, 1)$-robust PRG by taking the xor of $k + 1$ PRGs, each with the r-wise independence property. More precisely, letting $g : \{0,1\}^n \to \{0,1\}^m$, we let $G : \{0,1\}^{n \cdot (k+1)} \to \{0,1\}^m$:

$$G(x_1, \ldots, x_{k+1}) = g(x_1) \oplus g(x_2) \oplus \cdots \oplus g(x_{k+1})$$

where the xors are performed from left to right.

Lemma 2 (Strong robustness of G). *If g is an r-wise independent PRG, then G is a strong $(r, k, 1)$-robust PRG.*

Proof. Since there are at most k probes and $k + 1$ PRGs, there exists an index i^* such that $g(x_{i^*})$ has not been probed. In the following, we fix all inputs x_i except x_{i^*}.

Let $t \leq k$ be the number of probes. We consider the set T of indices $j \in [1, m]$ such that the j-th bit of any partial sum $g(x_1) \oplus \cdots \oplus g(x_i)$ is probed. We must have $|T| \leq t$. Since g is an r-wise independent PRG, by definition any set of r output bits of $g(x_i^{\star})$ is uniformly and independently distributed; this implies that any set of $r - t$ output bits of $g(x_i^{\star})$ with indices outside T are uniformly and independently distributed, even conditioned on the output bits in T and the other probes. Since we have fixed the inputs of all other PRGs, this also applies for the output of G. Therefore G is a strong $(r, k, 1)$-robust PRG.   □

Expander Graph Construction. Using an explicit construction of a bipartite expander graph [GUV09], the authors of [IKL+13] obtain a construction of a strong (r, k, q)-robust PRG with $r, k = n^{1-\eta}$ where n is the number of random input bits, for any $\eta > 0$. In the full version of our paper [CGZ19] we provide a simplified proof of strong robustness for expander graph based PRG, based

on the proof of weak robustness from [IKL+13]. We also argue that for minimizing the amount of input randomness, while asymptotically better than the
trivial construction, expander graph based constructions are actually impractical. Namely in our analysis the expander graph PRG construction based on
[GUV09] becomes better than the trivial construction only for $r \geq 2^{18}$ and at
least 2^{36} random input bits.

2.5   Application to Private Circuits

We recall below the main theorem from [IKL+13], showing that we can plug a
robust PRG in a private circuit to generate all randomness from a small random
seed, and the resulting construction remains secure against probing attacks.
Firstly an important parameter is the locality ℓ of the randomness in the circuit.

Definition 7 (Randomness locality [IKL+13]). *A circuit C is said to make
an ℓ-local use of its randomness if the value of each of its wires is determined by
its (original, unmasked) input and at most ℓ bits of the randomness used in the
circuit.*

Theorem 1 (Private circuit with PRG [IKL+13] (adapted)). *Suppose
$C(\hat{\omega}, \rho)$ is a qk-private implementation of f with encoder I and decoder O,
where C makes an ℓ-local use of its randomness, and uses at most m bits of
randomness. Let $G : \{0,1\}^n \to \{0,1\}^m$ be a strong (r, k, q)-robust linear PRG
with $r \geq k \cdot \max(\ell, q)$. Then, the circuit C' defined by $C'(\hat{\omega}, \rho') = C(\hat{\omega}, G(\rho'))$
is a k-private implementation of f with encoder I and decoder O which uses n
random bits.*

The proof of Theorem 1 is based on showing that the view of any adversary
who attacks with t probes an implementation in which the randomness is generated by a PRG, can be simulated given the view of an adversary with at most
qt probes who attacks an implementation with a true source of randomness; see
Fig. 3 for an illustration.

In the full version of our paper [CGZ19] we provide a proof that is essentially
the same as in [IKL+13, Theorem 30], except that we use our slightly weaker
definition of robustness. We recall the main steps of the proof below. We start
with the following Lemma, which is similar to [IKL+13, Lemma 29]. As illus-
trated in Fig. 2, any output of at most $r - q|S|$ bits of the robust PRG can be
replaced by a TRNG and any set S of at most k probes in the PRG can be per-
fectly simulated using a subset T of the output with $|T| \leq q|S|$. This means that
probing $|S|$ probes within the PRG is not better for the adversary than probing
$q|S|$ outputs of the TRNG. To simplify notation, we will use G to denote both
the function computed by a robust PRG and its circuit implementation. For a
set S of k wires in G, we denote by G_S the value of these wires; similarly, for a
subset T of output bits of G, we denote by G_T the values of these output bits.

$$X$$

$$k \text{ } \text{PRG} \quad \Longleftrightarrow \quad k \text{ } \text{SIM} \quad \text{TRNG}$$

$$Y \qquad\qquad\qquad\qquad Y$$

$$T$$

Fig. 2. With a strong (r, k, q)-robust PRG, any output of at most $r - q|S|$ bits of the PRG can be replaced by a TRNG and any set S of at most k probes can be perfectly simulated using a subset T of the output with $|T| \leq q|S|$.

Lemma 3 (Robust PRG). *Let $G : \{0,1\}^n \to \{0,1\}^m$ be a strong (r, k, q)-robust linear PRG with $r \geq kq$. Let S be any set of at most k wires in G. Let $L \subset [m]$ be any subset of $r - q|S|$ bits. There exists a subset T with $|T| \leq q|S|$ such that the distribution of $Y = G_{L \cup T}(X)$ is uniform in $\{0,1\}^{|L \cup T|}$ when $X \leftarrow \{0,1\}^n$ and moreover $G_S(X)$ can be efficiently simulated given Y_T only.*

Thanks to Lemma 3 we can now prove Theorem 1. As illustrated in Fig. 3, we can simulate any t probes within the PRG with a simulator SIM that uses qt random bits from the TRNG (see Fig. 2); these qt random bits can actually be queried by probing the original circuit C. This shows that when probing the PRG in C' the adversary does not learn more than by probing the circuit C with true randomness, as required; see the full version of our paper [CGZ19] for the details.

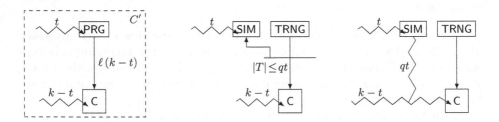

Fig. 3. Security proof when plugging a PRG into a private circuit.

2.6 Locality Refreshing

As recalled in Theorem 1, the r-wise independence parameter r of the PRG depends on the randomness locality ℓ of the circuit (see Definition 7). The goal is therefore to minimize the parameter ℓ. In the original ISW construction, the parameter ℓ would grow linearly with the circuit size; namely some wires can depend on almost all the randoms used in the circuit. To keep a small $\ell = \mathcal{O}(t^2)$, the authors of [IKL+13] use a mask refreshing at the end of each ISW gadget. Such locality refreshing, that we denote by LR, proceeds as described in Algorithm 1; see Fig. 4 for an illustration.

Algorithm 1. Locality refreshing LR

Input: shares $x_1, \ldots, x_n$,
Output: shares $y_1, \ldots, y_n$ such that $\bigoplus_{i=1}^{n} y_i = \bigoplus_{i=1}^{n} x_i$

1: $y_n \leftarrow x_n$
2: **for** $i = 1$ to $n - 1$ **do**
3:      $s \leftarrow \mathbb{F}_{2^k}$ # referred by s_i
4:      $y_i \leftarrow s$
5:      $y_n \leftarrow y_n \oplus (x_i \oplus s)$ # referred by $y_n^{(i)}$
6: **end for**
7: **return** $(y_1, \ldots, y_n)$

At the end of the algorithm, we have $y_i = s_i$ for all $1 \leq i \leq n - 1$, and $y_n = x \oplus s_1 \oplus \cdots \oplus s_{n-1}$ for the secret $x = x_1 \oplus \cdots \oplus x_n$. Therefore one can show recursively over the circuit that the internal variables of the ISW multiplication depend on at most $\ell = \mathcal{O}(t^2)$ randoms, and this actually holds for any variable in the circuit. The following Lemma shows that the LR gadget is PINI, so that it can be included in a circuit without degrading its security.

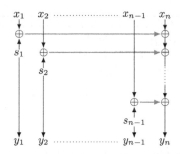

Fig. 4. Locality refreshing algorithm.

Lemma 4 (PINI security of LR). *Let* $(x_i)_{1 \leq i \leq n}$ *be the input shares of the mask refreshing Algorithm* LR. *For any* $t \in \mathbb{N}$, *any set of* t *intermediate variables and any subset* $\mathcal{O}$ *of output indices, there exists a subset* $I \subset [1, n]$ *of indices such the* t *intermediate variables and the output shares* $y_{|\mathcal{O}}$ *can be perfectly simulated from the input shares* $x_{|I \cup \mathcal{O}}$, *with* $|I| \leq t$.

Proof. We consider the following simple gadget $G: (x_1, x_n) \rightarrow (s_1, x_n \oplus (x_1 \oplus s_1))$, where s_1 is a random value. We start by showing that in Gadget G, we can always simulate t probes and $|\mathcal{O}|$ output variables from the input shares $x_{|I \cup \mathcal{O}}$, with $|I| \leq t$.

If $t + |\mathcal{O}| \geq 2$, we can let $I = \{1, n\} \setminus \mathcal{O}$ which gives $I \cup \mathcal{O} = \{1, n\}$ and all variables can be simulated from the input shares $x_{|I \cup \mathcal{O}}$. Moreover we have $|I| = |\{1, n\} \setminus \mathcal{O}| \leq 2 - |\mathcal{O}| \leq t$. If $t + |\mathcal{O}| = 1$, we distinguish two cases. If $|\mathcal{O}| = 1$

and $t = 0$, then we can simulate either s_1 or $x_n \oplus (x_1 \oplus s_1)$ by generating a random value. If $t = 1$ and $|\mathcal{O}| = 0$, we can simulate x_1 or x_n with $I = \{1\}$ or $I = \{n\}$; the other variables can be simulated by a random value.

We now consider the following gadget G_i for $1 \leq i \leq n - 1$:

$$G_i : (x_1, \ldots, x_i, \ldots, x_n) \to (x_1, \ldots, x_{i-1}, s_i, x_{i+1}, \ldots, x_n \oplus (x_i \oplus s_i))$$

which is similar to Gadget G, but with n input shares instead of 2, and $n - 2$ unmodified input shares. As previously, we can always simulate t probes and $|\mathcal{O}|$ output variables from the input shares $x_{|I \cup \mathcal{O}}$, with $|I| \leq t$. This implies that the gadget G_i is PINI. Since the LR gadget is the composition of $G_1, \ldots, G_{n-1}$, from Proposition 2 the LR gadget is also PINI. $\qquad \square$

In [IKL+13] the LR algorithm is then applied after each ISW gadget. In particular, for the SecMult gadget recalled in Appendix B, we obtain the following SecMultFLR gadget. Since the original SecMult is t-SNI, the SecMultFLR gadget is also t-SNI. The same LR algorithm is applied after the Xor gadget and the FullRefresh gadgets (see the full version of our paper [CGZ19]).

Algorithm 2. SecMultFLR

Input: shares a_i satisfying $\bigoplus_{i=1}^{n} a_i = a$, shares b_i satisfying $\bigoplus_{i=1}^{n} b_i = b$
Output: shares d_i satisfying $\bigoplus_{i=1}^{n} d_i = a \cdot b$
1: $c_1, \ldots, c_n \leftarrow$ SecMult$((a_i)_{1 \leq i \leq n}, (b_i)_{1 \leq i \leq n})$
2: $d_1, \ldots, d_n \leftarrow$ LR$(c_1, \ldots, c_n)$
3: **return** $(d_1, \ldots, d_n)$

Application to Private Circuits. We recall Claim 31 and Corollary 32 from [IKL+13]; we also recall the proof in the full version of our paper [CGZ19]. We use the notation $f(\lambda) = \tilde{\mathcal{O}}(g(\lambda))$ if $f(\lambda) = \mathcal{O}(g(\lambda) \log^k \lambda)$ for some $k \in \mathbb{N}$. We assume that the circuit size $s(\lambda)$ and the number of probes $t(\lambda)$ are both polynomial in the security parameter λ.

Lemma 5 (Private circuit with PRG [IKL+13]). *Any function f with circuit size s admits a t-private implementation (I, C, O) with the canonical encoder I and decoder O, where C uses $\mathcal{O}(t^2 s)$ random bits and makes an $\ell = \mathcal{O}(t^2)$-local use of its randomness. Consequently, f admits a t-private implementation (I, C', O), where C' uses $\tilde{\mathcal{O}}(t^4)$ bits of randomness, and runs in time $\tilde{\mathcal{O}}(t^6 s)$, using the trivial construction. Using the expander graph construction, for any $\varepsilon > 0$, it uses $\tilde{\mathcal{O}}(t^{3+\varepsilon})$ random bits and runs in time $\tilde{\mathcal{O}}(t^2 s)$.*

2.7 Composing ℓ-local Gadgets

In this section we provide an explicit definition of locality for a gadget, so that the locality property can be composed over a full circuit (as for the PINI definition for security against probing). As in [IKL+13], the basic technique is to perform a locality refresh (such as Algorithm 1) of the output of each gadget. We say that a set of wires $(y_i)_{1 \leq i \leq n}$ is locality refreshed if $y_i = s_i$ for all $1 \leq i \leq n-1$, for randoms s_i, and $y_n = y \oplus s_1 \oplus \cdots \oplus s_{n-1}$, where y is the original unmasked variable. In the definition below of gadget locality, we take into account the randomness of the (locality refreshed) inputs.

Definition 8 (ℓ-local gadget). *Let G be a gadget whose output is locality refreshed. Consider the circuit C where G is given locality refreshed inputs $x_{\star,\star}$. Let ρ be the randomness used by C, including the randomness from the inputs. The gadget G is said to make an ℓ-local use of its randomness if C makes an ℓ-local use of its randomness ρ.*

Theorem 2 (Composition of ℓ-local gadgets). *Any composite gadget made of ℓ-local gadgets is ℓ-local.*

Proof. We consider m gadgets $G_1, \cdots, G_m$ that we order as a direct acyclic graph from output to input in a reverse topological sort order. We assume that each gadget G_i makes an ℓ-local use of its randomness, with locality refreshed outputs. We prove by recurrence on n that the composition of ℓ-local gadgets is ℓ-local.

If $n = 1$, then there is only one gadget and this is straightforward since by assumption the gadget is ℓ-local. Now we assume that the composition of gadgets $G_1, \cdots, G_n$ is ℓ-local and we prove that the composition of gadgets $G_1, \cdots, G_{n+1}$ is still ℓ-local. Since the composition of gadgets $G_1, \cdots, G_n$ is ℓ-local, and since by definition the inputs of the gadget G_n are locality refreshed because they correspond to outputs of Gadget G_{n+1} which are locality refreshed, we get that the composition of both parts G_{n+1} and $G_1, \cdots, G_n$ does not increase the global locality. Namely, the global locality corresponds to the maximum locality between both parts. Since the composition of gadgets $G_1, \cdots, G_n$ is ℓ-local and since Gadget G_{n+1} is also ℓ-local, the maximum locality is ℓ and the composition of gadgets $G_1, \cdots, G_{n+1}$ is ℓ-local. $\qquad\square$

In the above definition, in order to determine the locality ℓ of a gadget, we must therefore assume that it receives locality refreshed inputs, and the randomness from this locality refreshed inputs must be taken into account when computing ℓ. Below we provide an example with the Xor gadget; the Xor gadget takes as input a_i and b_i for $1 \leq i \leq n$, and returns $c_i = a_i \oplus b_i$ for all $1 \leq i \leq n$.

Lemma 6 (Locality of Xor). *The Xor gadget followed by a locality refresh makes an ℓ-local use of its randomness, with $\ell = 2(n-1)$.*

Proof. The gadget takes as input a_i and b_i for $1 \leq i \leq n$, and then computes $c_i = a_i \oplus b_i$ for all $1 \leq i \leq n$, and finally $d_{n,j} = c_n \oplus (\oplus_{i=1}^{j} a_i \oplus b_i \oplus s_i)$ for $1 \leq j \leq n-1$, with outputs $d_i = s_i$ for $1 \leq i \leq n-1$ and $d_n = d_{n,n-1}$. We must consider $a_i = s_i^{(a)}$ for $1 \leq i \leq n-1$ and $a_n = a \oplus s_1^{(a)} \oplus \cdots \oplus s_{n-1}^{(a)}$, and similarly for b_i. Therefore c_n depends on $2(n-1)$ randoms, while $d_{n,j}$ depends on $2(n-1) - j$ randoms, which proves the lemma. $\qquad\square$

We also compute the concrete locality ℓ of the SecMultFLR algorithm introduced above; in [IKL+13] only the asymptotic bound $\ell = \mathcal{O}(n^2)$ was proved. Such concrete locality computations will be important when implementing the countermeasure for AES in Sect. 5; namely for a locality ℓ, from Theorem 1 the r-wise independence parameter of the PRG must be set to $r = \ell t$ for security against t probes. We refer to the full version of our paper [CGZ19] for the proof.

Lemma 7 (Locality of SecMultFLR). *The* SecMult *algorithm followed by a final locality refresh (*SecMultFLR*) is an ℓ-local gadget with $\ell = n^2/4 + 5n/2 - c$, where $c = 3$ for even n, and $c = 11/4$ for odd n.*

3   Improving the Locality of the Multiplication Gadget

In this section we describe two variants of the SecMult algorithm that improve the randomness locality of t-private circuits from $\ell = \mathcal{O}(t^2)$ to $\ell = \mathcal{O}(t)$. We show that this decreases the randomness complexity of private circuits from $\tilde{\mathcal{O}}(t^4)$ to $\tilde{\mathcal{O}}(t^3)$ using the trivial robust PRG construction. For our two new algorithms SecMultILR and SecMultILR2, we summarize in Table 3 below the number of required randoms and their locality ℓ. Since these randoms are eventually generated by a PRG, one should minimize their locality ℓ. We introduce SecMultILR first because the t-SNI proof of SecMultILR2 is significantly more complex.

Table 3. Summary of the multiplication gadgets, their locality and security. We have $c = 3$ for even n, and $c = 11/4$ for odd n.

	SecMult [ISW03]	SecMultFLR [IKL+13]	SecMultILR	SecMultILR2
Number of randoms	$n(n-1)/2$	$n(n-1)/2 + n - 1$	$n(n-1)$	$n(n-1)/2 + n - 1$
Locality ℓ	–	$n^2/4 + 5n/2 - c$	$4n - 5$	$4n - 6$
Security	t-SNI	t-SNI	t-SNI	t-SNI

3.1   First Construction with Internal Locality Refreshing (SecMultILR)

We describe below a variant of the SecMultFLR algorithm with locality $\ell = \mathcal{O}(t)$ instead of $\ell = \mathcal{O}(t^2)$. Our new SecMultILR is described below. The idea is to process the ISW matrix differently. In the original SecMult the final encoding is obtained by summing over all rows of the $n \times n$ ISW matrix. Instead we compute the partial sums over the rows of the successive $j \times j$ submatrices for $2 \le j \le n$. At each step we perform a locality refreshing of the j shares of the partial sum. In particular, the output of the algorithm is locality refreshed, so there is no need to apply the LR algorithm again.

Algorithm 3. SecMultILR

Input: shares a_i satisfying $\bigoplus_{i=1}^{n} a_i = a$, shares b_i satisfying $\bigoplus_{i=1}^{n} b_i = b$
Output: shares c_i satisfying $\bigoplus_{i=1}^{n} c_i = a \cdot b$

```
 1: for i = 1 to n do
 2:     c_i ← a_i · b_i
 3: end for
 4: for j = 2 to n do
 5:     for i = 1 to j − 1 do
 6:         r ← 𝔽_{2^k}                              # referred by r_{i,j}
 7:         c_i ← c_i ⊕ r                            # referred by c_{i,j}
 8:         r ← (a_i · b_j ⊕ r) ⊕ a_j · b_i          # referred by r_{j,i}
 9:         c_j ← c_j ⊕ r                            # referred by c_{j,i}
10:     end for
11:     for i = 1 to j − 1 do
12:         s ← 𝔽_{2^k}                              # referred by s_{i,j}
13:         c_j ← c_j ⊕ (c_i ⊕ s)                    # referred by c_{j,i}
14:         c_i ← s
15:     end for
16: end for
17: return (c_1, …, c_n)
```

We see that lines 6 to 9 are the same as in the original SecMult (see Appendix B), except that they are processed in a different order, since the loop starts with j instead of i. This implies that at Step 10 we have processed the $j \times j$ submatrix of the ISW matrix, and therefore the first j shares c_i must satisfy the equality:

$$c_1 \oplus \cdots \oplus c_j = (a_1 \oplus \cdots \oplus a_j) \cdot (b_1 \oplus \cdots \oplus b_j) \tag{2}$$

From lines 11 to 15 we then perform a locality refresh of these j shares $(c_i)_{i=1}^{j}$ using new randoms s_{ij}; therefore after the locality refresh the new shares c_i satisfy the same equality (2), but now they only depend on the $j - 1$ randoms s_{ij} for $1 \leq i \leq j - 1$, and not on the r_{ij}'s. This implies that at the next step of the loop (for index $j + 1$), the shares c_i will only depend on a linear number of randoms r_{ij}, instead of quadratic in the original SecMult. Thanks to these internal locality refreshings, the new locality parameter becomes $\ell = \mathcal{O}(t)$ instead of $\ell = \mathcal{O}(t^2)$.

Lemma 8 (Locality of SecMultILR). *The* SecMultILR *algorithm is an ℓ-local gadget with $\ell = 4n - 5$ for $n \geq 3$.*

Theorem 3 (Completeness of SecMultILR). *The* SecMultILR *algorithm, when taking $a_1, \ldots, a_n$ and $b_1, \ldots, b_n$ as inputs, outputs $c_1, \ldots, c_n$ such that $c_1 \oplus \cdots \oplus c_n = (a_1 \oplus \ldots \oplus a_n) \cdot (b_1 \oplus \ldots \oplus b_n)$.*

Theorem 4 (t-SNI of SecMultILR). *The* SecMultILR *algorithm is t-SNI for any $1 \leq t \leq n - 1$.*

One can therefore use a robust PRG with r-wise independence parameter $r = \ell \cdot t = \mathcal{O}(t^2)$ instead of $r = \mathcal{O}(t^3)$ in [IKL+13]. With the trivial construction of xoring $t + 1$ PRGs, the number of input randoms in the finite field becomes $r \cdot (t + 1) = \mathcal{O}(t^3)$ instead of $\mathcal{O}(t^4)$. This gives the following lemma, which improves over Lemma 5 from [IKL+13].

Lemma 9 (Efficiency properties of SecMultILR). *Any function of circuit size s admits a t-private implementation (I, C, O) with the canonic encoder I and decoder O, where C uses $\tilde{\mathcal{O}}(t^3)$ bits of randomness using the trivial construction, and runs in time $\tilde{\mathcal{O}}(s \cdot t^5)$.*

3.2 Second Construction with Less Randomness (SecMultILR2)

We describe in the full version of our paper [CGZ19] a variant called SecMultILR2 of the previous algorithm, that achieves the same locality ℓ as SecMultILR but with roughly half as many randoms. It uses the same number of randoms as SecMultFLR from [IKL+13], but with locality $\mathcal{O}(t)$ instead of $\mathcal{O}(t^2)$. Therefore it is strictly better than both SecMultFLR and SecMultILR; see Table 3.

Lemma 10 (Locality of SecMultILR2). *The SecMultILR2 gadget uses ℓ-local randomness, with $\ell = 4n - 6$ for $n \geq 3$.*

Theorem 5 (Completeness of SecMultILR2). *The SecMultILR2 algorithm, when taking $a_1, \ldots, a_n$ and $b_1, \ldots, b_n$ as inputs, outputs $c_1, \ldots, c_n$ such that $c_1 \oplus \cdots \oplus c_n = (a_1 \oplus \ldots \oplus a_n) \cdot (b_1 \oplus \ldots \oplus b_n)$.*

Theorem 6 (t-SNI of SecMultILR2). *The SecMultILR2 is t-SNI for any $1 \leq t \leq n - 1$.*

3.3 Formal Verification of Locality and Security

We have performed a formal verification of the above locality and security lemmas, using the CheckMasks tool [Cor18]. We refer to the full version of this paper [CGZ19] for the details.

4 Private Circuits with Multiple PRGs Without Robustness

In the previous section we have described two variants of SecMult where following the [IKL+13] paradigm a single robust PRG is used to generate all the randoms from the circuit; by improving the locality parameter from $\ell = \mathcal{O}(t^2)$ to $\ell = \mathcal{O}(t)$, we have decreased the number of input random bits from $\tilde{\mathcal{O}}(t^4)$ to $\tilde{\mathcal{O}}(t^3)$, that is independent of the circuit size s (up to logarithmic factors). In this section, we show that by using multiple independent PRGs instead of a single one, the robustness property of the PRG is not required anymore, and therefore much more efficient PRG constructions can be used; this allows to decrease the randomness complexity of private circuits down to $\tilde{\mathcal{O}}(t^2)$.

We start with a simple observation. In the security proof of ISW, if the attacker probes a given random r_{ij} in some SecMult gadget, then it is easy to see that we could give away to the attacker not only the probed r_{ij}, but actually *all* randoms $r_{ij}^{(k)}$ for the same i, j in all other SecMult gadgets k; namely in the ISW security proof with global index I, one would have $i \in I$, and therefore each $r_{ij}^{(k)}$ would then be simulated by letting $r_{ij}^{(k)} \leftarrow \mathbb{F}$ as in the original circuit, so it could be given to the attacker without requiring the knowledge of more input shares.

Now assume that for every pair (i, j) we use an independent PRG to generate the randoms $r_{ij}^{(k)}$ for all gadgets k. In that case the attacker has no advantage in probing the intermediate variables of the PRG circuit, since in our extended probing model he could get all corresponding randoms $r_{ij}^{(k)}$ with a single probe anyway. Therefore when each r_{ij} has a dedicated PRG (see Fig. 5 for an illustration), the robustness property of the PRG is not required anymore, and we can use a simple PRG with r-wise independence only, as for example the PRG based on polynomial evaluation from Sect. 2.3.

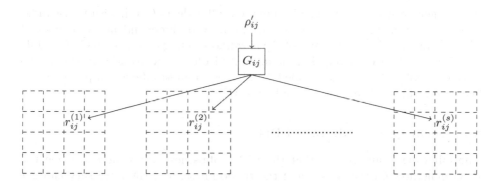

Fig. 5. In Construction 1, each r_{ij} has its dedicated PRG across all gadgets, from a random seed ρ'_{ij}.

Moreover, if a mask locality refreshing is performed at the end of each multiplication gadget, it is easy to see that any intermediate variable of the circuit can depend on at most a *single* random $r_{ij}^{(k)}$ for a fixed i, j, and therefore the locality with respect to each randomness subset $\rho_{ij} = \{r_{ij}^{(k)} : 1 \leq k \leq s\}$ is $\ell = 1$; this is because the locality refresh at the end of each multiplication gadget cancels the dependence on the internal $r_{ij}^{(k)}$. In that case, with t probes on intermediate variables the adversary can get information on at most t randoms within such set. Therefore these randoms can be generated by a PRG with r-wise independence parameter $r = t$. Since the robustness property is not required, we can use a PRG based on polynomial evaluation that requires only $r = t$ coefficients in a finite field, and therefore $\tilde{\mathcal{O}}(t)$ random bits per PRG. Since there are $\mathcal{O}(t^2)$ randoms r_{ij}, we need $\mathcal{O}(t^2)$ independent PRGs to generate all of them, and the total number of input random bits is therefore $\tilde{\mathcal{O}}(t^3)$, as in our single PRG constructions from Sect. 3. Note that the time to generate a pseudo-random is now $\tilde{\mathcal{O}}(t)$, instead of $\tilde{\mathcal{O}}(t^3)$ in Sect. 3.

We can improve the above randomness complexity as follows. Firstly, we observe as previously that in the security proof of ISW, whenever the attacker probes a random r_{ij}, we can actually give to the attacker the complete row of r_{ij}'s, that is for a given i, all r_{ij} with $i < j \leq n$; and more generally, for a fixed i, all randoms $r_{ij}^{(k)}$ with $i < j \leq n$ in all SecMult gadgets k. Therefore as previously we can use for each $1 \leq i < n$ a dedicated PRG to generate all $r_{ij}^{(k)}$ for all $i < j \leq n$ in all gadgets k, without needing the robustness property. Since we generate the complete row of r_{ij}'s (see Fig. 8 for an illustration), we only need $\mathcal{O}(t)$ independent PRGs, instead of $\mathcal{O}(t^2)$.

Moreover, if we perform internal mask refreshing as in the SecMultILR algorithm from Sect. 3 (instead of only at the end of the SecMult gadget), then no intermediate variable can depend on two distinct r_{ij}'s in the same row i. This implies that the locality with respect to the randomness subset $\rho_i = \{r_{ij}^{(k)} : i < j \leq n, 1 \leq k \leq s\}$ is still equal to 1. Therefore a PRG can be used to generate all $r_{ij}^{(k)}$ from a given row i in all gadgets k, still with r-wise independence parameter $r = t$. Since we need only $\mathcal{O}(t)$ independent PRGs instead of $\mathcal{O}(t^2)$ previously, the number of input random bits goes down to $\tilde{\mathcal{O}}(t^2)$, while the time to generate a pseudo-random is still $\tilde{\mathcal{O}}(t)$. Asymptotically this is the most efficient technique (see Table 1), and also the most efficient in practice (see Sect. 5 for our implementation results on AES).

4.1   Security with Multiple PRGs

The following lemma shows that the PRG robustness is not needed when the PRG generates only a subset ρ of the randomness, and the adversary can get ρ with a single probe; the lemma is analogous to Theorem 1 for a single robust PRG. We first consider a circuit C where we split the randomness in two parts ρ and $\bar{\rho}$, where only the randomness ρ will be replaced by pseudo-randoms. We consider an extended security model in which the attacker can get ρ with a single probe. Intuitively probing the PRG that generates ρ does not help the attacker, since in the extended security model he can get ρ with a single probe.

Lemma 11 (Security from r-wise independent PRG). *Suppose C is a t-private implementation of f with encoder I and decoder O, where $C(\hat{\omega}, \rho, \bar{\rho})$ uses m random bits ρ and makes an ℓ-local use of its randomness ρ, and the adversary can obtain ρ with a single probe. Let $G : \{0,1\}^{n_r} \rightarrow \{0,1\}^m$ be a linear ℓt-wise independent PRG. Then, the circuit C' defined by $C'(\hat{\omega}, \rho', \bar{\rho}) = C(\hat{\omega}, G(\rho'), \bar{\rho})$ is a t-private implementation of f with encoder I and decoder O which uses n_r random bits ρ' and random $\bar{\rho}$.*

Proof. We show that the view of an adversary A' who attacks $C'(\hat{\omega}, \rho', \bar{\rho})$ by probing a set S of $t' \leq t$ wires in G and a set of P of $t - t'$ wires in C is independent of the secret input ω. Since C is t-private, it suffices to show that the view of A' can be simulated given the view of an adversary A who probes at most t wires in $C(\hat{\omega}, \rho, \bar{\rho})$, and who can obtain the randomness ρ with a single probe.

Since C makes an ℓ-local use of its randomness ρ, the $t - t'$ probes from the set P in the circuit C can depend on at most $\ell(t - t') \leq \ell t$ bits of ρ. More precisely, for any $\hat{\omega}$ and $\bar{\rho}$, let $Q_{\hat{\omega}, \bar{\rho}}(\rho) = C_P(\hat{\omega}, \rho, \bar{\rho})$ be the value of these probes; the function $Q_{\hat{\omega}, \bar{\rho}}$ depends on at most ℓt bits of ρ. Let $T \subset [1, m]$ be the corresponding subset of bits of ρ on which $Q_{\hat{\omega}, \bar{\rho}}$ depends, with $|T| \leq \ell t$; we can write $Q_{\hat{\omega}, \bar{\rho}}(\rho) = Q'(\rho_T)$, where ρ_T is the corresponding subset of ρ.

We now proceed as follows. Instead of generating the PRG seed $X \leftarrow \{0,1\}^{n_r}$ and then the PRG output $G_T(X)$ corresponding to T, we can first generate the PRG output $\rho_T \leftarrow \{0,1\}^{|T|}$ and then sample the PRG seed; this is possible because G is a linear ℓt-wise independent PRG, and moreover $|T| \leq \ell t$. More precisely, since G is a linear ℓt-wise PRG, there exists a randomized simulator Sim that can perfectly sample the PRG input and therefore the probes within the PRG, given at most ℓt bits of PRG output; formally this means $(G_S(X), G_T(X)) \equiv (\mathsf{Sim}(\rho_T), \rho_T)$ where $X \leftarrow \{0,1\}^{n_r}$ and $\rho \leftarrow \{0,1\}^m$. We obtain:

$$(G_S(X), Q'(G_T(X))) \equiv (\mathsf{Sim}(\rho_T), Q'(\rho_T))$$

We now distinguish two cases. If the number of probes within the PRG is such that $t' \geq 1$, we let $\mathsf{Sim}'(\rho_T, v) = (\mathsf{Sim}(\rho_T), v)$ and we obtain:

$$(G_S(X), Q'(G_T(X))) \equiv (\mathsf{Sim}(\rho_T), Q'(\rho_T)) \equiv \mathsf{Sim}'(\rho_T, Q'(\rho_T))$$

which gives $(G_S(X), Q_{I(\omega), \bar{\rho}}(G(X))) \equiv \mathsf{Sim}'(\rho_T, Q_{I(\omega), \bar{\rho}}(\rho))$. In this case, the distribution to which Sim' is applied captures the view of an adversary A who corrupts a set $T \cup P$ of wires in C, where $|P| \leq t - t'$ and by definition ρ_T can be obtained with a single probe, which gives a total of at most $t - t' + 1 \leq t$ probes in C. Since by assumption C is t-private, this view is independent of the secret ω. Since the distribution on the left hand side captures the view of A', it follows that the view of A' is also independent of ω, as required.

In the second case, G is not probed by the adversary A'. Since G is ℓt-wise independent and the view of A' depends on at most ℓt bits of ρ, the view of A' is the same as the view of an adversary A probing the same wires in C. More precisely, we have from $G_T(X) \equiv \rho_T$:

$$Q_{I(\omega), \bar{\rho}}(G(X)) \equiv Q_{I(\omega), \bar{\rho}}(\rho)$$

As previously, the right hand side corresponds to the view of an adversary A who corrupts a set P of at most t wires in C and the distribution of the left hand side captures the view of A'; therefore the view of A' is independent of ω also in the second case.   □

We now consider the main theorem where the circuit randomness ρ can be split into $(\rho_i)_{i=1}^{k}$, and when considering each ρ_i separately, the circuit C makes an ℓ-local use of ρ_i; moreover we assume that C remains t-private even if the adversary can obtain each ρ_i with a single probe. The proof follows from a recursive application of Lemma 11.

Theorem 7 (Security with multiple PRGs). *Suppose C is a t-private implementation of f with encoder I and decoder O, where the circuit $C(\hat{\omega}, \rho_1, \ldots, \rho_k)$ uses for each $1 \leq i \leq k$, m random bits ρ_i, and makes an ℓ-local use of ρ_i, and the adversary can obtain each ρ_i with a single probe. Let $G : \{0,1\}^{n_r} \to \{0,1\}^m$ be a linear ℓt-wise independent PRG. Then, the circuit C' defined by $C'(\hat{\omega}, \rho'_1, \ldots, \rho'_k) = C(\hat{\omega}, G(\rho'_1), \ldots, G(\rho'_k))$ is a t-private implementation of f with encoder I and decoder O which uses $k \cdot n_r$ random bits.*

4.2 Extended Security Model: PINI-R

In Theorem 7 above we have considered an extended model of security, where the adversary can get any randomness subset ρ_i in the circuit with a single probe. Therefore, we define a variant of the PINI notion from [CS18], called PINI-R, in which the adversary can also get access to a subset of the randoms in a gadget, using a single probe.

Definition 9 (PINI-R). *Let G be a gadget with input shares $x_{i,\star}$ and output shares $y_{i,\star}$. Let $(\rho_i)_{1 \leq i \leq n}$ be a partition of the randoms used by G. The gadget G is PINI-R if for any $t_1 \in \mathbb{N}$, any set of t_1 intermediate variables, any subset $\mathcal{O}$ of output indices and any subset $R \subset [1,n]$, there exists a subset $I \subset [1,n]$ of input indices with $|I| \leq t_1$ such that the t_1 intermediate variables, the output shares $y_{|\mathcal{O} \cup R,\star}$ and the randoms ρ_i for $i \in R$ can be perfectly simulated from the input shares $x_{|I \cup \mathcal{O} \cup R,\star}$.*

The following proposition is analogous to Proposition 1. It shows that if a gadget with $n = t+1$ shares is PINI-R, then a t-probing adversary learns nothing about the underlying secrets, even in an extended model of security where the adversary can get each randomness subset ρ_i with a single probe. We provide the proof in the full version of our paper [CGZ19].

Proposition 4 (PINI-R security). *Let G be a gadget with input shares $x_{i,\star}$ and output shares $y_{i,\star}$ for $1 \leq i \leq n$. Let $(\rho_i)_{1 \leq i \leq n}$ be a partition of the randomness used by G. If G is PINI-R, then G is $(n-1)$-probing secure in an extended model of security where the adversary can get each ρ_i with a single probe.*

In the composition theorem below, the attacker can get the union of all corresponding subsets of randoms from all gadgets, still with a single probe; see the full version of our paper [CGZ19] for the proof.

Theorem 8 (Composition of PINI-R). *Any composite gadget made of PINI-R composing gadgets G_i for $i \in K$ is PINI-R, where for the composite gadget we take the randomness partition $\rho_i = \bigcup_{k \in K} \rho_i^{(k)}$ for $1 \leq i \leq n$.*

It is straightforward to prove the PINI-R property of the locality refreshing algorithm from Sect. 2.6, with the randomness partition $\rho_i = \{s_i\}$ for $1 \le i \le n-1$. In the full version of our paper [CGZ19] we consider an analogous extension of the t-SNI property, called t-SNI-R, which we prove for the SecMult and SecMultILR constructions, and the corresponding FullRefresh. More precisely, we show that those gadgets remain secure in an extended model of security where the adversary can get all randoms r_{ij} (and all randoms s_{ij} for SecMultILR) for a given i with a single probe. Moreover the "double-SNI" approach still works for the t-SNI-R and PINI-R notions. This implies that we can base our construction on t-SNI-R and PINI-R gadgets, and the resulting construction will be PINI-R. Note that the t-SNI security proof of SecMultILR2 is already complex, so we will not try to prove the t-SNI-R property of SecMultILR2; therefore we will use the multiple PRGs approach for SecMultFLR and SecMultILR only.

4.3   Constant Locality with Respect to a Randomness Subset

In this section we show that we can achieve constant locality, even $\ell = 1$, when we consider different subsets of randomness. Therefore we first provide a definition of gadget locality with respect to a subset of the gadget randomness only (and excluding the randomness of the inputs, as opposed to Sect. 2.7), and then a locality composition theorem as in Sect. 2.7.

Definition 10 (ℓ-local gadget with randomness subset). *Let G be a gadget and let ρ be a subset of the randomness used by G. The gadget G is said to make an ℓ-local use of its randomness ρ if any intermediate variable of G depends on at most ℓ bits of ρ.*

For example, the SecMult gadget makes a 1-local use of its randomness $\rho = \{r_{ij}\}$ for any $1 \le i < j \le n$; this is obvious, since ρ contains a single random bit. We can now state our composition theorem for locality with respect to a randomness subset. It shows that the gadget locality ℓ is kept the same in the composite gadget, while the locality of the randoms used for output refreshing is equal to 3 with respect to each subset $\{s_i^{(k)}, k \in K\}$ for $1 \le i \le n-1$. We refer to the full version of our paper [CGZ19] for the proof.

Theorem 9 (Locality composition with randomness subset). *Let G_k for $k \in K$ be a set of fan-in 2 gadgets which all make an ℓ-local use of a subset ρ_k of their randomness. Consider the gadgets G'_k for $k \in K$ where the output of G_k is locality refreshed with randoms $s_i^{(k)}$ for $1 \le i \le n-1$. Any composite gadget made of G'_k makes an ℓ-local use of the randomness $\bigcup_{k \in K} \rho_k$, and for any $1 \le i \le n-1$, it makes a 3-local use of the randoms in $\{s_i^{(k)} : k \in K\}$.*

For example if we compose a number of SecMultFLR gadgets, in the composite gadget the locality with respect to the randoms $r_{ij}^{(k)}$ for fixed i, j is $\ell = 1$, while the locality with respect to the randoms $s_i^{(k)}$ for fixed i from the output locality refreshing is $\ell = 3$. We stress that in the final implementation all the randomness (including the randomness from the locality refreshing) will be generated by the PRGs. Finally, we show in the full version of our paper [CGZ19] that the latter locality can be brought down to 1; for this it suffices to additionally perform a locality refreshing of the two inputs of each gadget, with independent sets of PRGs for the two inputs.

4.4   First Construction: Multiple PRGs with SecMultFLR

Our first construction is described in Fig. 6. It consists in using the SecMult algorithm and perform a locality refresh after each gadget; this includes the SecMult gadget, the Xor gadget and the FullRefresh gadget. For every $1 \le i < j \le n$, an independent PRG generates all randoms $r_{ij}^{(k)}$ in the SecMult and FullRefresh gadgets. Similarly, for each $1 \le i \le n - 1$, an independent PRG generates all randoms $s_i^{(k)}$ in all locality refreshing gadgets.

Construction 1: multiple PRGs with SecMultFLR

1. Given a circuit C, generate a private circuit (I, C', O) with $n = t + 1$ shares as follows:
   - replace every AND gate by the "double-SNI" gadget with SecMult and FullRefresh. Perform a locality refreshing LR after SecMult and FullRefresh.
   - replace every XOR gate by the Xor gadget. Perform a locality refreshing LR after each Xor gadget.
2. Initialize $n(n - 1)/2$ PRG functions G_{ij} for $1 \le i < j \le n$, each with r-wise independence parameter $r = t$.
3. Generate all randoms $r_{ij}^{(k)}$ in SecMult or FullRefresh gadget k with the PRG function G_{ij}.
4. Initialize $n - 1$ PRG functions G_i' for $1 \le i < n$, each with r-wise independence parameter $r = 3t$.
5. Generate all randoms $s_i^{(k)}$ in the LR algorithm from gadget k using the PRG function G_i'.

Fig. 6. Private circuit construction with multiple PRGs with SecMultFLR.

From the locality composition theorem (Theorem 9), in the global construction the locality with respect to the randoms $\{r_{ij}^{(k)} : k \in K\}$ is $\ell_r = 1$, while the locality with respect to the randoms $\{s_i^{(k)} : k \in K\}$ is $\ell_s = 3$. From the PINI-R property of the gadgets and Theorem 8, the full circuit is PINI-R. Therefore, from Proposition 4, it is secure in an extended model of security in which the adversary can get the previous randomness subsets with a single probe. From Lemma 11, the PRGs for the r_{ij}'s must be t-wise independent, while the PRGs for the s_i's must be $3t$-wise independent. Since one requires $n(n-1)/2$ independent PRGs for the r_{ij}'s, and $n-1$ independent PRGs for the s_i's, the number of input randoms in the finite field is therefore, with $n = t+1$, $n_r = n(n-1)/2 \cdot t + (n-1) \cdot 3t = \mathcal{O}(t^3)$. Thus we have shown the following lemma. Compared to Lemma 9 for a single robust PRG with our SecMultILR algorithm, the randomness complexity is the same but the total running time goes down from $\tilde{\mathcal{O}}(st^5)$ to $\tilde{\mathcal{O}}(st^3)$.

Lemma 12 (multiple PRGs with SecMultFLR). *Any function of circuit size s admits a t-private implementation (I, C, O) with the canonic encoder I and decoder O, where C uses $\mathcal{O}(t^3 \cdot \log(st))$ bits of randomness, and runs in time $\mathcal{O}(s \cdot t^3 \cdot \log^2(st))$.*

4.5 Second Construction: Multiple PRGs with SecMultILR

Our second construction is described in Fig. 7, based on the SecMultILR algorithm. As illustrated in Fig. 8, a dedicated PRG generates the r_{ij}'s for a given row i, in all gadgets. We first show that the SecMultILR algorithm makes a 1-local use of each row of randoms r_{ij} and a 2-local of each row of randoms s_{ij}; see the full version of our paper [CGZ19] for the proof.

Lemma 13 (Locality of SecMultILR). *The SecMultILR algorithm makes a 1-local use of each randomness set $\rho_i = \{r_{ij} : i < j \leq n\}$ and a 2-local use of each randomness set $\rho_i' = \{s_{ij} : i < j \leq n\}$.*

From Lemma 13 and Theorem 9, in the global construction the locality with respect to the subsets of randoms $\rho_i = \{r_{ij}^{(k)} : i < j \leq n, \, k \in K\}$ is equal to 1, the locality with respect to the subsets of randoms $\rho_i' = \{s_{ij}^{(k)} : i < j \leq n, \, k \in K\}$ is equal to 2, and the locality with respect to the subsets of randoms $\rho_i'' = \{s_i^{(k)} : k \in K\}$ is still equal to 3, for each $1 \leq i < n$. As previously, from the PINI-R property of the gadgets and Proposition 8, the full circuit is PINI-R. Therefore, it is secure in an extended model of security in which the adversary can get the previous randomness subsets with a single probe. From Lemma 11, the corresponding PRGs must therefore have r-wise independence parameter $r = t$, $r = 2t$ and $r = 3t$ respectively. The main difference is that now there are only $n-1$ independent PRGs to generate the $r_{ij}^{(k)}$ (instead of $n(n-1)/2$ previously), because a given PRG generates those randoms for all indices j. The total number of input randoms in the finite field is therefore $n_r = (n-1) \cdot t + (n-1) \cdot 2t + (n-1) \cdot 3t = \mathcal{O}(t^2)$. Thus we have shown the following lemma. Asymptotically this is the most efficient technique (see Table 1 for a comparison), and also the most efficient in practice (see the next section for our implementation results on AES).

Construction 2: multiple PRGs with SecMultILR

1. Given a circuit C, generate a private circuit (I, C', O) with $n = t + 1$ shares as follows:
   - replace every AND gate by the "double-SNI" gadget with SecMultILR and the corresponding FullRefreshILR. Perform a locality refreshing LR after each SecMultILR and FullRefreshILR.
   - replace every XOR gate by the Xor gadget. Perform a locality refreshing LR after each Xor gadget.
2. Initialize $n - 1$ PRG functions G_i for $1 \leq i < n$, each with r-wise independence parameter $r = t$.
3. Generate all randoms $r_{ij}^{(k)}$ in SecMultILR or FullRefreshILR gadget k with the PRG function G_i.
4. Initialize $n - 1$ PRG functions G_i' for $1 \leq i < n$, each with r-wise independence parameter $r = 2t$.
5. Generate all randoms $s_{ij}^{(k)}$ in SecMultILR or FullRefreshILR gadget k using the PRG function G_i'.
6. Initialize $n - 1$ PRG functions G_i'' for $1 \leq i < n$, each with r-wise independence parameter $r = 3t$.
7. Generate all randoms $s_i^{(k)}$ in the LR algorithm using the PRG function G_i''.

Fig. 7. Private circuit construction with multiple PRGs with SecMultILR.

Lemma 14 (multiple PRGs with SecMultILR). *Any function of circuit size s admits a t-private implementation (I, C, O) with the canonic encoder I and decoder O, where C uses $\mathcal{O}(t^2 \cdot \log(st))$ bits of randomness, and runs in time $\mathcal{O}(s \cdot t^3 \cdot \log^2(st))$.*

5 Application to AES

In this section we describe a concrete implementation of our techniques for AES; the goal is to minimize the total amount of randomness used to protect AES against t-th order attack. We provide the source code in C in [Cor19b].

5.1 The AES Circuit and the Rivain-Prouff Countermeasure

To implement the AES SBox, we need to perform 4 multiplications, and 2 mask refreshing per byte; see [RP10] for the sequence of operations. For the mask refreshing, we use the multiplication based refreshing FullRefresh recalled in the full version of our paper [CGZ19]. We refer to [BBD+16] for the proof that the x^{254} gadget is $(n-1)$-SNI; this implies that the gadget is PINI. Thus, this amounts to performing 6 multiplications per byte. Since there are 16 bytes to process per round, the number of required multiplications is $6 \times 16 = 96$ per round. Thus for the 10 rounds of the AES, one will perform $96 \times 10 = 960$ multiplications.

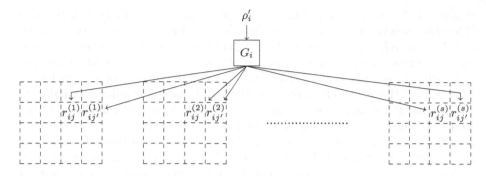

Fig. 8. In Construction 2, a dedicated PRG generates the r_{ij}'s for a given row i in all gadgets, from a random seed ρ'_i.

5.2 Implementation with Single Robust PRG

We first consider an implementation with a single robust PRG as in Sect. 3, with 3 possible algorithms: the original [IKL+13] construction with a locality refresh after each multiplication gadget (SecMultFLR), and our new SecMultILR and SecMultILR2 algorithms. For those three algorithms, we provide in Table 4 the total number of pseudo-randoms to be generated for the AES circuit, the corresponding locality parameter ℓ, and the number of 8-bit randoms from the TRNG to generate the seed of the PRG, as a function of the number of shares n, for security against t probes with $n = t + 1$.

Table 4. For AES, total number of pseudo-randoms and number of 8-bit TRNG calls, for a single robust PRG, as a function of the number of shares n. We have $c = 3$ for even n, and $c = 11/4$ for odd n. We assume that $n \leq 12$.

	SecMult [RP10]	SecMultFLR [IKL+13]	SecMultILR	SecMultILR2
Mult	$480n(n-1)$	$(480n+960)(n-1)$	$960n(n-1)$	$(480n+960)(n-1)$
Xor	–	$160(n-1)$		
Pseudo-rand	–	$(480n+1120)(n-1)$	$(960n+160)(n-1)$	$(480n+1120)(n-1)$
Locality ℓ	–	$\max(4(n-1),$ $n^2/4 + 5n/2 - c)$	$4(n-1)$	$4(n-1)$
True-rand	$480n(n-1)$	$2n(n-1)\cdot\max(4(n-1),$ $n^2/4 + 5n/2 - c)$	$8n(n-1)^2$	$8n(n-1)^2$

We now explain the content of Table 4. For each of the 3 algorithms, the number of pseudo-randoms is the number of randoms from Table 3 in Sect. 3, multiplied by 960, since one must perform 960 multiplications. Furthermore, the MixColumns operation requires 48 xors. Normally we should perform a locality refresh after each xor, but in the particular case of the AES, we can do the locality refresh only after the 3 xors of the MixColumns for each byte. In that case, the locality parameter with respect to MixColumns is then $4(n-1)$, instead of $2(n-1)$ for a single xor. The locality of the global circuit is then the max of locality parameter ℓ from Table 3 and $4(n-1)$. Equivalently, we can perform such locality refresh as input of the SubByte operation, which enables to keep the MixColumns unmodified. For the MixColumns, one therefore needs to perform 16 locality refresh per round, which gives a total of 160 locality refresh for the 10 rounds of the AES, which requires $160(n-1)$ pseudo-randoms. Finally, we assume that the round keys are already masked without PRG, and so we don't need to perform a locality refreshing after the AddRoundKey.

Let m the total number of pseudo-randoms over $\mathbb{F}_{2^8}$ that must be generated. To determine the finite field $\mathbb{F} = \mathbb{F}_{2^{8k}}$ used by the PRG, we must ensure $m \leq k \cdot |\mathbb{F}_{2^{8k}}| = k \cdot 2^{8k}$. Namely a single polynomial evaluation over $\mathbb{F}_{2^{8k}}$ generates k bytes of pseudo-random. One must then use a PRG with r-wise independence parameter $r = \ell \cdot (n-1)$. Using the trivial construction with the xor of $n = t+1$ polynomial evaluations (to provide resistance against t probes), the total number of fresh random values over $\mathbb{F}_{2^8}$ is then $n_r = k \cdot n \cdot r = k \cdot n(n-1) \cdot \ell$.

For the three algorithms one can work over $\mathbb{F}_{2^{16}}$ for $n \leq 12$; therefore for simplicity we take $k = 2$ in Table 4. For SecMultILR and SecMultILR2, the total number of TRNG calls over $\mathbb{F}_{2^8}$ is then $n_r = k \cdot n(n-1) \cdot 4(n-1) = 4k \cdot n(n-1)^2$ with $k = 2$ for $n \leq 12$, and $k = 3$ for $13 \leq n \leq 229$, instead of $480n(n-1)$ for the original Rivain-Prouff countermeasure; therefore one needs fewer TRNG calls than Rivain-Prouff for $n \leq 40$. We summarize in Table 6 below the number of input random bytes required for AES for small values of n, compared with the original Rivain-Prouff countermeasure.

5.3   Implementation with Multiple PRGs

We now consider an implementation of AES with multiple PRGs, as in Sect. 4. We consider the SecMultFLR algorithm corresponding to Construction 1, and the SecMultILR algorithm corresponding to Construction 2. As previously, we provide in Table 5 the total number of pseudo-randoms to be generated for the AES circuit, and the number of 8-bit randoms from the TRNG.

As previously, we only perform a locality refresh after the 3 xors of the Mix-Columns (equivalently, before each SubByte). Moreover we don't perform the LR algorithm after SecMultILR as in Construction 2, since the output of SecMultILR is already locality refreshed. Therefore the number of pseudo-randoms is the same as in the previous section. We use two classes of independent PRGs. The first class of independent PRGs is used to generate the r_{ij}'s from SecMultFLR and SecMultILR algorithms, with locality $\ell_r = 1$; therefore the PRGs must be $\ell_r t$-wise independent. We need $n(n-1)/2$ such PRGs for SecMultFLR, and only $n-1$ for SecMultILR. Working over $\mathbb{F}_{2^{16}}$, each PRG requires $2\ell_r t = 2(n-1)$ random bytes. Similarly, the second class of PRGs is used to generate randoms s_i from the locality refresh, and also the randoms s_{ij} for the internal locality refresh in SecMultILR, with locality $\ell_s = 5$. Namely we only perform the locality refresh after the 3 xors of the MixColumns, and therefore the locality is $\ell_s = 5$ (instead of $\ell_s = 3$). Note that for SecMultILR we can use the same class of PRGs to generate the randoms s_{ij}'s from SecMultILR and the randoms s_i's from LR,

Table 5. For AES, total number of Pseudo-random and True-random values to generate with the multiple PRGs approach, as a function of the number of shares n. Values for the Rivain-Prouff countermeasure are also recalled for comparison.

	SecMult [RP10]	SecMultFLR	SecMultILR
Pseudo-rand	–	$(480n + 1120)(n - 1)$	$(960n + 160)(n - 1)$
Locality ℓ_r of r_{ij}	–	1	1
Number of PRGs (r_{ij})	–	$n(n-1)/2$	$n - 1$
True-rand per PRG (r_{ij})	–	$2(n-1)$	$2(n-1)$
Locality ℓ_s of s_{ij} and s_i	–	5	5
Number of PRGs $(s_i$ and $s_{ij})$	–	$n - 1$	$n - 1$
True-rand per PRG $(s_{ij}$ and $s_i)$	–	$10(n-1)$	$10(n-1)$
Total True-Rand	$480n(n-1)$	$(n+10)(n-1)^2$	$12(n-1)^2$

instead of two classes in Construction 2 from Sect. 4; namely it is easy to see that the locality with respect to the corresponding randomness subsets is still equal to 5. Therefore the PRGs must be $\ell_s t$-wise independent; working over $\mathbb{F}_{2^{16}}$, each PRG requires $10(n-1)$ bytes of TRNG.

In summary, for SecMultFLR, the total number of 8-bit TRNG calls is therefore $n_r = n(n-1)/2 \cdot 2(n-1) + (n-1) \cdot 10(n-1) = (n+10)(n-1)^2$ and for SecMultILR, we get $n_r = (n-1) \cdot 2(n-1) + (n-1) \cdot 10(n-1) = 12(n-1)^2$ instead of $480n(n-1)$ in the original Rivain-Prouff countermeasure.

A Simple 3-wise Independent PRG. Finally, we consider the simple 3-wise independent PRG from Sect. 2.3:

$$G(x_1, \ldots, x_d, y_1, \ldots, y_d) = (x_i \oplus y_j)_{1 \le i, j \le d}$$

Since the PRG function G expands from $2d$ to d^2 bits (or bytes), the number of input randoms becomes $\mathcal{O}(\sqrt{s})$ instead of $\mathcal{O}(s)$, where s is the circuit size. Note that this is worse than the polynomial-based PRG used previously that requires only $\mathcal{O}(\log s)$ randoms, but the above function G is very fast since generating a pseudo-random only takes a single xor.

Since the above PRG only achieves 3-wise independence, we want to minimize the locality. Therefore, we perform a locality refresh of the 2 inputs of each gadget (with two distinct sets of independent PRGs), and we perform a locality refresh of the outputs of each gadget (SecMult, Xor and FullRefresh), using another distinct set of independent PRGs. As shown in the full version of our paper [CGZ19], the locality with respect to each subset of randoms is then always $\ell = 1$; therefore, we can use a PRG with r-wise independence $r = t = n - 1$. This implies that this specific PRG only works for $n = 3$ and $n = 4$ shares. We argue in the full version of our paper [CGZ19] that the total number of input bytes for AES is 642 for $n = 3$ and 1056 for $n = 4$, instead of 2880 and 5760 respectively for the original Rivain-Prouff countermeasure.

Table 6. For AES, total number of TRNG bytes to generate for single and multiple PRGs methods, depending of the number of shares n. We also provide the number of TRNG bytes for the original Rivain-Prouff countermeasure.

		Single robust PRG			Multiple PRGs		
	[RP10]	SecMultFLR	SecMultILR	SecMultILR2	SecMultFLR	SecMultILR	3-wise SecMultFLR
$n = 3$	2880	96	96	96	52	48	642
$n = 4$	5760	288	288	288	126	108	1056
$n = 5$	9600	640	640	640	240	192	−
$n = 6$	14400	1260	1200	1200	400	300	−
$n = 7$	20160	2268	2016	2016	612	432	−
$n = 8$	26880	3696	3136	3136	882	588	−
$n = 9$	34560	5760	4608	4608	1216	768	−
$n = 10$	43200	8460	6480	6480	1620	972	−

Summary. We summarize in Table 6 the number of input random bytes required for AES for all previous methods, as a function of the number of shares n, in order to achieve t-th order security, with $t = n - 1$. We see that the most efficient method (in terms of minimizing the number of TRNG calls) is the SecMultILR algorithm with multiple PRGs. Namely for small values of t we obtain almost two orders of magnitude improvement compared to the original Rivain-Prouff countermeasure. We provide in Appendix A the results of an implementation of our countermeasure on an ARM-based embedded device. We provide the source code in [Cor19b].

A   Concrete Implementation

We have implemented our constructions for AES in C, on a 44 MHz ARM-Cortex M3 processor. The processor is used in a wide variety of products such as passports, bank cards, SIM cards, secure elements, etc. The embedded TRNG module can run in parallel of the CPU, but it is relatively slow: according to our measurements on emulator, it outputs 32 bits of random in approximately 6000 cycles. Our results, obtained by running the code on emulator, are given in Table 7, and are compared with the classical Rivain-Prouff countermeasure.

We see that the most efficient countermeasure is the SecMultFLR algorithm with multiple PRGs, using the 3-wise independent PRG. For $n = 3$ and $n = 4$ we obtain a 52% and 61% speedup respectively, compared to Rivain-Prouff. We provide the source code in [Cor19b].

Table 7. Smart-card implementation results, on a 44 MHz ARM-Cortex M3 processor, with an embedded TRNG module. We provide the timings in millions of clock cycles, and the ratio with respect to the Rivain-Prouff countermeasure.

| | | [RP10] | Single robust PRG | | | Multiple PRGs | | |
			SecMultFLR	SecMultILR	SecMultILR2	SecMultFLR	SecMultILR	3-wise SecMultFLR
$n = 3$	Mcycles	20.6	65.6	76.8	65.4	12	14.1	9.8
	ratio	1	3.18	3.73	3.17	0.58	0.68	0.48
$n = 4$	Mcycles	40.2	235.1	425.1	324.9	24.6	34.7	15.5
	ratio	1	5.85	10.57	8.08	0.61	0.86	0.39
$n = 5$	Mcycles	65.8	1100	1541.5	1097.1	42.8	70	–
	ratio	1	16.72	23.43	16.67	0.65	1.06	–
$n = 6$	Mcycles	97.5	3042.1	4278.3	2898.5	67.2	124.1	–
	ratio	1	31.20	43.88	29.73	0.69	1.27	–

B   The SecMult Gadget

We recall in Algorithm 4 the SecMult gadget used in [RP10] for protecting AES against t-th order attacks. It is an extension to $\mathbb{F}_{2^k}$ of the original ISW countermeasure [ISW03] described in $\mathbb{F}_2$. The SecMult gadget was proven t-SNI in [BBD+16].

Algorithm 4. SecMult

Input: shares a_i satisfying $\bigoplus_{i=1}^{n} a_i = a$, shares b_i satisfying $\bigoplus_{i=1}^{n} b_i = b$
Output: shares c_i satisfying $\bigoplus_{i=1}^{n} c_i = a \cdot b$
1: **for** $i = 1$ **to** n **do**
2:     $c_i \leftarrow a_i \cdot b_i$
3: **end for**
4: **for** $i = 1$ **to** n **do**
5:     **for** $j = i + 1$ **to** n **do**
6:         $r \leftarrow \mathbb{F}_{2^k}$ # referred by $r_{i,j}$
7:         $c_i \leftarrow c_i \oplus r$ # referred by $c_{i,j}$
8:         $r \leftarrow (a_i \cdot b_j \oplus r) \oplus a_j \cdot b_i$ # referred by $r_{j,i}$
9:         $c_j \leftarrow c_j \oplus r$ # referred by $c_{j,i}$
10:     **end for**
11: **end for**
12: **return** $(c_1, \ldots, c_n)$

References

[AIS18] Ananth, P., Ishai, Y., Sahai, A.: Private circuits: a modular approach. In: Shacham, H., Boldyreva, A. (eds.) CRYPTO 2018, Part III. LNCS, vol. 10993, pp. 427–455. Springer, Cham (2018). https://doi.org/10.1007/978-3-319-96878-0_15. https://eprint.iacr.org/2018/566.pdf

[BBD+15] Barthe, G., Belaïd, S., Dupressoir, F., Fouque, P.-A., Grégoire, B., Strub, P.-Y.: Verified proofs of higher-order masking. In: Oswald, E., Fischlin, M. (eds.) EUROCRYPT 2015, Part I. LNCS, vol. 9056, pp. 457–485. Springer, Heidelberg (2015). https://doi.org/10.1007/978-3-662-46800-5_18

[BBD+16] Barthe, G., et al.: Strong non-interference and type-directed higher-order masking. In: Proceedings of the 2016 ACM SIGSAC Conference on Computer and Communications Security, Vienna, Austria, 24–28 October 2016, pp. 116–129 (2016). https://eprint.iacr.org/2015/506.pdf

[BBP+16] Belaïd, S., Benhamouda, F., Passelègue, A., Prouff, E., Thillard, A., Vergnaud, D.: Randomness complexity of private circuits for multiplication. In: Fischlin, M., Coron, J.-S. (eds.) EUROCRYPT 2016, Part II. LNCS, vol. 9666, pp. 616–648. Springer, Heidelberg (2016). https://doi.org/10.1007/978-3-662-49896-5_22

[CGZ19] Coron, J.-S., Greuet, A., Zeitoun, R.: Side-channel masking with pseudorandom generator. Full version of this paper. Cryptology ePrint Archive, Report 2019/1106 (2019). https://eprint.iacr.org/2019/1106

[Cor18] Coron, J.-S.: Formal verification of side-channel countermeasures via elementary circuit transformations. In: Preneel, B., Vercauteren, F. (eds.) ACNS 2018. LNCS, vol. 10892, pp. 65–82. Springer, Cham (2018). https://doi.org/10.1007/978-3-319-93387-0_4

[Cor19a] Coron, J.-S.: CheckMasks: formal verification of side-channel countermeasures (2019). https://github.com/coron/checkmasks

[Cor19b] Coron, J.-S.: Implementation of higher-order countermeasures (2019). https://github.com/coron/htable/

[CS18] Cassiers, G., Standaert, F.-X.: Trivially and efficiently composing masked gadgets with probe isolating non-interference. Cryptology ePrint Archive, Report 2018/438 (2018). https://eprint.iacr.org/2018/438

[DDF14] Duc, A., Dziembowski, S., Faust, S.: Unifying leakage models: from probing attacks to noisy leakage. In: Nguyen, P.Q., Oswald, E. (eds.) EUROCRYPT 2014. LNCS, vol. 8441, pp. 423–440. Springer, Heidelberg (2014). https://doi.org/10.1007/978-3-642-55220-5_24

[FPS17] Faust, S., Paglialonga, C., Schneider, T.: Amortizing randomness complexity in private circuits. In: Takagi, T., Peyrin, T. (eds.) ASIACRYPT 2017, Part I. LNCS, vol. 10624, pp. 781–810. Springer, Cham (2017). https://doi.org/10.1007/978-3-319-70694-8_27

[GUV09] Guruswami, V., Umans, C., Vadhan, S.P.: Unbalanced expanders and randomness extractors from Parvaresh-Vardy codes. J. ACM 56(4), 20:1–20:34 (2009)

[IKL+13] Ishai, Y., et al.: Robust pseudorandom generators. In: Fomin, F.V., Freivalds, R., Kwiatkowska, M., Peleg, D. (eds.) ICALP 2013, Part I. LNCS, vol. 7965, pp. 576–588. Springer, Heidelberg (2013). https://doi.org/10.1007/978-3-642-39206-1_49

[ISW03] Ishai, Y., Sahai, A., Wagner, D.: Private circuits: securing hardware against probing attacks. In: Boneh, D. (ed.) CRYPTO 2003. LNCS, vol. 2729, pp. 463–481. Springer, Heidelberg (2003). https://doi.org/10.1007/978-3-540-45146-4_27

[OMHT06] Oswald, E., Mangard, S., Herbst, C., Tillich, S.: Practical second-order DPA attacks for masked smart card implementations of block ciphers. In: Pointcheval, D. (ed.) CT-RSA 2006. LNCS, vol. 3860, pp. 192–207. Springer, Heidelberg (2006). https://doi.org/10.1007/11605805_13

[RP10] Rivain, M., Prouff, E.: Provably secure higher-order masking of AES. In: Mangard, S., Standaert, F.-X. (eds.) CHES 2010. LNCS, vol. 6225, pp. 413–427. Springer, Heidelberg (2010). https://doi.org/10.1007/978-3-642-15031-9_28

Non-Interactive Zero-Knowledge

Compact NIZKs from Standard Assumptions on Bilinear Maps

Shuichi Katsumata[1]($\boxtimes$), Ryo Nishimaki[2], Shota Yamada[1]($\boxtimes$), and Takashi Yamakawa[2]

[1] AIST, Tokyo, Japan
{shuichi.katsumata,yamada-shota}@aist.go.jp
[2] NTT Secure Platform Laboratories, Tokyo, Japan
{ryo.nishimaki.zk,takashi.yamakawa.ga}@hco.ntt.co.jp

Abstract. A non-interactive zero-knowledge (NIZK) protocol enables a prover to convince a verifier of the truth of a statement without leaking any other information by sending a single message. The main focus of this work is on exploring short pairing-based NIZKs for all **NP** languages based on standard assumptions. In this regime, the seminal work of Groth, Ostrovsky, and Sahai (J.ACM'12) (GOS-NIZK) is still considered to be the state-of-the-art. Although fairly efficient, one drawback of GOS-NIZK is that the proof size is *multiplicative* in the circuit size computing the **NP** relation. That is, the proof size grows by $O(|C|\kappa)$, where C is the circuit for the **NP** relation and κ is the security parameter. By now, there have been numerous follow-up works focusing on shortening the proof size of pairing-based NIZKs, however, thus far, all works come at the cost of relying either on a non-standard knowledge-type assumption or a non-static q-type assumption. Specifically, improving the proof size of the original GOS-NIZK under the same standard assumption has remained as an open problem.

Our main result is a construction of a pairing-based NIZK for all of **NP** whose proof size is *additive* in $|C|$, that is, the proof size only grows by $|C|+\mathsf{poly}(\kappa)$, based on the decisional linear (DLIN) assumption. Since the DLIN assumption is the same assumption underlying GOS-NIZK, our NIZK is a strict improvement on their proof size.

As by-products of our main result, we also obtain the following two results: (1) We construct a *perfectly zero-knowledge* NIZK (NIPZK) for **NP** relations computable in $\mathbf{NC}^1$ with proof size $|w| \cdot \mathsf{poly}(\kappa)$ where $|w|$ is the witness length based on the DLIN assumption. This is the first pairing-based NIPZK for a non-trivial class of **NP** languages whose proof size is independent of $|C|$ based on a standard assumption. (2) We construct a universally composable (UC) NIZK for **NP** relations computable in $\mathbf{NC}^1$ in the erasure-free adaptive setting whose proof size is $|w| \cdot \mathsf{poly}(\kappa)$ from the DLIN assumption. This is an improvement over the recent result of Katsumata, Nishimaki, Yamada, and Yamakawa (CRYPTO'19), which gave a similar result based on a non-static q-type assumption.

The main building block for all of our NIZKs is a constrained signature scheme with *decomposable online-offline efficiency*. This is a property which we newly introduce in this paper and construct from the DLIN assumption. We believe this construction is of an independent interest.

© International Association for Cryptologic Research 2020
A. Canteaut and Y. Ishai (Eds.): EUROCRYPT 2020, LNCS 12107, pp. 379–409, 2020.
https://doi.org/10.1007/978-3-030-45727-3_13

1   Introduction

1.1   Background

Zero-knowledge proof system [26] is an interactive protocol that allows a prover to convince a verifier about the validity of a statement without revealing anything beyond the fact that the statement is true. A variant of this, which is both practically and theoretically important, are *non-interactive* zero-knowledge (NIZK) proofs[1] [6] where the prover is only required to send one message to the verifier to prove the validity of the statement in question. Not only have NIZKs shown to be a ubiquitous building block for cryptographic primitives and protocols, but it has also shown to be a mine of theoretical questions with interesting technical challenges.

Unfortunately, it is known that NIZKs for non-trivial languages (i.e., **NP**) do not exist in the plain model where there is no trusted setup [25]. Therefore, NIZKs for non-trivial languages are typically constructed in the common reference string (CRS) model where the prover and verifier have access to a CRS generated by a trusted entity. We will call such NIZKs in the CRS model simply as NIZKs.

The most successful NIZK for all of **NP** is arguably the pairing-based NIZK of Groth, Ostrovsky, and Sahai [30] (GOS-NIZK). GOS-NIZKs are based on the standard decisional linear (DLIN) or the subgroup decision (SD) assumptions. Due to its simplicity and efficiency, pairing-based NIZKs have flourished into a research topic on its own, and the original GOS-NIZK has been followed by many subsequent works trying to improve on it through various approaches. For example, many works such as [31,37,38,42] aim to make GOS-NIZK more efficient by limiting the language to very specific pairing induced languages, while other works such as [14,20,28,29,45] aim to gain efficiency by relying on a much stronger assumption known as knowledge assumptions (i.e., a type of non-falsifiable [23,48] assumption). In fact, all works that achieve any notion of "better efficiency" compared to GOS-NIZK only succeeds by either restricting the language or by resorting to use stronger assumptions compared to DLIN or SD.

Similarly with many prior works, the main focus of "efficiency" in our work will be the *proof size* of the NIZK. Denoting C as the circuit computing the **NP** relation, GOS-NIZK requires a proof size as large as $O(|C|\kappa)$, where κ is the security parameter. Borrowing terminology from the recent work of Katsumata et al. [40,41], what we would like instead is a more *compact* proof size, that is, a proof size with only an additive overhead $|C| + \mathsf{poly}(\kappa)$ rather than a multiplicative overhead. For instance, the above latter approach using knowledge assumptions are known to achieve pairing-based NIZKs for **NP** with a significantly short proof size that only depends on the security parameter; in particular, the proof size does not even depend on the witness size. However, unfortunately, it is known that NIZKs with such an unusually short proof (i.e., proof size $\mathsf{poly}(\kappa) \cdot (|x| + |w|)^{o(1)}$ where x is the statement and w is the witness) inevitably require strong non-falsifiable assumptions [23]. The most compact

---

[1] In the introduction, we do not distinguish between proofs and arguments for simplicity.

NIZK based on any falsifiable assumption is due to [21,22] which achieves proof size $|w| + \mathsf{poly}(\kappa)$. However, since it uses (circular secure) fully homomorphic encryption (FHE) its instantiation is solely limited to lattice-based assumptions. Other than lattice-based constructions, Groth [27] proposed a NIZK based on the security of Naccache-Stern public key encryption scheme [47] with a proof size $|C| \cdot \mathsf{polylog}(\kappa)$, which is asymptotically shorter than that of GOS-NIZK. Very recently, Katsumata et al. [41] provided the first compact NIZK based on any falsifiable pairing-based assumption achieving a proof size of $|C| + \mathsf{poly}(\kappa)$. Their construction relies on a new primitive called homomorphic equivocal commitment (HEC), and they instantiate HEC using a *non-static* Diffie-Hellman type assumption recently introduced in [40]. Unfortunately, the construction of HEC seems to be tailored to their specific non-static assumption, and it seems quite difficult to construct HEC based on a clean static assumption such as DLIN.

In summary, despite the considerable work that has been put into paring-based NIZKs, improving the proof size of GOS-NIZK while simultaneously maintaining the language and assumption has shown to be elusive. Therefore, in this work, the main question we ask is:

Can we construct compact NIZKs for all of **NP** *based on standard assumptions over a pairing group?*

1.2 Our Result

In this work, we present the first compact pairing-based NIZK for all of **NP** with proof size $|C| + \mathsf{poly}(\kappa)$ based on the DLIN assumption.[2] Along the way, we also obtain several interesting compact variants of our NIZK such as non-interactive *perfect* zero-knowledge (NIPZK) and universally composable NIZK (UC-NIZK) [30] from the DLIN assumption. We provide a list of NIZKs which we achieve below and refer to Tables 1 and 2 for comparison between prior works. We note that the table only includes NIZKs for **NP** based on falsifiable assumptions.

1. We construct a compact NIZK for all of **NP** languages with proof size $|C| + \mathsf{poly}(\kappa)$ based on the DLIN assumption. This is the first NIZK to achieve a proof size shorter than that of GOS-NIZK under the same assumption required by GOS-NIZK. Moreover, if we assume the **NP** relation to be computable in $\mathbf{NC}^1$, the proof size can be made as small as $|w| + \mathsf{poly}(\kappa)$, which matches the state-of-the-art of compact NIZKs from any primitive based on (possibly non-pairing) falsifiable assumptions, e.g., fully-homomorphic encryption [22]. Our NIZK can also be seen as an improvement of the recently proposed compact NIZK of Katsumata et al. [41] in the following two aspects. First, our construction relies on a standard assumption, whereas theirs rely on a non-static q-type assumption. Second, our construction is fairly efficient since we only use pairing group operations in a black-box manner, whereas their construction is highly inefficient since they require pairing group operations in a non-black-box way.

---

[2] More precisely, we can base it on the weaker MDDH assumption, which includes the DLIN and symmetric external Diffie-Hellman (SXDH) assumptions as a special case.

2. We construct NIPZKs for **NP** languages that are computable in $\mathbf{NC}^1$ with proof size $|w| \cdot \mathsf{poly}(\kappa)$ from the DLIN assumption. This is the first pairing-based perfectly zero-knowledge NIZK for a non-trivial class of **NP** languages whose proof size is independent of $|C|$ based on a standard assumption.

3. We construct UC-NIZKs for **NP** languages that are computable in $\mathbf{NC}^1$ with proof size $|w| \cdot \mathsf{poly}(\kappa)$ from the DLIN assumption. This is an improvement over the recent result of Katsumata et al. [41], which gave a similar result based on a non-static q-type assumption.

The main building block for all of our NIZKs is a constrained signature scheme with *decomposable online-offline efficiency*. This is a property which we

Table 1. Comparison of CRS-NIZKs for **NP**.

Reference	CRS size	Proof size	Assumption (Misc.)
FLS [16]	$\mathsf{poly}(\kappa, |C|)$	$\mathsf{poly}(\kappa, |C|)$	trapdoor permutation[†]
Groth [27]	$|C| \cdot k_{\mathsf{tpm}} \cdot \mathsf{polylog}(\kappa)$ $+ \mathsf{poly}(\kappa)$	$|C| \cdot k_{\mathsf{tpm}} \cdot \mathsf{polylog}(\kappa)$ $+ \mathsf{poly}(\kappa)$	trapdoor permutation[†]
Groth [27]	$|C| \cdot \mathsf{polylog}(\kappa) + \mathsf{poly}(\kappa)$	$|C| \cdot \mathsf{polylog}(\kappa) + \mathsf{poly}(\kappa)$	Naccache-Stern PKE
GOS [30]	$\mathsf{poly}(\kappa)$	$O(|C|\kappa)$	DLIN/SD (Perfect ZK)
CHK, Abusalah [1, 11]	$\mathsf{poly}(\kappa, |C|)$	$\mathsf{poly}(\kappa, |C|)$	CDH (pairing group)
GGIPSS [22]	$\mathsf{poly}(\kappa)$	$|w| + \mathsf{poly}(\kappa)$	FHE and CRS-NIZK (circular security)
KNYY [41]	$\mathsf{poly}(\kappa, |C|)$	$|C| + \mathsf{poly}(\kappa)$	(n, m)-CDHER
KNYY [41]	$\mathsf{poly}(\kappa, |C|, 2^d)$	$|w| + \mathsf{poly}(\kappa)$	(n, m)-CDHER (limited to $\mathbf{NC}^1$ relation)
KNYY [41]	$\mathsf{poly}(\kappa, |x|, |w|, d)$	$\mathsf{poly}(\kappa, |x|, |w|, d)$	LFE and CRS-NIZK (prover-efficient, implied by sub-exp. LWE)
KNYY [41]	$(|x| + |w|) \cdot \mathsf{poly}(\kappa, d)$	$\tilde{O}(|x| + |w|) \cdot \mathsf{poly}(\kappa, d)$	LFE and CRS-NIZK[‡] (prover-efficient, implied by adaptive LWE)
Sect. 5.1	$\mathsf{poly}(\kappa, |C|)$	$|C| + \mathsf{poly}(\kappa)$	DLIN
Sect. 5.1	$\mathsf{poly}(\kappa, |C|, 2^d)$	$|w| + \mathsf{poly}(\kappa)$	DLIN (limited to $\mathbf{NC}^1$ relation)
Sect. 5.2	$\mathsf{poly}(\kappa, |C|, 2^d)$	$|w| \cdot \mathsf{poly}(\kappa)$	DLIN (perfect ZK, limited to $\mathbf{NC}^1$ relation)

In column "CRS size" and "Proof size", κ is the security parameter, $|x|, |w|$ is the statement and witness size, $|C|$ and d are the size and depth of the circuit computing the **NP** relation, and k_{tpm} is the length of the domain of the trapdoor permutation. In column "Assumption", (n, m)-CDHER stands for the (parameterized) computational DH exponent and ratio assumption, LFE stands for laconic functional evaluation, and sub-exp. LWE stands for sub-exponentially secure learning with errors (LWE).
[†]If the domain of the permutation is not $\{0, 1\}^n$, we further assume they are doubly enhanced [24].
[‡]We additionally require a mild assumption that the prover run time is linear in the size of the circuit computing the **NP** relation.

newly introduce in this paper and construct from the DLIN assumption. We believe this construction is of independent interest.

Table 2. Comparison of UC-NIZKs for **NP**.

Reference	Security (erasure-free)	CRS size	Proof size	Assumption (Misc.)
GOS [30]	adaptive ($\checkmark$)	$\mathsf{poly}(\kappa)$	$O(|C|\kappa)$	DLIN/SD
GGIPSS [22]	adaptive ($\boldsymbol{X}$)	$\mathsf{poly}(\kappa)$	$|w| + \mathsf{poly}(\kappa)$	FHE and UC-NIZK (circular security)
CsW [13]	adaptive ($\checkmark$)	$\mathsf{poly}(\kappa, d)$	$|w| \cdot \mathsf{poly}(\kappa, d)$	HTDF and UC-NIZK
KNYY [41]	adaptive ($\checkmark$)	$\mathsf{poly}(\kappa, |C|)$	$|w| \cdot \mathsf{poly}(\kappa)$	(n, m)-CDHER and UC-NIZK (limited to $\mathbf{NC}^1$ relation)
Sect. 5.2	adaptive ($\checkmark$)	$\mathsf{poly}(\kappa, |C|)$	$|w| \cdot \mathsf{poly}(\kappa)$	DLIN (limited to $\mathbf{NC}^1$ relation)

In column "CRS size" and "Proof size", κ is the security parameter, $|w|$ is the witness size, $|C|$ and d are the size and depth of circuit computing the **NP** relation. In column "Assumption", DLIN stands for the decisional linear assumption, SD stands for the subgroup decision assumption, HTDF stands for homomorphic trapdoor functions, and (n, m)-CDHER stands for the (parameterized) computational DH exponent and ratio assumption.

1.3   Technical Overview

Reviewing Previous Results. Here, we review definitions and previous results that are required for explaining our approach. We remark that we explain previous works [40,41,43] in terms of constrained signatures (CS) instead of homomorphic signatures, even though they are based on the latter primitive. This is because these primitives are actually equivalent as shown by Tsabary [52] and explaining in this way allows us to ignore small differences between our approach and previous ones that stem from the syntactic difference between them.

DP-NIZK and CS: We first explain the notion of designated prover NIZK (DP-NIZK), which is a relaxed notion of the standard notion of NIZK. In order to differentiate them, we call the latter CRS-NIZK in the following. In DP-NIZK, only a prover who possesses a secret proving key can generate a proof for an NP statement, and the verification can be done publicly by any entity. Here, the secret proving key is generated along with the CRS by a trusted entity. We require that soundness holds against a malicious prover who possesses the secret proving key and that zero-knowledge holds against a malicious verifier who only accesses the CRS and the proofs, but not the secret proving key. We then explain the notion of CS, which is a slightly simplified version of attribute-based signature [46]. CS is an advanced form of signature where a signing key is associated with some circuit $C : \{0,1\}^{\ell} \to \{0,1\}$ and using the signing key, one can sign on a message x if $C(x) = 1$. The signature can be verified by a public verification key. As for security, we require unforgeability and privacy. The former requires that one cannot forge a valid signature on a message x if it only has a signing key $\mathsf{CS.sk}_C$ for C such that $C(x) = 0$. The latter requires that an honestly generated signature reveals nothing about the circuit C associated with the signing key that is used for generating the signature. In addition to the above security notions, we also require CS to have compact signatures in the sense that the size of the signatures is a fixed polynomial that is independent of the size of the circuit C and the length of the message x.

DP-NIZK from CS [43]: We then explain the generic construction of DP-NIZK from CS shown by Kim and Wu [43]. This will serve as a good starting point for us because their conversion allows us to convert a compact CS into a compact DP-NIZK as we will see. Let us fix an NP language L that is verified by a circuit R that takes as input a statement x and a witness w and outputs $R(x, w) \in \{0, 1\}$. In their construction, they set the CRS of the DP-NIZK to be a verification key of the CS. Furthermore, they set the secret proving key for the DP-NIZK to be a secret key K of an SKE and a CS signing key $\mathsf{CS.sk}_{C_K}$ for circuit C_K. Here, C_K is a circuit that takes as input an SKE ciphertext $\mathsf{SKE.ct}$ and a statement x and outputs 1 if $R(x, \mathsf{SKE.Dec}(K, \mathsf{SKE.ct})) = 1$ and 0 otherwise. To generate a proof for an NP statement x corresponding to a witness w, the prover encrypts the witness w by the SKE to obtain $\mathsf{SKE.ct} = \mathsf{SKE.Enc}(K, w)$ and then signs on the message $(x, \mathsf{SKE.ct})$ using the CS signing key for C_K. By the correctness of the SKE, we have $C_K(x, \mathsf{SKE.ct}) = R(x, w) = 1$, which implies the completeness of the DP-NIZK. The soundness of the protocol follows from the unforgeability of the underlying CS. This is because any valid proof for an invalid statement $x^* \notin L$ is a valid signature on $(x^*, \mathsf{SKE.ct}^*)$ for some $\mathsf{SKE.ct}^*$, for which we have $C_K(x^*, \mathsf{SKE.ct}^*) = R(x^*, \mathsf{SKE.Dec}(K, \mathsf{SKE.ct}^*)) = 0$. The zero-knowledge property of the protocol follows from the following intuition. From the privacy of the CS, information of K hardwired into the circuit C_K is not leaked from the CS signature. We, therefore, can use the security of SKE to conclude that $\mathsf{SKE.ct}$ leaks no information of the witness w.

We now focus on the efficiency of the resultant DP-NIZK. If we instantiate the DP-NIZK with an SKE with additive ciphertext overhead and a CS with compact signatures, this gives us a compact DP-NIZK. Note that an SKE scheme with additive ciphertext overhead can be realized from very mild assumptions such as CDH. Therefore, their result suggests that it suffices to construct compact CS in order to construct a compact DP-NIZK.

Overview of Our Approach. Here, we provide an overview of our approach. In high level, we follow the same approach as Katsumata et al. [40,41], who constructed a compact CRS-NIZK from a non-static assumption over bilinear maps. Specifically, we will first construct a CS, then convert it into a DP-NIZK, and then modify it into a CRS-NIZK. However, our approach significantly differs from theirs in low level details. We will provide a comparison with their work after describing our approach in the following.

Compact DP-NIZK from a Standard Assumption: We set the construction of compact DP-NIZK from a static assumption as an intermediate goal. Thanks to the Kim-Wu conversion, the problem is reduced to the construction of a CS scheme with compact signatures from a static assumption. To achieve the goal, we follow the folklore conversion that converts an attribute-based encryption (ABE) into a CS that is somewhat reminiscent of the Naor conversion [7] (See e.g., [49]). In order to obtain the CS scheme with the desired properties, it turns out that we need to construct an adaptively secure ABE scheme whose ciphertext size is bounded by some fixed polynomial. Although there is no ABE scheme with the required properties from a static assumption in the literature, we are able to construct it by modifying the very recent ABE scheme proposed by Kowalczyk and Wee [44], who resolved the long-standing open problem of constructing adaptively secure ABE for $\mathbf{NC}^1$ whose ciphertext length is independent of the circuit size from a static assumption by cleverly adapting the piecewise guessing frameworks [17,18,32,35,36,44] to the setting of ABE. We modify their scheme so that it has even shorter ciphertexts by aggregating the ciphertext components and adding extra components to the secret keys as was done in previous works on ABE with short ciphertexts [2,33]. The security proof for the scheme is again similar to that of Kowalczyk and Wee, where we decompose the secret keys into smaller pieces and gradually randomize them via carefully chosen sequence of hybrid games. The additional challenge for the proof in our setting is to deal with the extra components in the secret keys. We handle this by observing that the originally proof strategy by Kowalczyk and Wee for randomizing the secret keys works even with these extra components. From this ABE scheme, we can obtain a CS scheme with the desired properties. Furthermore, by applying the Kim-Wu conversion to the CS scheme, we obtain a new compact DP-NIZK from a static assumption. Although this is not our main goal, we note that this improves the compact DP-NIZK scheme from a non-static assumption by Katsumata et al. [40].

Removing Secret Proving Key: We then try to remove the necessity of the secret proving key from the DP-NIZK described above to obtain a CRS-NIZK. Toward this goal, our first idea is to make the signing key of the CS scheme public by including it into the CRS. When we do so, we stop hardwiring the secret key K of the SKE into the circuit associated with the signing key and change the circuit so that it takes K as an input. The obvious reason for this is because we would like to use the security of SKE at some later point. More concretely, we include CS.sk_C into the CRS, where C is a circuit that takes as input the secret key K of SKE, a statement x, and a ciphertext SKE.ct of SKE and outputs $R(x, \mathsf{SKE.Dec}(K, \mathsf{SKE.ct}))$. When generating a proof, the prover chooses a random K on its own, computes $\mathsf{SKE.ct} \xleftarrow{\$} \mathsf{SKE.Enc}(K, w)$, and signs on the message $(x, \mathsf{SKE.ct}, K)$ by using CS.sk_C to obtain a signature CS.σ, which is possible because we have $C(x, \mathsf{SKE.ct}, K) = 1$ by the definition of C. The problem with this approach is that we do not know what components to publish as the final proof. More specifically, we run into the following deadlock: If we include K into the proof, then the scheme is not zero-knowledge anymore because one can decrypt SKE.ct by using K to retrieve w. On the other hand, if we do not include K into the proof, we can no longer verify the validity of CS.σ since K, which is now a part of the message, is required to verify the signature.

Introducing Non-Compact NIZK: We resolve the above issue by using a CRS-NIZK that is not necessarily compact (non-compact NIZK in the following) and change the scheme so that it proves the validity of the CS signature without revealing K nor the signature. In more detail, the prover generates $K, \mathsf{SKE.ct} \xleftarrow{\$}$ $\mathsf{SKE.Enc}(K, w), \mathsf{CS}.\sigma \xleftarrow{\$} \mathsf{CS.Sign}(\mathsf{CS.sk}_C, (x, \mathsf{SKE.ct}, K))$ as above. It then proves that there exists $(K, \mathsf{CS}.\sigma)$ such that CS.σ is a valid signature on a message $(x, \mathsf{SKE.ct}, K)$ under the verification key CS.vk by using the non-compact NIZK. It then outputs $(\mathsf{SKE.ct}, \mathsf{CS}.\sigma, \pi)$ as the final proof, where π is the non-compact proof for the above statement.

We then explain that the scheme satisfies soundness and zero-knowledge. To see this, we first observe that to break the soundness of the resultant NIZK scheme, it is necessary to break the soundness of the underlying non-compact NIZK or generate a valid CS signature on $(x^*, \mathsf{SKE.ct}^*, K^*)$ such that $x^* \notin L$. By our assumption, the former is impossible. Furthermore, the latter is also impossible, since we have $C(x^*, \mathsf{SKE.ct}^*, K^*) = 0$ for any choice of K^* and $\mathsf{SKE.ct}^*$ and thus it implies a forgery against the CS scheme. The zero-knowledge property of the scheme holds since the proof consists of the SKE ciphertext and the proof of the non-compact NIZK. Intuitively, since the latter does not leak the information about K, we can use the security of SKE to conclude that w is hidden from the adversary.

While this gives a secure construction, it is unclear whether this is a step forward at this point since we merely constructed a NIZK from a CS by further assuming a NIZK, which seems to be a vacuous statement. Furthermore, the construction we described so far is not compact since the relation proven by the underlying non-compact NIZK is verified by a circuit whose size depends on $|C|$. To see this, we recall that the verification circuit for the relation proven by the non-compact NIZK takes as input the statement $x' = (\mathsf{CS.vk}, x, \mathsf{SKE.ct})$ and witness $w' = (K, \mathsf{CS}.\sigma)$ and outputs 1 if and only if CS.σ is a valid signature on $(x, \mathsf{SKE.ct}, K)$. This circuit is not compact, since it takes as input x, which can be as large as $|C|$ in general and CS.vk, which is much larger than $|C|$ in our specific CS scheme.

Exploiting the Special Efficiency Property of the CS: We observe that what should be kept secret in the above construction are K and CS.σ,[3] and $(x, \mathsf{SKE.ct})$ can be made public without losing the zero-knowledge property. To get a clearer understanding of the problem, we slightly generalize and simplify the problem as follows. What we would like to do is to give a compact proof that we have a valid signature CS.σ on a message (y, z) for public y and secret z without revealing z nor CS.σ using a non-compact NIZK. Here, y is not compact while z and CS.σ are compact. In our context, $y = (x, \mathsf{SKE.ct})$ and $z = K$. In this generalized setting, the above approach is equivalent to proving that CS.σ is a valid signature on (y, z) under the verification key CS.vk. This relation is verified by a circuit

---

[3] Note that CS.σ should be kept secret since it reveals partial information of K.

that directly takes $(\mathsf{CS.vk}, (y, z), \mathsf{CS.\sigma})$ as inputs. This approach does not work simply because the input is not compact.

Our first observation is that if we were somehow able to compress the verification circuit size of the relation proven by the non-compact NIZK to be a fixed polynomial without changing the functionality, then the resultant NIZK scheme will have compact proofs. Fortunately, our CS scheme has a nice property that brings us closer to this goal. Namely, in the scheme, the verifier can aggregate the verification key $\mathsf{CS.vk}$ depending on a message m to obtain an aggregated verification key $\mathsf{CS.vk}_m$, which is of fixed polynomial size. Then, a signature $\mathsf{CS.\sigma}$ can be verified by using *only* the aggregated verification key $\mathsf{CS.vk}_m$. In particular, the verification circuit no longer takes m as an input. Typically, the aggregation of the verification key is done offline, where one is allowed to perform heavy computation, and the actual verification step is done online, where the computation is very fast even if m is a very long string. We call this property *online-offline efficiency*. We note that our CS scheme inherits this property from the underlying ABE scheme, where secret keys can be aggregated depending on an attribute in offline phase so that the decryption of a ciphertext corresponding to the same attribute in the online phase is very fast.

A natural approach to compress the verification circuit (for the non-compact NIZK) would be to replace the inputs $\mathsf{CS.vk}$ and (y, z) with its aggregated version $\mathsf{CS.vk}_{(y,z)}$. In particular, we replace the verification circuit which takes as input $\mathsf{CS.vk}$, (y, z), and $\mathsf{CS.\sigma}$ and verifies the signature with the corresponding online verification circuit which takes $\mathsf{CS.vk}_{(y,z)}$ and $\mathsf{CS.\sigma}$ as inputs. This circuit is compact thanks to the online-offline efficiency of the CS. However, since $\mathsf{CS.vk}_{(y,z)}$ cannot be publicly computed, we would have to move the term $\mathsf{CS.vk}_{(y,z)}$ into the witness. Furthermore, we additionally have to prove that $\mathsf{CS.vk}_{(y,z)}$ is honestly computed from $\mathsf{CS.vk}$ and (y, z) using the non-compact NIZK. The problem is that the resulting proof is not compact since this is a statement that involves non-compact terms. Put differently, even though we can compactly prove that we have a signature that passes the online verification under a compressed verification key, we cannot compactly prove that we honestly execute the offline phase to compute the compressed verification key.

As we saw above, the idea of compressing $\mathsf{CS.vk}$ depending on the entire string (y, z) does not work. Our idea is to "partially" compress $\mathsf{CS.vk}$ depending on the public part y and then use this compressed version of the verification key to construct the verification circuit for the non-compact NIZK. To enable the idea, let us assume that we can compress $\mathsf{CS.vk}$ with respect to a string y and obtain $\mathsf{CS.vk}_y$. Then, further assume that we can compress $\mathsf{CS.vk}_y$ into $\mathsf{CS.vk}_{(y,z)}$ using z, so that the verification of a message (y, z) is possible using $\mathsf{CS.vk}_{(y,z)}$. Furthermore, we require that the computational cost of compressing $\mathsf{CS.vk}_y$ into $\mathsf{CS.vk}_{(y,z)}$ depends only on $|z|$, not on $|y|$. Therefore if z is compact, we can compute $\mathsf{CS.vk}_{(y,z)}$ from $\mathsf{CS.vk}_y$ and z by a compact circuit. Assuming this property, we can solve the above generalized problem as follows: We first compress $\mathsf{CS.vk}$ depending on y to obtain $\mathsf{CS.vk}_y$. We then prove that there exists $\mathsf{CS.\sigma}$ and z such that $\mathsf{CS.\sigma}$ is a valid signature under $\mathsf{CS.vk}_{(y,z)}$, where $\mathsf{CS.vk}_{(y,z)}$

is obtained by compressing $\mathsf{CS.vk}_y$ depending on the string z. This statement can be proven compactly, since both verification under the verification key $\mathsf{CS.vk}_{(y,z)}$ and the compression of $\mathsf{CS.vk}_y$ into $\mathsf{CS.vk}_{(y,z)}$ can be done compactly. Furthermore, unlike the previous attempt, we do not have to prove that we honestly executed the offline computation. Namely, we do not have to prove the consistency between $\mathsf{CS.vk}$, y, and $\mathsf{CS.vk}_y$, since $\mathsf{CS.vk}_y$ is publicly computable from $\mathsf{CS.vk}$ and y. Therefore, it suffices to show that our CS scheme has the structure that allows one to compress the verification key in two steps. We name this property *online-offline decomposability* and show that our construction indeed has the property.[4]

Comparison with Katsumata et al. [41]. Here, we compare our approach with the one by Katsumata et al. [40,41], who showed a similar result from a non-static assumption. As we already mentioned, at the highest level, their approach is the same as ours in that they first construct a CS [40], then convert it into a DP-NIZK, and then modify it into a CRS-NIZK [41]. However, the way they obtained the CS, and the way they modify their DP-NIZK into a CRS-NIZK is significantly different from ours. We elaborate on this below.

Compact CS Scheme by Katsumata et al. [40]: Similarly to us, their approach is to construct an ABE scheme and then convert it into a CS scheme. However, the requirements for the ABE are different from ours. For the ABE scheme, they require short secret keys, whereas we require short ciphertexts. Furthermore, they require the ABE scheme to be secure following a so-called "single-shot" reduction, where the reduction algorithm runs the adversary only once and perfectly simulates the view of the game. Roughly, this is equivalent to saying that the proof cannot go through hybrid arguments. Therefore, their approach does not seem to be promising when we try to construct a compact CS scheme from a *static* assumption. Notably, their single-shot reduction requirement excludes the dual system encryption methodology [54], which is a powerful tool for proving the security of an ABE scheme from static assumptions. On the other hand, we manage to employ the dual system encryption methodology to obtain an ABE scheme with the desired properties from static assumptions.

From DP-NIZK to CRS-NIZK in Katsumata et al. [41]: They construct a DP-NIZK (as an intermediate goal) by applying the Kim-Wu conversion on their CS scheme. They then modify their DP-NIZK to a CRS-NIZK scheme by a non-generic technique. Here, we review their approach and compare it with ours. Recall that, in general, a DP-NIZK constructed from a CS via the Kim-Wu conversion, the CRS consists of the verification key of the CS $\mathsf{CS.vk}$, and the secret proving key consists of the secret key of an SKE K and a signing key of the CS $\mathsf{CS.sk}_{C_K}$. Their observation was that they can divide the CS verification key $\mathsf{CS.vk}$ into two components $\mathsf{CS.vk} := (\mathsf{CS.vk}_0, \mathsf{CSvk}_1)$ such that $\mathsf{CS.vk}_1$ is very short and anyone can compute $\mathsf{CS.vk}_1$ from $\mathsf{CS.sk}_{C_K}$ and K. Note that as

---

[4] Actually, the definition of online-offline decomposability is slightly different from the one in the main body, but the latter implies the former.

a stand-alone CS scheme, the secret key $\mathsf{CS.sk}_{C_K}$ is computed using the master key of the CS only *after* $\mathsf{CS.vk} = (\mathsf{vk}_0, \mathsf{vk}_1)$ is defined. What they observe is that the other direction of the computation is possible using the specific structure of their CS scheme. In order to construct a CRS-NIZK using this special structure, they remove $\mathsf{CS.vk}_1$ from the CRS. Then they let the prover pick K and $\mathsf{CS.sk}_{C_K}$ on their own and let it compute $\mathsf{CS.vk}_1$. At this point, the prover can generate a proof as in the original DP-NIZK. In order to prevent the adversary to maliciously choose K, $\mathsf{CS.sk}_{C_K}$, and $\mathsf{CS.vk}_1$, they let the prover prove consistency among the components using a non-compact NIZK and outputs the proof along with $\mathsf{CS.vk}_1$. The additional consistency proof by the non-compact NIZK as well as $\mathsf{CS.vk}_1$ appended to the final proof does not harm the compactness of the resulting NIZK, since all parameters involved are compact.

We note that their approach is not applicable to our specific CS scheme. The reason is that our signing key for the CS is as large as the circuit size and we cannot prove the consistency between K, $\mathsf{CS.sk}_{C_K}$, and $\mathsf{CS.vk}_1$ compactly no matter how we divide the CS verification key. We, therefore, take a different path from theirs and this entails several challenges that are not present in their approach.

1.4 Related Work

The first NIZK for **NP** was given by [16] based on the existence of trapdoor permutations (whose arguments were later refined by several works [3,24]). The next generation of NIZK following a completely different set of approaches were provided by Groth, Ostrovsky, and Sahai [30] (GOS-NIZK) based on pairings. Due to its simplicity and efficiency, pairing-based NIZKs have flourished into a research topic on its own, and the original GOS-NIZK has been followed by many subsequent works [20,27,28,31,45]. More than roughly a decade later, a new type of NIZKs based on indistinguishable obfuscation (iO) were proposed [4,5,12,51]. Finally, very recently, a different path for designing NIZKs based on correlation intractable hash functions (CIH) [9,10,39] have gained much attention and has finally lead to the closing of a long-standing problem of constructing NIZKs based on lattice-based assumptions [50].

2 Definitions

We omit definitions of standard cryptographic primitives due to limited space.

2.1 Preliminaries on Bilinear Maps

A bilinear group generator GGen takes as input 1^κ and outputs a group description $\mathbb{G} = (p, G_1, G_2, G_T, e, g_1, g_2)$, where p is a prime such that $p > 2^{2\kappa}$, G_1, G_2, and G_T are cyclic groups of order q, $e : G_1 \times G_2 \to G_T$ is a non-degenerate bilinear map, and g_1 and g_2 are generators of G_1 and G_2, respectively. We require that the group operations in G_1, G_2, and G_T as well as the bilinear map e can be efficiently computed. We employ the implicit representation of group elements: for a matrix $\mathbf{A}$ over $\mathbb{Z}_q$, we define $[\mathbf{A}]_1 := g_1^{\mathbf{A}}$, $[\mathbf{A}]_2 := g_2^{\mathbf{A}}$, $[\mathbf{A}]_T := g_T^{\mathbf{A}}$, where exponentiation is carried out component-wise.

Definition 2.1 (MDDH$_k$ assumption [15]). *Let GGen be a group generator. We say that the matrix DDH (MDDH$_k$) assumption holds on G_1 with respect to GGen, if for all PPT adversaries $\mathcal{A}$, we have*

$$\mathsf{Adv}_{\mathcal{A}}^{\mathsf{mddh}}(\lambda) := |\Pr\left[\mathcal{A}(\mathbb{G}, [\mathbf{M}]_1, [\mathbf{Ms}]_1) \rightarrow 1\right] - \Pr\left[\mathcal{A}(\mathbb{G}, [\mathbf{M}]_1, [\mathbf{u}]_1) \rightarrow 1\right]|$$

is negligible, where the probability is taken over the choice of $\mathbb{G} \xleftarrow{\$} \mathsf{GGen}(1^\kappa)$, $\mathbf{M} \xleftarrow{\$} \mathbb{Z}_p^{(k+1) \times k}$, $\mathbf{s} \xleftarrow{\$} \mathbb{Z}_p^k$, and $\mathbf{u} \xleftarrow{\$} \mathbb{Z}_p^{k+1}$. We can similarly define MDDH$_k$ assumption on G_2.

In fact, the above assumption is called MDDH$_k$ assumption for uniform distribution by Escala et al. [15] since $\mathbf{M}$ is chosen uniformly at random. As shown by them, MDDH$_k$ assumptions for uniform distribution is weaker than MDDH$_k$ assumption for all other distributions and in particular is implied by the k-LIN assumption.

2.2 Non-interactive Zero-Knowledge Arguments

Let $\mathcal{R} \subseteq \{0,1\}^* \times \{0,1\}^*$ be a polynomial time recognizable binary relation. For $(x, w) \in \mathcal{R}$, we call x as the statement and w as the witness. Let $\mathcal{L}$ be the corresponding **NP** language $\mathcal{L} = \{x \mid \exists w \text{ s.t. } (x, w) \in \mathcal{R}\}$. Below, we define non-interactive zero-knowledge arguments for **NP** languages.[5]

Definition 2.2 (NIZK Arguments). *A non-interactive zero-knowledge (NIZK) argument Π_{NIZK} for the relation $\mathcal{R}$ consists of PPT algorithms (Setup, Prove, Verify).*

$\mathsf{Setup}(1^\kappa) \rightarrow \mathsf{crs}$: *The setup algorithm takes as input the security parameter 1^κ and outputs a common reference string crs.*

$\mathsf{Prove}(\mathsf{crs}, x, w) \rightarrow \pi$: *The prover's algorithm takes as input a common reference string crs, a statement x, and a witness w and outputs a proof π.*

$\mathsf{Verify}(\mathsf{crs}, x, \pi) \rightarrow \top \text{ or } \bot$: *The verifier's algorithm takes as input a common reference string, a statement x, and a proof π and outputs $\top$ to indicate acceptance of the proof and $\bot$ otherwise.*

We consider the following requirements for a NIZK argument Π_{NIZK}, where the probabilities are taken over the random choice of the algorithms.

Completeness. *For all pairs $(x, w) \in \mathcal{R}$, if we run $\mathsf{crs} \xleftarrow{\$} \mathsf{Setup}(1^\kappa)$, then we have $\Pr[\pi \xleftarrow{\$} \mathsf{Prove}(\mathsf{crs}, x, w) : \mathsf{Verify}(\mathsf{crs}, x, \pi) = \top] = 1$.*

---

[5] We say it is a non-interactive zero-knowledge *proofs* when the soundness property holds for even unbounded adversaries. In this paper, we will only be interested in computationally bounded adversaries.

Adaptive Soundness. *For all PPT adversaries* $\mathcal{A}$, *if we run* $\mathsf{crs} \xleftarrow{\$} \mathsf{Setup}(1^\kappa)$, *then we have*

$$\Pr[(x, \pi) \xleftarrow{\$} \mathcal{A}(1^\kappa, \mathsf{crs}) : x \notin \mathcal{L} \wedge \mathsf{Verify}(\mathsf{crs}, x, \pi) = \top] = \mathsf{negl}(\kappa).$$

Non-Adaptive Soundness. *We also consider the slightly weaker variant of adaptive soundness above. For all PPT adversaries* $\mathcal{A}$ *and for all* $x \notin \mathcal{L}$, *if we run* $\mathsf{crs} \xleftarrow{\$} \mathsf{Setup}(1^\kappa)$, *then we have*

$$\Pr[\pi \xleftarrow{\$} \mathcal{A}(1^\kappa, \mathsf{crs}, x) : \mathsf{Verify}(\mathsf{crs}, x, \pi) = \top] = \mathsf{negl}(\kappa).$$

Zero-Knowledge. *For all adversaries* $\mathcal{A}$, *there exists a PPT simulator* $\mathcal{S} = (\mathcal{S}_1, \mathcal{S}_2)$ *such that if we run* $\mathsf{crs} \xleftarrow{\$} \mathsf{Setup}(1^\kappa)$ *and* $(\overline{\mathsf{crs}}, \bar{\tau}) \xleftarrow{\$} \mathcal{S}_1(1^\kappa)$, *then we have*

$$\left| \Pr[\mathcal{A}^{\mathcal{O}_0(\mathsf{crs}, \cdot, \cdot)}(1^\kappa, \mathsf{crs}) = 1] - \Pr[\mathcal{A}^{\mathcal{O}_1(\overline{\mathsf{crs}}, \bar{\tau}, \cdot, \cdot)}(1^\kappa, \overline{\mathsf{crs}}) = 1] \right| = \mathsf{negl}(\kappa),$$

where $\mathcal{O}_0(\mathsf{crs}, x, w)$ *outputs* $\mathsf{Prove}(\mathsf{crs}, x, w)$ *if* $(x, w) \in \mathcal{R}$ *and* $\perp$ *otherwise, and* $\mathcal{O}_1(\overline{\mathsf{crs}}, \bar{\tau}, x, w)$ *outputs* $\mathcal{S}_2(\overline{\mathsf{crs}}, \bar{\tau}, x)$ *if* $(x, w) \in \mathcal{R}$ *and* $\perp$ *otherwise. We say it is* computational *(resp.* statistical*) zero-knowledge if the adversary is computationally bounded (resp. unbounded). Moreover, we further say it is* perfect *zero-knowledge if the above r.h.s. equals 0 for computationally unbounded adversaries.*

We also define a stronger notion of soundness called *extractability* following [41].

Definition 2.3 (Extractability). *An NIZK argument is said to be extractable if the following is satisfied:*

Extractability. *There is a deterministic algorithm* $\mathsf{Extract}$ *(called extractor) such that for all PPT adversary* $\mathcal{A}$, *we have*

$$\Pr\left[\begin{array}{c} \mathsf{Verify}(\mathsf{crs}, x, \pi) = \top \\ (x, w) \notin \mathcal{R} \end{array} \middle| \begin{array}{c} \mathsf{crs} \xleftarrow{\$} \mathsf{Setup}(1^\kappa), (x, \pi) \xleftarrow{\$} \mathcal{A}(\mathsf{crs}), \\ w \xleftarrow{\$} \mathsf{Extract}(r_\mathsf{Setup}, \pi) \end{array} \right] \leq \mathsf{negl}(\kappa).$$

where r_Setup *is the randomness used in* Setup *to generate* crs.

We can convert any adaptively sound NIZK into an extractable one additionally assuming the existence of PKE [41].

Lemma 2.1. *If there exist an adaptively sound NIZK for all of* ***NP*** *and a CPA-secure PKE scheme, then there exists an extractable NIZK for all of* ***NP***.

2.3 $\mathbf{NC^1}$ Circuits and Monotone Formulae

Here, we define Monotone Boolean formula following Kowalczyk and Wee [44].

Monotone Boolean Formula. A monotone Boolean formula $f : \{0,1\}^n \to \{0,1\}$ is specified by a directed acyclic graph (DAG) with three kinds of nodes: input gate nodes, gate nodes, and a single output node. Input nodes have in-degree 0 and out-degree 1, AND/OR nodes have in-degree (fan-in) 2 and out-degree (fan-out) 1, and the output node has in-degree 1 and out-degree 0. We number the edges (wires) $1, 2, \ldots, m$, and each gate node is defined by a tuple (g, a_g, b_g, c_g) where $g : \{0,1\}^2 \to \{0,1\}$ is either AND or OR, a_g and b_g are the incoming wires, c_g is the outgoing wire and $a_g, b_g < c_g$. The size of a formula m is the number of edges in the underlying DAG and the depth of a formula d is the length of the longest path from the output node.

$\mathbf{NC^1}$ **and Boolean Formulae.** The following lemma summarizes the well-known equivalence between the monotone formulae and $\mathbf{NC^1}$ circuits.

Lemma 2.2. *Let $d = d(\kappa), n = n(\kappa)$, and $s = s(\kappa)$ be integers. There exist integer parameters $m = m(d, n, s)$ and deterministic algorithms EncInp and EncCir with the following properties.*

- *$\mathsf{EncInp}(x) \to \hat{x} \in \{0,1\}^{2n}$, where $x \in \{0,1\}^n$.*
- *$\mathsf{EncCir}(C) \to f$, where $C : \{0,1\}^n \to \{0,1\}$ is a circuit with depth and size bounded by d and s, respectively and f is a monotone Boolean formula of size m with input space being $\{0,1\}^{2n}$.*

We have $f(\hat{x}) = 1$ if and only if $C(x) = 1$. Furthermore, the running time of EncCir is $\mathsf{poly}(n, s, 2^d)$. In particular, if C is a polynomial-sized circuit with logarithmic depth (i.e., if the circuit is in $\mathbf{NC^1}$), EncCir runs in polynomial time and we have $m = \mathsf{poly}(\kappa)$. Furthermore, for $x \in \{0,1\}^n$, we have $\hat{x} = x_1 \bar{x}_1 x_2 \bar{x}_2 \cdots x_n \bar{x}_n$, where $\bar{x}_i$ is the flip of x_i.

See the full version for the details.

3 KP-ABE with Compact Ciphertexts

In this section, we give the construction of KP-ABE scheme for monotone Boolean formulae with constant-size ciphertexts by extending the scheme by Kowalczyk and Wee [44]. The scheme will be used in the construction of compact constrained signature scheme in Sect. 4, which will in turn be used for the construction of our compact NIZKs in Sect. 5. Our KP-ABE scheme would be of independent interest, since this is the first KP-ABE scheme for Boolean formulae with constant-size ciphertexts that is secure under a static assumption (rather than non-static q-type assumption).

3.1   Preliminaries

First, we review the secret sharing scheme for monotone Boolean formulae used by Kowalczyk and Wee, which is based on secret sharing schemes in [34,35,53].

Definition 3.1 (Secret Sharing). *A secret sharing scheme consists of two algorithms* (share, reconstruct).

share(f, μ): *This algorithm takes a (monotone) Boolean formula* $f : \{0, 1\}^n \to \{0, 1\}$ *and* $\mu \in \mathbb{Z}_p$ *and outputs shares* $\mu_1, \ldots, \mu_{\hat{m}} \in \mathbb{Z}_p$ *and a function* $\rho : [\hat{m}] \to \{0, 1, \ldots, n\}$. *We assume that* ρ *is deterministically determined from* f.
reconstruct$(f, x, \{\mu_j\}_{j \in S})$: *This algorithms takes an input* $x \in \{0, 1\}^n$ *for* f, f, *and a subset of shares* $\{\mu_j\}_{j \in S}$ *where* $S \subseteq [\hat{m}]$ *and outputs the original value* μ.

A secret sharing scheme satisfies the following properties.

Correctness: *For all* $x \in \{0, 1\}^n$, $f : \{0, 1\}^n \to \{0, 1\}$, $\mu \in \mathbb{Z}_p$, $(\{\mu_j\}_{j \in [\hat{m}]}, \rho) \leftarrow$ share(f, μ) *such that* $f(x) = 1$, *it holds that* reconstruct$(f, x, \{\mu_j\}_{\rho(j)=0 \vee x_{\rho(j)} = 1}) = \mu$.
Security: *For all* $x \in \{0, 1\}^n$, $f : \{0, 1\}^n \to \{0, 1\}$, $\mu, \mu' \in \mathbb{Z}_p$ *such that* $f(x) = 0$, *the following distributions are the same:*

$$\{\{\mu_j\}_{\rho(j)=0 \vee x_{\rho(j)}=1} \mid (\{\mu_j\}_{j \in [\hat{m}]}, \rho) \leftarrow \text{share}(f, \mu)\}$$
$$\equiv \{\{\mu'_j\}_{\rho(j)=0 \vee x_{\rho(j)}=1} \mid (\{\mu'_j\}_{j \in [\hat{m}]}, \rho) \leftarrow \text{share}(f, \mu')\}$$

Linearity: *The algorithm* reconstruct *is a linear function of the shares over* $\mathbb{Z}_p$. *That is, there exists* $\omega_j \in \mathbb{Z}_p$ *for* $j \in [\hat{m}]$ *and we can compute* $\mu = \sum_{\rho(j)=0 \vee x_{\rho(j)}=1} \omega_j \mu_j$.

We present their secret sharing scheme (share, reconstruct) in Fig. 1 as it is. The scheme satisfies Definition 3.1. As Kowalczyk and Wee observed, it is easy to extend the secret sharing scheme to treat vectors of secrets. That is, for a vector $\mathbf{v} \in \mathbb{Z}_p^k$, we define share$(f, \mathbf{v}) := (\{\mathbf{v}_j = (v_{1,j}, \ldots, v_{k,j})\}_{j \in [\hat{m}]}, \rho)$ where $(\{v_{i,j}\}_{j \in [\hat{m}]}, \rho) \leftarrow$ share(f, v_i) and reconstruct$(f, x, \{\mathbf{v}_j\}_{\rho(j)=0 \vee x_{\rho(j)}=1}) := \sum_{\rho(j)=0 \vee x_{\rho(j)}=1} \omega_j \mathbf{v}_j$ where $\{\omega_j\}_{j \in [\hat{m}]}$ is defined as above.

3.2   Construction

Here, we give the construction of KP-ABE with short ciphertext from the MDDH$_k$ assumption.

Setup$(1^\kappa, 1^n)$: Run $\mathbb{G} = (p, G_1, G_2, G_T, e) \xleftarrow{\$} \text{GGen}(1^\kappa)$. Sample $\mathbf{A} \xleftarrow{\$} \mathbb{Z}_p^{k \times (k+1)}$, $\mathbf{W}_i \xleftarrow{\$} \mathbb{Z}_p^{(k+1) \times k}$ for $i \in [n]$, $\mathbf{v} \xleftarrow{\$} \mathbb{Z}_p^{k+1}$ and output

$$\text{mpk} = ([\mathbf{A}]_1, [\mathbf{A}\mathbf{W}_1]_1, \ldots, [\mathbf{A}\mathbf{W}_n]_1, e([\mathbf{A}]_1, [\mathbf{v}]_2)), \quad \text{msk} = (\mathbf{v}, \mathbf{W}_1, \ldots, \mathbf{W}_n).$$

share(f, μ)

Input: A formula $f : \{0,1\}^n \to \{0,1\}$ of size m (that is, the number of edges in f is m) and a secret $\mu \in \mathbb{Z}_p$.

1. For each non-output wire $j = 1, \ldots, m-1$, choose a uniformly random $\hat{\mu}_j \xleftarrow{\$} \mathbb{Z}_p$. For the output wire, set $\hat{\mu}_m := \mu$.
2. For each outgoing wire j from input node i, add $\mu_j := \hat{\mu}_j$ to the output set of shares and set $\rho(j) := i$.
3. For each AND gate g with input wires a, b and output wire c, add $\mu_c := \hat{\mu}_c + \hat{\mu}_a + \hat{\mu}_b \in \mathbb{Z}_p$ to the output set of shares and set $\rho(c) := 0$.
4. For each OR gate g with input wires a, b and output wire c, add $\mu_{c_a} := \hat{\mu}_c + \hat{\mu}_a \in \mathbb{Z}_p$ and $\mu_{c_b} := \hat{\mu}_c + \hat{\mu}_b \in \mathbb{Z}_p$ to the output set of shares and set $\rho(c_a) := 0$ and $\rho(c_b) := 0$.
5. Output $(\{\mu_j\}_{j \in [\hat{m}]}, \rho)$.

reconstruct($f, x, \{\mu_j\}_{\rho(j)=0 \vee x_{\rho(j)}=1}$)

Input: A formula $f : \{0,1\}^n \to \{0,1\}$ of size m, $x \in \{0,1\}^n$, and $\{\mu_j\}_{\rho(j)=0 \vee x_{\rho(j)}=1}$.

From the leaves of the formula to the root, we compute the output wire value $\hat{\mu}_c$ at each node.

1. Given $\hat{\mu}_a, \hat{\mu}_b$ associated with the input wires a and b of an AND gate, we compute $\hat{\mu}_c = \mu_c - \hat{\mu}_a - \hat{\mu}_b$.
2. Given $\hat{\mu}_a$ (or $\hat{\mu}_b$) associated with the input wires a (or b) of an OR gate, we compute $\hat{\mu}_c = \mu_{c_a} - \hat{\mu}_a$ (or $\hat{\mu}_c = \mu_{c_b} - \hat{\mu}_b$).

Output $\mu = \hat{\mu}_m$.

Fig. 1. Information-theoretic linear secret sharing for monotone Boolean formulae by Kowalczyk and Wee [44]

Enc(mpk, x, M): To encrypt a message $M \in G_T$ for a string $x \in \{0,1\}^n$, sample $\mathbf{s} \xleftarrow{\$} \mathbb{Z}_p^k$ and output

$$\mathsf{ct}_x = \left(\mathsf{ct}_1 := [\mathbf{s}^\top \mathbf{A}]_1, \quad \mathsf{ct}_2 := \left[\mathbf{s}^\top \sum_{i:x_i=1} \mathbf{A}\mathbf{W}_i \right]_1, \quad \mathsf{ct}_3 := e([\mathbf{s}^\top \mathbf{A}]_1, [\mathbf{v}]_2) \cdot M \right).$$

KeyGen(msk, f): To generate a secret key for a Boolean formula f, sample $(\{\mathbf{v}_j\}_{j \in [\hat{m}]}, \rho) \xleftarrow{\$} \mathsf{share}(f, \mathbf{v})$, $\mathbf{r}_j \xleftarrow{\$} \mathbb{Z}_p^k$ and output sk_f, which consists of the following.

$$\left(\left\{ \mathsf{sk}_j := [\mathbf{r}_j]_2, \ \mathsf{sk}_{\rho(j),j} := [\mathbf{v}_j + \mathbf{W}_{\rho(j)}\mathbf{r}_j]_2, \ \{\mathsf{sk}_{i,j} := [\mathbf{W}_i \mathbf{r}_j]_2 \}_{i \in [n] \setminus \{\rho(j)\}} \right\}_{j \in [\hat{m}]} \right)$$

where $\mathbf{W}_0 = \mathbf{0}$ and $\hat{m}$ is the number of shares. We note that for j such that $\rho(j) = 0$, we have $[n] \setminus \{\rho(j)\} = [n]$.

$\mathsf{Dec}(\mathsf{mpk}, \mathsf{sk}_f, \mathsf{ct_x})$: Compute ω_j such that $\mathbf{v} = \sum_{j:\rho(j)=0 \vee x_{\rho(j)}=1} \omega_j \mathbf{v}_j$ and output

$$\mathsf{ct}_3 \cdot e \left(\mathsf{ct}_2, \prod_{j:\rho(j)=0 \vee x_{\rho(j)}=1} \mathsf{sk}_j^{\omega_j} \right) \cdot e \left(\mathsf{ct}_1, \prod_{j:\rho(j)=0 \vee x_{\rho(j)}=1} \left(\prod_{i:x_i=1} \mathsf{sk}_{i,j} \right)^{\omega_j} \right)^{-1} .$$

Correctness. The correctness follows since we have

$$\prod_{j:\rho(j)=0 \vee x_{\rho(j)}=1} \left(\prod_{i:x_i=1} \mathsf{sk}_{i,j} \right)^{\omega_j} = \left[\mathbf{v} + \sum_{i:\hat{x}_i=1} \mathbf{W}_i \mathbf{r} \right]_2 , \quad \prod_{j:\rho(j)=0 \vee x_{\rho(j)}=1} \mathsf{sk}_j^{\omega_j} = [\mathbf{r}]_2,$$

where $\mathbf{r} = \sum_{j:\rho(j)=0 \vee \hat{x}_{\rho(j)}=1} \omega_j \mathbf{r}_j$ for honestly generated secret key sk for f such that $f(x) = 1$ from the correctness of the secret sharing.

3.3 Security

We prove the following theorem.

Theorem 3.1. *The above construction is adaptively secure under the* MDDH_k *assumption.*

For proving this theorem, we first prove the following lemma.

Lemma 3.1. *Under the* MDDH_k *assumption,*

$$\left| \Pr \left[\begin{array}{c} \mu^{(0)}, \mu^{(1)} \xleftarrow{\$} \mathbb{Z}_p; \mathbf{w}_0 := \mathbf{0}, \mathbf{w}_1, \ldots, \mathbf{w}_n \xleftarrow{\$} \mathbb{Z}_p^k; \\ 1 \leftarrow \mathcal{A}^{\mathcal{O}_{\mathsf{F},0}(\cdot), \mathcal{O}_{\mathsf{X}}(\cdot), \mathcal{O}_{\mathsf{E}}(\cdot)}(\mu^{(0)}) \end{array} \right] \right.$$
$$\left. - \Pr \left[\begin{array}{c} \mu^{(0)}, \mu^{(1)} \xleftarrow{\$} \mathbb{Z}_p; \mathbf{w}_0 := \mathbf{0}, \mathbf{w}_1, \ldots, \mathbf{w}_n \xleftarrow{\$} \mathbb{Z}_p^k; \\ 1 \leftarrow \mathcal{A}^{\mathcal{O}_{\mathsf{F},1}(\cdot), \mathcal{O}_{\mathsf{X}}(\cdot), \mathcal{O}_{\mathsf{E}}(\cdot, \cdot)}(\mu^{(0)}) \end{array} \right] \right|$$

is negligible where $\mathcal{A}$ *adaptively interacts with three oracles:*

$$\mathcal{O}_{\mathsf{F},\beta}(f) := \left(\{\mu_j\}_{j:\rho(j)=0} \cup \left\{ [\mathbf{r}_j]_2, [\mu_j + \mathbf{w}_{\rho(j)}^\top \mathbf{r}_j]_2, \{[\mathbf{w}_i^\top \mathbf{r}_j]_2\}_{i \in [n] \setminus \{\rho(j)\}} \right\}_{j \in [\hat{m}]} \right)$$
where $(\{\mu_j\}_{j \in [\hat{m}]}, \rho) \leftarrow \mathsf{share}(f, \mu^{(\beta)})$
$$\mathcal{O}_{\mathsf{X}}(x) := (\{\mathbf{w}_i\}_{i:x_i=1})$$
$$\mathcal{O}_{\mathsf{E}}() := \left([\mathbf{r}]_2, \{[\mathbf{w}_i^\top \mathbf{r}]_2\}_{i \in [n]} \right) \text{ where } \mathbf{r} \xleftarrow{\$} \mathbb{Z}_p^k$$

with the restriction that (i) only one query is made to each of $\mathcal{O}_{\mathsf{F},\beta}(\cdot)$ *and* $\mathcal{O}_{\mathsf{X}}(\cdot)$, *and (ii) the queries* f *and* x *to* $\mathcal{O}_{\mathsf{F},\beta}(\cdot)$ *and* $\mathcal{O}_{\mathsf{X}}(\cdot)$ *respectively, satisfy* $f(x) = 0$.

Note that the statement of the lemma is similar to that of Theorem 2 in [44]. There, $\mathcal{O}_{\mathsf{F},\beta}(f)$ returns

$$\left(\{\mu_j\}_{j:\rho(j)=0} \cup \left\{ [\mathbf{r}_j]_2, [\mu_j + \mathbf{w}_{\rho(j)} \mathbf{r}_j]_2 \right\}_{j:\rho(j) \neq 0} \right)$$

and $\mathcal{O}_E$ takes as input $i \in [m]$ and returns $([\mathbf{r}]_2, [\mathbf{w}_i^\top \mathbf{r}]_2)$.[6] Since the answers by the oracles in [44] can be simulated by our oracles by just stripping off appropriate components, our statement is stronger than theirs. Nonetheless, we can prove the above lemma with very similar proof to that of Theorem 2 in [44]. See the full version for the details.

Then we prove Theorem 3.1. The proof of the theorem is again similar to the equivalent in [44], but with some appropriate adaptations.

Proof of Theorem 3.1. We prove the theorem by considering a sequence of hybrid games. To define the hybrid distributions, it would be helpful to first give names of various forms of ciphertext and secret keys that will be used. A ciphertext (of message M under attribute x) can be one of the following forms:

Normal: A normal ciphertext is generated as in the scheme.
SF: This is the same as normal ciphertext except that $\mathbf{s}^\top \mathbf{A}$ is replaced by a random vector $\mathbf{c}^\top \xleftarrow{\$} \mathbb{Z}_p^{k+1}$. That is,

$$\mathsf{ct}_x := \left(\mathsf{ct}_1 := \left[\boxed{\mathbf{c}^\top} \right]_1, \ \mathsf{ct}_2 := \left[\boxed{\mathbf{c}^\top} \sum_{i:x_i=1} \mathbf{W}_i \right]_1, \ \mathsf{ct}_3 := e\left(\left[\boxed{\mathbf{c}^\top} \right]_1, [\mathbf{k}]_2 \right) \cdot M \right).$$

A secret key (for a Boolean formula f) can be one of the following forms:

Normal: A normal key is generated by KeyGen.
SF: An SF key is sampled as a normal key except that $\mathbf{v}$ is replaced by $\mathbf{v} + \delta \mathbf{a}^\perp$, where a fresh δ is chosen per SF key and $\mathbf{a}^\perp$ is any fixed $\mathbf{a}^\perp \in \mathbb{Z}_p^{k+1} \setminus \{\mathbf{0}\}$. That is, sk_f consists of

$$\left(\left\{ \mathsf{sk}_j := [\mathbf{r}_j]_2, \ \mathsf{sk}_{\rho(j),j} := [\mathbf{v}_j + \mathbf{W}_{\rho(j)} \mathbf{r}_j]_2, \ \{\mathsf{sk}_{i,j} := [\mathbf{W}_i \mathbf{r}_j]_2 \}_{i \in [n] \setminus \{\rho(j)\}} \right\}_{j \in [\hat{m}]} \right)$$

where $(\{\mathbf{v}_j\}_{j \in [\hat{m}]}, \rho) \xleftarrow{\$} \mathsf{share}(f, \boxed{\mathbf{v} + \delta \mathbf{a}^\perp}), \ \mathbf{r}_j \xleftarrow{\$} \mathbb{Z}_p^k.$

We then define the following sequence of games to prove the security. Let the number of key generation queries made by an adversary be Q.

- H_0 : This is the real security game for adaptive security where all ciphertexts and keys are normal.
- H_1 : This game is the same as H_0 except that the challenge ciphertext is SF.
- $\mathsf{H}_{2,\ell}$: This game is the same as H_1 except that the first ℓ keys are SF and the remaining $Q - \ell$ keys are normal. The game is defined for $\ell = 0, 1, \ldots, Q$.
- H_3 : This is the same as H_Q except that the message to be encrypted is replaced by a random group element $\widetilde{M}$.

---

[6] More accurately, $\mathcal{O}_E$ takes as input $[M]_2 \in G_2$ in addition to i in [44]. But we can ignore the additional input $[M]_2$ without loss of generality.

Let us fix a PPT adversary $\mathcal{A}$ and denote the advantage of $\mathcal{A}$ in H_{xx} by Adv_{xx}. We can easily see that $\mathsf{H}_1 \equiv \mathsf{H}_{2,0}$ and $\mathsf{Adv}_3 = 0$. Therefore, to complete the proof of Theorem 3.1, it suffices to prove any neighboring games are computationally indistinguishable from the adversary's view. We omit proofs of them since they are proven similarly to their counterparts in [44] except that we need some adaptations for the analysis of the game hop from $\mathsf{H}_{2,\ell}$ to $\mathsf{H}_{2,\ell+1}$ by using Lemma 3.1. See the full version for the full proof.   □

4 Compact Constrained Signature

4.1 Constrained Signature

We provide definition of a constrained signature (CS) scheme. We also provide an additional feature (i.e., online/offline efficiency) for CS schemes which will play a vital role in our compact NIZK construction in Sect. 5.

Definition 4.1 (Constrained Signature). *A constrained signature (CS) scheme with message space $\{0,1\}^n$ for a circuit class $\mathcal{C} = \{\, C : \{0,1\}^n \to \{0,1\} \,\}$ consists of PPT algorithms (CS.Setup, CS.KeyGen, CS.Sign, CS.Vrfy).*

CS.Setup$(1^\kappa, 1^n) \to$ (msk, vk)*: The setup algorithm on input the security parameter 1^λ and the input length 1^n, outputs a master secret key msk and a verification key vk.*
CS.KeyGen(msk, C) $\to$ sk$_C$*: The key generation algorithm on input a master secret key msk and a circuit $C \in \mathcal{C}$, outputs a signing key sk$_C$.*
CS.Sign(sk$_C$, x) $\to \sigma$*: The signing algorithm on input the signing key sk$_C$ and message $x \in \{0,1\}^n$, outputs a signature σ.*
CS.Vrfy(vk, x, σ) $\to \top$ or $\bot$*: The verification algorithm on input the verification key vk, message x, and signature σ, outputs either $\bot$ (indicating the signature is valid) or $\top$ (indicating the signature is invalid).*

A CS scheme must satisfy the following requirements.

Correctness. For all $\kappa \in \mathbb{N}$, $n = n(\kappa) \in \mathbb{N}$, (msk, vk) $\xleftarrow{\$}$ CS.Setup$(1^\kappa, 1^n)$, $x \in \{0,1\}^n$, $C \in \mathcal{C}$ such that $C(x) = 1$, and sk$_C \xleftarrow{\$}$ CS.KeyGen(msk, C), we have

$$\Pr[\mathsf{CS.Vrfy}(\mathsf{vk}, x, \mathsf{CS.Sign}(\mathsf{sk}_C, x)) = \top] = 1$$

Unforgeability. We define (adaptive) unforgeability for a CS scheme. The security notion is defined by the following game between a challenger and an adversary $\mathcal{A}$.

Setup: The challenger runs (msk, vk) $\xleftarrow{\$}$ CS.Setup$(1^\kappa, 1^n)$ and gives vk to $\mathcal{A}$. It also prepares an empty list $\mathcal{Q}$.
Key Queries: $\mathcal{A}$ can adaptively make key queries unbounded polynomially many times throughout the game. When $\mathcal{A}$ queries $C \in \mathcal{C}$, the challenger runs sk$_C \xleftarrow{\$}$ CS.KeyGen(msk, C) and returns sk$_C$ to $\mathcal{A}$. Finally, the challenger updates $\mathcal{Q} \leftarrow \mathcal{Q} \cup \{\, C \,\}$.

Forgery: Eventually, $\mathcal{A}$ outputs (x^*, σ^*) as the forgery. We say $\mathcal{A}$ *wins* if $\mathsf{CS.Vrfy}(\mathsf{vk}, x^*, \sigma^*) = \top$ holds. Furthermore, we say that $\mathcal{A}$ is *admissible* if $C(x^*) = 0$ holds for all $C \in \mathcal{Q}$ at the end of the game.

We say the CS scheme is (adaptively) *unforgeable* if the winning probability for all admissible PPT adversaries $\mathcal{A}$ in the above game is $\mathsf{negl}(\kappa)$, where the probability is taken over the randomness of all algorithms.

The following property is optional in the sense that our CS scheme can achieve the following property, but the property is not strictly necessary for our application of CS to the construction of compact NIZKs.

Context-Hiding (optional). For all $\kappa, n \in \mathbb{N}$, $(\mathsf{mpk}, \mathsf{msk}) \xleftarrow{\$} \mathsf{Setup}(1^\kappa, 1^n)$, $x \in \{0,1\}^n$, $C_0, C_1 \in \mathcal{C}$, $(\mathsf{msk}, \mathsf{vk}) \xleftarrow{\$} \mathsf{CS.Setup}(1^\kappa, 1^n)$, $\mathsf{sk}_{C_0} \xleftarrow{\$} \mathsf{CS.KeyGen}(\mathsf{msk}, C_0)$, and $\mathsf{sk}_{C_1} \xleftarrow{\$} \mathsf{CS.KeyGen}(\mathsf{msk}, C_1)$, we need that the following distributions are statistically close:

$$\{\sigma \xleftarrow{\$} \mathsf{CS.Sign}(\mathsf{sk}_{C_0}, x)\} \overset{\text{stat}}{\approx} \{\sigma \xleftarrow{\$} \mathsf{CS.Sign}(\mathsf{sk}_{C_1}, x)\}$$

where the probability is only over the randomness used by $\mathsf{CS.Sign}$.

Additionally to the above essential requirements for CS, we introduce a natural notion of *decomposable online-offline efficiency*. At a high level, this notion states that if we (partially) knew the message x to be signed in advance, then we can modify the verification key vk to a message specific verification key vk_x which allows for an efficient verification of signature σ with running time independent of $|x|$. More formally, the notion is defined as follows.

Definition 4.2 (Decomposable Online-Offline Efficiency). *A constrained signature with message space $\{0,1\}^n$ for a circuit class $\mathcal{C} = \{C : \{0,1\}^n \to \{0,1\}\}$ is said to have decomposable online-offline efficiency if there further exists PPT algorithms $(\mathsf{CS.Aggrgt}, \mathsf{CS.VrfyOnL})$ exhibiting the following properties.*

- *The verification key vk can be decomposed into $\mathsf{vk} = (\mathsf{vk}_0, \{\mathsf{vk}_{i,b} \in \mathcal{VK}\}_{i \in [n], b \in \{0,1\}})$, where $\mathcal{VK}$ is a space of verification key component.*
- *Any component in $\mathcal{VK}$, any honestly generated vk_0, and any honestly generated signature σ can be represented as binary strings of fixed polynomial length $\mathsf{poly}(\kappa)$. In particular, length of these components are independent from n.*
- *Algorithm $\mathsf{CS.Aggrgt}$ takes as input an element of $\mathcal{VK}^* = \cup_{\ell \in \mathbb{N}} \mathcal{VK}^\ell$ and outputs an element in $\mathcal{VK}$. We require that for any $y, z \in \{0,1\}^*$ such that $x = y \| z \in \{0,1\}^n$, we have*

$$\mathsf{CS.Aggrgt}\left(\{\mathsf{vk}_{i,x_i}\}_{i \in [n]}\right)$$
$$= \mathsf{CS.Aggrgt}\left(\mathsf{CS.Aggrgt}\left(\{\mathsf{vk}_{i,y_i}\}_{i \in [|y|]}\right), \mathsf{CS.Aggrgt}\left(\{\mathsf{vk}_{|y|+i,z_i}\}_{i \in [|z|]}\right)\right).$$

- *Algorithm $\mathsf{CS.VrfyOnL}$ takes as input vk_0, a component in $\mathcal{VK}$ and a signature in σ, and outputs either $\top$ or $\bot$. We require that for any $x \in \{0,1\}^n$, for any honestly generated vk, and for any (possibly maliciously generated) σ, we have*

$$\mathsf{CS.Vrfy}(\mathsf{vk}, x, \sigma) = \mathsf{CS.VrfyOnL}\left(\mathsf{vk}_0, \mathsf{CS.Aggrgt}\left(\{\mathsf{vk}_{i,x_i}\}_{i \in [n]}\right), \sigma\right).$$

Observe that the input length of CS.VrfyOnL *is independent from* n*, which follows from the second item of this definition. We require that the running time of* CS.VrfyOnL *is independent from* n *as well.*

4.2   Construction and Security

Here, we give the construction of our constrained signature (CS) scheme that will be used for the construction of the compact NIZK. The CS scheme has very compact signature size and the decomposable online-offline efficiency defined in Definition 4.2. In order to get the CS scheme, we apply the folklore conversion that converts ABE into CS to our compact KP-ABE scheme in Sect. 3, where the signing key sk_f for the function f in the CS scheme is the same as the secret key sk_f for the same function f in the ABE scheme, and the signature on a string x in the CS scheme is certain "aggregated form" of the secret key that is derived when decrypting an ABE ciphertext encrypted for the attribute x. To verify a signature on x in the CS, we encrypt a random message for x in the underlying ABE and then see if the message is recovered or not when decrypting the ciphertext using the signature as an (aggregated form of) secret key.

The CS scheme obtained by the above conversion can only deal with monotone Boolean formulae, since the original ABE is for the same class of functions. For our purpose, we need CS scheme for $\mathbf{NC}^1$ circuits, which is more general class than monotone Boolean formulae. This gap can be filled using Lemma 2.2. We then provide the description of the construction.

$\mathsf{CS.Setup}(1^\kappa, 1^n)$: Run $\mathbb{G} = (p, G_1, G_2, G_T, e) \xleftarrow{\$} \mathsf{GGen}(1^\kappa)$. Sample $\mathbf{A} \xleftarrow{\$} \mathbb{Z}_p^{k \times (k+1)}$, $\mathbf{W}_i \xleftarrow{\$} \mathbb{Z}_p^{(k+1) \times k}$ for $i \in [2n]$ and $\mathbf{v} \xleftarrow{\$} \mathbb{Z}_p^{k+1}$ and output

$$\mathsf{vk} = ([\mathbf{A}]_1, [\mathbf{AW}_1]_1, \ldots, [\mathbf{AW}_{2n}]_1, e([\mathbf{A}]_1, [\mathbf{v}]_2)), \quad \mathsf{msk} = (\mathbf{v}, \mathbf{W}_1, \ldots, \mathbf{W}_{2n}).$$

$\mathsf{CS.KeyGen}(\mathsf{msk}, C)$: To generate a signing key for a circuit C, run $\mathsf{EncCir}(C) \to f$. Then sample $(\{\mathbf{v}_j\}_{j \in [\hat{m}]}, \rho) \xleftarrow{\$} \mathsf{share}(f, \mathbf{v})$ and $\mathbf{r}_j \xleftarrow{\$} \mathbb{Z}_p^k$ for $j \in [\hat{m}]$ and output sk_f, which consists of the following.

$$\left(\left\{ \mathsf{sk}_j := [\mathbf{r}_j]_2, \; \mathsf{sk}_{\rho(j),j} := [\mathbf{v}_j + \mathbf{W}_{\rho(j)}\mathbf{r}_j]_2, \; \{\mathsf{sk}_{i,j} := [\mathbf{W}_i \mathbf{r}_j]_2 \}_{i \in [2n] \setminus \{\rho(j)\}} \right\}_{j \in [\hat{m}]} \right)$$

where $\mathbf{W}_0 = \mathbf{0}$ and $\hat{m}$ is the number of shares that are generated by $\mathsf{share}(f, \mathbf{v})$.

$\mathsf{CS.Sign}(\mathsf{sk}_f, x)$: Set $\hat{x} := \mathsf{EncInp}(x)$ and compute ω_j such that $\mathbf{v} = \sum_{j: \rho(j)=0 \vee \hat{x}_{\rho(j)}=1} \omega_j \mathbf{v}_j$ and output

$$\sigma = \left(\sigma_1 = \prod_{j: \rho(j)=0 \vee \hat{x}_{\rho(j)}=1} \left(\prod_{i: \hat{x}_i=1} \mathsf{sk}_{i,j} \right)^{\omega_j}, \quad \sigma_2 = \prod_{j: \rho(j)=0 \vee \hat{x}_{\rho(j)}=1} \mathsf{sk}_j^{\omega_j} \right).$$

CS.Vrfy(vk, x, σ): Parse $\sigma \to (\sigma_1, \sigma_2) \in G_2^k \times G_2^k$ and output $\perp$ if the signature is not in this form. Otherwise, compute $\hat{x} = \mathsf{EncInp}(x)$ and

$$\mathsf{vk}' = \prod_{i:\hat{x}_i=1} [\mathbf{A}\mathbf{W}_i]_1. \tag{1}$$

Then output $\top$ if the following holds and $\perp$ otherwise:

$$e([\mathbf{A}]_1, \sigma_1) \cdot e(\mathsf{vk}', \sigma_2)^{-1} = e([\mathbf{A}]_1, [\mathbf{v}]_2).$$

Correctness. The correctness follows since we have $f(\hat{x}) = 1$ when $C(x) = 1$ from Lemma 2.2 and

$$\sigma_1 = \left[\mathbf{v} + \sum_{i:\hat{x}_i=1} \mathbf{W}_i \mathbf{r}\right]_2, \quad \sigma_2 = [\mathbf{r}]_2, \quad \text{where} \quad \mathbf{r} = \sum_{j:\rho(j)=0 \vee \hat{x}_{\rho(j)}=1} \omega_j \mathbf{r}_j. \tag{2}$$

Online-Offline Decomposability

Theorem 4.1. *The CS scheme above has decomposable online-offline efficiency defined as per Definition 4.2.*

Proof. To prove the theorem, we define $\mathcal{VK}$, vk_0, and $\mathsf{vk}_{i,b}$ for $i \in [n]$, $b \in \{0,1\}$ as

$$\mathcal{VK} := G_1^{k \times k}, \quad \mathsf{vk}_0 := ([\mathbf{A}]_1, e([\mathbf{A}]_1, [\mathbf{v}]_2)), \quad \mathsf{vk}_{i,b} := [\mathbf{A}\mathbf{W}_{2i-b}]_1.$$

It is easy to see that the first and the second items in Definition 4.2 are satisfied. We then define additional algorithms CS.VrfyOnL and CS.Aggrgt as follows:

CS.Aggrgt($\{\mathsf{vk}_i\}_{i \in [n']}$): If there exists $i \in [n']$ such that $\mathsf{vk}_i \notin \mathcal{VK} = G_1^{k \times k}$, output $\perp$. Otherwise, output $X := \prod_{i \in [n']} \mathsf{vk}_i$, where the product represents the component-wise multiplication in G_1.

CS.VrfyOnL($\mathsf{vk}_0, \mathsf{vk}', \sigma$): Parse $\mathsf{vk}_0 \to (A \in G_1^{k \times (k+1)}, V \in G_T^k)$, $\mathsf{vk}' \in G_1^{k \times k}$, and $\sigma \to (\sigma_1, \sigma_2) \in G_2^k \times G_2^k$. Then output $\top$ if the following holds and $\perp$ otherwise:

$$e(A, \sigma_1) \cdot e(\mathsf{vk}', \sigma_2)^{-1} = V.$$

The third item in Definition 4.2 follows from the fact that the following equation holds for any $x = y\|z \in \{0,1\}^n$:

$$\prod_{i \in [2n]} \underbrace{[\mathbf{A}\mathbf{W}_{i,2i-x_i}]}_{=\mathsf{vk}_{i,x_i}} = \prod_{i \in [|y|]} [\mathbf{A}\mathbf{W}_{i,2i-x_i}] \cdot \prod_{i \in [|y|+1,|y|+|z|]} [\mathbf{A}\mathbf{W}_{i,2i-x_i}]$$

$$= \prod_{i \in [|y|]} [\mathbf{A}\mathbf{W}_{i,2i-y_i}] \cdot \prod_{i \in [|y|+1,|y|+|z|]} [\mathbf{A}\mathbf{W}_{i,2i-z_{i-|y|}}]$$

$$= \prod_{i \in [|y|]} \underbrace{[\mathbf{A}\mathbf{W}_{i,2i-y_i}]}_{=\mathsf{vk}_{i,y_i}} \cdot \prod_{j \in [|z|]} \underbrace{[\mathbf{A}\mathbf{W}_{|y|+j,2(|y|+j)-z_j}]}_{=\mathsf{vk}_{|y|+j,z_j}} \cdot$$

To prove the fourth item, it suffices to show that vk' computed as Eq. 1 equals to $\mathsf{CS.Aggrgt}(\{\mathsf{vk}_{i,x_i}\}_{i\in[n]})$. This follows since the former is the product of $[\mathbf{AW}_i]_1$ over i in $S := \{i \in [2n] : \hat{x}_i = 1\}$ and the latter is over i in $S' := \{2j - x_j : j \in [n]\}$, and we have $S = S'$ by the definition of $\hat{x}$ (See Lemma 2.2). $\square$

Security. In the following, we show that the above construction is unforgeable and then discuss how to extend the scheme to satisfy context-hiding. While the latter property is not necessary for our application of CS in Sect. 5, this property may be useful when we use the CS scheme stand-alone.

Theorem 4.2. *The above construction is (adaptively) unforgeable under the* MDDH_k *assumption.*

Proof. For the sake of contradiction, suppose that there exists an adversary $\mathcal{A}$ that breaks unforgeability of the Π_{CS} with non-negligible probability ϵ. We then construct a PPT adversary $\mathcal{B}$ that breaks the adaptive security of the ABE with advantage ϵ for the attribute length $2n$ as follows.

$\mathcal{B}(\mathsf{mpk})$: It sets $\mathsf{vk} := \mathsf{mpk}$ and gives the master public key to $\mathcal{A}$. When $\mathcal{A}$ makes a signing key query for a circuit C, $\mathcal{B}$ runs $\mathsf{EncCir}(C) \to f$ and makes a key generation query for f to obtain sk_f. Then, $\mathcal{B}$ passes sk_f to $\mathcal{A}$. At some point, $\mathcal{A}$ outputs a forgery (x^*, σ^*). Then, $\mathcal{B}$ outputs a random bit and abort if $\mathsf{CS.Vrfy}(\mathsf{vk}, x^*, \sigma^*) = \bot$. Otherwise, $\mathcal{B}$ samples two random distinctive messages $M_0, M_1 \in G_T$ and makes a challenge query for $(\hat{x}^*, (M_0, M_1))$, where $\hat{x}^* = \mathsf{EncInp}(x^*)$. Given the challenge ciphertext ct, it first parses $\mathsf{ct} \to (\mathsf{ct}_1 \in G_1^{k+1}, \mathsf{ct}_2 \in G_1^k, \mathsf{ct}_3 \in G_T)$ and $\sigma^* \to (\sigma_1^* \in G_2^{k+1}, \sigma_2^* \in G_2^{k+1})$ and computes $M' := e(\mathsf{ct}_1, \sigma_1^*)^{-1} \cdot e(\mathsf{ct}_2, \sigma_2^*) \cdot \mathsf{ct}_3$. It outputs 0 if $M' = M_0$ and 1 otherwise.

We first check that $\mathcal{B}$ is an admissible adversary if so is $\mathcal{A}$, since we have $C(x^*) = 0$ iff $f(\hat{x}^*) = 0$ for any C and $f = \mathsf{EncCir}(C)$ from Lemma 2.2. We then claim that whenever $\mathsf{CS.Vrfy}(\mathsf{vk}, x^*, \sigma^*) = \top$, we have $M' = M_{\mathsf{coin}}$. To prove the claim, let us assume that $\mathsf{CS.Vrfy}(\mathsf{vk}, \hat{x}^*, \sigma^*) = \top$ holds. Then, we have

$$e([\mathbf{A}]_1, \sigma_1^*) \cdot e(\prod_{i:\hat{x}_i^*=1} [\mathbf{AW}_i]_1, \sigma_2^*)^{-1} = e([\mathbf{A}]_1, [\mathbf{v}]_2)$$

by the definition of $\mathsf{CS.Vrfy}$. Furthermore, there exists $\mathbf{s} \in \mathbb{Z}_p^k$ such that $\mathsf{ct}_1 = [\mathbf{s}^\top \mathbf{A}]_1$, $\mathsf{ct}_2 = [\mathbf{s}^\top \sum_{i:y_i^*=1} \mathbf{AW}_i]_1$, and $\mathsf{ct}_3 = e([\mathbf{s}^\top \mathbf{A}]_1, [\mathbf{v}]_2) \cdot M_{\mathsf{coin}}$ by the definition of Enc. Then, the above equation implies $e(\mathsf{ct}_1, \sigma_1^*) \cdot e(\mathsf{ct}_2, \sigma_2^*)^{-1} = e([\mathbf{s}^\top \mathbf{A}]_1, [\mathbf{v}]_2)$ which in turns implies $M' = M_{\mathsf{coin}}$. Thus, $\mathcal{B}$ correctly guesses coin when $\mathcal{A}$ breaks the unforgeability of Π_{CS} and outputs a random bit otherwise. This implies that the advantage of $\mathcal{B}$ is ϵ, which is non-negligible as desired. $\square$

Remark 1 (Adding Context-Hiding for the Scheme). We remark that it is possible to make the above scheme context-hiding by adding the following modification. Namely, we change the scheme so that it contains $[\mathbf{R}]_2, [\mathbf{W}_1\mathbf{R}]_2, \dots, [\mathbf{W}_{2n}\mathbf{R}]_2$, for random $\mathbf{R} \in \mathbb{Z}_p^{k\times k}$ in vk. This modification allows us to randomize $\mathbf{r}$ in Eq. 2, which makes the scheme context-hiding. The scheme remains adaptively unforgeable even with this change. For proving this, it suffices to show that our KP-ABE scheme in Sect. 3 remains adaptively secure even if we add $([\mathbf{R}]_2, [\mathbf{W}_1\mathbf{R}]_2, \ldots, [\mathbf{W}_n\mathbf{R}]_2)$ to the master public key. Although we need to slightly modify the proof of Theorem 3.1, the proof is not difficult. We omit it due to limited space. See the full version for the detail.

5 Compact NIZK from Compact Constrained Signatures

5.1 Main Construction

Here, we construct a compact NIZK based on the compact CS scheme which we constructed in Sect. 4. Let $\mathcal{L}$ be an **NP** language defined by a relation $\mathcal{R} \subseteq \{0,1\}^* \times \{0,1\}^*$. Let $n(\kappa)$ and $m(\kappa)$ be any fixed polynomials. Let C be a circuit that computes the relation $\mathcal{R}$ on $\{0,1\}^n \times \{0,1\}^m$, i.e., for $(x,w) \in \{0,1\}^n \times \{0,1\}^m$, we have $C(x,w) = 1$ if and only if $(x,w) \in \mathcal{R}$.

The construction will be given by combining following ingredients.

- A symmetric key encryption (SKE) scheme $\Pi_{\mathsf{SKE}} = (\mathsf{SKE.KeyGen}, \mathsf{SKE.Enc}, \mathsf{SKE.Dec})$ with message space $\{0,1\}^m$, key space $\{0,1\}^\ell$ and ciphertext space $\{0,1\}^{|\mathsf{ct}|}$. We require that its decryption circuit can be computed in $\mathbf{NC}^1$, and it has an additive ciphertext overhead (i.e., $|\mathsf{ct}| = m + \mathsf{poly}(\kappa)$).
- A constrained signature scheme $(\mathsf{CS.Setup}, \mathsf{CS.KeyGen}, \mathsf{CS.Sign}, \mathsf{CS.Vrfy}, \mathsf{CS.Aggrgt}, \mathsf{CS.VrfyOnL})$ we constructed in Sect. 4. The scheme should support the circuit f that computes $f(K, x, \mathsf{ct}) = C(x, \mathsf{SKE.Dec}(K, \mathsf{ct}))$.
- (Not necessarily compact) extractable NIZK scheme $\Pi_{\mathsf{NIZK}} = (\mathsf{Setup}, \mathsf{Prove}, \mathsf{Verify})$ for the language corresponding to the relation $\widetilde{\mathcal{R}}$ defined below:
  $((\mathsf{vk}_0, \{\mathsf{vk}_{i,b}\}_{i\in[\ell],b\in\{0,1\}}, Y), (K, \sigma)) \in \widetilde{\mathcal{R}}$ if and only if the followings are satisfied:
  1. $K \in \{0,1\}^\ell$,
  2. $\mathsf{CS.VrfyOnL}(\mathsf{vk}_0, Z, \sigma) = \top$ where $Z = \mathsf{CS.Aggrgt}(\mathsf{CS.Aggrgt}(\{\mathsf{vk}_{i,K_i}\}_{i\in[\ell]}), Y)$

Our compact NIZK is described as follows.

$\mathsf{Setup}'(1^\kappa)$:
  1. Generate $\mathsf{crs} \xleftarrow{\$} \mathsf{Setup}(1^\kappa)$.
  2. Generate $(\mathsf{vk} = (\mathsf{vk}_0, \{\mathsf{vk}_{i,b}\}_{i\in[\ell+n+|\mathsf{ct}|],b\in\{0,1\}}), \mathsf{msk}) \xleftarrow{\$} \mathsf{CS.Setup}(1^\kappa, 1^{\ell+n+|\mathsf{ct}|})$.
  3. Generate $\mathsf{sk}_f \xleftarrow{\$} \mathsf{CS.KeyGen}(\mathsf{msk}, f)$.
  4. Output $\mathsf{crs}' = (\mathsf{crs}, \mathsf{vk}, \mathsf{sk}_f)$.
$\mathsf{Prove}'(\mathsf{crs}', x, w)$:
  1. Abort if $\mathcal{R}(x,w) = 0$. Otherwise, do the following.
  2. Parse $\mathsf{crs}' \to (\mathsf{crs}, \mathsf{vk} = (\mathsf{vk}_0, \{\mathsf{vk}_{i,b}\}_{i\in[\ell+n+|\mathsf{ct}|],b\in\{0,1\}}), \mathsf{sk}_f)$.
  3. Generate $K \xleftarrow{\$} \mathsf{SKE.KeyGen}(1^\kappa)$ and $\mathsf{ct} \xleftarrow{\$} \mathsf{SKE.Enc}(K, w)$.

4. Compute $\sigma \xleftarrow{\$} \mathsf{CS.Sign}(\mathsf{sk}_f, (K, x, \mathsf{ct}))$.
5. Compute $Y := \mathsf{CS.Aggrgt}(\{\mathsf{vk}_{\ell+i, y_i}\}_{i \in [n+|\mathsf{ct}|]})$ where $y := (x, \mathsf{ct}) \in \{0, 1\}^{n+|\mathsf{ct}|}$.
6. Compute $\pi \xleftarrow{\$} \mathsf{Prove}((\mathsf{vk}_0, \{\mathsf{vk}_{i,b}\}_{i \in [\ell], b \in \{0,1\}}, Y), (K, \sigma))$.
7. Output $\pi' := (\mathsf{ct}, \pi)$.

$\mathsf{Verify}'(\mathsf{crs}', x, \pi')$:

1. Parse $\pi' \to (\mathsf{ct}, \pi)$. If it is not in this form, reject it. Otherwise, do the following.
2. Parse $\mathsf{crs}' \to (\mathsf{crs}, \mathsf{vk} = (\mathsf{vk}_0, \{\mathsf{vk}_{i,b}\}_{i \in [\ell+n+|\mathsf{ct}|], b \in \{0,1\}}), \mathsf{sk}_f)$.
3. Compute $Y := \mathsf{CS.Aggrgt}(\{\mathsf{vk}_{\ell+i, y_i}\}_{i \in [n+|\mathsf{ct}|]})$ where $y := (x, \mathsf{ct}) \in \{0, 1\}^{n+|\mathsf{ct}|}$.
4. Output $\top$ if $\mathsf{Verify}((\mathsf{vk}_0, \{\mathsf{vk}_{i,b}\}_{i \in [\ell], b \in \{0,1\}}, Y), \pi) = \top$ and otherwise $\bot$.

Correctness. Suppose that (ct, π) is an honestly generated proof on $(x, w) \in \mathcal{R}$. Then we have $\mathsf{ct} \xleftarrow{\$} \mathsf{SKE.Enc}(K, w)$ and $\pi \xleftarrow{\$} \mathsf{Prove}((\mathsf{vk}_0, \{\mathsf{vk}_{i,b}\}_{i \in [\ell], b \in \{0,1\}}, Y), (K, \sigma))$ where $K \xleftarrow{\$} \mathsf{SKE.KeyGen}(1^\kappa)$, $\sigma \xleftarrow{\$} \mathsf{CS.Sign}(\mathsf{sk}_f, (K, x, \mathsf{ct}))$, and

$$Y = \mathsf{CS.Aggrgt}(\{\mathsf{vk}_{\ell+i, y_i}\}_{i \in [n+|\mathsf{ct}|]}).$$

By the correctness of Π_{SKE}, we have $f(K, x, \mathsf{ct}) = 1$. Furthermore, by the correctness of Π_{CS}, we have $\mathsf{CS.Vrfy}(\mathsf{vk}, (K, x, \mathsf{ct}), \sigma) = \top$, which is equivalent to

$$\mathsf{CS.VrfyOnL}(\mathsf{vk}_0, Z, \sigma) = \top \quad \text{where} \quad Z = \mathsf{CS.Aggrgt}(\mathsf{CS.Aggrgt}(\{\mathsf{vk}_{i, K_i}\}_{i \in [\ell]}), Y).$$

Therefore we have $((\mathsf{vk}_0, \{\mathsf{vk}_{i,b}\}_{i \in [\ell], b \in \{0,1\}}, Y), (K, \sigma)) \in \widetilde{\mathcal{R}}$ and thus we have $\mathsf{Verify}((\mathsf{vk}_0, \{\mathsf{vk}_{i,b}\}_{i \in [\ell], b \in \{0,1\}}, Y), \pi) = \top$ by the correctness of Π_{NIZK}.

Efficiency. We first observe that the size of the verification circuit for the relation $\widetilde{\mathcal{R}}$ is $\mathsf{poly}(\kappa)$, which is independent of the size of the verification circuit for $\mathcal{R}$. This is because $Z = \mathsf{CS.Aggrgt}(\mathsf{CS.Aggrgt}(\{\mathsf{vk}_{i, K_i}\}_{i \in [\ell]}), Y)$ can be computed in polynomial time in κ and the length $\ell = \mathsf{poly}(\kappa)$ of K and the running time of $\mathsf{CS.VrfyOnL}(\mathsf{vk}_0, Z, \sigma)$ does not depend on the length of (x, ct) (and in particular the complexity of the circuit f) as required in Definition 4.2. Therefore, the size of π is $\mathsf{poly}(\kappa)$ and independent of $|x|$, $|w|$, or $|C|$ even though we do not require any compactness requirement for the underlying NIZK Π_{NIZK}. Since we assume $|\mathsf{ct}| = m + \mathsf{poly}(\kappa)$, the total proof size is $|w| + \mathsf{poly}(\kappa)$. We note that this scheme can be directly implemented only when the relation $\mathcal{R}$ can be verified in $\mathbf{NC}^1$. Otherwise, we have to first expand the witness to make the relation verifiable in $\mathbf{NC}^1$ similarly to [19,41]. This is done by considering all values corresponding to all gates when computing the circuit C on input (x, w) to be the new witness and have the new circuit verify the consistency of the values for all gates in C. In this case, the proof size becomes $|C| + \mathsf{poly}(\kappa)$.

Since the relation $\widetilde{R}$ is well-suited to be proven by the Groth-Sahai proof, a fairly efficient instantiation is possible based on the Groth-Sahai proof. Especially, a proof consists of $|C|$ bits, $6\kappa + 14$ elements of $\mathbb{G}_1$ and $7\kappa + 25$ elements of $\mathbb{G}_2$ when instantiated under the SXDH assumption. See the full version for the detail. We also note that if the relation $\mathcal{R}$ can be verified by a "leveled circuit" [8], we can further reduce the proof size to $|w| + |C|/\log\kappa + \mathsf{poly}(\kappa)$ which is sublinear in $|C|$ similarly to [41]. (See [41] for details.)

Security. In the following, we prove the soundness and the zero-knowledge property of Π'_{NIZK}.

Theorem 5.1 (Soundness). *The above NIZK scheme Π'_{NIZK} is computationally (adaptive) sound if Π_{NIZK} satisfies extractability and Π_{CS} is unforgeable.*

Proof. Suppose that there is a PPT adversary $\mathcal{A}$ that breaks soundness. Then we construct a PPT adversary $\mathcal{B}$ that breaks the unforgeability of Π_{CS} as follows.

$\mathcal{B}(\mathsf{vk})$: It queries f to the key generation oracle to obtain sk_f where f is the circuit as defined in the description of the scheme. Then it generates $\mathsf{crs} \xleftarrow{\$} \mathsf{Setup}(1^\kappa; r_{\mathsf{Setup}})$, runs $\mathcal{A}(\mathsf{crs}')$ to obtain $(x^*, \pi'^* = (\mathsf{ct}, \pi))$ where $\mathsf{crs}' := (\mathsf{crs}, \mathsf{vk}, \mathsf{sk}_f)$. Then it computes $(K, \sigma) \xleftarrow{\$} \mathsf{Extract}(r_{\mathsf{Setup}}, \pi)$ and outputs $((K, x^*, \mathsf{ct}), \sigma)$ as a forgery.

This completes the description of $\mathcal{B}$. In the following, we show that $\mathcal{B}$ breaks the unforgeability of Π_{CS}. Let $\mathsf{VK}_{[0,\ell]} := (\mathsf{vk}_0, \{\mathsf{vk}_{i,b}\}_{i\in[\ell], b\in\{0,1\}})$. Since we assume $\mathcal{A}$ breaks the soundness of Π'_{NIZK},

$$\Pr[x^* \notin \mathcal{L} \wedge \mathsf{Verify}((\mathsf{VK}_{[0,\ell]}, Y^*), \pi) = \top]$$

is non-negligible where $Y^* = \mathsf{CS.Aggrgt}(\{\mathsf{vk}_{\ell+i, y_i^*}\}_{i\in[n+|\mathsf{ct}|]})$ and $y^* := (x^*, \mathsf{ct}) \in \{0,1\}^{n+|\mathsf{ct}|}$. On the other hand, by the extractability of Π_{NIZK},

$$\Pr[\mathsf{Verify}((\mathsf{VK}_{[0,\ell]}, Y^*), \pi) = \top \wedge ((\mathsf{VK}_{[0,\ell]}, Y^*), (K, \sigma)) \notin \widetilde{\mathcal{R}}]$$

is negligible. Therefore

$$\Pr[x^* \notin \mathcal{L} \wedge \mathsf{Verify}((\mathsf{VK}_{[0,\ell]}, Y^*), \pi) = \top \wedge ((\mathsf{VK}_{[0,\ell]}, Y^*), (K, \sigma)) \in \widetilde{\mathcal{R}}]$$

is non-negligible. Suppose that this event happens. Since we have $x^* \notin \mathcal{L}$, we have $f(K, x^*, \mathsf{ct}) = 0$. On the other hand, $((\mathsf{VK}_{[0,\ell]}, Y^*), (K, \sigma)) \in \widetilde{\mathcal{R}}$ implies that we have $K \in \{0,1\}^\ell \wedge \mathsf{CS.VrfyOnL}(\mathsf{vk}_0, Z, \sigma) = \top$ where $Z = \mathsf{CS.Aggrgt}(\mathsf{CS.Aggrgt}(\{\mathsf{vk}_{i, K_i}\}_{i\in[\ell]}), Y^*)$, which implies $\mathsf{CS.Vrfy}(\mathsf{vk}, (K, x^*, \mathsf{ct}), \sigma) = \top$. This means that $\mathcal{B}$ succeeds in breaking the unforgeability of Π_{CS}. $\square$

Theorem 5.2 (Zero-Knowledge). *The above NIZK scheme Π'_{NIZK} is computationally zero-knowledge if Π_{NIZK} is computationally zero-knowledge and Π_{SKE} is CPA-secure.*

Proof. Let $(\mathcal{S}_1, \mathcal{S}_2)$ be the simulator for Π_{NIZK}. We describe the simulator $(\mathcal{S}_1', \mathcal{S}_2')$ for Π'_{NIZK} below.

$\mathcal{S}'_1(1^\kappa)$: It generates $(\mathsf{crs}, \tau_V) \overset{\$}{\leftarrow} \mathcal{S}_1(1^\kappa)$, $(\mathsf{vk} = (\mathsf{vk}_0,$ $\{\mathsf{vk}_{i,b}\}_{i\in[\ell+n+|\mathsf{ct}|],b\in\{0,1\}}), \mathsf{msk}) \overset{\$}{\leftarrow} \mathsf{CS.Setup}(1^\kappa, 1^{\ell+n+|\mathsf{ct}|})$, and $\mathsf{sk}_f \overset{\$}{\leftarrow}$ $\mathsf{CS.KeyGen}(\mathsf{msk}, f)$, and outputs $\mathsf{crs}' := (\mathsf{crs}, \mathsf{vk}, \mathsf{sk}_f)$ and $\tau'_V := \tau_V$.

$\mathcal{S}'_2(\mathsf{crs}' := (\mathsf{crs}, \mathsf{vk}, \mathsf{sk}_f), \tau'_V = \tau_V, x)$: It picks $K \overset{\$}{\leftarrow} \mathsf{SKE.KeyGen}(1^\kappa)$, computes $\mathsf{ct} \overset{\$}{\leftarrow} \mathsf{SKE.Enc}(K, 0^m)$, $Y := \mathsf{CS.Aggrgt}(\{\mathsf{vk}_{\ell+i,y_i}\}_{i\in[n+|\mathsf{ct}|]})$ where $y := (x, \mathsf{ct}) \in \{0,1\}^{n+|\mathsf{ct}|}$, and $\pi \overset{\$}{\leftarrow} \mathcal{S}_2(\mathsf{crs}, \tau_V, (\mathsf{vk}_0, \{\mathsf{vk}_{i,b}\}_{i\in[\ell],b\in\{0,1\}}, Y))$, and outputs $\pi' := (\mathsf{ct}, \pi)$.

This completes the description of the simulator. We prove that proofs simulated by the above simulator are computationally indistinguishable from the honestly generated proofs. To prove this, we consider the following sequence of games between a PPT adversary $\mathcal{A}$ and a challenger.

G_0: In this game, proofs are generated honestly. Namely,
1. The challenger generates $\mathsf{crs} \overset{\$}{\leftarrow} \mathsf{Setup}(1^\kappa)$, $(\mathsf{vk} = (\mathsf{vk}_0,$ $\{\mathsf{vk}_{i,b}\}_{i\in[\ell+n+|\mathsf{ct}|],b\in\{0,1\}}), \mathsf{msk}) \overset{\$}{\leftarrow} \mathsf{CS.Setup}(1^\kappa, 1^{\ell+n+|\mathsf{ct}|})$, and $\mathsf{sk}_f \overset{\$}{\leftarrow}$ $\mathsf{CS.KeyGen}(\mathsf{msk}, f)$, and gives $\mathsf{crs}' := (\mathsf{crs}, \mathsf{vk}, \mathsf{sk}_f)$ to $\mathcal{A}$.
2. $\mathcal{A}$ is given $(1^\kappa, \mathsf{crs}')$ and is allowed to query $\mathcal{O}(\mathsf{crs}', \cdot, \cdot)$, which works as follows. When $\mathcal{A}$ queries (x, w), if $(x, w) \notin \mathcal{R}$, then the oracle returns $\perp$. Otherwise, it picks $K \overset{\$}{\leftarrow} \mathsf{SKE.KeyGen}(1^\kappa)$, computes $\mathsf{ct} \overset{\$}{\leftarrow} \mathsf{SKE.Enc}(K, w)$, $\sigma \overset{\$}{\leftarrow} \mathsf{CS.Sign}(\mathsf{sk}_f, (K, x, \mathsf{ct}))$, $Y := \mathsf{CS.Aggrgt}(\{\mathsf{vk}_{\ell+i,y_i}\}_{i\in[n+|\mathsf{ct}|]})$ where $y := (x, \mathsf{ct}) \in \{0,1\}^{n+|\mathsf{ct}|}$, and $\pi \overset{\$}{\leftarrow} \mathsf{Prove}(\mathsf{crs}, (\mathsf{vk}_0, \{\mathsf{vk}_{i,b}\}_{i\in[\ell],b\in\{0,1\}}, Y), (K, \sigma))$, and returns a proof $\pi' := (\mathsf{ct}, \pi)$.
3. Finally, $\mathcal{A}$ returns a bit β.

G_1: This game is identical to the previous game except that crs and π are generated differently. Namely, the challenger generates $(\mathsf{crs}, \tau_V) \overset{\$}{\leftarrow} \mathcal{S}_1(1^\kappa)$ at the beginning of the game, and π is generated as $\pi \overset{\$}{\leftarrow} \mathcal{S}_2(\mathsf{crs}, \tau_V, (\mathsf{vk}_0, \{\mathsf{vk}_{i,b}\}_{i\in[\ell],b\in\{0,1\}}, Y))$ for each oracle query.

G_2: This game is identical to the previous game except that ct is generated as $\mathsf{ct} \overset{\$}{\leftarrow} \mathsf{SKE.Enc}(K, 0^m)$ for each oracle query.

Let T_i be the event that $\mathcal{A}$ returns 1 in G_i for $i = 0, 1, 2$. It is easy to see that proofs are generated by $\mathcal{S}' = (\mathcal{S}'_1, \mathcal{S}'_2)$ in G_2. Thus we have to prove that $|\Pr[T_0] - \Pr[T_2]|$ is negligible. The following lemmas are straightforward to prove.

Lemma 5.1. *If* Π_{NIZK} *satisfies computational zero-knowledge w.r.t. the simulator* $\mathcal{S}$, *then* $|\Pr[T_0] - \Pr[T_1]| = \mathsf{negl}(\kappa)$.

Proof. We observe that every proof π given to $\mathcal{A}$ is created for a correct statement in both games. Therefore, the indistinguishability of the games can be reduced to the zero-knowledge property of Π_{NIZK}. $\qquad\square$

Lemma 5.2. *If* Π_{SKE} *is CPA-secure, then* $|\Pr[T_1] - \Pr[T_2]| = \mathsf{negl}(\kappa)$.

Proof. Due to the change we introduced in G_1, the secret key K of SKE that is used to generate ct is not used anywhere else in both games. therefore, the indistinguishability of these games can be reduced to the CPA security of Π_{SKE}. $\qquad\square$

This completes the proof of Theorem 5.2. $\qquad\square$

5.2 Variants of Our NIZK

Perfect Zero-Knowledge Variant. Observe that the assumptions required to prove the zero-knowledge property of our NIZK was the zero-knowledge property of the underlying non-compact NIZK and the security of SKE. Therefore if we assume that the underlying non-compact NIZK is perfect zero-knowledge[7] and modify the scheme somehow so that we do not use an SKE anymore, the resulting NIZK can be made perfect zero-knowledge. Indeed, the latter can be done by using the witness w itself in place of the SKE key K in the definition of the circuit f supported by the CS scheme. By instantiating the non-compact NIZK with the Groth-Sahai proof, which is perfect zero-knowledge, we obtain the following theorem. (See the full version for the full detail.)

Theorem 5.3. *There exists a NIPZK for **NP** relations computable in $\boldsymbol{NC}^1$ with proof size $|w| \cdot \mathsf{poly}(\kappa)$ if the DLIN assumption holds.*

UC Variant. If we further modify the perfect zero-knowledge variant to have non-malleability by using one-time signatures and assume that the underlying non-compact NIZK is a UC-NIZK, then we can show that the resulting scheme is also UC-NIZK. In particular, we obtain the following theorem. (See the full version for the full detail.)

Theorem 5.4. *There exists a UC-NIZK for **NP** relations computable in $\boldsymbol{NC}^1$ with proof size $|w| \cdot \mathsf{poly}(\kappa)$ if the DLIN assumption holds.*

Acknowledgement. We thank anonymous reviewers of Eurocrypt 2020 for their helpful comments. The first and the third authors were supported by JST CREST Grant Number JPMJCR19F6. The third author was supported by JSPS KAKENHI Grant Number 16K16068.

References

1. Abusalah, H.: Generic instantiations of the hidden bits model for non-interactive zero-knowledge proofs for NP. Master's thesis, RWTH-Aachen University (2013)
2. Attrapadung, N., Libert, B., de Panafieu, E.: Expressive key-policy attribute-based encryption with constant-size ciphertexts. In: Catalano, D., Fazio, N., Gennaro, R., Nicolosi, A. (eds.) PKC 2011. LNCS, vol. 6571, pp. 90–108. Springer, Heidelberg (2011). https://doi.org/10.1007/978-3-642-19379-8_6
3. Bellare, M., Yung, M.: Certifying permutations: noninteractive zero-knowledge based on any trapdoor permutation. J. Cryptol. **9**(3), 149–166 (1996)
4. Bitansky, N., Paneth, O.: ZAPs and non-interactive witness indistinguishability from indistinguishability obfuscation. In: Dodis, Y., Nielsen, J.B. (eds.) TCC 2015, Part II. LNCS, vol. 9015, pp. 401–427. Springer, Heidelberg (2015). https://doi.org/10.1007/978-3-662-46497-7_16

---

[7] Actually, we have to assume the underlying non-compact NIZK is *dual-mode NIZK* for proving the soundness.

5. Bitansky, N., Paneth, O., Wichs, D.: Perfect structure on the edge of chaos. In: Kushilevitz, E., Malkin, T. (eds.) TCC 2016, Part I. LNCS, vol. 9562, pp. 474–502. Springer, Heidelberg (2016). https://doi.org/10.1007/978-3-662-49096-9_20

6. Blum, M., Feldman, P., Micali, S.: Non-interactive zero-knowledge and its applications (extended abstract). In: 20th ACM STOC, pp. 103–112 (1988)

7. Boneh, D., Franklin, M.: Identity-based encryption from the Weil pairing. In: Kilian, J. (ed.) CRYPTO 2001. LNCS, vol. 2139, pp. 213–229. Springer, Heidelberg (2001). https://doi.org/10.1007/3-540-44647-8_13

8. Boyle, E., Gilboa, N., Ishai, Y.: Breaking the circuit size barrier for secure computation under DDH. In: Robshaw, M., Katz, J. (eds.) CRYPTO 2016, Part I. LNCS, vol. 9814, pp. 509–539. Springer, Heidelberg (2016). https://doi.org/10.1007/978-3-662-53018-4_19

9. Canetti, R., et al.: Fiat-Shamir: from practice to theory. In: 51st ACM STOC, pp. 1082–1090 (2019)

10. Canetti, R., Chen, Y., Reyzin, L., Rothblum, R.D.: Fiat-Shamir and correlation intractability from strong KDM-secure encryption. In: Nielsen, J.B., Rijmen, V. (eds.) EUROCRYPT 2018, Part I. LNCS, vol. 10820, pp. 91–122. Springer, Cham (2018). https://doi.org/10.1007/978-3-319-78381-9_4

11. Canetti, R., Halevi, S., Katz, J.: A forward-secure public-key encryption scheme. J. Cryptol. 20(3), 265–294 (2007)

12. Canetti, R., Lichtenberg, A.: Certifying trapdoor permutations, revisited. In: Beimel, A., Dziembowski, S. (eds.) TCC 2018, Part I. LNCS, vol. 11239, pp. 476–506. Springer, Cham (2018). https://doi.org/10.1007/978-3-030-03807-6_18

13. Cohen, R., Shelat, A., Wichs, D.: Adaptively secure MPC with sublinear communication complexity. In: Boldyreva, A., Micciancio, D. (eds.) CRYPTO 2019, Part II. LNCS, vol. 11693, pp. 30–60. Springer, Cham (2019). https://doi.org/10.1007/978-3-030-26951-7_2

14. Danezis, G., Fournet, C., Groth, J., Kohlweiss, M.: Square span programs with applications to succinct NIZK arguments. In: Sarkar, P., Iwata, T. (eds.) ASIACRYPT 2014, Part I. LNCS, vol. 8873, pp. 532–550. Springer, Heidelberg (2014). https://doi.org/10.1007/978-3-662-45611-8_28

15. Escala, A., Herold, G., Kiltz, E., Ràfols, C., Villar, J.: An algebraic framework for Diffie–Hellman assumptions. J. Cryptol. 30(1), 242–288 (2015). https://doi.org/10.1007/s00145-015-9220-6

16. Feige, U., Lapidot, D., Shamir, A.: Multiple noninteractive zero knowledge proofs under general assumptions. SIAM J. Comput. 29(1), 1–28 (1999)

17. Fuchsbauer, G., Jafargholi, Z., Pietrzak, K.: A quasipolynomial reduction for generalized selective decryption on trees. In: Gennaro, R., Robshaw, M. (eds.) CRYPTO 2015, Part I. LNCS, vol. 9215, pp. 601–620. Springer, Heidelberg (2015). https://doi.org/10.1007/978-3-662-47989-6_29

18. Fuchsbauer, G., Konstantinov, M., Pietrzak, K., Rao, V.: Adaptive security of constrained PRFs. In: Sarkar, P., Iwata, T. (eds.) ASIACRYPT 2014, Part II. LNCS, vol. 8874, pp. 82–101. Springer, Heidelberg (2014). https://doi.org/10.1007/978-3-662-45608-8_5

19. Garg, S., Gentry, C., Halevi, S., Raykova, M., Sahai, A., Waters, B.: Candidate indistinguishability obfuscation and functional encryption for all circuits. SIAM J. Comput. 45(3), 882–929 (2016)

20. Gennaro, R., Gentry, C., Parno, B., Raykova, M.: Quadratic span programs and succinct NIZKs without PCPs. In: Johansson, T., Nguyen, P.Q. (eds.) EUROCRYPT 2013. LNCS, vol. 7881, pp. 626–645. Springer, Heidelberg (2013). https://doi.org/10.1007/978-3-642-38348-9_37

21. Gentry, C.: A fully homomorphic encryption scheme. Ph.D. thesis, Stanford University (2009)
22. Gentry, C., Groth, J., Ishai, Y., Peikert, C., Sahai, A., Smith, A.D.: Using fully homomorphic hybrid encryption to minimize non-interative zero-knowledge proofs. J. Cryptol. **28**(4), 820–843 (2015)
23. Gentry, C., Wichs, D.: Separating succinct non-interactive arguments from all falsifiable assumptions. In: 43rd ACM STOC, pp. 99–108 (2011)
24. Goldreich, O.: Foundations of Cryptography: Volume 2, Basic Applications (2004)
25. Goldreich, O., Oren, Y.: Definitions and properties of zero-knowledge proof systems. J. Cryptol. **7**(1), 1–32 (1994)
26. Goldwasser, S., Micali, S., Rackoff, C.: The knowledge complexity of interactive proof systems. SIAM J. Comput. **18**(1), 186–208 (1989)
27. Groth, J.: Short non-interactive zero-knowledge proofs. In: Abe, M. (ed.) ASIACRYPT 2010. LNCS, vol. 6477, pp. 341–358. Springer, Heidelberg (2010). https://doi.org/10.1007/978-3-642-17373-8_20
28. Groth, J.: Short pairing-based non-interactive zero-knowledge arguments. In: Abe, M. (ed.) ASIACRYPT 2010. LNCS, vol. 6477, pp. 321–340. Springer, Heidelberg (2010). https://doi.org/10.1007/978-3-642-17373-8_19
29. Groth, J.: On the size of pairing-based non-interactive arguments. In: Fischlin, M., Coron, J.-S. (eds.) EUROCRYPT 2016, Part II. LNCS, vol. 9666, pp. 305–326. Springer, Heidelberg (2016). https://doi.org/10.1007/978-3-662-49896-5_11
30. Groth, J., Ostrovsky, R., Sahai, A.: New techniques for noninteractive zero-knowledge. J. ACM **59**(3), 1–35 (2012)
31. Groth, J., Sahai, A.: Efficient noninteractive proof systems for bilinear groups. SIAM J. Comput. **41**(5), 1193–1232 (2012)
32. Hemenway, B., Jafargholi, Z., Ostrovsky, R., Scafuro, A., Wichs, D.: Adaptively secure garbled circuits from one-way functions. In: Robshaw, M., Katz, J. (eds.) CRYPTO 2016, Part III. LNCS, vol. 9816, pp. 149–178. Springer, Heidelberg (2016). https://doi.org/10.1007/978-3-662-53015-3_6
33. Hohenberger, S., Waters, B.: Attribute-based encryption with fast decryption. In: Kurosawa, K., Hanaoka, G. (eds.) PKC 2013. LNCS, vol. 7778, pp. 162–179. Springer, Heidelberg (2013). https://doi.org/10.1007/978-3-642-36362-7_11
34. Ishai, Y., Kushilevitz, E.: Perfect constant-round secure computation via perfect randomizing polynomials. In: Widmayer, P., Eidenbenz, S., Triguero, F., Morales, R., Conejo, R., Hennessy, M. (eds.) ICALP 2002. LNCS, vol. 2380, pp. 244–256. Springer, Heidelberg (2002). https://doi.org/10.1007/3-540-45465-9_22
35. Jafargholi, Z., Kamath, C., Klein, K., Komargodski, I., Pietrzak, K., Wichs, D.: Be adaptive, avoid overcommitting. In: Katz, J., Shacham, H. (eds.) CRYPTO 2017, Part I. LNCS, vol. 10401, pp. 133–163. Springer, Cham (2017). https://doi.org/10.1007/978-3-319-63688-7_5
36. Jafargholi, Z., Wichs, D.: Adaptive security of Yao's garbled circuits. In: Hirt, M., Smith, A. (eds.) TCC 2016, Part I. LNCS, vol. 9985, pp. 433–458. Springer, Heidelberg (2016). https://doi.org/10.1007/978-3-662-53641-4_17
37. Jutla, C.S., Roy, A.: Switching lemma for bilinear tests and constant-size NIZK proofs for linear subspaces. In: Garay, J.A., Gennaro, R. (eds.) CRYPTO 2014, Part II. LNCS, vol. 8617, pp. 295–312. Springer, Heidelberg (2014). https://doi.org/10.1007/978-3-662-44381-1_17
38. Jutla, C.S., Roy, A.: Shorter quasi-adaptive NIZK proofs for linear subspaces. J. Cryptol. **30**(4), 1116–1156 (2017)

39. Kalai, Y.T., Rothblum, G.N., Rothblum, R.D.: From obfuscation to the security of Fiat-Shamir for proofs. In: Katz, J., Shacham, H. (eds.) CRYPTO 2017, Part II. LNCS, vol. 10402, pp. 224–251. Springer, Cham (2017). https://doi.org/10.1007/978-3-319-63715-0_8

40. Katsumata, S., Nishimaki, R., Yamada, S., Yamakawa, T.: Designated verifier/prover and preprocessing NIZKs from Diffie-Hellman assumptions. In: Ishai, Y., Rijmen, V. (eds.) EUROCRYPT 2019, Part II. LNCS, vol. 11477, pp. 622–651. Springer, Cham (2019). https://doi.org/10.1007/978-3-030-17656-3_22

41. Katsumata, S., Nishimaki, R., Yamada, S., Yamakawa, T.: Exploring constructions of compact NIZKs from various assumptions. In: Boldyreva, A., Micciancio, D. (eds.) CRYPTO 2019, Part III. LNCS, vol. 11694, pp. 639–669. Springer, Cham (2019). https://doi.org/10.1007/978-3-030-26954-8_21

42. Kiltz, E., Wee, H.: Quasi-adaptive NIZK for linear subspaces revisited. In: Oswald, E., Fischlin, M. (eds.) EUROCRYPT 2015, Part II. LNCS, vol. 9057, pp. 101–128. Springer, Heidelberg (2015). https://doi.org/10.1007/978-3-662-46803-6_4

43. Kim, S., Wu, D.J.: Multi-theo preprocessing NIZKs from lattices. In: CRYPTO 2018, Part II, pp. 733–765 (2018)

44. Kowalczyk, L., Wee, H.: Compact adaptively secure ABE for NC^1 from k-Lin. In: Ishai, Y., Rijmen, V. (eds.) EUROCRYPT 2019, Part I. LNCS, vol. 11476, pp. 3–33. Springer, Cham (2019). https://doi.org/10.1007/978-3-030-17653-2_1

45. Lipmaa, H.: Progression-free sets and sublinear pairing-based non-interactive zero-knowledge arguments. In: Cramer, R. (ed.) TCC 2012. LNCS, vol. 7194, pp. 169–189. Springer, Heidelberg (2012). https://doi.org/10.1007/978-3-642-28914-9_10

46. Maji, H.K., Prabhakaran, M., Rosulek, M.: Attribute-based signatures. In: Kiayias, A. (ed.) CT-RSA 2011. LNCS, vol. 6558, pp. 376–392. Springer, Heidelberg (2011). https://doi.org/10.1007/978-3-642-19074-2_24

47. Naccache, D., Stern, J.: A new public key cryptosystem based on higher residues. In: ACM CCS 1998, pp. 59–66 (1998)

48. Naor, M.: On cryptographic assumptions and challenges. In: Boneh, D. (ed.) CRYPTO 2003. LNCS, vol. 2729, pp. 96–109. Springer, Heidelberg (2003). https://doi.org/10.1007/978-3-540-45146-4_6

49. Okamoto, T., Takashima, K.: Efficient attribute-based signatures for non-monotone predicates in the standard model. In: Catalano, D., Fazio, N., Gennaro, R., Nicolosi, A. (eds.) PKC 2011. LNCS, vol. 6571, pp. 35–52. Springer, Heidelberg (2011). https://doi.org/10.1007/978-3-642-19379-8_3

50. Peikert, C., Shiehian, S.: Noninteractive zero knowledge for NP from (plain) learning with errors. In: Boldyreva, A., Micciancio, D. (eds.) CRYPTO 2019, Part I. LNCS, vol. 11692, pp. 89–114. Springer, Cham (2019). https://doi.org/10.1007/978-3-030-26948-7_4

51. Sahai, A., Waters, B.: How to use indistinguishability obfuscation: deniable encryption, and more. In: 46th ACM STOC, pp. 475–484 (2014)

52. Tsabary, R.: An equivalence between attribute-based signatures and homomorphic signatures, and new constructions for both. In: Kalai, Y., Reyzin, L. (eds.) TCC 2017, Part II. LNCS, vol. 10678, pp. 489–518. Springer, Cham (2017). https://doi.org/10.1007/978-3-319-70503-3_16

53. Vinod, V., Narayanan, A., Srinathan, K., Rangan, C.P., Kim, K.: On the power of computational secret sharing. In: Johansson, T., Maitra, S. (eds.) INDOCRYPT 2003. LNCS, vol. 2904, pp. 162–176. Springer, Heidelberg (2003). https://doi.org/10.1007/978-3-540-24582-7_12

54. Waters, B.: Dual system encryption: realizing fully secure IBE and HIBE under simple assumptions. In: Halevi, S. (ed.) CRYPTO 2009. LNCS, vol. 5677, pp. 619–636. Springer, Heidelberg (2009). https://doi.org/10.1007/978-3-642-03356-8_36

New Constructions of Statistical NIZKs: Dual-Mode DV-NIZKs and More

Benoît Libert[1,2(✉)], Alain Passelègue[2,3(✉)], Hoeteck Wee[4], and David J. Wu[5]

[1] CNRS, Laboratoire LIP, Lyon, France
[2] ENS de Lyon, Laboratoire LIP (U. Lyon, CNRS, ENSL, Inria, UCBL),
Lyon, France
benoit.libert@ens-lyon.fr
[3] Inria, Paris, France
alain.passelegue@inria.fr
[4] CNRS, ENS, PSL, Paris, France
wee@di.ens.fr
[5] University of Virginia, Charlottesville, VA, USA
dwu4@virginia.edu

Abstract. Non-interactive zero-knowledge proofs (NIZKs) are important primitives in cryptography. A major challenge since the early works on NIZKs has been to construct NIZKs with a *statistical* zero-knowledge guarantee against unbounded verifiers. In the common reference string (CRS) model, such "statistical NIZK arguments" are currently known from k-Lin in a pairing-group and from LWE. In the (reusable) designated-verifier model (DV-NIZK), where a trusted setup algorithm generates a reusable verification key for checking proofs, we also have a construction from DCR. If we relax our requirements to *computational* zero-knowledge, we additionally have NIZKs from factoring and CDH in a pairing group in the CRS model, and from nearly *all* assumptions that imply public-key encryption (e.g., CDH, LPN, LWE) in the designated-verifier model. Thus, there still remains a gap in our understanding of statistical NIZKs in both the CRS and the designated-verifier models.

In this work, we develop new techniques for constructing statistical NIZK arguments. First, we construct statistical DV-NIZK arguments from the k-Lin assumption in *pairing-free* groups, the QR assumption, and the DCR assumption. These are the first constructions in pairing-free groups and from QR that satisfy statistical zero-knowledge. All of our constructions are secure even if the verification key is chosen maliciously (i.e., they are "malicious-designated-verifier" NIZKs), and moreover, they satisfy a "dual-mode" property where the CRS can be sampled from two computationally indistinguishable distributions: one distribution yields *statistical DV-NIZK arguments* while the other yields

B. Libert—Part of this research was supported by the French ANR ALAMBIC project (ANR-16-CE39-0006).

H. Wee—Supported in part by ERC Project aSCEND (H2020 639554).

D. J. Wu—Part of this work was done while visiting ENS de Lyon. Supported by NSF CNS-1917414 and a University of Virginia SEAS Research Innovation Award.

A. Canteaut and Y. Ishai (Eds.): EUROCRYPT 2020, LNCS 12107, pp. 410–441, 2020.
https://doi.org/10.1007/978-3-030-45727-3_14

computational DV-NIZK proofs. We then show how to adapt our k-Lin construction in a pairing group to obtain new *publicly-verifiable* statistical NIZK arguments from pairings with a *qualitatively weaker* assumption than existing constructions of pairing-based statistical NIZKs.

Our constructions follow the classic paradigm of Feige, Lapidot, and Shamir (FLS). While the FLS framework has traditionally been used to construct computational (DV)-NIZK proofs, we newly show that the same framework can be leveraged to construct dual-mode (DV)-NIZKs.

1 Introduction

Non-interactive zero-knowledge (NIZK) proofs [BFM88, GMR89] allow a prover to send a single message to convince a verifier that a statement is true without revealing anything beyond this fact. Although such NIZKs cannot exist in the plain model, they can be realized in the common reference string (CRS) model, where a trusted party generates and publishes a common reference string accessible to the prover and the verifier. Shortly after the introduction of NIZKs, numerous constructions have been developed in the CRS model from many classes of cryptographic assumptions such as factoring [BFM88, DMP87, FLS90, BY92, FLS99, DDO+01, Gro10, Gol11, GR13, CL18], pairing-based assumptions [CHK03, GOS06], and lattice-based assumptions [CCH+19, PS19]. We can also construct NIZKs in the random oracle model [FS86].

A major open problem since the early works on non-interactive zero-knowledge has been to construct NIZKs with a *statistical* zero-knowledge guarantee against *computationally-unbounded* verifiers (i.e., "statistical NIZK arguments"). Here, we only have constructions from the k-Lin family of assumptions over pairing groups [GOS06, GOS12] and LWE [PS19] (or circular-secure FHE [CCH+19]). If we relax the model and consider (reusable) designated-verifier NIZKs (DV-NIZKs), where the trusted party that generates the CRS also generates a *secret* verification key that is used to verify proofs, then the recent work of Chase et al. [CDI+19] provides an instantiation of a statistical DV-NIZK from the DCR assumption. In contrast, if we are satisfied with computational zero-knowledge, then we can additionally construct publicly-verifiable NIZKs in the CRS model from QR [BFM88], factoring [FLS99], and the CDH assumption over a pairing group [CHK03]. In the designated-verifier model, a recent line of works [QRW19, CH19, KNYY19a, KNYY19b, LQR+19] has provided constructions of computational DV-NIZKs from essentially all cryptographic assumptions known to imply public-key encryption. These include assumptions like CDH in a pairing-free group and LPN. Thus, there is still a gap in our understanding of statistical NIZKs in the CRS model, and especially in the designated-verifier model. In this work, we develop new techniques for constructing statistical NIZKs in both the standard CRS model as well as the (reusable) designated-verifier model, which we review below.

Reusable Designated-Verifier NIZKs. A key focus in this work is the designated-verifier model [PsV06, DFN06], where a trusted party generates the CRS together with a *secret* verification key that is used to verify proofs. In this work, we focus exclusively on *reusable* (i.e., multi-theorem) security where soundness holds even against a prover who has oracle access to the verification algorithm. We also consider the stronger *malicious-designated-verifier* model (MDV-NIZKs) introduced by Quach et al. [QRW19], where a trusted party only samples a common reference string,[1] and the verifier is allowed to choose its public and secret key-pair, which is used to generate and verify proofs, respectively. Here, we require that zero-knowledge should hold even if the verifier samples its public key maliciously. As discussed in [QRW19], MDV-NIZKs are equivalent to 2-round zero-knowledge protocols in the CRS model where the verifier's initial message is reusable. A recent line of works have shown how to construct (M)DV-NIZKs with *computational* zero-knowledge from nearly all assumptions known to imply public-key encryption (e.g., CDH, LWE, LPN) [QRW19, CH19, KNYY19a, KNYY19b, LQR+19].

Several recent works have also explored other relaxations of the standard notion of publicly-verifiable NIZKs such as the reusable designated-prover model (where there is a secret proving key and a public verification key) [KW18, KNYY19a] or the reusable preprocessing model (where both the proving and verifications keys are secret) [BCGI18, BCG+19]. In this work, our focus is on reusable designated-verifier NIZKs and publicly-verifiable NIZKs.

Dual-Mode NIZKs. An appealing feature of several existing NIZK constructions [GOS06, GOS12, PS19] is they satisfy a "dual-mode" property. Namely, the CRS in these schemes can be sampled from one of two computationally indistinguishable distributions. One distribution yields *computational NIZK proofs* while the other yields *statistical NIZK arguments*. Dual-mode NIZKs are powerful primitives and a recent work has also studied generic constructions from obfuscation [HU19]. Most of the constructions we develop in this work naturally satisfy this dual-mode property.

1.1 Our Results

In this work, we develop new techniques for constructing statistical NIZKs for general NP languages that yield new constructions in both the reusable designated-verifier model and the standard CRS model. Our techniques enable the following new constructions:

- Under the k-Lin assumption in a *pairing-free* group (for any $k \geq 1$; recall that 1-Lin $\equiv$ DDH), we obtain a statistical MDV-NIZK argument in the common

---

[1] In [QRW19], they require the stronger notion where the CRS is a *uniformly random string*. In some of our constructions in this work, the CRS will be a *structured* string. We believe that this model is still meaningful as the CRS just needs to be sampled once and can be reused by arbitrarily many verifiers, and zero-knowledge holds as long as the CRS is properly sampled.

random string model and a computational MDV-NIZK proof in the common *reference* string model.[2] This is the first construction of a statistical DV-NIZK argument (even ignoring malicious security) in a pairing-free group, and the first construction of a computational MDV-NIZK proof from a *static* assumption. Previously, computational MDV-NIZK proofs were only known from the interactive "one-more CDH" assumption [QRW19].

- Under the k-Lin assumption in $\mathbb{G}_1$ and the k-KerLin assumption in $\mathbb{G}_2$ of a pairing group (for any $k \geq 1$), we obtain a *publicly-verifiable* statistical NIZK argument in the common reference string model. Notably, the k-KerLin assumption is a *search* assumption that is implied by the standard k-Lin assumption [MRV15, KW15]. This is a *qualitatively weaker* assumption than existing pairing-based constructions of statistical NIZK arguments which rely on a *decisional* assumption (k-Lin) in *both* $\mathbb{G}_1$ and $\mathbb{G}_2$ [GOS06, GOS12].
- Under the QR assumption, we obtain a dual-mode MDV-NIZK in the common reference string model. Previously, we could only construct (publicly-verifiable) *computational* NIZKs from the QR assumption [BFM88] (or more generally, from factoring [FLS90, FLS99]), but nothing was known for statistical NIZKs or DV-NIZKs from these assumptions.
- Under the DCR assumption, we obtain a dual-mode MDV-NIZK in the common reference string model. This matches the recent construction described in [CDI+19], which realizes the result through a different approach (via reusable non-interactive secure computation).

We provide a detailed comparison of our constructions with existing NIZK constructions (in both the designated-verifier and the publicly-verifiable models) in Table 1. We describe the formal instantiations in Sect. 5.

From FLS to Statistical NIZKs. All of our constructions follow the classic paradigm of Feige, Lapidot, and Shamir (FLS) [FLS99] who provide a general compiler from a NIZK in an idealized model (i.e., the "hidden-bits" model) to a computational NIZK proof in the CRS model. To date, all existing instantiations of the [FLS99] paradigm have yielded *computational NIZK proofs* in either the CRS model [FLS90, BY92, FLS99, CHK03, Gro10, Gol11, GR13, CL18] or the designated-verifier model [QRW19, CII19, KNYY19a]. In this work, we show how to adapt the general FLS paradigm to obtain new constructions of *statistical NIZK arguments* and more generally, *dual-mode NIZKs*. We provide a general overview of our techniques in Sect. 1.2.

We further note that previous statistical NIZK arguments from pairings, LWE, and DCR follow very different approaches. Our work can also be viewed as providing a *unified* approach to realizing these existing results—both computational and statistical, with the sole exception of the LWE-based scheme—via the FLS paradigm, while also improving upon some of these prior results, and obtaining new ones.

---

[2] This is in fact a dual-mode NIZK, where one of the CRS distributions corresponds to the *uniform* distribution.

1.2   Technical Overview

We begin with a brief overview of the Feige-Lapidot-Shamir (FLS) framework [FLS90, FLS99] for constructing NIZK proofs for NP. We then describe how to adapt the main ideas from the FLS framework to obtain new constructions of (malicious) designated-verifier dual-mode NIZKs as well as publicly-verifiable statistical NIZK arguments.

Table 1. Comparison of our construction to existing multi-theorem NIZKs. We write "public" to denote the standard CRS model (with public proving and public verification), "DV" to denote the designated-verifier model, and "MDV" to denote the malicious-designated-verifier model. For soundness and zero-knowledge, we write "comp." to denote the computational variant of the property, "stat." to denote the statistical variant, and "perf." to denote the perfect variant. When a scheme supports a dual-mode CRS, we indicate the two modes by writing "stat./comp." For the pairing-based constructions, we list the necessary assumptions needed within each of the base groups $\mathbb{G}_1$ and $\mathbb{G}_2$ (assuming an asymmetric pairing).

Construction	Model	Soundness	ZK	Assumption
[BFM88]	public	stat.	comp.	QR
[FLS90, FLS99]	public	stat.	comp.	trapdoor permutation
[SW14]	public	comp.	perf.	$i\mathcal{O}$ + one-way function
[CHK03]*	public	stat.	comp.	CDH ($\mathbb{G}_2$)
[GOS06, GOS12]*	public	perf./comp.	comp./perf.	k-Lin ($\mathbb{G}_1, \mathbb{G}_2$)
This work*	**public**	**comp.**	**stat.**	k-Lin ($\mathbb{G}_1$), k-KerLin ($\mathbb{G}_2$)[†]
[PS19]	public	stat./comp.	comp./stat.	LWE
[QRW19, CH19, KNYY19a]	DV	stat.	comp.	CDH
[QRW19]	MDV	stat.	comp.	one-more CDH
[LQR+19]	MDV	comp.	comp.	CDH/LWE/LPN
[CDI+19]	MDV	stat./comp.	comp./stat.	DCR
This work	**MDV**	**stat./comp.**	**comp./stat.**	k-Lin[‡]/QR/DCR

*This is a *pairing-based* construction. In the assumption column, we enumerate all of the necessary hardness assumptions to instantiate the scheme (in an asymmetric setting).

†The k-KerLin refers to the kernel k-Lin assumption [MRV15, KW15], which can be viewed as the *search* analog of the classic k-Lin assumption [BBS04, HK07, Sha07].

‡This is over a *pairing-free* group. The special case where $k = 1$ corresponds to the standard DDH assumption. In addition, if we consider the vanilla DV-NIZK model (without malicious security), there is a simple instantiation (over elliptic-curve groups) that achieves *perfect* zero-knowledge.

The FLS Framework. The starting point of the FLS construction is a NIZK in an idealized model called the "hidden-bits model." In this model, a trusted party generates a string of uniformly random bits $r_1, \ldots, r_\rho \in \{0, 1\}$ and gives them to the prover. The prover then outputs a proof π along with a set of indices $I \subseteq [\rho]$. The verifier receives $(\pi, \{r_i\}_{i \in I})$ from the trusted party. The model guarantees that the prover cannot influence the value of any of the r_i's and the verifier does not learn anything about r_i for indices $i \notin I$. Feige et al. [FLS99] showed how to construct a NIZK with statistical soundness and perfect zero-knowledge in the hidden-bits model by adapting Blum's Σ-protocol for graph Hamiltonicity [Blu86]. Next, the FLS construction compiles a NIZK in the hidden-bits model into one in the CRS model by using the CRS to define the sequence of hidden bits. We recall the FLS compiler based on trapdoor permutations:

- The CRS contains the description of a *family* of trapdoor permutations over $\{0,1\}^\lambda$ together with ρ random strings $w_1, \ldots, w_\rho \in \{0,1\}^\lambda$ that are used to define a string of ρ hidden bits.
- A hidden-bits string is defined by sampling a permutation σ from the family of trapdoor permutations specified by the CRS, along with a trapdoor for computing σ^{-1}. In conjunction with w_i in the CRS, the permutation σ defines a hidden bit $r_i := \mathsf{hc}(\sigma^{-1}(w_i))$, where $\mathsf{hc}(\cdot)$ is a hard-core bit of σ. We refer to σ as a "commitment" to the hidden-bits string $r \in \{0,1\}^\rho$.
- The prover can open a commitment σ to a bit r_i by sending (i, r_i, u_i) where $u_i := \sigma^{-1}(w_i)$. The verifier checks that $\sigma(u_i) = w_i$ and that $\mathsf{hc}(u_i) = r_i$.

The security argument proceeds roughly as follows:

- Since hc is a hard-core bit, the value of any unopened bit r_i is *computationally hidden* given σ and w_i. The resulting NIZK satisfies computational zero-knowledge.
- The permutation σ and the string w_i *statistically determine* r_i, and the prover cannot open r_i to any value other than $\mathsf{hc}(\sigma^{-1}(w_i))$. The resulting NIZK satisfies statistical soundness. Note that a cheating prover can bias the bit r_i due to the adaptive choice of σ. The FLS construction works around this by leveraging the fact that if the commitment σ has length ℓ, then a malicious prover can bias at most ℓ of the ρ bits, and soundness holds as long as $\ell \ll \rho$.

Our Approach. In this work, we start by showing how to realize a *dual-mode* variant of the hidden-bits model in the *designated-verifier* setting where the underlying commitment to the random bits is either statistically binding or statistically hiding. This "dual-mode" property yields either a *computational DV-NIZK proof* or a *statistical DV-NIZK argument* depending on how the CRS is sampled (similar to previous dual-mode NIZKs [GOS06, GOS12, PS19]). We then show how to extend one of our constructions to the *publicly-verifiable* setting.

An Instantiation From DDH. We first sketch our construction from the DDH assumption. Here, we will work with a (multiplicative) group $\mathbb{G}$ of prime order p and generator g. For a vector $\mathbf{v} = (v_1, \ldots, v_n) \in \mathbb{Z}_p^n$, we write $g^{\mathbf{v}}$ to denote a vector of group elements $(g^{v_1}, \ldots, g^{v_n})$. Analogous to the FLS construction from trapdoor permutations, the CRS contains

- the description $g^{\mathbf{v}}$ of a function, where $\mathbf{v} \xleftarrow{\text{R}} \mathbb{Z}_p^{\rho+1}$ and $g^{\mathbf{v}}$ plays a role similar to the *family* of trapdoor permutations in the FLS construction;
- $g^{\mathbf{w}_1}, \ldots, g^{\mathbf{w}_\rho}$ where each $\mathbf{w}_i \in \mathbb{Z}_p^{\rho+1}$ plays a role similar to $w_i \in \{0,1\}^\lambda$.

In our construction, we will vary the distribution of $\mathbf{w}_i$ (but *not* $\mathbf{v}$) as follows:

- If we want *statistically-binding* "hidden bits," then we sample $\mathbf{w}_i \leftarrow s_i \mathbf{v}$, where $s_i \overset{R}{\leftarrow} \mathbb{Z}_p$.
- If we want *statistically-hiding* "hidden bits," then we sample $\mathbf{w}_i \overset{R}{\leftarrow} \mathbb{Z}_p^{\rho+1}$.

Thanks to the DDH assumption, $(g^{\mathbf{v}}, g^{s_i \mathbf{v}})$ is pseudorandom, and therefore, these two CRS distributions are computationally indistinguishable.[3] As with the construction from trapdoor permutations, the hidden bit r_i is a function of the CRS components $g^{\mathbf{v}}, g^{\mathbf{w}_i}$ together with an additional message σ from the prover. Concretely, the prover samples a random $\mathbf{y} \overset{R}{\leftarrow} \mathbb{Z}_p^{\rho+1}$ and sends $\sigma = g^{\mathbf{y}^\mathsf{T} \mathbf{v}} \in \mathbb{G}$. In conjunction with $g^{\mathbf{w}_i}$ in the CRS, the vector $\mathbf{y}$ defines a hidden bit $r_i := H(g^{\mathbf{y}^\mathsf{T} \mathbf{w}_i})$, where $H \colon \mathbb{G} \to \{0, 1\}$ is a universal hash function. Importantly, while the description $g^{\mathbf{v}}, g^{\mathbf{w}_1}, \ldots, g^{\mathbf{w}_\rho}$ in the CRS grows with ρ, the prover's message σ does not. Now, observe that:

- In binding mode where $\mathbf{w}_i = s_i \mathbf{v}$, we have $\mathbf{y}^\mathsf{T} \mathbf{w}_i = s_i \mathbf{y}^\mathsf{T} \mathbf{v}$. Then, $r_i = H(g^{\mathbf{y}^\mathsf{T} \mathbf{w}_i}) = H(g^{s_i \mathbf{y}^\mathsf{T} \mathbf{v}}) = H(\sigma^{s_i})$ is fully determined by the commitment $\sigma = g^{\mathbf{y}^\mathsf{T} \mathbf{v}}$ together with $g^{\mathbf{v}}, g^{\mathbf{w}_i}$ in the CRS.
- In hiding mode where $\mathbf{w}_i \overset{R}{\leftarrow} \mathbb{Z}_p^{\rho+1}$, the quantity $g^{\mathbf{y}^\mathsf{T} \mathbf{w}_i}$ is completely hidden given $g^{\mathbf{y}^\mathsf{T} \mathbf{v}}$ along with $g^{\mathbf{v}}, g^{\mathbf{w}_i}$ in the CRS, provided that $\mathbf{v}$ and $\mathbf{w}_i$ are linearly independent. More generally, perfect hiding holds as long as the vectors $\mathbf{v}, \mathbf{w}_1, \ldots, \mathbf{w}_\rho$ are linearly independent over $\mathbb{Z}_p^{\rho+1}$.

Next, to open the bit r_i, the prover will send along $g^{\mathbf{y}^\mathsf{T} \mathbf{w}_i}$. To ensure that a cheating prover computes this quantity correctly in the *designated-verifier* model, we rely on techniques using the Cramer-Shoup hash-proof system [CS98, CS02, CKS08] (and also used to construct computational DV-NIZK proofs from CDH [QRW19, CH19, KNYY19a]):

- The verifier's public key consists of components $g^{\mathbf{z}_i} := g^{a\mathbf{w}_i + b_i \mathbf{v}}$ where $a, b_i \overset{R}{\leftarrow} \mathbb{Z}_p$ are secret coefficients chosen by the verifier. The *secret* verification key is the scalars $(a, b_1, \ldots, b_\rho)$.
- The prover sends $g^{u_i} := g^{\mathbf{y}^\mathsf{T} \mathbf{z}_i} \in \mathbb{G}$ in addition to $\sigma = g^c := g^{\mathbf{y}^\mathsf{T} \mathbf{v}} \in \mathbb{G}$ and $g^{t_i} := g^{\mathbf{y}^\mathsf{T} \mathbf{w}_i} \in \mathbb{G}$.
- The verifier checks that $g^{u_i} = (g^{t_i})^a (g^c)^{b_i}$ using (a, b_i).

In the statistically-binding mode where $\mathbf{w}_i = s_i \mathbf{v}$, we have $\mathbf{z}_i = (as_i + b_i)\mathbf{v}$, so (a, b_i) has (statistical) entropy given $\mathbf{v}, \mathbf{w}_i, \mathbf{z}_i$. Roughly speaking, reusable soundness then follows from the analysis of the Cramer-Shoup CCA-secure encryption scheme [CS98, CS02, CKS08] to enforce the consistency check $t_i = s_i c$. In conjunction with a NIZK in the hidden-bits model, we thus obtain a dual-mode

---

[3] This idea of encoding either a full-rank matrix in the exponent or a rank-1 matrix in the exponent also featured in the construction of lossy public-key encryption from the Matrix Diffie-Hellman assumptions [HJR16].

DV-NIZK from the DDH assumption. This construction generalizes very naturally to the k-Lin family of assumptions [BBS04,HK07,Sha07,EHK+13] for any $k \geq 1$ (where in particular, 1-Lin is the DDH assumption). Concretely, we make the following substitutions to the above construction:

$$\mathbf{v} \in \mathbb{Z}_p^{\rho+1} \mapsto \mathbf{V} \in \mathbb{Z}_p^{(\rho+1) \times k}$$

$$s_i, b_i \in \mathbb{Z}_p \mapsto \mathbf{s}_i, \mathbf{b}_i \in \mathbb{Z}_p^k$$

$$t_i, u_i, c \in \mathbb{Z}_p \mapsto \mathbf{t}_i, \mathbf{u}_i, \mathbf{c} \in \mathbb{Z}_p^k$$

We provide the full details and security analysis in the full version.

Extending to QR/DCR. Our DDH construction readily generalizes to the subgroup indistinguishability family of assumptions [BG10] (which generalize the QR [GM82] and DCR [Pai99] assumptions). While there are some technical differences in our concrete instantiations from QR and DCR, all of the main ideas can be described via the conceptually-simpler language of subgroup indistinguishability. This is the approach we take in this overview, and we refer to the technical sections for the full details. First, the subgroup indistinguishability assumption says that the distributions (g, h, g^{r_1}) and $(g, h, g^{r_1} h^{r_2})$ are computationally indistinguishable, where g, h generate subgroups of co-prime order m_g, m_h, respectively, and $r_1 \xleftarrow{\text{R}} \mathbb{Z}_{m_g}$, $r_2 \xleftarrow{\text{R}} \mathbb{Z}_{m_h}$.

Similar to the DDH instantiation, the CRS contains a function $g^{\mathbf{v}}$ (where $\mathbf{v} \xleftarrow{\text{R}} \mathbb{Z}_{m_g m_h}^{\rho}$) together with additional components $g^{s_1 \mathbf{v}} h^{\hat{\mathbf{w}}_1}, \dots, g^{s_\rho \mathbf{v}} h^{\hat{\mathbf{w}}_\rho}$, where $\hat{\mathbf{w}}_i = \mathbf{0}$ in binding mode and $\hat{\mathbf{w}}_i = \mathbf{e}_i$ in hiding mode. Here $\mathbf{e}_i$ is the basis vector whose i^{th} index is 1. Under the subgroup indistinguishability assumption, these two distributions are computationally indistinguishable.

Next, the hidden bit r_i is a function of the CRS components $g^{\mathbf{v}}$ and $g^{s_i \mathbf{v}} h^{\hat{\mathbf{w}}_i}$ together with an additional commitment σ from the prover. Specifically, the prover samples a vector $\mathbf{y} = (y_1, \dots, y_\rho) \xleftarrow{\text{R}} \mathbb{Z}_{m_g m_h}^{\rho}$ and computes

$$\sigma := g^{\mathbf{y}^{\mathsf{T}} \mathbf{v}} \quad \text{and} \quad t_i := g^{s_i \mathbf{y}^{\mathsf{T}} \mathbf{v}} h^{\mathbf{y}^{\mathsf{T}} \hat{\mathbf{w}}_i} \quad \text{and} \quad r_i := H(t_i), \tag{1.1}$$

where H is a hash function. Now, observe that:

- In binding mode where $\hat{\mathbf{w}}_i = \mathbf{0}$, then $t_i = g^{s_i \mathbf{y}^{\mathsf{T}} \mathbf{v}} = \sigma^{s_i}$. Thus, t_i (and correspondingly, r_i) is fully determined by the commitment σ and the components $g^{\mathbf{v}}$, $g^{s_i \mathbf{v}} h^{\hat{\mathbf{w}}_i} = g^{s_i \mathbf{v}}$ in the CRS.
- In hiding mode where $\hat{\mathbf{w}}_i = \mathbf{e}_i$, then $t_i = g^{s_i \mathbf{w}^{\mathsf{T}} \mathbf{y}} h^{y_i}$. Since g and h generate subgroups of co-prime order m_g and m_h, respectively, we can appeal to the Chinese remainder theorem to argue that the commitment $\sigma = g^{\mathbf{y}^{\mathsf{T}} \mathbf{v}}$ *perfectly* hides the value of $\mathbf{y} \bmod m_h$. Since $\mathbf{y}$ is uniform over $\mathbb{Z}_{m_g m_h}$, this means that $t_1, \dots, t_i$ have at least $\log m_h$ bits of statistical entropy given σ (and the components of the CRS).
  In the DCR construction, $m_h = N$ is a product of two large primes, so we can use a standard universal hash function to extract a uniformly random bit [HILL99].

In the QR construction, $m_h = 2$, so each component t_i contains just one bit of entropy, and we cannot appeal to the leftover hash lemma. In this case, we adapt an idea from [DGI+19] (for constructing trapdoor hash functions from QR) and use a deterministic function to extract the bit from t_i.

Finally, to open a bit r_i, the prover provides σ, t_i, along with a proof that t_i and σ are consistent (i.e., there exists some $\mathbf{y}$ such that Eq. (1.1) hold). Here, we use the same techniques as in the DDH setting (i.e., using the Cramer-Shoup hash-proof system) to implement this. In the QR setting, we encounter some challenges because the order of the subgroup generated by h is polynomial-sized, which allows the adversary to break soundness with noticeable probability. To amplify soundness, we essentially embed multiple copies of the Cramer-Shoup hash-proof system and ensure that the proof verifies only if *all* copies verify (while retaining *reusable* soundness). We refer to the full version for the full analysis of the QR and DCR constructions.

Handling Malicious Verifiers. All of the constructions described thus far are zero-knowledge only if the verifier samples its public verification key *honestly*. However, if the verifier can choose its key *arbitrarily*, then it can break zero-knowledge. To see this, consider again the DDH construction (in hiding mode). There, the CRS contains elements $g^{\mathbf{v}}, g^{\mathbf{w}_1}, \ldots, g^{\mathbf{w}_\rho}$, and a verifier's public key is $(g^{\mathbf{z}_1}, \ldots, g^{\mathbf{z}_\rho})$ where $\mathbf{z}_i = a\mathbf{w}_i + b_i\mathbf{v}$. To generate a hidden-bits string r, the prover samples $\mathbf{y} \xleftarrow{\text{R}} \mathbb{Z}_p^{\rho+1}$ and sets $r_i = H(g^{\mathbf{y}^\top \mathbf{w}_i})$. To open a bit r_i, the prover computes $g^{t_i} = g^{\mathbf{y}^\top \mathbf{w}_i}$ and $g^{u_i} = g^{\mathbf{y}^\top \mathbf{z}_i}$. In order to appeal to security of the underlying NIZK in the hidden-bits model, we require that the commitment $\sigma = g^{\mathbf{y}^\top \mathbf{v}}$, the value of r_i, and the opening (g^{t_i}, g^{u_i}) do not leak information about any other (unopened) bit r_j. This is the case when all of the verification key components $\mathbf{z}_i$ are generated honestly. In this case, $\mathbf{v}, \mathbf{w}_1, \ldots, \mathbf{w}_\rho$ are linearly independent, and $\mathbf{z}_i$ is a function of only $\mathbf{v}$ and $\mathbf{w}_i$. However, a malicious verifier can choose $\mathbf{z}_i = \mathbf{w}_j$ for some $j \neq i$. Then, if the honest prover computes an opening to r_i, it will also compute $g^{u_i} = g^{\mathbf{y}^\top \mathbf{z}_i} = g^{\mathbf{y}^\top \mathbf{w}_j}$, which completely leaks the value of r_j. As such, the basic scheme is insecure against a malicious verifier.

This problem where an opening to r_i can leak information about the value r_j for $j \neq i$ is the same problem encountered in the basic DV-NIZK from [QRW19]. In this work, we adopt the same general strategy as them to defend against malicious verifiers. At a high-level, the approach of [QRW19] for achieving security against malicious verifiers is to use the basic scheme above to generate a hidden-bits string $r'_1, \ldots, r'_\ell$ of length $\ell \gg \rho$. Each of the ρ hidden bits $r_1, \ldots, r_\rho$ is then derived as a sparse pseudorandom combination of the bits $r'_1, \ldots, r'_\ell$. More specifically, the prover chooses a mapping φ that maps each index $i \in [\rho]$ onto a set $\varphi(i) \subseteq [\ell]$. Each bit r_i is a deterministic function of r'_j for $j \in \varphi(i)$. To open a bit r_i, the prover instead opens up all bits r'_j for $j \in \varphi(i)$. The length ℓ and the size $|\varphi(i)|$ of the sets are chosen so as to ensure that for all unopened bits $j \in [\rho]$, there is at least one index $k \in \varphi(j)$ such that r'_k is hidden from the verifier, which ideally, is sufficient to mask the value of r_j. Quach et al. show

how to implement this idea by relying on a one-more CDH assumption (in conjunction with somewhere equivocal PRFs [HJO+16]), and a complex rewinding argument in the security proof. In our setting, the algebraic structure of our construction enables us to make a conceptually-simpler *information-theoretic* argument (and only needing to assume a PRG). As such, we are able to obtain a *dual-mode* MDV-NIZK from the DDH (and more generally, k-Lin), QR, and DCR assumptions.

We give a brief overview of how we extend the basic DDH construction sketched above to achieve security against malicious verifiers. The same idea extends to the QR and DCR constructions. Specifically, we use our basic construction to generate a hidden-bits string of length $\ell \gg \rho$ as follows:

- The CRS (in hiding mode) consists of group elements $g^{\mathbf{v}}, g^{\mathbf{w}_1}, \ldots, g^{\mathbf{w}_\ell}$, where $\mathbf{v}, \mathbf{w}_1, \ldots, \mathbf{w}_\ell \xleftarrow{\text{R}} \mathbb{Z}_p^{\ell+1}$. With overwhelming probability, these vectors are linearly independent.
- The honest verifier's public key is $(g^{\mathbf{z}_1}, \ldots, g^{\mathbf{z}_\ell})$, constructed in the usual manner.
- The prover's commitment is a vector $\mathbf{y} \in \mathbb{Z}_p^{\ell+1}$ as well as a seed $\mathbf{s}$ for a PRG.[4] The PRG outputs a collection of ρ blocks, where each block consists of a set $S_i \subseteq [\ell]$ and a vector $\boldsymbol{\alpha} \in \mathbb{Z}_p^\ell$. The hidden bit r_i is determined by first computing $g^{t_j} = g^{\mathbf{y}^\mathsf{T}\mathbf{w}_j}$ for all $j \in S_i$ and defining $r_i := H(\prod_{j \in S_i} g^{\alpha_j t_j})$.
- The opening for r_i consists of $g^{t_j} = g^{\mathbf{y}^\mathsf{T}\mathbf{w}_j}$ and $g^{u_j} = g^{\mathbf{y}^\mathsf{T}\mathbf{z}_j}$ for all $j \in S_i$.

Our goal is to show that even for an adversarially-chosen verification key, the commitment σ and the opening $(\{g^{t_j}, g^{u_j}\}_{j \in S_i})$ to a bit r_i does not leak any information about r_j whenever $j \neq i$.[5] By construction, the opening to r_i is determined by $\mathbf{y}^\mathsf{T}\mathbf{v}$, $\mathbf{y}^\mathsf{T}\mathbf{w}_j$, and $\mathbf{y}^\mathsf{T}\mathbf{z}_j$ for $j \in S_i$ (where the set S_i is *pseudorandom*). Take any index $i^* \neq i$. Then, if there exists $j^* \in \varphi(i^*)$ such that $\mathbf{w}_{j^*}$ is linearly independent of $\{\mathbf{v}, \mathbf{w}_j, \mathbf{z}_j\}_{j \in S_i}$, then the value of $\mathbf{y}^\mathsf{T}\mathbf{w}_{j^*}$ is independent and uniformly random given the view of the adversary (since the honest prover samples $\mathbf{y} \xleftarrow{\text{R}} \mathbb{Z}_p^{\ell+1}$). In this case, the value $g^{t_{j^*}} = g^{\mathbf{y}^\mathsf{T}\mathbf{w}_{j^*}}$ remains uniformly random and statistically hides r_{i^*}. Thus, it suffices to set ℓ and $|S_i|$ so that there will always exist $j^* \in \varphi(i^*)$ where $\mathbf{w}_{j^*}$ is linearly independent of $\{\mathbf{v}, \mathbf{w}_j, \mathbf{z}_j\}_{j \in S_i}$ with overwhelming probability. In the case of our DDH construction, we can set $|S_i| = \lambda$, where λ is a security parameter, and $\ell = 3\rho^2\lambda$ to satisfy this property. We provide the details of our DDH (more generally, its generalization to the k-Lin assumption) in Sect. 4.3 and our QR and DCR constructions in the full version.

---

[4] We require a PRG because the prover's message needs to be *succinct* in order to argue soundness of the resulting NIZK in the FLS paradigm. Thus, we rely on a PRG for compression. Note that even though we rely on a computational assumption, we can still show *statistical* zero-knowledge. The security proof only requires that there are no efficient statistical tests that can distinguish the output of the PRG from a random string (which is implied by PRG security).

[5] To show adaptive, multi-theorem zero-knowledge, we in fact show an even stronger *simulation* property. We refer to Sect. 3 for more details.

Public Verifiability via Pairings. All of the constructions we have described so far operate in the designated-verifier model because our constructions rely on a Cramer-Shoup-style hash proof system to argue consistency between a commitment and the opening. If we can instead *publicly* check consistency between a commitment and its opening, then the resulting scheme becomes publicly verifiable. For the DDH construction, we can implement the consistency check using a pairing (this is the approach taken in [CHK03] to obtain a computational NIZK proof). In this work, we develop a similar approach to obtain a statistical NIZK argument from pairings.

In particular, let $e\colon \mathbb{G}_1 \times \mathbb{G}_2 \to \mathbb{G}_T$ be an (asymmetric) pairing. Let g_1, g_2 be generators of $\mathbb{G}_1$ and $\mathbb{G}_2$, respectively. At a high level, we implement the DDH scheme in $\mathbb{G}_1$ and use $\mathbb{G}_2$ for verification. More specifically, the CRS is $g_1^{\mathbf{v}}, g_1^{\mathbf{w}_1}, \ldots, g_1^{\mathbf{w}_\rho}$, and the verification key is $g_1^{(a\mathbf{w}_1 + b_1 \mathbf{v})}, \ldots, g_1^{(a\mathbf{w}_\rho + b_\rho \mathbf{v})}$. The commitment, hidden-bits sequence, and openings are defined as before:

$$\sigma = g_1^c = g_1^{\mathbf{y}^\mathsf{T}\mathbf{v}}, \quad r_i = H(g_1^{\mathbf{y}^\mathsf{T}\mathbf{w}_i}), \quad g_1^{t_i} = g_1^{\mathbf{y}^\mathsf{T}\mathbf{w}_i} \quad \text{and} \quad g_1^{u_i} = g_1^{\mathbf{y}^\mathsf{T}(a\mathbf{w}_i + b_i\mathbf{v})}.$$

In the designated-verifier setting, the verifier checks $g_1^{u_i} \stackrel{?}{=} (g_1^{t_i})^a (g_1^c)^{b_i}$. A direct approach for public verification is to include $g_2^a, g_2^{b_1}, \ldots, g_2^{b_\rho}$ as part of the verification key, and check the following:

$$e(g_1^{u_i}, g_2) \stackrel{?}{=} e(g_1^{t_i}, g_2^a) \cdot e(g_1^c, g_2^{b_i}).$$

While this approach is *correct*, it is unclear to argue soundness (even against computationally-bounded adversaries). In the designated-verifier setting, the soundness analysis critically relies on the verification coefficients a, b_i being hidden from the adversary, and it is unclear how to make such an argument when the adversary is given $g_2^a, g_2^{b_i}$.

To base hardness on a concrete cryptographic assumption, we leverage a technique from [KW15], who describe a general method to "securely publish" the verification key in the exponent (as we hoped to do in our initial attempt above) with a concrete security reduction to a *search* assumption in $\mathbb{G}_2$. This yields a general compiler from a designated-verifier scheme with unconditional soundness to a publicly-verifiable scheme with computational soundness, at the expense of requiring a pairing and a *search* assumption in $\mathbb{G}_2$. The compiler preserves zero-knowledge of the underlying scheme.

Concretely, instead of scalar verification coefficients a, b_i, we instead sample vectors $\mathbf{a}, \mathbf{b}_i \xleftarrow{R} \mathbb{Z}_p^2$, and publish $g_1^{\mathbf{w}_i \mathbf{a}^\mathsf{T} + \mathbf{v}\mathbf{b}_i^\mathsf{T}}$ for each $i \in [\rho]$ in the CRS. The public verification components will consist of $g_2^{\mathbf{d}}, g_2^{\mathbf{a}^\mathsf{T}\mathbf{d}}, g_2^{\mathbf{b}_1^\mathsf{T}\mathbf{d}}, \ldots, g_2^{\mathbf{b}_\rho^\mathsf{T}\mathbf{d}}$, where $\mathbf{d} \in \mathbb{Z}_p^2$. The key observation is that $\mathbf{a}, \mathbf{b}_1, \ldots, \mathbf{b}_\rho$ have *statistical entropy* even given the public components $g_2^{\mathbf{d}}, g_2^{\mathbf{a}^\mathsf{T}\mathbf{d}}, g_2^{\mathbf{b}_1^\mathsf{T}\mathbf{d}}, \ldots, g_2^{\mathbf{b}_\rho^\mathsf{T}\mathbf{d}}$. The commitment, hidden-bits sequence, and openings are still computed as before, except the verification component $g_1^{u_i}$ is replaced with $g_1^{\mathbf{u}_i^\mathsf{T}} = g_1^{\mathbf{y}^\mathsf{T}(\mathbf{w}_i \mathbf{a}^\mathsf{T} + \mathbf{v}\mathbf{b}_i^\mathsf{T})}$. The verification relation now checks

$$e(g_1^{\mathbf{u}_i^\mathsf{T}}, g_2^{\mathbf{d}}) \stackrel{?}{=} e(g_1^{t_i}, g_2^{\mathbf{a}^\mathsf{T}\mathbf{d}}) \cdot e(g_1^c, g_2^{\mathbf{b}_i^\mathsf{T}\mathbf{d}}).$$

Since the verification coefficients $\mathbf{a}, \mathbf{b}_1, \ldots, \mathbf{b}_\rho$ have statistical entropy given the public key, we can appeal to DDH in $\mathbb{G}_1$ and the 1-KerLin assumption (a *search* assumption that is *weaker* than DDH) over $\mathbb{G}_2$ to argue soundness of the resulting construction. This yields a publicly-verifiable statistical NIZK argument in the common *reference* string model. We provide the full description and analysis (generalized to the k-Lin and k-KerLin family of assumptions for any $k \geq 1$) in the full version.

Our pairing-based construction does not appear to have a dual mode and it is unclear how to modify this construction to obtain computational NIZK proofs. We do note that computational NIZK proofs can be built directly from pairings (under the CDH assumption in $\mathbb{G}_1$) also by following the FLS paradigm [CHK03]. At the same time, it is also unclear how to adapt the [CHK03] construction to obtain statistical NIZK arguments.

A Unifying Abstraction: Dual-Mode Hidden-Bits Generators. We unify the different algebraic constructions through the abstraction of a "dual-mode hidden-bits generator." Previously, Quach et al. [QRW19] introduced the notion of a *hidden-bits generator* (HBG) and showed how to use an HBG to implement the classic FLS paradigm in both the designated-verifier and the publicly-verifiable settings. Very briefly, an HBG with output size ρ consists of four main algorithms (Setup, KeyGen, GenBits, Verify):

- The Setup algorithm outputs a common reference string crs, and KeyGen generates a public key pk along with a (possibly secret) verification key sk.
- The GenBits algorithm outputs a short commitment σ together with a sequence of hidden bits $r \in \{0,1\}^\rho$ as well as openings $\{\pi_i\}_{i \in [\rho]}$.
- The Verify algorithm takes an index $i \in [\rho]$, a bit $r_i \in \{0,1\}$, and an opening π_i and either accepts or rejects the proof.

The main security requirements are *statistical binding* (i.e., no adversary can produce a commitment σ and valid openings π_i, π_i' that open to 0 and 1 for the same index) and *computational hiding* (i.e., an honestly-generated commitment σ and set of openings $\{r_i, \pi_i\}_{i \in I}$ should hide all unopened bits r_j for $j \notin I$ from any computationally-bounded adversary). Quach et al. show that an HBG with these properties can be combined directly with a NIZK in the hidden-bits model to obtain a computational NIZK proof in the CRS model. If the HBG is in the (malicious) designated-verifier model, then so is the resulting NIZK.

In this work, we extend this framework by introducing the notion of a dual-mode HBG where the CRS can be generated in one of two modes: a *binding* mode where the HBG satisfies statistical binding (as in [QRW19]) and a *hiding* mode where the HBG satisfies a stronger notion of *statistical hiding* (i.e., the unopened bits are statistically hidden given the CRS, the commitment σ and any subset of opened bits $\{(r_i, \pi_i)\}_{i \in I}$). In our case, we impose an even stronger equivocation property in the hiding mode: namely, given any set of indices $I \subseteq [\rho]$ and any assignment $r_I \in \{0,1\}^{|I|}$ to that set, it is possible to simulate a commitment σ and a set of openings $\{\pi_i\}_{i \in I}$ that is statistically indistinguishable from the output of the honest generator. This allows us to directly argue *adaptive* and *multi-theorem*[6] statistical zero-knowledge for the resulting NIZK construction. We give our formal definition in Sect. 3, and describe our construction of dual-mode (designated-verifier) NIZKs from dual-mode (designated-verifier) HBGs in Sect. 3.1. In Sect. 4 and the full version, we show how to construct dual-mode HBGs from the k-Lin, QR, and DCR assumptions.

2   Preliminaries

Throughout this work, we write λ (oftentimes implicitly) to denote the security parameter. For a positive integer $n \in \mathbb{N}$, we write $[n]$ to denote the set $\{1, \ldots, n\}$. We will typically use bold lowercase letters (e.g., $\mathbf{v}, \mathbf{w}$) to denote vectors and bold uppercase letters (e.g., $\mathbf{A}, \mathbf{B}$) to denote matrices. For a vector $\mathbf{v} \in \mathbb{Z}_p^n$, we will use non-boldface letters to refer to its components; namely, we write $\mathbf{v} = (v_1, \ldots, v_n)$. For a (sorted) set of indices $I = \{i_1, \ldots, i_m\} \subseteq [n]$, we write $\mathbf{v}_I$ to denote the sub-vector $(v_{i_1}, \ldots, v_{i_m})$.

We say that a function f is negligible in λ, denoted $\mathsf{negl}(\lambda)$, if $f(\lambda) = o(1/\lambda^c)$ for all $c \in \mathbb{N}$. We write $\mathsf{poly}(\lambda)$ to denote a function bounded by a fixed polynomial in λ. We say an event happens with negligible probability if the probability of the event happening is negligible, and that it happens with overwhelming probability if its complement occurs with negligible probability. We say that an algorithm is efficient if it runs in probabilistic polynomial-time in the length of its inputs. We say that two families of distributions $\mathcal{D}_1 = \{\mathcal{D}_{1,\lambda}\}_{\lambda \in \mathbb{N}}$ and $\mathcal{D}_2 = \{\mathcal{D}_{2,\lambda}\}_{\lambda \in \mathbb{N}}$ are computationally indistinguishable if no efficient adversary can distinguish samples from $\mathcal{D}_1$ and $\mathcal{D}_2$ except with negligible probability, and we denote this by writing $\mathcal{D}_1 \overset{c}{\approx} \mathcal{D}_2$. For two distributions $\mathcal{D}_1, \mathcal{D}_2$, we write $\Delta(\mathcal{D}_1, \mathcal{D}_2)$ to denote the statistical distance between $\mathcal{D}_1$ and $\mathcal{D}_2$. We write $\mathcal{D}_1 \overset{s}{\approx} \mathcal{D}_2$ to denote that $\mathcal{D}_1$ and $\mathcal{D}_2$ are statistically indistinguishable: namely, that $\Delta(\mathcal{D}_1, \mathcal{D}_2) = \mathsf{negl}(\lambda)$. For a finite set S, we write $x \overset{\mathrm{R}}{\leftarrow} S$ to denote that x is sampled uniformly at random from S. For a distribution $\mathcal{D}$, we write $x \leftarrow \mathcal{D}$ to denote that x is sampled from $\mathcal{D}$. We review additional preliminaries in the full version.

2.1   NIZKs in the Hidden-Bits Model

In this section, we recall the notion of a NIZK in the hidden-bits model [FLS99]. Our presentation is adapted from the description from [QRW19, CH19, KNYY19a].

---

[6] We can also use the transformation from [FLS99] to generically go from single-theorem zero-knowledge to multi-theorem zero-knowledge, but at the expense of making *non-black-box* use of a PRG. Our approach yields a direct construction of multi-theorem zero-knowledge without needing to make non-black-box use of cryptography. We discuss this in greater detail in Remark 2.5.

Definition 2.1 (NIZKs in the Hidden-Bits Model). *Let $\mathcal{L} \subseteq \{0,1\}^n$ be an NP language associated with an NP relation $\mathcal{R}$ with $n = n(\lambda)$. A non-interactive zero-knowledge proof in the hidden-bits model for $\mathcal{L}$ consists of a tuple $\Pi_{\mathsf{HBM}} = (\mathsf{Prove}, \mathsf{Verify})$ and a parameter $\rho = \rho(\lambda, n)$ with the following properties:*

- $\mathsf{Prove}(1^\lambda, r, x, w) \to (I, \pi)$: *On input the security parameter λ, a string $r \in \{0,1\}^\rho$, a statement $x \in \{0,1\}^n$ and a witness w, this algorithm outputs a set of indices $I \subseteq [\rho]$ and a proof π.*
- $\mathsf{Verify}(1^\lambda, I, r_I, x, \pi) \to \{0,1\}$: *On input the security parameter λ, a subset $I \subseteq [\rho]$, a string $r_I \in \{0,1\}^{|I|}$, a statement $x \in \{0,1\}^n$ and a proof π, the verification algorithm outputs a bit $b \in \{0,1\}$.*

Moreover, Π_{HBM} satisfies the following properties:

- **Completeness:** *For all $(x, w) \in \mathcal{R}$ and $r \in \{0,1\}^\rho$,*

$$\Pr[(I, \pi) \leftarrow \mathsf{Prove}(1^\lambda, r, x, w) : \mathsf{Verify}(1^\lambda, I, r_I, x, \pi) = 1] = 1.$$

- **Statistical soundness:** *For all unbounded provers $\mathcal{P}^*$, we have that for $r \xleftarrow{\text{R}} \{0,1\}^\rho$ and $(x, \pi, I) \leftarrow \mathcal{P}^*(1^\lambda, r)$,*

$$\Pr[x \notin \mathcal{L} \;\wedge\; \mathsf{Verify}(1^\lambda, I, r_I, x, \pi) = 1] = \mathsf{negl}(\lambda).$$

We will oftentimes refer to the above probability as the soundness error.

- **Perfect zero-knowledge:** *There exists an efficient simulator $\mathcal{S}$ such that for all unbounded verifiers $\mathcal{V}^*$, if we take $(x, w) \leftarrow \mathcal{V}^*(1^\lambda)$, $r \xleftarrow{\text{R}} \{0,1\}^\rho$, $(I, \pi) \leftarrow \mathsf{Prove}(1^\lambda, r, x, w)$, and $(\widetilde{I}, \widetilde{r_I}, \widetilde{\pi}) \leftarrow \mathcal{S}(1^\lambda, x)$, and moreover if $\mathcal{R}(x, w) = 1$, then the following two distributions are identically distributed:*

$$(I, r_I, \pi) \equiv (\widetilde{I}, \widetilde{r_I}, \widetilde{\pi}).$$

Theorem 2.2 (NIZKs in the Hidden-Bits Model [FLS99]). *For any $\varepsilon > 0$, every language $\mathcal{L} \in \mathsf{NP}$ has a NIZK in the hidden-bits model with soundness error ε and relying on a hidden-bits string of length $\rho = \mathsf{poly}(n, \log(1/\varepsilon))$.*

2.2 Designated-Verifier NIZKs and Dual-Mode NIZKs

We now review the notion of a *reusable* designated-verifier NIZK (DV-NIZK). Namely, we require that the same common reference string and verification state can be *reused* to prove and verify many statements without compromising either soundness or zero-knowledge. As in [LQR+19], we use the fine-grained notion with separate setup and key-generation algorithms. The setup algorithm samples the common reference string (CRS) while the key-generation algorithm generates a public key (used to generate proofs) along with a secret key (used to verify proofs). We allow the same CRS to be *reusable* by many verifiers, who each generate their own public/secret key-pairs. In the traditional notion of DV-NIZKs, the setup and key-generation algorithms would be combined into a single algorithm that outputs the CRS (which would include the public proving key) along with a secret verification key.

Definition 2.3 (Designated-Verifier NIZK). *Let* $\mathcal{L} \subseteq \{0,1\}^n$ *be an* NP *language associated with an* NP *relation* $\mathcal{R}$ *with* $n = n(\lambda)$. *A reusable* designated-verifier non-interactive zero-knowledge (DV-NIZK) *proof for* $\mathcal{L}$ *consists of a tuple of efficient algorithms* $\Pi_{\mathsf{dvNIZK}} = (\mathsf{Setup}, \mathsf{KeyGen}, \mathsf{Prove}, \mathsf{Verify})$ *with the following properties:*

- $\mathsf{Setup}(1^\lambda) \to \mathsf{crs}$: *On input the security parameter* λ, *this algorithm outputs a common reference string* crs. *If* Setup *outputs a* uniformly random string, *we say that the scheme is in the* common random string *model.*
- $\mathsf{KeyGen}(\mathsf{crs}) \to (\mathsf{pk}, \mathsf{sk})$: *On input the common reference string* crs, *the key-generation algorithm outputs a public key* pk *and a secret key* sk.
- $\mathsf{Prove}(\mathsf{crs}, \mathsf{pk}, x, w) \to \pi$: *On input the common reference string* crs, *a public key* pk, *a statement* $x \in \{0,1\}^n$, *and a witness* w, *this algorithm outputs a proof* π.
- $\mathsf{Verify}(\mathsf{crs}, \mathsf{sk}, x, \pi) \to \{0,1\}$: *On input the common reference string* crs, *a secret verification key* sk, *a statement* x, *and a proof* π, *the verification algorithm outputs a bit* $b \in \{0,1\}$.

Moreover, Π_{dvNIZK} *should satisfy the following properties:*

- **Completeness:** *For all* $(x, w) \in \mathcal{R}$, *and taking* $\mathsf{crs} \leftarrow \mathsf{Setup}(1^\lambda)$, $(\mathsf{pk}, \mathsf{sk}) \leftarrow \mathsf{KeyGen}(\mathsf{crs})$,

$$\Pr\left[\pi \leftarrow \mathsf{Prove}(\mathsf{crs}, \mathsf{pk}, x, w) : \mathsf{Verify}(\mathsf{crs}, \mathsf{sk}, x, \pi) = 1\right] = 1.$$

- *(Statistical)* **soundness:** *We consider two variants of soundness:*
  - **Non-adaptive soundness:** *For all* $x \notin \mathcal{L}$ *and all polynomials* $q = q(\lambda)$, *and all unbounded adversaries* $\mathcal{A}$ *making at most* q *verification queries, and sampling* $\mathsf{crs} \leftarrow \mathsf{Setup}(1^\lambda)$, $(\mathsf{pk}, \mathsf{sk}) \leftarrow \mathsf{KeyGen}(\mathsf{crs})$, *we have that*

$$\Pr\left[\pi \leftarrow \mathcal{A}^{\mathsf{Verify}(\mathsf{crs}, \mathsf{sk}, \cdot, \cdot)}(1^\lambda, \mathsf{crs}, \mathsf{pk}, x) : \mathsf{Verify}(\mathsf{crs}, \mathsf{sk}, x, \pi) = 1\right] = \mathsf{negl}(\lambda).$$

  - **Adaptive soundness:** *For all polynomials* $q = q(\lambda)$ *and all unbounded adversaries* $\mathcal{A}$ *making at most* q *verification queries, and sampling* $\mathsf{crs} \leftarrow \mathsf{Setup}(1^\lambda)$, $(\mathsf{pk}, \mathsf{sk}) \leftarrow \mathsf{KeyGen}(\mathsf{crs})$, *we have that*

$$\Pr\Big[(x, \pi) \leftarrow \mathcal{A}^{\mathsf{Verify}(\mathsf{crs}, \mathsf{sk}, \cdot, \cdot)}(1^\lambda, \mathsf{crs}, \mathsf{pk}) :$$
$$x \notin \mathcal{L} \wedge \mathsf{Verify}(\mathsf{crs}, \mathsf{sk}, x, \pi) = 1\Big] = \mathsf{negl}(\lambda).$$

  We also define the corresponding notions of computational soundness *where the above properties only need to hold against efficient adversaries* $\mathcal{A}$.
- *(Statistical)* **zero-knowledge:** *For all polynomials* $q = q(\lambda)$ *and all unbounded adversaries* $\mathcal{A}$ *making at most* q *oracle queries, there exists an efficient simulator* $\mathcal{S} = (\mathcal{S}_1, \mathcal{S}_2)$ *such that*

$$\left|\Pr[\mathcal{A}^{\mathcal{O}_0(\mathsf{crs}, \mathsf{pk}, \cdot, \cdot)}(\mathsf{crs}, \mathsf{pk}, \mathsf{sk}) = 1] - \Pr[\mathcal{A}^{\mathcal{O}_1(\mathsf{st}_\mathcal{S}, \cdot, \cdot)}(\widetilde{\mathsf{crs}}, \widetilde{\mathsf{pk}}, \widetilde{\mathsf{sk}}) = 1]\right| = \mathsf{negl}(\lambda),$$

where crs $\leftarrow$ Setup(1^λ), (pk, sk) $\leftarrow$ KeyGen(crs) *and* ($\mathsf{st}_\mathcal{S}, \widetilde{\mathsf{crs}}, \widetilde{\mathsf{pk}}, \widetilde{\mathsf{sk}}$) $\leftarrow$ $\mathcal{S}_1(1^\lambda)$, *the oracle* $\mathcal{O}_0$(crs, pk, x, w) *outputs* Prove(crs, pk, x, w) *if* $\mathcal{R}(x, w) = 1$ *and* $\perp$ *otherwise, and the oracle* $\mathcal{O}_1$($\mathsf{st}_\mathcal{S}, x, w$) *outputs* $\mathcal{S}_2(\mathsf{st}_\mathcal{S}, x)$ *if* $\mathcal{R}(x, w) = 1$ *and* $\perp$ *otherwise. Similar to soundness, we also consider* computational zero-knowledge *where the above property only needs to hold against efficient adversaries* $\mathcal{A}$.

Definition 2.4 (Publicly-Verifiable NIZKs). *A NIZK* Π_{NIZK} *is publicly-verifiable if the secret key output by* KeyGen *is empty. In this case, we can combine the* Setup *and* KeyGen *algorithms into a single algorithm that just outputs the CRS, and there is no notion of separate public/secret keys* pk *and* sk. *Both the* Prove *and* Verify *algorithms just take* crs *as input. We can define all of the properties analogously. In the publicly-verifiable setting, we do not need to provide the prover a separate verification oracle in the soundness game.*

Remark 2.5 (Single-Theorem vs. Multi-Theorem Zero-Knowledge). The zero-knowledge property in Definition 2.3 is *multi-theorem* in the sense that the adversary can see proofs of multiple statements. We can consider a weaker notion of single-theorem zero-knowledge where the adversary can only see a proof on a single (adaptively-chosen) statement. Previously, Feige et al. [FLS99] showed how to generically compile a single-theorem NIZK into a multi-theorem NIZK using a PRG. This transformation also applies in the designated-verifier setting [QRW19, CH19, KNYY19a]. One limitation of the [FLS99] transformation is that it requires making *non-black-box* use of a PRG. The constructions we present in this work directly achieve multi-theorem zero-knowledge without needing to go through the [FLS99] transformation. As such, our constructions do *not* require making non-black-box use of any cryptographic primitives.

Malicious DV-NIZKs. We also consider the notion of a malicious designated-verifier NIZK (MDV-NIZK) from [QRW19] where zero-knowledge holds even when the public key pk is chosen maliciously. In this case, the only trusted setup that we require is generating the common reference string (or, in some cases, a common random string), which can be reused by many verifiers.

We recall the formal definition in the full version.

Dual-Mode DV-NIZKs. Next, we recall the formal definition of a dual-mode (DV)-NIZK [GOS06, GOS12].

Definition 2.6 (Dual-Mode Designated-Verifier NIZK). *A dual-mode DV-NIZK* Π_{dvNIZK} = (Setup, KeyGen, Prove, Verify) *is a DV-NIZK with the following additional properties:*

- **Dual-mode:** *The* Setup *algorithm takes an additional argument* mode $\in$ {binding, hiding}, *and outputs a common reference string* crs.
- **CRS indistinguishability:** *The common reference string output by the two modes are computationally indistinguishable:*

$$\mathsf{Setup}(1^\lambda, \mathsf{binding}) \overset{c}{\approx} \mathsf{Setup}(1^\lambda, \mathsf{hiding}).$$

- **Statistical soundness in binding mode:** If crs ← Setup(1^λ, binding), *the designated-verifier NIZK satisfies statistical soundness.*
- **Statistical zero-knowledge in hiding mode:** If crs ← Setup(1^λ, hiding), *the designated-verifier NIZK satisfies statistical zero-knowledge.*

We define a dual mode MDV-NIZK analogously by requiring the stronger property of statistical zero-knowledge against malicious verifiers in hiding mode.

Remark 2.7 (Dual-Mode Designated-Verifier NIZKs). Let Π_{dvNIZK} = (Setup, KeyGen, Prove, Verify) be a dual-mode DV-NIZK for a language $\mathcal{L} \subseteq \{0, 1\}^n$. Then, the following properties hold:

- When the CRS is generated in binding mode, Π_{dvNIZK} satisfies statistical soundness and computational zero-knowledge (i.e., Π_{dvNIZK} is a "computational DV-NIZK proof").
- When the CRS is generated in hiding mode, Π_{dvNIZK} satisfies *non-adaptive* computational soundness and statistical zero-knowledge (i.e., Π_{dvNIZK} is a "statistical DV-NIZK argument").
- If Π_{dvNIZK} is a dual-mode MDV-NIZK, then the zero-knowledge properties in each of the above instantiations also hold against malicious verifiers.

The first two properties follow from CRS indistinguishability and the corresponding statistical properties of Π_{dvNIZK} in the two modes. Note though that even if Π_{dvNIZK} satisfies adaptive soundness in binding mode, we do not know how to argue *adaptive soundness* for Π_{dvNIZK} in hiding mode. At a high-level, this is because in the definition of adaptive soundness, checking whether the adversary succeeded or not requires deciding whether the statement x output by the adversary is contained in the language $\mathcal{L}$ or not. Unless NP $\subseteq$ P/poly, this is not an efficiently-checkable property in general, and as such, we are not able to directly argue adaptive soundness of the construction. We refer to [AF07] for more discussion on the challenges of using black-box reductions to argue adaptive soundness for statistical NIZK arguments.

Remark 2.8 (Adaptive Soundness via Complexity Leveraging). Using complexity leveraging [BB04] and relying on a sub-exponential hardness assumption (as in [GOS06, GOS12]), we can show that non-adaptive soundness implies adaptive soundness. A direct application of complexity leveraging to a dual-mode NIZK yields an adaptively-sound statistical NIZK argument for proving statements of a priori bounded length $n = n(\lambda)$. Using the method from [QRW19, §7], we can also obtain adaptive soundness for statements with arbitrary polynomial length, but still at the expense of a subexponential hardness assumption.

3   Dual-Mode Hidden-Bits Generators and Dual-Mode DV-NIZKs

In this section, we formally define a dual-mode hidden-bits generator. Our definition extends the notion of a hidden-bits generator from [QRW19] (and the similar notion of a designated-verifier PRG from [CH19]). Our definition differs from that in [QRW19] in the following respects:

- **Dual mode:** We require that the common reference string for the hidden-bits generator can be generated in two computationally indistinguishable modes: a *binding* mode where the commitment statistically binds to a sequence of hidden bits, and a *hiding* mode where the commitment (and the openings to any subset of the bits) statistically hide the remaining bits.
- **Statistical simulation in hiding mode.** Minimally, our hiding property requires that the commitment and openings to any subset of the bits output by the HBG *statistically* hide the unopened bits. Here, we require an even stronger *simulation* property where there is an efficient simulator that can simulate the commitment and openings to any (random) string, given *only* the values of the opened bits. Moreover, we allow the adversary to adaptively choose the subset of bits for which it wants to see openings, and we also allow *multiple* interactions with the simulator. This strong simulation property enables us to directly argue *adaptive* and *multi-theorem statistical zero-knowledge* for our NIZK constructions (Sect. 3.1).[7]

Definition 3.1 (Dual-Mode Hidden-Bits Generator). *Let λ be a security parameter and ρ be the output length. Let $\ell = \ell(\lambda, \rho)$ be a polynomial. A dual-mode (designated-verifier) hidden-bits generator (HBG) with commitments of length ℓ consists of a tuple of efficient algorithms $\Pi_{\mathsf{HBG}} = (\mathsf{Setup}, \mathsf{KeyGen}, \mathsf{GenBits}, \mathsf{Verify})$ with the following properties:*

- $\mathsf{Setup}(1^\lambda, 1^\rho, \mathsf{mode}) \to \mathsf{crs}$: *On input the security parameter λ, a length ρ, and a mode $\mathsf{mode} \in \{\mathsf{binding}, \mathsf{hiding}\}$, the setup algorithm outputs a common reference string crs.*
- $\mathsf{KeyGen}(\mathsf{crs}) \to (\mathsf{pk}, \mathsf{sk})$: *On input a common reference string crs, the key-generation algorithm outputs a public key pk and a secret key sk.*
- $\mathsf{GenBits}(\mathsf{crs}, \mathsf{pk}) \to (\sigma, r, \{\pi_i\}_{i \in [\rho]})$: *On input a common reference string crs and a public key pk, the bit-generation algorithm outputs a commitment $\sigma \in \{0,1\}^\ell$, a string $r \in \{0,1\}^\rho$, and a collection of proofs π_i for $i \in [\rho]$.*
- $\mathsf{Verify}(\mathsf{crs}, \mathsf{sk}, \sigma, i, r_i, \pi_i) \to \{0,1\}$: *On input a common reference string crs, a secret key sk, a commitment $\sigma \in \{0,1\}^\ell$, an index $i \in [\rho]$, a bit $r_i \in \{0,1\}$, and a proof π_i, the verification algorithm outputs a bit $b \in \{0,1\}$.*

In addition, we require that Π_{HBG} satisfy the following properties:

- *Correctness: For all integers $\lambda \in \mathbb{N}$, and all polynomials $\rho = \rho(\lambda)$, all indices $i \in [\rho]$ and both modes $\mathsf{mode} \in \{\mathsf{binding}, \mathsf{hiding}\}$, and sampling $\mathsf{crs} \leftarrow \mathsf{Setup}(1^\lambda, 1^\rho, \mathsf{mode})$, $(\mathsf{pk}, \mathsf{sk}) \leftarrow \mathsf{KeyGen}(\mathsf{crs})$, and $(\sigma, r, \{\pi_i\}_{i \in [\rho]}) \leftarrow \mathsf{GenBits}(\mathsf{crs}, \mathsf{pk})$, we have*

$$\Pr[\mathsf{Verify}(\mathsf{crs}, \mathsf{sk}, \sigma, i, r_i, \pi_i) = 1] = 1.$$

---

[7] The previous notion from [QRW19] was only sufficient for single-theorem non-adaptive computational zero-knowledge. Extending to adaptive multi-theorem computational zero-knowledge required imposing additional properties on the underlying NIZK in the hidden-bits model as well as making non-black-box use of cryptographic primitives [FLS99].

– **Succinctness:** *The length ℓ of the commitment depends only on the security parameter and not the length of the output: namely, $\ell = \mathsf{poly}(\lambda)$.[8]*
– **CRS indistinguishability:** *For all polynomials $\rho = \rho(\lambda)$, we have that*

$$\mathsf{Setup}(1^\lambda, 1^\rho, \mathsf{binding}) \overset{c}{\approx} \mathsf{Setup}(1^\lambda, 1^\rho, \mathsf{hiding}).$$

– **Statistically binding in binding mode:** *There exists a (possibly inefficient) deterministic algorithm $\mathsf{Open}(\mathsf{crs}, \sigma)$ such that for all polynomials $\rho = \rho(\lambda)$ and $q = q(\lambda)$ and all unbounded adversaries $\mathcal{A}$ making up to q oracle queries, and sampling $\mathsf{crs} \leftarrow \mathsf{Setup}(1^\lambda, 1^\rho, \mathsf{binding})$, $(\mathsf{pk}, \mathsf{sk}) \leftarrow \mathsf{KeyGen}(\mathsf{crs})$, $(\sigma^*, i^*, r^*, \pi^*) \leftarrow \mathcal{A}^{\mathsf{Verify}(\mathsf{crs}, \mathsf{sk}, \cdot, \cdot, \cdot, \cdot)}(1^\lambda, 1^\rho, \mathsf{crs}, \mathsf{pk})$, $r \leftarrow \mathsf{Open}(\mathsf{crs}, \sigma^*)$, we have*

$$\Pr[r_{i^*} \neq r^* \wedge \mathsf{Verify}(\mathsf{crs}, \mathsf{sk}, \sigma^*, i^*, r^*, \pi^*) = 1] = \mathsf{negl}(\lambda).$$

– **Statistical simulation in hiding mode:** *For all polynomials $\rho = \rho(\lambda)$, $q = q(\lambda)$, and all unbounded adversaries $\mathcal{A}$ making up to q queries, there exists an efficient simulator $\mathcal{S} = (\mathcal{S}_1, \mathcal{S}_2)$ such that*

$$\big| \Pr[\mathsf{ExptHide}[\mathcal{A}, \mathcal{S}, 0](1^\lambda, 1^\rho) = 1]$$
$$- \Pr[\mathsf{ExptHide}[\mathcal{A}, \mathcal{S}, 1](1^\lambda, 1^\rho) = 1] \big| = \mathsf{negl}(\lambda), \quad (3.1)$$

where for a bit $b \in \{0, 1\}$, the hiding experiment $\mathsf{ExptHide}[\mathcal{A}, \mathcal{S}, b](1^\lambda, 1^\rho)$ is defined as follows:

- **Setup phase:** *If $b = 0$, the challenger samples $\mathsf{crs} \leftarrow \mathsf{Setup}(1^\lambda, 1^\rho, \mathsf{hiding})$ and $(\mathsf{pk}, \mathsf{sk}) \leftarrow \mathsf{KeyGen}(\mathsf{crs})$, and gives $(\mathsf{crs}, \mathsf{pk}, \mathsf{sk})$ to $\mathcal{A}$. If $b = 1$, it samples $(\mathsf{st}_{\mathcal{S}}, \widetilde{\mathsf{crs}}, \widetilde{\mathsf{pk}}, \widetilde{\mathsf{sk}}) \leftarrow \mathcal{S}_1(1^\lambda, 1^\rho)$ and gives $(\widetilde{\mathsf{crs}}, \widetilde{\mathsf{pk}}, \widetilde{\mathsf{sk}})$ to $\mathcal{A}$.*
- **Query phase:** *The adversary $\mathcal{A}$ can now make up to q challenge queries. On each query, the challenger responds as follows:*
  - *If $b = 0$, the challenger computes $(\sigma, r, \{\pi_i\}_{i \in [\rho]}) \leftarrow \mathsf{GenBits}(\mathsf{crs}, \mathsf{pk})$ and gives r to the adversary. If $b = 1$, it responds with $\widetilde{r} \overset{R}{\leftarrow} \{0, 1\}^\rho$.*
  - *The adversary specifies a subset $I \subseteq [\rho]$.*
  - *If $b = 0$, then the challenger replies with the pair $(\sigma, \{\pi_i\}_{i \in [I]})$ it sampled above. If $b = 1$, it replies to $\mathcal{A}$ with $(\widetilde{\sigma}, \{\widetilde{\pi}_i\}_{i \in I}) \leftarrow \mathcal{S}_2(\mathsf{st}_{\mathcal{S}}, I, \widetilde{r}_I)$.*
- **Output phase:** *At the end of the experiment, the adversary outputs a bit $b \in \{0, 1\}$, which is the output of the experiment.*

When the difference in Eq. (3.1) is identically zero, we say that Π_{HBG} satisfies perfect simulation in hiding mode.

Definition 3.2 (Publicly-Verifiable Dual-Mode HBG). *A dual-mode HBG Π_{HBG} is publicly-verifiable if the secret key sk output by KeyGen is empty. In this case, we can combine the Setup algorithm and the KeyGen algorithm into a single algorithm that just outputs the crs, and there is no notion of separate*

---

[8] We remark that this is a *stronger* requirement than the corresponding requirement in [QRW19], which also allows ℓ to scale sublinearly with ρ. We use this definition because it is conceptually simpler and all of our constructions satisfy this stronger property.

public/secret keys pk *and* sk. *The* GenBits *and* Verify *algorithms just take* crs *as input. We define all of the other properties analogously. In the publicly-verifiable setting, we do not need to provide the verification oracle to the adversary in the statistical binding security definition.*

Definition 3.3 (Statistical Simulation for Malicious Keys). *Let* $\Pi_{\mathsf{HBG}} =$ (Setup, KeyGen, GenBits, Verify) *be a hidden-bits generator. We say that* Π_{HBG} *satisfies* statistical simulation for malicious keys *if it satisfies the following simulation property (where the adversary chooses* pk*) in hiding mode:*

- ***Statistical simulation for malicious keys:*** *For all polynomials* $\rho = \rho(\lambda)$, $q = q(\lambda)$, *and all unbounded adversaries* $\mathcal{A}$ *making up to* q *queries, there exists an efficient simulator* $\mathcal{S} = (\mathcal{S}_1, \mathcal{S}_2)$ *such that*

$$\big| \Pr[\mathsf{ExptHide}^*[\mathcal{A}, \mathcal{S}, 0](1^\lambda, 1^\rho) = 1]$$
$$- \Pr[\mathsf{ExptHide}^*[\mathcal{A}, \mathcal{S}, 1](1^\lambda, 1^\rho) = 1]\big| = \mathsf{negl}(\lambda),$$

where for a bit $b \in \{0,1\}$, *the hiding experiment* $\mathsf{ExptHide}^*[\mathcal{A}, \mathcal{S}, b](1^\lambda, 1^\rho)$ *is defined to be* $\mathsf{ExptHide}[\mathcal{A}, \mathcal{S}, b](1^\lambda, 1^\rho)$ *with the following differences:*
  - ***Setup phase:*** *If* $b = 0$, *the challenger samples* crs $\leftarrow$ Setup$(1^\lambda, 1^\rho, \mathsf{hiding})$ *and gives* crs *to* $\mathcal{A}$. *If* $b = 1$, *the challenger samples* $(\mathsf{st}_\mathcal{S}, \widetilde{\mathsf{crs}}) \leftarrow \mathcal{S}_1(1^\lambda, 1^\rho)$ *and gives* $\widetilde{\mathsf{crs}}$ *to* $\mathcal{A}$. *The adversary then chooses a public key* pk.
  - ***Query phase:*** *Same as in* $\mathsf{ExptHide}[\mathcal{A}, \mathcal{S}, b]$, *except when* $b = 1$, *the challenger also provides the (adversarially-chosen) public key* pk *to the simulator. In other words, when* $b = 1$, *the challenger's reply to* $\mathcal{A}$ *is computed as* $(\widetilde{\sigma}, \{\widetilde{\pi}_i\}_{i \in I}) \leftarrow \mathcal{S}_2(\mathsf{st}_\mathcal{S}, \mathsf{pk}, I, \widetilde{r}_I)$.
  - ***Output phase:*** *Same as in* $\mathsf{ExptHide}[\mathcal{A}, \mathcal{S}, b]$.

3.1   Dual-Mode DV-NIZK from Dual-Mode HBG

In this section, we give our construction of a dual-mode designated-verifier NIZK from a dual-mode designated-verifier HBG and a NIZK in the hidden-bits model. Our generic construction is essentially the same as the corresponding construction from [QRW19]. We do rely on a different argument to show adaptive, multi-theorem statistical zero-knowledge, and in particular, we appeal to the statistical simulation property of our dual-mode HBG that we introduced in Definition 3.1.

Construction 3.4 (Dual-Mode DV-NIZK from Dual-Mode HBG). Let $\mathcal{L} \subseteq \{0,1\}^n$ be an NP language with associated NP relation $\mathcal{R}$. We rely on the following building blocks:

- Let $\Pi_{\mathsf{HBM}} = $ (HBM.Prove, HBM.Verify) be a NIZK in the hidden-bits model for $\mathcal{L}$, and let $\rho = \rho(\lambda)$ be the length of the hidden-bits string for Π_{HBM}.
- Let $\Pi_{\mathsf{HBG}} = $ (HBG.Setup, HBG.KeyGen, HBG.GenBits, HBG.Verify) be a hidden-bits generator with commitments of length $\ell = \ell(\lambda, \rho)$, where λ is the security parameter and ρ is the output length of the generator.

We construct a dual-mode DV-NIZK $\Pi_{\mathsf{dvNIZK}} = (\mathsf{Setup}, \mathsf{KeyGen}, \mathsf{Prove}, \mathsf{Verify})$ for $\mathcal{L}$ as follows:

- $\mathsf{Setup}(1^\lambda, \mathsf{mode}) \to \mathsf{crs}$: On input λ and $\mathsf{mode} \in \{\mathsf{binding}, \mathsf{hiding}\}$, sample $s \xleftarrow{\text{R}} \{0,1\}^\rho$. Then, run $\mathsf{crs}_{\mathsf{HBG}} \leftarrow \mathsf{HBG}.\mathsf{Setup}(1^\lambda, 1^\rho, \mathsf{mode})$, and output $\mathsf{crs} = (\lambda, s, \mathsf{crs}_{\mathsf{HBG}})$.
- $\mathsf{KeyGen}(\mathsf{crs}) \to (\mathsf{pk}, \mathsf{sk})$: On input $\mathsf{crs} = (\lambda, s, \mathsf{crs}_{\mathsf{HBG}})$, the key-generation algorithm runs $(\mathsf{pk}_{\mathsf{HBG}}, \mathsf{sk}_{\mathsf{HBG}}) \leftarrow \mathsf{HBG}.\mathsf{KeyGen}(\mathsf{crs}_{\mathsf{HBG}})$ and outputs $\mathsf{pk} = \mathsf{pk}_{\mathsf{HBG}}$ and $\mathsf{sk} = \mathsf{sk}_{\mathsf{HBG}}$.
- $\mathsf{Prove}(\mathsf{crs}, \mathsf{pk}, x, w) \to \pi$: On input $\mathsf{crs} = (\lambda, s, \mathsf{crs}_{\mathsf{HBG}})$, $\mathsf{pk} = \mathsf{pk}_{\mathsf{HBG}}$, $x \in \{0,1\}^n$, and w, compute $(\sigma, r, \{\pi_{\mathsf{HBG},i}\}_{i \in [\rho]}) \leftarrow \mathsf{HBG}.\mathsf{GenBits}(\mathsf{crs}_{\mathsf{HBG}}, \mathsf{pk}_{\mathsf{HBG}})$, and an HBM proof $(I, \pi_{\mathsf{HBM}}) \leftarrow \mathsf{HBM}.\mathsf{Prove}(1^\lambda, r \oplus s, x, w)$. Output $\pi = (\sigma, I, r_I, \{\pi_{\mathsf{HBG},i}\}_{i \in I}, \pi_{\mathsf{HBM}})$.
- $\mathsf{Verify}(\mathsf{crs}, \mathsf{sk}, x, \pi)$: On input $\mathsf{crs} = (\lambda, s, \mathsf{crs}_{\mathsf{HBG}})$, $\mathsf{sk} = \mathsf{sk}_{\mathsf{HBG}}$, $x \in \{0,1\}^n$, and the proof $\pi = (\sigma, I, r_I, \{\pi_{\mathsf{HBG},i}\}_{i \in I}, \pi_{\mathsf{HBM}})$, output 1 if $\mathsf{HBM}.\mathsf{Verify}(1^\lambda, I, r_I \oplus s_I, x, \pi_{\mathsf{HBM}}) = 1$ and $\mathsf{HBG}.\mathsf{Verify}(\mathsf{crs}_{\mathsf{HBG}}, \mathsf{sk}_{\mathsf{HBG}}, \sigma, i, r_i, \pi_{\mathsf{HBG},i}) = 1$ for all $i \in I$. Otherwise, output 0.

Theorem 3.5 (Completeness). *If Π_{HBM} is complete and Π_{HBG} is correct, then Π_{dvNIZK} from Construction 3.4 is complete.*

Proof. Take any $\mathsf{mode} \in \{\mathsf{binding}, \mathsf{hiding}\}$, and sample $\mathsf{crs} \leftarrow \mathsf{Setup}(1^\lambda, \mathsf{mode})$, $(\mathsf{pk}, \mathsf{sk}) \leftarrow \mathsf{KeyGen}(\mathsf{crs})$. Here, $\mathsf{crs} = (\lambda, s, \mathsf{crs}_{\mathsf{HBG}})$, $\mathsf{pk} = \mathsf{pk}_{\mathsf{HBG}}$, and $\mathsf{sk} = \mathsf{sk}_{\mathsf{HBG}}$. Take any statement $(x, w) \in \mathcal{R}$, and let $\pi \leftarrow \mathsf{Prove}(\mathsf{crs}, \mathsf{pk}, x, w)$. Then $\pi = (\sigma, I, r_I, \{\pi_{\mathsf{HBG},i}\}_{i \in I}, \pi_{\mathsf{HBM}})$. Consider the behavior of $\mathsf{Verify}(\mathsf{crs}, \mathsf{sk}, x, \pi)$. By correctness of Π_{HBG}, $\mathsf{HBG}.\mathsf{Verify}(\mathsf{crs}_{\mathsf{HBG}}, \mathsf{sk}_{\mathsf{HBG}}, \sigma, i, r_i, \pi_{\mathsf{HBG},i}) = 1$ for all $i \in I$. By completeness of Π_{HBM}, $\mathsf{HBM}.\mathsf{Verify}(1^\lambda, I, r_I \oplus s_I, x, w) = 1$, and the verifier accepts. $\square$

Theorem 3.6 (CRS Indistinguishability). *If Π_{HBG} satisfies CRS indistinguishability, then Π_{dvNIZK} from Construction 3.4 satisfies CRS indistinguishability.*

Proof. The CRS in Construction 3.4 consists of a tuple $(\lambda, s, \mathsf{crs}_{\mathsf{HBG}})$. In both modes, the first two components are identically distributed, and $\mathsf{crs}_{\mathsf{HBG}}$ is computationally indistinguishable by CRS indistinguishability of Π_{HBG}. $\square$

Theorem 3.7 (Statistical Soundness in Binding Mode). *If Π_{HBM} is statistically sound with soundness error $\varepsilon(\lambda)$, Π_{HBG} is statistically binding in binding mode, and $2^\ell \cdot \varepsilon = \mathsf{negl}(\lambda)$ then Π_{dvNIZK} from Construction 3.4 satisfies adaptive statistical soundness.*

The proof of Theorem 3.7 is very similar to the corresponding proof of adaptive statistical soundness from [QRW19]. We include it in the full version.

Theorem 3.8 (Statistical Zero-Knowledge in Hiding Mode). *If Π_{HBM} satisfies statistical (resp., perfect) zero-knowledge and Π_{HBG} provides statistical (resp., perfect) simulation in hiding mode, then Π_{dvNIZK} from Construction 3.4 satisfies statistical (resp., perfect) zero-knowledge in hiding mode.*

We give the proof of Theorem 3.8 in the full version.

Theorem 3.9 (Statistical Zero-Knowledge against Malicious Verifiers). *If Π_{HBM} satisfies statistical zero-knowledge and Π_{HBG} provides statistical simulation for malicious keys, then Construction 3.4 is a MDV-NIZK. Namely, Construction 3.4 satisfies statistical zero-knowledge against malicious verifiers in hiding mode.*

The proof of Theorem 3.9 follows from a similar argument as Theorem 3.8 and is included in the full version.

4 Dual-Mode HBGs from the k-Lin Assumption

In this section, we show how to construct dual-mode hidden-bits generators from the k-Lin assumption. We begin with a basic construction from the k-Lin assumption (Sect. 4.1) and then show how to extend it to achieve public verifiability in a pairing group (Sect. 4.2) as well as how to achieve security against malicious verifiers in a pairing-free group (Sect. 4.3). In the full version, we also show how to construct dual-mode HBGs from the QR and DCR assumptions.

4.1 Dual-Mode Hidden-Bits Generator from k-Lin

In this section, we show how to construct a dual-mode hidden-bits generator from the k-linear (k-Lin) assumption [BBS04, HK07, Sha07, EHK+13] over *pairing-free* groups for any $k \geq 1$. We note that the 1-Lin assumption is precisely the decisional Diffie-Hellman (DDH) assumption. We begin by recalling some basic notation.

Notation. Throughout this section, we will work with cyclic groups $\mathbb{G}$ of prime order p. We will use multiplicative notation to denote the group operation. For $x \in \mathbb{Z}_p$, we often refer to g^x as an "encoding" of x. For a matrix $\mathbf{A} \in \mathbb{Z}_p^{n \times m}$, we write $g^{\mathbf{A}} \in \mathbb{G}^{n \times m}$ to denote the matrix of group elements formed by taking the element-wise encoding of each component of $\mathbf{A}$.

Definition 4.1 (Prime-Order Group Generator). *A prime-order group generator algorithm GroupGen is an efficient algorithm that on input the security parameter 1^λ outputs a description $\mathcal{G} = (\mathbb{G}, p, g)$ of a prime-order group $\mathbb{G}$ with order p and generator g. Throughout this work, we will assume that $1/p = \mathsf{negl}(\lambda)$.*

Construction 4.2 (Dual-Mode Hidden-Bits Generator from k-Lin). Let GroupGen be a prime-order group generator algorithm. We construct a dual-mode hidden-bits generator (HBG) as follows:

- $\mathsf{Setup}(1^\lambda, 1^\rho, \mathsf{mode}) \to \mathsf{crs}$: First, the setup algorithm samples $\mathcal{G} = (\mathbb{G}, p, g) \leftarrow$ GroupGen(1^λ) and a hash function $H \xleftarrow{\mathrm{R}} \mathcal{H}$, where $\mathcal{H}$ is a family of hash functions with domain $\mathbb{G}$ and range $\{0, 1\}$. Next, it samples $\mathbf{V} \xleftarrow{\mathrm{R}} \mathbb{Z}_p^{(\rho+k) \times k}$ and vectors $\mathbf{w}_1, \ldots, \mathbf{w}_\rho \in \mathbb{Z}_p^{\rho+k}$ as follows:

- If mode = hiding, sample $\mathbf{w}_i \xleftarrow{\text{R}} \mathbb{Z}_p^{\rho+k}$ for all $i \in [\rho]$.
- If mode = binding, sample $\mathbf{s}_i \xleftarrow{\text{R}} \mathbb{Z}_p^k$ and set $\mathbf{w}_i \leftarrow \mathbf{V}\mathbf{s}_i$ for all $i \in [\rho]$.

  Output $\mathsf{crs} = (\mathcal{G}, H, g^{\mathbf{V}}, g^{\mathbf{w}_1}, \ldots, g^{\mathbf{w}_\rho})$.

- KeyGen(crs) $\rightarrow$ (pk, sk): On input $\mathsf{crs} = (\mathcal{G}, H, g^{\mathbf{V}}, g^{\mathbf{w}_1}, \ldots, g^{\mathbf{w}_\rho})$, the key-generation algorithm samples $a \xleftarrow{\text{R}} \mathbb{Z}_p$ and $\mathbf{b}_1, \ldots, \mathbf{b}_\rho \xleftarrow{\text{R}} \mathbb{Z}_p^k$. For each $i \in [\rho]$, it sets $\mathbf{z}_i \leftarrow \mathbf{w}_i a + \mathbf{V}\mathbf{b}_i \in \mathbb{Z}_p^{\rho+k}$. It outputs

$$\mathsf{pk} = (g^{\mathbf{z}_1}, \ldots, g^{\mathbf{z}_\rho}) \quad \text{and} \quad \mathsf{sk} = (a, \mathbf{b}_1, \ldots, \mathbf{b}_\rho).$$

- GenBits(crs, pk) $\rightarrow$ $(\sigma, r, \{\pi_i\}_{i\in[\rho]})$: On input $\mathsf{crs} = (\mathcal{G}, H, g^{\mathbf{V}}, g^{\mathbf{w}_1}, \ldots, g^{\mathbf{w}_\rho})$ and $\mathsf{pk} = (g^{\mathbf{z}_1}, \ldots, g^{\mathbf{z}_\rho})$, sample $\mathbf{y} \xleftarrow{\text{R}} \mathbb{Z}_p^{\rho+k}$ and compute for each $i \in [\rho]$,

$$g^{t_i} \leftarrow g^{\mathbf{y}^\mathsf{T} \mathbf{w}_i} \quad \text{and} \quad g^{u_i} \leftarrow g^{\mathbf{y}^\mathsf{T} \mathbf{z}_i}.$$

  Next, let $\sigma = g^{\mathbf{y}^\mathsf{T} \mathbf{V}}$. For each $i \in [\rho]$, set $r_i \leftarrow H(g^{t_i})$ and $\pi_i \leftarrow (g^{t_i}, g^{u_i})$, and output σ, r, and $\{\pi_i\}_{i\in[\rho]}$.

- Verify(crs, sk, σ, i, r_i, π_i): On input $\mathsf{crs} = (\mathcal{G}, H, g^{\mathbf{V}}, g^{\mathbf{w}_1}, \ldots, g^{\mathbf{w}_\rho})$, the secret key $\mathsf{sk} = (a, \mathbf{b}_1, \ldots, \mathbf{b}_\rho)$, $\sigma = g^{\mathbf{c}^\mathsf{T}}$, $i \in [\rho]$, $r_i \in \{0, 1\}$, and $\pi_i = (g^{t_i}, g^{u_i})$, output 1 if $g^{u_i} = (g^{t_i a})(g^{\mathbf{c}^\mathsf{T} \mathbf{b}_i})$ and $r_i = H(g^{t_i})$. Otherwise, output 0.

Correctness and Security Analysis. We now state the correctness and security theorems for Construction 4.2 and give the proofs in the full version.

Theorem 4.3 (Correctness). *Construction 4.2 is correct.*

Theorem 4.4 (Succinctness). *Construction 4.2 is succinct.*

Theorem 4.5 (CRS Indistinguishability). *Suppose the k-Lin assumption holds for GroupGen. Then, Construction 3.4 satisfies CRS indistinguishability.*

Theorem 4.6 (Statistical Binding in Binding Mode). *Construction 4.2 satisfies statistical binding in binding mode.*

Theorem 4.7 (Statistical Simulation in Hiding Mode). *If $\mathcal{H}$ satisfies statistical uniformity, then Construction 4.2 satisfies statistical simulation in hiding mode.*

Remark 4.8 (Common Random String in Hiding Mode). Construction 4.2 has the property that in hiding mode, the CRS is a collection of *uniformly* random group elements; in other words, the CRS in hiding mode can be sampled as a common *random* string. In conjunction with Construction 3.4, we obtain a statistical NIZK argument in the common *random* string model (and a computational NIZK proof in the common *reference* string model).

4.2   Publicly-Verifiable Hidden-Bit Generators from Pairings

In this section, we describe a variant of our dual-mode hidden-bits generator from Sect. 4.1 to obtain a *publicly-verifiable* hidden-bits generator from pairings. Our resulting construction does not give a dual-mode hidden-bits generator. Instead, we obtain a standard HBG (where there is a *single* mode) that satisfies statistical simulation and computational binding. Using an analog of Construction 3.4, this suffices to construct a publicly-verifiable statistical NIZK argument. We refer to the full version for the details. Below, we define the computational binding property we use:

Definition 4.9 (Computational Binding). *A publicly-verifiable hidden bits generator* $\Pi_{\mathsf{HBG}} = (\mathsf{Setup}, \mathsf{GenBits}, \mathsf{Verify})$ *is computationally binding if the following property holds:*

- **Computational binding:** *There exists an efficient extractor* $\mathcal{E} = (\mathcal{E}_1, \mathcal{E}_2)$, *where* $\mathcal{E}_2$ *is deterministic, and for all polynomials* $\rho = \rho(\lambda)$, *the following two properties hold:*
  - **CRS indistinguishability:** *The following distributions are computationally indistinguishable:*

$$\{\mathsf{Setup}(1^\lambda, 1^\rho)\} \stackrel{c}{\approx} \{(\mathsf{st}_{\mathcal{E}}, \widetilde{\mathsf{crs}}) \leftarrow \mathcal{E}_1(1^\lambda, 1^\rho) : \widetilde{\mathsf{crs}}\}.$$

  - **Binding:** *For all efficient adversaries* $\mathcal{A}$, *and sampling* $(\mathsf{st}_{\mathcal{E}}, \widetilde{\mathsf{crs}}) \leftarrow \mathcal{E}_1(1^\lambda, 1^\rho)$ *followed by* $(\sigma^*, i^*, r^*, \pi^*) \leftarrow \mathcal{A}(1^\lambda, 1^\rho, \widetilde{\mathsf{crs}})$ *and* $r \leftarrow \mathcal{E}_2(\mathsf{st}_{\mathcal{E}}, \sigma^*)$, *we have that*

$$\Pr[r_{i^*} \neq r^* \wedge \mathsf{Verify}(\widetilde{\mathsf{crs}}, \sigma^*, i^*, r^*, \pi^*) = 1] = \mathsf{negl}(\lambda).$$

Pairing Groups. In this section, we work in (asymmetric) pairing groups. We review the notion of a pairing below. We review the kernel k-linear (k-KerLin) assumption from [MRV15, KW15] in the full version.

Definition 4.10 (Prime-Order Pairing-Group Generator). *A prime-order (asymmetric) pairing group generator algorithm* $\mathsf{PairingGroupGen}$ *is an efficient algorithm that on input the security parameter* 1^λ *outputs a description* $\mathcal{G} = (\mathbb{G}_1, \mathbb{G}_2, \mathbb{G}_T, p, g_1, g_2, e)$ *of two base groups* $\mathbb{G}_1$ *(generated by* g_1*),* $\mathbb{G}_2$ *(generated by* g_2*), and a target group* $\mathbb{G}_T$, *all of prime order* p, *together with an efficiently-computable mapping* $e: \mathbb{G}_1 \times \mathbb{G}_2 \rightarrow \mathbb{G}_T$ *(called the "pairing"). Finally, the mapping* e *is bilinear: for all* $x, y \in \mathbb{Z}_p$, $e(g_1^x, g_2^y) = e(g_1, g_2)^{xy}$.

Notation. For a matrix $\mathbf{A}$, we continue to write $g_1^{\mathbf{A}}$ and $g_2^{\mathbf{A}}$ to denote matrices of group elements (over $\mathbb{G}_1$ and $\mathbb{G}_2$, respectively). In addition, if we have two matrices $\mathbf{A} \in \mathbb{Z}^{m \times \ell}$ and $\mathbf{B} \in \mathbb{Z}^{\ell \times n}$, we write $e(g_1^{\mathbf{A}}, g_2^{\mathbf{B}})$ to denote the operation that outputs $e(g_1, g_2)^{\mathbf{AB}} \in \mathbb{G}_T^{m \times n}$. In particular, the $(i, j)^{\text{th}}$ entry of $e(g_1^{\mathbf{A}}, g_2^{\mathbf{B}})$ is computed as

$$[e(g_1^{\mathbf{A}}, g_2^{\mathbf{B}})]_{i,j} = \prod_{k \in [\ell]} e(g_1^{a_{i,k}}, g_2^{b_{k,j}}).$$

Construction 4.11 (Publicly-Verifiable Hidden-Bits Generator from Pairings). Let PairingGroupGen be a prime-order bilinear group generator algorithm. We construct a publicly-verifiable hidden-bits generator (HBG) as follow:

- Setup$(1^\lambda, 1^\rho) \to$ crs: The setup algorithm starts by sampling

$$\mathcal{G} = (\mathbb{G}_1, \mathbb{G}_2, \mathbb{G}_T, p, g_1, g_2, e) \leftarrow \mathsf{PairingGroupGen}(1^\lambda)$$

and a hash function $H \xleftarrow{\text{R}} \mathcal{H}$ where $\mathcal{H}$ is a family of hash functions with domain $\mathbb{G}_1$ and range $\{0, 1\}$. Next, it samples a matrix $\mathbf{V} \xleftarrow{\text{R}} \mathbb{Z}_p^{(\rho+k) \times k}$, vectors $\mathbf{w}_1, \ldots, \mathbf{w}_k \xleftarrow{\text{R}} \mathbb{Z}_p^{\rho+k}$, and verification components $\mathbf{a} \xleftarrow{\text{R}} \mathbb{Z}_p^{k+1}$, $\mathbf{B}_1, \ldots, \mathbf{B}_\rho \xleftarrow{\text{R}} \mathbb{Z}_p^{k \times (k+1)}$. In addition, it samples $\mathbf{d} \xleftarrow{\text{R}} \mathbb{Z}_p^k$, and constructs the matrix

$$\mathbf{D} = \left(\frac{\text{diag}(\mathbf{d})}{\mathbf{1}^\mathsf{T}} \right) \in \mathbb{Z}_p^{(k+1) \times k}. \tag{4.1}$$

It computes $\hat{\mathbf{a}}^\mathsf{T} \leftarrow \mathbf{a}^\mathsf{T} \mathbf{D} \in \mathbb{Z}_p^k$, and for each $i \in [\rho]$, it computes $\mathbf{Z}_i \leftarrow \mathbf{w}_i \mathbf{a}^\mathsf{T} + \mathbf{V} \mathbf{B}_i \in \mathbb{Z}_p^{(\rho+k) \times (k+1)}$ and $\hat{\mathbf{B}}_i \leftarrow \mathbf{B}_i \mathbf{D} \in \mathbb{Z}_p^{k \times k}$. It outputs

$$\mathsf{crs} = \left(\mathcal{G}, H, g_1^\mathbf{V}, g_2^{\hat{\mathbf{a}}^\mathsf{T}}, g_2^\mathbf{D}, \{ g_1^{\mathbf{w}_i}, g_1^{\mathbf{Z}_i}, g_2^{\hat{\mathbf{B}}_i} \}_{i \in [\rho]} \right).$$

- GenBits(crs) $\to (\sigma, r, \{\pi_i\}_{i \in [k]})$: On input

$$\mathsf{crs} = \left(\mathcal{G}, H, g_1^\mathbf{V}, g_2^{\hat{\mathbf{a}}^\mathsf{T}}, g_2^\mathbf{D}, \{ g_1^{\mathbf{w}_i}, g_1^{\mathbf{Z}_i}, g_2^{\hat{\mathbf{B}}_i} \}_{i \in [\rho]} \right),$$

sample $\mathbf{y} \xleftarrow{\text{R}} \mathbb{Z}_p^{\rho+k}$, and compute for each $i \in [\rho]$,

$$g_1^{t_i} \leftarrow g_1^{\mathbf{y}^\mathsf{T} \mathbf{w}_i} \quad \text{and} \quad g_1^{\mathbf{u}_i^\mathsf{T}} \leftarrow g_1^{\mathbf{y}^\mathsf{T} \mathbf{Z}_i}.$$

Next, let $\sigma = g_1^{\mathbf{y}^\mathsf{T} \mathbf{V}}$, and for each $i \in [\rho]$, set $r_i \leftarrow H(g_1^{t_i})$ and $\pi_i = (g_1^{t_i}, g_1^{\mathbf{u}_i^\mathsf{T}})$. Output σ, r, and $\{\pi_i\}_{i \in [\rho]}$.

- Verify(crs, σ, i, r_i, π_i): On input $\mathsf{crs} = \left(\mathcal{G}, H, g_1^\mathbf{V}, g_2^{\hat{\mathbf{a}}^\mathsf{T}}, g_2^\mathbf{D}, \{ g_1^{\mathbf{w}_i}, g_1^{\mathbf{Z}_i}, g_2^{\hat{\mathbf{B}}_i} \}_{i \in [\rho]} \right)$, $\sigma = g_1^{\mathbf{c}^\mathsf{T}}$, $i \in [\rho]$, $r_i \in \{0, 1\}$, and $\pi_i = (g_1^{t_i}, g_1^{\mathbf{u}_i^\mathsf{T}})$, output 1 if

$$e(g_1^{t_i}, g_2^{\hat{\mathbf{a}}^\mathsf{T}}) \cdot e(g_1^{\mathbf{c}^\mathsf{T}}, g_2^{\hat{\mathbf{B}}_i}) = e(g_1^{\mathbf{u}_i^\mathsf{T}}, g_2^\mathbf{D}) \tag{4.2}$$

and $r_i = H(g_1^{t_i})$. If either check fails, output 0.

Correctness and Security Analysis. We now state the correctness and security theorems for Construction 4.11 and provide the proofs in the full version.

Theorem 4.12 (Correctness). *Construction 4.11 is correct.*

Theorem 4.13 (Succinctness). *Construction 4.11 is succinct.*

Theorem 4.14 (Computational Binding). *Suppose* PairingGroupGen *outputs groups* $(\mathbb{G}_1, \mathbb{G}_2, \mathbb{G}_T)$ *such that the* k-Lin *assumption holds in* $\mathbb{G}_1$ *and the* k-KerLin *assumption holds in* $\mathbb{G}_2$. *Then, Construction 4.11 satisfies computational binding in binding mode.*

Theorem 4.15 (Statistical Simulation). *If* $\mathcal{H}$ *satisfies statistical uniformity, then Construction 4.11 satisfies statistical simulation.*

4.3   Dual-Mode HBG with Malicious Security from k-Lin

We now show how to modify the k-Lin construction from Sect. 4.1 (Construction 4.2) to obtain a hidden-bits generator with security against malicious verifiers. Combined with Construction 3.4, this yields a dual-mode MDV-NIZK (Theorem 3.9). We refer to Sect. 1.2 for a high-level description of our approach.

Construction 4.16 (Dual-Mode HBG with Malicious Security from k-Lin**).** Let ρ be the output length of the hidden-bits generator. We require the following primitives:

- Let GroupGen be a prime-order group generator algorithm.
- Let $\ell = 3\rho\lambda$ and define $\mathcal{T}_{\lambda,\ell} := \{S \subseteq [\ell] : |S| = \lambda\}$ to be the set of all subsets of $[\ell]$ that contains exactly λ elements. Let $G \colon \{0,1\}^\kappa \to \mathcal{T}_{\lambda,\ell}^\rho \times \mathbb{Z}_p^{\rho\ell}$ be a PRG with seed length $\kappa = \kappa(\lambda)$. Here, p is the order of the group $\mathbb{G}$ output by GroupGen (on input 1^λ).

  Constructing the PRG G. It is straightforward to construct a PRG with outputs in $\mathcal{T}_{\lambda,\ell}^\rho \times \mathbb{Z}_p^{\rho\ell}$ from a PRG with outputs in $\{0,1\}^{\rho\lambda\ell(1+\lceil\log p\rceil)}$. To see this, it suffices to give an efficient algorithm that maps from the uniform distribution on $\{0,1\}^{\lambda\ell(1+\lceil\log p\rceil)}$ to a distribution that is statistically close to uniform over $\mathcal{T}_{\lambda,\ell} \times \mathbb{Z}_p^\ell$. Take a string $\gamma \in \{0,1\}^{\lambda\ell(1+\lceil\log p\rceil)}$.
  - The first $\lambda\ell$ bits of γ are interpreted as ℓ blocks of λ-bit indices $i_1, \ldots, i_\ell \in \{0,1\}^\lambda$. These indices specify the set $S \subseteq \mathcal{T}_{\lambda,\ell}$ as follows. First, take $S_0 \leftarrow [\ell]$. For each $j \in [\lambda]$, take s_j to be the $(i_j \bmod |S_{j-1}|)^{\text{th}}$ element of S_{j-1} and define $S_j \leftarrow S_{j-1} \setminus \{s_j\}$. Define $S \leftarrow \{s_1, \ldots, s_\ell\} \in \mathcal{T}_{\lambda,\ell}$.
  - The remaining $\lambda\ell\lceil\log p\rceil$ bits of γ are taken to be the binary representation of a vector $\boldsymbol{\alpha} \in \mathbb{Z}^\ell$, where each component is a $\lambda\lceil\log p\rceil$-bit integer. The string $\gamma \in \{0,1\}^{\lambda\ell(1+\lceil\log p\rceil)}$ is mapped onto $(S, \boldsymbol{\alpha} \bmod p) \in \mathcal{T}_{\lambda,\ell} \times \mathbb{Z}_p^\ell$. By construction, this procedure maps from the uniform distribution over $\{0,1\}^{\lambda\ell(1+\lceil\log p\rceil)}$ to a distribution that is statistically uniform over $\mathcal{T}_{\lambda,\ell} \times \mathbb{Z}_p^\ell$.

We construct the dual-mode designated-verifier hidden-bits generator with malicious security as follows:

- Setup$(1^\lambda, 1^\rho, \text{mode}) \to \text{crs}$: Let $\ell' = \rho\ell$. Sample $\mathcal{G} = (\mathbb{G}, p, g) \leftarrow \text{GroupGen}(1^\lambda)$ and $H \xleftarrow{\text{R}} \mathcal{H}$, where $\mathcal{H}$ is a family of hash functions with domain $\mathbb{G}$ and range $\{0,1\}$. Next, it samples $\mathbf{V} \xleftarrow{\text{R}} \mathbb{Z}_p^{(\ell'+k)\times k}$ and $\mathbf{w}_1, \ldots, \mathbf{w}_{\ell'} \in \mathbb{Z}_p^{\ell'+k}$ as follows:
  - If mode = hiding, sample $\mathbf{w}_i \xleftarrow{\text{R}} \mathbb{Z}_p^{\ell'+k}$ for all $i \in [\ell']$.

- If mode = binding, sample $\mathbf{s}_i \xleftarrow{\text{R}} \mathbb{Z}_p^k$ and set $\mathbf{w}_i \leftarrow \mathbf{V}\mathbf{s}_i$ for all $i \in [\ell']$. Output crs $= (\mathcal{G}, H, g^{\mathbf{V}}, g^{\mathbf{w}_1}, \ldots, g^{\mathbf{w}_{\ell'}})$.
- KeyGen(crs) $\rightarrow$ (pk, sk): On input crs $= (\mathcal{G}, H, g^{\mathbf{V}}, g^{\mathbf{w}_1}, \ldots, g^{\mathbf{w}_{\ell'}})$, sample $a \xleftarrow{\text{R}} \mathbb{Z}_p$ and $\mathbf{b}_1, \ldots, \mathbf{b}_{\ell'} \xleftarrow{\text{R}} \mathbb{Z}_p^k$. For each $i \in [\ell']$, compute $\mathbf{z}_i \leftarrow \mathbf{w}_i a + \mathbf{V}\mathbf{b}_i \in \mathbb{Z}_p^{\ell'+k}$ and output

$$\text{pk} = (g^{\mathbf{z}_1}, \ldots, g^{\mathbf{z}_{\ell'}}) \quad \text{and} \quad \text{sk} = (a, \mathbf{b}_1, \ldots, \mathbf{b}_{\ell'}).$$

- GenBits(crs, pk) $\rightarrow$ $(\sigma, r, \{\pi_i\}_{i \in [\rho]})$: On input crs $= (\mathcal{G}, H, g^{\mathbf{V}}, g^{\mathbf{w}_1}, \ldots, g^{\mathbf{w}_{\ell'}})$ and pk $= (g^{\mathbf{z}_1}, \ldots, g^{\mathbf{z}_{\ell'}})$, sample $\mathbf{y} \xleftarrow{\text{R}} \mathbb{Z}_p^{\ell'+k}$ and compute for each $i \in [\ell']$

$$g^{t_i} \leftarrow g^{\mathbf{y}^\top \mathbf{w}_i} \quad \text{and} \quad g^{u_i} \leftarrow g^{\mathbf{y}^\top \mathbf{z}_i}.$$

Next, sample a PRG seed $\mathbf{s} \xleftarrow{\text{R}} \{0,1\}^\kappa$ and compute $(\hat{S}_1, \ldots, \hat{S}_\rho, \boldsymbol{\alpha}) \leftarrow G(\mathbf{s})$ where $\hat{S}_i \in \mathcal{T}_{\lambda, \ell}$ for all $i \in [\rho]$ and $\boldsymbol{\alpha} \in \mathbb{Z}_p^{\rho \ell}$. Compute the shifted sets $S_i \leftarrow \{j + \ell \cdot (i-1) \mid j \in \hat{S}_i\}$ for each $i \in [\rho]$. Finally, compute

$$r_i \leftarrow H\left(\prod_{j \in S_i} g^{\alpha_j t_j}\right) \quad \text{and} \quad \pi_i \leftarrow \{(j, g^{t_j}, g^{u_j})\}_{j \in S_i}.$$

Output $\sigma = (\mathbf{s}, g^{\mathbf{y}^\top \mathbf{V}})$, r, and $\{\pi_i\}_{i \in [\rho]}$.
- Verify(crs, sk, σ, i, r_i, π_i): On input crs $= (\mathcal{G}, H, g^{\mathbf{V}}, g^{\mathbf{w}_1}, \ldots, g^{\mathbf{w}_{\ell'}})$, the secret key sk $= (a, \mathbf{b}_1, \ldots, \mathbf{b}_{\ell'})$, $\sigma = (\mathbf{s}, g^{\mathbf{c}^\top})$, $i \in [\rho]$, $r_i \in \{0,1\}$, and $\pi_i = \{(j, g^{t_j}, g^{u_j})\}_{j \in S}$ for an implicitly-defined set $S \subseteq [\rho\ell]$, the verification algorithm performs the following checks:
  - Compute $(\hat{S}_1, \ldots, \hat{S}_\rho, \boldsymbol{\alpha}) \leftarrow G(\mathbf{s})$ and the shifted set $S_i \leftarrow \{j + \ell \cdot (i-1) \mid j \in \hat{S}_i\}$. It checks that $S = S_i$ and outputs 0 if not.
  - It checks that $g^{u_j} = (g^{t_j a})(g^{\mathbf{c}^\top \mathbf{b}_j})$ for all $j \in S$, and outputs 0 if not.
  - It checks that $r_i = H\left(\prod_{j \in S} g^{\alpha_j t_j}\right)$ and outputs 0 if not.

If all checks pass, the verification algorithm outputs 1.

Correctness and Security Analysis. We now state the correctness and security theorems for Construction 4.16 and provide the proofs in the full version.

Theorem 4.17 (Correctness). *Construction 4.16 is correct.*

Theorem 4.18 (Succinctness). *Construction 4.16 is succinct.*

Theorem 4.19 (CRS Indistinguishability). *Suppose the k-Lin assumption holds for GroupGen. Then, Construction 4.16 satisfies CRS indistinguishability.*

Theorem 4.20 (Statistical Binding in Binding Mode). *Construction 4.16 satisfies statistical binding in binding mode.*

Theorem 4.21 (Statistical Simulation in Hiding Mode), *If G is a secure PRG and $\mathcal{H}$ satisfies statistical uniformity, then Construction 4.16 satisfies statistical simulation in hiding mode against malicious verifiers.*

5   Instantiations and Extensions

In this section, we provide the main implications of our framework for construct-ing statistical (and more generally, dual-mode) NIZKs. In the full version, we describe two simple extensions to augment our NIZKs with additional properties.

Dual-Mode MDV-NIZKs. By instantiating Construction 3.4 with a dual-mode malicious designated-verifier hidden-bits generator, we obtain a dual-mode MDV-NIZK (Theorems 3.5, 3.7 and 3.9).

Corollary 5.1 (Dual-Mode MDV-NIZK from k-Lin). *Under the k-Lin assumption over pairing-free groups (for any $k \geq 1$), there exists a statistical MDV-NIZK argument (with non-adaptive soundness) in the common random string model, and a computational MDV-NIZK proof (with adaptive soundness) for* NP *in the common reference string model.*

Corollary 5.2 (Dual-Mode MDV-NIZK from QR or DCR). *Under the* QR *or* DCR *assumptions, there exists a statistical MDV-NIZK argument (with non-adaptive soundness) and a computational MDV-NIZK proof (with adaptive soundness) for* NP *in the common reference string model.*

Publicly-Verifiable Statistical NIZK Arguments. In the full version, we show how to obtain a publicly-verifiable statistical NIZK argument in the common reference string model using Construction 4.11:

Corollary 5.3 (Publicly-Verifiable Statistical NIZK Argument from Pairings). *Suppose that the k-Lin assumption holds in $\mathbb{G}_1$ and the k-KerLin assumption holds in $\mathbb{G}_2$ (for any $k \geq 1$) over a pairing group. Then, there exists a publicly-verifiable statistical NIZK argument for* NP *(with non-adaptive sound-ness) in the common reference string model.*

Acknowledgments. We thanks the anonymous Eurocrypt reviewers for helpful feed-back on this work.

References

[AF07]   Abe, M., Fehr, S.: Perfect NIZK with adaptive soundness. In: Vadhan, S.P. (ed.) TCC 2007. LNCS, vol. 4392, pp. 118–136. Springer, Heidelberg (2007). https://doi.org/10.1007/978-3-540-70936-7_7

[BB04]   Boneh, D., Boyen, X.: Efficient selective-ID secure identity-based encryp-tion without random oracles. In: Cachin, C., Camenisch, J.L. (eds.) EUROCRYPT 2004. LNCS, vol. 3027, pp. 223–238. Springer, Heidelberg (2004). https://doi.org/10.1007/978-3-540-24676-3_14

[BBS04] Boneh, D., Boyen, X., Shacham, H.: Short group signatures. In: Franklin, M. (ed.) CRYPTO 2004. LNCS, vol. 3152, pp. 41–55. Springer, Heidelberg (2004). https://doi.org/10.1007/978-3-540-28628-8_3

[BCG+19] Boyle, E., Couteau, G., Gilboa, N., Ishai, Y., Kohl, L., Scholl, P.: Efficient pseudorandom correlation generators: silent OT extension and more. In: Boldyreva, A., Micciancio, D. (eds.) CRYPTO 2019. LNCS, vol. 11694, pp. 489–518. Springer, Cham (2019). https://doi.org/10.1007/978-3-030-26954-8_16

[BCGI18] Boyle, E., Couteau, G., Gilboa, N., Ishai, Y.: Compressing vector OLE. In: ACM CCS (2018)

[BFM88] Blum, M., Feldman, P., Micali, S.: Non-interactive zero-knowledge and its applications (extended abstract). In: STOC (1988)

[BG10] Brakerski, Z., Goldwasser, S.: Circular and leakage resilient public-key encryption under subgroup indistinguishability (or: quadratic residuosity strikes back). In: Rabin, T. (ed.) CRYPTO 2010. LNCS, vol. 6223, pp. 1–20. Springer, Heidelberg (2010). https://doi.org/10.1007/978-3-642-14623-7_1

[Blu86] Blum, M.: How to prove a theorem so no one else can claim it. In: Proceedings of the International Congress of Mathematicians, vol. 1 (1986)

[BY92] Bellare, M., Yung, M.: Certifying cryptographic tools: the case of trapdoor permutations. In: Brickell, E.F. (ed.) CRYPTO 1992. LNCS, vol. 740, pp. 442–460. Springer, Heidelberg (1993). https://doi.org/10.1007/3-540-48071-4_31

[CCH+19] Canetti, R., et al.: Fiat-Shamir: from practice to theory. In: STOC (2019)

[CDI+19] Chase, M., et al.: Reusable non-interactive secure computation. In: Boldyreva, A., Micciancio, D. (eds.) CRYPTO 2019. LNCS, vol. 11694, pp. 462–488. Springer, Cham (2019). https://doi.org/10.1007/978-3-030-26954-8_15

[CH19] Couteau, G., Hofheinz, D.: Designated-verifier pseudorandom generators, and their applications. In: Ishai, Y., Rijmen, V. (eds.) EUROCRYPT 2019. LNCS, vol. 11477, pp. 562–592. Springer, Cham (2019). https://doi.org/10.1007/978-3-030-17656-3_20

[CHK03] Canetti, R., Halevi, S., Katz, J.: A forward-secure public-key encryption scheme. In: Biham, E. (ed.) EUROCRYPT 2003. LNCS, vol. 2656, pp. 255–271. Springer, Heidelberg (2003). https://doi.org/10.1007/3-540-39200-9_16

[CKS08] Cash, D., Kiltz, E., Shoup, V.: The twin Diffie-Hellman problem and applications. In: Smart, N. (ed.) EUROCRYPT 2008. LNCS, vol. 4965, pp. 127–145. Springer, Heidelberg (2008). https://doi.org/10.1007/978-3-540-78967-3_8

[CL18] Canetti, R., Lichtenberg, A.: Certifying trapdoor permutations, revisited. In: Beimel, A., Dziembowski, S. (eds.) TCC 2018. LNCS, vol. 11239, pp. 476–506. Springer, Cham (2018). https://doi.org/10.1007/978-3-030-03807-6_18

[CS98] Cramer, R., Shoup, V.: A practical public key cryptosystem provably secure against adaptive chosen ciphertext attack. In: Krawczyk, H. (ed.) CRYPTO 1998. LNCS, vol. 1462, pp. 13–25. Springer, Heidelberg (1998). https://doi.org/10.1007/BFb0055717

[CS02] Cramer, R., Shoup, V.: Universal hash proofs and a paradigm for adaptive chosen ciphertext secure public-key encryption. In: Knudsen, L.R. (ed.) EUROCRYPT 2002. LNCS, vol. 2332, pp. 45–64. Springer, Heidelberg (2002). https://doi.org/10.1007/3-540-46035-7_4

[DDO+01] De Santis, A., Di Crescenzo, G., Ostrovsky, R., Persiano, G., Sahai, A.:
          Robust non-interactive zero knowledge. In: Kilian, J. (ed.) CRYPTO 2001.
          LNCS, vol. 2139, pp. 566–598. Springer, Heidelberg (2001). https://doi.
          org/10.1007/3-540-44647-8_33
[DFN06]   Damgård, I., Fazio, N., Nicolosi, A.: Non-interactive zero-knowledge from
          homomorphic encryption. In: Halevi, S., Rabin, T. (eds.) TCC 2006.
          LNCS, vol. 3876, pp. 41–59. Springer, Heidelberg (2006). https://doi.org/
          10.1007/11681878_3
[DGI+19] Döttling, N., Garg, S., Ishai, Y., Malavolta, G., Mour, T., Ostrovsky, R.:
          Trapdoor hash functions and their applications. In: Boldyreva, A., Mic-
          ciancio, D. (eds.) CRYPTO 2019. LNCS, vol. 11694, pp. 3–32. Springer,
          Cham (2019). https://doi.org/10.1007/978-3-030-26954-8_1
[DMP87]   De Santis, A., Micali, S., Persiano, G.: Non-interactive zero-knowledge
          proof systems. In: Pomerance, C. (ed.) CRYPTO 1987. LNCS, vol. 293,
          pp. 52–72. Springer, Heidelberg (1988). https://doi.org/10.1007/3-540-
          48184-2_5
[EHK+13] Escala, A., Herold, G., Kiltz, E., Ràfols, C., Villar, J.: An algebraic
          framework for Diffie-Hellman assumptions. In: Canetti, R., Garay, J.A.
          (eds.) CRYPTO 2013. LNCS, vol. 8043, pp. 129–147. Springer, Heidel-
          berg (2013). https://doi.org/10.1007/978-3-642-40084-1_8
[FLS90]   Feige, U., Lapidot, D., Shamir, A.: Multiple non-interactive zero knowl-
          edge proofs based on a single random string (extended abstract). In: FOCS
          (1990)
[FLS99]   Feige, U., Lapidot, D., Shamir, A.: Multiple non-interactive zero knowl-
          edge proofs under general assumptions. SIAM J. Comput. 29(1), 1–28
          (1999)
[FS86]   Fiat, A., Shamir, A.: How to prove yourself: practical solutions to identi-
          fication and signature problems. In: Odlyzko, A.M. (ed.) CRYPTO 1986.
          LNCS, vol. 263, pp. 186–194. Springer, Heidelberg (1987). https://doi.
          org/10.1007/3-540-47721-7_12
[GM82]   Goldwasser, S., Micali, S.: Probabilistic encryption and how to play men-
          tal poker keeping secret all partial information. In: STOC (1982)
[GMR89]   Goldwasser, S., Micali, S., Rackoff, C.: The knowledge complexity of inter-
          active proof systems. SIAM J. Comput. 18(1), 186–208 (1989)
[Gol11]   Goldreich, O.: Basing non-interactive zero-knowledge on (enhanced) trap-
          door permutations: the state of the art. In: Goldreich, O. (ed.) Studies
          in Complexity and Cryptography. Miscellanea on the Interplay between
          Randomness and Computation. LNCS, vol. 6650, pp. 406–421. Springer,
          Heidelberg (2011). https://doi.org/10.1007/978-3-642-22670-0_28
[GOS06]   Groth, J., Ostrovsky, R., Sahai, A.: Perfect non-interactive zero knowl-
          edge for NP. In: Vaudenay, S. (ed.) EUROCRYPT 2006. LNCS, vol.
          4004, pp. 339–358. Springer, Heidelberg (2006). https://doi.org/10.1007/
          11761679_21
[GOS12]   Groth, J., Ostrovsky, R., Sahai, A.: New techniques for noninteractive
          zero-knowledge. J. ACM 59(3), 1–35 (2012)
[GR13]   Goldreich, O., Rothblum, R.D.: Enhancements of trapdoor permutations.
          J. Cryptol. 26(3), 484–512 (2013)
[Gro10]   Groth, J.: Short non-interactive zero-knowledge proofs. In: Abe, M. (ed.)
          ASIACRYPT 2010. LNCS, vol. 6477, pp. 341–358. Springer, Heidelberg
          (2010). https://doi.org/10.1007/978-3-642-17373-8_20

[HILL99] Håstad, J., Impagliazzo, R., Levin, L.A., Luby, M.: A pseudorandom generator from any one-way function. SIAM J. Comput. **28**(4), 1364–1396 (1999)

[HJO+16] Hemenway, B., Jafargholi, Z., Ostrovsky, R., Scafuro, A., Wichs, D.: Adaptively secure garbled circuits from one-way functions. In: Robshaw, M., Katz, J. (eds.) CRYPTO 2016. LNCS, vol. 9816, pp. 149–178. Springer, Heidelberg (2016). https://doi.org/10.1007/978-3-662-53015-3_6

[HJR16] Hofheinz, D., Jager, T., Rupp, A.: Public-key encryption with simulation-based selective-opening security and compact ciphertexts. In: Hirt, M., Smith, A. (eds.) TCC 2016. LNCS, vol. 9986, pp. 146–168. Springer, Heidelberg (2016). https://doi.org/10.1007/978-3-662-53644-5_6

[HK07] Hofheinz, D., Kiltz, E.: Secure hybrid encryption from weakened key encapsulation. In: Menezes, A. (ed.) CRYPTO 2007. LNCS, vol. 4622, pp. 553–571. Springer, Heidelberg (2007). https://doi.org/10.1007/978-3-540-74143-5_31

[HU19] Hofheinz, D., Ursu, B.: Dual-mode NIZKs from obfuscation. In: Galbraith, S.D., Moriai, S. (eds.) ASIACRYPT 2019. LNCS, vol. 11921, pp. 311–341. Springer, Cham (2019). https://doi.org/10.1007/978-3-030-34578-5_12

[KNYY19a] Katsumata, S., Nishimaki, R., Yamada, S., Yamakawa, T.: Designated verifier/prover and preprocessing NIZKs from Diffie-Hellman assumptions. In: Ishai, Y., Rijmen, V. (eds.) EUROCRYPT 2019. LNCS, vol. 11477, pp. 622–651. Springer, Cham (2019). https://doi.org/10.1007/978-3-030-17656-3_22

[KNYY19b] Katsumata, S., Nishimaki, R., Yamada, S., Yamakawa, T.: Exploring constructions of compact NIZKs from various assumptions. In: Boldyreva, A., Micciancio, D. (eds.) CRYPTO 2019. LNCS, vol. 11694, pp. 639–669. Springer, Cham (2019). https://doi.org/10.1007/978-3-030-26954-8_21

[KW15] Kiltz, E., Wee, H.: Quasi-adaptive NIZK for linear subspaces revisited. In: Oswald, E., Fischlin, M. (eds.) EUROCRYPT 2015. LNCS, vol. 9057, pp. 101–128. Springer, Heidelberg (2015). https://doi.org/10.1007/978-3-662-46803-6_4

[KW18] Kim, S., Wu, D.J.: Multi-theorem preprocessing NIZKs from lattices. In: Shacham, H., Boldyreva, A. (eds.) CRYPTO 2018. LNCS, vol. 10992, pp. 733–765. Springer, Cham (2018). https://doi.org/10.1007/978-3-319-96881-0_25

[LQR+19] Lombardi, A., Quach, W., Rothblum, R.D., Wichs, D., Wu, D.J.: New constructions of reusable designated-verifier NIZKs. In: Boldyreva, A., Micciancio, D. (eds.) CRYPTO 2019. LNCS, vol. 11694, pp. 670–700. Springer, Cham (2019). https://doi.org/10.1007/978-3-030-26954-8_22

[MRV15] Morillo, P., Ràfols, C., Villar, J.L.: Matrix computational assumptions in multilinear groups. IACR Cryptology ePrint Archive (2015)

[Pai99] Paillier, P.: Public-key cryptosystems based on composite degree residuosity classes. In: Stern, J. (ed.) EUROCRYPT 1999. LNCS, vol. 1592, pp. 223–238. Springer, Heidelberg (1999). https://doi.org/10.1007/3-540-48910-X_16

[PS19] Peikert, C., Shiehian, S.: Noninteractive zero knowledge for NP from (plain) learning with errors. In: Boldyreva, A., Micciancio, D. (eds.) CRYPTO 2019. LNCS, vol. 11692, pp. 89–114. Springer, Cham (2019). https://doi.org/10.1007/978-3-030-26948-7_4

[PsV06] Pass, R., Shelat, A., Vaikuntanathan, V.: Construction of a non-malleable encryption scheme from any semantically secure one. In: Dwork, C. (ed.) CRYPTO 2006. LNCS, vol. 4117, pp. 271–289. Springer, Heidelberg (2006). https://doi.org/10.1007/11818175_16

[QRW19] Quach, W., Rothblum, R.D., Wichs, D.: Reusable designated-verifier NIZKs for all NP from CDH. In: Ishai, Y., Rijmen, V. (eds.) EUROCRYPT 2019. LNCS, vol. 11477, pp. 593–621. Springer, Cham (2019). https://doi.org/10.1007/978-3-030-17656-3_21

[Sha07] Shacham, H.: A Cramer-Shoup encryption scheme from the linear assumption and from progressively weaker linear variants. IACR Cryptology ePrint Archive (2007)

[SW14] Sahai, A., Waters, B.: How to use indistinguishability obfuscation: deniable encryption, and more. In: STOC (2014)

Non-interactive Zero-Knowledge in Pairing-Free Groups from Weaker Assumptions

Geoffroy Couteau[1](✉), Shuichi Katsumata[2], and Bogdan Ursu[3]

[1] CNRS, IRIF, Université de Paris, Paris, France
geoffroy.couteau@irif.fr
[2] AIST, Tokyo, Japan
shuichi.katsumata@aist.go.jp
[3] ETH Zürich, Zürich, Switzerland
bogdan.ursu@inf.ethz.ch

Abstract. We provide new constructions of non-interactive zero-knowledge arguments (NIZKs) for NP from discrete-logarithm-style assumptions over cyclic groups, without relying on pairings. A previous construction from (Canetti et al., Eurocrypt'18) achieves such NIZKs under the assumption that no efficient adversary can break the key-dependent message (KDM) security of (additive) ElGamal with respect to all (even inefficient) functions over groups of size 2^λ, with probability better than $\mathsf{poly}(\lambda)/2^\lambda$. This is an extremely strong, non-falsifiable assumption. In particular, even mild (polynomial) improvements over the current best known attacks on the discrete logarithm problem would already contradict this assumption. (Canetti et al. STOC'19) describe how to improve the assumption to rely only on KDM security with respect to all efficient functions, therefore obtaining an assumption that is (in spirit) falsifiable.

Our first construction improves this state of affairs. We provide a construction of NIZKs for NP under the CDH assumption together with the assumption that no efficient adversary can break the key-dependent message one-wayness of ElGamal with respect to *efficient* functions over groups of size 2^λ, with probability better than $\mathsf{poly}(\lambda)/2^{c\lambda}$ (denoted $2^{-c\lambda}$-OW-KDM), for a constant $c = 3/4$. Unlike the previous assumption, our assumption leaves an exponential gap between the best known attack and the required security guarantee.

We also analyse whether we could build NIZKs when CDH does not hold. As a second contribution, we construct an *infinitely often* NIZK argument system for NP (where soundness and zero-knowledge are only guaranteed to hold for infinitely many security parameters), under the $2^{-c\lambda}$-OW-KDM security of ElGamal with $c = 28/29 + o(1)$, together with the existence of low-depth pseudorandom generators.

Keywords: Non-interactive zero-knowledge arguments · Pairing-free groups · KDM security

© International Association for Cryptologic Research 2020
A. Canteaut and Y. Ishai (Eds.): EUROCRYPT 2020, LNCS 12107, pp. 442–471, 2020.
https://doi.org/10.1007/978-3-030-45727-3_15

1   Introduction

Zero-knowledge proof systems, introduced in [21], are a fundamental crypto-graphic primitive, allowing a prover to convince a verifier of the veracity of a statement, while not divulging anything beyond whether the statement is true. When the proof consists of a single message from prover to the verifier, this results in a non-interactive zero-knowledge proof system (NIZK) [5]. Due to their large number of applications in cryptography, NIZKs enjoy particular interest, ranging from efficient implementations to feasibility results.

On Building NIZKs from Concrete Assumptions. While one-way functions are known to be necessary [36] and sufficient [20] for zero-knowledge proof systems, the exact relation of NIZKs to other cryptographic assumptions and primitives is considerably less clear. NIZKs are known to exist in the plain model only for trivial languages [35]. To circumvent this issue, cryptographers design NIZKs in the common reference string (CRS) model, where a common reference string is honestly generated beforehand in a setup phase and is given to both prover and verifier. A large body of work has been dedicated to the construction of NIZKs in the CRS model from various cryptographic assumptions. As a result, NIZKs are known to exist from a wide range of assumptions, from pairing groups [22,23], factorization assumptions [5,13], and indistinguishability obfuscation [40], to circularly-secure LWE [6] and plain LWE [37]. Yet, in spite of three decades of efforts, it remains an intriguing open question whether one can construct NIZKs from discrete-logarithm-style assumptions (without relying on pairing groups), which are among the most well-established assumptions in cryptography. Here, the only known result is the recent work of [7], which constructs NIZKs under the exponential key-dependent message security of ElGamal with respect to all (even inefficient) functions. While this is a remarkable stepping stone, it remains an extremely strong and non-standard assumption. Therefore, an important question remains open:

> "Is it possible to build NIZKs from (weaker) discrete-logarithm-style assumptions?"

NIZKs from Correlation Intractability. Our work follows the blueprint of a recent line of research, which seeks to compile interactive protocols into NIZKs using the Fiat-Shamir paradigm [15], by instantiating the underlying hash function by a correlation-intractable hash function. Informally, a correlation-intractable hash function (CIH) with respect to a relation R is a hash function such that it is infeasible to find an input x satisfying $(x, H(x)) \in R$. CIH have been introduced in [8], where it was also shown that correlation-intractability for all sparse relations suffices to instantiate the Fiat-Shamir paradigm. Despite some impossibility results [4], a recent line of work has shown how to construct CIH for various sparse relations of interest [6,7,24,25,37], obtaining NIZKs from new assumptions. Out of these works, [7] relies on the exponential key-dependent messages (KDM) security for all (even inefficient) functions of an encryption scheme with universal ciphertexts, which can be instantiated over pairing-free groups with a suitable variant of ElGamal; unfortunately, this is an extremely strong assumption, which has several undesirable features. In this paper, we seek to improve the result of [7] and to construct NIZKs for NP from weaker assumptions over pairing-free groups.

On the Strong-KDM Security Assumption of [7]. The construction of [7] relies on the following assumption over cyclic groups: let $\mathbb{G}$ be a group of order $p \approx 2^\lambda$ with a generator g. Then, for any probabilistic polynomial time adversary $\mathcal{A}$, any (possibly inefficient) function $f : \mathbb{Z}_p \mapsto \mathbb{Z}_p$, and any superpolynomial function s, it holds that

$$\Pr\left[(a, k) \leftarrow_r \mathbb{Z}_p^2 \ : \ \mathcal{A}\left(g^a, g^{ak+f(k)}\right) = k\right] \leq \frac{s(\lambda)}{2^\lambda}.$$

While this assumption is not contradicted by known attacks on the discrete logarithm over suitably chosen elliptic curves, it is an extremely strong assumption, with several undesirable features:

- **Optimality.** Optimal security means that every PPT adversary has advantage at most $\lambda^{O(1)}/2^\lambda$.[1] The above assumption requires *optimal* security, which is equivalent to assuming that no improvement (by more than polynomial factors) to the best known existing attack will ever be found. Hence, even mild cryptanalytic improvements would already contradict the above assumption.
- **Non-falsifiablity.** The above assumption is not *falsifiable*, in the sense of [17,33], since it might not be possible to efficiently check whether an adversary breaks the assumption with respect to some specific inefficient function. However, [6] notes that it is possible to construct NIZKs even when the functions f considered in the assumption are efficient.

Insecurity with Auxiliary Inputs. In the same spirit as knowledge of exponent assumptions, which are known to become insecure (under obfuscation-style assumptions) when auxiliary inputs are allowed, unfalsifiable flavors of KDM security have been recently shown to be insecure as soon as auxiliary inputs are allowed, assuming that LWE is hard and one-way permutations exist [16]. While this does not directly contradict the unfalsifiable flavour of the assumption above, it makes it very sensitive to any side information an adversary might have access to when it is used in a higher-level application.

1.1 Our Contribution

We propose new constructions of NIZKs, improving over the NIZK of [7] in terms of the underlying assumption. As noted in [6], the assumption in [7] can be

---

[1] In the case of DDH groups, the best known generic PPT adversary is Pollard's rho algorithm [38], which runs in time $O(2^{\lambda/2})$ and has constant success probability. However, restricted to polynomial time, it only provides a polynomial advantage over randomly guessing the discrete logarithm. Moreover, it is known [41] that no generic algorithm with T oracle queries can have better success probability than $O\left(\frac{T^2}{2^\lambda}\right)$.

improved to consider only efficient functions and thus construct NIZKs based on a *falsifiable*-style notion of KDM-security[2]. In this work, we remove the need of relying on optimal security of the underlying assumption, while maintaining the *falsifiable* flavor of KDM security.

We note that our second construction satisfies a weaker notion of security, infinitely-often security, where soundness and zero-knowledge are only required to hold for infinitely many security parameters. For a discussion on the notion of infinitely-often security and its usage in cryptography, please refer to the full version of the paper.

In more detail, the assumption at the core of our new construction is a strong flavor of the OW-KDM security of ElGamal: given a group $\mathbb{G}$ of size $\approx 2^\lambda$ with generator g, the $2^{-c\lambda}$-OW-KDM assumption states that for a family of (randomized) *efficient* functions $\mathcal{F}$, any PPT adversary receiving an ElGamal ciphertext encrypting $F(k)$ (in the exponent) with the key k is unable to recover the plaintext with advantage greater than $s(\lambda)/2^{c\lambda}$, for any superpolynomial function s:

$$\Pr_{\substack{(k,a)\leftarrow_r \mathbb{Z}_q^2 \\ m\leftarrow_r F(k)}}[\mathcal{A}(g^a, g^{ak+m}) = m] \leq s(\lambda)/2^{c\lambda} \text{ for some } c \in [0,1].$$

The value c determines the strength of the assumption: $c = 1$ corresponds to assuming optimal security (as in [7]), while smaller values of c leave a gap between the success probability of the best known attacks and the success probability that can be tolerated by the assumption. In particular, a constant $c < 1$ indicates that the assumption can stand even exponential improvements in the success probability of the best known attacks.

1. Assuming the hardness of CDH and the $2^{-c\lambda}$-OW-KDM security of ElGamal with $c = 3/4$, we propose an adaptively-sound multi-theorem NIZK for all of NP. Both soundness and zero knowledge are computational, the first is implied by OW-KDM, while the second is implied by CDH.
2. Our second construction aims at analysing the complementary landscape. More precisely, we investigate the possibility of building NIZKs in groups where CDH does *not* hold, building upon the fact that this implies (using known results) the existence of a self-bilinear map. We leverage this self-bilinear map to obtain an adaptively-sound, adaptively multi-theorem zero-knowledge (infinitely often) NIZK for all of NP, under the $2^{-c\lambda}$-OW-KDM security of ElGamal with $c = 28/29 + o(1)$, together with the assumption that Goldreich's PRG [18] instantiated under the Lombardi-Vaikuntanathan predicate [29] is secure up to some (arbitrarily small) polynomial stretch.[3] Combining this result with our first construction, we obtain a construction of (infinitely-often) NIZKs for NP under the same assumptions, independently of whether CDH holds.

---

[2] More precisely, these assumptions are falsifiable in spirit in the sense that they can be modeled as an efficient game with a challenger, but the winning condition can occur with exponentially small probability.

[3] The security of Goldreich's PRG is a well-established and widely studied assumption, which provably resists large classes of attacks [2,3,10,32,34].

In both constructions, an important effort is devoted to obtaining the smallest possible constant c, to minimize the strength of the underlying assumption. We view it as an interesting open problem to further minimize the value of c, especially in our second construction.

1.2 Our Techniques – First Construction

Both our constructions follow a similar footprint: we start from a Σ-protocol for a carefully chosen, but limited language. We compile this Σ-protocol using a correlation-intractable (CI) hash function into a NIZK for the same limited language. Then we use different techniques to bootstrap this restricted NIZK to NIZK for all of NP, by using them to build a verifiable pseudorandom generator (VPRG) [11,26,39], which in turns leads to NIZKs for NP. Our approach is inspired by [7], their strategy is to design a correlation-intractable (CI) hash function based on a scheme with universal ciphertexts, which they use to transform an underlying sigma protocol into a NIZK. In their case, the interactive protocol is the one in [14, Section 2.1]. We diverge from this approach by applying the CI hash function to a sigma protocol for a more restricted, but still expressive enough language (which we bootstrap later to a fully-fledged NIZK through VPRGs). Looking ahead, the parameters of the KDM security assumption are intrinsically tied to the ratio between the size of the first flow of the sigma protocol and its adaptive soundness. By allowing the underlying sigma protocol to support only a more restricted language, we expand the field of potential candidates and eventually identify a protocol with a better first flow/soundness ratio. Our initial attempt is to start with the standard Σ-protocol for the Diffie-Hellman relation $\mathcal{L}_{DH}$, described in Fig. 1. Choose a cyclic group $\mathbb{G}$ of prime order p, along with two generators g and h. The relation consists of all pairs of group elements of the form (g^x, h^x). To transform the sigma protocol into a NIZK for $\mathcal{L}_{DH}$, the idea of the CI framework is to apply the Fiat-Shamir transform, but instead of using random oracles, the random oracle is replaced with a CI hash function.

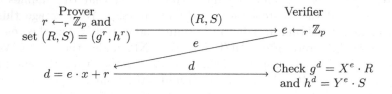

Fig. 1. Σ-protocol for the Diffie-Hellman language for the word $(g, h, X = g^x, Y = g^y)$. This is a variant of a protocol from [1]

CI Hash Functions. A CI hash function H for a specific relation $\mathcal{R}$ is a function for which it is hard to find an input α, such that $(\alpha, \mathsf{H}(\alpha)) \in \mathcal{R}$. Consider the case where the initial relation is sparse, meaning that for every α, the number of potential β's satisfying $(\alpha, \beta) \in \mathcal{R}$ is negligible. Then, the sigma protocol can be transformed into a NIZK by asking the prover to generate the second flow himself, by running $e = \mathsf{H}(R, S)$. The verifier will only accept if the resulting transcript is accepting and also $e = \mathsf{H}(R, S)$. From the correlation intractability of H, even a malicious prover will be unable to cheat by finding a properly chosen initial flow (R, S), such that $((R, S), \mathsf{H}(R, S)) \in \mathcal{R}$ (this also holds because the sparsity of the relation $\mathcal{R}$ is bounded by the soundness error of the sigma protocol, which is negligible).

Choice of H. To construct the hash, we choose a function closely related to the one used in [7], where $\mathsf{H}(x, K)$ interprets the input x as a decryption key, and the key K as a ciphertext, end returns $\mathsf{Dec}_x(K)$. For our instantiation, we crucially rely on a specific property of the additive variant of ElGamal (which is, informally, that keys and plaintexts are "interchangeable"). Since additive ElGamal does not provide efficient decryption (the decryption procedure recovers only $\tilde{G}^m$, and we cannot guarantee that m will be small in our construction), we modify the CI hash of [7] so that it returns $\mathsf{Trunc}(\tilde{G}^m)$, where Trunc is some function that parses its input as a bitstring and truncates it appropriately. More precisely, we pick a second cyclic group $\tilde{\mathbb{G}}$ of order q, generated by $\tilde{G}$ ($\lceil \log q \rceil = 2\lceil \log p \rceil$). The CI function is keyed by key $\tilde{C} = (\tilde{C}_0, \tilde{C}_1)$, where $(\tilde{C}_0, \tilde{C}_1) \leftarrow_r \tilde{\mathbb{G}}^2$. Then, we define:

$$\mathsf{H}_{(\tilde{C}_0, \tilde{C}_1)}(\alpha) \leftarrow \text{first } \lceil \log p \rceil \text{ bits of } \tilde{C}_1 / \tilde{C}_0^\alpha.$$

Parameters. This protocol has $\frac{1}{p}$ soundness and the size of the first flow is $2\lceil \log p \rceil$, which translates into a $2^{-\lambda/2}$-KDM assumption for the CI hash function. Unfortunately, this Σ-protocol does not satisfy adaptive soundness (given an honestly-generated first flow and challenge, there always exist words that are not in the relation, for which there exists an accepting third flow). Adaptive soundness is a crucial requirement for bootstrapping our first NIZK to cover all NP statements. Fortunately, performing a parallel repetition of the Σ-protocol yields adaptive soundness, albeit at the cost of worse parameters in our assumption ($c = 3/4$).

Reduction to KDM for Efficient Functions. The above construction reduces to the KDM security of ElGamal, but only with respect to an inefficient function f, which maps first flows to accepting challenges. From there, we leverage the fact that an ElGamal encryption $(\tilde{G}^r, \tilde{G}^{kr+m})$ of a plaintext m with key k, with respect to a generator $\tilde{G}$, can be equivalently seen as an ElGamal encryption of k with the key m with respect to the generator $\tilde{G}^r$. Building upon this observation and the fact that f^{-1} is efficient, we show that the security of our NIZK for the DDH language can in fact be reduced to the KDM security of ElGamal with respect to the *efficient* function f^{-1}.

From NIZK$_{\mathsf{DH}}$ for $\mathcal{L}_{\mathsf{DH}}$ to a NIZK for all of NP. In this step, we use an idea implicitly employed in [11,26,39]. We use the NIZK$_{\mathsf{DH}}$ for the $\mathcal{L}_{\mathsf{DH}}$ relation to construct a verifiable pseudo-random generator (VPRG), which we then in turn use to instantiate the hidden bits model of [14], to obtain NIZKs for all of NP.

Intuitively, a VPRG is a pseudo-random generator with the additional property that one can compute proofs for any individual bit of the output, certifying that the bit is consistent with a commitment of the initial seed. Let $\mathbb{G}$ be a cyclic group of order p, the VPRG public parameters will consist of $m + 1$ group elements $(g, h_1, \ldots, h_m)$. Seeds are elements $\tau \leftarrow_r \mathbb{Z}_p$, and commiting to a seed is $\mathsf{Commit}(\tau) = g^\tau$. The ith output bit of the VPRG is of the form $B(g^\tau, h_i^\tau)$, where B is the Goldreich-Levin hardcore bit. Now notice than we can actually certify this as a correctly computed bit, by noticing that $(g^\tau, h_i^\tau) \in \mathcal{L}_{\mathsf{DH}}$ and computing a proof using our $\mathsf{NIZK_{DH}}$. (additionally, we need to output h_i^τ as well, so that the verifier can compute $B(g^\tau, h_i^\tau)$ itself). Intuitively, this VPRG satisfies the following security properties:

1. Binding: If x_i is the ith output of the VPRG with respect to a seed τ, one should not be able to certify bit $1 - x_i$. This is implied in our construction by the soundness of $\mathsf{NIZK_{DH}}$.
2. Hiding: An adversary should not be able to recover the ith output of the VPRG, even if it received all the other output bits and proofs certifying that they are correct. In our construction, this property reduces to the CDH assumption.

NIZK for all of NP Through the Hidden-Bit Model. In this model [14], the prover and the verifier benefit from having access to a common reference string with special properties. The bits of the common reference string are initially hidden from the verifier. When proving a statement, the prover can decide to selectively reveal some bits of the common reference string, which allows the verifier to check the proof. The work of [14] has showed that NIZKs exist unconditionally in this model. The VPRG we construct allows us to simulate the hidden-bits model on the prover side. Initially, all bits are hidden from the verifier from the hiding property of the VPRG. Subsequently, the prover can decide to reveal several bits, which corresponds to computing VPRG proofs.

1.3   Our Techniques – Second Construction

The previous construction relies on the CDH assumption. In our second construction, we take the complementary road: we seek to construct NIZKs for NP (under the strong KDM security of ElGamal assuming that CDH does *not* hold. Together with our first construction, this implies a NIZK for NP that does not rely on the CDH assumption (albeit with an infinitely-often security notion). To this end, we also seek to build a VPRG.

Self-pairing. First, we notice that if CDH does not hold, there exists an efficient adversary solving it with non-negligible advantage. We use previous results by [31,41] to amplify the success probability of this adversary to obtain a self-pairing map. Since from the definition of CDH, the adversary is only guaranteed to succeed on infinitely-many security parameters, our NIZK will be secure only on infinitely-many security parameters. This self-pairing will allow us to perform homomorphic computations and to evaluate bounded integer arithmetic circuits in the exponent. Our core idea, informally, is to rely on this self-pairing to let the parties homomorphically evaluate a pseudorandom generator in the exponent: at a high level, given a (bit-by-bit) commitment c to the seed, the parties can homomorphically compute, using the self-pairing, a commitment c_i to the i-th output bit of the PRG (for all i). Then, the prover will open a given PRG value by providing a NIZK proof of correct opening.

A Commitment from Short-Exponent Discrete Logarithm. To instantiate this idea, we introduce a new commitment scheme which is perfectly binding, and which is hiding under the short-exponent discrete logarithm assumption (which states that given g^x for a random but *short* x, it is infeasible to retrieve x). This does not introduce any new assumption, as we further show that the short-exponent discrete logarithm assumption is implied by the strong OW-KDM security of ElGamal. Furthermore, we carefully design this commitment scheme so that it suffices, to convince the verifier that the opening was correct, to demonstrate that the randomness r of the commitment is *almost short*. By almost short, we mean that there exists short values (u, v) such that $v \cdot r = u \bmod p$. This turns out to be a crucial property, since the language of group elements with almost-short exponents is precisely one for which we are able to build a NIZK under the $2^{-c\lambda}$-OW-KDM security of ElGamal, for some $c < 1$.

A Σ-Protocol for Almost-Short Exponents. Let $\mathbb{G}$ be a cyclic group of p elements. We consider a simple Σ-protocol for proving that a word g^x has a short exponent, i.e. writing x as an integer yields a number $\leq 2^\ell$, for some carefully chosen $\ell < \lceil \log p \rceil$. Our protocol has a similar shape to the sigma protocol used in the previous construction, and is described in Fig. 3. However, we are unable to directly prove soundness, meaning that a malicious prover can convince the verifier of the validity of words g^x, where x is not short. Fortunately, we are able to ensure that if g^x is accepted, then $x = u \cdot v^{-1}$, where u and v are themselves short. We denote this as the language $\mathscr{L}_{\alpha,\beta}$ of (α, β)-almost-short elements:

$$\mathscr{L}_{\alpha,\beta} = \{g^x \mid x = u \cdot v^{-1} \in \mathbb{Z}_p, u \in [-2^\alpha, 2^\alpha], v \in [0, 2^\beta]\}.$$

Our Σ-protocol is somewhat atypical, in the honest run the prover must start with a word of the form g^x and a short witness x (notice that if x is short it belongs to the almost-short language). However, when proving soundness, we only safeguard membership to the larger almost-short set of words; therefore, there is a gap between the correctness requirement, and the soundness guarantees (this is similar to some lattice constructions, for example [30]).

NIZK^{AS} for the Language of Almost-Short Exponents. We will design another CI hash function, closely related to the one we built for the first construction, to transform the Σ-protocol above into a NIZK for the almost-short exponent language. This CI hash function will additionally employ a 2-universal hash function, which we use to reduce the security loss in our security analysis and achieve a better parameter c for the OW-KDM assumption. Now, equipped with our $\mathsf{NIZK}^{\mathsf{AS}}$, we only need one final tool before moving on to our VPRG.

A Low-Depth Local PRG. Equipped with the above tools, it remains to find a suitable PRG to be used in our construction. For correctness, we need to ensure that no overflow occurs during the homomorphic operations in the exponent; therefore, we must pick the group size large enough so that the homomorphic PRG evaluation does not cause an overflow. Since picking a larger group translates into a larger security loss in our reduction, we seek to rely on a PRG (with some arbitrary small polynomial stretch) that has a minimal *arithmetic degree*. Fortunately, such PRGs were recently studied in [29], which exhibits a PRG with arithmetic degree 3 which provably resists a large class of attacks for a stretch up to $1.25 - \varepsilon$. Combining this low-degree PRG with our new commitment scheme and our NIZK for the almost-short language yields a VPRG in groups where CDH does not hold, hence NIZKs for NP.

Wrapping Up. Combining our first and second construction, we get the following: assume that ElGamal is $2^{-c\lambda}$-OW-KDM secure with respect to efficient functions (with $c = 28/29 + o(1)$), and that the previous PRG is secure. Then either CDH holds, in which case our first construction implies a NIZK for NP, or CDH does *not* hold, in which case our second construction implies an (infinitely-often) NIZK for NP. Therefore, under a PRG assumption and the strong OW-KDM security of ElGamal, we prove the existence of an infinitely-often NIZK for NP (but our proof is non-constructive, in that it does not tell *which* of the two candidate constructions is actually secure; only that one is).

1.4 Organization

Section 2 introduces necessary preliminaries. Section 3 presents our first NIZK construction and Sect. 4 contains our second construction. Please consult the full version for supplementary material, on how to construct an algorithm for evaluating an arithmetic circuit in the exponent from groups where CDH is insecure, with bounds on the parameter growth when manipulating bounded-size exponents. The full version also contains all missing proofs of our theorems and a discussion on the notion of infinitely-often security.

2 Preliminaries

Notation. Throughout this paper, λ denotes the security parameter. A probabilistic polynomial time algorithm (PPT, also denoted *efficient* algorithm) runs in time polynomial in the (implicit) security parameter λ. A function f is *negligible* if for any positive polynomial p there exists a bound $B > 0$ such that, for any integer $k \geq B$, $|f(k)| \leq 1/|p(k)|$. We will write $f(\lambda) \approx 0$ to indicate that f is a negligible function of λ; we also write $f(\lambda) \approx g(\lambda)$ for $|f(\lambda) - g(\lambda)| \approx 0$. An event occurs with *overwhelming probability* p when $p \approx 1$. Given a finite set S, the notation $x \leftarrow_r S$ means a uniformly random assignment of an element of S to the variable x. For a positive integer n, m such that $n < m$, we denote by $[n]$ the set $\{1, \cdots, n\}$, by $[\pm n]$ the set $\{-n, \cdots, n\}$, and by $[n, m)$ the set $\{n, n+1, \cdots, m-1\}$. Given an element x of a set $\mathbb{Z}_p$, we denote by $\mathsf{int}(x)$ the integer $x' \in [\pm p/2]$ such that $x = x' \bmod p$. When manipulating elements (x, y) of $\mathbb{Z}_p$, we will generally abuse the notation and write $x \le y$ for $\mathsf{int}(x) \le \mathsf{int}(y)$.

The Computational Diffie-Hellman Assumption. Let DHGen be a deterministic algorithm that on input 1^λ returns a description $\mathcal{G} = (\mathbb{G}, p)$ where $\mathbb{G}$ is a cyclic group of prime order p. Then the computational Diffie-Hellman assumption is defined as follows.

Definition 1 (CDH Assumption). *We say that the computational Diffie-Hellman (CDH) assumption holds relative to DHGen if for all PPT adversaries $\mathcal{A}$,*

$$\Pr\left[\mathcal{G} \leftarrow DHGen(1^\lambda), g \leftarrow_r \mathbb{G}, \alpha, \beta \leftarrow_r \mathbb{Z}_p : g^{\alpha\beta} \leftarrow_r \mathcal{A}(1^\lambda, \mathcal{G}, g, g^\alpha, g^\beta)\right] \le \mathsf{negl}(\lambda).$$

Here, note that DHGen outputs a fixed group $\mathbb{G}$ per security parameter.

2.1 Non-interactive Zero-Knowledge

A (publicly-verifiable) non-interactive zero-knowledge (NIZK) argument system for an NP relation R, with associated language $\mathscr{L}(R) = \{x \mid \exists w, (x, w) \in R\}$ is a 3-tuple of efficient algorithms (Setup, Prove, Verify), where Setup outputs a common reference string, Prove(crs, x, w), given the crs, a word x, and a witness w, outputs a proof π, and Verify(crs, x, π), on input the crs, a word x, and a proof π, outputs a bit indicating whether the proof is accepted or not. A NIZK argument system satisfies the following: completeness, adaptive soundness, and selective single-theorem zero-knowledge properties: (we let R_λ denote the set $R \cap (\{0,1\}^\lambda \times \{0,1\}^*)$).

- A non-interactive argument system (Setup, Prove, Verify) for an NP relation R satisfies completeness if for every $(x, w) \in R$,

$$\Pr[\mathsf{crs} \leftarrow_r \mathsf{Setup}(1^{|x|}), \pi \leftarrow \mathsf{Prove}(\mathsf{crs}, x, w) : \mathsf{Verify}(\mathsf{crs}, x, \pi) = 1] \approx 1.$$

- A non-interactive argument system (Setup, Prove, Verify) for an NP relation R satisfies *adaptive soundness* if for any PPT $\mathcal{A}$,

$$\Pr\left[\begin{array}{l} \mathsf{crs} \leftarrow_r \mathsf{Setup}(1^\lambda), (x, \pi) \leftarrow_r \mathcal{A}(\mathsf{crs}) : \\ \mathsf{Verify}(\mathsf{crs}, x, \pi) = 1 \wedge x \notin \mathscr{L} \end{array}\right] \approx 0.$$

- A non-interactive argument system (Setup, Prove, Verify) for an NP relation R satisfies (computational, statistical) *selective single-theorem zero-knowledge* if there exists a PPT simulator Sim such that for every $(x, w) \in R$, the distribution $\{(\mathsf{crs}, \pi) : \mathsf{crs} \leftarrow_r \mathsf{Setup}(1^\lambda), \pi \leftarrow \mathsf{Prove}(\mathsf{crs}, x, w)\}$ and $\{(\mathsf{crs}, \pi) : (\mathsf{crs}, \pi) \leftarrow_r \mathsf{Sim}(x)\}$ are (computationally, statistically) indistinguishable.

Furthermore, we say that a NIZK for an NP relation R satisfies (computational, statistical) *adaptive multi-theorem zero-knowledge* if for all (computational, statistical) $\mathcal{A}$, there exists a PPT simulator $\mathsf{Sim} = (\mathsf{Sim}_1, \mathsf{Sim}_2)$ such that if we run $\mathsf{crs} \leftarrow_r \mathsf{Setup}(1^\lambda)$ and $\overline{\mathsf{crs}} \leftarrow_r \mathsf{Sim}_1(1^\lambda)$, then we have $|\Pr[\mathcal{A}^{\mathcal{O}_0(\mathsf{crs},\cdot,\cdot)}(\mathsf{crs}) = 1] - \Pr[\mathcal{A}^{\mathcal{O}_1(\overline{\mathsf{crs}},\cdot,\cdot)}(\mathsf{crs}) = 1]| \approx 0$, where $\mathcal{O}_0(\mathsf{crs}, x, w)$ outputs $\mathsf{Prove}(\mathsf{crs}, x, w)$ if $(x, w) \in R$ and $\perp$ otherwise, and $\mathcal{O}_1(\overline{\mathsf{crs}}, x, w)$ outputs $\mathsf{Sim}_2(\overline{\mathsf{crs}}, x)$ if $(x, w) \in R$ and $\perp$ otherwise.

We use the following result regarding the existence of NIZKs in the hidden-bits model (HBM). Since the full definition of NIZK in the HBM will not be required in our work, we refer the readers to [13] for more details.

Theorem 2 (NIZK for all of NP in the HBM). *Let λ denote the security parameter and let $k = k(\lambda)$ be any positive integer-valued function. Then, unconditionally, there exists NIZK proof systems for any NP language $\mathscr{L}$ in the HBM that uses $\mathsf{hb} = k \cdot \mathsf{poly}(\lambda)$ hidden bits with soundness error $\epsilon \leq 2^{-k \cdot \lambda}$, where λ denotes the security parameter and poly is a function related to the NP language $\mathscr{L}$.*

2.2 Verifiable Pseudorandom Generators

Definition 3 (Verifiable Pseudorandom Generator). *Let $\delta(\lambda)$ and $s(\lambda)$ be positive valued polynomials. A $(\delta(\lambda), s(\lambda))$-verifiable pseudorandom generator (VPRG) is a four-tuple of efficient algorithms $(\mathsf{Setup}, \mathsf{Stretch}, \mathsf{Prove}, \mathsf{Verify})$ such that*

- *$\mathsf{Setup}(1^\lambda, m)$, on input the security parameter (in unary) and a polynomial bound $m(\lambda) \geq s(\lambda)^{1+\delta(\lambda)}$, outputs a set of public parameters pp (which contains 1^λ);*
- *$\mathsf{Stretch}(\mathsf{pp})$, on input the public parameters pp, outputs a triple $(\mathsf{pvk}, x, \mathsf{aux})$, where pvk is a public verification key of length $s(\lambda)$, x is an m-bit pseudorandom string, and aux is an auxiliary information;*
- *$\mathsf{Prove}(\mathsf{pp}, \mathsf{aux}, i)$, on input the public parameters pp, auxiliary informations aux, an index $i \in [m]$, outputs a proof π;*
- *$\mathsf{Verify}(\mathsf{pp}, \mathsf{pvk}, i, b, \pi)$, on input the public parameters pp, a public verification key pvk, an index $i \in [m]$, a bit b, and a proof π, outputs a bit β;*

which is in addition complete, hiding, *and* binding, *as defined below.*

Definition 4 (Completeness of a VPRG). *For any $i \in [m]$, a complete DVPRG scheme $(\mathsf{Setup}, \mathsf{Stretch}, \mathsf{Prove}, \mathsf{Verify})$ satisfies:*

$$\Pr\left[\begin{array}{l} \mathsf{pp} \leftarrow_r \mathsf{Setup}(1^\lambda, m), \\ (\mathsf{pvk}, x, \mathsf{aux}) \leftarrow_r \mathsf{Stretch}(\mathsf{pp}), : \mathsf{Verify}(\mathsf{pp}, \mathsf{pvk}, i, x_i, \pi) = 1 \\ \pi \leftarrow_r \mathsf{Prove}(\mathsf{pp}, \mathsf{aux}, i), \end{array}\right] \approx 1.$$

Note that our definition of VPRG is slightly relaxed than what is considered in [11,12,39], in that, we do not require the size of $s(\lambda)$ to be independent of $m(\lambda)$. This relaxation still allows us to construct NIZKs for NP as long as the stretch $\delta(\lambda)$ is larger than some positive constant.

Definition 5 (Binding Property of a VPRG). *Let* (Setup, Stretch, Prove, Verify) *be a* VPRG. *A* VPRG *is* binding *if there exists a (possibly inefficient) extractor* Ext *such that for any PPT* $\mathcal{A}$, *it holds that*

$$\Pr \begin{bmatrix} \mathsf{pp} \leftarrow_r \mathsf{Setup}(1^\lambda, m), \\ (\mathsf{pvk}, i, \pi) \leftarrow_r \mathcal{A}(\mathsf{pp}), : \mathsf{Verify}(\mathsf{pp}, \mathsf{pvk}, i, 1 - x_i, \pi) = 1 \\ x \leftarrow \mathsf{Ext}(\mathsf{pp}, \mathsf{pvk}) \end{bmatrix} \approx 0.$$

Note that, following [11,26,39], we consider a significantly weaker flavor of binding compared to [12], which still allows to construct NIZKs for NP.

Definition 6 (Hiding Property of a VPRG). *A* VPRG *scheme* (Setup, Stretch, Prove, Verify) *is* hiding *if for any* $i \in [m]$ *and any PPT adversary* $\mathcal{A}$ *that outputs bits, it holds that:*

$$\Pr \begin{bmatrix} \mathsf{pp} \leftarrow_r \mathsf{Setup}(1^\lambda, m), \\ (\mathsf{pvk}, x, \mathsf{aux}) \leftarrow_r \mathsf{Stretch}(\mathsf{pp}), : \mathcal{A}(\mathsf{pp}, \mathsf{pvk}, i, (x_j, \pi_j)_{j \neq i}) = x_i \\ (\pi_j \leftarrow_r \mathsf{Prove}(\mathsf{pp}, \mathsf{aux}, j))_j \end{bmatrix} \approx 1/2.$$

The following shows that VPRG with a sufficient stretch is sufficient to construct NIZKs for all of NP.

Theorem 7 ($((\delta, s)$-VPRGs $\Rightarrow$ NIZKs for all of NP). *Fix an NIZK proof system for any NP language $\mathscr{L}$ in the HBM that uses* $\mathsf{hb} = \mathsf{hb}(\lambda)$ *hidden bits with soundness error $\epsilon \leq 2^{-\lambda}$ where* $\mathsf{hb} \geq \lambda$ *w.l.o.g. Suppose that a $(\delta(\lambda), s(\lambda))$-verifiable pseudorandom generator where $s(\lambda) \geq \max\{\lambda, (\mathsf{hb}^2/\lambda)^{1/\delta(\lambda)}\}$ exits. Then, there exist adaptively sound and adaptively multi-theorem zero-knowledge NIZK arguments for the NP relation $\mathscr{L}$.*

We provide a proof sketch in the full version. Since existence of an NIZK in the HBM for any NP language $\mathscr{L}$ is implied by Theorem 2, the above shows that VPRGs with some mild condition on $\delta(\lambda)$ and $s(\lambda)$ implies existence of an NIZK for any NP language $\mathscr{L}$.

2.3   Correlation-Intractable Hash Functions

We recall the definition of correlation intractability [9].

Definition 8 (Correlation Intractable Hash Function). *A collection* $\mathcal{H} = \{H_\lambda : K_\lambda \times I_\lambda \mapsto O_\lambda\}_{\lambda \in \mathbb{N}}$ *of (efficient) keyed hash functions is a $\mathcal{R}$-correlation intractable hash (CIH) family, with respect to a relation ensemble $\mathcal{R} = \{\mathcal{R}_\lambda \subseteq I_\lambda \times O_\lambda\}$, if for every (non-uniform) PPT adversary $\mathcal{A}$, it holds that*

$$\Pr_{\substack{k \leftarrow_r K_\lambda \\ x \leftarrow_r \mathcal{A}(k)}} [(x, H_\lambda(K, x)) \in \mathcal{R}_\lambda] = \mathsf{negl}(\lambda).$$

For CIH to be useful as a building block for NIZK, we require an additional property referred to as *programmability* [6].

Definition 9 (Programmability). *A collection* $\mathcal{H} = \{H_\lambda : K_\lambda \times I_\lambda \mapsto O_\lambda\}_{\lambda \in \mathbb{N}}$ *of (efficient) keyed hash functions is called* programmable *if there exists an efficient algorithm, which given* $x \in I_\lambda$ *and* $y \in O_\lambda$, *outputs a uniformly random key* k *from* K_λ, *such that* $H(k, x) = y$.

Finally, we define the standard notion of *sparsity*.

Definition 10 (Sparsity). *For any relation ensemble* $\mathcal{R} = \{\mathcal{R}_\lambda \subseteq I_\lambda \times O_\lambda\}$, *we say that* $\mathcal{R}$ *is* $\rho(\cdot)$-sparse *if for* $\lambda \in \mathbb{N}$ *and any* $x \in I_\lambda$, $\mathrm{Pr}_{y \leftarrow_r O_\lambda}[(x, y) \in \mathcal{R}_\lambda] \leq \rho(\lambda)$. *When* $\rho(\lambda) = \mathsf{negl}(\lambda)$, *we simply say it is* sparse.

2.4 Σ-Protocol

We recall the definition of Σ-protocols from [28]. A Σ-protocol is a three-move interactive proof between a prover P and a verifier V for a language $\mathscr{L}$, where the prover sends an initial message α, the verifier responds with a random $\beta \leftarrow_r S_\lambda$ for some challenge space S_λ, and the prover concludes with a message γ. Lastly, the verifier outputs 1, if it accepts and 0 otherwise. Three properties we require from a Σ-protocol are completeness, special honest-verifier zero-knowledge, and adaptive soundness.

Definition 11 (Completeness). *A Σ-protocol for a relation R with prover* P *and verifier* V *is* complete, *if* $\mathrm{Pr}[\mathsf{out}\langle \mathsf{P}(x, w), \mathsf{V}(x) \rangle = 1 | (x, w) \in R] = 1$.

Definition 12 (Special honest-verifier zero-knowledge). *A Σ-protocol for a relation R is* special honest-verifier zero-knowledge, *if there exists a polynomial-time simulator* Sim *such that the distributions* $\mathsf{Sim}(x, \beta)$ *and* $\langle \mathsf{P}(x, w), \mathsf{V}(x) \rangle$ *are statistically close for* $(x, w) \in R$, $\beta \in S_\lambda$.

Definition 13 (Adaptive soundness). *A Σ-protocol for a relation R is* $\rho(\cdot)$-adaptive sound, *if for any (possibly inefficient) cheating prover* P* *and any first flow* α, *it holds that* $\mathrm{Pr}[\beta \leftarrow_r S_\lambda; (x, \gamma) \leftarrow_r \mathsf{P}^*(\alpha, \beta) : \exists x \notin \mathscr{L} \wedge V(x, \alpha, \beta, \gamma) = 1] \leq \rho(\lambda)$. *When* $\rho(\lambda) = \mathsf{negl}(\lambda)$, *we simply say it is* adaptive sound.

In the above notion, when the cheating P* does not have the freedom to choose the word x, we say it is *selectively* sound. Note that a selective soundness is implied by the standard notion of special soundness of the Σ-protocol. The following lemma is due to [25], which at a high level claims that any adaptive sound Σ-protocol induces a natural sparse relation.

Lemma 14. *Let Π be an arbitrary* $\rho(\cdot)$-adaptive sound Σ-protocol for a language $\mathscr{L}$. *Then, the following relation induced by the Σ-protocol Π is* $\rho(\cdot)$-parse:

$$\mathcal{R}_{\mathsf{sparse}} = \{(\alpha, \beta) : \exists x, \gamma \text{ s.t. } x \notin \mathscr{L} \wedge V(x, \alpha, \beta, \gamma) = 1\}.$$

2.5   Secret Key Variant of ElGamal

Definition 15 (Secret Key ElGamal). *Let* $\tilde{\mathbb{G}} = \{\tilde{\mathbb{G}}_\lambda\}_{\lambda \in \mathbb{N}}$ *be an ensemble of groups where each group* $\tilde{\mathbb{G}}_\lambda$ *is of order* q *such that* $\lceil \log q \rceil = \lambda$. *The natural (secret-key) variant of additive ElGamal with message space* $\mathbb{Z}_q$ *consists of the following three PPT algorithms.*

- Setup(1^λ) : *output public-parameter* $\tilde{G} \leftarrow_r \tilde{\mathbb{G}}_\lambda$ *and secret key* $k \leftarrow_r \mathbb{Z}_q$.
- $\mathsf{Enc}_{\tilde{G}}(k, m)$: *pick* $\tilde{R} \leftarrow_r \tilde{G}$ *and output* $\tilde{\mathbf{C}} = (\tilde{R}, \tilde{R}^k \cdot \tilde{G}^m)$.
- $\mathsf{HalfDec}(k, \tilde{\mathbf{C}})$: *parse* $\tilde{\mathbf{C}}$ *as* $(\tilde{C}_0, \tilde{C}_1)$ *and output* $\tilde{C}_1/\tilde{C}_0^k$.

Throughout the paper, we omit the subscript when the meaning is clear. Note that the scheme does not allow for full decryption, but only for decryption "up to discrete logarithm": for every $(\tilde{G}, k, m)$, it holds that $\mathsf{HalfDec}(k, \mathsf{Enc}_{\tilde{G}}(k, m)) = \tilde{G}^m$. One important property of the scheme is that it enjoys the notion of *universality*. Informally, the notion claims that the ciphertexts are not associated with a specific key, but rather, could have been an output of *any* key.

Definition 16 (Universality). *For all* $\lambda \in \mathbb{N}$, $\tilde{G} \in \tilde{\mathbb{G}}_\lambda$, *and* $k^* \in \mathbb{Z}_q$, *the ciphertexts of ElGamal satisfies*

$$\{\tilde{\mathbf{C}} : (k, m) \leftarrow_r \mathbb{Z}_q^2, \tilde{\mathbf{C}} \leftarrow_r \mathsf{Enc}_{\tilde{G}}(k, m)\} = \{\tilde{\mathbf{C}} : m \leftarrow_r \mathbb{Z}_q, \tilde{\mathbf{C}} \leftarrow_r \mathsf{Enc}_{\tilde{G}}(k^*, m)\} = \mathcal{U}_{\tilde{\mathbb{G}}^2}.$$

Definition 17 (OW-KDM Security). *Let* $\mathcal{F} = \{\mathcal{F}_\lambda\}_{\lambda \in \mathbb{N}}$ *be an ensemble of sets of functions where each* $\mathcal{F}_\lambda = \{F_u\}_u$ *is a family of (possibly randomized) efficiently-computable functions. We say that ElGamal satisfies (one-query)* δ-*OW-KDM security with respect to* $\mathcal{F}$ *if for every* $F_u \in \mathcal{F}_\lambda$, *every superpolynomial function* s, *and every (non-uniform) PPT adversary* $\mathcal{A}$, *it holds that*

$$\Pr_{\substack{(\tilde{G}, k) \leftarrow_r \tilde{\mathbb{G}}_\lambda \times \mathbb{Z}_q \\ m \leftarrow F_u(\tilde{G}, k) \\ \tilde{\mathbf{C}} \leftarrow_r \mathsf{Enc}_{\tilde{G}}(k, m)}} [\mathcal{A}(\tilde{G}, \tilde{\mathbf{C}}) = m] \leq s(\lambda) \cdot \delta(\lambda).$$

If ElGamal satisfies δ-*OW-KDM security with* $\delta(\lambda) = 2^{-c\lambda}$ *for some constant* $c \in (0, 1]$, *then we say it is* strong OW-KDM *secure*.

2.6   Low-Depth Pseudorandom Generators

Definition. A pseudorandom generator is a deterministic process that expands a short random seed into a longer sequence, so that no efficient adversary can distinguish this sequence from a uniformly random string of the same length:

Definition 18 (Pseudorandom Generator). *A* $m(n)$-*stretch pseudorandom generator, for a polynomial* m, *is a pair of PPT algorithms* (PRG.Setup, PRG. Eval) *where* PRG.Setup(1^n) *outputs some public parameters* pp, *which are implicitly given as input to* PRG.Eval, *and* PRG.Eval(x), *on input a seed* $x \in \{0, 1\}^n$, *outputs a string* $y \in \{0, 1\}^{m(n)}$. *It satisfies the following security notion: for any probabilistic polynomial-time adversary* $\mathcal{A}$ *and every large enough* n,

$$\Pr[\text{pp} \leftarrow_r \text{PRG.Setup}(1^n), y \leftarrow_r \{0,1\}^{m(n)} : \mathcal{A}(\text{pp}, y) = 1]$$
$$\approx \Pr[\text{pp} \leftarrow_r \text{PRG.Setup}(1^n), x \leftarrow_r \{0,1\}^n, y \leftarrow \text{PRG.Eval}(x) : \mathcal{A}(\text{pp}, y) = 1]$$

A pseudorandom generator PRG *is d-local (for a function d) if for any* $n \in \mathbb{N}$, *every output bit of* PRG.Eval *on input a seed* $x \in \{0,1\}^n$ *depends on at most* $d(n)$ *input bits.*

Goldreich's Pseudorandom Generator. Goldreich's candidate local PRGs form a family $\mathcal{F}_{G,P}$ of local PRGs: $\text{PRG}_{G,P} : \{0,1\}^n \mapsto \{0,1\}^m$, parametrized by an (n, m, d)-hypergraph $G = (\sigma^1, \ldots, \sigma^m)$ (where $m = m(n)$ is polynomial in n), and a predicate $P : \{0,1\}^d \mapsto \{0,1\}$, defined as follows: on input $x \in \{0,1\}^n$, $\text{PRG}_{G,P}$ returns the m-bit string $(P(x_{\sigma_1^1}, \ldots, x_{\sigma_d^1}), \ldots, P(x_{\sigma_1^m}, \cdots, x_{\sigma_d^m}))$.

The Lombardi-Vaikuntanathan (LV) Predicate. For concreteness, we will rely on Goldreich PRG instantiated with the following predicate:

$$\mathsf{P}_{\mathsf{LV}}(x_1, x_2, x_3, x_4, x_5) = x_1 \oplus x_2 \oplus (x_1 \oplus x_3)(x_2 \oplus x_4) \oplus x_5 .$$

This predicate leads to a PRG with locality five. This predicate was introduced and studied in [29], were it was shown that it provably resists all $\mathbb{F}_2$-linear attacks, as well as all attacks using the SDP hierarchies (such as the Lassere-Parrilo sum-of-squares hierarchy), when stretching n bits to $n^{1.25-\varepsilon}$ bits. In addition, this predicate enjoys an optimaly low arithmetic degree, since it can be computed by the following degree 3 polynomial over the integers:

$$\mathsf{P}_{\mathsf{LV}}(x_1, x_2, x_3, x_4, x_5) = x_5 + (x_1(x_4 - 1) + x_2(x_1 + x_3 - 1) - x_3 x_4) \cdot (2x_5 - 1) .$$

3   NIZK Based on the Security of CDH and Strong OW-KDM Security of ElGamal

In this section, we describe a construction of a NIZK from the strong OW-KDM security of ElGamal with respect to efficient functions by assuming the CDH problem is *hard* to solve. We first provide a NIZK for the specific language of the Diffie-Hellman (DH) language. This is done by constructing a CIH based on the strong OW-KDM security of ElGamal for the natural sparse relation induced by the Σ-protocol for DH languages. We then show that such a NIZK for the DH language allows us to construct a VPRG, which in return, allows us to construct a NIZK for all of NP by Theorem 7.

3.1 Σ-Protocol for the Diffie-Hellman Language

Definition 19 (Diffie-Hellman Language). *Let* $\mathbb{G}$ *be a group with prime order* p. *We define the Diffie-Hellman (DH) language* $\mathscr{L}_{\mathsf{DH},t}$ *parameterized by* $t \in \mathbb{Z}_p^*$ *as* $\mathscr{L}_{\mathsf{DH},t} = \{(g, h, g^x, h^x) : g, h \in \mathbb{G}, x \in \mathbb{Z}_p, \mathsf{dlog}_g h = t\}$.

Prover   Verifier

$(r_1, r_2) \leftarrow_r \mathbb{Z}_p^2$ and
set $(R_1, S_1) = (g^{r_1}, h^{r_1})$ $\xrightarrow{\quad (R_1, S_1, R_2, S_2) \quad}$ $(e_1, e_2) \leftarrow_r (\mathbb{Z}_p^*)^2$
$(R_2, S_2) = (g^{r_2}, h^{r_2})$

$\xleftarrow{\qquad e_1, e_2 \qquad}$

$d_1 = e_1 \cdot x + r_1$ $\xrightarrow{\quad d_1, d_2 \quad}$ Check $g^{d_i} = X^{e_i} \cdot R_i$
$d_2 = e_2 \cdot x + r_2$ and $h^{d_i} = Y^{e_i} \cdot S_i$, for $i \in \{1, 2\}$

Fig. 2. Σ-protocol for the Diffie-Hellman language for the word $(g, h, X = g^x, Y = g^y)$.

Below we recall the standard Σ-protocol for the DH relation (with parallel repetition). Here, the word is $(g, h, X, Y) \in \mathscr{L}_{\mathsf{DH},t}$ where $(X, Y) = (g^x, h^x)$.

The above Σ-protocol achieves the standard notion of correctness and special honest-verifier zero-knowledge. Adaptive soundness is covered by the following lemma, the proof is standard and provided for completeness in the full version of the paper.

Lemma 20 (Adaptive Soundness). *The Σ-protocol in Fig. 2 satisfies $\frac{1}{p-1}$-adaptive soundness.*

3.2   Correlation-Intractable Hash Function H

Let λ be a security parameter. We consider a group $\tilde{\mathbb{G}}$ of order $q(\lambda)$ with $\lceil \log q \rceil \approx \lambda$. Let $\mathsf{Trunc} : \tilde{\mathbb{G}} \mapsto \{0, 1\}^{\lambda/2}$ be the function which, on input a group element $\tilde{G} \in \tilde{\mathbb{G}}$, parses it as a $\lceil \log q \rceil$-bit string and returns the first $\lambda/2$ bits of its input. We consider the following hash function $\mathsf{H} : \tilde{\mathbb{G}}^2 \times \mathbb{Z}_q \mapsto \{0, 1\}^{\lambda/2}$:

- Sampling the key: pick $(\tilde{G}, k, m) \leftarrow_r \tilde{\mathbb{G}} \times \mathbb{Z}_q^2$ and set $\tilde{\mathbf{C}} \leftarrow_r \mathsf{Enc}_{\tilde{G}}(k, m)$. Note that the key distribution is exactly the uniform distribution over $\tilde{\mathbb{G}}^2$.
- Evaluating $\mathsf{H}(\tilde{\mathbf{C}}, \cdot) : \mathsf{H}(\tilde{\mathbf{C}}, x) = \mathsf{Trunc}(\mathsf{HalfDec}(x, \tilde{\mathbf{C}}))$.

Correlation-Intractability of H. Consider a group $\mathbb{G}$ of order $p(\lambda)$ with $\lceil \log p \rceil \approx \lambda/4$. Then the output of H can be interpreted as two elements of $\mathbb{G}$. Fix a parameter $t \in \mathbb{Z}_p^*$. Define $\mathcal{R}_{\lambda,t}$ to be the natural sparse relation associated to the language $\mathscr{L}_{\mathsf{DH},t}$ (see Lemma 14). That is,

$$\mathcal{R}_{\lambda,t} = \{(\alpha, \beta) \in \mathbb{G}^4 \times (\mathbb{Z}_p^*)^2 : \exists x, \gamma \text{ s.t. } x \notin \mathscr{L}_{\mathsf{DH},t} \wedge V(x, \alpha, \beta, \gamma) = \mathsf{accept}\}.$$

Here, the above relation can also be described alternatively using the following (inefficient) randomized function:

$$f_t(a; z) : \begin{cases} \mathbb{G}^4 \times \mathbb{Z}_p^* \mapsto (\mathbb{Z}_p^*)^2 \\ (R_1, S_1, R_2, S_2) \times z \to (z, \log_{(R_1^t/S_1)}(R_2^t/S_2) \cdot z) \end{cases}.$$

The following is the main contribution of this section.

Theorem 21. *Assume that ElGamal satisfies* $2^{-3\lambda/4}$-OW-KDM *security with respect to efficient functions. Then the hash family* $\{H : H : \tilde{G}^2 \times \mathbb{Z}_q \mapsto \{0,1\}^{\lambda/2}\}_\lambda$ *is correlation-intractable with respect to* $\mathcal{R}^H := \{\mathcal{R}_\lambda := \{\mathcal{R}_{\lambda,t}\}_t\}_\lambda$.

Proof. We prove the theorem in two steps. We first show that an adversary against the correlation intractability of H can be shown to be an adversary against the OW-KDM security of ElGamal with respect to *inefficient* functions. We then show via the symmetry of messages and secret keys of ElGamal to conclude that such an adversary can indeed be used to break OW-KDM security of ElGamal with respect to *efficient* functions. The first step is summarized in the following lemma.

Lemma 22. *Let* $\mathcal{A}$ *be an adversary against the* $\mathcal{R}^H$-correlation intractability of H *with (non-negligible) advantage* $\varepsilon(\lambda)$. *Then, for some* $t \in \mathbb{Z}_p^*$, *it holds that:*

$$\Pr_{\substack{(\tilde{G},a^*,m)\leftarrow_r \tilde{G}\times\mathbb{Z}_q^2 \\ \tilde{C}\leftarrow_r \mathsf{Enc}_{\tilde{G}}(a^*,m)}}[\mathcal{A}(\tilde{G},\tilde{C}) = a^* | (a^*, H(\tilde{C},a^*)) \in \mathcal{R}_{\lambda,t}] \geq \frac{\varepsilon(\lambda)}{2^{3\lambda/4}}.$$

The proof follows closely the approach of [7], but simplifies some steps of the proof and makes the exact security loss explicit. We provide it in the full version of the paper. Given Lemma 22, it remains to show that this implies a contradiction to the OW-KDM security of ElGamal for *efficient* functions. The main difficulty here is that the above can be rewritten as

$$\Pr_{\substack{(\tilde{G},a^*)\leftarrow_r \tilde{G}\times\mathbb{Z}_q \\ m\leftarrow_r \alpha_t(\tilde{G},a^*) \\ \tilde{C}\leftarrow_r \mathsf{Enc}_{\tilde{G}}(a^*,m)}}[\mathcal{A}(\tilde{G},\tilde{C}) = a^*] \geq \frac{\varepsilon(\lambda)}{2^{3\lambda/4}}. \qquad (1)$$

with $\alpha_t : \tilde{G} \times \mathbb{Z}_q \times \{0,1\}^{\lambda/2} \times \mathbb{Z}_p^* \mapsto \mathbb{Z}_q$, such that $\alpha_t(\tilde{G}, a; z_1, z_2) = \mathsf{dlog}_{\tilde{G}}(f_t(a; z_2)||z_1)$. which naturally translates to an adversary against the KDM security of ElGamal where m is sampled as $\alpha_t(\tilde{G}, a^*; z_1, z_2)$, which is not an efficiently computable function. We show below how to get around this apparent issue. Define the (randomized) efficiently computable function f_t^{-1} as follows:

$$f_t^{-1}(e_1, e_2; r_1, r_2, s_1) := \begin{cases} (\mathbb{Z}_p^*)^2 \times \mathbb{G}^3 \mapsto \mathbb{G}^4 \\ (e_1, e_2; r_1, r_2, s_1) \to (g^{r_1}, g^{s_1}, g^{r_2}, g^{\frac{e_2(t \cdot r_1 - s_1)}{e_1} - t \cdot r_2}). \end{cases}$$

Furthermore, define F_t to be the following (efficient, randomized) function:

$$F_t : \begin{cases} \tilde{G} \times \mathbb{Z}_q \times \{0,1\}^{\lambda/2} \mapsto \mathbb{Z}_q \\ (\tilde{G}, m; z) \to f_t^{-1}(\mathsf{Trunc}(\tilde{G}^m); z), \end{cases}$$

where we assume in case the first $\lambda/4$-bits of $\mathsf{Trunc}(\tilde{G}^m)$ corresponds to $0 \in \mathbb{Z}_p$, then it outputs some fixed element in $\mathbb{Z}_q$. Consider now the distribution obtained by sampling $(\tilde{G}, a^*) \leftarrow_r \tilde{G} \times \mathbb{Z}_q$, $m \leftarrow_r \alpha_t(\tilde{G}, a^*)$, and outputting

$\tilde{\mathbf{C}} \leftarrow_r \mathsf{Enc}_{\tilde{G}}(a^*, m)$. Observe that we obtain the same distribution (up to some negligible difference) by first sampling $(\tilde{G}, m) \leftarrow_r \tilde{\mathbb{G}} \times \mathbb{Z}_q$, setting $k \leftarrow_r F_t(\tilde{G}, m)$, and outputting $\tilde{\mathbf{C}} \leftarrow_r \mathsf{Enc}_{\tilde{G}}(k, m)$. We build upon this observation to construct, using $\mathcal{A}$, an adversary against the one-query OW-KDM security of ElGamal with respect to the class of (efficient, randomized) functions $\{F_t\}_t$. Let $\mathcal{A}$ be the previous adversary, which satisfies Eq. 1. By our observation above, this can be rewritten as

$$\Pr_{\substack{(\tilde{G}, k) \leftarrow_r \tilde{\mathbb{G}} \times \mathbb{Z}_q \\ a^* \leftarrow_r F_t(\tilde{G}, k) \\ \tilde{\mathbf{C}} \leftarrow_r \mathsf{Enc}_{\tilde{G}}(a^*, k)}} [\mathcal{A}(\tilde{G}, \tilde{\mathbf{C}}) = a^*] \geq \frac{\varepsilon(\lambda)}{2^{3\lambda/4}}.$$

We build an adversary $\mathcal{B}$ against the OW-KDM security of ElGamal as follows: on input $(\tilde{G}, \tilde{\mathbf{C}})$, $\mathcal{B}$ parses $\tilde{\mathbf{C}}$ as $(\tilde{C}_0, \tilde{C}_1)$. $\mathcal{B}$ sets $\tilde{G}' \leftarrow \tilde{C}_0$ and $\tilde{\mathbf{C}}' \leftarrow (\tilde{G}, \tilde{C}_1)$. Then, $\mathcal{B}$ runs $\mathcal{A}(\tilde{G}', \tilde{\mathbf{C}}')$ and outputs whatever $\mathcal{A}$ outputs. Observe that the distributions

$$\{(\tilde{G}, \tilde{\mathbf{C}}) \; : \; (\tilde{G}, k) \leftarrow_r \tilde{\mathbb{G}} \times \mathbb{Z}_q, a^* \leftarrow_r F_t(\tilde{G}, k), \tilde{\mathbf{C}} \leftarrow_r \mathsf{Enc}_{\tilde{G}}(a^*, k)\},$$

which corresponds to the experiment in the previous probability, and

$$\{(\tilde{C}_0, (\tilde{G}, \tilde{C}_1)) \; : \; (\tilde{G}, k) \leftarrow_r \tilde{\mathbb{G}} \times \mathbb{Z}_q, a^* \leftarrow_r F_t(\tilde{G}, k), (\tilde{C}_0, \tilde{C}_1) \leftarrow_r \mathsf{Enc}_{\tilde{G}}(k, a^*)\}$$

are identical. Therefore,

$$\Pr_{\substack{(\tilde{G}, k) \leftarrow_r \tilde{\mathbb{G}} \times \mathbb{Z}_q \\ a^* \leftarrow_r F_t(\tilde{G}, k) \\ \tilde{\mathbf{C}} \leftarrow_r \mathsf{Enc}_{\tilde{G}}(k, a^*)}} [\mathcal{B}(\tilde{G}, \tilde{\mathbf{C}}) = a^*] \geq \frac{\varepsilon(\lambda)}{2^{3\lambda/4}},$$

which contradicts the (one-query) $2^{-3\lambda/4}$-OW-KDM security of ElGamal with respect to the family of (efficient, randomized) functions $\{F_t\}_t$.

3.3   NIZK for $\mathscr{L}_{\mathsf{DH}}$ via $\mathcal{R}^{\mathsf{H}}$-Correlation-Intractability

Lemma 23. *Our $\mathcal{R}^{\mathsf{H}}$-correlation intractable hash function family is programmable.*

The proof is given in the full version.

Theorem 24 (NIZK for $\mathscr{L}_{\mathsf{DH}}$). *Assume there exists a programmable correlation intractable hash family for relation $\mathcal{R}^{\mathsf{H}}$. Then, there exists an adaptively sound and selective single-theorem zero-knowledge NIZK argument system for the Diffie-Hellman language $\mathscr{L}_{\mathsf{DH},t}$ for any $t \in \mathbb{Z}_p^*$. Moreover, our NIZK is independent of the value t and all algorithms can be run oblivious of the value t.*

The proof follows in a relatively natural way by compiling the Σ-protocol for DDH with the correlation-intractable hash function H. We provide an explicit description of the proof system and a security analysis in the full version. As stated in Theorem 24, our NIZK for $\mathscr{L}_{\mathsf{DH},t}$ is agnostic of the value of $t \in \mathbb{Z}_p^*$, since the value of t is only significant during the security proof. Therefore, whenever the meaning is clear, we will drop the subscript t and simply state it as an NIZK for $\mathscr{L}_{\mathsf{DH}}$. The important thing to keep in mind is that for each crs generated by $\mathsf{Setup}^{\mathsf{DH}}$, it is only adaptive secure for $\mathscr{L}_{\mathsf{DH},t}$ with a *fixed* t.

3.4   VPRG from NIZK for $\mathscr{L}_{DH}$

Our construction relies on the CDH assumption and the NIZK argument system $(\mathsf{Setup}^{DH}, \mathsf{Prove}^{DH}, \mathsf{Verify}^{DH})$ for $\mathscr{L}_{DH}$ from the previous section. We prepare a predicate $B : \mathbb{G}^2 \mapsto \{0, 1\}$ satisfying the following property: given (g^a, g^b), computing $B(g^b, g^{ab})$ should be as hard (up to polynomial factors) as computing (g^b, g^{ab}). Note that this implies that distinguishing $B(g^b, g^{ab})$ from a random bit given random tuple (g^a, g^b) is as hard as solving CDH. One way to instantiate such a predicate is to use the Goldreich-Levin hard-core predicate [19].

Construction. Let $m := m(\lambda)$ be an arbitrary polynomial. Our construction of VPRG proceeds as follows:

- $\mathsf{Setup}(1^\lambda, m)$: run $\mathcal{G} = (\mathbb{G}, p) \leftarrow_r \mathsf{DHGen}(1^\lambda)$ and sample $g \leftarrow_r \mathbb{G}$. Further, for $i = 1$ to m, pick $h_i \leftarrow_r \mathbb{G}$ and generate $\mathsf{crs}_i \leftarrow_r \mathsf{Setup}^{DH}(1^\lambda)$. Finally, output $\mathsf{pp} = (g, (h_i, \mathsf{crs}_i)_{i \leq m})$.
- $\mathsf{Stretch}(\mathsf{pp})$: pick $\tau \leftarrow_r \mathbb{Z}_p$, set $\mathsf{pvk} \leftarrow g^\tau$, and for $i = 1$ to m, set $x_i \leftarrow B(\mathsf{pvk}, h_i^\tau)$. Output $(\mathsf{pvk}, x = (x_i)_{i \leq m}, \mathsf{aux} = \tau)$.
- $\mathsf{Prove}(\mathsf{pp}, \mathsf{aux}, i)$: set $\tau := \mathsf{aux}$ and run $\pi_i^{DH} \leftarrow_r \mathsf{Prove}^{DH}(\mathsf{crs}_i, (g, h_i, \mathsf{pvk}, h_i^\tau), \tau)$. Output $\pi = (h_i^\tau, \pi_i^{DH})$.
- $\mathsf{Verify}(\mathsf{pp}, \mathsf{pvk}, i, b, \pi)$: parse $(u, \pi^{DH}) \leftarrow \pi$. If $b = B(\mathsf{pvk}, u)$, then return $\mathsf{Verify}^{DH}(\mathsf{crs}_i, (g, h_i, \mathsf{pvk}, u), \pi^{DH})$. Otherwise, return 0.

Security Analysis. Correctness of the VPRG follows from the correctness of the underlying NIZK. In addition, the size of the verification key g^τ is p, and in particular, is independent of m. Hence, we can set the stretch $\delta := \delta(\lambda)$ to be an arbitrary polynomial, where we can set $m = s^{1+\delta}$ by definition.

Theorem 25. *If the CDH assumption holds relative to DHGen and the NIZK argument system for the Diffie-Hellman language $\mathscr{L}_{DH}$ is adaptive sound and selective single-theorem, then the above construction provides a (δ, s)-VPRG that is binding and hiding, where δ is an arbitrary polynomial in the security parameter λ and $s = |\mathbb{G}|$.*

The binding property is shown by guessing the position where the adversary forges an opening, and showing that this implies an adversary against the adaptive soundness of the NIZK for DDH. Hiding relies on a careful modification of the CRS generation, together with the zero-knowledge property of the NIZK for DDH. We provide a complete proof in the full version of the paper. As a direct consequence of Theorems 7, 31, 33, and 38, the following is obtained.

Theorem 26. *Assume that the CDH assumption holds relative to DHGen and that ElGamal satisfies $2^{-3\lambda/4}$-OW-KDM security with respect to efficient functions, then there exists an adaptive sound and adaptive multi-theorem NIZK for all of NP.*

4   NIZK from Insecurity of CDH and Strong OW-KDM Security of ElGamal

In this section, we describe a construction of an *infinitely often* NIZK from the strong OW-KDM security of ElGamal with respect with efficient functions by assuming that the CDH problem is *easy* to solve. We first provide a NIZK for the specific language of the *almost-short* language. This is done by constructing a CIH based on the strong OW-KDM security of ElGamal for the natural sparse relation induced by the Σ-protocol for the almost-short language. We then show that such a NIZK for the almost-short language along with the short-exponent discrete-log (SEDL) assumption allows us to construct a VPRG, which in return, allows us to construct an (infinitely often) NIZK for all of NP by Theorem 7. Note that, as we will show, SEDL is not an extra assumption since it follows from the strong OW-KDM security of ElGamal.

4.1 Σ-Protocol for the Language of Almost-Short Elements

In this section, we introduce the language $\mathscr{L}_{\alpha,\beta}$ of elements of $\mathbb{G}$ with (α,β)-*almost-short* exponents to be the subset of $\mathbb{G}$ containing elements of the form g^x where x is *almost-short*. We say that x is (α,β)-almost-short if there exists a short value $v \leq 2^\beta$ such that vx is short as well: $vx \in [\pm 2^\alpha]$. More formally:

Definition 27 ((α,β)-Almost-Shortness). *Let $\mathbb{G}$ be a group of prime order p. We define $\mathscr{L}_{\alpha,\beta}$ over $\mathbb{G}$ with respect to the generator $g \in \mathbb{G}$ to be the language of (α,β)-almost-short elements as:*

$$\mathscr{L}_{\alpha,\beta} = \{g^x \mid x = u \cdot v^{-1} \in \mathbb{Z}_p, \mathsf{int}(u) \subset [\pm 2^\alpha], \mathsf{int}(v) \in [2^\beta]\}.$$

A Σ-Protocol for the Almost-Short Language. We start by introducing a simple Σ-protocol for proving membership of an element $g^x \in \mathbb{G}$ to $\mathscr{L}_{\alpha,\beta}$. The protocol satisfies the following relaxed notion of correctness: an honest prover is guaranteed to produce an accepting proof if the input word g^x is such that $x \leq 2^\ell$ (with $\log p \gg \ell$), but soundness only guarantees that the word actually belongs to $\mathscr{L}_{\ell',c}$, where c is the challenge length, and $\ell' > c + \ell + \kappa$, for some statistical security parameter κ.[4] The protocol is represented on Fig. 3. Note that it only satisfies selective soundness.

In the full version, we prove the following lemmas:

Lemma 28 (Correctness). *If $x \in [0, 2^\ell]$, and $\ell' > \max\{c, \ell\} + \kappa$, then the Σ-protocol from Fig. 3 is correct (and the verifier accepts with probability greater than $1 - \frac{1}{2^\kappa}$).*

---

[4] This is similar in spirit to various Σ-protocols for lattice-based relations, where the Σ-protocol proves knowledge of a short preimage, but the protocol has some slackness, *i.e.*, a gap between the shortness needed for the honest proof to be accepted, and the shortness actually guaranteed by the soundness property; here, we have an additional "slackness" in that x is only guaranteed to be the product of a short value with the inverse of another short value.

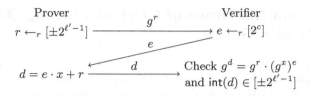

Fig. 3. Σ-protocol for the almost-shortness language, for the word g^x. In a honest run, the prover posseses a short witness $x \in [0, 2^\ell]$

Lemma 29 (Selective Soundness). *If $X \notin \mathscr{L}_{\ell',c}$, then the probability that the verifier accepts is at most $\frac{1}{2^c}$.*

Lemma 30 (Honest-Verifier Zero-Knowledge). *When $\ell' > c + \ell + \kappa$ and $x \in [0, 2^\ell)$, the Σ-protocol in Fig. 3 is honest-verifier zero-knowledge for words in $x \in [0, 2^\ell]$. In particular, the statistical distance between honest transcripts and those produced by the simulator described in the full version is $\frac{1}{2^\kappa}$.*[5]

Adaptive Soundness. The above protocol only enjoys selective soundness, which does not suffice in our context. As for our previous construction, however, adaptive soundness can be obtained using sufficiently many parallel repetitions of the underlying Σ-protocol, via standard complexity leveraging: since there are p possible words g^x, if the above Σ-protocol is amplified N-times with $N \geq \lceil \log p \rceil / c$, then it is $p/2^{N \cdot c}$-adaptively sound. We denote $\Pi_N(p, \ell, \kappa, c)$ the Σ-protocol obtained by repeating N times in parallel the above Σ-protocol for $\mathscr{L}_{\ell',c}$, with $\ell' = \ell + c + \kappa + 1$. When (p, ℓ, κ, c) are clear from the context, we simply denote it Π_N.

Admissible First Flow. Given a Σ-protocol for a language $\mathscr{L}$, we say that a candidate first flow a is *(adaptively) admissible* if there exists a word $X \notin \mathscr{L}$, a challenge e, and an answer d, such that (a, e, d) form an accepting transcript for X. Note that in Π_N, there are p^N possible first flows, but only $p \cdot 2^{N(\ell'+c)}$ admissible first flows, since an admissible first flow is of the form $(g^{d_i}/(g^x)^{e_i})_{i \leq N}$, for some $d_i \in [\pm 2^{\ell'-1}]$, $e_i \in [2^c]$, and $g^x \in \mathbb{G}$.

4.2 Correlation-Intractable Hash Function

Let λ be a security parameter and fix parameters $(N(\lambda), c(\lambda), p(\lambda), \ell(\lambda), \kappa(\lambda))$. We consider a group $\tilde{\mathbb{G}}$ of order $q(\lambda)$ with $\lceil \log q \rceil \approx \lambda$, and a group $\mathbb{G}$ of order $p(\lambda)$. Let $\mathsf{Trunc}' : \tilde{\mathbb{G}} \mapsto \{0,1\}^{N \cdot c}$ be the function which, on input a group element $\tilde{G} \in \tilde{\mathbb{G}}$, parses it as a $\lceil \log q \rceil$-bit string and returns the first $N \cdot c$ bits of its input. Let $\mathsf{h} : \mathbb{G}^N \to \{0,1\}^\lambda$ be a 2-universal hash function, for a security

---

[5] To be precise, this does not meet the definition of our honest-verifier zero-knowledge since we only consider a small set of $\mathscr{L}_{\ell',c}$. However, this notion suffices for our application.

parameter λ which will be defined afterward. We consider the following hash function $H'_\lambda : \tilde{\mathbb{G}}^2 \times \mathbb{G}^N \mapsto \{0,1\}^{N \cdot c}$:

- Sampling the key: pick $(\tilde{G}, k, m) \leftarrow_r \tilde{\mathbb{G}} \times \mathbb{Z}_q^2$ and set $\tilde{\mathbf{C}} \leftarrow_r \mathsf{Enc}_{\tilde{G}}(k, m)$. Note that the key distribution is exactly the uniform distribution over $\tilde{\mathbb{G}}^2$.
- Evaluating $H'_\lambda(\tilde{\mathbf{C}}, \cdot) : H'_\lambda(\tilde{\mathbf{C}}, x) = \mathsf{Trunc}'(\mathsf{HalfDec}(\mathsf{h}(x), \tilde{\mathbf{C}}))$.

Setting the Security Parameter λ. Let $\mathcal{R}_\lambda(N, c, p, \ell, \kappa) = \mathcal{R}_\lambda$ be the natural sparse relation associated to the language $\mathscr{L}_{\ell',c}$ over $\mathbb{G}$ with respect to a generator $g \in \mathbb{G}$, where $\ell' = \ell + c + \kappa$ (see Lemma 14). That is,

$$\mathcal{R}_\lambda = \{(a, b) \in \mathbb{G}^N \times \{0,1\}^{N \cdot c} : \exists X, d \text{ s.t. } X \notin \mathscr{L}_{\ell',c} \wedge V(X, a, b, c) = \mathsf{accept}\},$$

where V is the verifier from the Σ-protocol for the language $\mathscr{L}_{\ell',c}$ in Fig. 3. The purpose of the 2-universal hash function h in our correlation-intractable hash H'_λ is to compress the size of the first flow to λ bits, without significantly decreasing the winning probability of the adversary. The core observation is that when the adversary manages to output a such that $(a, H'_\lambda(\tilde{\mathbf{C}}, a)) \in \mathcal{R}_\lambda$, then a must at least be an admissible first flow. Since there are at most $p \cdot 2^{N(\ell'+c)}$ admissible first flows, we set $\lambda \leftarrow \lceil \log p \rceil + N(\ell'+c) + \kappa$, where κ is some statistical security parameter. Then, the 2-universality of h guarantees that, except with probability at most $2^{-\kappa}$ over the random choice of the hash key, all possible λ-bit strings will have at most a single admissible preimage a. In the following, we denote by Invh the (inefficient) function which, on input a λ-bit string s, outputs the unique admissible preimage of s (or $\perp$ if s has no admissible preimage).

Correlation-Intractability of H'

Theorem 31. *Fix parameters $(N(\lambda), c(\lambda), p(\lambda), \ell(\lambda), \kappa(\lambda))$. Assume that ElGamal satisfies $p^{-1} \cdot 2^{Nc-\lambda}$-OW-KDM security with respect to efficient functions. Then the hash family $\{H'_\lambda : \tilde{\mathbb{G}}^2 \times \mathbb{G}^N \mapsto \{0,1\}^{N \cdot c}\}_\lambda$ is correlation-intractable with respect to $\mathcal{R}^{H'} := \{\mathcal{R}_\lambda(N, c, p, \ell, \kappa)\}_\lambda = \{\mathcal{R}_\lambda\}_\lambda$.*

The structure of the proof is similar to the proof of Theorem 21, the core difference being that we rely on a 2-universal hash function to compress the size of the first flow, and only guess the compressed hash; then, we rely on the fact the 2-universal hash is injective with high probability over the set of admissible first flow. We provide a detailed proof in the full version.

4.3 NIZK for the Almost-Short Language via $\mathcal{R}^{H'}$-Correlation-Intractability

Lemma 32. *Our $\mathcal{R}^{H'}$-correlation intractable hash function family is programmable.*

The proof is essentially identical to the proof for $\mathcal{R}^H$.

Theorem 33 (NIZK for the almost-short language $\mathcal{L}_{\ell',c}$). *Assume there exists a programmable correlation intractable hash family for the relation $\mathcal{R}^{H'}$. Then, there exists an adaptive sound and selective single-theorem zero-knowledge NIZK argument system for the almost-short language $\mathcal{L}_{\ell',c}$.*

The proof of adaptive soundness and selective single-theorem zero-knowledge are essentially identical to the proof of Theorem 24. We provide an explicit description of the NIZK proof system in the full version.

4.4   A Commitment Scheme from the Short-Exponent Discrete Logarithm Assumption

Before providing our VPRG construction, we introduce one last set of tools. We first introduce the T-short-exponent discrete-logarithm (T-SEDL) assumption and then provide a simple commitment scheme based on T-SEDL.

Definition 34. *The T-SEDL assumption over an Abelian group $\mathbb{G}$ of order p with respect to the generator g states that for every PPT $\mathcal{A}$,*

$$\Pr[x \leftarrow_r [p/T], h \leftarrow g^x \; : \; \mathcal{A}(h) = x] \approx 0.$$

It is well known that under the T-SEDL assumption, it is infeasible to distinguish $\{g^x \mid x \leftarrow_r [p/T]\}$ from the uniform distribution over $\mathbb{G}$ [27].

A Commitment from T-SEDL. A commitment scheme is a pair of algorithms (Commit, Open) such that given $(c,d) \leftarrow_r$ Commit(m), c hides m (more formally, no adversary can distinguish whether c was output by Commit(m) or Commit(m'), for two messages (m,m') of their choice), but d binds the committer to m (more formally, no adversary can find (c,d,d',m,m') with $m \neq m'$ such that Open$(c,d,m) = $ Open$(c,d',m') = 1$). We now introduce the bit commitment scheme that will underly our construction. Let $\mathbb{G}$ be a group of order p. Fix some integers (ℓ, k). Commit(b), on input a bit b, picks $w \leftarrow_r \{0,1\}^\ell$ and outputs com $= g^{w+2^k b}$. Opening the commitment is done by revealing w. The commitment is perfectly binding, and hiding under the $p/2^\ell$-SEDL assumption.

From T-SEDL to Strong OW-KDM Security of ElGamal. In the full version of the paper, we show the following, which states that T-SEDL will be redundant with our other assumptions:

Lemma 35. *Assume that ElGamal satisfies $(1/T)$-OW-KDM security with respect to efficient functions. Then the T-SEDL assumption holds.*

Binding Property with Almost-Short Randomness. A useful property of the above commitment, which will play a crucial role in our construction, is that it remains computationally binding if instead of revealing w, the opener reveals b and proves (using any computationally binding argument) that com $\cdot g^{-2^k b} \in \mathcal{L}_{\alpha,\beta}$, provided that $k \geq \alpha + 2$ and under some condition on the size p of the group. We elaborate below.

Lemma 36. *Let* $\mathsf{com} = g^{w+2^{\alpha+2}b}$ *be a commitment to* b, *where* $g^w \in \mathscr{L}_{\alpha,\beta}$. *Further assume that* $p > 2^{\alpha+2\beta+4}$. *Then no computationally bounded prover can produce an accepting argument that* $g^{w+2^{\alpha+2}} \in \mathscr{L}_{\alpha,\beta}$.

Looking ahead, we will use this lemma together with a NIZK with relaxed correctness for the language $\mathscr{L}_{\alpha,\beta}$ to guarantee correct opening of the above commitment. The relaxed correctness requirement is the same as in Sect. 4.1 and will be satisfied when the commitment is constructed honestly.

Proof. Let $\mathsf{com} \in \mathbb{G}$ be any group element. We prove that it can never simultaneously hold that $\mathsf{com} \in \mathscr{L}_{\alpha,\beta}$ and $\mathsf{com} \cdot g^{2^{\alpha+2}} \in \mathscr{L}_{\alpha,\beta}$. Assume toward contradiction that both com and $\mathsf{com} \cdot g^{2^{\alpha+2}}$ belong to $\mathscr{L}_{\alpha,\beta}$. Let $x \leftarrow \mathsf{dlog}_g(\mathsf{com})$. Then we have:

$$x = u \cdot v^{-1} \bmod p \text{ for some } u \in [\pm 2^\alpha], v \in [2^\beta],$$
$$x + 2^{\alpha+2} = u' \cdot (v')^{-1} \bmod p \text{ for some } u' \in [\pm 2^\alpha], v' \in [2^\beta].$$

Hence, $uv^{-1} + 2^{\alpha+2} = u'(v')^{-1} \bmod p$, which gives $v'(u + 2^{\alpha+2}v) = u'v \bmod p$. However, since $p > 2^{\alpha+2\beta+4}$, we have that this equation holds over the integers as well. This implies (still using the bound on p) that $v'(u + 2^{\alpha+2}v) = u'v \le 2^\alpha v$. However, $u + 2^{\alpha+2}v \ge 2^{\alpha+2}v - 2^\alpha > 2^\alpha v$ (since $v \ge 1$). Therefore, we also get $2^\alpha v < v'(u + 2^{\alpha+2}v)$ (since $v' \ge 1$), which is a contradiction. Therefore, no bounded prover can provide an accepting argument of membership in $\mathscr{L}_{\alpha,\beta}$ (with any computationally sound argument system) for both com and $\mathsf{com} \cdot g^{2^{\alpha+2}}$. $\square$

4.5   A VPRG from NIZK for the Almost Short Language and the SEDL Assumption

With the tools we introduced, we are now ready to present our construction of a VPRG in a group where CDH is insecure.

Intuition of the Construction. Let DHGen be a deterministic algorithm that, on input 1^λ, returns a description $\mathcal{G} = (\mathbb{G}, p)$ where $\mathbb{G}$ is a cyclic group of prime order p. Assume that CDH does *not* hold with respect to DHGen. In the full version, we show that this means that there exists a strong CDH solver that allows to compute "self-pairings" over $(\mathbb{G}, p) = \mathsf{DHGen}(1^\lambda)$ with negligible error probability, for infinitely many security parameters λ. We denote (EvalCom, EvalOpen) the self-pairing algorithm, which evaluates integer arithmetic circuits (IAC) in the exponent, together with the evaluation algorithm "in the clear" EvalOpen, satisfying the following:

Theorem 37. *Let* $\{\mathcal{C}_\lambda\}_{\lambda \in \mathbb{N}}$ *be an ensemble of sets of IAC (with gates* $(+, \times, -)$*) where each circuit in* $\mathcal{C}_\lambda$ *has input length* $n = n(\lambda)$ *and size* $L = L(\lambda)$. *Let the CDH assumption relative to* DHGen *be easy. Moreover, let* $S \subset \mathbb{N}$ *be the infinite set of security parameters for which a strong CDH solver exists. Then there exists a PPT algorithm* EvalCom *and a deterministic polytime algorithm* EvalOpen *with the following properties for all* $\lambda \in S$:

- EvalCom$(C, g_1, \cdots, g_n) \to h$: *on input an IAC* $C \in \mathcal{C}_\lambda$ *and* $(g_1, \cdots, g_n) \in \mathbb{G}$, *it outputs* $h \in \mathbb{G}$.
- EvalOpen$(C, z_1, b_1, \cdots, z_n, b_n) \to z$: *on input an IAC* $C \in \mathcal{C}_\lambda$ *and* $((z_1, b_1), \cdots, (z_n, b_n)) \in (\mathbb{Z} \times \{0, 1\})^n$, *it outputs* $z \in \mathbb{Z}$.
- *Let* $(\ell, t) \in \mathbb{N}^2$ *such that* $\ell + t > 2L^2$. *Further, assume* $p = |\mathbb{G}|$ *to be greater than* $L(\ell + t) \cdot \log_2 B$ *where* $B = \max_{C \in \mathcal{C}_\lambda, (b_i \in \{0,1\})_i} C(b_1, \cdots, b_n)$. *Let* $b_i \in \{0, 1\}$ *and* $w_i \in [-2^\ell, 2^\ell]$ *for all* $i \in [n]$. *Then, for any* $C \in \mathcal{C}_\lambda$ *with degree* D *and* $g_i = g^{w_i + 2^{\ell+t} b_i}$, *if we run* $h \leftarrow_r$ EvalCom$(C, g_1, \cdots, g_n)$, *we have* $\mathsf{dlog}_g h = w^* + 2^{(D+1)(\ell+t)} \cdot C(b_1, \cdots, b_n)$, *where* $w^* \in [\pm(2^{D(\ell+L+t+2)})]$ *and* EvalOpen$(C, (w_i, b_i)_{i \leq n}) = w^*$, *except with negligible probability* $2^{-\lambda}$.

We will use this strong CDH solver to build a VPRG over DHGen, which will satisfy correctness, binding, and hiding for infinitely many security parameters. We set (PRG.Setup, PRG.Eval) to be Goldreich's PRG instantiated with the LV predicate; let PRG_i be IAC that computes, given a seed $(s_1, \cdots, s_n)$ as input, the i-th output bit of PRG.Eval$(s_1, \cdots, s_n)$. Observe that PRG_i is a degree-3 integer arithmetic circuit with 9 gates (ignoring the subtractions by a constant, which are "for free"), where all intermediate values belong to $[\pm 1]$ provided that the inputs to the IAC are bits. We fix an arbitrary small positive constant $\delta_{\mathsf{PRG}} < 0.25$, such that Goldreich's PRG instantiated with the LV predicate is conjectured to be secure when stretching n bits to $m = n^{1+\delta_{\mathsf{PRG}}}$ bits.

Fix integers (l, t, κ, c). The high-level intuition of our VPRG is relatively simple. The commitment to the seed $(s_1, \cdots, s_n)$ is a bit-by-bit commitment $(\mathsf{com}_1, \cdots, \mathsf{com}_n)$, with the commitment scheme given in Sect. 4.4, which computationally hides the seed under the short-exponent discrete logarithm assumption. The pseudorandom string is simply PRG.Eval$(\mathsf{pp}, (s_1, \cdots, s_n))$. Given the commitment to the seed, both parties will use the strong CDH solver, which exists since we assume that CDH does not hold over $\mathbb{G}$. In the full version, we prove a theorem that shows that the parties can both use EvalCom$(\mathsf{PRG}_i, \mathsf{com}_1, \cdots, \mathsf{com}_n)$ for $i = 1$ to $m = n^{1+\delta_{\mathsf{PRG}}}$. For each such i, denoting $\mathsf{com}_i = g^{w_i + 2^{l+t} s_i}$ with $w_i \in [\pm 2^l]$ and $s_i \in \{0, 1\}$, the parties get

$$\mathsf{com}_i^* \leftarrow \mathsf{EvalCom}(\mathsf{PRG}_i, (g^{w_j + 2^{l+t} s_j})_{j \leq n}) = g^{w_i^* + 2^{3(l+t)} \mathsf{PRG}_i(s_1, \cdots, s_n)},$$

with $w_i^* \in [\pm(2^{3l + 2t + 31})]$. Let $\ell \leftarrow 3l + 2t + 31$ and $\ell' \leftarrow \ell + \kappa + c + 1$. Let $b_i \leftarrow \mathsf{PRG}_i(s_1, \cdots, s_n)$. We set $t = 34 + \kappa + c$, which guarantees that $\ell' + 2 = 3(l + t)$. Therefore, we have $\mathsf{com}_i^* = g^{w_i^* + 2^{\ell'+2} b_i}$. To provably open the i-th bit of the pseudorandom string to the bit b_i, the prover reveals b_i, and both parties homomorphically compute $g^{w_i^*}$ from com_i^*. It remains for the prover to demonstrate that he revealed the right value b_i, which he does using a NIZK to prove that $g^{w_i^*}$ belongs to $\mathscr{L}_{\ell',c}$ (which he can do since $w_i^* \in [\pm 2^\ell]$). More precisely, we will use the CIH from Sect. 4.2 to compile the Σ-protocol for the language $\mathscr{L}_{\ell',c}$ from Sect. 4.1, with challenge length c, into a NIZK. Since $\ell' + 2 = 3(l + t)$, and using Lemma 36 from Sect. 4.4, this uniquely binds the prover to b_i.

Parameters and Assumptions. To apply Lemma 36, we must pick p such that $\log p > \ell' + 2c + 4 = 3l + 5c + 3\kappa + 104$, where l is such that the $p/2^l$-SEDL assumption holds over $\mathbb{G}$, and κ is a statistical security parameter. Choosing c to be polynomially larger than $l + \kappa$, we have $\ell' = 3c + o(c)$, and we can set p such that $\log p = 5c + o(c)$. Therefore, setting the number of parallel repetitions of the Σ-protocol for $\mathscr{L}_{\ell',c}$ to $N = 6$, we get $\lambda = 5c + 6(\ell' + c) + o(c) = 29c + o(c)$. In turns, this gives $p^{-1} \cdot 2^{Nc-\lambda} = 2^{-28c-o(c)} = 2^{-(28/29+o(1))\lambda}$. Therefore, the adaptive soundness of our NIZK for $\mathscr{L}_{\ell',c}$ reduces to the $2^{-(28/29+o(1))\lambda}$-OW-KDM security of ElGamal (over the group $\tilde{\mathbb{G}}$ of size $q \approx 2^\lambda$) w.r.t. efficient functions. Observe that with this choice of parameters, it holds that $p/2^l = 2^{O(\sqrt{\log p})}$, hence the $p/2^l$-SEDL assumption is implied by the $2^{-O(\sqrt{\log p})}$-OW-KDM security of ElGamal over $\mathbb{G}$, which is clearly implied by the $2^{-(28/29+o(1))\log p}$-OW-KDM security of ElGamal over $\mathbb{G}$. Due to the large number of parameters involved in our construction, and to make it more readable, we summarize our parameters and the constraints they must satisfy in the full version.

Construction. Let $\mathsf{NIZK}^{\mathsf{AS}} = (\mathsf{Setup}^{\mathsf{AS}}, \mathsf{Prove}^{\mathsf{AS}}, \mathsf{Verify}^{\mathsf{AS}})$ be a NIZK for the almost-short language $\mathscr{L}_{\ell',c}$ over the group generator DHGen where the CDH problem is insecure. Given a security parameter n for the VPRG, we set $l(n) = \kappa(n) = n$ and $c(n) = n^2$ (so that $\kappa + l = o(c)$). We set $(\ell(n), \ell'(n), \lambda(n), p(n))$ as described previously, and $s(n) = n \cdot \lceil \log p \rceil$. Let $m = m(n)$ be $n^{1+\delta_{\mathsf{PRG}}}$. Our construction of VPRG proceeds as follows:

- $\mathsf{Setup}(1^n, m)$: run $\mathcal{G} = (\mathbb{G}, p) \leftarrow_r \mathsf{DHGen}(1^{\lambda(n)})$ and sample $g \leftarrow_r \mathbb{G}$.[6] Further, for $i = 1$ to m, generate $\mathsf{crs}_i \leftarrow_r \mathsf{Setup}^{\mathsf{AS}}(1^{\lambda(n)})$ and $\mathsf{pp}_{\mathsf{PRG}} \leftarrow_r \mathsf{PRG.Setup}(1^n)$. Finally, output $\mathsf{pp} = (g, (\mathsf{crs}_i)_{i \leq m}, \mathsf{pp}_{\mathsf{PRG}})$.
- $\mathsf{Stretch}(\mathsf{pp})$: pick a seed $\mathsf{seed} = (s_1, \cdots, s_n) \leftarrow_r \{0,1\}^n$ for PRG. For $i = 1$ to n, pick $w_i \leftarrow_r [2^l]$ and compute $\mathsf{com}_i \leftarrow g^{w_i + 2^{l+t}s_i}$. Output $\mathsf{pvk} \leftarrow (\mathsf{com}_1, \cdots, \mathsf{com}_n)$, $x = \mathsf{PRG.Eval}(\mathsf{seed})$, and $\mathsf{aux} \leftarrow (\mathsf{seed}, w_1, \cdots, w_n)$.
- $\mathsf{Prove}(\mathsf{pp}, \mathsf{aux}, i)$: compute $\mathsf{com}_i^* \leftarrow \mathsf{EvalCom}(\mathsf{PRG}_i, (\mathsf{com}_1, \cdots, \mathsf{com}_n))$ and

$$w_i^* \leftarrow \mathsf{EvalOpen}(\mathsf{PRG}_i, (w_1, s_1), \cdots, (w_n, s_n)).$$

Set $x_i = \mathsf{PRG}_i(\mathsf{seed})$, $X_i = \mathsf{com}_i^*/g^{2^{l+t}x_i}$ and run $\pi_i^{\mathsf{AS}} \leftarrow \mathsf{Prove}^{\mathsf{AS}}(\mathsf{crs}_i, X_i, w_i^*)$. Output $\pi = \pi_i^{\mathsf{AS}}$.
- $\mathsf{Verify}(\mathsf{pp}, \mathsf{pvk}, i, b, \pi)$: compute $\mathsf{com}_i^* \leftarrow \mathsf{EvalCom}(\mathsf{PRG}_i, (\mathsf{com}_1, \cdots, \mathsf{com}_n))$ and set $X = \mathsf{com}_i^*/g^{2^{l+t}b}$. Output $\mathsf{Verify}^{\mathsf{AS}}(\mathsf{crs}_i, X, \pi)$.

Setting $(\delta(n), s(n))$ for VPRG. Before going into the security proofs, let us assess the parameter values of $\delta(n)$ and $s(n)$ of our VPRG. First, we have $m(n) = n^{1+\delta_{\mathsf{PRG}}}$ where the constant δ_{PRG} is the stretch of the underlying PRG that can be set arbitrary within $0 < \delta_{\mathsf{PRG}} < 0.25$. The size of the verification key is $s(n) := n \cdot \lceil \log p \rceil$, and in particular, $s(n) \leq n^{1+\delta_{\mathsf{PRG}}/2}$ for

---

[6] We remark that we assume the CDH problem is insecure over the group $\mathbb{G}$ for the specific parameter $\lambda(n)$.

all sufficiently large n. Therefore, by setting $\delta(n) := \delta_{PRG}/3$, we conclude $s(n)^{1+\delta(n)} \le (n^{1+\delta_{PRG}/2})^{1+\delta_{PRG}/3} = n^{1+\delta_{PRG}} = m(n)$. Specifically, we have a $(s(n) = n \cdot \lceil \log p \rceil, \delta(n) = \delta_{PRG}/3)$-VPRG.

Theorem 38. *If the $p/2^l$-SEDL assumption holds relative to DHGen, CDH does not hold relative to DHGen, PRG is a secure pseudorandom generator stretching n bits to $n^{1+\delta_{PRG}}$ bits for some arbitrarily small positive constant δ_{PRG}, and the NIZK argument system for the almost language $\mathcal{L}_{\ell'(n),c(n)}$ is adaptive sound and selective single-theorem zero-knowledge, where $\ell'(n)$ and $c(n)$ are chosen as described above, then our construction provides an $(s(n), \delta_{PRG}/3)$-VPRG (with $s(n) = n \cdot \lceil \log p \rceil$) that is binding and hiding.*

The proof of binding is very similar to the proof of Theorem 25. For the hiding property, in a first hybrids, we first simulate all NIZK proofs, still providing correct openings. Then, we replace the commitment to the seed by random group elements, which is indistinguishable from the previous hybrids under the short-exponent discrete logarithm assumption. Eventually, we replace the PRG values by random bits, which is indistinguishable under the pseudorandomness of the PRG. In the last game, the value of all opened bits is perfectly independent of the value of the unopened bit, hence the advantage of the adversary is 0. We provide a the full version. Since the above is an $(s(n), \delta(n))$-VPRG for a constant $\delta(n) = \delta_{PRG}/3$, by setting n large enough, we can satisfy the condition required in Theorem 7 for constructing NIZKs for all of NP. In particular, as a consequence of Theorems 7, 21, 24, and 25, the following is obtained.

Theorem 39. *Assume that the CDH assumption does not hold relative to DHGen, that ElGamal satisfies $2^{-(28/29+o(1))\lambda}$-OW-KDM security with respect to efficient functions, and that Goldreich's PRG instantiated with the LV predicate is secure for some (arbitrarily small) polynomial stretch. Then there exists an infinitely often adaptive sound and adaptive multi-theorem NIZK for all of NP.*

In the full version, we show that combining the results of Sect. 3 with the results of this section gives us the following theorem.

Theorem 40. *Assume that ElGamal satisfies $2^{-(28/29+o(1))\lambda}$-OW-KDM security with respect to efficient functions, and that Goldreich's PRG instantiated with the LV predicate is secure for some (arbitrarily small) polynomial stretch. Then there exists an adaptively sound and adaptive multi-theorem infinitely-often NIZK for NP, whose multi-theorem zero-knowledge property holds against uniform adversaries.*

Acknowledgements. Shuichi Katsumata was supported by JST CREST Grant Number JPMJCR19F6. Geoffroy Couteau and Bogdan Ursu were supported by ERC PREP-CRYPTO Grant Agreement ID 724307. We would like to thank Dennis Hofheinz for valuable discussions and contributions to the early stages of this work. We are also grateful for the comments received from the anonymous reviewers of this paper.

References

1. Abdalla, M., Fouque, P.A., Lyubashevsky, V., Tibouchi, M.: Tightly-secure signatures from lossy identification schemes. In: Pointcheval, D., Johansson, T. (eds.) EUROCRYPT 2012. LNCS, vol. 7237, pp. 572–590. Springer, Heidelberg (2012). https://doi.org/10.1007/978-3-642-29011-4_34
2. Alekhnovich, M., Hirsch, E.A., Itsykson, D.: Exponential lower bounds for the running time of DPLL algorithms on satisfiable formulas. J. Autom. Reason. **35**(1–3), 51–72 (2005)
3. Applebaum, B., Lovett, S.: Algebraic attacks against random local functions and their countermeasures. In: Wichs, D., Mansour, Y. (eds.) 48th ACM STOC, pp. 1087–1100. ACM Press, New York (2016)
4. Bitansky, N., et al.: Why "Fiat-Shamir for proofs" lacks a proof. In: Sahai, A. (ed.) TCC 2013. LNCS, vol. 7785, pp. 182–201. Springer, Heidelberg (2013). https://doi.org/10.1007/978-3-642-36594-2_11
5. Blum, M., Feldman, P., Micali, S.: Non-interactive zero-knowledge and its applications (extended abstract). In: 20th ACM STOC, pp. 103–112. ACM Press, May 1988
6. Canetti, R., et al.: Fiat-Shamir: from practice to theory. In: Charikar, M., Cohen, E. (eds.) 51st ACM STOC, pp. 1082–1090. ACM Press, New York (2019)
7. Canetti, R., Chen, Y., Reyzin, L., Rothblum, R.D.: Fiat-Shamir and correlation intractability from strong KDM-secure encryption. In: Nielsen, J.B., Rijmen, V. (eds.) EUROCRYPT 2018, Part I. LNCS, vol. 10820, pp. 91–122. Springer, Cham (2018). https://doi.org/10.1007/978-3-319-78381-9_4
8. Canetti, R., Goldreich, O., Halevi, S.: The random oracle methodology, revisited. Cryptology ePrint Archive, Report 1998/011 (1998). http://eprint.iacr.org/1998/011
9. Canetti, R., Goldreich, O., Halevi, S.: The random oracle methodology, revisited. J. ACM **51**(4), 557–594 (2004)
10. Couteau, G., Dupin, A., Méaux, P., Rossi, M., Rotella, Y.: On the concrete security of Goldreich's pseudorandom generator. In: Peyrin, T., Galbraith, S. (eds.) ASIACRYPT 2018, Part II. LNCS, vol. 11273, pp. 96–124. Springer, Cham (2018). https://doi.org/10.1007/978-3-030-03329-3_4
11. Couteau, G., Hofheinz, D.: Designated-verifier pseudorandom generators, and their applications. In: Ishai, Y., Rijmen, V. (eds.) EUROCRYPT 2019, Part II. LNCS, vol. 11477, pp. 562–592. Springer, Cham (2019). https://doi.org/10.1007/978-3-030-17656-3_20
12. Dwork, C., Naor, M.: Zaps and their applications. In: 41st FOCS, pp. 283–293. IEEE Computer Society Press, November 2000
13. Feige, U., Lapidot, D., Shamir, A.: Multiple non-interactive zero knowledge proofs based on a single random string (extended abstract). In: 31st FOCS, pp. 308–317. IEEE Computer Society Press, October 1990
14. Feige, U., Lapidot, D., Shamir, A.: Multiple noninteractive zero knowledge proofs under general assumptions. SIAM J. Comput. **29**(1), 1–28 (1999). https://doi.org/10.1137/S0097539792230010
15. Fiat, A., Shamir, A.: How to prove yourself: practical solutions to identification and signature problems. In: Odlyzko, A.M. (ed.) CRYPTO 1986. LNCS, vol. 263, pp. 186–194. Springer, Heidelberg (1987). https://doi.org/10.1007/3-540-47721-7_12
16. Freitag, C., Komargodski, I., Pass, R.: Impossibility of strong KDM security with auxiliary input. Cryptology ePrint Archive, Report 2019/293 (2019). https://eprint.iacr.org/2019/293

17. Gentry, C., Wichs, D.: Separating succinct non-interactive arguments from all falsifiable assumptions. In: Fortnow, L., Vadhan, S.P. (eds.) 43rd ACM STOC, pp. 99–108. ACM Press, New York (2011)

18. Goldreich, O.: Candidate one-way functions based on expander graphs. Cryptology ePrint Archive, Report 2000/063 (2000). http://eprint.iacr.org/2000/063

19. Goldreich, O., Levin, L.A.: A hard-core predicate for all one-way functions. In: 21st ACM STOC, pp. 25–32. ACM Press, May 1989

20. Goldreich, O., Micali, S., Wigderson, A.: Proofs that yield nothing but their validity and a methodology of cryptographic protocol design (extended abstract). In: 27th FOCS, pp. 174–187. IEEE Computer Society Press, October 1986

21. Goldwasser, S., Micali, S., Rackoff, C.: The knowledge complexity of interactive proof systems. SIAM J. Comput. $18(1)$, 186–208 (1989)

22. Groth, J., Ostrovsky, R., Sahai, A.: Perfect non-interactive zero knowledge for NP. In: Vaudenay, S. (ed.) EUROCRYPT 2006. LNCS, vol. 4004, pp. 339–358. Springer, Heidelberg (2006). https://doi.org/10.1007/11761679_21

23. Groth, J., Sahai, A.: Efficient non-interactive proof systems for bilinear groups. In: Smart, N. (ed.) EUROCRYPT 2008. LNCS, vol. 4965, pp. 415–432. Springer, Heidelberg (2008). https://doi.org/10.1007/978-3-540-78967-3_24

24. Holmgren, J., Lombardi, A.: Cryptographic hashing from strong one-way functions (or: one-way product functions and their applications). In: Thorup, M. (ed.) 59th FOCS, pp. 850–858. IEEE Computer Society Press, October 2018

25. Kalai, Y.T., Rothblum, G.N., Rothblum, R.D.: From obfuscation to the security of Fiat-Shamir for proofs. In: Katz, J., Shacham, H. (eds.) CRYPTO 2017, Part II. LNCS, vol. 10402, pp. 224–251. Springer, Cham (2017). https://doi.org/10.1007/978-3-319-63715-0_8

26. Katsumata, S., Nishimaki, R., Yamada, S., Yamakawa, T.: Designated verifier/prover and preprocessing NIZKs from Diffie-Hellman assumptions. In: Ishai, Y., Rijmen, V. (eds.) EUROCRYPT 2019, Part II. LNCS, vol. 11477, pp. 622–651. Springer, Cham (2019). https://doi.org/10.1007/978-3-030-17656-3_22

27. Koshiba, T., Kurosawa, K.: Short exponent Diffie-Hellman problems. In: Bao, F., Deng, R., Zhou, J. (eds.) PKC 2004. LNCS, vol. 2947, pp. 173–186. Springer, Heidelberg (2004). https://doi.org/10.1007/978-3-540-24632-9_13

28. Lindell, Y.: An efficient transform from sigma protocols to NIZK with a CRS and non-programmable random oracle. In: Dodis, Y., Nielsen, J.B. (eds.) TCC 2015, Part I. LNCS, vol. 9014, pp. 93–109. Springer, Heidelberg (2015). https://doi.org/10.1007/978-3-662-46494-6_5

29. Lombardi, A., Vaikuntanathan, V.: Minimizing the complexity of Goldreich's pseudorandom generator. Cryptology ePrint Archive, Report 2017/277 (2017). http://eprint.iacr.org/2017/277

30. Lyubashevsky, V., Neven, G.: One-shot verifiable encryption from lattices. In: Coron, J.-S., Nielsen, J.B. (eds.) EUROCRYPT 2017, Part I. LNCS, vol. 10210, pp. 293–323. Springer, Cham (2017). https://doi.org/10.1007/978-3-319-56620-7_11

31. Maurer, U.M., Wolf, S.: Diffie-Hellman oracles. In: Koblitz, N. (ed.) CRYPTO 1996. LNCS, vol. 1109, pp. 268–282. Springer, Heidelberg (1996). https://doi.org/10.1007/3-540-68697-5_21

32. Mossel, E., Shpilka, A., Trevisan, L.: On e-biased generators in NC0. In: 44th FOCS, pp. 136–145. IEEE Computer Society Press, October 2003

33. Naor, M.: On cryptographic assumptions and challenges. In: Boneh, D. (ed.) CRYPTO 2003. LNCS, vol. 2729, pp. 96–109. Springer, Heidelberg (2003). https://doi.org/10.1007/978-3-540-45146-4_6

34. ODonnell, R., Witmer, D.: Goldreich's PRG: evidence for near-optimal polynomial stretch. In: 2014 IEEE 29th Conference on Computational Complexity (CCC), pp. 1–12. IEEE (2014)

35. Oren, Y.: On the cunning power of cheating verifiers: some observations about zero knowledge proofs (extended abstract). In: 28th FOCS, pp. 462–471. IEEE Computer Society Press, October 1987

36. Ostrovsky, R., Wigderson, A.: One-way functions are essential for non-trivial zero-knowledge. In: Proceedings of the 2nd Israel Symposium on the Theory and Computing Systems, pp. 3–17. IEEE (1993)

37. Peikert, C., Shiehian, S.: Noninteractive zero knowledge for NP from (plain) learning with errors. In: Boldyreva, A., Micciancio, D. (eds.) CRYPTO 2019, Part I. LNCS, vol. 11692, pp. 89–114. Springer, Cham (2019). https://doi.org/10.1007/978-3-030-26948-7_4

38. Pollard, J.M.: A Monte Carlo method for factorization. BIT Numer. Math. **15**(3), 331–334 (1975). https://doi.org/10.1007/BF01933667

39. Quach, W., Rothblum, R.D., Wichs, D.: Reusable designated-verifier NIZKs for all NP from CDH. In: Ishai, Y., Rijmen, V. (eds.) EUROCRYPT 2019, Part II. LNCS, vol. 11477, pp. 593–621. Springer, Cham (2019). https://doi.org/10.1007/978-3-030-17656-3_21

40. Sahai, A., Waters, B.: How to use indistinguishability obfuscation: deniable encryption, and more. In: Shmoys, D.B. (ed.) 46th ACM STOC, pp. 475–484. ACM Press, New York (2014)

41. Shoup, V.: Lower bounds for discrete logarithms and related problems. In: Fumy, W. (ed.) EUROCRYPT 1997. LNCS, vol. 1233, pp. 256–266. Springer, Heidelberg (1997). https://doi.org/10.1007/3-540-69053-0_18

Public-Key Encryption

Everybody's a Target:
Scalability in Public-Key Encryption

Benedikt Auerbach[1]([⊠]) [iD], Federico Giacon[2]([⊠]), and Eike Kiltz[3] [iD]

[1] IST Austria, Klosterneuburg, Austria
benedikt.auerbach@ist.ac.at
[2] Gnosis Service GmbH, Berlin, Germany
federico.giacon@rub.de
[3] Ruhr-Universität Bochum, Bochum, Germany
eike.kiltz@rub.de

Abstract. For $1 \leq m \leq n$, we consider a natural m-out-of-n multi-instance scenario for a public-key encryption (PKE) scheme. An adversary, given n independent instances of PKE, wins if he breaks at least m out of the n instances. In this work, we are interested in the *scaling factor* of PKE schemes, SF, which measures how well the difficulty of breaking m out of the n instances scales in m. That is, a scaling factor SF $= \ell$ indicates that breaking m out of n instances is at least ℓ times more difficult than breaking one single instance. A PKE scheme with small scaling factor hence provides an ideal target for mass surveillance. In fact, the Logjam attack (CCS 2015) implicitly exploited, among other things, an almost constant scaling factor of ElGamal over finite fields (with shared group parameters).

For Hashed ElGamal over elliptic curves, we use the generic group model to describe how the scaling factor depends on the scheme's granularity. In low granularity, meaning each public key contains its independent group parameter, the scheme has optimal scaling factor SF $= m$; In medium and high granularity, meaning all public keys share the same group parameter, the scheme still has a reasonable scaling factor SF $= \sqrt{m}$. Our findings underline that instantiating ElGamal over elliptic curves should be preferred to finite fields in a multi-instance scenario.

As our main technical contribution, we derive new generic-group lower bounds of $\Omega(\sqrt{mp})$ on the complexity of both the m-out-of-n Gap Discrete Logarithm and the m-out-of-n Gap Computational Diffie-Hellman problem over groups of prime order p, extending a recent result by Yun (EUROCRYPT 2015). We establish the lower bound by studying the hardness of a related computational problem which we call the search-by-hypersurface problem.

A. Canteaut and Y. Ishai (Eds.): EUROCRYPT 2020, LNCS 12107, pp. 475–506, 2020.
https://doi.org/10.1007/978-3-030-45727-3_16

1   Introduction

For integers $1 \leq m \leq n$, consider the following natural m-out-of-n multi-instance attack scenario for a public-key encryption scheme PKE[1]. An attacker is given n independent instances (public keys) of PKE and would like to *simultaneously break semantic security at least m out of n instances*. Note that this is a different setting from the standard, well studied, multi-user attack scenario by Bellare et al. [7]. In the (security-wise) best possible scenario, running an m-out-of-n multi-instance attack is m times more difficult compared to a (standard) single-instance attack. However, there is no guarantee that breaking m-out-of-n instances is more difficult than breaking a single instance.

This motivates the following question:

How well does the difficulty of breaking m out of n instances of PKE scale with m?

In order to give a quantitative answer to this question, we define the scaling factor (relative to a fixed security notion) of PKE as

$$\mathrm{SF}_{\mathsf{PKE}}^{m,n} = \frac{\text{resources necessary to break } m \text{ out of } n \text{ instances}}{\text{resources necessary to break } 1 \text{ instance}}, \tag{1}$$

where "resources" refers to the running time to break PKE in the studied security notion. Clearly, the larger $\mathrm{SF}_{\mathsf{PKE}}$, the better are the security guarantees in the multi-instance setting. The best we can hope for is $\mathrm{SF}_{\mathsf{PKE}}^{m,n} = m$, meaning that breaking m out of n instances amounts to breaking m times a single instance of PKE.

SCALING FACTOR and MASS SURVEILLANCE. In 2012, James Bamford wrote in Wired:

> According to another top official also involved with the program, the NSA made an enormous breakthrough several years ago in its ability to cryptanalyze, or break, unfathomably complex encryption systems employed by not only governments around the world but also many average computer users in the US. The upshot, according to this official: **"Everybody's a target; everybody with communication is a target."**

This statement should appear as a surprise to the cryptographic community: Parameters for cryptographic schemes are usually chosen to make even compromising a single user a daunting challenge, meaning multi-instance attacks seem out of scope even for adversaries with nation-state capabilities. Unfortunately, the use of outdated parameters is a widespread occurrence in practice [2,19], either as a consequence of legacy infrastructure or hardware restrictions. In this case, a bad scaling factor would tip the scale from single compromised users to full-scale mass surveillance. Even more so, the hardness of several common number-theoretic problems is known to scale sub-optimally in the number of

---

[1] Formally, in this work we consider key-encapsulation mechanisms.

Table 1. Shared public system parameters and individual public keys for schemes $\text{HEG}[\text{GGen}_{\mathbb{E}(\mathbb{F}_\ell)}, \texttt{gran}]$ and $\text{HEG}[\text{GGen}_{\mathbb{F}_\ell^*}, \texttt{gran}]$ at different granularities. Here g generates a subgroup of prime order p of either an elliptic curve $\mathbb{E}(\mathbb{F}_\ell)$ or a finite field $\mathbb{F}_\ell^*$ and ℓ is a prime.

PKE	Setting	Shared param.	Public key pk_i
$\text{HEG}[\text{GGen}_{\mathbb{E}(\mathbb{F}_\ell)}, \texttt{high}]$	Elliptic curve	$\mathbb{E}(\mathbb{F}_\ell), p, g$	g^{x_i}
$\text{HEG}[\text{GGen}_{\mathbb{E}(\mathbb{F}_\ell)}, \texttt{med}]$	Elliptic curve	$\mathbb{E}(\mathbb{F}_\ell), p$	$g_i, g_i^{x_i}$
$\text{HEG}[\text{GGen}_{\mathbb{E}(\mathbb{F}_\ell)}, \texttt{low}]$	Elliptic curve	$-$	$\mathbb{E}_i(\mathbb{F}_{\ell_i}), p_i, g_i, g_i^{x_i}$
$\text{HEG}[\text{GGen}_{\mathbb{F}_\ell^*}, \texttt{high}]$	Finite field	$\mathbb{F}_\ell^*, p, g$	g^{x_i}
$\text{HEG}[\text{GGen}_{\mathbb{F}_\ell^*}, \texttt{med}]$	Finite field	$\mathbb{F}_\ell^*, p$	$g_i, g_i^{x_i}$
$\text{HEG}[\text{GGen}_{\mathbb{F}_\ell^*}, \texttt{low}]$	Finite field	$-$	$\mathbb{F}_{\ell_i}, p_i, g_i, g_i^{x_i}$

instances. Examples are factoring [11] and computing discrete logarithms in the finite-field [4,5] and elliptic-curve [18,20,22] setting. This sub-optimal scaling is typically inherited by the corresponding cryptographic schemes. It has been exploited in practice by the famous Logjam attack [2], where the authors break many Diffie-Hellman instances in TLS with nearly the same resources as to break a single Diffie-Hellman instance. Concretely, the Logjam attack could successfully break multiple 512-bit finite-field instances, and the authors also speculate about the feasibility of breaking 1024-bit instances. With our work we aim to deliver positive results by computing (non-trivial lower bounds on) the scaling factors of concrete encryption schemes that are currently employed in practice, thereby providing bounds on the hardness of performing mass surveillance.

CONSIDERED ENCRYPTION SCHEMES. We are able to provide non-trivial bounds on the scaling factor for Hashed ElGamal (HEG), also known as DHIES [1], in the elliptic curve ($\text{HEG}[\text{GGen}_{\mathbb{E}(\mathbb{F}_\ell)}]$) and the finite field ($\text{HEG}[\text{GGen}_{\mathbb{F}_\ell^*}]$) setting, the arguably most widely used discrete-logarithm-type encryption schemes. Here $\text{GGen}_{\mathbb{E}(\mathbb{F}_\ell)}$ and $\text{GGen}_{\mathbb{F}_\ell^*}$ are group-generating algorithms that generate prime-order subgroups of elliptic curves and finite fields respectively. In both cases, ℓ denotes randomly chosen primes of appropriate size. We consider both schemes instantiated in three different granularity settings (low, medium, and high), leading to six schemes, $\text{HEG}[\text{GGen}_{\mathbb{E}(\mathbb{F}_\ell)}, \texttt{low}]$, $\text{HEG}[\text{GGen}_{\mathbb{E}(\mathbb{F}_\ell)}, \texttt{med}]$, $\text{HEG}[\text{GGen}_{\mathbb{E}(\mathbb{F}_\ell)}, \texttt{high}]$, $\text{HEG}[\text{GGen}_{\mathbb{F}_\ell^*}, \texttt{low}]$, $\text{HEG}[\text{GGen}_{\mathbb{F}_\ell^*}, \texttt{med}]$, and $\text{HEG}[\text{GGen}_{\mathbb{F}_\ell^*}, \texttt{high}]$, which offer different trade-offs between public key sizes and scalability. The term *granularity* specifies which parts of the scheme's parameters belong to the global system parameters (shared among all n users), and which parts belong to the individual, user-specific public keys. Table 1 depicts the shared public system parameters and individual keys in a multi-instance setting with n parties for HEG at different granularities.

1.1   Our Results

FORMAL DEFINITIONS: MULTI-INSTANCE SECURITY. The notion of n-out-of-n multi-instance security for any $n \geq 1$ was first considered and formally defined by Bellare et al. [8] in the setting of secret-key encryption. As our first contribution, we extend their notion to m-out-of-n multi-instance security for public-key encryption, for arbitrary $1 \leq m \leq n$. In fact, we give two different notions, modeling (m,n)-CPA (passive) and (m,n)-CCA (active) security.

Our (m,n)-CPA experiment provides the adversary with n independent public keys $pk[1], \ldots, pk[n]$. Next, it picks n independent challenge bits $b[1], \ldots, b[n]$ and grants the adversary access to oracle $\mathrm{Enc}(\cdot, \cdot, \cdot)$ which, given i, M_0, M_1, returns an encryption of message $M_{b[i]}$ under $pk[i]$. The adversary outputs a single bit b' together with a list $L \subseteq \{1, \ldots, n\}$ of cardinality at least m. The advantage function is defined as

$$\mathrm{Adv}_{\mathsf{PKE}}^{(m,n)\text{-cpa}} = \Pr\left[b' = \bigoplus_{i \in L} b[i]\right] - \frac{1}{2}.$$

That is, the adversary wins if it guesses correctly the XOR of at least m (out of n) challenge bits. (Note that the standard multi-user security notion for PKE [7] is different: Most importantly, multi-user security involves only a single challenge bit, in particular limiting this notion to the case of $m = 1$.) Why using XOR for defining the winning condition? Bellare et al. [8] argue that this is a natural metric because its well-known "sensitivity" means that as long as at least one of the challenge bits looks random to the adversary so does their XOR. They further argue that other possible winning conditions such as using AND[2] are less natural and lead to inconsistencies. We refer to Bellare et al. [8] for an extensive discussion. In (m,n)-CCA security, the adversary is furthermore provided with a decryption oracle $\mathrm{Dec}(\cdot, \cdot)$ which given i, c returns a decryption of c under $sk[i]$. To expand on the characteristics of the multi-instance setting, we determine the relations between the security notions (m,n)-CPA and (m,n)-CCA for different values of m and n. The natural results we are able to show in this regard (among others, the intuitive idea that a single-instance adversary of advantage ϵ and running time t can be extended to an m-out-of-n adversary of advantage ϵ^m and running time mt; see Theorem 1) give us further confidence on the significance of the chosen multi-instance security definition, and enable us to present a formally sound definition of the scaling factor.

SCALING FACTOR OF $\mathsf{HEG}[\mathsf{GGen}_{\mathbb{E}(\mathbb{F}_\ell)}, \cdot]$ AND $\mathsf{HEG}[\mathsf{GGen}_{\mathbb{F}_\ell^*}, \cdot]$. In order to give a lower bound on $\mathrm{SF}_{\mathsf{PKE}}^{m,n}$ as defined in Eq. (1), we need to lower bound the numerator (i.e., resources required to break m out of n instances) for all possible adversaries and upper bound the denominator (i.e., resources needed to break one instance) by specifying a concrete adversary. Unfortunately, unless the famous P vs. NP problem is settled, all meaningful lower bounds on the resources will

---

[2] I.e., by letting the adversary output a vector $b'[1], \ldots, b'[n]$ and a set I and defining the advantage function as $\mathrm{Adv}_{\mathsf{PKE}}^{(m,n)\text{-cpa}} = \Pr[\bigwedge_{i \in I} b[i] = b'[i]] - 1/2^m$.

Table 2. Lower bounds on the scaling factor $\mathrm{SF}_{\mathsf{HEG}}^{m,n}$ relative to (m,n)-CCA security. $L_\ell(1/3, c)$ is defined as $\exp((c + o(1))(\log \ell)^{1/3}(\log \log \ell)^{2/3})$. In the finite field case $m = L_\ell(1/3, \delta)$ for some $\delta \geq 0$.

PKE	Setting	Scaling factor	
$\mathsf{HEG}[\mathsf{GGen}_{\mathbb{E}(\mathbb{F}_\ell)}, \{\texttt{high}, \texttt{med}\}]$	Elliptic curve	$\Theta(\sqrt{m})$	
$\mathsf{HEG}[\mathsf{GGen}_{\mathbb{E}(\mathbb{F}_\ell)}, \texttt{low}]$	Elliptic curve	$\Theta(m)$	
$\mathsf{HEG}[\mathsf{GGen}_{\mathbb{F}_\ell^*}, \{\texttt{high}, \texttt{med}\}]$	Finite field	$\begin{cases} 1 & \delta \leq 0.67 \\ L_\ell(1/3, \delta - 0.67) & \delta > 0.67 \end{cases}$	
$\mathsf{HEG}[\mathsf{GGen}_{\mathbb{F}_\ell^*}, \texttt{low}]$	Finite field	$\begin{cases} L_\ell(1/3, \delta) & 0 \leq \delta < 0.105 \\ L_\ell(1/3, 0.105) & 0.105 \leq \delta < 0.368 \\ L_\ell(1/3, -0.263 + \delta) & 0.368 \leq \delta \end{cases}$	

require either an unproven complexity assumption or a restricted model of computation. We rely on the generic group model [28] for $\mathsf{HEG}[\mathsf{GGen}_{\mathbb{E}(\mathbb{F}_\ell)}, \cdot]$ (which is considered to be meaningful for elliptic-curve groups) and on a hypothesis on the running time of variants of the number field sieve for $\mathsf{HEG}[\mathsf{GGen}_{\mathbb{F}_\ell^*}, \cdot]$ based on the fastest known attacks on finite fields.

Our main results regarding the scaling factor $\mathrm{SF}_{\mathsf{HEG}}^{m,n}$ in different granularities relative to (m, n)-CCA security are summarized in Table 2. In both considered group instantiations, HEG shows the same asymptotic scaling behavior for high and medium granularity. In both cases however, HEG scales better in the low-granularity case. Concretely, Hashed ElGamal over elliptic curves (modeled as generic groups) scales optimally for low-granularity parameters. For medium and high granularity, on the other hand, the scaling factor is of order $\Theta(\sqrt{m})$, where the constants hidden by the Θ-notation are small.

Let $L_\ell(1/3, c) := \exp((c + o(1))(\log \ell)^{1/3}(\log \log \ell)^{2/3})$. For HEG in the finite field setting with respect to high and medium granularity, we see that the scaling factor is roughly 1 for up to $m = L_\ell(1/3, 0.67)$ instances, the point starting from which the cumulative cost of breaking m individual instances outweighs the cost of the precomputation. Beyond, the KEM scales linearly with slope $L_\ell(1/3, -0.67)$. Note that $L_\ell(1/3, 0.67)$ is large for typical values of ℓ. Concretely, for 512 bit primes we get that $L_\ell(1/3, 0.67) \approx 2^{22}$ meaning that the effort of breaking 2^{22} instances roughly equals the effort to break a single instance. While the concrete number is obtained ignoring the $o(1)$ terms in L_ℓ, it still matches empirical results [2, Table 2]. For low granularity and for up to $L_\ell(1/3, 0.105)$ instances, $\mathsf{HEG}[\mathsf{GGen}_{\mathbb{F}_\ell^*}, \texttt{low}]$ scales optimally. For $L_\ell(1/3, 0.105) \leq m \leq L_\ell(1/3, 0.368)$, the scaling factor is roughly constant, and for larger numbers of instances, it scales linearly with slope $L_\ell(1/3, -0.263)$ which is far larger than the slope in the case of medium or high granularity.

Summing up, Hashed ElGamal instantiated with elliptic curve groups shows a better scaling behavior than the corresponding instantiation in the finite-field setting. Further, in both cases switching from the high granularity setting to the medium granularity setting does not improve the scaling behavior, while the

Table 3. Example values of scaling factor $\mathrm{SF}^{(m,m)\text{-cca}}_{\mathsf{HEG}[\mathsf{GGen},\mathsf{gran}]}$ for different values of m and ℓ, $\mathsf{GGen} \in \{\mathsf{GGen}_{\mathbb{E}(\mathbb{F}_\ell)}, \mathsf{GGen}_{\mathbb{F}_\ell^*}\}$, and $\mathsf{gran} \in \{\mathtt{high}, \mathtt{med}, \mathtt{low}\}$.

| | | Elliptic curve | | Finite field | |
m	ℓ	high, med	low	high, med	low
2^{20}	512	2^{10}	2^{20}	1.21	$2^{11.26}$
	1024	2^{10}	2^{20}	1.00	$2^{8.26}$
	2048	2^{10}	2^{20}	1.00	$2^{6.64}$
2^{30}	512	2^{15}	2^{30}	$2^{7.73}$	$2^{21.26}$
	1024	2^{15}	2^{30}	1.85	$2^{18.13}$
	2048	2^{15}	2^{30}	1.00	$2^{14.02}$

use of individual groups, i.e., low-granularity parameters does. To illustrate our findings we provide example values of the scaling factor for different numbers of instances m and prime sizes ℓ in Table 3.

While our results imply that the use of low-granularity parameters is preferable with respect to security scaling, we stress that generating cryptographically secure groups is a hard and error prone process. Delegating this task to the the individual user as part of the key generation might actually have a negative impact on the scheme's security in practice. Further, the use of individual groups negatively impacts the efficiency of the scheme, as key generation requires the sampling of secure groups, and key-sizes increase.

DERIVATION OF THE SCALING FACTORS. As we will explain below in more detail, the bounds from Table 2 are obtained in two steps. In a **first step**, we consider an m-out-of-n multi-instance version of the Gap Computational Diffie-Hellman problem, (m, n)-GapCDH[$\mathsf{GGen}, \mathsf{gran}$], where the term "gap" refers to the presence of a Decisional Diffie-Hellman (DDH) oracle. The following theorem holds for all $\mathsf{GGen} \in \{\mathsf{GGen}_{\mathbb{E}(\mathbb{F}_\ell)}, \mathsf{GGen}_{\mathbb{F}_\ell^*}\}$ and $\mathsf{gran} \in \{\mathtt{high}, \mathtt{med}, \mathtt{low}\}$.

Theorem. *The* (m, n)-*CCA security of* $\mathsf{HEG}[\mathsf{GGen}, \mathsf{gran}]$ *is tightly implied by the hardness of* (m, n)-GapCDH[$\mathsf{GGen}, \mathsf{gran}$].

The theorem (described formally in Sect. 4) is a somewhat straightforward generalization of the single-instance case [1]. We stress that tightness in our previous theorem is an essential ingredient to obtain overall tight bounds on the scaling factor.

In a **second step**, we provide bounds on the (m, n)-GapCDH[$\mathsf{GGen}, \mathsf{gran}$] problem. In the finite field case, we rely on the following hypothesis:

Hypothesis 1. *The fastest algorithms to break* (m, n)-GapCDH[$\mathsf{GGen}_{\mathbb{F}_\ell^*}, \mathsf{gran}$] *are variants of the number field sieve [4, 5] which require running time*

$$T = \begin{cases} L_\ell(1/3, 1.902) + m \cdot L_\ell(1/3, 1.232) & \mathsf{gran} \in \{\mathtt{high}, \mathtt{med}\} \\ \min\{m \cdot L_\ell(1/3, 1.902), L_\ell(1/3, 2.007) + m \cdot L_\ell(1/3, 1.639)\} & \mathsf{gran} = \mathtt{low} \end{cases}.$$

The lower bounds on $SF^{m,n}$ for $HEG[GGen_{\mathbb{F}_\ell^*}, gran]$ are obtained by combining the previous theorem and Hypothesis 1. The running times specified in the hypothesis stem from the multi-field NFS [5] (high/medium granularity) and the DLOG factory [4] (low granularity). Both variants first require an instance-independent precomputation. Then instances can be solved with a constant computational effort. The values $\delta = 0.67$ and $\delta = 0.368$ of Table 2 correspond to the number of instances starting from which the cumulative cost of breaking the instances outweighs the cost of the precomputation.

In the elliptic-curve case, we make the hypothesis that the fastest adversary attacking the system is a generic-group adversary. Concretely, we prove the following generic-group lower bounds for (m, n)-GapCDH$[GGen_{gg}, gran]$ in different granularities, where $GGen_{gg}$ generates a generic group [28] of prime order p, and the granularity $gran$ determines how much information about the used group is shared amongst the challenge instances (see Table 4).

Theorem. *The best generic algorithm to break (m, n)-GapCDH$[GGen_{gg}, gran]$ requires running time*

$$T = \begin{cases} \Theta(\sqrt{mp}) & gran \in \{high, med\} \\ \Theta(m\sqrt{p}) & gran = low \end{cases},$$

and the constants hidden by the Θ notation are small (between 0.1 and 6.6).

The lower bounds on $SF^{m,n}$ for $HEG[GGen_{\mathbb{E}(\mathbb{F}_\ell)}, gran]$ are obtained by combining our previous theorems and assuming that elliptic-curve groups behave like generic groups.

1.2 Generic Bounds on Multi-Instance GapCDH: Technical Details

We consider multi-instance variants of three different problems: the discrete logarithm problem $((m, n)$-DL$[GGen_{gg}, gran])$, the gap discrete logarithm problem $((m, n)$-GapDL$[GGen_{gg}, gran])$, and the gap computational Diffie-Hellman problem $((m, n)$-GapCDH$[GGen_{gg}, gran])$ in different granularities, see Table 4.

We now discuss the complexity column of Table 4. It is well known that the running time of solving (m, n)-DL$[GGen_{gg}, high]$ is $\Theta(\sqrt{mp})$, the lower bound being in the generic group model [29,30], the matching upper bound stemming from a concrete generic algorithm [22]. It is not hard to see that the bounds on (m, n)-DL$[GGen_{gg}, med]$ are basically the same because the generators g_i can be viewed as "high-granularity instances" g^{x_j}. Concerning low granularity, it is noteworthy to mention the bound for the case $m = n$ by Garay et al. [17]. Using different techniques, we are able to improve their bound from $\sqrt{mp}$ to $m\sqrt{p}$. In addition, our bound also holds in the case $m < n$ and in the gap setting.

Our **first main technical result** (Corollary 1) is a non-trivial extension of Yun's generic lower bound [30] to the gap setting, i.e., a new lower bound of $\Omega(\sqrt{mp})$ on solving (m, m)-GapDL$[GGen_{gg}, high]$. Based on this result, we also deduce bounds in the case of medium and low granularity.

Table 4. Definition and generic-group complexity of problems (m, n)-DL[GGen, gran], (m, n)-GapDL[GGen, gran], and (m, n)-GapCDH[GGen, gran], where **gran** belongs to $\{\text{high}, \text{med}, \text{low}\}$. $\mathbb{G}$ and $\mathbb{G}_i$ are generic groups of prime order p and p_i, with generators g and g_i, respectively. The third column defines the problem's winning condition. The Gap column indicates the presence of a DDH oracle.

m-out-of-n problem	Given	Break m out of	Gap?	Complexity	Ref.
DL[GGen, high]	$\mathbb{G}, p, g, g^{x_1}, \ldots, g^{x_n}$	$x_1, \ldots, x_n$	–	$\Theta(\sqrt{mp})$	[22,29,30]
DL[GGen, med]	$\mathbb{G}, p, g_1, g_1^{x_1}, \ldots, g_n, g_n^{x_n}$	$x_1, \ldots, x_n$	–	$\Theta(\sqrt{mp})$	full version [3]
DL[GGen, low]	$\mathbb{G}_1, p_1, g_1, g_1^{x_1}, \ldots, \mathbb{G}_n, p_n, g_n, g_n^{x_n}$	$x_1, \ldots, x_n$	–	$\Theta(m\sqrt{p})$	full version [3]
GapDL[GGen, high]	$\mathbb{G}, p, g, g^{x_1}, \ldots, g^{x_n}$	$x_1, \ldots, x_n$	✓	$\Theta(\sqrt{mp})$	§5.2
GapDL[GGen, med]	$\mathbb{G}, p, g_1, g_1^{x_1}, \ldots, g_n, g_n^{x_n}$	$x_1, \ldots, x_n$	✓	$\Theta(\sqrt{mp})$	full version [3]
GapDL[GGen, low]	$\mathbb{G}_1, p_1, g_1, g_1^{x_1}, \ldots, \mathbb{G}_n, p_n, g_n, g_n^{x_n}$	$x_1, \ldots, x_n$	✓	$\Theta(m\sqrt{p})$	full version [3]
GapCDH[GGen, high]	$\mathbb{G}, p, g, g^{x_1}, g^{y_1}, \ldots, g^{x_n}, g^{y_n}$	$g^{x_1 y_1}, \ldots, g^{x_n y_n}$	✓	$\Theta(\sqrt{mp})$	§6.1
GapCDH[GGen, med]	$\mathbb{G}, p, g_1, g_1^{x_1}, g_1^{y_1}, \ldots, g_n, g_n^{x_n}, g_n^{y_n}$	$g_1^{x_1 y_1}, \ldots, g_n^{x_n y_n}$	✓	$\Theta(\sqrt{mp})$	§6.2
GapCDH[GGen, low]	$\mathbb{G}_1, p_1, g_1, g_1^{x_1}, g_1^{y_1}, \ldots, \mathbb{G}_n, p_n, g_n, g_n^{x_n}, g_n^{y_n}$	$g_1^{x_1 y_1}, \ldots, g_n^{x_n y_n}$	✓	$\Theta(m\sqrt{p})$	§6.3

Our **second main technical result** (Theorem 4) states that, in high granularity, the (m, m)-GapDL and the (m, n)-GapCDH problems are essentially equally hard in the algebraic group model [16], hence implying the required bounds in the generic group model. The results in medium and low granularity follow as in the discrete logarithm setting.

MAIN TECHNICAL RESULT 1: LOWER BOUND ON (m, m)-GapDL[GGen$_{\text{gg}}$,high]. We define a new "hard" problem called the *polycheck discrete logarithm problem*: The security game is the same as that of standard multi-instance DL, but the adversary has additional access to an oracle Eval that behaves as follows: Given as input to Eval a polynomial $f \in \mathbb{Z}_p[X_1, \ldots, X_k]$ and group elements $g^{x_1}, \ldots, g^{x_k}$, it returns 1 if and only if $g^{f(x_1, \ldots, x_k)} = 1$. This problem is easier than GapDL: In fact, we can simulate the gap oracle $\text{DDH}(g^x, g^y, g^z)$ by querying $\text{Eval}(f := X_1 X_2 - X_3, g^x, g^y, g^z)$. In the generic group model, we can bound the advantage of an adversary against the m-out-of-m polycheck discrete logarithm problem that queries polynomial of degree at most d ((m, m)-d-PolyDL[GGen$_{\text{gg}}$, high]) as

$$\text{Adv}^{(m,m)\text{-}d\text{-polydl}} \lesssim \left(\frac{dq^2 + dq_{\text{Eval}}}{mp} \right)^m,$$

where q bounds the queries to the group-operation oracle, q_{Eval} to Eval, and p is the order of the generic group. The bound for high-granularity GapDL follows by setting $d = 2$.

The result is proven by extending the arguments by Yun [30] for the standard multi-instance DL problem. In line with Yun's approach, we define the *search-by-hypersurface* problem in dimension m (m-SHS$_d[p]$), which requires to find a uniformly sampled point $\boldsymbol{a} \in \mathbb{Z}_p^m$ while being able to check whether $\boldsymbol{a}$ is a zero of adaptively chosen polynomials in $\mathbb{Z}_p[X_1, \ldots, X_m]$ of degree at most d. Notably, Yun's *search-by-hyperplane-queries* problem in dimension m is equivalent to m-SHS$_1$. We stress that the more general case of $d \geq 1$ requires significantly different arguments from commutative algebra/algebraic geometry, compared to the linear algebra argument used for the DL bound.

We show that any generic adversary against (m, m)-d-PolyDL[GGen$_{gg}$, high] can be transformed into an adversary against m-SHS$_d$, and then proceed to bound the advantage of an adversary against m-SHS$_d$. The key step is observing that an adversary can make at most m useful hypersurface queries, that is, queries that return 1 (hence, identify a hypersurface on which the point a lies) and whose output is not easy to determine based on previous queries. The key difference between our result and Yun's lies in how useful queries are processed and counted. Since Yun considers only polynomials of degree 1, a hypersurface defined by a polynomial of degree 1 is a hyperplane of the affine space $\mathbb{Z}_p^m$. Each useful query identifies another hyperplane on which the sought point lies. When intersecting another hyperplane with the intersection of the hyperplanes previously found, the dimension of the intersection as an affine subspace is brought down by one. The dimension of the full affine space being m, at most m such queries can be made before identifying a single point (dimension 0). However, generalizing to hypersurfaces generated by polynomials of degree ≥ 2 requires to carry over more sophisticated arguments from commutative algebra. Firstly, intersecting m hypersurfaces does not, in general, identify a single point. Secondly, intersection of two hypersurfaces might give rise to the union of two or more irreducible components. Intersecting further with a hypersurface containing just one of those irreducible components would qualify as a useful query, however would not bring down the dimension of the intersection by one. This impasse is overcome by guessing the correct component at each step. Fortunately, Bézout's theorem and a discerning choice of the guessing probabilities at each useful query makes the argument go through with just an additional loss of d^m, which is absorbed by the exponential bound in the dimension.

MAIN TECHNICAL RESULT 2: (m, m)-GapDL[GGen, high] HARDNESS IMPLIES (m, n)-GapCDH[GGen, high]. The algebraic group model [16] is a technique used to extend existing bounds in the generic group model to different problems by means of generic reductions. Our second technical result (Theorem 4) presents a generic reduction between the problems (m, n)-GapCDH[GGen, high] and (m, m)-GapDL[GGen, high] with a tightness loss of 2^m in the algebraic group model. Combining this with the generic-group lower bound we prove as our first main technical result, we obtain, in the generic group model:

$$\text{Adv}_{\text{high}}^{(m,n)\text{-gcdh}} \overset{\text{Th. 4}}{\leq} 2^m \cdot \text{Adv}_{\text{high}}^{(m,m)\text{-gdl}} \overset{\text{Cor. 1}}{\lesssim} 2^m \left(\frac{q^2 + q_{\text{DDH}}}{mp} \right)^m \approx \left(\frac{2q^2}{mp} \right)^m,$$

where q bounds the queries to the group-operation oracle, q_{DDH} to the gap oracle, and p is the order of the generic group. Note that the reduction's exponential loss of 2^m gets swallowed by the (m, m)-GapDL[GGen$_{gg}$, high] bound. More importantly, by the above bound one requires $q \geq \Omega(\sqrt{mp})$ generic-group operations to break (m, n)-GapCDH[GGen$_{gg}$, high] with overwhelming advantage.

A natural approach to tackle the proof of Theorem 4 would be to adapt the single-instance proof presented by Fuchsbauer et al. [16] to the multi-instance setting. Following this strategy in a reduction, however, one would need to argue about the size of the solution set of a multivariate system of quadratic equations. In this work we employ significantly different proof techniques.

The path we pursue maintains, instead, the linear character of the system. The reduction distributes the i-th DL challenges in either the X or Y components of the i-th challenges to the CDH adversary. The intuition at the core of the proof is that an adversary finding the CDH solution for any one instance must provide the DL of at least one of the two corresponding challenge components (even if possibly depending on the remaining, unrecovered DLs). If the reduction manages to embed the m DL challenges at the right spot, then it is able to recover all logarithms. The reduction loss of 2^m is consequence of this guess. Moreover, expanding the m DL challenges into n CDH challenges adds a further layer of complexity.

1.3   Related Work and Future Directions

RELATED WORK. Multi-instance security in the sense of breaking m out of m instances was first formally considered in the setting of symmetric encryption by Bellare et al. [8]. We point out that the term is sometimes also used to describe multi-user, multi-challenge generalizations of single-instance security notions [21].

The (single-instance) GapCDH problem was introduced by Okamoto and Pointcheval [25]. Boneh et al. [12] and Rupp et al. [26] provide frameworks in the generic-group model that can be used to derive generic-group lower bounds on the hardness of many single-instance problems, gapCDH amongst others. The generic hardness of (m, m)-DL in the high-granularity setting was first analyzed by Yun [30], the result later generalized to (m, n)-DL by Ying and Kunihiro [29]. Kuhn and Struik [22], and Fouque et al. [15] give generic algorithms matching the lower bounds. The first bound for (m, m)-DL in the low granularity setting was derived by Garay et al. [17]. The algebraic-group model was introduced by Fuchsbauer et al. [16]. Mizuide et al. [24] provide a framework that can be used to reduce single-instance CDH-type problems to the discrete-logarithm problem in the algebraic-group model.

Bartusek et al. [6] and Sadeghi et al. [27] discuss differences between DL-type assumptions depending on whether the used group and group generator are fixed or sampled at random. We stress that in this work groups and group generators, while potentially shared amongst different users, are sampled at the beginning of the game and hence part of its probability space.

FUTURE DIRECTIONS. Corrigan-Gibbs and Kogan [14] consider the multi-instance discrete logarithm problem in a setting where the adversary is allowed to first perform unbounded preprocessing over the group to produce an advice string of bounded size, which in a second stage is used to solve multiple discrete logarithm instances. The resulting lower bounds in the generic group model were also derived by Coretti et al. [13] using a different technique. It would be interesting to compute scaling factors of the considered schemes taking preprocessing into account. Another possible direction is to derive lower bounds on the scaling factor for practical encryption schemes in the RSA setting (e.g., RSA-OAEP [9]) and in the post-quantum setting (e.g., based on lattices and codes).

2   Preliminaries

2.1   Notation

VECTOR NOTATION. We denote vectors with boldface fonts, for example v. The number of elements of a vector is represented by $|v|$. Element indexing starts from 1, and the entry at position i is accessed through square brackets: $v[i]$. To initialize all entries of a vector to some element a we write $v[\cdot] \leftarrow a$. We may initialize multiple vectors simultaneously, and moreover initialize them through running some (possibly randomized) routine. As an example, we could initialize a vector of public and of secret keys as $(\mathbf{pk}, \mathbf{sk})[\cdot] \leftarrow_\$ \mathsf{Gen}$ to indicate that for every index i we run Gen with fresh randomness and, denoting the output with (pk, sk), set $\mathbf{pk}[i] \leftarrow pk$ and $\mathbf{sk}[i] \leftarrow sk$. Given any set of indices I, we denote with $v[I]$ the vector that contains only the entries indexed with elements in I. For example, if $v = (a, b, c)$ then $v[\{1, 3\}] = (a, c)$. We slightly abuse this notation, writing $v[I] \leftarrow w$ when replacing each entry of v whose indices belong to I by the elements of w in their order. For example, if $v = (a, b, c)$ and we execute $v[\{1, 3\}] \leftarrow (d, e)$ then $v = (d, b, e)$.

GROUP NOTATION. In this paper we consider groups $\mathbb{G}$ of prime order p, generated by g. We call $\mathcal{G} = (\mathbb{G}, p, g)$ a group representation. A group-generating algorithm GGen is a randomized algorithm that outputs a group representation $\mathcal{G}$. We assume that all groups output by GGen are of the same bit length.

In this work we consider two instantiations $\mathsf{GGen}_{\mathbb{E}(\mathbb{F}_\ell)}$ and $\mathsf{GGen}_{\mathbb{F}_\ell^*}$ of group-generating algorithms. In both cases ℓ denotes a randomly sampled prime of appropriate size. Group descriptions $\mathcal{G}$ output by $\mathsf{GGen}_{\mathbb{E}(\mathbb{F}_\ell)}$ are prime-order p subgroups of elliptic curves defined over the field $\mathbb{F}_\ell$. Group descriptions output by the second considered group-generating algorithm $\mathsf{GGen}_{\mathbb{F}_\ell^*}$ are subgroups of the multiplicative group $\mathbb{F}_\ell^*$ of sufficiently large prime order.

Except for the group generators, all group elements will be denoted with uppercase letters, e.g., X. We use vectors and matrices of elements in $\mathbb{Z}_p$ to compute with group elements: If Y is a group element and x is a vector of elements in $\mathbb{Z}_p$, we write Y^x to denote the group element vector $(Y^{x[1]}, Y^{x[2]}, \ldots)$. Similarly, given some matrix $M = (m_{ij})_{i,j \in [1..n] \times [1..k]}$ and a vector of group elements Y of size k, we define Y^M to be the n-size vector $(Y[1]^{m_{11}} \ldots Y[k]^{m_{1k}}, \ldots, Y[1]^{m_{n1}} \ldots Y[k]^{m_{nk}})$. Note that if $Y = g^y$ then $Y^M = g^{My}$.

SECURITY GAMES. We define security notions via *code-based games* [10]. A game G consists of a main procedure and zero or more oracles that can be accessed from within the game. The game is defined with respect to an adversary $\mathcal{A}$, which is invoked within the main procedure. The adversary may have access to some of the oracles of the game: The ability to access oracle O is represented by invoking the adversary as $\mathcal{A}^O$. When the game stops, it outputs either a success (1) or a failure (0) symbol. With $\Pr[G(\mathcal{A})]$ we denote the probability that adversary $\mathcal{A}$ wins, i.e., that game G, executed with respect to $\mathcal{A}$, stops with output 1.

2.2   Generic/Algebraic Group Model

GENERIC GROUP MODEL. Intuitively, the Generic Group Model (GGM) is an abstraction to study the behavior of adversaries that do not exploit any specific structure of the group at play, but rather treat the group in a black-box fashion. This is usually modeled by representing group elements exclusively through "opaque" handles, which hide the structure of the group. These handles are used as input to a model-bound oracle, the group-operation oracle, which is the only interface to the group available to the adversary. An algorithm with such restrictions is referred to as a *generic algorithm*. The running time of generic adversaries is normally measured in number of calls to the group-operation oracle. For further details on the GGM we refer to the literature [23,28]. To derive bounds on the hardness of solving certain computational problems with respect to $\mathsf{GGen}_{\mathbb{E}(\mathbb{F}_\ell)}$ we model the output elliptic curves as generic groups. For clarity, in this case we denote the group-generating algorithm by $\mathsf{GGen}_{\mathsf{gg}}$.

ALGEBRAIC GROUP MODEL. For every group element Z it returns, an *algebraic algorithm* $\mathcal{A}$ must present a description of this element in terms of the elements it has previously seen. That is, if n is the order of the group and $X_1, \ldots, X_k$ are the elements that $\mathcal{A}$ received so far from the game, then $\mathcal{A}$ must return some elements $a_1, \ldots, a_k \in \mathbb{Z}_n$ such that $Z = X_1^{a_1} \ldots X_k^{a_k}$. We use the algebraic group model to analyze generic reductions:

Note that a generic reduction executed with respect to a generic adversary is itself a generic algorithm. Without loss of generality we may assume that generic adversaries are algebraic, which allows the reduction to exploit the useful algebraic representation of the input group elements. As demonstrated by Fuchsbauer et al. [16], this idea gives a handy technique for carrying over generic lower bounds through generic reductions, as seen in the following lemma.

Lemma 1. ([16, Lemma 1]). *Let α, Δ be constants and let $\mathcal{R}$ be a generic reduction $\mathcal{R}$ from game G_1 to G_0. Assume that for every generic adversary $\mathcal{A}$ that succeeds with probability ε and makes at most q group-operation queries, reduction $\mathcal{R}$ executed with respect to $\mathcal{A}$ makes at most $q + \Delta$ group-operation queries and succeeds with probability of at least $\alpha\varepsilon$. If there exists a function f such that $\Pr[\mathrm{G}_1(\mathcal{B})] \leq f(q)$ for every generic adversary $\mathcal{B}$ making at most q group-operation queries, then for every generic adversary $\mathcal{A}$ making at most q group-operation queries we obtain $\Pr[\mathrm{G}_0(\mathcal{A})] \leq \alpha^{-1}f(q + \Delta)$.*

2.3   Key-Encapsulation Mechanisms

A *key-encapsulation mechanism* (KEM) KEM specifies the following. Parameter generation algorithm Par generates public parameters *par* to be utilized by all users. Key-generation algorithm Gen gets the parameters as input and outputs a pair (pk, sk) consisting of a public and a secret key. Encapsulation algorithm Enc on input of the parameters and a public key outputs a pair (K, c) consisting of an encapsulated key K belonging to the encapsulated key space $\mathsf{KS}(par)$ and a ciphertext c belonging to the ciphertext space $\mathsf{CS}(par)$. Deterministic decapsulation algorithm Dec receives the parameters, a secret key sk and a ciphertext c as input and returns either the symbol $\perp$ indicating failure or an encapsulated key K. For *correctness* we require that for all par output of Par and for every (pk, sk) output of $\mathsf{Gen}(par)$ we obtain $K \leftarrow \mathsf{Dec}(par, sk, c)$ for $(K, c) \leftarrow_{\$} \mathsf{Enc}(par, pk)$.

3   Multi-Instance Security

In this section we investigate the m-out-of-n multi-instance security of key-encapsulation mechanisms. After giving security definitions in Sect. 3.1, in Sect. 3.2 we consider the relation between security notions for varying m and n. In Sect. 3.3 we define the scaling factor, which measures how well the security of KEMs scales with the number of users. Finally, in Sect. 3.4 we give security definitions for Diffie-Hellman type problems in the multi-instance setting, which will be used in the security analysis of the Hashed-ElGamal KEM in the next section.

3.1   Key Encapsulation in the Multi-Instance Setting

Below we give security definitions for key-encapsulation mechanisms in the multi-instance setting. Our definitions are in the xor metric introduced by Bellare et al. [8] for symmetric encryption schemes. We target m-out-of-n multi-instance indistinguishability of encapsulated keys from random against chosen-plaintext attacks ((m, n)-CPA) or chosen-ciphertext attacks ((m, n)-CCA).

In its most general form, the xor metric models the inability of an adversary to break m out of n instances of a decisional problem. The adversary receives as input n challenges, generated independently of each other with respect to n independent challenge bits $\boldsymbol{b}$. The adversary's task is to output a subset $L \subseteq [1 .. n]$ of size at least m (representing the "broken instances") together with a guess for $\bigoplus_{i \in L} \boldsymbol{b}[i]$; the intuition being that as long as at least one of the challenge bits contained in L is hidden to the adversary, so is $\bigoplus_{i \in L} \boldsymbol{b}[i]$, reducing the adversary to guessing the final output.

Formally, let KEM be a KEM and let $m, n \in \mathbb{N}$ such that $1 \leq m \leq n$. Consider games $\mathrm{G}_{\mathsf{KEM}}^{(m,n)\text{-cpa}}(\mathcal{A})$ and $\mathrm{G}_{\mathsf{KEM}}^{(m,n)\text{-cca}}(\mathcal{A})$ of Fig. 1 associated with KEM, m, n, and an adversary $\mathcal{A}$. In both games, $\boldsymbol{b}$ is a vector of n challenge bits, which corresponds to vectors $\boldsymbol{pk}, \boldsymbol{sk}$ of public and secret keys, which are set up using a single set of global parameters par. The adversary has access to a challenge oracle Enc, which on input of index $i \in [1 .. n]$ returns a pair consisting of an encapsulated key and a ciphertext generated with $\mathsf{Enc}(par, \boldsymbol{pk}[i])$ if the challenge bit $\boldsymbol{b}[i]$ equals 1, or, if $\boldsymbol{b}[i]$ equals 0, a ciphertext and a randomly sampled element of $\mathsf{KS}(par)$. At the end of the game, adversary $\mathcal{A}$ outputs a list of indices $L \subseteq [1 .. n]$ and a bit b'. $\mathcal{A}$ wins if L contains at least m elements and if $b' = \bigoplus_{i \in L} \boldsymbol{b}[i]$. In game $\mathrm{G}_{\mathsf{KEM}}^{(m,n)\text{-cca}}(\mathcal{A})$ the adversary additionally has access to

```
Games G_KEM^(m,n)-cpa(A), G_KEM^(m,n)-cca(A)          Oracle Enc(i)
00  C*[·] ← ∅                                          10  (K_1*, c*) ←$ Enc(par, pk[i])
01  b ←$ {0,1}^n                                       11  K_0* ←$ KS(par)
02  par ←$ Par                                         12  C*[i] ← C*[i] ∪ {c*}
03  for i ∈ [1..n]:                                    13  return (K_{b[i]}*, c*)
04      (pk[i], sk[i]) ←$ Gen(par)
05  (L, b') ←$ A^Enc(par, pk)       ∖(m, n)-CPA        Oracle Dec(i, c)
06  (L, b') ←$ A^{Enc,Dec}(par, pk) ∖(m, n)-CCA        14  if c ∈ C*[i]: return ⊥
07  if |L| < m: return 0                               15  K ← Dec(par, sk[i], c)
08  if ⊕_{i∈L} b[i] = b': return 1                     16  return K
09  else: return 0
```

Fig. 1. Games $G_{\mathsf{KEM}}^{(m,n)\text{-cpa}}$ and $G_{\mathsf{KEM}}^{(m,n)\text{-cca}}$ modeling m-out-of-n multi-instance indistinguishability of encapsulated keys from random. We assume that $L \subseteq [1..n]$.

a decapsulation oracle Dec, which on input of index $i \in [1..n]$ and ciphertext c returns the decapsulation of c under parameters par and secret key $sk[i]$ (unless c was output as response to a challenge query Enc(i) for index i).

We define $\mathcal{A}$'s advantage in game $G_{\mathsf{KEM}}^{(m,n)\text{-cpa}}$ and $G_{\mathsf{KEM}}^{(m,n)\text{-cca}}$ respectively as

$$\mathrm{Adv}_{\mathsf{KEM}}^{(m,n)\text{-cpa}}(\mathcal{A}) = 2\Pr[G_{\mathsf{KEM}}^{(m,n)\text{-cpa}}(\mathcal{A})] - 1,$$

$$\mathrm{Adv}_{\mathsf{KEM}}^{(m,n)\text{-cca}}(\mathcal{A}) = 2\Pr[G_{\mathsf{KEM}}^{(m,n)\text{-cca}}(\mathcal{A})] - 1.$$

The definition we have just presented lends itself naturally to a comparison with the standard multi-user security notion of Bellare et al. [7]. We describe the relationship between multi-user security and $(1, n)$-CCA in detail in the full version of the paper [3].

3.2 Advantage Relations for Different m and n

The relations between (m', n')-CPA and (m, n)-CPA security are summarized in Fig. 2. They are stated more formally in the following theorem. Its proof is in the full version of the paper [3]

Theorem 1. Let m, n, m', n' be positive integers such that $m \leq n$, $m' \leq n'$, and let KEM be any KEM scheme. Then for every adversary $\mathcal{A}$ against game $G_{\mathsf{KEM}}^{(m,n)\text{-cpa}}$ there exists an adversary $\mathcal{B}$ against game $G_{\mathsf{KEM}}^{(m',n')\text{-cpa}}$ such that:

1. If $m' \leq m$ and $m'n \leq mn'$ then $\mathcal{B}$ has roughly the same running time of $\mathcal{A}$ and

$$\mathrm{Adv}_{\mathsf{KEM}}^{(m',n')\text{-cpa}}(\mathcal{B}) \geq \frac{1}{2}\mathrm{Adv}_{\mathsf{KEM}}^{(m,n)\text{-cpa}}(\mathcal{A}).$$

Additionally, if $n'-m' \geq n-m$ then the reduction does not lose the factor $1/2$.

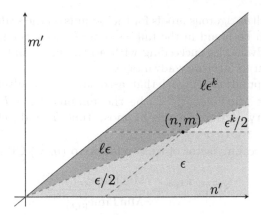

Fig. 2. Relations between (m', n')-CPA and (m, n)-CPA security. Given $\mathcal{A}$ against (m, n)-CPA with advantage ϵ, one can build $\mathcal{B}$ against (m', n')-CPA with advantage as shown in figure, depending on its position on the plane. The constants in the figure are $k = \lceil m'/m \rceil$ and $\ell = \frac{1}{2}\binom{n'}{m'}\binom{\lceil nm'/m \rceil}{m'}^{-1}$. The same result holds for CCA.

2. *If $m' \leq m$ and $m'n > mn'$ then $\mathcal{B}$ has roughly the same running time of $\mathcal{A}$ and*

$$\mathrm{Adv}_{\mathsf{KEM}}^{(m',n')\text{-cpa}}(\mathcal{B}) \geq \frac{1}{2}\binom{n'}{m'}\binom{\lceil nm'/m \rceil}{m'}^{-1} \mathrm{Adv}_{\mathsf{KEM}}^{(m,n)\text{-cpa}}(\mathcal{A}).$$

3. *If $m' > m$ and $m'n \leq mn'$ then $\mathcal{B}$ has roughly $k = \lceil m'/m \rceil$ times the running time of $\mathcal{A}$ and*

$$\mathrm{Adv}_{\mathsf{KEM}}^{(m',n')\text{-cpa}}(\mathcal{B}) \geq \frac{1}{2}\left(\mathrm{Adv}_{\mathsf{KEM}}^{(m,n)\text{-cpa}}(\mathcal{A})\right)^k.$$

   Additionally, if m divides m' then the reduction does not lose the factor $1/2$.

4. *If $m' > m$ and $m'n > mn'$ then $\mathcal{B}$ has roughly $k = \lceil m'/m \rceil$ times the running time of $\mathcal{A}$ and*

$$\mathrm{Adv}_{\mathsf{KEM}}^{(m',n')\text{-cpa}}(\mathcal{B}) \geq \frac{1}{2}\binom{n'}{m'}\binom{\lceil nm'/m \rceil}{m'}^{-1}\left(\mathrm{Adv}_{\mathsf{KEM}}^{(m,n)\text{-cpa}}(\mathcal{A})\right)^k.$$

An analogous statement holds between (m, n)-CCA and (m', n')-CCA. If $\mathcal{A}$ queries its decryption oracle q times, then adversary $\mathcal{B}$ queries its decryption oracle at most q, q, kq, and kq times respectively.

3.3 Scaling Factor

We now define the scaling factor of key-encapsulation mechanisms. To be able to give an intuitive and accessible definition we treat the running time and advantages of adversaries as if they were elements of $\mathbb{R}$ and $[0, 1]$ respectively. A formal definition that takes the asymptotic nature of running time and advantage into account as well as rigorous proofs for the bounds on the scaling factor derived in this section can be found in the full version of the paper [3]. We start with a definition for adversaries succeeding with advantage 1 and afterwards give a generalized version for arbitrary advantages.

We fix a computational model that associates each adversary $\mathcal{A}$ with its running time. Let $\mathrm{MinTime}_{\mathsf{KEM}}^{(m,n)\text{-cpa}}$ be the minimal time T for which there exists an adversary $\mathcal{A}$ that runs in at most time T and achieves advantage $\mathrm{Adv}_{\mathsf{KEM}}^{(m,n)\text{-cpa}}(\mathcal{A}) = 1$.

We define the scaling factor of KEM relative to (m, n)-CPA security as

$$\mathrm{SF}_{\mathsf{KEM}}^{(m,n)\text{-cpa}} := \frac{\mathrm{MinTime}_{\mathsf{KEM}}^{(m,n)\text{-cpa}}}{\mathrm{MinTime}_{\mathsf{KEM}}^{(1,1)\text{-cpa}}}.$$

The scaling factor of KEM relative to (m, n)-CCA security, $\mathrm{SF}_{\mathsf{KEM}}^{(m,n)\text{-cca}}$, is defined in the same way relative to advantage $\mathrm{Adv}_{\mathsf{KEM}}^{(m,n)\text{-cca}}(\mathcal{A})$. By the results of Sect. 3.2 we can give the following bounds on the scaling factor (which also hold in the CCA setting):

$$\mathrm{SF}_{\mathsf{KEM}}^{(m,n)\text{-cpa}} \leq \mathrm{SF}_{\mathsf{KEM}}^{(m,m)\text{-cpa}} \leq m$$

The lower bound follows since any adversary against (m, m)-CPA is also an adversary against (m, n)-CPA with the same advantage (Theorem 1, item 1). The upper bound follows from Theorem 1, item 3. Surprisingly, the scaling factor can be smaller than 1: Being able to choose which users to attack can make the task of breaking multiple instances easier than breaking a single one. An artificial example of a KEM with scaling factor of m/n is sketched in the full version of the paper [3]. This is, however, a phenomenon limited to the case $m \neq n$: For $n = m$, we know that $\mathrm{SF}_{\mathsf{KEM}}^{(n,m)\text{-cpa}} \geq 1$ by Theorem 1, item 1. Importantly, specific KEMs such as HEG or Cramer-Shoup are known to be "random self-reducible", which implies $\mathrm{MinTime}_{\mathsf{KEM}}^{(1,n)\text{-cpa}} = \mathrm{MinTime}_{\mathsf{KEM}}^{(1,1)\text{-cpa}}$, and hence by Theorem 1, item 1:

$$1 \leq \mathrm{SF}_{\mathsf{KEM}}^{(m,n)\text{-cpa}} \leq m.$$

The definition given above exclusively considers adversaries that achieve advantage 1. This definition generalizes naturally to encompass adversaries with arbitrary advantage as follows. Let $\mathrm{MinTime}_{\mathsf{KEM}}^{(m,n)\text{-cpa}}(\varepsilon)$, associated with $0 \leq \varepsilon \leq 1$, denote the running time of the fastest adversary achieving advantage at least ε in game (m, n)-CPA. Intuitively, an optimally scaling scheme requires m independent execution of a $(1, 1)$-CPA adversary in order to break m instances of the scheme. Hence, the advantage-dependent scaling factor for advantage ε is defined as

$$\mathrm{SF}_{\mathsf{KEM}}^{(m,n)\text{-cpa}}(\varepsilon) := \mathrm{MinTime}_{\mathsf{KEM}}^{(m,n)\text{-cpa}}(\varepsilon^m)/\mathrm{MinTime}_{\mathsf{KEM}}^{(1,1)\text{-cpa}}(\varepsilon).$$

Again, we can use Theorem 1 to show that, for every $0 \leq \varepsilon \leq 1$,

$$\mathrm{SF}_{\mathsf{KEM}}^{(m,n)\text{-cpa}}(\varepsilon) \leq \mathrm{SF}_{\mathsf{KEM}}^{(m,m)\text{-cpa}}(\varepsilon) \leq m.$$

3.4   Multi-Instance Diffie-Hellman-Type Problems

GAP DISCRETE LOGARITHM PROBLEM. The m-out-of-n multi-instance gap discrete logarithm problem $((m,n)$-GapDL) requires to find the discrete logarithms of at least m out of n input group elements given access to a decisional Diffie-Hellman oracle. We consider three variants of the problem, which differ in their granularity. For high granularity all discrete logarithm challenges are sampled with respect to a fixed group and group generator, while for medium granularity the challenges are elements of a fixed group but defined with respect to different group generators. Finally, in the case of low granularity a fresh group and generator is used for each challenge.

Formally, let $m, n \in \mathbb{N}$ such that $1 \leq m \leq n$ and consider game $\mathrm{G}^{(m,n)\text{-gdl}}_{\mathsf{GGen},\mathsf{gran}}(\mathcal{A})$ of Fig. 3 associated with adversary $\mathcal{A}$, group-generating algorithm GGen, and granularity $\mathsf{gran} \in \{\mathsf{high}, \mathsf{med}, \mathsf{low}\}$. In the game, a vector $\boldsymbol{\mathcal{G}}$ of n group descriptions is set up according to the desired level of granularity using parameter generation algorithm PGen[gran]. Each entry of $\boldsymbol{\mathcal{G}}$ is of the form $(\mathbb{G}, p, g)$ with $\mathbb{G}$ being a group of prime order p generated by g. After the setup of $\boldsymbol{\mathcal{G}}$ the three variants of the game proceed in the same way. A vector $\boldsymbol{x}$ of length n is sampled, where $\boldsymbol{x}[i]$ is uniformly distributed in $\mathbb{Z}_{\boldsymbol{p}[i]}$. The corresponding challenge vector contains the group elements $\boldsymbol{X}[i] = \boldsymbol{g}[i]^{\boldsymbol{x}[i]}$. At the end of the game, adversary $\mathcal{A}$ outputs a list of indices $L \subseteq [1 .. n]$ and a vector $\boldsymbol{x}'$ of length n, where the i-th entry is in $\mathbb{Z}_{\boldsymbol{p}[i]}$. The adversary wins if L contains at least m elements and if the vector $\boldsymbol{x}'$ coincides with $\boldsymbol{x}$ for all indices in L. Additionally, the adversary has access to an oracle DDH, which, on input of index $i \in [1 .. n]$ and three group elements $\hat{X}, \hat{Y}, \hat{Z}$, behaves as follows. The game computes the discrete logarithms $\hat{x}, \hat{y}$ of input $\hat{X}, \hat{Y}$ with respect to generator $\boldsymbol{g}[i]$, and then returns 1 if and only if $\boldsymbol{g}[i]^{\hat{x}\hat{y}} = \hat{Z}$.

We define $\mathcal{A}$'s advantage in game $\mathrm{G}^{(m,n)\text{-gdl}}_{\mathsf{GGen},\mathsf{gran}}(\mathcal{A})$ as

$$\mathrm{Adv}^{(m,n)\text{-gdl}}_{\mathsf{GGen},\mathsf{gran}}(\mathcal{A}) = \Pr[\mathrm{G}^{(m,n)\text{-gdl}}_{\mathsf{GGen},\mathsf{gran}}(\mathcal{A})].$$

The m-out-of-n multi-instance discrete logarithm $((m,n)$-DL) problem is defined as (m,n)-GapDL with the restriction that $\mathcal{A}$ cannot query DDH.

GAP COMPUTATIONAL DIFFIE-HELLMAN PROBLEM. The m-out-of-n multi-instance gap computational Diffie-Hellman problem $((m,n)$-GapCDH) requires, on input of vectors $g^{\boldsymbol{x}}$ and $g^{\boldsymbol{y}}$, to compute at least m elements of the form $g^{\boldsymbol{x}[i]\boldsymbol{y}[i]}$ for distinct $i \in [1 .. n]$. As in the corresponding DL game, the adversary has access to an oracle DDH which computes whether three given group elements are a Diffie-Hellman triple. As in the definition of (m,n)-GapDL, we consider three variants of the problem, which differ in their granularity.

Formally, for $m, n \in \mathbb{N}$ s.t. $1 \leq m \leq n$ consider game $\mathrm{G}^{(m,n)\text{-gcdh}}_{\mathsf{GGen},\mathsf{gran}}(\mathcal{A})$ of Fig. 4 associated with adversary $\mathcal{A}$, group-generating algorithm GGen, and granularity $\mathsf{gran} \in \{\mathsf{high}, \mathsf{med}, \mathsf{low}\}$. In the game, a vector $\boldsymbol{\mathcal{G}}$ of n group descriptions is set up according to parameter generation algorithm PGen[gran]. After the setup of $\boldsymbol{\mathcal{G}}$ the three variants of the game proceed in the same way. Two vectors $\boldsymbol{x}$, $\boldsymbol{y}$ of length n are sampled, where $\boldsymbol{x}[i]$, $\boldsymbol{y}[i]$ are uniformly distributed in $\mathbb{Z}_{\boldsymbol{p}[i]}$.

$$
\begin{array}{ll}
\textbf{Games } G_{\text{GGen,gran}}^{(m,n)\text{-gdl}}(\mathcal{A}) & \textbf{Oracle } \text{DDH}(i, \hat{X}, \hat{Y}, \hat{Z}) \\
00 \;\; \boldsymbol{\mathcal{G}} \leftarrow_\$ \text{PGen}[\text{gran}] & 06 \;\; \text{parse } \hat{X}, \hat{Y} \text{ as } \boldsymbol{g}[i]^{\hat{x}}, \boldsymbol{g}[i]^{\hat{y}} \\
01 \;\; \boldsymbol{x}[\cdot] \leftarrow_\$ \mathbb{Z}_{\boldsymbol{p}[\cdot]}; \; \boldsymbol{X}[\cdot] \leftarrow \boldsymbol{g}[\cdot]^{\boldsymbol{x}[\cdot]} & 07 \;\; \text{if } \boldsymbol{g}[i]^{\hat{x}\hat{y}} = \hat{Z}: \\
02 \;\; (L, \boldsymbol{x}') \leftarrow_\$ \mathcal{A}^{\text{DDH}}(\boldsymbol{\mathcal{G}}, \boldsymbol{X}) & 08 \;\;\;\;\; \text{return } 1 \\
03 \;\; \text{if } |L| < m: \text{return } 0 & 09 \;\; \text{else: return } 0 \\
04 \;\; \text{if } \boldsymbol{x}'[L] = \boldsymbol{x}[L]: \text{return } 1 & \\
05 \;\; \text{else: return } 0 &
\end{array}
$$

$$
\begin{array}{lll}
\textbf{Procedure } \text{PGen}[\text{high}] & \textbf{Procedure } \text{PGen}[\text{med}] & \textbf{Procedure } \text{PGen}[\text{low}] \\
10 \;\; \boldsymbol{\mathcal{G}} = (\mathbb{G}, p, g) \leftarrow_\$ \text{GGen} & 13 \;\; (\mathbb{G}, p, g) \leftarrow_\$ \text{GGen} & 17 \;\; \boldsymbol{\mathcal{G}}[\cdot] \leftarrow_\$ \text{GGen} \\
11 \;\; \boldsymbol{\mathcal{G}}[\cdot] \leftarrow \boldsymbol{\mathcal{G}} & 14 \;\; \boldsymbol{g} \leftarrow_\$ (\mathbb{G} \setminus \{1\})^n & 18 \;\; \text{return } \boldsymbol{\mathcal{G}} \\
12 \;\; \text{return } \boldsymbol{\mathcal{G}} & 15 \;\; \boldsymbol{\mathcal{G}}[\cdot] \leftarrow (\mathbb{G}, p, \boldsymbol{g}[\cdot]) & \\
& 16 \;\; \text{return } \boldsymbol{\mathcal{G}} &
\end{array}
$$

Fig. 3. Security game $G_{\text{GGen,gran}}^{(m,n)\text{-gdl}}(\mathcal{A})$ for $\text{gran} \in \{\text{high}, \text{med}, \text{low}\}$ modeling the m-out-of-n multi-instance gap discrete logarithm problem.

$$
\begin{array}{ll}
\textbf{Game } G_{\text{GGen,gran}}^{(m,n)\text{-gcdh}}(\mathcal{A}) & \textbf{Oracle } \text{DDH}(i, \hat{X}, \hat{Y}, \hat{Z}) \\
00 \;\; \boldsymbol{\mathcal{G}} \leftarrow_\$ \text{PGen}[\text{gran}] & 08 \;\; \text{parse } \hat{X}, \hat{Y} \text{ as } \boldsymbol{g}[i]^{\hat{x}}, \boldsymbol{g}[i]^{\hat{y}} \\
01 \;\; \boldsymbol{x}[\cdot] \leftarrow_\$ \mathbb{Z}_{\boldsymbol{p}[\cdot]}; \; \boldsymbol{X}[\cdot] \leftarrow \boldsymbol{g}[\cdot]^{\boldsymbol{x}[\cdot]} & 09 \;\; \text{if } \boldsymbol{g}[i]^{\hat{x}\hat{y}} = \hat{Z}: \\
02 \;\; \boldsymbol{y}[\cdot] \leftarrow_\$ \mathbb{Z}_{\boldsymbol{p}[\cdot]}; \; \boldsymbol{Y}[\cdot] \leftarrow \boldsymbol{g}[\cdot]^{\boldsymbol{y}[\cdot]} & 10 \;\;\;\;\; \text{return } 1 \\
03 \;\; \boldsymbol{Z}[\cdot] \leftarrow \boldsymbol{g}[\cdot]^{\boldsymbol{x}[\cdot]\boldsymbol{y}[\cdot]} & 11 \;\; \text{else: return } 0 \\
04 \;\; (L, \boldsymbol{Z}') \leftarrow_\$ \mathcal{A}^{\text{DDH}}(\boldsymbol{\mathcal{G}}, \boldsymbol{X}, \boldsymbol{Y}) & \\
05 \;\; \text{if } |L| < m: \text{return } 0 & \\
06 \;\; \text{if } \boldsymbol{Z}[L] = \boldsymbol{Z}'[L]: \text{return } 1 & \\
07 \;\; \text{else: return } 0 &
\end{array}
$$

Fig. 4. Security game $G_{\text{GGen,gran}}^{(m,n)\text{-gcdh}}(\mathcal{A})$ for $\text{gran} \in \{\text{high}, \text{med}, \text{low}\}$ modeling the m-out-of-n multi-instance gap computational Diffie-Hellman problem. PGen is defined in Fig. 3.

The corresponding challenge vectors contain the group elements $\boldsymbol{X}[i] = \boldsymbol{g}[i]^{\boldsymbol{x}[i]}$ and $\boldsymbol{Y}[i] = \boldsymbol{g}[i]^{\boldsymbol{y}[i]}$. Additionally, the adversary has access to an oracle DDH, which behaves as described for $G_{\text{GGen,gran}}^{(m,n)\text{-gdl}}(\mathcal{A})$. At the end of the game, adversary $\mathcal{A}$ outputs a list of indices $L \subseteq [1 .. n]$ and a vector $\boldsymbol{Z}'$ of length n, where the i-th entry is an element of the group represented by $\boldsymbol{\mathcal{G}}[i]$. The adversary wins if L contains at least m elements and if the vector $\boldsymbol{Z}'$ coincides with $\boldsymbol{Z}$ for all indices in L. We define $\mathcal{A}$'s advantage in game $G_{\text{GGen,gran}}^{(m,n)\text{-gcdh}}(\mathcal{A})$ as

$$
\text{Adv}_{\text{GGen,gran}}^{(m,n)\text{-gcdh}}(\mathcal{A}) = \Pr[G_{\text{GGen,gran}}^{(m,n)\text{-gcdh}}(\mathcal{A})].
$$

The m-out-of-n multi-instance computational Diffie-Hellman $((m, n)\text{-CDH})$ problem is defined as $(m, n)\text{-GapCDH}$ with the restriction that $\mathcal{A}$ cannot query oracle DDH.

4   Hashed ElGamal in the Multi-Instance Setting

We investigate the multi-instance security of the well-known Hashed-ElGamal key-encapsulation mechanism [1]. We consider three variants, HEG[GGen, high], HEG[GGen, med], and HEG[GGen, low], corresponding to high, medium, and low granularity respectively. After giving formal definitions of these variants in Sect. 4.1, in Sect. 4.2 we prove the main result of this section: The multi-instance security of each variant of the KEM in the random oracle model is tightly implied by the hardness of (m, n)-GapCDH[GGen, gran] for the corresponding granularity. Finally, in Sect. 4.3 we compute lower bounds on the scaling factor of HEG[GGen, gran] for GGen $\in \{$GGen$_{\mathbb{F}_\ell^*}$, GGen$_{\mathbb{E}(\mathbb{F}_\ell)}\}$ and gran $\in \{$high, med, low$\}$.

4.1   Hashed-ElGamal Key Encapsulation

We consider three variants of the Hashed-ElGamal KEM, defined relative to a hash function H and differing in the way parameters and key pairs are generated. For high granularity the parameters specify a group description $\mathcal{G} = (\mathbb{G}, p, g)$ with a fixed generator g. Key pairs (pk, sk) are of the form $pk = X = g^x$ and $sk = x$, where x is randomly sampled in $\mathbb{Z}_p$. For medium granularity the parameters consist of a group $\mathbb{G}$ of order p, but no fixed generator. In this case $pk = (g, g^x)$ and $sk = (g, x)$, where g is a randomly chosen generator of the group $\mathbb{G}$. Finally, for low granularity empty parameters are used. Correspondingly, in this case public keys are of the form $pk = (\mathcal{G}, g^x)$ and secret keys of the form $sk = (\mathcal{G}, x)$, where $\mathcal{G} = (\mathbb{G}, p, g)$ is a freshly sampled group description.

Note that in all three cases the parameters par and a key pair (pk, sk) generated with respect to par determine a group description $(\mathbb{G}, p, g)$ as well as x and X. In all three variants encapsulated keys are of the form $H(pk, g^y, X^y)$ with corresponding ciphertext g^y, where the y is sampled at random in $\mathbb{Z}_p$. The decapsulation of a ciphertext c is given by $H(pk, c, c^x)$. A formal description of the algorithms describing the Hashed-ElGamal key-encapsulation mechanism for each of the three considered variants can be found in Fig. 5.

4.2   Multi-Instance Security of Hashed ElGamal

The following theorem shows that (m, n)-GapCDH tightly reduces to the security against chosen-ciphertext attacks of HEG in the multi-instance setting for the corresponding granularity[3]. Its proof is a generalization of the single-instance version [1] and can be found in the full version of the paper [3].

Theorem 2. *Let $m, n \in \mathbb{N}$ with $1 \leq m \leq n$, let gran $\in \{$high, med, low$\}$, let GGen be a group-generating algorithm, and let HEG[GGen, gran] be the Hashed-ElGamal KEM of Fig. 5 relative to hash function H. If H is modeled as a random oracle and if the (m, n)-GapCDH[GGen, gran] problem is hard, then*

---

[3] The same result holds under the multi-instance version of the strong Diffie-Hellman assumption [1], a falsifiable assumption that is implied by (m, n)-GapCDH.

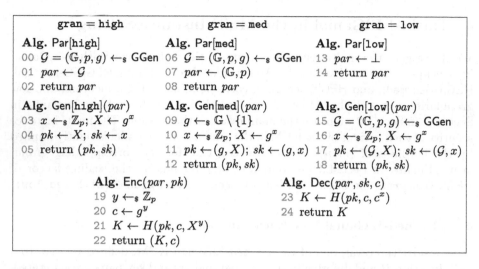

Fig. 5. Variants of Hashed-ElGamal KEM HEG[GGen, high], HEG[GGen, med], and HEG[GGen, low] relative to hash function H and group-generating algorithm GGen. The KEMs share the same encapsulation and decapsulation algorithms. Note that both (par, pk) or (par, sk) determine group description $(\mathbb{G}, p, g)$ and key pk.

HEG[GGen, gran] *is (m, n)-CCA secure. Formally, for every adversary $\mathcal{A}$ against game* $G_{\text{HEG[GGen,gran]}}^{(m,n)\text{-cca}}$ *making at most q queries to random oracle RO there exists an adversary $\mathcal{B}$ against game* $G_{\text{GGen,gran}}^{(m,n)\text{-gcdh}}$ *that makes at most q queries to DDH and runs in essentially the same time as $\mathcal{A}$ and satisfies*

$$\text{Adv}_{\text{GGen,gran}}^{(m,n)\text{-gcdh}}(\mathcal{B}) \geq \text{Adv}_{\text{HEG[GGen,gran]}}^{(m,n)\text{-cca}}(\mathcal{A}).$$

4.3   Scaling Factor of Hashed ElGamal for Different Parameters

Below we compute the scaling factor of Hashed-ElGamal key encapsulation for different parameter choices. Recall that the scaling factor is given by

$$\text{SF}_{\text{HEG[GGen,gran]}}^{(m,n)\text{-cca}} = \text{MinTime}_{\text{HEG[GGen,gran]}}^{(m,n)\text{-cca}} / \text{MinTime}_{\text{HEG[GGen,gran]}}^{(1,1)\text{-cca}}.$$

Note that the multi-instance security of HEG can be broken by computing m public keys, which corresponds to computing m DL instances. On the other hand, from Theorem 2 we know that the (m, n)-CCA-security of HEG is tightly implied by (m, n)-GapCDH. Thus,

$$\text{MinTime}_{\text{GGen,gran}}^{(m,n)\text{-gcdh}} \leq \text{MinTime}_{\text{HEG[GGen,gran]}}^{(m,n)\text{-cca}} \leq \text{MinTime}_{\text{GGen,gran}}^{(m,n)\text{-dl}}.$$

Hence, we can bound the scaling factor of Hashed ElGamal as

$$\text{SF}_{\text{HEG[GGen,gran]}}^{(m,n)\text{-cca}} \geq \text{MinTime}_{\text{GGen,gran}}^{(m,n)\text{-gcdh}} / \text{MinTime}_{\text{GGen,gran}}^{(1,1)\text{-dl}}.$$

Below we consider two instantiations of group-generating algorithms: $\mathsf{GGen}_{\mathbb{F}_\ell^*}$ and $\mathsf{GGen}_{\mathbb{E}(\mathbb{F}_\ell)}$. Due to either Hypothesis 1 from the introduction or the results of Sects. 5 and 6 respectively, for both instantiations solving (m,n)-GapCDH is as hard as (m,n)-GapDL. Thus, the lower bounds on the scaling factor derived below are sharp.

HASHED ELGAMAL IN THE FINITE-FIELD SETTING. Assuming the correctness of Hypothesis 1, we conclude that $\mathrm{MinTime}_{\mathbb{F}_\ell^*,\mathrm{gran}}^{(m,n)\text{-gcdh}} = \mathrm{MinTime}_{\mathbb{F}_\ell^*,\mathrm{gran}}^{(m,n)\text{-dl}}$ is given by

$$L_\ell(1/3, 1.902) + m \cdot L_\ell(1/3, 1.232) \quad \text{for } \mathrm{gran} \in \{\mathrm{high}, \mathrm{med}\}, \text{ and}$$

$$\min\{m \cdot L_\ell(1/3, 1.902), L_\ell(1/3, 2.007) + m \cdot L_\ell(1/3, 1.639)\} \quad \text{for } \mathrm{gran} = \mathrm{low}.$$

We obtain the scaling factor by dividing by $\mathrm{MinTime}_{\mathbb{F}_\ell^*,\mathrm{gran}}^{(1,1)\text{-dl}} = L_\ell(1/3, 1.902)$. Defining δ via $m = L_\ell(1/3, \delta)$ we can rewrite $m \cdot L_\ell(1/3, 1.232)$ as $L_\ell(1/3, \delta + 1.232)$. For $\delta \leq 0.67$ we get $L_\ell(1/3, 1.902) \geq L_\ell(1/3, \delta + 1.232)$. Hence for these values of δ the scaling factor for medium and high granularity is roughly 1. For larger m, on the other hand, it is of order $L_\ell(1/3, \delta - 0.67)$.

Summing up for $\mathrm{gran} \in \{\mathrm{med}, \mathrm{high}\}$ we obtain

$$\mathrm{SF}_{\mathrm{HEG}[\mathsf{GGen}_{\mathbb{F}_\ell^*},\mathrm{gran}]}^{(m,n)\text{-cca}} = \begin{cases} 1 & \delta \leq 0.67 \\ L_\ell(1/3, \delta - 0.67) & \delta > 0.67 \end{cases}.$$

Further, we get $L_\ell(1/3, \delta + 1.902) \leq L_\ell(1/3, 2.007)$ for $\delta \leq 0.105$. Hence in this case for low granularity the scaling factor is given by $m = L_\ell(1/3, \delta)$. Moreover, we obtain $L_\ell(1/3, \delta + 1.639) = L(1/3, 2.007)$ for $\delta = 0.368$ implying that for $0.105 \leq \delta \leq 0.368$ the scaling factor is of order $L_\ell(1/3, 2.007 - 1.902)$ and of order $L_\ell(1/3, \delta + 1.639 - 1.902)$ for larger values of δ. Summing up:

$$\mathrm{SF}_{\mathrm{HEG}[\mathsf{GGen}_{\mathbb{F}_\ell^*},\mathrm{low}]}^{(m,n)\text{-cca}} = \begin{cases} L_\ell(1/3, \delta) & 0 \leq \delta < 0.105 \\ L_\ell(1/3, 0.105) & 0.105 \leq \delta < 0.368 \\ L_\ell(1/3, -0.263 + \delta) & 0.368 \leq \delta \end{cases}.$$

Formally, the asymptotic behavior of the scaling factor computed above is linear[4] in m and hence, at first glance, seems optimal. However, as discussed in the introduction, the numbers of $L_\ell(1/3, 0.67)$ or $L_\ell(1/3, 0.368)$ instances starting from which the cumulative cost of breaking the instances outweighs the cost of the precomputation are typically large.

HASHED ELGAMAL IN THE ELLIPTIC-CURVE SETTING. Recall that $\mathsf{GGen}_{\mathbb{E}(\mathbb{F}_\ell)}$ generates elliptic curves of size $p \approx \ell$ defined over the field $\mathbb{F}_\ell$ for randomly chosen ℓ. If we model elliptic curves as generic groups we can derive the scaling factor as follows. Ignoring constants, a single DL instance can be solved in time $O(\sqrt{p})$.

---

[4] For fixed ℓ and very large values of m and n generic attacks start to outperform the NFS and the scaling factor actually becomes $\Theta(\sqrt{m})$.

The lower bounds derived in Sect. 6 (Corollaries 2 and 3 and Theorem 5) imply the following: A generic algorithm solving (m, n)-GapCDH for high and medium granularity performs at least $\Omega(\sqrt{mp})$ group operations; the low-granularity case requires at least $\Omega(m\sqrt{p})$ group operations. (In the low-granularity case we formally consider n groups of differing group orders $p_1, \ldots, p_n$, where all p_i are roughly of size p.) Summing up, we obtain

$$\text{SF}_{\text{HEG[GGen}_{\mathbb{E}(\mathbb{F}_\ell)},\text{gran]}}^{(m,n)\text{-cca}} = \begin{cases} \Theta(\sqrt{mp}/\sqrt{p}) = \Theta(\sqrt{m}) & \text{gran} \in \{\text{high, med}\} \\ \Theta(m\sqrt{p}/\sqrt{p}) = \Theta(m) & \text{gran} = \text{low} \end{cases}.$$

(The constants hidden within the Θ notation can be made explicit from our results, and are between 0.1 and 6.6.) In the full version of the paper [3] we additionally illustrate how the scaling factors computed above could be taken into account when choosing parameters for HEG.

5   Generic Hardness of the Multi-Instance Gap Discrete Logarithm Problem

In this section we define a new hard problem, namely the polycheck discrete logarithm problem (PolyDL), in the multi-instance setting. Then, we proceed to show a concrete bound on its security in the generic group model (Theorem 3). Most notably, from this bound we present a concrete bound on the security of GapDL. To prove the bound we define an additional problem, the *search-by-hypersurface* problem (SHS). In Sect. 5.1 we define the PolyDL and SHS problems. In Sect. 5.2 we derive the bound on the security of GapDL in the high granularity setting, and further argue that it is optimal. Bounds for the cases of medium and low granularity can be found in the full version of the paper [3].

5.1   Polycheck Discrete Logarithm and Search-by-Hypersurface Problem

POLYCHECK DISCRETE LOGARITHM PROBLEM. The m-out-of-n multi-instance polycheck discrete logarithm problem $((m, n)$-d-PolyDL) for polynomials of degree at most d requires to find the discrete logarithms of at least m out of n input group elements given access to a decisional oracle Eval which behaves as follows. Eval takes as input a polynomial $f \in \mathbb{Z}_p[X_1, \ldots, X_k]$ of degree at most d and a list of group elements $(g^{\hat{x}_1}, \ldots, g^{\hat{x}_k})$, where k is an arbitrary integer, and returns 1 if and only if $g^{f(\hat{x}_1, \ldots, \hat{x}_k)} = 1$. As usual, we consider three variants of the problem, which differ in their granularity.

Formally, let $m, n, d \in \mathbb{N}$ such that $1 \leq m \leq n$, $d \geq 1$, and consider game $\text{G}_{\text{GGen,gran}}^{(m,n)\text{-}d\text{-polydl}}(\mathcal{A})$ of Fig. 6 associated with adversary $\mathcal{A}$ and granularity $\text{gran} \in \{\text{high, med, low}\}$. In the game, a vector $\mathcal{G}$ of n group descriptions is set up according to the desired level of granularity using PGen[gran]. After the setup of $\mathcal{G}$ the three variants of the game proceed in the same way. A vector $\boldsymbol{x}$ of length n is sampled, where $\boldsymbol{x}[i]$ is uniformly distributed in $\mathbb{Z}_{\boldsymbol{p}[i]}$.

Game $G_{\mathsf{GGen,gran}}^{(m,n)\text{-}d\text{-}\mathrm{polydl}}(\mathcal{A})$	**Oracle** $\mathrm{Eval}(i, f, \hat{\boldsymbol{X}})$
00 $\boldsymbol{\mathcal{G}} \leftarrow_{\$} \mathsf{PGen[gran]}$	06 if $\deg f > d$: return 0
01 $\boldsymbol{x}[\cdot] \leftarrow_{\$} \mathbb{Z}_{\boldsymbol{p}[\cdot]};\; \boldsymbol{X}[\cdot] \leftarrow \boldsymbol{g}[\cdot]^{\boldsymbol{x}[\cdot]}$	07 parse $\hat{\boldsymbol{X}}$ as $\boldsymbol{g}[i]^{\hat{\boldsymbol{x}}}$
02 $(L, \boldsymbol{x}') \leftarrow_{\$} \mathcal{A}^{\mathrm{Eval}}(\boldsymbol{\mathcal{G}}, \boldsymbol{X})$	08 if $\boldsymbol{g}[i]^{f(\hat{\boldsymbol{x}})} = 1$:
03 if $|L| < m$: return 0	09 return 1
04 if $\boldsymbol{x}'[L] = \boldsymbol{x}[L]$: return 1	10 else: return 0
05 else: return 0	

Fig. 6. Security game $G_{\mathsf{GGen,gran}}^{(m,n)\text{-}d\text{-}\mathrm{polydl}}(\mathcal{A})$ relative to $\mathsf{GGen, gran}$, modeling the m-out-of-n multi-instance polycheck discrete logarithm problem for polynomials of degree at most d. We assume that polynomial f input to Eval has $|\hat{\boldsymbol{X}}|$ indeterminates. PGen is defined in Fig. 3.

The corresponding challenge vector contains the group elements $\boldsymbol{X}[i] = \boldsymbol{g}[i]^{\boldsymbol{x}[i]}$. At the end of the game, adversary $\mathcal{A}$ outputs a list of indices $L \subseteq [1 \mathinner{.\,.} n]$ and a vector $\boldsymbol{x}'$ of length n, where the i-th entry is in $\mathbb{Z}_{\boldsymbol{p}[i]}$. The adversary wins if L contains at least m elements and if the vector $\boldsymbol{x}'$ coincides with $\boldsymbol{x}$ for all indices in L. Additionally, the adversary has access to an evaluation oracle Eval, which on input of an index $i \in [1 \mathinner{.\,.} n]$, a polynomial $f \in \mathbb{Z}_p[X_1, \ldots, X_k]$, and a list of group elements $\hat{\boldsymbol{X}} = (\hat{\boldsymbol{X}}[1], \ldots, \hat{\boldsymbol{X}}[k])$, where k is an arbitrary integer which might be different on different calls, behaves as follows. If $\deg f > d$, then Eval returns 0. Otherwise, the game computes the discrete logarithms $\hat{\boldsymbol{x}}$ of the input elements $\hat{\boldsymbol{X}}$ with respect to generator $\boldsymbol{g}[i]$, and then returns 1 if and only if $\boldsymbol{g}[i]^{f(\hat{\boldsymbol{x}}[1],\ldots,\hat{\boldsymbol{x}}[k])} = 1$.

We define the advantage of $\mathcal{A}$ in game $G_{\mathsf{GGen,gran}}^{(m,n)\text{-}d\text{-}\mathrm{polydl}}(\mathcal{A})$ as

$$\mathrm{Adv}_{\mathsf{GGen,gran}}^{(m,n)\text{-}d\text{-}\mathrm{polydl}}(\mathcal{A}) = \Pr[G_{\mathsf{GGen,gran}}^{(m,n)\text{-}d\text{-}\mathrm{polydl}}(\mathcal{A})].$$

The next definition extends the search-by-hyperplane-query problem (SHQ) by Yun [30].

SEARCH-BY-HYPERSURFACE PROBLEM. The search-by-hypersurface problem in dimension n for polynomials of degree at most d (n-SHS_d) requires to find a randomly sampled point $\boldsymbol{a}$ of the space by adaptively checking whether point $\boldsymbol{a}$ is contained in the queried hypersurface (i.e., the set of zeroes of a polynomial).

Formally, let $n, d, p \in \mathbb{N}$ such that p is prime and $d, n \geq 1$, and consider game $G_p^{n\text{-}\mathrm{shs}_d}(\mathcal{A})$ of Fig. 7 associated with adversary $\mathcal{A}$. In the game, a vector $\boldsymbol{a}$ of length n is sampled, where $\boldsymbol{a}[i]$ is uniformly distributed in $\mathbb{Z}_p$. At the end of the game, adversary $\mathcal{A}$ outputs a vector $\boldsymbol{a}' \in \mathbb{Z}_p^n$. The adversary wins if $\boldsymbol{a}' = \boldsymbol{a}$. Additionally, the adversary has access to an evaluation oracle Eval, which on input of a polynomial $f \in \mathbb{Z}_p[X_1, \ldots, X_n]$ behaves as follows. If $\deg f > d$, then Eval returns 0. Otherwise, the oracle returns 1 if and only if $f(\boldsymbol{a}) = 0$.

We define the advantage of $\mathcal{A}$ in game $G_p^{n\text{-}\mathrm{shs}_d}(\mathcal{A})$ as

$$\mathrm{Adv}_p^{n\text{-}\mathrm{shs}_d}(\mathcal{A}) = \Pr[G_p^{n\text{-}\mathrm{shs}_d}(\mathcal{A})].$$

Game $G_p^{n\text{-shs}_d}(\mathcal{A})$	Oracle $\text{Eval}(f)$
00 $\boldsymbol{a} \leftarrow_\$ \mathbb{Z}_p^n$	04 if $\deg(f) > d$: return 0
01 $\boldsymbol{a}' \leftarrow_\$ \mathcal{A}^{\text{Eval}}(p)$	05 if $f(\boldsymbol{a}) = 0$: return 1
02 if $\boldsymbol{a}' = \boldsymbol{a}$: return 1	06 else: return 0
03 else: return 0	

Fig. 7. Security game $G_p^{n\text{-shs}_d}(\mathcal{A})$ with respect to integer d and prime p modeling the search-by-hypersurface problem on dimension n for polynomials of degree at most d. All inputs f to oracle Eval are elements of the polynomial ring $\mathbb{Z}_p[X_1, \ldots, X_n]$.

5.2   Generic Hardness of High-Granularity (m, n)-d-PolyDL

Below, we state the main result of this section, an explicit upper bound on the security of high-granularity (n, n)-d-PolyDL in the generic group model.

Note that this bound is of particular interest in the context of generic bilinear (or even multilinear) maps. In fact, a d-linear map yields a natural way to compute any answer of oracle Eval for polynomials of degree at most d in the base group.

Theorem 3. *Let n, d be positive integers and p a prime number. Let GGen_{gg} be a group-generating algorithm that generates generic groups of exactly size p. Then for every generic adversary $\mathcal{A}$ against (n, n)-d-PolyDL$[\mathsf{GGen}_{gg}, \mathsf{high}]$ that makes at most q queries to the group-operation oracle and q_{Eval} queries to oracle Eval:*

$$\text{Adv}_{\mathsf{GGen}_{gg}, \mathsf{high}}^{(n,n)\text{-}d\text{-polydl}}(\mathcal{A}) \leq \left(\frac{d}{p}\right)^n + \frac{1}{2}\left(\frac{ed(q+n+1)^2 + 2edq_{\text{Eval}}}{2np}\right)^n.$$

This extends [30, Corollary 2] from standard DL to the polycheck case. Most importantly, it allows us to prove the following corollary.

Corollary 1. *Let n be any positive integer and GGen_{gg} be a group-generating algorithm that generates generic groups of at least size p. Then for every generic adversary $\mathcal{A}$ against (n, n)-GapDL$[\mathsf{GGen}_{gg}, \mathsf{high}]$ that makes at most q queries to the group-operation oracle and q_{DDH} queries to the DDH oracle:*

$$\text{Adv}_{\mathsf{GGen}_{gg}, \mathsf{high}}^{(n,n)\text{-gdl}}(\mathcal{A}) \leq \left(\frac{2}{p}\right)^n + \frac{1}{2}\left(\frac{e(q+n+1)^2 + 2eq_{\text{DDH}}}{np}\right)^n \approx \left(\frac{q^2}{np}\right)^n.$$

Proof (Corollary 1). Note that oracle DDH of game (n, n)-GapDL can be simulated using oracle Eval from game (n, n)-2-PolyDL. In fact, $g^{xy} = g^z$ if and only if $g^{f(x,y,z)} = 1$, with $f(X_1, X_2, X_3) := X_1 X_2 - X_3$. Then apply Theorem 3 with $d = 2$. □

The result is optimal. Concretely, in the full version of the paper [3] we construct an algorithm that solves (n, n)-GapDL$[\mathsf{GGen}_{gg}, \mathsf{high}]$ in q group operations with success probability $(q^2/4np)^n$. Thus, for large p the fastest generic adversary solving (n, n)-GapDL$[\mathsf{GGen}_{gg}, \mathsf{high}]$ with overwhelming success probability requires $\sqrt{np/e} \leq q \leq 2\sqrt{np}$ group operations.

The proof of Theorem 3 follows a structure similar to Yun [30]. First we prove the equivalence of $n\text{-SHS}_d[p]$ and $(n,n)\text{-}d\text{-PolyDL}[\mathsf{GGen}_{\mathsf{gg}}, \mathtt{high}]$, and then we bound the success probability of an adversary against $n\text{-SHS}_d[p]$. The equivalence of the two problems corresponds to the lemma below.

Statement and proof closely follow [30, Theorem 1] while additionally handling Eval queries. The proof can be found the full version of the paper [3].

Lemma 2. *Let n, d be positive integers and p a prime number. Let $\mathsf{GGen}_{\mathsf{gg}}$ be a group-generating algorithm that generates generic groups of exactly size p. Then for every adversary $\mathcal{A}$ against game $(n,n)\text{-}d\text{-PolyDL}[\mathsf{GGen}_{\mathsf{gg}}, \mathtt{high}]$ there exists an adversary $\mathcal{B}$ against $n\text{-SHS}_d[p]$ such that*

$$\mathrm{Adv}_p^{n\text{-shs}_d}(\mathcal{B}) \geq \mathrm{Adv}_{\mathsf{GGen}_{\mathsf{gg}}, \mathtt{high}}^{(n,n)\text{-}d\text{-polydl}}(\mathcal{A}).$$

Moreover, if $\mathcal{A}$ makes q group-operation queries and q_{Eval} queries to Eval, then $\mathcal{B}$ makes at most $q_{\mathrm{Eval}} + (n+q)(n+q+1)/2$ queries to Eval.

We start working on $n\text{-SHS}_d[p]$ with the next lemma. Here we express that, up to a loss of d^n, an adversary against $n\text{-SHS}_d[p]$ does not need more than n hypersurface queries which return 1 to identify a solution.

Importantly, observe how we limit the resources of an adversary against $n\text{-SHS}_d[p]$ exclusively in terms of its queries to Eval. Our adversaries are otherwise unbounded. For this reason, the following reduction does not consider the computational resources needed by the adversary to perform its operations. The proof is in the full version of the paper [3].

Lemma 3. *Let n, d be positive integers and p a prime number. For every adversary $\mathcal{A}$ against $n\text{-SHS}_d[p]$ that makes at most q queries to Eval there exists an adversary $\mathcal{B}$ against $n\text{-SHS}_d[p]$ that makes at most q queries to Eval such that at most n of them return 1 and*

$$\mathrm{Adv}_p^{n\text{-shs}_d}(\mathcal{B}) \geq d^{-n}\mathrm{Adv}_p^{n\text{-shs}_d}(\mathcal{A}).$$

PROOF IDEA. Intuition for the proof is simple for the case $n = 1$: All queries of $\mathcal{A}$ to SimEval are forwarded to Eval. The first time $\mathrm{Eval}(g)$ returns 1, we know that the secret $\boldsymbol{a}$ must be a zero of g. Since g has degree at most d, there can be at most d distinct zeroes. The reduction guesses which zero is the correct one (this is the reduction loss) and then simulates the remaining queries of $\mathcal{A}$ to SimEval accordingly. The proof is similar for $n > 1$. We know that, in general, n polynomials in $\mathbb{Z}_p[X_1, \ldots, X_n]$ of degree d have at most d^n zeroes in common, one of which the reduction can use to simulate remaining queries to SimEval. However, the n queried polynomials must be in general position: For example, the zeroes of $x_1 + x_2$ are the same as those of $2x_1 + 2x_2$, and querying both polynomials would not help the reduction. To resolve this issue, the reduction keeps a set Z of common zeroes to all polynomials seen so far which, when forwarded to Eval, make the oracle return 1 (i.e., polynomials which vanish on $\boldsymbol{a}$). This set has a rich structure: In fact, the study of zero sets of polynomial is the raison d'être of the field of algebraic geometry. If the polynomial g queried by $\mathcal{A}$ carries no new information (i.e., $g(Z) = \{0\}$) then the simulated oracle returns 1 without forwarding. Otherwise, the polynomial is forwarded. If the answer is 1, then the reduction updates the set Z and then guesses which one of its irreducible components contains $\boldsymbol{a}$, which becomes the updated Z. The identification of irreducible components is made possible by the underlying structure of the set Z. Selecting an irreducible component guarantees that, on a following evaluation query, intersecting the now irreducible Z with another hypersurface not containing Z brings down the dimension of Z by 1. Since the dimension of $\mathbb{Z}_p^n$ is n, we can have at most n such queries. With a careful choice of the guessing probability of each irreducible component, Bézout's theorem ensures that the probability of always making the right guess is again d^{-n}. $\square$

Remark 1. The bound on the advantage against (n, n)-d-PolyDL[$\mathsf{GGen_{gg}}, \mathsf{high}$] of Theorem 3 extends to (m, n)-d-PolyDL[$\mathsf{GGen_{gg}}, \mathsf{high}$], for $m \lesssim n$. This is done by a simple tight reduction between problems (m, n)-d-PolyDL[$\mathsf{GGen_{gg}}, \mathsf{high}$] and (m, m)-d-PolyDL[$\mathsf{GGen_{gg}}, \mathsf{high}$]. The reduction extends the one for standard multi-instance discrete logarithm [29, Section 3] by also simulating oracle Eval: It simply forwards every query to its own oracle.

6   Generic Hardness of the Multi-Instance Gap Computational Diffie-Hellman Problem

In this section we derive lower bounds on the hardness of the m-out-of-n gap computational Diffie-Hellman problem in the generic group model for different granularities. We further argue that all derived bounds are optimal. Section 6.1 covers high, Sect. 6.2 medium, and Sect. 6.3 low granularity.

6.1   Generic Hardness of High-Granularity (m, n)-GapCDH

We work in the algebraic group model to show that the generic lower bound on the hardness of high-granularity (m, m)-GapDL carries over to high-granularity (m, n)-GapCDH. Concretely, in Theorem 4 we provide a generic reduction from (m, n)-GapCDH[$\mathsf{GGen}, \mathsf{high}$] to (m, m)-GapDL[$\mathsf{GGen}, \mathsf{high}$]. Then, an application of Corollary 1 establishes the desired bound on (m, n)-GapCDH.

In this section we work with high-granularity problems, in which the group description $\mathcal{G} = (\mathbb{G}, p, g)$ is shared by all instances. For ease of notation, we treat $\mathcal{G}$ as an implicit parameter of the system until the end of this section.

The generic reduction from (m, n)-GapCDH to (m, m)-GapDL in the high-granularity setting is sketched below. The full proof can be found in the full version of the paper [3].

Theorem 4. *Let* GGen *be a group-generating algorithm that generates groups of at least size* p, *and let* m, n *be two positive integers such that* $m \leq n \leq p$. *Then*

*there exists a generic reduction that constructs from any algebraic adversary $\mathcal{A}$
against game* $\mathrm{G}_{\mathsf{GGen},\mathsf{high}}^{(m,n)\text{-gcdh}}$ *an algebraic adversary* $\mathcal{B}$ *against* $\mathrm{G}_{\mathsf{GGen},\mathsf{high}}^{(m,m)\text{-gdl}}$ *such that*

$$\mathrm{Adv}_{\mathsf{GGen},\mathsf{high}}^{(m,m)\text{-gdl}}(\mathcal{B}) \geq 2^{-m}\,\mathrm{Adv}_{\mathsf{GGen},\mathsf{high}}^{(m,n)\text{-gcdh}}(\mathcal{A}).$$

Moreover, $\mathcal{B}$ *makes at most* $2n(m+2)(\log p + 1)$ *group operations in addition to
those made by* $\mathcal{A}$, *and the same amount of queries to* DDH.

Despite the seemingly sizeable reduction loss of 2^m, we argue that the factor
is small in the context of the final security bounds. In fact, as seen in Sect. 5,
the advantage in breaking (m, m)-GapDL decreases exponentially with m. This
renders the exponential contribution of the factor 2^m irrelevant, as the following concrete bound on the hardness of (m, n)-GapCDH[$\mathsf{GGen}_{\mathsf{gg}}$, high] shows. Its
proof can be found in the full version of the paper [3].

Corollary 2. *Let* $\mathsf{GGen}_{\mathsf{gg}}$ *be a group-generating algorithm that generates groups
of at least size* p, *and let* m, n *be two positive integers such that* $m \leq n \leq p$.
Then for every generic adversary $\mathcal{A}$ *against* (m, n)-GapCDH[$\mathsf{GGen}_{\mathsf{gg}}$, high] *that
makes at most* q *queries to the group-operation oracle and* q_{DDH} *queries to the
gap oracle:*

$$\mathrm{Adv}_{\mathsf{GGen}_{\mathsf{gg}},\mathsf{high}}^{(m,n)\text{-gcdh}}(\mathcal{A}) \leq \left(\frac{2e(q + 12mn\log p)^2 + 4eq_{\mathrm{DDH}}}{mp}\right)^m \approx \left(\frac{q^2}{mp}\right)^m.$$

Similarly to the bound for computing discrete logarithms, this result is opti-
mal. Namely, problem (m, n)-GapCDH[$\mathsf{GGen}_{\mathsf{gg}}$, high] can be solved computing q
group operations with success probability $(q^2/4mp)^m$ by using the generic adversary against high-granularity DL provided in the full version [3]. Thus, for large p
the fastest generic adversary solving (m, n)-GapCDH[$\mathsf{GGen}_{\mathsf{gg}}$, high] with overwhelming success probability requires $\sqrt{mp/2e} \leq q \leq 2\sqrt{mp}$ group operations.

PROOF IDEA OF THEOREM 4. This proof extends the following simple single-
instance reduction $\mathcal{B}$, in turn built from two reductions $\mathcal{B}_\emptyset$ and $\mathcal{B}_{\{1\}}$. The reductions build upon a CDH adversary $\mathcal{A}$. Adversary $\mathcal{A}$ receives $X = g^x$ and $Y = g^y$,
and is tasked with computing $W = g^{xy}$. In the algebraic group model, $\mathcal{A}$ must
return a representation of the output as a combination of its input, i.e., some
elements $a, b, c \in \mathbb{Z}_p$ such that $W = X^aY^bg^c$. Rewriting this expression in the
exponents, we obtain that, if $\mathcal{A}$ wins,

$$xy = ax + by + c.$$

Given a DL challenge $Z = g^z$, reduction $\mathcal{B}_\emptyset$ embeds the challenge as $X = Z$
and generates $Y = g^y$ by picking a random y. Then, $\mathcal{B}_\emptyset$ can compute the DL
as $z = x = (y - a)^{-1}(by + c)$. However, $y - a$ might not be invertible. In this
case, adversary $\mathcal{B}_{\{1\}}$ would be successful: It embeds the challenge as $Y = Z$ and
returns a, which is a correct solution if $y - a$ is not invertible. Reduction $\mathcal{B}$ picks
one of the two subsets $I \subseteq \{1\}$ at random and runs $\mathcal{B}_I$. If the CDH adversary is
successful, then $\mathcal{B}$ has at least probability $1/2$ of succeeding.

Case $n = m > 1$ is approached as follows. Again the reduction $\mathcal{B}$ is composed of components $\mathcal{B}_I$, where $I \subseteq [1..n]$. The DL challenge $\mathbf{Z}[i]$ is distributed as either $\mathbf{X}[i]$ or $\mathbf{Y}[i]$ according to whether $i \in I$, and all remaining values are picked by the reduction. The CDH adversary—if successful—returns square matrices A, B and vector $\mathbf{c}$ such that $\operatorname{diag}(\mathbf{y})\mathbf{x} = A\mathbf{x} + B\mathbf{y} + \mathbf{c}$, where $\operatorname{diag}(\mathbf{y})$ is the diagonal matrix with the elements of $\mathbf{y}$ on the diagonal. Rearranging, we obtain

$$(\operatorname{diag}(\mathbf{y}) - A)\mathbf{x} = B\mathbf{y} + \mathbf{c}.$$

Our goal is to iteratively decrease the dimension of this matrix equation. If $n \notin I$ adversary $\mathcal{B}_I$ expresses $\mathbf{x}[n]$ in terms of $\mathbf{x}[1..n-1]$. On the other hand, if $n \in I$ then it computes $\mathbf{y}[n]$. Whether this computation is correct depends on whether I is the right choice for A, B, and $\mathbf{c}$. More explicitly, from the last row of the previous matrix equation we get the expression

$$\mathbf{x}[n](\mathbf{y}[n] - A_{nn}) = (A_{n1}, \ldots, A_{n(n-1)})\mathbf{x}[1..n-1] + $$
$$+ (B_{n1}, \ldots, B_{n(n-1)})\mathbf{y}[1..n-1] + B_{nn}\mathbf{y}[n] + \mathbf{c}[n].$$

If the number $\mathbf{y}[n] - A_{nn}$ is not invertible (case $n \in I$), then adversary $\mathcal{B}_I$ can set $\mathbf{y}[n] = A_{nn}$. In the other case (case $n \notin I$) the adversary can replace the expression for $\mathbf{x}[n]$ into the remaining $n-1$ rows of the matrix. In this case, $\mathbf{y}[n]$ is known, and calling $\mathbf{x}' = (\mathbf{x}[1], \ldots, \mathbf{x}[n-1])$, $\mathbf{y}' = (\mathbf{y}[1], \ldots, \mathbf{y}[n-1])$, we have recovered again a matrix equation of the form

$$\operatorname{diag}(\mathbf{y}')\mathbf{x}' = A'\mathbf{x}' + B'\mathbf{y}' + \mathbf{c}'$$

of decreased dimension $n-1$. Repeating this argument, we arrive at an equation of dimension 1. At this point all elements of $\mathbf{y}$ are known to $\mathcal{B}_I$, which is then able to recover the elements of $\mathbf{x}$.

Note that there always exists, for every possible A, B, and $\mathbf{c}$, a set I for which the above procedure is successful, i.e., a set I such that, for every $i \in [1..n]$, the expression $i \in I$ is satisfied exactly if $\mathbf{y}[i] = (A_{(i)})_{ii}$, where $A_{(i)}$ is the i-th update of matrix A. Since adversary $\mathcal{B}$ picks $I \subseteq [1..n]$ at random and runs $\mathcal{B}_I$, the reduction loses a factor of 2^n.

The case $n \neq m$ adds more complexity to the proof. The reduction first expands the m DL challenges $\hat{\mathbf{Z}}$ to a vector $\mathbf{Z} = \hat{\mathbf{Z}}^V$ (plus some rerandomization) of length n. Here V is a $n \times m$ matrix for which each $m \times m$ submatrix is invertible.[5] This has two important consequences: Firstly, we can express any element of $\mathbf{Z}$ as a combination of any other fixed m elements of $\mathbf{Z}$. Secondly, retrieving any m DLs of $\mathbf{Z}$ allows the reduction to compute the DLs of the original $\hat{\mathbf{Z}}$. This has, however, an unintended side effect: We can still obtain an equation of the form $\operatorname{diag}(\mathbf{y})\mathbf{x} = A\mathbf{x} + B\mathbf{y} + \mathbf{c}$, where all terms are of size m (this is the role, in the reduction code, of the function reduceMatrices), but now $A, B, \mathbf{c}$ depend on the distribution of the challenges to $\mathbf{X}$ and $\mathbf{Y}$, that is, on the set I. This means that the reduction cannot simply compute the element $\mathbf{y}[i]$

---

[5] This expansion technique is originally from the work of Ying and Kunihiro [29].

as A_{ii} at each step. It has to answer the question: "Assuming the reduction was not trying to compute $\boldsymbol{y}[m]$, what would be the value for $\boldsymbol{y}[m]$ which would make it unable to compute $\boldsymbol{x}[m]$?" (In the reduction code, the answer is yielded by the function `computeDlog`.)

In the proof, the gap oracle of $\mathcal{A}$ is simply simulated by forwarding all queries to DDH.   □

Remark 2. Note that using Corollary 2 with $q_{\mathrm{DDH}} = 0$ yields a generic lower bound on the hardness of the "standard" multi-instance CDH problem.

Further, oracle DDH plays a modest role in the proof of Theorem 4. One could define a "polycheck CDH" problem in the same fashion as it is done for discrete logarithm in Sect. 5 (in short, (m, n)-d-PolyCDH). It is then immediate to extend Theorem 4 to show the equivalence of games (m, n)-d-PolyCDH[GGen, high] and (m, n)-d-PolyDL[GGen, high] in the algebraic group model with the same loss of 2^m. Hence, with an additional multiplicative factor of $(d/2)^m$ the advantage of any adversary against game (m, n)-d-PolyCDH[GGen$_{\mathrm{gg}}$, high] can be bounded as in Corollary 2.

6.2   Generic Hardness of Medium-Granularity (m, n)-GapCDH

We present an explicit bound on the concrete security of m-out-of-n gap computational Diffie-Hellman in the generic group model in the medium-granularity setting. The main result of this section is similar to that in Section 6.1. The bound follows from observing that we can simulate the medium-granularity game starting from the high-granularity one. Then, we can apply Corollary 2 after counting the additional group queries by the simulation. For more details, we refer to the full version of the paper [3].

Corollary 3. *Let* GGen$_{\mathrm{gg}}$ *be a group-generating algorithm that generates generic groups of at least size p, and let m, n be two positive integers such that $m \leq n \leq p$. Then for every generic adversary $\mathcal{A}$ against (m, n)-GapCDH[GGen$_{\mathrm{gg}}$, med] that makes at most q queries to the group-operation oracle and q_{DDH} queries to oracle DDH:*

$$\mathrm{Adv}_{\mathsf{GGen}_{\mathrm{gg}},\mathrm{med}}^{(m,n)\text{-gcdh}}(\mathcal{A}) \leq \left(\frac{2e(q + 6(q_{\mathrm{DDH}} + 5mn) \log p)^2}{mp} \right)^m \approx \left(\frac{q^2}{mp} \right)^m.$$

Similarly to the previous concrete bounds, this result is optimal, namely there exists a generic adversary against (m, n)-GapCDH[GGen$_{\mathrm{gg}}$, med] which needs $2\sqrt{2mp}$ group operations and achieves success probability 1. In fact, we can build an adversary against (m, n)-GapCDH[GGen$_{\mathrm{gg}}$, med] starting from an adversary against $(2m, 2m)$-DL[GGen$_{\mathrm{gg}}$, high] that requires about the same amount of oracle queries. Summing up, we obtain that for large p the fastest generic adversary achieving overwhelming success probability in game (m, n)-GapCDH[GGen$_{\mathrm{gg}}$, med] requires $\sqrt{mp/(2e)} \leq q \leq 2\sqrt{2mp}$ group operations.

6.3 Generic Hardness of Low-Granularity (m, n)-GapCDH

In this section we present an explicit bound on the concrete security of m-out-of-n gap computational Diffie-Hellman in the generic group model in the low-granularity setting. The bound is stated in the following theorem and is computed directly. The proof can be found in the full version of the paper [3].

Theorem 5. *Let $\mathsf{GGen}_{\mathsf{gg}}$ be a group-generating algorithm that generates generic groups of at least size p, and let m, n, q, q_{DDH} and q_i, $i \in [1 \mathbin{.\,.} n]$, be integers such that $1 \leq m \leq n$, $q = q_1 + \ldots + q_n$, and q_i is large ($q_i \geq 60 \log p$ and $4q_i^2 \geq q_{\mathrm{DDH}}$). Then for every generic adversary $\mathcal{A}$ against the low-granularity m-out-of-n multi-instance computational Diffie-Hellman problem that makes at most q_i queries to the i-th group-operation oracle and q_{DDH} queries to the gap oracle:*

$$\mathrm{Adv}_{\mathsf{GGen}_{\mathsf{gg}},\mathsf{low}}^{(m,n)\text{-gcdh}}(\mathcal{A}) \leq \left(\frac{4eq^2}{m^2 p} \right)^m.$$

Since the number of group operations performed by a (m, n)-GapCDH adversary is typically large, we reckon the requirements $q_i \geq 60 \log p$ and $4q_i^2 \geq q_{\mathrm{DDH}}$ are rather mild.

We argue that this result is optimal. In fact, each of the first m instances can be solved in time q/m with success probability $(q/m)^2/4p$ using the algorithm provided in the full version of the paper [3]. Thus, (m, n)-GapCDH[$\mathsf{GGen}_{\mathsf{gg}}, \mathsf{low}$] can be solved in time q by independently running the single-instance adversary on the first m instances which results in a success probability of $(q^2/4m^2p)^m$. Further, for large p the fastest generic adversary achieving overwhelming success probability in game (m, n)-GapCDH[$\mathsf{GGen}_{\mathsf{gg}}, \mathsf{low}$] requires $m\sqrt{p/8e} \leq q \leq 2m\sqrt{p}$ group operations.

Acknowledgments. The authors are grateful to Masayuki Abe, Razvan Barbulescu, Mihir Bellare, Dan Boneh, Nadia Heninger, Tanja Lange, Alexander May, Bertram Poettering, Maximilian Rath, Sven Schäge, Nicola Turchi, and Takashi Yamakawa for their helpful comments. Benedikt Auerbach was supported by the European Research Council, ERC consolidator grant (682815-TOCNeT), and conducted part of this work at Ruhr University Bochum, supported by the ERC Project ERCC (FP7/615074) and the NRW Research Training Group SecHuman. Federico Giacon conducted part of this work at Ruhr University Bochum, supported by the ERC Project ERCC (FP7/615074). Eike Kiltz was supported by the ERC Project ERCC (FP7/615074), DFG SPP 1736 Big Data, and the DFG Cluster of Excellence 2092 CASA.

References

1. Abdalla, M., Bellare, M., Rogaway, P.: The Oracle Diffie-Hellman assumptions and an analysis of DHIES. In: Naccache, D. (ed.) CT-RSA 2001. LNCS, vol. 2020, pp. 143–158. Springer, Heidelberg (2001). https://doi.org/10.1007/3-540-45353-9_12
2. Adrian, D., et al.: Imperfect forward secrecy: how Diffie-Hellman fails in practice. In: Ray, I., Li, N., Kruegel, C. (eds.) ACM CCS 2015, pp. 5–17. ACM Press, October 2015

3. Auerbach, B., Giacon, F., Kiltz, E.: Everybody's a target: scalability in public-key encryption. Cryptology ePrint Archive, Report 2019/364 (2019). https://eprint.iacr.org/2019/364

4. Barbulescu, R.: Algorithms for discrete logarithm in finite fields. Ph.D. thesis, University of Lorraine, Nancy, France (2013)

5. Barbulescu, R., Pierrot, C.: The multiple number field sieve for medium- and high-characteristic finite fields. LMS J. Computa. Math. **17**(A), 230–246 (2014)

6. Bartusek, J., Ma, F., Zhandry, M.: The distinction between fixed and random generators in group-based assumptions. In: Boldyreva, A., Micciancio, D. (eds.) CRYPTO 2019, Part II. LNCS, vol. 11693, pp. 801–830. Springer, Cham (2019). https://doi.org/10.1007/978-3-030-26951-7_27

7. Bellare, M., Boldyreva, A., Micali, S.: Public-key encryption in a multi-user setting: security proofs and improvements. In: Preneel, B. (ed.) EUROCRYPT 2000. LNCS, vol. 1807, pp. 259–274. Springer, Heidelberg (2000). https://doi.org/10.1007/3-540-45539-6_18

8. Bellare, M., Ristenpart, T., Tessaro, S.: Multi-instance security and its application to password-based cryptography. In: Safavi-Naini, R., Canetti, R. (eds.) CRYPTO 2012. LNCS, vol. 7417, pp. 312–329. Springer, Heidelberg (2012). https://doi.org/10.1007/978-3-642-32009-5_19

9. Bellare, M., Rogaway, P.: Optimal asymmetric encryption. In: De Santis, A. (ed.) EUROCRYPT 1994. LNCS, vol. 950, pp. 92–111. Springer, Heidelberg (1995). https://doi.org/10.1007/BFb0053428

10. Bellare, M., Rogaway, P.: The security of triple encryption and a framework for code-based game-playing proofs. In: Vaudenay, S. (ed.) EUROCRYPT 2006. LNCS, vol. 4004, pp. 409–426. Springer, Heidelberg (2006). https://doi.org/10.1007/11761679_25

11. Bernstein, D.J., Lange, T.: Batch NFS. In: Joux, A., Youssef, A. (eds.) SAC 2014. LNCS, vol. 8781, pp. 38–58. Springer, Cham (2014). https://doi.org/10.1007/978-3-319-13051-4_3

12. Boneh, D., Boyen, X., Goh, E.-J.: Hierarchical identity based encryption with constant size ciphertext. In: Cramer, R. (ed.) EUROCRYPT 2005. LNCS, vol. 3494, pp. 440–456. Springer, Heidelberg (2005). https://doi.org/10.1007/11426639_26

13. Coretti, S., Dodis, Y., Guo, S.: Non-uniform bounds in the random-permutation, ideal-cipher, and generic-group models. In: Shacham, H., Boldyreva, A. (eds.) CRYPTO 2018, Part I. LNCS, vol. 10991, pp. 693–721. Springer, Cham (2018). https://doi.org/10.1007/978-3-319-96884-1_23

14. Corrigan-Gibbs, H., Kogan, D.: The discrete-logarithm problem with preprocessing. In: Nielsen, J.B., Rijmen, V. (eds.) EUROCRYPT 2018, Part II. LNCS, vol. 10821, pp. 415–447. Springer, Cham (2018). https://doi.org/10.1007/978-3-319-78375-8_14

15. Fouque, P.-A., Joux, A., Mavromati, C.: Multi-user collisions: applications to discrete logarithm, even-Mansour and PRINCE. In: Sarkar, P., Iwata, T. (eds.) ASIACRYPT 2014, Part I. LNCS, vol. 8873, pp. 420–438. Springer, Heidelberg (2014). https://doi.org/10.1007/978-3-662-45611-8_22

16. Fuchsbauer, G., Kiltz, E., Loss, J.: The algebraic group model and its applications. In: Shacham, H., Boldyreva, A. (eds.) CRYPTO 2018, Part II. LNCS, vol. 10992, pp. 33–62. Springer, Cham (2018). https://doi.org/10.1007/978-3-319-96881-0_2

17. Garay, J.A., Johnson, D.S., Kiayias, A., Yung, M.: Resource-based corruptions and the combinatorics of hidden diversity. In: Kleinberg, R.D. (ed.) ITCS 2013, pp. 415–428. ACM, January 2013

18. Guillevic, A., Morain, F.: Discrete logarithms. In: Mrabet, N.E., Joye, M. (eds.) Guide to pairing-based cryptography. CRC Press/Taylor and Francis Group, December 2016
19. Heninger, N., Durumeric, Z., Wustrow, E., Halderman, J.A.: Mining your Ps and Qs: detection of widespread weak keys in network devices. In: 21st USENIX Security Symposium (2012)
20. Hitchcock, Y., Montague, P., Carter, G., Dawson, E.: The efficiency of solving multiple discrete logarithm problems and the implications for the security of fixed elliptic curves. Int. J.Inf. Secur. 3(2), 86–98 (2004). https://doi.org/10.1007/s10207-004-0045-9
21. Hofheinz, D., Nguyen, N.K.: On tightly secure primitives in the multi-instance setting. In: Lin, D., Sako, K. (eds.) PKC 2019, Part I. LNCS, vol. 11442, pp. 581–611. Springer, Cham (2019). https://doi.org/10.1007/978-3-030-17253-4_20
22. Kuhn, F., Struik, R.: Random walks revisited: extensions of Pollard's Rho algorithm for computing multiple discrete logarithms. In: Vaudenay, S., Youssef, A.M. (eds.) SAC 2001. LNCS, vol. 2259, pp. 212–229. Springer, Heidelberg (2001). https://doi.org/10.1007/3-540-45537-X_17
23. Maurer, U.: Abstract models of computation in cryptography. In: Smart, N.P. (ed.) Cryptography and Coding 2005. LNCS, vol. 3796, pp. 1–12. Springer, Heidelberg (2005). https://doi.org/10.1007/11586821_1
24. Mizuide, T., Takayasu, A., Takagi, T.: Tight reductions for Diffie-Hellman variants in the algebraic group model. In: Matsui, M. (ed.) CT-RSA 2019. LNCS, vol. 11405, pp. 169–188. Springer, Cham (2019). https://doi.org/10.1007/978-3-030-12612-4_9
25. Okamoto, T., Pointcheval, D.: The gap-problems: a new class of problems for the security of cryptographic schemes. In: Kim, K. (ed.) PKC 2001. LNCS, vol. 1992, pp. 104–118. Springer, Heidelberg (2001). https://doi.org/10.1007/3-540-44586-2_8
26. Rupp, A., Leander, G., Bangerter, E., Dent, A.W., Sadeghi, A.-R.: Sufficient conditions for intractability over black-box groups: generic lower bounds for generalized DL and DH Problems. In: Pieprzyk, J. (ed.) ASIACRYPT 2008. LNCS, vol. 5350, pp. 489–505. Springer, Heidelberg (2008). https://doi.org/10.1007/978-3-540-89255-7_30
27. Sadeghi, A.-R., Steiner, M.: Assumptions related to discrete logarithms: why subtleties make a real difference. In: Pfitzmann, B. (ed.) EUROCRYPT 2001. LNCS, vol. 2045, pp. 244–261. Springer, Heidelberg (2001). https://doi.org/10.1007/3-540-44987-6_16
28. Shoup, V.: Lower bounds for discrete logarithms and related problems. In: Fumy, W. (ed.) EUROCRYPT 1997. LNCS, vol. 1233, pp. 256–266. Springer, Heidelberg (1997). https://doi.org/10.1007/3-540-69053-0_18
29. Ying, J.H.M., Kunihiro, N.: Bounds in various generalized settings of the discrete logarithm problem. In: Gollmann, D., Miyaji, A., Kikuchi, H. (eds.) ACNS 2017. LNCS, vol. 10355, pp. 498–517. Springer, Cham (2017). https://doi.org/10.1007/978-3-319-61204-1_25
30. Yun, A.: Generic hardness of the multiple discrete logarithm problem. In: Oswald, E., Fischlin, M. (eds.) EUROCRYPT 2015, Part II. LNCS, vol. 9057, pp. 817–836. Springer, Heidelberg (2015). https://doi.org/10.1007/978-3-662-46803-6_27

Security Under Message-Derived Keys: Signcryption in iMessage

Mihir Bellare[1(✉)] and Igors Stepanovs[2(✉)]

[1] Department of Computer Science and Engineering, University of California San Diego, San Diego, USA
mihir@eng.ucsd.edu
[2] Department of Computer Science, ETH Zürich, Zürich, Switzerland
istepanovs@inf.ethz.ch

Abstract. At the core of Apple's iMessage is a signcryption scheme that involves symmetric encryption of a message under a key that is derived from the message itself. This motivates us to formalize a primitive we call Encryption under Message-Derived Keys (EMDK). We prove security of the EMDK scheme underlying iMessage. We use this to prove security of the signcryption scheme itself, with respect to definitions of signcryption we give that enhance prior ones to cover issues peculiar to messaging protocols. Our provable-security results are quantitative, and we discuss the practical implications for iMessage.

1 Introduction

Apple's iMessage app works across iOS (iPhone, iPad) and OS X (MacBook) devices. Laudably, it aims to provide end-to-end security. At its heart is a signcryption scheme.

The current scheme—we refer to the version in iOS 9.3 onwards, revised after the attacks of GGKMR [26] on the iOS 9.0 version—is of interest on two fronts. (1) *Applied*: iMessage encrypts (according to an Internet estimate) 63 quadrillion messages per year. It is important to determine whether or not the scheme provides the security expected by its users. (2) *Theoretical*: The scheme involves (symmetric) encryption of a message under a key that is derived from the message itself, an uncommon and intriguing technique inviting formalization and a foundational treatment.

CONTRIBUTIONS IN BRIEF. *Signcryption theory*: We extend the prior Signcryption definitions of ADR [3] to capture elements particular to messaging systems, and give general results that simplify the analysis of the candidate schemes. *EMDK*: We introduce, and give definitions (syntax and security) for, Encryption under Message Derived Keys. *iMessage EMDK scheme*: We extract from iMessage an EMDK scheme and prove its security in the random-oracle model. *Composition and iMessage Signcryption*: We give a way to compose EMDK, PKE and signatures to get signcryption, prove it works, and thereby validate the iMessage signcryption scheme for appropriate parameter choices.

A. Canteaut and Y. Ishai (Eds.): EUROCRYPT 2020, LNCS 12107, pp. 507–537, 2020.
https://doi.org/10.1007/978-3-030-45727-3_17

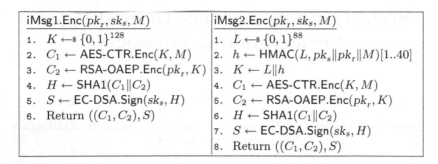

iMsg1.Enc(pk_r, sk_s, M)	iMsg2.Enc(pk_r, sk_s, M)
1. $K \leftarrow\!\!\$ \{0,1\}^{128}$	1. $L \leftarrow\!\!\$ \{0,1\}^{88}$
2. $C_1 \leftarrow$ AES-CTR.Enc(K, M)	2. $h \leftarrow$ HMAC($L, pk_s \| pk_r \| M$)[1..40]
3. $C_2 \leftarrow$ RSA-OAEP.Enc(pk_r, K)	3. $K \leftarrow L \| h$
4. $H \leftarrow$ SHA1($C_1 \| C_2$)	4. $C_1 \leftarrow$ AES-CTR.Enc(K, M)
5. $S \leftarrow$ EC-DSA.Sign(sk_s, H)	5. $C_2 \leftarrow$ RSA-OAEP.Enc(pk_r, K)
6. Return $((C_1, C_2), S)$	6. $H \leftarrow$ SHA1($C_1 \| C_2$)
	7. $S \leftarrow$ EC-DSA.Sign(sk_s, H)
	8. Return $((C_1, C_2), S)$

Fig. 1. Encryption in iMsg1 (left) and iMsg2 (right). Here pk_r is the recipient's public RSA encryption key, sk_s is the sender's ECDSA secret signing key and pk_s is the sender's ECDSA public verification key. Our analysis and proofs consider general schemes of which the above emerge as instantiations corresponding to particular choices of primitives and parameters.

BACKGROUND. By default, the iMessage chatting app encrypts communications between any two iMessage users. The encryption is end-to-end, under keys stored on the devices, meaning Apple itself cannot decrypt. In this way, iMessage joins Signal, WhatsApp and other secure messaging apps as a means to counter mass surveillance, but the cryptography used is quite different, and while the cryptography underlying Signal and WhatsApp, namely ratcheting, has received an extensive theoretical treatment [2, 12, 19, 22, 28, 29, 33], that underlying iMessage has not.

In 2016, Garman, Green, Kaptchuk, Miers and Rushanan (GGKMR) [26] gave chosen-ciphertext attacks on the then current, iOS 9 version, of iMessage that we will denote iMsg1. Its encryption algorithm is shown on the left in Fig. 1. In response Apple acknowledged the attack as CVE-2016-1788 [20], and revised the protocol for iOS 9.3. We'll denote this version iMsg2, its encryption algorithm is shown on the right in Fig. 1. It has been stable since iOS 9.3. It was this revision that, for the specific purpose of countering the GGKMR attack, introduced (symmetric) encryption with message-derived keys: message M at line 4 is encrypted under a key K derived, via lines 1–3, from M itself. The question we ask is, does the fix work?

IDENTIFYING THE GOAL. To meaningfully answer the above question we must first, of course, identify the formal primitive and security goal being targeted. Neither Apple's iOS Security Guide [4], nor GGKMR [26], explicitly do so. We suggest that it is signcryption. Introduced by Zheng [36], signcryption aims to simultaneously provide privacy of the message (under the receiver's public encryption key) and authenticity (under the sender's secret signing key), and can be seen as the asymmetric analogue of symmetric authenticated encryption. A formalization was given by An, Dodis and Rabin (ADR) [3]. They distinguish between outsider security (the adversary is not one of the users) and the stronger insider security (the adversary could be a sender or receiver).

Identifying the iMessage goal as signcryption gives some perspective on, and understanding of, the schemes and history. The iMessage schemes can be seen as using some form of ADR's Encrypt-then-Sign ($\mathcal{E}t\mathcal{S}$) method. The iMsg1 scheme turns out to be a simple scheme from ADR [3]. It may be outsider-secure, but ADR give an attack that shows it is not insider secure. (The adversary queries the sender encryption oracle to get a ciphertext $((C_1, C_2), S)$, substitutes S with a signature S' of $H = \mathsf{SHA1}(C_1\|C_2)$ under its own signing key, which it can do as an insider, and then queries this modified ciphertext to the recipient decryption oracle to get back the message underlying the original ciphertext.) The GGKMR [26] attack on iMsg1 is a clever improvement and real-world rendition of the ADR attack. That Apple acknowledged the GGKMR attack, and modified the scheme to protect against it, indicates that they want insider security, not just outsider security, for their modified iMsg2 scheme. So the question becomes whether this goal is achieved.

SIGNCRYPTION THEORY EXTENDED. We could answer the above question relative to ADR's (existing) definitions of insider-secure signcryption, but we do more, affirming the iMsg2 signcryption scheme under stronger definitions that capture elements particular to messaging systems, making our results of more applied value.

When you send an iMessage communication to Alice, it is encrypted to *all* her devices (her iPhone, MacBook, iPad, ...), so that she can chat seamlessly across them. To capture this, we *enhance signcryption syntax*, making the encryption algorithm multi-recipient. (It takes not one, but a list of receiver public encryption keys.) We also allow associated data as in symmetric authenticated encryption [35].

We give, like in prior work [3], a privacy definition (priv) and an authenticity definition (auth); but, unlike prior work, we also give a strong, unified definition (sec) that implies auth+priv. We show that (under certain conditions) sec is implied by auth+priv, mirroring analogous results for symmetric authenticated encryption [9,15]. Proving that a scheme satisfies sec (the definition more intuitively capturing the practical setting) now reduces to the simpler tasks of separately showing it satisfies auth and priv. These definitions and results are for both insider and outsider security, and parameterized by choices of *relaxing relations* that allow us to easily capture variants reflecting issues like plaintext or ciphertext integrity [8], gCCA2 [3] and RCCA [18].

EMDK DEFINITIONS. Recall that a scheme for conventional symmetric encryption specifies a key-generation algorithm that is run once, a priori, to return a key k; the encryption algorithm then takes k and message m to return a ciphertext. In our definition of a scheme for (symmetric) Encryption under Message-Derived Keys (EMDK), there is no dedicated key-generation algorithm. Encryption algorithm EMDK.Enc takes only a message m, returning both a key k and a ciphertext c, so that k may depend on m. Decryption algorithm EMDK.Dec takes k—in the overlying signcryption scheme, this is communicated to the receiver via asymmetric encryption—and c to return either m or $\perp$.

We impose two security requirements on an EMDK scheme. (1) The first, called ae, adapts the authenticated encryption requirement of symmetric encryption [35]. (Our game formalizing ae is in Fig. 8.) (2) The second, called rob, is a form of robustness or wrong-key detection [1,17,23,24]. (Our game formalizing rob is also in Fig. 8.) Of course one may define many other and alternative security goals for EMDK, so why these? We have focused on these simply because they suffice for our results.

EMDK is different from both (Symmetric) Encryption of Key-Dependent Messages (EKDM) [14,16] and (Symmetric) Encryption secure against Related-Key Attack (ERKA) [7]. To begin with, these definitions apply to *syntactically different objects*. Namely, both EKDM and ERKA are security metrics for the standard symmetric encryption syntax where the encryption algorithm takes a key and message as input and returns a ciphertext, while in EMDK the encryption algorithm takes only a message and itself produces a key along with the ciphertext. (Note that the latter is also different from the syntax of a Key-Encapsulation mechanism, where encryption does produce a key and ciphertext, but takes no input message.) These syntactic differences make comparison moot, but one can still discuss intuitively how the security requirements relate. In the security games for EKDM there is an honestly and randomly chosen target key k, and challenge messages to be encrypted may depend on k, but in our security games for EMDK, the key is not chosen honestly and could depend on the message being encrypted. In ERKA also, like EKDM but unlike EMDK, a target key k is chosen honestly and at random. One can now have the game apply the encryption algorithm under a key k' derived from k, but this does not capture the encryption algorithm not taking a key as input but itself producing it as a function of the message, as in EKDM.

DECONSTRUCTING iMESSAGE. Equipped with the above, we show how to cast the iMsg2 signcryption scheme as the result of a general transform (that we specify and call IMSG-SC) on a particular EMDK scheme (that we specify) and some standard auxiliary primitives (that we also specify). In Sect. 5, we prove that IMSG-SC works, reducing insider security (priv, auth, sec) of the signcryption scheme to the security of the constituents, leaving us with what is the main technical task, namely showing security of the EMDK scheme.

In more detail, IMSG-SC takes a scheme EMDK for encryption under message-derived keys, a public-key encryption scheme PKE and a digital signature scheme DS to return a signcryption scheme SC = IMSG-SC[EMDK, PKE, DS]. (In the body of the paper, this is done in two steps, with a multi-recipient public-key encryption scheme [6] as an intermediate point, but for simplicity we elide this here.) Both iMessage signcryption schemes (i.e. iMsg1 and iMsg2) can be seen as results of this transform. The two make the same choices of PKE and DS, namely RSA-OAEP and EC-DSA respectively, differing only in their choice of EMDK, which for iMsg1 is a trivial scheme that we call the basic scheme, and for iMsg2 a more interesting scheme that we denote IMSG-EMDK[F, SE] and discuss below. Our Sect. 5 result is that signcryption scheme SC = IMSG-SC[EMDK, PKE, DS]

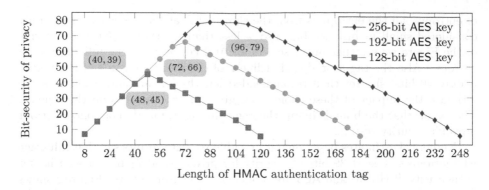

Fig. 2. Lower bounds for the bit-security of privacy achieved by iMessage, depending on the key size of AES-CTR and the length of the authentication tag returned by HMAC. iMessage 10 uses 128-bit AES key and 40-bit long HMAC authentication tag, and hence guarantees at least 39 bits of security for privacy. (Any choice of parameters guarantees 71 bits of security for authenticity.)

provides insider security (priv, auth, sec) assuming ae- and rob-security of EMDK and under standard assumptions on PKE and DS.

EMDK RESULTS. In Fig. 10 we specify an EMDK scheme IMSG-EMDK[F, SE] constructed from a given function family F and a given, ordinary one-time (assumed deterministic) symmetric encryption scheme SE. Setting F to HMAC and SE to AES-CTR recovers the EMDK scheme underlying iMsg2 signcryption. This EMDK scheme captures the heart of iMsg2 signcryption, namely lines 1–4 of the right side of Fig. 1.

The security analysis of IMSG-EMDK[F, SE] is somewhat complex. We prove ae-security of this EMDK scheme assuming F is a random oracle and SE has the following properties: one-time IND-CPA privacy, a property we define called uniqueness, and partial key recovery security. The latter strengthens key recovery security to say that, not only is it hard to recover the key, but it is hard to recover even a prefix, of a certain prescribed length, of this key. We prove rob-security of the EMDK scheme assuming F is a random oracle and SE satisfies uniqueness and weak robustness. The properties assumed of SE appear to be true for the AES-CTR used in iMessage, and could be shown in idealized models.

PRACTICAL IMPLICATIONS FOR IMESSAGE. What we have proved is that iMsg2 signcryption is secure in principle, in the sense that the underlying template is sound. (That is, the signcryption scheme given by our IMSG-SC transform is secure assuming the underlying primitives are secure.) For the practical implications, we must consider the quantitative security guaranteed by our theorems based on the particular choices of parameters and primitives made in iMsg2 signcryption scheme. Here, things seem a bit borderline, because iMsg2 signcryption has made some specific parameter choices that seem dangerous. Considering again the right side of Fig. 1, the 128-bit AES key K at line 3 has only 88 bits of entropy—all the entropy is from the choice of L at line 1—which is not only considered small in practice but also is less than for iMsg1. (On the left side of the Figure we see that line 1 selects an AES key K with the full 128 bits of entropy.) Also the tag h produced at line 2 of the right-hand-side of the Figure is only 40 bits, shorter than recommended lengths for authentication tags. To estimate the impact of these choices, we give concrete attacks on the scheme. They show that the bounds in our theorems are tight, but do not contradict our provable-security results.

Numerical estimates based on our provable-security results say that iMessage 10 guarantees at least 39 bits of security for privacy, and 71 bits of security for authenticity, if HMAC and AES are modeled as ideal primitives. Figure 2 shows the guaranteed bit-security of privacy for different choices of AES key length and HMAC tag length. For the small parameter choices made in iMsg2 signcryption, the attacks do approach feasibility in terms of computational effort, but we wouldn't claim they are practical, for two reasons. First, they only violate the very stringent security goals that are the target of our proofs. Second, following the GGKMR [26] attacks, Apple has implemented decryption-oracle throttling that will also curtail our attacks.

Still, ideally, a practical scheme would implement cryptography that meets even our stringent security goals without recourse to extraneous measures like throttling. We suggest that parameter and primitive choices in iMessage signcryption be revisited, for if they are chosen properly, our results do guarantee that the scheme provides strong security properties.

DISCUSSION. When a new primitive (like EMDK) is defined, the first question of a theoretical cryptographer is often, does it exist, meaning, can it be built, and under what assumptions? At least in the random-oracle model [10] in which our results are shown, it is quite easy to build, under standard assumptions, an EMDK scheme that provides the ae+rob-security we define, and we show such a scheme in Fig. 9. The issue of interest for us is less existence (to build some secure EMDK scheme) and more the security of the *particular* IMSG-EMDK[F, SE] scheme underlying iMsg2 signcryption. The motivation is mainly applied, stemming from this scheme running in security software (iMessage) that is used by millions.

But, one may then ask, WHY did Apple use their (strange) EMDK scheme instead of one like that in Fig. 9, which is simpler and provable under weaker assumptions? We do not know. In that vein, one may even ask, why did Apple use EMDK at all? The literature gives Signcryption schemes that are efficient and based on standard assumptions. Why did they not just take one of them? Again, we do not know for sure, but we can speculate. The EMDK-based template that we capture in our IMSG-SC transform provides *backwards decryption compatibility*; an iMsg1 implementation can decrypt an iMsg2 ciphertext. (Of course, security guarantees revert to those of the iMsg1 scheme under such usage, but this could be offset by operational gains.) Moving to an entirely new signcryption scheme would *not* provide this backwards compatibility. But we stress again that this is mere speculation; we did not find any Apple documents giving reasons for their choices.

RELATED WORK. We have discussed some related work above. However, signcryption is a big research area with a lot of work. We overview this in [13].

2 Preliminaries

In [13] we provide the following standard definitions. We state syntax, correctness and security definitions for function families, symmetric encryption, digital signatures, public-key encryption, and multi-recipient public-key encryption. We define the random oracle model, the ideal cipher model, and provide the birthday attack bounds. In this section we introduce the basic notation and conventions we use throughout the paper.

BASIC NOTATION AND CONVENTIONS. Let $\mathbb{N} = \{1, 2, \ldots\}$ be the set of positive integers. For $i \in \mathbb{N}$ we let $[i]$ denote the set $\{1, \ldots, i\}$. If X is a finite set, we let $x \leftarrow_\$ X$ denote picking an element of X uniformly at random and assigning it to x. Let ε denote the empty string. By $x \parallel y$ we denote the concatenation of strings x and y. If $x \in \{0, 1\}^*$ is a string then $|x|$ denotes its length, $x[i]$ denotes its i-th bit, and $x[i..j] = x[i] \ldots x[j]$ for $1 \le i \le j \le |x|$. If mem is a table, we use $\mathsf{mem}[i]$ to denote the element of the table that is indexed by i. We use a special symbol $\bot$ to denote an empty table position; we also return it as an error code indicating an invalid input to an algorithm or an oracle, including invalid decryption. We assume that adversaries never pass $\bot$ as input to their oracles.

UNIQUELY DECODABLE ENCODING. We write $\langle a, b, \ldots \rangle$ to denote a string that is a uniquely decodable encoding of $a, b, \ldots$, where each of the encoded elements can have an arbitrary type (e.g. string or set). For any $n \in \mathbb{N}$ let $x_1, \ldots, x_n$ and $y_1, \ldots, y_n$ be two sequences of elements such that for each $i \in [n]$ the following holds: either $x_i = y_i$, or both x_i and y_i are strings of the same length. Then we require that $|\langle x_1, \ldots, x_n \rangle| = |\langle y_1, \ldots, y_n \rangle|$, and that $\langle x_1, \ldots, x_{i-1}, x_i, x_{i+1}, \ldots, x_n \rangle \oplus \langle x_1, \ldots, x_{i-1}, y_i, x_{i+1}, \ldots, x_n \rangle = \langle x_1, \ldots, x_{i-1}, (x_i \oplus y_i), x_{i+1}, \ldots, x_n \rangle$ for all $i \in [n]$.

ALGORITHMS AND ADVERSARIES. Algorithms may be randomized unless otherwise indicated. Running time is worst case. If A is an algorithm, we let $y \leftarrow A(x_1, \ldots; r)$ denote running A with random coins r on inputs $x_1, \ldots$ and assigning the output to y. We let $y \leftarrow_\$ A(x_1, \ldots)$ be the result of picking r at random and letting $y \leftarrow A(x_1, \ldots; r)$. We let $[A(x_1, \ldots)]$ denote the set of all possible outputs of A when invoked with inputs $x_1, \ldots$. Adversaries are algorithms.

SECURITY GAMES AND REDUCTIONS. We use the code based game playing framework of [11]. (See Fig. 5 for an example.) We let $\Pr[G]$ denote the probability that game G returns true. In the security reductions, we omit specifying the running times of the constructed adversaries when they are roughly the same as the running time of the initial adversary.

IMPLICIT INITIALIZATION VALUES. In algorithms and games, uninitialized integers are assumed to be initialized to 0, Booleans to false, strings to the empty string, sets to the empty set, and tables are initially empty.

BIT-SECURITY OF CRYPTOGRAPHIC PRIMITIVES. Let prim be any cryptographic primitive, and let sec be any security notion defined for this primitive. We say that prim has n bits of security with respect to sec (or n bits of sec-security) if for every adversary $\mathcal{A}$ that has advantage $\epsilon_{\mathcal{A}}$ and runtime $T_{\mathcal{A}}$ against sec-security of prim it is true that $\epsilon_{\mathcal{A}}/T_{\mathcal{A}} < 2^{-n}$. In other words, if there exists an adversary $\mathcal{A}$ with advantage $\epsilon_{\mathcal{A}}$ and runtime $T_{\mathcal{A}}$ against sec-security of prim, then prim has at most $-\log_2(\epsilon_{\mathcal{A}}/T_{\mathcal{A}})$ bits of security with respect to sec. This is the folklore definition of bit-security for cryptographic primitives. Micciancio and Walter [31] recently proposed an alternative definition for bit-security.

BIT-SECURITY LOWER BOUNDS. Let $\mathcal{BS}(\text{prim}, \text{sec})$ denote the bit-security of cryptographic primitive prim with respect to security notion sec. Consider any security reduction showing $\mathsf{Adv}^{\text{sec}}_{\text{prim}}(\mathcal{A}) \leq \sum_i \mathsf{Adv}^{\text{sec}_i}_{\text{prim}_i}(\mathcal{B}_i^{\mathcal{A}})$ by constructing for any adversary $\mathcal{A}$ and for each i a new adversary $\mathcal{B}_i^{\mathcal{A}}$ with runtime roughly $T_{\mathcal{A}}$. Then we can lower bound the bit-security of prim with respect to sec as

$$\mathcal{BS}(\text{prim}, \text{sec}) = \min_{\forall \mathcal{A}} -\log_2\left(\frac{\epsilon_{\mathcal{A}}}{T_{\mathcal{A}}}\right) \geq \min_{\forall \mathcal{A}} -\log_2\left(\frac{\sum_i \mathsf{Adv}^{\text{sec}_i}_{\text{prim}_i}(\mathcal{B}_i^{\mathcal{A}})}{T_{\mathcal{A}}}\right)$$

$$\geq -\log_2\left(\sum_i 2^{-\mathcal{BS}(\text{prim}_i, \text{sec}_i)}\right).$$

3 Signcryption

In this section we define syntax, correctness and security notions for multi-recipient signcryption schemes. We assume that upon generating any signcryption key pair (pk, sk), it gets associated to some identity id. This captures a system where users can independently generate their cryptographic keys prior to registering them with a public-key infrastructure. We require that all identities are distinct values in $\{0, 1\}^*$. Depending on the system, each identity id serves as a label that uniquely identifies a device or a user. Note that pk cannot be used in place of the identity, because different devices can happen to use the same public keys (either due to generating the same key pairs by chance, or due to maliciously claiming someone's else public key). We emphasize that our syntax is not meant to capture identity-based signcryption, where a public key would have to depend on the identity. In [13] we provide an extensive summary of prior work on signcryption.

We focus on authenticity and privacy of signcryption in the *insider* setting, meaning that the adversary is allowed to adaptively compromise secret keys of any identities as long as that does not enable the adversary to trivially win the security games. Our definitions can also capture the *outsider* setting by considering limited classes of adversaries. We define our security notions with respect to *relaxing relations*. This allows us to capture a number of weaker security notions in a fine-grained way, by choosing an appropriate relaxing relation in each case.

$$\pi \leftarrow_{\$} \mathsf{SC.Setup}$$
$$(pk, sk) \leftarrow_{\$} \mathsf{SC.Kg}(\pi)$$
$$\mathcal{C} \leftarrow_{\$} \mathsf{SC.SigEnc}(\pi, id_s, pk_s, sk_s, \mathcal{R}, m, ad)$$
$$m \leftarrow \mathsf{SC.VerDec}(\pi, id_s, pk_s, id_r, pk_r, sk_r, c, ad)$$

Fig. 3. Syntax of the constituent algorithms of signcryption scheme SC.

$\mathsf{R_m.Vf}(z_0, z_1)$	$\mathsf{R_{id}.Vf}(z_0, z_1)$
$(x_0, y_0) \leftarrow z_0$; $(x_1, y_1) \leftarrow z_1$	Return $z_0 = z_1$
Return $x_0 = x_1$	

Fig. 4. Relaxing relations $\mathsf{R_m}$ and $\mathsf{R_{id}}$.

In [13] we define a *combined* security notion for signcryption that simultaneously encompasses authenticity and privacy, and prove that it is equivalent to the separate notions under certain conditions.

MULTI-RECIPIENT SIGNCRYPTION SCHEMES. A multi-recipient signcryption scheme SC specifies algorithms SC.Setup, SC.Kg, SC.SigEnc, SC.VerDec, where SC.VerDec is deterministic. Associated to SC is an identity space SC.ID. The setup algorithm SC.Setup returns public parameters π. The key generation algorithm SC.Kg takes π to return a key pair (pk, sk), where pk is a public key and sk is a secret key. The signcryption algorithm SC.SigEnc takes π, sender's identity $id_s \in$ SC.ID, sender's public key pk_s, sender's secret key sk_s, a set $\mathcal{R}$ of pairs (id_r, pk_r) containing recipient identities and public keys, a plaintext $m \in \{0,1\}^*$, and associated data $ad \in \{0,1\}^*$ to return a set $\mathcal{C}$ of pairs (id_r, c), each denoting that signcryption ciphertext c should be sent to the recipient with identity id_r. The unsigncryption algorithm SC.VerDec takes π, sender's identity id_s, sender's public key pk_s, recipient's identity id_r, recipient's public key pk_r, recipient's secret key sk_r, signcryption ciphertext c, and associated data ad to return $m \in \{0,1\}^* \cup \{\perp\}$, where $\perp$ indicates a failure to recover plaintext. The syntax used for the constituent algorithms of SC is summarized in Fig. 3.

CORRECTNESS OF SIGNCRYPTION. The correctness of a signcryption scheme SC requires that for all $\pi \in$ [SC.Setup], all $n \in \mathbb{N}$, all $(pk_0, sk_0), \ldots, (pk_n, sk_n) \in$ [SC.Kg(π)] all $id_0 \in$ SC.ID, all *distinct* $id_1, \ldots, id_n \in$ SC.ID, all $m \in \{0,1\}^*$, and all $ad \in \{0,1\}^*$ the following conditions hold. Let $\mathcal{R} = \{(id_i, pk_i)\}_{1 \le i \le n}$. We require that for all $\mathcal{C} \in$ [SC.SigEnc$(\pi, id_0, pk_0, sk_0, \mathcal{R}, m, ad)$]: (i) $|\mathcal{C}| = |\mathcal{R}|$; (ii) for each $i \in \{1, \ldots, n\}$ there exists a unique $c \in \{0,1\}^*$ such that $(id_i, c) \in \mathcal{C}$; (iii) for each $i \in \{1, \ldots, n\}$ and each c such that $(id_i, c) \in \mathcal{C}$ we have $m = $ SC.VerDec$(\pi, id_0, pk_0, id_i, pk_i, sk_i, c, ad)$.

RELAXING RELATIONS. A relaxing relation $\mathsf{R} \subseteq \{0,1\}^* \times \{0,1\}^*$ is a set containing pairs of arbitrary strings. Associated to a relaxing relation R is a membership

---

Games $G_{SC,R,\mathcal{F}}^{auth}$

$\pi \leftarrow_\$ \text{SC.Setup}$; $\mathcal{F}^{\text{NewH,NewC,Exp,SigEnc,VerDec}}(\pi)$; Return win

$\underline{\text{NewH}(id)}$
If initialized[id] then return $\perp$
initialized[id] $\leftarrow$ true ; $(pk, sk) \leftarrow_\$ \text{SC.Kg}(\pi)$; pk[id] $\leftarrow pk$; sk[id] $\leftarrow sk$; Return pk

$\underline{\text{NewC}(id, pk, sk)}$
If initialized[id] then return $\perp$
initialized[id] $\leftarrow$ true ; exp[id] $\leftarrow$ true ; pk[id] $\leftarrow pk$; sk[id] $\leftarrow sk$; Return true

$\underline{\text{Exp}(id)}$
If not initialized[id] then return $\perp$
exp[id] $\leftarrow$ true ; Return sk[id]

$\underline{\text{SigEnc}(id_s, \mathcal{I}, m, ad)}$
If (not initialized[id_s]) or ($\exists id \in \mathcal{I}$: not initialized[$id$]) then return $\perp$
$\mathcal{R} \leftarrow \emptyset$; For each $id \in \mathcal{I}$ do $\mathcal{R} \leftarrow \mathcal{R} \cup \{(id, \text{pk}[id])\}$
$\mathcal{C} \leftarrow_\$ \text{SC.SigEnc}(\pi, id_s, \text{pk}[id_s], \text{sk}[id_s], \mathcal{R}, m, ad)$
For each $(id_r, c) \in \mathcal{C}$ do $Q \leftarrow Q \cup \{((id_s, id_r, m, ad), c)\}$
Return $\mathcal{C}$

$\underline{\text{VerDec}(id_s, id_r, c, ad)}$
If (not initialized[id_s]) or (not initialized[id_r]) then return $\perp$
$m \leftarrow \text{SC.VerDec}(\pi, id_s, \text{pk}[id_s], id_r, \text{pk}[id_r], \text{sk}[id_r], c, ad)$; If $m = \perp$ then return $\perp$
$z_0 \leftarrow ((id_s, id_r, m, ad), c)$; If $\exists z_1 \in Q$: R.Vf(z_0, z_1) then return m
cheated $\leftarrow$ exp[id_s] ; If not cheated then win $\leftarrow$ true
Return m

Fig. 5. Game defining authenticity of signcryption scheme SC with respect to relaxing relation R.

verification algorithm R.Vf that takes inputs $z_0, z_1 \in \{0, 1\}^*$ to return a decision in {true, false} such that $\forall z_0, z_1 \in \{0, 1\}^*$: R.Vf($z_0, z_1$) = true iff $(z_0, z_1) \in$ R. We will normally define relaxing relations by specifying their membership verification algorithms. Two relaxing relations that will be used throughout the paper are defined in Fig. 4.

We define our security notions for signcryption with respect to relaxing relations. Relaxing relations are used to restrict the queries that an adversary is allowed to make to its unsigncryption oracle. The choice of different relaxing relations can be used to capture a variety of different security notions for signcryption in a fine-grained way. We will use relaxing relations R_{id} and R_m to capture strong vs. standard authenticity (or unforgeability) of signcryption, and IND-CCA vs. RCCA [18,27] style indistinguishability of signcryption. In Sect. 5.3 we will also define unforgeability of digital signatures with respect to relaxing relations, allowing to capture standard and strong unforgeability notions in a unified way.

AUTHENTICITY OF SIGNCRYPTION. Consider game G^{auth} of Fig. 5 associated to a signcryption scheme SC, a relaxing relation R and an adversary $\mathcal{F}$. The advantage of adversary $\mathcal{F}$ in breaking the AUTH-security of SC with respect to R is defined as $\mathsf{Adv}^{auth}_{SC,R}(\mathcal{F}) = \Pr[G^{auth}_{SC,R,\mathcal{F}}]$. Adversary $\mathcal{F}$ has access to oracles NEWH, NEWC, EXP, SIGENC, and VERDEC. The oracles can be called in any order. Oracle NEWH generates a key pair for a new honest identity id. Oracle NEWC associates a key pair (pk, sk) of adversary's choice to a new corrupted identity id; it permits malformed keys, meaning sk should not necessarily be a valid secret key that matches with pk. Oracle EXP can be called to expose the secret key of any identity. The game maintains a table exp to mark which identities are exposed; all corrupted identities that were created by calling oracle NEWC are marked as exposed right away. The signcryption oracle SIGENC returns ciphertexts produced by sender identity id_s to each of the recipient identities contained in set $\mathcal{I}$, encrypting message m with associated data ad. Oracle VERDEC returns the plaintext obtained as the result of unsigncrypting the ciphertext c sent from sender id_s to recipient id_r, with associated data ad. The goal of adversary $\mathcal{F}$ is to forge a valid signcryption ciphertext, and query it to oracle VERDEC. The game does not let adversary win by querying oracle VERDEC with a forgery that was produced for an exposed sender identity id_s, since the adversary could have trivially produced a valid ciphertext due to its knowledge of the sender's secret key. Certain choices of relaxing relation R can lead to another trivial attack.

A CHOICE OF RELAXING RELATION FOR AUTHENTICITY. When adversary $\mathcal{F}$ in game $G^{auth}_{SC,R,\mathcal{F}}$ calls oracle SIGENC on inputs $id_s, \mathcal{I}, m, ad$, then for each ciphertext c produced for a recipient $id_r \in \mathcal{I}$ the game adds a tuple $((id_s, id_r, m, ad), c)$ to set Q. This set is then used inside oracle VERDEC. Oracle VERDEC constructs $z_0 = ((id_s, id_r, m, ad), c)$ and prevents the adversary from winning the game if $R.\mathsf{Vf}(z_0, z_1)$ is true for any $z_1 \in Q$. If the relaxing relation is empty (meaning $R = \emptyset$ and hence $R.\mathsf{Vf}(z_0, z_1) = \mathsf{false}$ for all $z_0, z_1 \in \{0, 1\}^*$) then an adversary is allowed to trivially win the game by calling oracle SIGENC and claiming any of the resulting ciphertexts as a forgery (without changing the sender and recipient identities). Let us call this a "ciphertext replay" attack.

In order to capture a meaningful security notion, the AUTH-security of SC should be considered with respect to a relaxing relation that prohibits the above trivial attack. The strongest such security notion is achieved by considering AUTH-security of SC with respect to the relaxing relation R_{id} that is defined in Fig. 4; this relaxing relation prevents *only* the ciphertext replay attack. The resulting security notion captures the strong authenticity (or unforgeability) of signcryption. Alternatively, one could think of this notion as capturing the ciphertext integrity of signcryption.

Note that a relaxing relation R prohibits the ciphertext replay attack iff $R_{id} \subseteq R$. Now consider the relaxing relation R_m as defined in Fig. 4; it is a proper superset of R_{id}. The AUTH-security of SC with respect to R_m captures the standard authenticity (or unforgeability, or plaintext integrity) of signcryption. The resulting security notion does not let adversary win by merely replaying an encryption of (m, ad) from id_s to id_r for any fixed (id_s, id_r, m, ad), even if the adversary can produce a new ciphertext that was not seen before.

CAPTURING OUTSIDER AUTHENTICITY. Game $G^{auth}_{SC,R,\mathcal{F}}$ captures the authenticity of SC in the *insider* setting, because it allows adversary to win by producing a forgery from an honest sender identity to an *exposed* recipient identity. This, in particular, implies that SC assures non-repudiation, meaning that the sender cannot deny the validity of a ciphertext it sent to a recipient (since the knowledge of the recipient's secret key does not help to produce a forgery). In contrast, the *outsider* authenticity only requires SC to be secure when both the sender and the recipient are honest. Our definition can capture the notion of outsider authenticity by considering a class of *outsider* adversaries that never query VERDEC(id_s, id_r, c, ad) when $\exp[id_r] = $ true.

PRIVACY OF SIGNCRYPTION. Consider game G^{priv} of Fig. 6 associated to a signcryption scheme SC, a relaxing relation R and an adversary $\mathcal{D}$. The advantage of adversary $\mathcal{D}$ in breaking the PRIV-security of SC with respect to R is defined as $Adv^{priv}_{SC,R}(\mathcal{D}) = 2 \Pr[G^{priv}_{SC,R,\mathcal{D}}] - 1$. The game samples a challenge bit $b \in \{0, 1\}$, and the adversary is required to guess it. Adversary $\mathcal{D}$ has access to oracles NEWH, NEWC, EXP, LR, and VERDEC. The oracles can be called in any order. Oracles NEWH, NEWC, and EXP are the same as in the authenticity game (with the exception of oracle EXP also checking table ch, which is explained below). Oracle LR encrypts challenge message m_b with associated data ad, produced by sender identity id_s to each of the recipient identities contained in set $\mathcal{I}$. Oracle LR aborts if $m_0 \neq m_1$ and if the recipient set $\mathcal{I}$ contains an identity id_r that is exposed. Otherwise, the adversary would be able to trivially win the game by using the exposed recipient's secret key to decrypt a challenge ciphertext produced by this oracle. If $m_0 \neq m_1$ and none of the recipient identities is exposed, then oracle LR uses table ch to mark each of the recipient identities; the game will no longer allow to expose any of these identities by calling oracle EXP. Oracle VERDEC returns the plaintext obtained as the result of unsigncrypting the ciphertext c sent from id_s to id_r with associated data ad. We discuss the choice of a relaxing relation R below. However, note that oracle LR updates the set Q (used by relaxing relation) only when $m_0 \neq m_1$. This is because the output of LR does not depend on the challenge bit when $m_0 = m_1$, and hence such queries should not affect the set of prohibited queries to oracle VERDEC.

OUTPUTS OF ORACLE VERDEC. The output of oracle VERDEC in game G^{priv} is a pair containing the plaintext (or the incorrect decryption symbol $\bot$) as its first element, and the status message as its second element. This ensures that the adversary can distinguish whether VERDEC returned $\bot$ because it failed to decrypt the ciphertext (yields error message "dec"), or because the relaxing relation prohibits the query (yields error message "priv"). Giving more information to the adversary results in a stronger security definition, and will help us prove equivalence between the joint and separate security notions of signcryption in [13]. Note that an adversary can distinguish between different output branches of all other oracles used in our authenticity and privacy games.

Game $G_{\mathsf{SC},\mathsf{R},\mathcal{D}}^{\mathsf{priv}}$

$b \leftarrow_\$ \{0,1\}$; $\pi \leftarrow_\$ \mathsf{SC.Setup}$; $b' \leftarrow_\$ \mathcal{D}^{\mathrm{NEWH,NEWC,EXP,LR,VERDEC}}(\pi)$; Return $b' = b$

$\underline{\mathrm{NEWH}(id)}$
If initialized$[id]$ then return $\bot$
initialized$[id] \leftarrow$ true ; $(pk, sk) \leftarrow_\$ \mathsf{SC.Kg}(\pi)$; $\mathsf{pk}[id] \leftarrow pk$; $\mathsf{sk}[id] \leftarrow sk$; Return pk

$\underline{\mathrm{NEWC}(id, pk, sk)}$
If initialized$[id]$ then return $\bot$
initialized$[id] \leftarrow$ true ; $\exp[id] \leftarrow$ true ; $\mathsf{pk}[id] \leftarrow pk$; $\mathsf{sk}[id] \leftarrow sk$; Return true

$\underline{\mathrm{EXP}(id)}$
If (not initialized$[id]$) or ch$[id]$ then return $\bot$
$\exp[id] \leftarrow$ true ; Return $\mathsf{sk}[id]$

$\underline{\mathrm{LR}(id_s, \mathcal{I}, m_0, m_1, \mathsf{ad})}$
If (not initialized$[id_s]$) or ($\exists id \in \mathcal{I}$: not initialized$[id]$) or $|m_0| \neq |m_1|$ then return $\bot$
If $m_0 \neq m_1$ then
    If $\exists id \in \mathcal{I}$: $\exp[id]$ then return $\bot$
    For each $id \in \mathcal{I}$ do ch$[id] \leftarrow$ true
$\mathcal{R} \leftarrow \emptyset$; For each $id \in \mathcal{I}$ do $\mathcal{R} \leftarrow \mathcal{R} \cup \{(id, \mathsf{pk}[id])\}$
$\mathcal{C} \leftarrow_\$ \mathsf{SC.SigEnc}(\pi, id_s, \mathsf{pk}[id_s], \mathsf{sk}[id_s], \mathcal{R}, m_b, \mathsf{ad})$
For each $(id_r, c) \in \mathcal{C}$ do
    If $m_0 \neq m_1$ then
        $Q \leftarrow Q \cup \{((id_s, id_r, m_0, \mathsf{ad}), c)\}$
        $Q \leftarrow Q \cup \{((id_s, id_r, m_1, \mathsf{ad}), c)\}$
Return $\mathcal{C}$

$\underline{\mathrm{VERDEC}(id_s, id_r, c, \mathsf{ad})}$
If (not initialized$[id_s]$) or (not initialized$[id_r]$) then return $(\bot, \text{"init"})$
$m \leftarrow \mathsf{SC.VerDec}(\pi, id_s, \mathsf{pk}[id_s], id_r, \mathsf{pk}[id_r], \mathsf{sk}[id_r], c, \mathsf{ad})$
If $m = \bot$ then return $(\bot, \text{"dec"})$
$z_0 \leftarrow ((id_s, id_r, m, \mathsf{ad}), c)$; If $\exists z_1 \in Q$: $\mathsf{R.Vf}(z_0, z_1)$ then return $(\bot, \text{"priv"})$
Return $(m, \text{"ok"})$

Fig. 6. Games defining privacy of signcryption scheme SC with respect to relaxing relation R.

A CHOICE OF RELAXING RELATION FOR PRIVACY. Consider relaxing relations R_{id} and R_{m} that are defined in Fig. 4. We recover IND-CCA security of SC as the PRIV-security of SC with respect to R_{id}. And we capture the RCCA security of SC as the PRIV-security of SC with respect to R_{m}. Recall that the intuition behind the RCCA security [18, 27] is to prohibit the adversary from querying its decryption oracle with ciphertexts that encrypt a previously queried challenge message. In particular, this is the reason that two elements are added to set Q during each call to oracle LR, one for each of m_0 and m_1. Our definition of RCCA security for SC is very similar to that of IND-gCCA2 security as proposed by An, Dodis and Rabin [3]. The difference is that our definition passes the decrypted

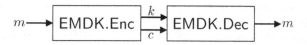

Fig. 7. Constituent algorithms of encryption scheme under message derived keys EMDK.

message as input to the relation, whereas IND-gCCA2 instead allows relations that take public keys of sender and recipient as input. It is not clear that having the relation take the public key would make our definition meaningfully stronger.

CAPTURING OUTSIDER PRIVACY. Game $G^{priv}_{SC,R,\mathcal{D}}$ captures the privacy of SC in the *insider* setting, meaning that the adversary is allowed to request challenge encryptions from id_s to id_r even when id_s is exposed. This implies some form of forward security because exposing the sender's key does not help the adversary win the indistinguishability game. To recover the notion of *outsider* privacy, consider a class of *outsider* adversaries that never query $LR(id_s, \mathcal{I}, m_0, m_1, ad)$ when $exp[id_s] = \text{true}$.

4 Encryption Under Message Derived Keys

We now define Encryption under Message Derived Keys (EMDK). It can be thought of as a special type of symmetric encryption allowing to use keys that depend on the messages to be encrypted. This type of primitive will be at the core of analyzing the security of iMessage-based signcryption scheme. In Sect. 4.1 we define syntax, correctness and basic security notions for EMDK schemes. In Sect. 4.2 we define the iMessage-based EMDK scheme and analyse its security.

4.1 Syntax, Correctness and Security of EMDK

We start by defining the syntax and correctness of encryption schemes under message derived keys. The interaction between constituent algorithms of EMDK is shown in Fig. 7. The main security notions for EMDK schemes are AE (authenticated encryption) and ROB (robustness). We also define the IND (indistinguishability) notion that will be used in Sect. 4.2 for an intermediate result towards showing the AE-security of the iMessage-based EMDK scheme.

ENCRYPTION SCHEMES UNDER MESSAGE DERIVED KEYS. An encryption scheme under message derived keys EMDK specifies algorithms EMDK.Enc and EMDK.Dec, where EMDK.Dec is deterministic. Associated to EMDK is a key length $EMDK.kl \in \mathbb{N}$. The encryption algorithm EMDK.Enc takes a message $m \in \{0,1\}^*$ to return a key $k \in \{0,1\}^{EMDK.kl}$ and a ciphertext $c \in \{0,1\}^*$. The decryption algorithm EMDK.Dec takes k, c to return message $m \in \{0,1\}^* \cup \{\bot\}$, where $\bot$ denotes incorrect decryption. Decryption correctness requires that $EMDK.Dec(k, c) = m$ for all $m \in \{0,1\}^*$, and all $(k, c) \in [EMDK.Enc(m)]$.

Game $G^{ind}_{EMDK,\mathcal{D}}$	Game $G^{ae}_{EMDK,\mathcal{D}}$	Game $G^{rob}_{EMDK,\mathcal{G}}$
$b \leftarrow_\$ \{0,1\}$; $b' \leftarrow_\$ \mathcal{D}^{LR}$ Return $b = b'$	$b \leftarrow_\$ \{0,1\}$; $b' \leftarrow_\$ \mathcal{D}^{LR,DEC}$ Return $b = b'$	$(i,k) \leftarrow_\$ \mathcal{G}^{ENC}$ If $i \notin [n]$ then return false $m \leftarrow EMDK.Dec(k, c[i])$ $win_1 \leftarrow (m \neq \bot)$
$\underline{LR(m_0, m_1)}$ If $|m_0| \neq |m_1|$ then return $\bot$ $(k,c) \leftarrow_\$ EMDK.Enc(m_b)$ Return c	$\underline{LR(m_0, m_1)}$ If $|m_0| \neq |m_1|$ then return $\bot$ $n \leftarrow n + 1$ $(k[n], c[n]) \leftarrow_\$ EMDK.Enc(m_b)$ Return $(n, c[n])$	$win_2 \leftarrow (m \neq m[i])$ Return win_1 and win_2 $\underline{ENC(m)}$ $(k,c) \leftarrow_\$ EMDK.Enc(m)$
	$\underline{DEC(i,c)}$ If $i \notin [n]$ or $c[i] = c$ then return $\bot$ $m \leftarrow EMDK.Dec(k[i], c)$ If $b = 1$ then return m Else return $\bot$	$n \leftarrow n + 1$; $m[n] \leftarrow m$; $c[n] \leftarrow c$ Return (k,c)

Fig. 8. Games defining indistinguishability, authenticated encryption security, and robustness of encryption scheme under message derived keys EMDK.

INDISTINGUISHABILITY OF EMDK. Consider game G^{ind} of Fig. 8, associated to an encryption scheme under message derived keys EMDK, and to an adversary $\mathcal{D}$. The advantage of $\mathcal{D}$ in breaking the IND security of EMDK is defined as $Adv^{ind}_{EMDK}(\mathcal{D}) = 2 \cdot \Pr[G^{ind}_{EMDK,\mathcal{D}}] - 1$. The game samples a random challenge bit b and requires the adversary to guess it. The adversary has access to an encryption oracle LR that takes two challenge messages m_0, m_1 to return an EMDK encryption of m_b.

AUTHENTICATED ENCRYPTION SECURITY OF EMDK. Consider game G^{ae} of Fig. 8, associated to an encryption scheme under message derived keys EMDK, and to an adversary $\mathcal{D}$. The advantage of $\mathcal{D}$ in breaking the AE security of EMDK is defined as $Adv^{ae}_{EMDK}(\mathcal{D}) = 2 \cdot \Pr[G^{ae}_{EMDK,\mathcal{D}}] - 1$. Compared to the indistinguishability game from above, game G^{ae} saves the keys and ciphertexts produced by oracle LR, and also provides a decryption oracle DEC to adversary $\mathcal{D}$. The decryption oracle allows to decrypt a ciphertext with any key that was saved by oracle Enc, returning either the actual decryption m (if $b = 1$) or the incorrect decryption symbol $\bot$ (if $b = 0$). To prevent trivial wins, the adversary is not allowed to query oracle DEC with a key-ciphertext pair that were produced by the same LR query.

ROBUSTNESS OF EMDK. Consider game G^{rob} of Fig. 8, associated to an encryption scheme under message derived keys EMDK, and to an adversary $\mathcal{G}$. The advantage of $\mathcal{G}$ in breaking the ROB security of EMDK is defined as $Adv^{rob}_{EMDK}(\mathcal{G}) = \Pr[G^{rob}_{EMDK,\mathcal{G}}]$. To win the game, adversary $\mathcal{G}$ is required to find (c, k_0, k_1, m_0, m_1) such that c decrypts to m_0 under key k_0, and c decrypts to m_1 under key k_1, but $m_0 \neq m_1$. Furthermore, the game requires that the ciphertext (along with one of the keys) was produced during a call to oracle ENC that takes a message m as input to return the output (k, c) of running $EMDK.Enc(m)$

EMDK.Enc$^{RO}(m)$	EMDK.Dec$^{RO}(k,c)$	RO(z,ℓ)
$k \leftarrow\!\!{}_\$ \{0,1\}^{\text{EMDK.kl}}$; $\ell \leftarrow |m|$	$(x,h) \leftarrow c$; $\ell \leftarrow |x|$	If $T[z,\ell] = \bot$ then
$x \leftarrow m \oplus \text{RO}(k,\ell)$	$m \leftarrow x \oplus \text{RO}(k,\ell)$	$T[z,\ell] \leftarrow\!\!{}_\$ \{0,1\}^\ell$
$h \leftarrow \text{RO}(k \parallel m, \ell)$	$h' \leftarrow \text{RO}(k \parallel m, \ell)$	Return $T[z,\ell]$
$c \leftarrow (x,h)$	If $h \neq h'$ then return $\bot$	
Return (k,c)	Else return m	

Fig. 9. Sample EMDK scheme EMDK = SIMPLE-EMDK in the ROM.

EMDK.Enc(m)	EMDK.Dec(k, c_{se})
$r_0 \leftarrow\!\!{}_\$ \{0,1\}^{\text{F.kl}}$; $r_1 \leftarrow \text{F.Ev}(r_0, m)$	$m \leftarrow \text{SE.Dec}(k, c_{se})$; If $m = \bot$ then return $\bot$
$k \leftarrow r_0 \parallel r_1$; $c_{se} \leftarrow\!\!{}_\$ \text{SE.Enc}(k, m)$	$r_0 \leftarrow k[1 \dots \text{F.kl}]$; $r_1 \leftarrow k[\text{F.kl} + 1 \dots \text{SE.kl}]$
Return (k, c_{se})	If $r_1 \neq \text{F.Ev}(r_0, m)$ then return $\bot$
	Return m

Fig. 10. iMessage-based EMDK scheme EMDK = IMSG-EMDK[F, SE].

with honestly generated random coins. The other key can be arbitrarily chosen by the adversary. In the symmetric encryption setting, a similar notion called *wrong-key detection* was previously defined by Canetti et al. [17]. The notion of robustness for public-key encryption was formalized by Abdalla et al. [1] and further extended by Farshim et al. [23].

SAMPLE EMDK SCHEME SIMPLE-EMDK. It is easy to build an EMDK scheme that is both AE-secure and ROB-secure. One example of such scheme is the construction SIMPLE-EMDK in the random oracle model (ROM) that is defined in Fig. 9. In the next section we will define the EMDK scheme used iMessage; it looks convoluted, and its security is hard to prove even in the ideal models. In [13] we define the EMDK scheme that was initially used in iMessage; it was replaced with the current EMDK scheme in order to fix a security flaw in the iMessage design. We believe that the design of the currently used EMDK scheme was chosen based on a requirement to maintain backward-compatibility across the initial and the current versions of iMessage protocol.

4.2 iMessage-Based EMDK Scheme

In this section we define the EMDK scheme IMSG-EMDK that is used as the core building block in the construction of iMessage (we use it to specify the iMessage-based signcryption scheme in Sect. 5). We will provide reductions showing the AE-security and the ROB-security of IMSG-EMDK. These security reductions will first require us to introduce two new security notions for symmetric encryption schemes: *partial key recovery* and *weak robustness*.

EMDK SCHEME IMSG-EMDK. Let SE be a symmetric encryption scheme. Let F be a function family with F.In $= \{0,1\}^*$ such that F.kl + F.ol = SE.kl. Then

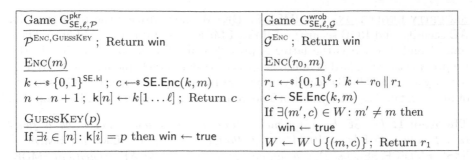

Fig. 11. Games defining partial key recovery security of symmetric encryption scheme SE with respect to prefix length ℓ, and weak robustness of deterministic symmetric encryption scheme SE with respect to randomized key-suffix length ℓ.

EMDK = IMSG-EMDK[F, SE] is the EMDK scheme as defined in Fig. 10, with key length EMDK.kl = SE.kl.

Informally, the encryption algorithm EMDK.Enc(m) samples a hash function key r_0 and computes hash $r_1 \leftarrow_\$ \mathsf{F.Ev}(r_0, m)$. It then encrypts m by running SE.Enc(k, m), where $k = r_0 \| r_1$ is a message-derived key. The decryption algorithm splits k into r_0 and r_1 and – upon recovering m – checks that $r_1 = \mathsf{F.Ev}(r_0, m)$. In the iMessage construction, SE is instantiated with AES-CTR using 128-bit keys and a fixed IV=1, whereas F is instantiated with HMAC-SHA256 using F.kl = 88 and F.ol = 40.

PARTIAL KEY RECOVERY SECURITY OF SE. Consider game $\mathsf{G}^{\mathsf{pkr}}$ of Fig. 11, associated to a symmetric encryption scheme SE, a prefix length $\ell \in \mathbb{N}$ and an adversary $\mathcal{P}$. The advantage of $\mathcal{P}$ in breaking the PKR-security of SE with respect to ℓ is defined as $\mathsf{Adv}^{\mathsf{pkr}}_{\mathsf{SE},\ell}(\mathcal{P}) = \Pr[\mathsf{G}^{\mathsf{pkr}}_{\mathsf{SE},\ell,\mathcal{P}}]$. The adversary $\mathcal{P}$ has access to oracle ENC that takes a message m and encrypts it under a uniformly random key k (independently sampled for each oracle call). The goal of the adversary is to recover the first ℓ bits of *any* secret key that was used in prior ENC queries.

WEAK ROBUSTNESS OF DETERMINISTIC SE. Consider game $\mathsf{G}^{\mathsf{wrob}}$ of Fig. 11, associated to a deterministic symmetric encryption scheme SE, a randomized key-suffix length $\ell \in \mathbb{N}$, and an adversary $\mathcal{G}$. The advantage of $\mathcal{G}$ in breaking the WROB-security of SE with respect to ℓ is defined as $\mathsf{Adv}^{\mathsf{wrob}}_{\mathsf{SE},\ell}(\mathcal{G}) = \Pr[\mathsf{G}^{\mathsf{wrob}}_{\mathsf{SE},\ell,\mathcal{G}}]$. The adversary has access to oracle ENC. The oracle takes a prefix of an encryption key $r_0 \in \{0,1\}^{\mathsf{SE.kl}-\ell}$ and message m as input. It then randomly samples the suffix of the key $r_1 \in \{0,1\}^\ell$ and returns it to the adversary. The adversary wins if it succeeds to query ENC on some inputs (r_0, m) and (r_0', m') such that $m \neq m'$ yet the oracle mapped both queries to the same ciphertext c. In other words, the goal of the adversary is to find k_0, m_0, k_1, m_1 such that SE.Enc$(k_0, m_0) = $ SE.Enc(k_1, m_1) and $m_0 \neq m_1$ (which also implies $k_0 \neq k_1$), and the adversary has only a partial control over the choice of k_0 and k_1. Note that this assumption can be validated in the ideal cipher model.

SECURITY REDUCTIONS FOR IMSG-EMDK. We now provide the reductions for AE-security and ROB-security of IMSG-EMDK. The former is split into Theorems 1 and 2, whereas the latter is provided in Theorem 3. Note that in [13] we provide the standard definitions for the random oracle model, the UNIQUE-security and the OTIND-security of symmetric encryption, and the TCR-security of function families. The proofs of Theorems 1, 2 and 3 are in the full version [13].

Theorem 1. *Let* SE *be a symmetric encryption scheme. Let* F *be a function family with* F.In $= \{0,1\}^*$, *such that* F.kl $+$ F.ol $=$ SE.kl. *Let* EMDK $=$ IMSG-EMDK[F, SE]. *Let* $\mathcal{D}_{AE}$ *be an adversary against the AE-security of* EMDK. *Then we build an adversary* $\mathcal{U}$ *against the UNIQUE-security of* SE, *an adversary* $\mathcal{H}$ *against the TCR-security of* F, *and an adversary* $\mathcal{D}_{IND}$ *against the IND-security of* EMDK *such that*

$$\mathsf{Adv}^{ae}_{EMDK}(\mathcal{D}_{AE}) \leq 2 \cdot \mathsf{Adv}^{unique}_{SE}(\mathcal{U}) + 2 \cdot \mathsf{Adv}^{tcr}_{F}(\mathcal{H}) + \mathsf{Adv}^{ind}_{EMDK}(\mathcal{D}_{IND}).$$

Theorem 2. *Let* SE *be a symmetric encryption scheme. Let* F *be a function family with* F.In $= \{0,1\}^*$ *and* F.kl $+$ F.ol $=$ SE.kl, *defined by* F.Ev$^{RO}(r,m) =$ RO$(\langle r,m \rangle, $F.ol$)$ *in the random oracle model. Let* EMDK $=$ IMSG-EMDK[F, SE]. *Let* $\mathcal{D}_{EMDK}$ *be an adversary against the IND-security of* EMDK *that makes* q_{LR} *queries to its* LR *oracle and* q_{RO} *queries to random oracle* RO. *Then we build an adversary* $\mathcal{P}$ *against the PKR-security of* SE *with respect to* F.kl, *and an adversary* $\mathcal{D}_{SE}$ *against the OTIND-security of* SE, *such that*

$$\mathsf{Adv}^{ind}_{EMDK}(\mathcal{D}_{EMDK}) \leq 2 \cdot \gamma + 2 \cdot \mathsf{Adv}^{pkr}_{SE,F.kl}(\mathcal{P}) + \mathsf{Adv}^{otind}_{SE}(\mathcal{D}_{SE}),$$

where

$$\gamma = \frac{(2 \cdot q_{RO} + q_{LR} - 1) \cdot q_{LR}}{2^{F.kl+1}}.$$

Theorem 3. *Let* SE *be a deterministic symmetric encryption scheme. Let* F *be a function family with* F.In $= \{0,1\}^*$ *and* F.kl $+$ F.ol $=$ SE.kl, *defined by* F.Ev$^{RO}(r,m) =$ RO$(\langle r,m \rangle, $F.ol$)$ *in the random oracle model. Let* EMDK $=$ IMSG-EMDK[F, SE]. *Let* $\mathcal{G}_{EMDK}$ *be an adversary against the ROB-security of* EMDK. *Then we build an adversary* $\mathcal{U}$ *against the UNIQUE-security of* SE, *and an adversary* $\mathcal{G}_{SE}$ *against the WROB-security of* SE *with respect to* F.ol *such that*

$$\mathsf{Adv}^{rob}_{EMDK}(\mathcal{G}_{EMDK}) \leq \mathsf{Adv}^{unique}_{SE}(\mathcal{U}) + \mathsf{Adv}^{wrob}_{SE,F.ol}(\mathcal{G}_{SE}).$$

5 Design and Security of iMessage

In this section we define a signcryption scheme that models the current design of iMessage protocol for end-to-end encrypted messaging, and we analyze its security. All publicly available information about the iMessage protocol is provided by Apple in *iOS Security Guide* [4] that is regularly updated but is very limited and vague. So in addition to the iOS Security Guide, we also reference work that attempted to reverse-engineer [32,34] and attack [26] the prior versions of iMessage. A message-recovery attack against iMessage was previously

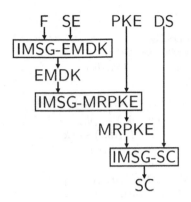

Scheme	Construction	Figure
EMDK	IMSG-EMDK[F, SE]	10
MRPKE	IMSG-MRPKE[EMDK, PKE]	14
SC	IMSG-SC[MRPKE, DS]	13

Scheme	Instantiation
F	HMAC-SHA256 (F.kl = 88, F.ol = 40)
SE	AES-CTR with 128-bit key and IV=1
PKE	RSA-OAEP with 1280-bit key
DS	ECDSA with NIST P-256 curve

Fig. 12. Modular design of iMessage-based signcryption scheme. The boxed nodes in the diagram denote transforms that build a new cryptographic scheme from two underlying primitives.

found and implemented by Garman et al. [26] in 2016, and subsequently fixed by Apple starting from version 9.3 of iOS, and version 10.11.4 of Mac OS X. The implemented changes to the protocol prevented the attack, but also made the protocol design less intuitive. It appears that one of the goals of the updated protocol design was to preserve backward-compatibility, and that could be the reason why the current design is a lot more more sophisticated than otherwise necessary. Apple has not formalized any claims about the security achieved by the initial or the current iMessage protocol, or the assumptions that are required from the cryptographic primitives that serve as the building blocks. We fill in the gap by providing precise claims about the security of iMessage design when modeled by our signcryption scheme. In this section we focus only on the current protocol design of iMessage. In [13] we provide the design of the initial iMessage protocol, we explain the attack proposed by Garman et al. [26], and we introduce the goal of backward-compatibility for signcryption schemes.

5.1   iMessage-Based Signcryption Scheme IMSG-SC

IDENTIFYING SIGNCRYPTION AS THE GOAL. The design of iMessage combines multiple cryptographic primitives to build an end-to-end encrypted messaging protocol. It uses HMAC-SHA256, AES-CTR, RSA-OAEP and ECDSA as the underlying primitives. Apple's *iOS Security Guide* [4] and prior work on reverse-engineering and analysis of iMessage [26,32,34] does not explicitly indicate what type of cryptographic scheme is built as the result of combining these primitives. We identify it as a signcryption scheme. We define the iMessage-based signcryption scheme IMSG-SC in a modular way that facilitates its security analysis. Figure 12 shows the order in which the underlying primitives are combined to build IMSG-SC, while also providing intermediate constructions along the way. We now explain this step by step.

SC.Setup	SC.Kg(π)
$\pi \leftarrow$ MRPKE.Setup ; Return π	$(vk, tk) \leftarrow\!\!\$ DS.Kg
	$(ek, dk) \leftarrow\!\!\$ MRPKE.Kg(π)
SC.SigEnc($\pi, id_s, pk_s, sk_s, \mathcal{R}, m, ad$)	$pk \leftarrow (vk, ek)$; $sk \leftarrow (tk, dk)$
$\mathcal{I} \leftarrow \emptyset$; $\mathcal{R}_{pke} \leftarrow \emptyset$; $\mathcal{C} \leftarrow \emptyset$	Return (pk, sk)
For each $(id_r, pk_r) \in \mathcal{R}$ do	
$\quad (vk_r, ek_r) \leftarrow pk_r$	SC.VerDec($\pi, id_s, pk_s, id_r, pk_r, sk_r, c, ad$)
$\quad \mathcal{I} \leftarrow \mathcal{I} \cup \{id_r\}$	$(c_{pke}, \sigma) \leftarrow c$; $(vk_s, ek_s) \leftarrow pk_s$
$\quad \mathcal{R}_{pke} \leftarrow \mathcal{R}_{pke} \cup \{(id_r, ek_r)\}$	$(vk_r, ek_r) \leftarrow pk_r$; $(tk_r, dk_r) \leftarrow sk_r$
$m_{pke} \leftarrow \langle m, id_s, \mathcal{I} \rangle$	$d \leftarrow$ DS.Ver($vk_s, \langle c_{pke}, ad \rangle, \sigma$)
$\mathcal{C}_{pke} \leftarrow\!\!\$ MRPKE.Enc($\pi, \mathcal{R}_{pke}, m_{pke}$)	If not d then return $\bot$
$(tk_s, dk_s) \leftarrow sk_s$	$m_{pke} \leftarrow$ MRPKE.Dec(π, ek_r, dk_r, c_{pke})
For each $(id_r, c_{pke}) \in \mathcal{C}_{pke}$ do	If $m_{pke} = \bot$ then return $\bot$
$\quad \sigma \leftarrow\!\!\$ DS.Sig($tk_s, \langle c_{pke}, ad \rangle$)	$\langle m, id_s^*, \mathcal{I} \rangle \leftarrow m_{pke}$
$\quad c \leftarrow (c_{pke}, \sigma)$; $\mathcal{C} \leftarrow \mathcal{C} \cup \{(id_r, c)\}$	If $id_s \neq id_s^*$ or $id_r \notin \mathcal{I}$ then return $\bot$
Return $\mathcal{C}$	Return m

Fig. 13. Signcryption scheme SC = IMSG-SC[MRPKE, DS].

MODULAR DESIGN OF IMSG-SC. Our construction starts from choosing a function family F and a symmetric encryption scheme SE (instantiated with HMAC-SHA256 and AES-CTR in iMessage). It combines them to build an encryption scheme under message derived keys EMDK = IMSG-EMDK[F, SE]. The resulting EMDK scheme is combined with public-key encryption scheme PKE (instantiated with RSA-OAEP in iMessage) to build a multi-recipient public-key encryption scheme MRPKE = IMSG-MRPKE[EMDK, PKE] (syntax and correctness of MRPKE schemes is defined in [13]). Finally, MRPKE and digital signature scheme DS (instantiated with ECDSA in iMessage) are combined to build the iMessage-based signcryption scheme SC = IMSG-SC[MRPKE, DS]. The definition of IMSG-EMDK was provided in Sect. 4.2. We now define IMSG-SC and IMSG-MRPKE.

SIGNCRYPTION SCHEME IMSG-SC. Let MRPKE be a multi-recipient public-key encryption scheme. Let DS be a digital signature scheme. Then SC = IMSG-SC[MRPKE, DS] is the signcryption scheme as defined in Fig. 13, with SC.ID = $\{0, 1\}^*$. In order to produce a signcryption of message m with associated data ad, algorithm SC.SigEnc performs the following steps. It builds a new message $m_{pke} = \langle m, id_s, \mathcal{I} \rangle$ as the unique encoding of $m, id_s, \mathcal{I}$, where $\mathcal{I}$ is the set of recipients. It then calls MRPKE.Enc to encrypt the same message m_{pke} for every recipient. Algorithm MRPKE.Enc returns a set $\mathcal{C}_{pke}$ containing pairs (id_r, c_{pke}), each indicating that an MRPKE ciphertext c_{pke} was produced for recipient id_r. For each recipient, the corresponding ciphertext c_{pke} is then encoded with the associated data ad into $\langle c_{pke}, ad \rangle$ and signed using the signing

MRPKE.Setup	MRPKE.Kg(π)
$\pi \leftarrow \varepsilon$; Return π	$(ek, dk) \leftarrow\!\!\$ \ PKE.Kg$; Return (ek, dk)
MRPKE.Enc($\pi, \mathcal{R}, m$)	MRPKE.Dec(π, ek, dk, c)
$\mathcal{C} \leftarrow \emptyset$; $(k, c_{se}) \leftarrow\!\!\$ \ EMDK.Enc(m)	$(c_{se}, c_{pke}) \leftarrow c$
For each $(id_r, ek_r) \in \mathcal{R}$ do	$k \leftarrow$ PKE.Dec(ek, dk, c_{pke})
$\quad c_{pke} \leftarrow\!\!\$ \ PKE.Enc(ek_r, k)	If $k = \perp$ then return $\perp$
$\quad c \leftarrow (c_{se}, c_{pke})$; $\mathcal{C} \leftarrow \mathcal{C} \cup \{(id_r, c)\}$	$m \leftarrow$ EMDK.Dec(k, c_{se})
Return $\mathcal{C}$	Return m

Fig. 14. Multi-recipient public-key encryption scheme MRPKE = IMSG-MRPKE [EMDK, PKE].

key tk_s of sender identity id_s, producing a signature σ. The pair $(id_r, (c_{pke}, \sigma))$ is then added to the output set of algorithm SC.SigEnc. When running the unsigncryption of ciphertext c sent from id_s to id_r, algorithm SC.VerDec ensures that the recovered MRPKE plaintext $m_{pke} = \langle m, id_s^*, \mathcal{I} \rangle$ is consistent with $id_s = id_s^*$ and $id_r \in \mathcal{I}$.

MULTI-RECIPIENT PUBLIC-KEY ENCRYPTION SCHEME IMSG-MRPKE. Let EMDK be an encryption scheme under message derived keys. Let PKE be a public-key encryption scheme with PKE.In = $\{0, 1\}^{\text{EMDK.kl}}$. Then MRPKE = IMSG-MRPKE[EMDK, PKE] is the multi-recipient public-key encryption scheme as defined in Fig. 14. Algorithm MRPKE.Enc first runs $(k, c_{se}) \leftarrow\!\!\$ \ EMDK.Enc(m) to produce an EMDK ciphertext c_{se} that encrypts m under key k. The obtained key k is then independently encrypted for each recipient identity id_r using its PKE encryption key ek_r, and the corresponding tuple $(id_r, (c_{se}, c_{pke}))$ is added to the output set of algorithm MRPKE.Enc.

COMBINING EVERYTHING TOGETHER. Let SC be the iMessage-based signcryption scheme that is produced by combining all of the underlying primitives described above. Then the data flow within the fully expanded algorithms SC.SigEnc and SC.VerDec is schematically displayed in Fig. 15. For simplicity, the diagrams show the case when a message m is sent to a single recipient id_r.

5.2   Parameter-Choice Induced Attacks on Privacy of iMessage

The iMessage-based signcryption scheme SC uses the EMDK scheme EMDK = IMSG-EMDK[F, SE] as one of its underlying primitives. Recall that in order to encrypt a payload $m' = \langle m, id_s, \mathcal{I} \rangle$, the EMDK scheme samples a function key $r_0 \leftarrow\!\!\$ \ \{0, 1\}^{\text{F.kl}}$, computes a hash of m' as $r_1 \leftarrow$ F.Ev(r_0, m'), sets the encryption key $k \leftarrow r_0 \| r_1$, and produces a ciphertext as $c_{se} \leftarrow\!\!\$ \ SE.Enc(k, m'). The implementation of iMessage uses parameters F.kl = 88 and F.ol = 40. In this section we provide three adversaries against the privacy of SC whose success depends on the choice of F.kl and F.ol. In next sections we will provide security proofs for SC.

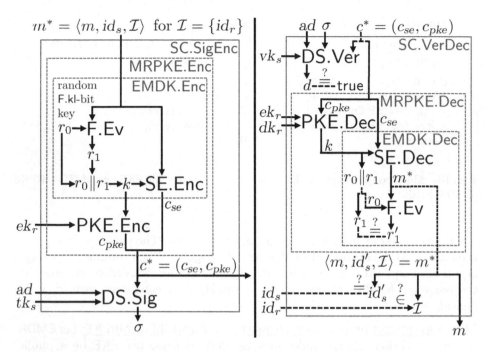

Fig. 15. Algorithms SC.SigEnc (left panel) and SC.VerDec (right panel) for SC = IMSG-SC[MRPKE, DS], where MRPKE = IMSG-MRPKE[EMDK, PKE] and EMDK = IMSG-EMDK[F, SE]. For simplicity, we let id_r be the only recipient, and we do not show how to parse inputs and combine outputs for the displayed algorithms. The dotted lines inside SC.VerDec denote equality check, and the dotted arrow denotes membership check.

We will show that each adversary in this section arises from an attack against a different step in our security proofs. We will be able to conclude that these are roughly the best attacks that arise from the choice of EMDK parameters. We will also explain why it is hard to construct any adversaries against the authenticity of SC. Now consider the adversaries of Fig. 16. The full version of this paper [13] provides a detailed explanation for each adversary.

FORMAL CLAIMS AND ANALYSIS. We provide the number of queries, the runtime complexity and the advantage of each adversary in Fig. 17. The assumptions necessary to prove the advantage are stated in Lemma 4 below. Note that $\mathcal{D}_{\text{birthday}}$ represents a purely theoretical attack, but both $\mathcal{D}_{\text{exhaustive}}$ and $\mathcal{D}_{\text{ADR02}}$ can lead to practical message-recovery attacks (the latter used by Garman et al. [26]).

Let EMDK = IMSG-EMDK[F, SE]. Adversary $\mathcal{D}_{\text{ADR02}}$ shows that EMDK can have at most F.ol bits of security with respect to PRIV, and adversary $\mathcal{D}_{\text{birthday}}$ shows that EMDK can have at most $\approx$ F.kl/2 + $\log_2$ F.kl bits of security with respect to PRIV. It follows that setting F.ol $\approx$ F.kl/2 is a good initial guideline, and roughly corresponds to the parameter choices made in iMessage. We will provide a more detailed analysis in Sect. 5.5. The proof of Lemma 4 is in the full version [13].

$$\mathcal{D}_{\text{exhaustive},n}^{\text{NewH,NewC,Exp,LR,VerDec}}(\pi)$$

$ids \leftarrow \text{"send"}$; $pk_s \leftarrow\!\!\$\ \text{NewH}(ids)$
$id_r \leftarrow \text{"recv"}$; $pk_r \leftarrow\!\!\$\ \text{NewH}(id_r)$
$\mathcal{I} \leftarrow \{id_r\}$; $ad \leftarrow \varepsilon$
$m_0 \leftarrow 0^n$; $m_1 \leftarrow\!\!\$\ \{0,1\}^n$
$\mathcal{C} \leftarrow\!\!\$\ \text{LR}(ids,\mathcal{I},m_0,m_1,ad)$
$\{(id_r,c)\} \leftarrow \mathcal{C}$; $((c_{se},c_{pke}),\sigma) \leftarrow c$
$m_1' \leftarrow \langle m_1, ids, \mathcal{I}\rangle$
For each $r_0 \in \{0,1\}^{\text{F.kl}}$ do
$\quad r_1 \leftarrow \text{F.Ev}(r_0, m_1')$; $k \leftarrow r_0 \,\|\, r_1$
$\quad$ If $\text{SE.Dec}(k, c_{se}) = m_1'$ then return 1
Return 0

$$\mathcal{D}_{\text{birthday}}^{\text{NewH,NewC,Exp,LR,VerDec}}(\pi)$$

$ids \leftarrow \text{"send"}$; $pk_s \leftarrow\!\!\$\ \text{NewH}(ids)$
$id_r \leftarrow \text{"recv"}$; $pk_r \leftarrow\!\!\$\ \text{NewH}(id_r)$
$\mathcal{I} \leftarrow \{id_r\}$; $ad \leftarrow \varepsilon$
$S \leftarrow \emptyset$; $p \leftarrow \lceil \text{F.kl}/2 \rceil$; $m_1 \leftarrow 0^p$
For each $m_0 \in \{0,1\}^p$ do
$\quad \mathcal{C} \leftarrow\!\!\$\ \text{LR}(ids,\mathcal{I},m_0,m_1,ad)$
$\quad \{(id_r,c)\} \leftarrow \mathcal{C}$; $((c_{se},c_{pke}),\sigma) \leftarrow c$
$\quad$ If $c_{se} \in S$ then return 1
$\quad S \leftarrow S \cup \{c_{se}\}$
Return 0

$$\mathcal{D}_{\text{ADR02}}^{\text{NewH,NewC,Exp,LR,VerDec}}(\pi)$$

$ids \leftarrow 0^{128}$; $pk_s \leftarrow\!\!\$\ \text{NewH}(ids)$; $id_r \leftarrow 1^{128}$; $pk_r \leftarrow\!\!\$\ \text{NewH}(id_r)$
$\mathcal{I} \leftarrow \{id_r\}$; $m_0 \leftarrow 0^{128}$; $m_1 \leftarrow 1^{128}$; $ad \leftarrow \varepsilon$
$\mathcal{C} \leftarrow\!\!\$\ \text{LR}(ids,\mathcal{I},m_0,m_1,ad)$; $\{(id_r,c)\} \leftarrow \mathcal{C}$; $((c_{se},c_{pke}),\sigma) \leftarrow c$
$id_c \leftarrow 0^{64}1^{64}$; $(pk_c,sk_c) \leftarrow\!\!\$\ \text{SC.Kg}(\pi)$; $\text{NewC}(id_c,pk_c,sk_c)$; $(tk_c,dk_c) \leftarrow sk_c$
$m_1' \leftarrow \langle m_1, ids, \{id_r\}\rangle$; $m_1'' \leftarrow \langle m_1, id_c, \{id_r\}\rangle$; $c_{se}' \leftarrow c_{se} \oplus (m_1' \oplus m_1'')$
$\sigma' \leftarrow\!\!\$\ \text{DS.Sig}(tk_c, \langle (c_{se}',c_{pke}),ad\rangle)$; $c' \leftarrow ((c_{se}',c_{pke}),\sigma')$
$(m,\text{err}) \leftarrow \text{VerDec}(id_c,id_r,c',ad)$; If $m = m_1$ then return 1 else return 0

Fig. 16. The resources used by adversaries $\mathcal{D}_{\text{exhaustive},n}$, $\mathcal{D}_{\text{birthday}}$ and $\mathcal{D}_{\text{ADR02}}$, and the advantage achieved by each of them. Columns labeled q_O denote the number of queries an adversary makes to oracle O. All adversaries make 2 queries to oracle NewH, and 0 queries to oracle Exp. See Lemma 4 for necessary assumptions.

Adversary	q_{LR}	q_{NewC}	q_{VerDec}	Runtime complexity	Advantage
$\mathcal{D}_{\text{exhaustive},n}$	1	0	0	$2^{\text{F.kl}}$ evaluations of F.Ev, SE.Enc	$\geq 1 - 2^{\text{SE.kl}-n}$
$\mathcal{D}_{\text{birthday}}$	$2^{\lceil \text{F.kl}/2\rceil}$	0	0	$2^p \cdot p$ for $p = \lceil \text{F.kl}/2 \rceil$	$> 1/8 - 2^{\text{F.kl}-128}$
$\mathcal{D}_{\text{ADR02}}$	1	1	1	1 evaluation of SC.Kg, DS.Sig	$= 2^{-\text{F.ol}}$

Fig. 17. Adversaries $\mathcal{D}_{\text{exhaustive},n}$, $\mathcal{D}_{\text{birthday}}$ and $\mathcal{D}_{\text{ADR02}}$ against the PRIV-security of $\text{SC} = \text{IMSG-SC}[\text{MRPKE}, \text{DS}]$, where $\text{MRPKE} = \text{IMSG-MRPKE}[\text{EMDK}, \text{PKE}]$ and $\text{EMDK} = \text{IMSG-EMDK}[\text{F}, \text{SE}]$. Adversary $\mathcal{D}_{\text{ADR02}}$ requires that SE is AES-CTR with a fixed IV.

Lemma 4. *Let* SE *be a symmetric encryption scheme. Let* F *be a function family with* $\text{F.In} = \{0,1\}^*$ *such that* $\text{F.kl} + \text{F.ol} = \text{SE.kl}$. *Let* $\text{EMDK} = \text{IMSG-EMDK}[\text{F}, \text{SE}]$. *Let* PKE *be a public-key encryption scheme with* $\text{PKE.In} = \{0,1\}^{\text{SE.kl}}$. *Let* $\text{MRPKE} = \text{IMSG-MRPKE}[\text{EMDK}, \text{PKE}]$. *Let* DS *be a digital signature scheme. Let* $\text{SC} = \text{IMSG-SC}[\text{MRPKE}, \text{DS}]$. *Let* $\text{R} \subseteq \{0,1\}^* \times \{0,1\}^*$ *be any relaxing relation. Then for any* $n > \text{SE.kl}$,

$$\text{Adv}_{\text{SC,R}}^{\text{priv}}(\mathcal{D}_{\text{exhaustive},n}) \geq 1 - 2^{\text{SE.kl}-n}.$$

Furthermore, for any $1 \leq \mathsf{F}.\mathsf{kl} \leq 124$, *if* SE *is AES-CTR with a fixed IV, and if AES is modeled as the ideal cipher, then*

$$\mathsf{Adv}^{\mathsf{priv}}_{\mathsf{SC},\mathsf{R}}(\mathcal{D}_{\mathsf{birthday}}) > 1/8 - 2^{\mathsf{F}.\mathsf{kl}-128}.$$

Let $\mathsf{R_m}$ *be the relaxing relation defined in Fig. 4. If* SE *is AES-CTR with a fixed IV, and if* F *is defined as* $\mathsf{F}.\mathsf{Ev}^{\mathrm{RO}}(r, m) = \mathrm{RO}(\langle r, m \rangle, \mathsf{F}.\mathsf{ol})$ *in the random oracle model, then*

$$\mathsf{Adv}^{\mathsf{priv}}_{\mathsf{SC},\mathsf{R_m}}(\mathcal{D}_{\mathsf{ADR02}}) = 2^{-\mathsf{F}.\mathsf{ol}}.$$

5.3 Authenticity of iMessage

In this section we reduce the authenticity of the iMessage-based signcryption scheme SC to the security of its underlying primitives. First we reduce the authenticity of $\mathsf{SC} = \mathsf{IMSG\text{-}SC[MRPKE, DS]}$ to the unforgeability of DS and to the robustness of MRPKE. And then we reduce the robustness of $\mathsf{MRPKE} = \mathsf{IMSG\text{-}MRPKE[EMDK, PKE]}$ to the robustness of *either* PKE or EMDK; it is sufficient that only one of the two is robust.

REDUCTION SHOWING AUTHENTICITY OF IMSG-SC. Recall that an SC ciphertext is a pair (c_{pke}, σ) that consists of an MRPKE ciphertext c_{pke} (encrypting some $\langle m, id_s, \mathcal{I} \rangle$) and a DS signature σ of $\langle c_{pke}, ad \rangle$. Intuitively, the authenticity of SC requires some type of unforgeability from DS in order to prevent the adversary from producing a valid signature on arbitrary c_{pke} and ad of its own choice. However, the unforgeability of DS is not a sufficient condition, because the adversary is allowed to win the game $\mathsf{G}^{\mathsf{auth}}$ by forging an SC ciphertext for a corrupted recipient identity that uses maliciously chosen SC keys. So an additional requirement is that the adversary should not be able to find an SC key pair (pk, sk) that successfully decrypts an honestly produced SC ciphertext (c_{pke}, σ) to an *unintended* message. To ensure this, we require that MRPKE is robust (as defined in the full version of this paper [13]). Note that finding a new key pair that decrypts the ciphertext to the *original* message will not help the adversary to win the game because then the decryption will fail by not finding the corrupted recipient's identity in recipient set $\mathcal{I}$.

We define unforgeability UF of a digital signature scheme with respect to a relaxing relation R, such that the standard unforgeability is captured with respect to $\mathsf{R_m}$ and the strong unforgeability is captured with respect to $\mathsf{R_{id}}$. The formal definition is in the full version [13]. We show that if DS is UF-secure with respect to a relaxing relation $\mathsf{R}^* \in \{\mathsf{R_m}, \mathsf{R_{id}}\}$ then SC is AUTH-secure with respect to the corresponding parameterized relaxing relation $\mathsf{IMSG\text{-}AUTH\text{-}REL[R^*]}$, which we define below. ECDSA signatures are not strongly unforgeable [25], so iMessage is AUTH-secure with respect to $\mathsf{IMSG\text{-}AUTH\text{-}REL[R_m]}$.

RELAXING RELATION IMSG-AUTH-REL. Let $\mathsf{R_m}$ and $\mathsf{R_{id}}$ be the relaxing relations defined in Sect. 3. Let $\mathsf{R}^* \in \{\mathsf{R_m}, \mathsf{R_{id}}\}$. Then $\mathsf{IMSG\text{-}AUTH\text{-}REL[R^*]}$ is the relaxing relation as defined in Fig. 18. Note that

$$\mathsf{R_{id}} = \mathsf{IMSG\text{-}AUTH\text{-}REL[R_{id}]} \subset \mathsf{IMSG\text{-}AUTH\text{-}REL[R_m]} \subset \mathsf{R_m},$$

IMSG-AUTH-REL[R*].Vf(z, z^*)

$((id_s, id_r, m, ad), (c_{pke}, \sigma)) \leftarrow z$; $z_0 \leftarrow ((id_s, id_r, m, ad, c_{pke}), \sigma)$
$((id_s^*, id_r^*, m^*, ad^*), (c_{pke}^*, \sigma^*)) \leftarrow z^*$; $z_1 \leftarrow ((id_s^*, id_r^*, m^*, ad^*, c_{pke}^*), \sigma^*)$
Return R*.Vf(z_0, z_1)

Fig. 18. Relaxing relation IMSG-AUTH-REL[R*].

where AUTH-security with respect to R_{id} captures the stronger security definition due to imposing the least number of restrictions regarding which queries
are permitted to oracle VERDEC. Relaxing relation IMSG-AUTH-REL[R_m] does
not allow adversary to win the authenticity game by only mauling the signature
σ and not changing anything else.

Theorem 5. *Let* MRPKE *be a multi-recipient public-key encryption scheme. Let*
DS *be a digital signature scheme. Let* SC $=$ IMSG-SC[MRPKE, DS]. *Let* R* $\in$
$\{R_m, R_{id}\}$. *Let* $\mathcal{F}_{SC}$ *be an adversary against the* AUTH-*security of* SC *with respect*
to relaxing relation R $=$ IMSG-AUTH-REL[R*]. *Then we build an adversary* $\mathcal{F}_{DS}$
against the UF-*security of* DS *with respect to* R*, *and an adversary* $\mathcal{G}$ *against*
the ROB-*security of* MRPKE *such that*

$$\mathsf{Adv}^{auth}_{SC,R}(\mathcal{F}_{SC}) \leq \mathsf{Adv}^{uf}_{DS,R^*}(\mathcal{F}_{DS}) + \mathsf{Adv}^{rob}_{MRPKE}(\mathcal{G}).$$

The proof of Theorem 5 is in the full version [13].

REDUCTION SHOWING ROBUSTNESS OF MRPKE. The ciphertext of MRPKE $=$
IMSG-MRPKE[EMDK, PKE] is a pair (c_{se}, c_{pke}), where c_{se} is an EMDK ciphertext
encrypting some $m^* = \langle m, id_s, \mathcal{I} \rangle$, and c_{pke} is a PKE ciphertext encrypting the
corresponding EMDK key k. The decryption algorithm of MRPKE first uses the
PKE key pair (ek, dk) to decrypt c_{pke}, and then uses the recovered EMDK key k to
decrypt c_{se}. We show that just one of PKE and EMDK being robust implies that
MRPKE is also robust. Our definition of robustness for public-key encryption
requires that it is hard to find a key pair (ek, dk) that decrypts an honestly
produced ciphertext to a plaintext that is different from the originally encrypted
message. If this condition holds for PKE, then clearly MRPKE is robust regardless
of whether EMDK is robust. On the other hand, if PKE is not robust, then the
robustness of EMDK (as defined in Sect. 4) would guarantee that the adversary
is unlikely to decrypt c_{se} to a message other than m^* even if it has full control
over the choice of EMDK key k. It is not known whether RSA-OAEP is robust,
so our concrete security analysis of iMessage in Sect. 5.5 will rely entirely on
the robustness of EMDK $=$ IMSG-EMDK. The formal definition of robustness for
PKE and the proof of Theorem 6 are in the full version [13].

Theorem 6. *Let* EMDK *be an encryption scheme under message derived keys.*
Let PKE *be a public-key encryption scheme with* PKE.In $= \{0, 1\}^{EMDK.kl}$. *Let*

IMSG-PRIV-REL.Vf(z, z^*)

$((id_s, id_r, m, ad), (c_{pke}, \sigma)) \leftarrow z$; $((id_s^*, id_r^*, m^*, ad^*), (c_{pke}^*, \sigma^*)) \leftarrow z^*$

Return $(id_s, id_r, m, c_{pke}) = (id_s^*, id_r^*, m^*, c_{pke}^*)$

Fig. 19. Relaxing relation IMSG-PRIV-REL.

MRPKE = IMSG-MRPKE[EMDK, PKE]. *Let* $\mathcal{G}_{MRPKE}$ *be an adversary against the* ROB-*security of* MRPKE. *Then we build an adversary* $\mathcal{G}_{EMDK}$ *against the* ROB-*security of* EMDK *such that*

$$\mathsf{Adv}_{MRPKE}^{rob}(\mathcal{G}_{MRPKE}) \leq \mathsf{Adv}_{EMDK}^{rob}(\mathcal{G}_{EMDK}),$$

and an adversary $\mathcal{G}_{PKE}$ *against the* ROB-*security of* PKE *such that*

$$\mathsf{Adv}_{MRPKE}^{rob}(\mathcal{G}_{MRPKE}) \leq \mathsf{Adv}_{PKE}^{rob}(\mathcal{G}_{PKE}).$$

5.4 Privacy of iMessage

In this section we reduce the PRIV-security of SC = IMSG-SC[MRPKE, DS] to the INDCCA-security of MRPKE, then reduce the INDCCA-security of MRPKE = IMSG-MRPKE[EMDK, PKE] to the AE-security of EMDK and the INDCCA-security of PKE. The reductions are straightforward.

An adversary attacking the PRIV-security of SC is allowed to query oracle LR and get a challenge ciphertext from an exposed sender as long as the recipient is honest. This means that the adversary can use the sender's DS signing key to arbitrarily change associated data ad and signature σ of any challenge ciphertext prior to querying it to oracle VERDEC. Our security reduction for PRIV-security of SC will be with respect to a relation that prohibits the adversary from trivially winning this way. Note that if IMSG-SC was defined to instead put ad inside $\langle m, id_s, \mathcal{I} \rangle$, then our security reduction would be able to show the PRIV-security of SC with respect to R_{id} assuming DS had *unique* signatures. However, ECDSA does not have this property (for the same reason it is not strongly unforgeable, as explained in [25]).

RELAXING RELATION IMSG-PRIV-REL. Let IMSG-PRIV-REL be the relaxing relation defined in Fig. 19. It first discards the associated data ad and the signature σ, and then compares the resulting tuples against each other. This reflects the intuition that an adversary can trivially change the values of ad and σ in any challenge ciphertext when attacking the PRIV-security of IMSG-SC.

Theorem 7. *Let* MRPKE *be a multi-recipient public-key encryption scheme. Let* DS *be a digital signature scheme. Let* SC = IMSG-SC[MRPKE, DS]. *Let* $\mathcal{D}_{SC}$ *be an adversary against the* PRIV-*security of* SC *with respect to the relaxing relation* R = IMSG-PRIV-REL. *Then we build an adversary* $\mathcal{D}_{MRPKE}$ *against the* INDCCA-*security of* MRPKE *such that*

$$\mathsf{Adv}_{SC,R}^{priv}(\mathcal{D}_{SC}) \leq \mathsf{Adv}_{MRPKE}^{indcca}(\mathcal{D}_{MRPKE}).$$

Theorem 8. *Let* EMDK *be an encryption scheme under message derived keys.*
Let PKE *be a public-key encryption scheme with input set* $\mathsf{PKE.In} = \{0,1\}^{\mathsf{EMDK.kl}}$.
Let $\mathsf{MRPKE} = \mathsf{IMSG\text{-}MRPKE}[\mathsf{EMDK}, \mathsf{PKE}]$. *Let* $\mathcal{D}_{\mathsf{MRPKE}}$ *be an adversary against*
the INDCCA-*security of* MRPKE. *Then we build an adversary* $\mathcal{D}_{\mathsf{PKE}}$ *against the*
INDCCA-*security of* PKE, *and an adversary* $\mathcal{D}_{\mathsf{EMDK}}$ *against the* AE-*security of*
EMDK *such that*

$$\mathsf{Adv}^{\mathsf{indcca}}_{\mathsf{MRPKE}}(\mathcal{D}_{\mathsf{MRPKE}}) \leq 2 \cdot \mathsf{Adv}^{\mathsf{indcca}}_{\mathsf{PKE}}(\mathcal{D}_{\mathsf{PKE}}) + \mathsf{Adv}^{\mathsf{ae}}_{\mathsf{EMDK}}(\mathcal{D}_{\mathsf{EMDK}}).$$

The proofs of Theorems 7 and 8 are in the full version [13].

5.5 Concrete Security of iMessage

In this section we summarize the results concerning the security of our iMessage-based signcryption scheme. For simplicity, we use the constructions and primitives from all across our work without formally redefining each of them.

COROLLARY FOR ABSTRACT SCHEMES. Let SC be the iMessage-based signcryption scheme, defined based on the appropriate underlying primitives. Let $\mathsf{R}_{\mathsf{auth}} = \mathsf{IMSG\text{-}AUTH\text{-}REL}[\mathsf{R}^*]$ and $\mathsf{R}_{\mathsf{priv}} = \mathsf{IMSG\text{-}PRIV\text{-}REL}$. Then for any adversary $\mathcal{F}_{\mathsf{SC}}$ attacking the AUTH-security of SC we can build new adversaries such that:

$$\mathsf{Adv}^{\mathsf{auth}}_{\mathsf{SC},\mathsf{R}_{\mathsf{auth}}}(\mathcal{F}_{\mathsf{SC}}) \leq \mathsf{Adv}^{\mathsf{uf}}_{\mathsf{DS},\mathsf{R}^*}(\mathcal{F}_{\mathsf{DS}}) + \min(\mathsf{Adv}^{\mathsf{rob}}_{\mathsf{PKE}}(\mathcal{G}_{\mathsf{PKE}}), \alpha),$$

where

$$\alpha = \mathsf{Adv}^{\mathsf{unique}}_{\mathsf{SE}}(\mathcal{U}_0) + \mathsf{Adv}^{\mathsf{wrob}}_{\mathsf{SE},\mathsf{F.ol}}(\mathcal{G}_{\mathsf{SE}}).$$

For any adversary $\mathcal{D}_{\mathsf{SC}}$ attacking the PRIV-security of SC, making q_{LR} queries to LR oracle and q_{RO} queries to RO oracle, we build new adversaries such that:

$$\mathsf{Adv}^{\mathsf{priv}}_{\mathsf{SC},\mathsf{R}_{\mathsf{priv}}}(\mathcal{D}_{\mathsf{SC}}) \leq 2 \cdot (\beta + \gamma) + \mathsf{Adv}^{\mathsf{otind}}_{\mathsf{SE}}(\mathcal{D}_{\mathsf{SE}}),$$

where

$$\beta = \mathsf{Adv}^{\mathsf{indcca}}_{\mathsf{PKE}}(\mathcal{D}_{\mathsf{PKE}}) + \mathsf{Adv}^{\mathsf{unique}}_{\mathsf{SE}}(\mathcal{U}_1) + \mathsf{Adv}^{\mathsf{tcr}}_{\mathsf{F}}(\mathcal{H}) + \mathsf{Adv}^{\mathsf{pkr}}_{\mathsf{SE},\mathsf{F.kl}}(\mathcal{P}),$$

$$\gamma = \frac{(2 \cdot q_{\mathrm{RO}} + q_{\mathrm{LR}} - 1) \cdot q_{\mathrm{LR}}}{2^{\mathsf{F.kl}+1}}.$$

BIT-SECURITY OF iMESSAGE. We now assess the concrete security of iMessage when the abstract schemes that constitute SC are instantiated with real-world primitives. First, note that $\mathsf{Adv}^{\mathsf{unique}}_{\mathsf{SE}}(\mathcal{U}) = 0$ for any $\mathcal{U}$ when SE is AES-CTR. We will approximate the bit-security of SC based on the other terms above.

We assume that ECDSA with 256-bit keys (on the NIST P-256 curve) has 128 bits of UF-security with respect to R_{m} [5,21]. We assume that RSA-OAEP with 1280-bit keys has 80 bits of INDCCA-security [21,30]. SE is AES-CTR with key length SE.kl; we assume that SE has SE.kl bits of OTIND-security.

For every other term used above, we approximate the corresponding bit-security based on the advantage ϵ and the runtime T of the best adversary we

SE.kl	F.kl	F.ol	PRIV bit-security	AUTH bit-security
	88	40	39	
128	80	48	45	
	72	56	41	
	128	64	63	
192	120	72	66	71
	112	80	62	
256	168	88	79	
	160	96	79	

Fig. 20. Lower bounds for bit-security of SC across different parameter choices.

can come up with. For simplicity, we model F as the random oracle and we model SE as the ideal cipher. This simplifies the task of finding the "best possible" adversary against each security notion and then calculating its advantage. In each case we consider either a constant-time adversary making a single guess in its security game (achieving some advantage ϵ in time $T \approx 1$), or an adversary that runs a birthday attack (achieving advantage $\epsilon \geq 0.3 \cdot \frac{q \cdot (q-1)}{N}$ in time $T \approx q \cdot \log_2 q$ for $q = \sqrt{2N}$). We use the following adversaries:

(i) Assume SE is AES-CTR where AES modeled as the ideal cipher with block length 128. In game $G_{\mathsf{SE},\mathsf{F}.\mathsf{ol},\mathcal{G}}^{\mathrm{wrob}}$ consider an adversary $\mathcal{G}$ that repeatedly queries its oracle ENC on inputs (r_0, m) where all $r_0 \in \{0,1\}^{\mathsf{F}.\mathsf{kl}}$ are distinct and all $m \in \{0,1\}^{128}$ are distinct. The adversary wins if a collision occurs across the 128-bit outputs of SE.Enc. Then $\epsilon = \mathsf{Adv}_{\mathsf{SE},\mathsf{F}.\mathsf{ol}}^{\mathrm{wrob}}(\mathcal{G}_{\mathsf{SE}}) \geq 0.3 \cdot \frac{q_{\mathrm{ENC}} * (q_{\mathrm{ENC}}-1)}{2^{128}}$ and $T = q_{\mathrm{ENC}} \cdot \log_2 q_{\mathrm{ENC}}$ for $q_{\mathrm{ENC}} = \sqrt{2^{128+1}}$.

(ii) In game $G_{\mathsf{F},\mathcal{H}}^{\mathrm{tcr}}$ consider an adversary $\mathcal{H}$ that queries its oracle NEWKEY(x_0) for any $x_0 \in \{0,1\}^*$ and then makes a guess $(1, x_1)$ for any $x_0 \neq x_1$. Then $\epsilon = \mathsf{Adv}_{\mathsf{F}}^{\mathrm{tcr}}(\mathcal{H}) = 2^{-\mathsf{F}.\mathsf{ol}}$ and $T \approx 1$ in the random oracle model.

(iii) In game $G_{\mathsf{SE},\mathsf{F}.\mathsf{kl},\mathcal{P}}^{\mathrm{pkr}}$ consider an adversary $\mathcal{P}$ that makes a single call to ENC and then randomly guesses any key prefix $p \in \{0,1\}^{\mathsf{F}.\mathsf{kl}}$. Then $\epsilon = \mathsf{Adv}_{\mathsf{SE},\mathsf{F}.\mathsf{kl}}^{\mathrm{pkr}}(\mathcal{P}) = 2^{-\mathsf{F}.\mathsf{kl}}$ and $T \approx 1$ in the ideal cipher model.

(iv) The term γ upper bounds the probability of an adversary finding a collision when running the birthday attack (in the random oracle model). The corresponding lower bound (for $q_{\mathrm{RO}} = 0$) is $\epsilon \geq 0.3 \cdot \frac{q_{\mathrm{LR}} \cdot (q_{\mathrm{LR}}-1)}{2^{\mathsf{F}.\mathsf{kl}}}$ with $T = q_{\mathrm{LR}} \cdot \log_2 q_{\mathrm{LR}}$ and $q_{\mathrm{LR}} = \sqrt{2^{\mathsf{F}.\mathsf{kl}+1}}$.

We wrote a script that combines all of the above to find the lower bound for the bit-security of SC (with respect to PRIV and AUTH security notions) for different choices of SE.kl, F.kl and F.ol. This assumes that the above adversaries are optimal, and computes the lower bound according to Sect. 2. Figure 2 (in Sect. 1) shows the bit-security lower bounds with respect to privacy, depending on the choice of symmetric key length SE.kl and authentication tag length F.ol. Figure 20 shows the choices of F.kl and F.ol that yield the best lower bounds for the bit-security of PRIV for each SE.kl $\in \{128, 192, 256\}$. According to our results, the security of the iMessage-based signcryption scheme would slightly improve if the value of F.ol was chosen to be 48 instead of 40. The bit-security of SC with respect to AUTH is constant because it does not depend on the values of SE.kl, F.kl, F.ol. The assumption that RSA-OAEP with 1280-bit long keys has 80 bits of INDCCA-security limits the bit-security that can be achieved when SE.kl = 256; otherwise, the PRIV bit-security for SE.kl = 256 would allow a lower bound of 86 bits. But note that using SE.kl ∈ {192, 256} is likely not possible while maintaining the backward-compatibility of iMessage.

Acknowledgments. The authors were supported in part by NSF grant CNS-1717640 and a gift from Microsoft. Igors Stepanovs's work was done while at UCSD. We thank Adina Wollner, Wei Dai and Joseph Jaeger for discussions and insights.

References

1. Abdalla, M., Bellare, M., Neven, G.: Robust encryption. In: Micciancio, D. (ed.) TCC 2010. LNCS, vol. 5978, pp. 480–497. Springer, Heidelberg (2010). https://doi.org/10.1007/978-3-642-11799-2_28
2. Alwen, J., Coretti, S., Dodis, Y.: The double ratchet: security notions, proofs, and modularization for the signal protocol. In: Ishai, Y., Rijmen, V. (eds.) EUROCRYPT 2019. LNCS, vol. 11476, pp. 129–158. Springer, Cham (2019). https://doi.org/10.1007/978-3-030-17653-2_5
3. An, J.H., Dodis, Y., Rabin, T.: On the security of joint signature and encryption. In: Knudsen, L.R. (ed.) EUROCRYPT 2002. LNCS, vol. 2332, pp. 83–107. Springer, Heidelberg (2002). https://doi.org/10.1007/3-540-46035-7_6
4. Apple. iOS security: iOS 12.3. Technical whitepaper, May 2019. https://www.apple.com/business/docs/site/iOS_Security_Guide.pdf
5. Barker, E.: Recommendation for key management part 1: general (revision 5). NIST special publication, 800(57), 1–174 (2019)
6. Bellare, M., Boldyreva, A., Kurosawa, K., Staddon, J.: Multirecipient encryption schemes: how to save on bandwidth and computation without sacrificing security. IEEE Trans. Inf. Theory **53**(11), 3927–3943 (2007)
7. Bellare, M., Kohno, T.: A theoretical treatment of related-key attacks: RKA-PRPs, RKA-PRFs, and applications. In: Biham, E. (ed.) EUROCRYPT 2003. LNCS, vol. 2656, pp. 491–506. Springer, Heidelberg (2003). https://doi.org/10.1007/3-540-39200-9_31
8. Bellare, M., Namprempre, C.: Authenticated encryption: relations among notions and analysis of the generic composition paradigm. In: Okamoto, T. (ed.) ASIACRYPT 2000. LNCS, vol. 1976, pp. 531–545. Springer, Heidelberg (2000). https://doi.org/10.1007/3-540-44448-3_41
9. Bellare, M., Ng, R., Tackmann, B.: Nonces are noticed: AEAD revisited. In: Boldyreva, A., Micciancio, D. (eds.) CRYPTO 2019. LNCS, vol. 11692, pp. 235–265. Springer, Cham (2019). https://doi.org/10.1007/978-3-030-26948-7_9
10. Bellare, M., Rogaway, P.: Random oracles are practical: a paradigm for designing efficient protocols. In: ACM CCS (1993)
11. Bellare, M., Rogaway, P.: The security of triple encryption and a framework for code-based game-playing proofs. In: Vaudenay, S. (ed.) EUROCRYPT 2006. LNCS, vol. 4004, pp. 409–426. Springer, Heidelberg (2006). https://doi.org/10.1007/11761679_25

12. Bellare, M., Singh, A.C., Jaeger, J., Nyayapati, M., Stepanovs, I.: Ratcheted encryption and key exchange: the security of messaging. In: Katz, J., Shacham, H. (eds.) CRYPTO 2017. LNCS, vol. 10403, pp. 619–650. Springer, Cham (2017). https://doi.org/10.1007/978-3-319-63697-9_21

13. Bellare, M., Stepanovs, I.: Security under message-derived keys: signcryption in imessage. Cryptology ePrint Archive, Report 2020/224 (2020)

14. Black, J., Rogaway, P., Shrimpton, T.: Encryption-scheme security in the presence of key-dependent messages. In: Nyberg, K., Heys, H. (eds.) SAC 2002. LNCS, vol. 2595, pp. 62–75. Springer, Heidelberg (2003). https://doi.org/10.1007/3-540-36492-7_6

15. Bose, P., Hoang, V.T., Tessaro, S.: Revisiting AES-GCM-SIV: multi-user security, faster key derivation, and better bounds. In: Nielsen, J.B., Rijmen, V. (eds.) EUROCRYPT 2018. LNCS, vol. 10820, pp. 468–499. Springer, Cham (2018). https://doi.org/10.1007/978-3-319-78381-9_18

16. Camenisch, J., Lysyanskaya, A.: An efficient system for non-transferable anonymous credentials with optional anonymity revocation. In: Pfitzmann, B. (ed.) EUROCRYPT 2001. LNCS, vol. 2045, pp. 93–118. Springer, Heidelberg (2001). https://doi.org/10.1007/3-540-44987-6_7

17. Canetti, R., Tauman Kalai, Y., Varia, M., Wichs, D.: On symmetric encryption and point obfuscation. In: Micciancio, D. (ed.) TCC 2010. LNCS, vol. 5978, pp. 52–71. Springer, Heidelberg (2010). https://doi.org/10.1007/978-3-642-11799-2_4

18. Canetti, R., Krawczyk, H., Nielsen, J.B.: Relaxing chosen-ciphertext security. In: Boneh, D. (ed.) CRYPTO 2003. LNCS, vol. 2729, pp. 565–582. Springer, Heidelberg (2003). https://doi.org/10.1007/978-3-540-45146-4_33

19. Cohn-Gordon, K., Cremers, C., Dowling, B., Garratt, L., Stebila, D.: A formal security analysis of the Signal messaging protocol. In: Proceedings of the IEEE European Symposium on Security and Privacy (EuroS&P) (2017)

20. Common Vulnerabilities and Exposures system. Cve-2016-1788. https://cve.mitre.org/cgi-bin/cvename.cgi?name=CVE-2016-1788

21. Damien, G.: Cryptographic key length recommendation. https://www.keylength.com

22. Durak, F.B., Vaudenay, S.: Bidirectional asynchronous ratcheted key agreement with linear complexity. In: Attrapadung, N., Yagi, T. (eds.) IWSEC 2019. LNCS, vol. 11689, pp. 343–362. Springer, Cham (2019). https://doi.org/10.1007/978-3-030-26834-3_20

23. Farshim, P., Libert, B., Paterson, K.G., Quaglia, E.A.: Robust encryption, Revisited. In: Kurosawa, K., Hanaoka, G. (eds.) PKC 2013. LNCS, vol. 7778, pp. 352–368. Springer, Heidelberg (2013). https://doi.org/10.1007/978-3-642-36362-7_22

24. Farshim, P., Orlandi, C., Roşie, R.: Security of symmetric primitives under incorrect usage of keys. IACR Trans. Symm. Cryptol. **2017**(1), 449–473 (2017)

25. Fersch, M., Kiltz, E., Poettering, B.: On the provable security of (EC)DSA signatures. In: ACM CCS (2016)

26. Garman, C., Green, M., Kaptchuk, G., Miers, I., Rushanan, M.: Dancing on the lip of the volcano: chosen ciphertext attacks on Apple iMessage. USENIX Security (2016)

27. Groth, J.: Rerandomizable and replayable adaptive chosen ciphertext attack secure cryptosystems. In: Naor, M. (ed.) TCC 2004. LNCS, vol. 2951, pp. 152–170. Springer, Heidelberg (2004). https://doi.org/10.1007/978-3-540-24638-1_9

28. Jaeger, J., Stepanovs, I.: Optimal channel security against fine-grained state compromise: the safety of messaging. In: Shacham, H., Boldyreva, A. (eds.) CRYPTO 2018. LNCS, vol. 10991, pp. 33–62. Springer, Cham (2018). https://doi.org/10.1007/978-3-319-96884-1_2

29. Jost, D., Maurer, U., Mularczyk, M.: Efficient ratcheting: almost-optimal guarantees for secure messaging. In: Ishai, Y., Rijmen, V. (eds.) EUROCRYPT 2019. LNCS, vol. 11476, pp. 159–188. Springer, Cham (2019). https://doi.org/10.1007/978-3-030-17653-2_6

30. Lenstra, A.K.: Key length. Contribution to the handbook of information security (2004)

31. Micciancio, D., Walter, M.: On the bit security of cryptographic primitives. In: Nielsen, J.B., Rijmen, V. (eds.) EUROCRYPT 2018. LNCS, vol. 10820, pp. 3–28. Springer, Cham (2018). https://doi.org/10.1007/978-3-319-78381-9_1

32. OpenIM wiki. iMessage. https://wiki.imfreedom.org/wiki/IMessage

33. Poettering, B., Rösler, P.: Towards bidirectional ratcheted key exchange. In: Shacham, H., Boldyreva, A. (eds.) CRYPTO 2018. LNCS, vol. 10991, pp. 3–32. Springer, Cham (2018). https://doi.org/10.1007/978-3-319-96884-1_1

34. Quarkslab. iMessage privacy, October 2013. https://blog.quarkslab.com/imessage-privacy.html

35. Rogaway, P.: Authenticated-encryption with associated-data. In: ACM CCS (2002)

36. Zheng, Y.: Digital signcryption or how to achieve cost(signature & encryption) ≪ cost(signature) + cost(encryption). In: Kaliski, B.S. (ed.) CRYPTO 1997. LNCS, vol. 1294, pp. 165–179. Springer, Heidelberg (1997). https://doi.org/10.1007/BFb0052234

Double-Base Chains for Scalar Multiplications on Elliptic Curves

Wei Yu[1,2(✉)], Saud Al Musa[3], and Bao Li[1,4]

[1] State Key Laboratory of Information Security, Institute of Information Engineering, Chinese Academy of Sciences, Beijing 100093, China
{yuwei,libao}@iie.ac.cn, yuwei_1_yw@163.com
[2] Data Assurance and Communications Security Research Center, Chinese Academy of Sciences, Beijing 100093, China
[3] College of Computer Science and Engineering, Taibah University, Medina, Saudi Arabia
smusa@taibahu.edu.sa
[4] School of Cyber Security, University of Chinese Academy of Sciences, Beijing 100049, China

Abstract. Double-base chains (DBCs) are widely used to speed up scalar multiplications on elliptic curves. We present three results of DBCs. First, we display a structure of the set containing all DBCs and propose an iterative algorithm to compute the number of DBCs for a positive integer. This is the first polynomial time algorithm to compute the number of DBCs for positive integers. Secondly, we present an asymptotic lower bound on average Hamming weights of DBCs $\frac{\log n}{8.25}$ for a positive integer n. This result answers an open question about the Hamming weights of DBCs. Thirdly, we propose a new algorithm to generate an optimal DBC for any positive integer. The time complexity of this algorithm is $\mathscr{O}\left((\log n)^2 \log\log n\right)$ bit operations and the space complexity is $\mathscr{O}\left((\log n)^2\right)$ bits of memory. This algorithm accelerates the recoding procedure by more than 6 times compared to the state-of-the-art Bernstein, Chuengsatiansup, and Lange's work. The Hamming weights of optimal DBCs are over 60% smaller than those of NAFs. Scalar multiplication using our optimal DBC is about 13% faster than that using non-adjacent form on elliptic curves over large prime fields.

Keywords: Elliptic curve cryptography · Scalar multiplication · Double-base chain · Hamming weight

1 Introduction

A double-base chain (DBC), as a particular double-base number system (DBNS) representation, represents an integer n as $\sum_{i=1}^{l} c_i 2^{b_i} 3^{t_i}$ where $c_i \in \{\pm 1\}$, b_i, t_i are non-increasing sequences. It is called an unsigned DBC when $c_i \in \{1\}$. A DBC was first used in elliptic curve cryptography for its sparseness by Dimitrov,

© International Association for Cryptologic Research 2020
A. Canteaut and Y. Ishai (Eds.): EUROCRYPT 2020, LNCS 12107, pp. 538–565, 2020.
https://doi.org/10.1007/978-3-030-45727-3_18

Imbert, and Mishra [1], and Ciet, Joye, Lauter, and Montgomery [2]. Scalar multiplication is the core operation in elliptic curve cryptosystems. A DBC allows one to represent an integer in a Horner-like fashion to calculate scalar multiplication such that all partial results can be reused. In the last decade, DBCs were widely investigated to speed up scalar multiplications [3–5] and pairings [6,7]. The generalizations of DBCs were also applied to the arithmetics of elliptic curves. The generalizations include simultaneously representing a pair of numbers to accelerate multi-scalar multiplications [8–10], using double-base representation to speed up scalar multiplication on Koblitz curves [11], and representing an integer in a multi-base number system to promote scalar multiplications [12–14].

Dimitrov, Imbert, and Mishra pointed out that DBC is highly redundant, and counting the exact number of DBCs is useful to generate optimal DBCs [1]. A precise estimate of the number of unsigned DBNS representation of a given positive integer was presented in [15]. 100 has exactly 402 unsigned DBNS representations and 1000 has 1295579 unsigned DBNS representations. For unsigned DBC, Imbert and Philippe [4] introduced an efficient algorithm to compute the number of unsigned DBCs for a given integer. By their algorithm, 100 has 7 unsigned DBCs and 1000 has 30 unsigned DBCs. DBCs are more redundant than unsigned DBCs. For a given integer n, Doche [16] proposed a recursion algorithm to calculate the number of DBCs with a leading term dividing $2^b 3^t$. His algorithm is efficient to find the number of DBCs with a leading term dividing $2^b 3^t$ for integers less than 2^{70} and b, $t < 70$. But it does not work for calculating the number of DBCs of a positive integer used in elliptic curve cryptography. We will show how to calculate the number of DBCs of a 256-bit integer or even a larger integer.

The Hamming weight is one of the most important factors that affect the efficiency of scalar multiplications. Dimitrov, Imbert, and Mishra proved an asymptotic upper bound $\mathscr{O}\left(\frac{\log n}{\log\log n}\right)$ on the Hamming weight of DBNS representation by a greedy approach [15]. Every integer n has a DBC with Hamming weight $\mathscr{O}(\log n)$. The upper bounds of DBNS representations and DBCs have been well investigated, in contrast, the precise lower bounds of DBCs can not be found in any literature. Doche and Habsieger [3] showed that the DBCs produced by the tree approach is shorter than those produced by greedy approach [1] for integers with several hundreds of bits experimentally. They observed that the average Hamming weight of the DBCs produced by the tree approach is $\frac{\log n}{4.6419}$. They also posed an open question that the average Hamming weight of DBCs generated by the greedy approach may be not $\mathscr{O}\left(\frac{\log n}{\log\log n}\right)$. We will give affirmation to this question.

Canonic DBCs are the DBCs with the lowest Hamming weight for a positive integer and were introduced by Dimitrov, Imbert, and Mishra [1]. Several algorithms were designed to produce near canonic DBCs such as greedy algorithm [1], binary/ternary approach [2], multi-base non-adjacent form (mbNAF)[13], and tree approach [3]. In Asiacrypt 2014, Doche proposed an algorithm to produce a canonic DBC [16]. As Doche's algorithm was in exponential time, Capuñay and

Thériault [7] improved Doche's algorithm to generate a canonic DBC or an optimal DBC. This is the first algorithm to generate an optimal DBC in polynomial time, explicitly $\mathscr{O}\left((\log n)^4\right)$ bit operations and $\mathscr{O}\left((\log n)^3\right)$ bits of memory. Bernstein, Chuengsatiansup, and Lange [17] presented a directed acyclic graph algorithm (DAG) to produce a canonic DBC or an optimal DBC. Their algorithm takes time $\mathscr{O}\left((\log n)^{2.5}\right)$ bit operations and $\mathscr{O}\left((\log n)^{2.5}\right)$ bits of memory. As scalar multiplication requires $\mathscr{O}\left((\log n)^2 \log\log n\right)$ when field multiplications use FFTs, we will focus on producing a canonic DBC or an optimal DBC in the same order of magnitude.

In this paper, we are concerned with the theoretical aspects of DBCs arising from their study to speed up scalar multiplication and producing a canonic DBC or an optimal DBC efficiently. The main contributions are detailed as follows.

1. As Doche's algorithm is in exponential time to compute the number of DBCs with a leading term dividing $2^b 3^t$ [16], we propose an iterative algorithm in $\mathscr{O}\left((\log n)^3\right)$ bit operations and in $\mathscr{O}\left((\log n)^2\right)$ bits of memory. Our algorithm is based on our new structure of the set containing all DBCs. It requires 10 milliseconds for 256-bit integers and 360 milliseconds for 1024-bit integers. Using the iterative algorithm, 100 has 2590 DBCs with a leading term dividing $2^{30} 3^4$ and 1000 has 28364 DBCs with a leading term dividing $2^{30} 3^6$. These results show that DBCs are redundant. We show that the number of DBCs with a leading term dividing $2^b 3^t$ is the same when $t \geq t_\tau$ for some t_τ. The number of DBCs with a leading term dividing $2^b 3^t$ minus the number of DBCs with a leading term dividing $2^{b_\tau} 3^t$ is $(b - b_\tau) C_\tau$ when $b \geq b_\tau$ for some b_τ and C_τ. We also present that the number of DBCs with a leading term dividing $2^b 3^t$ is $\mathscr{O}(\log n)$-bit when both b and t are $\mathscr{O}(\log n)$.

2. Doche and Habsieger posed an open question to decide whether the average Hamming weight of DBCs produced by the greedy approach is $\mathscr{O}\left(\frac{\log n}{\log\log n}\right)$ or not [3]. We show that an asymptotic lower bound of the average Hamming weight of the DBCs returned by any algorithm for a positive integer n is $\frac{\log n}{8.25}$. This theoretical result answers their open question. Experimental results show that the Hamming weight of canonic DBCs is $0.179822\log n$ for 3000-bit integers. It still has a distance from the theoretical bound.

3. We propose a dynamic programming algorithm to generate an optimal DBC. We introduce an equivalent representative for large integers to improve the efficiency of the dynamic programming algorithm. Our dynamic programming algorithm using equivalent representatives requires $\mathscr{O}\left((\log n)^2 \log\log n\right)$ bit operations and $\mathscr{O}\left((\log n)^2\right)$ bits of memory. It accelerates the recoding procedure by over 6 times compared to Bernstein, Chuengsatiansup, and Lange's algorithm. Many researches [1–3,6,7,16,17] indicate that the leading term of an optimal DBC is greater than $\frac{n}{2}$ and less than $2n$. We will prove it in this work.

4. Capuñay and Thériault's algorithm [7], Bernstein, Chuengsatiansup, and Lange's DAG algorithm [17], and our algorithms (Algorithms 2–4) can generate the same optimal DBC for a given integer. Using optimal DBCs to speed up pairing computations has been fully investigated by Capuñay and Thériault's algorithm in [7]. Using optimal DBCs to speed up scalar multiplication on Edwards curves has been studied by Bernstein, Chuengsatiansup, and Lange in [17]. We will study scalar multiplication on Weierstrass curves using optimal DBCs. Over large prime fields, both theoretical analyses and experimental results show that scalar multiplication protecting against simple side-channel attack using our optimal DBC is about 13% faster than that using NAF.

This paper is organized as follows. In Sect. 2, we present background of elliptic curves and DBCs. In Sect. 3, we show the structure of the set containing all DBCs, and give an iterative algorithm to compute the number of DBCs. In Sect. 4, we show an asymptotic lower bound of the average Hamming weights of DBCs. Section 5 shows a dynamic programming algorithm. Section 6 presents equivalent representatives for large numbers to improve our dynamic programming algorithm and presents the comparisons of several algorithms. Section 7 gives some comparisons of scalar multiplications. Finally, we conclude this work in Sect. 8.

2   Preliminaries

We give some basics about elliptic curves and DBCs.

2.1   Elliptic Curves

In what follows, point doubling ($2P$), tripling ($3P$), and mixed addition [18] ($P + Q$) are denoted by D, T, and A respectively where P and Q are rational points on an elliptic curve. Cost of scalar multiplications are expressed in terms of field multiplications ($\mathbf{M}$) and field squarings ($\mathbf{S}$). To allow easy comparisons, we disregard field additions/subtractions and multiplications/divisions by small constants. Moreover, we assume that $\mathbf{S} = 0.8\mathbf{M}$ as customary of software implementation (different CPU architectures usually imply different $\mathbf{S}$ and $\mathbf{M}$ ration) and that $\mathbf{S} = \mathbf{M}$ in the case of implementations on a hardware platform or protecting scalar multiplications against some simple side channel attack by side-channel atomicity [19].

Let $\mathcal{E}_W$ be an elliptic curve over a large prime field $\mathbb{F}_p$ defined by the Weierstrass equation in Jacobian projective coordinate: $Y^2 = X^3 + aXZ^4 + bZ^6$, where $a = -3$, $b \in \mathbb{F}_p$, and $4a^3 + 27b^2 \neq 0$. The respective cost of a doubling, a mixed addition, and a tripling are $3\mathbf{M}+5\mathbf{S}$, $7\mathbf{M}+4\mathbf{S}$, and $7\mathbf{M}+7\mathbf{S}$ on $\mathcal{E}_W$ respectively [20,21]. More about Weierstrass elliptic curves please refer to [22].

The cost of point operations on $\mathcal{E}_W$ are summarized in Table 1. $\mathcal{E}_W$ with $\mathbf{S}=0.8\mathbf{M}$ and $\mathcal{E}_W$ with $\mathbf{S}=\mathbf{M}$ are denoted by $\mathcal{E}_W$ 0.8 and $\mathcal{E}_W$ 1 respectively.

Table 1. Cost of elliptic curve point operations

operation	$\mathscr{E}_W$ 0.8	$\mathscr{E}_W$ 1
A	7M+4S(10.2M)	11M
D	3M+5S(7M)	8M
T	7M+7S(12.6M)	14M

2.2 DBCs

DBNS represents an integer as $\sum_{i=1}^{l} c_i 2^{b_i} 3^{t_i}$ where $c_i \in \{\pm 1\}$, and b_i, t_i are non-negative integers. It was first used in elliptic curve cryptography by Dimitrov, Imbert, and Mishra [1]. Meloni and Hasan proposed new algorithms using DBNS representation to speed up scalar multiplications [23, 24]. The drawback of DBNS representation to compute scalar multiplication is that it requires many pre-computations and space to compute scalar multiplication. A DBC is a special case of DBNS representations. It allows us to represent n in a Horner-like fashion such that all partial results can be reused. It is defined as follows.

Definition 1 (DBC [1]). *A DBC represents an integer n as $\sum_{i=1}^{l} c_i 2^{b_i} 3^{t_i}$ where $c_i \in \mathscr{C} = \{\pm 1\}, b_l \geq b_{l-1} \geq \ldots \geq b_1 \geq 0$ and $t_l \geq t_{l-1} \geq \ldots \geq t_1 \geq 0$. We call $2^{b_i} 3^{t_i}$ a term of the DBC, $2^{b_l} 3^{t_l}$ the leading term of the DBC, and l the Hamming weight of the DBC.*

If $\mathscr{C} = \{1\}$, the DBC is called an unsigned DBC. Since computing the negative of a point P can be done virtually at no cost, we usually set $\mathscr{C} = \{\pm 1\}$. The leading term of a DBC encapsulates the total number of point doublings and that of point triplings necessary to compute scalar multiplication nP whose total cost is $(l - 1) \cdot A + b_l \cdot D + t_l \cdot T$.

The number 0 has only one DBC that is 0. If a DBC does not exist, we denote it by NULL. We set the Hamming weight of 0 as 0 and that of NULL as a negative integer. A DBC for a negative integer is the negative of the DBC of its absolute value. Therefore, we usually investigate the DBCs of a positive integer.

Some properties of DBCs are useful. Let $n = \sum_{i=1}^{l} c_i 2^{b_i} 3^{t_i}$ be a DBC with $c_i \in \{\pm 1\}, b_l \geq b_{l-1} \geq \ldots \geq b_1$ and $t_l \geq t_{l-1} \geq \ldots \geq t_1$. We have

1. $2^{b_k} 3^{t_k}$ is a factor of $\sum_{i=k}^{l_0} c_i 2^{b_i} 3^{t_i}$, when $k \leq l_0 \leq l$;
2. $\sum_{i=k}^{l_0} c_i 2^{b_i} 3^{t_i}$ is not equal to 0 when $0 < k \leq l_0 \leq l$;
3. $\frac{2^{b_k+\varsigma} 3^{t_k+\varsigma}}{2^\varsigma - 1} > \sum_{i=1}^{k} c_i 2^{b_i} 3^{t_i} > -\frac{2^{b_k+\varsigma} 3^{t_k+\varsigma}}{2^\varsigma - 1}$, when $1 \leq \varsigma \leq l - k$;
4. $2^{b_l} 3^{t_l} > \frac{n}{2}$ [25];
5. $\sum_{i=1}^{\varsigma} c_i 2^{b_i} 3^{t_i} > 0$ if and only if $c_\varsigma = 1$, when $1 \leq \varsigma \leq l$.

Following from Dimitrov, Imbert, and Mishra's definition of canonic DBC,

Definition 2 (Canonic DBC [15]). *The canonic DBCs of a positive integer n are the ones with minimal Hamming weight.*

The canonic DBCs of a positive integer have the same Hamming weight. When we perform scalar multiplication using a DBC, its Hamming weight is not the only factor affecting the efficiency of scalar multiplication. The cost of point operations should also be considered. The works in [7,16,17] indicate the definition of an optimal DBC as follows.

Definition 3 (Optimal DBC). *Let* w *be a DBC of a positive integer* n *whose leading term is* $2^{b_l}3^{t_l}$ *and its Hamming weight is* l, *and the value function of* w *is defined by* $\text{val}(w) = (l-1) \cdot A + b_l \cdot D + t_l \cdot T$ *for given numbers* $A > 0$, $D \geq 0$, *and* $T \geq 0$. *An optimal DBC of* n *is the DBC with the smallest value in the set* $\{\text{val}(w)|w \in X\}$ *where* X *is the set containing all DBCs of* n.

Let minL $\{w_1, w_2, \ldots, w_m\}$ be a DBC with the smallest Hamming weight among these DBCs. If the Hamming weight of w is the smallest in a corresponding set, we say w is "minimal". Let minV$\{w_1, w_2, \ldots, w_m\}$ be a DBC with the smallest $\text{val}(w_i)$ in the set $\{\text{val}(w_1), \text{val}(w_2), \ldots, \text{val}(w_m)\}$. If more than one DBC has the same Hamming weight or the same value of its value function, we choose the one with the smallest position index i where i is the position index of w_i in the set of $\{w_1, w_2, \ldots, w_m\}$. minL is used to generate canonic DBCs, and minV is used to generate optimal DBCs.

An optimal DBC is associated with an elliptic curve. Let log denote binary logarithm. If the value of $\frac{T}{D}$ is log 3, then the optimal DBC is a canonic DBC. In this case, we usually set $D = T = 0$. For canonic DBCs of a positive integer, our concern is their Hamming weight.

3 The Number of DBCs

DBCs are special cases of DBNS representations. In 2008, Dimitrov, Imbert, and Mishra showed an accurate estimate of the number of unsigned DBNS representations for a given positive integer [15]. The number of signed DBNS representation is still an open question.

Dimitrov, Imbert, and Mishra pointed out that counting the exact number of DBCs is useful to show DBC is redundant [1] and to generate an optimal DBC. Dimitrov, Imbert, and Mishra [1] and Imbert and Philippe [4] both noticed that each positive integer has at least one DBC such as binary representation. Imbert and Philippe [4] proposed an elegant algorithm to compute the number of unsigned DBCs for a given integer and presented the first 400 values. These values behave rather irregularly. To determine the precise number of DBCs for a positive integer is usually hard, but we are convinced that this number is infinity. The number of DBCs with a leading term dividing 2^b3^t for a positive integer was first investigated by Doche [16]. His algorithm is very efficient for less than 70-bit integers with a leading term dividing 2^b3^t for the most b and t. The algorithm requires exponential time. Before we present a polynomial time algorithm to calculate the number of DBCs of large integers, a structure of the set containing all DBCs is introduced.

3.1 The Structure of the Set Containing All DBCs

Let $\Phi(b, t, n)$ be the set containing all DBCs of an integer $n \geq 0$ with a leading term strictly dividing 2^b3^t. "Strictly" indicates that the leading term of a DBC

$2^{b_l}3^{t_l}$ divides 2^b3^t but is not equal to 2^b3^t. Let $\bar{\Phi}(b,t,n)$ be the set containing all DBCs of an integer $n \leq 0$ with a leading term strictly dividing 2^b3^t. Both definitions of $\Phi(b,t,n)$ and $\bar{\Phi}(b,t,n)$ arise from Imbert and Philippe's structure of unsigned DBCs [4] and Capuñay and Thériault's definition of the set containing all DBCs (see Definition 5 of [7]).

Let z be $2^{b'}3^{t'}$ or $-2^{b'}3^{t'}$ with integers $b' \geq 0$ and $t' \geq 0$. The set $\{w + z |$ $w \in \Phi\}$ is denoted by $^z\Phi$ (the similar is for $\bar{\Phi}$). $^z\Phi$ is inspired by Imbert and Philippe's mark [4]. If $2^b3^t | z$, $^z\Phi(b,t,n)$ are the DBCs of $n + z$. Let $^{z_1,z_2}\Phi = {}^{z_1}({}^{z_2}\Phi)$. Take $\Phi(1,4,100) = \{3^4 + 3^3 - 3^2 + 1\}$ for example, $^{2 \cdot 3^4}\Phi(1,4,100) = \{2 \cdot 3^4 + 3^4 + 3^3 - 3^2 + 1\}$.

Some properties of Φ and $\bar{\Phi}$ are given.

1. If $\Phi = \emptyset$, then $^z\Phi = \emptyset$; if $\bar{\Phi} = \emptyset$, then $^z\bar{\Phi} = \emptyset$.
2. If $\Phi = \{0\}$, then $^z\Phi = \{z\}$; if $\bar{\Phi} = \{0\}$, then $^z\bar{\Phi} = \{z\}$.
3. If $n < 0$ or $n \geq 2^b3^t$ or $b < 0$ or $t < 0$, then $\Phi(b,t,n) = \bar{\Phi}(b,t,-n) = \emptyset$.
4. $\Phi(0,0,0) = \bar{\Phi}(0,0,0) = \{0\}$.
5. A DBC 0 plus z equals to z.
6. A DBC NULL plus z equals to NULL.

Imbert and Philippe's structure of the set containing unsigned DBCs [4] can be used to calculate the number of unsigned DBCs. Since the terms of DBCs of n may be larger than n, calculating the number of DBCs is usually difficult. Following from Capuñay and Thériault's definition [7],

$$n_{b,t} \equiv n \pmod{2^b3^t} \text{ where } 0 \leq n_{b,t} < 2^b3^t.$$

We redefine

$$\bar{n}_{b,t} = n_{b,t} - 2^b3^t.$$

To calculate the number of DBCs, $\Phi(b,t)$ and $\bar{\Phi}(b,t)$ are introduced to describe the structure of the set containing DBCs shown as Lemma 1 where $\Phi(b,t)$ and $\bar{\Phi}(b,t)$ represent $\Phi(b,t,n_{b,t})$ and $\bar{\Phi}(b,t,\bar{n}_{b,t})$ respectively.

Lemma 1. *Let n be a positive integer, $b \geq 0$, $t \geq 0$, and $b+t > 0$. The structure of $\Phi(b,t)$ and that of $\bar{\Phi}(b,t)$ are described as follows.*

1. If $n_{b,t} < 2^b3^{t-1}$, i.e., $n_{b,t} = n_{b-1,t} = n_{b,t-1}$, then

$$\Phi(b,t) = \Phi(b-1,t) \bigcup \left(^{2^{b-1}3^t}\bar{\Phi}(b-1,t)\right) \bigcup \Phi(b,t-1) \bigcup \left(^{2^b3^{t-1}}\bar{\Phi}(b,t-1)\right),$$
$$\bar{\Phi}(b,t) = \left(^{-2^{b-1}3^t}\bar{\Phi}(b-1,t)\right).$$

2. If $2^b3^{t-1} \leq n_{b,t} < 2^{b-1}3^t$, i.e., $n_{b,t} = n_{b-1,t} = n_{b,t-1} + 2^b3^{t-1}$, then

$$\Phi(b,t) = \Phi(b-1,t) \bigcup \left(^{2^{b-1}3^t}\bar{\Phi}(b-1,t)\right) \bigcup \left(^{2^b3^{t-1}}\Phi(b,t-1)\right),$$
$$\bar{\Phi}(b,t) = \left(^{-2^{b-1}3^t}\bar{\Phi}(b-1,t)\right) \bigcup \left(^{-2^b3^{t-1}}\bar{\Phi}(b,t-1)\right).$$

3. If $2^{b-1}3^t \leq n_{b,t} < 2 \cdot 2^b3^{t-1}$, i.e., $n_{b,t} = n_{b-1,t} + 2^{b-1}3^t = n_{b,t-1} + 2^b3^{t-1}$, then

$$\Phi(b,t) = \left(2^{b-1}3^t \Phi(b-1,t)\right) \bigcup \left(2^b 3^{t-1} \Phi(b,t-1)\right),$$

$$\bar{\bar{\Phi}}(b,t) = \left(-2^{b-1}3^t \Phi(b-1,t)\right) \bigcup \bar{\bar{\Phi}}(b-1,t) \bigcup \left(-2^b 3^{t-1} \bar{\bar{\Phi}}(b,t-1)\right).$$

4. If $n_{b,t} \geq 2 \cdot 2^b 3^{t-1}$, i.e., $n_{b,t} = n_{b-1,t} + 2^{b-1}3^t = n_{b,t-1} + 2 \times 2^b 3^{t-1}$, then

$$\Phi(b,t) = \left(2^{b-1}3^t \Phi(b-1,t)\right),$$

$$\bar{\bar{\Phi}}(b,t) = \left(-2^{b-1}3^t \Phi(b-1,t)\right) \bigcup \bar{\bar{\Phi}}(b-1,t) \bigcup \left(-2^b 3^{t-1} \Phi(b,t-1)\right) \bigcup \bar{\bar{\Phi}}(b,t-1).$$

The proofs, examples, and remarks can be found in the full version of this paper [26].

The definitions of $n_{b,t}$ and $\bar{n}_{b,t}$ indicate that both $n_{b,t} = n_{b-1,t} = n_{b,t-1} + 2^{b+1}3^{t-1}$ and $n_{b,t} = n_{b-1,t} + 2^{b-1}3^t = n_{b,t-1}$ are impossible. From Lemma 1, $\Phi(b,t)$ and $\bar{\bar{\Phi}}(b,t)$ only rely on $\Phi(b-1,t)$, $\bar{\bar{\Phi}}(b-1,t)$, $\Phi(b,t-1)$ and $\bar{\bar{\Phi}}(b,t-1)$. By the definitions of $n_{b,t}$ and $\bar{n}_{b,t}$, the structure of $\Phi(b,t)$ and that of $\bar{\bar{\Phi}}(b,t)$ still work for $n_{b,t} = 0$ in Case 1, $n_{b,t} = 2^b 3^{t-1}$ in Case 2, $n_{b,t} = 2^{b-1}3^t$ in Case 3, and $n_{b,t} = 2 \cdot 2^b 3^{t-1}$ in Case 4.

This is the first structure of the set containing all DBCs with a leading term strictly dividing $2^b 3^t$ in the literature. Based on this structure, we will show the number of DBCs with a leading term dividing $2^b 3^t$ for a positive integer n.

3.2   The Number of DBCs

Let $|\mathscr{S}|$ be the cardinality of the set $\mathscr{S}$. The number of DBCs with a leading term dividing $2^b 3^t$ for representing $n_{b,t}$ is $|\Phi(b,t)| + |\bar{\bar{\Phi}}(b,t)|$. We will provide some initial values of $|\Phi|$ and $|\bar{\bar{\Phi}}|$. If $n < 0$ or $n \geq 2^b 3^t$ or $b < 0$ or $t < 0$, $|\Phi(b,t,n)| = |\bar{\bar{\Phi}}(b,t,-n)| = 0$. $|\Phi(0,0,0)| = |\bar{\bar{\Phi}}(0,0,0)| = 1$.

Based on Lemma 1, the cardinality of $\Phi(b,t)$ and that of $\bar{\bar{\Phi}}(b,t)$ are shown as Theorem 1.

Theorem 1. *Let n be a positive integer, $b \geq 0$, $t \geq 0$, and $b + t > 0$. We have*

1. *If $n_{b,t} < 2^{b-1}3^{t-1}$, then*

$$|\Phi(b,t)| = |\Phi(b-1,t)| + |\bar{\bar{\Phi}}(b-1,t)| + |\Phi(b,t-1)| + |\bar{\bar{\Phi}}(b,t-1)|$$
$$- |\Phi(b-1,t-1)| - |\bar{\bar{\Phi}}(b-1,t-1)|,$$
$$|\bar{\bar{\Phi}}(b,t)| = |\bar{\bar{\Phi}}(b-1,t)|.$$

2. *If $2^{b-1}3^{t-1} \leq n_{b,t} < 2^b 3^{t-1}$, then*

$$|\Phi(b,t)| = |\Phi(b-1,t)| + |\bar{\bar{\Phi}}(b-1,t)| + |\Phi(b,t-1)|$$
$$+ |\bar{\bar{\Phi}}(b,t-1)| - |\Phi(b-1,t-1)|,$$
$$|\bar{\bar{\Phi}}(b,t)| = |\bar{\bar{\Phi}}(b-1,t)|.$$

3. *If $2^b 3^{t-1} \leq n_{b,t} < 2^{b-1}3^t$, then*

$$|\Phi(b,t)| = |\Phi(b-1,t)| + |\bar{\bar{\Phi}}(b-1,t)| + |\Phi(b,t-1)|,$$
$$|\bar{\bar{\Phi}}(b,t)| = |\bar{\bar{\Phi}}(b-1,t)| + |\bar{\bar{\Phi}}(b,t-1)|.$$

4. *If $2^{b-1}3^t \le n_{b,t} < 2 \cdot 2^b3^{t-1}$, then*

$$|\Phi(b,t)| = |\Phi(b-1,t)| + |\Phi(b,t-1)|,$$
$$|\bar{\bar{\Phi}}(b,t)| = |\Phi(b-1,t)| + |\bar{\bar{\Phi}}(b-1,t)| + |\bar{\bar{\Phi}}(b,t-1)|.$$

5. *If $2 \cdot 2^b3^{t-1} \le n_{b,t} < 5 \cdot 2^{b-1}3^{t-1}$, then*

$$|\Phi(b,t)| = |\Phi(b-1,t)|,$$
$$|\bar{\bar{\Phi}}(b,t)| = |\Phi(b-1,t)| + |\bar{\bar{\Phi}}(b-1,t)| + |\Phi(b,t-1)|$$
$$+ |\bar{\bar{\Phi}}(b,t-1)| - |\bar{\bar{\Phi}}(b-1,t-1)|.$$

6. *If $n_{b,t} \ge 5 \cdot 2^{b-1}3^{t-1}$, then*

$$|\Phi(b,t)| = |\Phi(b-1,t)|,$$
$$|\bar{\bar{\Phi}}(b,t)| = |\Phi(b-1,t)| + |\bar{\bar{\Phi}}(b-1,t) + |\Phi(b,t-1)|$$
$$+ |\bar{\bar{\Phi}}(b,t-1)| - |\bar{\bar{\Phi}}(b-1,t-1)| - |\Phi(b-1,t-1)|.$$

Based on Theorem 1, we have

Corollary 1. *1. If $b \ge 0$ and $t \ge 0$, then $|\Phi(b,t)| \ge |\Phi(b-1,t)|$, $|\Phi(b,t)| \ge |\Phi(b,t-1)|$, $|\bar{\bar{\Phi}}(b,t)| \ge |\bar{\bar{\Phi}}(b-1,t)|$, and $|\bar{\bar{\Phi}}(b,t)| \ge |\bar{\bar{\Phi}}(b,t-1)|$.*
2. If $b \ge 0$ and $t \ge 0$, then $|\Phi(b,t)| \le 4^{b+t}$ and $|\bar{\bar{\Phi}}(b,t)| \le 4^{b+t}$.

By Corollary 1, $|\Phi(b,t)|$ and $|\bar{\bar{\Phi}}(b,t)|$ are both $\mathscr{O}(\log n)$-bit integers when both b and t are $\mathscr{O}(\log n)$.

Based on Theorem 1, we employ an iterative algorithm to compute the number of DBCs with a leading term strictly dividing 2^b3^t for $n_{b,t}$ and $\bar{n}_{b,t}$ shown as Algorithm 1. The number of DBCs with a leading term dividing 2^b3^t for n is

1. $|\Phi(b,t)| + |\bar{\bar{\Phi}}(b,t)|$ when $2^b3^t > n$;
2. $|\Phi(b,t)|$ when $\frac{n}{2} < 2^b3^t \le n$;
3. 0 when $2^b3^t \le \frac{n}{2}$.

Algorithm 1. Iterative algorithm to compute the number of DBCs

Input: A positive integer n, $b \ge 0$, and $t \ge 0$
Output: The number of DBCs with a leading term strictly dividing 2^b3^t for $n_{b,t}$ and $\bar{n}_{b,t}$

1. $|\Phi(0,0)| \leftarrow 1$, $|\bar{\bar{\Phi}}(0,0)| \leftarrow 0$
2.   **For** i from 0 to b, $|\Phi(i,-1)| = |\bar{\bar{\Phi}}(i,-1)| \leftarrow 0$
3.   **For** j from 0 to t, $|\Phi(-1,j)| = |\bar{\bar{\Phi}}(-1,j)| \leftarrow 0$
4.   **For** j from 0 to t
5.   **For** i from 0 to b
6.   **If** $i + j > 0$, using Theorem 1 to compute $|\Phi(i,j)|$ and $|\bar{\bar{\Phi}}(i,j)|$
7.   **return** $|\Phi(b,t)|$, $|\bar{\bar{\Phi}}(b,t)|$

Table 2. Cost of Algorithm 1

bits of n	256	512	768	1024
b, t	$128, 81$	$256, 161$	$384, 242$	$512, 323$
cost(million cpu cycles)	34	177	551	1184

Algorithm 1 terminates in $\mathscr{O}\left((\log n)^3\right)$ bit operations and $\mathscr{O}\left((\log n)^2\right)$ bits of memory when b and t are both in $\mathscr{O}(\log n)$.

Miracl lib [27] is used to implement big number arithmetic. Our experiments in this paper are compiled and executed on Intel® Core™ i7–6567U 3.3 GHZ with Skylake architecture (our algorithms may have different running time on other architectures). Algorithm 1 requires 34, 177, 551, and 1184 million cpu cycles (10, 50, 170, and 360 ms) for 256-bit, 512-bit, 768-bit, and 1024-bit integers respectively. The details are shown in Table 2.

By Algorithm 1, the number of DBCs of $\lfloor \pi \times 10^{120} \rfloor$ with a leading term dividing $2^{240}3^{120}$ is 40569451268980332857047527244802033238443617954504672 7328 115784 367271984621308621154227072670259226179703610530387 8574879. The number of DBCs with a leading term dividing 2^b3^t for 100 when $b < 50$ and $t < 50$ is shown as Table 3. There exist 405 DBCs with a leading term dividing 2^73^4 for representing 100. These results all show a redundancy of DBCs for a positive integer. The number of DBCs with a leading term dividing 2^b3^t of 100 is the same for $4 \leq t < 50$. For the same b, we guess the number is the same when $t \geq 50$. For each $8 \leq b < 50$, the number of DBCs with a leading term dividing 2^b3^t of 100 minus the number of DBCs with a leading term dividing $2^{b-1}3^t$ of 100 is 7. We guess this result is still true for $b \geq 50$.

Table 3. Number of DBCs with a leading term dividing 2^b3^t for 100

	$t = 0$	$t = 1$	$t = 2$	$t = 3$	$t < 50$
$b = 0$	0	0	0	0	1
$b = 1$	0	0	0	0	7
$b = 2$	0	0	0	11	24
$b = 3$	0	0	18	51	70
$b = 4$	0	0	57	112	137
$b = 5$	0	13	111	188	219
$b = 6$	3	35	174	273	310
$b = 7$	10	61	241	362	405
$b < 50$	$10 + 7 * (b - 7)$	$61 + 26 * (b - 7)$	$241 + 67 * (b - 7)$	$362 + 89 * (b - 7)$	$405 + 95 * (b - 7)$

3.3   The Number of DBCs for Large b or t

If b or t is large, the number of DBCs are shown as Corollary 2.

Corollary 2. *Let n be a given positive integer, t_τ be a positive integer satisfying $3^{t_\tau-1} > n$ and $3^{t_\tau-2} \leq n$, and b_τ be a positive integer satisfying $2^{b_\tau} > 3n$ and $2^{b_\tau-1} \leq 3n$. Then*

1. *If $t \geq t_\tau$ and $b \in \mathbb{Z}$, then $|\Phi(b,t)| = |\Phi(b,t_\tau)|$.*
2. *If $b \geq b_\tau$ and $t \in \mathbb{Z}$, then $|\Phi(b,t)| = |\Phi(b_\tau,t)| + (b - b_\tau)C_\tau$ where $C_\tau = \sum_{i=0}^{t} |\bar{\Phi}(b_\tau, i)|$.*

3. *If $b \geq b_\tau$ and $t \geq t_\tau$, then $|\Phi(b,t)| = |\Phi(b_\tau, t)| + (b - b_\tau)C_\tau$ where $C_\tau = \sum_{i=0}^{t_\tau} |\bar{\Phi}(b_\tau, i)|$.*

These three properties of Corollary 2 are used to compute the number of DBCs with a leading term dividing $2^b 3^t$ for some large b and t. The number of DBCs with a leading term dividing $2^b 3^t$ is a constant when $t > t_\tau$. The number of DBCs with a leading term dividing $2^b 3^t$ adds a constant $\sum_{i=0}^{t} |\bar{\Phi}(b_\tau, i)|$ is the number of DBCs with a leading term dividing $2^{b+1} 3^t$ when $b > b_\tau$. Take 100 for example, 100 has 137 DBCs with a leading term dividing $2^4 3^t$ for each $t \geq t_\tau$, and has $405 + 95 * (b-7)$ DBCs with a leading term dividing $2^b 3^t$ for each $b \geq 9$ and $t \geq 6$. These results may be associated with that $1 = 2^b - \sum_{i=0}^{b-1} 2^i$ as b becomes larger and that $1 = 3^0$ can not be represented as other ternary representation with its coefficients in $\{\pm 1\}$.

4   Hamming Weight of DBCs

For a positive integer n, Chalermsook, Imai, and Suppakitpaisarn [28] showed that the Hamming weight of unsigned DBNS representations obtained from the greedy approach proposed by Dimitrov, Imbert, and Mishra [1] is $\theta\left(\frac{\log n}{\log \log n}\right)$. And they showed that the Hamming weight of unsigned DBCs produced by greedy approach [1] is $\theta(\log n)$.

For the Hamming weights of (signed) DBNS representations and DBCs, Dimitrov, Imbert, and Mishra [1] showed that every integer n has a DBNS representation with Hamming weight $\mathcal{O}\left(\frac{\log n}{\log \log n}\right)$. Every integer n has a DBC with Hamming weight $\mathcal{O}(\log n)$. These are upper bounds on the Hamming weight of DBNS representations and DBCs. The number of DBCs of a positive integer is infinite and the leading term of its DBC may be infinite. The range of the leading term of canonic DBCs is useful to show the lower bounds of the Hamming weight of DBCs.

4.1   The Range of the Leading Term of Optimal DBCs and Canonic DBCs

Doche [16] proved that a DBC with leading term $2^b 3^t$ belongs to the interval $\left[\frac{3^t+1}{2}, 2^{b+1} 3^t - \frac{3^t+1}{2}\right]$. His result showed the range of integers for a leading term. The leading term of a DBC $2^{b_l} 3^{t_l}$ for a positive integer does not have an upper bound for $1 = 2^{b_l} - 2^{b_l-1} - \ldots - 2 - 1$ where b_l is an arbitrary positive integer. We will show the range of the leading term of optimal DBCs and that of canonic DBCs for a given integer in Lemma 2.

Lemma 2. *Let n be a positive integer represented as* w : $\sum_{i=1}^{l} c_i 2^{b_i} 3^{t_i}$, $c_l = 1, c_i \in \{\pm 1\}$ *for $1 \leq i \leq l-1$. Then $\frac{n}{2} < 2^{b_l} 3^{t_l} < 2n$ when* w *is an optimal DBC, and $\frac{16n}{21} < 2^{b_l} 3^{t_l} < \frac{9n}{7}$ when* w *is a canonic DBC.*

The range of the leading term of optimal DBCs is useful to prove that the DBC produced by Capuñay and Thériault's algorithm [7] and that produced by Bernstein, Chuengsatiansup, and Lange's algorithm [17] both are optimal DBCs. The leading term of canonic DBCs of n is in the interval $\left(\frac{16n}{21}, \frac{9n}{7}\right)$. It is useful to prove that the DBCs generated by Doche's algorithm is a canonic DBC [16], and to prove the asymptotic lower bound on the Hamming weights of DBCs in the following.

4.2   A Lower Bound on the Hamming Weights of DBCs

Dimitrov and Howe proved that there exist infinitely many integers n whose shortest DBNS representations have Hamming weights $\Omega\left(\frac{\log n}{\log \log n \log \log \log n}\right)$ [29]. The minimum Hamming weight of DBCs for a positive integer n is also called Kolmogorov complexity [30] of a DBC of n, i.e., the Hamming weight of canonic DBCs of n. Lou, Sun, and Tartary [5] proved a similar result for DBCs: there exists at least one $\lfloor \log n \rfloor$-bit integer such that any DBC representing this integer needs at least $\Omega\left(\lfloor \log n \rfloor\right)$ terms. We will give a stronger result in Lemma 3.

Lemma 3. *For arbitrary $\alpha \in (0,1)$ and $0 < C < \frac{\alpha^2}{8.25}$, more than $n - n^\alpha$ integers in $[1, n]$ satisfy that the Hamming weight of the canonic DBCs of each integer is greater than $C \log n$ when $n > N$ (N is some constant shown as Claim 1).*

For convenience, we first give some conventions and definitions. $s(m)$ denotes the Hamming weight of canonic DBCs of m, and e is the base of the natural logarithm. Let φ_l be the number of DBCs $\sum_{i=1}^{l} c_i 2^{b_i} 3^{t_i}$ with $2^{b_l} 3^{t_l} < \frac{9n}{7}, c_i \in \{\pm 1\}$, and $c_l = 1$.

Definition 4 ($\varphi(L)$). *For a given positive integer n and a constant L, $\varphi(L) = \sum_{l=1}^{L} \varphi_l$, i.e., $\varphi(L)$ is the number of DBCs $\sum_{i=1}^{l} c_i 2^{b_i} 3^{t_i}$ with $2^{b_l} 3^{t_l} < \frac{9n}{7}, 1 \le l \le L$.*

By Lemma 2, in a canonic DBC, $\frac{16n}{21} < 2^{b_l} 3^{t_l} < \frac{9n}{7}$. Then, the number of integers of m in $[1, n]$ represented as a canonic DBC with Hamming weight no greater than L is not more than the number of integers of m in $[1, n]$ represented as a DBC with a leading term dividing $2^{b_l} 3^{t_l} < \frac{9n}{7}, l \le L$. Since every DBC corresponds to only one integer and each integer has at least one DBC, the number of integers in $[1, n]$ represented as a canonic DBC with Hamming weight no greater than L is no greater than $\varphi(L)$.

An outline of the proof of Lemma 3 is as follows. The number of integers of m in $[1, n]$ can not be represented as a DBC of Hamming weight j, $0 < j \le L$ is equal to n minus the number of integers of m in $[1, n]$ represented in that way. There are at least $n - \varphi(L)$ integers of m in $[1, n]$ can not be represented as a DBC of Hamming weight j with $2^{b_j} 3^{t_j} \le \frac{9n}{7}, 0 < j \le L$. Thus there are at least $n - \varphi(L)$ integers of m in $[1, n]$ satisfying $s(m) > L$. Hence, $\varphi(C \log n) < n^\alpha$ is enough to prove Lemma 3.

Since φ_j where $0 < j \leq C \log n$ is the number of DBCs of Hamming weight j with $2^{b_i} 3^{t_i} < \frac{9n}{7}$, we have

$$\varphi_j \leq 2^{j-1} \sum_{\alpha + \gamma \log 3 < \log \frac{9n}{7}} \binom{\alpha + j}{j - 1} \binom{\gamma + j}{j - 1}.$$

Then

$$\varphi(C \log n) = \sum_{j=1}^{C \log n} \varphi_j \leq \sum_{j=1}^{C \log n} \left(2^{j-1} \sum_{\alpha + \gamma \log 3 < \log \frac{9n}{7}} \binom{\alpha + j}{j - 1} \binom{\gamma + j}{j - 1} \right). \quad (1)$$

For this estimate of $\varphi(C \log n)$ is too complex to be dealt with, we simplify its estimate by Claim 1 and its proof requires the tools of Pascal's triangle and Stirling's formula.

Claim 1. *For any $0 < C < 1$, when $n > N$ where N satisfies that $N > 2^{10000 \cdot (3 - 0.5 \log_3 7)}$ and $\log N < 1.0001^{C \log N}$,*

$$\sum_{j=1}^{C \log n} \left(2^{j-1} \sum_{\alpha + \gamma \log_2 3 < \log \frac{9n}{7}} \binom{\alpha + j}{j - 1} \binom{\gamma + j}{j - 1} \right) < n^{C \log \left(\frac{2.0002 e^2 (0.5001 \log_3 2 + C)^2}{C^2} \right)}.$$

According to Eq. (1) and Claim 1, we have

$$\varphi(C \log n) < n^{C \log \left(\frac{2.0002 e^2 \log 3 \cdot (0.5001 \log_3 2 + C)^2}{C^2} \right)}.$$

For some larger N, the coefficients of $\log_3 2$ and e^2 will be smaller than 0.50001 and 2.0002 respectively in this inequation, and for some smaller N, the coefficients of $\log_3 2$ and e^2 will be larger than 0.50001 and 2.0002. The proof of Lemma 3 is as follows.

Proof. To prove Lemma 3, it is sufficient to show that the number of integers of m in $[1, n]$, represented as a DBC of Hamming weight j with $j \leq C \log n$ and $2^{b_j} 3^{t_j} < \frac{9n}{7}$, is no greater than n^α.

The number of integers of m in $[1, n]$ can be represented as DBCs of Hamming weight j with $2^{b_j} 3^{t_j} < \frac{9n}{7}$, $0 < j \leq C \log n$ is no greater than $\varphi(C \log n)$. This result is sufficient to show that $\varphi(C \log n) < n^\alpha$, i.e., the number of DBCs of Hamming weight j with $j \leq C \log n$ is less than n^α.

Since $\varphi(C \log n) < n^{C \log \left(\frac{2.0002 e^2 \log 3 \cdot (0.5001 \log_3 2 + C)^2}{C^2} \right)}$, then

$$n^{C \log \left(\frac{2.0002 e^2 \log 3 \cdot (0.5001 \log_3 2 + C)^2}{C^2} \right)} < n^\alpha. \text{ We have}$$

$$\frac{2.0002 e^2 \log 3 \cdot (0.5001 \log_3 2 + C)^2}{C^2} < 2^{\frac{\alpha}{C}}.$$

When $0 < C < \frac{\alpha^2}{8.25}$, this inequality holds.

Thus, for any real numbers α and C with $0 < \alpha < 1$ and $0 < C < \frac{\alpha^2}{8.25}$, when $n > N$, at least $n - n^\alpha$ integers of m in $[1, n]$ satisfy $s(m) > C \log n$.

As a corollary of Lemma 3, for any given positive number $\alpha < 1$, there exist two efficiently computable constants C and N, such that when $n > N$, there are at least $n - n^{\alpha}$ integers m in $[1, n]$ satisfying $s(m) > C \log n > C \log m$. This result is easy to understand and more advanced than Lou, Sun, and Tartary's result [5].

Doche and Habsieger [3] showed that the DBC produced by the tree approach is shorter than that produced by greedy approach experimentally. The average Hamming weight of the DBCs produced by the tree approach is $\frac{\log n}{4.6419}$. Then they posed an open question that the average Hamming weight of DBCs generated by the greedy approach may be not $\mathscr{O}\left(\frac{\log n}{\log \log n}\right)$. Lemma 3 is sufficient to solve this question.

The average Hamming weight of DBCs of $(\log n)$-bit integers is the average value of the Hamming weights of the DBCs of all $(\log n)$-bit integers where we choose one DBC for each integer. An asymptotic lower bound of the Hamming weights of DBCs is shown in Theorem 2.

Theorem 2. *An asymptotic lower bound of the average Hamming weights of canonic DBCs for $(\log n)$-bit integers is $\frac{\log n}{8.25}$.*

All existing algorithms confirm the asymptotic lower bound of Theorem 2. The average Hamming weight of binary representation is $0.5 \log n$, that of NAF is $\frac{\log n}{3}$, that of the DBC produced by binary/ternary approach is $0.2284 \log n$ [2], and that of the DBC produced by tree approach is $0.2154 \log n$ [3]. The Hamming weights of the DBCs produced by these algorithms are still a long way from the lower bound $\frac{\log n}{8.25}$ in Theorem 2.

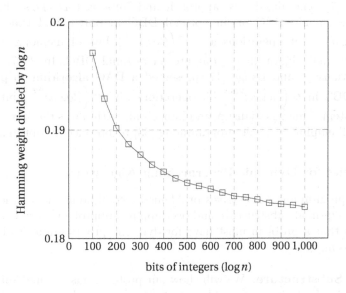

Fig. 1. The Hamming weight of canonic DBCs of integers

The average Hamming weight of canonic DBCs of integers is shown as Fig. 1. The data is gained by Algorithm 3 which will be given in Section 6 for 1000 random integers for each size. It is $0.19713 \log n$ for 100-bit integers, $0.190165 \log n$ for 200-bit integers, $0.18773 \log n$ for 300-bit integers, $0.186158 \log n$ for 400-bit integers, $0.185124 \log n$ for 500-bit integers, $0.184568 \log n$ for 600-bit integers, $0.183913 \log n$ for 700-bit integers, $0.183579 \log n$ for 800-bit integers, $0.183153 \log n$ for 900-bit integers, $0.182887 \log n$ for 1000-bit integers, $0.181867 \log n$ for 1500-bit integers, $0.181101 \log n$ for 2000-bit integers, $0.180495 \log n$ for 2500-bit integers, and $0.179822 \log n$ for 3000-bit integers. This value of the Hamming weight given for 3000-bit integers still has a distance from the lower bound given in Theorem 2. The Hamming weight divided by $\log n$ is decreased as the integers become larger.

Our method of calculating the asymptotic lower bound of the average Hamming weight of DBCs may be useful to calculate the asymptotic lower bound of the average Hamming weight of extended DBCs [31] where $\mathscr{C} = \{\pm 1, \pm 3, \ldots\}$.

We will propose an efficient algorithm to generate optimal DBCs.

5   Dynamic Programming Algorithm to Produce Optimal DBCs

Several algorithms were designed to produce near optimal DBCs such as greedy approach [1], binary/ternary approach [2], tree approach [3], and mbNAF [13]. Doche [16] generalized Erdös and Loxton's recursive equation of the number of unsigned chain partition [32] and presented an algorithm to produce a canonic DBC. As Doche's algorithm requires exponential time, in 2015, Capuñay and Thériault [7] generalized tree approach and improved Doche's algorithm to produce a canonic DBC or an optimal DBC in polynomial time, explicitly in $\mathscr{O}\left((\log n)^4\right)$ bit operations and $\mathscr{O}\left((\log n)^3\right)$ bits of memory. This is the first polynomial algorithm to compute an optimal DBC. In 2017, Bernstein, Chuengsatiansup, and Lange [17] presented a DAG algorithm to produce an optimal DBC in $\mathscr{O}\left((\log n)^{2.5}\right)$ bit operations and $\mathscr{O}\left((\log n)^{2.5}\right)$ bits of memory. Bernstein, Chuengsatiansup, and Lange's algorithm was the state-of-the-art.

We will employ dynamic programming [33] to produce an optimal DBC.

5.1   Basics for Dynamic Programming Algorithm

Dynamic programming [33] solves problems by combining the solutions of subproblems. Optimal substructure and overlapping subproblems are two key characteristics that a problem must have for dynamic programming to be a viable solution technique.

Optimal Substructure. We will show our problem has optimal substructure, i.e., an optimal solution to a problem contains optimal solutions to subproblems. First, we define sub-chain.

Definition 5 (Sub-chain). *A DBC* $\sum_{i=1}^{l} c_i 2^{b_i} 3^{t_i}$ *is a sub-chain of a DBC*
$\sum_{j=1}^{l_0} a_j 2^{d_j} 3^{e_j}$, *if it satisfies both of the following conditions:*

1. $b_l \leq d_{l_0}$, $t_l \leq e_{l_0}$, *and* $l \leq l_0$;
2. *For each* i *satisfies* $1 \leq i \leq l$, *there exists one* j *satisfying* $c_i = a_j, b_i = d_j$, *and* $t_i = e_j$.

Let $\mathrm{w}(b, t)$ (resp. $\bar{\mathrm{w}}(b, t)$) be one of the DBCs in $\Phi(b, t)$ (resp. $\bar{\Phi}(b, t)$) with the smallest Hamming weight. The optimal substructure of the problem of finding $\mathrm{w}(b, t)$ (resp. $\bar{\mathrm{w}}(b, t)$) is shown in Lemma 4.

Lemma 4. *Let* $\mathrm{w}(b, t)$ *be a minimal chain for* $n_{b,t}$ *in* $\Phi(b, t)$ *and* $\bar{\mathrm{w}}(b, t)$ *be a minimal chain for* $\bar{n}_{b,t}$ *in* $\bar{\Phi}(b, t)$. *If* $\mathrm{w}(b, t)$ *or* $\bar{\mathrm{w}}(b, t)$ *contains a sub-chain* $\mathrm{w}(i, j)$ *for* $n_{i,j}$, *then* $\mathrm{w}(i, j)$ *is minimal for* $n_{i,j}$ *in* $\Phi(i, j)$; *If* $\mathrm{w}(b, t)$ *or* $\bar{\mathrm{w}}(b, t)$ *contains a sub-chain* $\bar{\mathrm{w}}(i, j)$ *for* $\bar{n}_{i,j}$, *then* $\bar{\mathrm{w}}(i, j)$ *is minimal for* $\bar{n}_{i,j}$ *in* $\bar{\Phi}(i, j)$.

Lemma 4 shows that the problem of finding a minimal chain has optimal substructure. We can partition this problem into subproblems. These subproblems may share the same new problems. For example, subproblems for $n_{b,t-1}$ and subproblems for $n_{b-1,t}$ share the same problems for $n_{b-1,t-1}$ and for $\bar{n}_{b-1,t-1}$.

Overlapping Subproblems. When a recursive algorithm revisits the same problem over and over again rather than always generating new problems, we say that the optimization problem has overlapping subproblems. Dynamic programming algorithms typically take advantage of overlapping subproblems by solving each subproblem once and then storing the solution in a table where it can be looked up when needed.

Based on Lemma 1, using the range of the leading term of a canonic DBC in Lemma 2, we simplify the possible sources of $\mathrm{w}(b, t)$ and $\bar{\mathrm{w}}(b, t)$ shown as Lemma 5.

Lemma 5. *Let* n *be a positive integer*, $b \geq 0$, $t \geq 0$, *and* $b + t > 0$.

1. *If* $\frac{n_{b,t}}{2^{b-1} 3^{t-1}} < 2$, *then*

$$\mathrm{w}(b, t) = \mathrm{minL}\left\{\mathrm{w}(b-1, t), \mathrm{w}(b, t-1), 2^b 3^{t-1} + \bar{\mathrm{w}}(b, t-1)\right\},$$
$$\bar{\mathrm{w}}(b, t) = -2^{b-1} 3^t + \bar{\mathrm{w}}(b-1, t).$$

2. *If* $2 \leq \frac{n_{b,t}}{2^{b-1} 3^{t-1}} < 3$, *then*

$$\mathrm{w}(b, t) = \mathrm{minL}\left\{\mathrm{w}(b-1, t), 2^{b-1} 3^t + \bar{\mathrm{w}}(b-1, t), 2^b 3^{t-1} + \mathrm{w}(b, t-1)\right\},$$
$$\bar{\mathrm{w}}(b, t) = -2^{b-1} 3^t + \bar{\mathrm{w}}(b-1, t).$$

3. *If* $3 \leq \frac{n_{b,t}}{2^{b-1} 3^{t-1}} < 4$, *then*

$$\mathrm{w}(b, t) = 2^{b-1} 3^t + \mathrm{w}(b-1, t),$$
$$\bar{\mathrm{w}}(b, t) = \mathrm{minL}\left\{-2^{b-1} 3^t + \mathrm{w}(b-1, t), \bar{\mathrm{w}}(b-1, t), -2^b 3^{t-1} + \bar{\mathrm{w}}(b, t-1)\right\}.$$

4. If $\frac{n_{b,t}}{2^{b-1}3^{t-1}} \geq 4$, then

$$w(b,t) = 2^{b-1}3^t + w(b-1,t),$$
$$\bar{w}(b,t) = \text{minL}\left\{\bar{w}(b-1,t), -2^b3^{t-1} + w(b,t-1), \bar{w}(b,t-1)\right\}.$$

We give some conventions for initial values of $w(b,t)$ and $\bar{w}(b,t)$. If $b < 0$ or $t < 0$, $w(b,t) = \bar{w}(b,t) = \text{NULL}$. If $b \geq 0$, $t \geq 0$, and $n_{b,t} = 0$, then $w(b,t) = \{0\}$ and $\bar{w}(b,t) = \text{NULL}$.

Lemma 5 reveals the relationship between problems of finding $w(b,t)$ and $\bar{w}(b,t)$ and problems of finding their subproblems. Dynamic programming is efficient when a given subproblem may arise from more than one partial set of choices. Each problem of finding $w(b,t)$ and $\bar{w}(b,t)$ has at most 4 partial sets of choices. The key technique in the overlapping subproblems is to store the solution of each such subproblem in case it should reappear.

5.2 Dynamic Programming to Compute an Optimal DBC

The main blueprint of our dynamic programming algorithm to produce an optimal DBC contains four steps.

1. Characterize the structure of an optimal solution whose two key ingredients are optimal substructure and overlapping subproblems.
2. Recursively define the value of an optimal solution by minL.
3. Compute a DBC with the smallest Hamming weight and its leading term dividing 2^b3^t for each $n_{b,t}$ and $\bar{n}_{b,t}$ in a bottom-up fashion.
4. Construct an optimal DBC from computed information.

The dynamic programming algorithm to compute an optimal DBC is shown as Algorithm 2. In Algorithm 2, set $B = 2n$ in general cases, and set $B = \frac{9n}{7}$ in the case $D = T = 0$ by Lemma 2.

Algorithm 2. Dynamic programming to compute an optimal DBC

Input: a positive integer n, its binary representation n_{binary}, three non-negative constants $A > 0, D \geq 0, T \geq 0$
Output: an optimal DBC for n
1. **If** $D = 0$ and $T = 0$, $B \leftarrow \frac{9n}{7}$, **else** $B \leftarrow 2n$. $w(0,0) \leftarrow 0$, $\bar{w}(0,0) \leftarrow \text{NULL}$, $w_{\text{min}} \leftarrow n_{\text{binary}}$
2. **For** b from 0 to $\lfloor \log B \rfloor$, $w(b,-1) \leftarrow \text{NULL}$, $\bar{w}(b,-1) \leftarrow \text{NULL}$
3. **For** t **from** 0 **to** $\lfloor \log_3 B \rfloor$, $w(-1,t) \leftarrow \text{NULL}$, $\bar{w}(-1,t) \leftarrow \text{NULL}$, bBound$[t] \leftarrow \lfloor \log \frac{B}{3^t} \rfloor$
4. **For** t from 0 to $\lfloor \log_3 B \rfloor$
5.   **For** b from 0 to bBound$[t]$
6.   **If** $b + t > 0$, compute $w(b,t)$ and $\bar{w}(b,t)$ using Lemma 5
7.   **If** $n > n_{b,t}$, $w_{\text{min}} \leftarrow \text{minV}\left\{2^b3^t + w(b,t), w_{\text{min}}\right\}$
8.   **else if** $n = n_{b,t}$, $w_{\text{min}} \leftarrow \text{minV}\left\{w(b,t), 2^b3^t + \bar{w}(b,t), w_{\text{min}}\right\}$
9. **return** w_{min}

In Lines $1 - 3$ of Algorithm 2, the initial values of $w(0,0)$, $\bar{w}(0,0)$, w_{min}, $w(b,-1)$, $\bar{w}(b,-1)$, $w(-1,t)$ and $\bar{w}(-1,t)$ are given. w_{min} stores the resulting DBC for n whose initial value is n_{binary}, i.e., the binary representation of n.

In the Lines $4 - 8$ of Algorithm 2, a two-layer cycle computes a DBC w_{min}. Line 6 shows that the problem of computing $w(b,t)$ and $\bar{w}(b,t)$ are partitioned into subproblems of computing $w(b-1,t)$, $\bar{w}(b-1,t)$, $w(b,t-1)$, and $\bar{w}(b,t-1)$ using Lemma 5. This is a bottom-up fashion. For the same t, we compute $w(0,t)$ (the same for $\bar{w}(0,t)$); next, compute $w(1,t)$, ..., $w\left(\lfloor\log\frac{B}{3^t}\rfloor,t\right)$. Since $w(b,t-1)$ and $\bar{w}(b,t-1)$ have been computed by Lines 4 and 6 in the last loop of t and $w(b-1,t)$ and $\bar{w}(b-1,t)$ have been computed by Lines 5 and 6 in the last loop of b, we compute $w(b,t)$ and $\bar{w}(b,t)$ successfully. Using these results to solve the subproblems recursively, we can avoid calculating a problem twice or more.

By Lemma 4 and the bottom-up fashion, $w(b,t)$ and $\bar{w}(b,t)$ have been computed by Algorithm 2 for all b and t satisfying $2^b 3^t < B$. We will show that the DBC returned by Algorithm 2 is an optimal DBC in Theorem 3.

Theorem 3. *Algorithm 2 produces a canonic DBC when $D = T = 0$, and an optimal DBC when $D + T > 0$.*

If one wants to generate a different optimal DBC or canonic DBC, one possibility is to adjust the function minL and minV when two or more DBCs have the same value. Doing this, we can favor doubling or tripling. In our algorithm, we favor tripling.

Optimal DBCs are usually varied with Hamming weight by different costs of point operations. Canonic DBCs returned by Algorithm 2 are with the same Hamming weight and are not affected by the cost of point operations. Take a positive integer $\lfloor\pi\times 10^{20}\rfloor = 314159265358979323846$ for example. Its optimal DBC returned by Algorithm 2 is $2^{30}3^3 + 2^{28}3^2 + 2^{20}3^2 - 2^{17}3^1 - 2^{16}3^0 - 2^8 3^0 + 2^3 3^0 - 2^0 3^0$ with Hamming weight 8 for $\mathscr{E}_W$ 0.8. The value of the cost of this DBC is 319.2. Its optimal DBC returned by Algorithm 2 is $2^{19}3^{10} + 2^{13}3^{10} - 2^{12}3^8 + 2^9 3^6 + 2^6 3^5 + 2^3 3^2 - 2^0 3^0$ with Hamming weight 7 for $\mathscr{E}_W$ 1. The value of the cost of this DBC is 358. This DBC with Hamming weight 7 is one of the canonic DBCs of $\lfloor\pi\times 10^{20}\rfloor$.

5.3 The Time Complexity and Space Complexity of Algorithm 2

The running time of a dynamic programming algorithm depends on the product of two factors: the number of subproblems overall and how many choices we look at for each subproblem. Our dynamic programming algorithm has $(\log n + 1)(\log_3 n + 1)$ subproblems. If we store the value of $n_{b,t}$ and $n/(2^b 3^t)$ for the use of next cycle, each subproblems requires $\mathcal{O}(\log n)$ bit operations. Algorithm 2 terminates in $\mathcal{O}\left((\log n)^3\right)$ bit operations. The details are illustrated by Fig. 2. Each node (b,t) of computing $\lfloor\frac{n_{b,t}}{2^{b-1}3^{t-1}}\rfloor$, $w(b,t)$, and $\bar{w}(b,t)$ requires $\mathcal{O}(\log n)$ bit operations.

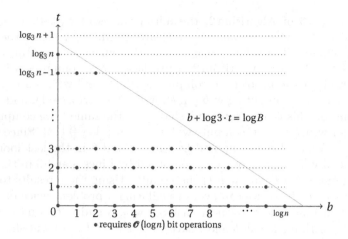

Fig. 2. The procedure of our dynamic programming algorithm

If the powers of 2 and 3 are recorded by their differences as Remark 5 of Capuñay and Thériault's work [7], our algorithm terminates in $\mathscr{O}\left((\log n)^2\right)$ bits of memory. The details are shown as follows. The term $c_i 2^{b_i} 3^{t_i}$ in the chain is stored as the pair (c_i, b_i, t_i). For example, $1000 = 2^{10} - 2^5 + 2^3$ is recorded as $(1, 3, 0)$, $(-1, 2, 0)$, and $(1, 5, 0)$. If DBCs are recorded as their difference with the previous term, then the memory requirement per chain is $\mathscr{O}(\log n)$. Thus, Algorithm 2 requires $\mathscr{O}\left((\log n)^2\right)$ bits of memory.

We will focus on improving the time complexity of Algorithm 2.

6 Equivalent Representatives for Large Numbers

The most time-consuming part of Lemma 5 is to compute $\frac{n_{b,t}}{2^{b-1}3^{t-1}}$. It can be improved by reduced representatives for large numbers [17]. Bernstein, Chuengsatiansup, and Lange [17] noticed that arbitrary divisions of $\mathscr{O}(\log n)$-bit numbers take time $(\log n)^{1+o(1)}$ shown in pages $81 - 86$ of "on the minimum computation time of functions" by Cook [34]. Based on this novel representative, the time complexity of dynamic programming algorithm is shown as Fig. 3. In Fig. 3, $\alpha' = (\log B)^{0.5}$ and $\beta' = (\log_3 B)^{0.5}$. Each node (b, t) satisfying $\alpha'|b$ or $\beta'|t$ is named a boundary node in Fig. 3. Each boundary node requires $\log n$ bit operations and each of the other nodes requires $(\log n)^{0.5}$ bit operations. Then Algorithm 2 terminates in $\mathscr{O}\left((\log n)^{2.5}\right)$ bit operations using reduced representatives.

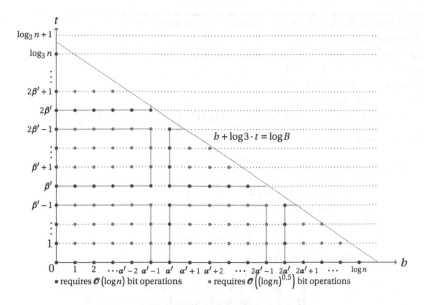

Fig. 3. The procedure of our dynamic programming algorithm using the trick in [17]

Motivated by their reduced representatives for large numbers, we will give a new representative named equivalent representative.

Definition 6 (Equivalent representative). *If one expression of an integer n' is equal to the value of $\left\lfloor \frac{n_{b,t}}{2^b-1 3^t-1} \right\rfloor$ in Lemma 5, then n' is an equivalent representative of n.*

Our equivalent representative is a generalization of Bernstein, Chuengsatiansup, and Lange's reduced representative. Reduced representatives for large numbers do not work for $\log n + \log_3 n$ boundary nodes. Our equivalent representatives will solve this problem.

6.1 Use Equivalent Representatives in Algorithm 2

We employ equivalent representatives to improve the recode procedure of Algorithm 2 shown as Algorithm 3. n_1 is an equivalent representative in Algorithm 3 shown by Claim 2.

Claim 2. *Let* $n_1' = \left\lfloor \frac{6 \cdot n}{2^{\text{ii}_1 \cdot \alpha_1^2 3^{\text{jj}_1 \cdot \beta_1^2}}} \right\rfloor \% \left(2^{\alpha_1^2+1} 3^{\beta_1^2+1}\right)$, $n_1 = \left\lfloor \frac{n_1'}{2^{i_1 \cdot \alpha_1} 3^{j_1 \cdot \beta_1}} \right\rfloor \%$ $\left(2^{\alpha_1+1} 3^{\beta_1+1}\right)$, $\alpha_1 = \left\lfloor (\log B)^{\frac{1}{3}} \right\rfloor$, $\beta_1 = \left\lfloor (\log B)^{\frac{1}{3}} \right\rfloor$, $b = \text{ii}_1 \cdot \alpha_1^2 + i_1 \cdot \alpha_1 + i$, $t = \text{jj}_1 \cdot \beta_1^2 + j_1 \cdot \beta_1 + j$, $i_1 \geq 0$, $j_1 \geq 0$, $0 \leq i < \alpha$, $0 \leq j < \beta$ *shown as Algorithm 3. Then* $\left(\left\lfloor \frac{n_1}{2^i 3^j} \right\rfloor \% 6\right) = \left\lfloor \frac{n_{b,t}}{2^b-1 3^t-1} \right\rfloor$.

Algorithm 3. Dynamic programming to compute an optimal DBC using equivalent representatives once

---

Input: a positive integer n and its binary representation n_{binary}, three non-negative constants $A > 0, D \geq 0, T \geq 0$

Output: an optimal DBC for n

1. Lines $1 - 3$ of Algorithm 2

2. $\alpha_0 \leftarrow \lfloor \log B \rfloor$, $\beta_0 \leftarrow \lfloor \log_3 B \rfloor$, $\alpha_1 \leftarrow \left\lfloor (\log B)^{\frac{1}{3}} \right\rfloor$, $\beta_1 \leftarrow \left\lfloor (\log B)^{\frac{1}{3}} \right\rfloor$

3. **For** jj_1 from 0 to $\left\lfloor \frac{\log_3 B}{\beta_1^2} \right\rfloor + 1$

4.   **For** ii_1 from 0 to $\left\lfloor \frac{\text{bBound}[j \cdot \beta_1^2]}{\alpha_1^2} \right\rfloor + 1$

5. $n_1' \leftarrow \left\lfloor \frac{6 \cdot n}{2^{\text{ii}_1 \cdot \alpha_1^2} 3^{\text{jj}_1 \cdot \beta_1^2}} \right\rfloor \% \left(2^{\alpha_1^2 + 1} 3^{\beta_1^2 + 1} \right)$

6.   **For** j_1 from 0 to $\beta_1 - 1$

7.   **For** i_1 from 0 to $\alpha_1 - 1$

8. $n_1 \leftarrow \left\lfloor \frac{n_1'}{2^{i_1 \cdot \alpha_1} 3^{j_1 \cdot \beta_1}} \right\rfloor \% \left(2^{\alpha_1 + 1} 3^{\beta_1 + 1} \right)$

9.   **For** j from 0 to $\beta_1 - 1$

10.   **For** i from 0 to $\alpha_1 - 1$

11. $t \leftarrow \text{jj}_1 \cdot \beta_1^2 + j_1 \cdot \beta_1 + j, b \leftarrow \text{ii}_1 \cdot \alpha_1^2 + i_1 \cdot \alpha_1 + i$

12.   **If** $b + t > 0 \& b < \text{bBound}[t] \& t \leq \lfloor \log_3 B \rfloor$

13.   compute $w(b, t), \bar{w}(b, t)$ using Lemma 5

                                ▷ $\left\lfloor \frac{n_{b,t}}{2^{b-1} 3^{t-1}} \right\rfloor$ is calculated by $\left(\left\lfloor \frac{n_1}{2^i 3^j} \right\rfloor \% 6 \right)$

14.   **else if** $b = \text{bBound}[t] \& t \leq \lfloor \log_3 B \rfloor$, Lines 7, 8 of Algorithm 2

15. **return** $\text{w}_{\min}$

Notice that $t = \text{jj}_1 \cdot \beta_1^2 + j_1 \cdot \beta_1 + j$, $b = \text{ii}_1 \cdot \alpha_1^2 + i_1 \cdot \alpha_1 + i$ in Line 11 of Algorithm 3. Algorithm 3 is similar as Algorithm 2 whose total cycles are at most $\log B \log_3 B$.

Algorithm 3 uses a trick of an equivalence representative n_1. The middle variable n_1' is used to calculate the equivalent representative n_1. Each n_1' is a $\mathcal{O}(\alpha_1^2)$-bit integers shown as Algorithm 3. There are at most $\left(\left\lfloor \frac{\log_3 B}{\beta_1^2} \right\rfloor + 1 \right) \left(\left\lfloor \frac{\log B}{\alpha_1^2} \right\rfloor + 1 \right)$ such numbers n_1', i.e., $\mathcal{O}(\alpha_1^2)$. Calculating each n_1' requires $\mathcal{O}(\log n)$ bit operations. Calculating all n_1' requires $\mathcal{O}\left((\log n)^{\frac{5}{3}} \right)$ bit operations. Calculating each representative n_1 requires $\mathcal{O}(\alpha_1^2)$ bit operations. Then calculating equivalent representatives requires $\mathcal{O}\left((\log n)^2 \right)$ bit operations.

Based on equivalent representatives, each node (b, t) requires $\mathcal{O}(\alpha_1)$ bit operations. $(\log B) \cdot (\log_3 B)$ nodes requiring $\mathcal{O}\left((\log n)^{\frac{7}{3}} \right)$ bit operations. The time complexity of Algorithm 3 is shown in Lemma 6.

Lemma 6. *Algorithm 3 terminates in $\mathcal{O}\left((\log n)^{2+\frac{1}{3}}\right)$ bit operations.*

The details of the time cost of Algorithm 3 are shown as Fig. 4.

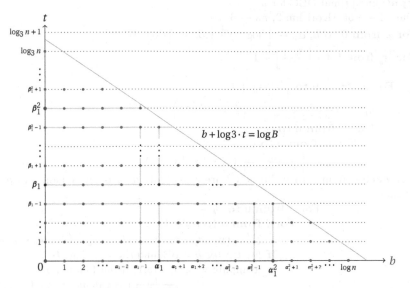

• requires $\mathcal{O}(\log n)$ bit operations • requires $\mathcal{O}\left((\log n)^{2/3}\right)$ bit operations • requires $\mathcal{O}\left((\log n)^{1/3}\right)$ bit operations

Fig. 4. The procedure of Algorithm 3 using equivalent representatives

Based on Algorithm 3, we will use equivalent representatives repeatedly.

6.2 Dynamic Programming Using Equivalent Representatives k-th

We generate Algorithm 3 and use equivalent representatives k-th in Algorithm 2 shown as Algorithm 4. $\left\lfloor \frac{n_{b,t}}{2^{b-1}3^{t-1}} \right\rfloor$ in Lemma 5 is calculated by $\left(\left\lfloor \frac{n_k}{2^i 3^j} \right\rfloor \% 6 \right)$. Algorithm 3 is a special case of Algorithm 4 with $k = 1$.

The time complexity of Algorithm 4 is shown in Theorem 4.

Theorem 4. *Algorithm 4 terminates in $\mathcal{O}\left((\log n)^2 \left((\log n)^{\frac{1}{3k}} + k + \log \log n\right)\right)$ bit operations. It requires $\mathcal{O}\left((\log n)^2 \log \log n\right)$ bit operations when $k = \log_3 \log n$.*

Notice that $\alpha_2 \leq 7$ when $n < 2^{134217728}$. Then k in Algorithm 4 is usually 1 or 2. Algorithms 2, 3, and 4 generate the same DBC with the same A, D, T, and n.

Algorithm 4. Dynamic programming to compute an optimal DBC using equivalent representatives k-th

---

Input: a positive integer n, a positive integer k, and its binary representation n_{binary}, three non-negative constants $A > 0, D \geq 0, T \geq 0$

Output: an optimal DBC for n

1. Lines $1 - 3$ of Algorithm 2, $n_0 \leftarrow 6 \cdot n$

2. **For** y from 0 to k, $\alpha_y \leftarrow \left\lfloor (\log B)^{\frac{1}{3y}} \right\rfloor, \beta_y \leftarrow \left\lfloor (\log_3 B)^{\frac{1}{3y}} \right\rfloor$

3. **For** jj_y from 0 to $\left\lfloor \frac{\beta_{y-1}}{\beta_y^2} \right\rfloor + 1$

4.   **For** ii_y from 0 to $\left\lfloor \frac{\alpha_{y-1}}{\alpha_y^2} \right\rfloor + 1$

5. $n_y' \leftarrow \left\lfloor \frac{n_{y-1}}{2^{ii_y} \cdot \alpha_y^2 3^{jj_y} \cdot \beta_y^2} \right\rfloor \% \left(2^{\alpha_y^2+1} 3^{\beta_y^2+1} \right)$

6.   **For** j_y from 0 to $\beta_y - 1$

7.   **For** i_y from 0 to $\alpha_y - 1$

8. $n_y \leftarrow \left\lfloor \frac{n_y'}{2^{i_y} \cdot \alpha_y 3^{j_y} \cdot \beta_y} \right\rfloor \% \left(2^{\alpha_y+1} 3^{\beta_y+1} \right)$

▷ **For each** y from 1 to k, Lines 3-8 are repeatedly as y is outer loop and $y + 1$ is inner loop

9.   **For** j from 0 to $\beta_k - 1$

10.   **For** i from 0 to $\alpha_k - 1$

11. $t \leftarrow \sum_{y=1}^k \left(jj_y \cdot \beta_y^2 + j_y \cdot \beta_y \right) + j, b \leftarrow \sum_{y=1}^k \left(ii_y \cdot \alpha_y^2 + i_y \cdot \alpha_y \right) + i$

12.   **If** $b + t > 0$& $b <$ bBound$[t]$& $t \leq \lfloor \log_3 B \rfloor$

13.   compute w(b,t), $\bar{w}(b,t)$ using Lemma 5

                                    ▷ $\left\lfloor \frac{n_{b,t}}{2^{b-1}3^{t-1}} \right\rfloor$ is calculated by $\left(\lfloor \frac{n_k}{2^i 3^j} \rfloor \%6 \right)$

14.   **else if** $b =$ bBound$[t]$ & $t \leq \lfloor \log_3 B \rfloor$, Lines 7, 8 of Algorithm 2

15. **return** w$_{\min}$

6.3 Comparison of These Algorithms

The time complexity, space complexity, and method of Doche's algorithm [16], Capuñay and Thériault's algorithm [7], Bernstein , Chuengsatiansup, and Lange's algorithm [17], and Algorithms 2–4 are summarized in Table 4. Table 4 shows the advantage of our dynamic programming algorithms.

Table 4. Comparison of algorithms to generate optimal DBCs

algorithm	time complexity ($\mathcal{O}$)	space complexity ($\mathcal{O}$)	method
Doche [16]	exponential	$(\log n)^2$	enumeration
CT [7]	$(\log n)^4$	$(\log n)^3$	two cycles
BCL [17]	$(\log n)^{2.5}$	$(\log n)^{2.5}$	DAG
Algorithm 2 (new)	$(\log n)^3$	$(\log n)^2$	dynamic programming
Algorithm 3 (new)	$(\log n)^{2+\frac{1}{3}}$	$(\log n)^2$	using equivalent representatives
Algorithm 4 (new)	$(\log n)^2 \log \log n$	$(\log n)^2$	using equivalent representatives $(\log_3 \log n)$−th

From the time costs of different algorithms to generate optimal DBCs in Table 5, Algorithm 4 is about $20, 25, 28, 32$, and 40 times faster than Capuñay and Thériault's algorithm and $6.1, 6.6, 7.7, 8.7$, and 9.3 times faster than Bernstein,

Chuengsatiansup and Lange's algorithm for each size ranges in 256, 384, 512, 640, and 768 respectively. As the integer becomes larger, Algorithm 4 will gain more compared to Bernstein, Chuengsatiansup and Lange's algorithm.

Table 5. Time Costs of different algorithms to generate optimal DBCs in million cpu cycles for integers with different size

	256-bit	384-bit	512-bit	640-bit	768-bit
CT [7]	41.9	106	217	386	645
BCL [17]	12.1	28.9	60.1	108	164
Algorithm 4 (new)	1.98	4.32	7.72	11.8	18.0

6.4 The Hamming Weights and Leading Terms of Canonic DBCs and Optimal DBCs

The Hamming weights and leading terms of the DBC produced by greedy approach [1] (greedy-DBC), canonic DBCs, and optimal DBCs are shown in Table 6 for the same 1000 integers by Algorithm 3. The Hamming weight of NAF is $\frac{\log n}{3}$. The Hamming weight of mbNAF, that of the DBC produced by binary/ternary approach(bt-DBC), and that of the DBC produced by tree approach (tree-DBC) are $0.2637 \log n$, $0.2284 \log n$, and $0.2154 \log n$ respectively and the leading terms are $2^{0.791 \log n} 3^{0.1318 \log n}$, $2^{0.4569 \log n} 3^{0.3427 \log n}$, and $2^{0.5569 \log n} 3^{0.2796 \log n}$ respectively. The Hamming weights of canonic DBCs are usually smaller than those of optimal DBCs. By Table 6, the Hamming weights of optimal DBCs are over 60% smaller than those of NAFs. As the integer becomes larger, the Hamming weight dividing $\log n$ will be smaller with a limitation $\frac{1}{8.25}$ by Theorem 2. Please refer to Fig. 1 to get more details of the Hamming weight of canonic DBCs.

Table 6. Hamming weights and leading terms of optimal DBCs on elliptic curves with different size

		256-bit	384-bit	512-bit	640-bit	768-bit
greedy-DBC[1]	Hamming weight	62.784	94.175	125.48	155.307	188.764
	leading term(b_l, t_l)	124.282, 82.168	183.256, 125.779	258.908, 159.309	314.954, 204.158	384.604, 240.957
canonic DBC	Hamming weight	48.319	71.572	94.75	118.108	141.097
	leading term(b_l, t_l)	128.275, 80.316	197.183, 117.582	261.227, 157.903	328.541, 196.231	396.162, 234.330
optimal DBC $\mathscr{E}_W$ 0.8	Hamming weight	50.027	74.163	98.234	122.544	146.403
	leading term(b_l, t_l)	176.675, 49.750	265.369, 74.549	353.175, 99.895	444.538, 123.015	532.690, 148.162
optimal DBC $\mathscr{E}_W$ 1	Hamming weight	49.393	73.210	96.993	121.134	144.684
	leading term(b_l, t_l)	169.026, 54.578	253.989, 81.731	338.509, 109.154	426.218, 134.577	509.540, 162.764

We will discuss scalar multiplications using our optimal DBCs.

7 Comparison of Scalar Multiplications

The scalar multiplication algorithm using a DBC is a Horner-like scheme for the evaluation of nP utilizing the DBC of $n = \sum_{i=1}^{l} c_i 2^{b_i} 3^{t_i}$ as $nP = \sum_{i=1}^{l} c_i 2^{b_i} 3^{t_i} P$. Theoretical cost of scalar multiplications on elliptic curves using NAF, greedy-DBC, bt-DBC, mbNAF, tree-DBC, canonic DBC, and optimal DBC on $\mathscr{E}_W$ 0.8 and $\mathscr{E}_W$ 1 are shown in Table 7.

Table 7 shows that scalar multiplication using an optimal DBC is more efficient than that using a canonic DBC. Scalar multiplication using an optimal DBC on $\mathscr{E}_W$ 0.8 and $\mathscr{E}_W$ 1 is about 13% and 13% faster than that using NAF, 7.5% and 7.1% faster than that using greedy-DBC, 6.5% and 6% faster than that using bt-DBC, 7% and 7% faster than that using mbNAF, 4% and 4% faster than that using a tree-DBC, and 0.9% and 0.7% faster than that using a canonic DBC respectively. Scalar multiplication using an optimal DBC is usually faster than that using a canonic DBC. Take $\lfloor \pi \times 10^{240} \rfloor$ on $\mathscr{E}_W$ 1 for example, scalar multiplication using our optimal DBC is 14% faster and 3.8% faster than that using NAF and tree-DBC respectively.

Table 7. Theoretical costs of scalar multiplications on elliptic curves using optimal DBC, canonic DBC, tree-DBC, and NAF in **M**

bits of n	representation	256-bit	384-bit	512-bit	640-bit	768-bit
	NAF	2652	3983	5315	6646	7977
	greedy-DBC [1]	2535	3818	5089	6351	7643
	bt-DBC [2]	2510	3771	5031	6291	7552
$\mathscr{E}_W$ 0.8	mbNAF [13]	2521	3787	5052	6318	7583
	tree-DBC [3]	2452	3683	4914	6146	7377
	canonic DBC(this work)	2393	3582	4774	5967	7155
	optimal DBC(this work)	2364	3543	4722	5902	7080
	NAF	2976	4469	5962	7456	8949
	greedy-DBC [1]	2824	4252	5671	7075	8516
	bt-DBC [2]	2796	4200	5603	7007	8410
$\mathscr{E}_W$ 1	mbNAF [13]	2824	4241	5659	7076	8494
	tree-DBC [3]	2738	4113	5488	6862	8237
	canonic DBC(this work)	2671	4000	5332	6664	7991
	optimal DBC(this work)	2649	3970	5292	6615	7936

In Table 7, the value of $\frac{T}{D}$ on $\mathscr{E}_W$ 0.8 is greater than that on $\mathscr{E}_W$ 1. The ratio of the cost of scalar multiplication using an optimal DBC to that using NAF on $\mathscr{E}_W$ 0.8 is greater than that on $\mathscr{E}_W$ 1 for integers of each size in Table 7. The ratio of the improvement of scalar multiplication using an optimal DBC compared to NAF is increasing as the value of $\frac{T}{D}$ becomes larger.

A constant-time software implementation is used to protect the scalar multiplication algorithms for avoiding some side-channel attacks by side channel atomicity. Multiplication and squaring are both executed by one multiplication and two additions. For each size ranges in $256, 384, 512, 640,$ and 768, we generate a prime number p with the same size and create a random curve for $\mathscr{E}_W$ over a finite field $\mathbb{F}_p$. Scalar multiplications using NAF, greedy-DBC, bt-DBC, mbNAF, tree-DBC, canonic DBC, and optimal DBC are shown in Table 8.

Experimental results show that scalar multiplication using an optimal DBC is 13% faster than that using NAF, 7% faster than that using greedy-DBC, 6% faster than that using bt-DBC, 7% faster than that using mbNAF, and 4.1% faster than that using a tree-DBC on $\mathscr{E}_W$ respectively. Within the bounds of the errors, the practical implementations are consistent with these theoretical analyses. The theoretical analyses and practical implementations both show that the Hamming weight is not the only factor affecting the efficiency of scalar multiplications and that scalar multiplications using optimal DBCs are the fastest.

Those computations do not take the time of producing the expansions into account. The recoding of our optimal DBC takes up a small amount of time to

Table 8. Experimental cost of scalar multiplications on elliptic curves using optimal DBC, canonic DBC, tree-DBC, and NAF on $\mathscr{E}_W$ in million cpu cycles

representation	256-bit	384-bit	512-bit	640-bit	768-bit
NAF	4.038	8.151	13.94	22.34	34.05
greedy-DBC [1]	3.836	7.751	13.27	21.23	32.43
bt-DBC [2]	3.798	7.656	13.12	21.02	32.03
mbNAF[13]	3.837	7.731	13.25	21.23	32.35
tree-DB [3]	3.734	7.575	12.92	20.68	31.54
canonic DBC(this work)	3.624	7.279	12.44	19.95	30.35
optimal DBC(this work)	3.594	7.168	12.37	19.83	30.17

compute scalar multiplication where both take time $\mathscr{O}\left((\log n)^2 \log\log n\right)$ when field multiplications use FFTs. It can't be ignored. Optimal DBCs are suitable for computing scalar multiplications when the multiplier n is fixed.

8 Conclusion

We first proposed a polynomial time algorithm to compute the number of DBCs for a positive integer with a leading term dividing $2^b 3^t$. We showed theoretical results of the number of DBCs for large b and t and gave an estimate of this number. The asymptotic lower bound of the Hamming weights of DBCs produced by any algorithm for n is linear $\frac{\log n}{8.25}$. This result changed the traditional idea that the asymptotic lower bound of the Hamming weight of a DBC produced by any algorithm may be sub-linear $\frac{\log n}{\log\log n}$. The time complexity and the space complexity of our dynamic programming algorithm to produce an optimal DBC were both the state-of-the-art. The recoding procedure of our algorithm was more than 20 times faster than Capuñay and Thériault's algorithm and more than 6 times faster than Bernstein, Chuengsatiansup, and Lange's algorithm.

Let $S(i)$ denote the smallest positive integer whose Hamming weight of its canonic DBCs is i. Our dynamic programming algorithm allowed us to find $S(i)$ for $i \leq 12$ immediately where $S(1) = 1$, $S(2) = 5$, $S(3) = 29$, $S(4) = 173$, $S(5) = 2093$, $S(6) = 14515$, $S(7) = 87091$, $S(8) = 597197$, $S(9) = 3583181$, $S(10) = 34936013$, $S(11) = 263363789$, and $S(12) = 1580182733$. This numerical fact provides a good impression about the sparseness of DBCs.

The cost function in this study was associated with $P + Q$, $2P$, and $3P$ for scalar multiplications. A direct promotion of the cost function is defined by $P + Q$, $P - Q$, $2P$, $2P + Q$, $3P$, and $3P + Q$. As the cost function is defined more precisely, an optimal DBC will improve scalar multiplications more. The optimal DBC can be directly generalized to a DBC with a large coefficient set of integers. Algorithm 1 can be generated to calculate the number of triple-base chains, and Algorithms 2–4 can be extended to produce optimal extended DBCs and optimal triple-base chains.

Acknowledgments. The authors would like to thank the anonymous reviewers for many helpful comments and thank Guangwu Xu, Kunpeng Wang, Song Tian and Bei Liang for their helpful suggestions, especially for Guangwu Xu's suggestions on the parts of "Abstract" and "Introduction". This work is supported by the National Natural Science Foundation of China (Grants 61872442, 61502487, and 61772515) and the

National Cryptography Development Fund (No. MMJJ20180216). W. Yu is supported by China Scholarship Council (No. 201804910201) and Study of Practical Cryptanalytic Approaches based on Combining Information Leakages and Mathematical and Structural Properties of Real-World Cryptosystems (No.U1936209).

References

1. Dimitrov, V., Imbert, L., Mishra, P.K.: Efficient and secure elliptic curve point multiplication using double-base chains. In: Roy, B. (ed.) ASIACRYPT 2005. LNCS, vol. 3788, pp. 59–78. Springer, Heidelberg (2005). https://doi.org/10.1007/11593447_4
2. Ciet, M., Joye, M., Lauter, K., Montgomery, P.L.: Trading inversions for multiplications in elliptic curve cryptography. Designs, Codes Crypt. **39**(6), 189–206 (2006)
3. Doche, C., Habsieger, L.: A tree-based approach for computing double-base chains. In: Mu, Y., Susilo, W., Seberry, J. (eds.) ACISP 2008. LNCS, vol. 5107, pp. 433–446. Springer, Heidelberg (2008). https://doi.org/10.1007/978-3-540-70500-0_32
4. Imbert, L., Philippe, F.: Strictly chained (p, q)-ary partitions. Contrib. Discrete Math. **2010**, 119–136 (2010)
5. Lou, T., Sun, X., Tartary, C.: Bounds and trade-offs for double-base number systems. Inf. Process. Lett. **111**(10), 488–493 (2011)
6. Zhao, C.A., Zhang, F.G., Huang, J.W.: Efficient Tate pairing computation using double-base chains. Sci. China Ser. F **51**(8), 1096–1105 (2008)
7. Capuñay, A., Thériault, N.: Computing optimal 2-3 chains for pairings. In: Lauter, K., Rodríguez-Henríquez, F. (eds.) LATINCRYPT 2015. LNCS, vol. 9230, pp. 225–244. Springer, Cham (2015). https://doi.org/10.1007/978-3-319-22174-8_13
8. Doche, C., Kohel, D.R., Sica, F.: Double-base number system for multi-scalar multiplications. In: Joux, A. (ed.) EUROCRYPT 2009. LNCS, vol. 5479, pp. 502–517. Springer, Heidelberg (2009). https://doi.org/10.1007/978-3-642-01001-9_29
9. Adikari, J., Dimitrov, V.S., Imbert, L.: Hybrid binary ternary number system for elliptic curve cryptosystems. IEEE Trans. Comput. **60**, 254–265 (2011)
10. Doche, C., Sutantyo, D.: New and improved methods to analyze and compute double-scalar multiplications. IEEE Trans. Comput. **63**(1), 230–242 (2014)
11. Avanzi, R., Dimitrov, V., Doche, C., Sica, F.: Extending scalar multiplication using double bases. In: Lai, X., Chen, K. (eds.) ASIACRYPT 2006. LNCS, vol. 4284, pp. 130–144. Springer, Heidelberg (2006). https://doi.org/10.1007/11935230_9
12. Mishra, P.K., Dimitrov, V.: Efficient quintuple formulas for elliptic curves and efficient scalar multiplication using multibase number representation. In: Garay, J.A., Lenstra, A.K., Mambo, M., Peralta, R. (eds.) ISC 2007. LNCS, vol. 4779, pp. 390–406. Springer, Heidelberg (2007). https://doi.org/10.1007/978-3-540-75496-1_26
13. Longa, P., Gebotys, C.: Fast multibase methods and other several optimizations for elliptic curve scalar multiplication. In: Jarecki, S., Tsudik, G. (eds.) PKC 2009. LNCS, vol. 5443, pp. 443–462. Springer, Heidelberg (2009). https://doi.org/10.1007/978-3-642-00468-1_25
14. Yu, W., Wang, K., Li, B., Tian, S.: Triple-base number system for scalar multiplication. In: Youssef, A., Nitaj, A., Hassanien, A.E. (eds.) AFRICACRYPT 2013. LNCS, vol. 7918, pp. 433–451. Springer, Heidelberg (2013). https://doi.org/10.1007/978-3-642-38553-7_26
15. Dimitrov, V.S., Imbert, L., Mishra, P.K.: The double-base number system and its application to elliptic curve cryptography. Math. Comput. **77**(262), 1075–1104 (2008)

16. Doche, C.: On the enumeration of double-base chains with applications to elliptic curve cryptography. In: Sarkar, P., Iwata, T. (eds.) ASIACRYPT 2014. LNCS, vol. 8873, pp. 297–316. Springer, Heidelberg (2014). https://doi.org/10.1007/978-3-662-45611-8_16

17. Bernstein, D.J., Chuengsatiansup, C., Lange, T.: Double-base scalar multiplication revisited. http://eprint.iacr.org/2017/037

18. Cohen, H., Miyaji, A., Ono, T.: Efficient elliptic curve exponentiation using mixed coordinates. In: Ohta, K., Pei, D. (eds.) ASIACRYPT 1998. LNCS, vol. 1514, pp. 51–65. Springer, Heidelberg (1998). https://doi.org/10.1007/3-540-49649-1_6

19. Chevallier-Mames, B., Ciet, M., Joye, M.: Low-cost solutions for preventing simple side-channel analysis: side-channel atomicity. IEEE Trans. Comput. **53**(6), 760–768 (2004)

20. Longa, P., Miri, A.: Fast and flexible elliptic curve point arithmetic over prime fields. IEEE Trans. Comput. **57**(3), 289–302 (2008)

21. Bernstein, D.J., Lange, T.: Explicit-formulas database. http://www.hyperelliptic.org/EFD/

22. Renes, J., Costello, C., Batina, L.: Complete addition formulas for prime order elliptic curves. In: Fischlin, M., Coron, J.-S. (eds.) EUROCRYPT 2016. LNCS, vol. 9665, pp. 403–428. Springer, Heidelberg (2016). https://doi.org/10.1007/978-3-662-49890-3_16

23. Méloni, N., Hasan, M.A.: Elliptic curve scalar multiplication combining Yao's algorithm and double bases. In: Clavier, C., Gaj, K. (eds.) CHES 2009. LNCS, vol. 5747, pp. 304–316. Springer, Heidelberg (2009). https://doi.org/10.1007/978-3-642-04138-9_22

24. Meloni, N., Hasan, M.: Efficient double bases for scalar multiplication. IEEE Trans. Comput. **64**(8), 2204–2212 (2015)

25. Disanto, F., Imbert, L., Philippe, F.: On the maximal weight of (p, q)-ary chain partitions with bounded parts. https://www.emis.de/journals/INTEGERS/vol14.html

26. Yu, W., Musa, S., Li, B.: Double-base chains for scalar multiplications on elliptic curves. http://eprint.iacr.org/2020/144

27. Scott, M.: MIRACL-multiprecision integer and rational arithmetic cryptographic library, C/C++ Library. ftp://ftp.computing.dcu.ie/pub/crypto/miracl.zip

28. Chalermsook, P., Imai, H., Suppakitpaisarn, V.: Two lower bounds for shortest double-base number system. IEICE Trans. Fundam. Electron. Commun. Comput. Sci. **98–A**(6), 1310–1312 (2015)

29. Dimitrov, V.S., Howe, E.W.: Lower bounds on the lengths of double-base representations. Proc. Am. Math. Soc. **139**(10), 3423–3430 (2011)

30. Kolmogorov, A.N.: On tables of random numbers. Theor. Comput. Sci. **207**, 387–395 (1998)

31. Doche, C., Imbert, L.: Extended double-base number system with applications to elliptic curve cryptography. In: Barua, R., Lange, T. (eds.) INDOCRYPT 2006. LNCS, vol. 4329, pp. 335–348. Springer, Heidelberg (2006). https://doi.org/10.1007/11941378_24

32. Erdös, P., Loxton, J.H.: Some problems in partitio numerorum. J. Aust. Math. Soc. Ser. A **27**(3), 319–331 (1979)

33. Cormen, T.H., Leiserson, C.E., Rivest, R.L., Stein, C.: Introduction to Algorithms, 3rd edn. The MIT Press, Cambridge (2009)

34. Cook, S.A.: On the minimum computation time of functions. Harvard University, Department of Mathematics (1966). https://cr.yp.to/bib/1966/cook.html

Zero-Knowledge

Stacked Garbling for Disjunctive Zero-Knowledge Proofs

David Heath[(✉)] and Vladimir Kolesnikov[(✉)]

Georgia Institute of Technology, Atlanta, GA, USA
{heath.davidanthony,kolesnikov}@gatech.edu

Abstract. Zero-knowledge (ZK) proofs (ZKP) have received wide attention, focusing on non-interactivity, short proof size, and fast verification time. We focus on the fastest total proof time, in particular for large Boolean circuits. Under this metric, Garbled Circuit (GC)-based ZKP (Jawurek et al., [JKO], CCS 2013) remained the state-of-the-art technique due to the low-constant linear scaling of computing the garbling.

We improve GC-ZKP for proof statements with conditional clauses. Our communication is proportional to the longest branch rather than to the entire proof statement. This is most useful when the number m of branches is large, resulting in up to factor $m\times$ improvement over JKO.

In our proof-of-concept **illustrative application**, prover P demonstrates knowledge of a bug in a codebase consisting of *any number* of snippets of **actual C code**. Our computation cost is linear in the size of the codebase and communication is *constant in the number of snippets*. That is, we require only enough communication for a single largest snippet!

Our **conceptual contribution** is *stacked garbling for ZK*, a privacy-free circuit garbling scheme that can be used with the JKO GC-ZKP protocol to construct more efficient ZKP. Given a Boolean circuit $\mathcal{C}$ and computational security parameter κ, our garbling is $L \cdot \kappa$ bits long, where L is the length of the longest execution path in $\mathcal{C}$. All prior concretely efficient garbling schemes produce garblings of size $|\mathcal{C}| \cdot \kappa$. The computational cost of our scheme is not increased over prior state-of-the-art.

We implement our GC-ZKP and demonstrate significantly improved ($m\times$ over JKO) ZK performance for functions with branching factor m. Compared with recent ZKP (STARK, Libra, KKW, Ligero, Aurora, Bulletproofs), our scheme offers much better proof times for larger circuits (35–1000$\times$ or more, depending on circuit size and compared scheme).

For our illustrative application, we consider four C code snippets, each of about 30–50 LOC; one snippet allows an invalid memory dereference. The entire proof takes 0.15 s and communication is 1.5 MB.

Keywords: Garbled circuits · Inactive branch elimination · ZK ·
Proof of C bugs

Electronic supplementary material The online version of this chapter (https://doi.org/10.1007/978-3-030-45727-3_19) contains supplementary material, which is available to authorized users.

A. Canteaut and Y. Ishai (Eds.): EUROCRYPT 2020, LNCS 12107, pp. 569–598, 2020.
https://doi.org/10.1007/978-3-030-45727-3_19

1   Introduction

Zero-knowledge (ZK) proofs (ZKP) have a number of practical applications; reducing their cost is an active research direction. Many efficient schemes were recently proposed, focusing on small proofs and fast verification. These works are largely motivated by blockchain applications [AHIV17, BCR+19, BBB+18, WTs+18, XZZ+19, BBHR19, etc.] and also by post-quantum signatures [CDG+17, KKW18].

Our focus, in contrast, is on the classical setting of *fastest total proof time*, including (possibly interactive) proof generation, transmission, and verification. In this total-time metric, Yao's garbled circuits (GC) is the fastest and one of the most popular techniques for proving general NP statements (expressed as Boolean circuits) in ZK. GC offers low-overhead linear prover complexity, while other techniques' provers are either superlinear or have high constants.

[JKO13] and [FNO15] demonstrate how to use GC for ZK without the costly cut-and-choose technique, while [ZRE15] proposes an efficient garbling technique that requires only 1 cryptographic ciphertext per AND gate in the ZK setting. As a result, GC-ZKP can process 20 million AND gates per second or more on a regular laptop (XOR gates are essentially free [KS08]). Unfortunately, while the computational cost of GC-ZKP is low, the communication is high. Even a fast 1 Gbps LAN can support only ≈6 million AND gates per second (XOR gates are free in communication). While this rate is higher than all recent NIZK systems, further communication improvements would make the approach even stronger.

In this work we achieve such a communication improvement. We reduce the cost of sending a GC when the proof statement contains logically disjoint clauses (i.e. conditional branches in `if` or `switch` constructs). In particular, if a logical statement contains disjoint clauses, then the cost to transmit the GC is bounded by the size of the largestclause rather than the total size of all clauses.

Our key idea is that the proof verifier (who is the GC generator) garbles from seeds all the clauses and then XORs together, or *stacks*, the garblings before sending them to the prover for evaluation. The prover receives via OT the seeds for the inactive clauses, reconstructs their garblings, and then XORs them out to obtain the target clause's garbling. By stacking the garblings, we decrease the cost to transmit the GC from the verifier to the prover.

In Sect. 3, we formally present our approach as a garbling scheme, which we call Privacy-Free Stacked (PFS) garbling. Accompanying proofs are in Sect. 4. We implement our approach in C++ and evaluate its performance against state-of-the-art techniques in Sect. 6 (see also discussion in Sect. 1.6).

1.1   Use Cases: Hash Trees and Existence of Bugs in Program Code

Our technique is useful for proving in ZK one of several statements.

Consider proving arbitrary statements in ZK, represented as Boolean circuits. These can be straightline programs or, more generally and quite typically, will include logical combinations of basic clauses. Several lines of work consider ZK of general functions, including MPC-in-the-head, SNARKs/STARKs, JKO, Sigma protocols [CDS94]; the latter specifically emphasizes proving disjoint statements, e.g., [Dam10, CDS94, CPS+16, GK14].

We now briefly present our two main applications (cf. Sects. 6 and 7):

App 1: Existence of Bugs. Our most exciting application allows a prover P to demonstrate knowledge of a bug in a potentially large codebase. We stress that ours is not a full-strength automated application, but rather a proof of concept. Still, we are able to handle C code with pointers, standard library calls, and simple data structures (see Sect. 7).

We consider a number of code snippets motivated by real code used in operating systems, standard algorithms, etc. The snippets we consider contain between 30 and 50 lines of code, but this number can be easily increased. We manually instrument each snippet with program assertions. Each snippet outputs a single bit that indicates if any assertion failed, and hence whether there is a bug.

We used and extended the EMP toolkit [WMK16] to compile instrumented snippets to Boolean circuits. Now, P can demonstrate she knows an input to a snippet, resulting in output 1. We envision that the mechanical tasks of instrumenting a codebase and splitting it into snippets will be automated in a practical tool; we leave further development as important and imminent future work.

Our approach excels in this use case because it features (1) high concrete performance and (2) communication that is constant in the number of code snippets. We further elaborate on this use case in Sect. 7.

App 2: Merkle Tree Membership. We wish to compare the performance of our PFS garbling to recent ZKP systems. We therefore consider a typical application considered in the literature: proof of membership in a Merkle tree.

Specifically, Alice wishes to assert properties of her record R embedded in a certificate signed by one of several acceptable authorities (CAs). Each CA A_i includes a number of different players' records $R_1^i, ..., R_n^i$ in a Merkle tree, and securely publishes its root. Alice receives her record R_j^k (which may embed a secret) and the Merkle tree hashes on the path to root. Now, Alice can prove statements in ZK about R_j^k with respect to any set of the published roots. CAs may use different hash functions for Merkle trees, or, in general, differ in other aspects of the proof, thus creating a use case for proving one of many clauses. In Sect. 6, we compare our performance to recent work based on this use case.

1.2   Key Contributions

- Conceptual contribution: A novel GC technique, which we call *stacked*, or PFS, garbling, requiring garbled material linear in the longest execution path, rather than in the full size of the circuit. Specifically, the same material sent from the verifier to the prover can represent the execution of any of the disjoint clauses. Note, Free IF technique [Kol18] *does not* work in our setting.
- High concrete performance, improving over the state-of-the art baseline (JKO+half-gates) approximately by the function branching factor; improvement over recent SNARKs is 35× – 1000× or more, depending on function size, branching, and compared scheme. Our technique has low RAM requirements (146 MB for 7M gate circuit).

- A proof of concept system that allows proving knowledge of a bug in C code. We use realistic C code snippets, which include pointers and standard library calls, and prove a bug related to incorrect use of **sizeof()** on a pointer.

1.3 Preliminaries

Free IF review: First, we review Kolesnikov's Free IF approach [Kol18]. Free IF decouples circuit topology (i.e. wire connections among the gates) from cryptographic material used to evaluate gates (i.e. encrypted gate tables). While a topology is needed to evaluate a circuit, it is assumed to be conveyed to the evaluator, Eval, separately from the garbled tables, or by implicit agreement between the participants Eval and GC generator Gen.

Let $S = \{C_1, ..., C_m\}$ be a set of Boolean circuits. Let (only) Gen know which circuit in S is evaluated, and let C_t be this target circuit. The key idea of [Kol18] is that Gen constructs cryptographic material for C_t, but does *not* construct material for the other circuits. Let $\widehat{C}$ be the constructed cryptographic material. The circuits in S may have varying topologies, but $\widehat{C}$ is a collection of garbled tables that can be interpreted as the garbling of any of these topologies. Eval knows S, but does not know which circuit is the target. For each $C_i \in S$, Eval interprets $\widehat{C}$ as cryptographic material for C_i and evaluates, obtaining garbled output. Only the output labels of C_t encrypt truth values; the other output labels are garbage. Eval cannot distinguish the garbage labels from the valid labels, and hence cannot distinguish which of the circuits in S is the target circuit C_t.

Next, Eval obliviously propagates (only) the target output labels to Gen via an *output selection* protocol. As input to the protocol, Eval provides all output labels (including the garbage outputs), and Gen provides the index t as well as C_t's zero labels on output wires. The output selection protocol outputs (re-encoded) labels corresponding to the output of C_t.

While our technique is different, PFS garbling is inspired by the key ideas from Free IF: (1) Separating the topology of a circuit from its garbled tables and (2) using the same garbling to securely evaluate several topologies.

Superficially, both [Kol18] and we omit inactive clauses when one of the players (Gen in [Kol18] and Eval in our work) knows the target clause. Indeed, in GC ZK, Gen *must not* know the evaluated branch. This is a critical distinction that requires a different approach. We present this new approach in this work.

Garbled Circuits for Zero Knowledge: Until the work of Jawurek et al. [JKO13], ZK research focused on proofs of algebraic statements. Generic ZKP techniques were known, but were based on generic NP reductions and were inefficient. [JKO13] provides an efficient generic ZKP technique based on garbled circuits.

The construction works as follows: The Verifier, V, and the Prover, P, run a passively-secure Yao's GC protocol, where V acts as the circuit generator and P acts as the circuit evaluator. The agreed upon Boolean circuit, C, is an encoding of the proof relation where (1) the input is a witness supplied by P, (2) the output is a single bit, and (3) if the output bit is 1, then the witness satisfies the relation. V garbles C and sends the garbling to P. P evaluates the GC and sends V the output label. The security of Yao's protocol (namely the authenticity property [BHR12]) ensures that a computationally bounded P can only produce the correct output label by running the circuit with a valid witness as input. By computing $\mathcal{C}$, P and V have achieved a ZK proof in the honest verifier setting.

A malicious V can violate ZK security by sending an invalid circuit or invalid OT inputs, which can leak P's inputs. [JKO13] solves this as follows: P does not immediately send the output label to V, but instead commits to it. Then V sends the seed used to generate the GC. P uses the seed to verify that the GC was honestly constructed. If so, P can safely open the commitment to the output label, completing the proof. [JKO13] consider a generalization of the above that does not require V to construct GCs from seeds. Instead, they define the notion of *verifiable* garbling. Verifiability prevents V from distinguishing different witnesses used by the prover, and therefore from learning something about P's input. Specifically, a garbling scheme is verifiable if there is a verification procedure such that even a malicious V cannot create circuits that both (1) satisfy the procedure and (2) output different values depending on the evaluator's witness.

In this work, we deal with explicit randomness and generate GCs from seeds. It is possible to generalize our work to the verifiable formulation of [JKO13].

Subsequent to the [JKO13] work, [FNO15] observes that weaker *privacy-free* garbling schemes are sufficient for the ZK construction of [JKO13]. [FNO15] construct a more efficient privacy-free garbling, whose cost is between 1 and 2 ciphertexts per AND gate. Zahur et al. [ZRE15] present a privacy-free variant of their half gates scheme, which requires only 1 ciphertext per AND gate, and is compatible with the JKO/FNO schemes. In our implementation, we use these state-of-the-art constructions. Because our work leverages the protocol from [JKO13], we will include their protocol in the full version of this paper.

1.4   High-Level Approach

Our main contribution is a new ZKP technique in the [JKO13] paradigm. The key characteristic of our construction is that for proof relations with disjoint clauses (i.e. conditional branches), communication is bounded by the size of the largest clause rather than the total size of the clauses. In Sect. 3, we present our approach in technical detail as a garbling scheme which can be plugged into the [JKO13] protocol. For now, we explain our approach at a high level.

Consider the proof of a statement represented by a Boolean circuit $\mathcal{C}$ with conditional evaluation of one of several clauses. In Sect. 1.3, we reviewed existing work that demonstrates how to efficiently evaluate $\mathcal{C}$ if the circuit *generator* knows the active clause. However, the [JKO13] ZK approach requires the generator to be V. Unfortunately, V has no input and therefore does not know the target clause. Instead, P must select the target clause.

As a naïve first attempt, P can select 1-out-of-m garbled circuits via OT. However, this involves transferring all GC clauses, resulting in no improvement.

Instead, we propose the following idea, inspired by a classic two-server private information retrieval approach [CGKS95].[1] Let $\mathcal{S} = \{\mathcal{C}_1, .., \mathcal{C}_m\}$ be the set of

---

[1] [CGKS95] includes a PIR protocol where two non-colluding servers separately respond to a client's two random, related queries by XORing elements of their result sets (and the client XORs out the true answer).

circuits implementing clauses of the ZK relation. Let $\mathcal{C}_t \in \mathcal{S}$ be the target clause that P wants to evaluate. For simplicity, suppose all clauses $\mathcal{C}_i$ are of the same size, meaning that they each generate GCs of equal size. Our approach naturally generalizes to clauses of different sizes (we discuss this in more detail in Sect. 3.7). The players proceed as follows.

V generates m random seeds $s_1..s_m$ and generates from them m GCs, $\widehat{\mathcal{C}}_1..\widehat{\mathcal{C}}_m$. V then computes $\widehat{\mathcal{C}} = \bigoplus \widehat{\mathcal{C}}_1..\widehat{\mathcal{C}}_m$ and sends $\widehat{\mathcal{C}}$ to P. Informally, computing $\widehat{\mathcal{C}}$ can be understood as *stacking* the different garbled circuits for space efficiency.

The key idea is that we will allow P to reconstruct (from seeds received via OT) all but one of the stacked GCs and then XOR these reconstructions out to retrieve the target GC, which P can evaluate with the witness she has. We must prevent P from receiving all m GCs and thus forging the proof. To do so, we introduce the notion of a 'proof of retrieval' string PoR. P receives PoR via OT only when she *does not* choose to receive a clause seed. P proves that she has not forged the proof by showing that she knows PoR. This is put together as follows.

V generates a random proof of retrieval string PoR. For each $i \in \{1..m\}$, the players run 1-out-of-2 OT, where V is the sender and P is the receiver. Players use *committing* OT for this phase [KS06]. For the ith OT, V's input is a pair (s_i, PoR). P selects 0 as her input in all instances, except for instance t, where she selects 1. Therefore P receives PoR and seeds $s_{i \neq t}$, from which P can reconstruct all GCs $\widehat{\mathcal{C}}_{i \neq t}$. P reconstructs the garbled material for the target clause by computing $\widehat{\mathcal{C}}_t = \widehat{\mathcal{C}} \oplus (\bigoplus_{i \neq t} \widehat{\mathcal{C}}_i)$.

Now, P received the garbling of the target clause, but we have not yet described how P receives input encodings for the target clause. We again simplify by specifying that each clause must have the same number, n, of input bits. Our approach generalizes to clauses with different numbers of inputs, as we discuss in Sect. 3.7. V's random seed s_i is used to generate the n pairs of input labels for each corresponding clause $\widehat{\mathcal{C}}_i$. Let X_i be the vector of n label pairs used to encode the input bits for clause i. V generates m such vectors, $X_1..X_m$. As an optimization similar to stacking the garbled circuits, V computes $X = \bigoplus X_1..X_m$. V and P now perform n committing 1-out-of-2 OTs, where in each OT V provides the two (stacked) possible input labels for a bit (a label corresponding to 0 and to a 1) and P provides the bit for that input. P uses the seeds obtained in the first step to reconstruct each $X_{i \neq t}$ and computes $X_t = X \oplus (\bigoplus_{i \neq t} X_i)$.

P now has the garbling $\widehat{\mathcal{C}}_t$ and appropriate input labels X_t. Therefore, P can evaluate $\widehat{\mathcal{C}}_t$ with the input labels and receive a single output label Y_t. For security, we must prevent V from learning t, so we must hide which clause P received output from. We accomplish this by allowing P to compute the correct output label for *every* clause. Recall that P has the seeds for every non-target clause. P can use the garblings constructed from these seeds to obtain the output labels $Y_{i \neq t}$. P computes $Y = \text{PoR} \oplus (\bigoplus Y_1..Y_m)$ and commits to this value (as suggested in [JKO13]). Next, V opens all commitments made during rounds of OT. From this, P checks that PoR is consistent across all seed OTs and obtains the final seed s_t. P checks that the circuits are properly constructed by regarbling them from the seeds (and checking the input labels and garbled material) and, if so, completes the proof by opening the output commitment.

1.5   Generality of Top-Level Clauses

Our approach optimizes for *top-level* clauses. That is, possible execution paths of the proof relation must be represented by separate clauses. Top-level clauses are general: Even nested conditionals can be represented by performing program transformations that lift inner conditionals into top-level conditionals.

Unfortunately, over-optimistically lifting conditionals can sometimes lead to an exponential number of clauses. In particular, if two conditionals occur sequentially in the relation, then the number of possible execution paths is the product of the number of paths through both conditionals. Of course, it is not necessary to fully lift all conditionals in a program; individual clauses can include (unstacked) conditional logic. Our approach will yield improvement for any separation of top level clauses. Improving the described protocol to handle nested and sequential conditionals directly is a potential direction for improvement.

We emphasize that the notion of top-level clauses matches nicely with the target use case of proving the existence of program bugs: Programs can be split into various snippets, each of which may contain a bug. Each snippet can then be presented as a top-level proof clause.

1.6   Related Work

Our work is a novel extension of GC-based ZK [JKO13] which we reviewed in Sect. 1.3. Here we review other related work and provide brief comparisons in Sect. 1.7. We focus on recent concrete-efficiency protocols.

ZK. ZKP [GMR85, GMW91] is a fundamental cryptographic primitive. ZK proofs of knowledge (ZKPoKs) [GMR85, BG93, DP92] allow a prover to convince a verifier, who holds a circuit C, that the prover knows an input, or *witness*, w for which $C(w) = 1$. There are several flavors of ZK proofs. In this work we do not distinguish between computational and information-theoretic soundness, and thus refer to both arguments and proofs simply as 'proofs.'

ZK proofs were investigated both theoretically and practically in largely non-intersecting bodies of work. Earlier practical ZK protocols focused on algebraic relations, motivated mainly by signatures and identification schemes, e.g. [Sch90, CDS94]. More recently, these two directions have merged. Today, ZKPoKs and non-interactive ZKPoK (NIZKPoK) for arbitrary circuits are efficient in practice. Two lines of work stand out:

Garbled RAM combines GC with ORAM to repeatedly perform individual processor cycles instead of directly computing the program as a circuit [LO13]. Because the circuit needed to handle a cycle has fixed size, this groundbreaking technique has cost proportional to the program execution rather than to the full program. Garbled RAM must interface the GC with ORAM, making it not concretely efficient. While our approach is not as general as Garbled RAM, we achieve high concrete efficiency for conditions.

Efficient ZK from MPC. Ishai et al. (IKOS) [IKOS07], introduced the 'MPC-in-the-head' approach. Here, the prover emulates MPC evaluation of $C(w)$ among several virtual players, where w is secret-shared among the players. The verifier checks that the evaluation outputs 1 and asks the prover to open the views of some virtual players. A prover who does not have access to w must cheat to output 1; opening random players ensures a cheating prover is caught with some probability. At the same time, ZK is preserved because (1) not all virtual players are opened, (2) the witness is secret shared among the virtual players, and (3) MPC protects the inputs of the unopened virtual players.

Based on the IKOS approach, Giacomelli et al. [GMO16] implemented a protocol called ZKBoo that supports efficient NIZKPoKs for arbitrary circuits. Concurrently, Ranellucci et al. [RTZ16] proposed a NIZKPoK with similar asymptotics. Chase et al. [CDG+17] introduced ZKB++, which improves the performance of ZKBoo; they also showed that ZKB++ could be used to construct an efficient signature scheme based on symmetric-key primitives alone. Katz et al. [KKW18] further improved the performance of this approach by using MPC with precomputation. A version of the [CDG+17] scheme called *Picnic* [ZCD+17] was submitted to the NIST post-quantum standardization effort. The Picnic submission was since updated and is now based on [KKW18].

Ligero [AHIV17] offers proofs of length $O(\sqrt{|C|})$, and asymptotically outperforms ZKBoo, ZKB++ and [KKW18] in communication. The break-even point between [KKW18] and Ligero depends on function specifics, and is estimated in [KKW18] to be $\approx$100K gates.

SNARKs/STARKs. Succinct non-interactive arguments of knowledge (SNARK) [GGPR13,PHGR13,BCG+13,CFH+15,Gro16] offer proofs that are particularly efficient in both communication and verification time. They construct proofs that are shorter than the input itself. Prior work demonstrated the feasibility of ZK proofs with size sublinear in the input [Kil92,Mic94], but were concretely inefficient. Earlier SNARKs require that their public parameters be generated and published by some semi-trusted party. This disadvantage motivated development of STARKs (succinct transparent arguments of knowledge) [BBHR18]. STARKs do not require trusted set up and rely on more efficient primitives. STARKs are succinct ZKP, and thus are SNARKs. In this work, we do not separate them; rather we see them as a body of work focused on sublinear proofs. Thus, Ligero [AHIV17], which is an MPC-in-the-head ZKP, is a SNARK.

In our comparisons, we focus on JKO, [KKW18], and recent SNARKs Ligero, Aurora, Bulletproofs [BBB+18], STARK [BBHR19], and Libra [XZZ+19].

1.7 Comparison with Prior Work

We present detailed experiment results in Sect. 6; here we reiterate that our focus and the main metric is *fastest total proof time*, including (possibly interactive) proof generation, transmission and verification. In this total-time metric, GC is the fastest technique for proving statements expressed as Boolean circuits. This is because GC offers low-overhead linear prover complexity, while other techniques' provers are superlinear, have high constants, or both.

In Sect. 1.1, we presented an exciting application where a prover demonstrates knowledge of a program bug. However, for comparison with prior work, the Merkle hash tree evaluation is most convenient, since many other works report on it. In Sect. 6, we implement our GC-ZK of Merkle hash tree and compare the results to JKO (which we reimplement as JKO was measured on older hardware), as well as to a variety of modern ZKP systems: KKW, Ligero, Aurora, Bulletproofs, STARK, and Libra.

As expected, our total time is improved over [JKO13] by a factor approximately equal to the branching factor. Indeed, our communication cost is linear in the longest execution path, while [JKO13, KKW18] are linear in $|\mathcal{C}|$, and our constants are similar to that of [JKO13] and significantly smaller than [KKW18].

Our total time outperforms current SNARKS by $35\times - 1,000\times$ or more. Like JKO, and unlike KKW and SNARKs, our technique is interactive and requires higher bandwidth.

2   Notation

The following are variables related to a given disjoint proof statement:

- t is the *target* index. It specifies the clause for which the prover has a witness.
- m is the number of clauses.
- n is the number of inputs. Unless stated otherwise, each clause has n inputs.

We simplify much of our notation by using $\oplus$ to denote a slight generalization of XOR: Specifically, if one of the inputs to XOR is longer than the other, the shorter input is padded by appending 0s until both inputs have the same length. We use $\bigoplus x_i..x_j$ as a vectorized version of this length-aware XOR:

$$\bigoplus x_i..x_j = x_i \oplus x_{i+1} \oplus \ldots x_{j-1} \oplus x_j$$

We discuss in Sect. 3.7 that this generalization is not detrimental to security in the context of our approach.

$x \parallel y$ refers to the concatenation of strings x and y. We use κ as the computational security parameter. We use V, he, him, his, etc. to refer to the verifier and P, she, her, etc. to refer to the prover. We use . for namespacing; `pack.proc` refers to a procedure `proc` defined as part of the package `pack`.

3   Our Privacy-Free Stacked Garbling Construction

We optimize the performance of ZK proofs for circuits that include disjoint clauses. In this section, we present our approach in technical detail.

We present our approach as a *verifiable garbling scheme* [BHR12, JKO13]. A verifiable garbling scheme is a tuple of functions conforming to a specific interface and satisfying certain properties such that protocols can be defined with the garbling scheme left as a parameter. Thus, new garbling schemes can

1 Proc *Stack.Gb* $(1^\kappa, f, R)$:
2     $(f_1..f_m) \leftarrow f$
3     $(\text{PoR}||s_1..s_m) \leftarrow R$
4   **for** $i \in 1..m$ **do**
5         $(F_i, e_i, d_i) \leftarrow \text{Base.Gb}(1^\kappa, f_i, s_i)$
6     $F \leftarrow f \,||\, \left(\bigoplus F_1..F_m\right)$
7     $d \leftarrow \text{PoR} \oplus \left(\bigoplus d_1..d_m\right)$
8     $e \leftarrow \text{PoR}||s_1..s_m||e_1..e_m$
9   **return** (F, e, d)

1 Proc *Stack.En* (e, x):
2     $(\text{PoR} \,||\, s_1..s_m \,||\, e_1..e_m) \leftarrow e$
3     $(t \,||\, x_t) \leftarrow x$
4   **for** $i \in 1..m$ **do**
5   **if** $i \neq t$ **then**
6             $r_i \leftarrow s_i$
7   **else**
8             $r_i \leftarrow \text{PoR}$
9         $X_i \leftarrow \text{Base.En}(e_i, x_t)$
10     $X \leftarrow r_1..r_m \,||\, \left(\bigoplus X_1..X_m\right)$
11   **return** X

1 Proc *Stack.De* (Y, d):
2     $y \leftarrow Y = d$
3   **return** y

1 Proc *Stack.ev* (f, x):
2     $(f_1..f_m) \leftarrow f$
3     $(t \,||\, x_t) \leftarrow x$
4     $y \leftarrow \text{Base.ev}(f_t, x_t)$
5   **return** y

1 Proc *Stack.Ev* (F, X, x):
2     $(f_1..f_m \,||\, F) \leftarrow F$
3     $(r_1..r_m \,||\, X) \leftarrow X$
4     $(t \,||\, x_t) \leftarrow x$
5   **for** $i \in 1..m$ **do**
6   **if** $i \neq t$ **then**
7             $(F_i, e_i, d_i) \leftarrow \text{Base.Gb}(1^\kappa, f_i, r_i)$
8             $X_i \leftarrow \text{Base.En}(e_i, x_t)$
9   **else**
10             $(F_i, d_i, X_i) \leftarrow (0, 0, 0)$
11     $F_t \leftarrow F \oplus \left(\bigoplus F_1..F_m\right)$
12     $X_t \leftarrow X \oplus \left(\bigoplus X_1..X_m\right)$
13     $Y_t \leftarrow \text{Base.Ev}(F_t, X_t)$
14     $Y \leftarrow Y_t \oplus \left(\bigoplus d_1..d_m\right) \oplus r_t$
15   **return** Y

1 Proc *Stack.Ve* (f, F, e):
2     $(\text{PoR} \,||\, s_1..s_m \,||\, \cdot) \leftarrow e$
3     $(F', e', d') \leftarrow$
        $\text{Stack.Gb}(1^\kappa, f, \text{PoR} \,||\, s_1..s_m)$
4   **return** $e = e' \wedge F = F'$

Fig. 1. PFS garbling scheme Stack. Stack is defined as six procedures: Stack.Gb, Stack.Ev, Stack.ev, Stack.En, Stack.De, and Stack.Ve.

be easily plugged into existing protocols. That is, a garbling scheme *does not* specify a protocol. Instead, it specifies a modular building block.

We specify an efficient verifiable garbling scheme, where the function encoding, F, is proportional to the longest program execution path, rather than to the entire program[2]. Our scheme satisfies the security properties required by existing

---

[2] To be more precise, in the notation of Kolesnikov [Kol18], the function encoding $F = (T, E)$ consists of function topology T (thought of as the Boolean circuit) and cryptographic material E (e.g., garbled tables). In our work, the cryptographic material E is proportional to the longest execution path.

For the reader familiar with the BHR notation, we provide the following discussion. In BHR, the function encoding F must (implicitly) include a full description of the function, i.e., it must include a description of each clause. In this sense, F is also proportional to the full size of the function. However, compared to the cryptographic material needed for the longest clause, this function description (which can be thought of as a Boolean circuit $\mathcal{C}$ computing f) is small. Formally, the size of the circuit description is constant in κ. Most importantly, implementations can assume that circuit descriptions are known to both players, and therefore need not transmit them (or treat them separately).

ZK constructions [JKO13, FNO15]. This results in an efficient ZK scheme whose communication is proportional to the longest program execution path.

A verifiable garbling scheme is a tuple of six algorithms:

$$(\mathsf{ev}, \mathsf{Gb}, \mathsf{En}, \mathsf{Ev}, \mathsf{De}, \mathsf{Ve})$$

The first five algorithms define a garbling scheme [BHR12], while the sixth adds verifiability [JKO13]. In the ZK context, a garbling scheme can be seen as a specification of the functionality computed by V and P. Loosely speaking, V uses Gb to construct the garbled circuit sent to P. V defines input labels by using En, and decodes the output label received from P by using De. P uses Ev to compute the garbled circuit with encrypted inputs and uses Ve to check that the circuit was honestly constructed. Finally, ev provides a reference against which the other algorithms can be compared. The key idea is that if (1) a garbling is constructed using Gb, (2) the inputs are encoded using En, (3) the encoded output is computed using Ev, and (4) the output is decoded using De, then the resulting bit should be the same as calling ev directly.

A verifiable garbling scheme must satisfy the formal definitions of **correctness**, **soundness**, and **verifiability**. We present these definitions, as well as formal proofs that our scheme satisfies these properties in Sect. 4.

Since we are primarily concerned with reducing the cost of disjoint clauses, we can offload the remaining work (i.e. processing a single clause) to another garbling scheme. Therefore, our scheme is parameterized over another garbling scheme, Base. We place the following requirements on this underlying scheme:

- The scheme must be **correct** and **sound**.
- The scheme must be *projective* [BHR12]. In a projective garbling scheme, each bit of the prover's input is encoded by one of two cryptographic labels. The truth value of that bit is used to decide which label the prover will receive. Projectivity allows us to stack input labels from different clauses. We can lift this requirement by compromising on efficiency: The verifier can send an input encoding for *each* clause rather than a stacked encoding.
- The scheme must output a single cryptographic label and decoding must be based on an equality check of this label. This property is important because it allows us to stack the output labels from each clause. Again, we can lift this requirement by compromising efficiency: The prover can send each output label rather than the stacked value.

These requirements are reasonable and are realized by existing schemes, including state-of-the-art privacy-free half gates [ZRE15].

In the following text, we describe our construction, the PFS verifiable garbling scheme Stack. Pseudocode for each of our algorithms is given in Fig. 1.

3.1   Reference Evaluation

ev maps the computed function f and an input x to an output bit. Informally, ev provides a specification that the garbled evaluation can be compared to: The garbled evaluation should yield the same output as running ev. In our setting, the input can be split into a clause selection index t and the remaining input. Stack.ev delegates to Base.ev on the t-th clause. For many practical choices of Base (including privacy-free half gates) the procedure Base.ev simply applies the function to the input: That is, it returns $f(x)$.

3.2   Garble

Gb maps the given function, f, to a garbled function F, an encoding string e, and a decoding string d. At a high level, Gb corresponds to the actions taken by V to construct the proof challenge for P. Typically, e contains input labels (conveyed to P via OT), F contains cryptographic material needed to evaluate the individual logic gates, and in the ZK setting d contains a single label corresponding to a secret that will convince the verifier that the prover has a witness. The objective of the prover is to use her witness to construct d.

Gb is usually described as an algorithm with implicit randomness. However, for the purposes of our scheme it is important that Gb is explicitly parameterized over its randomness. Gb takes as parameters the unary string 1^κ, the desired function f, and a random string, R. It generates a three-tuple of strings, (F, e, d).

At a high level, Stack.Gb (Fig. 1) delegates to Base.Gb for each clause and XORs[3] the obtained garbling strings, thus reducing the GC length to that of a single (largest) clause. First, it deconstructs f into its various clauses and extracts from the randomness (1) m different random seeds and (2) the random string PoR which we refer to as the *proof of retrieval*. The proof of retrieval is a security mechanism that allows our approach to cleanly interact with existing MPC protocols. Later, in Sect. 3.3 we will see that the prover receives via OT the garbling seed for each of m clauses, except for the target clause. PoR prevents P from simply taking *all* m seeds and trivially constructing a proof (we enforce that if P takes all seeds, then she will not obtain PoR). Next, each seed is used to garble its respective clause using the underlying scheme (Stack.Gb line 5). The cryptographic material from each clause is XORed together and concatenated with the function description[4] (Stack.Gb line 6). This is a key step in our approach: Since the cryptographic material has been XORed together, we have reduced the cost of sending the garbling F compared to sending each garbling separately. Similarly, the output labels from each clause are XORed together. The PoR string is also XORed onto the latter value. Finally, the encoding string e contains PoR, each random string s_i, and each encoding string e_i.

---

[3] As discussed in Sect. 2, by XOR we mean length-aware XOR, where shorter clauses are padded with zeros so that all clauses are bitstrings of the same length.

[4] Including the function description f is a formality to fit the BHR interface. In practice, f is often known to both parties and need not be explicitly handled/transmitted.

3.3 Encode

En maps the encoding string, e, and the function input, x, to an encoded input, X. En describes which input encoding the verifier should send to the prover. Typically, En is implemented by OT.

Stack.En ensures that the prover receives (1) the proof of retrieval string PoR, (2) each random seed $s_{i \neq t}$, and (3) stacked garbled inputs for the target clause. Section 3.2 described how e contains PoR, $s_1..s_m$, and $e_1..e_m$.

First, Stack.En deconstructs e into the above parts. It also deconstructs the circuit input into t (the target clause index) and x_t (the input for the target clause). Next, a vector of secrets, $r_1..r_m$ is constructed. This vector contains PoR and $s_{i \neq t}$. Finally, we use the underlying scheme to construct m encodings of x_t and XOR the encodings together (Stack.En line 10). Stack.En outputs the vector of secrets and the stacked input encodings.

We remark that Stack.En defines the encoding functionality, not an implementation. As mentioned earlier, Stack.En is implemented using OT. Our implementation realizes this functionality in the following way:

- For each clause, V generates n pairs of labels, one pair for each bit and one label for each configuration of that bit.[5]
- V stacks these labels, yielding n pairs of stacked labels.
- For each $i \in 1..m$, V constructs the pair (s_i, PoR).
- Now, P and V participate in $m + n$ executions of 1-out-of-2 OT, such that P receives PoR, non-target seeds, and stacked garbled inputs according to En.

By running this protocol, V obliviously transfers encoded input, including the seeds and PoR, to P.

3.4 Evaluate

Ev maps an encoded function, F, and encoded inputs, X, to the encoded output, Y. In the ZK setting we (as do [JKO13] and [FNO15]) allow Ev to take the unencoded input, x, as a parameter (in practice Ev is run by P who knows the witness). Informally, Ev describes the actions of the prover to construct a proof string, given the garbling of the function and input labels.

The bulk of the work done by Stack.Ev is concerned with 'undoing' the stacking of the encoded functions $F_1..F_m$ and of the encoded inputs $X_1..X_m$, in order to extract the encoded function F_t, and inputs X_t for the target clause. First, Stack.Ev deconstructs all inputs into their constituent parts. It then uses the random strings included in the encoded input to re-garble each non-target clause by calling Base.Gb (Stack.Ev line 7). Note that since Base.Gb is called with the same random strings in both Stack.Ev and Stack.Gb, the resulting encodings are the

---

[5] In fact, since we use half gates we can use the Free XOR extension [KS08]. Therefore, each clause has only one label for each input bit and one global Δ value that separates 0 bit labels from 1 bit labels. Our implementation stacks the Δ from each clause as part of the stacked projective garbling.

same. Stack.Ev cannot call Base.Gb on the target clause because the input encoding does not include the corresponding random string. Instead, r_t is the proof of retrieval POR. Stack.Ev XORs out the garblings of the non-target clauses to obtain the encoded function (Stack.Ev line 11) and encoded input (Stack.Ev line 12) for the target clause. Now, the prover can use F_t and X_t to compute the output Y_t by calling Base.Ev. Finally, the prover XORs together Y_t, $d_1..d_m$, and POR and returns the result.

3.5 Decode

De maps an encoded output, Y, and an output encoding string, d, to an unencoded output. In the ZK setting, both Y and d are labels encoding a single bit. Stack.De checks that the values are the same, and if so returns 1 (and 0 if not).

3.6 Verify

Ve maps an input function f, the garbled function F, and the encoding string e to a bit. Informally, the function should return 1 if (F, e) is correctly constructed.

Stack.Ve extracts the proof of retrieval POR and input seeds $s_1..s_m$ from e. It uses these strings to garble the computed functions and checks that it indeed matches the provided garbling.

In our implementation, we take advantage of an optimization available in Stack.Ve. To verify V's messages, the prover must reconstruct the garbling of each clause. However, the prover *already* garbled each circuit except the target while computing Ev, so we simply reuse these already computed values and only garble the target during verification. This is noteworthy because our approach not only transmits less information, it involves less computation on the part of P as well: Under previously defined ZK garbling schemes (e.g. [ZRE15]), P must both garble and evaluate *every* clause. Under our scheme the prover needs to garble every clause, but need only evaluate the target clause.

3.7 Generalizing to Diverse Clauses

In Sect. 1.4, we simplified the discussion by presenting our approach as handling clauses of the same size and with the same number of inputs. However, our formal presentation does not need these simplifications. Here, we discuss generalization to clauses with different sizes and numbers of inputs.

Our approach supports clauses of various sizes. The only implementation detail that relates to the size of the clauses is the XOR stacking of the garbled material from each clause (Stack.Gb line 6 and Stack.Ev line 11). In Sect. 2, we describe how we use $\oplus$ to denote a *length-aware* variant of XOR (i.e. the shorter string is padded with 0 s). Therefore, there is no correctness concern with stacking mismatched length of material. The only potential concern is security. Our proofs formally alleviate this concern; informally, stacking material is secure because we can safely allow the prover to obtain material for each clause F_i.

Indeed, even sending each clause F_i separately is secure, although inefficient. Giving P access to the garbled material provides no aid in constructing a proof. Specifically, only having a witness and *running* the garbled circuit will allow P to construct the correct Y_t. Therefore, clause stacking does not hinder security.

We support clauses with different numbers of inputs. Regardless of her clause choice t, the prover will append the input string x_t with 0s until x_t is appropriate for an input of length n. This is secure for a similar reason as having cryptographic material of different lengths. Our technique allows P to learn every input encoding $X_{i \neq t}$ and therefore to learn X_t. This is desirable: We must allow P to learn X_t in order to evaluate the target clause on their input.

4   Proofs of Security

Jawurek et al. [JKO13] introduced a methodology for using garbling schemes to build maliciously secure ZKP protocols. In this section, we prove that our construction satisfies the [JKO13] requirements. Thus, we can directly leverage the work of [JKO13] to construct a maliciously secure ZKP scheme with efficient disjoint clause handling.

[JKO13] requires the garbling scheme to be **correct**, **sound**, and **verifiable**. We use slightly simpler formulations of these definitions presented in [FNO15], a follow-up work on [JKO13].

We now explicitly state the definitions of these properties in our notation. We prove our garbling scheme Stack (Fig. 1) satisfies each property (Theorems 1 to 3) if the underlying scheme Base is **correct** and **sound** (We do not require Base to be verifiable, since we explicitly manage the scheme's randomness).

4.1   Correctness

Correctness ensures that the prover can construct a valid proof if she, in fact, has a valid witness. More precisely, Definition 1 states that if a garbling is constructed by calling Gb, then Ev will *always*[6] yield the correct output label, d, when called with the encoding of a valid witness. Recall, we work with explicit randomness. Thus, Gb takes a random string R as an additional input.

Definition 1 (Correctness). *A garbling scheme is* **correct** *if for all* $n = poly(\kappa)$, *all functions* $f : \{0,1\}^n \rightarrow \{0,1\}$, *all inputs* $x \in \{0,1\}^n$ *such that* $ev(f,x) = 1$, *and all random strings* $R \in_R \{0,1\}^{\kappa}$:

$$(F, e, d) = Gb(1^{\kappa}, f, R) \Rightarrow Ev(F, En(e, x), x) = d$$

Theorem 1. *If the underlying garbling scheme* Base *is correct, then the garbling scheme* Stack *(Fig. 1) is correct (Definition 1).*

---

[6] In the full version of this paper, we will discuss *probabilistic* correctness and the changes to our approach that are necessary to account for this probabilistic notion.

Proof. By correctness of the underlying garbling scheme. Stack.Gb constructs the output label d by XORing together the output label of each clause, d_i, and the proof of retrieval string, POR. Therefore, it suffices to show that a prover, P, with satisfying input obtains each d_i and POR. Recall that P's input includes the bits that select a clause, t, concatenated with her remaining input x. We show that she obtains each output label d_i and POR in three steps:

1. P obtains d_i for all $i \neq t$ by garbling f_i. This is immediate from the fact that P receives every seed s_i for $i \neq t$ as a part of her encoded input (Stack.En, line 6). P garbles clause f_i with seed s_i and obtains d_i (Stack.Ev, line 7).
2. P obtains d_t by evaluating f_t on her input x. We show this in three parts: (1) P obtains the garbling of the selected clause, F_t, (2) P obtains encoded inputs for the selected clause, X_t, and (3) P computes d_t.
   First, Stack.Gb constructs the XOR sum of the garbling of each clause, F_i (Stack.Gb, line 6). Therefore, to show that P obtains F_t, it suffices to show that she obtains F_i for all $i \neq t$ and F. F is given as a parameter to Stack.Ev and so is trivially available. P obtains the garblings of all clauses F_i by calling Stack.Gb with the seeds in her encoded input.
   Second, Stack.En constructs X by XORing together the encodings of each clause X_i (Stack.En, line 10). Similar to the previous step, P computes each X_i by garbling clause i with s_i. She then uses the encoding e_i to compute $X_i = \mathsf{Base.En}\,(e_i, x)$ (Stack.Ev, line 8). She XORs these encodings with X to get the appropriate input for clause t, X_t.
   Finally, P computes $Y_t = \mathsf{Base.Ev}(F_t, X_t, x)$. The underlying garbling scheme is correct by assumption. Therefore, $Y_t = d_t$.
3. P obtains POR. This string is immediately available as r_t (Stack.En line 8).

P XORs together each of these elements (Stack.Ev line 14), obtaining the output Y which has the same value as d. That is, $\mathsf{Stack.Ev}\,(F, \mathsf{Stack.En}\,(e, x)\,, x) = d$. Therefore, Stack is correct. $\qquad\square$

4.2   Soundness

Definition 2 (Soundness). *A garbling scheme is **sound** if for all $n = \mathsf{poly}(\kappa)$, all functions $f : \{0,1\}^n \to \{0,1\}$, all inputs $x \in \{0,1\}^n$ such that $\mathsf{ev}(f,x) = 0$, and all probabilistic polynomial time adversaries $\mathcal{A}$ the following probability is negligible in κ:*

$$Pr(\mathcal{A}\,(F, \mathsf{En}\,(e, x)\,, x) = d : (F, e, d) \leftarrow \mathsf{Gb}\,(1^\kappa, f))$$

Soundness is a more succinct version of authenticity [BHR12], restricted to the ZK setting. Informally, soundness ensures that a prover who does *not* have a valid witness cannot convince the verifier otherwise. More specifically, we require that no malicious evaluator can extract the garbling scheme's secret d unless she knows an input x such that $f(x) = 1$.

In our garbling scheme, d combines 1-labels of all clauses and the proof of retrieval POR. We show that an adversarial P who is given $(F, \mathsf{Stack.En}\,(e, x)\,, x)$, such that $\mathsf{Stack.ev}\,(f, x) = 0$, cannot obtain at least one of the components of d and hence cannot output d, except with negligible probability.

Theorem 2. *If the underlying garbling scheme* Base *is sound, then the garbling scheme* Stack *(Fig. 1) is sound (Definition 2).*

Proof. By soundness of the underlying garbling scheme. Recall that $d = (\bigoplus d_1..d_m) \oplus \mathrm{POR}$. That is, the output label is the XOR sum of the output labels for each clause and the proof of retrieval. Consider an arbitrary input $(t \parallel x_t) \leftarrow x$, such that $\mathsf{Stack.ev}\,(f, x) = 0$. We proceed by case analysis on t.

Suppose t is invalid (i.e., $t \notin [1..m]$) and thus $\mathsf{Stack.En}(x)$ outputs all seeds $s_1..s_m$. Then by the definition of $\mathsf{Stack.En}$, $\mathcal{A}$ will *not* receive POR and hence cannot construct d (except with negligible probability).

Suppose that $t \in [1..m]$, i.e. t is valid. Because $\mathsf{Stack.ev}\,(f, x) = 0$, it must be that $\mathsf{Base.ev}\,(f_t, x_t) = 0$. Now, $\mathcal{A}$'s input includes the proof of retrieval POR, as well as the seeds for each clause except for clause t. Therefore, an adversary can easily obtain each output label except d_t. We must therefore demonstrate that our scheme prevents an adversary without a witness from successfully constructing d_t, and thereby prevent construction of d. d_t is independent of all values in the scheme except for the values related to the clause itself: s_t, f_t, F_t, X_t, and e_t. By assumption, Base is sound. Therefore, since x_t is not a witness for clause t, the adversary cannot obtain d_t (except with negligible probability), and therefore cannot construct d (except with negligible probability).

Therefore Stack is sound.   ☐

4.3   Verifiability

Definition 3 (Verifiability). *A garbling scheme is* **verifiable** *if there exists an expected polynomial time algorithm* Ext *such that for all* x *where* $f(x) = 1$, *the following probability is negligible in* κ:

$$\Pr\left(\mathsf{Ext}(F, e) \neq \mathsf{Ev}(F, \mathsf{En}(e, x), x) : (F, e, \cdot) \leftarrow \mathcal{A}(1^\kappa, f), \mathsf{Ve}(f, F, e) = 1\right)$$

Informally, verifiability prevents even a malicious verifier from learning the prover's inputs. In the ZK protocol, the prover checks the construction of the garbling via Ve. Verifiability ensures that this check is reliable. That is, it guarantees that if $f(x) = 1$, then the output value $\mathsf{Ev}\,(F, \mathsf{En}\,(e, x), x)$ is unique and moreover can be efficiently extracted given the encoding. This implies that the verifier has access to the secret d ahead of time. Therefore, V learns nothing by receiving d from the prover, except for the fact that $f(x) = 1$. This holds also for maliciously generated circuits, as long as they pass the verification procedure.

Theorem 3. *If the underlying garbling scheme* Base *is correct, then the garbling scheme* Stack *is verifiable (Definition 3).*

Proof. By correctness of Stack. Let (F', e') be a garbling of f constructed by $\mathcal{A}$. Let x satisfy $f(x) = 1$. Let Y be the value obtained by evaluating this garbling:

```
1 Proc Stack.Ext (F, e):
2    (f₁..fₘ || ·) ← F
3    (POR || s₁..sₘ || ·) ← e
4    (·, ·, d) ← Stack.Gb (1ᴷ, f₁..fₘ, POR || s₁..sₘ)
5    return d
```

Fig. 2. The Stack.Ext algorithm that demonstrates verifiability of Stack.

$$Y = \mathsf{Ev}\,(F', \mathsf{En}\,(e', x)\,, x)$$

Let R be the randomness included in e' (i.e. $R = \text{POR} \parallel s_1..s_m$). Let (F, e, d) be the result of calling Stack.Gb on this randomness:

$$(F, e, d) = \mathsf{Stack.Gb}\,(1^\kappa, f, R)$$

We first claim that Y must be equal to d.

Suppose not, i.e. suppose $Y \neq d$. By correctness (Theorem 1), Ev always returns d; therefore it must be the case that (F', e') is different from (F, e), i.e. either $F' \neq F$ or $e' \neq e$. But if so, Stack.Ve would have returned 0 (Stack.Ve line 4). Verifiability assumes that Stack.Ve returns 1, so we have a contradiction. Therefore $Y = d$.

Now, we must prove that there exists a poly-time extraction algorithm Stack.Ext, which probabilistically extracts the output label from (F', e'). This construction and proof is immediate: Stack.Ext delegates to Stack.Gb. Namely (see Fig. 2 for full description of Stack.Ext), on input (F, e), Stack.Ext parses $(R, \cdot) \leftarrow e'$, runs $(\cdot, \cdot, d) \leftarrow \mathsf{Stack.Gb}\,(1^\kappa, f, R)$ and outputs d. We have already shown that d constructed this way satisfies $Y = d$.

Therefore Stack is verifiable.   □

5   Instantiating Our Scheme

We built our implementation on the publicly available EMP-Toolkit [WMK16]. We use privacy-free half gates as the underlying garbling scheme [ZRE15]. That is, XOR gates are free (requiring no cryptographic material or operations) and all AND gates are implemented using fixed-key AES [BHKR13]. Each AND gate costs 1 ciphertext in cryptographic material, 2 AES encryptions to garble, and 1 AES encryption to evaluate. We use security parameter $\kappa = 128$.

We instantiate all [JKO13] ingredients, including committing OT. We use the maliciously-secure OT extension of [ALSZ15] in our implementation both because it is efficient and because an implementation with support for committing OT is available in EMP.

6   Performance Evaluation

Recent advances in non-interactive ZK proofs (NIZK) are astounding. The blockchain use case motivates intense focus on small proof size (as short as

work		Experiment 1. Fig. 4		Experiment 2. [XZZ+19]	
		time (s)	comm. (MB)	time (s)	comm. (MB)
	LAN	0.395		4.205	
Stack [this work]	sh. LAN	2.473	13.426	32.04	182.2
	WAN	3.525		24.52	
	LAN	0.782		4.205	
[JKO13]	sh. LAN	5.567	31.180	32.04	182.2
	WAN	6.208		24.52	
[KKW18]		140	20	840	120
Ligero [AHIV17]		60	0.3	404	1.5
Aurora [BCR+19]		1,000	0.15	3,214	0.174
Bulletproofs [BBB+18]		1,800	0.002	13,900	0.006
STARK [BBHR19]		40	0.5	300	0.6
Libra [XZZ+19]		15	0.03	202	0.051

Fig. 3. Experimental performance of our approach compared to state-of-the-art ZKP systems. **1.** We compare circuit C from Fig. 4 which makes calls to AES, SHA-1 and SHA-256 and has 7,088,734 gates (1,887,628 AND). **2.** We compare based on an experiment from [XZZ+19] where the prover builds a depth 8 Merkle tree from the leaves. The circuit invokes SHA-256 511 times. Resulting timings include prover computation, verifier computation, and all communication. For our and the [JKO13] GC-based approaches we separate timing results for LAN, Shared LAN, and WAN networks. Results for works other than ours and [JKO13] are either approximate interpolations from related works [KKW18,BBHR19] or taken directly from the reporting of [XZZ+19].

several hundred bytes!) and fast verifier computation time. Prover computation time is usually superlinear ($O(|\mathcal{C}| \log |\mathcal{C}|)$) or higher in most schemes, with Libra and Bulletproofs offering linear time) with relatively large constants. As proof circuits grow larger, the high constants and superlinear computational scaling becomes burdensome and GC-based proof systems become more efficient thanks to linear computation scaling with small constants.

We focus our performance comparison on JKO and the fastest NIZK systems, such as [KKW18,BBHR19], Bulletproofs [BBB+18], Ligero [AHIV17], Aurora [BCR+19], and Libra [XZZ+19]. Figure 3 shows that GC-based approaches (Stack and JKO) scale better than current NIZKs at the cost of interactivity, and Fig. 5 shows how Stack improves on JKO w.r.t. the branching factor.

A reader familiar with recent GC research and related work discussed in Sect. 1.6 may already have a very good sense for the performance of our scheme Stack, both in computation and communication. Indeed, Stack simply calls privacy-free half gates and XORs the results. Compared to Free IF [Kol18] (a GC protocol using topology-decoupling, not a ZK scheme), our communication is 2× smaller, since we use 1-garbled-row privacy free garbling.

Our and the Baseline Systems. We implemented and ran our scheme Stack and [JKO13] instantiated with privacy-free half gates [ZRE15], as the state-of-the-art baseline. Most of the code (except for handling stacking) is shared between the two systems. By comparing the performance of these two protocols, we isolate the effect of stacking garbled material. In addition, we include detailed comparison to performance numbers reported by other state-of-the-art systems [BBB+18, KKW18, AHIV17, BCR+19, BBHR19, XZZ+19] in Sect. 6.2.

Boolean vs Arithmetic/R1CS representations are difficult to compare. Arithmetic operations are costly in Boolean world; program control flow and other operations (e.g., bit operations in hash functions and ciphers) often cannot be done in arithmetic, and a costly bit decomposition is required. Because of this, we focus on the benchmark that emerged as universal in recent literature: SHA-256 evaluations. We use standard SHA-256 Boolean circuits available as part of EMP, and other works use R1CS representations optimized for their work.

System and Experiment Setup. We implemented our and JKO protocols based on EMP [WMK16]. We ran both P and V *single-threaded* on the same machine, a ThinkPad^{TM} Carbon X1 laptop with an Intel® Core^{TM} i7-6600U CPU @ 2.60 GHz and 16 GB of RAM. We record the total communication and the total wall clock time. Each experimental result was averaged over 5 runs. We use the Linux command tc to simulate three network settings (shared LAN models the setting where LAN is shared with other traffic):

Network Setting	bandwidth (mbps)	latency (ms)
LAN	1000	2
Shared LAN	50	2
WAN	100	100

RAM and CPU Consumption. GC-based ZK proofs can be performed with very low RAM and CPU. This is because GC generation and evaluation is a highly serializable and streamlined process: Gen only needs to keep in RAM the amount of material proportional to the largest cross-section of the GC. Wire labels and garbled gates can be discarded once they no longer appear in future gates. Further, each AND gate garbling requires only 2 AES calls.

In contrast, recent NIZK systems are resource-hungry. They execute their experiments on high-end machines with very high RAM. For example, STARK was run on a powerful server with 32 3.2 GHz AMD cores and 512 GB RAM. In Experiment 2, Libra uses 24.7 GB of RAM while running on 64 GB machine [Zha19].

We execute all our experiments on a standard laptop with 16 GB RAM (of which 146 MB is used in Experiment 1, as reported by Linux time command). We *do not* adjust our numbers to account for the hardware differences.

6.1   Experiment 1: Merkle Tree Proof (JKO Comparison Focus)

We first evaluate our approach against prior work using a Merkle tree membership benchmark, discussed in Sect. 1.1. This experiment is designed to show how our scheme compares to JKO. We include comparison to state-of-the-art NIZK as an additional point of reference.

Circuit	# AND	# XOR	# INV
Clause C1: proof w.r.t. tree 1	812936	519699	986677
Clause C2: proof w.r.t. tree 2	546089	2243643	55237
Clause C3: proof w.r.t. tree 3	528601	944039	451828
C = (C1 ∨ C2 ∨ C3)	1887628	3707381	1493725

Fig. 4. Clause and circuit sizes in our experiment. Clauses are defined in Sect. 6.1.

For the sake of concreteness, we constructed a scenario whereby P's record is certified by inclusion in a Merkle tree whose root is published by an authority. There are several such roots published, and P wishes to hide which root certifies her. P's record, in addition to arbitrary data fields, contains a 128-bit secret key, which P may use as a witness to prove statements about its record.In our experiment, P wishes to prove membership of her record in one of three Merkle trees, as well as properties of her record. We will explain the exact details of this benchmark in the full version of this paper.

The resulting circuit C (cf. Fig. 4) consists of three conditional branches, each clause corresponding to a proof for a specific Merkle tree. The clauses execute various combinations of calls to SHA256, SHA-1 and AES. Total circuit size (i.e. what JKO and other ZK systems would evaluate) is over 7 million gates.

Figure 3 tabulates results and includes the estimated performance of the NIZK systems [BBB+18, KKW18, AHIV17, BCR+19, BBHR19, XZZ+19]. The larger proof statement sizes we consider were not reported in prior works (e.g., [KKW18, BCR+19]); we estimate their performance by considering their asymptotic complexity and extrapolating their reported numbers. The tabulation includes 4 metrics. This experiment explores JKO comparison, and below we discuss metrics w.r.t. JKO. (We discuss at length other NIZKs in Sect. 6.2.)

- **Total communication** (in MB). Our reported communication includes performing commitments, OTs, and sending the circuit garbled material.
  Discussion. Stacking yields a 2.3× improvement over JKO. This is optimal for stacked garbling: total circuit size is 2.3× larger than the largest clause.
- **Total LAN wall clock time** used to complete each protocol in a simulated LAN setting. The simulated LAN has 1 gbps bandwidth and 2 ms latency.
  Discussion. Our approach yields a 2.0× speedup over JKO, due to reduced communication. Our total speedup does not quite match the 2.3× proof size improvement because our computation cost is same as JKO. As 1 gbps is extremely fast, computation takes a noticeable portion of the overall time.
- **Total shared LAN wall clock time** in a setting where LAN is shared with other traffic and approximately 50 Mbps of bandwidth is available.
  Discussion. Our approach yields a 2.25× speedup, close to the optimal 2.3×. In shared LAN the cost of computation becomes less important.
- **Total WAN wall clock time** with 100 mbps bandwidth and 100 ms latency.
  Discussion. Our approach yields a 1.76× speedup. As network latency increases, the number of rounds becomes important. Both [JKO13] and our approach have the same number of rounds, and hence our performance improvement is less pronounced than in the shared LAN setting.

6.2 Experiment 2: Merkle Tree Building (NIZK Comparison Focus)

As discussed above, Boolean/arithmetic/R1CS representations each have their advantages, and their comparison is highly nuanced. SHA-256 evaluation has become an informal standard by which recent NIZKs compare their performance. We use a standard Boolean circuit for SHA-256 that is included with EMP.

Libra [XZZ+19] includes a benchmark where P computes the root of a depth-8 Merkle tree (256 leaves; total 511 SHA-256 evaluations) as part of a proof. When compiled as a Boolean circuit, this benchmark includes ≈60 million gates. Figure 3 includes results for this benchmark; our focus is on the relative efficiency of our approach against Libra and other state-of-the-art NIZKs. Performance numbers for NIZKs were obtained from [XZZ+19], except in the case of [KKW18] and [BBHR19] which were not tabulated by [XZZ+19]. The numbers for these two works were extrapolated based on their reported performance.

Discussion. This experiment does not present an opportunity to take advantage of stacking since there is no conditional branching. Therefore, our approach reduces to [JKO13] equipped with privacy-free half gates. Still, this helps to demonstrate the high concrete efficiency of the GC-based ZKP approach. We (and [JKO13]) are several orders of magnitude faster (over LAN; one or more orders over WAN) in this second benchmark than each reported NIZKs except Libra. We outperform Libra by 6× over WAN and nearly 50× over LAN.

We now present more detailed comparison of Fig. 3 results with the individual NIZK schemes, each of which offers different advantages and trade offs.

- Ligero, Aurora and STARK are NIZK proof systems in the 'interactive oracle proof' paradigm (IOP). Among these three superlinear-runtime works, STARK is most competitive in total runtime due to better constants. Our work outperforms STARK by 10–100×, depending on the network. Our advantage would be higher for cases with branching (cf. Sects. 6.1 and 6.3).
- [KKW18] is linear both in computation and proof size with moderate constants. It may be preferable for smaller-size statements ([KKW18] suggest their scheme can be used as a signature scheme based on AES or LowMC cipher), or for proofs of very large statements due to linear scaling of the prover work. Our work outperforms [KKW18] in the proof time metric because [KKW18] has constants much higher than us: [KKW18] simulates 40-100-player MPC and also repeats the proof multiple times. We are two orders of magnitude faster than [KKW18]. Further, our approach yields smaller proof size in Experiment 1 due to our ability to stack the three clauses.
- Bulletproofs [BBB+18] features linear proof time and staggeringly small proofs, logarithmic in the size of the witness! It has high constants due the use of public key operations. We are 1,000 s of times faster than Bulletproofs.
- Libra [XZZ+19] not only constructs small proofs (with size second only to Bulletproofs amongst the considered works), but also features linear prover time with low-moderate constants. Notably (and unlike all other considered works), Libra requires one time trusted setup, which somewhat limits its applicability. We outperform Libra by 6× over WAN and nearly 50× over LAN. Our advantage will increase as the branching increases.

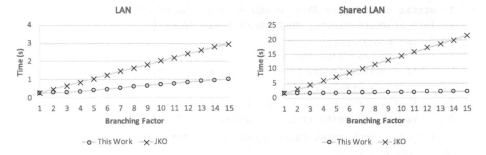

Fig. 5. Plotted results of Experiment 2, evaluating 1-out-of-n randomly generated clauses each of size 500K AND/2M total gates. Each data point plots the total wall clock time needed to perform a proof.

6.3 Experiment 3: Scaling to Many Clauses

We explore how our approach scales in overall proof time as the number of proof disjuncts increases. This metric helps quantify our advantage over [JKO13]. In this experiment, we measure performance of proof statements with different numbers of disjoint clauses and plot total proof times in Fig. 5. To ensure there are no shortcuts in proofs (e.g. exploiting common subcircuits across the branches), we generate all clauses randomly (details will be included in the full version of this paper). Each circuit has 500,000 AND gates and 2 million total gates. We focus on total proof time, and compare our performance to [JKO13].

Discussion. This experiment shows the benefit of reduced communication and its relative cost to computation. In a *single-thread execution* on a LAN, our approach can complete the 1-out-of-15 clause proof (8M AND gates and 30M total gates) in 1 s. This is less than 15× communication improvement over [JKO13] due to relatively high computation cost. As we scale up computation relative to communication (by multi-threading, or, as in our experiment, by consuming only 50 Mbps bandwidth on a shared LAN), our performance relative to [JKO13] increases. In single-threaded execution on shared LAN we are 10× faster than [JKO13] with 15× smaller communication.

7 Proving Existence of Bugs in Program Code

We present a compelling application where our approach is particularly effective: P can demonstrate in ZK the existence of a bug in V's program code. In particular, V can arrange a corpus of C code into various snippets, annotated with assertions. Some assertions, such as array bounds checks and division by zero checks can be automatically inserted. In general, assertions can include arbitrary Boolean statements about the program state. Once the program is annotated, P can demonstrate that she knows an input that causes a program assertion in a snippet to fail. We stress that the instrumentation alone, which can be automated, does not help V to find the bug. P's secret is the snippet ID and input which exercises the error condition caught by an assertion.

```
1: static const char* SMALL_BOARD = "small_board_v11";
2: int* alloc_resources(const char* board_type) {
3:     int block_size;
4:     // The next line has a bug!!
5:     if (!strncmp(board_type, SMALL_BOARD, sizeof(SMALL_BOARD))) {
6:         block_size = 10;
7:     } else { block_size = 100; }
8:     return malloc(block_size * sizeof(int));  }
9: int incr_clock(const char* board_type, int* resources) {
10:     int clock_loc;
11:     if (!strncmp(board_type, SMALL_BOARD, strlen(SMALL_BOARD))) {
12:         clock_loc = 0;
13:     } else { clock_loc = 64 }
14:     (*(resources + clock_loc))++;
15:     return resources[clock_loc];  }
16: void snippet(const char* board_type) {
17:     int* res = alloc_resources(board_type);
18:     incr_clock(board_type, res);  }
```

Fig. 6. An example C snippet that the prover can demonstrate has a bug. Lines 5 and 11 contain inconsistent string comparisons that can cause undefined behavior.

As a simple example, consider the following piece of C code:

```
1: char example(const char* s) { return s[1]; }
```

Once the program has been instrumented to detect invalid memory dereferences, the prover can submit the input " " (the empty string) as proof that this program has a bug: The input is empty, but the program attempts to access index 1.

Ours is the best-in-class ZK approach to this application for two reasons:

1. Common programs contain seemingly innocuous constructs, such as pointer dereferences and array accesses, that compile to very large circuits and hence result in very large proof statements. As we have demonstrated, the JKO paradigm, and hence our proof system, is particularly well suited for proving large statements as quickly as possible.
2. Many organizations have truly enormous repositories of code. This is problematic even for fast interactive techniques like JKO because larger code bases require more communication.

   In contrast, our approach remains realistic as the repository grows larger: Communication is constant in the number of snippets (it is proportional to the maximum snippet length). We believe that this advantage opens the possibility of implementing this application in industrial settings.

We include a proof of concept of this use case. Further expanding this is an exciting direction for future work, both in the area of cryptography and of software engineering/compiler design.

experiment	LAN time (s)	WAN time (s)	comm. (MB)	compilation (s)
4 snippets	0.107	2.327	1.542	0.054
1,000 snippets	4.953	6.716	1.600	10.468

Fig. 7. Results for running `Stack` for the bug proving application with 4 and 1,000 snippets. We record LAN and WAN time to complete the proof, total communication, and the time to compile all snippets to Boolean circuits.

At the same time, we can already handle relatively complex code. One of the snippets we implemented (Fig. 6) contains a mistake inspired by a real-world bug in the in MITRE Common Weakness Enumeration (CWE) CWE-467 [cwe19]. This bug is potentially dangerous: For example, MITRE illustrates how it can lead to overly permissive password checking code. We implemented this C code snippet and three others that range between 30 and 50 lines of code.

Consider Fig. 6 Lines 5 and 11. These two lines both perform string comparisons using **strncmp**. However, Line 5 incorrectly compares the first n characters where n is the result of the **sizeof** call. This call returns the size of a pointer (8 on 64 bit systems) rather than the length of the string. The comparison should have used **strlen** in place of **sizeof**. An observant prover can notice that a malicious input like "small_boERROR" will cause inconsistent behavior that leads to a dereference of unallocated memory.

We instrumented this snippet and three others. Together, these four snippets exercise everyday programming tasks such as user input validation, string parsing, nontrivial memory allocation, and programming against a specification. We will include the source code for all four snippets in the full version of this paper. When compiled to Boolean circuits, these four snippets range between 70,000 and 90,000 AND gates. The number of AND gates is largely determined by the operations performed; e.g. dereferencing memory (array lookup) is expensive while adding integers is cheap. We use the snippets to exercise `Stack` in two experiments:

1 First, we had P demonstrate that she knows a bug in at least 1 out of the 4 snippets. In particular, her input is the string "small_boERROR" and triggers an assertion in the code shown in Fig. 6.
2 Second, we simulated a larger code base with 1,000 snippets of 30-50 LOC. Ideally, this code base would contain 1,000 or more *unique* snippets, but since in this work we hand-code instrumentations, this would be an unrealistic effort. We approximate real performance by including multiple copies of each of our four snippets (250 copies each) in the proof disjunction and carefully ensuring that we don't take replication-related shortcuts. P proves the existence of the bug in the first copy of the snippet from Fig. 6.

In both experiments we recorded (1) the total LAN proof time, (2) the total WAN proof time, (3) the total message transmission, and (4) the total time to compile each snippet to a Boolean circuit using the EMP toolkit [WMK16]. The results reflect our expectations and are tabulated in Fig. 7. Note, the 1,000 snippet experiment is less than 250× slower than the 4 snippet experiment due to constant costs such as setting up a channel and evaluating OTs.

Communication stays nearly constant between the two experiments despite a large increase in the size of the proof challenge. This is a direct result of our contribution of clause stacking. The small change in communication is a result of additional OTs needed for P to select 1 target out of 1,000. Because of the relatively small proof size, both experiments run fast, even on our modest hardware: The 4-snippet proof takes a tenth of a second and the 1,000 snippet proof takes fewer than 5 s. We also ran the same two experiments against [JKO13]. In the 4 snippet experiment, JKO took 0.2211 s on LAN and 3.056 s on WAN, consuming 5.253 MB of communication. The 1,000 snippet experiment crashed our modest hardware as JKO tried to allocate an enormous piece of memory to hold the garblings of the large circuit. Therefore, we tried again with only 500 snippets. Here, JKO took 13.868 s on LAN and 86.356 s on WAN, using 645.9 MB of communication. Again, our approach significantly outperforms [JKO13] due to clause stacking. Performance may already be realistic for some use cases and will likely improve through future work.

Compiling C programs into Boolean circuits is currently the slowest part of our proof. Compilation speed has largely been ignored in prior work; it is unsurprising that the EMP-toolkit is not heavily optimized for it. We believe future work will significantly improve compilation.

7.1   Snippet Instrumentation

We instrument the snippets by extending EMP [WMK16] with pointers (and arrays to facilitate pointers) and implementations of C standard library functions. These features are critical to handling realistic program code and Fig. 6 prominently uses them. We briefly discuss how these features are implemented.

First, we examine pointers and arrays. Our implementation of pointers is greatly simplified, and we leave more general and efficient handling of pointers for future work. In our implementation, a pointer consists of a triple of:

1. A cleartext pointer to an array. This array is allocated to a fixed publicly known size by calls to our instrumentation of **malloc**.
2. An encrypted index into the array. Pointer operations (e.g., pointer offset by an integer) operate over this index. Calls to **malloc** set this index to 0.
3. An encrypted maximum index. **malloc** determines this maximum value based on the size argument.

Pointer dereferences contain an instrumented assertion that checks that the private index is ≥ 0 and is less than the maximum index. It is this assertion that allows the prover to demonstrate Fig. 6 has a bug: The dereference on Line 14 triggers this assertion on particular inputs. After this assertion is checked, the pointer dereference is implemented as a linear scan over the array. For each index of the array, we perform an equality check against the encrypted index. We multiply the output of each equality check by the array entry at that index. Therefore, the result of each multiplication is 0, except for at the target index, where the result is the dereferenced value. We add all multiplication results together using XOR, which returns the dereferenced value.

This pointer handling is limited. For example, we cannot handle a program that conditionally assigns a pointer to one of two different memory locations constructed by different calls to **malloc**: Each pointer can only hold one cleartext array pointer. Additionally, it is likely possible to concretely improve over linearly scanning the entire cleartext array.

Second, we discuss C standard library functions. In fact, with the availability of pointers this instrumentation is mostly uninteresting. The implementations are relatively straightforward pieces of C code that we instrument in a manner similar to the snippets. For example, our instrumentation of **strlen** takes an instrumented pointer as an argument. It walks the cleartext array of the pointer and increments an encrypted counter until the null character is reached.

Notably, we allow functions to contain loops, but place hard-coded upper bounds on the number of allowed iterations for any loop.

Acknowledgment. This work was supported in part by NSF award #1909769 and by the Office of the Director of National Intelligence (ODNI), Intelligence Advanced Research Projects Activity (IARPA), via 2019-1902070008. The views and conclusions contained herein are those of the authors and should not be interpreted as necessarily representing the official policies, either expressed or implied, of ODNI, IARPA, or the U.S. Government. The U.S. Government is authorized to reproduce and distribute reprints for governmental purposes notwithstanding any copyright annotation therein. This work was also supported in part by Sandia National Laboratories, a multi-mission laboratory managed and operated by National Technology and Engineering Solutions of Sandia, LLC., a wholly owned subsidiary of Honeywell International, Inc., for the U.S. Department of Energy's National Nuclear Security Administration under contract DE-NA-0003525.

References

[AHIV17] Ames, S., Hazay, C., Ishai, Y., Venkitasubramaniam, M.: Ligero: lightweight sublinear arguments without a trusted setup. In: Bhavani, M.T., Evans, D., Malkin, T., Xu, D. (ed.) ACM CCS 2017, pp. 2087–2104. ACM Press, October/November 2017

[ALSZ15] Asharov, G., Lindell, Y., Schneider, T., Zohner, M.: More efficient oblivious transfer extensions with security for malicious adversaries. In: Oswald, E., Fischlin, M. (eds.) EUROCRYPT 2015. LNCS, vol. 9056, pp. 673–701. Springer, Heidelberg (2015). https://doi.org/10.1007/978-3-662-46800-5_26

[BBB+18] Bünz, B., Bootle, J., Boneh, D., Poelstra, A., Wuille, P., Maxwell, G.: Bulletproofs: short proofs for confidential transactions and more. In: 2018 IEEE Symposium on Security and Privacy, pp. 315–334. IEEE Computer Society Press, May 2018

[BBHR18] Ben-Sasson, E., Bentov, I., Horesh, Y., Riabzev, M.: Scalable, transparent, and post-quantum secure computational integrity. Cryptology ePrint Archive, Report 2018/046 (2018). https://eprint.iacr.org/2018/046

[BBHR19] Ben-Sasson, E., Bentov, I., Horesh, Y., Riabzev, M.: Scalable zero knowledge with no trusted setup. In: Boldyreva, A., Micciancio, D. (eds.) CRYPTO 2019. LNCS, vol. 11694, pp. 701–732. Springer, Cham (2019). https://doi.org/10.1007/978-3-030-26954-8_23

[BCG+13] Ben-Sasson, E., Chiesa, A., Genkin, D., Tromer, E., Virza, M.: SNARKs for C: verifying program executions succinctly and in zero knowledge. In: Canetti, R., Garay, J.A. (eds.) CRYPTO 2013. LNCS, vol. 8043, pp. 90–108. Springer, Heidelberg (2013). https://doi.org/10.1007/978-3-642-40084-1_6

[BCR+19] Ben-Sasson, E., Chiesa, A., Riabzev, M., Spooner, N., Virza, M., Ward, N.P.: Aurora: transparent succinct arguments for R1CS. In: Ishai, Y., Rijmen, V. (eds.) EUROCRYPT 2019. LNCS, vol. 11476, pp. 103–128. Springer, Cham (2019). https://doi.org/10.1007/978-3-030-17653-2_4

[BG93] Bellare, M., Goldreich, O.: On defining proofs of knowledge. In: Brickell, E.F. (ed.) CRYPTO 1992. LNCS, vol. 740, pp. 390–420. Springer, Heidelberg (1993). https://doi.org/10.1007/3-540-48071-4_28

[BHKR13] Bellare, M., Hoang, V.T., Keelveedhi, S., Rogaway, P.: Efficient garbling from a fixed-key blockcipher. In: 2013 IEEE Symposium on Security and Privacy, pp. 478–492. IEEE Computer Society Press, May 2013

[BHR12] Bellare, M., Hoang, V.T., Rogaway, P.: Foundations of garbled circuits. In: Yu, T., Danezis, G., Gligor, V.D. (eds.) ACM CCS 2012, pp. 784–796. ACM Press, October 2012

[CDG+17] Chase, M., et al.: Post-quantum zero-knowledge and signatures from symmetric-key primitives. In: Thuraisingham, B.M., Evans, D., Malkin, T., Xu, D. (eds.) ACM CCS 2017, pp. 1825–1842. ACM Press, October/November 2017

[CDS94] Cramer, R., Damgård, I., Schoenmakers, B.: Proofs of partial knowledge and simplified design of witness hiding protocols. In: Desmedt, Y.G. (ed.) CRYPTO 1994. LNCS, vol. 839, pp. 174–187. Springer, Heidelberg (1994). https://doi.org/10.1007/3-540-48658-5_19

[CFH+15] Costello, C., et al.: Geppetto: versatile verifiable computation. In: 2015 IEEE Symposium on Security and Privacy, pp. 253–270. IEEE Computer Society Press, May 2015

[CGKS95] Chor, B., Goldreich, O., Kushilevitz, E., Sudan, M.: Private information retrieval. In: 36th FOCS, pp. 41–50. IEEE Computer Society Press, October 1995

[CPS+16] Ciampi, M., Persiano, G., Scafuro, A., Siniscalchi, L., Visconti, I.: Improved OR-composition of sigma-protocols. In: Kushilevitz, E., Malkin, T. (eds.) TCC 2016. LNCS, vol. 9563, pp. 112–141. Springer, Heidelberg (2016). https://doi.org/10.1007/978-3-662-49099-0_5

[cwe19] Common weakness enumeration (2019). https://cwe.mitre.org/

[Dam10] Damgård, I.: On Σ-protocols (2010). http://www.cs.au.dk/~ivan/Sigma.pdf. Accessed 11 May 2019

[DP92] De Santis, A., Persiano, G.: Zero-knowledge proofs of knowledge without interaction (extended abstract). In: 33rd FOCS, pp. 427–436. IEEE Computer Society Press, October 1992

[FNO15] Frederiksen, T.K., Nielsen, J.B., Orlandi, C.: Privacy-free garbled circuits with applications to efficient zero-knowledge. In: Oswald, E., Fischlin, M. (eds.) EUROCRYPT 2015. LNCS, vol. 9057, pp. 191–219. Springer, Heidelberg (2015). https://doi.org/10.1007/978-3-662-46803-6_7

[GGPR13] Gennaro, R., Gentry, C., Parno, B., Raykova, M.: Quadratic Span programs and succinct NIZKs without PCPs. In: Johansson, T., Nguyen, P.Q. (eds.) EUROCRYPT 2013. LNCS, vol. 7881, pp. 626–645. Springer, Heidelberg (2013). https://doi.org/10.1007/978-3-642-38348-9_37

[GK14] Groth, J., Kohlweiss, M.: One-out-of-many proofs: or how to leak a secret and spend a coin. Cryptology ePrint Archive, Report 2014/764 (2014). http://eprint.iacr.org/2014/764

[GMO16] Giacomelli, I., Madsen, J., Orlandi, C.: ZKBoo: faster zero-knowledge for Boolean circuits. In: Holz, T., Savage, S. (eds.) USENIX Security 2016, pp. 1069–1083. USENIX Association, August 2016

[GMR85] Goldwasser, S., Micali, S., Rackoff, C.: The knowledge complexity of interactive proof-systems (extended abstract). In: 17th ACM STOC, pp. 291–304. ACM Press, May 1985

[GMW91] Goldreich, O., Micali, S., Wigderson, A.: Proofs that yield nothing but their validity or all languages in NP have zero-knowledge proof systems. J. ACM 38(3), 690–728 (1991)

[Gro16] Groth, J.: On the size of pairing-based non-interactive arguments. In: Fischlin, M., Coron, J.-S. (eds.) EUROCRYPT 2016. LNCS, vol. 9666, pp. 305–326. Springer, Heidelberg (2016). https://doi.org/10.1007/978-3-662-49896-5_11

[IKOS07] Ishai, Y., Kushilevitz, E., Ostrovsky, R., Sahai, A.: Zero-knowledge from secure multiparty computation. In: Johnson, D.S., Feige, U. (eds.) 39th ACM STOC, pp. 21–30. ACM Press, June 2007

[JKO13] Jawurek, M., Kerschbaum, F., Orlandi, C.: Zero-knowledge using garbled circuits: how to prove non-algebraic statements efficiently. In: Sadeghi, A.-R., Gligor, V.D., Yung, M., (eds.) ACM CCS 2013, pp. 955–966. ACM Press, November 2013

[Kil92] Kilian, J.: A note on efficient zero-knowledge proofs and arguments (extended abstract). In: 24th ACM STOC, pp. 723–732. ACM Press, May 1992

[KKW18] Katz, J., Kolesnikov, V., Wang, X.: Improved non-interactive zero knowledge with applications to post-quantum signatures. In: Lie, D., Mannan, M., Backes, M., Wang, X. (eds.) ACM CCS 2018, pp. 525–537. ACM Press, October 2018

[Kol18] Kolesnikov, V.: Free IF: how to omit inactive branches and implement S-universal garbled circuit (almost) for free. In: Peyrin, T., Galbraith, S. (eds.) ASIACRYPT 2018. LNCS, vol. 11274, pp. 34–58. Springer, Cham (2018). https://doi.org/10.1007/978-3-030-03332-3_2

[KS06] Kiraz, M.S., Schoenmakers, B.: A protocol issue for the malicious case of Yao's garbled circuit construction. In: Proceedings of 27th Symposium on Information Theory in the Benelux, pp. 283–290 (2006)

[KS08] Kolesnikov, V., Schneider, T.: Improved garbled circuit: free XOR gates and applications. In: Aceto, L., Damgård, I., Goldberg, L.A., Halldórsson, M.M., Ingólfsdóttir, A., Walukiewicz, I. (eds.) ICALP 2008. LNCS, vol. 5126, pp. 486–498. Springer, Heidelberg (2008). https://doi.org/10.1007/978-3-540-70583-3_40

[LO13] Lu, S., Ostrovsky, R.: How to garble RAM programs? In: Johansson, T., Nguyen, P.Q. (eds.) EUROCRYPT 2013. LNCS, vol. 7881, pp. 719–734. Springer, Heidelberg (2013). https://doi.org/10.1007/978-3-642-38348-9_42

[Mic94] Micali, S.: CS proofs (extended abstracts). In: 35th FOCS, pp. 436–453. IEEE Computer Society Press, November 1994

[PHGR13] Parno, B., Howell, J., Gentry, C., Raykova, M.: Pinocchio: nearly practical verifiable computation. In: 2013 IEEE Symposium on Security and Privacy, pp. 238–252. IEEE Computer Society Press, May 2013

[RTZ16] Ranellucci, S., Tapp, A., Zakarias, R.: Efficient generic zero-knowledge proofs from commitments (extended abstract). In: Nascimento, A.C.A., Barreto, P. (eds.) ICITS 2016. LNCS, vol. 10015, pp. 190–212. Springer, Cham (2016). https://doi.org/10.1007/978-3-319-49175-2_10

[Sch90] Schnorr, C.-P.: Efficient identification and signatures for smart cards. In: Brassard, G. (ed.) CRYPTO 1989. LNCS, vol. 435, pp. 239–252. Springer, New York (1990). https://doi.org/10.1007/0-387-34805-0_22

[WMK16] Wang, X., Malozemoff, A.J., Katz, J.: EMP-toolkit: efficient multiparty computation toolkit (2016). https://github.com/emp-toolkit

[WTs+18] Wahby, R.S., Tzialla, I., Shelat, A., Thaler, J., Walfish, M.: Doubly-efficient zkSNARKs without trusted setup. In: 2018 IEEE Symposium on Security and Privacy, pp. 926–943. IEEE Computer Society Press, May 2018

[XZZ+19] Xie, T., Zhang, J., Zhang, Y., Papamanthou, C., Song, D.: Libra: succinct zero-knowledge proofs with optimal prover computation. In: Boldyreva, A., Micciancio, D. (eds.) CRYPTO 2019. LNCS, vol. 11694, pp. 733–764. Springer, Cham (2019). https://doi.org/10.1007/978-3-030-26954-8_24

[ZCD+17] Zaverucha, G., et al.: Picnic. Technical report, National Institute of Standards and Technology (2017). https://csrc.nist.gov/projects/post-quantum-cryptography/round-1-submissions

[Zha19] Zhang, Y.: Personal communication (2019)

[ZRE15] Zahur, S., Rosulek, M., Evans, D.: Two halves make a whole. In: Oswald, E., Fischlin, M. (eds.) EUROCRYPT 2015. LNCS, vol. 9057, pp. 220–250. Springer, Heidelberg (2015). https://doi.org/10.1007/978-3-662-46803-6_8

Which Languages Have 4-Round Fully Black-Box Zero-Knowledge Arguments from One-Way Functions?

Carmit Hazay[1]([⊠]), Rafael Pass[2],
and Muthuramakrishnan Venkitasubramaniam[3]([⊠])

[1] Bar-Ilan University, Ramat Gan, Israel
carmit.hazay@biu.ac.il
[2] Cornell Tech, New York, USA
[3] University of Rochester, Rochester, USA
muthuv@cs.rochester.edu

Abstract. We prove that if a language $\mathcal{L}$ has a 4-round fully black-box zero-knowledge argument with negligible soundness based on one-way functions, then $\overline{\mathcal{L}} \in$ MA. Since coNP $\subseteq$ MA implies that the polynomial hierarchy collapses, our result implies that NP-complete languages are unlikely to have 4-round fully black-box zero-knowledge arguments based on one-way functions. In TCC 2018, Hazay and Venkitasubramaniam, and Khurana, Ostrovsky, and Srinivasan demonstrated 4-round fully black-box zero-knowledge arguments for all languages in NP based on injective one-way functions. Their results also imply a 5-round protocol based on one-way functions. In essence, our result resolves the round complexity of fully black-box zero-knowledge arguments based on one-way functions.

Keywords: One-way functions · Zero-knowledge arguments · Black-box constructions

1 Introduction

Zero-knowledge (ZK) interactive proofs [11] are paradoxical constructs that allow one player (called the prover) to convince another player (called the verifier) of the validity of a mathematical statement $x \in \mathcal{L}$, while providing zero additional knowledge to the verifier. Security against a cheating prover is formalized via soundness, which bounds its success probability to convince of the truthfulness of an incorrect statement. Whereas the zero-knowledge property is formalized by requiring that the view of every "efficient" adversary verifier $\mathcal{V}^*$ interacting with the honest prover $\mathcal{P}$ be simulated by an "efficient" machine $\mathcal{S}$ (a.k.a. the simulator). The idea behind this definition is that whatever $\mathcal{V}^*$ might have learned from interacting with $\mathcal{P}$, it could have actually learned by itself (by running the simulator $\mathcal{S}$). As "efficient" adversaries are typically modeled as probabilistic polynomial-time machines (PPT), the traditional definition of ZK models both the verifier and the simulator as PPT machines.

© International Association for Cryptologic Research 2020
A. Canteaut and Y. Ishai (Eds.): EUROCRYPT 2020, LNCS 12107, pp. 599–619, 2020.
https://doi.org/10.1007/978-3-030-45727-3_20

Several different flavors of ZK systems have been studied in the literature. In this work, we are interested in *computational ZK argument systems with black-box simulation*, where the soundness is required to hold only against non-uniform PPT provers whereas the zero-knowledge property holds against PPT verifiers which get an auxiliary input. Such systems are referred to as computational zero-knowledge argument systems. We will further focus on the case of fully black-box constructions[1] and black-box simulation.[2] The main question we are interested in this work is the round-complexity of computational zero-knowledge argument systems based on minimal assumptions via a fully black-box construction.

We begin with a survey of prior work in this area. Goldreich, Micali and Wigderson [9] constructed the first zero-knowledge proof system for all of NP based on any commitment scheme (which can be instantiated via a 2-round protocol based on one-way functions [12,19]), where they required polynomially many rounds to achieve negligible soundness. For arguments, Feige and Shamir [6] provided a 4-round zero-knowledge system based on algebraic assumptions. In [3], Bellare, Jackobson and Yung, showed how to achieve the same assuming only one-way functions.

In this work, we are interested in fully black-box constructions based on the underlying assumptions. Pass and Wee [21] provided the first black-box construction of a 6-round zero-knowledge argument for NP based on one-way permutations,[3] and seven rounds based argument on one-way functions. Ishai, Mahmoody and Sahai provided the first black-box zero-knowledge arguments based on collision-resistant hash-functions that has total sublinear communication complexity [15]. Ostrovsky, Richelson and Scafuro [20] showed how to construct black-box two-party secure computation protocols in four rounds where only one party receives the output, based on enhanced trapdoor permutations. More recently, in two independent works by Hazay and Venkitasubramaniam [13] and Khurana, Ostrovsky and Srinivasan [17], 4-round fully black-box zero-knowledge arguments based on injective one-way function were demonstrated for all of NP.

On the negative side, Goldreich and Oren [10] demonstrated that three rounds are necessary for designing zero-knowledge arguments for any non-trivial language (i.e. outside BPP) against non-uniform verifiers. When further restricting to black-box simulation, Goldreich and Krawczyk [8] showed that four rounds are necessary for achieving zero-knowledge arguments of non-trivial languages. For the specific case of proofs, Katz [16] showed that only languages in MA can have 4-round zero-knowledge proof systems. As such, the works of [3] and [8] identify the round-complexity of zero-knowledge arguments as four, when restricting to black-box simulation. The sequence of prior works leaves the following fundamental question regarding zero-knowledge arguments open:

---

[1] Where the construction is agnostic of the specific implementation and relies only on its input/output behavior.

[2] Where the simulator is only allowed to make black-box use of the verifier's code.

[3] Where injective one-way functions are sufficient.

What is the weakest hardness assumption for a fully black-box construction of a 4-round zero-knowledge argument system for all of NP?
or
Is there an inherent black-box barrier to design 4-round ZK arguments for all of NP *based on one-way functions?*

We remark that when considering non-black-box simulation, a recent work due to Bitansky, Tauman Kalai and Paneth [5] demonstrated how to obtain 3-round zero-knowledge arguments for NP based on multi-collision resistant hash functions. On the negative side, Fleischhacker, Goyal and Jain [7] proved that 3-round private-coin ZK proofs for NP do not exist, even with respect to non-black-box simulation assuming the existence of certain program obfuscation primitives.

Our Results. In this work we prove the infeasibility of 4-round black-box ZK arguments for all of NP from one-way functions. More formally, the main theorem we prove in this work is:

Theorem 11 (Main result). *If $\mathcal{L}$ has a fully black-box construction of 4-round computational zero-knowledge argument for $\mathcal{L}$ with negligible soundness based on one-way functions, then $\overline{\mathcal{L}} \in$ MA.*

We remark that our result is essentially optimal on several fronts. In particular, if we relax the requirement of a black-box construction, then the work of [3] showed how to construct 4-round ZK argument based on one-way functions. If we only required inverse polynomial soundness (as opposed to negligible soundness), then the classic GMW protocol [9] when repeated in parallel a logarithmic number of times gives a 4-round ZK proof based on one-way functions with inverse polynomial soundness. If we relaxed one-way functions to injective one-way functions, then the works of [13,17] demonstrates a 4-round zero-knowledge arguments for all of NP that is fully black-box based on one-way permutations. We highlight here that our impossibility result only requires that the zero-knowledge property holds w.r.t. one-way functions. In other words, we can show $\overline{\mathcal{L}} \in$ MA even if the soundness of the underlying argument is based on one-way permutations. This matches the construction of [13]. Finally, we cannot hope to improve the theorem from MA to BPP as there exist languages (that are believed to be) outside of BPP (e.g., graph non-isomorphism) that have unconditional 4-round ZK proofs.

1.1 Our Techniques

On a high-level, our technique follows very closely the lower bound result of Katz [16]. In this work, Katz proves that if a language $\mathcal{L}$ has a 4-round black-box zero-knowledge proof, then $\overline{\mathcal{L}} \in$ MA. As a warmup, we begin with an overview of this proof.

Suppose that we have a 4-round zero-knowledge proof for a language $\mathcal{L}$. The main idea is to design a malicious verifier $\mathcal{V}^*$ that satisfies the following properties:

– On a true statement $x \in \mathcal{L}$, $\mathcal{S}^{\mathcal{V}^*}$ will output an accepting transcript with high probability, where $\mathcal{S}$ is the simulator for this argument system.
– On a false statement $x \notin \mathcal{L}$, $\mathcal{S}^{\mathcal{V}^*}$ outputs an accepting transcript with a small probability.

Given such an algorithm $\mathcal{V}^*$, one can consider the following procedure to decide $\overline{\mathcal{L}}$: Run $\mathcal{S}^{\mathcal{V}^*}$. Then, reject if it outputs an accepting transcript and accept otherwise. If this procedure can be carried out via a PPT algorithm then it would imply $\mathcal{L} \in$ BPP. Since we know there are languages outside BPP which have 4-round zero-knowledge proofs (e.g., languages in SZKP), it is unlikely that we will be able to construct a $\mathcal{V}^*$ for which this decision procedure will be efficiently computable. Indeed, the algorithm $\mathcal{V}^*$ that is constructed in [16] cannot be sampled via a PPT algorithm. Recall that the goal is to design an MA proof system for $\overline{\mathcal{L}}$. Katz shows that with some limited help from an unbounded Merlin, Arthur will be able to run the decision procedure, namely $\mathcal{S}^{\mathcal{V}^*}$. More concretely, Merlin will sample a string m from a prescribed distribution and send it to Arthur. Using m, Arthur will be able to run $\mathcal{S}^{\mathcal{V}^*}$. On a true statement (i.e. $x \in \overline{\mathcal{L}}$), Merlin will (honestly) provide the single message with the right distribution and Arthur will be able to decide correctly. Soundness, on the other hand, will require to argue that, for any *arbitrary* message sent by Merlin, Arthur rejects the statement with high probability. If the underlying zero-knowledge argument system admits perfect completeness then it becomes easy to argue that Merlin cannot provide "bad" messages that will make Arthur accept a false statement. The imperfect completeness case is more challenging. To make the proof system sound in the case of imperfect completeness, Katz showed a mechanism for Arthur to discard "bad" messages from Merlin. We now proceed to describe in more detail the lower bound in the case of imperfect completeness as we follow the ideas in this case closely.

We begin with a description of the malicious verifier $\mathcal{V}^*$ and then give our MA proof system. Roughly speaking, the malicious verifier $\mathcal{V}^*$ generates the first message according to the honest verifier $\mathcal{V}$ and will generate the third message depending on the second message of the prover by randomly sampling a random tape consistent with its first message. In more detail, we will consider $\mathcal{V}^*$ that takes as an auxiliary input random strings $r_1, \ldots, r_s$ under the promise that for every i, $\mathcal{V}(x; r_i)$ generates the same first message α. $\mathcal{V}^*$ then sends α as the first message and upon receiving the second message β from the prover, applies a pseudo-random function (a poly-wise independent hash-function is sufficient) on β to obtain an index $i \in [s]$. Finally, $\mathcal{V}^*$ uses r_i to generate the third message γ by running $\mathcal{V}$ with random tape r_i and the partial transcript so far.

We will need a procedure to sample a uniform α that is in the support of the verifier's first messages and then sample $r_1, \ldots, r_s$ uniformly over all consistent random tapes. This procedure will not be PPT computable (as otherwise, it would imply $\mathcal{S}^{\mathcal{V}^*}$ is efficiently computable and consequently $L \in$ BPP). As we only need to design an MA proof system, we will have Merlin (who is computationally unbounded) sample $r_1, \ldots, r_s$ and send these to Arthur. Before we describe the MA proof system, we first argue two properties:

1. If α is distributed according to the honest verifier algorithm with a uniform random tape, and r_i's are uniformly sampled conditioned on α, then the marginal distribution of any r_i will be uniform. This implies that, for $x \in \mathcal{L}$, if the r_i's were sampled correctly then for any i, $\mathcal{S}^{\mathcal{V}(x;r_i)}$ will output an accepting transcript with high probability. We show below that by the zero-knowledge property of the proof system, this implies that $\mathcal{S}^{\mathcal{V}^*(x,r_1,...,r_s)}$ outputs an accepting transcript with high probability.

2. For $x \notin \mathcal{L}$ and r_i's sampled correctly, $\mathcal{S}^{\mathcal{V}^*}$ does not output an accepting transcript with high probability. This is argued by showing that if $\mathcal{S}^{\mathcal{V}^*(x,r_1,...,r_s)}$ outputs an accepting transcript with high probability, then there exists a cheating prover $\mathcal{P}^*$ that can break soundness on input x with non-negligible probability. The idea here is, $\mathcal{P}^*$ will emulate $\mathcal{S}^{\mathcal{V}^*(x,r_1,...,r_s)}$ internally and forward the outside execution inside in one of the rewinding sessions made by $\mathcal{S}$. In more detail, upon receiving the first message α from the verifier, $\mathcal{P}^*$ first samples $r_1, \ldots, r_s$ that are consistent with α as explained above. Next, it internally emulates $\mathcal{S}^{\mathcal{V}^*(x,r_1,...,r_s)}$, with the exception that it forwards the messages of a random rewinding session to an external verifier. Now, if the chosen session is an accepting session then $\mathcal{P}^*$ convinces the external verifier to accept. Specifically, the analysis shows that $\mathcal{P}^*$ will convince the external verifier with probability at least μ/s where μ is the probability that $\mathcal{S}^{\mathcal{V}^*(x,r_1,...,r_s)}$ outputs an accepting transcript.

Now consider the following MA proof system for $\overline{\mathcal{L}}$: Merlin samples a random first message α for the honest verifier and then samples several consistent random tapes $r_1 \ldots, r_s$, and sends them to Arthur. Arthur will run $\mathcal{S}^{\mathcal{V}^*(x,r_1,...,r_s)}$. If $\mathcal{S}$ outputs an accepting transcript, Arthur rejects and accepts otherwise. Completeness follows directly from Item 2, as Merlin will follow its actions honestly, making Arthur accept. Soundness, as mentioned before, requires that $r_1 \ldots, r_s$ are generated with the right distribution. If the underlying zero-knowledge protocol had perfect completeness, then arguing soundness becomes easy because for any set of random tapes $r_1, \ldots, r_s$ sent by Merlin, if they all are consistent with the same first message for the verifier, then by perfect completeness we will have that $\mathcal{S}^{\mathcal{V}^*}$ will output an accepting transcript with high probability. We discuss the case of imperfect completeness as it is more relevant to our techniques.

Handling Imperfect Completeness. If the original zero-knowledge system has imperfect completeness, then Merlin could select random tapes $r_1 \ldots, r_s$ that makes $\mathcal{S}^{\mathcal{V}^*}$ not output an accepting transcript, causing Arthur to accept.

To tackle this issue, as mentioned before, Katz introduces a procedure with which Arthur checks whether the r_i values are "good". First, we observe that if these strings were sampled correctly, then the marginal distribution of any of the r_i's will be uniform (Item 1). This implies that when running the simulator with the honest verifier with random tape r_i on a true statement, the simulator is expected to output an accepting transcript with high-probability.

Second, from the zero-knowledge property we have that for every set of random tapes $r_1, \ldots, r_s$:

$$\{i \leftarrow [t] : \mathcal{S}^{\mathcal{V}(x; r_i)}\} \approx \{i \leftarrow [t] : \langle \mathcal{P}(x), \mathcal{V}(x; r_i) \rangle\} \text{ and,}$$
$$\{\mathcal{S}^{\mathcal{V}^*(x, r_1, \ldots, r_s)}\} \approx \{\langle \mathcal{P}(x), \mathcal{V}^*(x, r_1, \ldots, r_s) \rangle\}.$$

Since the Verifier chooses r_i in its second round via pseudo-random function, we have that:[4]

$$\{i \leftarrow [t] : \langle \mathcal{P}(x), \mathcal{V}(x; r_i) \rangle\} \approx \{\langle \mathcal{P}(x), \mathcal{V}^*(x, r_1, \ldots, r_s) \rangle$$

This implies that, for any message $r_1, \ldots, r_s$ received from Merlin, if $\mathcal{S}^{\mathcal{V}(x; r_i)}$ outputs an accepting transcript for a randomly chosen i with high-probability, then $\mathcal{S}^{\mathcal{V}^*(x, r_1, \ldots, r_s)}$ must output an accepting transcript with high-probability. This gives rise to a checking procedure that can now be incorporated into the MA proof system. In more detail, the MA proof system is modified by asking Arthur to first check if $\mathcal{S}^{\mathcal{V}(x; r_i)}$ outputs an accepting transcript for a random i and reject otherwise. Only if the check passes, namely $\mathcal{S}^{\mathcal{V}(x; r_i)}$ outputs an accepting transcript, Arthur runs $\mathcal{S}^{\mathcal{V}^*(x, r_1, \ldots, r_s)}$ and decides accordingly. This gives an MA proof system that is sound. However, this modification alters the completeness of the proof system, as $x \notin L$ could imply that $\mathcal{S}^{\mathcal{V}(x; r_i)}$ might not output an accepting transcript causing Arthur to reject immediately. This can be fixed by having Arthur first check if the simulator outputs an accepting transcript with the honest verifier on a uniformly sampled random tape by Arthur. More precisely, the final MA proof system has Arthur perform the following:

1. Run $\mathcal{S}^{\mathcal{V}(x; r)}$ several times. If $\mathcal{S}$ fails to output an accepting transcript with high probability where r is uniformly chosen in each trial, then accept and halt. Otherwise, proceed to the next step.
2. Pick a random index i and run $\mathcal{S}^{\mathcal{V}(x; r_i)}$. If $\mathcal{S}$ does not output an accepting transcript then reject and halt. Otherwise, proceed to the next step.
3. Run $\mathcal{S}^{\mathcal{V}^*(x, r_1, \ldots, r_s)}$. If $\mathcal{S}$ outputs an accepting transcript with high probability then reject, otherwise accept.

Our Approach. We now discuss how we extend this lower bound to our setting where we have a fully black-box construction of a 4-round zero-knowledge argument for $\mathcal{L}$. First, we observe that to consider the malicious verifier $\mathcal{V}^*$ as in Katz's proof, we need to provide $r_1, \ldots, r_s$ consistent with the first message in the presence of a one-way function oracle. Given an arbitrary oracle, we will not be able to sample randomness $r_1, \ldots, r_s$ even in unbounded time, if we are only allowed to make polynomially many queries to the oracle (which will be required as eventually, we want to use $\mathcal{V}^*$ to break soundness which is computational based on the one-wayness of the oracle). Instead, we will prescribe a joint distribution over $r_1, \ldots, r_s$ and random oracles for which we can carry out the

---

[4] In fact, the distributions are identical if the verifier uses poly-wise independent hash-functions.

proof. More precisely, given a statement x, we will specify a joint distribution over random oracles $\mathcal{O}$ and $r_1, \ldots, r_s$ such that for all i, $\mathcal{V}^{\mathcal{O}}(x; r_i)$ will output the same message and the following two properties hold:

Property P1. On a true statement x, $\mathcal{S}^{\mathcal{O}, \mathcal{V}^{*\mathcal{O}}(x, r_1, \ldots, r_s)}$ will output an accepting transcript with high probability, where $\mathcal{S}$ is the simulator for this argument system.

Property P2. On a false statement x, $\mathcal{S}^{\mathcal{O}, \mathcal{V}^{*\mathcal{O}}(x, r_1, \ldots, r_s)}$ outputs an accepting transcript with negligible probability.

Description of a Malicious Verifier Strategy $\mathcal{V}^*$. We now proceed to describe our malicious verifier strategy and the corresponding random oracle distribution.

1. Run $\mathcal{V}^{\mathcal{O}}(x; r)$ where we emulate $\mathcal{O}$ as a random oracle and choose the verifier's random tape uniformly at random. Let α be the message output by $\mathcal{V}$. Discard r and the oracle $\mathcal{O}$.
2. Consider the oracle PPT algorithm $\mathcal{A}^\bullet$ that on random tape (r, r') outputs whatever $\mathcal{S}^{\bullet, \mathcal{V}^\bullet(x; r)}(x; r')$ outputs. We will next rely on the "heavy-query" learning procedure due to Barak and Mahmoody [2] who give a procedure to identify the most frequent queries made by an algorithm to the random oracle conditioned on its output being fixed to a particular message. We apply the heavy query learning procedure to the honest verifier algorithm $\mathcal{V}$ subject to the condition that it outputs α as its first message. Let $\mathcal{Q}$ be the set of queries output by this procedure for some oracle $\mathcal{O}'$ sampled as a random oracle.
3. Let R_α be the set that contains all the pairs $(r', \mathcal{Q}')$ such that $\mathcal{V}(x; r')$ outputs α as its first message while making queries only in $\mathcal{Q} \cup \mathcal{Q}'$ (where $\mathcal{Q}'$ are the non-frequent queries). Now, sample s elements $\{(r_i, \mathcal{Q}_i)\}_{i \in [s]}$ from R_α uniformly at random.
4. Output $(r_1, \ldots, r_s)$ and $(\mathcal{Q}, \mathcal{Q}_1, \ldots, \mathcal{Q}_s)$.

Given a sample $(r_1, \ldots, r_s)$ and $(\mathcal{Q}, \mathcal{Q}_1, \ldots, \mathcal{Q}_s)$, the distribution of oracles will be random oracles whose queries in $(\mathcal{Q}, \mathcal{Q}_1, \ldots, \mathcal{Q}_s)$ are fixed and set to be random on all other points. Such oracles were previously considered in [18] and referred to as partially-fixed random oracles. The malicious verifier $\mathcal{V}^*$ is specified as a PPT algorithm that takes as auxiliary information $(r_1, \ldots, r_s)$ and proceeds as follows. For the first message, it runs $\mathcal{V}(x; r_1)$ and outputs whatever $\mathcal{V}$ does, say α. Given a second message β sent by the prover $\mathcal{V}^*$ applies a poly-wise independent hash function (also supplied as auxiliary information) $h(\beta)$ to a chosen index $i \in [s]$. Then it runs $\mathcal{V}(x; r_i)$ on the partial transcript α, β to output the third message δ and forwards that to the prover. Any oracle query made by $\mathcal{V}$ is forwarded to the oracle attached to $\mathcal{V}^*$.

Proving P1 follows essentially the same way as in [16]. So we argue P2 next.

Proving P2. Just as in [16], we will show that if the simulator can simulate $\mathcal{V}^*$ on a false statement with non-negligible probability, then there exists a cheating prover $\mathcal{P}^*$ that can break the soundness of the zero-knowledge argument, which, in turn, establishes the property P2 specified at the beginning of the outline. As before, in the security reduction, $\mathcal{P}^*$ will internally emulate the simulator with $\mathcal{V}^*$ and forward the message from the external interaction inside, for one of the random rewindings made by the simulator. Recall that $\mathcal{P}^*$ and the external verifier are equipped with an oracle $\mathcal{O}$ (for the one-way function).

Observe that $\mathcal{P}^*$ will not be able to use $\mathcal{O}$ for internally emulating $\mathcal{S}^{\mathcal{V}^*}$, as in the internal execution $\mathcal{P}^*$ it needs to run $\mathcal{S}$ and $\mathcal{V}^*$ from a prescribed distribution over $r_1, \ldots, r_s$ and random oracles. By applying the same learning heavy-query algorithm we can show that $\mathcal{P}^*$ will be able to sample $\mathcal{Q}, \mathcal{Q}_1, \ldots, \mathcal{Q}_s$ and $r_1, \ldots, r_s$ and an oracle $\mathcal{O}'$ where

- $\mathcal{Q}$ is consistent with $\mathcal{O}$.
- $\mathcal{O}'$ is consistent with $\mathcal{Q} \cup \mathcal{Q}_1 \cup \cdots \cup \mathcal{Q}_s$ and with $\mathcal{O}$ everywhere else.
- If $\mathcal{O}$ is sampled according to a random oracle, then the distribution of $\mathcal{O}'$ and $r_1, \ldots, r_s$ is identical to the prescribed distribution.

Next, if the random rewinding chosen by $\mathcal{P}^*$ is the one that the simulator outputs as an accepting transcript, then we want to conclude that $\mathcal{P}^*$ succeeds in convincing the external verifier. There are two (related) issues to make this argument work:

- First, forwarding the messages from the external verifier internally in a random rewinding session could result in skewing the distribution internally simulated by $\mathcal{P}^*$.
- Second, the external oracle $\mathcal{O}$ and the internally emulated oracle $\mathcal{O}'$ are not identical. In particular, they could be different on $\mathcal{Q}_1, \ldots, \mathcal{Q}_s$.

We argue that the first item is not an issue and the distribution is, in fact, correct because we can view the random tape and queries made by the outside verifier as one of the elements in R_α. The second issue is problematic because if the messages generated by the simulator in the forwarded session makes the external verifier make one of the conflicting queries (namely a query on $\mathcal{Q}_1 \cup \cdots \cup \mathcal{Q}_s$), then we cannot claim that the external verifier will accept if the internal emulation results in an accepting transcript on that session. To resolve this issue, we weaken property P2 as follows:

P2' On a false statement x, $\mathcal{S}^{\mathcal{O}, \mathcal{V}^{*\mathcal{O}}(x, r_1, \ldots, r_s)}$ outputs an accepting transcript *while not making conflicting queries* with negligible probability. In particular, if a particular rewinding session (where r_j was used as the random tape) is the accepting transcript then the verifier on that transcript should not make any query to $\mathcal{Q}_i$ for $i \neq j$.

This modification will be the crux of making our MA proof system work.

MA Proof System. Upon receiving $r_1, \ldots, r_s, \mathcal{Q}, \mathcal{Q}_1, \ldots, \mathcal{Q}_s$, Arthur continues as follows:

1. Emulate $\mathcal{S}^{\mathcal{O},\mathcal{V}^{\mathcal{O}}(x;r)}$ where r is chosen at random and $\mathcal{O}$ according to the random oracle. If it does not output an accepting transcript, then accept and halt. Otherwise proceed.
2. Pick a random $i \leftarrow [s]$ and emulate $\mathcal{S}^{\mathcal{O},\mathcal{V}^{\mathcal{O}}(x;r_i)}$ where $\mathcal{O}$ is sampled according to a partially fixed random oracle, fixed on the set $\mathcal{Q} \cup \mathcal{Q}_1 \cup \cdots \cup \mathcal{Q}_s$. If it either does not output an accepting transcript or outputs an accepting transcript with conflicting queries, then reject and halt. Otherwise, proceed.
3. Emulate $\mathcal{S}^{\mathcal{O},\mathcal{V}^{*\mathcal{O}}(x,r_1,\ldots,r_s)}$. If it either does not output a transcript or an accepting transcript is output with conflicting queries then accept. Otherwise, reject.

2 Preliminaries

Basic Notations. We denote the security parameter by n. We say that a function $\mu : \mathbb{N} \to \mathbb{N}$ is *negligible* if for every positive polynomial $p(\cdot)$ and all sufficiently large n it holds that $\mu(n) < \frac{1}{p(n)}$. We use the abbreviation PPT to denote probabilistic polynomial-time. We further denote by $a \leftarrow A$ the random sampling of a from a distribution A, and by $[n]$ the set of elements $\{1,\ldots,n\}$. For an NP relation $\mathcal{R}$, we denote by $\mathcal{R}_x$ the set of witnesses of x and by $\mathcal{L}_\mathcal{R}$ its associated language. That is, $\mathcal{R}_x = \{\omega \mid (x,\omega) \in \mathcal{R}\}$ and $\mathcal{L}_\mathcal{R} = \{x \mid \exists \omega \text{ s.t. } (x,\omega) \in \mathcal{R}\}$. We specify next the definition of computationally indistinguishable.

Definition 21. *Let* $X = \{X(a,n)\}_{a \in \{0,1\}^*, n \in \mathbb{N}}$ *and* $Y = \{Y(a,n)\}_{a \in \{0,1\}^*, n \in \mathbb{N}}$ *be two distribution ensembles. We say that* X *and* Y *are* computationally indistinguishable, *denoted* $X \overset{c}{\approx} Y$, *if for every* PPT *machine* $\mathcal{D}$, *every* $a \in \{0,1\}^*$, *every positive polynomial* $p(\cdot)$ *and all sufficiently large* n:

$$\left| \Pr\left[\mathcal{D}(X(a,n),1^n,a) = 1\right] - \Pr\left[\mathcal{D}(Y(a,n),1^n,a) = 1\right] \right| < \frac{1}{p(n)}.$$

We assume familiarity with the basic notions of an Interactive Turing Machine (ITM for brevity) and a protocol (in essence a pair of ITMs). We denote by PPT the class of probabilistic polynomial-time Turing machines. We denote by $M^{\bullet}$ an oracle machine; we sometimes drop $\bullet$ when it is clear from the context. As usual, if $M^{\bullet}$ is an oracle machine, $M^{\mathcal{O}}$ denotes the joint execution of M with oracle access to $\mathcal{O}$.

Definition 22 (Random Oracle). *A* random oracle **RO** *is a randomized stateful oracle that given a query* $x \leftarrow \{0,1\}^n$ *outputs* y *if the pair* (x,y) *is stored or outputs a random element* y' *from* $\{0,1\}^{|x|}$ *and stores* (x,y').

Following [4,18], we use randomized oracles as opposed to fixing a random oracle by sampling it once as in [14] as this is sufficient for refuting black-box constructions.

We recall the properties of the "heavy-query" learning algorithm (verbatim) from [2] that have typically been used in separation from one-way functions [14,18].

Lemma 21 (Learning Heavy Queries Efficiently [2]**).** *Let $\mathcal{A}$ be a randomized oracle algorithm which asks up to m oracle queries, denoted by $\mathcal{Q}(\mathcal{A}^{\mathcal{O}})$ and outputs some message C. Let $0 < \varepsilon < 1$ be a given parameter. There is a learning algorithm G in* PSPACE *(in fact,* BPP^{NP}*) which learns a list of $\mathcal{Y}$ of query-answer pairs from the oracle $\mathcal{O}$ such that:*

1. *$|\mathcal{Y}| \leq 10m/\varepsilon^2$.*
2. *With probability at least $1 - \varepsilon$ over the choice of $\mathcal{O}$ from* **RO** *and the random coins of $\mathcal{A}$ and G, for every u that is not part of any query-answer pair in $\mathcal{Y}$, it holds that $\Pr[u \in \mathcal{Q}(\mathcal{A})|(C, \mathcal{Y})] < \varepsilon$ where the latter probability is over the remaining randomness of* **RO** *and $\mathcal{A}$ conditioned on $(C, \mathcal{Y})$.*

Next, we recall the property about random oracles that they cannot be inverted by any oracle algorithm (possibly unbounded) that makes only polynomially many queries to the oracle. The following is repeated verbatim from [18].

Definition 23 (Security Threshold). *A primitive P has security threshold τ_P if an adversary "breaking" P has to "win" in the security game of P with probability $\tau_P + \varepsilon$ for a non-negligible ε.*

Lemma 22 ([2,18])**.** *Let P and Q be two cryptographic primitives and P has security threshold zero. For a randomized oracle $\mathcal{O}$, suppose one can break the black-box security of any implementation $Q^{\mathcal{O}}$ of Q with non-negligible probability and asking poly(n) oracle queries to $\mathcal{O}$. Suppose also that there exists a black-box secure implementation $P^{\mathcal{O}}$ of P from $\mathcal{O}$. Then there is no black-box construction of Q from P.*

Definition 24 (Partially-Fixed Random Oracles). *We call a randomized function f a $k(n)$-partially-fixed random oracle if it is fixed over some subdomain S and chooses its answers similarly to the random oracle* **RO** *at any point q out of S and it holds that $|S \cap \{0,1\}^n| \leq k(n)$ for every n. We simply call f partially-fixed random if it is $2^{o(n)}$-partially-fixed random.*

Lemma 23 ([18])**.** *One-way functions can be black-box securely realized from all partially-fixed random oracles.*

2.1 Fully Black-Box Constructions

Following the terminology of [22], we consider fully black-box constructions of zero-knowledge arguments from the underlying primitive.

Definition 25 (Fully black-box construction). *A black-box implementation of a primitive $\mathcal{Q}$ from a primitive $\mathcal{P}$ is an oracle algorithm Q (referred to as the implementation) such that Q^P is an implementation of $\mathcal{Q}$ whenever P is an implementation of $\mathcal{P}$. Q^P is said to have a black-box proof of security, if there exists an efficient machine $\mathcal{R}$ such that for any oracle P implementing $\mathcal{P}$ and machine $\mathcal{A}$ that breaks Q^P with non-negligible advantage for some security parameter n, then $\mathcal{R}^{P,\mathcal{A}}$ breaks the security of P over some security parameter $n' = \mathsf{poly}(n)$. A black-box construction $\mathcal{Q}$ from $\mathcal{P}$ requires a black-box implementation Q and a black-box proof of security $\mathcal{R}$.*

2.2   Interactive Systems

We denote by $\langle A(\omega), B(z)\rangle(x)$ the random variable representing the (local) output of machine B when interacting with machine A on common input x, when the random-input to each machine is uniformly and independently chosen, and A (resp., B) has auxiliary input ω (resp., z).

A round of an interactive proof system consists of a message sent from one party to the other, and we assume that the prover and the verifier speak in alternating rounds. Following [1], we let MA denote the class of languages having a 1-round proof system and in this case refer to the prover as Merlin and the verifier as Arthur; that is:

Definition 26 (MA). $\mathcal{L} \in$ MA *if there exists a probabilistic polynomial-time verifier* $\mathcal{V}$, *a non-negative function* s, *and a polynomial* p *such that the following hold for all sufficiently-long* x:

- *If* $x \in \mathcal{L}$ *then there exists a string* w *(that can be sent by Merlin) such that*

$$\Pr[\mathcal{V}(x, w) = 1] \geq s(|x|) + 1/p(|x|).$$

- *If* $x \notin \mathcal{L}$ *then for all* w *(sent by a cheating Merlin) it holds that*

$$\Pr[\mathcal{V}(x, w) = 1] \leq s(|x|).$$

Definition 27 (Interactive argument system). *A pair of* PPT *interactive machines* $(\mathcal{P}, \mathcal{V})$ *is called an* interactive proof system *for a language* $\mathcal{L}$ *if there exists a negligible function* $\mu(\cdot)$ *such that the following two conditions hold:*

1. COMPLETENESS: *For every* $x \in \mathcal{L}$ *there exists a string* ω *such that for every* $z \in \{0, 1\}^*$,
$$\Pr[\langle \mathcal{P}(\omega), \mathcal{V}(z)\rangle(x) = 1] \geq c(|x|)$$
   where c *is the acceptance probability.*
2. SOUNDNESS: *For every* $x \notin \mathcal{L}$, *every interactive* PPT *machine* $\mathcal{P}^*$, *and every* $\omega, z \in \{0, 1\}^*$
$$\Pr[\langle \mathcal{P}^*(\omega), \mathcal{V}(z)\rangle(x) = 1] \leq s(|x|).$$
   where s *is the soundness error and will be negligible in this paper.*

Definition 28 (Computational zero-knowledge (CZK)). *Let* $(\mathcal{P}, \mathcal{V})$ *be an interactive proof system for some language* $\mathcal{L}$. *We say that* $(\mathcal{P}, \mathcal{V})$ *is a computational zero-knowledge with respect to an auxiliary input if for every* PPT *interactive machine* $\mathcal{V}^*$ *there exists a* PPT *algorithm* $\mathcal{S}$, *running in time polynomial in the length of its first input, such that*

$$\{\langle \mathcal{P}(\omega), \mathcal{V}^*(z)\rangle(x)\}_{x \in \mathcal{L}, \omega \in \mathcal{R}_x, z \in \{0,1\}^*} \overset{c}{\approx} \{\langle \mathcal{S}\rangle(x, z)\}_{x \in \mathcal{L}, z \in \{0,1\}^*}$$

(when the distinguishing gap is considered as a function of $|x|$*). Specifically, the left term denotes the output of* $\mathcal{V}^*$ *after it interacts with* $\mathcal{P}$ *on common input* x *whereas, the right term denotes the output of* $\mathcal{S}$ *on* x.

Black-Box Construction of Zero-Knowledge Arguments

Definition 29. *A black-box construction of a zero-knowledge argument system for a language $\mathcal{L}$ from one-way functions is a tuple of oracle algorithms $(\mathcal{P}, \mathcal{V}, \mathcal{S})$ such that for any oracle $f = \{f_m : \{0,1\}^m \to \{0,1\}^m\}$, $\mathcal{P}, \mathcal{V}$ and $\mathcal{S}$ are oracle algorithms where completeness holds w.r.t to any oracle $\mathcal{O}$ and the soundness and zero-knowledge property are proved via a reduction to the underlying function f as follows:*

Soundness: *There is an efficient oracle reduction algorithm $\mathcal{R}_s$, such that for every oracle f, every malicious prover $\mathcal{P}^*$ (that could arbitrarily depend on f), if $\mathcal{P}^*$ convinces the verifier on input $x \in \{0,1\}^n \backslash \mathcal{L}$ with probability $1/p(n)$ for some polynomial $p(\cdot)$, $\mathcal{R}_s^{f,\mathcal{P}^{*f}}$ inverts f with probability $1/q(m)$ for some polynomial $q(\cdot)$ over a polynomially related $m = n^{\theta(1)}$, namely,*

$$\Pr[y \leftarrow f(U^m) : \mathcal{R}_s^{f,\mathcal{P}^{*f}}(y) \in f^{-1}(y)] \geq \frac{1}{q(m)}$$

Zero Knowledge: *This is defined analogously to the soundness property. There is an efficient oracle reduction algorithm $\mathcal{R}_{zk}$, such that for every oracle f, every malicious verifier $\mathcal{V}^*$ (that could arbitrarily depend on f), if $\mathcal{V}^*$ distinguishes the real execution from the simulation on input $x \in \mathcal{L} \cap \{0,1\}^n$ with probability $\frac{1}{p(n)}$ for some polynomial $p(\cdot)$, $\mathcal{R}_{zk}^{f,\mathcal{V}^{*f}}$ inverts f with probability $1/q(m)$ for some polynomial $q(\cdot)$ over a polynomially related $m = n^{\theta(1)}$, namely,*

$$\Pr[y \leftarrow f(U^m) : \mathcal{R}_{zk}^{f,\mathcal{V}^{*f}}(y) \in f^{-1}(y)] \geq \frac{1}{q(m)}$$

We remark that, by view of the verifier we include the transcript of the messages, random tape and the query and answers obtained by the verifier from its oracle.

Terminology. We will be concerned with 4-round CZK argument systems, where the verifier sends the first message and the prover sends the final message. We use $\alpha, \beta, \gamma, \delta$ to denote the first, second, third, and fourth messages, respectively. We let $\mathcal{P}$ (resp., $\mathcal{V}$) denote the honest prover (resp., honest verifier) algorithm when the common input is x.

3   Implausibility of 4-Round BB ZK Arguments from OWFs

We begin with an outline of the proof. Recall that any separation cannot rule out the existence of 4-round arguments with a random oracle, as a random oracle with high probability acts as a "one-way permutation" and we do know 4-round arguments based on one-way permutations [13,17]. Instead, we follow the approach of [18], by considering partially-fixed random oracles that crucially rely on the fact that the distribution of oracles is not a permutation. A partially fixed random oracle behaves essentially as a random oracle with the exception that for a pre-specified subset $\mathcal{F}$ of its domain the answers are fixed.

3.1   Main Result

We are ready to prove our main result.

Theorem 31. *If $\mathcal{L}$ has a fully black-box construction of 4-round computational zero-knowledge argument for $\mathcal{L}$ with negligible soundness based on one-way functions, then $\overline{\mathcal{L}} \in$ MA.*

Proof. Assume for contradiction, there is a fully black-box construction of a 4-round ZK argument $(\mathcal{P}, \mathcal{V})$ from a one-way function with black-box simulator $\mathcal{S}$.

In the proof system, Merlin (namely, the prover) and Arthur (namely, the verifier) share in advance an input x of length n. Let $c(\cdot)$ be the completeness of $\langle \mathcal{P}, \mathcal{V} \rangle$. The soundness of $\langle \mathcal{P}, \mathcal{V} \rangle$ is negligible. Let $T_s(n)$ be a bound on the expected running time of the simulator. Let $m(n)$ be the total number of queries made by the prover and the verifier on inputs of length n. Let $T_v(n)$ be a bound on the runtime of the honest verifier. Let $\eta(n)$ denote the length of the prover's second message. We set $\varepsilon(n) = c(n)/20$, and $s'(n) = 4(T_s(n))^2(\varepsilon)^{-3}$. For sake of succinctness, we define $m = m(n)$, $c = c(n)$, $T = T_s(n)$, $\ell = T_v(n)$, $\eta = \eta(n)$, $\varepsilon = \varepsilon(n)$ and $s = s'(n)$. Finally, let $\widetilde{\mathcal{S}}$ be the algorithm that proceeds identically to $\mathcal{S}$ with the exception that it halts after $2T/\varepsilon$ steps on inputs of length n.

We will first describe a distribution of a malicious verifier $\mathcal{V}^*$ and oracles $\mathcal{O}$ and then describe and analyze the MA proof system.

Specifying the Distribution of Malicious Verifier and the Oracle.

1. Run $\mathcal{V}^{\mathcal{O}}(x; r)$ where we emulate $\mathcal{O}$ as a random oracle and choose the verifier's random tape uniformly at random. Let α be the message output by $\mathcal{V}$. Discard r and the oracle $\mathcal{O}$.
2. Consider the oracle PPT algorithm $\mathcal{A}$ that on random tape (r, r') outputs what $\mathcal{S}^{\bullet, \mathcal{V}^\bullet(x; r)}(x; r')$ outputs. We execute the heavy-query learning procedure for the algorithm $\mathcal{A}$ from Lemma 21 with parameter $\frac{\varepsilon}{(2s^2 \cdot \ell)}$ subject to the condition that the output contains the view of the verifier where the first message generated by $\mathcal{V}$ is α. Let $\mathcal{Q}$ be the set of queries output by this procedure.
3. Let R_α be the set that contains all the pairs $(r', \mathcal{Q}')$ such that $\mathcal{V}(x; r')$ outputs α as its first message while only making oracle queries inside $\mathcal{Q} \cup \mathcal{Q}'$. Now sample s elements $\{(r_i, \mathcal{Q}_i)\}_{i \in [s]}$ from R_α uniformly at random.
4. Output $(r_1, \ldots, r_s)$ and $(\mathcal{Q}, \mathcal{Q}_1, \ldots, \mathcal{Q}_s)$.

Description of a Malicious Verifier Strategy $\mathcal{V}^*$: Given $r_1, \ldots, r_s$ from the distribution above, we consider an oracle PPT algorithm $\mathcal{V}^*$, that given an input x and auxiliary input $r_1, \ldots, r_s, h$, where r_i represents random coins for the honest verifier algorithm and h is a hash function, proceeds as follows:

1. $\mathcal{V}^*$ internally emulates the honest verifier oracle algorithm $\mathcal{V}$ on input x and random tape r_1 to generate its first message α which it forwards externally to the prover. If at any point during the emulation, $\mathcal{V}$ makes a query to its oracle, $\mathcal{V}^*$ forwards that query to its oracle and the response back to $\mathcal{V}$.

2. Upon receiving a message β from the prover, the verifier computes $i = h(\beta)$ and emulates $\mathcal{V}$ on input x with random tape r_i. It obtains α as $\mathcal{V}$'s first message and feeds β as the prover's message. It then obtains γ as the third message and $\mathcal{V}^*$ forwards γ to the external prover.

3. $\mathcal{V}^*$ receives the last message δ from the prover. Finally, $\mathcal{V}^*$ outputs its view.

Description of the Family of Oracles. Given $\mathcal{Q}, \mathcal{Q}_1, \ldots, \mathcal{Q}_s$, we consider a partially-fixed random oracle $\tilde{\mathbf{O}}$ that is defined as follows. It contains oracles that are fixed over the queries in $\mathcal{Q} \cup \mathcal{Q}_1 \cup \ldots \cup \mathcal{Q}_s$ and chooses its answers similarly to the random oracle $\mathbf{RO}$ at any point q not in the subdomain defined by $\mathcal{Q} \cup \mathcal{Q}_1 \cup \ldots \cup \mathcal{Q}_s$. We remark that such a family is well defined only if no two sets among $\mathcal{Q}, \mathcal{Q}_1, \ldots, \mathcal{Q}_s$ have *conflicting queries*, where a query u is conflicting for query-answer sets A and B, if there exists v_1, v_2 (possibly equal) such that $(u, v_1) \in A$ and $(u, v_2) \in B$. Looking ahead, by the properties of the learning algorithm employed in the sampling procedure described above, we will have that there will be no conflicting queries with high probability.

Before proceeding with the proof we introduce some notation, borrowed verbatim from [16]. For a given randomized experiment Expt that can be run in polynomial-time and outputs a bit, we let $\mathsf{Estimate}_\varepsilon(\Pr[\mathsf{Expt}])$ denote a procedure that outputs an estimate to the given probability (taken over randomness used in the Expt) to within an additive factor of ε, except with probability at most ε. That is:

$$| \Pr \left[\mathsf{Estimate}_\varepsilon(\Pr[\mathsf{Expt} = 1]) - \Pr[\mathsf{Expt} = 1] \right| \geq \varepsilon] \leq \varepsilon.$$

This can be done in the standard way using $\Theta(\varepsilon^{-2} \log \frac{1}{\varepsilon})$ independent executions of Expt. Observe that if ε is non-negligible then the estimation runs in polynomial time whenever Expt is a polynomial-time sampleable.

Description of the MA Proof System: We are now ready to describe an MA proof for $\overline{\mathcal{L}}$. On input x, Arthur proceeds as follows:

1. Upon receiving Merlin's first message, Arthur interprets the message as strings $r_1, \ldots, r_s \in \{0,1\}^\ell$ and sets of query-answer pairs $\mathcal{Q}, \mathcal{Q}_1, \ldots, \mathcal{Q}_s$. Next, it proceeds as follows:

   (a) Estimate the probability:

$$p_1 = \mathsf{Estimate}_\varepsilon \left(\Pr_{r', r, \mathcal{O}} \left[\tilde{\mathcal{S}}^{\mathcal{O}, \mathcal{V}^{\mathcal{O}}(x; r')}(x; r) \text{ outputs an accepting transcript} \right] \right)$$

   where r and r' are chosen uniformly at random from $\{0,1\}^T$ and $\{0,1\}^\ell$ respectively, and $\mathcal{O}$ is sampled according to $\mathbf{RO}$. We remark that the estimation procedure requires sampling a random execution of $\tilde{\mathcal{S}}^{\mathcal{O}, \mathcal{V}^{\mathcal{O}}(x; r')}(x; r)$ and this can be done in polynomial time by emulating $\mathcal{O}$ distributed according to a random oracle $\mathbf{RO}$. If $p_1 < c - 2\varepsilon$ then accept and halt. Otherwise, proceed to the next step.

(b) If any pair of the sets $\mathcal{Q}, \mathcal{Q}_1, \ldots, \mathcal{Q}_s$ have conflicting queries then reject and halt. Else, emulate the honest verifier algorithm $\mathcal{V}$ on input x and random tape r_1 until it generates its first message α. In this emulation, if $\mathcal{V}$ makes a query inside $\mathcal{Q} \cup \mathcal{Q}_1$ we respond with the corresponding answer from the set. If $\mathcal{V}$ makes a query outside $\mathcal{Q} \cup \mathcal{Q}_1$, then Arthur rejects. For every $i \in [s]$, internally emulate $\mathcal{V}(x; r_i)$ and reject if it does not output the same α as its first message or makes a query outside $\mathcal{Q} \cup \mathcal{Q}_i$.

(c) Denote by $\widetilde{\mathbf{O}}$ the distribution of partially-fixed random oracles fixed on the set $\mathcal{Q} \cup \mathcal{Q}_1 \cup \cdots \cup \mathcal{Q}_s$. Let $E(v)$ denote the event when a view v of the verifier is consistent with $\mathcal{V}(x; r_i)$ for some $i \in [s]$ and contains no query from $\mathcal{Q}_j$ for any $j \neq i$ (where consistent with $\mathcal{V}(x; r_i)$ means that transcript in v can be regenerated when the prover messages in v are fed to the honest verifier's code on input x and randomness r_i). Pick a random $i \in [s]$ and emulate $\widetilde{\mathcal{S}}^{\mathcal{O}, \mathcal{V}^{\mathcal{O}}(x; r_i)}(x; r)$ where the oracle $\mathcal{O}$ is emulated according to $\widetilde{\mathbf{O}}$. Such an oracle can be emulated by answering all queries in the fixed set according to the query-answer pair and any other query randomly (but consistently). If either $\widetilde{\mathcal{S}}$ does not output an accepting transcript or $E(v)$ does not hold for the view v output by $\widetilde{\mathcal{S}}$, then reject.

(d) Let H denote a family of $2T/\varepsilon$-wise independent hash function $h : \{0,1\}^\eta \rightarrow \{1, \ldots, s\}$. We next estimate:

$$p_2 =$$

$$\mathsf{Estimate}_\varepsilon \left(\Pr_{r,h,\mathcal{O}} \left[v \leftarrow \widetilde{\mathcal{S}}^{\mathcal{O}, \mathcal{V}^{*\mathcal{O}}(x, r_1, \ldots, r_s, h)}(x; r) : v \text{ is accepting } \wedge E(v) \right] \right),$$

where $r \leftarrow \{0,1\}^T$, $h \leftarrow H$ and $\mathcal{O} \leftarrow \widetilde{\mathbf{O}}$. If $p_2 < c - 10\varepsilon$ accept, otherwise reject.

We now proceed to proving the completeness and soundness arguments of the above proof.

Lemma 31. *For any $x \notin \overline{\mathcal{L}} \cap \{0,1\}^n$ and sufficiently large n, and any message $r_1, \ldots, r_s, \mathcal{Q}, \mathcal{Q}_1, \ldots, \mathcal{Q}_s$ sent by Merlin, the probability that Arthur accepts is at most $c - 6\varepsilon$.*

Proof: In this case, we have $x \in \mathcal{L}$, so it must hold that for any oracle $\mathcal{O}$ that the probability with which the honest prover convinces the honest verifier on input x and oracle $\mathcal{O}$ is at least c. From the zero-knowledge property we have that, for sufficiently large n, $x \in \{0,1\}^n \cap \mathcal{L}$, we have

$$\Pr_{r,r',\mathcal{O}} \left[\widetilde{\mathcal{S}}^{\mathcal{O}, \mathcal{V}^{\mathcal{O}}(x; r')}(x; r) \text{ outputs an accepting transcript} \right] \geq c - \varepsilon$$

This means that with probability at most ε, the estimate p_1 obtained by Arthur will be smaller than $c - 2\varepsilon$. In other words, Arthur accepts the statement with probability at most ε in Step 1a.

Next recall that if the message sent by Merlin does not meet the conditions in Step 1b, then it rejects. Thus we will assume that these conditions hold. Now consider the following probability

$$\hat{p} = \Pr_{i,r,h,\mathcal{O}} \left[v \leftarrow \widetilde{\mathcal{S}}^{\mathcal{O}, \mathcal{V}^{\mathcal{O}}(x;r_i)}(x;r) : \mathsf{v} \text{ is accepting } \wedge E(\mathsf{v}) \right]$$

where $i \leftarrow [s]$, $r \leftarrow \{0,1\}^T$, $h \leftarrow H$ and $\mathcal{O} \leftarrow \widetilde{\mathbf{O}}$. Recall that if $p_2 < c - 10\varepsilon$ then Arthur accepts, and otherwise rejects. There are two cases depending on $\hat{p}$.

Case $\hat{p} < c - 7\varepsilon$: Recall that, in Step 1c, Arthur picks a random i, emulates $\widetilde{\mathcal{S}}^{\mathcal{O}, \mathcal{V}^{\mathcal{O}}(x;r_i)}(x;r)$ and rejects if the simulator does not output an accepting transcript. Therefore, in this case, the probability with which Arthur accepts is at most the probability that Arthur proceeds beyond Step 1c which is at most $c - 7\varepsilon$.

Case $\hat{p} \geq c - 7\varepsilon$: In this case, by the zero-knowledge property, we have that the probability that the honest prover convinces the verifier with $\mathcal{O}$ and E does not occur, is at least $c - 8\varepsilon$. In other words,

$$\Pr_{i,\mathcal{O}} \left[v \leftarrow \mathbf{View}_{\mathcal{V}}(\langle \mathcal{P}^{\mathcal{O}}, \mathcal{V}^{\mathcal{O}}(r_i) \rangle(x)) : v \text{ is accepting } \wedge E(v) \right] \geq c - 8\varepsilon.$$

where $i \leftarrow [s]$ and $\mathcal{O} \leftarrow \widetilde{\mathbf{O}}$. Recall that $\widetilde{\mathbf{O}}$ is partially-fixed random oracle fixed over a polynomial-sized subdomain and from Lemma 23 (as shown in [18]) we know it implies one-way functions. We remark that here we rely on the fact that the zero-knowledge property holds w.r.t such one-way functions. By our construction of $\mathcal{V}^*$ and $2T/\varepsilon$-wise independence of H, it holds that

$$\Pr_{h,\mathcal{O}} \left[v \leftarrow \mathbf{View}_{\mathcal{V}^*}(\langle \mathcal{P}^{\mathcal{O}}, \mathcal{V}^{*\mathcal{O}}(r_1, \ldots, r_s, h) \rangle(x)) : v \text{ is accepting } \wedge E(v) \right]$$
$$= \Pr_{i,\mathcal{O}} \left[v \leftarrow \mathbf{View}_{\mathcal{V}}(\langle \mathcal{P}^{\mathcal{O}}, \mathcal{V}^{\mathcal{O}}(r_i) \rangle(x)) : v \text{ is accepting } \wedge E(v) \right]$$

where $i \leftarrow [s]$, $h \leftarrow H$ and $\mathcal{O} \leftarrow \widetilde{\mathbf{O}}$.
Using the zero-knowledge property again, but, with $\mathcal{V}^*$ this time we have that

$$\Pr_{r,h,\mathcal{O}} \left[v \leftarrow \widetilde{\mathcal{S}}^{\mathcal{O}, \mathcal{V}^{*\mathcal{O}}(x,r_1,\ldots,r_s,h)}(x;r) : v \text{ is accepting } \wedge E(v) \right] \geq c - 9\varepsilon$$

where $r \leftarrow \{0,1\}^T$, $h \leftarrow H$ and $\mathcal{O} \leftarrow \widetilde{\mathbf{O}}$. This means that the probability with which Arthur accepts in Step 1d is at most ε.

Overall, the probability with which Arthur accepts is at most $\varepsilon + \max\{c - 7\varepsilon, \varepsilon\} = c - 6\varepsilon$ and this concludes the proof of the lemma. □

Lemma 32. *For any $x \in \overline{\mathcal{L}} \cap \{0,1\}^n$ and sufficiently large n, there is a strategy for Merlin that makes Arthur accept with probability is at least $c - 5\varepsilon$.*

Proof: We first define Merlin's strategy. Merlin will internally maintain the state of an oracle $\mathcal{O}$ that is sampled according to **RO**. It chooses $\tilde{r} \leftarrow \{0,1\}^\ell$ uniformly at random and emulates $\mathcal{V}^{\mathcal{O}}(x; \tilde{r})$ and computes the verifier's first message α. Next, it runs the simulator with the honest verifier and tries to learn all the heavy queries made by the algorithm $\widetilde{S}^{\bullet, \mathcal{V}^\bullet(x; r')}(x; r)$ subject to the verifier's first message being α and the oracle being $\mathcal{O}$ where the learning parameter is set to $\frac{\varepsilon}{(2s^2 \cdot \ell)}$. Let $\mathcal{Q}$ be the set of the queries that Merlin learns. Let R_α be the set that contains all the pairs $(r', \mathcal{Q}')$ such that $\mathcal{V}^{\mathcal{Q} \cup \mathcal{Q}'}(x; r')$ outputs α as its first message. Then Merlin samples s elements $\{(r_i, \mathcal{Q}_i)\}_{i \in [s]}$ from R_α uniformly at random and sends $r_1, \ldots, r_s, \mathcal{Q}, \mathcal{Q}_1, \ldots, \mathcal{Q}_s$ to the Arthur.

We now proceed to analyze the probability Arthur accepts. Recall that in Step 1a, Arthur accepts if the estimate $p_1 < c - 2\varepsilon$. Let

$$\hat{p} = \Pr_{r, r', \mathcal{O}} \left[\widetilde{S}^{\mathcal{O}, \mathcal{V}^{\mathcal{O}}(x; r')}(x; r) \text{ outputs an accepting transcript} \right]$$

where $r \leftarrow \{0,1\}^T$, $r' \leftarrow \{0,1\}^\ell$, $\mathcal{O} \leftarrow$ **RO**. We consider two cases:

Case $\hat{p} < c - 3\varepsilon$: In this case, by our estimation algorithm, we have that except with probability ε, Arthur will accept at the end of Step 1a.

Case $\hat{p} \geq c - 3\varepsilon$: In this case, we consider Step 1b, where Arthur checks if there are no conflicting queries. Since Merlin honestly samples from the right distribution, we have that for each $i \in [s]$, the Verifier $\mathcal{V}$ outputs α with random tape r_i while making queries only in $\mathcal{Q} \cup \mathcal{Q}_i$ where $\mathcal{Q}$ and $\mathcal{Q}_i$ dont have any conflicting queries. Second, it follows from the properties of the learning algorithm as stated in Lemma 21 and the parameters that was set, that the probability that any query from $\mathcal{Q}_i$ occurs in $\mathcal{Q}_j$ for $j \neq i$ with probability at most $\frac{\varepsilon}{(2s^2 \cdot \ell)}$. Using a union bound we have that the probability that some two sets in $\mathcal{Q}_1, \ldots, \mathcal{Q}_s$ have conflicting queries can be bounded by $s \times (|\mathcal{Q}_i| \times s \times \frac{\varepsilon}{2s^2 \cdot \ell}) < \frac{\varepsilon}{2}$. Therefore, the probability that Arthur rejects in Step 1b is at most $\frac{\varepsilon}{2}$.

In Step 1c, Arthur emulates $\widetilde{S}^{\mathcal{O}, \mathcal{V}^{\mathcal{O}}(x; r_i)}$ for a randomly chosen i and aborts if it either does not output a transcript or the $E(v)$ holds for the view output by the simulator.

First, we observe that, from Merlin's algorithm, the following two distributions are identical:

- $\{\widetilde{S}^{\mathcal{O}, \mathcal{V}^{\mathcal{O}}(x; r_i)}(x; r)\}$ where $r_1, \ldots, r_s, \mathcal{Q}, \mathcal{Q}_1, \ldots, \mathcal{Q}_s$ are sampled according to Merlin's algorithm, $i \leftarrow [s]$, $\mathcal{O} \leftarrow \widetilde{\mathbf{O}}$, $r \leftarrow \{0,1\}^T$
- $\{\widetilde{S}^{\mathcal{O}, \mathcal{V}^{\mathcal{O}}(x; r')}(x; r)\}$ where $r \leftarrow \{0,1\}^T$, $r' \leftarrow \{0,1\}^\ell$, and $\mathcal{O} \leftarrow$ **RO**

This implies that

$$\Pr_{i, r, \mathcal{O}} \left[v \leftarrow \widetilde{S}^{\mathcal{O}, \mathcal{V}^{\mathcal{O}}(x; r_i)}(x; r) : v \text{ is accepting} \right] = \hat{p}$$

where $r_1, \ldots, r_s, \mathcal{Q}, \mathcal{Q}_1, \ldots, \mathcal{Q}_s$ are sampled according to Merlin's algorithm, $i \leftarrow [s]$, $\mathcal{O} \leftarrow \widetilde{\mathbf{O}}$, $r \leftarrow \{0,1\}^T$.

Next, we compute the probability $E(v)$ holds, namely, the probability $\widetilde{\mathcal{S}}^{\mathcal{O},\mathcal{V}^{\mathcal{O}}(x;r_i)}$ makes no query in $\mathcal{Q}_j$ for $j \neq i$. From Lemma 21, we have that each query in $\mathcal{Q}_j$ could occur in an emulation of $\widetilde{\mathcal{S}}^{\mathcal{O},\mathcal{V}^{\mathcal{O}}(x;r_i)}(x;r)$ with probability at most $\frac{\varepsilon}{(2s^2 \cdot \ell)}$. Therefore, applying a union bound, we have that the probability $E(v)$ does not hold is at most $\frac{\varepsilon}{(2s^2 \cdot \ell)} \cdot |\cup_{j\in[s]/i} \mathcal{Q}_j| < \frac{\epsilon}{2}$.

This means that the probability with which Arthur rejects in Steps 1b or 1c is at most $1 - \hat{p} + \frac{\varepsilon}{2} + \frac{\varepsilon}{2} \leq 1 - c + 3\varepsilon + \epsilon = 1 - c + 4\epsilon$.

Next, we compute the probability with which it rejects in Step 1d. Recall that, this happens if the final estimate exceeds $c - 10\varepsilon$. We will show that the real probability is at most $c - 11\varepsilon$, which means the estimate fails with probability at most ε and Arthur therefore rejects with probability at most ϵ. This means the overall probability Arthur rejects in this case is at most $1 - c + 4\varepsilon + \varepsilon = 1 - c + 5\varepsilon$. Therefore, Arthur accepts with probability at least $c - 5\varepsilon$ and concludes the proof of the Lemma.

It only remains to show that

$$\Pr\left[v \leftarrow \widetilde{\mathcal{S}}^{\mathcal{O},\mathcal{V}^{*\mathcal{O}}(x,r_1,\ldots,r_s,h)}(x;r) : v \text{ is accepting } \wedge E(v)\right] < c - 11\varepsilon \quad (1)$$

where $r_1,\ldots,r_s, \mathcal{Q}, \mathcal{Q}_1,\ldots,\mathcal{Q}_s$ is sampled according to Merlin's algorithm, $r \leftarrow \{0,1\}^T$, $h \leftarrow H$ and $\mathcal{O} \leftarrow \mathbf{O}$. In fact, we will show this is at most ε which is less than $c - 11\varepsilon$ as ε was chosen to be less than $c/20$.

First, we consider the event coll if in the simulation by $\widetilde{\mathcal{S}}$ for two different rewindings (α, β_i) and (α, β_j) it holds that $h(\beta_i) = h(\beta_j)$. Since $\widetilde{\mathcal{S}}$ makes at most s queries and H is a family of $2T/\varepsilon$-wise independent hash functions, we have

$$\Pr[\text{coll}] < \binom{2T/\varepsilon}{2} \cdot \frac{1}{s} < (2T/\varepsilon)^2/(2s) = \varepsilon/2.$$

where the last equality follows from the fact that $s = 4T^2/\varepsilon^3$. We can now upper bound the probability in Eq. 1 by

$$\Pr\left[v \leftarrow \widetilde{\mathcal{S}}^{\mathcal{O},\mathcal{V}^{*\mathcal{O}}(x,r_1,\ldots,r_s,h)}(x;r) : v \text{ is accepting } \wedge E(v)|\overline{\text{coll}}\right] + \Pr[\text{coll}]$$

Next, we will show that the probability of the first term in the above expression is at most $\varepsilon/2$. Then we can conclude the proof of completeness as it implies Eq. 1. More formally we prove the following claim.

Claim 33

$$\Pr\left[v \leftarrow \widetilde{\mathcal{S}}^{\mathcal{O},\mathcal{V}^{*\mathcal{O}}(x,r_1,\ldots,r_s,h)}(x;r) : v \text{ is accepting } \wedge E(v)|\overline{\text{coll}}\right] < \frac{\varepsilon}{2}$$

Proof: We begin by defining,

$$\Pr\left[v \leftarrow \widetilde{\mathcal{S}}^{\mathcal{O},\mathcal{V}^{*\mathcal{O}}(x,r_1,\ldots,r_s,h)}(x;r) : v \text{ is accepting } \wedge E(v)|\overline{\text{coll}}\right] = \mu$$

where the probability is over $r_1, \ldots, r_s, \mathcal{Q}, \mathcal{Q}_1, \ldots, \mathcal{Q}_s$ are sampled according to Merlin's algorithm, $r \leftarrow \{0,1\}^T$, $h \leftarrow H$ and $\mathcal{O} \leftarrow \tilde{\mathbf{O}}$.

On a high-level, we will construct a cheating unbounded prover $\mathcal{P}^*$ that makes at most polynomially many queries to the oracle and convinces an honest verifier with probability at least $\frac{\mu}{T}$ when the oracle is sampled according to **RO**. Since we have a black-box reduction from a cheating prover to inverting the oracle, we have from Lemma 22 and Lemma 23 that $\frac{\mu}{T}$ must be negligible. This means that for sufficiently large n, it will be at most $\frac{\varepsilon}{2}$ and concludes the proof of the Claim.

We now proceed to describe our malicious prover $\mathcal{P}^*$. On input x, $\mathcal{P}^*$ proceeds as follows:

1. $\mathcal{P}^*$ will internally begin an emulation of $\tilde{\mathcal{S}}$ with $\mathcal{V}^*$. Externally $\mathcal{P}^*$ interacts with the honest verifier. Both $\mathcal{P}^*$ and the external verifier are equipped with an oracle $\mathcal{O}$.

2. Upon receiving the first message α from the external verifier, $\mathcal{P}^*$ uses a **PSPACE** algorithm to learn all the heavy queries made by the algorithm $\tilde{\mathcal{S}}^{\bullet, \mathcal{V}^*(x;r')}(x;r)$ conditioned on the verifier's first message in the transcript output being α where $\mathcal{P}^*$ uses its oracle $\mathcal{O}$ to learn the responses of the heavy queries. Let $\mathcal{Q}$ be the set of queries $\mathcal{P}^*$ learns.

3. Next, using a **PSPACE** algorithm it samples $r_i, \mathcal{Q}_i$ for $i \in [s]$ from R_α similar to Merlin's algorithm. Namely, it samples t views for $\mathcal{V}$ from the distribution where it outputs α as its first message and oracle queries are consistent with $\mathcal{Q}$. Let r_i be the verifier's random tape and $\mathcal{Q}_i$ be the query-answer pairs made in this view. By construction, we have that $\mathcal{Q}$ is consistent with the oracle $\mathcal{O}$, however, $\mathcal{Q}_i$ might not be consistent with $\mathcal{O}$.

4. Next, $\mathcal{P}^*$ continues the emulation of $\tilde{\mathcal{S}}$ where it feeds α as $\mathcal{V}^*$'s first message and internally emulates a random oracle $\mathcal{O}'$ which answers according to $\mathcal{Q}_1 \cup \cdots \cup \mathcal{Q}_s$ for the queries in this set of query-answer pairs and according to $\mathcal{O}$ otherwise. $\mathcal{P}^*$ picks a random index j from $[s]$ to forward the external execution internally in the jth rewinding session. More precisely, in the internal emulation, $\mathcal{P}^*$ follows $\mathcal{V}^*$ strategy of selecting $i = h(\beta)$ and using r_i to generate the third message in all rewindings except the jth rewinding. In the jth rewinding, it sends β externally to $\mathcal{V}$ and the forwards γ received from $\mathcal{V}$ internally in that rewinding. If $\tilde{\mathcal{S}}$ concludes its simulation outputting a transcript that does not corresponds to the jth rewinding, then $\mathcal{P}^*$ halts. Otherwise, $\mathcal{P}^*$ takes the fourth message δ generated in that rewinding session and forwards externally to $\mathcal{V}$.

We will now argue that the probability with which $\mathcal{P}^*$ succeeds is at least μ/T.

1. Recall that, each of $(r_i, \mathcal{Q}_i)$ were uniformly sampled from R_α. Let r' be the external verifier's random tape and $\mathcal{Q}'$ be the set of query-answer pairs made to generate α. By construction, we have that $(r', \mathcal{Q}'/\mathcal{Q})$ is an element of R_α. This means that, unless the event coll occurs (i.e. for some two rewinding sessions i and i', we have $h(\beta_i) = h(\beta_{i'})$), the distribution of $\mathcal{V}^*$'s messages

emulated internally by P^* is identically distributed to

$$\{\widetilde{\mathcal{S}}^{\mathcal{O}',\mathcal{V}^{*\mathcal{O}'}}(x,r_1,\ldots,r_s,h)\}$$

where $r_1,\ldots,r_s,\mathcal{Q},\mathcal{Q}_1,\ldots,\mathcal{Q}_s$ sampled according to Merlin's algorithm and oracle $\mathcal{O}'$ is according to the partially-fixed random oracle fixed on $\mathcal{Q}\cup\mathcal{Q}_1\cup\cdots\cup\mathcal{Q}_s$. This means that the probability that the simulator outputs the jth rewinding session as the accepting transcript is $\frac{1}{T}$.

2. Whenever $E(v)$ occurs, it means that on the accepting transcript the honest verifier will not query any $\mathcal{Q}_i$ for $i \neq j$. This means that the only queries made by the verifier will be consistent with $\mathcal{O}$.

Therefore, we have that, $\mathcal{P}^*$ succeeds in convincing the external verifier with the probability at least μ as long as its guess for the accepting session j is correct. Therefore, the overall probability $\mathcal{P}^*$ succeeds is at least $\frac{\mu}{T}$.   □

Acknowledgements. The first author is supported by the BIU Center for Research in Applied Cryptography and Cyber Security in conjunction with the Israel National Cyber Bureau in the Prime Minister's Office, and by ISF grant 1316/18. The second author is supported in part by NSF Award SATC-1704788, NSF Award RI-1703846, and AFOSR Award FA9550-18-1-0267, and in part by the Office of the Director of National Intelligence (ODNI), Intelligence Advanced Research Projects Activity (IARPA), via 2019-19-020700006. The views and conclusions contained herein are those of the authors and should not be interpreted as necessarily representing the official policies, either expressed or implied, of ODNI, IARPA, or the U.S. Government. The U.S. Government is authorized to reproduce and distribute reprints for governmental purposes notwithstanding any copyright annotation therein. The third author is supported by Google Faculty Research Grant and NSF Award CNS-1618884. The views expressed are those of the authors and do not reflect the official policy or position of Google, the Department of Defense, the National Science Foundation, or the U.S. Government.

References

1. Babai, L., Moran, S.: Arthur-Merlin games: a randomized proof system, and a hierarchy of complexity classes. J. Comput. Syst. Sci. **36**(2), 254–276 (1988)
2. Barak, B., Mahmoody-Ghidary, M.: Lower bounds on signatures from symmetric primitives. In: FOCS, pp. 680–688 (2007)
3. Bellare, M., Jakobsson, M., Yung, M.: Round-optimal zero-knowledge arguments based on any one-way function. In: Fumy, W. (ed.) EUROCRYPT 1997. LNCS, vol. 1233, pp. 280–305. Springer, Heidelberg (1997). https://doi.org/10.1007/3-540-69053-0_20
4. Bellare, M., Rogaway, P.: Random oracles are practical: a paradigm for designing efficient protocols. In: CCS, pp. 62–73 (1993)
5. Bitansky, N., Kalai, Y.T., Paneth, O.: Multi-collision resistance: a paradigm for keyless hash functions. In: STOC (2018)
6. Feige, U., Shamir, A.: Zero knowledge proofs of knowledge in two rounds. In: Brassard, G. (ed.) CRYPTO 1989. LNCS, vol. 435, pp. 526–544. Springer, New York (1990). https://doi.org/10.1007/0-387-34805-0_46

7. Fleischhacker, N., Goyal, V., Jain, A.: On the existence of three round zero-knowledge proofs. In: Nielsen, J.B., Rijmen, V. (eds.) EUROCRYPT 2018. LNCS, vol. 10822, pp. 3–33. Springer, Cham (2018). https://doi.org/10.1007/978-3-319-78372-7_1
8. Goldreich, O., Krawczyk, H.: On the composition of zero-knowledge proof systems. SIAM J. Comput. **25**(1), 169–192 (1996)
9. Goldreich, O., Micali, S., Wigderson, A.: Proofs that yield nothing but their validity for all languages in NP have zero-knowledge proof systems. J. ACM **38**(3), 691–729 (1991)
10. Goldreich, O., Oren, Y.: Definitions and properties of zero-knowledge proof systems. J. Cryptol. **7**(1), 1–32 (1994). https://doi.org/10.1007/BF00195207
11. Goldwasser, S., Micali, S., Rackoff, C.: The knowledge complexity of interactive proof systems. SIAM J. Comput. **18**(1), 186–208 (1989)
12. Håstad, J., Impagliazzo, R., Levin, L.A., Luby, M.: A pseudorandom generator from any one-way function. SIAM J. Comput. **28**(4), 1364–1396 (1999)
13. Hazay, C., Venkitasubramaniam, M.: Round-optimal fully black-box zero-knowledge arguments from one-way permutations. In: Beimel, A., Dziembowski, S. (eds.) TCC 2018. LNCS, vol. 11239, pp. 263–285. Springer, Cham (2018). https://doi.org/10.1007/978-3-030-03807-6_10
14. Impagliazzo, R., Rudich, S.: Limits on the provable consequences of one-way permutations. In: STOC, pp. 44–61 (1989)
15. Ishai, Y., Mahmoody, M., Sahai, A.: On efficient zero-knowledge PCPs. In: Cramer, R. (ed.) TCC 2012. LNCS, vol. 7194, pp. 151–168. Springer, Heidelberg (2012). https://doi.org/10.1007/978-3-642-28914-9_9
16. Katz, J.: Which languages have 4-round zero-knowledge proofs? J. Cryptol. **25**(1), 41–56 (2012). https://doi.org/10.1007/s00145-010-9081-y
17. Khurana, D., Ostrovsky, R., Srinivasan, A.: Round optimal black-box "commit-and-prove". In: Beimel, A., Dziembowski, S. (eds.) TCC 2018. LNCS, vol. 11239, pp. 286–313. Springer, Cham (2018). https://doi.org/10.1007/978-3-030-03807-6_11
18. Mahmoody, M., Pass, R.: The curious case of non-interactive commitments – on the power of black-box vs. non-black-box use of primitives. In: Safavi-Naini, R., Canetti, R. (eds.) CRYPTO 2012. LNCS, vol. 7417, pp. 701–718. Springer, Heidelberg (2012). https://doi.org/10.1007/978-3-642-32009-5_41
19. Naor, M.: Bit commitment using pseudorandomness. J. Cryptol. **4**(2), 151–158 (1991). https://doi.org/10.1007/BF00196774
20. Ostrovsky, R., Richelson, S., Scafuro, A.: Round-optimal black-box two-party computation. In: Gennaro, R., Robshaw, M. (eds.) CRYPTO 2015. LNCS, vol. 9216, pp. 339–358. Springer, Heidelberg (2015). https://doi.org/10.1007/978-3-662-48000-7_17
21. Pass, R., Wee, H.: Black-box constructions of two-party protocols from one-way functions. In: Reingold, O. (ed.) TCC 2009. LNCS, vol. 5444, pp. 403–418. Springer, Heidelberg (2009). https://doi.org/10.1007/978-3-642-00457-5_24
22. Reingold, O., Trevisan, L., Vadhan, S.: Notions of reducibility between cryptographic primitives. In: Naor, M. (ed.) TCC 2004. LNCS, vol. 2951, pp. 1–20. Springer, Heidelberg (2004). https://doi.org/10.1007/978-3-540-24638-1_1

Statistical ZAPR Arguments
from Bilinear Maps

Alex Lombardi[1]($\boxtimes$), Vinod Vaikuntanathan[1]($\boxtimes$), and Daniel Wichs[2,3]

[1] MIT, Cambridge, MA, USA
{alexjl,vinodv}@mit.edu
[2] Northeastern University, Boston, MA, USA
wichs@ccs.neu.edu
[3] NTT Research Inc., Palo Alto, CA, USA

Abstract. Dwork and Naor (FOCS '00) defined ZAPs as 2-message witness-indistinguishable proofs that are public-coin. We relax this to *ZAPs with private randomness* (ZAPRs), where the verifier can use private coins to sample the first message (independently of the statement being proved), but the proof must remain publicly verifiable given only the protocol transcript. In particular, ZAPRs are *reusable*, meaning that the first message can be reused for multiple proofs without compromising security.

Known constructions of ZAPs from trapdoor permutations or bilinear maps are only computationally WI (and statistically sound). Two recent results of Badrinarayanan-Fernando-Jain-Khurana-Sahai and Goyal-Jain-Jin-Malavolta [EUROCRYPT '20] construct the first *statistical ZAP arguments*, which are statistically WI (and computationally sound), from the quasi-polynomial LWE assumption. Here, we construct *statistical ZAPR arguments* from the quasi-polynomial decision-linear (DLIN) assumption on groups with a bilinear map. Our construction relies on a combination of several tools, including the Groth-Ostrovsky-Sahai NIZK and NIWI [EUROCRYPT '06, CRYPTO '06, JACM '12], "sometimes-binding statistically hiding commitments" [Kalai-Khurana-Sahai, EUROCRYPT '18] and the "MPC-in-the-head" technique [Ishai-Kushilevitz-Ostrovsky-Sahai, STOC '07].

A. Lombardi—Research supported in part by an NDSEG fellowship. Research supported in part by NSF Grants CNS-1350619 and CNS-1414119, and by the Defense Advanced Research Projects Agency (DARPA) and the U.S. Army Research Office under contracts W911NF-15-C-0226 and W911NF-15-C-0236.

V. Vaikuntanathan—Research was supported in part by NSF Grants CNS-1350619 and CNS-1414119, an NSF-BSF grant CNS-1718161, the Defense Advanced Research Projects Agency (DARPA) and the U.S. Army Research Office under contracts W911NF-15-C-0226 and W911NF-15-C-0236, an IBM-MIT grant and a Microsoft Trustworthy and Robust AI grant.

D. Wichs—Research supported by NSF grants CNS-1314722, CNS-1413964, CNS-1750795 and the Alfred P. Sloan Research Fellowship.

A. Canteaut and Y. Ishai (Eds.): EUROCRYPT 2020, LNCS 12107, pp. 620–641, 2020.
https://doi.org/10.1007/978-3-030-45727-3_21

1   Introduction

Zero-Knowledge and Witness-Indistinguishability. Zero-knowledge (ZK) proofs, introduced in the ground-breaking paper of Goldwasser, Micali, and Rackoff [GMR85], have found countless uses in cryptography. Unfortunately, such protocols are known to require at least 3 rounds of interaction [GO94] in the plain model without additional setup, which is the model that we consider throughout this work. Witness indistinguishable (WI) proofs [FS90] are a natural relaxation of zero-knowledge, which has turned out to be extremely useful. A WI proof generated using any witnesses w for an NP statement x is indistinguishable from a proof generated with any other possible witness w' for x. Unlike in the case of ZK, there are no lower bounds on the round complexity of WI proofs.

ZAPs and Non-Interactive WI (NIWI). The work of Dwork and Naor [DN00, DN07] constructed two-message public-coin WI proofs, which they called *ZAPs*. By now, we have constructions of ZAPs under any of: trapdoor permutations (factoring) [FLS99, DN00]; the decision-linear assumption (DLIN) in bilinear maps [GOS06a]; indistinguishability obfuscation [BP15]; or learning with errors [BFJ+20, GJJM20, LVW19]. In fact, we can even get completely noninteractive WI proofs (NIWI) assuming either trapdoor permutations and a mild complexity-theoretic derandomization assumption [BOV03] or the bilinear DLIN assumption [GOS06a].

ZAPs and ZAPRs. The original definition of ZAPs from [DN00, DN07] required that they are public coin, meaning that the first message from the verifier to the prover consists of uniform randomness. The main advantage of such protocols is that they are *publicly verifiable*, meaning that anybody can decide whether the proof is accepting or rejecting by only looking at the protocol transcript. Moreover, in such publicly verifiable protocols, the first message is inherently *reusable* for multiple different proofs of different statements, and security holds even if the cheating prover learns whether the verifier accepts or rejects various proofs with the same first message (since this decision only depends on the public transcript). This is in contrast to *secret-coin* two-message WI proofs, which may be insecure under such reuse.

In this work, we introduce an intermediate notion that we call *ZAPs with private randomness* (ZAPRs). ZAPRs allow the verifier to use secret coins to generate the first message, but we still require the proofs to be *publicly verifiable*, and we require that the first message is sampled independently of the statement being proved. Therefore, ZAPRs have essentially the same advantages as ZAPs, and the two can be used interchangeably in most applications.[1]

Statistical WI. Most prior constructions of ZAPs (and 2-message WI protocols in general) only achieve computational WI security, often with statistical soundness [DN00, GOS06a, BP15]. However, it is arguably more important for WI security

---

[1] One notable exception where the "public coin" nature of ZAPs is used essentially is for *derandomization* of the verifier message [BOV03]; however, this seems to require ZAPs satisfying statistical soundness, while we focus on computationally sound, statistically WI protocols in this work.

tu hold statistically than it is for soundness. In particular, we want privacy to be preserved long into the future after the protocols have finished executing, despite the potential that computational assumptions may become broken in the long term. On the other hand, soundness is only relevant during the protocol execution itself and, even if the underlying assumptions are broken after the protocol finished executing, it is too late for the adversary to take advantage of this.

Interestingly, 2-message statistically WI protocols were unknown until recently. The first progress on this problem was only made by Kalai, Khurana and Sahai [KKS18], who constructed a *secret-coin* 2-message statistical WI protocol under standard quasi-polynomial assumptions (DDH or QR or Nth residuosity). Unfortunately, their protocol is not publicly verifiable and the first message is not reusable (a simple attack breaks soundness under such reuse). Even more recently, Badrinarayanan et al. [BFJ+20] along with Goyal et al. [GJJM20][2] constructed the first statistical ZAP arguments under the quasi-polynomial LWE assumption. These last two results rely on recent constructions of NIZKs from LWE [CLW18, CCH+19, PS19] via *correlation-intractable hash functions*, which in turn rely on fully homomorphic encryption/commitments from LWE. This left open the question of whether we can achieve such statistical ZAP or ZAPR arguments under other assumptions, without relying on LWE or "fully homomorphic cryptography".

Our Results. In this work, we construct statistical ZAPR arguments from the quasi-polynomial decision-linear (DLIN) assumption in groups with a bilinear map. More generally, we construct ZAPR arguments using three generic ingredients:

- *Non-interactive statistical ZK (NISZK) arguments in the common-reference string (CRS) model.* We need the scheme to have the additional property that every *valid* CRS in the support of the setup algorithm ensures that the resulting arguments are statistically WI. This is guaranteed, for example, if the NISZK argument system satisfies perfect zero knowledge, as in [GOS06b, GOS12]. One can think of this property as ensuring WI security even if the CRS is chosen "semi-maliciously" using adversarial randomness *but still from the support of the setup algorithm.*
- *Non-interactive WI proofs (NIWI) in the plain model,* where the WI property is computational and soundness is statistical. As mentioned above, we know how to construct such NIWI proofs assuming either trapdoor permutations and a mild complexity-theoretic derandomization assumption [BOV03] or the bilinear DLIN assumption [GOS06a].
- *Sometimes binding, statistically hiding (SBSH) commitments.* This is a relaxation of a notion introduced recently by [KKS18].[3] It is a 2-round commitment protocol where the receiver chooses a random α in the first round, and the

---

[2] The conference paper [GJJM20] subsumes the construction of statistical ZAP arguments in a preprint of Jain and Jin [JJ19].

[3] The main difference is that their commitment needed to be "sometimes extractable" whereas ours only needs to be "sometimes statistically binding".

sender sends a random β and uses $\mathsf{ck} = (\alpha, \beta)$ as a commitment key to create a commitment $\mathsf{Com}(\mathsf{ck}, m)$ to his message m in the second round. Even if the receiver chooses α maliciously, the commitment key ck is statistically hiding with overwhelming probability over a random choice of β. However, there is some inverse quasi-polynomial probability ϵ such that, even if the sender chooses β maliciously after seeing α, the commitment key $\mathsf{ck} = (\alpha, \beta)$ makes the commitment statistically binding. Furthermore, the sender cannot tell whether this rare event occurs or not.

The first two primitives can be constructed under the bilinear DLIN assumption using the techniques of [GOS06a]. (We will require that the primitives satisfy quasi-polynomial security and therefore need to rely on quasi-polynomial DLIN.) The last primitive can be constructed under a variety of quasi-polynomial assumptions such as DDH or QR or N'th residuosity [KKS18], and we show it can also be done under quasi-polynomial DLIN.

Our construction broadens the set of assumptions from which we can build statistical ZAPR arguments (previously only quasi-polynomial LWE was known) and gives an alternate approach for achieving them without relying on correlation intractability.

What About Adaptive Soundness? We show that our statistical ZAPR arguments, under the quasi-polynomial bilinear DLIN assumption, satisfy *non-adaptive soundness*: for any false statement x, a (quasi-poly time) cheating prover P^* cannot find proof π^* for x that the verifier would accept. One could potentially ask for the stronger security notion of *adaptive soundness*: informally, a protocol is adaptively sound if a cheating prover P^* cannot find *any false statement* $x^* \notin L$ along with an accepting proof π^* for x^*.

As is standard for adaptive security notions, if we strengthen our assumption to the *subexponential* security of bilinear DLIN, we can make use of complexity leveraging [BB04] and obtain a statistical ZAPR argument that is adaptively sound for statements of a priori bounded length. More formally, for every length $\ell(\lambda)$, there is a statistical ZAPR argument $\Pi^{(\ell)}$ that is adaptively sound for statements of length $\ell(\lambda)$.

One would ideally hope for a protocol satisfying adaptive soundness for unbounded (poly-length) statements. However, there is some evidence that such a protocol would be difficult to obtain. In particular, in the context of *NISZK arguments*, a result of Pass [Pas16] shows that there is no black-box reduction from the adaptive soundness of a NISZK protocol to a "falsifiable assumption" [Nao03]. There is additionally no known non-black-box construction overcoming this impossibility result (without relying on non-falsifiable assumptions, as in [AF07]).

Given the similarity between NISZK arguments and statistical ZAPR arguments (if anything, the latter seem harder to achieve), we consider this to be a barrier to constructing adaptively sound statistical ZAPR arguments. However, no formal impossibility result is known; indeed, we do not even know how to rule out the existence of *statistical ZAP proofs* (ZAPs satisfying both statistical soundness and statistical WI) for all of NP.

1.1   Technical Overview

We now describe our construction using the above primitives. We start with a very simple construction, which already gives a 2-message (publicly verifiable) statistical WI protocol for NP ∩ coNP and conveys some of the intuition.

Interestingly, our warm-up protocol relies on only the *polynomial hardness* of bilinear DLIN (rather than quasi-polynomial hardness), yielding a 2-message statistical WI protocol for a broad class of languages without relying on super-polynomial assumptions.

We then describe our more complex construction, which works for all of NP.

Warm-Up: A Simple Protocol for NP ∩ coNP. As a warm up, we describe a very simple 2-message statistical WI argument for languages $L \in$ NP ∩ coNP. In this warm-up construction, the first message depends on the statement x being proved, but we remove this in the full construction. The construction makes use of NISZK arguments and NIWI as above (but does not require SBSH commitments). The main ideas behind the construction are that:

1. The prover uses the [GOS12] NISZK argument system to prove that $x \in L$, where we let the verifier chooses the CRS. This already provides "semi-malicious" WI security. To get full WI, we need to ensure that the CRS is valid (in the support of the setup algorithm).
2. The verifier uses a NIWI to prove that the CRS is valid. The challenge is to only rely on WI security rather than full ZK. To do so, we let the verifier prove that either the CRS is valid or $x \notin L$.

In more detail, the protocol proceeds as follows.

Verifier → Prover: The verifier samples a CRS of a NISZK argument. He then uses a NIWI to prove that either the CRS is valid (i.e., in the support of the setup algorithm, using the random coins of the setup algorithm as a witness) or $x \notin L$. The first message consists of the CRS along with the NIWI proof.

Prover → Verifier: The prover verifies the NIWI proof (aborting if it does not accept) and then uses the NISZK argument with the received CRS to prove that $x \in L$.

For $x \in L$, the statistical WI security of the ZAPR follows from the statistical soundness of the NIWI, which ensures that the CRS is valid, together with the statistical WI of the NISZK, which holds for all valid CRS.

For $x \notin L$, the computational soundness of the ZAPR follows by first relying on the computational WI security of the NIWI to argue that the prover cannot notice if we modify the NIWI proof to use the witness for $x \notin L$ instead of the randomness of the setup algorithm. With this change, we can then rely on the computational soundness of the NISZK argument to argue that the prover cannot produced a valid NISZK proof for $x \in L$.

The Full Construction. The full construction is more involved. In addition to the three primitives mentioned previously (NISZK, NIWI, and SBSH commitments), we also rely on an additional information-theoretic tool that we now describe.

Locally-ZK Proofs (LZK) via "MPC in the Head". We introduce a new tool called *locally ZK proofs* (LZK). An LZK proof consists of a probabilistic encoding that maps a witness w for a statement x into a proof string $\pi \in \Sigma^\ell$ for some alphabet Σ. There is also a polynomial size set $\{S_1, \ldots, S_Q\}$ of "queries" $S_i \subseteq [\ell]$ and a verification algorithm $\mathsf{Verify}(x, i, \pi[S_i])$ that locally verifies that π is consistent on the positions S_i. The proof satisfies two statistical security properties:

- Global Soundness: If there exists some proof $\pi \in \Sigma^\ell$ such that $\mathsf{Verify}(x, i, \pi[S_i]) = 1$ for all $i \in [Q]$ then $x \in L$.
- t-Local-ZK: For any t queries $S_{a_1}, \ldots, S_{a_t}$ the values $\pi[S_{a_1}], \ldots, \pi[S_{a_t}]$ can be simulated without knowing the witness.

We can think of LZK proofs as a relaxation of ZK-PCPs [KPT97] where the verifier needs to make *all* the queries to be convinced of soundness but ZK holds locally. We construct such LZK proofs for any Q and $t < Q/2$ using the "MPC in the head" technique [IKOS07]. In particular, to construct the proof π, the encoding algorithm runs a (semi-honest information-theoretic) MPC protocol with Q parties and security against t corruptions. Each party has as input a secret share (in an additive secret sharing) of the witness w and the MPC outputs 1 to each party iff the shares add up to a valid witness for x. The proof π is of length $\ell = Q + Q(Q-1)/2$ and contains the view of each party $i \in [Q]$ in the protocol, as well as the contents of the $Q(Q-1)/2$ communication channels between each pair of parties $\{i, j\}$. Each query set S_i contains locations that correspond to the view of party i and all of the communication channels that involve party i. The verification algorithm for i checks that the view of the party i and the communication channels involving party i correspond to an honest execution of the protocol and that the output of the protocol is 1. It is easy to check that this satisfies global soundness and t-local ZK.

ZAPR Construction. We now describe our ZAPR construction using NIWIs, NISZKs, sometimes binding statistically hiding commitments, and LZK proofs. To rely on quasi-polynomial assumptions, we choose the parameter Q of the LZK proof to be $\mathrm{poly}(\log \lambda)$.

Verifier $\rightarrow$ Prover: The verifier samples $3Q$ CRS's of the NISZK. We interpret this as Q bundles of 3 CRS's each. The verifier then gives a NIWI proof that, in each bundle, at least 2 out of 3 of the CRS's are valid. He does so by choosing a random 2 of the 3 CRS's in each bundle and using the corresponding randomness of the setup algorithm for them as the witness. Lastly, the verifier also sends the first message α of the SBSH commitment scheme.

Prover → Verifier: The prover verifier the NIWI proofs and aborts if any of them do not accept. The prover then samples an LZK proof $\pi \in \Sigma^\ell$ for the statement $x \in L$. It samples the SBSH commitment component β and uses the commitment key $\mathsf{ck} = (\alpha, \beta)$ to commit to each of the ℓ blocks of π separately. Lastly, it chooses a random CRS in each bundle $i \in [Q]$ and uses it to give an NISZK argument showing that the LZK verifier outputs $\mathsf{Verify}(x, i, \pi[S_i]) = 1$, where $\pi[S_i]$ is contained in the committed values. It sends back β, all the commitments, and the NISZK arguments.

We first argue that the above construction is statistically WI. By the statistical hiding of the commitment scheme, the commitments do not reveal anything about the committed values. By the statistical soundness of the NIWI, we know that at least 2 of the 3 CRS's in each bundle are valid. Since the prover chooses a random CRS in each bundle, on expectation at least $2Q/3$ of the chosen CRS's are valid and, by Chernoff, at least $Q/2$ of them are valid with overwhelmingly probability. The NISZK arguments for the valid CRS's are statistically WI and hence do not reveal any information about the committed values. The remaining $t < Q/2$ NISZK arguments may reveal some information about the committed values $\pi[S_i]$. But, by the locally-ZK property of the proof π, this does not reveal anything about w.

Next, we argue that the construction is computationally sound. Assume that the adversarial prover succeeds in proving a false statement with non-negligible probability δ. The commitment scheme ensures that there is a ϵ probability that $\mathsf{ck} = (\alpha, \beta)$ is binding and, because the prover cannot tell whether this occurred or not, the probability that (1) *the commitment is binding* and (2) *the prover succeeds in proving a false statement* is $\epsilon \cdot \delta$, which is inverse quasi-polynomial. Next, we rely on the (quasi-polynomial) computational WI security of the NIWI argument to argue that the prover cannot learn which 2 of the 3 CRS's in each bundle had their setup randomness used as a witness in the NIWI. Therefore, even if we condition on (1) and (2), there is an inverse quasi-polynomial $(1/3)^Q$ chance that (3) *in each bundle, the prover chooses the one CRS whose setup randomness was not used in the NIWI.* Altogether there is an inverse quasi-poly probability of (1), (2) and (3) occurring simultaneously. But if this happens, then (as guaranteed by the global soundness of the LZK proof) at least one of the statements proved via the NISZK is false and therefore the prover breaks the (quasi-polynomial) soundness of the NISZK arguments.

In our presentation, we assume quasi-polynomial hardness of the underlying primitives, but only ensure that the statistical WI holds with a quasi-polynomial error. We could analogously assume sub-exponential hardness and ensure that statistical WI holds with a sub-exponentially small error.

1.2 Organization

The rest of the paper is organized as follows. In Sect. 2, we describe basic preliminaries on witness indistinguishability and ZAPRs. In Sect. 3, we introduce and discuss some of the main tools used in our construction: NISZK arguments, locally zero knowledge proofs, and sometimes-binding statistically hiding commitments. Finally, in Sect. 4, we present our construction of statistical ZAPR arguments from these building blocks.

2 Preliminaries

We say that a function $\mu(\lambda)$ is *negligible* if $\mu(\lambda) = O(\lambda^{-c})$ for every constant c, and that two distribution ensembles $X = \{X_\lambda\}$ and $Y = \{Y_\lambda\}$ are computationally indistinguishable ($X \approx_c Y$) if for all polynomial-sized circuit ensembles $\{\mathcal{A}_\lambda\}$,

$$\left| \Pr\left[\mathcal{A}_\lambda(X_\lambda) = 1\right] - \Pr\left[\mathcal{A}_\lambda(Y_\lambda) = 1\right] \right| = \mathrm{negl}(\lambda).$$

More generally, for any function $\delta(\lambda)$, we say that X and Y are δ-computationally indistinguishable ($X \approx_{c,\delta} Y$) if for all polynomial-sized circuit ensembles $\{\mathcal{A}_\lambda\}$,

$$\left| \Pr\left[\mathcal{A}_\lambda(X_\lambda) = 1\right] - \Pr\left[\mathcal{A}_\lambda(Y_\lambda) = 1\right] \right| = O(\delta(\lambda)).$$

2.1 Witness Indistinguishable Arguments

Definition 1. *A* witness indistinguishable arugment system Π *for an* NP *relation R consists of ppt interactive algorithms (P, V) with the following syntax.*

- $P(x, w)$ *is an interactive algorithm that takes as input an instance x and witness w that $(x, w) \in R$.*
- $V(x)$ *is an interactive algorithm that takes as input an instance x. At the end of an interaction, it outputs a bit b. If $b = 1$, we say that V* accepts, *and otherwise we say that V* rejects.

The proof system Π must satisfy the following requirements for every polynomial function $n = n(\lambda)$. Recall that $\mathcal{L}(R)$ denotes the language $\{x : \exists w \text{ s.t. } (x, w) \in R\}$ and R_n denotes the set $R \cap (\{0,1\}^n \times \{0,1\}^*)$.

- **Completeness.** *For every $(x, w) \in R$, it holds with probability 1 that V accepts at the end of an interaction $\langle P(x, w), V(x) \rangle$.*
- **Soundness.** *For every $\{x_{n(\lambda)} \in \{0,1\}^{n(\lambda)} \backslash \mathcal{L}(R)\}_\lambda$ and every polynomial size $P^* = \{P_\lambda^*\}$, there is a negligible function ν such that V accepts with probability $\nu(\lambda)$ at the end of an interaction $\langle P^*(x), V(x) \rangle$.*
- **Witness Indistinguishability.** *For every ppt (malicious) verifier V^* and every ensemble $\left\{ (x_n, (w_{0,n}, w_{1,n}), z_n) : (x_n, w_{0,n}), (x_n, w_{1,n}) \in R_n \right\}_\lambda$, the distribution ensembles*

$$\mathsf{view}_{V^*} \langle P(x, w_0), V^*(x, w_0, w_1, z) \rangle$$

and

$$\mathsf{view}_{V^*} \langle P(x, w_1), V^*(x, w_0, w_1, z) \rangle$$

are computationally indistinguishable.

In the work, we focus on obtaining two message WI arguments for NP. A (two message) WI argument system can also satisfy various stronger properties. We describe the variants relevant to this work below.

- **Public Verification:** A WI argument system is publicly verifiable if the verifier's accept/reject algorithm is an efficiently computable function of the transcript (independent of the verifier's internal state).
- **Delayed Input:** A *two-message* WI argument system is *delayed input* if the (honestly sampled) verifier message $\alpha \leftarrow V(1^\lambda, x) = V(1^\lambda, 1^n)$ depends only on the length $n = |x|$.
- **Statistical Soundness.** For every $\{x_n \in \{0,1\}^n \backslash \mathcal{L}(R)\}$ and every (*unbounded*) $P^* = \{P_\lambda^*\}$, there is a negligible function ν such that V accepts with probability $\nu(\lambda)$ at the end of an interaction $\langle P^*(x), V(x) \rangle$.
- **Statistical Witness Indistinguishability.** For every polynomial function $n(\lambda)$, every (*unbounded*) (malicious) verifier V^*, and every ensemble $\left\{ (x_n, (w_{0,n}, w_{1,n}), z_n) : (x_n, w_{0,n}), (x_n, w_{1,n}) \in R_n \right\}_\lambda$, the distribution ensembles

$$\text{view}_{V^*} \langle P(x, w_0), V^*(x, w_0, w_1, z) \rangle$$

and

$$\text{view}_{V^*} \langle P(x, w_1), V^*(x, w_0, w_1, z) \rangle$$

are *statistically* indistinguishable.

Our goal is to construct a 2-message argument system that is publicly verifiable, delayed input, and satisfies statistical witness indistinguishability. We call such protocols *statistical ZAPR arguments*.

Definition 2 (Statistical ZAPR Arguments). *A 2-message argument system* (P, V) *is a* statistical ZAPR argument system *if it is a delayed-input, publicly verifiable protocol satisfying statistical witness indistinguishability.*

As a tool towards our construction, we make use of another variant of WI arguments: non-interactive witness indistinguishable proofs (NIWIs).

Definition 3 (NIWI Proofs). *A one-message proof system is a* non-interactive witness indistinguishable *proof system if it satisfies statistical soundness and (computational) witness indistinguishability.*

By [GOS06a], we know that NIWIs exist based on the decision linear assumption on groups with bilinear maps.

Lemma 1 ([GOS06a]). *Under the DLIN assumption, there exists a NIWI proof system for* NP.

3   Tools for the Main Construction

3.1   Non-Interactive Statistical Zero Knowledge Arguments

We make use of non-interactive statistical zero knowledge arguments in the *common reference string model*, as constructed by [GOS06b] under the DLIN assumption on bilinear groups. Moreover, we make use of the fact that the GOS protocol satisfies *statistical witness indistinguishability* in the presence of semi-malicious setup, which we describe below.

Definition 4. *A non-interactive statistical zero knowledge* (NISZK) *argument system* Π *for an* NP *relation* R *consists of three ppt algorithms* (Setup, P, V) *with the following syntax.*

- Setup$(1^n, 1^\lambda)$ *takes as input a statement length* n *and a security parameter* λ. *It outputs a common reference string* crs.
- $P(\text{crs}, x, w)$ *takes as input the common reference string, as well as* x *and* w *such that* $(x, w) \in R$. *It outputs a proof* π.
- $V(\text{crs}, x, \pi)$ *takes as input the common reference string, a statement* x, *and a proof* π. *It outputs a bit* b. *If* $b = 1$, *we say that* V accepts, *and otherwise we say that* V rejects.

The proof system Π *must satisfy the following requirements for every polynomial function* $n = n(\lambda)$.

- **Completeness.** *For every* $(x, w) \in R$, *it holds with probability* 1 *that* $V(\text{crs}, x, \pi) = 1$ *in the probability space defined by sampling* crs $\leftarrow$ Setup$(1^{|x|}, 1^\lambda)$ *and* $\pi \leftarrow P(\text{crs}, x, w)$,
- **(Non-adaptive) Soundness.** *For every* $\{x_n \in \{0,1\}^n \backslash \mathcal{L}(R)\}$ *and every polynomial size* $P^* = \{P_\lambda^*\}$, *there is a negligible function* ν *such that*

$$\Pr_{\substack{\text{crs} \leftarrow \text{Setup}(1^n, 1^\lambda) \\ \pi \leftarrow P_\lambda^*(\text{crs})}} \left[V(\text{crs}, x_n, \pi) = 1 \right] \leq \nu(\lambda).$$

- **Statistical Zero Knowledge.** *There is a ppt simulator* Sim *such that for every ensemble* $\{(x_n, w_n) \in R_n\}$, *the distribution ensembles*

$$\left\{ \left(\text{crs}_{\lambda, n}, P(\text{crs}_{\lambda, n}, x_n, w_n) \right) \right\}_\lambda$$

and

$$\left\{ \text{Sim}(x_n, 1^\lambda) \right\}_\lambda$$

are statistically indistinguishable in the probability space defined by sampling crs$_{\lambda, n} \leftarrow$ Setup$(1^n, 1^\lambda)$ *(and evaluating* P *and* Sim *with independent and uniform randomness).*

In this work, we consider a strengthening of statistical zero knowledge[4] to a setting where the CRS is chosen in a semi-malicious way.

---

[4] Technically, it is only a strengthening of witness indistinguishability.

Definition 5 (Semi-Malicious Statistical Witness Indistinguishability).
We say that a NISZK argument system (Setup, P, V) *is statistically witness indistinguishable in the presence of semi-malicious setup if for every polynomial function* $n(\lambda)$ *and every ensemble* $\Big\{ (\mathsf{crs}_{\lambda,n}, x_n, (w_{0,n}, w_{1,n}), z_n) \ :$
$\mathsf{crs}_{\lambda,n} \in \mathsf{Supp}(\mathsf{Setup}(1^\lambda, 1^n))$ *and* $(x_n, w_{0,n}), (x_n, w_{1,n}) \in R_n \Big\}_\lambda$, *the distribution ensembles*

$$\Big\{ \big(\mathsf{crs}_{\lambda,n}, P(\mathsf{crs}_n, x_n, w_{0,n})\big), z_n \Big\}_\lambda$$

and

$$\Big\{ \big(\mathsf{crs}_{\lambda,n}, P(\mathsf{crs}_n, x_n, w_{1,n})\big), z_n \Big\}_\lambda$$

are statistically indistinguishable.

In other words, witness indistinguishability is guaranteed for *any* CRS that can be output by the $\mathsf{Setup}(1^\lambda, 1^n)$ algorithm. Moreover, we have the following:

Remark 1. Any NISZK argument system satisfying perfect zero knowledge (or perfect WI) satisfies semi-malicious statistical (and even perfect) WI.

Therefore, we obtain the following conclusion from [GOS12]:

Lemma 2. *Under the DLIN assumption on groups with a bilinear map, there exists an NISZK argument system for* NP *satisfying semi-malicious statistical WI.*

3.2   Locally Zero Knowledge Proofs

In this section, we define "locally zero knowledge proofs", which one can think of as a weak kind of zero-knowledge PCP [KPT97] that captures the "MPC in the head" paradigm [IKOS07].

Definition 6 (*t*-Local Zero Knowledge Proof). *For an* NP *language L (with witness relation R), a t-local zero-knowledge proof* lzkp = (Prove, Verify) *is a pair of PPT algorithms with the following syntax.*

- Prove(x, w) *takes as input a statement* $x \in L$ *and witness* $w \in R_x$; *it outputs a proof* $\pi = (\pi_1, \ldots, \pi_\ell) \in \Sigma^\ell$ *for some alphabet* Σ.
- Queries $= \{S_1, \ldots, S_Q\} \subset \{0,1\}^{[\ell]}$ *is a set of "allowable queries"; we require that it is possible to enumerate* Queries *in time* $\mathrm{poly}(n, Q)$.
- Verify(x, i, π_{S_i}) *takes as input a statement* x, *index* i *(describing some set* $S_i \in$ Queries*), and string* $\pi_{S_i} \in \Sigma^{|S_i|}$; *it outputs a bit* $b \in \{0,1\}$.

We say that lzkp *has* $Q = |$Queries$|$ *possible queries and* block length Σ. *Moreover, we require that the following properties hold.*

- ***Completeness:*** *for any valid pair* (x, w) *and any index* $i \in [Q]$, *we have that* Verify$(x, i, \pi_{S_i}) = 1$ *with probability 1 over the randomness of* $\pi \leftarrow$ Prove(x, w).

- **Soundness:** *for any* $x \notin L$ *and any proof* π*, there exists some index* $i \in Q$ *such that* $\mathsf{Verify}(x, i, \pi_{S_i}) = 0$.
- **Perfect Zero Knowledge for** t **Queries:** *there exists a PPT simulator* $\mathsf{Sim}(x, i_1, \ldots, i_t) \to \tilde{\pi}_{S^*}$ *such that for every valid pair* (x, w) *and every collection of* t *indices* $i_1, \ldots, i_t \in [Q]$*, the distribution on* $\tilde{\pi}_{S^*}$ *is identical to the marginal distribution of an honestly generated proof* π *on the subset* $S^* = S_{i_1} \cup \ldots \cup S_{i_t}$.

Lemma 3. *For any* $t > 0$*, there exists a* t*-local zero knowledge proof for Circuit-SAT with* $Q = 2t + 1$ *possible queries.*

Proof (sketch). Let Π denote an MPC protocol for distributed Circuit-SAT (that is, the functionality $(w_1, \ldots, w_T) \mapsto C(\bigoplus w_i)$ for an arbitrary input circuit C) for $T = 2t + 1$ parties satisfying information theoretic security against a collection of t semi-honest parties. Following [IKOS07], we define the following proof system:

- $\mathsf{Prove}(x, w)$: interpret $x = C$ as a circuit; set $(w_i)_{i=1}^T$ to be a T-out-of-T secret sharing of w, and let $\pi = ((\mathsf{view}_i)_{i=1}^T, (\tau_{ij})_{i \neq j})$ denote the following information regarding an honest execution of Π (evaluating $C(\bigoplus w_i)$): view_i denotes the view of party i in this execution, and τ_{ij} denotes the communication transcript between party i and party j.
- Queries: for every $i \in [T]$, we define the set $S_i \subset [T + \binom{T}{2}]$ to be $\{\mathsf{view}_i\} \cup \{\tau_{i,j}\}_{j=1}^T$.
- $\mathsf{Verify}(x, i, \pi_{S_i})$ outputs 1 if and only if (for $S_i = \{\mathsf{view}_i\} \cup \{\tau_{i,j}\}_{j=1}^T$):
  - view_i is internally consistent and outputs 1.
  - For every j, view_i is consistent with $\tau_{i,j}$.

It was implicitly shown in [IKOS07] that this protocol satisfies the desired properties. Completeness holds assuming that Π is perfectly complete; soundness holds because if $x \notin L$, then there is no valid witness for x, and hence any consistent collection of views and transcripts $((\mathsf{view}_i)_{i=1}^T, (\tau_{ij})_{i \neq j})$ for Π must correspond to a global execution of Π outputting 0. Perfect zero knowledge for t joint queries holds by the perfect security of Π against t semi-honest parties.

3.3 Sometimes-Binding Statistically Hiding (SBSH) Commitments

For simplicity, we focus on two-message commitment schemes with the following form:

- **Key Agreement:** The sender and receiver execute a two-message protocol in which they publicly agree on a commitment key ck (the transcript of the protocol). We require that the sender message be *public-coin*[5] (i.e., it simply outputs a string β). In other words,

---

[5] Equivalently, we require that the commitment scheme is hiding even given a "partial opening", i.e., the randomness used in this phase.

- The receiver $R(\rho) \rightarrow \alpha$ outputs a message α using randomness ρ.
- The (honest) sender S samples and sends a uniformly random string $\beta \leftarrow \{0,1\}^{\ell}$.
- The commitment key is defined to be $\mathsf{ck} = (\alpha, \beta)$.
- **Non-Interactive Commitment:** The sender commits to a message m using a (non-interactive) PPT algorithm $\mathsf{Com}(\mathsf{ck}, m)$.

We call these schemes "non-interactive commitment schemes with key agreement." We will denote a transcript of this commitment scheme $(\alpha, \beta, \mathsf{com})$.

We say that a commitment key ck is binding if the non-interactive commitment scheme Com with hardwired key ck is perfectly binding.

Definition 7 (Sometimes-Binding Statistically Hiding (SBSH) Commitments). *A non-interactive commitment scheme with key agreement (R, S, Com) is a sometimes-binding statistically hiding (SBSH) commitment scheme with parameters (ϵ, δ) if the following three properties hold.*

- **Statistical hiding:** *for any malicious PPT receiver R^* (using randomness ρ and outputting message α), the view of R^* in an interaction with an honest sender statistically hides the sender's message m; that is,*

$$\{(\rho, \alpha, \beta, \mathsf{Com}(\mathsf{ck}, 0))\} \approx_s \{(\rho, \alpha, \beta, \mathsf{Com}(\mathsf{ck}, 1))\}$$

for $\alpha = R^*(\rho)$, $\beta \leftarrow \{0,1\}^{\ell}$, and $\mathsf{ck} = (\alpha, \beta)$.
- **Sometimes statistical binding:** *for any malicious PPT sender $S^*(\alpha) \rightarrow (\beta^*, \mathsf{st})$ for the key agreement phase, and for any PPT distinguisher $D(\mathsf{st}) \rightarrow b \in \{0,1\}$, we have that*

$$\Pr[D(\mathsf{st}) = 1 \wedge \mathsf{ck} := (\alpha, \beta^*) \text{ is binding}] = \epsilon \cdot \Pr[D(\mathsf{st}) = 1] \pm \delta \cdot \mathsf{negl}(\lambda),$$

where the probability is taken over $\alpha \leftarrow R(1^{\lambda})$, $(\beta^*, \mathsf{st}) \leftarrow S^*(\alpha)$, and the randomness of D.

In other words, it is a statistically hiding commitment scheme such that, even for malicious PPT senders S^*, the commitment key ck is binding with probability roughly ϵ, and moreover any event that S^* produces (with sufficiently high probability) occurs "independently" of the event that ck is binding.

Constructions. The works [KKS18, BFJ+20, GJJM20] construct variants of SBSH commitment schemes (for ϵ and δ both inverse quasi-polynomial in the security parameter) from (quasi-polynomially secure) 2-message OT satisfying IND-based security against PPT senders and statistical sender privacy against unbounded receivers.[6] This leads to instantiations based on DDH [NP05], QR/DCR [HK12] and LWE [BD18]. In fact, the [NP05] oblivious transfer scheme can be generalized to a variant that relies on the DLIN assumption (rather than DDH) on (not necessarily bilinear) cryptographic groups, which then yields SBSH commitments based on DLIN as well.

---

[6] All three of these works use slightly different security definitions than we use here, but the [BFJ+20, GJJM20] instantiations can easily be shown to satisfy our variant of the security property.

Extending Naor-Pinkas OT to DLIN

Definition 8 (DLIN [BBS04]). *Let $\mathbb{G}$ a group of prime order q with generator g (all parametrized by the security parameter λ), where the tuple $(\mathbb{G}, g, q)$ is public. The DLIN assumption states that*

$$(g^a, g^b, g^c, g^{ar_1}, g^{ar_2}, g^{c(r_1+r_2)}) \ : \ a, b, c, r_1, r_2 \leftarrow \mathbb{Z}_q$$

is computationally indistinguishable from a uniformly random distribution over $\mathbb{G}^6$.

It will be convenient for us to work with "matrix in the exponent" notation, where for a matrix $M \in \mathbb{Z}_q^{n \times m}$ we let g^M denote the matrix of group elements $(g^{M_{i,j}})$. We define the set $\mathcal{D}$ of matrices

$$\mathcal{D} = \left\{ \begin{bmatrix} a & 0 & c \\ 0 & b & c \end{bmatrix} \ : \ a, b, c \in \mathbb{Z}_q^* \right\}$$

Then the DLIN assumption can be equivalently written as

$$((g^{\mathbf{D}}, g^{\mathbf{rD}}) \ : \ \mathbf{D} \leftarrow \mathcal{D}, \mathbf{r} \leftarrow \mathbb{Z}_q^2) \approx_c ((g^{\mathbf{D}}, g^{\mathbf{u}}) \ : \ \mathbf{D} \leftarrow \mathcal{D}, \mathbf{u} \leftarrow \mathbb{Z}_q^3))$$

We also define $g^{\mathcal{D}}$ to be the set $\{g^{\mathbf{D}} \ : \ \mathbf{D} \in \mathcal{D}\}$. Membership in $g^{\mathcal{D}}$ can be checked efficiently.

OT Construction and Security. We define a 2-round oblivious transfer scheme $(\mathsf{OT}_1, \mathsf{OT}_2, \mathsf{Rec})$ where the receiver computes $(\mathsf{ot}_1, \mathsf{st}) \leftarrow \mathsf{OT}_1(b)$ with the choice bit $b \in \{0, 1\}$, the sender computes $\mathsf{ot}_2 \leftarrow \mathsf{OT}_2(\mathsf{ot}_1, m_0, m_1)$ and receiver recovers $m_b = \mathsf{Rec}(\mathsf{ot}_2, \mathsf{st})$. We define the functions as follows:

- $\mathsf{ot}_1 \leftarrow \mathsf{OT}_1(b)$: Sample $\mathbf{D} \leftarrow \mathcal{D}$, $\mathbf{r} \leftarrow \mathbb{Z}_q^2$ and define $\mathbf{v}_b = \mathbf{rD}$, $\mathbf{v}_{1-b} = (0, 0, 1) - \mathbf{v}_b$. Output $\mathsf{ot}_1 = (g^{\mathbf{D}}, g^{\mathbf{v}_0}, g^{\mathbf{v}_1})$, $\mathsf{st} = (b, \mathbf{r})$.
- $\mathsf{OT}_2(\mathsf{ot}_1, m_0, m_1)$: Parse $\mathsf{ot}_1 = (g^{\mathbf{D}}, g^{\mathbf{v}_0}, g^{\mathbf{v}_1})$ and $m_0, m_1 \in \mathbb{G}$. Check that $g^{\mathbf{D}} \in g^{\mathcal{D}}$ and that $g^{\mathbf{v}_0 + \mathbf{v}_1} = g^{(0,0,1)}$; if not then abort. Sample $\mathbf{a}_0 \leftarrow \mathbb{Z}_q^3, \mathbf{a}_1 \leftarrow \mathbb{Z}_q^3$ and output $\mathsf{ot}_2 = (g^{\mathbf{D}\mathbf{a}_0^T}, g^{\mathbf{D}\mathbf{a}_1^T}, g^{\mathbf{v}_0 \cdot \mathbf{a}_0^T} \cdot m_0, g^{\mathbf{v}_1 \cdot \mathbf{a}_1^T} \cdot m_1)$.
- $\mathsf{Rec}(\mathsf{ot}_2, \mathsf{st})$: Parse $\mathsf{ot}_2 = (g^{\mathbf{z}_0}, g^{\mathbf{z}_1}, h_0, h_1)$ and $\mathsf{st} = (b, \mathbf{r})$. Output $h_b \cdot g^{-\mathbf{r} \cdot \mathbf{z}_b^T}$.

We now show that this scheme satisfies the same properties as Naor-Pinkas OT.

- *Correctness:* For any b, m_0, m_1 it holds that if $(\mathsf{ot}_1, \mathsf{st}) \leftarrow \mathsf{OT}_1(b), \mathsf{ot}_2 \leftarrow \mathsf{OT}_2(\mathsf{ot}_1, m_0, m_1), m = \mathsf{Rec}(\mathsf{ot}_2, \mathsf{st})$ then $m = m_b$ with probability 1.
  Proof. This is because, using the notation of the scheme, we have $g^{\mathbf{v}_b} = g^{\mathbf{rD}}$, $g^{\mathbf{z}_b} = g^{\mathbf{D}\mathbf{a}_b^T}$ and hence

  $$h_b = g^{\mathbf{v}_b \cdot \mathbf{a}_b^T} \cdot m_b = g^{\mathbf{rD} \cdot \mathbf{a}_b^T} \cdot m_b = g^{\mathbf{r} \cdot \mathbf{z}_b^T} \cdot m_b.$$

  So $h_b \cdot g^{-\mathbf{r} \cdot \mathbf{z}_b^T} = m_b$.

- *Computational Receiver Security:* We have

$$(\mathsf{ot}_1 \; : \; (\mathsf{ot}_1, \mathsf{st}) \leftarrow \mathsf{OT}_1(0)) \approx (\mathsf{ot}_1 \; : \; (\mathsf{ot}_1, \mathsf{st}) \leftarrow \mathsf{OT}_1(1)).$$

Proof. This follows from DLIN. In particular, we can modify the OT_1 algorithm to sample $\mathbf{v}_b \leftarrow \mathbb{Z}_q^3$ instead of $\mathbf{v}_b \leftarrow \mathbf{rD}$ and the distribution of ot_1 is indistinguishable. But in this case the bit b is statistically hidden since in either case the vectors $\mathbf{v}_0, \mathbf{v}_1$ are just uniformly random subject to $\mathbf{v}_0 + \mathbf{v}_1 = (0, 0, 1)$.

- *Statistical Sender Security: There exists an inefficient function* Extract *such that, for any* ot_1*, if* $b = \mathsf{Extract}(\mathsf{ot}_1)$ *then* $\mathsf{OT}_2(\mathsf{ot}_1, m_0, m_1)$ *statistically hides* m_{1-b}*: for any* m_0, m_1, m_0', m_1' *such that* $m_b = m_b'$ *we have* $\mathsf{OT}_2(\mathsf{ot}_1, m_0, m_1)$ *is statistically close to* $\mathsf{OT}_2(\mathsf{ot}_1, m_0', m_1')$*.*

Proof. We define $\mathsf{Extract}(\mathsf{ot}_1 = (g^{\mathbf{D}}, g^{\mathbf{v}_0}, g^{\mathbf{v}_1}))$ to output 0 if $\mathbf{v}_0$ is in the row-space of $\mathbf{D}$ and 1 otherwise. If it does not hold that $g^{\mathbf{D}} \in g^{\mathcal{D}}$ and that $g^{\mathbf{v}_0 + \mathbf{v}_1} = g^{(0,0,1)}$ then $\mathsf{OT}_2(\mathsf{ot}_1, \ldots)$ aborts and we are done. Otherwise, at most one of $\mathbf{v}_0, \mathbf{v}_1$ is in the row-space of $\mathbf{D}$ since $(0, 0, 1)$ is not in the row space. Therefore $\mathbf{v}_{1-b}$ is not in the row-space of $\mathbf{D}$. But this means that $g^{\mathbf{Da}_{1-b}^T}, g^{\mathbf{v}_{1-b} \cdot \mathbf{a}_{1-b}^T}$ are mutually random and independent over the choice of $\mathbf{a}_{1-b}$ and therefore the message m_{1-b} is perfectly hidden.

This completes the construction of statistically sender private (2-message) OT from DLIN. Moreover, quasi-polynomial security of the scheme is inherited from the (quasi-polynomial) DLIN assumption, so we additionally obtain SBSH commitments from quasi-polynomial DLIN.

SBSH Commitments via NIWI. In this section, we present another construction of SBSH commitments from bilinear DLIN using a proof technique similar to that of our main construction in Sect. 4.

The OT-based commitment schemes above satisfy a stronger security property than "sometimes statistical binding": informally, they are "sometimes extractable". We write down a construction that does not involve any extraction using two generic building blocks (both instantiable based on DLIN): NIWI proofs along with a slight strengthening of dual-mode commitments in the CRS model.

Definition 9 (Semi-Malicious Secure Dual-Mode Commitment). *A non-interactive commitment scheme* Com(ck, m) *in the CRS model is a semi-malicious secure dual-mode commitment if there are two additional algorithms* (BindingSetup, HidingSetup) *satisfying the following properties.*

- BindingSetup$(1^\lambda) \rightarrow$ ck *and* HidingSetup$(1^\lambda) \rightarrow$ ck *both output a commitment key.*
- ***Key Indistinguishability:*** *Commitment keys output by* BindingSetup *and* HidingSetup *are computationally indistinguishable.*

- **Honest Binding:** (BindingSetup, Com) *is a statistically binding commitment scheme in the CRS model.*
- **Semi-Malicious Hiding:** *For* any *commitment key* ck *in the support of* HidingSetup, *the commitment distribution* Com(ck, m) *(with* ck *hardwired) statistically hides the message m.*

That is, a semi-malicious secure dual-mode commitment satisfies the property that commitments using semi-maliciously chosen "hiding keys" still statistically hide the underlying message. We say that a key ck "is a hiding key" if ck is in the support of HidingSetup.

Remark 2. The [GOS06a] homomorphic commitment scheme based on DLIN is a semi-malicious secure dual-mode commitment scheme. It was explicitly shown to be a dual-mode commitment, but by inspection, we see that it is statistically hiding for an arbitrary (hardwired) key from the "hiding" distribution.

We now show how to construct a sometimes-binding statistically hiding commitment scheme using NIWI proofs and a semi-malicious secure dual-mode commitment; this in particular yields such a scheme based on the DLIN assumption on bilinear groups. Our construction is inspired by the construction of [KKS18, BFJ+20, GJJM20].

Construction 1. *Let* (BindingSetup, HidingSetup, Com) *denote a semi-malicious secure dual-mode commitment scheme, and let* (niwi.Prove, niwi.Verify) *denote a NIWI proof system. We then define the following two-message commitment scheme:*

- **Receiver message:** *for* $\ell = \log(\frac{1}{\epsilon})$, *the receiver samples a random string* $r \leftarrow \{0,1\}^\ell$ *along with* ℓ *pairs of commitment keys* $\{ck_{i,b}\}_{i \in [\ell], b \in \{0,1\}}$, *such that*
  - ck_{i,r_i} *is sampled using* BindingSetup(1^λ); *and*
  - $ck_{i,1-r_i}$ *is sampled using* HidingSetup(1^λ) *with randomness* $tk_{i,1-r_i}$.
  The receiver then outputs $\{ck_{i,b}\}_{i \in [\ell], b \in \{0,1\}}$ *along with a NIWI proof that for every* $i \in [\ell]$, *at least one out of* $(ck_{i,0}, ck_{i,1})$ *is a hiding key (using witness* $tk_{i,1-r_i}$)).
- **Sender Key Selection:** *the sender first verifies the NIWI above and aborts if the check fails. The sender then samples and outputs a uniformly random string* $s \leftarrow \{0,1\}^\ell$.
- **Non-Interactive Commitment:** *to commit to a bit m, the sender samples* 2ℓ *uniformly random bits* $\{\sigma_{i,b}\}$. *The sender then outputs* $\{com_{i,b} \leftarrow$ Com($ck_{i,b}, \rho_{i,b}$)} *along with* $c := m \oplus \bigoplus_i \sigma_{i,s_i}$.

It now remains to show that this commitment scheme satisfies the desired security properties.

- **Statistical hiding:** without loss of generality, consider a fixed first message $(\{ck_{i,b}\}, \pi)$ sent by a (potentially malicious) receiver R^*. In order for hiding to be broken, this proof π must be accepted by the sender S, so by the soundness of our NIWI, we know that there exists a string r^* such that $\mathsf{ck}_{i,1-r_i^*}$ is in the support of $\mathsf{HidingSetup}(1^\lambda)$. Now, we note that if the sender S picks any $s \neq r^*$, the commitment $(\{\mathsf{com}_{i,b}\}, c)$ statistically hides the underlying message m; this is because for any i such that $s_i \neq r_i^*$, we have that com_{i,s_i} statistically hides σ_{i,s_i} and hence $c = m \oplus \bigoplus \sigma_{i,s_i}$ statistically hides m. Since S only picks $s = r^*$ with probability $2^{-\ell} = \epsilon$, we conclude that this commitment is statistically hiding.

- **Sometimes statistical binding:** we claim that (ϵ, δ) sometimes statistical binding holds assuming (1) the dual-mode commitment satisfies $\delta \cdot \mathsf{negl}(\lambda)$-key indistinguishability, and (2) the NIWI is $\delta \cdot \mathsf{negl}(\lambda)$-witness indistinguishable. Equivalently, we want to show that the following two distributions are $\delta \cdot \mathsf{negl}(\lambda)$-computationally indistinguishable for any malicious PPT sender S^*:

$$\{(\alpha, S^*(\alpha), r)\} \approx_{c, \delta \cdot \mathsf{negl}(\lambda)} \{(\alpha, S^*(\alpha), r')\}$$

where $r, r' \leftarrow \{0,1\}^\ell$ are i.i.d. and α is computed using r. To prove the above indistinguishability, consider the following sequence of hybrids.

- H_0: This is the LHS, $\{(\alpha, S^*(\alpha), r)\}$.
- H_1: Same as H_0, except that the receiver samples ck_{i,r_i} using $\mathsf{HidingSetup}$ (instead of $\mathsf{BindingSetup}$). In other words, in H_1, all keys $\mathsf{ck}_{i,b}$ are sampled from $\mathsf{HidingSetup}$. We have that $H_0 \approx_{c, \delta \cdot \mathsf{negl}(\lambda)} H_1$ by the key indistinguishability of the dual-mode commitment.
- H_2: Same as H_1, except that the proof π is sampled using a random ℓ-tuple of witnesses (as opposed to witnesses $\{\mathsf{tk}_{i,1-r_i}\}$). We have that $H_1 \approx_{c, \delta \cdot \mathsf{negl}(\lambda)} H_2$ by the witness indistinguishability of the NIWI.
- H_3: Same as H_2, except that r is replaced by r' in the third slot. We have that $H_2 \equiv H_3$ because r and r' are i.i.d. conditioned on $(\alpha, S^*(\alpha))$ as computed in H_2/H_3.
- H_4: Same as H_3, except that π is sampled using witnesses $\{\mathsf{tk}_{i,1-r_i}\}$; indistinguishability is the same as H_1/H_2.
- H_5: Same as H_4, except that the receiver samples ck_{i,r_i} using $\mathsf{BindingSetup}$ (instead of $\mathsf{HidingSetup}$); indistinguishability is the same as H_0/H_1. This is the RHS.

This completes the proof of indistinguishability.

4 Construction of Statistical ZAPR Arguments

We now give our construction of statistical ZAPR arguments, which are proven sound under the quasi-polynomial DLIN assumption in bilinear groups.

4.1 Description

Our construction uses the following ingredients. Let $\epsilon = \epsilon(\lambda)$ denote a fixed negligible function.

- Let lzkp $=$ (lzkp.Prove, lzkp.Queries, lzkp.Verify) denote a t-local zero knowledge proof with $Q = 2t + 1 = \log_3(\frac{1}{\epsilon})$.
- Let sbsh $=$ (sbsh.R, sbsh.S, sbsh.Com) denote a SBSH commitment scheme with parameters (ϵ, ϵ^2).
- Let niwi $=$ (niwi.Prove, niwi.Verify) denote a NIWI proof system for NP that satisfies $\epsilon(\lambda)^3 \cdot \mathsf{negl}(\lambda)$-witness indistinguishability.
- Let niszk $=$ (niszk.Setup, niszk.Prove, niszk.Verify) denote a NISZK argument system with $\epsilon(\lambda)^3 \cdot \mathsf{negl}(\lambda)$ (computational) soundness error along with semi-malicious statistical witness indistinguishability.

Construction 2. *With* niwi, niszk, lzkp, sbsh *as above, we define the following two-message argument system* zapr $=$ (zapr.V, zapr.Prove, zapr.Verify) *as follows*

- **Verifier message:** zapr.$V(1^n, 1^\lambda)$ *does the following.*
  - *Sample a commitment first message* $\alpha \leftarrow$ sbsh.$R(1^\lambda)$.
  - *Sample* $3Q$ *common reference strings* $\mathsf{crs}_{i,a} \leftarrow$ niszk.Setup$(1^n, 1^\lambda; \rho_{i,a})$ *(using randomness $\rho_{i,a}$).*
  - *Sample a random string* $r \leftarrow \{0, 1, 2\}^Q$.
  - *Sample a proof*

    $$\mathsf{niwi}.\pi \leftarrow \mathsf{niwi.Prove}(\varphi, \{\mathsf{crs}_{i,a}\}_{i \in [Q], a \in [3]}, \{\rho_{i,r_i+1}, \rho_{i,r_i+2}\}_{i \in [Q]}),$$

    where sums $r_i + 1, r_i + 2$ are computed mod 3, and $\varphi(\{\mathsf{crs}_{i,a}\}_{i \in [t], a \in [3]})$ denotes the statement "for every $i \in [Q]$, at least two out of $\{\mathsf{crs}_{i,0}, \mathsf{crs}_{i,1}, \mathsf{crs}_{i,2}\}$ are in the support of niszk.Setup$(1^n, 1^\lambda)$.
  - *Output* $(\alpha, \{\mathsf{crs}_{i,a}\}_{i \in [Q], a \in [3]}, \mathsf{niwi}.\pi)$.
- **Prover message:** *Given a verifier message $(\alpha, \{\mathsf{crs}_{i,a}\}_{i \in [Q], a \in [3]}, \mathsf{niwi}.\pi)$ and an instance-witness pair $(x, w) \in R_L$,* zapr.Prove *does the following.*
  - *Verify the proof* niwi.π *with respect to $\{\mathsf{crs}_{i,a}\}_{i \in [Q], a \in [3]}$ and abort if the check fails.*
  - *Sample a (uniformly random)* sbsh *second message β and set* ck $= (\alpha, \beta)$.
  - *Sample a locally zero knowledge proof*

    $$(\mathsf{lzkp}.\pi_1, \ldots, \mathsf{lzkp}.\pi_\ell) \leftarrow \mathsf{lzkp.Prove}(x, w).$$

  - *For $j \in [\ell]$, sample commitments* $\mathsf{com}_j \leftarrow$ sbsh.Com(ck, lzkp.π_j); σ_j) *to the symbol* lzkp.π_j.
  - *Sample a random string* $s \leftarrow \{0, 1, 2\}^Q$.
  - *For every $i \in [Q]$ sample a NISZK proof*

    $$\mathsf{niszk}.\pi_i \leftarrow \mathsf{niszk.Prove}(\mathsf{crs}_{i,s_i}, \psi, i, \mathsf{ck}, \mathsf{com}_{S_i}, \sigma_{S_i})$$

    for the statement $\psi(\mathsf{ck}, i, \mathsf{com}_{S_i})$ denoting "com_{S_i} is a commitment (under ck*) to a string π_{S_i} such that* lzkp.Verify(x, i, π_{S_i}) *outputs 1."*
  - *Output* $(\beta, \{\mathsf{com}_j\}_{j \in [\ell]}, s, \{\mathsf{niszk}.\pi_i\}_{i \in [Q]})$.

- **Proof Verification:** *given a statement* x *and transcript*

$$\tau = \Big(\alpha, \{\mathsf{crs}_{i,a}\}_{i\in[Q],a\in[3]}, \mathsf{niwi}.\pi, \beta, \{\mathsf{com}_j\}_{j\in[\ell]}, s, \{\mathsf{niszk}.\pi_i\}_{i\in[Q]}\Big),$$

zapr.Verify *does the following: for every* $i \in [Q]$, *verify the proof* $\mathsf{niszk}.\pi_i$ *using* crs_{i,s_i}; *output* 1 *if all* Q *proofs are accepted.*

We now proceed to prove the following theorem about Construction 2.

Theorem 3. *If* lzkp, sbsh, niwi, *and* niszk *satisfy the hypotheses stated in Sect. 4.1, then* zapr *is a ZAPR argument system with* $\epsilon^{\Omega(1)}$ *(computational) soundness error and* $\epsilon^{\Omega(1)}$-*statistical witness indistinguishability.*

This has the following implication for bilinear DLIN-based statistical ZAPR arguments.

Corollary 1. *Under the bilinear DLIN assumption (ruling out inverse quasi-polynomial advantage), there exist statistical ZAPR arguments for* NP *with inverse quasi-polynomial soundness error and satisfying inverse quasi-polynomial statistical indistinguishability.*

Under the (inverse) subexponential bilinear DLIN assumption, there exist statistical ZAPR arguments for NP *with inverse subexponential soundness error and satisfying inverse subexponential statistical indistinguishability.*

4.2   Proof of Theorem 3

Completeness of our protocol follows from the completeness of niwi, niszk, lzkp, and the correctness of sbsh. Moreover, the protocol is delayed input and publicly verifiable by construction. In the rest of this section, we prove that the protocol is computationally sound and statistically witness indistinguishable.

Statistical Witness Indistinguishability. Let (x, w_0, w_1) denote a statement x along with two witnesses w_0, w_1 for $x \in L$. Let V^* denote a malicious (unbounded) verifier, which without loss of generality we may assume to be deterministic and outputs a message $m_1 = (\alpha, \{\mathsf{crs}_{i,a}\}_{i\in[Q],a\in[3]}, \mathsf{niwi}.\pi)$. We want to show that a proof zapr.Prove(m_1, x, w_0) is statistically indistinguishable from a proof zapr.Prove(m_1, x, w_1).

To do so, we first note that if $\mathsf{niwi}.\mathsf{Verify}(\varphi, \{\mathsf{crs}_{i,a}\}_{i\in[Q],a\in[3]}, \mathsf{niwi}.\pi)$ outputs 0, then the zapr prover aborts and hence indistinguishability trivially holds. Hence, we assume that the NIWI verification passes.

In this case, the perfect soundness of niwi implies that there exists a string $r^* \in \{0,1,2\}^Q$ such that for all $i \in [Q]$, crs_{i,r_i^*+1} and crs_{i,r_i^*+2} are in the support of $\mathsf{niszk}.\mathsf{Setup}(1^n, 1^\lambda)$. Since the prover samples $s \leftarrow \{0,1,2\}^Q$ uniformly at random, we know that the agreement between s and r^* is at most $t = \frac{Q-1}{2}$ with probability $\geq 1 - 2^{-\Omega(Q)} = 1 - \epsilon^{\Omega(1)} = 1 - \mathsf{negl}(\lambda)$ by a Chernoff bound. Therefore, we assume that this event holds in the following analysis.

We now consider the following sequence of hybrids; let USim denote the unbounded simulator for niszk corresponding to the semi-malicious witness indistinguishability property. For $s \in \{0, 1, 2\}^Q$, let $\mathsf{Good}(s) \subset [Q]$ denote the set of $j \in [Q]$ such that $s_j \neq r_j^*$, and let $\mathsf{Bad}(s)$ denote the remaining set.

- $H_{0,b}$: this is an honest proof $\mathsf{zapr.Prove}(m_1, x, w_b)$.
- $H_{1,b}$: this is the same as $H_{0,b}$, except that for all $j \in \mathsf{Good}(s)$, we sample $\mathsf{niszk}.\pi_i \leftarrow \mathsf{USim}(\mathsf{crs}_{i,s_i}, \psi, \mathsf{ck}, \mathsf{com}_{S_i})$. We have that $H_{1,b} \approx_s H_{0,b}$ by the semi-malicious witness indistinguishability of niszk (and the fact that crs_{s_i} is in the support of $\mathsf{niszk.Setup}(1^n, 1^\lambda)$ for all $i \in \mathsf{Good}(s)$).
- $H_{2,b}$: this is the same as $H_{1,b}$, except that for all $j \notin \bigcup_{i \in \mathsf{Bad}(s)} S_i$, we sample $\mathsf{com}_j \leftarrow \mathsf{sbsh.Com}(\mathsf{ck}, 0)$ to be a commitment to an all 0s string. We have that $H_{1,b} \approx_s H_{2,b}$ by the statistical hiding of sbsh (which can be invoked because the commitment randomness used to sample com_j is not used anywhere in these hybrids).
- $H_{3,b}$: this is the same as $H_{2,b}$, except that for all $j \in \bigcup_{i \in \mathsf{Bad}(s)}$, we instead sample $\mathsf{lzkp}.\pi_j \leftarrow \mathsf{lzkp.Sim}(x, \mathsf{Bad}(s))$ using the lzkp simulator. We have that $H_2 \approx_s H_3$ by the perfect zero knowledge of lzkp (which can be invoked because the symbols $\mathsf{lzkp}.\pi_j$ for $j \notin \bigcup_{i \in \mathsf{Bad}(s)} S_i$ do not appear in these hybrids).

Finally, we note that H_3 is defined independently of the bit b; hence, statistical witness indistinguishability holds.

Computational Soundness.

We claim that our argument system has computational soundness error at most ϵ.

To see this, let $r \notin L$ be a false statement, and suppose that an efficient cheating prover $P^*(\alpha, \{\mathsf{crs}_{i,a}\}_{i \in [Q], a \in [3]}, \mathsf{niwi}_\pi)$ successfully breaks the soundness of zapr with probability at least ϵ. We then make the following sequence of claims about P^*.

- $P^*(\alpha, \{\mathsf{crs}_{i,a}\}_{i \in [Q], a \in [3]}, \mathsf{niwi}_\pi)$ breaks the soundness of zapr *and* outputs a message β^* such that $\mathsf{ck} = (\alpha, \beta^*)$ is binding with probability $\epsilon^2(1 - \mathsf{negl}(\lambda))$. This follows directly from the $(\epsilon, \epsilon^2 \cdot \mathsf{negl}(\lambda))$ "sometimes statistical binding" property of sbsh.
- $P^*(\alpha, \{\mathsf{crs}_{i,a}\}_{i \in [Q], a \in [3]}, \mathsf{niwi}_\pi)$ simultaneously:
  - breaks the soundness of zapr,
  - outputs β^* such that ck is a binding key, and
  - outputs $s = r$ (the verifier's random string)
  with probability $\epsilon^3(1 - \mathsf{negl}(\lambda))$. This holds by the $\epsilon^3 \cdot \mathsf{negl}(\lambda)$-witness indistinguishability of niwi, using the following argument. Consider an alternative experiment in which the verifier samples $r, r' \leftarrow \{0, 1, 2\}^Q$ i.i.d. and uses the r'-witness when computing $\mathsf{niwi}.\pi$ instead of the r-witness; in this experiment, P^* indeed satisfies the above three conditions with probability $\epsilon^3(1 - \mathsf{negl}(\lambda))$, since here, r is independent of the rest of the experiment (and so $s = r$ with probability ϵ conditioned on the rest of the experiment). Then, the same holds true in the real soundness experiment by the $\epsilon^3 \cdot \mathsf{negl}(\lambda)$-witness indistinguishability of niwi.

This last claim about P^* contradicts the $\epsilon^3 \cdot \text{negl}(\lambda)$-soundness of niszk. This is because when ck is a binding key, the soundness of lzkp implies that for any collection of commitments $(\text{com}_1, \ldots, \text{com}_\ell)$, there exists some index i such that the statement $\psi(\text{ck}, i, \text{com}_{S_i})$ is false. By randomly guessing which of the Q statements is false, P^* can therefore be used to contradict the $\epsilon^3 \cdot \text{negl}(\lambda)$-soundness of niszk.

Acknowledgements. We thank the anonymous reviewers for their helpful comments and suggestions.

References

[AF07] Abe, M., Fehr, S.: Perfect NIZK with adaptive soundness. In: Vadhan, S.P. (ed.) TCC 2007. LNCS, vol. 4392, pp. 118–136. Springer, Heidelberg (2007). https://doi.org/10.1007/978-3-540-70936-7_7

[BB04] Boneh, D., Boyen, X.: Efficient selective-ID secure identity-based encryption without random oracles. In: Cachin, C., Camenisch, J.L. (eds.) EURO-CRYPT 2004. LNCS, vol. 3027, pp. 223–238. Springer, Heidelberg (2004). https://doi.org/10.1007/978-3-540-24676-3_14

[BBS04] Boneh, D., Boyen, X., Shacham, H.: Short group signatures. In: Franklin, M. (ed.) CRYPTO 2004. LNCS, vol. 3152, pp. 41–55. Springer, Heidelberg (2004). https://doi.org/10.1007/978-3-540-28628-8_3

[BD18] Brakerski, Z., Döttling, N.: Two-message statistically sender-private OT from LWE. In: Beimel, A., Dziembowski, S. (eds.) TCC 2018. LNCS, vol. 11240, pp. 370–390. Springer, Cham (2018). https://doi.org/10.1007/978-3-030-03810-6_14

[BFJ+20] Badrinarayan, S., Fernando, R., Jain, A., Khurana, D., Sahai, A.: Statistical zap arguments. In: Canteaut, A., Ishai, Y. (eds.) EUROCRYPT 2020. LNCS, vol. 12107, pp. 642–667. Springer, Cham (2020). https://eprint.iacr.org/2019/780

[BOV03] Barak, B., Ong, S.J., Vadhan, S.: Derandomization in cryptography. In: Boneh, D. (ed.) CRYPTO 2003. LNCS, vol. 2729, pp. 299–315. Springer, Heidelberg (2003). https://doi.org/10.1007/978-3-540-45146-4_18

[BP15] Bitansky, N., Paneth, O.: ZAPs and non-interactive witness indistinguishability from indistinguishability obfuscation. In: Dodis, Y., Nielsen, J.B. (eds.) TCC 2015. LNCS, vol. 9015, pp. 401–427. Springer, Heidelberg (2015). https://doi.org/10.1007/978-3-662-46497-7_16

[CCH+19] Canetti, R., et al.: Fiat-Shamir: from practice to theory. In: Proceedings of the 51st Annual ACM SIGACT Symposium on Theory of Computing. ACM (2019)

[CLW18] Canetti, R., Lombardi, A., Wichs, D.: Fiat-Shamir: from practice to theory, part II (non-interactive zero knowledge and correlation intractability from circular-secure FHE). IACR Cryptology ePrint Archive 2018 (2018)

[DN00] Dwork, C., Naor, M.: Zaps and their applications. In: Proceedings of the 41st Annual Symposium on Foundations of Computer Science, pp. 283–293. IEEE (2000)

[DN07] Dwork, C., Naor, M.: Zaps and their applications. SIAM J. Comput. **36**(6), 1513–1543 (2007)

[FLS99] Feige, U., Lapidot, D., Shamir, A.: Multiple noninteractive zero knowledge proofs under general assumptions. SIAM J. Comput. **29**(1), 1–28 (1999)

[FS90] Feige, U., Shamir, A.: Witness indistinguishable and witness hiding protocols. In: Proceedings of the Twenty-Second Annual ACM Symposium on Theory of Computing, pp. 416–426. Citeseer (1990)

[GJJM20] Goyal, V., Jain, A., Jin, Z., Malavolta, G.: Statistical zaps and new oblivious transfer protocols. In: Canteaut, A., Ishai, Y. (eds.) EUROCRYPT 2020. LNCS, vol. 12107, pp. 668–699. Springer, Cham (2020). Subsumes [JJ19]

[GMR85] Goldwasser, S., Micali, S., Rackoff, C.: The knowledge complexity of interactive proof-systems. In: Proceedings of the Seventeenth Annual ACM Symposium on Theory of Computing, pp. 291–304. ACM (1985)

[GO94] Goldreich, O., Oren, Y.: Definitions and properties of zero-knowledge proof systems. J. Cryptology **7**(1), 1–32 (1994). https://doi.org/10.1007/BF00195207

[GOS06a] Groth, J., Ostrovsky, R., Sahai, A.: Non-interactive zaps and new techniques for NIZK. In: Dwork, C. (ed.) CRYPTO 2006. LNCS, vol. 4117, pp. 97–111. Springer, Heidelberg (2006). https://doi.org/10.1007/11818175_6

[GOS06b] Groth, J., Ostrovsky, R., Sahai, A.: Perfect non-interactive zero knowledge for NP. In: Vaudenay, S. (ed.) EUROCRYPT 2006. LNCS, vol. 4004, pp. 339–358. Springer, Heidelberg (2006). https://doi.org/10.1007/11761679_21

[GOS12] Groth, J., Ostrovsky, R., Sahai, A.: New techniques for noninteractive zero-knowledge. J. ACM **59**(3), 11:1–11:35 (2012)

[HK12] Halevi, S., Kalai, Y.T.: Smooth projective hashing and two-message oblivious transfer. J. Cryptology **25**(1), 158–193 (2012). https://doi.org/10.1007/s00145-010-9092-8

[IKOS07] Ishai, Y., Kushilevitz, E., Ostrovsky, R., Sahai, A.: Zero-knowledge from secure multiparty computation. In: Proceedings of the Thirty-Ninth Annual ACM Symposium on Theory of Computing, pp. 21–30. ACM (2007)

[JJ19] Jain, A., Jin, Z.: Statistical zap arguments from quasi-polynomial LWE. Cryptology ePrint Archive, Report 2019/839 (2019). https://eprint.iacr.org/2019/839

[KKS18] Kalai, Y.T., Khurana, D., Sahai, A.: Statistical witness indistinguishability (and more) in two messages. In: Nielsen, J.B., Rijmen, V. (eds.) EUROCRYPT 2018. LNCS, vol. 10822, pp. 34–65. Springer, Cham (2018). https://doi.org/10.1007/978-3-319-78372-7_2

[KPT97] Kilian, J., Petrank, E., Tardos, G.: Probabilistically checkable proofs with zero knowledge. In: STOC, vol. 97, pp. 496–505. Citeseer (1997)

[LVW19] Lombardi, A., Vaikuntanathan, V., Wichs, D.: 2-message publicly verifiable WI from (subexponential) LWE. Cryptology ePrint Archive, Report 2019/808 (2019). https://eprint.iacr.org/2019/808

[Nao03] Naor, M.: On cryptographic assumptions and challenges. In: Boneh, D. (ed.) CRYPTO 2003. LNCS, vol. 2729, pp. 96–109. Springer, Heidelberg (2003). https://doi.org/10.1007/978-3-540-45146-4_6

[NP05] Naor, M., Pinkas, B.: Computationally secure oblivious transfer. J. Cryptology **18**(1), 1–35 (2005). https://doi.org/10.1007/s00145-004-0102-6

[Pas16] Pass, R.: Unprovable security of perfect NIZK and non-interactive non-malleable commitments. Comput. Complex. **25**(3), 607–666 (2016). https://doi.org/10.1007/s00037-016-0122-2

[PS19] Peikert, C., Shiehian, S.: Noninteractive zero knowledge for NP from (plain) learning with errors. Technical report, IACR Cryptology ePrint Archive (2019)

Statistical ZAP Arguments

Saikrishna Badrinarayanan[1($\boxtimes$)], Rex Fernando[2($\boxtimes$)], Aayush Jain[2],
Dakshita Khurana[3], and Amit Sahai[2]

[1] VISA Research, Palo Alto, USA
bsaikrishna7393@gmail.com
[2] UCLA, Los Angeles, USA
{rex,aayushjain,sahai}@cs.ucla.edu
[3] University of Illinois Urbana-Champaign, Champaign, USA
dakshita@illinois.edu

Abstract. Dwork and Naor (FOCS'00) first introduced and constructed
two message public coin witness indistinguishable proofs (ZAPs) for
NP based on trapdoor permutations. Since then, ZAPs have also been
obtained based on the decisional linear assumption on bilinear maps, and
indistinguishability obfuscation, and have proven extremely useful in the
design of several cryptographic primitives.

However, all known constructions of two-message public coin (or even
publicly verifiable) proof systems only guarantee witness indistinguishability against computationally bounded verifiers. In this paper, we construct the first public coin two message witness indistinguishable (WI)
arguments for NP with *statistical* privacy, assuming quasi-polynomial
hardness of the learning with errors (LWE) assumption. We also show
that the same protocol has a super-polynomial simulator (SPS), which
yields the first public-coin SPS statistical zero knowledge argument. Prior
to this, there were no known constructions of two-message publicly verifiable WI protocols under lattice assumptions, even satisfying the weaker
notion of computational witness indistinguishability.

1 Introduction

Witness indistinguishability (WI) is one of the most widely used notions of privacy for proof systems. Informally, WI protocols [13] allow a prover to convince a
verifier that some statement X belongs to an NP language L, with the following
privacy guarantee: if there are two witnesses w_0, w_1 that both attest to the fact
that $X \in L$, then a verifier should not be able to distinguish an honest prover
using witness w_0 from an honest prover using witness w_1. WI is a relaxation of
zero-knowledge and has proven to be surprisingly useful. Since WI is a relaxation, unlike zero-knowledge, there are no known lower bounds on the rounds of
interaction needed to build WI protocols in the plain model.

Indeed, Dwork and Naor [10,12] introduced the notion of two-message public-
coin witness indistinguishable proofs (ZAPs) without any setup assumptions, and
also constructed it assuming trapdoor permutations. We observe that the public-
coin feature of ZAPs yield public verifiability of the resulting proof system, since

© International Association for Cryptologic Research 2020
A. Canteaut and Y. Ishai (Eds.): EUROCRYPT 2020, LNCS 12107, pp. 642–667, 2020.
https://doi.org/10.1007/978-3-030-45727-3_22

a third party can use the public coins of the verifier to determine whether or not the prover's response constitutes a valid proof. Subsequently, Groth et al. [15] constructed ZAPs assuming the decisional linear assumption, and Bitansky and Paneth [2] constructed ZAPs from indistinguishability obfuscation and one way functions.

Our Goal: ZAPs with Statistical Privacy. As originally introduced, ZAPs satisfied soundness against unbounded provers (i.e. were *proofs*), and witness indistinguishability against computationally bounded verifiers. In this work, we examine whether these requirements can be reversed: can we achieve witness indistinguishability against computationally unbounded verifiers, while achieving soundness against computationally bounded cheating provers? We call such objects *statistical ZAP arguments*.

An analogue of this question has a long history of study in the context of zero-knowledge protocols. Indeed, zero-knowledge protocols for NP were originally achieved guaranteeing privacy to hold only against computationally bounded verifiers [14]. In the case of zero-knowledge, the notion of *statistical* zero-knowledge arguments was achieved soon after [6,8], that strengthened the privacy requirement to hold against computationally unbounded verifiers, while requiring soundness to hold only against computationally bounded provers.

Because ZAPs require a single message each from the verifier and the prover, a better comparison would perhaps be to non-interactive zero-knowledge (NIZK) [4]. Even in the case of NIZKs, we have had arguments for NP satisfying statistical zero-knowledge since 2006 [15]. And yet, the following natural question has remained open since the introduction of ZAPs nearly two decades ago.

Do there exist statistical ZAP arguments for NP in the plain model?

Statistical witness indistinguishability, just like its zero-knowledge counterpart, guarantees *everlasting privacy* against malicious verifiers, long after protocols have completed execution. Of course, to achieve statistical privacy, we must necessarily sacrifice soundness against unbounded provers. But such a tradeoff could often be desirable, since soundness is usually necessary only in an online setting: in order to convince a verifier of a false statement, a cheating prover must find a way to cheat *during* the execution of the protocol.

The Main Challenge: Achieving a Public-coin Protocol. The recent work of Kalai et al. [20] constructed the first two message statistically witness indistinguishable arguments in the plain model under standard sub-exponential assumptions. However, their arguments are only *privately verifiable*.

The blueprint of [20], which builds on other similar approaches in the computational witness indistinguishability setting [1,18], uses oblivious transfer (OT) to reduce interaction in a Σ-protocol. In all these approaches, the verifier obtains the third message of the Σ-protocol via the output of the OT, and therefore these approaches fundamentally require the use of private coins for verification. It is also worth noting that these protocols are not sound against provers that have access to the private coins of the verifier, which restricts their applicability.

Additionally, the verifier's message is *not reusable*, which means that soundness is not guaranteed if the same verifier message is reused across multiple executions.

On the other hand, a *public coin* argument, which is the focus of this work, does not suffer from any of these limitations. In fact, where the verifier's message only needs to be a uniformly random string. Such a string can easily be generated, for example, via an MPC protocol, and can then be reused across multiple executions with no loss in soundness.

We stress that prior to our work, even two message statistically witness indistinguishable arguments that were only publicly verifiable (and not necessarily public coin) were not known.

1.1 Our Results

In this paper, we construct the first two message public coin statistically witness indistinguishable arguments for NP in the plain model. Our constructions assume quasi-polynomial hardness of the learning with errors (LWE) problem. In fact, these are the first known two-message public coin (or even publicly verifiable) arguments based on lattice assumptions, satisfying *any notion of witness indistinguishability* (computational/statistical). We provide an informal theorem below.

Informal Theorem 1. *Assuming quasi-polynomial hardness of the learning with errors (LWE) assumption, there exist two message public-coin statistically witness indistinguishable arguments for NP in the plain model.*

Our results are obtained by combining two recent results in a new way: recent constructions of correlation-intractable hash functions based on LWE [7] and the statistically hiding extractable commitments of [20] (which are built upon [21]). This yields a new method of using correlation intractable hash functions to instantiate the Fiat-Shamir transform, by extracting messages from *statistically hiding commitments*, instead of from statistically binding trapdoor commitments – that we believe may be of independent interest.

Additionally, we observe that the same protocol has a super-polynomial zero knowledge simulator assuming subexponential LWE, giving the following theorem.

Informal Theorem 2. *Assuming subexponential hardness of the learning with errors (LWE) assumption, there exist two message public-coin super-polynomial simulation statistical zero knowledge arguments for NP in the plain model.*

2 Overview of Techniques

In this section, we provide a brief overview of the techniques we use to build a two message public coin statistical WI argument (henceforth referred to as a ZAP).

Our starting point is the popular technique to construct ZAPs for NP, due to Dwork and Naor [11]. Their construction makes use of a statistically sound NIZK in the common random string model, and can be described as follows.

- In the first round, the verifier picks uniformly random strings $crs_1, ..., crs_\lambda$, where λ denotes the security parameter, and sends them to the prover.
- In the second round, the prover samples a uniformly random string crs'. It computes proofs $(\pi_1, ..., \pi_\ell)$ where π_i is a NIZK proof for the instance x that verifies under $crs'_i = crs' \oplus crs_i$ The prover sends crs' along with proof strings $(\pi_1, ..., \pi_\ell)$ to the verifier.

The soundness of this protocol can be proven based on the statistical soundness of NIZK, in the following way. Fix an instance $x \notin L$. Statistical soundness of the NIZK implies that with probability at least $1/2$ over the choice of crs from the domain of the common random string of NIZK, *there does not exist a proof* π that verifies for instance x with respect to crs. Put another way, for fixed x, for at least $1/2$ of the strings in the domain of the common random string of the NIZK, *there does not exist a proof for x*. One can use this fact to argue combinatorially that over the choice of random $crs_1, ..., crs_\lambda$, the probability that there exists crs' for which there exist proofs with respect to every member of the set $\{crs'_i = crs' \oplus crs_i\}_{i \in [\ell]}$, is negligible.

The proof of witness indistinguishability follows quite simply, by switching the witness in each of the proofs one by one.

But when applied to our context, this approach immediately encounters the following problems.

1. The soundness argument outlined above crucially requires that with high probability over the CRS of the NIZK, there just should not exist a proof for any fixed false instance. This translates to requiring *statistical soundness* of the underlying NIZK.
2. One cannot hope to get a WI argument secure against unbounded verifiers via this transform, unless the underlying NIZK also satisfies privacy against unbounded verifiers, i.e. satisfies statistical zero-knowledge.
3. It is believed that statistically sound and statistical zero-knowledge NIZKs for all of NP cannot exist.
4. Even if we only desired *computational* witness indistinguishability based on lattice assumptions, no statistically sound NIZKs in the common random string model are known from lattice assumptions.

As an intermediate objective, we will first try to tackle problem #4 and build a publicly verifiable computational WI argument based on LWE.

2.1   A Simple Two-Message Public-Coin Computational WI Argument

We make a few modifications to the template above so as to obtain a publicly verifiable computational WI argument based on LWE.

Before we describe these modifications, we list a few ingredients. We will assume that there exists a dense public key encryption scheme PKE, that is, a scheme for which every string in $\{0,1\}^{|pk|}$ corresponds to a valid public key (and therefore every string has a valid secret key). We will further assume the existence of a correlation intractable hash function family. Informally, a hash function family $\mathcal{H}$ is correlation-intractable for a function family $\mathcal{F}$ if:

- Given a fixed function $f \in \mathcal{F}$, and a randomly generated key K (that can depend on f), the probability that an adversary outputs x such that $(x, \mathcal{H}(K, x)) = (x, f(x))$ is at most ϵ.
- The hash key K statistically hides the function f, such that adversaries cannot distinguish a random key from a key for f with advantage better than ϵ.

We will set $\epsilon = 2^{-2|pk|}$. We will use Π to denote a parallel repetition of Blum's Σ-protocol for Graph Hamiltonicity, represented as $\{a_i = \mathsf{com}(\hat{a}_i)\}_{i \in [\lambda]}, \{e_i\}_{i \in [\lambda]}, \{z_i\}_{i \in [\lambda]}\}$, where $\{a_i\}_{i \in [\lambda]}$ represents the first commitments sent by the prover, $\{e_i\}_{i \in [\lambda]}$ is a challenge string sent by the verifier and $\{z_i\}_{i \in [\lambda]}$ represents the corresponding third message by the prover. Let the instance be x and its witness be w. Then, the protocol is described as follows.

1. In the first round, the verifier randomly samples a key K for the correlation intractable hash function $\mathcal{H}$ for bounded size NC_1 functions.
2. In the second round, the prover picks a key pair (pk, sk) for the scheme PKE. Then the prover uses $\mathsf{PKE.Enc}(pk, \cdot)$ as a commitment scheme to compute the commitments $\{a_i\}_{i \in [\lambda]}$. Next, the prover computes $e = \mathcal{H}(K, x, \{a_i\}_{i \in [\lambda]}) \in \{0, 1\}^\lambda$, and uses (x, w, a, e) to compute $z = (z_1, ..., z_\lambda)$ according to the protocol Π. It outputs $(pk, \{a_i = \mathsf{PKE.Enc}(pk, \hat{a}_i)\}_{i \in [\lambda]}, e, z)$

While witness indistinguishability of this protocol is easy to see, arguing soundness is trickier. In order to argue soundness, the reduction will simple try to *guess* the public key pk^* that the prover will use, and will abort if this guess is not correct. Note that such a guess is correct with probability at least $2^{-|pk^*|}$.

Suppose a cheating prover convinces a verifier to accept false statements with probability $\frac{1}{p(\lambda)}$ for some polynomial $p(\cdot)$. Then, with probability at least $\frac{1}{p(\cdot)} \cdot 2^{-|pk^*|}$, the reduction guesses pk^* correctly, and the prover provides a convincing proof of a false statement using pk^*.

In the next hybrid, the challenger guesses pk^* together with the corresponding secret key sk^*, and then samples a correlation intractable hash key for a specific function $f_{sk^*}(\cdot)$. The function $f_{sk^*}(\cdot)$ on input x, along with a (the messages committed in the Σ-protocol), outputs the only possible string e_{bad} for which there exists a string z such that (a, e_{bad}, z) verifies for $x \notin L$.[1] Note that this function is in NC_1. By ϵ-security of the correlation intractable hash family (where $\epsilon = 2^{-2|pk|}$), with probability at least $\left(\frac{1}{p(\cdot)} - 2^{-|pk|}\right) \cdot 2^{-|pk|}$, the reduction guesses pk^* correctly, and the prover provides a convincing proof of a false statement using pk^*.

Finally, since the correlation intractable hash function is ϵ-secure, in the final hybrid adversary cannot produce a proof for x with probability greater than ϵ, as this will mean that he output a^*, e^*, z^* such that $e^* = f_{bad}(x, a^*)$.

---

[1] Note that this property is satisfied by any Σ-Protocol with a $1/2-$special soundness where the bad challenge e_{bad} can be computed efficiently from the precommitted values $\{\hat{a}_i\}$, such as Blum's Σ-protocol.

The protocol sketched above is public-coin, because when we instantiate the correlation-intractable hash family with the LWE-based one by [24], the hash keys are statistically close to uniform.

In the description above, we also relied on a dense public key encryption scheme, which is unfortunately not known to exist based on LWE. However, we note that we can instead use a scheme with the property that at least $1/2$ of the strings in $\{0,1\}^{\ell_{\mathsf{PKE}}}$ correspond to correct encryption keys with a valid secret key, and the property that public keys are pseudorandom. Then, the verifier sends λ public keys $pk_1, \ldots, pk_\lambda$, and the prover outputs pk', and then uses the public keys $\{(pk' \oplus pk_i)\}_{i \in [\lambda]}$ to compute λ proofs. Soundness can be obtained by arguing that with overwhelming probability, there will exist an index $i \in [\lambda]$ such that $(pk' \oplus pk_i)$ has a secret key, just like the [11] technique described at the beginning of this overview.

However, the construction above falls short of achieving statistical witness indistinguishability against malicious verifiers. The reason is the following: arguing that the construction described above satisfies soundness requires relying on correlation intractability of the hash function. In order to invoke the correlation intractable hash function, it is crucial that the prover be "committed" to a well-defined, unique message $\{a_i\}_{i \in [\lambda]}$, that can be extracted using the secret key sk^* of the public key encryption scheme. At first, statistical hiding, together with such extraction, may appear to be contradictory objectives.

Indeed, we will try obtain a weaker version of these contradictory objectives, and specifically, we will rely on a two-message statistically hiding extractable commitment scheme [20].

2.2 Using Correlation-Intractable Hashing with Statistically Hiding Extractable Commitments

In the recent exciting work on using LWE-based correlation-intractable hashing [7,24] for achieving soundness, as well as in the "warm up" ZAP protocol described above, the correlation-intractable hash function is used as follows. Because the LWE-based CI-hash function is designed to avoid an *efficiently computable* function f of the prover's first message, it is used together with a public-key encryption scheme: the prover's first message is encrypted using the public key, and the function f is built to contain the secret key of the encryption scheme, so that it can decrypt the prover's first message in order to calculate the challenge that must be avoided.

Our work imagines a simple modification of this strategy of using correlation-intractable hashing for arguing soundness. The main idea is that we want to replace the encryption scheme (which necessarily can only at most provide computational hiding) with an *extractable* statistically hiding commitment scheme. We will describe what this object entails in more detail very shortly, but the main observation is that such an extractable commitment in fact reveals the value being committed to with a tiny (but tunable) probability – crucially in a way that prevents a malicious prover from learning whether the commitment will reveal the committed value or not. With such a commitment scheme, the efficient function f underlying the correlation-intractable hash function will only "work" in the rare case that the commitment reveals the value being committed. But since a cheating prover can't tell whether its committed values will be revealed or not, soundness will still hold overall, even though the actual guarantee of the correlation-intractable hash function is only invoked with a tiny probability in the proof of soundness. We now elaborate.

2.3   Statistically Hiding Extractable Commitments

Any statistically hiding commitment must lose all information about the committed message, except with negligible probability. This makes it challenging to define notions of extraction for statistically hiding commitments. In 4 rounds or more, this notion is easier to define, as extraction is possible even from statistically hiding commitments, simply by rewinding the adversary. However, traditional rewinding techniques break down completely when considering two-message commitments.

Nevertheless, the recent work of [20], building on [21], defined and constructed two-message statistically hiding extractable commitments, which they used to construct two-message statistical WI arguments, that were *privately verifiable*. In what follows, we abstract out the properties of a statistically hiding extractable commitment. A more formal description can be found in Sect. 5. We point out that we only need to rely on significantly simpler definitions than the ones in [20], and we give much simpler proofs that the constructions in [20] according to our new definitions. This may be of independent interest.

Defining Statistically Hiding Extractable Commitments. We start with an important observation about statistically hiding commitments, which gives a hint about how one can possibly define (and construct) two-message statistically hiding extractable commitments. Namely, any statistically hiding commitment must lose all information about the committed message, *but may retain this information with some small negligible probability.* Specifically,

- A commitment that leaks the committed message with probability ϵ (where ϵ is a fixed negligible function in the security parameter) and statistically hides the message otherwise, will continue to be statistically hiding.
- At the same time, one could ensure that no matter the behavior of the committer, the message being committed *does get leaked to the honest receiver with probability at least* ϵ.
- Moreover, the committer does not know whether or not the committed message was leaked to the receiver. This property is important and will be crucially used in our proofs.

In spirit, this corresponds to establishing an erasure channel over which the committer transmits his message to the receiver. This channel almost always erases the committed message, but is guaranteed to transmit the committed message with a very small probability (ϵ). Moreover, just like cryptographic erasure channels, the committer does not know whether or not his message was transmitted.

Additionally, because this is a commitment, we require computational binding: once the committer transmits his message (that is, commits), he should not be able to change his mind about the message, *even if* the message did not get transmitted. Finally, we say that "extraction occurs" whenever the message does get transmitted, and we require that extraction occur with probability at least ϵ, even against a malicious committer.

Next, we describe how we interface these commitments with correlation intractable hash functions to obtain two-message statistical ZAP arguments.

2.4 Statistical ZAP Arguments

With this tool in mind, we make the following observations:

1. We would like to replace the encryption scheme used for generating the first message a for the sigma protocol, sent by the prover in the second round, with a statistically hiding commitment.
2. The first message of this commitment will be generated by the verifier. Furthermore, because we want a public coin protocol, we require this message to be pseudorandom.
3. We will require that with some small probability (say $\lambda^{-\omega(\log \lambda)}$), *all* messages committed by the prover get transmitted to the verifier, that is with probability $\lambda^{-\omega(\log \lambda)}$, the verifier can recover all the messages committed by the prover in polynomial time given his secret state. Next, using an insight from the simple protocol in Sect. 2.1, we will set the security of the correlation intractable hash function, so that it is infeasible for any polynomially sized adversary to break correlation intractability with probability $\lambda^{-\omega(\log \lambda)}$.

The protocol is then as follows:

- In the first round, the verifier samples a hash key K for the correlation intractable hash function $\mathcal{H}$, for the same function family $\mathcal{F}$ as Sect. 2.1. The verifier also samples strings $q = \{c_{1,j}\}_{j \in [\mathsf{poly}(\lambda)]}$ uniformly at random, where poly is a polynomial denoting the number of commitments made by the prover. The verifier sends q and K over to the prover.
- In the second round, the prover computes the first message of the sigma protocol a (where the number of parallel repetitions equals the output length of correlation intractable hash function). This message a is generated using the statistically hiding extractable commitment scheme com with q as the first message. The prover computes $e = \mathcal{H}(K, x, q, a)$ and uses e to compute the third message z of the sigma protocol, by opening some subset of the commitments made by the prover. The prover outputs (a, e, z).

We now provide some intuition for the security of this protocol.

- **Soundness:** To argue soundness, we follow an approach that is similar to the soundness proof for the computational ZAP argument described in Sect. 2.1 (although with some additional technical subtleties). We discuss one such subtlety here:

Let $\ell = |e|$. Then, the correlation-extractable hash function can be at most $2^{-\ell^\delta}$-secure[2]. For this reason, we require the commitments to be *jointly* extractable in polynomial time with probability at least $2^{-\ell^\delta}$. Note that the total number of commitments is $N = \ell \cdot \mathsf{poly}(\lambda)$.

However, statistically hiding commitments, as originally constructed in [20], are such that if a single commitment can be extracted with probability ϵ, then N commitments can be extracted with probability roughly ϵ^N. Setting $N = \ell \cdot \mathsf{poly}(\lambda)$ as above implies that trivially, the probability of extraction will be roughly $O(2^{-\ell \cdot \mathsf{poly}(\lambda)})$, which is smaller than the required probability $2^{-\ell^\delta}$.

However, we observe that the commitments constructed in [20] can be modified very slightly so that the probability of extraction can be $2^{-g(\lambda)}$ for any efficiently computable function g that is bounded by any polynomial in λ. Thus, for example, the probability of extraction can be made to be $\lambda^{-\log(\lambda)}$. In other words, this extraction probability can be made to be *independent of the total number of commitments, N*. We describe this modification in additional detail in Sect. 4.2.

Using commitments that satisfy the property stated above, we observe that we can switch to a hybrid where the challenger samples the commitment messages on behalf of the verifier, and hardwires the secret state used for extraction inside the hash key. The function is defined such that in the event that extraction occurs (given the secret state), the verifier can use the extracted values to compute the bad challenge e_{bad} (just as in Sect. 2.1), by evaluating a depth bounded function f_{bad} on the extracted values, and otherwise e_{bad} is set to 0. If the adversary breaks soundness with noticeable probability ϵ, then with probability roughly at least $2^{-g(\lambda)} \cdot \epsilon$, the outputs of the adversary satisfy $\mathcal{H}(K, x, q, a) = e_{bad}$. As already alluded to previously, we set the function g and the (quasi-polynomial) security of the hash function such that the event above suffices to contradict correlation intractability.

- **Statistical Witness Indistinguishability:** Statistical witness indistinguishability composes under parallel repetition, and therefore can be proven index-by-index based on the statistical hiding property of the commitment. Additional details about the construction and the proof can be found in Sect. 5.

Super-Polynomial Simulation (SPS) Zero Knowledge. We show that the protocol above has a super-polynomial simulator which provides statistical zero knowledge. At a very high level, we do this by showing that the extractable commitment scheme can be equivocated in exponential time, and then by using complexity leveraging. We refer to the full version of the paper for details.

Concurrent and Independent Works. In a concurrent and independent work, [17] also constructed a 2-message public-coin statistically witness

---

[2] More formally, if the output of the hash function is ℓ bits long, then even if we rely on sub-exponential assumptions, we cannot hope to have the guessing advantage be smaller than $2^{-\ell^\delta}$ for a small positive constant $\delta < 1$.

indistinguishable argument from quasipolynomial LWE. Another concurrent and independent work is that of [22], who construct a 2-message computationally witness indistinguishable public-coin argument from subexponential LWE.

2.5   Organization

The rest of this paper is organized as follows. In Sect. 3, we describe some of the preliminaries such as correlation intractability, oblivious transfer and proof systems. In Sect. 4, we define a simplified variant and present a slightly modified construction of extractable statistically hiding commitments, first proposed by [20]. Finally, in Sect. 5, we construct and prove the security of our statistical ZAP argument.

3   Preliminaries

Notation. Throughout this paper, we will use λ to denote the security parameter, and $\mathsf{negl}(\lambda)$ to denote any function that is asymptotically smaller than $\frac{1}{\mathsf{poly}(\lambda)}$ for any polynomial $\mathsf{poly}(\cdot)$.

The statistical distance between two distributions D_1, D_2 is denoted by $\Delta(D_1, D_2)$ and defined as:

$$\Delta(D_1, D_2) = \frac{1}{2} \Sigma_{v \in V} |\mathrm{Pr}_{x \leftarrow D_1}[x = v] - \mathrm{Pr}_{x \leftarrow D_2}[x = v]|.$$

We say that two families of distributions $D_1 = \{D_{1,\lambda}\}, D_2 = \{D_{2,\lambda}\}$ are statistically indistinguishable if $\Delta(D_{1,\lambda}, D_{2,\lambda}) = \mathsf{negl}(\lambda)$. We say that two families of distributions $D_1 = \{D_{1,\lambda}\}, D_2 = \{D_{2,\lambda}\}$ are computationally indistinguishable if for all non-uniform probabilistic polynomial time distinguishers $\mathcal{D}$,

$$\left| \mathrm{Pr}_{r \leftarrow D_{1,\lambda}}[\mathcal{D}(r) = 1] - \mathrm{Pr}_{r \leftarrow D_{2,\lambda}}[\mathcal{D}(r) = 1] \right| = \mathsf{negl}(\lambda).$$

Let Π denote an execution of a protocol. We use $\mathsf{View}_A(\Pi)$ denote the view, including the randomness and state of party A in an execution Π. We also use $\mathsf{Output}_A(\Pi)$ denote the output of party A in an execution of Π.

Remark 1. In what follows we define several 2-party protocols. We note that in all these protocols both parties take as input the security parameter 1^λ. We omit this from the notation for the sake of brevity.

Definition 1 (Σ-protocols). *Let $L \in \mathsf{NP}$ with corresponding witness relation R_L. A protocol $\Pi = \langle P, V \rangle$ is a Σ-protocol for relation R_L if it is a three-round public-coin protocol which satisfies:*

- **Completeness:** *For all $(x, w) \in R_L$, $\mathrm{Pr}[\mathsf{Output}_V \langle P(x, w), V(x) \rangle = 1] = 1 - \mathsf{negl}(\lambda)$, assuming P and V follow the protocol honestly.*
- **Special Soundness:** *There exists a polynomial-time algorithm A that given any x and a pair of accepting transcripts $(a, e, z), (a, e', z')$ for x with the same first prover message, where $e \neq e'$, outputs w such that $(x, w) \in R_L$.*

- **Honest verifier zero-knowledge:** *There exists a probabilistic polynomial time simulator S_Σ such that for all $(x, w) \in R_L$, the distributions $\{S_\Sigma(x, e)\}$ and $\{\text{View}_V \langle P(x, w(x)), V(x, e)\rangle\}$ are statistically indistinguishable. Here $S_\Sigma(x, e)$ denotes the output of simulator S upon input x and e, such that V's random tape (determining its query) is e.*

3.1 Correlation Intractable Hash Functions

We adapt definitions of a correlation intractable hash function family from [7,24].

Definition 2. *For any polynomials $k, (\cdot), s(\cdot) = \omega(k(\cdot))$ and any $\lambda \in \mathbb{N}$, let $\mathcal{F}_{\lambda, s(\lambda)}$ denote the class of NC^1 circuits of size $s(\lambda)$ that on input $k(\lambda)$ bits output λ bits. Namely, $f : \{0, 1\}^{k(\lambda)} \to \{0, 1\}^\lambda$ is in $\mathcal{F}_{\lambda, s}$ if it has size $s(\lambda)$ and depth bounded by $O(\log \lambda)$.*

Definition 3. *[Quasi-polynomially Correlation Intractable Hash Function Family] A hash function family $\mathcal{H} = (\text{Setup}, \text{Eval})$ is quasi-polynomially correlation intractable (CI) with respect to $\mathcal{F} = \{\mathcal{F}_{\lambda, s(\lambda)}\}_{\lambda \in \mathbb{N}}$ as defined in Definition 2, if the following two properties hold:*

- **Correlation Intractability:** *For every $f \in \mathcal{F}_{\lambda, s}$, every non-uniform polynomial-size adversary $\mathcal{A}$, every polynomial s, and every large enough $\lambda \in \mathbb{N}$,*

$$\Pr_{K \leftarrow \mathcal{H}.\text{Setup}(1^\lambda, f)} \Big[\mathcal{A}(K) \to x \text{ such that } (x, \mathcal{H}.\text{Eval}(K, x)) = (x, f(x)) \Big] \leq \frac{1}{\lambda^{\log \lambda}}.$$

- **Statistical Indistinguishability of Hash Keys:** *Moreover, for every $f \in \mathcal{F}_{\lambda, s}$, for every unbounded adversary $\mathcal{A}$, and every large enough $\lambda \in \mathbb{N}$,*

$$\Big| \Pr_{K \leftarrow \mathcal{H}.\text{Setup}(1^\lambda, f)}[\mathcal{A}(K) = 1] - \Pr_{K \leftarrow \{0,1\}^\ell}[\mathcal{A}(K) = 1] \Big| \leq 2^{-\lambda^{\Omega(1)}},$$

where ℓ denotes the size of the output of $\mathcal{H}.\text{Setup}(1^\lambda, f)$.

The work of [24] gives a construction of correlation intractable hash functions with respect to $\mathcal{F} = \{\mathcal{F}_{\lambda, s(\lambda)}\}_{\lambda \in \mathbb{N}}$, based on polynomial LWE with polynomial approximation factors. We observe that their construction also satisfies Definition 3, assuming quasi-polynomial LWE with polynomial approximation factors.

3.2 Oblivious Transfer

Definition 4 (Oblivious Transfer). *Oblivious transfer is a protocol between two parties, a sender S with input messages (m_0, m_1) and receiver R with input a choice bit b. The correctness requirement is that R obtains output m_b at the end of the protocol (with probability 1). We let $\langle S(m_0, m_1), R(b)\rangle$ denote an execution of the OT protocol with sender input (m_0, m_1) and receiver input bit b. We require OT that satisfies the following properties:*

- **Computational Receiver Security.** *For any non-uniform PPT sender S^* and any $(b, b') \in \{0, 1\}$, the views* $\mathsf{View}_{S^*}(\langle S^*, R(b) \rangle)$ *and* $\mathsf{View}_{S^*}(\langle S^*, R(b') \rangle)$ *are computationally indistinguishable.*
  We say that the OT scheme is T-secure if all PPT malicious senders have distinguishing advantage less than $\frac{1}{T}$.
- **Statistical Sender Security.** *This is defined using the real-ideal paradigm, and requires that for any distribution on the inputs (m_0, m_1) and any unbounded adversarial receiver R^*, there exists a (possibly unbounded) simulator Sim_{R^*} that interacts with an ideal functionality $\mathcal{F}_{ot}$ on behalf of R^*. Here $\mathcal{F}_{ot}$ is an oracle that obtains the inputs (m_0, m_1) from S and b from Sim_{R^*} (simulating the malicious receiver), and outputs m_b to Sim_{R^*}. Then $\mathsf{Sim}_{R^*}^{\mathcal{F}_{ot}}$ outputs a receiver view that is statistically indistinguishable from the real view of the malicious receiver $\mathsf{View}_{R^*}(\langle S(m_0, m_1), R^* \rangle)$. We say that the OT protocol satisfies $(1-\delta)$ statistical sender security if the statistical distance between the real and ideal distributions is at most δ.*

We use the following sender security property in our protocols (which follows from the definition of sender security in Definition 4 above).

Claim. For any two-message OT protocol satisfying Definition 4, for every malicious receiver R^* and every first message m_{R^*} generated by R^*, we require that there exists an unbounded machine E which extracts b such that either of the following statements is true:

- For all m_0, m_1, m_2, $\mathsf{View}_{R^*}\langle S(m_0, m_1), R^* \rangle$ and $\mathsf{View}_{R^*}\langle S(m_0, m_2), R^* \rangle$ are statistically indistinguishable and $b = 0$, or,
- For all m_0, m_1, m_2, $\mathsf{View}_{R^*}\langle S(m_0, m_1), R^* \rangle$ and $\mathsf{View}_{R^*}\langle S(m_2, m_1), R^* \rangle$ are statistically indistinguishable and $b = 1$.

Proof. From the (unbounded) simulation property of the two-message OT, there exists a simulator that extracts a receiver input bit b from the first message of R^*, sends it to the ideal functionality, obtains m_b and generates an indistinguishable receiver view. Then, by the definition of sender security, when $b = 0$, the simulated view must be close to both $\mathsf{View}_{R^*}\langle S(m_0, m_1), R^* \rangle$, and $\mathsf{View}_{R^*}\langle S(m_0, m_2), R^* \rangle$. Similarly, when $b = 1$, the simulated view must be statistically close to both $\mathsf{View}_{R^*}\langle S(m_0, m_1), R^* \rangle$, and $\mathsf{View}_{R^*}\langle S(m_2, m_1), R^* \rangle$.

Throughout the paper, we focus on two-message oblivious transfer. We now discuss an additional specific property of two-message OT protocols.

Property 1. The message sent by the receiver is pseudorandom - in particular, this means that the receiver can just sample and send a uniformly random string as a valid message to the sender.

Such two-message OT protocols with this additional property have been constructed based on the DDH assumption [23], LWE assumption [5], and a stronger variant of smooth-projective hashing, which can be realized from DDH as well as the Nth-residuosity and Quadratic Residuosity assumptions [16,19]. Such two-message protocols can also be based on witness encryption or indistinguishability obfuscation (iO) together with one-way permutations [25].

3.3   Proof Systems

An n-message interactive protocol for deciding a language L with associated relation R_L proceeds in the following manner:

- At the beginning of the protocol, P and V receive the size of the instance and security parameter, and execute the first $n-1$ messages.
- At some point during the protocol, P receives input $(x, w) \in R_L$. P sends x to V together with the last message of the protocol. Upon receiving the last message from P, V outputs 1 or 0.

An execution of this protocol with instance x and witness w is denoted by $\langle P(x, w), V(x) \rangle$. One can consider both proofs – with soundness against unbounded provers, and arguments – with soundness against computationally bounded provers.

Definition 5 (Two-Message Interactive Arguments). *A two-message delayed-input interactive protocol (P, V) for deciding a language L is an interactive argument for L if it satisfies the following properties:*

- **Completeness:** *For every $(x, w) \in R_L$, $\Pr[\mathsf{Output}_V \langle P(x, w), V(x) \rangle = 1] = 1 - \mathsf{negl}(\lambda)$, where the probability is over the random coins of P and V, and where in the protocol P receives (x, w) right before computing the last message of the protocol, and V receives x together with the last message of the protocol.*
- **Non-adaptive Soundness:** *For every (non-uniform) PPT prover P^* that on input 1^λ (and without access to the verifier's message) outputs a length $1^{p(\lambda)}$ and $x \in \{0, 1\}^{p(\lambda)} \setminus L$, $\Pr[\mathsf{Output}_V \langle P^*, V \rangle(x) = 1] = \mathsf{negl}(\lambda)$, where the probability is over the random coins of V.*

Witness Indistinguishability. A proof system is witness indistinguishable if for any statement with at least two witnesses, proofs computed using different witnesses are indistinguishable. In this paper, we only consider statistical witness indistinguishability, which we formally define below.

Definition 6 (Statistical Witness Indistinguishability). *A delayed-input interactive argument (P, V) for a language L is said to be statistical witness-indistinguishable if for every unbounded verifier V^*, every polynomially bounded function $n = n(\lambda) \leq \mathsf{poly}(\lambda)$, and every $(x_n, w_{1,n}, w_{2,n})$ such that $(x_n, w_{1,n}) \in R_L$ and $(x_n, w_{2,n}) \in R_L$ and $|x_n| = n$, the following two ensembles are statistically indistinguishable:*

$$\big\{ \mathsf{View}_{V^*} \langle P(x_n, w_{1,n}), V^*(x_n) \rangle \big\} \quad and \quad \big\{ \mathsf{View}_{V^*} \langle P(x_n, w_{2,n}), V^*(x_n) \rangle \big\}$$

Definition 7 (T_{Sim}-Statistical Zero Knowledge). *A delayed-input interactive argument (P, V) for a language L is said to be a T_{Sim}-super-polynomial simulation (SPS) statistical zero-knowledge argument for L if there exists a (uniform) simulator Sim that runs in time T_{Sim}, such that for every x, every unbounded verifier V^*, the two distributions $\mathsf{View}_{V^*}[\langle P, V^* \rangle (x, w)]$ and $S^{V^*}(x, z)$ are statistically close.*

4   Extractable Commitments

4.1   Definitions

We take the following definition of statistically hiding extractable commitments from [20]. As before, we use λ to denote the security parameter, and we let $p = \mathsf{poly}(\lambda)$ be an arbitrary fixed polynomial such that the message space is $\{0,1\}^{p(\lambda)}$.

We restrict ourselves to commitments with non-interactive decommitment, and where the (honest) receiver is not required to maintain any state at the end of the commit phase in order to execute the decommit phase. Our construction will satisfy this property and this will be useful in our applications to constructing statistically private arguments.

Definition 8 (Statistically Hiding Commitment Scheme). *A commitment $\langle C, R \rangle$ is a two-phase protocol between a committer C and receiver R, consisting of algorithms* Commit, Decommit *and* Verify. *At the beginning of the protocol, C obtains as input a message $M \in \{0,1\}^p$. Next, C and R execute the commit phase, and obtain a commitment transcript, denoted by τ, together with private states for C and R, denoted by* $\mathsf{state}_{C,\tau}$ *and* $\mathsf{state}_{R,\tau}$ *respectively. We use the notation*

$$(\tau, \mathsf{state}_{C,\tau}, \mathsf{state}_{R,\tau}) \leftarrow \mathsf{Commit}\langle C(M), R \rangle.$$

Later, C and R possibly engage in a decommit phase, where the committer C computes and sends message $y = \mathsf{Decommit}(\tau, \mathsf{state}_{C,\tau})$ to R. At the end, R computes $\mathsf{Verify}(\tau, y)$ to output $\perp$ or a message $\widetilde{M} \in \{0,1\}^p$.[3]

A statistically hiding commitment scheme is required to satisfy three properties: perfect completeness, statistical hiding and computational binding. We formally define these in the full version of the paper.

We also define an extractor $\mathcal{E}$ that given black-box access to C^*, and then without executing any decommitment phase with C^*, outputs message $\widetilde{M}$ committed by C^* with probability at least ϵ: we require "correctness" of this extracted message $\widetilde{M}$. We also require that no PPT adversary can distinguish transcripts where extraction is successful from those where it is unsuccessful. This is formally described in Definition 9.

Definition 9 (ϵ-Extractable Statistically Hiding Commitment). *We say that a statistically hiding commitment scheme is ϵ-extractable if the following holds: Denote $(\tau, \mathsf{state}_{C,\tau}, \mathsf{state}_{R,\tau}) \leftarrow \mathsf{Commit}\langle C^*, R \rangle$. We require that there exists a deterministic polynomial time extractor $\mathcal{E}$ that on input $(\tau, \mathsf{state}_{R,\tau})$ outputs $\widetilde{M}$ such that the following properties hold.*

---

[3] We note that in our definition, R *does not* need to use private state $\mathsf{state}_{R,\tau}$ from the commitment phase in order to execute the Verify algorithm in the decommitment phase.

- **Frequency of Extraction.** *For every PPT committer* $\mathcal{C}^*$,

$$\Pr[\mathcal{E}(\tau, \mathsf{state}_{\mathcal{R},\tau}) \neq \bot] = \epsilon$$

  where the probability is over $(\tau, \mathsf{state}_{\mathcal{C},\tau}, \mathsf{state}_{\mathcal{R},\tau}) \leftarrow \mathsf{Commit}\langle \mathcal{C}^*, \mathcal{R} \rangle$.
- **Correctness of Extraction.** *For every PPT committer* $\mathcal{C}^*$, *every execution* $(\tau, \mathsf{state}_{\mathcal{C},\tau}, \mathsf{state}_{\mathcal{R},\tau}) \in \mathsf{Supp}(\mathsf{Commit}\langle \mathcal{C}^*, \mathcal{R} \rangle)$, *and every* y, *denoting* $\widetilde{M} = \mathcal{E}(\tau, \mathsf{state}_{\mathcal{R},\tau})$ *and* $M = \mathsf{Verify}(\tau, y)$, *if* $\widetilde{M} \neq \bot$ *and* $M \neq \bot$, *then* $\widetilde{M} = M$.
- **Indistinguishability of Extractable Transcripts.** *For every* $\mathcal{C}^*$,

$$\left| \Pr[\mathcal{C}^*(\tau) = 1 \mid \mathcal{E}(\tau, \mathsf{state}_{\mathcal{R},\tau}) \neq \bot] - \Pr[\mathcal{C}^*(\tau) = 1 \mid \mathcal{E}(\tau, \mathsf{state}_{\mathcal{R},\tau}) = \bot] \right| = \mathsf{negl}(\lambda)$$

  where the probability is over $(\tau, \mathsf{state}_{\mathcal{R},\tau}) \leftarrow \mathsf{Commit}\langle \mathcal{C}^*, \mathcal{R} \rangle$.

We also consider a stronger definition, of ϵ-extractable statistically hiding ℓ multi-commitments, where we require that an entire sequence of ℓ commitments can be extracted with probability ϵ, that is independent of ℓ. We will also modify the Verify algorithm so that it obtains as input the transcript $\tau := (\tau_1, \tau_2, \dots \tau_\ell)$ of all ℓ commitments, together with an index $i \in [\ell]$ and the decommitment $\mathsf{state}_{\mathcal{C},\tau,i}$ to a single commitment. We defer their formal description to the full version of the paper.

4.2   Protocol

In this section, we construct two-message statistically hiding, extractable commitments according to Definition 9 assuming the existence of two message oblivious transfer (OT). Our construction is described in Fig. 1.

Primitives Used. Let $\mathsf{OT} = (\mathsf{OT}_1, \mathsf{OT}_2)$ denote a two-message string oblivious transfer protocol according to Definition 4, also satisfying Property 1. Let $\mathsf{OT}_1(b; r_1)$ denote the first message of the OT protocol with receiver input b and randomness r_1, and let $\mathsf{OT}_2(M_0, M_1; r_2)$ denote the second message of the OT protocol with sender input strings M_0, M_1 and randomness r_2.[4]

Observe that the protocol satisfies the property mentioned in the definition that the verify algorithm in the decommitment phase does not require the private randomness used by the receiver in the commit phase. Further, observe that if the oblivious transfer protocol satisfies Property 1, the receiver's message can alternately be generated by just sampling a uniformly random string. Thus, this would give an extractable commitment protocol where the receiver's algorithms are public coin.

We will now prove the following main theorem.

Theorem 1. *Assuming that the underlying OT protocol is* $\lambda^{-\log \lambda}$*-secure against malicious senders,* $(1 - \delta_{\mathsf{OT}})$ *secure against malicious receivers according to Definition 4, and satisfies Property 1, there exists a setting of* $m = O(\log^2 \lambda)$

---

[4] Note that OT_2 also depends on OT_1. We omit this dependence in our notation for brevity.

Extraction parameter: m.

Committer Input: Message $M \in \{0,1\}^p$.

Commit Stage:

Receiver Message.

1. Pick challenge string $\mathsf{ch} \overset{\$}{\leftarrow} \{0,1\}^m$.
2. Sample uniform randomness $\{r_{1,i}\}_{i \in [m]}$.
3. Compute and send $\{\mathsf{OT}_1(\mathsf{ch}_i, r_{1,i})\}_{i \in [m]}$ using m instances of two-message OT.

Committer Message.

1. Sample a random string $r \overset{\$}{\leftarrow} \{0,1\}^m$.

   For every $i \in [m]$ and every $b \in \{0,1\}$, sample $M_i^b \overset{\$}{\leftarrow} \{0,1\}^p$ subject to $\bigoplus_{i \in [m]} M_i^{r_i} = M$.
2. For every $i \in [m]$ compute $o_{2,i} = \mathsf{OT}_2(M_i^0, M_i^1; r_{2,i})$ with uniform randomness $r_{2,i}$.
3. Send $(r, \{o_{2,i}\}_{i \in [m]})$.

Reveal Stage: The committer reveals M, and all values $\{M_i^0, M_i^1\}_{i \in [m]}$ as well as the randomness $r_{2,i}$. The receiver accepts the decommitment to message M if and only if:

1. For all $i \in [m]$, $o_{2,i} = \mathsf{OT}_2(M_i^0, M_i^1; r_{2,i})$,
2. $\bigoplus_{i \in [m]} M_i^{r_i} = M$.

Fig. 1. Extractable commitments

for which the scheme in Fig. 1 is a $(1 - 2^{-m} - \delta_{\mathsf{OT}})$ statistically hiding, $\lambda^{-\log^{1/2} \lambda}$-extractable commitment scheme according to Definition 9. Further, the receiver's algorithms are public coin.

We relegate the proof of Theorem 1 to the full version of the paper.

5 Our Statistical WI Protocol

5.1 Modified Blum Protocol

We begin by describing a very simple modification to the Blum Σ-protocol for Graph Hamiltonicity. The protocol we describe will have soundness error $\frac{1}{2} - \mathsf{negl}(\lambda)$ against adaptive PPT provers, and will satisfy *statistical* zero-knowledge. Since Graph Hamiltonicity is NP-complete, this protocol can also be used to prove any statement in NP via a Karp reduction. This protocol is described in Fig. 2.

We give an overview of the protocol here. Note that the only modification to the original protocol of Blum [3] is that we use two message statistically hiding,

---

Modified Blum Argument

1. **Verifier Message:** The verifier does the following:
   ○ Sample the first message $\mathsf{extcom}_{1,i,j}$ for independent instances of the extractable commitment, where $i,j \in [p(\lambda)] \times [p(\lambda)]$, *uniformly at random.*
   ○ Send an additional first message $\mathsf{extcom}_{1,P}$ for another independent instance of the extractable commitment, again sampled *uniformly at random.*
2. **Prover Message:** The prover gets input graph $G \in \{0,1\}^{p(\lambda) \times p(\lambda)}$ represented as an adjacency matrix, with $(i,j)^{th}$ entry denoted by $G[i][j]$), Hamiltonian cycle $H \subseteq G$. Here $p(\cdot)$ is an a-priori fixed polynomial. The prover does the following:
   ○ Sample a random permutation π on $p(\lambda)$ nodes, and compute $c_P = \mathsf{extcom}_{2,P}(\pi)$ as a commitment to π using extcom.
   ○ Compute $\pi(G)$, which is the adjacency matrix corresponding to the graph G when its nodes are permuted according to π. Compute $c_{i,j} = \mathsf{extcom}_{2,i,j}(\pi(G)[i][j])$ for $(i,j) \in [p(\lambda)] \times [p(\lambda)]$.
   ○ Send $G, c_P, c_{i,j}$ for $(i,j) \in [p(\lambda)] \times [p(\lambda)]$.
3. **Verifier Message:** Sample and send $c \xleftarrow{\$} \{0,1\}$ to the prover.
4. **Prover Message:** The prover does the following:
   ○ If $c = 0$, send π and the decommitments of $\mathsf{extcom}_P, \mathsf{extcom}_{i,j}$ for $(i,j) \in [p(\lambda)] \times [p(\lambda)]$.
   ○ If $c = 1$, send the decommitment of $\mathsf{extcom}_{i,j}$ for all (i,j) such that $\pi(H)[i][j] = 1$.
5. **Verifier Output:** The verifier does the following:
   ○ If $c = 0$, accept if and only if all extcom openings were accepted and $\pi(G)$ was computed correctly by applying π on G.
   ○ If $c = 1$, accept if and only if all extcom openings were accepted and all the opened commitments form a Hamiltonian cycle.

Remark: Observe that since the receiver's algorithms in the extractable commitment scheme are public coin, the above protocol is also public coin.

Fig. 2. Modified blum SZK argument

extractable commitments instead of non-interactive statistically binding commitments. The proofs of soundness and statistical honest-verifier zero-knowledge are fairly straightforward. They roughly follow the same structure as [3], replacing statistically binding commitments with statistically hiding commitments.

Lemma 1. *Assuming that* extcom *is computationally binding, the protocol in Fig. 2 satisfies soundness against PPT provers that may choose x adaptively in the second round of the protocol.*

Proof. The proof of soundness follows by the computational binding property of extcom and the soundness of the (original) Blum protocol.

Let L denote the language consisting of all graphs that have a Hamiltonian cycle. Consider a cheating prover P^* that convinces a malicious verifier about a statement $x \notin L$ with probability $\frac{1}{2} + h(n)$, where $h(\cdot) > \frac{1}{\mathsf{poly}(\cdot)}$ for some polynomial $\mathsf{poly}(\cdot)$. By an averaging argument, this means that there exists at least one transcript prefix τ consisting of the first two messages of the protocol, where for $G \notin L$ sent by the prover in the third message, $\Pr[V \text{ accepts}|\tau, G \notin L] > \frac{1}{2}$. This implies that there exists a cheating prover that generates a transcript prefix τ, for which it provides an accepting opening corresponding to both $b = 0$ and $b = 1$, with probability at least $h(n)$. Next, we argue that such a cheating prover must break the (computational) binding of com.

Since $G \notin L$, it is information theoretically impossible for any cheating prover to generate a commitment to a unique string $\pi, \pi(G)$ such that there exists a Hamiltonian cycle in $\pi(G)$. Therefore, any prover that opens a transcript prefix τ, G corresponding to both $b = 0$ and $b = 1$ for $G \notin L$, must open at least one commitment in the set $\{\mathsf{extcom}_P, \{\mathsf{extcom}_{i,j}\}_{i,j\in p\times p}\}$ to two different values, thereby giving a contradiction to the binding of the commitment scheme. □

Lemma 2. *Assuming that* extcom *is statistically hiding, the protocol in Fig. 2 satisfies honest-verifier statistical zero-knowledge.*

Proof. The simulation strategy is identical to that of [3]. The simulator Sim first guesses the challenge bit c'. It begins an interaction with the malicious verifier. On obtaining the first message from the verifier, if $c' = 0$, it samples π uniformly at random and generates a commitment to $\pi, \pi(G)$ following honest prover strategy to generate the commitment. If $c' = 1$, it samples π, H' uniformly at random where H' is an arbitrary hamiltonian cycle, and generates a commitment to $\pi, \pi(H')$ following honest prover strategy to generate the commitment. Next, it waits for the verifier to send c, and if $c \neq c'$, it aborts and repeats the experiment. If $c = c'$, then it decommits to the commitments according to honest prover strategy.

Note that when $c = c' = 1$, the resulting simulation is perfect zero-knowledge since the simulated view of the verifier is identical to the view generated by an honest prover. On the other hand when $c = c' = 0$, it follows from the statistical hiding property of the commitment extcom that the verifier cannot distinguish the case where extcom is a commitment to $\pi, \pi(G)$ and a hamiltonian cycle is opened in $\pi(G)$, from the case where extcom is not a commitment to $\pi(G)$, but instead to some $\pi(H')$ for a hamiltonian cycle H'. □

Since honest-verifier zero-knowledge composes under parallel repetition, we can repeat the protocol several times in parallel to get negligible soundness error. Formally, we have the following lemma:

Lemma 3. *Assuming that* extcom *is statistically hiding, the protocol in Fig. 2 satisfies honest verifier statistical zero-knowledge under parallel repetition.*

Finally, Cramer et al. [9] showed that honest verifier zero knowledge where the receiver's algorithms are public coin implies witness indistinguishability even against malicious verifiers. As a result, we get the following lemma:

Lemma 4. *Assuming that* extcom *is statistically hiding, the protocol in Fig. 2 satisfies statistical witness indistinguishability under parallel repetition.*

5.2 Statistical ZAPs

In this section, we prove the following theorem:

Theorem 2. *There exists a two message public-coin statistical witness indistinguishable argument system for NP in the plain model assuming that the following primitives exist:*

- *Two-message oblivious transfer (OT) that is quasi-polynomially secure against malicious senders, satisfying Definition 4 and Property 1, and,*
- *Quasi-polynomially correlation intractable hash functions.*

Recall from previous sections that we can use the above OT to build the extractable commitment which is then used to build a four message Σ-protocol that is a modification to Blum's protocol. As mentioned before, we can instantiate both the OT and the correlation intractable hash function assuming the learning with errors (LWE) assumption. Therefore, instantiating both the primitives in the above theorem gives us the following:

Theorem 3. *Assuming quasi-polynomially secure LWE, there exists a two message public-coin statistical witness indistinguishable argument system for NP in the plain model.*

Notations and Primitives Used

- Let λ be the security parameter.
- Let $\Sigma := (\Sigma_1, \ldots, \Sigma_\lambda)$ denote λ parallel repetitions of the modified Blum Sigma protocol constructed in Sect. 5.1, where for $i \in [\ell]$, $\Sigma_i = (q_i, a_i, e_i, z_i)$. Let the underlying commitment scheme be instantiated with extraction success probability $\epsilon = \lambda^{-\log^{1/2} \lambda}$.
- Let $\mathcal{H}$ be a correlation intractable hash function with respect to $\{\mathcal{F}_{\lambda, s(\lambda)}\}_{\lambda \in \mathbb{N}}$ according to Definition 3 that outputs strings of length λ, where $s(\lambda) = 2s_1(\lambda)$ where s_1 is the size of the extractor $\mathcal{E}$ used in the commitment scheme and $\mathcal{F}$ denotes the class of all NC^1 circuits of size $s(\lambda)$ as defined in Definition 2. Recall the correlation-intractability advantage is assumed to be at most $\frac{1}{\lambda^{\log \lambda}}$.

Construction. Let x be any instance in $\{0, 1\}^\lambda$ and let w be the corresponding witness for the statement $x \in L$.

1. **Verifier's message to the Prover:**
   - Sample $q := \{q_i\}_{i \in [\lambda]}$.
   - Sample $K \leftarrow \mathcal{H}.\mathsf{Setup}(1^\lambda, 0^\ell)$.
   - Output (q, K).
2. **Prover's message to the Verifier:**
   - Compute $\{a_i\}_{i \in [\lambda]}$ as a response to $\{q_i\}_{i \in [\lambda]}$.
   - Compute $e \leftarrow \mathcal{H}.\mathsf{Eval}(K, x, (q, a))$.
   - Compute $\{z_i\}_{i \in [\lambda]}$ with respect to the challenge string e.
   - Output (x, a, e, z).

3. **Verification:** The verifier does the following:
   - If $\mathcal{H}.\mathsf{Eval}(K, x, a) \neq e$, output reject.
   - Else if (x, q, a, e, z) does not verify according to the Σ protocol, output reject.
   - Else output accept.

Completeness. Completeness of the protocol can be easily observed from the correctness of the underlying primitives: the protocol Σ and the hash function H.

Public Coin. Recall from the statistical indistinguishability of hash keys property that an honest verifier can just sample a uniformly random string as the hash key K. This, along with the fact that the underlying protocol Σ is public coin results in the above protocol also being public coin.

Soundness. We now prove computational soundness of the protocol above. Towards a contradiction, fix any adversary $\mathcal{A}$ that breaks soundness of the protocol with probability $\frac{1}{p(\lambda)}$ for some polynomial $p(\cdot)$.

We consider a sequence of hybrids where the first hybrid corresponds to the real soundness experiment.

- Hybrid_0 : This hybrid corresponds to the experiment where the challenger behaves identically to the verifier in the actual protocol.
- Hybrid_1: In this hybrid, instead of generating the verifier's first message as uniformly random string, the challenger Ch now computes the first message of the extractable commitment scheme used in the underlying protocol Σ as done in the protocol description in Fig. 1. In particular, the underlying OT receiver messages are not sampled as uniformly random strings but instead are computed by running the OT receiver algorithm. As a result, Ch now has some internal state r_{state} as part of the extractable commitment scheme that is not public.
- Hybrid_2: This hybrid is the same as the previous hybrid except that the hash key K is generated as follows. $K \leftarrow \mathcal{H}.\mathsf{Setup}(1^\lambda, R)$ where the relation R consists of tuples of the form $((x, q, a), y)$ where y is computed by an efficient function f_{bad} described below. f_{bad} has the verifier's secret state r_{state} hardwired, takes as input the statement x, the verifier's message q, the prover's message a and does the following.
  1. Run the extractor algorithm $\mathcal{E}$ on input $(r_{\mathsf{state}}, \tau = (q, a))$ to compute m. Note that $\mathcal{E}$ can be represented by an NC^1 circuit of size $s_1(\lambda)$ for some polynomial s_1.
  2. If $m \neq \bot$, this means that m is the tuple of messages committed to in the set of λ commitment tuples $(c_P, \{c_{i,j}\})$. For each $k \in [\lambda]$, check whether the message committed to by the tuple $\{c_{i,j}\}$ is indeed equal to $\pi(G)$ where π is the permutation committed to in c_P. If so, then set $e_k = 0$ and else set $e_k = 1$. Set $y = (e_1, \ldots, e_\lambda)$.[5]
  3. If $m = \bot$, set $y = 0^\lambda$.

---

[5] Essentially, since $x \notin L$, if the cheating prover has to succeed, it can either generate a successful response z_k for verifier's query bit $e_k = 0$ or $e_k = 1$ and this function determines which bit it is.

Before proving the soundness of the protocol using the hybrids, we define an event that helps us in the proof.

Event E: Let τ denote the transcript of an execution of the above protocol and let τ_C denote the transcript of the commitment scheme in the execution. Let $\mathsf{state}_{\mathcal{R}}$ denote the state of the verifier when it runs the receiver algorithm of the commitment scheme. We will say that the event **E** occurs if for any honest verifier V:

$$[V(\tau) = 1 \wedge \mathcal{E}(\tau_C, \mathsf{state}_{\mathcal{R}}) \neq \bot].$$

We now continue the proof of soundness with the following claims.

Lemma 5. *Assuming the pseudorandomness of receiver messages of the OT protocol used in the underlying extractable commitment scheme (Property 1),* $|\Pr[V(\tau) = 1|\mathsf{Hybrid}_1] - \Pr[V(\tau) = 1|\mathsf{Hybrid}_0]| = \mathsf{negl}(\lambda)$

Proof. The only difference between the two hybrids is that in Hybrid_0, the OT receiver messages in the extractable commitment scheme used in the underlying protocol Σ are generated as uniformly random strings while in Hybrid_1, they are generated by running the algorithm OT_1 on behalf of the OT receiver. It is easy to see that if the difference in the adversary's success probability in breaking soundness between these two hybrids is non-negligible, we can break the pseudorandomness of receiver messages property (Property 1) of the underlying two message OT protocol, which is a contradiction. □

Lemma 6. *Assuming the frequency of extraction property and the indistinguishability of extractable transcripts property of the extractable commitment scheme, there exists a polynomial $p(\cdot)$ such that $\Pr[\mathbf{E} \text{ occurs in } \mathsf{Hybrid}_1] \geq \epsilon \cdot \frac{1}{p(\lambda)}$, where the probability is over the randomness of V, and where $\epsilon = \lambda^{-\log^{1/2} \lambda}$ is the extraction probability of the underlying commitment scheme.*

Proof. Fix $x \notin L$. We will consider a reduction $\mathcal{B}$ that interacts with the adversary and relies on the frequency of extraction property and the indistinguishability of extractable transcripts property of the extractable commitment scheme to prove the lemma.

$\mathcal{B}$ interacts with a challenger Ch for the commitment scheme and receives a first round message com_1 for the ℓ-extractable commitment scheme. It then interacts with the adversary $\mathcal{A}$ as the verifier in the ZAP protocol, setting com_1 as its message on behalf of the receiver in the underlying commitment scheme, and sampling the hash key $K \leftarrow \mathcal{H}.\mathsf{Setup}(1^\lambda, 0^\ell)$. After completing the protocol execution with $\mathcal{A}$, $\mathcal{B}$ forwards the commitments sent by $\mathcal{A}$ as its message com_2 of the commitment scheme to the challenger Ch. Further, $\mathcal{B}$ outputs 1 in its interaction with Ch if the proof provided by $\mathcal{A}$ verifies, and 0 otherwise.

Let τ denote the transcript of the ZAP protocol and τ_C the transcript of the underlying commitment scheme. Let state_r be the state of the receiver in the commitment scheme as sampled by the challenger Ch.

First, we observe that by Lemma 5, there exists a polynomial $p(\cdot)$ such that adversary $\mathcal{A}$ breaks the soundness property in Hybrid_1 with non-negligible probability $\frac{1}{p(\lambda)}$. This implies that $\Pr[\mathcal{B}(\tau_C) = 1] \geq \frac{1}{p(\lambda)}$ over the random coins of $\mathcal{B}, \mathsf{Ch}$. This gives us the following equation.

$$\Pr[\mathcal{B}(\tau_C) = 1] = (\Pr[\mathcal{B}(\tau_C) = 1 \mid \mathcal{E}(\tau_C, \mathsf{state}_\mathcal{R}) \neq \bot] \cdot \Pr[\mathcal{E}(\tau_C, \mathsf{state}_\mathcal{R}) \neq \bot]$$
$$+\Pr[\mathcal{B}(\tau_C) = 1 \mid \mathcal{E}(\tau_C, \mathsf{state}_\mathcal{R}) = \bot] \cdot \Pr[\mathcal{E}(\tau_C, \mathsf{state}_\mathcal{R}) = \bot]) \geq \frac{1}{p(\lambda)} \quad (1)$$

From the indistinguishability of extractable transcripts property, we have that:

$$\left| \Pr[\mathcal{B}(\tau_C) = 1 \mid \mathcal{E}(\tau_C, \mathsf{state}_\mathcal{R}) \neq \bot] - \Pr[\mathcal{B}(\tau_C) = 1 \mid \mathcal{E}(\tau_C, \mathsf{state}_\mathcal{R}) = \bot] \right| = \mathsf{negl}(\lambda) \quad (2)$$

From the frequency of extraction property, we have that :

$$\Pr[\mathcal{E}(\tau_C, \mathsf{state}_\mathcal{R}) \neq \bot] \geq \epsilon \quad (3)$$

where all equations are over the random coins of the challenger Ch and reduction $\mathcal{B}$. Combining Eqs. (1) and (2) implies that there exists a polynomial $q(\cdot)$ such that $\Pr[\mathcal{B}(\tau_C) = 1 \mid \mathcal{E}(\tau_C, \mathsf{state}_\mathcal{R}) \neq \bot] \geq \frac{1}{q(\lambda)}$, which, by Eq. (3), implies that

$$\Pr[\mathcal{B}(\tau) = 1 \wedge \mathcal{E}(\tau_C, \mathsf{state}_\mathcal{R}) \neq \bot]$$
$$= \Pr[\mathcal{B}(\tau_C) = 1 \mid \mathcal{E}(\tau_C, \mathsf{state}_\mathcal{R}) \neq \bot] \cdot \Pr[\mathcal{E}(\tau_C, \mathsf{state}_\mathcal{R}) \neq \bot]$$
$$\geq \frac{1}{q(\lambda)} \cdot \epsilon.$$

Thus we have $\Pr[\mathbb{E} \text{ occurs in } \mathsf{Hybrid}_1] \geq \epsilon \cdot \frac{1}{q(\lambda)}$. This completes the proof of the Lemma. $\qquad\square$

Lemma 7. *Assuming the statistical indistinguishability of hash keys of the correlation intractable hash function, there exists a polynomial $p(\cdot)$ such that*

$$\Pr[\mathbb{E} \text{ occurs in } \mathsf{Hybrid}_2] \geq \epsilon \cdot \frac{1}{p(\lambda)},$$

where the probability is over the randomness of V, and where $\epsilon = \lambda^{-\log^{1/2}\lambda}$ is the extraction probability of the underlying commitment.

Proof. Assume for the sake of contradiction that the lemma is not true. We will show that we can break the statistical indistinguishability of hash keys property of the correlation intractable hash function.

We will design a reduction $\mathcal{B}$ that interacts with $\mathcal{A}$, where $\mathcal{B}$ acts as verifier in the above ZAP protocol. $\mathcal{B}$ interacts with a challenger Ch for the correlation intractable hash function. Initially, $\mathcal{B}$ samples the first round message q for the underlying Sigma protocol just as in Hybrid_1, along with associated receiver state $\mathsf{state}_\mathcal{R}$ for the commitment scheme, and sends both to Ch. $\mathcal{B}$ obtains a hash key K sampled either uniformly at random (as in Hybrid_1) or by running the setup algorithm of the hash function as described in Hybrid$_2$. $\mathcal{B}$ uses this key K in its interaction with the adversary $\mathcal{A}$ and completes executing the ZAP protocol. Observe that if Ch sampled a hash key uniformly at random, the interaction between $\mathcal{A}$ and $\mathcal{B}$ is identical to Hybrid$_1$ and if Ch sampled as hash key as described in Hybrid$_2$, the interaction between $\mathcal{A}$ and $\mathcal{B}$ is identical to Hybrid$_2$.

Now, $\mathcal{B}$ tests if event $\mathbf{E}$ occurs. That is, it checks if the ZAP protocol verifies and if so, runs the extractor $\mathcal{E}(\tau_C, \mathsf{state}_\mathcal{R})$ using the transcript τ_C for the commitment scheme. If the extractor cE does not output $\bot$, then event $\mathbf{E}$ occurs and $\mathcal{B}$ guesses that the hash key was uniformly sampled in its interaction with the challenger Ch. Otherwise, it guesses that the hash key was not uniformly sampled. Thus, if the event $\mathbf{E}$ occurs with probability $\geq \epsilon \cdot \frac{1}{p(\lambda)}$ in Hybrid$_1$, and occurs with probability $\epsilon \cdot \mathsf{negl}(\lambda)$ in Hybrid$_2$, $\mathcal{B}$ can distinguish between the hash keys with advantage $\frac{\epsilon}{q(\lambda)}$ for some polynomial q. This is a contradiction, and this completes the proof of the lemma. $\qquad\square$

Lemma 8. *Assuming the quasi-polynomial correlation intractable property of the hash function, the soundness of the underlying protocol Σ and the correctness of extraction of the extractable commitment scheme,*

$$\Pr[\mathbf{E} \ occurs \ in \ \mathsf{Hybrid}_2] \leq \epsilon \cdot \mathsf{negl}(\lambda).$$

Proof. Suppose the claim is not true. This implies that $\Pr[V(\tau) = 1 \wedge \mathcal{E}(\tau_C, \mathsf{state}_\mathcal{R}) \neq \bot] = \epsilon \cdot \frac{1}{p(\lambda)}$ for some polynomial p. Let us consider any transcript on which event $\mathbf{E}$ occurs. Let (q, K) denote the verifier's message and (x, a, e, z) denote the prover's message. Then, from the correctness of the ZAP protocol, it must be the case that (q, a, e, z) verifies according to protocol Σ and $e = H(K, q, x, a)$. Further, since the extractor $\mathcal{E}$ succeeds on this transcript, the commitment scheme is statistically binding. Therefore, we can invoke the special soundness of the underlying modified Blum Σ protocol (as in the case of the regular Blum protocol) to state that for the statement $x \notin L$ and prefix (q, a) there can exist at most one pair (e^*, z^*) such that (q, a, e^*, z^*) verifies successfully. Therefore, the adversary's message e must be equal to this value e^*.

Now, from the description of the relation R used in defining the hash key K in Hybrid$_2$, we observe that, by the correctness of extraction, $f_{bad}(q, x, a) = e^* = H(K, q, x, a)$. Thus, for any transcript that satisfies the conditions in event $\mathbf{E}$, $f_{bad}(q, x, a) = e^* = H(K, q, x, a)$.

Thus, we can build a reduction $\mathcal{B}$ that, using the adversary $\mathcal{A}$, produces (x, q, a) such that $f_{bad}(q, x, a) = e^* = H(K, q, x, a)$ with probability at least $\epsilon \cdot \frac{1}{p(\lambda)} = \frac{1}{\lambda^{\log^{1/2} \lambda} \cdot p(\lambda)}$. Since by Definition 3 the advantage of any polynomial-time adversary in this game must be at most $\frac{1}{\lambda^{\log \lambda}}$, this yields a contradiction. $\qquad\square$

Note that Lemmas 7 and 8 contradict each other, and therefore the adversary does not break soundness in the real experiment. This completes the proof of soundness. $\qquad\square$

Statistical Witness Indistinguishability. Let $\mathcal{A}$ denote the unbounded time adversarial verifier and Ch denote the challenger. Let x be the challenge instance of length λ and w_0 and w_1 be a pair of witnesses for $x \in L$. Consider a pair of hybrids where the first hybrid Hybrid_0 corresponds to Ch running the honest prover algorithm with witness w_0 being used and the second hybrid Hybrid_1 corresponds to Ch running the honest prover algorithm with witness w_1 being used. We now show that these two hybrids are statistically indistinguishable to complete the proof.

Claim. Assuming the Σ-protocol is statistically witness indistinguishable, Hybrid_0 is statistically indistinguishable from Hybrid_1.

Proof. We now show that if there exists an unbounded time adversary $\mathcal{A}$ for which the two hybrids are not statistically indistinguishable, we can build a reduction $\mathcal{B}$ that can break the witness indistinguishability of the underlying modified Blum's Sigma protocol which is a contradiction to Lemma 4. $\mathcal{B}$ acts as the challenger in its interaction with the adversary $\mathcal{A}$ that is trying to distinguish between these two hybrids. Further, $\mathcal{B}$ acts as the adversary in its interaction with a challenger $\mathcal{C}$ in trying to break the WI property of the modified Blum Sigma protocol. Initially, $\mathcal{A}$ sends a statement x, a pair of witnesses (w_0, w_1) and a first round message (q, K) for the above ZAP construction. $\mathcal{B}$ forwards (x, w_0, w_1) to the challenger $\mathcal{C}$ and sends q as its first message of the underlying protocol Σ. $\mathcal{C}$ responds with its round two message a on behalf of the prover. $\mathcal{B}$ computes $e \leftarrow \mathcal{H}.\mathsf{Eval}(K, x, (q, a))$ and sends it to $\mathcal{C}$. Finally, $\mathcal{C}$ responds with the last round message z on behalf of the prover. Now, $\mathcal{B}$ sends the tuple (x, a, e, z) to $\mathcal{A}$ as the prover message for the above ZAP protocol. Observe that if the challenger $\mathcal{C}$ interacted using witness w_0, then the interaction between the reduction $\mathcal{B}$ and the adversary $\mathcal{A}$ is identical to Hybrid_0 and if the challenger $\mathcal{C}$ interacted using witness w_1, then the interaction between the reduction $\mathcal{B}$ and the adversary $\mathcal{A}$ is identical to Hybrid_1. Thus, if these two hybrids are not statistically indistinguishable to $\mathcal{A}$, $\mathcal{B}$ can use the same guess used by $\mathcal{A}$ to distinguish them, to break the statistical witness indistinguishability property of the protocol Σ which is a contradiction. $\square$

5.3   Statistical SPS Zero Knowledge

We achieve the following theorem:

Theorem 4. *For any $c > 0$, there exists a two message public-coin T_{Sim}-SPS statistical zero knowledge argument system for NP in the plain model, where $T_{\mathsf{Sim}} = 2^{\lambda^c}$, assuming two-message oblivious transfer (OT) that is subexponentially secure against malicious senders, and quasi-polynomially correlation intractable hash functions.*

Note that we can instantiate the CI hash function and the OT protocol assuming subexponential LWE. We refer to the full version of the paper for the proof of Theorem 4.

Acknowledgements. Rex Fernando, Aayush Jain and Amit Sahai were supported in part by the following: a DARPA/ARL SAFEWARE award, NSF Frontier Award 1413955, NSF grants 1619348, 1228984, 1136174, and 1065276, BSF grant 2012378, a Xerox Faculty Research Award, a Google Faculty Research Award, an equipment grant from Intel, and an Okawa Foundation Research Grant. Aayush Jain was also supported by a Google PhD Fellowship (2018) in the area of Privacy and Security. This material is based upon work supported by the Defense Advanced Research Projects Agency through the ARL under Contract W911NF-15-C-0205. The views expressed are those of the authors and do not reflect the official policy or position of the Department of Defense, the National Science Foundation, the U.S. Government, or Google.

References

1. Badrinarayanan, S., Garg, S., Ishai, Y., Sahai, A., Wadia, A.: Two-message witness indistinguishability and secure computation in the plain model from new assumptions. In: Takagi, T., Peyrin, T. (eds.) ASIACRYPT 2017. LNCS, vol. 10626, pp. 275–303. Springer, Cham (2017). https://doi.org/10.1007/978-3-319-70700-6_10
2. Bitansky, N., Paneth, O.: ZAPs and non-interactive witness indistinguishability from indistinguishability obfuscation. In: Dodis, Y., Nielsen, J.B. (eds.) TCC 2015. LNCS, vol. 9015, pp. 401–427. Springer, Heidelberg (2015). https://doi.org/10.1007/978-3-662-46497-7_16
3. Blum, M.: How to prove a theorem so no one else can claim it. In: Proceedings of the International Congress of Mathematicians, Berkeley, CA, pp. 1444–1451 (1986)
4. Blum, M., Feldman, P., Micali, S.: Non-interactive zero-knowledge and its applications (extended abstract). In: STOC, pp. 103–112 (1988)
5. Brakerski, Z., Döttling, N.: Two-message statistically sender-private OT from LWE. In: Beimel, A., Dziembowski, S. (eds.) TCC 2018. LNCS, vol. 11240, pp. 370–390. Springer, Cham (2018). https://doi.org/10.1007/978-3-030-03810-6_14
6. Brassard, G., Crépeau, C., Robert, J.: Information theoretic reductions among disclosure problems. In: FOCS (1986)
7. Canetti, R., et al.: Fiat-Shamir: from practice to theory. In: STOC (2019)
8. Chaum, D.: Demonstrating that a public predicate can be satisfied without revealing any information about how. In: Odlyzko, A.M. (ed.) CRYPTO 1986. LNCS, vol. 263, pp. 195–199. Springer, Heidelberg (1987). https://doi.org/10.1007/3-540-47721-7_13
9. Cramer, R., Damgård, I., Schoenmakers, B.: Proofs of partial knowledge and simplified design of witness hiding protocols. In: Desmedt, Y.G. (ed.) CRYPTO 1994. LNCS, vol. 839, pp. 174–187. Springer, Heidelberg (1994). https://doi.org/10.1007/3-540-48658-5_19
10. Dwork, C., Naor, M.: Zaps and their applications. In: FOCS (2000)
11. Dwork, C., Naor, M.: Zaps and their applications. Electronic Colloquium on Computational Complexity (ECCC) (001) (2002)
12. Dwork, C., Naor, M.: Zaps and their applications. SIAM J. Comput. **36**(6), 1513–1543 (2007). https://doi.org/10.1137/S0097539703426817
13. Feige, U., Shamir, A.: Witness indistinguishable and witness hiding protocols. In: STOC (1990)
14. Goldreich, O., Micali, S., Wigderson, A.: Proofs that yield nothing but their validity and a methodology of cryptographic protocol design (extended abstract). In: FOCS (1986)

15. Groth, J., Ostrovsky, R., Sahai, A.: Non-interactive zaps and new techniques for NIZK. In: Dwork, C. (ed.) CRYPTO 2006. LNCS, vol. 4117, pp. 97–111. Springer, Heidelberg (2006). https://doi.org/10.1007/11818175_6
16. Halevi, S., Kalai, Y.T.: Smooth projective hashing and two-message oblivious transfer. J. Cryptol. **25**(1), 158–193 (2012). https://doi.org/10.1007/s00145-010-9092-8
17. Jain, A., Jin, Z.: Statistical zap arguments from quasi-polynomial LWE. Cryptology ePrint Archive, Report 2019/839 (2019). https://eprint.iacr.org/2019/839
18. Jain, A., Kalai, Y.T., Khurana, D., Rothblum, R.: Distinguisher-dependent simulation in two rounds and its applications. In: Katz, J., Shacham, H. (eds.) CRYPTO 2017. LNCS, vol. 10402, pp. 158–189. Springer, Cham (2017). https://doi.org/10.1007/978-3-319-63715-0_6
19. Kalai, Y.T.: Smooth projective hashing and two-message oblivious transfer. In: Cramer, R. (ed.) EUROCRYPT 2005. LNCS, vol. 3494, pp. 78–95. Springer, Heidelberg (2005). https://doi.org/10.1007/11426639_5
20. Kalai, Y.T., Khurana, D., Sahai, A.: Statistical witness indistinguishability (and more) in two messages. In: Nielsen, J.B., Rijmen, V. (eds.) EUROCRYPT 2018. LNCS, vol. 10822, pp. 34–65. Springer, Cham (2018). https://doi.org/10.1007/978-3-319-78372-7_2
21. Khurana, D., Sahai, A.: Two-message non-malleable commitments from standard sub-exponential assumptions. IACR Cryptology ePrint Archive 2017, 291 (2017). http://eprint.iacr.org/2017/291
22. Lombardi, A., Vaikuntanathan, V., Wichs, D.: 2-message publicly verifiable WI from (subexponential) LWE. Cryptology ePrint Archive, Report 2019/808 (2019). https://eprint.iacr.org/2019/808
23. Naor, M., Pinkas, B.: Efficient oblivious transfer protocols. In: SODA (2001)
24. Peikert, C., Shiehian, S.: Noninteractive zero knowledge for NP from (plain) learning with errors (2010)
25. Sahai, A., Waters, B.: How to use indistinguishability obfuscation: deniable encryption, and more. In: STOC (2014)

Statistical Zaps and New Oblivious Transfer Protocols

Vipul Goyal[1], Abhishek Jain[2(✉)], Zhengzhong Jin[2(✉)], and Giulio Malavolta[1,3]

[1] Carnegie Mellon University, Pittsburgh, PA, USA
vipul@cmu.edu, giulio.malavolta@hotmail.it
[2] Johns Hopkins University, Baltimore, MD, USA
abhishek@cs.jhu.edu, zzjin@cs.jhu.edu
[3] UC Berkeley, Berkeley, USA

Abstract. We study the problem of achieving *statistical privacy* in interactive proof systems and oblivious transfer – two of the most well studied two-party protocols – when limited rounds of interaction are available.

- **Statistical Zaps:** We give the first construction of statistical Zaps, namely, two-round statistical witness-indistinguishable (WI) protocols with a *public-coin* verifier. Our construction achieves computational soundness based on the quasi-polynomial hardness of learning with errors assumption.
- **Three-Round Statistical Receiver-Private Oblivious Transfer:** We give the first construction of a three-round oblivious transfer (OT) protocol – in the plain model – that achieves statistical privacy for receivers and computational privacy for senders against malicious adversaries, based on *polynomial-time* assumptions. The round-complexity of our protocol is optimal.

We obtain our first result by devising a public-coin approach to compress sigma protocols, without relying on trusted setup. To obtain our second result, we devise a general framework via a new notion of *statistical hash commitments* that may be of independent interest.

1 Introduction

We study the problem of achieving statistical privacy in two-party cryptographic protocols. Statistical privacy is very appealing in cryptography since it guarantees *everlasting security* – even if the adversary is computationally unbounded during the protocol execution and later post-processes the protocol transcript for as long as it wants, it cannot violate the privacy guarantee. For this reason, perhaps unsurprisingly, statistical privacy is typically much harder to achieve than computational privacy. For example, achieving statistical privacy for *both* participants in two-party protocols is impossible in general.

Nevertheless, in many scenarios, "one-sided" statistical privacy is possible to achieve. In other words, it is typically possible to design protocols that guarantee statistical privacy for one participant and computational privacy for the other. In

© International Association for Cryptologic Research 2020
A. Canteaut and Y. Ishai (Eds.): EUROCRYPT 2020, LNCS 12107, pp. 668–699, 2020.
https://doi.org/10.1007/978-3-030-45727-3_23

this work, we investigate the possibility of achieving such asymmetric guarantees when *limited* rounds of interaction are available. We narrow the focus of our study on interactive proof systems [2,24] and oblivious transfer [17,39], two of the most well-studied two-party protocols in the cryptography literature.

Statistical Zaps. The notion of witness-indistinguishable (WI) proofs [19] allows a prover to convince a verifier about the validity of a statement (say) x in a manner such that the proof does not reveal which one of possibly multiple witnesses that attest to the validity of x was used in the computation. More specifically, if w_1, w_2 are both witnesses for x, then the verifier should not be able to distinguish between an honest prover using w_1 from an honest prover using w_2. Despite offering a weaker privacy guarantee than zero-knowledge (ZK) proofs [24], WI has found wide applications in cryptography. One reason for its appeal is that most known round-complexity lower bounds for ZK do not apply to WI.

The seminal work of Dwork and Naor [15] proved that unlike ZK [23], WI can be achieved in two rounds, without relying on a trusted setup. They constructed two-round WI protocols with a *public-coin* verifier message, which they termed *Zaps*, from non-interactive zero-knowledge (NIZK) proofs in the common random string model [12,18]. By relying on known constructions of such NIZKs, their methodology can be used to obtain Zaps from quadratic residuosity [12], trapdoor permutations [18] and the decisional linear assumption over bilinear groups [26]. More recently, Zaps were also constructed based on indistinguishability obfuscation [6].

Over the years, Zaps have found numerous applications in cryptography. Part of their appeal is due to the public-coin verifier property which is crucial to many applications. In particular, it implies *public verifiability*, a property which is often used in the design of round-efficient secure multiparty computation protocols (see, e.g., [27]). Moreover, it also allows for the verifier message to be *reusable* across multiple proofs, a property which is often used, for example, in the design of resettably-secure protocols (see, e.g., [13]).

Remarkably, all known constructions of Zaps (as well as non-interactive WI [5,6,25]) only achieve *computational* WI property. Despite several years of research, the following fundamental question has remained open:

Do there exist statistical Zaps?

In fact, even two-round statistical WI that only satisfy public-verifiability or reusability, in isolation, are not known currently. This is in contrast to NIZKs, which are indeed known with statistical privacy [8,38] or even perfect privacy [26]. One reason for this disparity is that the methodology of [15] for constructing Zaps is not applicable in the statistical case.

The recent work of Kalai, Khurana and Sahai [31] comes close to achieving this goal. They constructed two round statistical WI with *private-coin* verifier message based on two round statistical sender-private oblivious transfer (OT) [1,7,28,30,36]. The use of a private-coin verifier message is, in fact, instrumental to their approach (which builds on [4,29]). As such, a different approach is required for constructing statistical Zaps with a public-coin verifier.

Statistical Receiver-Private Oblivious Transfer. An oblivious transfer (OT) [17,39] protocol allows a "sender" to transfer one of its two inputs to a "receiver" without learning which of the inputs was obtained by the receiver. OT is of special importance to the theory and practice of secure computation [22,41] since OT is both necessary and complete [33].

Nearly two decades ago, the influential works of works of Naor and Pinkas [36] and Aiello et al. [1] constructed two-round OT protocols that achieve game-based security against malicious adversaries in the plain model. An important property of these protocols is that they guarantee *statistical privacy for senders* (and computational privacy for receivers). Subsequent to these works, new constructions of such protocols were proposed based on a variety of assumptions (see, e.g., [7,28,30]). Over the years, such OT protocols have found many applications such as constructions of two-round (statistical) WI [4,29,31], non-malleable commitments [32], and more.

A natural question is whether it is possible to construct such OT protocols with a "reverse" guarantee, namely, *statistical privacy for receivers* (and computational privacy for senders). As observed in [31], two rounds are insufficient for this task: statistical receiver privacy implies that there exists different randomness tapes for receiver that explains a fixed receiver message for both input bits 0 and 1. Thus, a non-uniform malicious PPT receiver could simply start a two-round protocol with non-uniform advice that consists of such a message and randomness tapes, and then use both random tapes to learn *both* inputs of the sender, thereby violating sender privacy.

In the same work, [31] also proved that three rounds are sufficient for this task. Namely, they constructed three round statistical receiver-private OT with game-based security against malicious adversaries, in the plain model. However, they achieve this result by relying upon *super-polynomial-time* hardness assumptions. In contrast, two-round statistical sender-private OT protocols are known from polynomial-time assumptions. This leaves open the following important question:

Does there exist three-round statistical receiver-private OT in the plain model based on polynomial-time assumptions?

1.1 Our Results

In this work, we resolve both of the aforementioned questions in the affirmative.

I. Statistical Zap Arguments. We give the first construction of statistical Zaps with computational soundness, a.k.a. *statistical Zap arguments*. The soundness of our protocol is based on the quasi-polynomial hardness of the learning with errors (LWE) assumption. While we focus on achieving statistical privacy, we note that our construction, in fact, also yields the first computational Zap argument system based on (quasi-polynomial) LWE.

Theorem 1 (Informal). *Assuming quasi-polynomial LWE, there exists a statistical Zap argument system.*

In order to obtain our result, we depart significantly from prior approaches for constructing Zaps. Specifically, our approach combines the recent statistical NIZK arguments of Peikert and Shiehian [38] in a non-black-box manner with a two-round *public-coin* statistically-hiding extractable commitment scheme (see Sect. 4.1). Previously, such a commitment scheme in the private-coin setting was constructed by [31].

Roughly speaking, while the work of [38] (following [8]) instantiates the Fiat-Shamir methodology [19] for compressing sigma protocols [10] into a NIZK using collision-intractable hash (CIH) functions [9], our approach can be seen as a way to compress sigma protocols into statistical Zaps using CIH and two-round public-coin statistically-hiding extractable commitments, without using a trusted setup. Importantly, while prior approaches for compressing sigma protocols into two-round WI [4,29,31] lose the public-coin property of the sigma protocol, our approach retains it. We refer the reader to Sect. 2.1 for more details on our technical approach.

Related Work. In a concurrent and independent work, Badrinarayanan et al. [3] also construct statistical Zap arguments from quasi-polynomial LWE. In another concurrent and independent work, Lombardi et al. [34] construct computational Zap arguments from quasi-polynomial LWE. In a follow up work, Lombardi et al. [35] construct statistical Zaps with private verifier randomness from quasi-polynomial decisional linear assumption over groups with bilinear maps.

II. Three-Round Statistical Receiver-Private Oblivious Transfer. We devise a general framework for constructing three-round statistical receiver-private OT via a new notion of *statistical hash commitments* (SHC). This notion is inspired by hash proof systems [11] that were previously used to design two-round statistical sender-private OT [28,30]. Roughly speaking, an SHC scheme is a two-round statistically hiding commitment scheme where the opening verification simply involves an equality check with a hash output (computed w.r.t. a hashing algorithm associated with the scheme).

We devise a generic transformation from any SHC scheme with statistical hiding property to three-round statistical receiver-private OT. The resulting OT scheme achieves game-based security against malicious adversaries in the plain model. For the case of senders, we in fact, achieve a stronger notion of distinguisher-dependent simulation security [16,29]. Next, we provide two instantiations of an SHC scheme:

- A direct construction based on a search assumption, specifically, the computational Diffie-Hellman (CDH) problem. This construction, in fact, achieves *perfect* hiding property.
- We provide another construction of SHC based on any two-round statistical sender-private OT. Such schemes are known based on a variety of assumptions, including DDH, Quadratic (or N^{th}) Residuosity, and LWE. This yields a new approach for *OT reversal* [40] in the context of game-based security.

Putting these together, we obtain the following result:

Theorem 2 (Informal). *Assuming the existence of any two-round statistical sender-private OT (resp., polynomial hardness of CDH), there exists a three-round statistical (resp., perfect) receiver-private OT in the plain model.*

2   Technical Overview

2.1   Statistical Zap Arguments

We now prove a high-level overview of the main ideas underlying our construction of statistical Zaps. Roughly speaking, we devise a strategy to compress sigma protocols into statistical Zaps. While the idea of compressing sigma protocols to two-round WI arguments has been considered before [4,29,31], the resulting protocol in these works were inherently private coin as they use oblivious transfer to "hide" the verifier message in the underlying sigma protocol. To obtain a public-coin protocol, we take a different approach.

Our starting point is the recent construction of NIZKs from LWE [8,38] that compresses any "trapdoor" sigma protocol into a NIZK by instantiating the Fiat-Shamir transformation [19] in the CRS model. We start by briefly recalling these constructions.

Recent Constructions of NIZKs from LWE. The main tool underlying the constructions of NIZK in [8,38] is the notion of Correlation Intractable Hash (CIH) functions. Roughly speaking, correlation intractability means that for any multi-bit-output circuit f, if we sample a hash function $H_k(\cdot)$ from the CIH function family, it is hard to find an input x such that $H_k(x)$ coincides with $f(x)$.

The work of [38] construct a NIZK for the Graph Hamiltonian Language[1] starting from a sigma protocol for the same language. Recall that the first round prover message in the sigma protocol consists of commitments to some random cycle graphs. Let α denote the cycle graphs. The compression strategy works as follows: first, the prover prepares commitments to α by using a public-key encryption scheme, where the public-key is a part of the CRS setup. Next, the prover computes the verifier's challenge in the sigma protocol by evaluating the CIH function over the first round message, where the CIH key is also fixed by the CRS setup. Given this challenge, the prover finally computes the third round message of the sigma protocol. The NIZK proof simply consists of this transcript.

Roughly speaking, the zero knowledge property of this construction relies on the semantic security of the public key encryption scheme (used to commit α) as well as the programmability of the CIH. Moreover, when the public key is *lossy*, then the NIZK in fact achieves *statistical zero knowledge* property.

The soundness property crucially relies upon the ability to *extract* the values α from the commitments by using the secret key corresponding to the public-key fixed by the CRS, as well as the correlation intractability of the CIH. Specifically,

---

[1] Their construction, in fact, works for any trapdoor sigma protocol.

for any instance that is not in the language, given the secret key of the public key encryption, one can extract α from the commitment by decrypting it using the secret key, and then check if α corresponds to cycle graphs or not. Note that this checking procedure can be viewed as a function f. Then, if the malicious prover can find an accepting proof for the false statement, it implies that the output of the function f (with the secret key hardwired) evaluated over first round prover message coincides with the verifier's challenge bits, which are outputted by the CIH function. However, from the correlation intractability of CIH, such a prover shouldn't exist.

Starting Observations. Towards constructing statistical Zaps in the plain model, a naive first idea would be to simply let the verifier generate and send the CRS of the (statistical) NIZK in the first round, and then require the prover to compute and send the NIZK proof based on this CRS in the second round. This attempt, however, fails immediately since the verifier may use the trapdoor corresponding to the CRS (specifically, the secret key corresponding to the public-key encryption) to extract the prover's witness.

One natural idea to address this issue is to replace the public-key encryption scheme with a two-round statistically-hiding commitment scheme. However, while this seems to address witness privacy concerns, it is no longer clear how to argue soundness since the proof of soundness (as discussed above) crucially requires the ability to extract the α values.

Achieving Weak Privacy. In order to devise a solution to the above problems, let us first consider a significantly weaker goal of constructing a two-round protocol that achieves computational soundness but only a very weak form of privacy guarantee, namely, that the verifier can learn the prover's witness with probability at most one-half. Moreover, we do not require the protocol to be public-coin, but only satisfy the weaker property of public verifiability.

To obtain such a protocol, we rely on a 2-round statistical sender-private oblivious transfer protocol in plain model [7,28,30,36]. In such an OT scheme, even if the receiver is malicious, at least one of the sender's messages remains statistically hidden from the receiver. Given such an OT scheme, we construct the desired two-round protocol as follows:

- In the first round, the verifier acts as the OT receiver, and sends a first round OT message with a random input bit b.
- In the second round, the prover prepares a transcript of the sigma protocol in the same manner as in the NIZK construction earlier, with the following key difference: it flips a coin b' and instead of computing the first round prover message as encryptions of α values, it computes OT sender messages where in each message, he uses inputs m_0, m_1, where $m_{b'} = \alpha$ and $m_{1-b'} = \bot$.

With probability one-half, the random bit b of the verifier and the random coin b' of the prover are *different*. In this case, the statistical sender-privacy of the OT ensures that the α values remain hidden from the verifier. As such, the construction satisfies weak privacy, as required.

For computational soundness, consider any instance that is not in the language. Suppose we have an efficient cheating prover that can generate an accepting proof with non-negligible probability. In this case, we can run the cheating prover multiple times to estimate the distribution of the random coin b'. Note that at least one side of the random coin appears with probability no less than half. Without loss of generality, let assume such side is 0. Now we can switch the verifier's random hidden bit b in the first round message of OT to 0. Since the first round message of OT computationally hides b, the efficient cheating prover should not notice the switch, and hence the two random bits coincide with constant probability. However, when the two bits coincide, we can extract α by using the receiver's trapdoor of the OT. This allows us to contradict the correlation intractability of CIH, in the same manner as before.

Finally, note that the verifier does not need to use the randomness of the OT receiver to verify the proof; as such the above construction is publicly verifiable.

Amplifying Privacy. In order to amplify the privacy guarantee of the above scheme, we consider a modified approach where we replace the random bits b and b' – which collide with probability one-half – with random strings of length ℓ that collide with $\frac{1}{2^\ell}$ probability. Specifically, consider a two-round protocol where the receiver's input is a random string $\mathbf{b}$ of length ℓ, while the sender also chooses a random string $\mathbf{b}'$ of length and "encrypts" some message m. Suppose that the protocol satisfies the following "extractability" property, namely, if $\mathbf{b}$ and $\mathbf{b}'$ are equal, then the receiver can extract the encrypted message; otherwise, m remains statistically hidden.

Now consider a modified version of our weakly-private two-round argument system where we replace the two-round OT with the above "string" variant. Note that with probability $1 - 2^\ell$, $\mathbf{b}$ and $\mathbf{b}'$ chosen by the prover and the verifier would be different, in which case, the α values would remain statistically hidden. This observation can, in fact, be turned into a formal proof for statistical witness indistinguishability.

The proof of computational soundness, however, now requires more work. Specifically, we now run the cheating prover for $\approx 2^\ell$ times, and estimate a $\mathbf{b}'_0$ that the cheating prover is most likely to output (with probability $\geq 1/2^\ell$). We then switch $\mathbf{b}$ to $\mathbf{b}'_0$. If the first round message of the receiver is secure against 2^ℓ-time adversaries, then the cheating prover would not notice the switch. We can now extract α values and derive a contradiction in a similar manner as before.

Two Round Public-Coin Statistical-Hiding Extractable Commitments. A two-round protocol that achieves statistical hiding property for the sender as well as extractability property of the aforementioned form was first formalized as a *statistical-hiding extractable commitment scheme* in the work of [31]. Their construction, however, is private coin for the receiver. Below, we briefly recall their construction, and then discuss how it can be adapted to the public-coin setting.

– In the first round, the receiver samples a uniformly random string $\mathbf{b}$ of length ℓ. For each bit of the $\mathbf{b}$, the receiver sends a first round 1-out-of-2 OT message with the input bit specified by $\mathbf{b}$.

- The committer first samples a uniformly random string $\mathbf{b}'$ of length ℓ. To commit to a message m, the committer firstly uses the xor secret sharing to share m to ℓ shares. It then generates ℓ second round OT messages: for the i-th second round OT message, if the i-th bit of $\mathbf{b}'$ is 0, then the committer puts the share in the first input slot, and puts a random value in the second slot. Otherwise, the committer puts the share in the second slot, and put a random value in the first slot.

From statistical sender-privacy of the underlying OT, the above construction achieves statistically hiding with probability $1 - 2^\ell$, even if the first round messages are maliciously generated.

Let us now explain the extractability property. For any committer, there exists a string $\mathbf{b}_0$ of length ℓ, such that the second string coincides with $\mathbf{b}_0$ with probability no less than $2^{-\ell}$. Therefore, we can switch the first round message of the commitment to hide $\mathbf{b}_0$. If we set ℓ to be sub-linear, and assume the first round message is secure against sub-exponential-time adversaries, then the committer would not notice the switching. Hence, when the two strings coincide, we can extract the committed message.

The aforementioned statistical-hiding extractable commitment scheme is a private coin scheme. To obtain a public-coin scheme, we rely on the fact that in many known statistical sender-private OT schemes, the first round message is pseudorandom. For example, in the recent construction of two-round statistical sender-private OT from LWE [7], the first round message is either statistical close to uniformly random, or is an LWE instance, which is computationally indistinguishable from the uniform distribution.

Putting It All Together. Our final construction combines the above ideas to obtain a statistical Zap argument system:

- In the first round, the receiver simply sends the first round message of a two-round public-coin statistical-hiding extractable commitment scheme.
- Next, the prover samples a random string $\mathbf{b}'$ and computes a transcript of the sigma protocol in the same manner as before, except that it commits to α values within the second round messages of the public-coin statistical-hiding extractable commitment scheme.

We argue the statistical WI property by relying on the statistical-hiding property of the commitment scheme. The proof of soundness relies on the ideas discussed above. In order to base security on quasi-polynomial hardness assumptions, we set the parameter ℓ for the commitment scheme to be super-logarithmic rather than sub-linear. Given any cheating prover with inverse polynomial advantage, we run the cheating prover several times to estimate a string $\mathbf{b}_0$ of length ℓ such that the string chosen by the prover coincides with $\mathbf{b}_0$ with some inverse quasi-polynomial probability. This estimation takes quasi-polynomial time. Next, we switch the first round verifier message to one that is computed using $\mathbf{b}_0$. This switch is not noticeable to the prover since the first round message hides $\mathbf{b}_0$ even from adversaries that run in time 2^ℓ. This allows us to extract the α values and then invoke the correlation intractability of the CIH function as before. Note that we can construct the function f for CIH explicitly by using the receiver randomness for the first round message.

2.2 Three Round Statistical Receiver-Private OT

In this section, we describe our main ideas for constructing statistical receiver-private OT in three rounds in the plain model.

Prior Work Based on Super-Polynomial Time Assumptions. We start by briefly recalling the recent work of [31] who investigated the problem of statistical receiver-private OT in three rounds. Since security w.r.t. black-box polynomial-time simulation is known to be impossible to achieve in three rounds [20], [31] settled for the weaker goal of achieving security w.r.t. super-polynomial time simulation [37]. To achieve their goal, [31] implemented an OT reversal approach, starting from a two-round statistical sender-private OT to obtain a three-round statistical receiver-private OT based on super-polynomial-time hardness assumptions. In fact, the use of super-polynomial-time hardness assumptions seems somewhat inherent to their approach.

Motivated by our goal of basing security on standard polynomial-time hardness assumptions, we take a different approach, both in our security definition as well as techniques. On the definitional side, we consider distinguisher-dependent simulation security [16,29] for senders. On the technical side, we develop a general framework for three round statistical receiver-private OT via a new notion of *statistical hash commitment*. We elaborate on both of these aspects below.

Defining Security. In the setting of interactive proof systems, a well-studied security notion is weak zero-knowledge [16] which relaxes the standard notion of zero knowledge by reversing the order of quantifiers, namely, by allowing the simulator to depend upon the distinguisher. A recent work of [29] dubbed this idea as *distinguisher-dependent simulation* and studied it for proof systems and some other two-party functionalities. Following their approach, in this work, we formalize security for senders in three round OT via distinguisher-dependent simulation. Roughly speaking, this notion requires that for every malicious PPT receiver and PPT distinguisher, there must exist a PPT simulator that can simulate an indistinguishable view of the receiver.

Towards achieving distinguisher-dependent simulation security for senders, we first consider (computational) game-based security definition for senders. Interestingly, it is not immediately clear how to define game-based security for senders when we also require statistical receiver privacy. This is because in any protocol that achieves statistical receiver privacy, the protocol transcript does not fix the receiver message in an information-theoretic sense. As such, unlike the case of two-round computational receiver-private OT (where the receiver's input is information-theoretically fixed by the transcript), we cannot simply require indistinguishability of views generated using (say) sender inputs (m_b, m_{1-b}) and (m_b, m'_{1-b}), where b is presumably the input bit of the receiver.

We resolve this conundrum by using an observation from [29]. In order to build proof systems with distinguisher-dependent simulation security, the work of [29] used the following natural property of two-round OT with computational privacy for senders and receivers – the distribution over receiver views generated using (say) sender inputs (m_0, m_1) must be indistinguishable from at least one of the following:

- Distribution over receiver views generated using sender inputs (m_0, m_0).
- Distribution over receiver views generated using sender inputs (m_1, m_1).

Intuitively, the first case corresponds to receiver input bit 0, while the second case corresponds to receiver input bit 1.

It is not difficult to see that the above stated property is, in fact, meaningful even when the receiver's input is only fixed in a computational sense by the protocol transcript, which is the case in our setting. A recent work of [14] formulated a game-based security definition for senders that captures the above intuition, and we adopt it in this work. We also show that for our three round setting, game-based security for senders can be used to achieve distinguisher-dependent simulation security for senders.

So far, we have focused on formalizing security for senders. Formalizing security for receivers is easier; we consider game-based security that requires statistical/perfect indistinguishability of views generated with receiver inputs 0 and 1, against unbounded-time malicious senders.

In the remainder of this section, we describe our main ideas for constructing three-round OT with game-based security for senders and receivers.

A General Framework via Statistical Hash Commitment. We introduce a new notion of an statistical hash commitment (SHC) scheme a two-round statistically hiding commitment scheme where the decommitment verification simply involves an equality check with a hash output (computed w.r.t. a hashing algorithm associated with the scheme). We start by informally defining this notion and then discuss how it can be used to construct three-round OT with our desired security properties.

An SHC scheme is a two-round commitment scheme between a committer $\mathcal{C}$ and a receiver $\mathcal{R}$, that comes equipped with three additional algorithms – a key generation algorithm KGen, a commitment algorithm Com, and a hash algorithm H.

- In the first round, the Receiver $\mathcal{R}$ samples a key pair $(\mathsf{pk}, \mathsf{k}) \leftarrow \mathsf{KGen}$ and sends pk to the committer $\mathcal{C}$.
- In the second round, to commit a bit $b \in \{0, 1\}$, the committer $\mathcal{C}$ executes $(c, \rho) \leftarrow \mathsf{Com}(\mathsf{pk}, b)$, and sends c to the receiver $\mathcal{R}$.
- In the opening phase, the committer $\mathcal{C}$ sends (b, ρ) to the receiver $\mathcal{R}$.
- The verification algorithm only involves an equality check: $\mathcal{R}$ computes the hash algorithm H using the private key k on input (c, b) and then matches the resulting value against ρ. If the check succeeds, then $\mathcal{R}$ accepts the opening, else it rejects.

Computational Binding This property requires that no PPT malicious committer $\mathcal{C}$ can successfully compute a commitment c, and a opening ρ_0 and ρ_1 for *both* bits $b = 0$ and $b = 1$. Put differently, for an instance x and a second round message α, a PPT malicious committer cannot compute $H(k, c, b)$ for both $b = 0$ and $b = 1$.

- **Statistical (Perfect) Hiding** This property requires that, every (possibly maliciously computed) public key pk, the commitment of 0 and 1 are statistically close.

Looking ahead, we use computational binding property of SHC to achieve computational game-based security for senders in our construction of three-round OT. The statistical (resp., perfect) hiding property, on the other hand, is used to achieve statistical (resp., perfect) game-based security for receivers.

From SHC to Three-Round OT. We next describe a generic transformation from an SHC scheme statistical/perfect receiver-private OT. In our protocol design, the OT sender plays the role of the receiver in SHC, while the OT receiver plays the role of the committer for SHC. In the discussion below, let b denote the input bit of the OT receiver and let (m_0, m_1) denote the input bits of the OT sender.

- In the first round, the sender samples a key pair $(\mathsf{pk}, \mathsf{k})$ using the key generation algorithm KGen for SHC, and sends pk to the sender.
- In the second round, it runs the commitment algorithm Com for SHC on input (pk, b) to compute a second round message c and an opening ρ, and sends c to the sender.
- In the last round, the sender samples two random strings (r_0, r_1) and then computes two "mask" bits z_0 and z_1, one each for its inputs m_0, m_1. The mask z_i (for $i \in \{0, 1\}$) is computed as $\mathsf{hc}\big(\mathsf{H}(\mathsf{k}, c, i), r_i\big)$, where $\mathsf{hc}(\cdot, \cdot)$ is the Goldreich-Levin universal hardcore predicate [21].

To argue computational game-based security for senders, we crucially rely upon the strong soundness of SHC. In particular, the strong soundness of SHC, coupled with the security of the hardcore predicate ensures that at least one of the two mask bits z_i must be hidden from a malicious PPT receiver when the instance x is sampled from a hard distribution. Statistical (resp., perfect) security for receivers, on the other hand, follows from the statistical (resp., perfect) hiding property of the commitment.

We next discuss two different constructions of SHC.

Instantiating SHC from CDH. We first describe a construction of SHC that achieves *perfect* hiding property, based on CDH.

Let $\mathbf{M} = \begin{pmatrix} 1 & 0 \\ y & 1 \end{pmatrix}$, which must be full rank. Note that $g^{\mathbf{M}}$ can be computed using g^y.

- In the first round, the receiver $\mathcal{R}$ samples a random 2-by-1 column vector k as the secret key of the hash function, and sets the public key pk to be $\mathsf{pk} = (g^y, g^{\mathbf{M} \cdot \mathsf{k}})$. It then sends pk to the committer $\mathcal{C}$.

- The committer $\mathcal{C}$ (with input bit $b \in \{0, 1\}$) samples a random 2-by-1 matrix $\boldsymbol{\alpha}$, and uses pk to compute $c = g^{\boldsymbol{\alpha}^T \cdot \mathbf{M}} \cdot g^{[0,b]}$. The committer sends c to the verifier, and then compute $\rho = g^{\boldsymbol{\alpha}^T \mathbf{M} \cdot \mathsf{k}}$.
- The receiver $\mathcal{R}$ parse $c = g^{\mathbf{z}}$, and computes $\mathsf{H}(\mathsf{k}, c, b) = g^{(\mathbf{z} - [0,b]) \cdot \mathsf{k}}$. If $\mathsf{H}(\mathsf{k}, c, b) = \rho$, then accept, otherwise reject.

We next informally argue the security of the above construction. Let us first consider computational binding property. Intuitively, for any prover who wants to compute two accepting last round messages ρ_0, ρ_1 for both $b = 0$ and $b = 1$, it must compute the inverse of $\mathbf{M}$, which requires that the prover knows the witness y. More formally, to prove the computational binding property, we build a PPT extractor that extracts y to derive a contradiction. Specifically, for any cheating committer who can output two accepting ρ_0, ρ_1 for $b = 0$ and $b = 1$, we can divide them to derive $g^{[0,1] \cdot \mathsf{k}}$. If we parse k as $\mathsf{k} = (s, t)$, then this implies that given $(g^y, g^{\mathbf{M}\mathsf{k}}) = (g^y, g^{sy}, g^{sy+t})$, an efficient algorithm can compute $g^{[0,1] \cdot \mathsf{k}} = g^t$. We can then divide it from g^{sy+t} and derive g^{sy}. This gives us an efficient adversary for CDH.

To prove statistical hiding property, for any (potentially maliciously computed) pk, the commitment of bit $b \in \{0, 1\}$ is $c = g^{\boldsymbol{\alpha}^T \cdot \mathbf{M} + [0,b]}$. Since the matrix $\mathbf{M}$ is full rank, and $\boldsymbol{\alpha}$ is uniformly random, we have that c is uniformly random. Hence, the commitment statistically hides b.

Instantiating SHC from Statistical Sender-Private 2-round OT. We next show a construction of SHC from any statistical sender-private 2-round OT protocol $(\mathsf{OT}_1, \mathsf{OT}_2, \mathsf{OT}_3)$, where OT_3 denotes the receiver output computation algorithm.

- In the first round, the receiver $\mathcal{R}$ samples a random string r of length ℓ. Then for each bit $r[i]$, it invokes OT_1 to generate a first round OT message $(\mathsf{ot}_{1,i}, \mathsf{st}_i) \leftarrow \mathsf{OT}_1(1^\lambda, r[i])$. The public key pk is set to be the tuple of messages $\{\mathsf{ot}_{1,i}\}_{i \in [\ell]}$, while the private key k is set to be the tuple of private states $\{\mathsf{st}_i\}_{i \in [\ell]}$.
- The committer $\mathcal{C}$ receives pk, and its input is a bit b. It first samples a random string r' of length ℓ. For each position $i \in [\ell]$, it generates the second round OT messages $\mathsf{ot}_{2,i} = \mathsf{OT}_2(\mathsf{ot}_{1,i}, r'[i], r'[i] \oplus b)$. The commitment c is set to be the tuple of second round OT messages $\{\mathsf{ot}_{2,i}\}_{i \in [\ell]}$, and the opening $\rho = r'$.
- The verification process first computes $\mathsf{H}(\mathsf{k}, c, b)$ as follows: parse k as $\{\mathsf{st}_i\}_{i \in [\ell]}$, and the commitment c as $\{\mathsf{ot}_{2,i}\}_{i \in [\ell]}$. Then, compute $\rho_{0,i} \leftarrow \mathsf{OT}_3(\mathsf{ot}_{2,i}, \mathsf{st}_i)$, set $\rho_{1,i} = \rho_{0,i} \oplus r[i]$ for each $i \in [\ell]$, and set $\{\rho_{b,i}\}_{i \in [\ell]}$ to be the output of $\mathsf{H}(\mathsf{k}, c, b)$. If this output equals ρ, accept, otherwise, reject.

To show the completeness of this protocol, from the construction of the committer, we know that $\rho_{0,i} = r'[i] \oplus (r[i] \cdot b)$. From the computation of $\mathsf{H}(\mathsf{k}, c, b)$, we have that $\rho_{b,i} = \rho_{0,i} \oplus (r[i] \cdot b) = (r'[i] \oplus (r[i] \cdot b)) \oplus (r[i] \cdot b) = r'[i] = \rho$. The statistical hiding property follows from the statistical hiding property of the underlying OT. Finally, to show the construction is computational binding, our observation is that the construction of H always satisfies $\mathsf{H}(\mathsf{k}, c, 0) \oplus \mathsf{H}(\mathsf{k}, c, 1) = r$.

Hence, any adversary breaking the computational binding property can also find $\rho_0 \oplus \rho_1 = \mathsf{H}(\mathsf{k}, c, 0) \oplus \mathsf{H}(\mathsf{k}, c, 1) = r$, given only the first round messages $\mathsf{ot}_{1,i}$. This breaks the computational receiver privacy of the OT.

3   Preliminaries

For any two (discrete) probability distributions P and Q, let $\mathsf{SD}(P, Q)$ denote *statistical distance* between P, Q. Let $\mathbb{Z}$ denote the set containing all integers. For any positive integer q, let $\mathbb{Z}_q$ denote the set $\mathbb{Z}/q\mathbb{Z}$. Let S be a discrete set, and let $\mathcal{U}(S)$ denote the uniform distribution over S. Throughout the paper, unless specified otherwise, we use λ to denote the security parameter.

3.1   Learning with Errors

We first recall the learning with errors (LWE) distribution.

Definition 1 (LWE distribution). *For positive integer n and modulus q, and an error distribution χ over $\mathbb{Z}$, the LWE distribution $A_{\mathbf{s},\chi}$ is the following distribution. First sample a uniform random vector $\mathbf{a} \leftarrow \mathbb{Z}_q^n$, and an error $e \leftarrow \chi$, then output $(\mathbf{a}, \langle \mathbf{a}, \mathbf{s} \rangle + e) \in \mathbb{Z}_q^n \times \mathbb{Z}_q$.*

Standard instantiations of LWE distribution usually choose χ to be discrete Gaussian distribution over $\mathbb{Z}$.

Definition 2 (Quasi-polynomial LWE Assumption). *There exists a polynomial $n = n(\lambda)$ and a small real constant $c \in (0, 1/2)$ such that for any non-uniform probabilistic oracle adversary $\mathcal{D}^{(\cdot)}(\cdot)$ that runs in time $2^{O(\log^4 \lambda)}$, we have*

$$\mathsf{Adv}_\lambda(\mathcal{D}) = \left| \Pr\left[\mathcal{D}^{\mathcal{U}(\mathbb{Z}_q^n \times \mathbb{Z}_q)}(1^\lambda) = 1 \right] - \Pr\left[\mathbf{s} \leftarrow \mathbb{Z}_q^n : \mathcal{D}^{A_{\mathbf{s},\chi}}(1^\lambda) = 1 \right] \right| < c$$

Where the adversary is given oracle access to the uniform distribution $\mathcal{U}(\mathbb{Z}_q^n \times \mathbb{Z}_q)$ or the LWE distribution $A_{\mathbf{s},\chi}$.

In the following Lemma 1, we show that quasi-polynomial LWE assumption implies that any adversary running in a slower quasi-polynomial time can only have inverse quasi-polynomial advantage. We defer the proof to the full version.

Lemma 1. *Assuming quasi-polynomial hardness of LWE, for any non-uniform probabilistic adversary $\mathcal{D}$ that runs in time $2^{O(\log^2 \lambda)}$, we have*

$$\mathsf{Adv}_\lambda(\mathcal{D}) = \left| \Pr\left[\mathcal{D}^{\mathcal{U}(\mathbb{Z}_q^n \times \mathbb{Z}_q)}(1^\lambda) = 1 \right] - \Pr\left[\mathbf{s} \leftarrow \mathbb{Z}_q^n : \mathcal{D}^{A_{\mathbf{s},\chi}}(1^\lambda) = 1 \right] \right| < 2^{-\Omega(\log^4 \lambda)}$$

3.2   Computational Diffie-Hellman Assumption

Definition 3. *Let G be a cyclic group of order q generated by g, where each element of G can represented in a polynomial $n = n(\lambda)$ number of bits. The CDH assumption states that for any non-uniform PPT adversary $\mathcal{A}$, there exists an negligible function $\nu(\lambda)$ such that*

$$\Pr[x \leftarrow \mathbb{Z}_q, y \leftarrow \mathbb{Z}_q, z \leftarrow \mathcal{A}(1^\lambda, g^x, g^y) : z = g^{xy}] < \nu(\lambda)$$

3.3   Goldreich-Levin Hardcore Predicate

Definition 4. *Let f be an one-way function from $\{0,1\}^n \rightarrow \{0,1\}^m$, where $n = n(\lambda)$ and $m = m(\lambda)$ are polynomials of λ. The Goldreich-Levin hardcore predicate hc is defined as $\mathsf{hc}(x,r) = \langle x, r \rangle_2$, where $x, r \in \{0,1\}^n$, and $\langle \cdot, \cdot \rangle_2$ is the inner product function modulo 2.*

Theorem 3 (Goldreich-Levin Theorem [21], modified). *If there exists an PPT adversary $\mathcal{A}$ such that*

$$\Pr[x \leftarrow \{0,1\}^n, r \leftarrow \{0,1\}^n, b \leftarrow \mathcal{A}(1^\lambda, (f(x), r)) : b = \mathsf{hc}(x,r)] > 1/2 + \epsilon(\lambda)$$

where $\epsilon(\lambda)$ is an non-negligible function of λ, then there exits a PPT inverter $\mathcal{A}'$ s.t.

$$\Pr[x \leftarrow \{0,1\}^n, x' \leftarrow \mathcal{A}'(1^\lambda, f(x)) : x' = x] > \epsilon'(\lambda)$$

where $\epsilon'(\lambda)$ is also an non-negligible function λ.

3.4   Statistical Zap Arguments

Zaps [15] are two-round witness indistinguishable proof systems with a public-coin verifier message. Below, we define statistical Zap arguments, i.e., Zaps that achieve statistical WI property and computational soundness.

Let $\mathcal{P}$ denote the prover and $\mathcal{V}$ denote the verifier. We use $\mathsf{Trans}(\mathcal{P}(1^\lambda, x, \omega) \leftrightarrow \mathcal{V}(1^\lambda, x))$ to denote the transcript of an execution between $\mathcal{P}$ and $\mathcal{V}$, where $\mathcal{P}$ and $\mathcal{V}$ both have input a statement x and P also has a witness ω for x.

Definition 5. *Let L be a language in NP. We say that a two round protocol $\langle \mathcal{P}, \mathcal{V} \rangle$ with a public-coin verifier message is a statistical Zap argument for L if it satisfies the following properties:*

Completeness *For every $x \in L$, and witness ω for x, we have that*

$$\Pr\left[\mathsf{Trans}(\mathcal{P}(1^\lambda, x, \omega) \leftrightarrow \mathcal{V}(1^\lambda, x)) \text{ is accepted by } \mathcal{V}\right] = 1$$

Computational Soundness *For any non-uniform probabilistic polynomial time (cheating) prover $\mathcal{P}^*$, there exists a negligible function $\nu(\cdot)$ such that for any $x \notin L$, we have that $\Pr\left[\mathsf{Trans}(\mathcal{P}^*(1^\lambda, x) \leftrightarrow \mathcal{V}(1^\lambda, x)) \text{ is accepted by } \mathcal{V}\right] < \nu(\lambda)$.*

Statistical Witness Indistinguishability *For any (unbounded cheating) verifier $\mathcal{V}^*$, there exists a negligible function $\nu(\cdot)$ such that for every $x \in L$, and witnesses ω_1, ω_2 for x, we have that*

$$\mathsf{SD}\left(\mathsf{Trans}(\mathcal{P}(1^\lambda, x, \omega_1) \leftrightarrow \mathcal{V}^*(1^\lambda, x)), \mathsf{Trans}(\mathcal{P}(1^\lambda, x, \omega_2) \leftrightarrow \mathcal{V}^*(1^\lambda, x))\right) < \nu(\lambda)$$

3.5   Statistical Sender-Private Oblivious Transfer

Definition 6. *A statistical sender-private oblivious transfer (OT) is a tuple of algorithms* $(\mathsf{OT}_1, \mathsf{OT}_2, \mathsf{OT}_3)$:

$\mathsf{OT}_1(1^\lambda, b)$: *On input security parameter λ, a bit $b \in \{0,1\}$, OT_1 outputs the first round message ot_1 and a state st.*

$\mathsf{OT}_2(1^\lambda, \mathsf{ot}_1, m_0, m_1)$: *On input security parameter λ, a first round message ot_1, two bits $m_0, m_1 \in \{0,1\}$, OT_2 outputs the second round message ot_2.*

$\mathsf{OT}_3(1^\lambda, \mathsf{ot}_2, \mathsf{st})$: *On input security parameter λ, the second round message ot_2, and the state generated by OT_1, OT_3 outputs a message m.*

We require the following properties:

Correctness *For any $b, m_0, m_1 \in \{0,1\}$,*

$$\Pr\left[{}^{(\mathsf{ot}_1,\mathsf{st})\leftarrow\mathsf{OT}_1(1^\lambda,b),\mathsf{ot}_2\leftarrow\mathsf{OT}_2(1^\lambda,\mathsf{ot}_1,m_0,m_1),}_{m\leftarrow\mathsf{OT}_3(1^\lambda,\mathsf{ot}_2,\mathsf{st})} : m = m_b\right] = 1$$

Statistical Sender Privacy *There exists a negligible function $\nu(\lambda)$ and an deterministic exponential time extractor OTExt such that for any (potential maliciously generated) ot_1, $\mathsf{OTExt}(1^\lambda, \mathsf{ot}_1)$ outputs a bit $b \in \{0,1\}$. Then for any $m_0, m_1 \in \{0,1\}$, we have $\mathsf{SD}\left(\mathsf{OT}_2(1^\lambda, \mathsf{ot}_1, m_0, m_1), \mathsf{OT}_2(1^\lambda, \mathsf{ot}_1, m_b, m_b)\right) < \nu(\lambda)$.*

Quasi-polynomial Pseudorandom Receiver's Message *For any $b \in \{0,1\}$, let ot_1 be the first round message generated by $\mathsf{OT}_1(1^\lambda, b)$. For any non-uniform probabilistic adversary $\mathcal{D}$ that runs in time $2^{O(\log^2 \lambda)}$, we have*

$$\mathsf{Adv}_\lambda(\mathcal{D}) = \left|\Pr\left[\mathcal{D}(1^\lambda, \mathsf{ot}_1) = 1\right]\right.$$

$$\left. - \Pr\left[u \leftarrow \{0,1\}^{|\mathsf{ot}_1|} : \mathcal{D}(1^\lambda, u) = 1\right]\right| < 2^{-\Omega(\log^4 \lambda)}$$

Lemma 2. *Assuming quasi-polynomial hardness of LWE, there exists a statistical sender private oblivious transfer scheme.*

A statistical sender-private OT scheme from LWE was recently constructed by [7]. Their construction satisfies correctness and statistical sender-privacy. Further, the receiver's message in their scheme is pseudorandom, assuming LWE. We observe that assuming quasi-polynomial LWE and using Lemma 1, their scheme also satisfies quasi-polynomially pseudorandom receiver's message property.

3.6   Correlation Intractable Hash Function

The following definition is taken verbatim from [38].

Definition 7 (Searchable Relation [38]). *We say that a relation $R \subseteq \mathcal{X} \times \mathcal{Y}$ is searchable in size S if there exists a function $f : \mathcal{X} \to \mathcal{Y}$ that is implementable as a Boolean circuit of size S, such that if $(x, y) \in R$ then $y = f(x)$.*

Correlation intractable hash function is a family of keyed hash functions satisfying the following property: for any searchable relation R, it is hard for a computationally unbounded adversary to find an element x such that $(x, f(x)) \in R$.

Definition 8 (Correlation Intractable Hash Function, slightly modified from [38]). Correlation Intractable Hash Function *(CIH) is a triple of algorithms* $(\mathsf{KGen}, \mathsf{FakeGen}, \mathsf{H}_{(\cdot)}(\cdot))$*, with the following properties:*
   Let $s = s(\lambda), \ell = \ell(\lambda), d = d(\lambda)$ be $\mathsf{poly}(\lambda)$-bounded functions. Let $\{\mathcal{R}_{\lambda,s,\ell,d}\}_\lambda$ be a family of searchable relations, where each relation $R \in \mathcal{R}_{\lambda,s,\ell,d}$ is searchable by a circuit of size $s(\lambda)$, output length $\ell(\lambda)$ and depth $d(\lambda)$.

Statistical Correlation Intractable *There exists a negligible function $\nu(\cdot)$ such that, for any relation $R \in \mathcal{R}_{\lambda,s,\ell,d}$, and circuit C_λ that searches for a witness for R, we have $\Pr[k \leftarrow \mathsf{FakeGen}(1^\lambda, 1^{|C_\lambda|}, C_\lambda) : \exists x \text{ s.t. } (x, \mathsf{H}_k(x)) \in R] < \nu(\lambda)$.*

Quasi-polynomial Pseudorandom Fake Key *For any circuit C_λ with size s, output length ℓ, and depth d, $\mathsf{KGen}(1^\lambda, 1^{|C_\lambda|})$ outputs an uniform random string. Furthermore, for any non-uniform adversary $\mathcal{D}$ that runs in time $2^{O(\log^2 \lambda)}$, we have*

$$\left| \Pr\left[\mathcal{D}(1^\lambda, 1^{|C_\lambda|}, \mathsf{KGen}(1^\lambda, 1^{|C_\lambda|})) = 1 \right] \right.$$
$$\left. - \Pr\left[\mathcal{D}(1^\lambda, 1^{|C_\lambda|}, \mathsf{FakeGen}(1^\lambda, 1^{|C_\lambda|}, C_\lambda)) = 1 \right] \right| \leq 2^{-\Omega(\log^4 \lambda)}$$

Theorem 4. *Assuming quasi-polynomial hardness of LWE, there exists a construction of correlation intractable hash function with quasi-polynomial pseudorandom fake key.*

The construction of such a function is given in [8, 38]. Specifically, we use the construction of [38], which satisfies *statistical correlation intractability*. Moreover, the FakeGen algorithm in their construction simply consists of some ciphertexts that are pseudorandom assuming LWE. Thus, if we assume quasi-polynomial hardness of LWE, their construction satisfies quasi-polynomial pseudorandom fake key property.

For our application, we require a slightly stronger property than statistical correlation intractability as defined above. Specifically, we require that the distinguishing probability in statistical correlation intractability is $2^{-\lambda}$ for a special class of relations.

We show in Lemma 3 that by using parallel repetition, we can construct a CIH with the above property from any CIH.

Lemma 3 (Amplification of Statistical Correlation Intractability).
There exists a correlation intractable hash function $(\mathsf{KGen}, \mathsf{FakeGen}, \mathsf{H}_{(\cdot)}(\cdot))$ *such that the following additional property holds.*

$2^{-\lambda}$**-Statistical Correlation Intractability** *Let* $\{C_\lambda\}_\lambda$ *be a family of* Boolean *circuits, where* C_λ *has polynomial size* $s(\lambda)$, *polynomial depth* $d(\lambda)$, *and outputs a single bit. There exists a polynomial* $\ell = \ell(\lambda)$ *such that the following holds. Let* $\overrightarrow{C_{\lambda,\ell}}$ *be the circuit* $\overrightarrow{C_\lambda}(c_1, c_2, \ldots, c_\ell) = (C_\lambda(c_1), C_\lambda(c_2), \ldots, C_\lambda(c_\ell))$, *then for large enough* λ,

$$\Pr\left[k \leftarrow \mathsf{FakeGen}\left(1^\lambda, 1^{|\overrightarrow{C_{\lambda,\ell}}|}, \overrightarrow{C_{\lambda,\ell}}\right) : \exists x \text{ s.t. } \mathsf{H}_k(x) = \overrightarrow{C_{\lambda,\ell}}(x)\right] < 2^{-\lambda}$$

The CIH in [38] already satisfies the above property. In the full version, we describe a generic transformation from any CIH to one that achieves the above property.

4 Statistical Zap Arguments

4.1 Public Coin Statistical-Hiding Extractable Commitments

In this section, we start by defining and constructing a key building block in our construction of statistical Zaps, namely, a statistical-hiding extractable commitment scheme. The notion and its construction are adapted from [31], with some slight modifications to fit in our application. The main difference between our definition and that of [31] is that we require the first round message to be public coin as opposed to private-coin.

Our syntax departs from the classical definition of commitment schemes. We consider a tuple of four algorithms $(\mathsf{Com}_1, \mathsf{FakeCom}_1, \mathsf{Com}_2, \mathsf{Dec})$, where Com_1 corresponds to the honest receiver's algorithm that simply outputs a uniformly random string. Com_2 corresponds to the committer's algorithm that takes as input a message m as well as a random string $\mathbf{b}'$ of length μ and outputs a commitment string. We require two additional algorithms: (1) $\mathsf{FakeCom}_1$ that takes a binary string $\mathbf{b}$ of length μ as input and produces a first round message that "hides" the string $\mathbf{b}$, and (2) Dec that takes as input a transcript generated using $\mathsf{FakeCom}_1$ and Com_2 and outputs the committed message if the strings $\mathbf{b}$ and $\mathbf{b}'$ used for computing the transcript are equal.

Let $\mathcal{C}$, $\mathcal{R}$ denote the committer and the receiver, respectively. We now proceed to give a formal definition.

Definition 9. *A public coin statistical-hiding extractable commitment is a tuple* $(\mathsf{Com}_1, \mathsf{FakeCom}_1, \mathsf{Com}_2, \mathsf{Dec})$. *The commit phase and open phase are defined as follows.*

Commitment Phase

Round 1 *On input parameters* $(1^\lambda, 1^\mu)$, $\mathcal{R}$ *executes* Com_1 *to sample a uniform random string* com_1. $\mathcal{R}$ *sends* com_1 *to* $\mathcal{C}$.

Round 2 *On input* $(1^\lambda, m)$, $\mathcal{C}$ *chooses* $\mathbf{b}' \leftarrow \{0,1\}^\mu$ *uniformly at random and computes* $\mathsf{com}_2 \leftarrow \mathsf{Com}_2(1^\lambda, 1^\mu, \mathsf{com}_1, \mathbf{b}', m; r)$ *with randomness* r. $\mathcal{C}$ *sends* $(\mathbf{b}', \mathsf{com}_2)$ *to* $\mathcal{R}$.

Opening Phase
$\mathcal{C}$ *sends the message and the randomness* (m, r) *to* $\mathcal{R}$. $\mathcal{R}$ *checks if* $\mathsf{com}_2 = \mathsf{Com}_2(1^\lambda, 1^\mu, \mathsf{com}_1, \mathbf{b}', m; r)$.

We require the following properties of the commitment scheme.

Statistical Hiding *There exists a negligible function* $\nu(\cdot)$, *a deterministic exponential time algorithm* ComExt, *and a randomized simulator* Sim, *such that for any fixed (potentially maliciously generated)* com_1, $\mathsf{ComExt}(1^\lambda, 1^\mu, \mathsf{com}_1)$ *outputs* $\mathbf{b} \in \{0,1\}^\mu$, *and for any* $\mathbf{b}' \neq \mathbf{b}$, *and* $m \in \{0,1\}$, *we have*

$$\mathsf{SD}\left(\mathsf{Com}_2(1^\lambda, 1^\mu, \mathsf{com}_1, \mathbf{b}', m), \mathsf{Sim}(1^\lambda, 1^\mu, \mathsf{com}_1)\right) < \mu \cdot \nu(\lambda) \tag{1}$$

Quasi-polynomial Pseudorandom Receiver's Message *For any* $\mathbf{b} \in \{0,1\}^\mu$, $\mathsf{FakeCom}_1(1^\lambda, 1^\mu, \mathbf{b})$ *and a uniform random string outputted by* $\mathsf{Com}(1^\lambda, 1^\mu)$ *are quasi-polynomially indistinguishable. Specifically, for any non-uniform adversary* $\mathcal{D}$ *that runs in time* $2^{O(\log^2 \lambda)}$, *we have*

$$\left| \Pr[\mathcal{D}(1^\lambda, 1^\mu, \mathsf{Com}_1(1^\lambda, 1^\mu)) = 1] \right.$$

$$\left. - \Pr[\mathcal{D}(1^\lambda, 1^\mu, \mathsf{FakeCom}_1(1^\lambda, 1^\mu, \mathbf{b})) = 1] \right| \leq \mu \cdot 2^{-\Omega(\log^4 \lambda)}$$

Extractable $\mathsf{FakeCom}_1$ *and* Dec *satisfy the following property. For any* $\mathbf{b} \in \{0,1\}^\mu$, *we have*

$$\Pr\left[\begin{matrix} (\mathsf{com}_1, \mathsf{st}) \leftarrow \mathsf{FakeCom}_1(1^\lambda, 1^\mu, \mathbf{b}), \\ \mathsf{com}_2 \leftarrow \mathsf{Com}_2(1^\lambda, 1^\mu, \mathsf{com}_1, \mathbf{b}, m) \end{matrix} : \mathsf{Dec}(1^\lambda, 1^\mu, \mathsf{st}, \mathsf{com}_2) = m \right] = 1$$

Lemma 4. *Assuming quasi-polynomial hardness of LWE, there exists a public coin statistical-hiding extractable commitment scheme.*

In the full version, we construct a public coin statistical hiding extractable commitment by slightly modifying the commitment scheme of [31]. Their construction already satisfies extractability and statistical hiding properties. However, their construction, as originally described, is private coin. We note that the receiver's message in their scheme simply consists of multiple receiver messages of a statistical sender-private OT scheme. Then, by instantiating their construction with an OT scheme that satisfies quasi-polynomial pseudorandom receiver's message property (see Sect. 3.5), their scheme can be easily adapted to obtain a *public coin* statistical-hiding extractable commitment. Specifically, in the modified construction, the honest receiver's algorithm $\mathsf{Com}(1^\lambda, 1^\mu)$ simply computes a uniform random string, while $\mathsf{FakeCom}_1$ corresponds to the receiver algorithm in the construction of [31].

4.2   Our Construction

In this section, we describe our construction of a statistical Zap argument system for Graph Hamiltonicity, which is an NP-Complete problem.

Notation. We describe some notation that is used in our construction. Let L_{HAM} denote the Graph Hamiltonicity language over graphs $G = (V, E)$ of n vertices, where V denotes the set of vertices and E denotes the set of edges in G. We slightly abuse notation and use G to denote its adjacency matrix $G = (G_i[s, t])_{s,t\in[n]}$.

Let $(\mathsf{Com}_1, \mathsf{FakeCom}_1, \mathsf{Com}_2, \mathsf{Dec})$ be a public coin statistical-hiding extractable commitment scheme (Definition 9). We set the parameter μ of the commitment scheme as $\Theta(\log^2 \lambda)$. Let $(\mathsf{KGen}, \mathsf{FakeGen}, \mathsf{H}_{(\cdot)}(\cdot))$ be a family of CIH (Definition 8). We choose the polynomial $\ell = \ell(\lambda)$ in Lemma 3 such that the CIH is $2^{-\lambda}$-statistical correlation intractable.

Circuit C_{st}. Let C_{st} denote the following Boolean circuit.

> Input: a $n \times n$ matrix $c = (c_{s,t})_{s,t\in[n]}$.
> Output: a boolean value.

1. For any $s, t \in [n]$, execute $G[s, t] = \mathsf{Dec}(1^\lambda, 1^\mu, \mathsf{st}, c_{s,t})$.
2. If $G = (G_i[s, t])_{s,t\in[n]}$ is a cycle graph, then output 0. Otherwise output 1.

For ease of exposition, we extend the notation C_{st} to a series of matrices $(c_1, c_2, \ldots, c_\ell)$. Specifically, $C_{\mathsf{st}}(c_1, c_2, \ldots, c_\ell)$ is defined as $(C_{\mathsf{st}}(c_1), C_{\mathsf{st}}(c_2), \ldots, C_{\mathsf{st}}(c_\ell))$.

Construction. The verifier $\mathcal{V}$ and prover $\mathcal{P}$ are both given input the security parameter λ and a graph $G = (V, E)$ of n vertices. The prover is additionally given as input a witness ω for G.

Round 1 Verifier $\mathcal{V}$ computes and sends uniform random strings $(\mathsf{com}_1 \leftarrow \mathsf{Com}_1(1^\lambda, 1^\mu), k \leftarrow \mathsf{KGen}(1^\lambda, 1^{|C_{\mathsf{st}}|})$, where C_{st} takes ℓ separate $n \times n$ matrices as input, and outputs ℓ bits.

Round 2 Prover $\mathcal{P}$ does the following:
1. Choose a random $\mathbf{b}' \leftarrow \{0, 1\}^\mu$.
2. Compute ℓ first round messages of Blum's sigma protocol for Graph Hamiltonicity. Specifically, for every $i \in [\ell]$, first sample a random cycle graph $G_i = (G_i[s, t])_{s,t\in[n]}$. Next, for each $s, t \in [n]$, compute $c_i[s, t] \leftarrow \mathsf{Com}_2(1^\lambda, 1^\mu, \mathsf{com}_1, \mathbf{b}', G_i[s, t]; r_i^{(s,t)})$ using randomness $r_i^{(s,t)}$. Finally let $c_i = (c_i[s, t])_{s,t\in[n]}$.
3. Compute $(b_1, b_2, \ldots, b_\ell) = \mathsf{H}_k(c_1, \ldots, c_\ell)$.
4. For every $i \in [\ell]$, compute the answer to challenge b_i in Blum's sigma protocol. Specifically, if $b_i = 0$, then set $z_i = (G_i, (r_i^{(s,t)})_{s,t\in[n]})$. Else, if $b_i = 1$, then compute a one-to-one map $\phi : G \to G_i$ such that $\phi(w)$ is the cycle G_i, and set $z_i = (\phi, (r_i^{(s,t)})_{(s,t)=\phi(e),e\notin E})$.
5. Send $\Pi = (\mathbf{b}', (c_i)_{i\in[\ell]}, (z_i)_{i\in[\ell]})$ to the verifier.

Verification Upon receiving the proof $\Pi = (\mathbf{b}', (c_i)_{i\in[\ell]}, (z_i)_{i\in[\ell]})$, the verifier first computes $(b_1, b_2, \cdots, b_\ell) = H_k(c_1, c_2, \ldots, c_\ell)$, and then verifies each copy (c_i, b_i, z_i) of the proof as in Blum's protocol. Specifically, if $b_i = 0$, then parse $z_i = (G_i, (r_i^{(s,t)})_{s,t\in[n]})$ and check if $c_i = (\mathsf{Com}_2(1^\lambda, 1^\mu, \mathsf{com}_1,$ $\mathbf{b}', G_i[s,t]; r_i^{(s,t)})_{s,t\in[n]}$ and G_i is a cycle graph. Otherwise if $b_i = 1$, then parse $z_i = (\phi, (r_i^{(s,t)})_{(s,t)=\phi(e), e\notin E})$ and check if ϕ is a one-to-one map, and for each $e \notin E$, and $(s,t) = \phi(e)$, check if $c_i[s,t] = \mathsf{Com}_2(1^\lambda, 1^\mu, \mathsf{com}_1, \mathbf{b}', 0; r_i^{(s,t)})$. If all of the checks succeed, then accept the proof, otherwise reject.

This completes the description of our construction. We defer the proof of completeness and statistical witness indistinguishability to the full version. We next prove that our construction satisfies computational soundness.

Theorem 5. *The construction in Sect. 4.2 satisfies computational soundness.*

Suppose $G \notin L_{\mathsf{HAM}}$ and there exists a cheating prover $\mathcal{P}^*$ such that $\Pr[\mathcal{P}^* \text{ succeeds}] \geq 1/\lambda^c$ for infinite many λ. Then for each such λ, there must exist a $\mathbf{b}'_0$ such that $\Pr[\mathcal{P}^* \text{ succeeds} \wedge \mathbf{b}' = \mathbf{b}'_0] \geq \lambda^{-c} 2^{-\mu}$, where $\mathbf{b}'$ is outputted by the cheating prover $\mathcal{P}^*$ in the second round.

$\mathbf{b}'_0$**-Extractor** Ext. We first describe an algorithm Ext that extracts a $\mathbf{b}'_0$ from any cheating prover $\mathcal{P}^*$, such that $\Pr[\mathcal{P}^* \text{ succeeds} \wedge \mathbf{b}' = \mathbf{b}'_0] \geq \lambda^{-c} 2^{-\mu-1}$. Ext receives oracle access to $\mathcal{P}^*$.

1. Initialize an empty multiset $S = \{\}$.
2. For $j \in [2^{1.5\mu}]$, set fresh random tape for $\mathcal{P}^*$. Compute and send uniformly random first round message $(\mathsf{Com}_1(1^\lambda, 1^\mu), k \leftarrow \mathsf{KGen}(1^\lambda, 1^{|C_{\mathsf{st}}|}))$ to $\mathcal{P}^*$. Let $(\mathbf{b}'^{(j)}, (c_i^{(j)})_{i\in[\ell]}, (z_i^{(j)})_{i\in[\ell]})$ be the response of $\mathcal{P}^*$. Execute the verifier algorithm; if verification succeeds, then append multiset $S = S \cup \{\mathbf{b}'^{(j)}\}$.
3. Output $\mathbf{b}'_0$ that appears for the maximum number of times in the multiset S.

In the sequel, we denote $p_\lambda = \Pr[\mathcal{P}^* \text{ succeeds}]$.

Lemma 5. *The algorithm* Ext *runs in time* $O(2^{1.5\mu}) = 2^{O(\log^2 \lambda)}$. *Furthermore, with probability* $1 - \exp(-\Omega(2^{0.5\mu}p_\lambda))$, *it outputs a* $\mathbf{b}'_0$ *such that* $\Pr[\mathcal{P}^* \text{ succeeds} \wedge \mathbf{b}' = \mathbf{b}'_0] \geq p_\lambda/2^{-\mu-1}$.

We defer the proof of the Lemma 5 to the full version. Now we use the extractor Ext to build the following hybrids.

Hybrid H_0: Compute $\mathbf{b}'_0 \leftarrow \mathsf{Ext}(\mathcal{P}^*)$. Generate uniformly random string $(\mathsf{com}_1 \leftarrow \mathsf{Com}_1(1^\lambda, 1^\mu), k \leftarrow \mathsf{KGen}(1^\lambda, 1^{|C_{\mathsf{st}}|}))$. Send (com_1, k) to $\mathcal{P}^*$. Let $(\mathbf{b}', (c_i)_{i\in[\ell]}, (z_i)_{i\in[\ell]})$ be the output of $\mathcal{P}^*$.
If $\mathbf{b}' = \mathbf{b}'_0$ and $(\mathbf{b}', (c_i)_{i\in[\ell]}, (z_i)_{i\in[\ell]})$ passes the verification, then the hybrid outputs 1, otherwise outputs 0.

Hybrid H_1: Compute $b'_0 \leftarrow \text{Ext}(\mathcal{P}^*)$. ~~Generate~~ $(\text{com}_1, \text{st}) \leftarrow \text{FakeCom}(1^\lambda, 1^\mu, b'_0)$, $k \leftarrow \text{KGen}(1^\lambda, 1^{|C_{st}|})$. Send (com_1, k) to $\mathcal{P}^*$. Let $(b', (c_i)_{i \in [\ell]}, (z_i)_{i \in [\ell]})$ be the output of $\mathcal{P}^*$.
If $b' = b'_0$ and $(b', (c_i)_{i \in [\ell]}, (z_i)_{i \in [\ell]})$ passes the verification, then the hybrid outputs 1, otherwise output 0.

Hybrid H_2: Compute $b'_0 \leftarrow \text{Ext}(\mathcal{P}^*)$. Generate $(\text{com}_1, \text{st}) \leftarrow \text{FakeCom}(1^\lambda, 1^\mu, b'_0), k \leftarrow \overline{\text{FakeGen}(1^\lambda, 1^{|C_{st}|}, C_{st})}$. Send (com_1, k) to $\mathcal{P}^*$. Let $(b', (c_i)_{i \in [\ell]}, (z_i)_{i \in [\ell]})$ be the output of $\mathcal{P}^*$.
If $b' = b'_0$ and $(b', (c_i)_{i \in [\ell]}, (z_i)_{i \in [\ell]})$ passes the verification, then the hybrid outputs 1, otherwise outputs 0.

This completes the description of the hybrids. We now prove Lemmas 6 and 7 to establish the indistinguishability of the hybrids.

Lemma 6. $|\Pr[H_0 = 1] - \Pr[H_1 = 1]| < 2^{-\Omega(\log^4 \lambda)}$.

Proof. We prove this Lemma by relying on *quasi-polynomial pseudorandom receiver's message* property of the commitment scheme (Definition 9). We build the following adversary $\mathcal{D}$ trying to distinguish the receiver's message of commitment scheme from random string.

$\mathcal{D}$ takes as input $(1^\lambda, 1^\mu, \text{com}_1)$. Firstly, $\mathcal{D}$ computes $b'_0 \leftarrow \text{Ext}(\mathcal{P}^*)$. Then, it generates $k \leftarrow \text{KGen}(1^\lambda, 1^{|C_{st}|})$ and sends (com_1, k) to $\mathcal{P}^*$. Let $(b', (c_i)_{i \in [\ell]}, (z_i)_{i \in [\ell]})$ be the response of $\mathcal{P}^*$. If $b' = b'_0$ and $(b, (c_i)_{i \in [\ell]}, (z_i)_{i \in [\ell]})$ passes the verification, then output 1. Otherwise output 0.

Now $\mathcal{D}(1^\lambda, 1^\mu, \text{Com}_1(1^\lambda, 1^\mu))$ simulates the environment of H_0 for $\mathcal{P}^*$. Hence, $\Pr[\mathcal{D}(1^\lambda, 1^\mu, \text{Com}_1(1^\lambda, 1^\mu)) = 1] = \Pr[H_0 = 1]$. Also, $\mathcal{D}(1^\lambda, 1^\mu, \text{FakeCom}(1^\lambda, 1^\mu, b'_0))$ simulates the environment of H_1. Hence, $\Pr[\mathcal{D}(1^\lambda, 1^\mu, \text{FakeCom}_1(1^\lambda, 1^\mu, b'_0)) = 1] = \Pr[H_1 = 1]$.

From Lemma 5, $\mathcal{D}$ runs in time $2^{O(\log^2 \lambda)}$. Since the distributions $\text{Com}(1^\lambda, 1^\mu)$ and $\text{FakeCom}(1^\lambda, 1^\mu, b'_0)$ are quasi-polynomially indistinguishable,

$$|\Pr[\mathcal{D}(1^\lambda, 1^\mu, \text{Com}_1(1^\lambda, 1^\mu)) = 1]$$
$$- \Pr[\mathcal{D}(1^\lambda, 1^\mu, \text{FakeCom}_1(1^\lambda, 1^\mu, b'_0)) = 1]| < 2^{-\Omega(\log^4 \lambda)}$$

Thus, we derive that $|\Pr[H_0 = 1] - \Pr[H_1 = 1]| \leq 2^{-\Omega(\log^4 \lambda)}$. $\qquad\square$

Lemma 7. $|\Pr[H_1 = 1] - \Pr[H_2 = 1]| < 2^{-\Omega(\log^4 \lambda)}$.

Proof. We prove this lemma by relying on *quasi-polynomial pseudorandom fake key* property of CIH. We build adversary $\mathcal{D}$ trying to distinguish the fake CIH key from uniform random string.

$\mathcal{D}$ takes as input $(1^\lambda, 1^\mu, k)$. It first computes $b'_0 \leftarrow \text{Ext}(\mathcal{P}^*)$. Next, it generates $\text{com}_1 \leftarrow \text{FakeCom}_1(1^\lambda, 1^\mu, b'_0)$ and sends (com_1, k) to $\mathcal{P}^*$. Let $(b', (c_i)_{i \in [\ell]}, (z_i)_{i \in [\ell]})$ be the response of $\mathcal{P}^*$. If $b' = b'_0$ and $(b, (c_i)_{i \in [\ell]}, (z_i)_{i \in [\ell]})$ passes the verification, then output 1. Otherwise output 0.

Now $\mathcal{D}(1^\lambda, 1^{|C_{st}|}, k \leftarrow \mathsf{KGen}(1^\lambda, 1^{|C_{st}|}))$ simulates the environment of H_1 for $\mathcal{P}^*$. Hence, $\Pr[\mathcal{D}(1^\lambda, 1^{|C_{st}|}, k \leftarrow \mathsf{KGen}(1^\lambda, 1^{|C_{st}|})) = 1] = \Pr[H_1 = 1]$.

Also, $\mathcal{D}(1^\lambda, 1^{|C_{st}|}, k \leftarrow \mathsf{FakeGen}(1^\lambda, 1^{|C_{st}|}, C_{st}))$ simulates the environment of H_2. Hence, $\Pr[\mathcal{D}(1^\lambda, 1^{|C_{st}|}, k \leftarrow \mathsf{FakeGen}(1^\lambda, 1^{|C_{st}|}, C_{st})) = 1] = \Pr[H_2 = 1]$.

From Lemma 5, $\mathcal{D}$ runs in time $2^{O(\log^2 \lambda)}$. Since the distributions $\mathsf{KGen}(1^\lambda, 1^{|C_{st}|})$ and $\mathsf{FakeGen}(1^\lambda, 1^{|C_{st}|}, C_{st})$ are quasi-polynomially indistinguishable, we have

$$| \Pr[\mathcal{D}(1^\lambda, 1^{|C_{st}|}, k \leftarrow \mathsf{KGen}(1^\lambda, 1^{|C_{st}|})) = 1]$$
$$- \Pr[\mathcal{D}(1^\lambda, 1^{|C_{st}|}, k \leftarrow \mathsf{FakeGen}(1^\lambda, 1^{|C_{st}|}, C_{st})) = 1]| < 2^{-\Omega(\log^4 \lambda)}$$

Thus, we derive $| \Pr[H_1 = 1] - \Pr[H_2 = 1]| \leq 2^{-\Omega(\log^4 \lambda)}$. $\square$

We now prove the following lemma to lower bound the probability that the output of H_2 is 1.

Lemma 8. $\Pr[H_2 = 1] \geq \lambda^{-c} 2^{-\mu-2} - 2 \cdot 2^{-\Omega(\log^4 \lambda)}$

Proof. From Lemma 5, we have

$$\Pr[H_0 = 1] = \Pr[b_0' \leftarrow \mathsf{Ext}(\mathcal{P}^*) : \mathcal{P}^* \text{ succeeds } \wedge \mathbf{b}' = \mathbf{b}_0']$$
$$\geq \Pr\left[b_0' \leftarrow \mathsf{Ext}(\mathcal{P}^*) : \mathcal{P}^* \text{ succeeds } \wedge \mathbf{b}' = \mathbf{b}_0' \wedge \right.$$
$$\left. \Pr[\mathcal{P}^* \text{ succeeds } \wedge \mathbf{b}' = \mathbf{b}_0'] > p_\lambda 2^{-\mu-1}\right]$$
$$= \Pr[\mathcal{P}^* \text{ succeeds } \wedge \mathbf{b}' = \mathbf{b}_0' | \Pr[\mathcal{P}^* \text{ succeeds } \wedge \mathbf{b}' = \mathbf{b}_0'] > p_\lambda 2^{-\mu-1}]$$
$$\cdot \Pr[b_0' \leftarrow \mathsf{Ext}(\mathcal{P}^*) : \Pr[\mathcal{P}^* \text{ succeeds } \wedge \mathbf{b}' = \mathbf{b}_0'] > p_\lambda 2^{-\mu-1}]$$
$$> \lambda^{-c} 2^{-\mu-1} \cdot \left(1 - \exp\left(-\Omega(2^{0.5\mu} p_\lambda)\right)\right) \geq \lambda^{-c} 2^{-\mu-2}$$

Combining the above with the Lemmas 6 and 7, we have $\Pr[H_2 = 1] \geq \lambda^{-c} 2^{-\mu-2} - 2 \cdot 2^{-\Omega(\log^4 \lambda)}$. $\square$

In the remainder of the proof, we use the $2^{-\lambda}$-correlation intractability property of the CIH to reach a contradiction. Towards this, we first show in the following lemma that $H_2 = 1$ implies that there exists a 'collision' for CIH and C_{st}. Specifically, we show that any accepting proof in hybrid H_2 such that $\mathbf{b}' = \mathbf{b}_0'$, we can find a 'collision' for CIH and C_{st}.

Lemma 9. *If hybrid H_2 outputs 1, denote $\mathsf{COM} = (c_1, c_2, \ldots, c_\ell)$ in the accepting proof. Then $H_k(\mathsf{COM}) = C_{st}(\mathsf{COM})$.*

Proof. We will prove by contradiction. Denote $(b_1, b_2, \ldots, b_\ell) = H_k(\mathsf{COM})$. Suppose there is an $i \in [\ell]$ such that $b_i \neq C_{st}(c_i)$. Now we consider two cases: (1). $b_i = 0, C_{st}(c_i) = 1$, (2). $b_i = 1, C_{st}(c_i) = 0$.

For case (1), since $b_i = 0$, z_i must be of the form $(G_i, (r_i^{(s,t)})_{s,t \in [n]})$, where G_i is a cycle graph, and $c_i[s,t] = \mathsf{Com}_2(1^\lambda, 1^\mu, \mathsf{com}_1, \mathbf{b}', G_i[s,t]; r_i^{(s,t)})$ for each $s, t \in [n]$. From the extractability property of the commitment scheme and $\mathbf{b}' = \mathbf{b}_0'$, we have $\mathsf{Dec}(1^\lambda, 1^\mu, \mathsf{st}, \mathsf{c}_i[s,t]) = G_i[s,t]$. Since G_i is a cycle graph, $C_{\mathsf{st}}(\mathsf{c}_i) = 0$. Therefore, we reach a contradiction.

For case (2), since $b_i = 1$, z_i must be the form $(\phi, (r_i^{(s,t)})_{e \notin E, (s,t) = \phi(e)})$, where ϕ is a one-to-one map, and $\mathsf{c}_i[s,t] = \mathsf{Com}_2(1^\lambda, 1^\mu, \mathsf{com}_1, \mathbf{b}', 0; r_i^{(s,t)})$ for each $e \notin E, (s,t) = \phi(e)$. Let $G_i[s,t] = \mathsf{Dec}(1^\lambda, 1^\mu, \mathsf{st}, \mathsf{c}_i[s,t])$ for each $s,t \in [n]$. Since $C_{\mathsf{st}}(\mathsf{c}_i) = 0$, G_i is a cycle graph. For each edge $e' = (s',t')$ of the cycle graph, $G_i[s',t'] = 1$. Now we will show that $(\phi^{-1}(s'), \phi^{-1}(t')) \in E$. We show this by contradiction. Suppose $(\phi^{-1}(s'), \phi^{-1}(t')) \notin E$, then $\mathsf{c}_i[s',t'] = \mathsf{Com}_2(1^\lambda, 1^\mu, \mathsf{com}_1, \mathbf{b}', 0; r_i^{(s',t')})$. From extractable property of commitment scheme, $\mathsf{Dec}(1^\lambda, 1^\mu, \mathsf{st}, \mathsf{c}_i[s',t']) = 0$, which implies $G_i[s',t'] = 0$. Thus, we find a contradiction. Hence, for each edge e in cycle graph G_i, $\phi^{-1}(e)$ is an edge in G. Now we have found a Hamiltonian cycle $\phi^{-1}(G_i) \subseteq G$, which is a contradiction to $G \notin L_{\mathsf{HAM}}$. □

Combining Lemmas 8 and 9, we derive that

$$\Pr\left[k \leftarrow \mathsf{FakeGen}(1^\lambda, 1^{|C_{\mathsf{st}}|}, C_{\mathsf{st}}) : \exists \mathsf{COM}, \mathsf{H}_k(\mathsf{COM}) = C_{\mathsf{st}}(\mathsf{COM})\right]$$
$$\geq \lambda^{-c} 2^{-\mu-2} - 2 \cdot 2^{-\Omega(\log^4 \lambda)}$$

However, the above contradicts the $2^{-\lambda}$-statistical correlation intractability of CIH.

5   Statistical Hash Commitments

Intuitively speaking, a statistical hash commitment (SHC) scheme is a two-round *statistical hiding* commitment scheme, where the verification of the decommitment is a simple equality check with a hash output (computed w.r.t. a hashing algorithm associated with the scheme).

Definition 10. *A statistical hash commitment scheme is a tuple of algorithms* $(\mathsf{KGen}, \mathsf{Com}, \mathsf{H}, \mathcal{C}, \mathcal{R})$. *It proceeds as follows.*

Round 1 $\mathcal{R}$ *executes* $(\mathsf{pk}, \mathsf{k}) \leftarrow \mathsf{KGen}(1^\lambda)$, *and sends* pk *to* $\mathcal{C}$.
Round 2 $\mathcal{C}$*'s input is a bit* $b \in \{0,1\}$. *Compute* $(c, \rho) \leftarrow \mathsf{Com}(\mathsf{pk}, b)$ *and send* c *to* $\mathcal{R}$.
Opening $\mathcal{C}$ *sends* (b, ρ) *to the* $\mathcal{R}$.
Verification $\mathcal{R}$ *accepts iff* ρ *is equal to* $\mathsf{H}(\mathsf{k}, c, b)$.

We require the scheme to satisfy the following properties.

Completeness For any $b \in \{0,1\}$, we have

$$\Pr\left[(\mathsf{pk}, \mathsf{k}) \leftarrow \mathsf{KGen}(1^\lambda), (c, \rho) \leftarrow \mathsf{Com}(\mathsf{pk}, b) : \rho = \mathsf{H}(\mathsf{k}, c, b)\right] = 1$$

Computational Binding We say that the commitment scheme is computational binding, if for any non-uniform probabilistic polynomial time adversary $\mathcal{A}$, there exists a negligible function $\nu(\cdot)$ such that

$$\mathsf{Adv}(\mathcal{A}) \triangleq \Pr\left[(\mathsf{pk}, \mathsf{k}) \leftarrow \mathsf{KGen}(1^\lambda), (c, \rho_0, \rho_1) \leftarrow \mathcal{A}(1^\lambda, \mathsf{pk}) : \begin{smallmatrix} \rho_0 = \mathsf{H}(\mathsf{k},c,0) \wedge \\ \rho_1 = \mathsf{H}(\mathsf{k},c,1) \end{smallmatrix}\right] < \nu(\lambda)$$

Statistical Hiding For any (maliciously generated) pk, there exists a negligible function $\nu(\lambda)$ such that $\mathsf{SD}\,(c_0, c_1) \leq \nu(\lambda)$, where $(c_b, \rho_b) \leftarrow \mathsf{Com}(\mathsf{pk}, b)$ for every $b \in \{0, 1\}$. If $\nu(\lambda) = 0$, then we say that the scheme is perfectly hiding.

5.1   Construction from CDH

Let q be an integer, and $G = \langle g \rangle$ be a cyclic group generated by g of order q.

Construction. We describe our construction of the SHC scheme.

$\mathsf{KGen}(1^\lambda)$ Randomly sample $s, t \leftarrow \mathbb{Z}_q$, and $x \leftarrow G$. Output $(\mathsf{pk} = (x, g^s, x^s \cdot g^t), \mathsf{k} = (s, t))$.

$\mathsf{Com}(\mathsf{pk}, b)$ Parse pk as $(x, a_1, a_2) \in G \times G$. Randomly sample $u, v \leftarrow \mathbb{Z}_q$. Output $(c = (g^u \cdot x^v, g^v \cdot g^b), \rho = a_1^u \cdot a_2^v)$.

$\mathsf{H}(\mathsf{k}, c, b)$ Parse c as $(z_1, z_2) \in G \times G$, and parse k as (s, t). Output $z_1^s \cdot (z_2 \cdot g^{-b})^t$.

We now prove the properties of this construction. We defer the proof of completeness to the full version.

Lemma 10 (Computational Binding). *Assuming CDH, the above construction of SHC is computational binding.*

Proof. For any n.u. probabilistic polynomial time adversary $\mathcal{A}$, we construct the following adversary $\mathcal{A}'$ for CDH problem.

Adversary $\mathcal{A}'(1^\lambda, g^s, g^y)$. Sample $u \leftarrow \mathbb{Z}_q$ uniformly at random. Set $x = g^y$, $\mathsf{pk} = (x, g^s, g^u)$. Execute $(c, \rho_0, \rho_1) \leftarrow \mathcal{A}(1^\lambda, \mathsf{pk})$. Output $g^u \cdot \rho_0^{-1} \cdot \rho_1$.

We now prove that $\Pr[a \leftarrow \mathcal{A}'(1^\lambda, g^s, g^y) : a = g^{sy}] \geq \mathsf{Adv}(\mathcal{A})$. Since in our construction, $\mathsf{pk} = (x, g^s, x^s \cdot g^t)$, where t is uniformly random. The second component of pk is uniformly random over G. Hence, the distributions of pk in real execution and the adversary $\mathcal{A}'$ are identical.

Now for any $u \in \mathbb{Z}_q$, there exists an unique $t' \in \mathbb{Z}_q$ such that $x^s \cdot g^{t'} = g^u$. Then, for adversary $\mathcal{A}'$, we have

$$\Pr[a = g^{sy}] = \Pr[g^u \cdot \rho_0^{-1} \cdot \rho_1 = g^{sy}] = \Pr[g^{t'} = \rho_0 \cdot \rho_1^{-1}]$$
$$\geq \Pr\left[\rho_0 = \mathsf{H}(\mathsf{k}, c, 0) \wedge \rho_1 = \mathsf{H}(\mathsf{k}, c, 1)\right] = \mathsf{Adv}(\mathcal{A})$$

where $\mathsf{k} = (s, t')$. By the hardness of CDH, we conclude that $\mathsf{Adv}(\mathcal{A})$ is negligible. $\qquad\square$

Lemma 11 (Perfect Hiding). *The Construction 5.1 is perfect hiding.*

Proof. For any fixed $\mathsf{pk} = (x, a_1, a_2)$, since v is uniformly random, $g^v \cdot g^b$ is uniformly random. Furthermore, conditioned on $g^v \cdot g^b$, since u is uniformly random, $g^u \cdot x^v$ is also uniformly random. Hence, c is uniformly random over $G \times G$. $\qquad\square$

5.2   Construction from Any 2-round Statistical Sender-Private OT

We now describe our construction of SHC from statistical sender-private OT. Let $\ell = \ell(\lambda)$ be a polynomial in λ, and let (OT_1, OT_2, OT_3) be any statistical sender private 2-round OT scheme.

$\mathsf{KGen}(1^\lambda)$ Randomly sample $r \leftarrow \{0,1\}^\ell$.
For $i \in [\ell]$, execute $(\mathsf{ot}_{1,i}, \mathsf{st}_i) \leftarrow OT_1(1^\lambda, r[i])$.
Output $\mathsf{pk} = ((\mathsf{ot}_{1,i})_{i \in [\ell]}, \mathsf{k} = (\mathsf{st}_i)_{i \in [\ell]})$.
$\mathsf{Com}(\mathsf{pk}, b \in \{0,1\})$ Parse pk as $(\mathsf{ot}_{1,i})_{i \in [\ell]}$. Randomly sample $r' \leftarrow \{0,1\}^\ell$.
For $i \in [\ell]$, execute $\mathsf{ot}_{2,i} \leftarrow OT_2(\mathsf{ot}_{1,i}, r'[i], r'[i] \oplus b)$.
Output $(c = (\mathsf{ot}_{2,i})_{i \in [\ell]}, \rho = r')$.
$\mathsf{H}(\mathsf{k}, c, b)$ Parse $\mathsf{k} = (\mathsf{st}_i)_{i \in [\ell]}, c = (\mathsf{ot}_{2,i})_{i \in [\ell]}$.
For $i \in [\ell]$, Let $\rho_{0,i} \leftarrow OT_3(\mathsf{st}_i, \mathsf{ot}_{2,i})$.
Let $\rho_b = (\rho_{0,i} \oplus (r[i] \cdot b))_{i \in [\ell]}$.
Output ρ_b.

We defer the proof of completeness and statistical hiding property to the full version Below, we prove computational binding.

Lemma 12 (Computational Binding). *Assuming computational indistinguishability of* OT_1, *the above construction of SHC is computational binding.*

Proof. For any PPT adversary $\mathcal{A}$ trying to break the computational binding property, we construct the following hybrids.

Hybrid H_0 Randomly sample $r \leftarrow \{0,1\}^\ell$. For $i \in [\ell]$, execute $(\mathsf{ot}_{1,i}, \mathsf{st}_i) \leftarrow OT_1(1^\lambda, r[i])$. Let $\mathsf{pk} = (\mathsf{ot}_{1,i})_{i \in [\ell]}$. Execute $(c, \rho_0, \rho_1) \leftarrow \mathcal{A}(1^\lambda, \mathsf{pk})$. If $\rho_0 \oplus \rho_1 = r$, then output 1, otherwise output 0.
Hybrid $H_{0.5}^{i^*}$ Randomly sample $r \leftarrow \{0,1\}^\ell$. For $1 \leq i \leq i^*$, execute $(\mathsf{ot}_{1,i}, \mathsf{st}_i) \leftarrow OT_1(1^\lambda, 0)$. For $i^* < i \leq \ell$, execute $(\mathsf{ot}_{1,i}, \mathsf{st}_i) \leftarrow OT_1(1^\lambda, r[i])$. Let $\mathsf{pk} = (\mathsf{ot}_{1,i})_{i \in [\ell]}$. Execute $(c, \rho_0, \rho_1) \leftarrow \mathcal{A}(1^\lambda, \mathsf{pk})$. If $\rho_0 \oplus \rho_1 = r$, then output 1, otherwise output 0.
Hybrid H_1 Randomly sample $r \leftarrow \{0,1\}^\ell$. For $i \in [\ell]$, execute $(\mathsf{ot}_{1,i}, \mathsf{st}_i) \leftarrow OT_1(1^\lambda, 0)$. Let $\mathsf{pk} = (\mathsf{ot}_{1,i})_{i \in [\ell]}$. Execute $(c, \rho_0, \rho_1) \leftarrow \mathcal{A}(1^\lambda, \mathsf{pk})$. If $\rho_0 \oplus \rho_1 = r$, then output 1, otherwise output 0.

Lemma 13. $\Pr[H_0 = 1] \geq \mathsf{Adv}(\mathcal{A})$.

Proof. From the construction of H, we now that $\mathsf{H}(\mathsf{k}, c, 0) \oplus \mathsf{H}(\mathsf{k}, c, 1) = r$. Hence, when $\mathcal{A}$ wins the security game, $(c, \rho_0, \rho_1) \leftarrow \mathcal{A}(1^\lambda, \mathsf{pk})$ with $\rho_0 = \mathsf{H}(\mathsf{k}, x, 0) \wedge \rho_1 = \mathsf{H}(\mathsf{k}, x, 1)$ implies $\rho_0 \oplus \rho_1 = \mathsf{H}(\mathsf{k}, x, 0) \oplus \mathsf{H}(\mathsf{k}, x, 1) = r$. □

Lemma 14. *Hybrid H_0 and Hybrid $H_{0.5}^0$ are identical. Furthermore, there exits a negligible function $\nu(\lambda)$ such that for each $i = 0, \ldots, \ell - 1$, $|\Pr[H_{0.5}^{i^*} = 1] - \Pr[H_{0.5}^{i^*+1} = 1]| < \nu(\lambda)$.*

Proof. When $i^* = 0$, all $\mathsf{ot}_{1,i}$ are generated in the same way as in Hybrid H_0, for all $i \in [\ell]$. Hence, Hybrid H_0 and Hybrid $\mathsf{H}_{0.5}^0$ are identical.

To show $\mathsf{H}_{0.5}^{i^*} \approx \mathsf{H}_{0.5}^{i^*+1}$, we consider the following adversary $\mathcal{D}$ for receiver's computational privacy.

$\mathcal{D}(1^\lambda, \mathsf{ot}_1)$ Randomly sample $r \leftarrow \{0,1\}^\ell$. For $i \in [\ell] \setminus \{i^*+1\}$, let $(\mathsf{ot}_{1,i}, \mathsf{st}_i) \leftarrow \mathsf{OT}_1(1^\lambda, r[i])$. If $r[i^*+1] = 0$, then let $(\mathsf{ot}_{1,i^*+1}, \mathsf{st}_{i^*+1}) \leftarrow \mathsf{OT}_1(1^\lambda, 0)$, otherwise let $\mathsf{ot}_{1,i^*+1} = \mathsf{ot}_1$. Let $\mathsf{pk} = (\mathsf{ot}_{1,i})_{i \in [\ell]}$. Execute $(c, \rho_0, \rho_1) \leftarrow \mathcal{A}(1^\lambda, \mathsf{pk})$. If $\rho_0 \oplus \rho_1 = r$, then output 1, otherwise output 0.

If ot_1 is generated from $\mathsf{OT}_1(1^\lambda, 0)$, then $\mathcal{D}$ simulates the environment of $\mathsf{H}_{0.5}^{i^*+1}$ for $\mathcal{A}$. Hence, $\Pr[\mathsf{H}_{0.5}^{i^*+1} = 1] = \Pr[(\mathsf{ot}_1, \mathsf{st}) \leftarrow \mathsf{OT}_1(1^\lambda, 0) : \mathcal{D}(1^\lambda, \mathsf{ot}_1) = 1]$.

If ot_1 is generated from $\mathsf{OT}_1(1^\lambda, 1)$, then $\mathcal{D}$ simulates the environment of $\mathsf{H}_{0.5}^{i^*}$ for $\mathcal{A}$. Hence, $\Pr[\mathsf{H}_{0.5}^{i^*} = 1] = \Pr[(\mathsf{ot}_1, \mathsf{st}) \leftarrow \mathsf{OT}_1(1^\lambda, 1) : \mathcal{D}(1^\lambda, \mathsf{ot}_1) = 1]$.

From the indistinguishability of ot_1, we know that the right hand ot_1^0 generated by $\mathsf{OT}_1(1^\lambda, 0)$ and ot_1^1 generated by $\mathsf{OT}_1(1^\lambda, 1)$ are indistinguishable. Hence, there exits a negligible function $\nu(\lambda)$ such that $|\Pr[\mathsf{H}_{0.5}^{i^*} = 1] - \Pr[\mathsf{H}_{0.5}^{i^*+1} = 1]| < \nu(\lambda)$. $\square$

Lemma 15. *Hybrid $\mathsf{H}_{0.5}^\ell$ is identical to H_1. Furthermore, $\Pr[\mathsf{H}_1 = 1] = 1/2^\ell$.*

Proof. When $i^* = \ell$, we know that all $\mathsf{ot}_{1,i}$ are generated in the same way as in Hybrid H_1. Hence, $\mathsf{H}_{0.5}^\ell$ and H_1 are identical.

In Hybrid H_1, pk is completely independent of r. Hence, $\Pr[\mathsf{H}_1 = 1] = \Pr[\rho_0 \oplus \rho_1 = r] = 1/2^\ell$. $\square$

By the hybrid argument, combining Lemmas 13, 14, and 15, we have $\mathsf{Adv}(\mathcal{A}) < \mathsf{neg}(\lambda)$. $\square$

We defer the proof of statistical hiding property to the full version.

6   Three Round Statistical Receiver-Private Oblivious Transfer

We start by presenting the definition for 3-round statistical receiver-private oblivious transfer. We capture statistical receiver privacy via a game-based definition. We consider two definitions to capture computational sender privacy: a game-based definition that intuitively requires that any malicious receiver who interacts with an honest sender can only learn one of its two inputs, and a distinguisher-dependent simulation based definition. We defer the formal treatment of the latter as well as the proof of implication from the former to the latter definition to the full version.

Definition 11 (3-round Statistical Receiver-Private Oblivious Transfer). *A 3-round oblivious transfer is a tuple of algorithms $(\mathsf{OT}_1, \mathsf{OT}_2, \mathsf{OT}_3, \mathsf{OT}_4)$, which specify the following protocol.*

Round 1 *The sender $\mathcal{S}$ computes $(\mathsf{ot}_1, \mathsf{st}_S) \leftarrow \mathsf{OT}_1(1^\lambda)$ and sends ot_1 to the receiver $\mathcal{R}$.*

Round 2 *The receiver* $\mathcal{R}$ *with input* $\beta \in \{0,1\}$, *computes* $(\text{ot}_2, \text{st}_R) \leftarrow \text{OT}_2(1^\lambda, \text{ot}_1, \beta)$ *and sends* ot_2 *to* $\mathcal{S}$.

Round 3 $\mathcal{S}$ *with input* $(m_0, m_1) \in \{0,1\}^2$ *computes* $\text{ot}_3 \leftarrow \text{OT}_3(1^\lambda, \text{ot}_2, \text{st}_S, m_0, m_1)$ *and sends* ot_3 *to the receiver.*

Message Decryption *The receiver computes* $m' \leftarrow \text{OT}_4(1^\lambda, \text{ot}_1, \text{ot}_3, \text{st}_R)$.

We require the protocol to satisfy the following properties.

Correctness[2] *For any* $\beta \in \{0,1\}, (m_0, m_1) \in \{0,1\}^2$, *we have*

$$\Pr\left[\begin{array}{l} (\text{ot}_1, \text{st}_S) \leftarrow \text{OT}_1(1^\lambda) \\ (\text{ot}_2, \text{st}_R) \leftarrow \text{OT}_2(1^\lambda, \text{ot}_1, \beta) \\ \text{ot}_3 \leftarrow \text{OT}_3(1^\lambda, \text{ot}_2, \text{st}_S, m_0, m_1) \\ m' \leftarrow \text{OT}_4(1^\lambda, \text{ot}_1, \text{ot}_3, \text{st}_R) \end{array} : m' = m_\beta \right] = 1$$

Game-Based Statistical Receiver-Privacy *For any (potentially maliciously generated)* ot_1^*, *denote* $(\text{ot}_2^{(0)}, \text{st}_R^{(0)}) \leftarrow \text{OT}_2(1^\lambda, \text{ot}_1^*, 0)$, *and* $(\text{ot}_2^{(1)}, \text{st}_R^{(1)}) \leftarrow \text{OT}_2(1^\lambda, \text{ot}_1^*, 1)$. *Then we have* $\text{SD}(\text{ot}_2^{(0)}, \text{ot}_2^{(1)}) < \nu(\lambda)$, *where* $\nu(\cdot)$ *is a negligible function.*

Game-Based Computational Sender-Privacy *For any probabilistic polynomial time distinguisher* $\mathcal{A}_0, \mathcal{A}_1$, *and any probabilistic polynomial time malicious receiver* $\mathcal{R}^*$, *we define the following games.*

  Interact with $\mathcal{R}^*$ *The challenger plays the role of an honest sender for the first round and the second round with the malicious receiver* $\mathcal{R}^*$. *Specifically, the challenger executes* $(\text{ot}_1, \text{st}_S) \leftarrow \text{OT}_1(1^\lambda)$. *Then send* ot_1 *to* $\mathcal{R}^*$. *Then the receiver* $\mathcal{R}^*$ *sends* ot_2^* *to the challenger.*

  Game $\mathsf{G}_0(m_0, m_1)$ *This game interact with adversary* $\mathcal{A}_0$. *In the beginning, the adversary* $\mathcal{A}_0$ *is given input* $\text{View}(\mathcal{R}^*)$. *Then the challenger samples* $b_0 \leftarrow \{0,1\}$ *at random, and send* $\text{ot}_3 \leftarrow \text{OT}_3(1^\lambda, \text{ot}_2^*, \text{st}_S, m_{b}, m_1)$ *to* $\mathcal{A}_0$. *Finally* $\mathcal{A}_0$ *outputs a bit* b_0'. *If* $b_0 = b_0'$, *then we say* $\mathcal{A}_0$ *wins the game.*

  Game $\mathsf{G}_1(m_0, m_1)$ *This game interact with adversary* $\mathcal{A}_1$. *In the beginning, the adversary* $\mathcal{A}_1$ *is given input* $\text{View}(\mathcal{R}^*)$. *Then the challenger samples* $b_1 \leftarrow \{0,1\}$ *at random, and send* $\text{ot}_3 \leftarrow \text{OT}_3(1^\lambda, \text{ot}_2^*, \text{st}_S, m_0, m_{b})$ *to* $\mathcal{A}_1$. *Finally* $\mathcal{A}_1$ *outputs a bit* b_1'. *If* $b_1 = b_1'$, *then we say* $\mathcal{A}_1$ *wins the game.*

We define the following advantage

$$\text{Adv}(\mathcal{A}_0, \mathcal{A}_1, \mathcal{R}^*) \triangleq \mathbb{E}_{\text{View}(\mathcal{R}^*)}\left[\min \Big\{ \right.$$

$$\max_{m_0, m_1 \in \{0,1\}} \left(\left| \Pr[\mathcal{A}_0(\text{View}(\mathcal{R}^*)) \text{ wins } \mathsf{G}_0(m_0, m_1)] - \frac{1}{2} \right| \right),$$

$$\left. \max_{m_0, m_1 \in \{0,1\}} \left(\left| \Pr[\mathcal{A}_1(\text{View}(\mathcal{R}^*)) \text{ wins } \mathsf{G}_1(m_0, m_1)] - \frac{1}{2} \right| \right) \Big\} \right]$$

We say the oblivious transfer scheme is game-based computational sender-secure, if for any probabilistic polynomial time distinguisher $\mathcal{A}_0, \mathcal{A}_1$, *and any probabilistic polynomial time malicious receiver* $\mathcal{R}^*$, *there exist a negligible function* $\nu(\cdot)$ *such that* $\text{Adv}(\mathcal{A}_0, \mathcal{A}_1, \mathcal{R}^*) < \nu(\lambda)$.

---

[2] We can relax the definition to be statistical correctness, which only requires the probability to be $1 - \text{negl}(\lambda)$.

6.1 Our Construction

We now describe a generic transformation from SHC scheme to three-round statistical receiver-private oblivious transfer.

Construction. Let $(\mathsf{KGen}, \mathsf{Com}, \mathsf{H}, \mathcal{C}, \mathcal{R})$ be an SHC scheme. Let hc denote the Goldreich-Levin hardcore predicate [21]. The 3-round statistical receiver-private oblivious transfer proceeds as follows.

$\mathsf{OT}_1(1^\lambda)$ Execute $(\mathsf{pk}, \mathsf{k}) \leftarrow \mathsf{KGen}(1^\lambda)$. Let $\mathsf{ot}_1 = \mathsf{pk}, \mathsf{st}_S = \mathsf{k}$.

$\mathsf{OT}_2(1^\lambda, \mathsf{ot}_1, \beta)$ Parse $\mathsf{ot}_1 = \mathsf{pk}$. Run $(c, \rho) \leftarrow \mathsf{Com}(\mathsf{pk}, \beta)$. Output $\mathsf{ot}_2 = c, \mathsf{st}_R = \rho$.

$\mathsf{OT}_3(1^\lambda, \mathsf{ot}_2, \mathsf{st}_S, m_0, m_1)$ Parse $\mathsf{ot}_2 = c$, and $\mathsf{st}_S = \mathsf{k}$. For any $b \in \{0,1\}$, sample $r_b \leftarrow \{0,1\}^\lambda$, encrypt m_b as $c_b = (\mathsf{hc}(\mathsf{H}(\mathsf{k}, c, b), r_b) \oplus m_b, r_b)$. Output $\mathsf{ot}_3 = (c_0, c_1)$.

$\mathsf{OT}_4(1^\lambda, \mathsf{ot}_1, \mathsf{ot}_3, \mathsf{st}_R)$ Parse $\mathsf{ot}_1 = \mathsf{pk}$, $\mathsf{ot}_3 = (c_0, c_1)$, and $\mathsf{st}_R = \rho$. Parse c_β as $c_\beta = (u_\beta, r_\beta)$. Output $m' = u_\beta \oplus \mathsf{hc}(\rho, r_\beta)$.

We now prove the required properties of the protocol. We defer the proof of correctness to the full version.

Lemma 16 (Statistical Receiver-Privacy). *If the underlying SHC is statistical (resp. perfect) hiding, then the construction above is statistical (resp. perfect) receiver-private.*

Proof. From the statistical hiding property of the SHC scheme, for any pk, we have $\mathsf{SD}(\mathsf{ot}_2^0, \mathsf{ot}_2^1) \leq \mathsf{neg}(\lambda)$, where $(\mathsf{ot}_2^b, \rho^b) \leftarrow \mathsf{Com}(\mathsf{pk}, b)$ for any $b \in \{0,1\}$. Hence, for any ot_1, $\mathsf{OT}_2(1^\lambda, \mathsf{ot}_1, 0)$ and $\mathsf{OT}_2(1^\lambda, \mathsf{ot}_1, 1)$ are statistically (resp. perfectly) close. □

Lemma 17 (Game-based Computational Sender-Privacy). *If the underlying SHC scheme is computational binding, then the 3-round oblivious transfer constructed above is game-based computational sender-private.*

Proof. For any probabilistic polynomial time adversary $\mathcal{A}_0, \mathcal{A}_1$ and any probabilistic polynomial time malicious receiver $\mathcal{R}^*$ with $\mathsf{Adv}(\mathcal{A}_0, \mathcal{A}_1, \mathcal{R}^*) > \delta$, where δ is a non-negligible function of λ. Then, with probability at least $\delta/2$ over $\mathsf{View}(\mathcal{R}^*)$,

$$\exists\, \mathbf{m}_0 \in \{0,1\}^2, \mathbf{m}_1 \in \{0,1\}^2 : \left| \Pr[\mathcal{A}_0(\mathsf{View}(\mathcal{R}^*)) \text{ wins } \mathsf{G}_0(\mathbf{m}_0)] - \frac{1}{2} \right| > \frac{\delta}{2} \wedge$$

$$\left| \Pr[\mathcal{A}_1(\mathsf{View}(\mathcal{R}^*)) \text{ wins } \mathsf{G}_1(\mathbf{m}_1)] - \frac{1}{2} \right| > \frac{\delta}{2}$$

Denote this fraction of $\mathsf{View}(\mathcal{R}^*)$ as GOOD. Randomly sample $\overline{m}_0, \overline{m}_1 \leftarrow \{0,1\}^2$. With probability $1/16$, we have $\overline{\mathbf{m}}_0 = \mathbf{m}_0 \wedge \overline{\mathbf{m}}_1 = \mathbf{m}_1$.

From Goldreich-Levin Theorem [21], there exits two inverters $\mathcal{A}'_0, \mathcal{A}'_1$ such that $\mathcal{A}'_0$ takes input $(\mathsf{View}(\mathcal{R}^*), r_0, \mathsf{hc}(\mathsf{H}(\mathsf{k}, c, 1), r_1) \oplus m_1, r_1)$, output x'_0. $\mathcal{A}'_1$ takes input $(\mathsf{View}(\mathcal{R}^*), r_1, \mathsf{hc}(\mathsf{H}(\mathsf{k}, c, 0), r_0) \oplus m_0, r_0)$, output x'_1. Furthermore, the inverters $\mathcal{A}_0', \mathcal{A}_1'$ satisfy the property that for any $v \in$ GOOD and $\overline{m}_0 = m_0 \wedge \overline{m}_1 = m_1$, $\Pr[x_0' = \mathsf{H}(k, c, 0)] > \delta'$ and $\Pr[x_1' = \mathsf{H}(k, c, 1)] > \delta'$, where $\delta' = \delta'(\lambda)$ is a non-negligible function. We construct the following adversary $\mathcal{A}$ to attack the computational binding property of the SHC scheme.

Adversary $\mathcal{A}(1^\lambda, \mathsf{pk})$. Set random coins and execute $\mathcal{R}^*$. Send $\mathcal{R}^*$ the first round message $\mathsf{ot}_1 = \mathsf{pk}$, then $\mathcal{R}^*$ replies ot_2^*. Sample $r_0 \leftarrow \{0,1\}^\lambda, b_1 \leftarrow \{0,1\}, r_1 \leftarrow \{0,1\}^\lambda$, then execute $x_0' \leftarrow \mathcal{A}_0'(\mathsf{View}(\mathcal{R}^*), r_0, b_1, r_1)$. Sample $r_1' \leftarrow \{0,1\}^\lambda, b_0 \leftarrow \{0,1\}, r_0' \leftarrow \{0,1\}^\lambda$, then execute $x_1' \leftarrow \mathcal{A}_1'(\mathsf{View}(\mathcal{R}^*), r_1', b_0, r_0')$. Output $(c = \mathsf{ot}_2^*, x_0', x_1')$. We now prove that the advantage of $\mathcal{A}$ satisfies

$$\mathsf{Adv}(\mathcal{A}) = \Pr\left[(\mathsf{pk}, k) \leftarrow \mathsf{KGen}(1^\lambda), (c, \rho_0, \rho_1) \leftarrow \mathcal{A}(1^\lambda, \mathsf{pk}) : \begin{smallmatrix} \rho_0 = \mathsf{H}(k,c,0) \wedge \\ \rho_1 = \mathsf{H}(k,c,1) \end{smallmatrix}\right] \geq \frac{\delta \cdot \delta'^2}{128}$$

Hybrids H_0 $(\mathsf{pk}, k) \leftarrow \mathsf{KGen}(1^\lambda)$. Set random coins and execute $\mathcal{R}^*$. $\mathcal{R}^*$ replies ot_2^*. Sample $r_0 \leftarrow \{0,1\}^\lambda, r_1 \leftarrow \{0,1\}^\lambda$. Let $b_1 = \mathsf{hc}(\mathsf{H}(k, c, 1), r_1) \oplus m_1$. Execute $x_0' \leftarrow \mathcal{A}_0'(\mathsf{View}(\mathcal{R}^*), r_0, b_1, r_1)$. Sample $r_0' \leftarrow \{0,1\}^\lambda, r_1' \leftarrow \{0,1\}^\lambda$. Let $b_0 = \mathsf{hc}(\mathsf{H}(k, c, 0), r_0') \oplus m_0$. Execute $x_1' \leftarrow \mathcal{A}_1'(\mathsf{View}(\mathcal{R}^*), r_1', b_0, r_0')$. If $\rho_0 = \mathsf{H}(k, c, 0) \wedge \rho_1 = \mathsf{H}(k, c, 1)$, then output 1; else output 0.

Hybrids H_1 $(\mathsf{pk}, k) \leftarrow \mathsf{KGen}(1^\lambda)$. Set random coins and execute $\mathcal{R}^*$. $\mathcal{R}^*$ replies ot_2^*. Sample $r_0 \leftarrow \{0,1\}^\lambda, r_1 \leftarrow \{0,1\}^\lambda$. <u>Let $b_1 \leftarrow \{0,1\}$</u>. Execute $x_0' \leftarrow \mathcal{A}_0'(\mathsf{View}(\mathcal{R}^*), r_0, b_1, r_1)$. Sample $r_0' \leftarrow \{0,1\}^\lambda, r_1' \leftarrow \{0,1\}^\lambda$. <u>Let $b_0 \leftarrow \{0,1\}$</u>. Execute $x_1' \leftarrow \mathcal{A}_1'(\mathsf{View}(\mathcal{R}^*), r_1', b_0, r_0')$. If $\rho_0 = \mathsf{H}(k, c, 0) \wedge \rho_1 = \mathsf{H}(k, c, 1)$, then output 1; else output 0.

Hybrids H_2 $(\mathsf{pk}, k) \leftarrow \mathsf{KGen}(1^\lambda), (c, \rho_0, \rho_1) \leftarrow \mathcal{A}(1^\lambda, \mathsf{pk})$. If $\rho_0 = \mathsf{H}(k, c, 0) \wedge \rho_1 = \mathsf{H}(k, c, 1)$, then output 1; else output 0.

From the construction of $\mathcal{A}$, the hybrids H_1 and H_2 are identical. Hence, $\mathsf{Adv}(\mathcal{A}) = \Pr[\mathsf{H}_2 = 1] = \Pr[\mathsf{H}_1 = 1]$. Furthermore, in hybrids H_1, with probability $1/4$, $b_1 = \mathsf{hc}(\mathsf{H}(k, c, 1), r_1) \oplus m_1 \wedge b_0 = \mathsf{hc}(\mathsf{H}(k, c, 0), r_0') \oplus m_0$. Conditioned on such event, H_0 and H_1 are identical. Hence, $\Pr[\mathsf{H}_1 = 1] \geq \Pr[\mathsf{H}_0 = 1]/4$. In hybrid H_0, the fraction of $\mathsf{View}(\mathcal{R}^*) \in$ GOOD is at least $\delta/2$. With probability $1/16$, the guess of m_0, m_1 is correct. With probability δ'^2, both $\mathcal{A}_0'$ and $\mathcal{A}_1'$ inverts correctly. Hence, $\mathsf{Adv}(\mathcal{A}) \geq \frac{\delta}{2} \cdot \frac{1}{16} \cdot \delta'^2 \cdot \frac{1}{4} = \delta \cdot \delta'^2/128$. If $\delta(\lambda)$ is non-negligible, then $\mathsf{Adv}(\mathcal{A})$ is also non-negligible. This contradicts with the computational binding property of the SHC scheme.   □

Acknowledgement. The first author was supported in part by the NSF award 1916939, a gift from Ripple, a JP Morgan Faculty Fellowship, a PNC center for financial services innovation award, and a Cylab seed funding award. The second and third author were supported in part by NSF SaTC award 1814919 and DARPA Safeware W911NF-15-C-0213. The last author conducted part of the research while at the Simons Institute for the Theory of Computing.

References

1. Aiello, B., Ishai, Y., Reingold, O.: Priced oblivious transfer: how to sell digital goods. In: Pfitzmann, B. (ed.) EUROCRYPT 2001. LNCS, vol. 2045, pp. 119–135. Springer, Heidelberg (2001). https://doi.org/10.1007/3-540-44987-6_8

2. Babai, L.: Trading group theory for randomness. In: 17th ACM STOC, Providence, RI, USA, 6–8 May 1985, pp. 421–429. ACM Press (1985). https://doi.org/10.1145/22145.22192
3. Badrinarayanan, S., Fernando, R., Jain, A., Khurana, D., Sahai, A.: Statistical ZAP arguments. In: Canteaut, A., Ishai, Y. (eds.) EUROCRYPT 2020. LNCS, vol. 12107, pp. 642–667. Springer, Heidelberg (2020)
4. Badrinarayanan, S., Garg, S., Ishai, Y., Sahai, A., Wadia, A.: Two-message witness indistinguishability and secure computation in the plain model from new assumptions. In: Takagi, T., Peyrin, T. (eds.) ASIACRYPT 2017, Part III. LNCS, vol. 10626, pp. 275–303. Springer, Cham (2017). https://doi.org/10.1007/978-3-319-70700-6_10
5. Barak, B., Ong, S.J., Vadhan, S.: Derandomization in cryptography. In: Boneh, D. (ed.) CRYPTO 2003. LNCS, vol. 2729, pp. 299–315. Springer, Heidelberg (2003). https://doi.org/10.1007/978-3-540-45146-4_18
6. Bitansky, N., Paneth, O.: ZAPs and non-interactive witness indistinguishability from indistinguishability obfuscation. In: Dodis, Y., Nielsen, J.B. (eds.) TCC 2015, Part II. LNCS, vol. 9015, pp. 401–427. Springer, Heidelberg (2015). https://doi.org/10.1007/978-3-662-46497-7_16
7. Brakerski, Z., Döttling, N.: Two-message statistically sender-private OT from LWE. In: Beimel, A., Dziembowski, S. (eds.) TCC 2018, Part II. LNCS, vol. 11240, pp. 370–390. Springer, Cham (2018). https://doi.org/10.1007/978-3-030-03810-6_14
8. Canetti, R., et al.: Fiat-Shamir: from practice to theory. In: Charikar, M., Cohen, E. (eds.) 51st ACM STOC, Phoenix, AZ, USA, 23–26 June 2019, pp. 1082–1090. ACM Press (2019). https://doi.org/10.1145/3313276.3316380
9. Canetti, R., Goldreich, O., Halevi, S.: The random oracle methodology, revisited (preliminary version). In: 30th ACM STOC, Dallas, TX, USA, 23–26 May 1998, pp. 209–218. ACM Press (1998). https://doi.org/10.1145/276698.276741
10. Cramer, R., Damgård, I., Schoenmakers, B.: Proofs of partial knowledge and simplified design of witness hiding protocols. In: Desmedt, Y.G. (ed.) CRYPTO 1994. LNCS, vol. 839, pp. 174–187. Springer, Heidelberg (1994). https://doi.org/10.1007/3-540-48658-5_19
11. Cramer, R., Shoup, V.: Universal hash proofs and a paradigm for adaptive chosen ciphertext secure public-key encryption. In: Knudsen, L.R. (ed.) EUROCRYPT 2002. LNCS, vol. 2332, pp. 45–64. Springer, Heidelberg (2002). https://doi.org/10.1007/3-540-46035-7_4
12. De Santis, A., Micali, S., Persiano, G.: Non-interactive zero-knowledge proof systems. In: Pomerance, C. (ed.) CRYPTO 1987. LNCS, vol. 293, pp. 52–72. Springer, Heidelberg (1988). https://doi.org/10.1007/3-540-48184-2_5
13. Deng, Y., Goyal, V., Sahai, A.: Resolving the simultaneous resettability conjecture and a new non-black-box simulation strategy. In: 50th FOCS, Atlanta, GA, USA, 25–27 October 2009, pp. 251–260. IEEE Computer Society Press (2009). https://doi.org/10.1109/FOCS.2009.59
14. Döttling, N., Garg, S., Hajiabadi, M., Masny, D., Wichs, D.: Two-round oblivious transfer from CDH or LPN. IACR Cryptology ePrint Archive 2019, 414 (2019)
15. Dwork, C., Naor, M.: Zaps and their applications. In: 41st FOCS, Redondo Beach, CA, USA, 12–14 November 2000, pp. 283–293. IEEE Computer Society Press (2000). https://doi.org/10.1109/SFCS.2000.892117
16. Dwork, C., Naor, M., Reingold, O., Stockmeyer, L.J.: Magic functions. In: 40th FOCS, New York, NY, USA, 17–19 October 1999, pp. 523–534. IEEE Computer Society Press (1999). https://doi.org/10.1109/SFFCS.1999.814626

17. Even, S., Goldreich, O., Lempel, A.: A randomized protocol for signing contracts. Commun. ACM **28**(6), 637–647 (1985)
18. Feige, U., Lapidot, D., Shamir, A.: Multiple non-interactive zero knowledge proofs based on a single random string (extended abstract). In: 31st FOCS, St. Louis, MO, USA, 22–24 October 1990, pp. 308–317. IEEE Computer Society Press (1990). https://doi.org/10.1109/FSCS.1990.89549
19. Fiat, A., Shamir, A.: How to prove yourself: practical solutions to identification and signature problems. In: Odlyzko, A.M. (ed.) CRYPTO 1986. LNCS, vol. 263, pp. 186–194. Springer, Heidelberg (1987). https://doi.org/10.1007/3-540-47721-7_12
20. Goldreich, O., Krawczyk, H.: On the composition of zero-knowledge proof systems. SIAM J. Comput. **25**(1), 169–192 (1996)
21. Goldreich, O., Levin, L.A.: A hard-core predicate for all one-way functions. In: 21st ACM STOC, Seattle, WA, USA, 15–17 May 1989, pp. 25–32. ACM Press (1989). https://doi.org/10.1145/73007.73010
22. Goldreich, O., Micali, S., Wigderson, A.: How to play any mental game or a completeness theorem for protocols with honest majority. In: Aho, A. (ed.) 19th ACM STOC, New York City, NY, USA, 25–27 May 1987, pp. 218–229. ACM Press (1987). https://doi.org/10.1145/28395.28420
23. Goldreich, O., Oren, Y.: Definitions and properties of zero-knowledge proof systems. J. Cryptol. **7**(1), 1–32 (1994). https://doi.org/10.1007/BF00195207
24. Goldwasser, S., Micali, S., Rackoff, C.: The knowledge complexity of interactive proof-systems (extended abstract). In: 17th ACM STOC, Providence, RI, USA, 6–8 May 1985, pp. 291–304. ACM Press (1985). https://doi.org/10.1145/22145.22178
25. Groth, J., Ostrovsky, R., Sahai, A.: Non-interactive zaps and new techniques for NIZK. In: Dwork, C. (ed.) CRYPTO 2006. LNCS, vol. 4117, pp. 97–111. Springer, Heidelberg (2006). https://doi.org/10.1007/11818175_6
26. Groth, J., Ostrovsky, R., Sahai, A.: Perfect non-interactive zero knowledge for NP. In: Vaudenay, S. (ed.) EUROCRYPT 2006. LNCS, vol. 4004, pp. 339–358. Springer, Heidelberg (2006). https://doi.org/10.1007/11761679_21
27. Halevi, S., Hazay, C., Polychroniadou, A., Venkitasubramaniam, M.: Round-optimal secure multi-party computation. In: Shacham, H., Boldyreva, A. (eds.) CRYPTO 2018, Part II. LNCS, vol. 10992, pp. 488–520. Springer, Cham (2018). https://doi.org/10.1007/978-3-319-96881-0_17
28. Halevi, S., Kalai, Y.T.: Smooth projective hashing and two-message oblivious transfer. J. Cryptol. **25**(1), 158–193 (2012). https://doi.org/10.1007/s00145-010-9092-8
29. Jain, A., Kalai, Y.T., Khurana, D., Rothblum, R.: Distinguisher-dependent simulation in two rounds and its applications. In: Katz, J., Shacham, H. (eds.) CRYPTO 2017, Part II. LNCS, vol. 10402, pp. 158–189. Springer, Cham (2017). https://doi.org/10.1007/978-3-319-63715-0_6
30. Kalai, Y.T.: Smooth projective hashing and two-message oblivious transfer. In: Cramer, R. (ed.) EUROCRYPT 2005. LNCS, vol. 3494, pp. 78–95. Springer, Heidelberg (2005). https://doi.org/10.1007/11426639_5
31. Kalai, Y.T., Khurana, D., Sahai, A.: Statistical witness indistinguishability (and more) in two messages. In: Nielsen, J.B., Rijmen, V. (eds.) EUROCRYPT 2018, Part III. LNCS, vol. 10822, pp. 34–65. Springer, Cham (2018). https://doi.org/10.1007/978-3-319-78372-7_2

32. Khurana, D., Sahai, A.: How to achieve non-malleability in one or two rounds. In: Umans, C. (ed.) 58th FOCS, Berkeley, CA, USA, 15–17 October 2017, pp. 564–575. IEEE Computer Society Press (2017). https://doi.org/10.1109/FOCS.2017.58
33. Kilian, J.: Founding cryptography on oblivious transfer. In: 20th ACM STOC, Chicago, IL, USA, 2–4 May 1988, pp. 20–31. ACM Press (1988). https://doi.org/10.1145/62212.62215
34. Lombardi, A., Vaikuntanathan, V., Wichs, D.: 2-message publicly verifiable WI from (subexponential) LWE. IACR Cryptology ePrint Archive 2019, 808 (2019)
35. Lombardi, A., Vaikuntanathan, V., Wichs, D.: Statistical ZAPR arguments from bilinear maps. In: Canteaut, A., Ishai, Y. (eds.) EUROCRYPT 2020. LNCS, vol. 12107, pp. 620–641. Springer, Heidelberg (2020)
36. Naor, M., Pinkas, B.: Efficient oblivious transfer protocols. In: Kosaraju, S.R. (ed.) 12th SODA, Washington, DC, USA, 7–9 January 2001, pp. 448–457. ACM-SIAM (2001)
37. Pass, R.: Simulation in quasi-polynomial time, and its application to protocol composition. In: Biham, E. (ed.) EUROCRYPT 2003. LNCS, vol. 2656, pp. 160–176. Springer, Heidelberg (2003). https://doi.org/10.1007/3-540-39200-9_10
38. Peikert, C., Shiehian, S.: Noninteractive zero knowledge for NP from (plain) learning with errors. In: Boldyreva, A., Micciancio, D. (eds.) CRYPTO 2019, Part I. LNCS, vol. 11692, pp. 89–114. Springer, Cham (2019). https://doi.org/10.1007/978-3-030-26948-7_4
39. Rabin, M.O.: How to exchange secrets by oblivious transfer. Technical report TR-81, Harvard University (1981)
40. Wolf, S., Wullschleger, J.: Oblivious transfer is symmetric. In: Vaudenay, S. (ed.) EUROCRYPT 2006. LNCS, vol. 4004, pp. 222–232. Springer, Heidelberg (2006). https://doi.org/10.1007/11761679_14
41. Yao, A.C.C.: How to generate and exchange secrets (extended abstract). In: 27th FOCS, Toronto, Ontario, Canada, 27–29 October 1986, pp. 162–167. IEEE Computer Society Press (1986). https://doi.org/10.1109/SFCS.1986.25

Quantum II

Measure-Rewind-Measure: Tighter Quantum Random Oracle Model Proofs for One-Way to Hiding and CCA Security

Veronika Kuchta[1], Amin Sakzad[1(✉)], Damien Stehlé[2,3], Ron Steinfeld[1(✉)], and Shi-Feng Sun[1,4]

[1] Faculty of Information Technology, Monash University, Melbourne, Australia
{amin.sakzad,ron.steinfeld}@monash.edu
[2] Univ. Lyon, EnsL, UCBL, CNRS, Inria, LIP, 69342 Lyon Cedex 07, France
[3] Institut Universitaire de France, Paris, France
[4] Data61, CSIRO, Canberra, Australia

Abstract. We introduce a new technique called 'Measure-Rewind-Measure' (MRM) to achieve tighter security proofs in the quantum random oracle model (QROM). We first apply our MRM technique to derive a new security proof for a variant of the 'double-sided' quantum One-Way to Hiding Lemma (O2H) of Bindel et al. [TCC 2019] which, for the first time, avoids the square-root advantage loss in the security proof. In particular, it bypasses a previous 'impossibility result' of Jiang, Zhang and Ma [IACR eprint 2019]. We then apply our new O2H Lemma to give a new tighter security proof for the Fujisaki-Okamoto transform for constructing a strong (IND-CCA) Key Encapsulation Mechanism (KEM) from a weak (IND-CPA) public-key encryption scheme satisfying a mild injectivity assumption.

Keywords: QROM · Security proof · Public-key encryption

1 Introduction

Background. Correctly selecting secure parameters for quantum-resistant cryptosystems requires understanding both the concrete quantum cost of attacks against the underlying intractability assumption (e.g., LWE [20]), as well as the concrete quantum cost of attacks against the cryptosystem itself. Ideally, one would like a cryptosystem whose security is *tightly* related via a *security proof* (or security reduction) to the intractability of a well-studied problem, so that attacks against the cryptosystem of lower cost than those against the problem are ruled out. Such tight proofs give confidence in the concrete security of practical parameter choices based on the best known attacks against the underlying problem. Unfortunately, due to existing gaps in the understanding of security proofs in the context of quantum adversaries, there are many practical post-quantum cryptosystem candidates that lack such tight security proofs.

A. Canteaut and Y. Ishai (Eds.): EUROCRYPT 2020, LNCS 12107, pp. 703–728, 2020.
https://doi.org/10.1007/978-3-030-45727-3_24

A case in point is the Fujisaki-Okamoto (FO) CCA transform [9], which is commonly applied in the design of practical public-key cryptosystems to strengthen their security from chosen-plaintext security (IND-CPA) to chosen-ciphertext security (IND-CCA), assuming the random oracle model (ROM) for the underlying cryptographic hash functions. This transform and its variants [8,10,21,22] are used in all public-key encryption schemes and key-establishment algorithms of the second round of the NIST PQC standardisation process [19]. Tight security proofs are known for FO variants against classical adversaries (in the classical ROM), meaning that an adversary breaking the FO-transformed scheme in time T and advantage ε can be used to break the underlying scheme in time $\approx T$ and advantage $\approx \varepsilon$. Oppositely, no such tight security proof for an all-purpose FO transform is known against *quantum* attacks in the quantum random oracle model [6]. In the QROM, the adversary is given *quantum* access to those hash functions modeled by random oracles. Note that [21,26] described a transform from a deterministic encryption scheme that enjoys a so-called disjoint simulatability property, to an IND-CCA public-key encryption scheme, which is tight in the QROM. The assumptions for this tight QROM transform are more stringent than those of the all-purpose FO transform: only 2.5 out of 17 second round NIST proposals for public-key encryption schemes claim that it is applicable to them [3,4,7],[1] and at the cost of additional assumptions.

Although a series of works [5,10–13,15,22] have provided improved analyses of the FO transform, the existing QROM reductions are still not tight. The state-of-the-art reductions essentially preserve the runtime, but the advantage degradation only satisfies $\mathsf{Adv}(\mathcal{A}_{\mathrm{CCA}}) \leq O(q^c \cdot (\mathsf{Adv}(\mathcal{B}_{\mathrm{CPA}}))^\delta)$, where $(c, \delta) = (1/2, 1/2)$ (versus the ideal tight result $(c, \delta) = (0, 1)$ that one could hope for), where $\mathsf{Adv}(\mathcal{A}_{\mathrm{CCA}})$ and $\mathsf{Adv}(\mathcal{B}_{\mathrm{CPA}})$ respectively denote the distinguishing advantages of the IND-CCA attack against the FO-transformed scheme and IND-CPA attack against the original scheme, and q denotes the number of QROM queries made by the attacker $\mathcal{A}$. We note that previous techniques have mainly improved the value of c, reducing it gradually from $c = 3/2$ down to $c = 1/2$. Regarding δ, while it has been improved from $1/4$ to $1/2$, going further towards $\delta = 1$ has seemed challenging. Recently, it has even been conjectured infeasible, based on an 'impossibility result' [14].

At the heart of these prior results has been the use of the 'One-way to Hiding' (O2H) lemma, first given in [24]. All its versions so far inherently lead to a 'square-root advantage' loss in the proofs of the FO transforms. The O2H lemma can be formulated informally as follows. A quantum distinguisher $\mathcal{A}_{\mathrm{O2H}}$ is given quantum access to an oracle O that implements either a random oracle $H : X \to Y$ or a modified random oracle $G : X \to Y$, where H and G are identical on all except a single secret point $x \in X$: we have $H(x') = G(x')$ for all $x' \neq x$ and $H(x) = y_H$ and $G(x) = y_G$ where y_H, y_G are independent uniformly chosen random strings. The distinguisher is also given $z = (z_x =$

---

[1] In the case of [4], this holds for Streamlined NTRU Prime, but not for NTRU LPRime.

$\mathsf{enc}(x), z_H = y_H, z_G = y_G)$, where enc is a one-way function (a deterministic encryption scheme in the FO scenario).[2] The goal of $\mathcal{A}_{\mathrm{O2H}}$ is to distinguish whether the oracle O implements G or H, while making up to q queries to O with depth at most d (where a depth of d means that $\mathcal{A}_{\mathrm{O2H}}$ splits its queries into d bunches and all queries within each bunch are queried in *parallel*, so queries in each bunch may depend on the answer to $d-1$ previous query bunches, and the total number of queries over all d bunches is at most q). An algorithm that computes x from z_x (by breaking the one-wayness of enc), queries $O(x)$ and compares the result to z_H achieves an advantage $\mathsf{Adv}(\mathcal{A}_{\mathrm{O2H}}^O)$ negligibly close to 1. In the case of a classical access to O, no algorithm can do better. In the quantum access case, all variants of the O2H lemma known so far suffer from a square-root advantage loss. For example, the recent [5, Lemma 5] states that $\mathsf{Adv}(\mathcal{A}_{\mathrm{O2H}}^O) \leq 2 \cdot \sqrt{\mathsf{Adv}(\mathcal{B}_{\mathrm{OW}}^{G,H})}$. Here $\mathcal{B}_{\mathrm{OW}}^{G,H}(z)$ is a quantum attacker against the one-wayness of enc, which is given oracle access for both G and H (these oracles can be simulated given z_x, and thus such an attacker implies an attacker against the one-wayness of enc). The one-wayness attacker $\mathcal{B}_{\mathrm{OW}}^{G,H}$ constructed in the proof of this O2H lemma (and all prior variants thereof) 'only' runs $\mathcal{A}_{\mathrm{O2H}}$ and measures its queries. In particular, it does not 'rewind' $\mathcal{A}_{\mathrm{O2H}}$ to an earlier state. Rewinding the state of an attacker to an earlier state is often considered tricky in the quantum setting, due to the fact that measurement operations are not reversible. The 'impossibility result' of [14] states that any O2H lemma based on a one-wayness attacker that runs the distinguisher only once and involves no rewinding, must incur a square-root advantage loss. Thus, it has been suggested in [5,14] that the square-root advantage loss in the O2H lemma may be unavoidable in the quantum setting.

Contributions. We present a novel quantum O2H lemma that, for the first time, does not suffer from the square-root advantage loss in the reduction. Concretely, we obtain a security bound of the form $\mathsf{Adv}(\mathcal{A}) \leq 4 \cdot d \cdot \mathsf{Adv}(\mathcal{B}^{G,H})$, where $\mathcal{B}$ is the one-wayness attacker against the underlying one-way function enc.

To circumvent the 'impossibility result' of [14], we introduce a Measure-Rewind-Measure (MRM) proof technique, which provides a new way to extract the one-wayness secret x from the distinguisher. Rather than extracting x directly by measuring the oracle queries of the distinguisher (as in prior works), the MRM technique may also extract x from the *distinguishing measurement* of the distinguisher. The latter distinguishing measurement knowledge extraction is achieved by letting the distinguisher perform its distinguishing measurement, and then rewinding *the collapsed measured state* back to the state of the oracle query stage, to perform a second measurement and extract x. A comparison of our O2H lemma security bounds and features with earlier O2H lemma variants is provided in Table 1.

---

[2] We use this definition of z for simplicity in this introduction. The actual formulation of most prior O2H lemmas, as well as our new one, is more general and allows z to have an arbitrary joint distribution with G, H, x, as well as allowing a set S of any number of x's on which G and H may differ, rather than just one.

Table 1. Comparison of security bounds and features of our new O2H lemma with earlier variants of the O2H lemma. The 'Bound' column shows the dependence of the upper bound on the distinguisher advantage $\mathsf{Adv}(\mathcal{A})$ in terms of the One-Wayness attacker advantage ε and $\mathcal{A}$'s oracle query depth $d \leq q$ (where q is the total number of queries). The '$|S|$' column indicates the number of points on which G and H may differ, the '$\mathcal{B}_{\mathrm{OW}}$ must know' column shows the oracles available to the one-wayness attacker, and the 'Event' column indicates the type of event used to define $\mathcal{A}$'s advantage. Here $H \setminus S$ (resp. $G \setminus S$) refers to the restriction of H (resp. G) to the complementary set of S, and 1_S refers to the indicator function of S.

O2H variant	Bound	$|S|$	$\mathcal{B}_{\mathrm{OW}}$ must know	Event
Original [1,24]	$2d\varepsilon^{1/2}$	Arbitrary	H or G	Arbitrary
Semi-classical [1]	$2d^{1/2}\varepsilon^{1/2}$	Arbitrary	$(H \setminus S$ or $G \setminus S)$ and 1_S	Arbitrary
Double-sided [5]	$2\varepsilon^{1/2}$	One	H and G	Arbitrary
This work	$4d\varepsilon$	Arbitrary	H and G	Efficiently checkable

Compared to prior O2H lemmas, our variant is the first to avoid the square-root advantage loss. On the other hand, it constructs a one-wayness attacker which in general requires oracle accesses to both G and H. Therefore, our lemma is in the same setting as the 'double-sided' O2H lemma of [5], which makes it less general than the semi-classical or original O2H lemmas. Nevertheless, it still suffices for important applications (see below). Compared to the 'double-sided' O2H lemma in [5], our variant is slightly less general in one respect and more general in another. On the one hand, the classical event distinguished by the O2H attacker $\mathcal{A}$ in [5] can be arbitrary, while we assume this event to be efficiently checkable by $\mathcal{A}$. 'Efficiently checkable' means that the distinguishing advantage in the definition of the O2H Lemma is defined as the advantage of $\mathcal{A}$ in the usual way, i.e., $\mathsf{Adv}(\mathcal{A}) = |\Pr[1 \leftarrow \mathcal{A}^G(z)] - \Pr[1 \leftarrow \mathcal{A}^H(z)]|$. This is in contrast to the more general definition used in [5], which uses the advantage $|\Pr[\mathsf{Ev} : \mathcal{A}^G(z)] - \Pr[\mathsf{Ev} : \mathcal{A}^H(z)]|$ for any classical event Ev over the view of $\mathcal{A}$. There may not exist a computationally efficient algorithm to check whether Ev has occurred. On the other hand, our O2H variant allows $|S|$ (the number of points on which G and H may differ) to be arbitrary, while in [5] it must contain a single point.

As an important application of our O2H lemma, we present the first security proof for the FO transform in the QROM which does not suffer from a 'square-root' advantage loss for non-deterministic schemes, i.e., it has the form $\mathsf{Adv}(\mathcal{A}_{\mathrm{CCA}}) \leq O(q^c \cdot \mathsf{Adv}(\mathcal{B}_{\mathrm{CPA}})^\delta)$, where $\delta = 1$ rather than $\delta = 1/2$ as in previous results (on the other hand, our proof currently gives a larger value of c compared to earlier works, see below). A comparison of our FO security proof bounds with earlier ones starting from IND-CPA non-deterministic weak schemes is provided in Table 2. The 'Security loss' column of that table shows the number of extra bits of security required for the 'weak scheme' in order to guarantee (via the security proof bound) a desired bit security of λ for the FO-transformed scheme. To obtain the 'security loss' L, we define the indistinguishability bit security of a scheme (against distinguishers that never output $\perp$, which is the class of attacks considered here) [17] as λ if the time to squared (conditional) advantage ratio T/ε^2 of any attack with time $T \leq 2^\lambda$ is $\geq 2^\lambda$.[3] We then choose the smallest bit security S_{weak} of the 'weak scheme' so that the CCA security bound for the CCA scheme implies a CCA bit security of the FO scheme to be $\geq \lambda$, and define the 'security loss' as $L := S_{weak} - \lambda$. We remark that our bit security loss estimates in Table 2 assume that the classical bit security definitions in [17] are appropriate in the quantum setting, as we are not aware of any research on bit security notions in the quantum setting. Note also that this latter assumption does not impact the security bounds we prove in this paper (which do not depend on this assumption); it only affects their interpretation in Table 2 in terms of bit security.

We make the following remarks about Table 2. Whereas all previous proofs for FO applied to non-deterministic IND-CPA weak schemes incurred at least a λ bit security loss (due to the square-root advantage loss in the CCA bound), our proof removes this λ bit overhead, and instead incurs a loss $4 \log d$ that depends only on the query depth d of the CCA distinguisher. In particular, this means that our security proof is nearly tight for low query depth attacks (i.e., when $\log d$ is much smaller than λ), its loss is less than λ bits for $\log d < \lambda/4$. The case of (relatively) low query depth attacks ruled out by our proof tends to be of high practical interest, since it corresponds, for instance, to massively parallelized attacks, which are the standard approach to deal with high computation costs in practical cryptanalyses. An additional requirement of our scheme is injectivity, but it turns out that it is commonly satisfied by many practical weak schemes, as argued in [5]. We leave a detailed investigation of injectivity of the second round PQC NIST KEM candidates [19] to future work (see [5, Appendix D] for a short discussion). We also remark that although our work and [5] need the extra injectiveness assumption, it gives a better bound than prior works for *modular* FO proofs (those that decompose into a composition of two proofs: one for the T transform and one for the U transform). The prior works in Table 2 can get the same bound overall for FO but only via a direct proof for whole FO transform (combining the T and U transforms). The reason we do not adapt prior FO proofs that do not rely on the injectiveness property is that those proofs also seem to require an O2H Lemma where the extractor works with single-sided oracles for either G *or* H, rather than the G *and* H requirement we (and [5]) have in our 'double-sided' O2H Lemma.

Techniques. To explain our MRM security proof technique, we consider the following example and explain the difficulty encountered by previous O2H proofs, and then our observations leading to our MRM technique for resolving this difficulty.

---

[3] We note that [17] calls ε the 'conditional advantage' while ε^2 is referred to as the 'advantage'; we always refer to 'conditional advantage' ε as 'advantage'.

Table 2. Comparison of security bounds for FO-type non-deterministic IND-CPA to IND-CCA transforms in the QROM. The 'CCA bound' column shows the dependence of the upper bound on CCA attacker advantage $\mathsf{Adv}(\mathcal{A})$ against the FO-transformed scheme in terms of the attacker advantage ε against the weak scheme transformed by FO, and $\mathcal{A}$'s oracle query depth $d \leq q$ (where q is the total number of random oracle queries). For simplicity, in this table, we only take into account the dependence in ε, and neglect other additive terms and (small) multiplicative constants. In all cases listed, the run-time of the weak scheme attacker is within a constant factor of the run-time of the CCA scheme. The required weak scheme security notion is shown in column 'Weak scheme'. The 'Security loss' column indicates the bit security loss of the CCA bound (see text). Note that all the weak schemes are not required to enjoy perfect correctness of decryption.

	|CCA bound|	|Security loss|	Weak scheme
[10]	$q^{3/2} \cdot \varepsilon^{1/4}$	$3\lambda + 9\log q$	IND-CPA
[11,13,15]	$d^{1/2} \cdot \varepsilon^{1/2}$	$\lambda + \log d$	IND-CPA
[5]	$d^{1/2} \cdot \varepsilon^{1/2}$	$\lambda + \log d$	IND-CPA injective
This work	$d^2 \cdot \varepsilon$	$4\log d$	IND-CPA injective

Consider the following O2H distinguisher $\mathcal{A}^O$ that makes 1 query (with depth 1) to its quantum oracle and makes a measurement on the resulting state to distinguish whether $O = H$ or $O = G$. The oracle input (first) and output (second) registers are denoted by in and out. Given $z = (\mathsf{enc}(x), H(x))$, the distinguisher $\mathcal{A}^O$ prepares in the input register in a superposition of the form $\sum_{x' \in X} \sqrt{p_{x'}} |x'\rangle$ and queries O to get the state

$$|\psi^O\rangle = \sum_{x' \in X} \sqrt{p_{x'}} |x', O(x')\rangle = \sqrt{p_x} |x, O(x)\rangle + \sum_{x' \neq x} \sqrt{p_{x'}} |x', O(x')\rangle,$$

where $\sum_{x' \in X} p_{x'} = 1$. Let $|\psi_{\neq x}\rangle := \sum_{x' \neq x} \sqrt{\frac{p_{x'}}{1 - p_x}} |x', H(x')\rangle$. Recalling that G and H differ only on x, we are in one of the following two cases:

$$|\psi^H\rangle = \sqrt{p_x} |\psi_x^H\rangle + \sqrt{1 - p_x} |\psi_{\neq x}\rangle \text{ and } |\psi^G\rangle = \sqrt{p_x} |\psi_x^G\rangle + \sqrt{1 - p_x} |\psi_{\neq x}\rangle,$$

with $|\psi_x^H\rangle := |x, H(x)\rangle$ and $|\psi_x^G\rangle := |x, G(x)\rangle$.

Since the amplitude of $in = |x\rangle$ in $|\psi^H\rangle$ is $\sqrt{p_x}$, measuring the input register in for $\mathcal{A}$'s query would give the secret x with probability $\mathsf{Adv}(\mathcal{B}) = \Pr[M_{in=|x\rangle}|\psi^O\rangle] = p_x$. This is in fact the strategy of the one-wayness adversary $\mathcal{B}$ constructed from $\mathcal{A}$ in prior O2H security proofs.

On the other hand, as observed in [14], the trace distance between $|\psi^G\rangle$ and $|\psi^H\rangle$ is $\sqrt{1 - (\langle\psi^G\rangle, |\psi^H\rangle)^2} = \sqrt{p_x}$ and therefore there exists a projective measurement $\mathbb{M}_V = (M_V, I - M_V)$ (where M_V is a projector on a subspace V of the state space)[4] that $\mathcal{A}$ can perform on $|\psi^O\rangle$ to distinguish the case $O = H$ from

---

[4] Here, we assume that $\mathcal{A}$ outputs 1 when the result of measurement space is a state in subspace V.

$O = G$ with distinguishing advantage $\mathsf{Adv}(\mathcal{A}) = \|M_V|\psi^H\rangle\|^2 - \|M_V|\psi^G\rangle\|^2 = \sqrt{p_x}$ (see [18, Chapter 9]). The existence of such a distinguisher with a square root advantage $\sqrt{p_x}$ led the authors of [5,14] to the suggestion that removing the square-root loss from the O2H security reduction may be impossible in the quantum setting.

Let us exhibit such the worst-case M_V that $\mathcal{A}$ could use. Consider $M_V = |v\rangle\langle v|$ that projects the state on a single unit vector $|v\rangle$, with $|v\rangle$ defined as lying on the plane spanned by $|\psi^G\rangle$ and $|\psi^H\rangle$, and at angle $\pi/4 + \theta/2$ from $|\psi^G\rangle$ if $|\psi^H\rangle$ is at angle θ from $|\psi^G\rangle$. Then $\mathsf{Adv}(\mathcal{A}) = \cos^2(\pi/4 + \theta/2) - \cos^2(\pi/4 - \theta/2) = \sin\theta = \sqrt{p_x}$.

Our MRM technique for resolving the above conundrum stems from the observation that to achieve its high $\sqrt{p_x}$ advantage, the above example distinguisher $\mathcal{A}$ uses a measurement M_V that itself *encodes the secret* x. Indeed, in the measurement vector $|v\rangle$ the state $in = |x\rangle$ has amplitude $\approx 1/\sqrt{2}$ when p_x is small. Hence, as $\mathcal{A}$ can measure along $|v\rangle$, it must somehow store it and we should be able to extract x from $\mathcal{A}$ with high probability by simply measuring in of $|v\rangle$ in the computational basis.

The above idea raises the question of how to set up the system state to be $|v\rangle$. The answer is simply to let $\mathcal{A}$ perform its distinguishing measurement M_V on $|\psi^H\rangle$.[5] If the measurement is M_V, the state collapses to the state $M_V|\psi^H\rangle/\|M_V|\psi^H\rangle\|$. In the above example, this is $|v\rangle$ with probability $\approx 1/2$ when p_x is small. In the standard quantum computational model, since $\mathcal{A}$'s measurement M_V is not performed with respect to the computational basis (note that $|v\rangle$ is a superposition of computational basis vectors), applying M_V to the oracle output state is implemented by $\mathcal{A}$ as a composition of a unitary U_V followed by a computational basis measurement M_β of a qubit register β corresponding to $\mathcal{A}$'s output bit (where U_V is designed so that it maps the state $|v\rangle$ to a state with $\beta = 1$). Then, setting up the system state to be $|v\rangle$ actually consists in running $\mathcal{A}$ with oracle H to obtain the state $|\psi^H\rangle$, applying U_V followed by $\mathcal{A}$'s output qubit measurement M_β, and if the result of the latter measurement is $\beta = 1$, then *rewinding* the collapsed output state of $\mathcal{A}$ to the step before the measurement by applying the inverse unitary U_V^{-1} (so that effectively the measurement projector $M_V = U_V^{-1}M_{\beta=|1\rangle}U_V$ is applied on the state $|\psi^H\rangle$).

Overall, we obtain an efficient MRM-based quantum algorithm $\mathcal{C}$ to extract x from $\mathcal{A}$ that works as follows for $q = d = 1$: run $\mathcal{A}^H$ and query the H oracle to set up the state $|\psi^H\rangle$, continue running $\mathcal{A}$ until it performs its measurement $M_\beta U_V$ and, if the result is $\beta = |1\rangle$, rewind $\mathcal{A}$ back to just after the query by running U_V^{-1} and apply measurement M_{in} on the in register to extract x, achieving overall success probability $\approx 1/4$ for the above example distinguisher $\mathcal{A}$ when p_x is small.

In our new O2H security proof, we show that (a slight variant of) the above MRM extraction technique works for $q = d = 1$ in the case where M_V is a general measurement. More precisely, we show that the advantage of any distinguisher $\mathcal{A}$

---

[5] Our actual general reduction applies it to a uniform superposition $\frac{1}{2}(|\psi^H\rangle + |\psi^G\rangle)$; see below.

cannot exceed $4 \cdot \max(\mathsf{Adv}(\mathcal{B}), \mathsf{Adv}(\mathcal{C}))$, where $\mathsf{Adv}(\mathcal{C})$ is the probability that our MRM-based extractor recovers x, and $\mathsf{Adv}(\mathcal{B}) = p_x$ is the probability that the direct query measurement algorithm $\mathcal{B}$ recovers x. Our actual extraction algorithm $\mathcal{D}$ therefore runs $\mathcal{A}$ *twice*: in the first run of $\mathcal{A}$, algorithm $\mathcal{D}$ runs the direct query measurement algorithm $\mathcal{B}$ to attempt to compute x, and in the second run of $\mathcal{A}$, algorithm $\mathcal{D}$ runs our MRM-based algorithm $\mathcal{C}$ to attempt to compute x. By the above bound, the advantage of $\mathcal{A}$ is at most 4 times the success probability of $\mathcal{D}$.

The proof of our new O2H bound is based on re-writing $\mathsf{Adv}(\mathcal{A}) := \left| \|M_V|\psi^G\rangle\|^2 - \|M_V|\psi^H\rangle\|^2 \right|$ as an inner product of the form

$$\mathsf{Adv}(\mathcal{A}) \leq \left| \left(|\psi^G\rangle - |\psi^H\rangle, M_V(|\psi^G\rangle + |\psi^H\rangle) \right) \right|.$$

At this point, we use the crucial fact that since G and H differ only on x, $|\psi^G\rangle - |\psi^H\rangle = |\psi_x^G\rangle + |\psi_x^H\rangle$ is a vector in the subspace $E_{|x\rangle}$ of vectors with $in = |x\rangle$, so it is unchanged by applying a projection $M_{in=|x\rangle}$ onto $E_{|x\rangle}$. Consequently, the inner-product above can be rewritten as

$$\mathsf{Adv}(\mathcal{A}) \leq \left| \left(M_{in=|x\rangle}(|\psi^G\rangle - |\psi^H\rangle), M_{in=|x\rangle}M_V(|\psi^G\rangle + |\psi^H\rangle) \right) \right|.$$

Now, we observe that the norm $\|M_{in=|x\rangle}(|\psi^G\rangle - |\psi^H\rangle)\|$ of the vector on the left of the inner-product is (up to a factor of 2) the square-root of the advantage p_x of the direct measurement extraction algorithm $\mathcal{B}$, whereas the norm

$$\|M_{in=|x\rangle}M_V(|\psi^G\rangle + |\psi^H\rangle)\| = \|M_{in=|x\rangle}U_V^{-1}M_{\beta=|1\rangle}U_V(|\psi^G\rangle + |\psi^H\rangle)\|$$

of the vector on the right of the inner-product is (up to a factor of 2) the square-root of the advantage of a variant of the MRM-based extraction algorithm $\mathcal{C}$. Applying the Cauchy-Schwarz inequality gives our bound

$$\mathsf{Adv}(\mathcal{A}) \leq 4 \cdot \sqrt{\mathsf{Adv}(\mathcal{B})} \cdot \sqrt{\mathsf{Adv}(\mathcal{C})} \leq 4 \cdot \max(\mathsf{Adv}(\mathcal{B}), \mathsf{Adv}(\mathcal{C})),$$

for $q = d = 1$. We extend our O2H security proof to the case of any depth $d \geq 1$ by applying a standard hybrid argument over d hybrid distributions in which the oracle O is used only to answer the i-th depth of $\mathcal{A}$, which leads to an additional loss of a factor d in our bound on $\mathsf{Adv}(\mathcal{A})$.

We apply the new O2H lemma to the FO transform, by showing that a slight variant of the proof of security for the $\mathsf{FO}^{\not\perp}$ ('implicit rejection') variant based on the 'double-sided' O2H lemma from [5] suffices for use with our new O2H lemma, without any significant reduction cost. The reason we cannot directly plug in our new 'double-sided' O2H lemma in the FO security proof of [5] is the limitation of our new O2H lemma to 'efficiently checkable' events for the definition of distinguisher $\mathcal{A}$. Our modified proof applies the lemma with the event '$\mathcal{A}$ outputs 1' instead. By the general tight equivalence results of [5, Theorem 5], we also obtain an improved security proof for other variants $\mathsf{FO}^\perp$ ('explicit rejection') and $\mathsf{FO}_m^{\not\perp}$ (key derived from message only).

Open problems. Our new O2H security proof for $q = d = 1$ oracle queries crucially makes use of the fact that $|\psi^G\rangle - |\psi^H\rangle$ is in the subspace of vectors with $in = |x\rangle$. This property may no longer be satisfied after $q > 1$ queries, and currently, we handle this difficulty via a hybrid argument that loses a factor q in the advantage (in the presentation of our reduction we actually only lose a factor $d \leq q$ that is the query depth, but in the worst-case we have $d = q$). The security proofs of [1,5] make use of semi-classical oracles or a variant of Zhandry's quantum query recording technique [27] to reduce (or even eliminate) the loss factor q in the advantage, but they do not seem to be easily compatible with our MRM technique. An interesting open problem is to find an even tighter security proof that combines our MRM technique with those techniques to give a fully tight reduction for O2H in the quantum setting. Relaxing the 'double-sided' aspect of our O2H Lemma to a 'single-sided' variant (like the original O2H Lemma [24]) is also left as an interesting question. Removing the injectivity assumption and finding other applications for our O2H Lemma and the underlying MRM technique are further questions left open by our work.

Additional related work. To the best of our knowledge, the use of quantum circuit rewinding is novel in the context of the O2H Lemma, but there is a body of work using different forms of quantum circuit rewinding in other applications, notably in the analysis of quantum security of zero-knowledge protocols. Watrous [25] presented a *quantum rewinding lemma*, which is a procedure involving multiple 'measure-rewind' iterations with interleaved unitary gates, in order to approximate a desired collapsed measured state with any desired fidelity. The procedure assumes a near independence of the measurement probabilities on the input state, which suffices to prove the zero-knowledge property of certain protocols. Our MRM technique does not make such near independence assumptions (indeed the measurement distribution of the distinguisher may strongly depend on the input state), but only applies one 'measure-rewind-measure' iteration. Unruh [23] presented a form of rewinding extraction technique for proving soundness of zero-knowledge proof of knowledge protocols against quantum attacks. However, the purpose of rewinding there is to approximate the previous state of the attacker while minimising the disturbance of the measurement, whereas in our MRM technique, we actually *want* the measurement to disturb the state in order to extract knowledge from the measurement vector. Later work by Ambianis et al. [2] showed the necessity of restrictions of Unruh's rewinding in the context of quantum-secure proofs of knowledge.

2 Preliminaries

For a finite set $\mathcal{H}$, we denote by $H \xleftarrow{\$} \mathcal{H}$ the sampling of a uniformly random element H from $\mathcal{H}$. If $\mathcal{A}$ is an algorithm, we denote by $b \leftarrow \mathcal{A}(z)$ the assignment to b of the output of $\mathcal{A}$ run on input z.

Let $\mathbb{C}$ denote the set of complex numbers. For $z \in \mathbb{C}$, we denote the absolute value of z by $|z|$ and the complex conjugate of z by $\bar{z}$. The (complex) inner product between two vectors $|u\rangle = (u_0, \ldots, u_{n-1})$ and $|v\rangle = (v_0, \ldots, v_{n-1})$ in $\mathbb{C}^n$ is denoted by $(|u\rangle, |v\rangle) := \sum_i \bar{u}_i \cdot v_i$. Let $|v\rangle \in \mathbb{C}^n$, then $\||v\rangle\| = \sqrt{(|v\rangle, |v\rangle)}$ denotes its Euclidean norm. For a linear transformation M, the Hermitian (adjoint) operation on M is denoted by $M^\dagger$.

2.1 Quantum Computations

A qubit is a quantum system defined over $\{0, 1\}$. Given two orthonormal vectors $|0\rangle, |1\rangle$, let $\mathbb{S}$ be the state space of a single qubit, namely

$$\mathbb{S} = \left\{ \alpha_0|0\rangle + \alpha_1|1\rangle : |\alpha_0|^2 + |\alpha_1|^2 = 1, \ \alpha_0, \alpha_1 \in \mathbb{C} \right\}.$$

For an integer $N \geq 1$, the state space of a quantum system (register) of N qubits is the N-fold tensor product of $\mathbb{S}$ and is denoted by

$$\mathbb{S}^{\otimes N} = \left\{ \sum_{\mathbf{in} \in \{0,1\}^N} \alpha_{\mathbf{in}}|in_1\rangle \cdots |in_N\rangle : \sum_{\mathbf{in} \in \{0,1\}^N} |\alpha_{\mathbf{in}}|^2 = 1, \ \alpha_{\mathbf{in}} \in \mathbb{C} \right\}.$$

For $\mathbf{x} = (x_1, \ldots, x_N) \in \{0,1\}^N$, the associated *computational basis vector* of $\mathbb{S}^{\otimes N}$ is $\mathbf{x} = |x_1\rangle|x_2\rangle \cdots |x_N\rangle$, and is denoted by $|\mathbf{x}\rangle$. The set of all 2^N computational basis states $\{|\mathbf{x}\rangle\}$ forms an orthonormal basis for $\mathbb{S}^{\otimes N}$. A linear combination $|\phi\rangle = \sum_{\mathbf{x} \in \{0,1\}^N} \alpha_{\mathbf{x}}|\mathbf{x}\rangle$ of computational basis states $|\mathbf{x}\rangle$ is referred to as a *superposition* of computational basis states. We refer to the weight $\alpha_{\mathbf{x}}$ as the *amplitude* of $|\mathbf{x}\rangle$ in state $|\phi\rangle$.

Given the state $|\phi_{in}\rangle \in \mathbb{S}^{\otimes N}$ of an N-qubit register in and a value $y \in \{0,1\}^N$, we denote by $M_{in=|y\rangle} : \mathbb{S}^{\otimes N} \to \mathbb{S}^{\otimes N}$ the operator that applies the projection $|y\rangle\langle y|$ map to the state $|\phi_{in}\rangle$ of register in to get the new state $|y\rangle\langle y||\phi_{in}\rangle$. This projector can be generalized to a projector M_{E_V} onto a subspace $E_V = \{\sum_{in \in V} \alpha_{in}|in\rangle : \alpha_{in} \in \mathbb{C}\}$ defined by a subset $V \subseteq \{0,1\}^N$, which applies the projection map $\sum_{y \in V} |y\rangle\langle y|$ to a state $|\phi_{in}\rangle \in \mathbb{S}^{\otimes N}$. For example, for a subset $S \subseteq \{0,1\}^N$, we define $S^{\oplus n} := \{\mathbf{in} \in (\{0,1\}^N)^n : \exists\, i \text{ with } in_i \in S\}$, and then $M_{E_{S^{\oplus n}}}$ is the projector onto subspace $E_{S^{\oplus n}} := \{\sum_{\mathbf{in} \in S^{\oplus n}} \alpha_{\mathbf{in}}|\mathbf{in}\rangle : \alpha_{\mathbf{in}} \in \mathbb{C}\}$. We use the same notation for operators and projectors even if they are applied to non-normalized vectors in $\mathbb{C}^N$. It can be checked that any projector operator M_{E_V} is Hermitian (i.e., we have $M^\dagger = M$) and idempotent (i.e., we have $M^2 = M$).

A *measurement* in the computational basis on a register in that is in state $|\phi_{in}\rangle \in \mathbb{S}^{\otimes N}$ returns the measurement result $y \in \{0,1\}^N$ with probability $P = \|M_{in=|y\rangle}|\phi_{in}\rangle\|^2$ and changes ('collapses') the state of in to $|\phi'_{in}\rangle = \frac{M_{in=|y\rangle}|\phi_{in}\rangle}{\|M_{in=|y\rangle}|\phi_{in}\rangle\|}$. Such a measurement of register in is denoted by $\mathbb{M}_{in}$. A general projective measurement is defined by a set of projection operators $\{M_1, \ldots, M_n\}$ where M_i's project onto subspaces V_i that are mutually orthogonal and whose sum is the whole state space. For example, for any subspace V of $\mathbb{S}^{\otimes N}$, we can define the projective measurement $\mathbb{M}_V = (M_V, I - M_V)$ where M_V is the projector onto V and $I - M_V$ is the projector onto the orthogonal complement of V. Any general projective measurement can be implemented by composing a unitary operation followed by a measurement in computational basis. Each measurement costs one time unit.

A quantum algorithm executes a sequence of unitary gate operations for a fixed set F containing Hadamard, phase, CNOT and $\pi/8$ gates. Each gate is also counted as one unit of time. The overall time taken to perform a quantum algorithm $\mathcal{A}$ is denoted by $\mathcal{T}_{\mathcal{A}}$. An efficient quantum algorithm runs a polynomial-time (in N) sequence of gate operations or measurements.

Given a function $H : X \to Y = \{0,1\}^N$, a quantum-accessible oracle O of H is modeled by a unitary transformation U_H operating on two registers *in*, *out* with state spaces $\mathbb{S}^{\otimes N}$, in which $|x, y\rangle$ is mapped to $|x, y \oplus H(x)\rangle$, where $\oplus$ denotes XOR group operation on Y. A quantum algorithm with quantum random oracle O performs a mix of classical and quantum unitary algorithms. This can be efficiently converted, up to a constant factor overhead and same number of oracle queries [18], to a purely unitary algorithm that applies a unitary followed by a final set of measurements. A purely unitary algorithm making q oracle queries to O is denoted by $(OU_i)_{i=1}^q$, where U_i is a unitary operation applied before the i-th call to oracle O. Following [5], we model a quantum algorithm $\mathcal{A}$ making parallel queries to a quantum oracle O as a quantum algorithm making $d \leq q$ queries to an oracle $O^{\otimes n}$ consisting of $n = q/d$ parallel copies of oracle O. Given an input state of n pairs of *in/out* registers $|x_1\rangle|y_1\rangle \cdots |x_n\rangle|y_n\rangle$, the oracle of $O^{\otimes n}$ maps it to the state $|x_1\rangle|y_1 \oplus O(x_1)\rangle \cdots |x_n\rangle|y_n \oplus O(x_n)\rangle$. We call d the algorithm's *query depth*, n the parallelization factor, and $q = n \cdot d$ the total number of oracle queries.

2.2   Original One-Way to Hiding (O2H) Lemma

We now recall the One-Way to Hiding (O2H) Lemma, as stated in [1] (this formulation generalizes Unruh's original O2H Lemma [24]).

Lemma 2.1. ([1, **Theorem 3**]). *Let $G, H \colon X \to Y$ be random functions, z be a random value, and $S \subseteq X$ be a random set such that $G(x) = H(x)$ for every $x \notin S$. The tuple (G, H, S, z) may have an arbitrary joint distribution. Furthermore, let $\mathcal{A}^H$ be a quantum oracle algorithm which queries H with depth at most d. Let* Event *be an arbitrary classical event. Define the oracle algorithm $\mathcal{B}^H(z)$ as follows: sample $i \xleftarrow{\$} \{0, \ldots, d-1\}$; run $\mathcal{A}^H(z)$ until just before its i-th round of queries to H; measure all query input registers in the computational basis, and output the set T of measurement outcomes. Then*

$$\mathsf{Adv}(\mathcal{A}) \leq 2d\sqrt{\mathsf{Adv}(\mathcal{B})} \quad and \quad |\sqrt{P_{\text{left}}} - \sqrt{P_{\text{right}}}| \leq 2d\sqrt{\mathsf{Adv}(\mathcal{B})},$$

where $\mathsf{Adv}(\mathcal{A}) := |P_{\text{left}} - P_{\text{right}}|$ *with*

$$P_{\text{left}} := \Pr[\text{Event} : \mathcal{A}^H(z)], \quad P_{\text{right}} := \Pr[\text{Event} : \mathcal{A}^G(z)],$$

and

$$\mathsf{Adv}(\mathcal{B}) := \Pr[S \cap T \neq \emptyset : T \leftarrow \mathcal{B}^H(z)].$$

3   Main Results

The following result will prove useful later on in the proof of Lemma 3.2.

Lemma 3.1. *For any vectors $|\phi_1\rangle$ and $|\phi_2\rangle$, we have*

$$\left| \|\,|\phi_1\rangle\|^2 - \|\,|\phi_2\rangle\|^2 \right| \leq |(|\phi_1\rangle - |\phi_2\rangle, |\phi_1\rangle + |\phi_2\rangle)|.$$

Proof. Let $x_1 = |\phi_1\rangle - |\phi_2\rangle$ and $x_2 = |\phi_1\rangle + |\phi_2\rangle$. Then, we have:

$$\left| \frac{\|x_1 + x_2\|^2}{4} - \frac{\|x_1 - x_2\|^2}{4} \right| = \frac{|(x_1 + x_2, x_1 + x_2) - (x_1 - x_2, x_1 - x_2)|}{4}$$

$$= |\mathsf{Real}((x_1, x_2))| \leq |(x_1, x_2)|,$$

where $\mathsf{Real}(z)$ denotes the real part of a complex number z. $\qquad\square$

3.1   O2H with Measure-Rewind-Measure (MRM)

We first describe the fixed input version of our result, where G, H, S, z are all fixed, and then we extend it to case of random G, H, S, z. Note that below, the value z can depend on G, H, S, so can serve to provide the adversary with a 'hint' about G, H, S (for instance, in our application later on, the value z contains an encryption of S).

Lemma 3.2 (Fixed O2H with MRM). *Let $G, H: X \to Y$ be fixed functions, z be a fixed value, and $S \subseteq X$ be a fixed set such that $G(x) = H(x)$ for every $x \notin S$. Furthermore, let $\mathcal{A}^O$ be a quantum oracle algorithm which queries an oracle O with depth d. Then we can construct unitary algorithms $\{\mathcal{A}_i^O(z)\}_{0 \leq i < d}$, $\{\mathcal{B}_i^{G,H}(z)\}_{0 \leq i < d}$, and $\{\mathcal{C}_i^{G,H}(z)\}_{0 \leq i < d}$ with $T_{\mathcal{A}_i^O} \approx T_{\mathcal{A}^O}$, $T_{\mathcal{B}_i^{G,H}} \lesssim T_{\mathcal{A}_i^O}$ and $T_{\mathcal{C}_i^{G,H}} \approx 2 \cdot T_{\mathcal{A}_i^O}$ (for all i) and such that*

$$\mathsf{Adv}(\mathcal{A}^O) \leq \sum_{i=0}^{d-1} \mathsf{Adv}(\mathcal{A}_i^O), \tag{1}$$

and (for all i):

$$\mathsf{Adv}(\mathcal{A}_i^O) \leq 4\sqrt{\mathsf{Adv}(\mathcal{B}_i^{G,H}) \cdot \mathsf{Adv}(\mathcal{C}_i^{G,H})}$$

$$\leq 4 \max\{\mathsf{Adv}(\mathcal{B}_i^{G,H}), \mathsf{Adv}(\mathcal{C}_i^{G,H})\}. \tag{2}$$

Here $\mathsf{Adv}(\mathcal{A}^O) := |P_{\mathsf{left}} - P_{\mathsf{right}}|$ with

$$P_{\mathsf{left}} := \Pr[1 \leftarrow \mathcal{A}^H(z)], \; P_{\mathsf{right}} := \Pr[1 \leftarrow \mathcal{A}^G(z)],$$
$$\mathsf{Adv}(\mathcal{A}_i^O) := |\Pr[1 \leftarrow \mathcal{A}_i^H(z)] - \Pr[1 \leftarrow \mathcal{A}_i^G(z)]|,$$
$$\mathsf{Adv}(\mathcal{B}_i^{G,H}) := \Pr[S \cap T_{\mathcal{B}_i} \neq \emptyset : T_{\mathcal{B}_i} \leftarrow \mathcal{B}_i^{G,H}(z)],$$

and

$$\mathsf{Adv}(\mathcal{C}_i^{G,H}) := \Pr[S \cap T_{\mathcal{C}_i} \neq \emptyset : T_{\mathcal{C}_i} \leftarrow \mathcal{C}_i^{G,H}(z)].$$

Proof. Let $O_G^{\otimes n}$ and $O_H^{\otimes n}$ be the n-wise parallel quantum oracles for G and H, respectively. As in [5, Lemma 5], we define another quantum oracle $O_{G,H}^{\otimes n}$, which is used to put the sum and difference of $O_G^{\otimes n}$ and $O_H^{\otimes n}$ in superposition, entangled with another bit b. This can be configured so that the additional bit register b decides which oracle is in use. Concretely, we define

$$O_{G,H}^{\otimes n} := (O_H^{\otimes n} \otimes |+\rangle\langle+|) + (O_G^{\otimes n} \otimes |-\rangle\langle-|),$$

where $|+\rangle = \frac{|0\rangle + |1\rangle}{\sqrt{2}}$ and $|-\rangle = \frac{|0\rangle - |1\rangle}{\sqrt{2}}$. Therefore, the oracle $O_{G,H}^{\otimes n}$ maps the state $|\psi\rangle|+\rangle$ to the state $O_H^{\otimes n}(|\psi\rangle)|+\rangle$ and the state $|\psi\rangle|-\rangle$ to the state $O_G^{\otimes n}(|\psi\rangle)|-\rangle$. As observed in [5], it can be efficiently implemented by applying a Hadamard gate before and after a conditional evaluation map that applies O_H if $b = 0$ and O_G if $b = 1$. By setting the b bit register to start in the superposition state $\frac{|+\rangle + |-\rangle}{\sqrt{2}} = |0\rangle$, and applying $O_{G,H}^{\otimes n}$ we get a state with the sum and differences of the oracle output states entangled with the bit b:

$$
\begin{aligned}
O_{G,H}^{\otimes n}(|\psi\rangle|0\rangle) &= \frac{1}{\sqrt{2}} \cdot \left(O_H^{\otimes n}(|\psi\rangle)|+\rangle + O_G^{\otimes n}(|\psi\rangle)|-\rangle\right) \\
&= \frac{1}{2} \cdot \left(O_H^{\otimes n}|\psi\rangle + O_G^{\otimes n}|\psi\rangle\right) \otimes |0\rangle \\
&\quad + \frac{1}{2} \cdot \left(O_H^{\otimes n}|\psi\rangle - O_G^{\otimes n}|\psi\rangle\right) \otimes |1\rangle.
\end{aligned}
\tag{3}
$$

Looking ahead, we will use the above bit b in algorithms $\mathcal{B}_i$ and $\mathcal{C}_i$ and aim to measure $b = 1$ in the former and $b = 0$ in the latter, so that we get the difference and sum states, respectively, in the remaining registers.

We now present our hybrid algorithms for $i \in \{0, \ldots, d-1\}$. The i-th hybrid pair of algorithms for $\mathcal{A}$ corresponds to running $\mathcal{A}$ with its first i oracle calls answered with $O_H^{\otimes n}$, $\mathcal{A}$'s $(i+1)$-th call answered by $O_O^{\otimes n}$ where $O \in \{G, H\}$ is $\mathcal{A}$'s oracle, and $\mathcal{A}$'s final $d - (i+1)$ calls answered using $O_G^{\otimes n}$. The extraction algorithms $\mathcal{B}_i$ and $\mathcal{C}_i$ detailed below will run $\mathcal{A}$ similarly except with the $(i+1)$-th query answered with the superposition oracle $O_{G,H}^{\otimes n}$. We define the four hybrid algorithms below. Recall that the total number of quantum oracle queries of $\mathcal{A}$ equals $q = n \cdot d$, where n is the parallelization factor, and that $\mathcal{A}$ applies a unitary U_j in between its $(j-1)$-th and j-th oracle call.

- Algorithm $\mathcal{A}_i^O$ for $O \in \{O_H^{\otimes n}, O_G^{\otimes n}\}$. This algorithm starts with 0's in registers $|aux\rangle \bigotimes_{i=1}^{n}(|in_i\rangle|out_i\rangle)|\beta\rangle$, where aux is $\mathcal{A}$'s auxiliary working register, and $\beta \in \{0,1\}$ is $\mathcal{A}$'s output bit. Algorithm $\mathcal{A}_i^O$ first runs $(O_H^{\otimes n}U_j)_{j=1}^i$ to get to state $|st_{2i,i}\rangle$, then runs OU_{i+1} to get to state $|st_{2i+2,i}\rangle$, and finally performs $(O_G^{\otimes n}U_j)_{j=i+2}^d$, which takes us to state $|st_{2d,i}\rangle$. This is finalized by a unitary operation U_{d+1}, which gives state $|st_{2d+1,i}\rangle$, to which the output bit measurement $\mathbb{M}_\beta$ is applied. The algorithm outputs the measurement result bit β.
- Algorithm $\mathcal{B}_i^{G,H}$. This algorithm starts with one extra bit register as input compared to previous algorithm. The first $2n + 2$ registers are exactly the

same as those in $\mathcal{A}_i^O$ and the last register is devoted to bit b to implement $O_{G,H}^{\otimes n}$. All registers are initialized to 0. Then, this algorithm runs $(O_H^{\otimes n} U_j)_{j=1}^i$ (giving a state $|st'_{2i,i}\rangle$), then applies $O_{G,H}^{\otimes n} U_{i+1}$ (giving a state $|st'_{2i+2,i}\rangle$), and then performs a measurement $\mathbb{M}_b$ of the b register (i.e., just after the $(i+1)$-th oracle call). If the result of this measurement is 1, then a measurement $\mathbb{M}_{\mathbf{in}}$ of the oracle's input register $\mathbf{in} = (in_1, \ldots, in_n)$ is conducted. This can also be seen as n parallel measurements $\mathbb{M}_{in_1} \ldots \mathbb{M}_{in_n}$. The algorithm terminates by outputting the results of the measurements.

- Algorithm $\mathcal{C}_i^{G,H}$. This algorithm has the same registers as the previous one. All registers are initialized to 0. This algorithm applies $(O_H^{\otimes n} U_j)_{j=1}^i$, $O_{G,H}^{\otimes n} U_{i+1}$, $(O_G^{\otimes n} U_j)_{j=i+2}^d$ and U_{d+1}. The states after applying those operations are called $|st''_{2i,i}\rangle$, $|st''_{2i+2,i}\rangle$, $|st''_{2d,i}\rangle$ and $|st''_{2d+1,i}\rangle$, respectively. Then the measurements $\mathbb{M}_b$, and $\mathbb{M}_\beta$ are applied. If the result of $\mathbb{M}_b$ equals 0 and the result of $\mathbb{M}_\beta$ equals 1, then the following (rewinding) transformations are applied back to the point just after the $(i+1)$-th oracle call: $U_{d+1}^\dagger$, $((O_G^{\otimes n} U_j)^\dagger)_{j=i+2}^d$, resulting in states called $|st'''_{2d,i}\rangle$, and $|st'''_{2i+2,i}\rangle$, respectively. Finally, a measurement with respect to $\mathbf{in}$ is performed, and the algorithm outputs the result of the measurement.

One can check that $\mathcal{T}_{\mathcal{A}_i^O} \approx \mathcal{T}_{\mathcal{A}^O}$, $\mathcal{T}_{\mathcal{B}_i^{G,H}} \lesssim \mathcal{T}_{\mathcal{A}_i^O}$ and that $\mathcal{T}_{\mathcal{C}_i^{G,H}} \approx \mathcal{T}_{\mathcal{B}_i^{G,H}} + 2(\mathcal{T}_{\mathcal{A}_i^O} - \mathcal{T}_{\mathcal{B}_i^{G,H}}) \leq 2 \cdot \mathcal{T}_{\mathcal{A}_i^O}$.

We have $\mathcal{A}_0^{O=G} = \mathcal{A}^G$, $\mathcal{A}_{d-1}^{O=H} = \mathcal{A}^H$ and $\mathcal{A}_i^{O=H} = \mathcal{A}_{i+1}^{O=G}$ for $0 \leq i \leq d-2$ (here and in the following, we use the shorthand $O = G$ and $O = H$ for $O = O_G^{\otimes n}$ and $O = O_H^{\otimes n}$ respectively). This implies that:

$$
\begin{aligned}
\mathsf{Adv}(\mathcal{A}) &= |\Pr[1 \leftarrow \mathcal{A}^G] - \Pr[1 \leftarrow \mathcal{A}^H]| \\
&= |\Pr[1 \leftarrow \mathcal{A}_0^{O=G}] - \Pr[1 \leftarrow \mathcal{A}_{d-1}^{O=H}]| \\
&= \left| \sum_{i=0}^{d-1} \left(\Pr[1 \leftarrow \mathcal{A}_i^{O=G}] - \Pr[1 \leftarrow \mathcal{A}_i^{O=H}] \right) \right| \\
&\leq \sum_{i=0}^{d-1} |\Pr[1 \leftarrow \mathcal{A}_i^{O=G}] - \Pr[1 \leftarrow \mathcal{A}_i^{O=H}]| \\
&= \sum_{i=0}^{d-1} \mathsf{Adv}(\mathcal{A}_i^O),
\end{aligned}
$$

where the first and the last equalities are obtained based on the definitions, the second equality is the result of a simple telescopic argument, and the only inequality follows from the triangle inequality. This proves (1).

We now proceed to prove (2). Fix $0 \leq i \leq d-1$. Let

$$
\begin{aligned}
W_i &:= U_{d+1}(O_G^{\otimes n} U_j)_{j=i+2}^d, \\
|\psi_{i,F}\rangle &:= |st_{2i+2,i}^{O=H}\rangle - |st_{2i+2,i}^{O=G}\rangle, \\
|\psi_{i,B}\rangle &:= W_i^\dagger M_{\beta=|1\rangle} W_i(|st_{2i+2,i}^{O=H}\rangle + |st_{2i+2,i}^{O=G}\rangle).
\end{aligned}
$$

We first study $\mathsf{Adv}(\mathcal{A}_i^O)$. We have:

$$|\Pr[1 \leftarrow \mathcal{A}_i^{O=H}] - \Pr[1 \leftarrow \mathcal{A}_i^{O=G}]|$$

$$= \left| \|M_{\beta=|1\rangle}|st_{2d+1,i}^{O=H}\rangle\|^2 - \|M_{\beta=|1\rangle}|st_{2d+1,i}^{O=G}\rangle\|^2 \right|$$

$$\leq \left| (M_{\beta=|1\rangle}(|st_{2d+1,i}^{O=H}\rangle - |st_{2d+1,i}^{O=G}\rangle), M_{\beta=|1\rangle}(|st_{2d+1,i}^{O=H}\rangle + |st_{2d+1,i}^{O=G}\rangle)) \right| \quad (4)$$

$$= \left| (M_{\beta=|1\rangle}W_i|\psi_{i,F}\rangle, M_{\beta=|1\rangle}W_i(|st_{2i+2,i}^{O=H}\rangle + |st_{2i+2,i}^{O=G}\rangle)) \right| \quad (5)$$

$$= \left| \left(|\psi_{i,F}\rangle, W_i^\dagger M_{\beta=|1\rangle}^\dagger M_{\beta=|1\rangle}W_i(|st_{2i+2,i}^{O=H}\rangle + |st_{2i+2,i}^{O=G}\rangle) \right) \right|$$

$$= |(|\psi_{i,F}\rangle, |\psi_{i,B}\rangle)| \quad (6)$$

$$= |(M_{\mathbf{in}\in S^{\oplus n}}|\psi_{i,F}\rangle, |\psi_{i,B}\rangle)| \quad (7)$$

$$= \left| \left(M_{\mathbf{in}\in S^{\oplus n}}|\psi_{i,F}\rangle, M_{\mathbf{in}\in S^{\oplus n}}^\dagger|\psi_{i,B}\rangle \right) \right| \quad (8)$$

$$\leq \|M_{\mathbf{in}\in S^{\oplus n}}|\psi_{i,F}\rangle\| \cdot \|M_{\mathbf{in}\in S^{\oplus n}}^\dagger|\psi_{i,B}\rangle\|, \quad (9)$$

where (4) follows from Lemma 3.1, (5) is obtained based on the definitions of $\mathcal{A}_i^O$ and $|\psi_{i,F}\rangle$, (6) employs the fact that $M_{\beta=|1\rangle}$ is a Hermitian and idempotent transformation and the definition of $|\psi_{i,B}\rangle$, (8) uses the fact that $M_{\mathbf{in}\in S^{\oplus n}}$ is idempotent, and (9) follows from the Cauchy-Schwarz inequality. Finally, the equality in (7) exploits the fact that $|\psi_{i,F}\rangle$ may have non-zero amplitudes only for computational basis vectors $\mathbf{in} \in S^{\oplus n}$ (we recall that $S^{\oplus n}$ is the set of n-dimensional vectors $\mathbf{in}$ having at least one component in the set S on which H and G differ). To see the latter fact, one can write

$$|st_{2i+2,i}^O\rangle = \sum_{\mathbf{in}\in S^{\oplus n},\mathbf{out}} \alpha_{\mathbf{in},\mathbf{out}}|in_1\rangle|out_1 \oplus O(in_1)\rangle \cdots |in_n\rangle|out_n \oplus O(in_n)\rangle$$

$$+ \sum_{\mathbf{in}\in \overline{S^{\oplus n}},\mathbf{out}} \alpha_{\mathbf{in},\mathbf{out}}|in_1\rangle|out_1 \oplus O(in_1)\rangle \cdots |in_n\rangle|out_n \oplus O(in_n)\rangle,$$

with $\overline{S^{\oplus n}} = \{0,1\}^{N\cdot n} \setminus S^{\oplus n}$. From this, we deduce that difference vector $|\psi_{i,F}\rangle$ only has a component along $S^{\oplus n}$, as the sum over $\overline{S^{\oplus n}}$ (and $\mathbf{out}$) is identical for both $|st_{2i+2,i}^G\rangle$ and $|st_{2i+2,i}^H\rangle$.

Based on the definitions of $O_{G,H}^{\otimes n}$, $\mathcal{B}_i^{G,H}$ and $\mathcal{C}_i^{G,H}$, and the superposition property (3), the following holds:

$$|st'_{2i+2,i}\rangle = |st''_{2i+2,i}\rangle = \frac{1}{2}\left(|\psi_{i,F}\rangle|1\rangle + (|st_{2i+2,i}^{O=H}\rangle + |st_{2i+2,i}^{O=G}\rangle)|0\rangle\right). \quad (10)$$

On the one hand, we have

$$\mathsf{Adv}(\mathcal{B}_i^{G,H}) = \Pr[S \cap T_{\mathcal{B}_i} \neq \emptyset, \ T_{\mathcal{B}_i} \leftarrow \mathcal{B}_i^{G,H}(z)]$$

$$= \left\| M_{\mathbf{in}\in S^{\oplus n}} \frac{M_{b=|1\rangle}|st'_{2i+2,i}\rangle}{\|M_{b=|1\rangle}|st'_{2i+2,i}\rangle\|} \right\|^2 \cdot \|M_{b=|1\rangle}|st'_{2i+2,i}\rangle\|^2$$

$$= \left\| M_{\mathbf{in}\in S^{\oplus n}} \frac{|\psi_{i,F}\rangle|1\rangle}{\||\psi_{i,F}\rangle|1\rangle\|} \right\|^2 \cdot \left\| \frac{1}{2}|\psi_{i,F}\rangle|1\rangle \right\|^2 \quad (11)$$

$$= \frac{1}{4}\|M_{\mathbf{in}\in S^{\oplus n}}|\psi_{i,F}\rangle\|^2, \quad (12)$$

where (11) follows from (10). On the other hand, by definition of $\mathcal{C}_i^{G,H}$, we have that:

$$|st_{2i+2,i}'''\rangle = \frac{W_i^\dagger M_{\beta=|1\rangle} M_{b=|0\rangle} W_i |st_{2i+2,i}''\rangle}{\|M_{\beta=|1\rangle} M_{b=|0\rangle} W_i |st_{2i+2,i}''\rangle\|}$$

$$= \frac{W_i^\dagger M_{\beta=|1\rangle} W_i M_{b=|0\rangle} |st_{2i+2,i}''\rangle}{\|M_{\beta=|1\rangle} W_i M_{b=|0\rangle} |st_{2i+2,i}''\rangle\|}, \tag{13}$$

$$= \frac{|\psi_{i,B}\rangle |0\rangle}{\||\psi_{i,B}\rangle |0\rangle\|}, \tag{14}$$

where (13) holds since $M_{b=|0\rangle}$ does not have any effect on U_{d+1} nor on $(U_j O_G^{\otimes n})_{j=i+2}^d$ and hence it commutes with W_i, and (14) is obtained using (10) and the definition of $|\psi_{i,R}\rangle$. Finally, one can write:

$$\begin{aligned}
\mathsf{Adv}(\mathcal{C}_i^{G,H}) &= \Pr[S \cap T_{\mathcal{C}_i} \neq \emptyset, \; T_{\mathcal{C}_i} \leftarrow \mathcal{C}_i^{G,H}(z)] \\
&= \|M_{\mathbf{in} \in S \oplus n}^\dagger |st_{2i+2,i}'''\rangle\|^2 \cdot \|M_{\beta=|1\rangle} M_{b=|0\rangle} W_i |st_{2i+2,i}''\rangle\|^2 \\
&= \|M_{\mathbf{in} \in S \oplus n}^\dagger |st_{2i+2,i}'''\rangle\|^2 \cdot \|W_i^\dagger M_{\beta=|1\rangle} W_i M_{b=|0\rangle} |st_{2i+2,i}''\rangle\|^2 \tag{15} \\
&= \left\| M_{\mathbf{in} \in S \oplus n}^\dagger \frac{|\psi_{i,B}\rangle |0\rangle}{\||\psi_{i,B}\rangle |0\rangle\|} \right\|^2 \cdot \left\| \frac{1}{2} |\psi_{i,B}\rangle |0\rangle \right\|^2 \tag{16} \\
&= \frac{1}{4} \|M_{\mathbf{in} \in S \oplus n}^\dagger |\psi_{i,B}\rangle\|^2, \tag{17}
\end{aligned}$$

where (15) holds true as $W_i^\dagger$ is a unitary operation and $M_{b=|0\rangle}$ commutes with W_i, and (16) follows from (14). Substituting (12) and (17) into (9) proves (2). $\qquad\square$

We now extend our O2H Lemma to the random case.

Lemma 3.3 (Random O2H with MRM). *Let $G, H: X \to Y$ be random functions, z be a random value, and $S \subseteq X$ be a random set such that $G(x) = H(x)$ for every $x \notin S$. The tuple (G, H, S, z) may have arbitrary joint distribution. Furthermore, let $\mathcal{A}^O$ be a quantum oracle algorithm which queries oracle O with query depth d. Then we can construct an algorithm $\mathcal{D}^{G,H}(z)$ such that $T_{\mathcal{D}^{G,H}} \lesssim 3 \cdot T_{\mathcal{A}^O}$ and*

$$\mathsf{Adv}(\mathcal{A}^O) \leq 4d \cdot \mathsf{Adv}(\mathcal{D}^{G,H}).$$

Here $\mathsf{Adv}(\mathcal{A}^O) := |P_{\mathsf{left}} - P_{\mathsf{right}}|$ with

$$P_{\mathsf{left}} := \Pr_{H,z}[1 \leftarrow \mathcal{A}^H(z)], \quad P_{\mathsf{right}} := \Pr_{G,z}[1 \leftarrow \mathcal{A}^G(z)],$$

and

$$\mathsf{Adv}(\mathcal{D}^{G,H}) := \Pr_{G,H,S,z}[T \cap S \neq \emptyset : T \leftarrow \mathcal{D}^{G,H}(z)].$$

Proof. We first construct $\mathcal{D}^{G,H}$ on input z as follows:

- Sample $i \overset{\$}{\leftarrow} \{0, \ldots, d-1\}$,
- Run $\mathcal{B}_i^{G,H}(z)$ and $\mathcal{C}_i^{G,H}(z)$ to obtain $T_{\mathcal{B}_i}$ and $T_{\mathcal{C}_i}$, respectively, and
- Return $T := T_{\mathcal{B}_i} \cup T_{\mathcal{C}_i}$.

The run-time bound follows from Lemma 3.2, which states that $T_{\mathcal{B}_i^{G,H}} \lesssim T_{\mathcal{A}^O}$ and $T_{\mathcal{C}^{G,H}} \approx 2 \cdot T_{\mathcal{A}^O}$. In the following, when we do not explicitly state the subscripts of probabilities or expectations, it means that they are over the internal randomness of the quantum algorithms only. Now, for fixed G, H, S, z, let

$$P_i^{\mathcal{B}_i \vee \mathcal{C}_i}(G, H, S, z) := \Pr[(T_{\mathcal{B}_i} \cap S \neq \emptyset) \vee (T_{\mathcal{C}_i} \cap S \neq \emptyset) :$$
$$T_{\mathcal{B}_i} \leftarrow \mathcal{B}_i^{G,H}(z), T_{\mathcal{C}_i} \leftarrow \mathcal{C}_i^{G,H}(z)].$$

With the above definition, we can write:

$$\underset{G,H,S,z}{\mathbb{E}}\left[P_i^{\mathcal{B}_i \vee \mathcal{C}_i}(G, H, S, z) \right] \geq \underset{G,H,S,z}{\mathbb{E}}\left[\max\left\{ \mathsf{Adv}(\mathcal{B}_i^{G,H}), \mathsf{Adv}(\mathcal{C}_i^{G,H}) \right\} \right]$$
$$\geq \frac{1}{4}\underset{G,H,S,z}{\mathbb{E}}[\mathsf{Adv}(\mathcal{A}_j^O)], \tag{18}$$

where the first inequality uses the fact that, for any two events E_1 and E_2, we have $\Pr[E_1 \vee E_2] \geq \max\{\Pr[E_1], \Pr[E_2]\}$, and the second one follows from Lemma 3.2. We now investigate the advantage of algorithm $\mathcal{D}$:

$$\mathsf{Adv}(\mathcal{D}^{G,H}) = \sum_j \Pr[i = j] \cdot \underset{G,H,S,z}{\mathbb{E}}\left[P_j^{\mathcal{B}_j \vee \mathcal{C}_j}(G, H, S, z) \right]$$
$$\geq \frac{1}{4d}\sum_j \underset{G,H,S,z}{\mathbb{E}}[\mathsf{Adv}(\mathcal{A}_j^O)]$$
$$\geq \frac{1}{4d} \cdot \mathsf{Adv}(\mathcal{A}^O),$$

where the first and second inequalities follow from (18) and Lemma 3.2, respectively. $\square$

4   Tighter IND-CCA Proofs for Fujisaki-Okamoto KEMs

Here, we apply our results from Sect. 3 to prove IND-CCA security of the Fujisaki-Okamoto $\mathsf{FO}^{\not\perp}$ transform, which takes an IND-CPA secure public-key encryption scheme (PKE) and applies a composition of the T transform [10] and the $U^{\not\perp}$ transform [10,13] to produce an IND-CCA secure Key Encapsulation Mechanism (KEM). Our QROM security proof for $\mathsf{FO}^{\not\perp}$ is obtained by adapting the proof in [5] to work with our new O2H lemma.

4.1   Security Definitions

We recall standard definitions related to PKEs, KEMs and pseudo-random functions (PRFs) in the full version of the paper [16]. Here we recall less standard definitions that will be needed in the analysis of the transform to an IND-CCA KEM.

We start with the definitions of a valid ciphertext and a security property called "finding failing ciphertext" (FFC). The latter was introduced in [5] to capture a decryption error requirement on the dPKE scheme needed for the IND-CCA security of the $U^{\not\perp}$ transform (recalled below). Notice that the success event of the FFC experiment is *not* efficiently checkable, which may at first sight seem incompatible with our O2H lemma; looking ahead, this event corresponds to the Fail event in the proof of Theorem 4.6, which we handle without invoking our O2H lemma.

Definition 4.1 (Valid Ciphertext). *Let* P = (KeyGen, Encr, Decr) *be a deterministic* PKE. *We call a ciphertext* $c \in C$ *valid for a public key* pk *if there exists a message* $m \in M$ *such that* $c = $ Encr(pk, m).

Definition 4.2 (Finding Failing Ciphertext). *Let* P = (KeyGen, Encr, Decr) *be a* PKE *and* A *be an adversary executing an attack against the finding failing ciphertext property (FFC), as specified by the following experiment:*

1. $H \xleftarrow{\$} \mathcal{H}$
2. (pk, sk) $\leftarrow$ KeyGen(λ)
3. $L \leftarrow A^H$(pk)
4. *return* $[\exists m \in \mathcal{M}, c \in L : $ Encr(pk, m) = $c \land$ Decr(sk, c) $\neq m]$

The advantage of A *in the above experiment is defined as:*

$$\mathsf{Adv}_\mathsf{P}^\mathsf{FFC}(A) := \Pr[1 \leftarrow \mathsf{Expt}_\mathsf{P}^\mathsf{FFC}(A)].$$

In the analysis of the $U^{\not\perp}$ transform, we will also need a dPKE satisfying the following injectivity property.

Definition 4.3 (Injectivity of a dPKE). *Let* $\eta \geq 0$. *A* dPKE *scheme* P = (KeyGen, Encr, Decr) *is* η-*injective if*

$$\Pr[\mathsf{Encr}(\mathsf{pk}, \cdot) \text{ *is not injective*: } (\mathsf{pk}, \mathsf{sk}) \leftarrow \mathsf{KeyGen}(1^\lambda), H \xleftarrow{\$} \mathcal{H}] \leq \eta.$$

4.2 Transforms

In [10], the authors showed how to build a transform T which converts any rPKE scheme P = (KeyGen, Encr, Decr) into a dPKE scheme $T(\mathsf{P}, G) = $ (KeyGen, Encr$_d$, Decr) using a hash function $G : \mathcal{M} \to \mathcal{R}$, where $\mathcal{R}$ is the space of random coins of rPKE's Encr algorithm. In [5], the authors proved the following security reduction from IND-CPA security of rPKE to OW-CPA security of $T(\mathsf{P}, G)$. We use this result as is, since it does not suffer from a square-root advantage loss.

Theorem 4.4 ([5, Theorem 1]). *Let P be an rPKE with message space $\mathcal{M}$ and randomness space $\mathcal{R}$. Let $G : \mathcal{M} \to \mathcal{R}$ be a quantum-accessible random oracle. Let $\mathcal{A}$ be a OW-CPA adversary against $P' = T(P, G)$. Suppose that $\mathcal{A}$ queries G at most q times with query depth at most d. Then we can construct an IND-CPA adversary $\mathcal{B}$, running in time $\approx \mathcal{T}_{\mathcal{A}}$, such that:*

$$\mathsf{Adv}_{P'}^{\mathsf{OW\text{-}CPA}}(\mathcal{A}) \leq (d+2) \cdot \left(\mathsf{Adv}_{P}^{\mathsf{IND\text{-}CPA}}(\mathcal{B}) + \frac{8 \cdot (q+1)}{|\mathcal{M}|} \right).$$

The following result provides a bound on the FFC advantage for a scheme obtained via the transform above.

Lemma 4.5 ([5, Lemma 6]). *Let $P = (\mathsf{KeyGen}, \mathsf{Encr}, \mathsf{Decr})$ be a δ-correct rPKE with messages in $\mathcal{M}$ and randomness in $\mathcal{R}$. Let $G : \mathcal{M} \to \mathcal{R}$ be a random oracle, so that $T(P, G) := (\mathsf{KeyGen}, \mathsf{Encr}_1, \mathsf{Decr})$ is a derandomized version of P. Suppose that $T(P, G)$ is η-injective. Let $\mathcal{A}$ be an FFC adversary against $T(P, G)$ which makes at most q queries to G with query depth at most d and returns a list of at most q_{dec} ciphertexts. Then*

$$\mathsf{Adv}_{T(P,G)}^{\mathsf{FFC}}(\mathcal{A}) \leq ((4d+1)\delta + \sqrt{3\eta}) \cdot (q + q_{dec}) + \eta.$$

We now recall the $U^{\not\perp}$ transform from [10]. It converts a dPKE $P = (\mathsf{KeyGen}_P, \mathsf{Encr}, \mathsf{Decr})$ into a KEM $K = (\mathsf{KeyGen}, \mathsf{Encaps}, \mathsf{Decaps})$ using a pseudo-random function $F : \mathcal{K}_F \times \mathcal{C} \to \mathcal{K}$ and a hash function $H : \mathcal{M} \times \mathcal{C} \to \mathcal{K}$ for given key spaces $\mathcal{K}_F$ and $\mathcal{K}$. Here $\mathcal{M}$ and $\mathcal{C}$ denote the message and cipher spaces of P. The PRF is used in case the ciphertext happens to be invalid. The transform is defined by the following three algorithms:

- $\mathsf{KeyGen}(1^\lambda)$. On input a security parameter λ, this algorithm runs $(\mathsf{pk}, \mathsf{sk}_P) \leftarrow \mathsf{KeyGen}_P(1^\lambda)$, samples a random key $\mathsf{prfk} \xleftarrow{\$} \mathcal{K}_F$ and sets $\mathsf{sk} = (\mathsf{sk}_P, \mathsf{prfk})$. The algorithm returns a pair of public and secret keys $(\mathsf{pk}, \mathsf{sk})$.
- $\mathsf{Encaps}(\mathsf{pk})$. On input a public key pk, this algorithm samples a random message $m \xleftarrow{\$} \mathcal{M}$, encrypts it running the encryption algorithm of P, i.e., $c \leftarrow \mathsf{Encr}(\mathsf{pk}, m)$, and computes a hash value $\mathsf{k} \leftarrow H(m, c)$. It outputs (k, c).
- $\mathsf{Decaps}(\mathsf{sk}, c)$. This algorithm parses sk as $\mathsf{sk} = (\mathsf{sk}_P, \mathsf{prfk})$ and runs the decryption algorithm of P to decrypt c, i.e., $m' \leftarrow \mathsf{Decr}(\mathsf{sk}_P, c)$. If $m' = \bot$, then it returns $F(\mathsf{prfk}, c)$. If $m' \neq \bot$ but $\mathsf{Encr}(\mathsf{pk}, m') \neq c$, then it also returns $F(\mathsf{prfk}, c)$. In all other cases (i.e., if $m' \neq \bot$ and $\mathsf{Encr}(\mathsf{pk}, m') = c$), it returns $H(m', c)$.

4.3 Analysis of the $U^{\not\perp}$ Transform

We are now ready to state our main application of the O2H lemma from Sect. 3. In the following theorem, we state that $U^{\not\perp}(P, F, H)$ is an IND-CCA secure KEM as long as the following four conditions are satisfied: (i) the dPKE scheme P is OW-CPA secure, (ii) it is η-injective for a negligible η, (iii) it is FFC secure, and (iv) F is a secure PRF. The latter is as in prior works: the improvement is in the security loss.

Theorem 4.6. *Let* $H : \mathcal{M} \times \mathcal{C} \to \mathcal{K}$ *be a quantum-accessible random oracle,* $F : \mathcal{K}_F \times \mathcal{C} \to \mathcal{K}$ *be a* PRF *and* P *be an* η-*injective* dPKE *which does not depend of* H. *Let* $U^{\not\perp}(\mathsf{P}, \mathsf{F}, H)$ *be the* KEM *obtained by applying the* $U^{\not\perp}$ *transform to* P, F *and* H. *Let* $\mathcal{A}$ *be an adversary against the* IND-CCA *security of* $U^{\not\perp}(\mathsf{P}, \mathsf{F}, H)$ *issuing at most* q *(quantum oracle) queries to* H *with query depth at most* d, *and* q_{dec} *classical queries to the decapsulation oracle.*

Then, we can construct three algorithms whose run-times are $\lesssim 3T_{\mathcal{A}}$. *These algorithms are:*

- *a* OW-CPA-*adversary* $\mathcal{B}_1$ *against* P,
- *an* FFC-*adversary* $\mathcal{B}_2$ *against* P, *returning a list of at most* q_{dec} *ciphertexts,*
- *a* PRF-*adversary* $\mathcal{B}_3$ *against* F *making* q_{dec} *queries.*

These algorithms satisfy the following:

$$\mathsf{Adv}^{\mathsf{IND\text{-}CCA}}_{U^{\not\perp}(\mathsf{P},\mathsf{F},H)}(\mathcal{A}) \leq 4d \cdot \mathsf{Adv}^{\mathsf{OW\text{-}CPA}}_{\mathsf{P}}(\mathcal{B}_1) + 6\mathsf{Adv}^{\mathsf{FFC}}_{\mathsf{P}}(\mathcal{B}_2) + 2\mathsf{Adv}^{\mathsf{PRF}}_{\mathsf{F}}(\mathcal{B}_3)$$
$$+ (4d + 6) \cdot \eta.$$

Proof. Our proof uses a sequence of games. All six games in our proof are essentially the same as in the proof of [5, Theorem 2], the only difference being the analysis of Game 5 to apply our new O2H lemma instead of the O2H lemma from [5]. For the sake of completeness, we present all the games.

In each of the following games, the probability space is partitioned into three mutually exclusive classical outcomes (events) called Win, Lose and Draw, respectively corresponding to $\mathcal{A}$ succeeding in its IND-CCA attack ($b' = b$), failing ($b' \neq b$) and a kind of intermediate outcome between the two, defined precisely in Game 2. Outcome Draw is defined to have probability 0 in Games 0 and 1, but in later games, whenever Draw occurs, the game continues and returns a Draw in the end regardless of b and b'. In Game i (for $i \in \{0, \ldots, 5\}$), we define the attacker's 'score' w_i as

$$w_i := \Pr[\mathsf{Win} : \mathsf{Game}\ i] + \frac{1}{2}\Pr[\mathsf{Draw} : \mathsf{Game}\ i]$$
$$= \frac{1}{2} + \frac{1}{2}\left(\Pr[\mathsf{Win} : \mathsf{Game}\ i] - \Pr[\mathsf{Lose} : \mathsf{Game}\ i]\right),$$

where the last equality comes from the fact that Win, Lose and Draw partition the probability space in each game.

Game 0 (IND-CCA). This game is the original IND-CCA experiment against $U^{\not\perp}(\mathsf{P}, \mathsf{F}, H)$.

Game 1 (PRF is random). This game is the same as Game 0, except that the simulator replaces the PRF $\mathsf{F}(\mathsf{prfk}, \cdot)$ in the decapsulation algorithm by a random function $\mathsf{R} \xleftarrow{\$} \mathcal{K}^{\mathcal{C}}$. We construct a PRF adversary $\mathcal{B}_3$ by replacing calls to $\mathsf{F}(\mathsf{prfk}, \cdot)$ by calls to $\mathcal{B}_3$'s oracle. Adversary $\mathcal{B}_3$ runs $\mathcal{A}$ and outputs 1 if $\mathcal{A}$ wins the IND-CCA game and 0 otherwise. If $\mathcal{B}_3$'s oracle is F, then it simulates Game 0, and if $\mathcal{B}_3$'s oracle is R, then it simulates Game 1. Therefore, we have

$\Pr[\mathcal{B}_3^{\mathsf{F}(k,\cdot)} = 1] = \Pr[\mathsf{Win} : \mathsf{Game} \ 0]$ and $\Pr[\mathcal{B}_3^{\mathsf{R}(\cdot)} = 1] = \Pr[\mathsf{Win} : \mathsf{Game} \ 1]$, and hence

$$|w_1 - w_0| = \mathsf{Adv}_{\mathsf{F}}^{\mathsf{PRF}}(\mathcal{B}_3).$$

Game 2 (Draw on fail). We let Fail be the (classical) event that at least one query of $\mathcal{A}$ to the decapsulation oracle $\mathcal{O}^D$ fails to decrypt a valid ciphertext., i.e., adversary $\mathcal{A}$ queries a c such that there exists some message $m \in \mathcal{M}$ such that $c = \mathsf{Encr}(\mathsf{pk}, m)$, but with $\mathsf{Decr}(\mathsf{sk}, c) \neq m$. We also let Inj denote the (classical) event that the encryption mapping $\mathsf{Encr}(\mathsf{pk}, \cdot)$ is injective over the message space $\mathcal{M}$. In Game 2 and the subsequent games, we define the Draw event as $\mathsf{Draw} := \mathsf{Fail} \vee \neg\mathsf{Inj}$ (which implies $\neg\mathsf{Draw} := \neg\mathsf{Fail} \wedge \mathsf{Inj}$). We define $d_i := \Pr[\mathsf{Draw} : \mathsf{Game} \ i]$, for $i \geq 2$. For $i < 2$, we define Draw as the empty event and $d_i = 0$.

We have:

$$|w_2 - w_1| = \left| \Pr[\mathsf{Win} : \mathsf{Game} \ 2] - \Pr[\mathsf{Win} : \mathsf{Game} \ 1] + \frac{d_2}{2} \right| \leq \frac{d_2}{2},$$

where the first equality holds since $d_1 = 0$ and the inequality holds true as $-d_2 \leq \Pr[\mathsf{Win} : \mathsf{Game} \ 2] - \Pr[\mathsf{Win} : \mathsf{Game} \ 1] \leq 0$. Note that the simulator may not be able to efficiently check whether Draw occurs, but the games will not require the simulator to perform this check.

Game 3 (Reprogram $H(m, c)$ to $\mathsf{R}(c)$). This game differs from Game 2 by reprogramming the hash function return value $H(m, c)$ on input (m, c) to $\mathsf{R}(c)$ if $c = \mathsf{Encr}(\mathsf{pk}, m)$.

The change from Game 2 to Game 3 does not affect the probability of Win and Draw so that $w_3 = w_2$ and $d_3 = d_2$. This is because in Game 3, the joint distribution of the oracle H and the attacker's view remains the same as in Game 2, as long as Draw does not occur. In particular, the distribution of $H(m, c)$ for each (m, c) remains uniformly random thanks to the uniformly random choice of $\mathsf{R}(c)$. The $H(m, c)$ values also remain independent for distinct pairs $(m, c) \neq (m', c')$ if Draw does not occur, since the latter implies that Inj occurs (i.e., there do not exist two distinct messages $m \neq m'$ with $c = \mathsf{Encr}(\mathsf{pk}, m) = \mathsf{Encr}(\mathsf{pk}, m') = c'$). Also, if Draw does not occur, then for any ciphertext c queried to and failing decryption by the Decaps oracle (meaning that $\mathsf{Encr}(\mathsf{pk}, \mathsf{Decr}(sk, c)) \neq c$), the Decaps oracle returns a value $\mathsf{R}(c)$ that is statistically independent of the value of $H(m, c)$ for all messages $m \in \mathcal{M}$ (since if there would exist some m with $H(m, c) = \mathsf{R}(c)$, i.e., $\mathsf{Encr}(\mathsf{pk}, m) = c$, it would imply that c is a valid ciphertext which failed to decrypt in Decaps, so that Draw occurred).

Game 4 (Decapsulation oracle returns $\mathsf{R}(c)$). This game is the same as Game 3 except that Decaps is modified to output $\mathsf{R}(c)$ for all ciphertexts but the challenge ciphertext (for the challenge ciphertext, it still outputs $\perp$). Since in Game 3, Decaps already responds in this way (as both F and H have been reprogrammed to respond with $\mathsf{R}(c)$), the values of w_4, d_4 are not affected, i.e., $w_4 = w_3$ and $d_4 = d_3$. The only change is that in Game 4 and onwards, the secret key is not used anymore in the simulation. We conclude that all probabilities d_i of Draw in Games 2 to 4 are the same.

To bound this Draw probability, we construct an adversary $\mathcal{B}_2$ which, given a public key pk, simulates Game 4 with $\mathcal{A}$, and outputs the list L of $\mathcal{A}$'s decapsulation queries. Note that if the event Fail occurs, then L contains a valid ciphertext c that fails decryption by Decr. Therefore, according to Definition 4.2, algorithm $\mathcal{B}_2$ is an FFC adversary against P which runs in almost the same time as $\mathcal{A}$ and has FFC advantage

$$
\begin{aligned}
\mathsf{Adv}_\mathsf{P}^\mathsf{FFC}(\mathcal{B}_2) &= \Pr[\mathsf{Fail} : \mathsf{Game}\ 4] \\
&\geq \Pr[\mathsf{Draw} : \mathsf{Game}\ 4] - \Pr[\neg\mathsf{Inj} : \mathsf{Game}\ 4] \\
&= d_4 - \eta,
\end{aligned}
$$

using the fact that P is η-injective. We conclude that

$$
d_2 = d_3 = d_4 \leq \mathsf{Adv}_\mathsf{P}^\mathsf{FFC}(\mathcal{B}_2) + \eta. \tag{19}
$$

Game 5 (Change shared secret). This game differs from Game 4 by changing the challenge shared secret k_b^* given to $\mathcal{A}$ to always be an independent uniformly random value r (whereas in Game 4, the challenge shared secret k_b^* was chosen as an independent random value $r = \mathsf{k}_1^*$ if $b = 1$ but chosen as $\mathsf{R}(c^*)$ if $b = 0$). Additionally, if $b = 0$ then $\mathsf{R}(c^*)$ is reprogrammed to return r (i.e., $H(m, c^*) = r$ for all messages m such that $\mathsf{Encr}(\mathsf{pk}, m) = c^*$; we denote by S^* the set of such messages m), but if $b = 1$ then $\mathsf{R}(c^*)$ is not reprogrammed.

In fact, the change from Game 4 to Game 5 is purely conceptual and does not change the joint distribution of the view of $\mathcal{A}$. Indeed, in both games, if $b = 0$, the input shared key k_0^* to $\mathcal{A}$ is uniformly random and equal to $H(m, c^*) = \mathsf{R}(c^*)$ for all $m \in S^*$. And in both games, if $b = 1$, the input shared key k_1^* to $\mathcal{A}$ is uniformly random and statistically independent of the uniformly random value of $H(m, c^*) = \mathsf{R}(c^*)$ for all $m \in S^*$. Therefore, we have $w_5 = w_4$ and $d_5 = d_4$.

In Game 5, the distribution of the input $z = (\mathsf{pk}, c^*, \mathsf{k}_b^* = r)$ to $\mathcal{A}$ is independent of b, and the random oracle queried by $\mathcal{A}$ and the simulator is either H if $b = 1$ (where $H(m, c) = \mathsf{R}(c)$ if $\mathsf{Encr}(\mathsf{pk}, m) = c$) or H' if $b = 0$, where H' is equal to H on all inputs except those in the set $S := \{(m, c^*) : m \in S^*\}$; for inputs in S, H' returns r. The simulation in Game 5 runs in time $\approx \mathcal{T}_\mathcal{A}$. Therefore, the algorithm $\mathcal{A}$ together with the simulator in Game 5 constitutes an O2H distinguisher algorithm for distinguishing oracle H from H' with runtime $\approx \mathcal{T}_\mathcal{A}$. Therefore, applying Lemma 3.3, we can construct algorithm $\mathcal{D}$, with run-time $\lesssim 3\mathcal{T}_\mathcal{A}$ and making oracle calls to H' and H, such that

$$
\begin{aligned}
\varDelta &:= |\Pr[0 \leftarrow \mathcal{A} : b = 0] - \Pr[0 \leftarrow \mathcal{A} : b = 1]| \\
&= \left| \Pr[0 \leftarrow \mathcal{A}^{H'}] - \Pr[0 \leftarrow \mathcal{A}^H] \right| \\
&\leq 4d \cdot \Pr[T \cap S \neq \emptyset : T \xleftarrow{\$} \mathcal{D}^{H',H}(z)]. \tag{20}
\end{aligned}
$$

Using $\mathcal{D}$, we can construct an algorithm $\mathcal{B}_1$ against the OW-CPA security of P that given (pk, c^*, r), runs $\mathcal{D}^{H',H}$ and when $\mathcal{D}$ returns its output set T of candidates for m^*, algorithm $\mathcal{B}_1$ tests each $m \in T$ to check whether $m \in S$, i.e., whether $\mathsf{Encr}(\mathsf{pk}, m) = c^*$, and returns any such m if it is found. Note that $\mathcal{T}_{\mathcal{B}_1} \approx \mathcal{T}_{\mathcal{D}}$. Further, algorithm $\mathcal{B}_1$ succeeds (i.e., outputs m^*) if $T \cap S \neq \emptyset$, unless $\neg\mathsf{Inj}$ occurs (in the latter case, the output of $\mathcal{B}_1$ may be a different decryption of c^* than m^*). Since P is η-injective, we have

$$\Pr[T \cap S \neq \emptyset : T \xleftarrow{\$} \mathcal{D}^{H',H}(\mathsf{pk}, c^*)] \leq \mathsf{Adv}_\mathsf{P}^{\mathsf{OW\text{-}CPA}}(\mathcal{B}_1) + \eta. \tag{21}$$

On the other hand, in Game 5 we have:

$$2\left|w_5 - \frac{1}{2}\right| = |\Pr[\mathsf{Win} : \mathsf{Game}\ 5] - \Pr[\mathsf{Lose} : \mathsf{Game}\ 5]|$$

$$= \left|\frac{1}{2}\Pr[0 \leftarrow \mathcal{A} \wedge \neg\mathsf{Draw} : b = 0] + \frac{1}{2}\Pr[0 \leftarrow \mathcal{A} \wedge \neg\mathsf{Draw} : b = 1]\right.$$

$$\left. - \frac{1}{2}\Pr[0 \leftarrow \mathcal{A} \wedge \neg\mathsf{Draw} : b = 1] - \frac{1}{2}\Pr[1 \leftarrow \mathcal{A} \wedge \neg\mathsf{Draw} : b = 0]\right|$$

$$\leq \frac{1}{2}|\Delta_{0,\neg\mathsf{Draw}}| + \frac{1}{2}|\Delta_{1,\neg\mathsf{Draw}}|, \tag{22}$$

where we define, for $v \in \{0, 1\}$,

$$\Delta_{v,\neg\mathsf{Draw}} := \Pr[v \leftarrow \mathcal{A} \wedge \neg\mathsf{Draw} : b = 0] - \Pr[v \leftarrow \mathcal{A} \wedge \neg\mathsf{Draw} : b = 1].$$

We further define:

$$\Delta_{v,\mathsf{Draw}} := \Pr[v \leftarrow \mathcal{A} \wedge \mathsf{Draw} : b = 0] - \Pr[v \leftarrow \mathcal{A} \wedge \mathsf{Draw} : b = 1],$$

which satisfies

$$|\Delta_{v,\mathsf{Draw}}| \leq \Pr[v \leftarrow \mathcal{A} \wedge \mathsf{Draw} : b = 0] + \Pr[v \leftarrow \mathcal{A} \wedge \mathsf{Draw} : b = 1]$$

$$= 2 \cdot (\Pr[v \leftarrow \mathcal{A} \wedge \mathsf{Draw} \wedge b = 0] + \Pr[v \leftarrow \mathcal{A} \wedge \mathsf{Draw} \wedge b = 1])$$

$$\leq 4 \cdot \Pr[\mathsf{Draw}] = 4 \cdot d_5. \tag{23}$$

Now, for $v \in \{0, 1\}$, observe that $\Delta_{v,\neg\mathsf{Draw}} + \Delta_{v,\mathsf{Draw}} = \Delta$, so we have, by the triangle inequality, (23), (20) and (21):

$$\Delta_{v,\neg\mathsf{Draw}} \leq |\Delta| + |\Delta_{v,\mathsf{Draw}}|$$

$$\leq 4d \cdot \left(\mathsf{Adv}_\mathsf{P}^{\mathsf{OW\text{-}CPA}}(\mathcal{B}_1) + \eta\right) + 4d_5. \tag{24}$$

and plugging (24) into (22) for $v \in \{0, 1\}$ gives

$$\left|w_5 - \frac{1}{2}\right| \leq 2d \cdot \left(\mathsf{Adv}_\mathsf{P}^{\mathsf{OW\text{-}CPA}}(\mathcal{B}_1) + \eta\right) + 2d_5.$$

Summing up the differences of w_i's over all games, we get

$$\mathsf{Adv}_{\mathsf{U}^{\not\perp}(\mathsf{P},\mathsf{F},\mathsf{H})}^{\mathsf{IND\text{-}CCA}}(\mathcal{A}) = 2|w_0 - 1/2|$$

$$\leq 4d \cdot \left(\mathsf{Adv}_\mathsf{P}^{\mathsf{OW\text{-}CPA}}(\mathcal{B}_1) + \eta\right) + 4d_5 + 2d_2 + 2\mathsf{Adv}_\mathsf{F}^{\mathsf{PRF}}(\mathcal{B}_3)$$

$$\leq 4d \cdot \mathsf{Adv}_\mathsf{P}^{\mathsf{OW\text{-}CPA}}(\mathcal{B}_1) + 6\mathsf{Adv}_\mathsf{P}^{\mathsf{FFC}}(\mathcal{B}_2) + 2\mathsf{Adv}_\mathsf{F}^{\mathsf{PRF}}(\mathcal{B}_3)$$

$$+ (4d + 6) \cdot \eta,$$

where in the last line we plugged in the bound on $d_5 = d_2$ from (19). □

Combining Theorem 4.6 with Theorem 4.4 and Lemma 4.5, we immediately obtain the following result for the IND-CCA security of the FO-transformed scheme $\mathsf{FO}^{\not\perp}(\mathsf{P},\mathsf{F},G,H) = \mathsf{U}^{\not\perp}(T(\mathsf{P},G),\mathsf{F},H)$ from the IND-CPA security of scheme P.

Corollary 4.7. *Let* P *be a δ-correct rPKE with message space $\mathcal{M}$ and randomness space $\mathcal{R}$. Let $G : \mathcal{M} \to \mathcal{R}$ and $H : \mathcal{M} \times \mathcal{C} \to \mathcal{K}$ be quantum-accessible random oracles, and $\mathsf{F} : \mathcal{K}_\mathsf{F} \times \mathcal{C} \to \mathcal{K}$ be a PRF. Suppose that $\mathsf{P}' = T(\mathsf{P},G)$ is η-injective and let $\mathsf{FO}^{\not\perp}(\mathsf{P},\mathsf{F},G,H) = \mathsf{U}^{\not\perp}(T(\mathsf{P},G),\mathsf{F},H)$. Let $\mathcal{A}$ be an adversary against the IND-CCA security of $\mathsf{FO}^{\not\perp}(\mathsf{P},\mathsf{F},G,H)$ issuing at most q_G (resp. q_H) quantum queries to G (resp. H) with query depth at most d_G (resp. d_H) and at most q_{dec} classical queries to the decapsulation oracle of $\mathsf{FO}^{\not\perp}(\mathsf{P},\mathsf{F},G,H)$.*

Then, we can construct two algorithms whose run-times are $\lesssim 3T_\mathcal{A}$. These algorithms are:

- *an IND-CPA-adversary $\mathcal{B}_1$ against* P,
- *a PRF-adversary $\mathcal{B}_2$ against* F *issuing at most q_{dec} queries.*

These algorithms satisfy the following:

$$\mathsf{Adv}^{\mathsf{IND\text{-}CCA}}_{\mathsf{FO}^{\not\perp}(\mathsf{P},\mathsf{F},G,H)}(\mathcal{A}) \leq 8d_H \cdot (d_G + 1) \cdot \left(\mathsf{Adv}^{\mathsf{IND\text{-}CPA}}_{\mathsf{P}}(\mathcal{B}_1) + \frac{8 \cdot (3q_G + 1)}{|\mathcal{M}|} \right)$$
$$+ 6 \cdot (3q_G + q_{dec}) \cdot \left((8d_G + 1) \cdot \delta + \sqrt{3\eta} \right)$$
$$+ (4d_H + 12) \cdot \eta + 2\mathsf{Adv}^{\mathsf{PRF}}_{\mathsf{F}}(\mathcal{B}_2).$$

Acknowledgments. This work was supported in part by BPI-France in the context of the national project RISQ (P141580), by the European Union PROMETHEUS project (Horizon 2020 Research and Innovation Program, grant 780701) and the Australian Research Council Discovery Grant DP180102199. Part of this work was done while Damien Stehlé was visiting the Simons Institute for the Theory of Computing.

References

1. Ambainis, A., Hamburg, M., Unruh, D.: Quantum security proofs using semi-classical oracles. In: Boldyreva, A., Micciancio, D. (eds.) CRYPTO 2019. LNCS, vol. 11693, pp. 269–295. Springer, Cham (2019). https://doi.org/10.1007/978-3-030-26951-7_10
2. Ambainis, A., Rosmanis, A., Unruh, D.: Quantum attacks on classical proof systems: the hardness of quantum rewinding. In: 55th IEEE Annual Symposium on Foundations of Computer Science, FOCS 2014, pp. 474–483 (2014)
3. Bernstein, D.J., et al.: Classic McEliece - supporting documentation. Submitted to [19] (2019). https://classic.mceliece.org/nist/mceliece-20190331.pdf
4. Bernstein, D.J., Chuengsatiansup, C., Lange, T., van Vredendaal, C.: NTRU prime: round 2 - supporting documentation. Submitted to [19] (2019). https://ntruprime.cr.yp.to/nist/ntruprime-20190330.pdf

5. Bindel, N., Hamburg, M., Hövelmanns, K., Hülsing, A., Persichetti, E.: Tighter proofs of CCA security in the quantum random oracle model. In: Hofheinz, D., Rosen, A. (eds.) TCC 2019. LNCS, vol. 11892, pp. 61–90. Springer, Cham (2019). https://doi.org/10.1007/978-3-030-36033-7_3

6. Boneh, D., Dagdelen, Ö., Fischlin, M., Lehmann, A., Schaffner, C., Zhandry, M.: Random oracles in a quantum world. In: Lee, D.H., Wang, X. (eds.) ASIACRYPT 2011. LNCS, vol. 7073, pp. 41–69. Springer, Heidelberg (2011). https://doi.org/10.1007/978-3-642-25385-0_3

7. Chen, C., et al.: NTRU - supporting documentation. Submitted to [19] (2019). https://ntru.org/f/ntru-20190330.pdf

8. Dent, A.W.: A designer's guide to KEMs. In: Paterson, K.G. (ed.) Cryptography and Coding 2003. LNCS, vol. 2898, pp. 133–151. Springer, Heidelberg (2003). https://doi.org/10.1007/978-3-540-40974-8_12

9. Fujisaki, E., Okamoto, T.: Secure integration of asymmetric and symmetric encryption schemes. In: Wiener, M. (ed.) CRYPTO 1999. LNCS, vol. 1666, pp. 537–554. Springer, Heidelberg (1999). https://doi.org/10.1007/3-540-48405-1_34

10. Hofheinz, D., Hövelmanns, K., Kiltz, E.: A modular analysis of the Fujisaki-Okamoto transformation. In: Kalai, Y., Reyzin, L. (eds.) TCC 2017. LNCS, vol. 10677, pp. 341–371. Springer, Cham (2017). https://doi.org/10.1007/978-3-319-70500-2_12

11. Hövelmanns, K., Kiltz, E., Schäge, S., Unruh, D.: Generic authenticated key exchange in the quantum random oracle model. IACR Cryptology ePrint Archive 2018/928 (2018)

12. Jiang, H., Zhang, Z., Chen, L., Wang, H., Ma, Z.: IND-CCA-secure key encapsulation mechanism in the quantum random oracle model, revisited. In: Shacham, H., Boldyreva, A. (eds.) CRYPTO 2018. LNCS, vol. 10993, pp. 96–125. Springer, Cham (2018). https://doi.org/10.1007/978-3-319-96878-0_4

13. Jiang, H., Zhang, Z., Ma, Z.: Key encapsulation mechanism with explicit rejection in the quantum random oracle model. In: Lin, D., Sako, K. (eds.) PKC 2019. LNCS, vol. 11443, pp. 618–645. Springer, Cham (2019). https://doi.org/10.1007/978-3-030-17259-6_21

14. Jiang, H., Zhang, Z., Ma, Z.: On the non-tightness of measurement-based reductions for key encapsulation mechanism in the quantum random oracle model. IACR Cryptology ePrint Archive 2019/494 (2019)

15. Jiang, H., Zhang, Z., Ma, Z.: Tighter security proofs for generic key encapsulation mechanism in the quantum random oracle model. In: Ding, J., Steinwandt, R. (eds.) PQCrypto 2019. LNCS, vol. 11505, pp. 227–248. Springer, Cham (2019). https://doi.org/10.1007/978-3-030-25510-7_13

16. Kuchta, V., Sakzad, A., Stehlé, D., Steinfeld, R., Sun, S.-F.: Measure-rewind-measure: tighter quantum random oracle model proofs for one-way to hiding and CCA security. IACR Cryptology ePrint Archive 2020/xxx (2020). Full version of this paper

17. Micciancio, D., Walter, M.: On the bit security of cryptographic primitives. In: Nielsen, J.B., Rijmen, V. (eds.) EUROCRYPT 2018. LNCS, vol. 10820, pp. 3–28. Springer, Cham (2018). https://doi.org/10.1007/978-3-319-78381-9_1

18. Nielsen, M.A., Chuang, I.L.: Quantum Computation and Quantum Information: 10th Anniversary Edition, 10th edn. Cambridge University Press, New York (2011)

19. NIST: Post-quantum cryptography standardization. https://csrc.nist.gov/Projects/post-quantum-cryptography/

20. Regev, O.: On lattices, learning with errors, random linear codes, and cryptography. In: 37th Annual ACM Symposium on Theory of Computing, pp. 84–93 (2005)

21. Saito, T., Xagawa, K., Yamakawa, T.: Tightly-secure key-encapsulation mechanism in the quantum random oracle model. In: Nielsen, J.B., Rijmen, V. (eds.) EUROCRYPT 2018. LNCS, vol. 10822, pp. 520–551. Springer, Cham (2018). https://doi.org/10.1007/978-3-319-78372-7_17

22. Targhi, E.E., Unruh, D.: Post-quantum security of the Fujisaki-Okamoto and OAEP transforms. In: Hirt, M., Smith, A. (eds.) TCC 2016. LNCS, vol. 9986, pp. 192–216. Springer, Heidelberg (2016). https://doi.org/10.1007/978-3-662-53644-5_8

23. Unruh, D.: Quantum proofs of knowledge. In: Pointcheval, D., Johansson, T. (eds.) EUROCRYPT 2012. LNCS, vol. 7237, pp. 135–152. Springer, Heidelberg (2012). https://doi.org/10.1007/978-3-642-29011-4_10

24. Unruh, D.: Revocable quantum timed-release encryption. In: Nguyen, P.Q., Oswald, E. (eds.) EUROCRYPT 2014. LNCS, vol. 8441, pp. 129–146. Springer, Heidelberg (2014). https://doi.org/10.1007/978-3-642-55220-5_8

25. Watrous, J.: Zero-knowledge against quantum attacks. SIAM J. Comput. **39**(1), 25–58 (2009)

26. Xagawa, K., Yamakawa, T.: (Tightly) QCCA-secure key-encapsulation mechanism in the quantum random oracle model. In: Ding, J., Steinwandt, R. (eds.) PQCrypto 2019. LNCS, vol. 11505, pp. 249–268. Springer, Cham (2019). https://doi.org/10.1007/978-3-030-25510-7_14

27. Zhandry, M.: How to record quantum queries, and applications to quantum indifferentiability. In: Boldyreva, A., Micciancio, D. (eds.) CRYPTO 2019. LNCS, vol. 11693, pp. 239–268. Springer, Cham (2019). https://doi.org/10.1007/978-3-030-26951-7_9

Secure Multi-party Quantum Computation with a Dishonest Majority

Yfke Dulek[1,2]($\boxtimes$), Alex B. Grilo[1,3]($\boxtimes$), Stacey Jeffery[1,3]($\boxtimes$),
Christian Majenz[1,3]($\boxtimes$), and Christian Schaffner[1,2]($\boxtimes$)

[1] QuSoft, Amsterdam, The Netherlands
yfkedulek@gmail.com, abgrilo@gmail.com, smjeffery@gmail.com,
c.majenz@uva.nl
[2] University of Amsterdam, Amsterdam, The Netherlands
c.schaffner@uva.nl
[3] Centrum voor Wiskunde en Informatica, Amsterdam, The Netherlands

Abstract. The cryptographic task of secure multi-party (classical) computation has received a lot of attention in the last decades. Even in the extreme case where a computation is performed between k mutually distrustful players, and security is required even for the single honest player if all other players are colluding adversaries, secure protocols are known. For quantum computation, on the other hand, protocols allowing arbitrary dishonest majority have only been proven for $k = 2$. In this work, we generalize the approach taken by Dupuis, Nielsen and Salvail (CRYPTO 2012) in the two-party setting to devise a secure, efficient protocol for multi-party quantum computation for any number of players k, and prove security against up to $k - 1$ colluding adversaries. The quantum round complexity of the protocol for computing a quantum circuit of $\{\mathsf{CNOT}, \mathsf{T}\}$ depth d is $O(k \cdot (d + \log n))$, where n is the security parameter. To achieve efficiency, we develop a novel public verification protocol for the Clifford authentication code, and a testing protocol for magic-state inputs, both using classical multi-party computation.

1 Introduction

In secure multi-party computation (MPC), two or more players want to jointly compute some publicly known function on their private data, without revealing their inputs to the other players. Since its introduction by Yao [Yao82], MPC has been extensively developed in different setups, leading to applications of both theoretical and practical interest (see, e.g., [CDN15] for a detailed overview).

With the emergence of quantum technologies, it becomes necessary to understand its consequences in the field of MPC. First, classical MPC protocols have to be secured against quantum attacks. But also, the increasing number of applications where quantum computational power is desired motivates protocols enabling multi-party *quantum* computation (MPQC) on the players' private (possibly quantum) data. In this work, we focus on the second task. Informally,

A. Canteaut and Y. Ishai (Eds.): EUROCRYPT 2020, LNCS 12107, pp. 729–758, 2020.
https://doi.org/10.1007/978-3-030-45727-3_25

we say a MPQC protocol is secure if the following two properties hold: 1. Dishonest players gain no information about the honest players' private inputs. 2. If the players do not abort the protocol, then at the end of the protocol they share a state corresponding to the correct computation applied to the inputs of honest players (those that follow the protocol) and some choice of inputs for the dishonest players.

MPQC was first studied by Crépeau, Gottesman and Smith [CGS02], who proposed a k-party protocol based on verifiable secret sharing that is information-theoretically secure, but requires the assumption that at most $k/6$ players are dishonest. The fraction $k/6$ was subsequently improved to $<k/2$ [BOCG+06] which is optimal for secret-sharing-based protocols due to no-cloning. The case of a dishonest majority was thus far only considered for $k = 2$ parties, where one of the two players can be dishonest [DNS10, DNS12, KMW17][1]. These protocols are based on different cryptographic techniques, in particular quantum authentication codes in conjunction with classical MPC [DNS10, DNS12] and quantum-secure bit commitment and oblivious transfer [KMW17].

In this work, we propose the first secure MPQC protocol for any number k of players in the dishonest majority setting, i.e., the case with up to $k - 1$ colluding adversarial players.[2] We remark that our result achieves *composable security*, which is proven according to the standard ideal-vs.-real definition. Like the protocol of [DNS12], on which our protocol is built, our protocol assumes a classical MPC that is secure against a dishonest majority, and achieves the same security guarantees as this classical MPC. In particular, if we instantiate this classical MPC with an MPC in the *pre-processing model* (see [BDOZ11, DPSZ12, KPR18, CDE+18]), our construction yields a MPQC protocol consisting of a classical "offline" phase used to produce authenticated shared randomness among the players, and a second "computation" phase, consisting of our protocol, combined with the "computation" phase of the classical MPC. The security of the "offline" phase requires computational assumptions, but assuming no attack was successful in this phase, the second phase has information-theoretic security.

1.1 Prior Work

Our protocol builds on the two-party protocol of Dupuis, Nielsen, and Salvail [DNS12], which we now describe in brief. The protocol uses a classical MPC protocol, and involves two parties, Alice and Bob, of whom at least one is honestly following the protocol. Alice and Bob encode their inputs using a technique called *swaddling*: if Alice has an input qubit $|\psi\rangle$, she first encodes it using the n-qubit Clifford code (see Definition 2.5), resulting in $A(|0^n\rangle \otimes |\psi\rangle)$, for some random $(n+1)$-qubit Clifford A sampled by Alice, where n is the security parameter.

---

[1] In Kashefi and Pappa [KP17], they consider a non-symmetric setting where the protocol is secure only when some specific sets of $k - 1$ players are dishonest.

[2] In the case where there are k adversaries and no honest players, there is nobody whose input privacy and output authenticity is worth protecting.

Then, she sends the state to Bob, who puts another encoding on top of Alice's: he creates the "swaddled" state $B(A(|0^n\rangle \otimes |\psi\rangle) \otimes |0^n\rangle)$ for some random $(2n+1)$-qubit Clifford B sampled by Bob. This encoded state consists of $2n + 1$ qubits, and the data qubit $|\psi\rangle$ sits in the middle.

If Bob wants to test the state at some point during the protocol, he simply needs to undo the Clifford B, and test that the last n qubits (called traps) are $|0\rangle$. However, if Alice wants to test the state, she needs to work together with Bob to access her traps. Using classical multi-party computation, they jointly sample a random $(n+1)$-qubit Clifford B' which is only revealed to Bob, and compute a Clifford $T := (\mathbb{I}^{\otimes n} \otimes B')(A^\dagger \otimes \mathbb{I}^{\otimes n})B^\dagger$ that is only revealed to Alice. Alice, who will not learn any relevant information about B or B', can use T to "flip" the swaddle, revealing her n trap qubits for measurement. After checking that the first n qubits are $|0\rangle$, she adds a fresh $(2n + 1)$-qubit Clifford on top of the state to re-encode the state, before computation can continue.

Single-qubit Clifford gates are performed simply by classically updating the inner key: if a state is encrypted with Cliffords BA, updating the decryption key to $BAG^\dagger$ effectively applies the gate G. In order to avoid that the player holding the inner key B skips this step, both players keep track of their keys using a classical commitment scheme. This can be encapsulated in the classical MPC, which we can assume acts as a trusted third party with a memory [BOCG+06].

CNOT operations and measurements are slightly more involved, and require both players to test the authenticity of the relevant states several times. Hence, the communication complexity scales linearly with the number of CNOTs and measurements in the circuit.

Finally, to perform T gates, the protocol makes use of so-called magic states. To obtain reliable magic states, Alice generates a large number of them, so that Bob can test a sufficiently large fraction. He decodes them (with Alice's help), and measures whether they are in the expected state. If all measurements succeed, Bob can be sufficiently certain that the untested (but still encoded) magic states are in the correct state as well.

Extending two-party computation to multi-party computation. A natural question is how to lift a two-party computation protocol to a multi-party computation protocol. We discuss some of the issues that arise from such an approach, making it either infeasible or inefficient.

Composing ideal functionalities. The first naive idea would be trying to split the k players in two groups and make the groups simulate the players of a two-party protocol, whereas internally, the players run $\frac{k}{2}$-party computation protocols for all steps in the two-party protocol. Those $\frac{k}{2}$-party protocols are in turn realized by running $\frac{k}{4}$-party protocols, etc., until at the lowest level, the players can run actual two-party protocols.

Trying to construct such a composition in a black-box way, using the *ideal functionality* of a two-party protocol, one immediately faces a problem: at the lower levels, players learn intermediate states of the circuit, because they receive plaintext outputs from the ideal two-party functionality. This would immediately break the privacy of the protocol. If, on the other hand, we require the ideal two-party functionality to output encoded states instead of plaintexts, then the size of the ciphertext will grow at each level. The overhead of this approach would be $O(n^{\log k})$, where $n \geqslant k$ is the security parameter of the encoding, which would make this overhead super-polynomial in the number of players.

Naive extension of DNS to multi-party. One could also try to extend [DNS12] to multiple parties by adapting the subprotocols to work for more than two players. While this approach would likely lead to a correct and secure protocol for k parties, the computational costs of such an extension could be high.

First, note that in such an extension, each party would need to append n trap qubits to the encoding of each qubit, causing an overhead in the ciphertext size that is linear in k. Secondly, in this naive extension, the players would need to create $\Theta(2^k)$ magic states for T gates (see Sect. 2.5), since each party would need to sequentially test at least half of the ones approved by all previous players.

Notice that in both this extension and our protocol, a state has to pass by the honest player (and therefore all players) in order to be able to verify that it has been properly encoded.

1.2 Our Contributions

Our protocol builds on the work of Dupuis, Nielsen, and Salvail [DNS10, DNS12], and like it, assumes a classical MPC, and achieves the same security guarantees as this classical MPC. In contrast to a naive extension of [DNS12], requiring $\Theta(2^k)$ magic states, the complexity of our protocol, when considering a quantum circuit that contains, among other gates, g gates in $\{\mathsf{CNOT}, \mathsf{T}\}$ and acts on w qubits, scales as $O((g + w)k)$.

In order to efficiently extend the two-party protocol of [DNS12] to a general k-party protocol, we make two major alterations to the protocol:

Public authentication test. In [DNS12], given a security parameter n, each party adds n qubits in the state $|0\rangle$ to each input qubit in order to authenticate it. The size of each ciphertext is thus $2n + 1$. The extra qubits serve as check qubits (or "traps") for each party, which can be measured at regular intervals: if they are non-zero, somebody tampered with the state.

In a straightforward generalization to k parties, the ciphertext size would become $kn + 1$ per input qubit, putting a strain on the computing space of each player. In our protocol, the ciphertext size is constant in the number of players: it is usually $n + 1$ per input qubit, temporarily increasing to $2n + 1$ for qubits that are involved in a computation step. As an additional advantage, our protocol does not require that all players measure their traps every time a state needs to be checked for its authenticity.

To achieve this smaller ciphertext size, we introduce a *public authentication test.* Our protocol uses a single, shared set of traps for each qubit. If the protocol calls for the authentication to be checked, the player that currently holds the state cannot be trusted to simply measure those traps. Instead, she temporarily adds extra trap qubits, and fills them with an encrypted version of the content of the existing traps. Now she measures only the newly created ones. The encryption ensures that the measuring player does not know the expected measurement outcome. If she is dishonest and has tampered with the state, she would have to guess a random n-bit string, or be detected by the other players. We design a similar test that checks whether a player has honestly created the first set of traps for their input at encoding time.

Efficient magic-state preparation. For the computation of non-Clifford gates, the [DNS12] protocol requires the existence of authenticated "magic states", auxiliary qubits in a known and fixed state that aid in the computation. In a two-party setting, one of the players can create a large number of such states, and the other player can, if he distrusts the first player, test a random subset of them to check if they were honestly initialized. Those tested states are discarded, and the remaining states are used in the computation.

In a k-party setting, such a "cut-and-choose" strategy where all players want to test a sufficient number of states would require the first party to prepare an exponential number (in k) of authenticated magic states, which quickly gets infeasible as the number of players grows. Instead, we need a testing strategy where dishonest players have no control over which states are selected for testing. We ask the first player to create a polynomial number of authenticated magic states. Subsequently, we use classical MPC to sample random, disjoint subsets of the proposed magic states, one for each player. Each player continues to decrypt and test their subset of states. The random selection process implies that, conditioned on the test of the honest player(s) being successful, the remaining registers indeed contain encrypted states that are reasonably close to magic states. Finally, we use standard magic-state distillation to obtain auxiliary inputs that are exponentially close to magic states.

1.3 Overview of the Protocol

We describe some details of the k-player quantum MPC protocol for circuits consisting of classically-controlled Clifford operations and measurements. Such circuits suffice to perform Clifford computation and magic-state distillation, so that the protocol can be extended to arbitrary circuits using the technique described above. The protocol consists of several subprotocols, of which we highlight four here: input encoding, public authentication test, single-qubit gate application, and CNOT application. In the following description, the classical MPC is treated as a trusted third party with memory[3]. The general idea is to first ensure that initially all inputs are properly encoded into the Clifford authentication code, and to test the encoding after each computation step that exposes the encoded

---

[3] The most common way to achieve classical MPC against dishonest majority is in the so called pre-processing model, as suggested by the SPDZ [BDOZ11] and MAS-COT [KOS16] families of protocols. We believe that these protocols can be made post-quantum secure, but that is beyond the scope of this paper.

qubit to an attack. During the protocol, the encryption keys for the Clifford authentication code are only known to the MPC.

Input encoding. For an input qubit $|\psi\rangle$ of player i, the MPC hands each player a circuit for a random $(2n + 1)$-qubit Clifford group element. Now player i appends $2n$ "trap" qubits initialized in the $|0\rangle$-state and applies her Clifford. The state is passed around, and all other players apply their Clifford one-by-one, resulting in a Clifford-encoded qubit $F(|\psi\rangle |0^{2n}\rangle)$ for which knowledge of the encoding key F is distributed among all players. The final step is our *public authentication test*, which is used in several of the other subprotocols as well. Its goal is to ensure that all players, including player i, have honestly followed the protocol.

The public authentication test (details). The player holding the state $F(|\psi\rangle |0^{2n}\rangle)$ (player i) will measure n out of the $2n$ trap qubits, which should all be 0. To enable player i to measure a random subset of n of the trap qubits, the MPC could instruct her to apply $(E \otimes X^r)(\mathbb{I} \otimes U_\pi)F^\dagger$ to get $E(|\psi\rangle |0^n\rangle) \otimes |r\rangle$, where U_π permutes the $2n$ trap qubits by a random permutation π, and E is a random $(n + 1)$ qubit Clifford, and $r \in \{0, 1\}^n$ is a random string. Then when player i measures the last n trap qubits, if the encoding was correct, she will obtain r and communicate this to the MPC. However, this only guarantees that the remaining traps are correct up to polynomial error.

To get a stronger guarantee, we replace the random permutation with an element from the sufficiently rich yet still efficiently samplable group of invertible transformations over $\mathbb{F}^{2n}$, $\mathrm{GL}(2n, \mathbb{F}_2)$. An element $g \in \mathrm{GL}(2n, \mathbb{F}_2)$ maybe be viewed as a unitary U_g acting on computational basis states as $U_g |x\rangle = |gx\rangle$ where $x \in \{0, 1\}^{2n}$. In particular, $U_g |0^{2n}\rangle = |0^{2n}\rangle$, so if all traps are in the state $|0\rangle$, applying U_g does not change this, whereas for non-zero x, $U_g |x\rangle = |x'\rangle$ for a *random* $x' \in \{0, 1\}^{2n}$. Thus the MPC instructs player i to apply $(E \otimes X^r)(\mathbb{I} \otimes U_g)F^\dagger$ to the state $F(|\psi\rangle |0^{2n}\rangle)$, then measure the last n qubits and return the result, aborting if it is not r. Crucially, $(E \otimes X^r)(\mathbb{I} \otimes U_g)F^\dagger$ is given as an element of the Clifford group, hiding the structure of the unitary and, more importantly, the values of r and g. So if player i is dishonest and holds a corrupted state, she can only pass the MPC's test by guessing r. If player i correctly returns r, we have the guarantee that the remaining state is a Clifford-authenticated qubit with n traps, $E(|\psi\rangle |0^n\rangle)$, up to exponentially small error.

Single-qubit Clifford gate application. As in [DNS12], this is done by simply updating encryption key held by the MPC: If a state is currently encrypted with a Clifford E, decrypting with a "wrong" key $EG^\dagger$ has the effect of applying G to the state.

CNOT application. Applying a CNOT gate to two qubits is slightly more complicated: as they are encrypted separately, we cannot just implement the CNOT via a key update like in the case of single qubit Clifford gates. Instead, we bring the two encoded qubits together, and then run a protocol that is similar to input encoding using the $(2n + 2)$-qubit register as "input", but using $2n$

additional traps instead of just n, and skipping the final authentication-testing step. The joint state now has $4n + 2$ qubits and is encrypted with some Clifford F only known to the MPC. Afterwards, CNOT can be applied via a key update, similarly to single-qubit Cliffords. To split up the qubits again afterwards, the executing player applies $(E_1 \otimes E_2)F^\dagger$, where E_1 and E_2 are freshly sampled by the MPC. The two encoded qubits can then be tested separately using the public authentication test.

1.4 Open Problems

Our results leave a number of exciting open problems to be addressed in future work. Firstly, the scope of this work was to provide a protocol that reduces the problem of MPQC to classical MPC in an information-theoretically secure way. Hence we obtain an information-theoretically secure MPQC protocol *in the preprocessing model*, leaving the post-quantum secure instantiation of the latter as an open problem.

Another class of open problems concerns applications of MPQC. For instance, classically, MPC can be used to devise zero-knowledge proofs [IKOS09] and digital signature schemes [CDG+17].

An interesting open question concerning our protocol more specifically is whether the CNOT sub-protocol can be replaced by a different one that has round complexity independent of the total number of players, reducing the quantum round complexity of the whole protocol. We also wonder if it is possible to develop more efficient protocols for narrower classes of quantum computation, instead of arbitrary (polynomial-size) quantum circuits.

Finally, it would be interesting to investigate whether the public authentication test we use can be leveraged in protocols for specific MPC-related tasks like oblivious transfer.

1.5 Outline

In Sect. 2, we outline the necessary preliminaries and tools we will make use of in our protocol. In Sect. 3, we give a precise definition of MPQC. In Sect. 4, we describe how players encode their inputs to setup for computation in our protocol. In Sect. 5 we describe our protocol for Clifford circuits, and finally, in Sect. 6, we show how to extend this to universal quantum circuits in Clifford+T.

2 Preliminaries

2.1 Notation

We assume familiarity with standard notation in quantum computation, such as (pure and mixed) quantum states, the Pauli gates X and Z, the Clifford gates H and CNOT, the non-Clifford gate T, and measurements.

We work in the quantum circuit model, with circuits C composed of elementary unitary gates (of the set Clifford+T), plus computational basis measurements. We consider those measurement gates to be destructive, i.e., to destroy the post-measurement state immediately, and only a classical wire to remain. Since subsequent gates in the circuit can still classically control on those measured wires, this point of view is as general as keeping the post-measurement states around.

For a set of quantum gates $\mathcal{G}$, the $\mathcal{G}$-depth of a quantum circuit is defined as the minimal number of layers such that in every layer, gates from $\mathcal{G}$ do not act on the same qubit.

For two circuits C_1 and C_2, we write $C_2 \circ C_1$ for the circuit that consists of executing C_1, followed by C_2. Similarly, for two protocols Π_1 and Π_2, we write $\Pi_2 \diamond \Pi_1$ for the execution of Π_1, followed by the execution of Π_2.

We use capital letters for both quantum registers (M, R, S, T, ...) and unitaries (A, B, U, V, W, ...). We write $|R|$ for the dimension of the Hilbert space in a register R. The registers in which a certain quantum state exists, or on which some map acts, are written as gray superscripts, whenever it may be unclear otherwise. For example, a unitary U that acts on register A, applied to a state ρ in the registers AB, is written as $U^A \rho^{AB} U^\dagger$, where the registers $U^\dagger$ acts on can be determined by finding the matching U and reading the grey subscripts. Note that we do not explicitly write the operation $\mathbb{I}^B$ with which U is in tensor product. The gray superscripts are purely informational, and do not signify any mathematical operation. If we want to denote, for example, a partial trace of the state ρ^{AB}, we use the conventional notation ρ_A.

For an n-bit string $s = s_1 s_2 \cdots s_n$, define $U^s := U^{s_1} \otimes U^{s_2} \otimes \cdots \otimes U^{s_n}$. For an n-element permutation $\pi \in S_n$, define P_π to be the unitary that permutes n qubits according to π:

$$P_\pi |\psi_1\rangle ... |\psi_n\rangle = |\psi_{\pi(1)}\rangle ... |\psi_{\pi(n)}\rangle .$$

We use $[k]$ for the set $\{1, 2, \ldots, k\}$. For a projector Π, we write $\overline{\Pi}$ for its complement $\mathbb{I} - \Pi$. We use $\tau^R := \mathbb{I}/|R|$ for the fully mixed state on the register R.

Write $GL(n, F)$ for the general linear group of degree n over a field F. We refer to the Galois field of two elements as $\mathbb{F}_2$, the n-qubit Pauli group as $\mathscr{P}_n$, and the n-qubit Clifford group as $\mathscr{C}_n$. Whenever a protocol mandates handing an element from one of these groups, or more generally, a unitary operation, to an agent, we mean that a (classical) description of the group element is given, e.g. as a normal-form circuit.

Finally, for a quantum operation that may take multiple rounds of inputs and outputs, for example an environment $\mathcal{E}$ interacting with a protocol Π, we write $\mathcal{E} \leftrightarrows \Pi$ for the final output of $\mathcal{E}$ after the entire interaction.

2.2   Classical Multi-party Computation

At this point, we are unaware of any formal analysis of the post-quantum security of existing classical multi-party computation schemes. Establishing full post-quantum security of classical multi-party computation is outside the scope of this paper, but we discuss some possible directions in the full version. For the purpose of this paper, we assume that a post-quantum secure classical multi-party computation is available.

Throughout this paper, we will utilize the following ideal MPC functionality as a black box:

Definition 2.1 (Ideal classical k-party stateful computation with abort). *Let $f_1, ..., f_k$ and f_S be public classical deterministic functions on $k + 2$ inputs. Let a string s represent the internal state of the ideal functionality. (The first time the ideal functionality is called, s is empty.) Let $A \subsetneq [k]$ be a set of corrupted players.*

1. *Every player $i \in [k]$ chooses an input x_i of appropriate size, and sends it (securely) to the trusted third party.*
2. *The trusted third party samples a bit string r uniformly at random.*
3. *The trusted third party computes $f_i(s, x_1, ..., x_k, r)$ for all $i \in [k] \cup \{S\}$.*
4. *For all $i \in A$, the trusted third party sends $f_i(s, x_1, ..., x_k, r)$ to player i.*
5. *All $i \in A$ respond with a bit b_i, which is 1 if they choose to abort, or 0 otherwise.*
6. *If $b_j = 0$ for all j, the trusted third party sends $f_i(s, x_1, ..., x_k, r)$ to the other players $i \in [k] \backslash A$ and stores $f_S(s, x_1, ..., x_k, r)$ in an internal state register (replacing s). Otherwise, he sends an **abort** message to those players.*

2.3   Pauli Filter

In our protocol, we use a technique which alters a channel that would act jointly on registers S and T, so that its actions on S are replaced by a flag bit into a separate register. The flag is set to 0 if the actions on S belong to some set $\mathcal{P}$, or to 1 otherwise. This way, the new channel "filters" the allowed actions on S.

Definition 2.2 (Pauli filter). *For registers S and T with $|T| > 0$, let U^{ST} be a unitary, and let $\mathcal{P} \subseteq \left(\{0,1\}^{\log |S|}\right)^2$ contain pairs of bit strings. The $\mathcal{P}$-filter of U on register S, denoted $\mathsf{PauliFilter}_{\mathcal{P}}^S(U)$, is the map $T \to TF$ (where F is some single-qubit flag register) that results from the following operations:*

1. *Initialize two separate registers S and S' in the state $|\Phi\rangle\langle\Phi|$, where $|\Phi\rangle := \left(\frac{1}{\sqrt{2}}(|00\rangle + |11\rangle)\right)^{\otimes \log |S|}$. Half of each pair is stored in S, the other in S'.*
2. *Run U on ST.*
3. *Measure SS' with the projective measurement $\{\Pi, \mathbb{I} - \Pi\}$ for*

$$\Pi := \sum_{(a,b) \in \mathcal{P}} \left(\mathsf{X}^a \mathsf{Z}^b\right)^S |\Phi\rangle\langle\Phi| \left(\mathsf{Z}^b \mathsf{X}^a\right).$$

If the outcome is Π, set the F register to $|0\rangle\langle 0|$. Otherwise, set it to $|1\rangle\langle 1|$.

The functionality of the Pauli filter becomes clear in the following lemma, which we prove in the full version by straightforward calculation:

Lemma 2.3. *For registers S and T with $|T| > 0$, let U^{ST} be a unitary, and let $\mathcal{P} \subseteq \left(\{0,1\}^{\log|S|}\right)^2$. Write $U = \sum_{x,z}(\mathsf{X}^x\mathsf{Z}^z)^S \otimes U_{x,z}^T$. Then $\mathsf{PauliFilter}_{\mathcal{P}}^S(U)$ equals the map*

$$(\cdot) \mapsto \sum_{(a,b)\in\mathcal{P}} U_{a,b}^T(\cdot)U_{a,b}^{\dagger} \otimes |0\rangle\langle 0|^F + \sum_{(a,b)\notin\mathcal{P}} U_{a,b}^T(\cdot)U_{a,b}^{\dagger} \otimes |1\rangle\langle 1|^F$$

A special case of the Pauli filter for $\mathcal{P} = \{(0^{\log|S|}, 0^{\log|S|})\}$ is due to Broadbent and Wainewright [BW16]. This choice of $\mathcal{P}$ represents only identity: the operation $\mathsf{PauliFilter}_{\mathcal{P}}$ filters out any components of U that do not act as identity on S. We will denote this type of filter with the name $\mathsf{IdFilter}$.

In this work, we will also use $\mathsf{XFilter}^S(U)$, which only accepts components of U that act trivially on register S in the computational basis. It is defined by choosing $\mathcal{P} = \{0^{\log|S|}\} \times \{0,1\}^{\log|S|}$.

Finally, we note that the functionality of the Pauli filter given in Definition 2.2 can be generalized, or weakened in a sense, by choosing a different state than $|\Phi\rangle\langle\Phi|$. In this work, we will use the $\mathsf{ZeroFilter}^S(U)$, which initializes SS' in the state $|00\rangle^{\log|S|}$, and measures using the projector $\Pi = |00\rangle\langle 00|$. It filters U by allowing only those Pauli operations that leave the computational-zero state (but not necessarily any other computational-basis states) unaltered:

$$(\cdot) \mapsto U_0^T(\cdot)U_0^{\dagger} \otimes |0\rangle\langle 0|^F + \sum_{a\neq 0} U_a^T(\cdot)U_a^{\dagger} \otimes |1\rangle\langle 1|^F,$$

where we abbreviate $U_a := \sum_b U_{a,b}$. Note that for $\mathsf{ZeroFilter}^S(U)$, the extra register S' can also be left out.

2.4   Clifford Authentication Code

The protocol presented in this paper will rely on quantum authentication. The players will encode their inputs using a quantum authentication code to prevent the other, potentially adversarial, players from making unauthorized alterations to their data. That way, they can ensure that the output of the computation is in the correct logical state.

A quantum authentication code transforms a quantum state (the *logical* state or *plaintext*) into a larger quantum state (the *physical* state or *ciphertext*) in a way that depends on a secret key. An adversarial party that has access to the ciphertext, but does not know the secret key, cannot alter the logical state without being detected at decoding time.

More formally, an authentication code consists of an encoding map $\mathsf{Enc}_k^{M \to MT}$ and a decoding map $\mathsf{Dec}_k^{MT \to M}$, for a secret key k, which we usually assume that the key is drawn uniformly at random from some key set $\mathcal{K}$. The message register M is expanded with an extra register T to accommodate for the fact that the ciphertext requires more space than the plaintext.

An authentication code is correct if $\mathsf{Dec}_k \circ \mathsf{Enc}_k = \mathbb{I}$. It is secure if the decoding map rejects (e.g., by replacing the output with a fixed reject symbol $\perp$) whenever an attacker tried to alter an encoded state:

Definition 2.4 (Security of authentication codes [DNS10]**).** *Let* $(\mathsf{Enc}_k^{M \to MT},$ $\mathsf{Dec}_k^{MT \to M})$ *be a quantum authentication scheme for k in a key set $\mathcal{K}$. The scheme is ε-secure if for all CPTP maps $\mathcal{A}^{MTR}$ acting on the ciphertext and a side-information register R, there exist CP maps Λ_{acc} and Λ_{rej} such that $\Lambda_{\mathsf{acc}} + \Lambda_{\mathsf{rej}}$ is trace-preserving, and for all ρ^{MR}:*

$$\left\| \mathbb{E}_{k \in \mathcal{K}} \left[\mathsf{Dec}_k \left(\mathcal{A} \left(\mathsf{Enc}_k (\rho) \right) \right) \right] - \left(\Lambda_{\mathsf{acc}}^R (\rho) + |\perp\rangle\langle\perp|^M \otimes \mathrm{Tr}_M \left[\Lambda_{\mathsf{rej}}^R (\rho) \right] \right) \right\|_1 \leqslant \varepsilon.$$

A fairly simple but powerful authentication code is the Clifford code:

Definition 2.5 (Clifford code [ABOE10]**).** *The n-qubit Clifford code is defined by a key set $\mathscr{C}_{n+1}$, and the encoding and decoding maps for a $C \in \mathscr{C}_{n+1}$:*

$$\mathsf{Enc}_C(\rho^M) := C(\rho^M \otimes |0^n\rangle\langle 0^n|^T)C^\dagger,$$

$$\mathsf{Dec}_C(\sigma^{MT}) := \langle 0^n|^T C^\dagger \sigma C |0^n\rangle + |\perp\rangle\langle\perp|^M \otimes \mathrm{Tr}_M \left[\sum_{x \neq 0^n} \langle x| C^\dagger \sigma C |x\rangle \right].$$

Note that, from the point of view of someone who does not know the Clifford key C, the encoding of the Clifford code looks like a Clifford twirl (see the full version) of the input state plus some trap states.

We prove the security of the Clifford code in the full version.

2.5 Universal Gate Sets

It is well known that if, in addition to Clifford gates, we are able to apply *any* non-Clifford gate G, then we are able to achieve universal quantum computation. In this work, we focus on the non-Clifford T gate (or $\pi/8$ gate).

In several contexts, however, applying non-Clifford gates is not straightforward for different reasons: common quantum error-correcting codes do not allow transversal implementation of non-Clifford gates, the non-Clifford gates do not commute with the quantum one-time pad and, more importantly in this work, neither with the Clifford encoding.

In order to concentrate the hardness of non-Clifford gates in an offline pre-processing phase, we can use techniques from computation by teleportation if we have so-called *magic states* of the form $|T\rangle := T|+\rangle$. Using a single copy of this state as a resource, we are able to implement a T gate using the circuit in Fig. 1. The circuit only requires (classically controlled) Clifford gates.

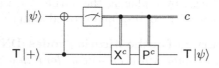

Fig. 1. Using a magic state $|T\rangle = T|+\rangle$ to implement a T gate.

The problem is how to create such magic states in a fault-tolerant way. Bravyi and Kitaev [BK05] proposed a distillation protocol that allows to create states that are δ-close to true magic states, given $\mathrm{poly}(\log(1/\delta))$ copies of *noisy* magic-states. Let $|T^\perp\rangle = T|-\rangle$. Then we have:

Theorem 2.6 (Magic-state distillation [BK05]). *There exists a circuit of CNOT-depth $d_{\mathrm{distill}}(n) \leqslant O(\log(n))$ consisting of $p_{\mathrm{distill}}(n) \leqslant \mathsf{poly}\,(n)$ many classically controlled Cliffords and computational-basis measurements such that for any $\varepsilon < \frac{1}{2}\left(1 - \sqrt{3/7}\right)$, if ρ is the output on the first wire using input*

$$\left((1-\varepsilon)\,|T\rangle\,\langle T| + \varepsilon\,|T^\perp\rangle\,\langle T^\perp|\right)^{\otimes n}, \tag{1}$$

then $1 - \langle T|\,\rho\,|T\rangle \leqslant O\left((5\varepsilon)^{n^c}\right)$, where $c = (\log_2 30)^{-1} \approx 0.2$.

As we will see in Sect. 6, our starting point is a bit different from the input state required by Theorem 2.6. We now present a procedure that will allow us to prepare the states necessary for applying Theorem 2.6 (see Circuit 2.8). We prove Lemma 2.7 in the full version.

Lemma 2.7. *Let $V_{LW} = \mathrm{span}\{P_\pi(|T\rangle^{\otimes m-w}\,|T^\perp\rangle^w) : w \leqslant \ell, \pi \in S_m\}$, and let Π_{LW} be the orthogonal projector onto V_{LW}. Let Ξ denote the CPTP map induced by Circuit 2.8. If ρ is an m-qubit state such that $\mathrm{Tr}(\Pi_{LW}\rho) \geqslant 1 - \varepsilon$, then*

$$\left\|\,\Xi(\rho) - (|T\rangle\,\langle T|)^{\otimes t}\,\right\|_1 \leqslant O\left(m\sqrt{t}\left(\frac{\ell}{m}\right)^{O((m/t)^c/2)} + \varepsilon\right),$$

for some constant $c > 0$.

Circuit 2.8 (Magic-state distillation). *Given an m-qubit input state and a parameter $t < m$:*

1. To each qubit, apply $\hat{Z} := PX$ with probability $\frac{1}{2}$.
2. Permute the qubits by a random $\pi \in S_m$.

> *3. Divide the m qubits into t blocks of size m/t, and apply magic-state distillation from Theorem 2.6 to each block.*

Remark 2.9. Circuit 2.8 can be implemented with (classically controlled) Clifford gates and measurements in the computational basis.

3 Multi-party Quantum Computation: Definitions

In this section, we describe the ideal functionality we aim to achieve for multi-party quantum computation (MPQC) with a dishonest majority. As noted in Sect. 2.2, we cannot hope to achieve fairness: therefore, we consider an ideal functionality with the option for the dishonest players to abort.

Definition 3.1 (Ideal quantum k-party computation with abort). *Let C be a quantum circuit on $W \in \mathbb{N}_{>0}$ wires. Consider a partition of the wires into the players' input registers plus an ancillary register, as $[W] = R_1^{\text{in}} \sqcup \cdots \sqcup R_k^{\text{in}} \sqcup R^{\text{ancilla}}$, and a partition into the players' output registers plus a register that is discarded at the end of the computation, as $[W] = R_1^{\text{out}} \sqcup \cdots \sqcup R_k^{\text{out}} \sqcup R^{\text{discard}}$. Let $I_A \subsetneq [k]$ be a set of corrupted players.*

1. *Every player $i \in [k]$ sends the content of R_i^{in} to the trusted third party.*
2. *The trusted third party populates R^{ancilla} with computational-zero states.*
3. *The trusted third party applies the quantum circuit C on the wires $[W]$.*
4. *For all $i \in I_A$, the trusted third party sends the content of R_i^{out} to player i.*
5. *All $i \in I_A$ respond with a bit b_i, which is 1 if they choose to abort, or 0 otherwise.*
6. *If $b_i = 0$ for all i, the trusted third party sends the content of R_i^{out} to the other players $i \in [k] \backslash I_A$. Otherwise, he sends an* `abort` *message to those players.*

In Definition 3.1, all corrupted players individually choose whether to abort the protocol (and thereby to prevent the honest players from receiving their respective outputs). In reality, however, one cannot prevent several corrupted players from actively working together and sharing all information they have among each other. To ensure that our protocol is also secure in those scenarios, we consider security against a general adversary that corrupts all players in I_A, by replacing their protocols by a single (interactive) algorithm $\mathcal{A}$ that receives the registers $R_{\mathcal{A}}^{\text{in}} := R \sqcup \bigsqcup_{i \in I_A} R_i^{\text{in}}$ as input, and after the protocol produces output in the register $R_{\mathcal{A}}^{\text{out}} := R \sqcup \bigsqcup_{i \in I_A} R_i^{\text{out}}$. Here, R is a side-information register in which the adversary may output extra information.

We will always consider protocols that fulfill the ideal functionality with respect to some gate set $\mathcal{G}$: the protocol should then mimic the ideal functionality only for circuits C that consist of gates from $\mathcal{G}$. This security is captured by the definition below.

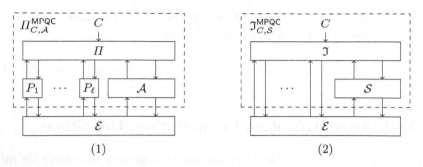

Fig. 2. (1) The environment interacting with the protocol as run by honest players $P_1, \ldots, P_\ell$, and an adversary who has corrupted the remaining players. (2) The environment interacting with a simulator running the ideal functionality.

Definition 3.2 (Computational security of quantum k-party computation with abort). *Let $\mathcal{G}$ be a set of quantum gates. Let Π^{MPQC} be a k-party quantum computation protocol, parameterized by a security parameter n. For any circuit C, set $I_{\mathcal{A}} \subsetneq [k]$ of corrupted players, and adversarial (interactive) algorithm $\mathcal{A}$ that performs all interactions of the players in $I_{\mathcal{A}}$, define $\Pi^{\mathsf{MPQC}}_{C,\mathcal{A}} : R^{\mathsf{in}}_{\mathcal{A}} \sqcup \bigsqcup_{i \notin I_{\mathcal{A}}} R^{\mathsf{in}}_i \to R^{\mathsf{out}}_{\mathcal{A}} \sqcup \bigsqcup_{i \notin I_{\mathcal{A}}} R^{\mathsf{out}}_i$ to be the channel that executes the protocol Π^{MPQC} for circuit C by executing the honest interactions of the players in $[k] \setminus I_{\mathcal{A}}$, and letting $\mathcal{A}$ fulfill the role of the players in $I_{\mathcal{A}}$ (See Fig. 2, (1)).*

For a simulator S that receives inputs in $R^{\mathsf{in}}_{\mathcal{A}}$, then interacts with the ideal functionalities on all interfaces for players in $I_{\mathcal{A}}$, and then produces output in $R^{\mathsf{out}}_{\mathcal{A}}$, let $\mathfrak{I}^{\mathsf{MPQC}}_{C,S}$ be the ideal functionality described in Definition 3.1, for circuit C, simulator S for players $i \in I_{\mathcal{A}}$, and honest executions (with $b_i = 0$) for players $i \notin I_{\mathcal{A}}$ (See Fig. 2, (2)). We say that Π^{MPQC} is a computationally ε-secure quantum k-party computation protocol with abort, *if for all $I_{\mathcal{A}} \subsetneq [k]$, for all quantum polynomial-time (QPT) adversaries $\mathcal{A}$, and all circuits C comprised of gates from $\mathcal{G}$, there exists a QPT simulator S such that for all QPT environments $\mathcal{E}$,*

$$\left| \Pr\left[1 \leftarrow (\mathcal{E} \leftrightarrows \Pi^{\mathsf{MPQC}}_{C,\mathcal{A}}) \right] - \Pr\left[1 \leftarrow (\mathcal{E} \leftrightarrows \mathfrak{I}^{\mathsf{MPQC}}_{C,S}) \right] \right| \leqslant \varepsilon.$$

Here, the notation $b \leftarrow (\mathcal{E} \leftrightarrows (\cdot))$ represents the environment $\mathcal{E}$, on input 1^n, interacting with the (real or ideal) functionality $(\cdot)$, and producing a single bit b as output.

Remark 3.3. In the above definition, we assume that all QPT parties are polynomial in the size of circuit $|C|$, and in the security parameter n.

We show in Sect. 6.2 the protocol Π^{MPQC} implementing the ideal functionality described in Definition 3.1, and we prove its security in Theorem 6.5.

4 Setup and Encoding

4.1 Input Encoding

In the first phase of the protocol, all players encode their input registers qubit-by-qubit. For simplicity of presentation, we pretend that player 1 holds a single-qubit input state, and the other players do not have input. In the actual protocol, multiple players can hold multiple-qubit inputs: in that case, the initialization is run several times in parallel, using independent randomness. Any other player i can trivially take on the role of player 1 by relabeling the player indices.

Definition 4.1 (Ideal functionality for input encoding). *Without loss of generality, let R_1^{in} be a single-qubit input register, and let $\dim(R_i^{\text{in}}) = 0$ for all $i \neq 1$. Let $I_A \subsetneq [k]$ be a set of corrupted players.*

1. *Player 1 sends register R_1^{in} to the trusted third party.*
2. *The trusted third party initializes a register T_1 with $|0^n\rangle\langle 0^n|$, applies a random $(n+1)$-qubit Clifford E to MT_1, and sends these registers to player 1.*
3. *All players $i \in I_A$ send a bit b_i to the trusted third party. If $b_i = 0$ for all i, then the trusted third party stores the key E in the state register S of the ideal functionality. Otherwise, it aborts by storing $\perp$ in S.*

The following protocol implements the ideal functionality. It uses, as a black box, an ideal functionality MPC that implements a classical multi-party computation with memory.

Protocol 4.2 *(Input encoding). Without loss of generality, let $M := R_1^{\text{in}}$ be a single-qubit input register, and let $\dim(R_i^{\text{in}}) = 0$ for all $i \neq 1$.*

1. *For every $i \in [k]$, MPC samples a random $(2n+1)$-qubit Clifford F_i and tells it to player i.*
2. *Player 1 applies the map $\rho^M \mapsto F_1 \left(\rho^M \otimes |0^{2n}\rangle\langle 0^{2n}|^{T_1 T_2} \right) F_1^\dagger$ for two n-qubit (trap) registers T_1 and T_2, and sends the registers MT_1T_2 to player 2.*
3. *Every player $i = 2, 3, ..., k$ applies F_i to MT_1T_2, and forwards it to player $i+1$. Eventually, player k sends the registers back to player 1.*
4. *MPC samples a random $(n+1)$-qubit Clifford E, random n-bit strings r and s, and a random classical invertible linear operator $g \in GL(2n, \mathbb{F}_2)$. Let U_g be the (Clifford) unitary that computes g in-place, i.e., $U_g |t\rangle = |g(t)\rangle$ for all $t \in \{0,1\}^{2n}$.*
5. *MPC gives[a]*

$$V := (E^{MT_1} \otimes (\mathsf{X}^r \mathsf{Z}^s)^{T_2})(\mathbb{I} \otimes (U_g)^{T_1 T_2})(F_k \cdots F_2 F_1)^\dagger$$

to player 1, who applies it to MT_1T_2.
6. *Player 1 measures T_2 in the computational basis, discarding the measured wires, and keeps the other $(n+1)$ qubits as its output in $R_1^{\text{out}} = MT_1$.*

7. *Player 1 submits the measurement outcome r' to* MPC, *who checks whether $r = r'$. If so,* MPC *stores the key E in its memory-state register S. If not, it aborts by storing $\perp$ in S.*

---

[a] As described in Sect. 2.1, the MPC gives V as a group element, and the adversary cannot decompose it into the different parts that appear in its definition.

If MPC aborts the protocol in step 7, the information about the Clifford encoding key E is erased. In that case, the registers MT_1 will be fully mixed. Note that this result differs slightly from the 'reject' outcome of a quantum authentication code as in Definition 2.4, where the message register M is replaced by a dummy state $|\perp\rangle\langle\perp|$. In our current setting, the register M is in the hands of (the possibly malicious) player 1. We therefore cannot enforce the replacement of register M with a dummy state: we can only make sure that all its information content is removed. Depending on the application or setting, the trusted MPC can of course broadcast the fact that they aborted to all players, including the honest one(s).

To run Protocol 4.2 in parallel for multiple input qubits held by multiple players, MPC samples a list of Cliffords $F_{i,q}$ for each player $i \in [k]$ and each qubit q. The $F_{i,q}$ operations can be applied in parallel for all qubits q: with k rounds of communication, all qubits will have completed their round past all players.

We will show that Protocol 4.2 fulfills the ideal functionality for input encoding:

Lemma 4.3. *Let Π^{Enc} be Protocol 4.2, and $\mathfrak{I}^{\mathsf{Enc}}$ be the ideal functionality described in Definition 4.1. For all sets $I_{\mathcal{A}} \subsetneq [k]$ of corrupted players and all adversaries $\mathcal{A}$ that perform the interactions of players in $I_{\mathcal{A}}$ with Π, there exists a simulator $\mathcal{S}$ (the complexity of which scales polynomially in that of the adversary) such that for all environments $\mathcal{E}$,*

$$| \Pr[1 \leftarrow (\mathcal{E} \leftrightarrows \Pi_{\mathcal{A}}^{\mathsf{Enc}})] - \Pr[1 \leftarrow (\mathcal{E} \leftrightarrows \mathfrak{I}_{\mathcal{S}}^{\mathsf{Enc}})]| \leqslant \mathsf{negl}\,(n)\,.$$

Note that the environment $\mathcal{E}$ also receives the state register S, which acts as the "output" register of the ideal functionality (in the simulated case) or of MPC (in the real case). It is important that the environment cannot distinguish between the output states even given that state register S, because we want to be able to compose Protocol 5.4 with other protocols that use the key information inside S. In other words, it is important that, unless the key is discarded, the states *inside* the Clifford encoding are also indistinguishable for the environment.

We provide just a sketch of the proof for Lemma 4.3, and refer to the full version for its full proof.

Proof (sketch). We divide our proof into two cases: when player 1 is honest, or when she is dishonest.

For the case when player 1 is honest, we know that she correctly prepares the expected state before the state is given to the other players. That is, she appends $2n$ ancilla qubits in state $|0\rangle$ and applies the random Clifford instructed by the classical MPC. When the encoded state is returned to player 1, she performs the Clifford V as instructed by the MPC. By the properties of the Clifford encoding, if the other players acted dishonestly, the tested traps will be non-zero with probability exponentially close to 1.

The second case is a bit more complicated: the first player has full control over the state and, more importantly, the traps that will be used in the first encoding. In particular, she could start with nonzero traps, which could possibly give some advantage to the dishonest players later on the execution of the protocol.

In order to prevent this type of attack, the MPC instructs the first player to apply a random linear function U_g on the traps, which is hidden from the players inside the Clifford V. If the traps were initially zero, their value does not change, but otherwise, they will be mapped to a random value, unknown by the dishonest parties. As such, the map U_g removes any advantage that the dishonest parties could have in step 7 by starting with non-zero traps. Because *any* nonzero trap state in $T_1 T_2$ is mapped to a random string, it suffices to measure only T_2 in order to be convinced that T_1 is also in the all-zero state (except with negligible probability). This intuition is formalized in the full version.

Other possible attacks are dealt with in a way that is similar to the case where player 1 is honest (but from the perspective of another honest player).

In the full proof (see the full version), we present two simulators, one for each case, that tests (using Pauli filters from Sect. 2.3) whether the adversary performs any such attacks during the protocol, and chooses the input to the ideal functionality accordingly. See Fig. 3 for a pictorial representation of the structure of the simulator for the case where player 1 is honest.

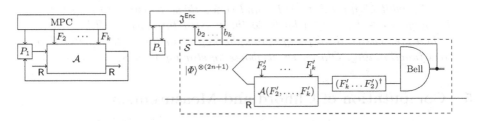

Fig. 3. On the left, the adversary's interaction with the protocol Π^{Enc}, $\Pi_{\mathcal{A}}^{\mathsf{Enc}}$ in case player 1 is the only honest player. On the right, the simulator's interaction with $\mathfrak{J}^{\mathsf{Enc}}$, $\mathfrak{J}_{\mathcal{S}}^{\mathsf{Enc}}$. It performs the Pauli filter $\mathsf{IdFilter}^{MT_1 T_2}$ on the adversary's attack on the encoded state.

4.2   Preparing Ancilla Qubits

Apart from encrypting the players' inputs, we also need a way to obtain encoded ancilla-zero states, which may be fed as additional input to the circuit. Since none of the players can be trusted to simply generate these states as part of their input, we need to treat them separately.

In [DNS12], Alice generates an encoding of $|0\rangle\langle 0|$, and Bob tests it by entangling (with the help of the classical MPC) the data qubit with a separate $|0\rangle\langle 0|$ qubit. Upon measuring that qubit, Bob then either detects a maliciously generated data qubit, or collapses it into the correct state. For details, see [DNS12, Appendix E].

Here, we take a similar approach, except with a public test on the shared traps. In order to guard against a player that may lie about the measurement outcomes during a test, we entangle the data qubits with *all* traps. We do so using a random linear operator, similarly to the encoding described in the previous subsection.

Essentially, the protocol for preparing ancilla qubits is identical to Protocol 4.2 for input encoding, except that now we do not only test whether the $2n$ traps are in the $|0\rangle\langle 0|$ state, but also the data qubit: concretely, the linear operator g acts on $2n + 1$ elements instead of $2n$. That is,

$$V := (E \otimes P)U_g(F_k \cdots F_2 F_1)^\dagger.$$

As a convention, Player 1 will always create the ancilla $|0\rangle\langle 0|$ states and encode them. In principle, the ancillas can be created by any other player, or by all players together.

Per the same proof as for Lemma 4.3, we have implemented the following ideal functionality, again making use of a classical MPC as a black box.

Definition 4.4 (Ideal functionality for encoding of $|0\rangle\langle 0|$). *Let $I_{\mathcal{A}} \subsetneq [k]$ be a set of corrupted players.*

1. *The trusted third party initializes a register T_1 with $|0^n\rangle\langle 0^n|$, applies a random $(n + 1)$-qubit Clifford E to MT_1, and sends these registers to player 1.*
2. *All players $i \in I_{\mathcal{A}}$ send a bit b_i to the trusted third party. If $b_i = 0$ for all i, then the trusted third party stores the key E in the state register S of the ideal functionality. Otherwise, it aborts by storing $\perp$ in S.*

5   Computation of Clifford and Measurement

After all players have successfully encoded their inputs and sufficiently many ancillary qubits, they perform a quantum computation gate-by-gate on their joint inputs. In this section, we will present a protocol for circuits that consist only of Clifford gates and computational-basis measurements. The Clifford gates may be classically controlled (for example, on the measurement outcomes that appear earlier in the circuit). In Sect. 6, we will discuss how to expand the protocol to general quantum circuits.

Concretely, we wish to achieve the functionality in Definition 3.1 for all circuits C that consist of Clifford gates and computational-basis measurements. As an intermediate step, we aim to achieve the following ideal functionality, where the players only receive an *encoded* output, for all such circuits:

Definition 5.1 (Ideal quantum k-party computation without decoding). *Let C be a quantum circuit on W wires. Consider a partition of the wires into the players' input registers plus an ancillary register, as $[W] = R_1^{in} \sqcup \cdots \sqcup R_k^{in} \sqcup R^{ancilla}$, and a partition into the players' output registers plus a register that is discarded at the end of the computation, as $[W] = R_1^{out} \sqcup \cdots \sqcup R_k^{out} \sqcup R^{discard}$. Let $I_A \subsetneq [k]$ be the set of corrupted players.*

1. *All players i send their register R_i^{in} to the trusted third party.*
2. *The trusted third party instantiates $R^{ancilla}$ with $|0\rangle\langle 0|$ states.*
3. *The trusted third party applies C to the wires $[W]$.*
4. *For every player i and every output wire $w \in R_i^{out}$, the trusted third party samples a random $(n+1)$-qubit Clifford E_w, applies $\rho \mapsto E_w(\rho \otimes |0^n\rangle\langle 0^n|)E_w^\dagger$ to w, and sends the result to player i.*
5. *All players $i \in I_A$ send a bit b_i to the trusted third party.*
   (a) *If $b_i = 0$ for all i, all keys E_w and all measurement outcomes are stored in the state register S.*
   (b) *Otherwise, the trusted third party **aborts** by storing $\perp$ in S.*

To achieve the ideal functionality, we define several subprotocols. The subprotocols for encoding the players' inputs and ancillary qubits have already been described in Sect. 4. It remains to describe the subprotocols for (classically-controlled) single-qubit Clifford gates (Sect. 5.1), (classically controlled) CNOT gates (Sect. 5.2), and computational-basis measurements (Sect. 5.3).

In Sect. 5.5, we show how to combine the subprotocols in order to compute any polynomial-sized Clifford+measurement circuit. Our approach is inductive in the number of gates in the circuit. The base case is the identity circuit, which is essentially covered in Sect. 4. In Sects. 5.1–5.3, we show that the ideal functionality for any circuit C, followed by the subprotocol for a gate G, results in the ideal functionality for the circuit $G \circ C$ (C followed by G). As such, we can chain together the subprotocols to realize the ideal functionality in Definition 5.1 for any polynomial-sized Clifford+measurement circuit. Combined with the decoding subprotocol we present in Sect. 5.4, such a chain of subprotocols satisfies Definition 3.1 for ideal k-party quantum Clifford+measurement computation with abort.

In Definition 5.1, all measurement outcomes are stored in the state register of the ideal functionality. We do so to ensure that the measurement results can be used as a classical control to gates that are applied after the circuit C, which can be technically required when building up to the ideal functionality for C inductively. Our protocols can easily be altered to broadcast measurement results as they happen, but the functionality presented in Definition 5.1 is the most general: if some player is supposed to learn a measurement outcome m_ℓ, then the circuit can contain a gate X^{m_ℓ} on an ancillary zero qubit that will be part of that player's output.

5.1   Subprotocol: Single-Qubit Cliffords

Due to the structure of the Clifford code, applying single-qubit Clifford is simple: the classical MPC, who keeps track of the encoding keys, can simply update the key so that it includes the single-qubit Clifford on the data register. We describe the case of a single-qubit Clifford that is classically controlled on a previous measurement outcome stored in the MPC's state. The unconditional case can be trivially obtained by omitting the conditioning.

> **Protocol 5.2 (Single-qubit Cliffords).** *Let G^{m_ℓ} be a single-qubit Clifford to be applied on a wire w (held by a player i), conditioned on a measurement outcome m_ℓ. Initially, player i holds an encoding of the state on that wire, and the classical MPC holds the encoding key E.*
>
> 1. *MPC reads result m_ℓ from its state register S, and updates its internally stored key E to $E((G^{m_\ell})^\dagger \otimes I^{\otimes n})$.*

If $m_\ell = 0$, nothing happens. To see that the protocol is correct for $m_\ell = 1$, consider what happens if the state $E(\rho \otimes |0^n\rangle\langle 0^n|)E^\dagger$ is decoded using the updated key: the decoded output is

$$(E(G^\dagger \otimes I^{\otimes n}))^\dagger E(\rho \otimes |0^n\rangle\langle 0^n|)E^\dagger(E(G^\dagger \otimes I^{\otimes n})) = G\rho G^\dagger \otimes |0^n\rangle\langle 0^n|.$$

Protocol 5.2 implements the ideal functionality securely: given an ideal implementation $\mathfrak{I}^C$ for some circuit C, we can implement $G^{m_\ell} \circ C$ (i.e., the circuit C followed by the gate G^{m_ℓ}) by performing Protocol 5.2 right after the interaction with $\mathfrak{I}^C$.

Lemma 5.3. *Let G^{m_ℓ} be a single-qubit Clifford to be applied on a wire w (held by a player i), conditioned on a measurement outcome m_ℓ. Let $\Pi^{G^{m_\ell}}$ be Protocol 5.2 for the gate G^{m_ℓ}, and $\mathfrak{I}^C$ be the ideal functionality for a circuit C as described in Definition 5.1. For all sets $I_A \subsetneq [k]$ of corrupted players and all adversaries A that perform the interactions of players in I_A, there exists a simulator S (the complexity of which scales polynomially in that of the adversary) such that for all environments $\mathcal{E}$,*

$$\Pr[1 \leftarrow (\mathcal{E} \leftrightarrows (\Pi^{G^{m_\ell}} \diamond \mathfrak{I}^C)_A)] = \Pr[1 \leftarrow (\mathcal{E} \leftrightarrows \mathfrak{I}_S^{G^{m_\ell} \circ C})].$$

Proof (sketch). In the protocol $\Pi^{G^{m_\ell}} \diamond \mathfrak{I}^C$, an adversary has two opportunities to attack: once before its input state is submitted to $\mathfrak{I}^C$, and once afterwards. We define a simulator that applies these same attacks, except that it interacts with the ideal functionality $\mathfrak{I}^{G^{m_\ell} \circ C}$.

Syntactically, the state register S of $\mathfrak{I}^C$ is provided as input to the MPC in $\Pi^{G^{m_\ell}}$, so that the MPC can update the key as described by the protocol. As such, the output state of the adversary and the simulator are exactly equal. We provide a full proof in in the full version.

5.2 Subprotocol: CNOT Gates

The application of two-qubit Clifford gates (such as CNOT) is more complicated than the single-qubit case, for two reasons.

First, a CNOT is a *joint* operation on two states that are encrypted with *separate* keys. If we were to classically update two keys E_1 and E_2 in a similar fashion as in Protocol 5.2, we would end up with a new key $(E_1 \otimes E_2)(\text{CNOT}_{1,n+2})$, which cannot be written as a product of two separate keys. The keys would become 'entangled', which is undesirable for the rest of the computation.

Second, the input qubits might belong to separate players, who may not trust the authenticity of each other's qubits. In [DNS12], authenticity of the output state is guaranteed by having both players test each state several times. In a multi-party setting, both players involved in the CNOT are potentially dishonest, so it might seem necessary to involve all players in this extensive testing. However, because all our tests are publicly verified, our protocol requires less testing. Still, interaction with all other players is necessary to apply a fresh 'joint' Clifford on the two ciphertexts.

Protocol 5.4 (CNOT). *This protocol applies a CNOT gate to wires w_i (control) and w_j (target), conditioned on a measurement outcome m_ℓ. Suppose that player i holds an encoding of the first wire, in register $M^i T_1^i$, and player j of the second wire, in register $M^j T_1^j$. The classical MPC holds the encoding keys E_i and E_j.*

1. *If $i \neq j$, player j sends their registers $M^j T_1^j$ to player i. Player i now holds a $(2n + 2)$-qubit state.*
2. *Player i initializes the registers T_2^i and T_2^j both in the state $|0^n\rangle\langle 0^n|$.*
3. *For all players h, MPC samples random $(4n + 2)$-qubit Cliffords D_h, and gives them to the respective players. Starting with player i, each player h applies D_h to $M^{ij} T_{12}^{ij}$,[a] and sends the state to player $h + 1$. Eventually, player i receives the state back from player $i - 1$. MPC remembers the applied Clifford*

$$D := D_{i-1} D_{i-2} \cdots D_1 D_k D_{k-1} \cdots D_i.$$

4. *MPC samples random $(2n + 1)$-qubit Cliffords F_i and F_j, and tells player i to apply*

$$V := (F_i \otimes F_j)\text{CNOT}_{1,2n+2}^{m_i}(E_i^\dagger \otimes I^{\otimes n} \otimes E_j^\dagger \otimes I^{\otimes n})D^\dagger.$$

Here, the CNOT acts on the two data qubits inside the encodings.

5. *If $i \neq j$, player i sends $M^j T_{12}^j$ to player j.*
6. *Players i and j publicly test their encodings. The procedures are identical, we describe the steps for player i:*
   (a) *MPC samples a random $(n + 1)$-qubit Clifford E_i', which will be the new encoding key. Furthermore, MPC samples random n-bit strings s_i and r_i, and a random classical invertible linear operator g_i on $\mathbb{F}_2^{2n}$.*

(b) MPC *tells player i to apply*

$$W_i := (E'_i \otimes (\mathsf{X}^{r_i}\mathsf{Z}^{s_i})^{T_2^i})U_{g_i}^{T_{12}^i}F_i^\dagger.$$

Here, U_{g_i} is as defined in Protocol 4.2.

(c) Player i measures T_2^i in the computational basis and reports the n-bit measurement outcome r'_i to the MPC.

(d) MPC *checks whether $r'_i = r_i$. If it is not,* MPC *sends* abort *to all players. If it is, the test has passed, and* MPC *stores the new encoding key E'_i in its internal memory.*

---

^{a} We combine subscripts and superscripts to denote multiple registers: e.g., T_{12}^{ij} is shorthand for $T_1^i T_2^i T_1^j T_2^j$.

Lemma 5.5. *Let $\Pi^{\mathsf{CNOT}^{m_\ell}}$ be Protocol 5.4, to be executed on wires w_i and w_j, held by players i and j, respectively. Let $\mathfrak{I}^C$ be the ideal functionality for a circuit C as described in Definition 5.1. For all sets $I_A \subsetneq [k]$ of corrupted players and all adversaries A that perform the interactions of players in I_A, there exists a simulator S (the complexity of which scales polynomially in that of the adversary) such that for all environments $\mathcal{E}$,*

$$\left| \Pr[1 \leftarrow (\mathcal{E} \leftrightarrows (\Pi^{\mathsf{CNOT}^{m_\ell}} \diamond \mathfrak{I}^C)_A)] = \Pr[1 \leftarrow (\mathcal{E} \leftrightarrows \mathfrak{I}_S^{\mathsf{CNOT}^{m_\ell} \circ C})] \right| \leqslant \mathsf{negl}\,(n)\,.$$

Proof (sketch). There are four different cases, depending on which of players i and j are dishonest. In the full version, we provide a full proof by detailing the simulators for all four cases, but in this sketch, we only provide an intuition for the security in the case where both players are dishonest.

It is crucial that the adversary does not learn any information about the keys (E_i, E_j, E'_i, E'_j), nor about the randomizing elements $(r_i, r_j, s_i, s_j, g_i, g_j)$. Even though the adversary learns W_i, W_j, and V explicitly during the protocol, all the secret information remains hidden by the randomizing Cliffords F_i, F_j, and D.

We consider a few ways in which the adversary may attack. First, he may prepare a non-zero state in the registers T_2^i (or T_2^j) in step 2, potentially intending to spread those errors into $M^i T_1^i$ (or $M^j T_1^j$). Doing so, however, will cause U_{g_i} (or U_{g_j}) to map the trap state to a random non-zero string, and the adversary would not know what measurement string r'_i (or r'_j) to report. Since g_i is unknown to the adversary, it suffices to measure T_2^i in order to detect any errors in T_{12}^i.

Second, the adversary may fail to execute its instructions V or $W_i \otimes W_j$ correctly. Doing so is equivalent to attacking the state right before or right after these instructions. In both cases, however, the state in $M^i T_1^i$ is Clifford-encoded (and the state in T_2^i is Pauli-encoded) with keys unknown to the adversary, so the authentication property of the Clifford code prevents the adversary from altering the outcome.

The simulator we define in the full version tests the adversary exactly for the types of attacks above. By using Pauli filters (see Definition 2.2), the simulator checks whether the attacker leaves the authenticated states and the trap states T_2^i and T_2^j (both at initialization and before measurement) unaltered. In the full proof, we show that the output state of the simulator approximates, up to an error negligible in n, the output state of the real protocol.

5.3   Subprotocol: Measurement

Measurement of authenticated states introduces a new conceptual challenge. For a random key E, the result of measuring $E(\rho \otimes |0^n\rangle\langle 0^n|)E^\dagger$ in a fixed basis is in no way correlated with the logical measurement outcome of the state ρ. However, the measuring player is also not allowed to learn the key E, so they cannot perform a measurement in a basis that depends meaningfully on E.

In [DNS10, Appendix E], this challenge is solved by entangling the state with an ancilla-zero state on a logical level. After this entanglement step, Alice gets the original state while Bob gets the ancilla state. They both decode their state (learning the key from the MPC), and can measure it. Because those states are entangled, and at least one of Alice and Bob is honest, they can ensure that the measurement outcome was not altered, simply by checking that they both obtained the same outcome. The same strategy can in principle also be scaled up to k players, by making all k players hold part of a big (logically) entangled state. However, doing so requires the application of $k-1$ logical CNOT operations, making it a relatively expensive procedure.

We take a different approach in our protocol. The player that performs the measurement essentially entangles, with the help of the MPC, the data qubit with a random subset of the traps. The MPC later checks the consistency of the outcomes: all entangled qubits should yield the same measurement result.

Our alternative approach has the additional benefit that the measurement outcome can be kept secret from some or all of the players. In the description of the protocol below, the MPC stores the measurement outcome in its internal state. This allows the MPC to classically control future gates on the outcome. If it is desired to instead reveal the outcome to one or more of the players, this can easily be done by performing a classically-controlled X operation on some unused output qubit of those players.

Protocol 5.6 (Computational-basis measurement). *Player i holds an encoding of the state in a wire w in the register MT_1. The classical MPC holds the encoding key E in the register S.*

1. *MPC samples random strings $r, s \in \{0,1\}^{n+1}$ and $c \in \{0,1\}^n$.*
2. *MPC tells player i to apply*

$$V := \mathsf{X}^r \mathsf{Z}^s \mathsf{CNOT}_{1,c} E^\dagger$$

to the register MT_1, where $\mathsf{CNOT}_{1,c}$ denotes the unitary $\prod_{i \in [n]} \mathsf{CNOT}_{1,i}^{c_i}$ (that is, the string c dictates with which of the qubits in T_1 the M register will be entangled).

3. *Player i measures the register MT_1 in the computational basis, reporting the result r' to MPC.*
4. *MPC checks whether $r' = r \oplus (m, m \cdot c)$ for some $m \in \{0,1\}$.[a] If so, it stores the measurement outcome m in the state register S. Otherwise, it aborts by storing $\perp$ in S.*
5. *MPC removes the key E from the state register S.*

---

[a] The $\cdot$ symbol represents scalar multiplication of the bit m with the string c.

Lemma 5.7. *Let C be a circuit on W wires that leaves some wire $w \leqslant W$ unmeasured. Let $\mathfrak{I}^C$ be the ideal functionality for C, as described in Definition 5.1, and let $\Pi^{\swarrow}$ be Protocol 5.6 for a computational-basis measurement on w. For all sets $I_A \subsetneq [k]$ of corrupted players and all adversaries A that perform the interactions of players in I_A, there exists a simulator S (the complexity of which scales polynomially in that of the adversary) such that for all environments $\mathcal{E}$,*

$$\left| \Pr[1 \leftarrow (\mathcal{E} \leftrightarrows (\Pi^{\swarrow} \diamond \mathfrak{I}^C)_A)] - \Pr[1 \leftarrow (\mathcal{E} \leftrightarrows \mathfrak{I}_S^{\swarrow \circ C})] \right| \leqslant \mathsf{negl}\,(n)\,.$$

Proof (sketch). The operation $\mathsf{CNOT}_{1,c}$ entangles the data qubit in register M with a random subset of the trap qubits in register T_1, as dictated by c. In step 4 of Protocol 5.6, the MPC checks both for consistency of all the bits entangled by c (they have to match the measured data) *and* all the bits that are not entangled by c (they have to remain zero).

In the full version, we show that checking the consistency of a measurement outcome after the application of $\mathsf{CNOT}_{1,c}$ is as good as measuring the logical state: any attacker that does not know c will have a hard time influencing the measurement outcome, as he will have to flip all qubits in positions i for which $c_i = 1$ without accidentally flipping any of the qubits in positions i for which $c_i = 0$. See the full version for a full proof that the output state in the real and simulated case are negligibly close.

5.4   Subprotocol: Decoding

After the players run the computation subprotocols for all gates in the Clifford circuit, all they need to do is to decode their wires to recover their output. At this point, there is no need to check the authentication traps publicly: there is nothing to gain for a dishonest player by incorrectly measuring or lying about their measurement outcome. Hence, it is sufficient for all (honest) players to apply the regular decoding procedure for the Clifford code.

Below, we describe the decoding procedure for a single wire held by one of the players. If there are multiple output wires, then Protocol 5.8 can be run in parallel for all those wires.

Protocol 5.8 (Decoding). *Player i holds an encoding of the state w in the register MT_1. The classical MPC holds the encoding key E in the state register S.*

1. MPC *sends E to player i, removing it from the state register S.*
2. *Player i applies E to register* MT_1.
3. *Player i measures* T_1 *in the computational basis. If the outcome is not* 0^n, *player i discards M and aborts the protocol.*

Lemma 5.9. *Let C be a circuit on W wires that leaves a single wire* $w \leqslant W$ *(intended for player i) unmeasured. Let* $\mathcal{J}^C$ *be the ideal functionality for C, as described in Definition 5.1, and let* $\mathcal{J}_C^{\mathsf{MPQC}}$ *be the ideal MPQC functionality for C, as described in Definition 3.1. Let* Π^{Dec} *be Protocol 5.8 for decoding wire w. For all sets* $I_A \subsetneq [k]$ *of corrupted players and all adversaries A that perform the interactions of players in* I_A, *there exists a simulator S (the complexity of which scales polynomially in that of the adversary) such that for all environments* $\mathcal{E}$,

$$\Pr[1 \leftarrow (\mathcal{E} \leftrightarrows (\Pi^{\mathsf{Dec}} \diamond \mathcal{J}^C)_A)] = \Pr[1 \leftarrow (\mathcal{E} \leftrightarrows \mathcal{J}_{C,S}^{\mathsf{MPQC}})].$$

Proof (sketch). If player i is honest, then he correctly decodes the state received from the ideal functionality $\mathcal{J}^C$. A simulator would only have to compute the adversary's abort bit for $\mathcal{J}_C^{\mathsf{MPQC}}$ based on whether the adversary decides to abort in either $\mathcal{J}^C$ or the MPC computation in Π^{Dec}.

If player i is dishonest, a simulator S runs the adversary on the input state received from the environment before inputting the resulting state into the ideal functionality $\mathcal{J}_C^{\mathsf{MPQC}}$. The simulator then samples a key for the Clifford code and encodes the output of $\mathcal{J}_C^{\mathsf{MPQC}}$, before handing it back to the adversary. It then simulates Π^{Dec} by handing the sampled key to the adversary. If the adversary aborts in one of the two simulated protocols, then the simulator sends abort to the ideal functionality $\mathcal{J}_C^{\mathsf{MPQC}}$.

5.5 Combining Subprotocols

We show in this section how to combine the subprotocols of the previous sections in order to perform multi-party quantum Clifford computation.

Recalling the notation defined in Definition 3.1, let C be a quantum circuit on $W \in \mathbb{N}_{>0}$ wires, which are partitioned into the players' input registers plus an ancillary register, as $[W] = R_1^{\mathsf{in}} \sqcup \cdots \sqcup R_k^{\mathsf{in}} \sqcup R^{\mathsf{ancilla}}$, and a partition into the players' output registers plus a register that is discarded at the end of the computation, as $[W] = R_1^{\mathsf{out}} \sqcup \cdots \sqcup R_k^{\mathsf{out}} \sqcup R^{\mathsf{discard}}$. We assume that C is decomposed in a sequence $G_1, ..., G_m$ of operations where each G_i is one of the following operations:

- a single-qubit Clifford on some wire $j \in [M]$;
- a CNOT on wires $j_1, j_2 \in [M]$ for $j_1 \neq j_2$;
- a measurement of the qubit on wire j in the computational basis.

In Sects. 4 and 5.1–5.3, we have presented subprotocols for encoding single qubits and perform these types of operations on single wires. The protocol for all players to jointly perform the bigger computation C is simply a concatenation of those smaller subprotocols:

Protocol 5.10 (Encoding and Clifford+measurement computation). *Let C be a Clifford+measurement circuit composed of the gates $G_1, \ldots, G_m$ on wires $[W]$ as described above.*

1. *For all $i \in [k]$ and $j \in R_i^{\mathsf{in}}$, run Protocol 4.2 for the qubit in wire j.*
2. *For all $j \in R^{\mathsf{ancilla}}$, run Protocol 4.2 (with the differences described in Sect. 4.2).*
3. *For all $j \in [m]$:*
   (a) If G_j is a single-qubit Clifford, run Protocol 5.2 for G_j.
   (b) If G_j is a CNOT, run Protocol 5.4 for G_j.
   (c) If G_j is a computational-basis measurement, run Protocol 5.6 for G_j.
4. *For all $i \in [k]$ and $j \in R_i^{\mathsf{out}}$, run Protocol 5.8 for the qubit in wire j.*

Lemma 5.11. *Let Π^{Cliff} be Protocol 5.10, and $\mathfrak{I}^{\mathsf{Cliff}}$ be the ideal functionality described in Definition 3.1 for the special case where the circuit consists of (a polynomial number of) Cliffords and measurements. For all sets $I_A \subsetneq [k]$ of corrupted players and all adversaries $\mathcal{A}$ that perform the interactions of players in I_A with Π, there exists a simulator $\mathcal{S}$ (the complexity of which scales polynomially in that of the adversary) such that for all environments $\mathcal{E}$,*

$$|\Pr[1 \leftarrow (\mathcal{E} \leftrightarrows \Pi_{\mathcal{A}}^{\mathsf{Cliff}})] - \Pr[1 \leftarrow (\mathcal{E} \leftrightarrows \mathfrak{I}_{\mathcal{S}}^{\mathsf{Cliff}})]| \leqslant \mathsf{negl}\,(n)\,.$$

Proof. The proof by induction on m is given in the full version.

6   Protocol: MPQC for General Quantum Circuits

In this section, we show how to lift the MPQC for Clifford operations (as laid out in Sects. 4 and 5) to MPQC for general quantum circuits.

The main idea is to use magic states for T gates, as described in Sect. 2.5. Our main difficulty here is that the magic states must be supplied by the possibly dishonest players themselves. We solve this problem in Sect. 6.1 and then in Sect. 6.2, we describe the MPQC protocol for universal computation combining the results from Sects. 5 and 6.1.

6.1   Magic-State Distillation

We now describe a subprotocol that allows the players to create the encoding of exponentially good magic states, if the players do not abort.

Our subprotocol can be divided into two parts. In the first part, player 1 is asked to create many magic states, which the other players will test. After this step, if none of the players abort during the testing, then with high probability the resource states created by player 1 are at least somewhat good. In the second part of the subprotocol, the players run a distillation procedure to further increase the quality of the magic states.

Protocol 6.1 (Magic-state creation). *Let t be the number of magic states we wish to create. Let $\ell := (t+k)n$.*

1. *Player 1 creates ℓ copies of $|T\rangle$ and encodes them separately using Protocol 4.2 (jointly with the other players).*
2. *MPC picks random disjoint sets $S_2, \ldots, S_k \subseteq [\ell]$ of size n each.*
3. *For each $i \in 2, \ldots, k$, player i decodes the magic states indicated by S_i (see Protocol 5.8), measures in the $\{|T\rangle, |T^\perp\rangle\}$-basis and aborts if any outcome is different from $|T\rangle$.*
4. *On the remaining encoded states, the players run Protocol 5.10 for multi-party computation of Clifford circuits (but skipping the input-encoding step) to perform the magic-state distillation protocol described in Protocol 2.8. Any randomness required in that protocol is sampled by the classical MPC.*

We claim that Protocol 6.1 implements the following ideal functionality for creating t magic states, up to a negligible error:

Definition 6.2 (Ideal functionality for magic-state creation). *Let t be the number of magic states we wish to create. Let $I_A \subsetneq [k]$ be a set of corrupted players.*

1. *For every $i \in I_A$, player i sends a bit b_i to the trusted third party.*
   (a) If $b_i = 0$ for all i, the trusted third party samples t random $(n+1)$-qubit Clifford E_j for $1 \leqslant j \leqslant t$, and sends $E_j(|T\rangle \otimes |0^n\rangle)$ to Player 1.
   *(b) Otherwise, the trusted third party sends **abort** to all players.*
2. *Store the keys E_j, for $1 \leqslant j \leqslant t$ in the state register S of the ideal functionality.*

Lemma 6.3. *Let Π^{MS} be Protocol 6.1, and $\mathfrak{I}^{MS}$ be the ideal functionality described in Definition 6.2. For all sets $I_A \subsetneq [k]$ of corrupted players and all adversaries A that perform the interactions of players in I_A with Π, there exists a simulator S (the complexity of which scales polynomially in that of the adversary) such that for all environments $\mathcal{E}$,*

$$\left| \Pr[1 \leftarrow (\mathcal{E} \leftrightarrows \Pi_A^{MS})] - \Pr[1 \leftarrow (\mathcal{E} \leftrightarrows \mathfrak{I}_S^{MS})] \right| \leqslant \mathsf{negl}\,(n).$$

We prove this lemma in the full version.

6.2   MPQC Protocol for Universal Quantum Computation

Finally, we present our protocol for some arbitrary quantum computation. For this setting, we extend the setup of Sect. 5.5 by considering quantum circuits $C = G_m...G_1$ where G_i can be single-qubit Cliffords, CNOTs, measurements or, additionally, T gates.

For that, we will consider a circuit C' where each gate $G_i = T$ acting on qubit j is then replaced by the T-gadget presented in Fig. 1, acting on the qubit j and a fresh new T magic state.

Protocol 6.4 (Protocol for universal MPQC). *Let C be a polynomial-sized quantum circuit, and t be the number of* T*-gates in C.*

1. *Run Protocol 6.1 to create t magic states.*
2. *Run Protocol 5.10 for the circuit C', which is equal to the circuit C, except each* T *gate is replaced with the* T*-gadget from Fig. 1.*

Theorem 6.5. *Let* Π^{MPQC} *be Protocol 6.4, and* $\mathfrak{I}^{\mathsf{MPQC}}$ *be the ideal functionality described in Definition 3.1. For all sets* $I_A \subsetneq [k]$ *of corrupted players and all adversaries* A *that perform the interactions of players in* I_A *with* Π*, there exists a simulator* S *(the complexity of which scales polynomially in that of the adversary) such that for all environments* $\mathcal{E}$*,*

$$| \Pr[1 \leftarrow (\mathcal{E} \leftrightarrows \Pi_A^{\mathsf{MPQC}})] - \Pr[1 \leftarrow (\mathcal{E} \leftrightarrows \mathfrak{I}_S^{\mathsf{MPQC}})]| \leqslant \mathsf{negl}\,(n)\,.$$

Proof. Direct from Lemmas 5.11 and 6.3.

6.3 Round Complexity and MPC Calls

Recall that we are assuming access to an ideal (classical) MPC functionality defined in Definition 2.1. One MPC call can produce outputs to all players simultaneously. In this section, we analyze the number of rounds of quantum communication, and the number of calls to the classical MPC. The actual implementation of the classical MPC is likely to result in additional rounds of classical communication.

In the way we describe it, Lemma 4.2 encodes a single-qubit input (or an ancilla $|0\rangle$ state) using k rounds of quantum communication and $O(1)$ MPC calls. Note that this protocol can be run in parallel for all input qubits per player, simultaneously for all players. Hence, the overall number of communication rounds for the encoding phase remains k, and the total number of calls to the MPC is $O(w)$ where w is the total number of qubits.

Lemma 5.2 for single-qubit Cliffords, Lemma 5.6 for measuring in the computational basis and Lemma 5.8 for decoding do not require quantum communication and use $O(1)$ MPC calls each, whereas Lemma 5.4 for CNOT requires at most $k+2$ rounds of quantum communication, and makes $O(1)$ MPC calls. Overall, Lemma 5.10 for encoding and Clifford+measurement computation require $O(dk)$ rounds of quantum communication and $O(w+g)$ calls to the MPC, where d is the CNOT-depth of the quantum circuit, and g is the total number of gates in the circuit.

Lemma 6.1 for magic-state creation encodes $\ell := (t + k)n$ qubits in parallel using k rounds of quantum communication (which can be done in parallel with the actual input encoding) and $O((t + k)n)$ MPC calls. Then a circuit of size $p_{\text{distill}}(n)$ and CNOT-depth $d_{\text{distill}}(n)$ classically controlled Cliffords and measurements is run on each of the t blocks of n qubits each, which can be done in parallel for the t blocks, requiring $O(k \cdot d_{\text{distill}}(n))$ rounds of quantum communication and $O(tn \cdot p_{\text{distill}}(n))$ calls to the MPC.

Eventually, all T-gate operations in the original circuit C are replaced by the T-gadget from Fig. 1, resulting in one CNOT and classically controlled Cliffords. Overall, our Lemma 6.4 for universal MPQC requires $O(k \cdot (d_{\text{distill}}(n)+d))$ rounds of quantum communication and $O(tn \cdot p_{\text{distill}}(n) + w + g)$ calls to the classical MPC, where d is the $\{\text{CNOT}, \text{T}\}$-depth of the circuit, w is the total number of qubits and g is the total number of gates in the circuit.

We notice that instead of evaluating each Clifford operation gate-by-gate, we could evaluate a general w-qubit Clifford using $O(k)$ rounds of quantum communication, similarly to the CNOT protocol. This could improve the parameter d to be the T depth of the circuit, at the cost of requiring significantly more communication per round.

Acknowledgments. We thank Frédéric Dupuis, Florian Speelman, and Serge Fehr for useful discussions, and the anonymous EUROCRYPT referees for helpful comments and suggestions. CM is supported by an NWO Veni Innovational Research Grant under project number VI.Veni.192.159. SJ is supported by an NWO WISE Fellowship, an NWO Veni Innovational Research Grant under project number 639.021.752, and QuantERA project QuantAlgo 680-91-03. SJ is a CIFAR Fellow in the Quantum Information Science Program. CS and CM were supported by a NWO VIDI grant (Project No. 639.022.519). Part of this work was done while YD, AG and CS were visiting the Simons Institute for the Theory of Computing.

References

[ABOE10] Aharonov, D., Ben-Or, M., Eban, E.: Interactive proofs for quantum computations. In: ICS 2010 (2010)

[DDOZ11] Bendlin, R., Damgård, I., Orlandi, C., Zakarias, S.: Semi-homomorphic encryption and multiparty computation. In: Paterson, K.G. (ed.) EURO-CRYPT 2011. LNCS, vol. 6632, pp. 169–188. Springer, Heidelberg (2011). https://doi.org/10.1007/978-3-642-20465-4_11

[BK05] Bravyi, S., Kitaev, A.: Universal quantum computation with ideal Clifford gates and noisy ancillas. Phys. Rev. A **71**, 022316 (2005)

[BOCG+06] Ben-Or, M., Crépeau, C., Gottesman, D., Hassidim, A., Smith, A.: Secure multiparty quantum computation with (only) a strict honest majority. In: FOCS 2006 (2006)

[BW16] Broadbent, A., Wainewright, E.: Efficient simulation for quantum message authentication. In: Nascimento, A.C.A., Barreto, P. (eds.) ICITS 2016. LNCS, vol. 10015, pp. 72–91. Springer, Cham (2016). https://doi.org/10.1007/978-3-319-49175-2_4

[CDE+18] Cramer, R., Damgård, I., Escudero, D., Scholl, P., Xing, C.: SPDZ$_{2^k}$: efficient MPC mod 2^k for dishonest majority. In: Shacham, H., Boldyreva, A. (eds.) CRYPTO 2018. LNCS, vol. 10992, pp. 769–798. Springer, Cham (2018). https://doi.org/10.1007/978-3-319-96881-0_26

[CDG+17] Chase, M., et al.: Post-quantum zero-knowledge and signatures from symmetric-key primitives. In: CCS 2017 (2017)

[CDN15] Cramer, R., Damgård, I., Nielsen, J.B.: Secure Multiparty Computation and Secret Sharing. Cambridge University Press, Cambridge (2015)

[CGS02] Crépeau, C., Gottesman, D., Smith, A.: Secure multi-party quantum computation. In: STOC 2002 (2002)

[DNS10] Dupuis, F., Nielsen, J.B., Salvail, L.: Secure two-party quantum evaluation of unitaries against specious adversaries. In: Rabin, T. (ed.) CRYPTO 2010. LNCS, vol. 6223, pp. 685–706. Springer, Heidelberg (2010). https://doi.org/10.1007/978-3-642-14623-7_37

[DNS12] Dupuis, F., Nielsen, J.B., Salvail, L.: Actively secure two-party evaluation of any quantum operation. In: Safavi-Naini, R., Canetti, R. (eds.) CRYPTO 2012. LNCS, vol. 7417, pp. 794–811. Springer, Heidelberg (2012). https://doi.org/10.1007/978-3-642-32009-5_46

[DPSZ12] Damgård, I., Pastro, V., Smart, N., Zakarias, S.: Multiparty computation from somewhat homomorphic encryption. In: Safavi-Naini, R., Canetti, R. (eds.) CRYPTO 2012. LNCS, vol. 7417, pp. 643–662. Springer, Heidelberg (2012). https://doi.org/10.1007/978-3-642-32009-5_38

[IKOS09] Ishai, Y., Kushilevitz, E., Ostrovsky, R., Sahai, A.: Zero-knowledge proofs from secure multiparty computation. SIAM J. Comput. **39**(3), 1121–1152 (2009)

[KMW17] Kashefi, E., Music, L., Wallden, P.: The quantum cut-and-choose technique and quantum two-party computation. arXiv preprint arXiv:1703.03754 (2017)

[KOS16] Keller, M., Orsini, E., Scholl, P.: MASCOT: faster malicious arithmetic secure computation with oblivious transfer. In: CCS 2016 (2016)

[KP17] Kashefi, E., Pappa, A.: Multiparty delegated quantum computing. Cryptography **1**(2), 12 (2017)

[KPR18] Keller, M., Pastro, V., Rotaru, D.: Overdrive: making SPDZ great again. In: Nielsen, J.B., Rijmen, V. (eds.) EUROCRYPT 2018. LNCS, vol. 10822, pp. 158–189. Springer, Cham (2018). https://doi.org/10.1007/978-3-319-78372-7_6

[Yao82] Yao, A.C.-C.: Protocols for secure computations (extended abstract). In: FOCS 1982 (1982)

Efficient Simulation of Random States
and Random Unitaries

Gorjan Alagic[1,2]([⊠]), Christian Majenz[3,4]([⊠]), and Alexander Russell[5]

[1] QuICS, University of Maryland, College Park, MD, USA
galagic@gmail.com
[2] NIST, Gaithersburg, MD, USA
[3] QuSoft, Amsterdam, The Netherlands
[4] Centrum Wiskunde & Informatica, Amsterdam, The Netherlands
christian.majenz@cwi.nl
[5] Department of Computer Science and Engineering,
University of Connecticut, Storrs, CT, USA
acr@cse.uconn.edu

Abstract. We consider the problem of efficiently simulating random quantum states and random unitary operators, in a manner which is convincing to unbounded adversaries with black-box oracle access.

This problem has previously only been considered for restricted adversaries. Against adversaries with an a priori bound on the number of queries, it is well-known that t-designs suffice. Against polynomial-time adversaries, one can use pseudorandom states (PRS) and pseudorandom unitaries (PRU), as defined in a recent work of Ji, Liu, and Song; unfortunately, no provably secure construction is known for PRUs.

In our setting, we are concerned with unbounded adversaries. Nonetheless, we are able to give stateful quantum algorithms which simulate the ideal object in both settings of interest. In the case of Haar-random states, our simulator is polynomial-time, has negligible error, and can also simulate verification and reflection through the simulated state. This yields an immediate application to quantum money: a money scheme which is information-theoretically unforgeable and untraceable. In the case of Haar-random unitaries, our simulator takes polynomial space, but simulates both forward and inverse access with zero error.

These results can be seen as the first significant steps in developing a theory of lazy sampling for random quantum objects.

1 Introduction

1.1 Motivation

Efficient simulation of randomness is a task with countless applications, ranging from cryptography to derandomization. In the setting of classical probabilistic computation, such simulation is straightforward in many settings. For example, a random function which will only be queried an a priori bounded number of times t can be perfectly simulated using a t-wise independent function [30]. In the case of unbounded queries, one can use pseudorandom functions (PRFs), provided

© International Association for Cryptologic Research 2020
A. Canteaut and Y. Ishai (Eds.): EUROCRYPT 2020, LNCS 12107, pp. 759–787, 2020.
https://doi.org/10.1007/978-3-030-45727-3_26

the queries are made by a polynomial-time algorithm [16]. These are examples of *stateless* simulation methods, in the sense that the internal memory of the simulator is initialized once (e.g., with the PRF key) and then remains fixed regardless of how the simulator is queried. Against arbitrary adversaries, one must typically pass to *stateful* simulation. For example, the straightforward and well-known technique of *lazy sampling* suffices to perfectly simulate a random function against arbitrary adversaries; however, the simulator must maintain a list of responses to all previous queries.

Each of these techniques for simulating random classical primitives has a plethora of applications in theoretical cryptography, both as a proof tool and for cryptographic constructions. These range from constructing secure cryptosystems for encryption and authentication, to proving security reductions in a wide range of settings, to establishing security in idealized models such as the Random Oracle Model [7].

Quantum randomness. As is well-known, quantum sources of randomness exhibit dramatically different properties from their classical counterparts [8,23]. Compare, for example, uniformly random n-bit classical states (i.e., n-bit strings) and uniformly random n-qubit (pure) quantum states. A random string x is obviously trivial to sample perfectly given probabilistic classical (or quantum) computation, and can be copied and distributed arbitrarily. However, it is also (just as obviously) deterministic to all parties who have examined it before. By contrast, a random state $|\varphi\rangle$ would take an unbounded amount of information to describe perfectly. Even if one manages to procure such a state, it is then impossible to copy due to the no-cloning theorem. On the other hand, parties who have examined $|\varphi\rangle$ many times before, can *still* extract almost exactly n bits of randomness from any fresh copy of $|\varphi\rangle$ they receive – even if they use the *exact same measurement procedure* each time.

The differences between random classical and random quantum maps are even more stark. The outputs of a classical random function are of course classical random strings, with all of the aforementioned properties. Outputs which have already been examined become effectively deterministic, while the rest remain uniformly random and independent. This is precisely what makes efficient simulation possible via lazy sampling. A Haar-random unitary U queried on two inputs $|\psi\rangle$ and $|\phi\rangle$ also produces (almost) independent and uniformly random states when queried, but only if the queries are *orthogonal*, i.e., $\langle \psi \mid \phi \rangle = 0$. Unitarity implies that overlapping queries must be answered consistently, i.e., if $\langle \psi \mid \phi \rangle = \delta$ then $\langle (U\psi) \mid (U\phi) \rangle = \delta$. This possibility of querying with a distinct pure state which is not linearly independent from previous queries simply doesn't exist for classical functions.

We emphasize that the above differences should not be interpreted as quantum random objects simply being "stronger" than their classical counterparts. In the case of classical states, i.e. strings, the ability to copy is quite useful, e.g., in setting down basic security definitions [2,3,9] or when rewinding an algorithm [14,28,29]. In the case of maps, determinism is also quite useful, e.g., for verification in message authentication.

1.2   The Problem: Efficient Simulation

Given the dramatic differences between classical and quantum randomness, and the usefulness of both, it is reasonable to ask if there exist quantum analogues of the aforementioned efficient simulators of classical random functions. In fact, given the discussion above, it is clear that we should begin by asking if there even exist efficient simulators of random quantum states.

Simulating random states. The first problem of interest is thus to efficiently simulate the following ideal object: an oracle $\mathfrak{JS}(n)$ which contains a description of a perfectly Haar-random n-qubit pure state $|\varphi\rangle$, and which outputs a copy of $|\varphi\rangle$ whenever it is invoked. We first make an obvious observation: the classical analogue, which is simply to generate a random bitstring $x \leftarrow \{0,1\}^n$ and then produce a copy whenever asked, is completely trivial. In the quantum case, efficient simulation is only known against limited query algorithms (henceforth, adversaries.)

If the adversary has an a priori bound on the number of queries, then *state t-designs* suffice. These are indexed families $\{|\varphi_{k,t}\rangle : k \in K_t\}$ of pure states which perfectly emulate the standard uniform "Haar" measure on pure states, up to the first t moments. State t-designs can be sampled efficiently, and thus yield a stateless simulator for this case [5]. A recent work of Ji, Liu and Song considered the case of polynomial-time adversaries [18]. They defined a notion of *pseudorandom states* (PRS), which appear Haar-random to polynomial-time adversaries who are allowed as many copies of the state as they wish. They also showed how to construct PRS efficiently, thus yielding a stateless simulator for this class of constrained adversaries [18]; see also [10].

The case of arbitrary adversaries is, to our knowledge, completely unexplored. In particular, before this work it was not known whether simulating $\mathfrak{JS}(n)$ against adversaries with no a priori bound on query or time complexity is possible, even if given polynomial space (in n and the number of queries) and unlimited time. Note that, while the state family constructions from [10,18] could be lifted to the unconditional security setting by instantiating them with random instead of pseudorandom functions, this would require space exponential in n regardless of the number of queries.

Simulating random unitaries. In the case of simulating random unitaries, the ideal object is an oracle $\mathfrak{JU}$ (n) which contains a description of a perfectly Haar-random n-qubit unitary operator U, and applies U to its input whenever it is invoked. The classical analogue is the well-known Random Oracle, and can be simulated perfectly using the aforementioned technique of lazy sampling. In the quantum case, the situation is even less well-understood than in the case of states.

For the case of query-limited adversaries, we can again rely on design techniques: (approximate) *unitary t-designs* can be sampled efficiently, and suffice for the task [11,21]. Against polynomial-time adversaries, Ji, Liu and Song defined the natural notion of a *pseudorandom unitary* (or PRU) and described candidate constructions [18]. Unfortunately, at this time there are no provably secure constructions of PRUs. As in the case of states, the case of arbitrary adversaries is completely unexplored. Moreover, one could a priori plausibly conjecture that simulating $\mathfrak{IU}$ might even be impossible. The no-cloning property seems to rule out examining input states, which in turn seems to make it quite difficult for a simulator to correctly identify the overlap between multiple queries, and then answer correspondingly.

Extensions. While the above problems already appear quite challenging, we mention several natural extensions that one might consider. First, for the case of repeatedly sampling a random state $|\varphi\rangle$, one would ideally want some additional features, such as the ability to apply the two-outcome measurement $\{|\varphi\rangle\langle\varphi|, \mathbb{1} - |\varphi\rangle\langle\varphi|\}$ (*verification*) or the reflection $\mathbb{1} - 2|\varphi\rangle\langle\varphi|$. In the case of pseudorandom simulation, these additional features can be used to create a (computationally secure) quantum money scheme [18]. For the case of simulating random unitaries, we might naturally ask that the simulator for a unitary U also has the ability to respond to queries to $U^{-1} = U^\dagger$.

1.3 This Work

In this work, we make significant progress on the above problems, by giving the first simulators for both random states and random unitaries, which are convincing to arbitrary adversaries. We also give an application of our sampling ideas: the construction of a new quantum money scheme, which provides information-theoretic security guarantees against both forging and tracing.

We begin by remarking that our desired simulators must necessarily be stateful, for both states and unitaries. Indeed, since approximate t-designs have $\Omega((2^{2n}/t)^{2t})$ elements (see, e.g., [25] which provides a more fine-grained lower bound), a stateless approach would require superpolynomial space simply to store an index from a set of size $\Omega((2^{2n}/t(n))^{2t(n)})$ for all polynomials $t(n)$.

In the following, we give a high-level overview of our approach for each of the two simulation problems of interest.

Simulating random states. As discussed above, we wish to construct an efficient simulator $\mathfrak{ES}(n)$ for the ideal oracle $\mathfrak{IS}(n)$. For now we focus on simulating the procedure which generates copies of the fixed Haar-random state; we call this $\mathfrak{IS}(n).\mathsf{Gen}$. We first note that the mixed state observed by the adversary after t queries to $\mathfrak{IS}(n).\mathsf{Gen}$ is the expectation of the projector onto t copies of $|\psi\rangle$. Equivalently, it is the (normalized) projector onto the *symmetric subspace* $\mathbf{Sym}_{n,t}$ of $(\mathbb{C}^{2^n})^{\otimes t}$:

$$\tau_t = \mathbb{E}_{\psi \sim \text{Haar}} |\psi\rangle\langle\psi|^{\otimes t} \propto \Pi_{\text{Sym}^t \mathbb{C}^{2^n}}. \tag{1}$$

Recall that $\mathbf{Sym}_{n,t}$ is the subspace of $(\mathbb{C}^{2^n})^{\otimes t}$ of vectors which are invariant under permutations of the t tensor factors. Our goal will be to maintain an entangled state between the adversary $\mathcal{A}$ and our oracle simulator $\mathfrak{CS}$ such that the reduced state on the side of $\mathcal{A}$ is τ_t after t queries. Specifically, the joint state will be the maximally entangled state between the $\mathbf{Sym}_{n,t}$ subspace of the t query output registers received by $\mathcal{A}$, and the $\mathbf{Sym}_{n,t}$ subspace of t registers held by $\mathfrak{CS}$. If we can maintain this for the first t queries, then it's not hard to see that there exists an isometry $V^{t \to t+1}$ which, by acting only on the state of $\mathfrak{CS}$, implements the extension from the t-fold to the $(t+1)$-fold joint state.

The main technical obstacle, which we resolve, is showing that $V^{t \to t+1}$ can be performed efficiently. To achieve this, we develop some new algorithmic tools for working with symmetric subspaces, including an algorithm for coherent preparation of its basis states. We let A denote an n-qubit register, A_j its indexed copies, and $A^t = A_1 \cdots A_t$ t-many indexed copies (and likewise for B.) We also let $\{|\mathrm{Sym}(\alpha)\rangle : \alpha \in S^\uparrow_{n,t}\}$ denote a particular orthonormal basis set for $\mathbf{Sym}_{n,t}$, indexed by some set $S^\uparrow_{n,t}$ (see Sect. 3 for definitions of these objects.)

Theorem 1. *For each n and t, there exists a polynomial-time quantum algorithm which implements an isometry $V = V^{t \to t+1}$ from B^t to $A_{t+1}B^{t+1}$ such that, up to negligible trace distance,*

$$(\mathbb{1}_{A^t} \otimes V) \sum_{\alpha \in S^\uparrow_{n,t}} |\mathrm{Sym}(\alpha)\rangle_{A^t} |\mathrm{Sym}(\alpha)\rangle_{B^t} = \sum_{\beta \in S^\uparrow_{n,t+1}} |\mathrm{Sym}(\beta)\rangle_{A^{t+1}} |\mathrm{Sym}(\beta)\rangle_{B^{t+1}}.$$

Above, V is an operator defined to apply to a specific subset of registers of a state. When no confusion can arise, in such settings we will abbreviate $\mathbb{1} \otimes V$—the application of this operator on the entire state—as simply V.

It will be helpful to view $V^{t \to t+1}$ as first preparing $|0^n\rangle_{A_{t+1}}|0^n\rangle_{B_{t+1}}$ and then applying a unitary $U^{t \to t+1}$ on $A_{t+1}B^{t+1}$. Theorem 1 then gives us a way to answer Gen queries efficiently, as follows. For the first query, we prepare a maximally entangled state $|\phi^+\rangle_{A_1 B_1}$ across two n-qubit registers A_1 and B_1, and reply with register A_1. Note that $\mathbf{Sym}_{n,1} = \mathbb{C}^{2^n}$. For the second query, we prepare two fresh registers A_2 and B_2, both in the $|0^n\rangle$ state, apply $U^{1 \to 2}$ on $A_2 B_1 B_2$, return A_2, and keep $B_1 B_2$. For the t-th query, we proceed similarly, preparing fresh blank registers $A_{t+1}B_{t+1}$, applying $U^{t \to t+1}$, and then outputting the register A_{t+1}.

With this approach, as it turns out, there is also a natural way to respond to verification queries Ver and reflection queries Reflect. The ideal functionality $\mathfrak{IS}.\mathsf{Ver}$ is to apply the two-outcome measurement $\{|\varphi\rangle\langle\varphi|, \mathbb{1} - |\varphi\rangle\langle\varphi|\}$ corresponding to the Haar-random state $|\varphi\rangle$. To simulate this after producing t samples, we apply the inverse of $U^{t-1 \to t}$, apply the measurement $\{|0^{2n}\rangle\langle 0^{2n}|, \mathbb{1} - |0^{2n}\rangle\langle 0^{2n}|\}$ to $A_t B_t$, reapply $U^{t-1 \to t}$, and then return A_t together with the measurement outcome (i.e., yes/no). For $\mathfrak{IS}.\mathsf{Reflect}$, the ideal functionality is to apply the reflection $\mathbb{1} - 2|\varphi\rangle\langle\varphi|$ through the state. To simulate this, we perform a sequence of operations analogous to Ver, but apply a phase of -1 on the $|0^{2n}\rangle$ state of $A_t B_t$ instead of measuring.

Our main result on simulating random states is to establish that this collection of algorithms correctly simulates the ideal object $\mathfrak{IS}$, in the following sense.

Theorem 2. *There exists a stateful quantum algorithm* $\mathfrak{ES}(n, \epsilon)$ *which runs in time polynomial in* n, $\log(1/\epsilon)$, *and the number of queries* q *submitted to it, and satisfies the following. For all oracle algorithms* $\mathcal{A}$,

$$\left| \Pr\left[\mathcal{A}^{\mathfrak{IS}(n)} = 1 \right] - \Pr\left[\mathcal{A}^{\mathfrak{ES}(n,\epsilon)} = 1 \right] \right| \leq \epsilon.$$

A complete description of our construction, together with the proofs of Theorems 1 and 2, are given in Sect. 3.

We remark that, if one can give a certain mild a-priori bound on the number of queries that will be made to the state sampler, an alternative construction[1] based on the compressed oracle technique of Zhandry [31] and the aforementioned work by Ji, Liu and Song [18] becomes possible. We describe this construction in Sect. 3.3.

Application: untraceable quantum money. To see that the efficient state sampler leads to a powerful quantum money scheme, consider building a scheme where the bank holds the ideal object $\mathfrak{IS}$. The bank can mint bills by $\mathfrak{IS}.\mathsf{Gen}$, and verify them using $\mathfrak{IS}.\mathsf{Ver}$. As each bill is guaranteed to be an identical and Haar-random state, it is clear that this scheme should satisfy perfect unforgeability and untraceability, under quite strong notions of security.

By Theorem 7, the same properties should carry over for a money scheme built on $\mathfrak{ES}$, provided ϵ is sufficiently small. We call the resulting scheme *Haar money*. Haar money is an information-theoretically secure analogue of the scheme of [18], which is based on pseudorandom states. We remark that our scheme requires the bank to have quantum memory and to perform quantum communication with the customers. However, given that quantum money already requires customers to have large-scale, high-fidelity quantum storage, these additional requirements seem reasonable.

The notions of correctness and unforgeability (often called completeness and soundness) for quantum money are well-known (see, e.g., [1].) Correctness asks that honestly generated money schemes should verify, i.e., Ver(Mint) should always accept. Unforgeability states that an adversary with k bills and oracle access to Ver should not be able to produce a state on which $\mathsf{Ver}^{\otimes k+1}$ accepts. In this work, we consider untraceable quantum money (also called "quantum coins" [24].) We give a formal security definition for untraceability, which states that an adversary $\mathcal{A}$ with oracle access to Ver and Mint cannot do better than random guessing in the following experiment:

1. $\mathcal{A}$ outputs some candidate bill registers $\{M_j\}$ and a permutation π;
2. $b \leftarrow \{0, 1\}$ is sampled, and if $b = 1$ the registers $\{M_j\}$ are permuted by π; each candidate bill is verified and the failed ones are discarded;
3. $\mathcal{A}$ receives the rest of the bills and the entire internal state of the bank, and outputs a guess b' for b.

Theorem 3. *The Haar money scheme* $\mathfrak{HM}$, *defined by setting*

---

[1] We thank Zvika Brakerski for pointing out this alternative approach.

1. $\mathfrak{H}\mathfrak{M}.\mathsf{Mint} = \mathfrak{E}\mathfrak{G}(n, \mathsf{negl}(n)).\mathsf{Gen}$
2. $\mathfrak{H}\mathfrak{M}.\mathsf{Ver} = \mathfrak{E}\mathfrak{G}(n, \mathsf{negl}(n)).\mathsf{Ver}$

is a correct quantum money scheme which satisfies information-theoretic unforgeability and untraceability.

One might reasonably ask if there are even stronger definitions of security for quantum money. Given its relationship to the ideal state sampler, we believe that Haar money should satisfy almost any notion of unforgeability and untraceability, including composable notions. We also remark that, based on the structure of the state simulator, which maintains an overall pure state supported on two copies of the symmetric subspace of banknote registers, it is straightforward to see that the scheme is also secure against an "honest but curious" or "specious" [15, 26] bank. We leave the formalization of these added security guarantees to future work.

Sampling Haar-random unitaries. Next, we turn to the problem of simulating Haar-random unitary operators. In this case, the ideal object $\mathfrak{J}\mathfrak{U}(n)$ initially samples a description of a perfectly Haar-random n-qubit unitary U, and then responds to two types of queries: $\mathfrak{J}\mathfrak{U}.\mathsf{Eval}$, which applies U, and $\mathfrak{J}\mathfrak{U}.\mathsf{Invert}$, which applies $U^{\dagger}$. In this case, we are able to construct a stateful simulator that runs in space polynomial in n and the number of queries q, and is *exactly indistinguishable* from $\mathfrak{J}\mathfrak{U}(n)$ to arbitrary adversaries. Our result can be viewed as a polynomial-space quantum analogue of the classical technique of lazy sampling for random oracles.

Our high-level approach is as follows. For now, suppose the adversary $\mathcal{A}$ only makes parallel queries to Eval. If the query count t of $\mathcal{A}$ is a priori bounded, we can simply sample an element of a unitary t-design. We can also do this coherently: prepare a quantum register I in uniform superposition over the index set of the t-design, and then apply the t-design controlled on I. Call this efficient simulator $\mathfrak{E}\mathfrak{U}_t$. Observe that the effect of t parallel queries is just the application of the t-*twirling channel* $\mathcal{T}^{(t)}$ to the t input registers [11], and that $\mathfrak{E}\mathfrak{U}_t$ simulates $\mathcal{T}^{(t)}$ faithfully. What is more, it applies a *Stinespring dilation*[2] [27] of $\mathcal{T}^{(t)}$ with dilating register I.

Now suppose $\mathcal{A}$ makes an "extra" query, i.e., query number $t+1$. Consider an alternative Stinespring dilation of $\mathcal{T}^{(t)}$, namely the one implemented by $\mathfrak{E}\mathfrak{U}_{t+1}$ when queried t times. Recall that all Stinespring dilations of a quantum channel are equivalent, up to a partial isometry on the dilating register. It follows that there is a partial isometry, acting on the private space of $\mathfrak{E}\mathfrak{U}_t$, that transforms the dilation of $\mathcal{T}^{(t)}$ implemented by $\mathfrak{E}\mathfrak{U}_t$ into the dilation of $\mathcal{T}^{(t)}$ implemented by $\mathfrak{E}\mathfrak{U}_{t+1}$. If we implement this transformation, and then respond to $\mathcal{A}$ as prescribed by $\mathfrak{E}\mathfrak{U}_{t+1}$, we have achieved perfect indistinguishability against the additional query. By iterating this process, we see that the a priori bound on the

---

[2] The Stinespring dilation of a quantum channel is an isometry with the property that the quantum channel can be implemented by applying the isometry and subsequently discarding an auxiliary register.

number of queries is no longer needed. We let $\mathfrak{EU}$ denote the resulting simulator. The complete construction is described in Construction 4 below.

Our high-level discussion above did not take approximation into account. All currently known efficient constructions of t-designs are approximate. Here, we take a different approach: we will implement our construction using *exact t-designs*. This addresses the issue of adaptive queries: if there exists an adaptive-query distinguisher with nonzero distinguishing probability, then by post-selection there also exists a parallel-query one via probabilistic teleportation. This yields that the ideal and efficient unitary samplers are perfectly indistinguishable to arbitrary adversaries.

Theorem 4. *For all oracle algorithms $\mathcal{A}$,* $\Pr\left[\mathcal{A}^{\mathfrak{JU}(n)} = 1\right] = \Pr\left[\mathcal{A}^{\mathfrak{EU}(n)} = 1\right].$

The existence of exact unitary t-designs for all t is a fairly recent result. It follows as a special case of a result of Kane [19], who shows that designs exist for all finite-dimensional vector spaces of well-behaved functions on path-connected topological spaces. He also gives a simpler result for homogeneous spaces when the vector space of functions is invariant under the symmetry group action. Here, the number of elements of the smallest design is bounded just in terms of the dimension of the space of functions. The unitary group is an example of such a space, and the dimension of the space of homogeneous polynomials of degree t in both U and $U^\dagger$ can be explicitly derived, see e.g. [25]. This yields the following.

Corollary 1. *The space complexity of $\mathfrak{EU}(n)$ for q queries is bounded from above by* $2q(2n + \log e) + O(\log q)$.

An alternative approach. We now sketch another potential approach to lazy sampling of unitaries. Very briefly, this approach takes a representation-theoretic perspective and suggests that the Schur transform [6] could lead to a polynomial-time algorithm for lazy sampling Haar-random unitaries. The discussion below uses tools and language from quantum information theory and the representation theory of the unitary and symmetric groups to a much larger extent than the rest of the article, and is not required for understanding our main results.

We remark that the analogous problem of lazy sampling a quantum oracle for a random classical function was recently solved by Zhandry [31]. One of the advantages of Zhandry's technique is that it partly recovers the ability to inspect previously made queries, an important feature of classical lazy sampling. The key insight is that the simulator can implement the Stinespring dilation of the oracle channel, and thus record the output of the *complementary channel*.[3] As the classical function is computed via XOR, changing to the $\mathbb{Z}_2^n$-Fourier basis makes the recording property explicit. It also allows for an efficient implementation.

In the case of Haar-random unitary oracles, we can make an analogous observation. Consider an algorithm that makes t parallel queries to U. The relevant Fourier transform is now over the unitary group, and is given by the Schur

---

[3] The complementary channel of a quantum channel maps the input to the auxiliary output of the Stinespring dilation isometry.

transform [6]. By Schur-Weyl duality (see e.g. [13]), the decomposition of $\left(\mathbb{C}^{2^n}\right)^{\otimes t}$ into irreducible representations is given by

$$\left(\mathbb{C}^d\right)^{\otimes t} \cong \bigoplus_{\lambda \vdash_d t} [\lambda] \otimes V_{\lambda,d}. \tag{2}$$

Here $\lambda \vdash_d t$ means λ is any partition of t into at most d parts, $[\lambda]$ is the Specht module of S_t, and $V_{\lambda,d}$ is the Weyl module of $U(d)$, corresponding to the partition λ, respectively. By Schur's lemma, the t-twirling channel acts as

$$\mathcal{T}^{(t)} = \bigoplus_{\lambda \vdash_d t} \mathrm{id}_{[\lambda]} \otimes \Lambda_{V_{\lambda,d}}, \tag{3}$$

where id is the identity channel, and $\Lambda = \mathrm{Tr}(\cdot)\tau$ with the maximally mixed state τ is the depolarizing channel. We therefore obtain a Stinespring dilation of the t-twirling channel as follows. Let $\tilde{B}, \tilde{B}'$ be registers with Hilbert spaces

$$\mathcal{H}_{\tilde{B}} = \mathcal{H}_{\tilde{B}'} = \bigotimes_{\lambda \vdash_d t} V_{\lambda,d} \tag{4}$$

and denote the subregisters by $\tilde{B}_\lambda$ and $\tilde{B}'_\lambda$, respectively. Let further $|\phi^+\rangle_{\tilde{B}\tilde{B}'}$ be the standard maximally entangled state on these registers, and let C be a register whose dimension is the number of partitions of t (into at most 2^n parts). Define the isometry

$$\hat{V}_{A^t \tilde{B} \to A^t \tilde{B} C} = \bigoplus_{\lambda \vdash_d t} F_{V_{\lambda,d} \tilde{B}_\lambda} \otimes \mathbb{I}_{[\lambda]} \otimes |\lambda\rangle_C \tag{5}$$

In the above equation $V_{\lambda,d}$ and $[\lambda]$ are understood to be subspaces of A^t, the identity operators on $\tilde{B}_\mu, \mu \neq \lambda$ are omitted and F is the swap operator. By (3), a Stinespring dilation of the t-twirling channel is then given by

$$V_{A^t \to A^t \tilde{B} \tilde{B}' C} = \hat{V}_{A^t \tilde{B} \to A^t \tilde{B} C} |\phi^+\rangle_{\tilde{B}\tilde{B}'}. \tag{6}$$

By the equivalence of all Stinespring dilations, the exists an isometry $W_{\hat{B}_t \to \tilde{B}\tilde{B}'C}$ that transforms the state register of $\mathfrak{CU}(n)$ after t parallel queries so that the global state is the same as if the Stinespring dilation above had been applied to the t input registers. But now the quantum information that was contained in the subspace $V_{\lambda,d}$ of the algorithm's query registers can be found in register $\tilde{B}_\lambda$.

1.4 Organization

The remainder of the paper is organized as follows. In Sect. 2, we recall some basic notation and facts, and some lemmas concerning coherent preparation of certain generic families of quantum states. The proofs for these lemmas are given in the full version [4]. We also describe stateful machines, which will be our model for thinking about the aforementioned ideal objects and their efficient simulators. In Sect. 3 we describe our efficient simulator for Haar-random states, and in Sect. 4 we describe our polynomial-space simulator for Haar-random unitaries. We end by describing the Haar money scheme and establishing its security in Sect. 5.

2 Preliminaries

Given a fixed-size (e.g., n-qubit) register A, we will use $A_1, A_2, \ldots$ to denote indexed copies of A. We will use A^t to denote a register consisting of t indexed copies of A, i.e., $A^t = A_1 A_2 \cdots A_t$. Unless stated otherwise, distances of quantum states are measured in the trace distance, i.e., $d(\rho, \sigma) = \frac{1}{2}\|\rho - \sigma\|_1$ where $\|X\|_1 = \mathrm{Tr}\left[\sqrt{X^\dagger X}\right]$. Distances of unitary operators are measured in the operator norm.

We will frequently apply operators to some subset of a larger collection of registers. In that context, we will use register indexing to indicate which registers are being acted upon, and suppress identities to simplify notation. The register indexing will also be suppressed when it is clear from context. For example, given an operator $X_{A \to B}$ and some state ρ on registers A and C, we will write $X(\rho)$ in place of $(X \otimes \mathbb{1}_C)(\rho)$ to denote the state on BC resulting from applying X to the A register of ρ.

We let $|\phi^+\rangle_{AA'}$ denote the maximally entangled state on registers A and A'. For a linear operator X and some basis choice, we denote its transpose by X^T.

Lemma 1 (Mirror lemma; see, e.g., [22]). *For $X_{A \to B}$ a linear operator,*

$$X_{A \to B}|\phi^+\rangle_{AA'} = \sqrt{\frac{\dim(B)}{\dim(A)}} X^T_{B' \to A'}|\phi^+\rangle_{BB'}.$$

2.1 Unitary Designs

Let μ_n be the Haar measure on the unitary group $\mathrm{U}(2^n)$. We define the Haar t-twirling channel $\mathcal{T}_{\mathrm{Haar}}^{(t)}$ by

$$\mathcal{T}_{\mathrm{Haar}}^{(t)}(X) = \int_{\mathrm{U}(2^n)} U^{\otimes t} X \left(U^{\otimes t}\right)^\dagger \mathrm{d}\mu(U). \tag{7}$$

For a finite subset $D \subset \mathrm{U}(2^n)$, we define the t-twirling map with respect to D as

$$\mathcal{T}_D^{(t)}(X) = \frac{1}{|D|} \sum_{U \in D} U^{\otimes t} X \left(U^{\otimes t}\right)^\dagger. \tag{8}$$

An n-qubit unitary t-design is a finite set $D \subset \mathrm{U}(2^n)$ such that

$$\mathcal{T}_D^{(t)} = \mathcal{T}_{\mathrm{Haar}}^{(t)}(X) \tag{9}$$

Another twirling channel is the mixed twirling channels with ℓ applications of the unitary and $t - \ell$ applications of it's inverse,

$$\mathcal{T}_{\mathrm{Haar}}^{(\ell, t-\ell)}(\Gamma) = \int_{\mathrm{U}(2^n)} U^{\otimes \ell} \otimes \left(U^{\otimes(t-\ell)}\right)^\dagger \Gamma \left(U^{\otimes \ell}\right)^\dagger \otimes U^{\otimes(t-\ell)} \mathrm{d}\mu(U). \tag{10}$$

The mixed twirling channel $\mathcal{T}_D^{(\ell, t-\ell)}$ for a finite set $D \subset \mathrm{U}(2^n)$ is also defined analogous to Eq. (8). As our definition of unitary t-designs is equivalent to one based on the expectation values of polynomials (see, e.g., [21]), we easily obtain the following.

Proposition 1. *Let D be an n-qubit unitary t-design and $0 \le \ell \le t$. Then*

$$\mathcal{T}_{\text{Haar}}^{(\ell, t-\ell)} = \mathcal{T}_D^{(\ell, t-\ell)} \tag{11}$$

Finite exact unitary t-designs exist. In particular, one can apply the following theorem to obtain an upper bound on their minimal size. Here, a design for a function space W on a topological space X with measure μ is a finite set $D \subset X$ such that the expectation of a function $f \in W$ is the same whether it is taken over X according to μ or over the uniform distribution on D.

Theorem 5 ([19], Theorem 10). *Let X be a homogeneous space, μ an invariant measure on X and W a M-dimensional vector subspace of the space of real functions on X that is invariant under the symmetry group of X, where $M > 1$. Then for any $N > M(M-1)$, there exists a W-design for X of size N. Furthermore, there exists a design for X of size at most $M(M-1)$.*

The case of unitary t-designs is the one where $X = U(2^n)$ is acting on itself (e.g., on the left), μ is the Haar measure, and W is the vector space of homogeneous polynomials of degree t in both U and $U^{\dagger}$[4]. The dimension of this space is

$$M_t = \binom{2^{2n} + t - 1}{t}^2 \le \left(\frac{e(2^{2n} + t - 1)}{t} \right)^t, \tag{12}$$

see e.g. [25]. We therefore get

Corollary 2. *For all n, there exists an exact n-qubit unitary t-design with a number of elements which is at most*

$$\left(\frac{e(2^{2n} + t - 1)}{t} \right)^{2t}.$$

2.2 Real and Ideal Stateful Machines

We will frequently use stateful algorithms with multiple "interfaces" which allow a user to interact with the algorithm. We will refer to such objects as *stateful machines*. We will use stateful machines to describe functionalities (and implementations) of collections of oracles which relate to each other in some way. For example, one oracle might output a fixed state, while another oracle reflects about that state.

Definition 1 (Stateful machine). *A stateful machine $\mathcal{S}$ consists of:*

- *A finite set Λ, whose elements are called interfaces. Each interface $\mathcal{I} \in \Lambda$ has two fixed parameters $n_{\mathcal{I}} \in \mathbb{N}$ (input size) and $m_{\mathcal{I}} \in \mathbb{N}$ (output size), and a variable $t_{\mathcal{I}}$ initialized to 1 (query counter.)*

---

[4] The output of the twirling channel (7) is a matrix of such polynomials.

- *For each interface $\mathcal{I} \in \Lambda$, a sequence of quantum algorithms $\{S.\mathcal{I}_j : j = 1, 2, \dots\}$. Each $S.\mathcal{I}_j$ has an input register of $n_{\mathcal{I}}$ qubits, an output register of $m_{\mathcal{I}}$ qubits, and is allowed to act on an additional shared work register R (including the ability to add/remove qubits in R.) In addition, each $S.\mathcal{I}_j$ increments the corresponding query counter $t_{\mathcal{I}}$ by one.*

The typical usage of a stateful machine S is as follows. First, the work register R is initialized to be empty, i.e., no qubits. After that, whenever a user invokes an interface $S.\mathcal{I}$ and supplies $n_{\mathcal{I}}$ qubits in an input register M, the algorithm $S.\mathcal{I}_{t_{\mathcal{I}}}$ is invoked on registers M and R. The contents of the output register are returned to the user, and the new, updated work register remains for the next invocation. We emphasize that the work register is shared between all interfaces.

We remark that we will also sometimes define *ideal machines*, which behave outwardly like a stateful machine but are not constrained to apply only maps which are implementable in finite space or time. For example, an ideal machine can have an interface that implements a perfectly Haar-random unitary U, and another interface which implements $U^{\dagger}$.

2.3   Some State Preparation Tools

We now describe some algorithms for efficient coherent preparation of certain quantum state families. The proofs for the following lemmas can be found in the full version [4]. We begin with state families with polynomial support.

Lemma 2. *Let $|\varphi\rangle = \sum_{x \in \{0,1\}^n} \varphi(x)|x\rangle$ be a family of quantum states whose amplitudes φ have an efficient classical description $\tilde{\varphi}$, and such that $|\{x : \varphi(x) \neq 0\}| \leq \mathsf{poly}(n)$. Then there exists a quantum algorithm $\mathcal{P}$ which runs in time polynomial in n and $\log(1/\epsilon)$ and satisfies $\||\mathcal{P}|\tilde{\varphi}\rangle|0^n\rangle - |\tilde{\varphi}\rangle|\varphi\rangle\|_2 \leq \epsilon$.*

Given a set $S \subset \{0,1\}^n$, we let

$$|S\rangle := \frac{1}{\sqrt{|S|}} \sum_{x \in S} |x\rangle \qquad \text{and} \qquad |\bar{S}\rangle := \frac{1}{\sqrt{2^n - |S|}} \sum_{x \in \{0,1\} \setminus S} |x\rangle$$

denote the states supported only on S and its set complement $\bar{S}$, respectively. Provided that S has polynomial size, we can perform coherent preparation of both state families efficiently: the former by Lemma 2 and the latter via the below.

Lemma 3. *Let $S \subset \{0,1\}^n$ be a family of sets of size $\mathsf{poly}(n)$ with efficient description $\tilde{S}$, and let $\epsilon > 0$. There exists a quantum algorithm $\mathcal{P}$ which runs in time polynomial in n and $\log(1/\epsilon)$ and satisfies*

$$\left\| \mathcal{P}|\tilde{S}\rangle_A |0^n\rangle_B - |\tilde{S}\rangle_A |\bar{S}\rangle_B \right\|_2 \leq \epsilon.$$

Finally, we show that if two orthogonal quantum states can be prepared, then so can an arbitrary superposition of the two.

Lemma 4. *Let* $|\zeta_{0,j}\rangle, |\zeta_{1,j}\rangle$ *be two familes of n-qubit quantum states such that* $\langle \zeta_{0,j} \mid \zeta_{1,j} \rangle = 0$ *for all j, and such that there exists a quantum algorithm $\mathcal{P}_b$ which runs in time polynomial in n and $\log(1/\epsilon)$ and satisfies $\| \mathcal{P}_b |j\rangle |0^n\rangle - |j\rangle |\zeta_{b,j}\rangle \|_2 \leq \epsilon$ for $b \in \{0,1\}$.*

For $z_0, z_1 \in \mathbb{C}$ such that $|z_0|^2 + |z_1|^2 = 1$, let $\tilde{z}$ denote a classical description of (z_0, z_1) to precision at least ϵ. There exists a quantum algorithm $\mathcal{Q}$ which runs in time polynomial in n and $\log(1/\epsilon)$ and satisfies

$$\left\| \mathcal{Q} |j\rangle |\tilde{z}\rangle |0^n\rangle - |j\rangle |\tilde{z}\rangle \big(z_0 |\zeta_{0,j}\rangle + z_1 |\zeta_{1,j}\rangle \big) \right\|_2 \leq \epsilon. \tag{13}$$

3   Simulating a Haar-Random State Oracle

3.1   The Problem, and Our Approach

We begin by defining the ideal object we'd like to emulate. Here we deviate slightly from the discussion above, in that we ask for the reflection oracle to also accept a (quantum) control bit.

Construction 1 (Ideal state sampler). *The ideal n-qubit state sampler is an ideal machine $\mathfrak{IS}(n)$ with interfaces* (Init, Gen, Ver, CReflect), *defined as follows.*

1. $\mathfrak{IS}(n)$.Init: *takes no input; samples a description $\tilde{\varphi}$ of an n-qubit state $|\varphi\rangle$ from the Haar measure.*
2. $\mathfrak{IS}(n)$.Gen: *takes no input; uses $\tilde{\varphi}$ to prepare a copy of $|\varphi\rangle$ and outputs it.*
3. $\mathfrak{IS}(n)$.Ver: *receives n-qubit input; uses $\tilde{\varphi}$ to apply the measurement $\{|\varphi\rangle\langle\varphi|, \mathbb{1} - |\varphi\rangle\langle\varphi|\}$; return the post-measurement state and output* acc *in the first case and* rej *in the second.*
4. $\mathfrak{IS}(n)$.CReflect: *receives $(n+1)$-qubit input; uses $\tilde{\varphi}$ to implement the controlled reflection $R_\varphi := |0\rangle\langle 0| \otimes \mathbb{1} + |1\rangle\langle 1| \otimes (\mathbb{1} - 2|\varphi\rangle\langle\varphi|)$ about $|\varphi\rangle$.*

We assume that Init is called first, and only once; the remaining oracles can then be called indefinitely many times, and in any order. If this is inconvenient for some application, one can easily adjust the remaining interfaces to invoke Init if that has not been done yet. We remark that Ver can be implemented with a single query to CReflect.

Lemma 5. Ver *can be simulated with one application of* CReflect.

Proof. Prepare an ancilla qubit in the state $|+\rangle$ and apply reflection on the input controlled on the ancilla. Then apply H to the ancilla qubit and measure it. Output all the qubits, with the ancilla interpreted as $1 = $ acc and $0 = $ rej. □

Our goal is to devise a stateful simulator for Construction 1 which is efficient. Efficient here means that, after t total queries to all interfaces (i.e., Init, Gen, Ver, and CReflect), the simulator has expended time polynomial in n, t, and $\log(1/\epsilon)$.

As described in Sect. 1.3, our approach will be to ensure that, for every t, the state shared between the adversary $\mathcal{A}$ and our stateful oracle simulator $\mathfrak{CS}$ will be maximally entangled between two copies of the t-fold symmetric subspace

$\mathbf{Sym}_{n,t}$: one held by $\mathcal{A}$, and the other by $\mathfrak{E}\mathfrak{G}$. The extension from the t-fold to the $(t+1)$-fold joint state will be performed by an isometry $V^{t\to t+1}$ which acts only on the state of $\mathfrak{E}\mathfrak{G}$ and two fresh n-qubit registers A_{t+1} and B_{t+1} initialized by $\mathfrak{E}\mathfrak{G}$. After V is applied, A_{t+1} will be given to $\mathcal{A}$. As we will show, V can be performed efficiently using some algorithmic tools for working with symmetric subspaces, which we will develop in the next section. This will yield an efficient way of simulating Gen. Simulation of Ver and CReflect will follow without much difficulty, as outlined in Sect. 1.3.

3.2   Some Tools for Symmetric Subspaces

A basis for the symmetric subspace. We recall an explicit orthonormal basis of the symmetric subspace (see, e.g., [18] or [17].) Let

$$S_{n,t}^{\uparrow} = \left\{ \alpha \in (\{0,1\}^n)^t \,\big|\, \alpha_1 \leq \alpha_2 \leq \dots \leq \alpha_t \right\} \tag{14}$$

be the set of lexicographically-ordered t-tuples of n bit strings. For each $\alpha \in S_{n,t}^{\uparrow}$, define the unit vector

$$|\mathrm{Sym}(\alpha)\rangle = \left(t! \prod_{x \in \{0,1\}^n} f_x(\alpha)! \right)^{-\frac{1}{2}} \sum_{\sigma \in S_t} |\alpha_{\sigma(1)}\rangle |\alpha_{\sigma(2)}\rangle \dots |\alpha_{\sigma(t)}\rangle. \tag{15}$$

Here, $f_x(\alpha)$ is the number of times the string x appears in the tuple α. The set $\{|\mathrm{Sym}(\alpha)\rangle : \alpha \in S_{n,t}^{\uparrow}\}$ is an orthonormal basis for $\mathrm{Sym}^t \mathbb{C}^{2^n}$. We remark that the Schmidt decomposition of $|\mathrm{Sym}(\alpha)\rangle$ with respect to the bipartition formed by the t-th register vs. the rest is given by

$$|\mathrm{Sym}(\alpha)\rangle = \sum_{x \in \{0,1\}^n} \sqrt{\frac{f_x(\alpha)}{t}} |\mathrm{Sym}(\alpha^{-x})\rangle |x\rangle, \tag{16}$$

where $\alpha^{-x} \in S_{n,t-1}^{\uparrow}$ is the tuple α with one copy of x removed.

Some useful algorithms. We now describe some algorithms for working in the above basis. Let A and B denote n-qubit registers. Recall that A_j denotes indexed copies of A and that A^t denotes $A_1 A_2 \cdots A_t$, and likewise for B. In our setting, the various copies of A will be prepared by the oracle simulator and then handed to the query algorithm at query time. The copies of B will be prepared by, and always remain with, the oracle simulator.

Proposition 2. *For each n, t and $\epsilon = 2^{-\mathrm{poly}(n,t)}$, there exists an efficiently implementable unitary $U_{n,t}^{\mathrm{Sym}}$ on A^t such that for all $\alpha \in S_{n,t}^{\uparrow}$, $U_{n,t}^{\mathrm{Sym}} |\alpha\rangle = |\mathrm{Sym}(\alpha)\rangle$ up to trace distance ϵ.*

Proof. Clearly, the operation

$$|\text{Sym}(\alpha)\rangle|\beta\rangle \mapsto |\text{Sym}(\alpha)\rangle|\beta \oplus \alpha\rangle \tag{17}$$

is efficiently implementable exactly, by XORing the classical sort function of the first register into the second register.

Let us now show that the operation $|\alpha\rangle \mapsto |\alpha\rangle|\text{Sym}(\alpha)\rangle$ is also efficiently implementable (up to the desirable error) by exhibiting an explicit algorithm. We define it recursively in t, as follows. For $t = 1$, $\text{Sym}(x) = x$ for all $x \in \{0,1\}^n$, so this case is simply the map $|x\rangle \mapsto |x\rangle|x\rangle$. Suppose now the operation $|\alpha\rangle \mapsto |\alpha\rangle|\text{Sym}(\alpha)\rangle$ can be implemented for any $\alpha \in S_{n,t-1}^\uparrow$. The t-th level algorithm will begin by applying

$$|\alpha\rangle \mapsto |\alpha\rangle \sum_{x \in \{0,1\}^n} \sqrt{\frac{f_x(\alpha)}{t}} |x\rangle.$$

Since $f_x(\alpha)$ is nonzero for only t-many $x \in \{0,1\}^n$, this can be implemented efficiently by Lemma 2. Next, we perform $|\alpha\rangle|x\rangle \mapsto |\alpha\rangle|x\rangle|\alpha^{-x}\rangle$. Using the algorithm for $t - 1$, we then apply $|\alpha\rangle|x\rangle|\alpha^{-x}\rangle \mapsto |\alpha\rangle|x\rangle|\alpha^{-x}\rangle|\text{Sym}(\alpha^{-x})\rangle$, and uncompute α^{-x}. By (16), we have in total applied $|\alpha\rangle \mapsto |\alpha\rangle|\text{Sym}(\alpha)\rangle$ so far. To finish the t-th level algorithm for approximating $|\alpha\rangle \mapsto |\text{Sym}(\alpha)\rangle$, we simply apply (17) to uncompute α from the first register. □

Theorem 6 (Restatement of Theorem 1). *For each n, t and $\epsilon = 2^{-\text{poly}(n,t)}$, there exists an efficiently implementable isometry $V^{t \to t+1}$ from B^t to $A_{t+1}B^{t+1}$ such that, up to trace distance ϵ,*

$$V : \sum_{\alpha \in S_{n,t}^\uparrow} |\text{Sym}(\alpha)\rangle_{A^t} |\text{Sym}(\alpha)\rangle_{B^t} \longmapsto \sum_{\beta \in S_{n,t+1}^\uparrow} |\text{Sym}(\beta)\rangle_{A^{t+1}} |\text{Sym}(\beta)\rangle_{B^{t+1}}.$$

We expect the techniques used here to generalize to other irreducible representations of the unitary group.

Proof. We describe the algorithm assuming all steps can be implemented perfectly. It is straightforward to check that each step can be performed to a sufficient accuracy that the accuracy of the entire algorithm is at least ϵ.

We will need a couple of simple subroutines. First, given $\alpha \in S_{n,t}^\uparrow$ and $x \in \{0,1\}^n$, we define α^{+x} to be the element of $S_{n,t+1}^\uparrow$ produced by inserting x at the first position such that the result is still lexicographically ordered. One can perform this reversibly via $|\alpha\rangle|0^n\rangle|x\rangle \mapsto |\alpha\rangle|x\rangle|x\rangle \mapsto |\alpha^{+x}\rangle|x\rangle$. Second, we will need to do coherent preparation of the state

$$|\psi_\alpha\rangle = \sum_{x \in \{0,1\}^n} \sqrt{\frac{1 + f_x(\alpha)}{2^n + t}} |x\rangle. \tag{18}$$

For any given $\alpha \in S_{n,t}^\uparrow$, the state $|\psi_\alpha\rangle$ can be prepared via the preparation circuit for the two orthogonal components of the state whose supports are

$\{x : f_x(\alpha) > 0\}$ and $\{x : f_x(\alpha) = 0\}$. These two components can be prepared coherently using Lemmas 2 and 3, respectively. Their superposition can be prepared with Lemma 4. All together, we get an algorithm for $|\alpha\rangle|0^n\rangle \mapsto |\alpha\rangle|\psi_\alpha\rangle$.

The complete algorithm is a composition of several efficient routines. We describe this below, explicitly calculating the result for the input states of interest. For readability, we omit overall normalization factors.

$$\sum_\alpha |\mathrm{Sym}(\alpha)\rangle_{A^t}|\mathrm{Sym}(\alpha)\rangle_{B^t}$$

$$\longmapsto \sum_\alpha |\mathrm{Sym}(\alpha)\rangle_{A^t}|0^n\rangle|\mathrm{Sym}(\alpha)\rangle_{B^t}|0^n\rangle \qquad\qquad \text{add working registers}$$

$$\longmapsto \sum_\alpha |\mathrm{Sym}(\alpha)\rangle_{A^t}|0^n\rangle|\alpha\rangle_{B^t}|0^n\rangle \qquad\qquad \text{apply } (U_{n,t}^{\mathrm{Sym}})^\dagger \text{ to } B^t$$

$$\longmapsto \sum_{\alpha,x} \sqrt{\frac{1+f_x(\alpha)}{2^n+t}}|\mathrm{Sym}(\alpha)\rangle_{A^t}|x\rangle|\alpha\rangle_{B^t}|0^n\rangle \qquad\qquad \text{prepare } |\psi_\alpha\rangle$$

$$\longmapsto \sum_{\alpha,x} \sqrt{\frac{1+f_x(\alpha)}{2^n+t}}|\mathrm{Sym}(\alpha)\rangle_{A^t}|x\rangle|\alpha^{+x}\rangle_{B^{t+1}} \qquad\qquad \text{insert } x \text{ into } \alpha$$

$$\longmapsto \sum_{\alpha,x} \sqrt{\frac{1+f_x(\alpha)}{2^n+t}}|\mathrm{Sym}(\alpha)\rangle_{A^t}|x\rangle_{A_{t+1}}|\mathrm{Sym}(\alpha^{+x})\rangle_{B^{t+1}} \quad \text{apply } U_{n,t+1}^{\mathrm{Sym}} \text{ to } B^{t+1}$$

To see that the last line above is the desired result, we observe that we can index the sum in the last line above in a more symmetric fashion: the sum is just taken over all pairs (α, β) such that the latter can be obtained from the former by adding one entry (i.e., the string x). But that is the same as summing over all pairs (α, β), such that the former can be obtained from the latter by *removing* one entry.

$$\sum_{\alpha,x} \sqrt{\frac{1+f_x(\alpha)}{2^n+t}}|\mathrm{Sym}(\alpha)\rangle_{A^t}|x\rangle_{A_{t+1}}|\mathrm{Sym}(\alpha^{+x})\rangle_{B^{t+1}}$$

$$= \sum_{\beta,x} \sqrt{\frac{f_x(\beta)}{2^n+t}}|\mathrm{Sym}(\beta^{-x})\rangle_{A^t}|x\rangle_{A_{t+1}}|\mathrm{Sym}(\beta)\rangle_{B^{t+1}}$$

$$= \sqrt{\frac{t}{2^n+t}} \sum_\beta \left(\sum_x \sqrt{\frac{f_x(\beta)}{t}}|\mathrm{Sym}(\beta^{-x})\rangle_{A^t}|x\rangle_{A_{t+1}} \right) |\mathrm{Sym}(\beta)\rangle_{B^{t+1}}$$

$$= \sqrt{\frac{t}{2^n+t}} \sum_\beta |\mathrm{Sym}(\beta)\rangle_{A^{t+1}}|\mathrm{Sym}(\beta)\rangle_{B^{t+1}}.$$

Here, the last equality is (16), and the prefactor is the square root of the quotient of the dimensions of the t- and $(t+1)$-copy symmetric subspaces, as required for a correct normalization of the final maximally entangled state. □

3.3 State Sampler Construction and Proof

Construction 2 (Efficient state sampler). *Let n be a positive integer and ϵ a negligible function of n. The efficient n-qubit state sampler with precision ϵ is a stateful machine $\mathfrak{ES}(\epsilon, n)$ with interfaces (Init, Gen, Reflect), defined below. For convenience, we denote the query counters by $t = t_{\mathsf{Gen}}$ and $q = t_{\mathsf{Reflect}}$ in the following.*

1. $\mathfrak{ES}(\epsilon, n)$.Init: *prepares the standard maximally entangled state $|\phi^+\rangle_{A_1 B_1}$ on n-qubit registers A_1 and B_1, and stores both A_1 and B_1.*
2. $\mathfrak{ES}(\epsilon, n)$.Gen: *On the first query, outputs register A_1. On query t, takes as input registers B^{t-1} and produces registers $A_t B^t$ by applying the isometry $V^{t-1 \to t}$ from Theorem 6 with accuracy $\epsilon 2^{-(t+2q)}$; then it outputs A_t and stores B^t.*
3. $\mathfrak{ES}(\epsilon, n)$.CReflect: *On query q with input registers CA^*, do the following controlled on the qubit register C: apply $\left(U^{t-1 \to t}\right)^\dagger$, a unitary implementation of $V^{t-1 \to t}$, with accuracy $\epsilon 2^{-(t+2(q-1))}$, in the sense that $V^{t-1 \to t} = U^{t-1 \to t}|0^{2n}\rangle_{A_t B_t}$, with A^* playing the role of A_t. Subsequently, apply a phase -1 on the all-zero state of the ancilla registers A_t and B_t, and reapply $U^{t-1 \to t}$, this time with accuracy $\epsilon 2^{-(t+2(q-1)+1)}$.*

We omitted defining $\mathfrak{ES}$.Ver since it is trivial to build from CReflect, as described in Lemma 5. By Theorem 6, the runtime of $\mathfrak{ES}(\epsilon, n)$ is polynomial in n, $\log(1/\epsilon)$ and the total number of queries q that are made to its various interfaces.

We want to show that the above sampler is indistinguishable from the ideal sampler to any oracle algorithm, in the following sense. Given a stateful machine $\mathcal{C} \in \{\mathfrak{IS}(n), \mathfrak{ES}(n, \epsilon)\}$ and a (not necessarily efficient) oracle algorithm $\mathcal{A}$, we define the process $b \leftarrow \mathcal{A}^{\mathcal{C}}$ as follows:

1. $\mathcal{C}$.Init is called;
2. $\mathcal{A}$ receives oracle access to $\mathcal{C}$.Gen and $\mathcal{C}$.CReflect;
3. $\mathcal{A}$ outputs a bit b.

Theorem 7. *For all oracle algorithms $\mathcal{A}$ and all $\epsilon > 0$ that can depend on n in an arbitrary way,*

$$\left| \Pr\left[\mathcal{A}^{\mathfrak{IS}(n)} = 1 \right] - \Pr\left[\mathcal{A}^{\mathfrak{ES}(n,\epsilon)} = 1 \right] \right| \leq \epsilon. \tag{19}$$

Proof. During the execution of $\mathfrak{ES}(\epsilon, n)$, the i-th call of $V^{t-1 \to t}$ (for any t) incurs a trace distance error of at most $\epsilon 2^{-i}$. The trace distance between the outputs of $\mathcal{A}^{\mathfrak{ES}}(\epsilon, n)$ and $\mathcal{A}^{\mathfrak{ES}}(0, n)$ is therefore bounded by $\sum_{i=1}^{\infty} \epsilon 2^{-i} = \epsilon$. It is thus sufficient to establish the theorem for $\mathfrak{ES}(0, n)$.

For any fixed q, there exists a stateful machine $\hat{\mathfrak{ES}}(0, q, n)$ which is perfectly indistinguishable from $\mathfrak{IS}(n)$ to all adversaries who make a maximum total number q of queries. The Init procedure of $\hat{\mathfrak{ES}}(0, q, n)$ samples a random element U_i from an exact unitary $2q$-design $D^{2q} = \{U_i\}_{i \in I}$. Queries to Gen are answered with a copy of $U_i|0\rangle$, and Reflect is implemented by applying $\mathbb{1} - 2U_i|0\rangle\langle0|U_i^\dagger$. It will be helpful to express $\mathfrak{E}\mathfrak{S}(0, q, n)$ in an equivalent isometric form. In this form, the initial oracle state is $|\eta\rangle = |I|^{-1/2} \sum_{i\in I} |i\rangle_{\hat{B}}$. Gen queries are answered using the $\hat{B}$-controlled isometry

$$\hat{V}^{t\to t+1}_{\hat{B}\to\hat{B}A_{t+1}} = \sum_{i\in I} |i\rangle\langle i|_{\hat{B}} \otimes U_i|0\rangle_{A_{t+1}}. \tag{20}$$

Reflect queries are answered by

$$\hat{V}^{\text{Reflect}}_{\hat{B}A^*\to\hat{B}A^*} = \mathbb{1} - 2\sum_{i\in I} |i\rangle\langle i|_{\hat{B}} \otimes U_i|0\rangle\langle0|_{A^*}U_i^\dagger \tag{21}$$

$$= \mathbb{1} - 2\hat{V}^{t\to t+1}_{\hat{B}\to\hat{B}A^*} \left(\hat{V}^{t\to t+1}\right)^\dagger_{\hat{B}A^*\to\hat{B}}. \tag{22}$$

Now suppose $\mathcal{A}$ is an arbitrary (i.e., not bounded-query) algorithm making only Gen queries. We will show that after q queries, the oracles $\mathfrak{E}\mathfrak{S}(0, n)$ and $\mathfrak{E}\mathfrak{S}(0, q, n)$ are equivalent, and that this holds for all q. We emphasize that $\mathfrak{E}\mathfrak{S}(0, n)$ does not depend on q; we can thus apply the equivalence for the appropriate total query count q_{total} after $\mathcal{A}$ has produced its final state, even if q_{total} is determined only at runtime. It will follow that $\mathfrak{E}\mathfrak{S}(0, n)$ is equivalent to $\mathfrak{I}\mathfrak{S}(n)$.

To show the equivalence betwen $\mathfrak{E}\mathfrak{S}(0, n)$ and $\mathfrak{E}\mathfrak{S}(0, q, n)$, we will demonstrate partial isometry $V^{\text{switch},t}$ that transforms registers B^t of $\mathfrak{E}\mathfrak{S}(0, n)$ (after t Gen queries and no Reflect queries) into the register $\hat{B}$ of $\mathfrak{E}\mathfrak{S}(0, q, n)$, in such a way that the corresponding global states on $A^t B^t$ and $A^t \hat{B}$ are mapped to each other. The isometry is partial because its domain is the symmetric subspace of $\mathbb{C}^{2^n \otimes t}$. It is defined as follows:

$$V^{\text{switch},t}_{B^t\to\hat{B}} = \sqrt{\frac{d_{\text{Sym}^t\mathbb{C}^{d2^n}}}{|I|}} \sum_{i\in I} \left(\langle0|U_i^T\right)^{\otimes t}_{B^t} \otimes |i\rangle_{\hat{B}}. \tag{23}$$

To verify that this is indeed the desired isometry, we calculate:

$$\left(\langle0|U_i^T\right)^{\otimes t}_{B^t} |\phi^+_{\text{Sym}}\rangle_{A^t B^t} = \sqrt{\frac{2^{nt}}{d_{\text{Sym}^t\mathbb{C}^{2n}}}} \left(\langle0|U_i^T\right)^{\otimes t}_{B^t} \Pi^{\text{Sym}}_{B^t} |\phi^+\rangle_{A^t B^t} \tag{24}$$

$$= \sqrt{\frac{2^{nt}}{d_{\text{Sym}^t\mathbb{C}^{2n}}}} \left(\langle0|U_i^T\right)^{\otimes t}_{B^t} |\phi^+\rangle_{A^t B^t} \tag{25}$$

$$= \sqrt{\frac{2^{nt}}{d_{\text{Sym}^t\mathbb{C}^{2n}}}} \left(\langle0|\right)^{\otimes t}_{B^t} \otimes (U_i)^{\otimes t}_{A^t} |\phi^+\rangle_{A^t B^t} \tag{26}$$

$$= \sqrt{\frac{1}{d_{\text{Sym}^t\mathbb{C}^{2n}}}} \left(U_i|0\rangle\right)^{\otimes t}_{A^t}. \tag{27}$$

Here we have used the fact that $\left(\langle0|U_i^T\right)^{\otimes t}$ is in the symmetric subspace in the second equality, and the third and forth equality are applications of the Mirror Lemma (Lemma 1) with $d = d' = 2^{nt}$, and $d = 1$, $d' = 2^{nt}$, respectively.

We have hence proven the exact correctness of $\mathfrak{ES}(0,n)$ without the Reflect interface. Note that the global state after t queries to $\mathfrak{ES}(0,n)$.Gen is the maximally entangled state of two copies of the t-fold symmetric subspace; of course, this is only true up to actions performed by the adversary, but those trivially commute with maps applied only to the oracle registers. As the global state is in the domain of $V^{\mathrm{switch},t}_{B^t \to \hat{B}}$, we obtain the equation

$$\hat{V}^{t \to t+1}_{\hat{B} \to \hat{B}A_{t+1}} V^{\mathrm{switch},t}_{B^t \to \hat{B}} = V^{\mathrm{switch},t+1}_{B^{t+1} \to \hat{B}} V^{t \to t+1}_{B^t \to B^{t+1}A_{t+1}}. \tag{28}$$

More precisely, we observe that the two sides of the above have the same effect on the global state, and then conclude that they must be the same operator by the Choi-Jamoiłkowski isomorphism.

Recalling that $V^{\mathrm{switch},t}$ is partial with the symmetric subspace as its domain, we see that Eq. (28) is equivalent to

$$\left(V^{\mathrm{switch},t+1}_{B^{t+1} \to \hat{B}}\right)^{\dagger} \hat{V}^{t \to t+1}_{\hat{B} \to \hat{B}A_{t+1}} V^{\mathrm{switch},t}_{B^t \to \hat{B}} = \Pi^{\mathrm{Sym}^{t+1}\mathbb{C}^{2^n}}_{B^{t+1}} V^{t \to t+1}_{B^t \to B^{t+1}A_{t+1}} \tag{29}$$

$$= V^{t \to t+1}_{B^t \to B^{t+1}A_{t+1}} \Pi^{\mathrm{Sym}^t\mathbb{C}^{2^n}}_{B^t}. \tag{30}$$

By taking the above equality times its adjoint, we arrive at

$$\left(V^{\mathrm{switch},t}_{B^t \to \hat{B}}\right)^{\dagger} \left(\hat{V}^{t \to t+1}_{\hat{B} \to \hat{B}A_{t+1}}\right)^{\dagger} V^{\mathrm{switch},t+1}_{B^{t+1} \to \hat{B}} \left(V^{\mathrm{switch},t+1}_{B^{t+1} \to \hat{B}}\right)^{\dagger} \hat{V}^{t \to t+1}_{\hat{B} \to \hat{B}A_{t+1}} V^{\mathrm{switch},t}_{B^t \to \hat{B}}$$

$$= \Pi^{\mathrm{Sym}^t\mathbb{C}^{2^n}}_{B^t} \left(V^{t \to t+1}_{B^t \to B^{t+1}A_{t+1}}\right)^{\dagger} V^{t \to t+1}_{B^t \to B^{t+1}A_{t+1}} \Pi^{\mathrm{Sym}^t\mathbb{C}^{2^n}}_{B^t}. \tag{31}$$

By Eq. (28), the range of $\hat{V}^{t \to t+1}_{\hat{B} \to \hat{B}A_{t+1}} V^{\mathrm{switch},t}_{B^t \to \hat{B}}$ is contained in the range of $V^{\mathrm{switch},t+1}_{B^{t+1} \to \hat{B}} \otimes \mathbb{1}_{A_{t+1}}$. We can thus simplify as follows:

$$\left(V^{\mathrm{switch},t}_{B^t \to \hat{B}}\right)^{\dagger} \left(\hat{V}^{t \to t+1}_{\hat{B} \to \hat{B}A_{t+1}}\right)^{\dagger} \hat{V}^{t \to t+1}_{\hat{B} \to \hat{B}A_{t+1}} V^{\mathrm{switch},t}_{B^t \to \hat{B}}$$

$$= \Pi^{\mathrm{Sym}^t\mathbb{C}^{2^n}}_{B^t} \left(V^{t \to t+1}_{B^t \to B^{t+1}A_{t+1}}\right)^{\dagger} V^{t \to t+1}_{B^t \to B^{t+1}A_{t+1}} \Pi^{\mathrm{Sym}^t\mathbb{C}^{2^n}}_{B^t}. \tag{32}$$

Now observe that both sides of the above consist of a projection operator "sandwiched" by some operation. These two projection operators are precisely the projectors which define the reflection operators of $\hat{\mathfrak{ES}}(0,q,n)$ (on the left-hand side) and $\mathfrak{ES}(0,n)$ (on the right-hand side.) We thus see that Eq. (32) shows that applying $\mathfrak{ES}(0,n)$.Reflect is the same as switching to $\hat{\mathfrak{ES}}(0,q,n)$, applying $\hat{\mathfrak{ES}}(0,q,n)$.Reflect, and then switching back to $\mathfrak{ES}(0,n)$. The same holds for the controlled versions $\mathfrak{ES}(0,n)$.CReflect and $\hat{\mathfrak{ES}}(0,n)$.CReflect.

This completes the proof of the exact equality between the stateful machines $\mathfrak{IS}(n)$ and $\mathfrak{ES}(0,n)$. The approximate case follows as argued above. $\qquad\square$

It turns out that if we have an a priori bound of the form $q = O(\sqrt{2^n \epsilon})$ on the number of queries that will be made to our state sampler, in relation to the number of qubits n and the desired accuracy ϵ, there is also an alternative protocol, due to Zvika Brakerski. The approach is based on Zhandry's compressed oracle technique and the work by Ji, Liu and Song. In [18] and in [10] one can find the following theorem for the two mentioned phase variants, respectively.

Theorem 8 (Lemma 1 in [18], respectively Theorem 1.2 in [10]). *Let* $H :$ $\{0,1\}^n \to \{0,1\}^n$ *be a random function. Then* k *copies of the* n-*qubit quantum state*

$$|\psi^H\rangle = 2^{-n/2} \sum_{x \in \{0,1\}^n} \omega^{H(x)}|x\rangle \tag{33}$$

are statistically indistinguishable from k *copies of a Haar random quantum state up to error* $O(k^2/2^n)$, *for* $\omega = e^{\frac{2\pi i}{2^n}}$, *respectively* $\omega = -1$.

Let now $\mathfrak{EF}(n,n)$ be the stateful machine with interfaces Init and Query simulating a random function from n bits to n bits that was given in [31]. Then we get the following

Corollary 3. *Let* $\mathfrak{EG}'(n)$ *be the following stateful machine:*

- $\mathfrak{EG}'(n)$.Init *is equal to* $\mathfrak{EF}(n,n)$.Init.
- $\mathfrak{EG}'(n)$.Gen *produces a copy of* $|\psi^H\rangle$, *simulating* H *using a single query to* $\mathfrak{EF}(n,n)$.Query.
- $\mathfrak{EG}'(n)$.CCReflect *implements the controlled reflection about* $|\psi^H\rangle$, *simulating* H *using two queries to* $\mathfrak{EF}(n,n)$.Query.

For all oracle algorithms $\mathcal{A}$ *making* q *that make* q *queries and that can depend on* n *in an arbitrary way,*

$$\left| \Pr\left[\mathcal{A}^{\mathfrak{IG}(n)} = 1\right] - \Pr\left[\mathcal{A}^{\mathfrak{EG}'(n)} = 1\right] \right| \leq O(q^2/2^n). \tag{34}$$

4   Simulating a Haar-Random Unitary Oracle

4.1   The Problem, and Our Approach

We begin by defining the ideal object we'd like to emulate. This ideal object samples a Haar-random unitary U, and then answers two types of queries: queries to U, and queries to its inverse $U^\dagger$.

Construction 3 (Ideal unitary sampler). *Let* n *be a positive integer. The ideal unitary sampler is an ideal machine* $\mathfrak{IU}(n)$ *with interfaces* (Init, Eval, Invert), *defined as follows.*

1. $\mathfrak{IU}(n)$.Init: *takes no input; samples a description* $\tilde{U}$ *of a Haar-random* n-*qubit unitary operator* U.
2. $\mathfrak{IU}(n)$.Eval: *takes* n-*qubit register as input, applies* U *and responds with the output;*
3. $\mathfrak{IU}(n)$.Invert: *takes* n-*qubit register as input, applies* U^{-1} *and responds with the output.*

Below, we construct a stateful machine that runs in polynomial *space* (and the runtime of which we don't characterize), and that is indistinguishable from $\mathfrak{IU}(n)$ for arbitrary query algorithms.

Our approach. It turns out that the solution of a much easier task comes to our help, namely simulating a Haar random unitary for an algorithm that makes an *a priori* polynomially bounded number t of queries. In this case we can just pick a unitary t-design, sample an element from it and answer the up to t queries using this element. As in the proof of Theorem 7, we can also construct an isometric stateful machine version of this strategy: Instead of sampling a random element from the t-design, we can prepare a quantum register in a superposition, e.g. over the index set of the t-design (Init), and then apply the t-design element (Eval) or its inverse (Invert) controlled on that register.

Now consider an algorithm that makes t parallel queries to a Haar random unitary (for ease of exposition let us assume here that the algorithm makes no inverse queries). The effect of these t parallel queries is just the application of the t-twirling channel (or the mixed twirling channel defined in Eq. (10)) to the t input registers. The t-design-based isometric stateful machine simulates this t-twirling channel faithfully. What is more, it applies a Stinespring dilation of the t-twirling channel, the dilating register being the one created by initialization.

Now suppose we have answered t queries using the t-design-based machine, and are now asked to answer another, still parallel, query. Of course we cannot, in general, just answer it using the t-design, as its guarantees only hold for t applications of the unitary. But all Stinespring dilations of a quantum channel are equivalent in the sense that there exists a (possibly partial) isometry acting on the dilating register of one given dilation, that transforms it into another given dilation. So we can just apply an isometry that transforms our t-design based Stinespring dilation into a $t+1$-design based one, and subsequently answer the $t + 1$st query using a controlled unitary.

4.2   Construction and Proof

We continue to describe a stateful machine that simulates $\mathfrak{IU}(n)$ exactly and has a state register of size polynomial in n and the total number of queries q that an algorithm makes to its Eval and Invert interfaces. The existence of the required unitary t-designs is due to Corollary 2.

We recall our conventions for dealing with many copies of fixed-sized registers. We let A denote an n-qubit register, we let A_j denote indexed copies of A, and we let A^t denote $A_1 A_2 \cdots A_t$. In this case, the various copies of A will be the input registers of the adversary, on which the simulator will act. The oracle will now hold a single register $\hat{B}_t$ whose size will grow with the number of queries t. This register holds an index of an element in a t-design.

For the construction below, we need the following quantum states and operators. For a positive integer n, choose a family of n-qubit unitary designs $\{D_t\}_{t \in \mathbb{N}}$, where $D_t = \{U_{t,i}\}_{i \in I_t}$ is a unitary t-design. Let $\hat{B}_t$ be a register of dimension $|I_t|$ and define the uniform superposition over indices

$$|\eta_t\rangle_{\hat{B}_t} = \frac{1}{\sqrt{|I_t|}} \sum_{i \in I_t} |i\rangle_{\hat{B}_t}. \tag{35}$$

For nonnegative integers t, t', ℓ, define the unitaries

$$V^{(t,t',\ell)}_{A^{t'}\hat{B}_t} = \sum_{i \in I_t} (U_{t,i})^{\otimes \ell}_{A_1 A_2 \ldots A_\ell} \otimes \left(U^\dagger_{t,i}\right)^{\otimes t'-\ell}_{A_{\ell+1} A_{\ell+2} \ldots A_{t'}} \otimes |i\rangle\langle i|_{\hat{B}_t}. \qquad (36)$$

These isometries perform the following: controlled on an index i of a t-design $U_{t,i}$, apply $U_{t,i}$ to ℓ registers and $U^\dagger_{t,i}$ to $t' - \ell$ registers. For us it will always be the case that $t' \leq t$, since otherwise the t-design property no longer makes the desired guarantees on the map V.

We also let $W^{(t,\ell)}_{\hat{B}_t \to \hat{B}_{t+1}}$ be an isometry such that

$$V^{(t+1,t,\ell)}_{A^t \hat{B}_{t+1}} |\eta_{t+1}\rangle_{\hat{B}_{t+1}} = W_{\hat{B}_t \to \hat{B}_{t+1}} V^{(t,t,\ell)}_{A^t \hat{B}_t} |\eta_t\rangle_{\hat{B}_t} \qquad (37)$$

for $\ell = 0, \ldots, t$. The isometry W always exists, as all Stinespring dilations are isometrically equivalent, and both $V^{(t,t,\ell)}_{A^t \hat{B}_t} |\eta_t\rangle_{\hat{B}_t}$ and $V^{(t+1,t,\ell)}_{A^t \hat{B}_{t+1}} |\eta_{t+1}\rangle_{\hat{B}_{t+1}}$ are Stinespring dilations of the mixed twirling channel $\mathcal{T}^{(t,\ell)}$ by the t-design property.

We are now ready to define the space-efficient unitary sampler.

Construction 4 (Space-efficient unitary sampler). *Let n be a positive integer and $\{D_t\}_{t \in \mathbb{N}}$ a family of n-qubit unitary t-designs $D_t = \{U_{t,i}\}_{i \in I_t}$, with $|I_t| = 2^{\text{poly}(n,t)}$. Define a stateful machine $\mathfrak{EU}(n, \epsilon)$ with interfaces (Init, Eval, Invert) as follows. The machine will maintain counters t_e (the number of Eval queries), t_i (the number of Invert queries), and $t := t_e + t_i$.*

1. $\mathfrak{EU}(n).\text{Init}$: *Prepares the state $|\eta_1\rangle_{\hat{B}_1}$ and stores it.*
2. $\mathfrak{EU}(n).\text{Eval}$:
   - *If $t = 0$, apply $V^{(1,1,1)}_{A_1 \hat{B}_1}$, where A_1 is the input register.*
   - *If $t > 0$, apply $W^{(t,t_e)}_{\hat{B}_t \to \hat{B}_{t+1}}$ to the state register and subsequently apply $V^{t+1,1,1}_{A_{t+1} \hat{B}_{t+1}}$, where A_{t+1} is the input register.*
3. $\mathfrak{IU}(n).\text{Invert}$:
   - *If $t = 0$, apply $V^{(1,1,0)}_{A_1 \hat{B}_1}$, where A_1 is the input register.*
   - *If $t > 0$, apply $W^{(t,t_e)}_{\hat{B}_t \to \hat{B}_{t+1}}$ to the state register and subsequently apply $V^{t+1,1,0}_{A_{t+1} \hat{B}_{t+1}}$, where A_{t+1} is the input register.*

We want to show that the above sampler is indistinguishable from the ideal sampler to any oracle algorithm, in the following sense. Given a stateful machine $\mathcal{C} \in \{\mathfrak{IU}(n), \mathfrak{EU}(n, \epsilon)\}$ and a (not necessarily efficient) oracle algorithm $\mathcal{A}$, we define the process $b \leftarrow \mathcal{A}^\mathcal{C}$ as follows:

1. $\mathcal{C}.\text{Init}$ is called;
2. $\mathcal{A}$ receives oracle access to $\mathcal{C}.\text{Eval}$ and $\mathcal{C}.\text{Invert}$;
3. $\mathcal{A}$ outputs a bit b.

Theorem 9. *For all oracle algorithms $\mathcal{A}$*

$$\Pr\left[\mathcal{A}^{\mathfrak{IU}(n)} = 1\right] = \Pr\left[\mathcal{A}^{\mathfrak{EU}(n,\epsilon)} = 1\right]. \qquad (38)$$

Proof. We begin by proving the following claim by induction. The claim states that the theorem holds for adversaries who only make parallel queries.

Claim. For all $x \in \{0,1\}^t$, let $V^{(x)}_{A^t \to A^t \hat{B}_t}$ be the isometry that is implemented by making t parallel queries to $\mathfrak{CU}(n, \epsilon)$, where the i-th query is made to the Eval interface if $x_i = 1$ and to the Invert interface if $x_i = 0$. Let further $\sigma \in S_t$ be a permutation such that $\sigma.x = 11...100...0$, where the lower dot denotes the natural action of S_t on strings of length t. Then

$$V^{(x)}_{A^t \to A^t \hat{B}_t} = \sigma^{-1}_{A^t} V^{(t,t,\ell)}_{A^t \hat{B}_t} |\eta_t\rangle_{\hat{B}_t}, \tag{39}$$

where σ acts by permuting the t registers.

Proof. For $t = 1$, the claim trivially holds. Now suppose the claim holds for $t-1$. By definition of the Eval and Invert interfaces,

$$V^{(x)}_{A^t \to A^t \hat{B}_t} = V^{t,1,x_t}_{A_t \hat{B}_t} W^{(t,\ell)}_{\hat{B}_{t-1} \to \hat{B}_t} V^{(x_{[1;t-1]})}_{A^{t-1} \to A^{t-1} \hat{B}_{t-1}}, \tag{40}$$

where $x_{[a,b]} = x_a x_{a+1}...x_b$. By the induction hypothesis, we have

$$V^{(x_{[1;t-1]})}_{A^{t-1} \to A^{t-1} \hat{B}_{t-1}} = \hat{\sigma}^{-1}_{A^{t-1}} V^{(t-1,t-1,\ell-x_t)}_{A^{t-1} \hat{B}_{t-1}} |\eta_{t-1}\rangle_{\hat{B}_{t-1}} \tag{41}$$

for an appropriate permutation $\hat{\sigma} \in S_{t-1}$. By the design property of D_j for $j = t, t-1$ and the definition of $W^{(t,\ell)}$ we obtain

$$T^{(t-1,\ell-x_t)}_{D_{t-1}} = T^{(t-1,\ell-x_t)}_{D_t}$$

$$\Leftrightarrow \quad W^{(t-1,\ell)}_{\hat{B}_{t-1} \to \hat{B}_t} V^{(t-1,t-1,\ell-x_t)}_{A^{t-1} \hat{B}_{t-1}} |\eta_{t-1}\rangle_{\hat{B}_{t-1}} = V^{(t,t-1,\ell-x_t)}_{A^{t-1} \hat{B}_t} |\eta_{t-1}\rangle_{\hat{B}_t}$$

$$\Leftrightarrow \quad W^{(t,\ell)}_{\hat{B}_{t-1} \to \hat{B}_t} \hat{\sigma}^{-1}_{A^{t-1}} V^{(t-1,t-1,\ell-x_t)}_{A^{t-1} \hat{B}_{t-1}} |\eta_{t-1}\rangle_{\hat{B}_{t-1}} = \hat{\sigma}^{-1}_{A^{t-1}} V^{(t,t-1,\ell-x_t)}_{A^{t-1} \hat{B}_t} |\eta_{t-1}\rangle_{\hat{B}_t}. \tag{42}$$

Here we have used the fact that the permutation and $W^{(t-1,\ell)}$ commute because they act on disjoint sets of registers. Putting Eqs. (40), (41) and (42) together, it follows that

$$V^{(x)}_{A^t \to A^t \hat{B}_t} = V^{t,1,x_t}_{A_t \hat{B}_t} \hat{\sigma}^{-1}_{A^{t-1}} V^{(t,t-1,\ell-x_t)}_{A^{t-1} \hat{B}_t} |\eta_t\rangle_{\hat{B}_t}. \tag{43}$$

But clearly

$$V^{t,1,x_t}_{A_t \hat{B}_t} \hat{\sigma}^{-1}_{A^{t-1}} V^{(t,t-1,\ell-x_t)}_{A^{t-1} \hat{B}_t} = \sigma^{-1}_{A^t} V^{(t,t,\ell)}_{A^t \hat{B}_t} \tag{44}$$

For an appropriate permutation σ that consists of applying $\hat{\sigma}$ and then sorting in x_t correctly.

The generalization to adaptive algorithms is done via *post-selection*: Given an algorithm $\mathcal{A}$ with some oracles $O_1, O_2, ..., O_k$, consider non-adaptive algorithm $\tilde{\mathcal{A}}$ that first queries the oracles a sufficient number of times, each of the queries being made with the first half of a maximally entangled state as input. Subsequently the adaptive adversary is run, answering the queries by performing the sender's part of the standard quantum teleportation with the input playing the role of the state to be teleported, and the second half of one of the maximally entangled states playing the role of the sender's half of the entangled resource state for teleportation. Conditioned on the event that all the Pauli corrections in all the teleportation protocols are equal to the identity, the output of $\tilde{\mathcal{A}}$ is equal to the output of $\mathcal{A}$.

Now consider the case where $k = 2$ and O_1 and O_2 are the Eval and Invert interfaces of $\mathfrak{CU}(n, 0)$, or $\mathfrak{IU}(n)$. As the output of $\tilde{\mathcal{A}}$ is *exactly* the same in the two cases, the same holds for the version of $\tilde{\mathcal{A}}$ where we condition, on the outcome that all the Pauli corrections in all the teleportation protocols are equal to the identity, which proves the theorem.   □

Using Corollary 2 and the above, we get the following upper bound on the space complexity of lazy sampling Haar random unitaries.

Corollary 4. *The space complexity S of simulating $\mathfrak{IU}(n)$ as a function of n and the number of queries q is bounded from above by the logarithm of number of elements in any family of exact n-qubit unitary q-designs, and hence*

$$S(n, q) \leq 2q(2n + \log e) + O(\log q). \tag{45}$$

Proof. According to Corollary 2, There exists an exact unitary q-design such that $2q \log \left(\frac{e(2^{2n} + q - 1)}{q} \right) \leq 2q(2n + \log e)$ qubits suffice to coherently store the index of an element from it. The only additional information that $\mathfrak{CU}(n)$ needs to store is how many direct and inverse queries have been answered, which can be done using $\log q$ bits.   □

Our results suggest two possible approaches to devise a time-efficient lazy sampler for Haar random unitaries. The most promising one is to use the same approach as for the state sampler and explicitly constructing the update isometry, possibly using explicit bases for the irreducible representations of $U(2^n)$, or using the Schur transform [6]. The other one would be to use the t-design update method described above, but using efficient approximate t-designs, e.g. the ones constructed in [11]. This would, however, likely require a generalization of the Stinespring dilation continuity result from [20] to so-called quantum combs [12]. In addition, we would need to show that the transition isometries, i.e. the approximate analogue of the isometries $W^{(t,\ell)}$ from Construction 4, are efficiently implementable. We leave the exploration of these approaches for future work.

5 Application: Untraceable Quantum Money

5.1 Untraceable Quantum Money

Our definition of quantum money deviates somewhat from others in the literature [1,18]. We allow the bank to maintain an internal quantum register, we do not require that the money states are pure, and we allow adversaries to apply arbitrary (i.e., not necessarily efficiently implementable) channels.

Definition 2 (Quantum money). *A quantum money scheme is a family of stateful machines $\mathfrak{M}$ indexed by a security parameter λ, and having two interfaces:*

1. Mint: *receives no input, outputs an n-qubit register;*
2. Ver: *receives an n-qubit register as input, outputs an n-qubit register together with a flag $\{\mathsf{acc}, \mathsf{rej}\}$,*

satisfying the following two properties:

- *correctness:* $\|\mathsf{Ver} \circ \mathsf{Mint} - \mathbb{1} \otimes |\mathsf{acc}\rangle\langle\mathsf{acc}|\| \leq \mathsf{negl}(\lambda)$;[5]
- *unforgeability: for all channels Λ with oracle, and all $k \geq 0$,*

$$\Pr\left[\mathsf{acc}^{k+1} \leftarrow {}_{\mathsf{flag}}|\mathsf{Ver}^{\otimes k+1} \circ \Lambda^{\mathsf{Ver}} \circ \mathsf{Mint}^{\otimes k}\right] \leq \mathsf{negl}(\lambda),$$

where $_{\mathsf{flag}}|$ denotes discarding all registers except Ver flags.

It is implicit in the definition that n is a fixed polynomial function of λ, and that all relevant algorithms are uniform in λ.

Next, we define untraceability for quantum money schemes.

Definition 3 (Untraceability game). *The untraceability game* $\mathsf{Untrace}_\lambda$ *$[\mathfrak{M}, \mathcal{A}]$ between an adversary $\mathcal{A}$ and a quantum money scheme $\mathfrak{M}$ at security parameter λ proceeds as follows:*

1. **set up the trace:** *$\mathcal{A}(1^\lambda)$ receives oracle access to* Ver *and* Mint, *and outputs registers $M_1, M_2, \ldots, M_k$ and a permutation $\pi \in S_k$;*
2. **permute and verify bills:** *$b \leftarrow \{0,1\}$ is sampled, and if $b = 1$ the registers $M_1 \cdots M_k$ are permuted by π.* Ver *is invoked on each M_j; the accepted registers are placed in a set $\mathcal{M}$ while the rest are discarded;*
3. **complete the trace:** *$\mathcal{A}$ receives $\mathcal{M}$ and the entire internal state of $\mathfrak{M}$, and outputs a guess $b' \in \{0,1\}$.*

The output of $\mathsf{Untrace}_\lambda[\mathfrak{M}, \mathcal{A}]$ *is $\delta_{bb'}$; in the case $b = b'$, we say that $\mathcal{A}$ wins.*

Definition 4 (Untraceable quantum money). *A quantum money scheme $\mathfrak{M}$ is untraceable if, for every algorithm $\mathcal{A}$,*

$$\Pr\left[1 \leftarrow \mathsf{Untrace}_\lambda[\mathfrak{M}, \mathcal{A}]\right] \leq \frac{1}{2} + \mathsf{negl}(\lambda).$$

The intuition behind the definition is as follows. In general, one might consider a complicated scenario involving many honest players and many adversaries, where the goal of the adversaries is to trace the movement of at least one

---

[5] Note that it is understood that this inequality should hold no matter which interfaces have been called in between the relevant Mint and Ver calls.

bill in transactions involving at least one honest player. Tracing in transactions involving only adversaries is of course trivial. The first natural simplification is to view all the adversaries as a single adversarial party; if that party cannot trace, then neither can any individual adversary. Next, we assume that honest players will verify any bills they receive immediately; obviously, if they do not do this, and then participate in transactions with the adversary, then tracing is again trivial. We thus arrive at the situation described in the game: the adversary is first allowed to create candidate bills arbitrarily, including storing information about them and entangling them with additional registers, before handing them to honest players who may or may not perform some transactions; the goal of the adversary is to decide which is the case, with the help of the bank. Note that one round of this experiment is sufficient in the security game, as an adversary can always use the Ver and Mint oracles to simulate additional rounds.

One might reasonably ask if there are even stronger definitions of untraceability than the above. Given its relationship to the ideal state sampler, we believe that Haar money, defined below, should satisfy almost any notion of untraceability, including composable notions. We also remark that, based on the structure of the state simulator, which maintains an overall pure state supported on two copies of the symmetric subspace of banknote registers, it is straightforward to see that the scheme is also secure against an "honest but curious" or "specious" [15,26] bank. We leave the formalization of these added security guarantees to future work.

5.2   Haar Money

Next, we show how the lazy state sampler (Construction 2) yields untraceable quantum money. The construction follows the idea of [18] sample a single (pseudo)random quantum state and hand out copies of it as banknotes.

Construction 5 (Haar money). *Let n be a positive integer and $\epsilon > 0$. The Haar scheme $\mathfrak{HM}(n, \epsilon)$ is defined as follows:*

- Mint: *on first invocation, instantiate $\mathfrak{CS} := \mathfrak{CS}(n, \epsilon)$ by running $\mathfrak{CS}$.Init. On all invocations, output result of $\mathfrak{CS}$.Gen;*
- Ver: *apply $\mathfrak{CS}$.Ver; in the* acc *case, call* Mint *and output the result; in the* rej *case, output 0^n.*

We remark that, while Construction 2 does not explicitly include a Ver interface, one can easily be added by Lemma 5.

Proposition 3. *Haar money is an untraceable quantum money scheme.*

Proof. We need to show three properties: completeness, unforgeability, and untraceability. For the completeness and unforgeability properties, observe that Theorem 7 implies that the adversary's view is indistinguishable (up to negligible terms) if we replace the efficient state sampler $\mathfrak{CS}$ with the ideal $\mathfrak{IS}$. Once we've made that replacement, completeness follows from the definition of

$\mathfrak{IG}$.Gen and $\mathfrak{IG}$.Ver, and unforgeability follows from the complexity-theoretic no-cloning theorem [1].

For untraceability, it is of course true that $\mathfrak{IG}$ is obviously untraceable. However, we cannot simply invoke Theorem 7 to conclude the same about $\mathfrak{CG}$, since the adversary will receive the state of the bank at the end of the game. Instead, we argue as follows. Consider step 2 (permute and verify bills) in the untraceability game Untrace$_\lambda[\mathfrak{HM}, \mathcal{A}]$. An equivalent way to perform this step is to (i) verify all the registers first, (ii) discard the ones that fail verification, and then (iii) apply the permutation, conditioned on the challenge bit b. Steps (i) and (ii) are applied always and in particular do not depend on b. However, after (i) and (ii) have been applied, by the definition of $\mathfrak{CG}$ the joint state of the bank and all the $M_j \in \mathcal{M}$ (and indeed all verified bills in existence) is negligibly far from the state $|\phi_{\mathrm{Sym}}^+\rangle$, i.e., the maximally entangled state on the symmetric subspace. This state is clearly invariant under permutation of the money registers, and in particular under the permutation of the registers in $\mathcal{M}$ selected by the adversary. We emphasize that this invariance holds for the entire state (including the bank.) As the remainder of the game experiment is simply some channel applied to that state, and this channel does not depend on b, the result follows.   □

While Haar money is an information-theoretically unforgeable and untraceable quantum money scheme, it is easy to see that the quantum money scheme devised in [18] is *computationally* unforgeable and untraceable.

Acknowledgments. The authors thank Zvika Brakerski for suggesting the alternative construction based on compressed oracles. We thank Yi-Kai Liu, Carl Miller, and Fang Song for helpful comments on an earlier draft. CM thanks Michael Walter for discussions about t-designs. CM was funded by a NWO VIDI grant (Project No. 639.022.519) and a NWO VENI grant (Project No. VI.Veni.192.159). GA acknowledges support from NSF grant CCF-1763736. GA was supported by the Dutch Research Council (NWO) through a travel grant - 040.11.708. AR acknowledges support from NSF grant CCF-1763773.

References

1. Aaronson, S., Christiano, P.: Quantum money from hidden subspaces. In: Proceedings of the Forty-Fourth Annual ACM Symposium on Theory of Computing, pp. 41–60. ACM (2012)
2. Alagic, G., Gagliardoni, T., Majenz, C.: Can you sign a quantum state. Cryptology ePrint Archive, Report 2018/1164 (2018). https://eprint.iacr.org/2018/1164
3. Alagic, G., Gagliardoni, T., Majenz, C.: Unforgeable quantum encryption. In: Nielsen, J.B., Rijmen, V. (eds.) EUROCRYPT 2018. LNCS, vol. 10822, pp. 489–519. Springer, Cham (2018). https://doi.org/10.1007/978-3-319-78372-7_16
4. Alagic, G., Majenz, C., Russell, A.: Efficient simulation of random states and random unitaries. arXiv preprint arXiv:1910.05729 (2019)
5. Ambainis, A., Emerson, J.: Quantum t-designs: t-wise independence in the quantum world. In: Proceedings of the Twenty-Second Annual IEEE Conference on Computational Complexity, CCC 2007, pp. 129–140. IEEE Computer Society, Washington, DC (2007)

6. Bacon, D., Chuang, I.L., Harrow, A.W.: Efficient quantum circuits for Schur and Clebsch-Gordan transforms. Phys. Rev. Lett. **97**, 170502 (2006)
7. Bellare, M., Rogaway, P.: Random oracles are practical: a paradigm for designing efficient protocols. In: Proceedings of the 1st ACM Conference on Computer and Communications Security, CCS 1993, pp. 62–73. ACM, New York (1993)
8. Bennett, C., Brassard, G.: Quantum cryptography: public key distribution and coin tossing. In: Proceedings of the International Conference on Computers, Systems, and Signal Processing, pp. 175–179 (1984)
9. Boneh, D., Zhandry, M.: Quantum-secure message authentication codes. In: Johansson, T., Nguyen, P.Q. (eds.) EUROCRYPT 2013. LNCS, vol. 7881, pp. 592–608. Springer, Heidelberg (2013). https://doi.org/10.1007/978-3-642-38348-9_35
10. Brakerski Z., Shmueli O.: (Pseudo) random quantum states with binary phase. arXiv preprint arXiv:1906.10611 (2019)
11. Brandão, F.G.S.L., Harrow, A.W., Horodecki, M.: Local random quantum circuits are approximate polynomial-designs. Commun. Math. Phys. **346**(2), 397–434 (2016). https://doi.org/10.1007/s00220-016-2706-8
12. Chiribella, G., D'Ariano, G.M., Perinotti, P.: Quantum circuit architecture. Phys. Rev. Lett. **101**, 060401 (2008)
13. Christandl, M.: The structure of bipartite quantum states-insights from group theory and cryptography. Ph.D. thesis, University of Cambridge (2006)
14. Don, J., Fehr, S., Majenz, C., Schaffner, C.: Security of the Fiat-Shamir transformation in the quantum random-oracle model. In: Boldyreva, A., Micciancio, D. (eds.) CRYPTO 2019. LNCS, vol. 11693, pp. 356–383. Springer, Cham (2019). https://doi.org/10.1007/978-3-030-26951-7_13
15. Dupuis, F., Nielsen, J.B., Salvail, L.: Secure two-party quantum evaluation of unitaries against specious adversaries. In: Rabin, T. (ed.) CRYPTO 2010. LNCS, vol. 6223, pp. 685–706. Springer, Heidelberg (2010). https://doi.org/10.1007/978-3-642-14623-7_37
16. Goldreich, O., Goldwasser, S., Micali, S.: How to construct random functions. J. ACM **33**(4), 792–807 (1986)
17. Harrow, A.W.: The church of the symmetric subspace. arXiv e-prints arXiv:1308.6595, August 2013
18. Ji, Z., Liu, Y.-K., Song, F.: Pseudorandom quantum states. In: Shacham, H., Boldyreva, A. (eds.) CRYPTO 2018. LNCS, vol. 10993, pp. 126–152. Springer, Cham (2018). https://doi.org/10.1007/978-3-319-96878-0_5
19. Kane, D.: Small designs for path-connected spaces and path-connected homogeneous spaces. Trans. Am. Math. Soc. **367**(9), 6387–6414 (2015)
20. Kretschmann, D., Schlingemann, D., Werner, R.F.: The information-disturbance tradeoff and the continuity of Stinespring's representation. IEEE Trans. Inf. Theory **54**(4), 1708–1717 (2008)
21. Low, R.A.: Pseudo-randomness and learning in quantum computation. arXiv preprint arXiv:1006.5227 (2010)
22. Majenz, C.: Entropy in quantum information theory - communication and cryptography. arXiv e-prints arXiv:1810.10436, October 2018
23. Mayers, D., Yao, A.: Self testing quantum apparatus. Quantum Inf. Comput. **4**(4), 273–286 (2004)
24. Mosca, M., Stebila, D.: Quantum coins. In: Error-Correcting Codes, Finite Geometries and Cryptography, vol. 523, pp. 35–47 (2010)
25. Roy, A., Scott, A.J.: Unitary designs and codes. Des. Codes Cryptogr. **53**(1), 13–31 (2009). https://doi.org/10.1007/s10623-009-9290-2

26. Salvail, L., Schaffner, C., Sotáková, M.: On the power of two-party quantum cryptography. In: Matsui, M. (ed.) ASIACRYPT 2009. LNCS, vol. 5912, pp. 70–87. Springer, Heidelberg (2009). https://doi.org/10.1007/978-3-642-10366-7_5
27. Stinespring, W.F.: Positive functions on C*-algebras. Proc. Am. Math. Soc. **6**(2), 211–216 (1955)
28. Unruh, D.: Quantum proofs of knowledge. In: Pointcheval, D., Johansson, T. (eds.) EUROCRYPT 2012. LNCS, vol. 7237, pp. 135–152. Springer, Heidelberg (2012). https://doi.org/10.1007/978-3-642-29011-4_10
29. Watrous, J.: Zero-knowledge against quantum attacks. SIAM J. Comput. **39**(1), 25–58 (2009)
30. Wegman, M.N., Carter, J.L.: New hash functions and their use in authentication and set equality. J. Comput. Syst. Sci. **22**(3), 265–279 (1981)
31. Zhandry, M.: How to record quantum queries, and applications to quantum indifferentiability. In: Boldyreva, A., Micciancio, D. (eds.) CRYPTO 2019. LNCS, vol. 11693, pp. 239–268. Springer, Cham (2019). https://doi.org/10.1007/978-3-030-26951-7_9

Quantum-Access-Secure Message Authentication via Blind-Unforgeability

Gorjan Alagic[1]($\boxtimes$), Christian Majenz[2]($\boxtimes$), Alexander Russell[3], and Fang Song[4]

[1] QuICS, University of Maryland, and NIST, Gaithersburg, MD, USA
galagic@gmail.com
[2] QuSoft and Centrum Wiskunde & Informatica, Amsterdam, The Netherlands
c.majenz@uva.nl
[3] Department of Computer Science and Engineering, University of Connecticut,
Storrs, CT, USA
acr@cse.uconn.edu
[4] Department of Computer Science and Engineering, Texas A&M University,
College Station, TX, USA
fang.song@tamu.ed

Abstract. Formulating and designing authentication of classical messages in the presence of adversaries with quantum query access has been a longstanding challenge, as the familiar classical notions of unforgeability do not directly translate into meaningful notions in the quantum setting. A particular difficulty is how to fairly capture the notion of "predicting an unqueried value" when the adversary can query in quantum superposition.

We propose a natural definition of unforgeability against quantum adversaries called *blind unforgeability*. This notion defines a function to be predictable if there exists an adversary who can use "partially blinded" oracle access to predict values in the blinded region. We support the proposal with a number of technical results. We begin by establishing that the notion coincides with EUF-CMA in the classical setting and go on to demonstrate that the notion is satisfied by a number of simple guiding examples, such as random functions and quantum-query-secure pseudorandom functions. We then show the suitability of blind unforgeability for supporting canonical constructions and reductions. We prove that the "hash-and-MAC" paradigm and the Lamport one-time digital signature scheme are indeed unforgeable according to the definition. To support our analysis, we additionally define and study a new variety of quantum-secure hash functions called *Bernoulli-preserving*.

Finally, we demonstrate that blind unforgeability is strictly stronger than a previous definition of Boneh and Zhandry [EUROCRYPT '13, CRYPTO '13] and resolve an open problem concerning this previous definition by constructing an explicit function family which is forgeable yet satisfies the definition.

1 Introduction

Large-scale quantum computers will break widely-deployed public-key cryptography, and may even threaten certain post-quantum candidates [6,9,10,12,23].

© International Association for Cryptologic Research 2020
A. Canteaut and Y. Ishai (Eds.): EUROCRYPT 2020, LNCS 12107, pp. 788–817, 2020.
https://doi.org/10.1007/978-3-030-45727-3_27

Even elementary symmetric-key constructions like Feistel ciphers and CBC-MACs become vulnerable in quantum attack models where the adversary is presumed to have quantum query access to some part of the cryptosystem [16–18,22]. As an example, consider encryption in the setting where the adversary has access to the unitary operator $|x\rangle|y\rangle \mapsto |x\rangle|y \oplus f_k(x)\rangle$, where f_k is the encryption or decryption function with secret key k. While it is debatable if this model reflects physical implementations of symmetric-key cryptography, it appears necessary in a number of generic settings, such as public-key encryption and hashing with public hash functions. It could also be relevant when private-key primitives are composed in larger protocols, e.g., by exposing circuits via obfuscation [21]. Setting down appropriate security definitions in this quantum attack model is the subject of several threads of recent research [8,13].

In this article, we study authentication of classical information in the quantum-secure model. Here, the adversary is granted quantum query access to the signing algorithm of a message authentication code (MAC) or a digital signature scheme, and is tasked with producing valid forgeries. In the purely classical setting, we insist that the forgeries are fresh, i.e., distinct from previous queries to the oracle. When the function may be queried in superposition, however, it's unclear how to meaningfully reflect this constraint that a forgery was previously "unqueried." For example, it is clear that an adversary that simply queries with a uniform superposition and then measures a forgery—a feasible attack against any function—should not be considered successful. On the other hand, an adversary that uses the same query to discover some structural property (e.g., a superpolynomial-size period in the MAC) should be considered a break. Examples like these indicate the difficulty of the problem. How do we correctly "price" the queries? How do we decide if a forgery is fresh? Furthermore, how can this be done in a manner that is consistent with these guiding examples? In fact, this problem has a natural interpretation that goes well beyond cryptography: *What does it mean for a classical function to appear unpredictable to a quantum oracle algorithm?*[1]

Previous approaches. The first approach to this problem was suggested by Boneh and Zhandry [7]. They define a MAC to be unforgeable if, after making q queries to the MAC, no adversary can produce $q + 1$ valid input-output pairs except with negligible probability. We will refer to this notion as "PO security" (PO for "plus one," and k-PO when the adversary is permitted a maximum of k queries). Among a number of results, Boneh and Zhandry prove that this notion can be realized by a quantum-secure pseudorandom function (qPRF).

Another approach, due to Garg, Yuen and Zhandry [14] (GYZ), considers a function *one-time* unforgeable if only a trivial "query, measure in computational basis, output result" attack[2] is allowed. Unfortunately, it is not clear how to

---

[1] The related notion of "appearing *random* to quantum oracle algorithms" has a satisfying definition, which can be fulfilled efficiently [29].

[2] Technically, the *Stinespring dilation* [25] of a computational basis measurement is the most general attack.

extend GYZ to two or more queries. Furthermore, the single query is allowed in a limited query model with an non-standard restriction.[3] Zhandry recently showed a separation between PO and GYZ by means of the powerful tool of obfuscation [31].

It is interesting to note that similar problems arise in encryption schemes of *quantum* data and a convincing solution was recently found [2,3]. However, it relies on the fact that for quantum messages, *authentication implies secrecy*. This enables "tricking" the adversary by replacing their queries with "trap" plaintexts to detect replays. As unforgeability and secrecy are orthogonal in the classical world, adversaries would easily recognize the spoofed oracle. This renders the approach of [2,3] inapplicable in this case.

Unresolved issues. PO security, the only candidate definition of quantum-secure unforgeability in the general, multi-query setting, appears to be insufficient for several reasons. First, as observed in [14], it is a priori unclear if PO security rules out forging on a message region A while making queries to a signing oracle supported on a disjoint message region B. Second, there may be unique features of quantum information, such as the destructiveness of quantum measurement, which PO does not capture. In particular, quantum algorithms must sometimes "consume" (i.e., fully measure) a state to extract some useful information, such as a symmetry in the oracle. There might be an adversary that makes one or more quantum queries but then must consume the post-query states completely in order to make a single, but convincing, forgery.

Surprisingly, prior to this work none of these plausible attack strategies have been exploited to give a separation between PO and "intuitive security."

2   Summary of Results

A new definition: Blind-unforgeability. To address the above mentioned issues, and in light of the concrete "counterexample" presented below as Construction 8, we develop a new definition of many-time unforgeability we call "blind-unforgeability" (or BU). In this approach we examine the behavior of adversaries in the following experiment. The adversary is granted quantum oracle access to the MAC, "blinded" at a random region B. Specifically, we set B to be a random ϵ-fraction of the message space, and declare that the oracle function will output $\perp$ on all of B.

$$B_\epsilon \mathsf{Mac}_k(x) := \begin{cases} \perp & \text{if } x \in B_\epsilon, \\ \mathsf{Mac}_k(x) & \text{otherwise.} \end{cases}$$

Given a MAC (Mac, Ver), an adversary $\mathcal{A}$, and $\mathcal{A}$-selected parameter ϵ, the "blind forgery experiment" is:

---

[3] Compared to the standard quantum oracle for a classical function, GYZ require the output register to be empty prior to the query.

1. Generate key k and random blinding B_ϵ;
2. Produce candidate forgery $(m, t) \leftarrow \mathcal{A}^{B_\epsilon \mathsf{Mac}_k}(1^n)$.
3. Output win if $\mathsf{Ver}_k(m, t) = \mathsf{acc}$ and $m \in B_\epsilon$; otherwise output rej.

Definition 1. *A MAC is blind-unforgeable* (BU) *if for every adversary* $(\mathcal{A}, \epsilon)$, *the probability of winning the blind forgery experiment is negligible.*

In this work, BU will typically refer to the case where $\mathcal{A}$ is an efficient quantum algorithm (QPT) and the oracle is quantum, i.e., $|x\rangle|y\rangle \mapsto |x\rangle|y \oplus B_\epsilon \mathsf{Mac}_k(x)\rangle$. We will also consider q-BU, the information-theoretic variant where the total number of queries is a priori fixed to q. We remark that the above definition is also easy to adapt to other settings, e.g., classical security against PPT adversaries, quantum or classical security for digital signatures, etc.

We remark that one could define a variant of the above where the adversary is allowed to describe the blinding distribution, rather than it being uniform. However, this is not a stronger notion. By a straightforward argument, an adversary wins in the chosen-blinding BU game if and only if it wins with a uniform ϵ-blinding for inverse-polynomial ϵ. Indeed, the adversary can just simulate its chosen blinding herself, and this still succeeds with inverse polynomial probability when interacting with a standard-blinded oracle (see Theorem 2 below).

Results about blind-unforgeability. To solidify our confidence in the new notion, we collect a series of results which we believe establish BU as a definition of unforgeability that captures the desired intuitive security requirement. In particular, we show that BU is strictly stronger than previous candidate definitions, and that it classifies a wide range of representative examples (in fact, all examples examined thus far) as either forgeable or unforgeable in a way that agrees with cryptographic intuition.

Relations and characterizations. First, we show that BU correctly classifies unforgeability in the classical-query setting: it is equivalent to the classical unforgeability notion of EUF-CMA (existential unforgeability against chosen-message attack). Then, we show that it implies PO.

Theorem 1. *If a function family is* BU-*unforgeable, then it is* PO-*unforgeable.*

One key technical component of the proof is a general simulation theorem, which tightly controls the deviation in the behavior of an algorithm when subjected to the BU experiment.

Theorem 2. *Let* $\mathcal{A}$ *be a quantum query algorithm making at most* T *queries. Let* $f : X \to Y$ *be a function,* B_ϵ *a random* ϵ-*blinding subset of* X, *and for each* $B \subset X$, *let* g_B *a function with support* B. *Then*

$$\mathop{\mathbb{E}}_{B_\epsilon} \left\| \mathcal{A}^f(1^n) - \mathcal{A}^{f \oplus g_{B_\epsilon}}(1^n) \right\|_1 \leq 2T\sqrt{\epsilon}.$$

This result can be viewed as strong evidence that algorithms that produce "good forgeries" in any reasonable sense will also win the BU experiment.

Specifically, adversaries that produce "good forgeries" will not be disturbed too much by blinding, and will thus in fact also win the BU experiment with non-negligible probability.

We can formulate and prove this intuition explicitly for a wide class of adversaries, as follows. Given an oracle algorithm $\mathcal{A}$, we let $\mathsf{supp}(\mathcal{A})$ denote the union of the supports of all the queries of $\mathcal{A}$, taken over all choices of oracle function.

Theorem 3 (informal). *Let $\mathcal{A}$ be QPT and $\mathsf{supp}(\mathcal{A}) \cap R = \emptyset$ for some $R \neq \emptyset$. Let* Mac *be a MAC, and suppose $\mathcal{A}^{\mathsf{Mac}_k}(1^n)$ outputs a valid pair $(m, \mathsf{Mac}_k(m))$ with $m \in R$ with noticeable probability. Then* Mac *is not BU secure.*

Blind-unforgeable MACs. Next, we show that several natural constructions satisfy BU. We first show that a random function is blind-unforgeable.

Theorem 4. *Let $R : X \to Y$ be a random function such that $1/|Y|$ is negligible. Then R is a blind-unforgeable MAC.*

By means of results of Zhandry [29] and Boneh and Zhandry [7], this leads to efficient BU-secure constructions.

Corollary 1. *Quantum-secure pseudorandom functions (qPRF) are BU-secure MACs, and (4q+1)-wise independent functions are q-BU-secure MACs.*

We can then invoke a recent result about the quantum-security of domain-extension schemes such as NMAC and HMAC [24], and obtain variable-length BU-secure MACs from any qPRF.

In the setting of public verification, we show that the one-time Lamport signature scheme [19] is BU-secure, provided that the underlying hash function family $\mathcal{R} : X \to Y$ is modeled as a random oracle.

Theorem 5. *Let $\mathcal{R} : X \to Y$ be a random function family. Then the Lamport scheme $L_\mathcal{R}$ is BU against adversaries which make one quantum query to $L_\mathcal{R}$ and poly-many quantum queries to $\mathcal{R}$.*

Hash-and-MAC. Consider the following natural variation on the blind-forgery experiment. To blind $F : X \to Y$, we first select a hash function $h : X \to Z$ and a blinding set $B_\epsilon \subseteq Z$; we then declare that F will be blinded on $x \in X$ whenever $h(x) \in B_\epsilon$. We refer to this as "hash-blinding." We say that a hash function h is a Bernoulli-preserving hash if, for every oracle function F, no QPT can distinguish between an oracle that has been hash-blinded with h, and an oracle that has been blinded in the usual sense. Recall the notion of *collapsing* from [27].

Theorem 6. *Let $h : X \to Y$ be a hash function. If h is Bernoulli-preserving hash, then it is also collapsing. Moreover, against adversaries with classical oracle access, h is a Bernoulli-preserving hash if and only if it is collision-resistant.*

We apply this new notion to show security of the Hash-and-MAC construction $\Pi^h = (\mathsf{Mac}^h, \mathsf{Ver}^h)$ with $\mathsf{Mac}_k^h(m) := \mathsf{Mac}_k(h(m))$.

Theorem 7. *Let $\Pi = (\mathsf{Mac}_k, \mathsf{Ver}_k)$ be a BU-secure MAC with $\mathsf{Mac}_k : X \to Y$, and let $h : Z \to X$ a Bernoulli-preserving hash. Then Π^h is a BU-secure MAC.*

We also show that the Bernoulli-preserving property can be satisfied by pseudorandom constructions, as well as a (public-key) hash based on *lossy functions* from LWE [20,26].

A concrete "counterexample" for PO. Supporting our motivation to devise a new unforgeability definition, we present a construction of a MAC which is forgeable (in a strong intuitive sense) and yet is classified by PO as secure.

Construction 8. *Given a triple* $k = (p, f, g)$ *where* $p \in \{0,1\}^n$ *and* $f, g : \{0,1\}^n \to \{0,1\}^n$, *define* $M_k : \{0,1\}^{n+1} \to \{0,1\}^{2n}$ *by*

$$
M_k(x) = \begin{cases} 0^{2n} & x = 0\|p, \\ 0^n\|f(x') & x = 0\|x', \ x' \neq p, \\ g(x' \bmod p)\|f(x') & x = 1\|x'. \end{cases}
$$

Define $g_p(x) := g(x \bmod p)$ and consider an adversary that queries only on messages starting with 1, as follows:

$$
\sum_{x,y} |1,x\rangle_X |0^n\rangle_{Y_1} |y\rangle_{Y_2} \longmapsto \sum_{x,y} |1,x\rangle_X |g_p(x)\rangle_{Y_1} |y \oplus f(x)\rangle_{Y_2} ; \tag{1}
$$

discarding the first qubit and Y_2 then yields $\sum_x |x\rangle |g_p(x)\rangle$, as $\sum_y |y \oplus f(x)\rangle_{Y_2} = \sum_y |y\rangle_{Y_2}$. One can then recover p via period-finding and output $(0\|p, 0^{2n})$. We emphasize that the forgery was queried with *zero* amplitude. In practice, we can interpret it as, e.g., the attacker queries only on messages starting with "From: Alice" and then forges a message starting with "From: Bob". Despite this, we can show that it is PO-secure.

Theorem 9. *The family* M_k *(for uniformly random* $k = (p, f, g)$*) is* PO*-secure.*

The PO security of M relies on a dilemma the adversary faces at each query: either learn an output of f, or obtain a superposition of $(x, g(x))$-pairs for Fourier sampling. Our proof shows that, once the adversary commits to one of these two choices, the other option is irrevocably lost. Our result can thus be understood as a refinement of an observation of Aaronson: quantumly learning a property sometimes requires *uncomputing* some information [1]. Note that, while Aaronson could rely on standard (asymptotic) query complexity techniques, our problem is quite fragile: PO security describes a task which should be hard with q queries, but is completely trivial given $q + 1$ queries. Our proof makes use of a new quantum random oracle technique of Zhandry [30].

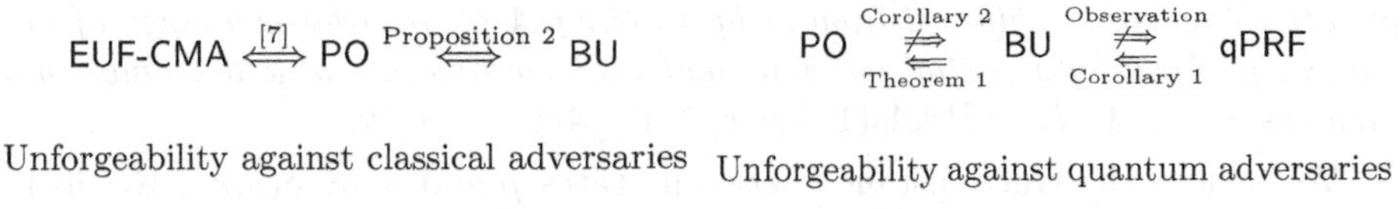

$$
\text{EUF-CMA} \xLeftrightarrow{[7]} \text{PO} \xLeftrightarrow{\text{Proposition 2}} \text{BU} \qquad\qquad \text{PO} \underset{\text{Theorem 1}}{\overset{\text{Corollary 2}}{\rightleftarrows}} \text{BU} \underset{\text{Corollary 1}}{\overset{\text{Observation}}{\rightleftarrows}} \text{qPRF}
$$

Unforgeability against classical adversaries   Unforgeability against quantum adversaries

Fig. 1. Relationship between different unforgeability notions

A straightforward application of Theorem 3 shows that Construction 8 is BU-insecure. In particular, we have the following.

Corollary 2. *There exists a* PO-*secure MAC which is* BU-*insecure.*

The relationship between BU, PO some other notions are visualized in Fig. 1.

3   Preliminaries

Basic notation, conventions. Given a finite set X, the notation $x \in_R X$ will mean that x is a uniformly random element of X. Given a subset B of a set X, let $\chi_B : X \to \{0,1\}$ denote the characteristic function of B, i.e., $\chi_B(x) = 1$ if $x \in B$ and $\chi_B(x) = 0$ else. When we say that a classical function F is efficiently computable, we mean that there exists a uniform family of deterministic classical circuits which computes F. We will consider three classes of algorithms: (i) unrestricted algorithms, modeling computationally unbounded adversaries, (ii) probabilistic poly-time algorithms (PPTs), modeling classical adversaries, and (iii) quantum poly-time algorithms (QPTs), modeling quantum adversaries. We assume that the latter two are given as polynomial-time uniform families of circuits. For PPTs, these are probabilistic circuits. For QPTs, they are quantum circuits, which may contain both unitary gates and measurements. We will often assume (without loss of generality) that the measurements are postponed to the end of the circuit, and that they take place in the computational basis. Given an algorithm $\mathcal{A}$, we let $\mathcal{A}(x)$ denote the (in general, mixed) state output by $\mathcal{A}$ on input x. In particular, if $\mathcal{A}$ has classical output, then $\mathcal{A}(x)$ denotes a probability distribution. Unless otherwise stated, the probability is taken over all random coins and measurements of $\mathcal{A}$, and any randomness used to select the input x. If $\mathcal{A}$ is an oracle algorithm and F a classical function, then $\mathcal{A}^F(x)$ is the mixed state output by $\mathcal{A}$ equipped with oracle F and input x; the probability is now also taken over any randomness used to generate F.

We will distinguish between two ways of presenting a function $F : \{0,1\}^n \to \{0,1\}^m$ as an oracle. First, the usual "classical oracle access" simply means that each oracle call grants one classical invocation $x \mapsto F(x)$. This will always be the oracle model for PPTs. Second, "quantum oracle access" will mean that each oracle call grants an invocation of the $(n+m)$-qubit unitary gate $|x\rangle|y\rangle \mapsto |x\rangle|y \oplus F(x)\rangle$. For us, this will always be the oracle model for QPTs. Note that both QPTs and unrestricted algorithms could in principle receive either oracle type.

We will need the following lemma. We use the formulation from [8, Lemma 2.1], which is a special case of a more general "pinching lemma" of Hayashi [15].

Lemma 1. *Let $\mathcal{A}$ be a quantum algorithm and $x \in \{0,1\}^*$. Let $\mathcal{A}_0$ be another quantum algorithm obtained from $\mathcal{A}$ by pausing $\mathcal{A}$ at an arbitrary stage of execution, performing a partial measurement that obtains one of k outcomes, and then resuming $\mathcal{A}$. Then $\Pr[\mathcal{A}_0(1^n) = x] \geq \Pr[\mathcal{A}(1^n) = x]/k$.*

We denote the trace distance between states ρ and σ by $\delta(\rho, \sigma)$. Recall its definition via the trace norm, i.e., $\delta(\rho, \sigma) = (1/2)\|\rho - \sigma\|_1$. When ρ and σ are classical states, the trace distance is equal to the total variation distance.

Quantum-secure pseudorandomness. A quantum-secure pseudorandom function (qPRF) is a family of classical, deterministic, efficiently-computable functions which appear random to QPT adversaries with quantum oracle access.

Definition 2. *An efficiently computable function family* $f : K \times X \to Y$ *is a quantum-secure pseudorandom function* (qPRF) *if, for all QPTs* $\mathcal{D}$,

$$\left| \Pr_{k \in_R K}\left[\mathcal{D}^{f_k}(1^n) = 1\right] - \Pr_{g \in_R \mathcal{F}_X^Y}\left[\mathcal{D}^g(1^n) = 1\right] \right| \leq \mathrm{negl}(n).$$

Here $\mathcal{F}_X^Y$ denotes the set of all functions from X to Y. The standard "GGM+GL" construction of a PRF yields a qPRF when instantiated with a quantum-secure one-way function [29]. One can also construct a qPRF directly from the Learning with Errors assumption [29]. If we have an a priori bound on the number of allowed queries, then a computational assumption is not needed.

Theorem 10. (Lemma 6.4 in [7]). *Let* $q, c \geq 0$ *be integers, and* $f : K \times X \to Y$ *a* $(2q+c)$*-wise independent family of functions. Let* $\mathcal{D}$ *be an algorithm making no more than* q *quantum oracle queries and* c *classical oracle queries. Then*

$$\Pr_{k \in_R K}\left[\mathcal{D}^{f_k}(1^n) = 1\right] = \Pr_{g \in_R \mathcal{F}_X^Y}\left[\mathcal{D}^g(1^n) = 1\right].$$

PO-unforgeability. Boneh and Zhandry define unforgeability (against quantum queries) for classical MACs as follows [7]. They also show that random functions satisfy this notion.

Definition 3. *Let* $\Pi = (\mathsf{KeyGen}, \mathsf{Mac}, \mathsf{Ver})$ *be a MAC with message set* X. *Consider the following experiment with an algorithm* $\mathcal{A}$:

1. Generate key: $k \leftarrow \mathsf{KeyGen}(1^n)$.
2. Generate forgeries: $\mathcal{A}$ *receives quantum oracle for* Mac_k, *makes* q *queries, and outputs a string* s;
3. Outcome: *output* win *if* s *contains* $q + 1$ *distinct input-output pairs of* Mac_k, *and* fail *otherwise.*

We say that Π *is* PO-*secure if no adversary can succeed at the above experiment with better than negligible probability.*

The Fourier Oracle. Our separation proof will make use of a new technique of Zhandry [30] for analyzing random oracles. We briefly describe this framework.

A random function f from n bits to m bits can be viewed as the outcome of a quantum measurement. More precisely, let $\mathcal{H}_F = \bigotimes_{x \in \{0,1\}^n} \mathcal{H}_{F_x}$, where $\mathcal{H}_{F_x} \cong \mathbb{C}^{2^m}$. Then set $f(x) \leftarrow \mathcal{M}_{F_x}(\eta_F)$ with $\eta_F = |\phi_0\rangle\langle\phi_0|^{\otimes 2^n}$, $|\phi_0\rangle = 2^{-\frac{m}{2}} \sum_{y \in \{0,1\}^m} |y\rangle$, and where $\mathcal{M}_{F_x}$ denotes the measurement of the register F_x in the computational basis. This measurement commutes with any $\mathrm{CNOT}_{A:B}$ gate with control qubit A in F_x and target qubit B outside F_x. It follows that, for any quantum algorithm making queries to a random oracle, the output distribution is identical if the algorithm is instead run with the following oracle:

1. Setup: prepare the state η_F.
2. Upon a query with query registers X and Y, controlled on X being in state $|x\rangle$, apply $(\text{CNOT}^{\otimes m})_{F_x:Y}$.
3. After the algorithm has finished, measure F to determine the success of the computation.

We denote the oracle unitary defined in step 2 above by U^{O}_{XYF}. Having defined this oracle representation, we are free to apply any unitary U_H to the oracle state, so long as we then also apply the conjugated query unitary $U_H(\text{CNOT}^{\otimes m})_{F_x:Y}U_H^\dagger$ in place of U^{O}_{XYF}. We choose $U_H = H^{\otimes m2^n}$, which means that the oracle register starts in the all-zero state now. Applying Hadamard to both qubits reverses the direction of CNOT, i.e., $H_A \otimes H_B \text{CNOT}_{A:B} H_A \otimes H_B = \text{CNOT}_{B:A}$, so the adversary-oracle-state after a first query with query state $|x\rangle_X|\phi_y\rangle_Y$ is

$$|x\rangle_X|\phi_y\rangle_Y|0^m\rangle^{\otimes 2^n} \longmapsto |x\rangle_X|\phi_y\rangle_Y|0^m\rangle^{\otimes(\text{lex}(x)-1)}|y\rangle_{F_x}|0^m\rangle^{\otimes(2^n-\text{lex}(x))}, \quad (2)$$

where $\text{lex}(x)$ denotes the position of x in the lexicographic ordering of $\{0,1\}^n$, and we defined the Fourier basis state $|\phi_y\rangle = H^{\otimes m}|y\rangle$. In the rest of this section, we freely change the order in which tensor products are written, and keep track of the tensor factors through the use of subscripts. This adjusted representation is called the *Fourier oracle* (FO), and we denote its oracle unitary by

$$U^{\text{FO}}_{XYF} = \left(H^{\otimes m2^n}\right)_F U^{O}_{XYF} \left(H^{\otimes m2^n}\right)_F.$$

An essential fact about the FO is that each query can only change the number of non-zero entries in the FO's register by at most one. To formalize this idea, we define the "number operator" $N_F = \sum_{x\in\{0,1\}^n}(\mathbb{1} - |0\rangle\langle 0|)_{F_x} \otimes \mathbb{1}^{\otimes(2^n-1)}$. The number operator can also be written in its spectral decomposition,

$$N_F = \sum_{l=0}^{2^n} lP_l \qquad \text{where} \qquad P_l = \sum_{r\in S_l}|r\rangle\langle r|,$$
$$S_l = \left\{r \in (\{0,1\}^m)^{2^n} \,\middle|\, |\{x\in\{0,1\}^n|r_x \neq 0\}| = l\right\}.$$

Note that the initial joint state of a quantum query algorithm and the oracle (in the FO-oracle picture described above) is in the image of P_0. The following fact is essential in working with the Fourier Oracle; the proof is given in Appendix A.

Lemma 2. *The number operator satisfies* $\left\|[N_F, U^{\text{FO}}_{XYF}]\right\|_\infty = 1$. *In particular, the joint state of a quantum query algorithm and the oracle after the q-th query is in the kernel of P_l for all $l > q$.*

4   The New Notion: Blind-Unforgeability

Formal definition. For ease of exposition, we begin by introducing our new security notion in a form analogue to the standard notion of existential unforgeability under chosen-message attacks, EUF-CMA. We will also later show how to extend our approach to obtain a corresponding analogue of strong unforgeability. We begin by defining a "blinding" operation. Let $f : X \to Y$ and $B \subseteq X$. We let

$$Bf(x) = \begin{cases} \bot & \text{if } x \in B, \\ f(x) & \text{otherwise.} \end{cases}$$

We say that f has been "blinded" by B. In this context, we will be particularly interested in the setting where elements of X are placed in B independently at random with a particular probability ϵ; we let B_ϵ denote this random variable. (It will be easy to infer X from context, so we do not reflect it in the notation.)

Next, we define a security game in which an adversary is tasked with using a blinded MAC oracle to produce a valid input-output pair in the blinded set.

Definition 4. *Let $\Pi = (\mathsf{KeyGen}, \mathsf{Mac}, \mathsf{Ver})$ be a MAC with message set X. Let $\mathcal{A}$ be an algorithm, and $\epsilon : \mathbb{N} \to \mathbb{R}_{\geq 0}$ an efficiently computable function. The blind forgery experiment $\mathsf{BlindForge}_{\mathcal{A},\Pi}(n, \epsilon)$ proceeds as follows:*

1. Generate key: $k \leftarrow \mathsf{KeyGen}(1^n)$.
2. Generate blinding: *select $B_\epsilon \subseteq X$ by placing each m into B_ϵ independently with probability $\epsilon(n)$.*
3. Produce forgery: $(m, t) \leftarrow \mathcal{A}^{B_\epsilon \mathsf{Mac}_k}(1^n)$.
4. Outcome: *output 1 if $\mathsf{Ver}_k(m, t) = \mathsf{acc}$ and $m \in B_\epsilon$; otherwise output 0.*

We say that a scheme is blind-unforgeable if, for any efficient adversary, the probability of winning the game is negligible. The probability is taken over the choice of key, the choice of blinding set, and any internal randomness of the adversary. We remark that specifying an adversary requires specifying (in a uniform fashion) both the algorithm $\mathcal{A}$ and the blinding fraction ϵ.

Definition 5. *A MAC Π is blind-unforgeable (BU) if for every polynomial-time uniform adversary $(\mathcal{A}, \epsilon)$, $\Pr\left[\mathsf{BlindForge}_{\mathcal{A},\Pi}(n, \epsilon(n)) = 1\right] \leq \mathsf{negl}(n)$.*

We also define the "q-time" variant of the blinded forgery game, which is identical to Definition 4 except that the adversary is only allowed to make q queries to $B_\epsilon \mathsf{Mac}_k$ in step (3). We call the resulting game $\mathsf{BlindForge}^q_{\mathcal{A},\Pi}(n, \epsilon)$, and give the corresponding definition of q-time security (now against computationally unbounded adversaries).

Definition 6. *A MAC Π is q-time blind-unforgeable (q-BU) if for every q-query adversary $(\mathcal{A}, \epsilon)$, we have $\Pr\left[\mathsf{BlindForge}^q_{\mathcal{A},\Pi}(n, \epsilon(n)) = 1\right] \leq \mathsf{negl}(n)$.*

The above definitions are agnostic regarding the computational power of the adversary and the type of oracle provided. For example, selecting PPT adversaries and classical oracles in Definition 5 yields a definition of classical unforgeability; we will later show that this is equivalent to standard EUF-CMA. The main focus of our work will be on BU against QPTs with quantum oracle access, and q-BU against unrestricted adversaries with quantum oracle access.

Some technical details. We now remark on a few details in the usage of BU. First, strictly speaking, the blinding sets in the security games above cannot be generated efficiently. However, a pseudorandom blinding set will suffice. Pseudorandom blinding sets can be generated straightforwardly using an appropriate pseudorandom function, such as a PRF against PPTs or a qPRF against QPT. A precise description of how to perform this pseudorandom blinding is given in the proof of Corollary 3. Note that simulating the blinding requires computing and uncomputing the random function, so we must make two quantum queries for each quantum query of the adversary. Moreover, verifying whether the forgery is in the blinding set at the end requires one additional classical query. This means that $(4q + 1)$-wise independent functions are both necessary and sufficient for generating blinding sets for q-query adversaries (see [7, Lemma 6.4]). In any case, an adversary which behaves differently in the random-blinding game versus the pseudorandom-blinding game immediately yields a distinguisher against the corresponding pseudorandom function.

The Blinding Symbol. There is some flexibility in how one defines the blinding symbol $\perp$. In situations where the particular instantiation of the blinding symbol might matter, we will adopt the convention that the blinded version Bf of $f : \{0,1\}^n \rightarrow \{0,1\}^\ell$ is defined by setting $Bf : \{0,1\}^n \rightarrow \{0,1\}^{\ell+1}$, where $Bf(m) = 0^\ell \| 1$ if $m \in B$ and $Bf(m) = f(m)\|0$ otherwise. One advantage of this convention (i.e., that $\perp = 0^\ell\|1$) is that we can compute on and/or measure the blinded bit (i.e., the $(\ell + 1)$-st bit) without affecting the output register of the function. This will also turn out to be convenient for uncomputation.

Strong Blind-Unforgeability. The security notion BU given in Definition 5 is an analogue of simple unforgeability, i.e., EUF-CMA, for the case of a quantum-accessible MAC/Signing oracle. It is, however, straightforward to define a corresponding analogue of strong unforgeability, i.e., SUF-CMA, as well.

The notion of strong blind-unforgeability, sBU, is obtained by a simple adjustment compared to BU: we blind (message, tag) pairs rather than just messages. We briefly describe this for the case of MACs. Let $\Pi = (\mathsf{KeyGen}, \mathsf{Mac}, \mathsf{Ver})$ be a MAC with message set M, randomness set R and tag set T, so that $\mathsf{Mac}_k : M \times R \rightarrow T$ and $\mathsf{Ver}_k : M \times T \rightarrow \{\mathsf{acc}, \mathsf{rej}\}$ for every $k \leftarrow \mathsf{KeyGen}$. Given a parameter ϵ and an adversary $\mathcal{A}$, the strong blind forgery game proceeds as follows:

1. Generate key: $k \leftarrow \mathsf{KeyGen}$; generate blinding: select $B_\epsilon \subseteq M \times T$ by placing pairs (m, t) in B_ϵ independently with probability ϵ;
2. Produce forgery: produce (m, t) by executing $\mathcal{A}(1^n)$ with quantum oracle access to the function

$$B_\epsilon \mathsf{Mac}_{k;r}(m) := \begin{cases} \perp & \text{if } (m, \mathsf{Mac}_k(m; r)) \in B_\epsilon, \\ \mathsf{Mac}_k(m; r) & \text{otherwise.} \end{cases}$$

where r is sampled uniformly for each oracle call.
3. Outcome: output 1 if $\mathsf{Ver}_k(m, t) = \mathsf{acc} \wedge (m, t) \in B_\epsilon$; otherwise output 0.

Security is then defined as before: Π is sBU-secure if for all adversaries $\mathcal{A}$ (and their declared ϵ), the success probability at winning the above game is negligible. Note that, for the case of canonical MACs, this definition coincides with Definition 5, just as EUF-CMA and SUF-CMA coincide in this case.

5   Intuitive Security and the Meaning of BU

In this section, we gather a number of results which build confidence in BU as a correct definition of unforgeability in our setting. We begin by showing that a wide range of "intuitively forgeable" MACs (indeed, all such examples we have examined) are correctly characterized by BU as insecure.

Intuitively forgeable schemes. As indicated earlier, BU security rules out any MAC schemes where an attacker can query a subset of the message space and forge outside that region. To make this claim precise, we first define the *query support* $\mathsf{supp}(\mathcal{A})$ of an oracle algorithm $\mathcal{A}$. Let $\mathcal{A}$ be a quantum query algorithm with oracle access to the quantum oracle O for a classical function from n to m bits. Without loss of generality $\mathcal{A}$ proceeds by applying the sequence of unitaries $OU_q OU_{q-1}...U_1$ to the initial state $|0\rangle_{XYZ}$, followed by a POVM $\mathcal{E}$. Here, X and Y are the input and output registers of the function and Z is the algorithm's workspace. Let $|\psi_i\rangle$ be the intermediate state of of $\mathcal{A}$ after the application of U_i. Then $\mathsf{supp}(\mathcal{A})$ is defined to be the set of input strings x such that there exists a function $f : \{0,1\}^n \to \{0,1\}^m$ such that $\langle x|_X|\psi_i\rangle \neq 0$ for at least one $i \in \{1,...,q\}$ when $\mathcal{O} = \mathcal{O}_f$.

Theorem 11. *Let $\mathcal{A}$ be a QPT such that $\mathsf{supp}(\mathcal{A}) \cap R = \emptyset$ for some $R \neq \emptyset$. Let Mac be a MAC, and suppose $\mathcal{A}^{\mathsf{Mac}_k}(1^n)$ outputs a valid pair $(m, \mathsf{Mac}_k(m))$ with $m \in R$ with non-negligible probability. Then Mac is not BU-secure.*

To prove Theorem 11, we will need the following theorem, which controls the change in the output state of an algorithm resulting from applying a blinding to its oracle. Given an oracle algorithm $\mathcal{A}$ and two oracles F and G, the trace distance between the output of $\mathcal{A}$ with oracle F and $\mathcal{A}$ with oracle G is denoted by $\delta(\mathcal{A}^F(1^n), \mathcal{A}^G(1^n))$. Given two functions $F, P : \{0,1\}^n \to \{0,1\}^m$, we define the function $F \oplus P$ by $(F \oplus P)(x) = F(x) \oplus P(x)$.

Theorem 12. *Let $\mathcal{A}$ be a quantum query algorithm making at most T queries, and $F : \{0,1\}^n \to \{0,1\}^m$ a function. Let $B \subseteq \{0,1\}^n$ be a subset chosen by independently including each element of $\{0,1\}^n$ with probability ϵ, and $P : \{0,1\}^n \to \{0,1\}^m$ be any function with support B. Then*

$$\mathbb{E}_B\left[\delta\left(\mathcal{A}^F(1^n), \mathcal{A}^{F \oplus P}(1^n)\right)\right] \leq 2T\sqrt{\epsilon}.$$

The proof is a relatively straightforward adaptation of a hybrid argument in the spirit of the lower bound for Grover search [5]. We provide the complete proof in the full version [4]. We are now ready to prove Theorem 11.

Proof (of Theorem 11). Let $\mathcal{A}$ be a quantum algorithm with $\mathsf{supp}(\mathcal{A})$ for any oracle. By our hypothesis,

$$\tilde{p} := \Pr\nolimits_{k,(m,t)\leftarrow\mathcal{A}^{\mathsf{Mac}_k}(1^n)} [\mathsf{Mac}_k(m) = t \wedge m \notin \mathsf{supp}(\mathcal{A})] \geq n^{-c},$$

for some $c > 0$ and sufficiently large n. Since $\mathsf{supp}(A)$ is a fixed set, we can think of sampling a random B_ε as picking $B_0 := B_\varepsilon \cap \mathsf{supp}(A)$ and $B_1 := B_\varepsilon \cap \overline{\mathsf{supp}(A)}$ independently. Let "blind" denote the random experiment of $\mathcal{A}$ running on Mac_k blinded by a random B_ε: $k, B_\varepsilon, (m,t) \leftarrow \mathcal{A}^{B_\varepsilon \mathsf{Mac}_k}(1^n)$, which is equivalent to $k, B_0, B_1, (m,t) \leftarrow \mathcal{A}^{B_0 \mathsf{Mac}_k}(1^n)$. The probability that $\mathcal{A}$ wins the BU game is

$$
\begin{aligned}
p := {}& \Pr_{\text{blind}}[f(m) = t \wedge m \in B_\varepsilon] \geq \Pr_{\text{blind}}[f(m) = t \wedge m \in B'] \\
\geq {}& \Pr_{\text{blind}}[f(m) = t \wedge m \in B' \mid m \notin \mathsf{supp}(A)] \cdot \Pr_{\text{blind}}[m \notin \mathsf{supp}(A)] \\
= {}& \Pr_{\substack{f,B_0 \\ (m,t)\leftarrow\mathcal{A}^{Bf}}}[f(m) = t \wedge m \notin \mathsf{supp}(A)] \cdot \Pr_{\substack{f,B' \\ (m,t)\leftarrow\mathcal{A}^{Bf}}}[m \in B' \mid m \notin \mathsf{supp}(A)] \\
\geq {}& \left(\tilde{p} - 2T\sqrt{\varepsilon}\right)\varepsilon \geq \frac{\tilde{p}^3}{27T^2}.
\end{aligned}
$$

Here the second-to-last step follows from Theorem 12; in the last step, we chose $\varepsilon = (\tilde{p}/3T)^2$. We conclude that $\mathcal{A}$ breaks the BU security of the MAC. $\qquad\square$

Relationship to other definitions. As we will show in Sect. 7, PO fails to capture certain prediction algorithms. It does, however, capture a natural family of attacks and should hence be implied by a good security notion. In this section we show that our new definition, BU, indeed implies PO. To this end, we first introduce a natural weaker variant of BU that we call measured BU, or mBU.

Definition 7. *The* measured ε-blinded oracle *for a function* $f : \{0,1\}^n \to \{0,1\}^m$ *is the oracle that first applies the ε-blinded oracle for f and then performs the projective measurement* $|\bot\rangle\langle\bot|$ *vs.* $\mathbb{1} - |\bot\rangle\langle\bot|$. *A scheme Π is* measured-BU, *or* mBU, *secure, if for all $\varepsilon > 0$ and all QPT adversaries $\mathcal{A}$, the winning probability in the* BU *game when provided with a measured ε-blinded oracle instead of a ε-blinded oracle, is negligible.*

A straightforward reduction argument shows that BU implies mBU.

Proposition 1. *Let Π be a BU $(k - BU)$-secure MAC. Then Π is* mBU $(k - mBU)$-secure.

Proof. Let $\mathcal{A}$ be an mBU-adversary against Π. We construct a BU-adversary $\mathcal{A}'$ against Π as follows. $\mathcal{A}'$ runs $\mathcal{A}$. For each query that $\mathcal{A}$ makes to the measured ε-blinded oracle, $\mathcal{A}'$ queries the ε-blinded oracle and performs the "blinded or not" measurement before returning the answer to $\mathcal{A}$. Clearly the probabilities for $\mathcal{A}'$ winning the BU and for $\mathcal{A}$ winning the mBU game are the same. $\qquad\square$

For the following proof we need a generalization of Zhandry's superposition oracle technique to functions drawn from a non-uniform distribution. Such has been developed in detail in [11]. As for the proof of Theorem 21, we do not need the more complicated (but efficiently implementable) compressed oracle. Hence we introduce only the basic non-uniform superposition oracle. The generalization is straight-forward. In [30], a uniformly random function $f : \{0,1\}^n \to \{0,1\}^m$ is sampled by preparing 2^n m-qubit uniform superposition states. The measurement that performs the actual sampling is delayed, which allows for new ways of analyzing the behavior of a query algorithm by inspecting the oracle registers. Here, we woudl like to use the superposition oracle representation for the indicator function $\mathbb{1}_{B_\epsilon} : \{0,1\}^n \to \{0,1\}$ of the blinding set B_ϵ. This is a Boolean function with $\Pr\left[\mathbb{1}_{B_\epsilon}(x) = 1\right] = \epsilon$ independently for all $x \in \{0,1\}^n$.

We will sample $\mathbb{1}_{B_\epsilon}$ by preparing 2^n qubits in the state

$$|\eta_0^\epsilon\rangle = \sqrt{1-\epsilon}|0\rangle + \sqrt{\epsilon}|1\rangle, \tag{3}$$

i.e., we prepare the 2^n-qubit oracle register F in the state

$$\left(|\eta_0^\epsilon\rangle^{\otimes 2^n}\right)_F = \bigotimes_{x\in\{0,1\}^{\otimes n}} |\eta_0^\epsilon\rangle_{F_x}. \tag{4}$$

We will refrain from fourier-transforming any registers, so if the adversaries query registers are X and B (the input register and the blinding bit register), the oracle unitary is just given by

$$U_{\mathrm{StO}} = \sum_{x\in\{0,1\}^n} |x\rangle\langle x|_X \otimes \mathrm{CNOT}_{F_x:B}. \tag{5}$$

We can also define the generalization of the projectors P_ℓ. To this end we complete $|\eta_0^\epsilon\rangle$ to an orthonormal basis by introducing the state

$$|\eta_1^\epsilon\rangle = \sqrt{\epsilon}|0\rangle - \sqrt{1-\epsilon}|1\rangle. \tag{6}$$

Let further U_ϵ be the unitary such that $U_\epsilon|i\rangle = |\eta_i^\epsilon\rangle$. The generalization of P_ℓ is now defined by $P_\ell^\epsilon = U_\epsilon P_\ell U_\epsilon^\dagger$. As U_{StO} is a sum of terms that each act non-trivially only on one out of the 2^n F_x registers, the analogue of Lemma 2 clearly holds, i.e., if $|\psi_q\rangle$ is the joint algorithm-oracle state after q queries to the superposition oracle for $\mathbb{1}_{B_\epsilon}$, then $P_\ell^\epsilon|\psi_q\rangle = 0$ for all $\ell > q$.

We are now ready to prove that BU security implies PO security.

Theorem 13. *Let Π be a BU-secure MAC. Then Π is PO-secure.*

Proof. According to Proposition 1, Π is mBU secure. It therefore suffices to find a reduction from breaking mBU to breaking PO. Let $\mathcal{A}$ be a q query PO adversary against Π, i.e., an algorithm that makes q queries and outputs $q+1$ pairs (x_i, t_i) with the goal that $t_i = \mathrm{Mac}_k(x_i)$ for all $i = 1, ..., q+1$. We construct an mBU-adversary $\mathcal{A}'$ as follows. The adversary $\mathcal{A}'$ runs $\mathcal{A}$, answering the queries using the measured ϵ-blinded oracle for Mac_k. If for any of the queries the result is $\perp$,

$\mathcal{A}'$ aborts. In this case we formally define $\mathcal{A}$'s output to be $\perp$. After (and if) $\mathcal{A}$ has finished by outputting $q+1$ candidate message-tag pairs (m_i, t_i), $\mathcal{A}'$ chooses $i \in_R \{1, ..., q+1\}$ and outputs (m_i, t_i).

According to Theorem 2, the trace distance between the distribution of the $q+1$ candidate message tag pairs that $\mathcal{A}$ outputs only changes by $\delta = 2q\sqrt{\epsilon}$ in total variational distance when run with the measured ϵ-blinded oracle as done as a subroutine of $\mathcal{A}'$. It follows that with at least probability $p_{\text{succ}}^{\mathcal{A}} - \delta$, all $q+1$ outputs of $\mathcal{A}$ ar valid message-tag-pairs, where $p_{\text{succ}}^{\mathcal{A}}$ is the probability with which $\mathcal{A}$ wins the PO game when provided with an unblinded Mac_k-oracle.

For the rest of the proof we instantiate the blinding set using the superposition oracle described above. In this case, the measured ϵ-blinded oracle is implemented as follows. On input registers X and Y, create a blank qubit register B and query the blinding function $\mathbb{1}_{B_\epsilon}$ on XB. Measure B to obtain b (the blinding bit). If $b = 1$, query the Mac_k-oracle on XY, otherwise add $\perp$ to Y. For the q-query algorithm $\mathcal{A}'$, q queries are made to the superposition blinding oracle. Afterwards the oracle register F is measured in the computational basis to determine whether the output is blinded or not.

We continue by finding a lower bound on the probability that the message output by $\mathcal{A}'$ is blinded. To that end, consider the modified game, where after $\mathcal{A}'$ has finished, but before measuring the oracle register F, we compute the smallest index $i \in \{1, ..., q+1\}$ such that F_{x_i} is in state $|\eta_0^{(\varepsilon)}\rangle$ in superposition into an additional register. Such an index always exists. This is because $P_\ell^\epsilon |\psi\rangle = 0$ for all $\ell > q$, where $|\psi\rangle$ is the joint adversary-oracle state after the execution of $\mathcal{A}'$. Hence $|\psi\rangle$ is a superposition of states $|\beta\rangle = \bigotimes_{x \in \{0,1\}^n} |\eta_{\beta_x}^\epsilon\rangle$ for strings $\beta \in \{0,1\}^{2^n}$ of Hamming weight at most q. Now we measure the register to obtain an outcome i_0. But given outcome i_0, the register $F_{m_{i_0}}$ is in state $|\eta_0^\epsilon\rangle$. Now the oracle register is measured to determine the blinding set $B_\epsilon \subset \{0,1\}^n$. The computation together with the measurement implements a $(q+1)$-outcome projective measurement on F. The probability that m_{i_0} is blinded is ε independently, so the success probability in the modified game is

$$\tilde{p}_{\text{succ}}^{\mathcal{A}'} \geq \frac{\epsilon \left(p_{\text{succ}}^{\mathcal{A}} - 2q\sqrt{\epsilon}\right)}{q+1}. \tag{7}$$

Finally, we can apply Lemma 1 to conclude that adding the measurement has not decreased the success probability by more than a factor $1/(q+1)$, to conclude that the success probability of $\mathcal{A}'$ in the unmodified mBU game is lower-bounded by

$$p_{\text{succ}}^{\mathcal{A}'} \geq \frac{\epsilon \left(p_{\text{succ}}^{\mathcal{A}} - 2q\sqrt{\epsilon}\right)}{(q+1)^2}. \tag{8}$$

Choosing $\epsilon = \left(p_{\text{succ}}^{\mathcal{A}}/3q\right)^2$ we obtain

$$p_{\text{succ}}^{\mathcal{A}'} \geq \frac{\left(p_{\text{succ}}^{\mathcal{A}}\right)^3}{27q^2(q+1)^2}. \tag{9}$$

In particular we have that $p_{\text{succ}}^{\mathcal{A}'}$ is non-negligible if p_{succ} was non-negligible. $\square$

1-BU also implies the notion by Garg et al. [14], see the full version [4].

In the purely classical setting, our notion is equivalent to EUF-CMA. Also, sBU from Sect. 4 implies SUF-CMA.

Proposition 2. *A MAC is* EUF-CMA *if and only if it is blind-unforgeable against classical adversaries.*

Proof. Set $F_k = \mathsf{Mac}_k$. Consider an adversary $\mathcal{A}$ which violates EUF-CMA. Such an adversary, given 1^n and oracle access to F_k (for $k \in_R \{0,1\}^n$), produces a forgery (m,t) with non-negligible probability $s(n)$; in particular, $|m| \geq n$ and m is not among the messages queried by $\mathcal{A}$. This same adversary (when coupled with an appropriate ϵ) breaks the system under the blind-forgery definition. Specifically, let $p(n)$ be the running time of $\mathcal{A}$, in which case $\mathcal{A}$ clearly makes no more than $p(n)$ queries, and define $\epsilon(n) = 1/p(n)$. Consider now a particular $k \in \{0,1\}^n$ and a particular sequence r of random coins for $\mathcal{A}^{F_k}(1^n)$. If this run of $\mathcal{A}$ results in a forgery (m,t), observe that with probability at least $(1-\epsilon)^{p(n)} \approx c^{-1}$ in the choice of B_ϵ, we have $F_k(q) = B_\epsilon F_k(q)$ for every query q made by $\mathcal{A}$. On the other hand, $B_\epsilon(m) = \perp$ with (independent) probability ϵ. It follows $\phi(n, \epsilon_n)$ is at least $\epsilon s(n)/e = \Omega(s(n)/p(n))$.

On the the other hand, suppose that $(\mathcal{A}, \epsilon)$ is an adversary that breaks blind-unforgeability. Consider now the EUF-CMA adversary $\mathcal{A}'^{F_k}(1^n)$ which simulates the adversary $\mathcal{A}^{(\cdot)}(1^n)$ by answering oracle queries according to a locally-simulated version of $B_\epsilon F_k$; specifically, the adversary $\mathcal{A}'$ proceeds by drawing a subset $B_{\epsilon(n)} \subseteq \{0,1\}^*$ as described above and answering queries made by $\mathcal{A}$ according to $B_\epsilon F$. Two remarks are in order:

- When $x \in B_\epsilon$, this query is answered without an oracle call to $F(x)$.
- $\mathcal{A}'$ can construct the set B_ϵ "on the fly," by determining, when a particular query q is made by $\mathcal{A}$, whether $q \in B_\epsilon$ and "remembering" this information in case the query is asked again ("lazy sampling").

With probability $\phi(n, \epsilon(n))$ $\mathcal{A}$ produces a forgery on a point which was not queried by $\mathcal{A}'$, as desired. It follows that $\mathcal{A}$ produces a (conventional) forgery with non-negligible probability when given F_k for $k \in_R \{0,1\}^n$. $\square$

6 Blind-Unforgeable Schemes

Random schemes. We now show that suitable random and pseudorandom function families satisfy our notion of unforgeability.

Theorem 14. *Let $R: X \to Y$ be a uniformly random function such that $1/|Y|$ is negligible in n. Then R is a blind-forgery secure MAC.*

Proof. For simplicity, we assume that the function is length-preserving; the proof generalizes easily. Let $\mathcal{A}$ be an efficient quantum adversary. The oracle $B_\epsilon R$ supplied to $\mathcal{A}$ during the blind-forgery game is determined entirely by B_ϵ and the restriction of R to the complement of B_ϵ. On the other hand, the forgery event

$$\mathcal{A}^{B_\epsilon F_k}(1^n) = (m,t) \wedge |m| \geq n \wedge F_k(m) = t \wedge B_\epsilon F_k(m) = \perp$$

depends additionally on values of R at points in B_ϵ. To reflect this decomposition, given R and B_ϵ define $R_\epsilon : B_\epsilon \to Y$ to be the restriction of R to the set B_ϵ and note that—conditioned on $B_\epsilon R$ and B_ϵ—the random variable R_ϵ is drawn uniformly from the space of all (length-preserving) functions from B_ϵ into Y. Note, also, that for every n the purported forgery $(m,t) \leftarrow \mathcal{A}^{B_\epsilon R}(1^n)$ is a (classical) random variable depending only on $B_\epsilon R$. In particular, conditioned on B_ϵ, (m,t) is independent of R_ϵ. It follows that, conditioned on $m \in B_\epsilon$, that $t = R_\epsilon(m)$ with probability no more than $1/2^n$ and hence $\phi(n,\epsilon) \leq 2^{-n}$, as desired. □

Next, we show that a qPRF is a blind-unforgeable MAC.

Corollary 3. *Let m and t be $\mathsf{poly}(n)$, and $F : \{0,1\}^n \times \{0,1\}^m \to \{0,1\}^t$ a qPRF. Then F is a blind-forgery-secure fixed-length MAC (with length $m(n)$).*

Proof. For a contradiction, let $\mathcal{A}$ be a QPT which wins the blind forgery game for a certain blinding factor $\varepsilon(n)$, with running time $q(n)$ success probability $\delta(n)$. We will use $\mathcal{A}$ to build a quantum oracle distinguisher $\mathcal{D}$ between the qPRF F and the perfectly random function family $\mathcal{F}_m^t$ with the same domain and range.

First, let $k = q(n)$ and let $\mathcal{H}$ be a family of $(4k + 1)$-wise independent functions with domain $\{0,1\}^m$ and range $\{0, 1, \ldots, 1/\varepsilon(n)\}$. The distinguisher $\mathcal{D}$ first samples $h \in_R \mathcal{H}$. Set $B_h := h^{-1}(0)$. Given its oracle $\mathcal{O}_f$, $\mathcal{D}$ can implement the function $B_h f$ (quantumly) as follows:

$$|x\rangle|y\rangle \mapsto |x\rangle|y\rangle|H_x\rangle|\delta_{h(x),0}\rangle \mapsto |x\rangle|y\rangle|H_x\rangle|\delta_{h(x),0}\rangle|f(x)\rangle$$
$$\mapsto |x\rangle|y \oplus f(x) \cdot (1 - \delta_{h(x),0})\rangle|H_x\rangle|\delta_{h(x),0}\rangle|f(x)\rangle$$
$$\mapsto |x\rangle|y \oplus f(x) \cdot (1 - \delta_{h(x),0})\rangle.$$

Here we used the CCNOT (Toffoli) gate from step 2 to 3 (with one control bit reversed), and uncomputed both h and f in the last step. After sampling h, the distinguisher $\mathcal{D}$ will execute $\mathcal{A}$ with the oracle $B_h f$. If $\mathcal{A}$ successfully forges a tag for a message in B_h, $\mathcal{A}'$ outputs "pseudorandom"; otherwise "random."

Note that the function $B_h f$ is perfectly ϵ-blinded if h is a perfectly random function. Note also that the entire security experiment with $\mathcal{A}$ (including the final check to determine if the output forgery is blind) makes at most $2k$ quantum queries and 1 classical query to h, and is thus (by Theorem 10) identically distributed to the perfect-blinding case.

Finally, by Theorem 14, the probability that $\mathcal{D}$ outputs "pseudorandom" when $f \in_R \mathcal{F}_m^t$ is negligible. By our initial assumption about $\mathcal{A}$, the probability that $\mathcal{D}$ outputs "pseudorandom" becomes $\delta(n)$ when $f \in_R F$. It follows that $\mathcal{D}$ distinguishes F from perfectly random. □

Next, we give a information-theoretically secure q-time MACs (Definition 6).

Theorem 15. *Let $\mathcal{H}$ be a $(4q+1)$-wise independent function family with range Y, such that $1/|Y|$ is a negligible function. Then $\mathcal{H}$ is a q-time BU-secure MAC.*

Proof. Let $(\mathcal{A}, \epsilon)$ be an adversary for the q-time game $\mathsf{BlindForge}^q_{\mathcal{A},h}(n, \epsilon(n))$, where h is drawn from $\mathcal{H}$. We will use $\mathcal{A}$ to construct a distinguisher $\mathcal{D}$ between $\mathcal{H}$ and a random oracle. Given access to an oracle $\mathcal{O}$, $\mathcal{D}$ first runs $\mathcal{A}$ with the blinded oracle $B\mathcal{O}$, where the blinding operation is performed as in the proof of Corollary 3 (i.e., via a $(4q+1)$-wise independent function with domain size $1/\epsilon(n)$). When $\mathcal{A}$ is completed, it outputs (m, σ). Next, $\mathcal{D}$ queries $\mathcal{O}$ on the message m and outputs 1 if and only if $\mathcal{O}(m) = \sigma$ and $m \in B$. Let $\gamma_{\mathcal{O}}$ be the probability of the output being 1.

We consider two cases: (i) $\mathcal{O}$ is drawn as a random oracle R, and (ii) $\mathcal{O}$ is drawn from the family $\mathcal{H}$. By Theorem 10, since $\mathcal{D}$ makes only $2q$ quantum queries and one classical query to $\mathcal{O}$, its output is identical in the two cases. Observe that γ_R (respectively, $\gamma_{\mathcal{H}}$) is exactly the success probability of $\mathcal{A}$ in the blind-forgery game with random oracle R (respectively, $\mathcal{H}$). We know from Theorem 14 that γ_R is negligible; it follows that $\gamma_{\mathcal{H}}$ is as well. $\qquad\square$

Several domain-extension schemes, including NMAC (a.k.a. encrypted cascade), HMAC, and AMAC, can transform a fixed-length qPRF to a qPRF that takes variable-length inputs [24]. As a corollary, starting from a qPRF, we also obtain a number of quantum blind-unforgeable variable-length MACs.

Lamport one-time signatures. The Lamport signature scheme [19] is a EUF-1-CMA-secure signature scheme, specified as follows.

Construction 16 (Lamport signature scheme, [19]). *For the Lamport signature scheme using a hash function family $h : \{0,1\}^n \times \{0,1\}^n \to \{0,1\}^n$, the algorithms $\mathsf{KeyGen}, \mathsf{Sign}$ and Ver are specified as follows. KeyGen, on input 1^n, outputs a pair $(\mathsf{pk}, \mathsf{sk})$ with*

$$\mathsf{sk} = (s_i^j)_{i \in \{1,\ldots,n\}, j=0,1}, \ \text{with } s_i^j \in_R \{0,1\}^n, \ \text{and} \tag{10}$$

$$\mathsf{pk} = \left(k, \left(p_i^j\right)_{i \in \{1,\ldots,n\}, j=0,1}\right), \ \text{with } k \in \{0,1\}^n \ \text{and } p_i^j = h_k\left(s_i^j\right). \tag{11}$$

The signing algorithm is defined by $\mathsf{Sign}_{\mathsf{sk}}(x) = (s_i^{x_i})_{i \in \{1,\ldots,n\}}$ where x_i, $i = 1,\ldots,n$ are the bits of x. The verification procedure checks the signature's consistency with the public key, i.e., $\mathsf{Ver}_{\mathsf{pk}}(x, s) = 0$ if $p_i^{x_i} = h_k(s_i)$ and $\mathsf{Ver}_{\mathsf{pk}}(x, s) = 0$ else.

We now show that the Lamport scheme is 1-BU secure in the quantum random oracle model.

Theorem 17. *If in Construction 16, h is modeled as a quantum-accessible random oracle, it is 1-BU secure.*

We give a brief sketch of the proof; for details, see Appendix A. The proof uses arguments analogous to the classical proof. This is made possible through the use of the Fourier oracle technique (from Sect. 3) for both h and sk. The latter can be understood as a uniformly random function $\mathsf{sk} : \{0, ..., n-1\} \times \{0, 1\} \to \{0, 1\}^n$. Subsequently we perform "forensics" on the oracle database after the adversary has finished, in a similar way as in the proof of Theorem 21. Let us first argue that an adversary $\mathcal{A}$ that makes a signing query but no queries to h and outputs (m, σ) does not succeed except with negligible probability. If m is blinded, then there is at least one bit of m where the corresponding part of sk (and hence the correct signature) is independent of σ. While this is only true in superposition, we can break this superposition using an n-outcome measurement on the sk-register, which does not change the success probability by much according to Lemma 1.

For the general case, we observe that queries to h do not help, because they will only have negligible support on the unqueried parts of sk. Concretely, we show that the commutator of the oracle unitary for h and the projector on the uniform superposition state (the initial state of the oracle register holding a part of sk) is small in operator norm, which implies that an untouched sk register remains untouched except with negligible amplitude, even in superposition.

A simple proof of the PO-security of a random function can be given using a similar idea; see the full version [4].

Hash-and-MAC. To authenticate messages of arbitrary length with a fixed-length MAC, it is common practice to first compress a long message by a *collision-resistant* hash function and then apply the MAC. This is known as Hash-and-MAC. However, when it comes to BU-security, collision-resistance may not be sufficient. We therefore propose a new notion, Bernoulli-preserving hash, generalizing collision-resistance in the quantum setting, and show that it is sufficient for Hash-and-MAC with BU security. Recall that, given a subset B of a set X, $\chi_B : X \to \{0, 1\}$ denotes the characteristic function of B.

Definition 8 (Bernoulli-preserving hash). *Let $\mathcal{H} : X \to Y$ be an efficiently computable function family. Define the following distributions on subsets of X:*

1. *$\mathcal{B}_\epsilon$: generate $B_\epsilon \subseteq X$ by placing $x \in B_\epsilon$ independently with probability ϵ. Output B_ϵ.*
2. *$\mathcal{B}_\epsilon^{\mathcal{H}}$: generate $C_\epsilon \subseteq Y$ by placing $y \in C_\epsilon$ independently with probability ϵ. Sample $h \in \mathcal{H}$ and define $B_\epsilon^h := \{x \in X : h(x) \in C_\epsilon\}$. Output B_ϵ^h.*

We say that $\mathcal{H}$ is a Bernoulli-preserving hash if for all adversaries $(\mathcal{A}, \epsilon)$,

$$\left| \Pr_{B \leftarrow \mathcal{B}_\epsilon} [\mathcal{A}^{\chi_B}(1^n) = 1] - \Pr_{B \leftarrow \mathcal{B}_\epsilon^{\mathcal{H}}} [\mathcal{A}^{\chi_B}(1^n) = 1] \right| \leq \mathsf{negl}(n).$$

The motivation for the name Bernoulli-preserving hash is simply that selecting $\mathcal{B}_\epsilon$ can be viewed as a Bernoulli process taking place on the set X, while $\mathcal{B}_\epsilon^h$ can be viewed as the pullback (along h) of a Bernoulli process taking place on Y.

We show that the standard, so-called "Hash-and-MAC" construction will work w.r.t. to BU security, if we instantiate the hash function with a Bernoulli-preserving hash. Recall that, given a MAC $\Pi = (\mathsf{Mac}_k, \mathsf{Ver}_k)$ with message set X and a function $h : Z \to X$, there is a MAC $\Pi^h := (\mathsf{Mac}_k^h, \mathsf{Ver}_k^h)$ with message set Z defined by $\mathsf{Mac}_k^h = \mathsf{Mac}_k \circ h$ and $\mathsf{Ver}_k^h(m, t) = \mathsf{Ver}_k(h(m), t)$.

Theorem 18 (Hash-and-MAC with Bernoulli-preserving hash).
Let $\Pi = (\mathsf{Mac}_k, \mathsf{Ver}_k)$ be a BU-secure MAC with $\mathsf{Mac}_k : X \to Y$, and let $h : Z \to X$ a Bernoulli-preserving hash. Then Π^h is a BU-secure MAC.

The proof follows in a straightforward way from the definitions of BU and Bernoulli-preserving hash; the details are in the full version [4].

In Appendix B, we also provide a number of additional results about Bernoulli-preserving hash functions. These results can be summarized as follows.

Theorem 19. *We prove the following about Bernoulli-preserving hash functions.*

- *If H is a random oracle or a qPRF, then it is a Bernoulli-preserving hash.*
- *If H is 4q-wise independent, then it is a Bernoulli-preserving hash against q-query adversaries.*
- *Under the* LWE *assumption, there is a (public-key) family of Bernoulli-preserving hash functions.*
- *If we only allow classical oracle access, then the Bernoulli-preserving property is equivalent to standard collision-resistance.*
- *Bernoulli-preserving hash functions are* collapsing *(another quantum generalization of collision-resistance proposed in [27]).*

7   The Problem with PO-Unforgeability

Our search for a new definition of unforgeability for quantum-secure authentication is partly motivated by concerns about the PO security notion [7]. In this section, we make these concerns concrete by pointing out a significant security concern not addressed by this definition. Specifically, we demonstrate a MAC which is readily broken with an efficient attack, and yet is PO secure. The attack queries the MAC with a superposition over a particular subset S of the message space, and then forges a valid tag for a message lying outside S.

One of the intuitive issues with PO is that it might rule out adversaries that have to measure, and thereby destroy, one or more post-query states to produce an interesting forgery. Constructing such an example seems not difficult at first. For instance, let us look at one-time PO, and construct a MAC from a qPRF f by sampling a key k for f and a superpolynomially-large prime p, and setting

$$\mathsf{Mac}_{k,p}(m) = \begin{cases} 0^n & \text{if } m = p, \\ (f_k(m \bmod p)) & \text{otherwise.} \end{cases} \tag{12}$$

This MAC is forgeable: a quantum adversary can use a single query to perform period-finding on the MAC, and then forge at 0^n. Intuitively, it seems plausible that the MAC is 1-PO secure as period-finding uses a full measurement. This is incorrect for a somewhat subtle reason: identifying the hidden symmetry does not necessarily consume the post-query state completely, so an adversary can learn the period and a random input-output-pair of the MAC simultaneously. As shown in the full version [4] this is a special case of a fairly general situation, which makes establishing a proper PO "counterexample" difficult.

A counterexample to PO. Another intuitive problem with PO is that using the contents of a register can necessitate *uncomputing* the contents of another one. We exploit this insufficiency in the counterexample below. Consider the following MAC construction.

Construction 20. *Given $k = (p, f, g, h)$ where $p \in \{0,1\}^n$ is a random period and $f, g, h : \{0,1\}^n \to \{0,1\}^n$ are random functions, define $M_k : \{0,1\}^{n+1} \to \{0,1\}^{2n}$ by*

$$
M_k(x) = \begin{cases} g(x' \bmod p) \| f(x') & x = 1\|x', \\ 0^n \| h(x') & x = 0\|x', \ x' \neq p, \\ 0^{2n} & x = 0\|p. \end{cases}
$$

Consider an adversary that queries as follows

$$
\sum_{x,y} |1, x\rangle_X |0^n\rangle_{Y_1} |y\rangle_{Y_2} \longmapsto \sum_{x,y} |1, x\rangle_X |g_p(x)\rangle_{Y_1} |y \oplus f(x)\rangle_{Y_2}, \tag{13}
$$

and then discards the first qubit and the Y_2 register; this yields $\sum_x |x\rangle |g_p(x)\rangle$. The adversary can extract p via period-finding from polynomially-many such states, and then output $(0\|p, 0^{2n})$. This attack only queries the MAC on messages starting with 1 (e.g., "from Alice"), and then forges at a message which starts with 0 (e.g., "from Bob.") We emphasize that the forgery was never queried, not even with negligible amplitude. It is thus intuitively clear that this MAC does not provide secure authentication. And yet, despite this obvious and intuitive vulnerability, this MAC is in fact PO-secure.

Theorem 21. *The MAC from Construction 20 is PO-secure.*

The proof of this theorem can be found in the full version [4]. The proof idea is as follows. The superposition oracle technique outlined in Sect. 3 achieves something that naively seems impossible due to the quantum no-cloning theorem: it records on which inputs the adversary has made non-trivial[4] queries. The information recorded in this way cannot, in general be utilized in its entirety – after all, the premise of the superposition oracle is that the measurement $\mathcal{M}_F$ that samples the random function is delayed until after the algorithm has finished, but it still has to be performed. Any measurement $\mathcal{M}'$ that does not commute

---

[4] For the standard unitary oracle for a classical function, a query has no effect when the output register is initialized in the uniform superposition of all strings.

with $\mathcal{M}_F$ and is performed before $\mathcal{M}_F$, can disturb the outcome of $\mathcal{M}_F$. If however, $\mathcal{M}'$ only has polynomially many possible outcomes, that disturbance is at most inverse polynomial according to Lemma 1.

Here, we sample the random function f using a superposition oracle, and we chose to use a measurement $\mathcal{M}'$ to determine the *number* of nontrivial queries that the adversary has made to f, which is polynomial by assumption. Random functions are PO-secure [7], so the only way to break PO security is to output $(0\|p, 0^{2n})$ and q other input-output-pairs. Querying messages that start with 0 clearly only yields a negligible advantage in guessing p by the Grover lower bound, so we consider an adversary querying only on strings starting with 1. We distinguish two cases, either the adversary makes or exactly q non-trivial queries to f, or less than that. In the latter case, the success probability is negligible by the PO-security of f and h. In the former case, we have to analyze the probability that the adversary guesses p correctly. f is not needed for that, so the superposition oracle register can be used to measure the set of q queries that the adversary made. Using an inductive argument reminiscent of the hybrid method [5] we show that this set is almost independent of p, and hence the period is equal to the difference of two of the queried inputs only with negligible probability. But if that is not the case, the periodic version of g is indistinguishable from a random function for that adversary which is independent of p.

It's not hard to see that the MAC from Construction 20 is not GYZ-secure. Indeed, observe that the forging adversary described above queries on messages starting with 0 only, and then forges successfully on a message starting with 1. If the scheme was GYZ secure, then in the accepting case, the portion of this adversary between the query and the final output would have a simulator which leaves the computational basis invariant. Such a simulator cannot change the first bit of the message from 0 to 1, a contradiction.

By Theorem 11, this PO-secure MAC is also not BU-secure.

Corollary 4. *The MAC from Construction 20 is* BU-*insecure.*

Acknowledgements. CM thanks Ronald de Wolf for helpful discussions on query complexity. GA acknowledges support from NSF grant CCF-1763736. CM was funded by a NWO VIDI grant (Project No. 639.022.519) and a NWO VENI grant (Project No. VI.Veni.192.159). FS acknowledges support from NSF grant CCF-1901624. AR acknowledges support from NSF grant CCF-1763773.

A   Technical Proofs

The Fourier Oracle number operator. We now restate and prove Lemma 2.

Lemma 3. *The number operator satisfies* $\left\| \left[N_F, U_{XYF}^{FO} \right] \right\|_\infty = 1$. *In particular, the joint state of a quantum query algorithm and the oracle after the q-th query is in the kernel of P_l for all $l > q$.*

Proof. Let $|\psi\rangle_{XYEF}$ be an arbitrary query state, where X and Y are the query input and output registers, E is the algorithm's internal register and F is the FO register. We expand the state in the computational basis of X,

$$|\psi\rangle_{XYEF} = \sum_{x\in\{0,1\}^n} p(x)|x\rangle_X|\psi_x\rangle_{YEF}. \tag{14}$$

Now observe that $U^{\mathrm{FO}}_{XYF}|x\rangle_X|\psi_x\rangle_{YEF} = |x\rangle_X \left(\widetilde{\mathrm{CNOT}}^{\otimes m}\right)_{Y:F_x}|\psi_x\rangle_{YEF}$ with $\widetilde{\mathrm{CNOT}}_{A:B} = H_A \mathrm{CNOT}_{A:B} H_A$, and therefore

$$\left[N_F, U_{XYF}\right]|x\rangle_X|\psi_x\rangle_{YEF} = |x\rangle_X \left[N_F, \left(\widetilde{\mathrm{CNOT}}^{\otimes m}\right)_{Y:F_x}\right]|\psi_x\rangle_{YEF}$$

$$= |x\rangle_X \left[(\mathbb{1} - |0\rangle\langle 0|)_{F_x}, \left(\widetilde{\mathrm{CNOT}}^{\otimes m}\right)_{Y:F_x}\right]|\psi_x\rangle_{YEF}.$$

It follows that

$$\left\|\left[N_F, U_{XYF}\right]|\psi\rangle_{XYEF}\right\|_2 \tag{15}$$

$$= \sum_{x\in\{0,1\}^n} p(x)\left\|[N_F, U_{XYF}]|\psi_x\rangle_{YEF}\right\|_2$$

$$= \sum_{x\in\{0,1\}^n} p(x)\left\|\left[(\mathbb{1} - |0\rangle\langle 0|)_{F_x}, \left(\widetilde{\mathrm{CNOT}}^{\otimes m}\right)_{Y:F_x}\right]|\psi_x\rangle_{YEF}\right\|_2$$

$$\leq \left\|\left[(\mathbb{1} - |0\rangle\langle 0|)_{F_{0^n}}, \left(\widetilde{\mathrm{CNOT}}^{\otimes m}\right)_{Y:F_{0^n}}\right]\right\|_\infty, \tag{16}$$

where we have used the definition of the operator norm and the normalization of $|\psi\rangle_{XYEF}$ in the last line. For a unitary U and a projector P, it is easy to see that $\|[U, P]\|_\infty \leq 1$, as $[U, P] = PU(\mathbb{1} - P) - (\mathbb{1} - P)UP$ is a sum of two operators that have orthogonal support and singular values smaller or equal to 1. We therefore get $\left\|[N_F, U_{XYF}]|\psi\rangle_{XYEF}\right\|_2 \leq 1$, and as the state $|\psi\rangle$ was arbitrary, this implies $\left\|[N_F, U_{XYF}]\right\|_\infty \leq 1$. The example from Eq. (2) shows that the above is actually an equality. The observation that $P_l\eta_F = 0$ for all $l > 0$ and an induction argument proves the second statement of the lemma. $\square$

BU-security of Lamport. In this section, we provide the full proof of Theorem 17, showing that the Lamport construction is BU-secure in the QROM.

Proof. We implement the random oracle h as a superposition oracle with register F. In the 1-BlindForge experiment we execute the sampling part of the key generation by preparing a superposition as well. More precisely, we can just prepare $2n$ n-qubit registers S_i^j in a uniform superposition, with the intention of measuring them to sample s_i^j in mind. We are talking about a classical one-time signature scheme, and all computation that uses the secret key is done by an honest party, and is therefore classical. It follows that the measurement that samples s_i^j commutes with all other operations which are implemented as quantum-controlled operations controlled on the secret key registers, i.e., we can postpone it to the very end of the 1-BlindForge experiment, just like the measurement that samples an actual random oracle using a superposition oracle. The joint state $|\psi_0\rangle$ with oracle register F and secret key register $SK = (S_i^j)_{i \in \{1,...,n\}, j=0,1}$ is now in a uniform superposition, i.e.,

$$|\psi_0\rangle_{SKF} = |\phi_0\rangle_{SK}^{\otimes 2n} \otimes |\phi_0\rangle_F^{\otimes 2^n}. \tag{17}$$

To subsequently generate the public key, the superposition oracle for h is queried on each of the S_i^j with an empty output register P_i^j, producing the state $|\psi_1\rangle_{SKPKF}$ equal to

$$2^{-2n^2} \sum_{\substack{s_i^j \in \{0,1\}^n \\ p_i^j \in \{0,1\}^n \\ i \in \{1,...,n\}, j=0,1}} \left(\bigotimes_{\substack{i \in \{1,...,n\} \\ j=0,1}} |s_i^j\rangle_{S_i^j} \right) \otimes \left(\bigotimes_{\substack{i \in \{1,...,n\} \\ j=0,1}} |p_i^j\rangle_{P_i^j} \right) \otimes |f_{\mathsf{sk},\mathsf{pk}}\rangle_F,$$

where $|f_{\mathsf{sk},\mathsf{pk}}\rangle_F$ is the superposition oracle state where $F_{s_i^j}$ is in state $|p_i^j\rangle$ and all other registers are still in state $|\phi_0\rangle$. Then the registers P_i^j are measured to produce an actual, classical, public key that can be handed to the adversary. Note that there is no hash function key k now, as it has been replaced by the random oracle. Treating the public key as classical information from now on and removing the registers PK, the state takes the form

$$|\psi_2(\mathsf{pk})\rangle_{SKF} = 2^{-n^2} \sum_{\substack{s_i^j \in \{0,1\}^n \\ i \in \{1,...,n\}, j=0,1}} \left(\bigotimes_{\substack{i \in \{1,...,n\} \\ j=0,1}} |s_i^j\rangle_{S_i^j} \right) \otimes |f_{\mathsf{sk},\mathsf{pk}}\rangle_F, \tag{18}$$

Now the interactive phase of the 1-BlindForge experiment can begin, and we provide both the random oracle h and the signing oracle (that can be called exactly once) as superposition oracles using the joint oracle state $|\psi_2(\mathsf{pk})\rangle$ above. The random oracle answers queries as described in Sect. 3. The signing oracle, when queried with registers XZ with $Z = Z_1...Z_n$, applies $\mathrm{CNOT}_{S_i^{x_i}:Z_i}^{\otimes n}$, $i = 1,...,n$ controlled on X being in the state $x \notin B_\varepsilon$.

Now suppose $\mathcal{A}$, after making at most one query to Sign and an arbitrary polynomial number of queries to h, outputs a candidate message signature pair (x^0, z^0) with $z^0 = z_1^0 \| ... \| z_n^0$. If $x^0 \notin B_\varepsilon$, $\mathcal{A}$ has lost. Suppose therefore that $x^0 \in B_\varepsilon$. We will now make a measurement on the oracle register to find an index i such that $S_i^{x_i^0}$ has not been queried. To this end we first need to decorrelate SK and F. This is easily done, as the success test only needs computational basis measurement results from the register SK, allowing us to perform any controlled operation on F controlled on SK. Therefore we can apply the operation $\oplus p_i^j$ followed by $H^{\otimes n}$ to the register $F_{s_i^j}$ controlled on S_i^j being in state $|s_i^j\rangle$, for all $i = 1, ..., n$ and $j = 0, 1$. For an adversary that does not make any queries to h, this has the effect that all F-registers are in state $|\phi_0\rangle$ again now.

We can equivalently perform this restoring procedure before the adversary starts interaction, and answer the adversary's h-queries as follows. Controlled on the adversary's input being equal to one of the parts s_i^j of the secret key, answer with the corresponding public key, otherwise use the superposition oracle for h.

For any fixed secret key register S_i^j, the unitary that is applied upon an h-query has hence the form

$$U_h' = U_\perp + \sum_{x \in \{0,1\}^n} (U_x - U_\perp)|x\rangle\langle x|_X |x\rangle\langle x|_{S_i^j} \tag{19}$$

$$= U_\perp + \sum_{x \in \{0,1\}^n} |x\rangle\langle x|_X |x\rangle\langle x|_{S_i^j} (U_x - U_\perp), \tag{20}$$

where the second equality follows because the unitaries $U_\perp$ and U_x are controlled unitaries with X and S_i^j part of the control register. Using the above equation we derive a bound on the operator norm of the commutator of this unitary and the projector onto $|\phi_0\rangle$,

$$\|[U_h', |\phi_0\rangle\langle\phi_0|]\|_\infty$$

$$= 2^{-n/2} \left\| \sum_{x \in \{0,1\}^n} \left((U_x - U_\perp)|x\rangle\langle x|_X |x\rangle\langle\phi_0|_{S_i^j} - |x\rangle\langle x|_X |\phi_0\rangle\langle x|_{S_i^j} (U_x - U_\perp) \right) \right\|_\infty$$

$$= 2^{-n/2} \max_{x \in \{0,1\}^n} \left\| \left((U_x - U_\perp)|x\rangle\langle x|_X |x\rangle\langle\phi_0|_{S_i^j} - |x\rangle\langle x|_X |\phi_0\rangle\langle x|_{S_i^j} (U_x - U_\perp) \right) \right\|_\infty$$

$$\leq 2 \cdot 2^{-n/2},$$

where the second equality follows again because $U_\perp$ and U_x are controlled unitaries with X and S_i^j part of the control register.

It follows that a query to h does not decrease the number of registers S_i^j that are in state $|\phi_0\rangle$, except with probability $8n \cdot 2^{-n}$.

As we assume that x^0 is blinded, we have that for any message $x \notin B_\varepsilon$, there exists an $i \in \{1, ..., n\}$ such that $x_i \neq x_i^0$. But $\mathcal{A}$ interacts with a blinded signing oracle, i.e., controlled on his input being not blinded, it is forwarded to the signing oracle, otherwise $\perp$ is XORed into his output register. Therefore only non-blinded queries have been forwarded to the actual signing oracle, so the final state is a superposition of states in which the register SK has at least n subregisters S_i^j are in state $|\phi_0\rangle$, and at least one of them is such that $x_i^0 = j$. We can therefore apply an n-outcome measurement to the oracle register to obtain an index i_0 such that $S_{i_0}^{x_{i_0}^0}$ is in state $|\phi_0\rangle$. By Lemma 1, this implies that $\mathcal{A}$'s forgery is independent of s_{i_0}, so $\mathcal{A}$'s probability of succeeding in BlindForge is negligible. $\qquad\square$

B   More on Bernoulli-Preserving Hash

In this section, we prove several results about Bernoulli-preserving hash functions. Recalling Definition 8, we refer to blinding according to $\mathcal{B}_\epsilon$ as "uniform blinding," and blinding according to $\mathcal{B}_\epsilon^{\mathcal{H}}$ as "hash blinding." First, we show that random and pseudorandom functions are Bernoulli-preserving, and that this property is equivalent to collision-resistance against classical queries.

Lemma 4. *Let $H : X \to Y$ be a function such that $1/|Y|$ is negligible. Then*

1. *If H is a random oracle or a qPRF, then it is a Bernoulli-preserving hash.*
2. *If H is 4q-wise independent, then it is a Bernoulli-preserving hash against q-query adversaries.*

Proof. The claim for random oracles is obvious: by statistical collision-resistance, uniform blinding is statistically indistinguishable from hash-blinding. The remaining claims follow from the observation that one can simulate one quantum query to $\chi_{B_\epsilon^h}$ using two quantum queries to h (see, e.g., the proof of Corollary 3).   □

Theorem 22. *A function $h : \{0,1\}^* \to \{0,1\}^n$ is Bernoulli-preserving against classical-query adversaries if and only if it is collision-resistant.*

Proof. First, the Bernoulli-preserving hash property implies collision-resistance: testing whether two colliding inputs are either (i) both not blinded or both blinded, or (ii) exactly one of them is blinded, yields always outcome (i) when dealing with a hash-blinded oracle and a uniformly random outcome for a blinded oracle and $\varepsilon = 1/2$. On the other hand, consider an adversary $\mathcal{A}$ that has inverse polynomial distinguishing advantage between blinding and hash-blinding, and let $x_1, ..., x_q$ be it's queries. Assume for contradiction that with overwhelming probability $h(x_i) \neq h(x_j)$ for all $x_i \neq x_j$. Then with that same overwhelming probability the blinded and hash blinded oracles are both blinded independently with probability ε on each x_i and are hence statistically indistinguishable, a contradiction. It follows that with non-negligible probability there exist two queries $x_i \neq x_j$ such that $h(x_i) = h(x_j)$, i.e., $\mathcal{A}$ has found a collision.   □

Bernoulli-preserving hash from LWE. We have observed that any qPRF is a Bernoulli-preserving hash function, which can be constructed from various quantum-safe computational assumption (e.g., LWE). Nonetheless, qPRF typically does not give short digest, which would result in long tags, and it requires a secret key.[5]

Here we point out an alternative construction of a public Bernoulli-preserving hash function based on the quantum security of LWE. In fact, we show that the collapsing hash function in [26] is also Bernoulli-preserving hash. This constructions relies on a lossy function family $F : X \to Y$ and a universal hash function

---

[5] In practice, it is probably more convenient (and more reliable) to instantiate a qPRF from block ciphers, which may not be ideal for message authentication.

$G = \{g_k : Y \to Z\}_{k \in \mathcal{K}}$. A lossy function family admits two types of keys: a lossy key $s \leftarrow \mathcal{D}_{los}$ and an injective key $s \leftarrow \mathcal{D}_{inj}$, which are computationally indistinguishable. $F_s : X \to Y$ under a lossy key s is compressing, i.e., $|im(F_s)| \ll |Y|$; whereas under an injective key s, F_s is injective. We refer a formal definition to [26, Definition 2], and an explicit construction based on LWE to [20]. There exist efficient constructions for universal hash families by various means [28]. Then one constructs a hash function family $H = \{h_{s,k}\}$ by $h_{s,k} := g_k \circ F_s$ with public parameters generated by $s \leftarrow \mathcal{D}_{los}, k \leftarrow \mathcal{K}$. The proof of Bernoulli-preserving for this hash function is similar to Unruh's proof that H is collapsing; see the full version [4].

Relationship to collapsing. Finally, we relate Bernoulli-preserving hash to another quantum generalization of classical collision-resistance: the collapsing property. Collapsing hash functions are particularly relevant to post-quantum signatures. We first define the collapsing property (slightly rephrasing Unruh's original definition [27]) as follows. Let $h : X \to Y$ be a hash function, and let $\mathcal{S}_X$ and $\mathcal{S}_{XY}$ be the set of quantum states (i.e., density operators) on registers corresponding to the sets X and $X \times Y$, respectively. We define two channels from $\mathcal{S}_X$ to $\mathcal{S}_{XY}$. First, $\mathcal{O}_h$ receives X, prepares $|0\rangle$ on Y, applies $|x\rangle|y\rangle \mapsto |x\rangle|y \oplus h(x)\rangle$, and then measures Y fully in the computational basis. Second, $\mathcal{O}_h'$ first applies $\mathcal{O}_h$ and then also measures X fully in the computational basis.

$$\mathcal{O}_h : \quad |x\rangle_X \xrightarrow{h} |x, h(x)\rangle_{X,Y} \xrightarrow{\text{measure } Y} (\rho_X^y, y),$$

$$\mathcal{O}_h' : \quad |x\rangle_X \xrightarrow{h} |x, h(x)\rangle_{X,Y} \xrightarrow{\text{measure } X\&Y} (x, y).$$

If the input is a pure state on X, then the output is either a superposition over a fiber $h^{-1}(s) \times \{s\}$ of h (for $\mathcal{O}_h$) or a classical pair $(x, h(x))$ (for $\mathcal{O}_h'$).

Definition 9 (Collapsing). *A hash function h is collapsing if for any single-query QPT $\mathcal{A}$, it holds that $\left| \Pr[\mathcal{A}^{\mathcal{O}_h}(1^n) = 1] - \Pr[\mathcal{A}^{\mathcal{O}_h'}(1^n) = 1] \right| \leq \mathsf{negl}(n)$.*

To prove that Bernoulli-preserving hash implies collapsing, we need a technical fact. Recall that any subset $S \subseteq \{0,1\}^n$ is associated with a two-outcome projective measurement $\{\Pi_S, \mathbb{1} - \Pi_S\}$ on n qubits defined by $\Pi_S = \sum_{x \in S} |x\rangle\langle x|$. We will write Ξ_S for the channel (on n qubits) which applies this measurement.

Lemma 5. *Let $S_1, S_2, \ldots, S_{cn}$ be subsets of $\{0,1\}^n$, each of size 2^{n-1}, chosen independently and uniformly at random. Let Ξ_{S_j} denote the two-outcome measurement defined by S_j, and denote their composition $\tilde{\Xi} := \Xi_{S_{cn}} \circ \Xi_{S_{cn-1}} \circ \cdots \circ \Xi_{S_1}$. Let Ξ denote the full measurement in the computational basis. Then $\Pr[\tilde{\Xi} = \Xi] \geq 1 - 2^{-\varepsilon n}$, whenever $c \geq 2 + \varepsilon$ with $\varepsilon > 0$,*

A proof is given in the full version [4]. We remark that, to efficiently implement each Ξ_S with a random subset S, we can sample $h_i : [M] \to [N]$ from a pairwise-independent hash family (sampling an independent h_i for each i), and then define $x \in S$ iff. $h(x) \leq N/2$. For any input state $\sum_{x,z} \alpha_{x,z}|x, z\rangle$, we can compute

$$\sum_{x,z} \alpha_{x,z} |x, z\rangle \mapsto \sum_{x,z} |x, z\rangle |b(x)\rangle, \quad \text{where } b(x) := h(x) \overset{?}{\le} N/2,$$

and then measure $|b(x)\rangle$. Pairwise independence is sufficient by Theorem 10 because only one quantum query is made.

Theorem 23. *If $h : X \to Y$ is Bernoulli-preserving, then it is collapsing.*

Proof. Let $\mathcal{A}$ be an adversary with inverse-polynomial distinguishing power in the collapsing game. Choose n such that $X = \{0, 1\}^n$. We define $k = cn$ hybrid oracles $H_0, H_1, \dots, H_k$, where hybrid H_j is a channel from $\mathcal{S}_X$ to $\mathcal{S}_{XY}$ which acts as follows: (1) adjoin $|0\rangle_Y$ and apply the unitary $|x\rangle_X |y\rangle_Y \mapsto |x\rangle_X |y \oplus h(x)\rangle_Y$; (2) measure the Y register in the computational basis; (3) repeat j times: (i) select a uniformly random subset $S \subseteq X$ of size 2^{n-1}; (ii) apply the two-outcome measurement Ξ_S to the X register; (4) output registers X and Y.

Clearly, H_0 is identical to the $\mathcal{O}_h$ channel in the collapsing game. By Lemma 5, H_k is indistinguishable from the $\mathcal{O}'_h$. By our initial assumption and the triangle inequality, there exists a j such that

$$\left| \Pr[\mathcal{A}^{H_j}(1^n) = 1] - \Pr[\mathcal{A}^{H_{j+1}}(1^n) = 1] \right| \ge 1/\mathsf{poly}(n). \tag{21}$$

We now build a distinguisher $\mathcal{D}$ against the Bernoulli-preserving property (with $\epsilon = 1/2$) of h. It proceeds as follows: (1) run $\mathcal{A}(1^n)$ and place its query state in register X; (2) simulate oracle H_j on XY (use 2-wise independent hash to select sets S); (3) prepare an extra qubit in the $|0\rangle$ state in register W, and invoke the oracle for χ_B on registers X and W; (4) measure and discard register W; (5) return XY to $\mathcal{A}$, and output what it outputs.

We now analyze $\mathcal{D}$. After the first two steps of H_j (compute h, measure output register) the state of $\mathcal{A}$ (running as a subroutine of $\mathcal{D}$) is given by

$$\sum_z \sum_{x \in h^{-1}(s)} \alpha_{xz} |x\rangle_X |s\rangle_Y |z\rangle_Z.$$

Here Z is a side information register private to $\mathcal{A}$. Applying the j measurements (third step of H_j) results in a state of the form $\sum_z \sum_{x \in M} \beta_{xz} |x\rangle |s\rangle |z\rangle$, where M is a subset of $h^{-1}(s)$. Applying the oracle for χ_B into an extra register now yields

$$\sum_z \sum_{x \in M} \beta_{xz} |x\rangle |s\rangle |z\rangle |\chi_B(x)\rangle_W.$$

Now consider the two cases of the Bernoulli-preserving game.

First, in the "hash-blinded" case, $B = h^{-1}(C)$ for some set $C \subseteq Y$. This implies that $\chi_B(x) = \chi_C(h(x)) = \chi_C(s)$ for all $x \in M$. It follows that W simply contains the classical bit $\chi_C(s)$; computing this bit, measuring it, and discarding it will thus have no effect. The state returned to $\mathcal{A}$ will then be identical to the output of the oracle H_j. Second, in the "uniform blinding" case, B is a random subset of X of size 2^{n-1}, selected uniformly and independently of everything else in the algorithm thus far. Computing the characteristic function of B into an extra qubit and then measuring and discarding that qubit implements the channel Ξ_B, i.e., the measurement $\{\Pi_B, \mathbb{1} - \Pi_B\}$. It follows that the state returned to $\mathcal{A}$ will be identical to the output of oracle H_{j+1}.

By (21), it now follows that $\mathcal{D}$ is a successful distinguisher in the Bernoulli-preserving hash game for h, and that h is thus not a Bernoulli-preserving hash.

$\square$

References

1. Aaronson, S.: Quantum lower bound for recursive Fourier sampling. Quantum Inf. Comput. **3**(2), 165–174 (2003)
2. Alagic, G., Gagliardoni, T., Majenz, C.: Can you sign a quantum state? arXiv preprint arXiv:1811.11858 (2018)
3. Alagic, G., Gagliardoni, T., Majenz, C.: Unforgeable quantum encryption. In: Nielsen, J.B., Rijmen, V. (eds.) EUROCRYPT 2018. LNCS, vol. 10822, pp. 489–519. Springer, Cham (2018). https://doi.org/10.1007/978-3-319-78372-7_16
4. Alagic, G., Majenz, C., Russell, A., Song, F.: Quantum-secure message authentication via blind-unforgeability. arXiv preprint arXiv:1803.03761 (2020)
5. Bennett, C.H., Bernstein, E., Brassard, G., Vazirani, U.V.: Strengths and weaknesses of quantum computing. SIAM J. Comput. **26**(5), 1510–1523 (1997)
6. Biasse, J.-F., Song, F.: Efficient quantum algorithms for computing class groups and solving the principal ideal problem in arbitrary degree number fields. In: Proceedings of the Twenty-Seventh Annual ACM-SIAM Symposium on Discrete Algorithms. SODA 2016, Philadelphia, PA, USA, pp. 893–902. Society for Industrial and Applied Mathematics (2016)
7. Boneh, D., Zhandry, M.: Quantum-secure message authentication codes. In: Johansson, T., Nguyen, P.Q. (eds.) EUROCRYPT 2013. LNCS, vol. 7881, pp. 592–608. Springer, Heidelberg (2013). https://doi.org/10.1007/978-3-642-38348-9_35
8. Boneh, D., Zhandry, M.: Secure signatures and chosen ciphertext security in a quantum computing world. In: Canetti, R., Garay, J.A. (eds.) CRYPTO 2013. LNCS, vol. 8043, pp. 361–379. Springer, Heidelberg (2013). https://doi.org/10.1007/978-3-642-40084-1_21
9. Chen, L., et al.: Report on post-quantum cryptography. Technical report, National Institute of Standards and Technology (2016)
10. Cramer, R., Ducas, L., Peikert, C., Regev, O.: Recovering short generators of principal ideals in cyclotomic rings. In: Fischlin, M., Coron, J.-S. (eds.) EUROCRYPT 2016. LNCS, vol. 9666, pp. 559–585. Springer, Heidelberg (2016). https://doi.org/10.1007/978-3-662-49896-5_20
11. Czajkowski, J., Majenz, C., Schaffner, C., Zur, S.: Quantum lazy sampling and game-playing proofs for quantum indifferentiability. Cryptology ePrint Archive, Report 2019/428 (2019). https://eprint.iacr.org/2019/428
12. Eisenträger, K., Hallgren, S., Kitaev, A., Song, F.: A quantum algorithm for computing the unit group of an arbitrary degree number field. In: Proceedings of the 46th Annual ACM Symposium on Theory of Computing. STOC 2014, pp. 293–302. ACM, New York (2014)
13. Gagliardoni, T., Hülsing, A., Schaffner, C.: Semantic security and indistinguishability in the quantum world. In: Robshaw, M., Katz, J. (eds.) CRYPTO 2016. LNCS, vol. 9816, pp. 60–89. Springer, Heidelberg (2016). https://doi.org/10.1007/978-3-662-53015-3_3

14. Garg, S., Yuen, H., Zhandry, M.: New security notions and feasibility results for authentication of quantum data. In: Katz, J., Shacham, H. (eds.) CRYPTO 2017. LNCS, vol. 10402, pp. 342–371. Springer, Cham (2017). https://doi.org/10.1007/978-3-319-63715-0_12

15. Hayashi, M.: Optimal sequence of quantum measurements in the sense of Stein's lemma in quantum hypothesis testing. J. Phys. A: Math. Gen. **35**(50), 10759 (2002)

16. Kaplan, M., Leurent, G., Leverrier, A., Naya-Plasencia, M.: Breaking symmetric cryptosystems using quantum period finding. In: Robshaw, M., Katz, J. (eds.) CRYPTO 2016. LNCS, vol. 9815, pp. 207–237. Springer, Heidelberg (2016). https://doi.org/10.1007/978-3-662-53008-5_8

17. Kuwakado, H., Morii, M.: Quantum distinguisher between the 3-round Feistel cipher and the random permutation. In: Proceedings of IEEE International Symposium on Information Theory, pp. 2682–2685, June 2010

18. Kuwakado, H., Morii, M.: Security on the quantum-type Even-Mansour cipher. In: Proceedings of the International Symposium on Information Theory and Its Applications, pp. 312–316. IEEE Computer Society (2012)

19. Lamport, L.: Constructing digital signatures from a one way function. Technical report SRI-CSL-98, SRI International Computer Science Laboratory (1979)

20. Peikert, C., Waters, B.: Lossy trapdoor functions and their applications. In: Proceedings of the Fortieth Annual ACM Symposium on Theory of Computing, STOC 2008, pp. 187–196. ACM, New York (2008)

21. Sahai, A., Waters, B.: How to use indistinguishability obfuscation: deniable encryption, and more. In: Proceedings of the 46th Annual ACM Symposium on Theory of Computing, STOC 2014, pp. 475–484. ACM (2014)

22. Santoli, T., Schaffner, C.: Using Simon's algorithm to attack symmetric-key cryptographic primitives. Quantum Inf. Comput. **17**(1&2), 65–78 (2017)

23. Shor, P.W.: Polynomial-time algorithms for prime factorization and discrete logarithms on a quantum computer. SIAM J. Comput. **26**(5), 1484–1509 (1997)

24. Song, F., Yun, A.: Quantum security of NMAC and related constructions. In: Katz, J., Shacham, H. (eds.) CRYPTO 2017. LNCS, vol. 10402, pp. 283–309. Springer, Cham (2017). https://doi.org/10.1007/978-3-319-63715-0_10

25. Forrest Stinespring, W.: Positive functions on c*-algebras. Proc. Am. Math. Soc. **6**(2), 211–216 (1955)

26. Unruh, D.: Collapse-binding quantum commitments without random oracles. In: Cheon, J.H., Takagi, T. (eds.) ASIACRYPT 2016. LNCS, vol. 10032, pp. 166–195. Springer, Heidelberg (2016). https://doi.org/10.1007/978-3-662-53890-6_6

27. Unruh, D.: Computationally binding quantum commitments. In: Fischlin, M., Coron, J.-S. (eds.) EUROCRYPT 2016. LNCS, vol. 9666, pp. 497–527. Springer, Heidelberg (2016). https://doi.org/10.1007/978-3-662-49896-5_18

28. Vadhan, S.P.: Pseudo randomness. Found. Trends® Theor. Comput. Sci. **7**(1–3), 1–336 (2012)

29. Zhandry, M.: How to construct quantum random functions. In: Proceedings of the 53rd Annual Symposium on Foundations of Computer Science, FOCS 2012, pp. 679–687. IEEE Computer Society, Washington, DC (2012)

30. Zhandry, M.: How to record quantum queries, and applications to quantum indifferentiability. In: Boldyreva, A., Micciancio, D. (eds.) CRYPTO 2019. LNCS, vol. 11693, pp. 239–268. Springer, Cham (2019). https://doi.org/10.1007/978-3-030-26951-7_9

31. Zhandry, M.: Quantum lightning never strikes the same state twice. In: Ishai, Y., Rijmen, V. (eds.) EUROCRYPT 2019. LNCS, vol. 11478, pp. 408–438. Springer, Cham (2019). https://doi.org/10.1007/978-3-030-17659-4_14

Author Index

Printed in the United States
By Bookmasters